THE
RISE AND FALL
OF
FREEDOM OF CONTRACT

BY

P. S. ATIYAH, D.C.L., F.B.A.

CLARENDON PRESS . OXFORD

*This book has been printed digitally and produced in a standard specification
in order to ensure its continuing availability*

OXFORD
UNIVERSITY PRESS

Great Clarendon Street, Oxford OX2 6DP

Oxford University Press is a department of the University of Oxford.
It furthers the University◌ objective of excellence in research, scholarship,
and education by publishing worldwide in

Oxford New York

Auckland Bangkok Buenos Aires Cape Town Chennai
Dar es Salaam Delhi Hong Kong Istanbul Karachi Kolkata
Kuala Lumpur Madrid Melbourne Mexico City Mumbai Nairobi
S‹o Paulo Shanghai Taipei Tokyo Toronto

Oxford is a registered trade mark of Oxford University Press
in the UK and in certain other countries

Published in the United States
by Oxford University Press Inc., New York

© Oxford University Press 1979

ISBN 0-19-825527-6

Printed in Great Britain by

Antony Rowe Ltd., Eastbourne

'A study of the history of opinion is a necessary preliminary to the emancipation of the mind.'
J. M. Keynes, *The End of Laissez-Faire.*

PREFACE

THIS is the first volume in a projected two-part study of the theory of contractual and promissory liability. I hope to follow it with a volume devoted to the contemporary scene in which I will explore the interrelationship of modern contract law with the underlying theories and values of modern England. The book is primarily a study in the history of ideas although it also attempts to explore the interrelationship between social and economic conditions and those ideas. This kind of study raises many well-known methodological difficulties, and much of the work must be read as offering a series of hypotheses rather than as proposing definitive solutions. This is particularly the case because the magnitude of the theme, and the quantity of material available, mean that in my attempt to delineate the main outlines of the story, I may have overlooked detailed evidence about this or that episode or problem. Evidence of this kind may come to light, or may even now be available, overlooked by me, which contradicts, or requires modifications to be made to some of my hypotheses; in other respects I am confident that further evidence will confirm my conclusions.

An inter-disciplinary subject of this nature poses many problems for an author. Nobody could hope to be equally proficient in all the disciplines encompassed in a work of this kind. Ideally, this book should have been written by someone qualified not only as a lawyer, but also as an economist, a social and economic historian, and a student of political theory and philosophy. I need not say that I make no claim to these qualifications, and I am acutely aware of the dangers of venturing into this work without them.

I am also uneasily conscious of the difficulties involved in gauging the level of sophistication required in a work addressed to readers of so many disciplines. Some of my historical material on the background to the law will, I suspect, appear elementary and unexciting to historians, much of my economic material will seem unsophisticated to economists, while some of my legal material will be found difficult, if not incomprehensible to those without a legal background. On the other hand, the non-legal material will be much less familiar to lawyers and I felt that its inclusion was an indispensable preliminary to the theories I had to offer concerning the development of the law itself. In attempting to strike the right balance on this difficult question I have generally taken as my guide the probable needs of the contemporary English-speaking lawyer. Nevertheless, I hope that the work will contain sufficient of interest to students of other disciplines, and that even the legal material will, in some degree, be found intelligible and useful to them.

A brief word is in order about the scope of the work. The movement whose history I have here attempted to trace was, of course, not confined to England. A parallel movement took place in the United States, and also in Europe, and here and there I have drawn on the work of American scholars and historians to illuminate some of the themes I have dealt with in relation to England. But the book is, nevertheless, confined to the English experience. To have broadened the theme still further would have turned the work into an encyclopedia, and would, anyhow, have been far beyond my competence. Although, no doubt, much that is discussed here is also relevant to Scotland, the differences between English and Scots law, and my ignorance of the latter, compel me to add that in this work England is not deemed to include Scotland.

I should, perhaps, add a word about the relationship between this book and some of my earlier works. The historical research which led to this book has modified my opinions on many important points concerning contractual liabilities, the relationship between contractual and other forms of liability, and above all the central role of promises and consideration. In general, however, I hope it is right to say that this book represents a development of former ideas, rather than a contradiction of them.

It remains to acknowledge the debts I have accumulated in writing this book. Intellectually, my greatest debt is to John Dwyer who discussed innumerable points in this book while it was in gestation and while it was being written, as well as contributing many valuable suggestions on the first draft. To Professor A. W. B. Simpson also, I owe more than I can say. His detailed comments on Part I have saved me from many egregious errors, and I have also derived enormous benefit from reading his *History of the Common Law of Contract*. I believe that the general story I tell in this work is broadly in line with Professor Simpson's *History*, though I am not confident that he himself would endorse that view. Among others who have read and commented on part of the book, or with whom I have profitably discussed some of its themes, my thanks are due to Sir Otto Kahn-Freund, Professor S. F. C. Milsom, Mr Michael Hurst, Professor Grant Gilmore, Professor Arthur Leff, Professor Duncan Kennedy, and Professor Richard Danzig. Finally I owe debts of a different character to the Trustees of the Nuffield Foundation for two small grants which assisted me with the research and the typing expenses for the book, and to the Social Science Research Council for a personal research grant which enabled me to take leave of absence for the whole academic year 1976/7.

The opportunity has been taken in this paper edition to correct a number of misprints and to revise and enlarge the index.

P. S. ATIYAH

CONTENTS

PART III. THE DECLINE AND FALL OF FREEDOM OF CONTRACT:
1870–1970

1

INTRODUCTION

THIS book is an attempt to trace the history of one of the great intellectual movements of modern times, but although its main theme is historical, it has been necessary to re-examine the nature of contractual, and of promissory, liability in order to understand the historical developments with which I am primarily concerned. This re-examination has led me to the conclusion that the nature of contractual and promissory liability have been largely misunderstood by lawyers, philosophers, and others.[1] This is indeed a large claim to make, and of its justification I must leave the reader to judge. But it may make the historical story I have to tell somewhat more intelligible if I begin by sketching out the theory of contractual and promissory liability at which I have arrived and which forms the basis for many of the following pages.

In order to understand this theory it is necessary at the outset to distinguish three situations in which contracts may be held legally binding, or promises may be found morally binding:

(1) In the first situation a contract or a promise may be found binding after a price has been paid for it. For example, a person may borrow £100 from a friend and may simultaneously promise to repay it. In this situation there would, both legally and morally, be a liability to repay even if there were no promise. The promise may, indeed, be said to be 'implied' but my contention is that in this situation the primary justification for imposing a legal or moral obligation on the party borrowing the money is that he has received a benefit at the expense of the other party, and that is, in a property-owning society, usually sufficient to establish a liability. I express this conclusion by saying that the liability is benefit-based in this type of case; it could also be said to arise from broad notions of unjust enrichment. If it should be asked what is the function of the promise in such circumstances, one answer might be that the promise has evidentiary value. It is evidence that the promisor has received a benefit (for if it was not a benefit would he have promised to pay for it?) and it may be evidence of many ancillary matters such as the precise terms of the arrangement, the date of repayment and so on.

(2) In the second situation, a contract or promise may be enforced where

---

[1] But I must express my great indebtedness to the article by Fuller and Perdue, 'The Reliance Interest in Contract Damages', 46 *Yale Law Journal* 52 and 373 (1936). In many respects, this article has been the starting-point for the whole of this book.

the promisee has acted in reliance on the promise, or on the promisor's conduct, and would in consequence be in a worse situation than if no promise had ever been made. The case of a simple loan discussed above may, of course, also be a case of such action in reliance, for the lender may only have lent his money in reliance on the borrower's promise to repay. But cases of action in reliance may arise without any element of benefit or unjust enrichment. In the law, a common example is to be found in the typical contract of guarantee, as where A promises to guarantee repayment of a loan to be made by B to C. In this situation if B acts in reliance on the guarantee, he will lend money to C and may (if C is himself not good for the money) thus make his position worse than it would be if there had been no promise. In my terminology I would refer to liability in such a case as reliance-based. As in the previous case, I suggest that many forms of reliance-based liability arise, or would arise even in the absence of a promise. The party relying may be relying, not on a promise, but on other words, or mere conduct. Such reliance is a commonplace in modern societies and often gives rise to liabilities even in the absence of a promise. For instance, a person who buys a new house, in reliance on the proper performance by the local authority of its duties of ensuring compliance with the Building Regulations, may have a remedy against the authority for malperformance even though they give no promise. Here again, as with benefit-based liability, the result may be justified or explained by saying that there is an 'implied' promise. But it will be observed that in such circumstances the liability comes first, and the implication is made subsequently to justify the decision already arrived at. Once the liability itself is well established (whether in law or in social custom) it is easy to make the implication. But in the first instance, it is the conduct of one party, followed by the action in reliance of the other, which creates the liability. As with the case of benefit-based liability, it is likely that an actual, express promise, will serve a useful evidentiary role in reliance-based liability. Whether the party acting did in fact rely on the other (or, for example, on his own judgment) and if so, whether in so acting, he acted reasonably by the standards of the society in question, are questions whose answer may be greatly assisted by the presence of an express promise. But again, it does not follow that it is the promise which creates the liability.

(3) The third situation concerns a promise or a contract which has not been paid for, and which has not yet been relied upon. In the law such a contract or promise would be called 'wholly executory'.[2] If such a promise or contract generates any liability, the liability must be promise-based, since it cannot be benefit-based or reliance-based. In the first two

---

[2] It should be made clear that in this book I do not treat a promise which has been relied upon as wholly executory, even though in strict law this might sometimes be the case.

cases, distinct grounds exist for imposing the liability, apart altogether from the promise. In this case, no such distinct grounds exist. If the promise is held to be 'binding' or to create some liability, it must be for some reason which is inherent in the promise itself. The principal grounds which (it is suggested) can be found for imposing such liability in this case are these. First, it may be said that a promise, even while executory, creates expectations, and that these expectations will be disappointed if the promise is not performed. In this sense, there is a similarity between a promise-based and a reliance-based liability. The promisee whose expectations are disappointed may feel he is worse off than he would have been if no promise had been made at all. Psychologically this may be true; but in a pecuniary sense, it is not. The party who acts in reliance may spend money which he would lose if he could not claim recompense from the party on whose conduct he relied. But the promisee who has not yet acted in reliance on a promise, and not yet paid any price for it, will not be worse off in a pecuniary sense merely because his expectations are disappointed.

Secondly, it may be said that contracts and promises are essentially risk-allocation devices, like simple bets. The nature of this device is such that the transaction must generally remain executory prior to the occurrence of the risk, and the whole point of the transaction would be lost if the arrangement could not be made binding for the future.

The third possible ground for the enforcement of executory promises or contracts is that it may be desirable to uphold the *principle* of promissory liability, even in cases where the non-performance of the promise has little practical effect. The argument here comes to this, that if executory promises are held binding (whether in law or in social custom and morality) then people are more likely to perform promises which have been paid for, or relied upon.

Now it will be seen that many promises and contracts are likely to be wholly executory at the outset, but may quickly pass into one or other of the first two situations discussed above. A promise may be given which is at first executory, and only subsequently is it acted upon by the promisee, or paid for by the promisee. In this book I suggest that once this happens, the ground for imposing a liability shifts.[3] The liability becomes benefit-based or reliance-based, where it was previously promise-based. This may seem strange, and indeed, it is precisely because this seems so strange that it has not generally been recognized, either in law or in general discussion of the nature of promissory liability. This, I suggest, is because promise-based liability is seen as the paradigm case for discussion

[3] I pass over here the legal issues as to the quantum of damages which are awarded in such circumstances. Even in benefit-based and reliance-based liabilities, the damages awarded are often calculated as though the liability was promise-based.

both in law and among philosophers, and perhaps in ordinary discourse. One of the purposes of this book is to suggest that this is itself part of our cultural and legal heritage, and that an alternative perspective may be possible and even preferable. If benefit-based and reliance-based liabilities are taken as the paradigm cases of obligation, whether legal or moral, it may be suggested that promise-based liabilities are neither paradigmatic nor of central importance. Far from being the typical case of obligation, a promise-based liability may be a projection of liabilities normally based on benefit or reliance. Because these are normally found such powerful grounds for imposing obligations, it has been thought that the element of promise (express or implied) which is often combined with benefit-based and reliance-based liability, is itself the ground for the obligation. And from this, it has been an easy move to the inference that promise-based liability, even without any element of benefit or reliance, carries its own justification.

Much of this book is based on the conviction that this traditional attitude to promise-based obligations is misconceived, and that the grounds for the imposition of such liabilities are, by the standards of modern values, very weak compared with the grounds for the creation of benefit-based and reliance-based obligations. The protection of mere expectations cannot (it is suggested) rank equally with the protection of restitution interests (arising from benefit-based liability) or reliance interests (arising from reliance-based liability). A person whose expectations are disappointed, but who suffers no pecuniary or other loss from the failure to perform a promise, has surely a relatively weak claim for complaint or redress. No doubt if there is *no* excuse or justification at all for the failure to perform the promise or contract, the promisee may be felt entitled to some redress, but even then it does not follow that he should be entitled to demand full performance of the promise, or redress based on such an entitlement. Frequently, a promise-based claim is based on relatively short-lived expectations; for it is where the promisor has (for instance) made some mistake, or overlooked some fact, that he is most likely to attempt to withdraw a promise.[4] Where the promisor does not do this, the probability is that some action in reliance (or some payment) will soon be performed by the promisee, and he can then claim the much greater protection due to reliance interests or restitution interests. Adoption of this alternative approach would, of course, have a profound effect on the conceptual pattern of moral and legal obligation, but to argue, as I do, that the justification for creating promise-based obligations is usually weak, does not mean that this approach would involve a serious undercutting of typical moral or legal obligations. For in practice, even liabilities which are usually perceived as promise-based

[4] See, e.g., the case put by Stephen J. in 1 *Law Q. Rev.* 1 (1885) which is discussed below, p. 658.

in law or social custom, are, in my terminology not exclusively promise-based at all. In fact most such liabilities are, or rapidly become, reliance-based or benefit-based, and the period during which they remain promise-based is usually relatively short. Indeed, in practical terms, the approach I advocate would tend chiefly to affect those relatively marginal cases in which promises are revoked shortly after they are given, and before they have been paid for or relied upon.

The second ground for maintaining the binding force of an executory contract is, as I have suggested, that such a contract is essentially a way of allocating a risk, or perhaps of transferring a risk from one party to another in advance. Where this is indeed the case (as for example, with bets, or some forms of insurance) it seems that the arrangement must, if it is to have any point at all, be binding on the parties at the outset. But this argument is open to two possible answers. One is that most contracts are not in fact entered into for the purpose of transferring or allocating risks. If contracts are construed as being risk-allocation mechanisms, this is because they are often seen as such in the eye of the beholder. Pure risk-allocation contracts are relatively rare, and it may be that special considerations do apply to them. The second possible answer is that even in contracts of this nature an element of reliance is still needed before it becomes essential to maintain the integrity of the transaction. Even an executory insurance arrangement, for instance, could be made cancell-able so long as the insured still has time to find alternative cover. A person might, in principle, be given the right to withdraw from a bet on a race before the race is run, so long as the other party has time to place his own bet elsewhere at similar odds. There would be nothing logically impossible about such a possibility though it might be inconvenient.

The third ground for the creation of promise-based liabilities is also, I suggest, very weak in comparison with the grounds for the creation of benefit-based and reliance-based obligations. For this ground is, in effect, nothing more than an argument for the use of promise-based liability as a subsidiary method of ensuring compliance with benefit-based and reliance-based obligations. There are, of course, great difficulties in arguing that promise-based liabilities should be observed even though there is no independent justification for their observance, in order that reliance-based and benefit-based obligations should be better observed. Now it cannot be claimed that the case for the enforcement of promise-based liabilities is entirely vitiated by these difficulties, because the fact that my approach is so unorthodox itself testifies to the practical strength of this argument. Both morally and legally, promise-based liabilities *have* traditionally been thought worthy of protection, even where there has been no element of reliance or reciprocal benefit. It seems certain, therefore, that where there is some element of reliance or benefit, the case for redress has been felt *a fortiori* to be the more powerful. This too, I suggest, is part of the cultural heritage which I explore further in this book, and it is enough to say here that the whole trend of modern times is against arguments of principle of this character. It appears more in accord with contemporary beliefs to reject the argument of principle, and to insist upon the difference (for example) between maintaining the sanctity of a promise or contract because it has been relied upon, and because it might have been (but was not) relied upon. What is lacking is a theoretical or conceptual (and perhaps even linguistic) recognition of these differences.

In suggesting that these ideas are, at least intuitively or implicitly, gaining much ground today, and in advocating open recognition of these facts, it does not follow that I approve or disapprove of them. The nature of the conflict of values which underlies this question will become clear during the course of this book, but in its essentials the conflict is perfectly plain. Promise-based liability rests upon a belief in the traditional liberal values of free choice. Many still admire these values but they bring with them, inescapably, many other consequences which are today less admired, especially in England. They bring, in particular, the recognition that some individuals are better equipped to exercise free choice than others, through natural aptitude, education, or the possession of wealth. And the greater is the scope for the exercise of free choice, the stronger is the tendency for these original inqualities to perpetuate themselves by maintaining or even increasing economic inequalities. For example, in contracts which really are risk-allocation arrangements, to hold the contract binding must, in general, favour the party who has the better skill and knowledge for assessing future risks.

By contrast, other forms of liability rest on different values. Even benefit-based liability, though it may tend to perpetuate existing inequalities of wealth, does at least militate against increasing those inequalities in the way in which promise-based liabilities may do. For where liabilities are benefit-based, the law (or the moral norms) strive for a reasonable or just balance in the reciprocity of benefit; where liabilities are promise-based the free choice of the parties determines this balance, and it is inevitable that this will tend to favour those better able to exercise free choice.

Reliance-based liabilities are still more hostile to the values of free choice. As soon as liabilities come to be placed upon a person in whom another has reposed trust or reliance, even though there is no explicit promise or agreement to bear that liability, the door is opened to a species of liability which does not depend upon a belief in individual responsibility and free choice. Not only is the party relied upon held liable without his promise, but the party relying is relieved from the consequences of his own actions. The values involved in this type of liability are therefore closely associated with a paternalist social philosophy, and a redistributive economic system. This book is not the place for a full exploration of these questions, but it claims at least to offer some explanations for the origins of the present traditional approach to promissory and contractual obligations.

Part I

The Beginnings of Freedom of Contract: The Story to 1770

2

THE CONDITION OF ENGLAND IN 1770

THE POLITICAL BACKGROUND

By 1770 the central features of the Revolution settlement of 1688 had become an unquestioned part of the firmament. George III had been on the throne for ten years, and though he may not have enjoyed great personal popularity, he was at least a Protestant, and he was (what neither of the first two Georges had been) manifestly an Englishman. A man would have had to be some 60 years old to remember a pre-Hanoverian monarch, and it was twenty-five years since the Stuarts had been finally disposed of as a serious threat to the political order. Politically, England enjoyed a solid and stable system of government. 'The conflicts over sovereignty which had made seventeenth-century history had been settled by the demonstration in the years following 1688 that parliament, the king, lords and commons in parliament assembled, was a legally sovereign body.'[1] Even the Parliamentary wrangles, the political and personality squabbles—one can hardly call them party divisions—which had characterized political affairs since the resignation of Walpole some thirty years earlier, had not seriously weakened or even threatened the basic constitutional order. Parliament's prestige had never been higher. The presence of a great galaxy of orators and debaters, and the relative weakness of the executive branch of government, divided as its powers were between the king and a succession of office holders without modern party supporters, meant that major political decisions were actually made openly in Parliament as the result of debate and discussion.

It is true that—at the lower order of things—there had been what today one would be tempted to call political instability, as one short-lived administration succeeded another. But in the absence of a serious party system, this instability had arisen primarily as a result of personalities, of fluctuations in the royal favour, and of conflicts over foreign policy. Fundamental domestic discord in terms of national policy was not an important feature of eighteenth-century politics, precisely because the basic causes of domestic discord of the previous century had been so largely removed by the Revolution settlement. Moreover, even this degree of instability was now coming to an end. In 1770 Lord North began his twelve-year period of office as the King's Chief Minister, and when he finally fell, he was succeeded, after a short turbulent

[1] J. Steven Watson, *The Reign of George III 1760–1815* (Oxford, 1960), p. 55.

interregnum, by the young William Pitt. Pitt held office for the last sixteen years of the eighteenth century, and, after a brief interval, from 1801 to 1804, he was back in office from 1804 to 1806. During Pitt's terms of office, the party divisions largely re-established themselves (despite the later split among the Whigs), and fear of the new revolutionary ideologies from France itself proved a powerful impetus to stability.

Throughout this period there was never any doubt what class of the people held political power. The influence of the King might ebb and flow, the influence of Ministers amongst themselves, and as between themselves and Parliament, might fluctuate, but taken over all there is no question but that the central political power in the nation was in the hands of the landed aristocracy. By far the greater part of the country's wealth still consisted of its land, and a very large part of this land was still held by the great magnates who sat in the House of Lords. The upper House was, of course, politically more influential then than it became in the twentieth century, but even the House of Commons was to a substantial degree dominated by the great landowners. Many peers' sons sat in the Commons, and a large number of seats, especially in the rural areas, were in effect at the complete disposal of the great landowners. And if the great landowners dominated the national political scene, it was the small landowners—the country gentry—who ran local affairs in the country areas. Most effective local power in the country had been in the hands of the Justices of the Peace since Tudor times. The country justices combined a role of social leadership with a general administrative, judicial, and police function which in practice made them local despots. Lack of modern means of communication and travel left them very largely free of central government supervision, and though the Secretary of State had a vague oversight of their activities, he was unlikely to act on his own initiative unless moved by some serious complaint. But there was, in fact, little need for the central government to supervise the local justices. As Crown appointees, and as themselves small landowners, their interests were apt to coincide with those of the great landowners. Many of them sat as M.P.s where they rubbed shoulders with the great. And it must be remembered, too, that much of the land occupied by the local gentry was only rented by them and actually belonged to the great lords. This was, after all, a time when the only significant class barrier was that which divided those who owned property from those who did not. Those who did own property were an extraordinarily small number, much of whose strength derived from their cohesiveness. 'Everybody who counted at all in society or the government of the country was known to everybody else in the same circle.'[2]

[2] Basil Williams, *The Whig Supremacy 1714–1760*, 2nd edn., by C. H. Stuart (Oxford, 1962), p. 146.

Moreover, it would be naïve in the extreme to conclude that this state of affairs was somehow an untoward result of the Revolution of 1688. It is unnecessary to adopt a crude Marxist version of history to recognize that the seventeenth-century struggles were just as much about property rights as they were about constitutional power; indeed, it is impossible to separate the two matters, since one of the principal motives which drove the propertied classes to fight for constitutional power was the desire to protect what they conceived of as their property. It is true that, in the eighteenth century, the 'glorious revolution' came to be celebrated more because it preserved the 'liberties of Englishmen' than because it preserved their property, but that is hardly surprising. The number of property owners was so very small in proportion to the total population that the Revolution of 1688 would have seemed a good deal less 'glorious' to the mass of the people had they been told that one of its primary objectives was to preserve the property rights of the aristocracy.

That is not to say, of course, that the Revolution of 1688 did not greatly enhance the liberties of Englishmen. Quite apart from the reduction in the power of the Crown which was implicit in the very Revolution itself, civil and political liberties had been greatly strengthened by a number of constitutional and legal developments around the same time. Amongst these were, of course, the Habeas Corpus Act 1679, *Bushel's* case in 1671,[3] holding juries not to be accountable for their verdicts, the provisions of the Act of Settlement ensuring the independence of the judges, and the prohibition of the maintenance of a standing army without Parliamentary authorization. As Christopher Hill has said, England after 1688 was 'for the propertied class an exceptionally free society by contemporary European standards.'[4]

As the eighteenth century wore on, and the landed aristocracy itself became increasingly associated with the executive branch of government, the very measures they had obtained to protect themselves against the Crown began to be used against them by the people. No doubt traditional and legal and 'Whig' historians may have exaggerated the impartiality of the judges and the integrity of the rule of law, but neither was wholly mythical.[5] There must have been many occasions when eighteenth-century Ministers regretted the independence of the judiciary and the non-accountability of juries. If the propertied classes had fooled the people into thinking that it was *their* liberties which were at stake in 1688, the London mob had no doubt whose liberties were involved when they shouted 'Wilkes and Liberty' or when juries awarded huge damages

[3] Vaughan 135; 124 E.R. 1006.

[4] Christopher Hill, *Reformation to Industrial Revolution* (Pelican Economic History of Britain, vol. ii, revised ed., Harmondsworth, 1969), p. 144.

[5] See, especially, E. P. Thompson, *Whigs and Hunters* (London, 1975).

against the Secretary of State for authorizing an illegal search of Wilkes's house.[6] Habeas corpus, jury trial, and (despite all government efforts) a relatively free press did make England—even for the poor—the freest country in Europe, perhaps the world. Most Englishmen in 1770 would have heartily concurred in Blackstone's encomiums on the law and constitution as protectors of freedom.

But it is, in any event, probably misleading to separate the ideas of liberty and property in this way. It was not for their civil liberties that the city merchants feared when Charles I seized their money on deposit in the Mint and treated it as a loan; it was not merely for political purposes that the propertied classes complained about the Crown's rights of 'purveyance' (i.e. the right to purchase goods for Royal and Court consumption at below market price);[7] it was not merely their respect for due process of law which led them to protest at huge and arbitrary fines being imposed upon them,[8] it was not merely a hostility to royal monopolists which led landowners to object to prerogative claims over mineral rights on their land.[9] The truth was that the propertied class trembled for their property under the Stuarts.

But it is true also that the very concept of property was itself changing. The freedom of property which the Whigs had wrested from the Crown had no more ancient and respectable a lineage than the constitutional rights which they had obtained. What had happened in both cases was that men's ideas had changed; just as changing ideas about the relative rights of Kings, Lords, and Commons had brought to a head questions to which there had never been a clear legal answer, so also changing ideas about the nature of property rights had brought to a head questions concerning the relationship between Crown and subject. In medieval times the relation between the Crown and its tenants had been both governmental and, in a sense, contractual. The rents paid by the Crown's tenants were both taxes and recompense for the value of the land. Only gradually was the economic-rent idea separated from the tax idea. The abolition of feudal tenures in 1660 and the creation of new excise taxes marked a fundamental shift in ideas about land as private property. It was this change which 'truly created modern landed property . . . [The great lords] resolved themselves from tenants into owners.'[10] And the smaller landowners were also benefiting by parallel changes. For

---

[6] *Wilkes* v. *Wood* (1763) 1 Lofft 1; 98 E.R. 489; *Huckle* v. *Money* (1763) 2 Wils. K.B. 205; 95 E.R. 768. In both cases the real defendant was Lord Halifax.

[7] Christopher Hill, *Reformation to Industrial Revolution*, pp. 105, 173.

[8] For example, £3,000 for calling Laud 'a treasonable papist', and £10,000 for slandering the Lord Keeper and the Court of Star Chamber: Hill, op. cit., pp. 114, 122.

[9] Ibid., p. 173.

[10] J. Commons, *Legal Foundations of Capitalism* (Madison, Milwaukee, London, 1968), pp. 219–20; Hill, op. cit., p. 145.

inflation was destroying the value of old feudal rents payable by freeholders. A freeholder now began to see himself as an owner.

But although it may have been the propertied classes who now held the political power and who made the rules, at least they did abide by rule, and not by arbitrary fiat.[11] As had happened with liberty, it became possible, in particular cases, for the laws of property to be used against the great and powerful, and even, occasionally, for them to be used by the weak and poor. Every law student has heard of *Armory* v. *Delamirie*[12] in which the Court of King's Bench in 1722 enforced the right of a chimney sweeper's boy to a jewel which he had found, against the defendant goldsmith to whom the boy had taken it to be valued. Such cases were, of course, rare. And when the rights of the poor were a serious threat or nuisance to the governing classes it was possible, though not always easy, to legislate them out of existence, as with the Enclosure Acts. But what was significant about the Enclosure Acts was not that so many of them were readily passed by a property-owning Parliament, but that in general, a meticulous respect for fair compensation and due process was in fact observed. The Enclosure Acts did not provide for simple confiscation of the rights of common of which the poor were generally deprived. Whatever the Enclosure Acts may demonstrate about the attitudes of the propertied classes to the rights of the poor, they certainly did not demonstrate any lack of respect for rights of property.[13]

The English class system, and the place of the aristocracy in it, had never been a rigid caste system even in the Middle Ages. It had always been relatively easy to rise at least to the rank of a gentleman, to become a member of the gentry, although it was less easy to rise into the aristocracy itself. Even in the sixteenth century there was a sense in which 'blue blood was purchasable'.[14] In the seventeenth century the convulsions produced by the civil war had greatly loosened up the existing divisions in all classes of society, and the growing importance of trade as a source of wealth led to the rise of the merchants. The difficulty of drawing a line between the gentry and those below them became steadily more marked. 'The upward tracks to gentility through the Church, the law and the counting-house were more frequented than

[11] See E. P. Thompson, *Whigs and Hunters*, pp. 263–4.

[12] (1722) 1 Stra. 505, 93 E.R. 664.

[13] The Marxist view of the Enclosure Acts as ruthless expropriation of the property rights of the poor was largely adopted by the Hammonds in *The Village Labourer 1760–1832* (London, 1911). This 'classic study' unfortunately overlooks a mass of evidence, much of which was already available in 1911, showing, for example, that in very many parishes the smallest landowners had largely disappeared even before the eighteenth century, and also showing that the work of enclosure was generally done fairly and with due respect for the rights of the poor. See, generally, G. E. Mingay's Introduction to the 2nd edition (London, 1966) of E. C. K. Gonner, *Common Land and Enclosure* (1st edn., London 1912) and works there cited.

[14] Christopher Hill, *Reformation to Industrial Revolution*, p. 51.

ever, and they grew broader as the nation's business grew more complicated.'[15] By the seventeenth century many merchants were richer than the great landowners, and throughout the eighteenth century these *nouveaux riches* aspired, through marriage, or the purchase of land, to the social status of the aristocracy, while preserving their political and commercial independence. Even in the middle of the eighteenth century, the heyday of the Whig aristocracy, when luxury and ostentation appeared everywhere in the great new palaces of the magnates, and when the social rank of a peer counted for more than it has perhaps ever done, before or since, the English nobility seemed a poor thing by comparison with the French. And it was certainly less based on birth.[16]

There was another important point. As the collective power of the landed classes had grown, there is a sense in which their individual powers had declined. In earlier periods, the legal and social privileges of the great lords, not to mention the physical powers they could wield with the aid of bands of retainers, had given them an important role as powerful 'protectors' of individuals less fortunately placed. Merchants and city burgesses often thrived or languished according to the power and favour of some great protector. By the mid-eighteenth century this situation had almost totally disappeared. 'High connections' or friends in 'high places' could still be invaluable in a great variety of ways—this remained true for many years after 1770—but this was not the lawless protection of the great lords of old. Eighteenth-century patronage operated in a more structured way, against the background of settled laws and conventions. Of course, part of the reason for this change was, once again, the fact that the landed magnates, having acquired the political power in the state, themselves largely made the laws and conventions under which they operated. But, as with liberties, and as with property, the rules and conventions, though made by the propertied class, could occasionally be used against them. Perhaps this did not happen to any significant degree before the end of the eighteenth century, in the case of patronage (as it had, for instance, with liberties and property). Indeed, not until the second half of the nineteenth century did 'connections' and patronage begin to have that association with bribery and corruption which they have today; but even so, the fact that they operated within a fairly settled framework of conventions was not unimportant. For it all helped to create that sense of stability, order, and regularity, as opposed to unpredictability and arbitrariness in government and law which were the very essence of eighteenth-century England; and even if this stability, order, and regularity was sometimes

---

[15] Sir George Clark, *The Wealth of England* (London, New York, Toronto, 1946, reprinted 1965), p. 160.
[16] Christopher Hill, *Reformation to Industrial Revolution*, p. 139.

a sham, even if the rules and conventions could be bent to suit some individual interest, the appearance gradually transmuted into the reality. People who habitually behaved as if they were subject to laws and conventions of their own making gradually came to accept their subservience as a fact.

THE MACHINERY OF GOVERNMENT

In modern times the words 'the Government' have come to be used almost exclusively to signify the Ministers of the Crown who collectively and individually are responsible for supervising the execution of the policy of the governing party. Sometimes the term is more loosely used to embrace Parliament as well. Except in this extended sense there was no real Government at all in 1770; the office of Prime Minister had still not really come into being, there was certainly no collective responsibility in the modern sense, and Ministers could still be drawn from differing parties. Moreover, the King still played a much more important role in the selection both of his chief minister and of the other office holders. But it is nevertheless easy to recognize at least in embryonic form the modern machinery of Government if we use the words in their widest modern sense. The sovereign, the House of Lords, the House of Commons, the first lord of the Treasury and the Secretaries of State are still with us. The House of Lords is still presided over by the Lord Chancellor and the Commons by Mr. Speaker. The formal processes involved in the enactment of legislation have changed little; even the courtesies of debate—the 'honourable member', the 'noble lord'—are still much the same. If we extend the concept of 'the Government' a little further so as to include the law courts, here too, on the surface, little has changed. Here too, many of the titles are still recognizable—the Queen's Bench, the Chancery; the styles of dress and address have changed little—'my learned friend' still makes his submissions 'with great respect' to 'his lordship' on the Bench. Judges and jurymen still divide responsibility for trials on indictment in a way which is at least recognizable as that which prevailed two hundred years ago. The office of Lord Chief Justice is still the greatest judicial office in England. Judges still acknowledge the supremacy of Parliament in the law-making process. And so on. But there is a wider sense to the term 'Government' in which the changes have been profound.

In a very broad sense, the term 'Government' includes the whole machinery of Government of the State; it includes the whole process by which the people are governed, by which authority is exercised, order is maintained, and the physical power of the State can, if need arise, be brought to bear on the recalcitrant. In the modern democratic State this machinery of Government is almost invariably characterized by three principal features. First, there is the existence of a large centralized bureaucracy, directly employed by and under the control of, the executive branch of the Government. Secondly, legal power is diffused throughout a considerable number of persons and institutions, each of which has some clearly allotted function, a fairly well-defined legal authority, and its own bureaucratic staff.[17] And thirdly, the telephone, the police force, and the car, mean that the physical power of the State can be brought to bear in almost any inch of the country in a very short space of time. The nearest policeman is rarely more than a few minutes away from the nearest telephone. These three essential features of the modern Governmental machine were almost entirely absent in 1770 England. There *was* no vast bureaucracy then or for many years to come. There was not even a proper Home Office until 1782.[18] There was no careful and rational allocation of legal power to offices and institutions through the country. Actual power, of a traditional kind, some lawful, some of dubious legality, and some downright illegal, was certainly exercised by a variety of officials and institutions; but they themselves lacked a supporting bureaucracy, they had no role as part of any overall planned governmental machinery, and sometimes the same functions were placed under the jurisdiction of two or more bodies, while others were the responsibility of none. The result was 'an amazing hotch-potch of authorities and conflicting institutions, on all and every one of which parliament tended periodically to impose new duties with hardly any provision for the due performance of these or any of the older functions.'[19] And the absence of the third essential feature of the modern State—the ability to bring physical power to bear anywhere, any time—was, of course, due to the absence of precisely those things which make it such a simple matter today—the telephone, the police, and the car.

The absence in 1770 of so much of what is taken for granted today as part of the machinery of Government, is, in many respects, one of the most profound differences between eighteenth- and twentieth-century society; and it is likely that it also had a great impact on ideas. It was Lord Shelburne, and no nineteenth-century statesman, who declared

[17] I do not, of course, mean to imply that in the swollen Governmental machine of the 1970s there may not be some office or institutions whose functions are unclear or whose legal authority may be difficult to ascertain. But over all the present position simply bears no comparison with that of the 1770s.

[18] Until that date there had normally been two Secretaries of State, one for the Northern Department in charge of business relating to Northern Europe, and one for the Southern Department who looked after France and the southern countries. Home Affairs went indifferently to either. 'The arrangement led to endless confusion and difficulties; and nothing but an obstinate conservatism could have retained it for more than a hundred years after it had become useless.' Sir Edward Troup, *The Home Office*, 2nd edn. (London and New York, 1926), p. 18.

[19] Basil Williams, *The Whig Supremacy*, p. 45.

that 'Providence has so ordered the world that very little government is necessary.'[20] It is, therefore, worth pausing to reflect on the implications of these differences.

The first point that needs to be made is that if a Government does not have a staff under its own immediate control there is very little that it can actually *do* itself. If Government wants something done, it will have to contract for it, or farm the task out to someone else who can contract for it. But in the first part of George III's reign there was no distinct public purse out of which payments could be made to contractors. In 1760, when George III succeeded to the throne, Parliament voted him £800,000 per annum for the duration of his reign, out of which he was expected to defray the entire cost of the civil and foreign service.[21] Except for the armed services and one or two exceptional items all Government expenditure was expected to be paid for out of this sum. The very idea of public money—as distinguished from the King's private revenue—had not yet been developed. It is, therefore, not surprising that the idea of public services being provided at the public expense was slow in developing. It seemed much more natural to farm out the jobs that needed to be done to officials or institutions who could then raise the money needed to defray the cost of the services by charging for their use. This was, in fact, a common feature of eighteenth-century government. Large numbers of Private Acts were passed setting up Commissioners to carry out various 'public' works, such as paving or lighting streets, building roads and bridges, laying drains and sewers, and giving them the power to levy tolls or rates to defray the cost of the works. Even workhouses and prisons were often farmed out to contractors.[22] Commissioners, or contractors, did it matter which they were called? Were they public or private bodies? The question is largely meaningless. In many respects they acted as private bodies; certainly it was often on their own initiatives that the necessary local or private legislation was passed. No Government department stood beside them, or supported them, or bailed them out if they overspent, or stood behind them if they were sued. No Government department planned, or co-ordinated their activities; who was to do the work of planning and co-ordination? Where was the necessary information, expertise, and money to come from? After all, in many cities it was still thought to be the responsibility of each householder to pave the road in front of his door, and remove his own filth and sewage.[23] If a few citizens co-operated in securing a Private Act

---

[20] J. Steven Watson, *The Reign of George III*, p. 9. Lord Shelburne later the Marquis of Lansdowne, was the great-grandson of Sir William Petty (1623–87) one of England's earliest economic liberals, and in all respects a very remarkable man.

[21] J. Steven Watson, op. cit., p. 61.   [22] Basil Williams, *The Whig Supremacy*, p. 135.

[23] Dorothy George, 'London and the Life of the Town', in *Johnson's England*, ed. A. S. Turberville (Oxford, 1933), p. 169.

to enable them to do the work a little more efficiently, and to compel the shirkers, or freeriders, to pay their share of the cost, this did not mean that the Government was taking over the job. In retrospect, we know that these early Commissioners represented in many respects the beginnings of modern English local government authorities; but it did not seem so at the time.

All this may help to explain why, even when real social evils were known to exist, little or nothing often seems to have been done. Two notable examples concern the dreadful fate of pauper children in early eighteenth-century London, and the appalling evils associated with drink in the first half of the century. The drink problem was to some extent brought under control by taxes and licensing by the end of George II's reign—passing laws was relatively easy and cheap—but virtually nothing was done over the problem of pauper children. That would have required administrative machinery, a bureaucracy, to enforce, and no such machinery existed. The principal features of Parliamentary Government may have been settled by the Revolution of 1688, but the problems of *administration* had not even been seriously perceived a hundred years later. And the reasons for this were in large part twofold. First, the problems themselves were generally far less acute prior to the industrialization and urbanization of the country, processes which had barely begun by 1770. England, at this time, it is hard to appreciate, was still a simple agricultural community; its urban centres consisted of one large metropolis, one other city of around one hundred thousand people (Bristol), and a dozen or so small market towns with populations of perhaps 10,000 to 30,000; the remainder of the population lived in the country or in small villages of which the largest and most prosperous numbered barely three or four thousand persons.[24] Descriptions of London life in mid-eighteenth century, while no doubt real enough and grim enough, may seriously mislead the modern reader who may fail to remember the uniqueness of London at this period. The problems of governing and administering a city the size of London in 1770 were beyond the administrative and perhaps the scientific skills and resources of the time; but the rest of the country largely ran itself.

The second reason for the failure to deal with, or even largely to perceive, the administrative problems of the time owed much more to the state of mind of the propertied classes, and to their ideas about the proper role of Government in society. This is a theme to which I will return, but it is necessary to grasp the fact that—naturally enough—Government

[24] G. D. H. Cole, 'Town Life in the Provinces', in *Johnson's England*, pp. 203-4. The population of Manchester in 1769 was about 30,000, of Liverpool about 34,500, of Birmingham (1770) about 30,000. Hull, Sheffield, and Norwich each had between 20,000 to 30,000 inhabitants, Nottingham, Leeds, and Chester, some 15,000 to 17,000. Few other towns had a population exceeding 10,000 at this time.

did not seem to these people to be something separate from, and imposed on the nation from outside, as it were. It was *their* Government, created *by* them, for *their* purposes. This way of looking at things was, of course, supported by historical truth, as well as by the ideas of Locke, to whose influence I will return later. Here it is enough to stress a few key points. First, English political institutions were at this time largely built on the supposition that England was a property owners' association. Government and Parliament were the organs of the property owners, much as the executive committee and annual general meeting are the organs of many lesser associations. The judges were appointed to punish crime (which threatened the lives and security of the property owners) and to settle disputes between property owners. We have already seen how one very natural result of this attitude of mind was the belief that only the propertied classes were entitled to participate in Government at all; those who had no property had no vote. Not only did they have nothing to protect, and hence have no need to participate in Government, but it was also assumed that it was very largely against the propertiless classes that protection was needed anyhow. If they did have the vote, what was to stop them plundering the property of those who possessed it? Another very natural result of this was that the property owners were very much more conscious of the cost of their self-protecting association. If it was their property which was being defended, they knew, or at least they thought, that they were bearing the cost of its protection. This also affected the attitudes of these people to administrative problems.

There was another factor, too: a somewhat circular one. Inefficient and corrupt administration—and wherever there *was* administration in the eighteenth century it was nearly always inefficient and (by our standards) corrupt—tends to breed a distrust of more administration. Much of the inefficiency and even the corruption were the result of the very system of nepotism and patronage that the aristocratic social structure necessitated. The system of land tenure which the great Whigs developed after 1688—especially the 'strict settlement' about which more will be said later—helped to preserve the great landed estates in the hands of eldest sons, and to prevent their fragmentation and dispersal through the normal processes of succession. The same system made it necessary to find other openings, and other sources of income, for younger sons. These openings were found in the Church, the law, the armed services, and in nepotism and patronage. Those who played the game according to the rules of the time probably saw little wrong in doing so. In many cases, patronage was itself seen as a form of property right which could be bought and sold. And if a man purchased with hard cash the right to appoint a younger son to an office he naturally looked upon this as a form of investment, a property right, which one day he could sell in his turn. But although the propertied classes may have seen little wrong in all this, the inevitable result was inefficient administration. The appointment of unqualified, perhaps incompetent, and frequently irremovable relatives and friends to minor administrative offices was clearly no way to create a modern and efficient administrative system. Whenever anyone brought forward proposals for change or reform which would have the effect of creating new offices, the cynical assumed that the primary purpose of the change was to provide new outlets for patronage. Naturally, at any given moment, those who would benefit from these outlets were fewer than those who would have to pay the cost. Naturally, therefore, even those who played the game according to the rules, were apt to look unfavourably on such proposals for change. This attitude prevailed until well into the nineteenth century.

The second chief implication of the general absence of an adequate machinery of Government at this period concerned the very foundations of society itself—the maintenance of law and order. It is today difficult to appreciate the very thin line which separated—and was perceived to separate—the civilized, elegant, and cultured society of the eighteenth-century aristocracy from the darkness and chaos of mob rule. If the property owners tenaciously protected their property—clung to their privileges, as many would say today—it was partly at least because they knew how precariously they were held, and how easy it would be to dislodge them. There was, it must be remembered, no organized police force, and no permanent standing army on English soil, throughout the eighteenth century. The physical force available to Government—especially at short notice—was by modern standards unbelievably feeble. The rebellion of 1745—the last Stuart attempt to restore their fortunes—had shown how a ragged, ill-equipped, and undisciplined force could march half-way across England without serious opposition. In the country areas the absence of a police force may not have been a serious problem. Strangers were readily recognized, and the social status of the local squire meant that it was usually easy for him, with a handful of picked and loyal stalwarts, to quell most minor disorders. In peaceful times—and the eighteenth century was generally a very peaceful time in England—the country was easily controlled. But if times were troubled, if harvests were bad, and the poor were short of food, disorders and violence (for example, in poaching) were frequent and not easily controlled.

In London the position was infinitely worse. The London mob was a significant force in eighteenth-century England. Though generally good-natured, the populace expected to be humoured, and, any attempt to curtail what they regarded as their customary rights, could spark off a riot which would not easily be quelled.[25] The worst of the eighteenth-century London riots still lay in the future in 1770—those terrible days in 1780 when the whole of London was given over to the destruction and plunder of the mob, when the lords and members of Parliament went in danger of their lives, and the house of the Lord Chief Justice of the King's Bench was burned to the ground. But lesser riots were a commonplace, and even these were enough to make the governing classes aware of the delicate knife edge on which their civilization constantly trembled. After the outbreak of the French Revolution, they were, of course, even more aware of it, but in 1770 that still lay many years in the future.

It was not only mobs and riots that threatened property. Petty thieving and robbery were also commonplace, especially in parts of London. Nobody, however highly placed, was safe from the threat of molestation, especially after dark in isolated places. In 1753 the King himself had been relieved of his watch, money, and shoe buckles while strolling alone in the gardens of Kensington Palace.[26] And the highwaymen who intercepted travellers on their way to and from London certainly did not have, to their victims, the romantic associations which later ages have bestowed upon them, any more than the muggers of today.

What is so remarkable about eighteenth-century England is that despite these dangers, despite the absence of police, of proper machinery for the maintenance of law and order, the country was generally so peaceful. The general impression one has of mid-eighteenth-century England is that of a country accustoming itself to stability and solidity.[27] If there were deep-rooted and underlying conflicts they remained latent and did not result in major change. Law and order, too, were becoming better secured. Organized and long-lived lawlessness had disappeared, although unorganized and short-lived lawlessness continued to be a serious social problem until the middle of the nineteenth century. In other respects, also, the irregularity, insecurity, and unpredictability of life was lessening. The threats to overseas trade of piracy, shipwreck, or the hostility of distant powers, was growing less all the time as the Royal Navy began to acquire world-wide command of the seas; the natural calamities of life at home, such as fire, famine, and pestilence seemed to strike less frequently—and not entirely by chance. London had been rebuilt after the Great Fire in the past century in a way which paid some regard to the need to prevent a similar conflagration. And in 1772 a new Code of building regulations for London was enacted in the Metropolitan Building Act. Even the streets of London, despite the mob, seemed

[25] Dorothy George, 'London and the Life of the Town', pp. 184–5.
[26] Basil Williams, The Whig Supremacy, p. 138, n.1.
[27] For a somewhat different view, see E. P. Thompson, Whigs and Hunters.

generally more peaceful than those in many a European town. Foreigners who visited England were impressed by the paradox that London without police was on the whole more law-abiding than Paris or other European cities which were heavily policed.[28] That this sense of security, and of the ability to plan for the future, was becoming continuously stronger, is as important for present purposes as how it came about. But, in the absence of police and an adequate machinery of government, that too is an important and puzzling question. Was there, in fact, a reign of terror behind the bland façade, a mailed fist behind the velvet glove? The bloody penal code of eighteenth-century law may seem to give an affirmative answer to these questions. But this is a question which needs to be deferred until we turn our attention to the Law.

THE STATE OF THE ECONOMY

What sort of society was it over which the landed classes presided? What was the source of this wealth and property which they were so concerned about? We have seen that England was still in 1770 a fundamentally agricultural country, and its economy largely reflected this fact. It was still a sparsely populated country; in 1760 England and Wales probably numbered some seven million persons, about one-seventh of the modern population; by 1770 this number must have increased slightly on its way up to the figure of some nine million revealed by the first (not wholly reliable) census of 1801. We have already seen that, except for London and Bristol, the country did not support any towns exceeding 100,000, or indeed 50,000, in number. Nevertheless, things were already changing rapidly in all directions. In 1688 nearly 90 per cent of the people were still engaged in agriculture;[29] by the 1760s Arthur Young estimated the figure at 2·8 million, or rather under 50 per cent.[30] These figures give some indication of the radical changes which were already taking place in the country's economic system. It would be beyond the scope of this work to explore these changes in detail, but some idea of their nature must be sketched because they were nearly all associated with the growth of trade and of the beginnings of a market economy.

Already in the sixteenth and early seventeenth centuries the expansion

---

[28] Dorothy George, 'London and the Life of the Town', pp. 184-5. Compare E. P. Thompson, *The Making of the English Working Class* (London, 1963) p. 62: 'The British people were noted throughout Europe for their turbulence, and the people of London astonished foreign visitors by their lack of deference.' Thompson sees this as a sign of oppression, while contemporary observers saw it as a sign of liberty (or even licence).

[29] Christopher Hill, *Reformation to Industrial Revolution*, p. 61.

[30] Basil Williams, *The Whig Supremacy*, p. 105. Arthur Young was a farmer who left a record of his travels in the 1760s in which he carefully noted a great many observations concerning agricultural wages and costs, as well as many other social and industrial matters.

of London had created a large market for agricultural produce grown within reach of the capital; and as other cities grew, and more of the people moved into non-agricultural work, the demand for the production of food for sale naturally grew apace. The meeting of this demand and other changes associated with it, all involved steady movement to a market economy. First, the improvements in transport and communication were becoming very noticeable by 1770. Apart from the expansion of coastal shipping, the first major development had been the increase, through clearance, in the mileage of the navigable rivers; the second major development, proceeding apace by 1770, was the considerable improvements being effected in the roads by the new Turnpike Trusts; and the third was the beginning of the canal era around 1760. The canals played a most important role in reducing the costs of transport of bulky articles; they halved the price of coal in Manchester. These changes helped to create a national market throughout the country, a market already enlarged by the union with Scotland in 1707 which had created 'the largest free trade area in the world'.[31]

The changes in the institutional relationships of those involved with the land were also proceeding in the same direction. On the one hand, as we have already seen, the relationship of the landlord and tenant of agricultural land had changed. The older feudal type relationship had been obsolete for many years even before the abolition of feudal dues in 1660. As these dues had waned in importance, the great inflation of the early seventeenth century had led to their replacement by economic rents. And the relationship between the tenant and the agricultural labourer was also changing, or perhaps it would be more accurate to say, was coming to affect a much larger number of people. The landless agricultural labourer—who began increasingly to be the typical 'working class' person of the eighteenth century—was coming to be a person who sold his labour to the tenant farmer in an impersonal, if free, economy. Already in the seventeenth century something like half the adult male population were full-time wage earners, while many 'cottagers' engaged in domestic industrial labour, were part-time wage earners. Well before the end of the seventeenth century the majority of those later to be known as the 'working class' were life-long wage earners.[32] These changes did not, of course, occur without stress. When labour became increasingly a market commodity something had to be done for those who could not labour; and by 1700 over 20 per cent of the population was on poor relief.[33]

By the middle of the eighteenth century the three-tiered pattern of

[31] Christopher Hill, *Reformation to Industrial Revolution*, p. 224.
[32] Godfrey Davies, *The Early Stuarts* (Oxford, 1945), p. 271.
[33] Christopher Hill, *Reformation to Industrial Revolution*, pp. 258-9.

English agriculture was becoming established. '[I]t is clear', writes E. J. Hobsbawm,

that by 1750 the characteristic structure of English landownership was already discernible: a few thousand landowners, leasing out their land to some tens of thousand of tenant farmers, who in turn operated it with the labour of some hundreds of thousands of farm labourers, servants or dwarf holders who hired themselves out for much of their time. This fact in itself implied a very substantial system of cash-incomes and cash sales.[34]

At the same time, there was a trend towards larger holdings by the farmers in the middle tier. The older idea that a holding should be sufficient to maintain a family and no more was giving way to belief in larger units, more responsive to substantial capital investment. Leases too were changing in a way that encouraged rational planning and investment. Covenants designed to maintain traditional but 'obsolete farming practices were tending to disappear. The old lease for three lives, frequently at a low rent, which the landlord might make good by a somewhat arbitrarily levied charge on renewal, was giving way to the fixed lease for seven, fourteen, or twenty-one years at fixed rentals.[35]

But if labour was becoming increasingly a marketable commodity, certain of the older social attitudes and legal restrictions still restricted the growth of a national market in labour. The difficulties and costs of personal travel were no less than those associated with the transport of goods before the great improvements which began around the mid-eighteenth century. Naturally these inhibited any significant movement of labourers. But in addition the Act of Settlement of 1662 made a labourer subject to removal to his former parish by order of the local justices merely because he might become chargeable to the parish. Despite this draconian legislation—which was not mitigated until 1795—there was some mobility of labour; indeed, it has been said that the Act of Settlement did not so much prohibit mobility as regulate it in the interests of the governing classes.[36]

These changes in the relationships between those concerned with agriculture were closely associated with changing methods of agricultural production. I have already referred to the Enclosure Acts, and it is necessary to bear in mind the great revolution, both socially and economically, which these Acts involved. In 1770 the enclosure movement was well under way. Over a thousand Enclosure Acts were

[34] *Industry and Empire* (Harmondsworth, 1974), p. 29. But the figures are somewhat misleading because the proportion of labourers to farmers was much smaller than this, perhaps seven to four in 1700, and eleven to four in 1830: J. D. Chambers and E. G. Mingay, *The Agricultural Revolution 1750–1880* (London, 1969), p. 18.

[35] T. S. Ashton, *Economic History of England in the Eighteenth Century* (London, 1955, reprinted, 1972), p. 35.

[36] Christopher Hill, *Reformation to Industrial Revolution*, pp. 177–9.

passed between 1761 and 1780, and another nine hundred between 1781 and 1800.[37] These Acts killed off the vestigial remains of the old communal system of farming, and greatly stimulated the incentive to invest in modern agricultural techniques. Expenditure on draining, research and experimentation in different crops and fertilizing methods, great advances in animal breeding, all these and many other improvements added up to an 'Agricultural Revolution' which preceded and in some respects contributed to the subsequent Industrial Revolution. From our point of view the importance of this Revolution lies in the fact that it represented part of the process by which agriculture was converted into a series of economic relationships. It came to be seen that capital could be profitably invested in land; that what was profitable could be the subject, despite all the uncertainties of farming, of rational economic calculations; that these calculations depended, among other things, on the market price of the produce, on the one hand, and of rents and the cost of labour, on the other hand.[38] By 1770 most of those concerned in this Agricultural Revolution would surely have agreed with the lament of Sir John Mason who had protested in 1550 about controlled prices in a letter to Cecil: 'For who will keep a cow that may not sell the milk for so much as the merchant and he can agree upon?'[39]

The growth of internal trade had, since 1688, also been paralleled by the growth of overseas trade. Cromwell's Navigation Act of 1651 had inaugurated a real national economic policy on overseas trade; henceforth merchants had been left to trade substantially free of economic regulation but within the general protective framework of national legislation. The day of the old monopolistic companies was also over for the Navigation Act represented 'the victory of a *national* trading interest over the separate interests and privileges of the old companies'.[40] By the 1760s the relationship of overseas trade and war potential was the key factor in the economy. The result was a pattern of trade imposed from Westminster by means of trade laws, embargoes, and duties. 'But within such a framework there was greater scope for free enterprise. Government was able to exercise less supervision of the conduct of either trade or industry at this time than in the later period of theoretical *laissez-faire*.'[41] By the mid-eighteenth century Britain's overseas trade had multiplied many times over, trade with the colonies surpassed trade with Europe, and England had outstripped even the Dutch as the greatest trading nation in the world. Commercial machinery was being developed, and obtaining legal recognition, to enable the merchants

[37] Basil Williams, *The Whig Supremacy*, p. 108.
[38] See J. D. Chambers and E. G. Mingay, *The Agricultural Revolution*.
[39] Tawney and Power, *Tudor Economic Documents* (London, 1924), ii. 188.
[40] Christopher Hill, *Reformation to Industrial Revolution*, p. 157; and see works there cited.
[41] J. Steven Watson, *The Reign of George III*, p. 25.

engaged in overseas trade to turn their capital over more rapidly. Adam Smith, it is true, was still remarking in 1776 that capital employed in foreign trade could only be turned over once a year, or even less frequently, while capital employed in home trade could be turned over a dozen times a year, although he also insisted that it was the opportunity to make large profits from overseas trade which nevertheless encouraged merchants to invest their capital in it.[42] Trade was becoming a major source of national, as of individual, wealth. By 1770, Britain was a rich country, perhaps the richest in the world. Foreign observers associated this prosperity with Britain's growth of trade, as well as with her political freedom, lack of regulation, and her relatively bourgeois aristocracy.[43]

Throughout the eighteenth century—indeed, almost from the very beginnings of the reign of William and Mary—another important economic process had been under way. This was the beginnings of the modern monetary, banking, and credit system, which by 1770 had reached a high degree of sophistication. Credit itself was, of course, nothing new. Personal loans and retail credit are probably as old as money and retail selling. But what was happening in the eighteenth century was the creation of a whole national credit economy whose function was the proper organization and use of the large quantity of capital now becoming available. Once again, any detailed account of these developments would be beyond my scope,[44] but some reference to them, however sketchy, is a necessary part of my theme. Here too the story is one of steadily increasing stability in financial affairs. Shortly after the Revolution of 1688 a great recoinage was carried out, and Governments began to accept the view of the City men that the value of money should be kept constant; the older idea that the value of money should be deliberately manipulated to suit the economic needs of the moment fell into disfavour.[45] In 1717 the value of the pound was defined in terms of a fixed quantity of the precious metals.[46] This was the real beginning of stability in the value of the currency although for another half-century varying relative prices of gold and silver meant that much silver was melted down and illegally exported. In 1774 the crucial step was taken of limiting silver as legal tender and this (together with a fixed gold-silver parity which had existed for some years) meant that 'the gold standard was silently established'.[47] This was, in a sense, the first and most essential precondition to the establishment of a credit economy; for

[42] *Wealth of Nations*, Book II, Chapter V.
[43] E. J. Hobsbawm, *Industry and Empire*, pp. 23–8.
[44] See P. G. M. Dickson, *The Financial Revolution in England 1688–1756* (London, Melbourne, Toronto, 1967).
[45] Sir George Clark, *The Wealth of England*, p. 183.
[46] Ibid., p. 184.
[47] T. S. Ashton, *Economic History of England in the Eighteenth Century*, p. 177.

a credit economy depends on the expectation and confidence of the creditor that what he ultimately receives will not be worth less than that which he now forgoes. Although we have discovered in recent years that an established credit economy can continue to survive despite persistent changes in the value of money, it has also become increasingly evident that in periods of violent and unpredictable fluctuations the credit system comes under considerable stress; and what is true of an established system is infinitely more true of one in process of being established.

The second precondition to the credit economy was the existence of an adequate banking system. This, too, largely came into existence during the century following the Revolution of 1688. Indeed, the beginnings are clearly discernible before the Revolution. By the 1670s it is possible to identify the three essential characteristics of banking in the activities of the Goldsmiths, that is, the taking of deposits, the discounting of bills, and the issuing of notes.[48] Cheques were known by 1675.[49] In 1694 the Bank of England was established, and in the eighteenth century banking developed fast. In 1750 there were scarcely a dozen 'bankers' shops' outside London; by 1793 there were nearly four hundred provincial banks in existence in embryonic form;[50] most of these early provincial bankers were primarily engaged in other forms of business which necessitated their having accounts with the Bank of England in London. In turn they offered intermediary banking facilities to smaller local tradesmen and in due course many of them evolved into proper banks themselves.[51] At the same time as the internal banking system was becoming established, a sophisticated system of international credit was growing up for the financing of overseas trade. In the latter half of the seventeenth century an elaborate payments mechanism came into existence, based on Amsterdam and London, which furnished facilities for short-term lending, and by use of bills of exchange enabled overseas liabilities to be discharged without the need for large international movements of gold.[52]

The third precondition to the establishment of a complex credit economy was confidence. In normal times nobody will voluntarily be a creditor who has not confidence in the willingness and ability of the debtor to discharge his obligations. But confidence was one of the most difficult things to establish in the turbulent and insecure years of the seventeenth century. Real confidence in the ability of debtors to pay

[48] Christopher Hill, *Reformation to Industrial Revolution*, p. 183; E. Lipson, *Economic History of England* (reprinted London, 1949), iii. 227 *et seq.*
[49] Christopher Hill, *Reformation to Industrial Revolution*, p. 186.
[50] J. Steven Watson, *The Reign of George III*, p. 28.
[51] E. Lipson, *Economic History of England*, iii. 245–6.
[52] J. Sperling, 'The International Payments Mechanism in the Seventeenth and Eighteenth Centuries', 14 *Economic History Review* (N.S.) 446 (1961–2).

required the creation of Banks who could be supported by such massive quantities of capital that their credit would be assured. And there were many suggestions for the establishment of a National Bank in the seventeenth century. But it was necessary to get rid of the Stuarts before the Bank of England could be created for too many men remembered the way in which Charles I had seized the bullion in the Mint in 1640. As Pepys wrote in his diary in 1666, 'it sticks in the memory of most merchants . . . the thing will never be forgot.'[53] And as though that were not enough there had also been the occasion in 1672 when Charles II had closed the Exchequer and defaulted on his loans so that the Goldsmiths, his creditors, had in turn defaulted on their loans. But once the Whigs had finally got rid of the Stuarts it was possible for them to set up the Bank of England as a sort of 'Whig Finance Company'[54] and the Bank was immensely successful almost from the first. After an initial crisis of confidence had been overcome in 1696 the Bank rapidly created a powerful sense of financial stability; it helped to encourage trade by discounting bills and it greatly expanded available credit by issuing notes beyond the value of its deposits. Although it was not owned or even managed by the Government, its stability also helped to establish the credit of the new Government securities which began to be issued on a regular basis after 1688—the 'Funds' as they came to be called at first until they were consolidated in the nineteenth century when they became 'Consols'.

The Funds soon came to be an important part of the national financial scene. Their great success was due partly to the increasing volume of capital seeking either a short-term outlet, or a long-term and really safe and liquid outlet (for the Funds were 'the first *safe* long-term investment other than land') ;[55] but it was also due to another critical factor. The Government was absolutely punctilious in the discharge of its liabilities for the payment of interest. Commonplace though this may seem today, it was something of a novelty in the early eighteenth century.[56] The Whig landowners had made the interesting discovery that even Governments are subject to the laws of the market place when it comes to borrowing money; that is to say, they discovered that it was very much cheaper for them to discharge their liabilities promptly and fully. Enlightened self-interest indeed worked. Interest rates for the Funds dropped steadily, from 14 per cent in the 1690s to under 4 per cent in the 1750s.[57]

[53] Pepys's *Diary*, 17 August 1666.
[54] The phrase is Bagehot's, cited by Holdsworth, *History of English Law* (reprinted London, 1966) (hereafter cited as *H.E.L.*), viii. 188.
[55] Christopher Hill, *Reformation to Industrial Revolution*, p. 244.
[56] Dickson, *The Financial Revolution in England*, p. 92.
[57] Ibid., p. 470.

Ironically, it was the Government's new-found financial integrity which very nearly led to the downfall of the whole system with the South Sea crisis in 1721. For one of the objects of that ill-fated scheme, at least from the Government's point of view, was to get rid of a number of irredeemable annuities which had been issued at a time when interest rates were higher than they were in 1721. It is to be observed that in 1721 the traditional attitude to such a situation—illustrated by the Court of Chancery's rules as to mortgages—was that there was nothing wrong or unreasonable in redeeming the debt at par. The fact that the debt had been declared irredeemable would have made no difference to the attitude of the Chancery in a case involving a mortgage. The view of the Court of Chancery was fundamentally that if the creditor received back what he had lent, together with interest, he had no cause for complaint, a view (one might say) which stressed the proprietary, as opposed to the contractual, aspects of the transaction. But in 1721 the Government was not willing to pay off the irredeemable annuitants without their consent, and one of the objects of the South Sea scheme had been to offer a tempting bait to these annuitants.[58] The South Sea Act accordingly gave the company power to replace the irredeemable annuities but 'without any compulsion on any of the said proprietors ... at such prices ... as shall be agreed.'[59] And, of course, as the price of South Sea stock was driven higher and higher by the manipulations of the directors most of the hapless annuitants agreed to accept South Sea stock in place of the irredeemable annuities. Despite their furious complaints, they were subsequently held to their bargain by the Government. The Government felt entitled to insist that the rules which it assumed itself must be applied to those who dealt with it.

Fortunately the public credit recovered astonishingly quickly from the débâcle which followed the inevitable collapse of the bubble. By mid-century the 'scrupulous exactitude' with which British Government interest payments were made was a source of much comment among foreigners, and British public finance remained for the rest of the century 'more honest as well as more efficient than that of any country in Europe'.[60]

The development of public credit had also been accompanied by attempts to apply the same principles to private companies; indeed, the South Sea company was itself a private company. The concept of the 'joint-stock' company had, by the late seventeenth century, triumphed over earlier forms of corporate activity.[61] The joint-stock was a 'fund of credit' which could be used several times over to generate new wealth. By the 1690s the growth of commercial corporate activity had brought

<hr/>

[58] Ibid., pp. 92–7. [59] Ibid., p. 104.
[60] Ibid., p. 198. [61] Holdsworth, *H.E.L.*, viii. 206–11.

with it dealings in stocks and shares, options, time bargains, and the emergence of brokers, as well as of the inevitable fraudulent manipulators. It has been estimated that some fifty million pounds had been invested in joint-stock companies by 1720.[62] Much of this commercial activity suffered a severe and prolonged setback after the collapse of the South Sea scheme, and the Bubble Act which preceded it. Private commercial credit took a long time to re-establish confidence in its integrity and it was not until very late in the century that the public began to invest again on a wide scale in such commercial enterprises. But in the meantime, some parts of the institutional debris re-established themselves after the bursting of the bubble. In particular a *market* was coming into existence for the Funds, a new impersonal market where prices rose and fell, and everyone dealing of necessity took the same chance as everyone else. By the middle of the century a Stock Exchange was in process of formation and in 1773 a formal body was instituted. Various new types of transaction began to appear, all involving risks of loss or gain through market movements. Some were simply wagering contracts, but others were sensible commercial transactions. For example, a person with money in the Funds who was asked to lend a sum involving sale of his stock, might stipulate that he should be repaid such a sum as would replace the stock he had had to sell. Such transactions seem to have become quite common, and they began to raise new legal problems.

One other important commercial development of the eighteenth century needs to be mentioned—the growth of insurance. Although various forms of insurance had existed long before this period, insurance as a modern, scientifically based institution, had its beginnings in the late seventeenth century. It was not until the publication of mortality statistics began in London in the latter half of the seventeenth century that it became possible for actuarial tables to be compiled. By the eighteenth century actuarial skills were rapidly developing and life insurance and annuity business was placed on a firm footing. Marine insurance, too, was rapidly developing as merchants strove to minimize the risks to which overseas trade was inevitably subject, and modern fire insurance was also well established by mid-eighteenth century, having originated after the Great Fire of London in 1666. Two points in connection with the early developments in the insurance industry are of particular relevance. The first is that although insurance is designed to shift the risks of untoward events, or at least of events whose timing is uncertain, the uncertainty must not be too great. Insurers cannot properly cover risks except on the assumption that the future will largely follow the pattern of the past. Some change in the pattern of losses can be absorbed, and the greater the industry, and the wider is the spread of

[62] E. Lipson, *Economic History of England*, iii. 217.

risks achieved, the greater is the degree to which the industry can cope with fluctuations in the course of events. Today, with a world-wide reinsurance market, the risks of catastrophic losses are generally spread so widely that the most extreme changes in the pattern of losses in one country can usually be absorbed because they are unlikely to be repeated on a world-wide basis. But a nascent insurance industry with a limited market and without extensive reinsurance facilities, is much more vulnerable to violent fluctuations in the pattern of losses. It is likely that the rapid development of insurance in eighteenth-century England was not unrelated to the general stability of the times.

The second point of interest concerns the extent to which the success of eighteenth-century insurers depended on their reputation and integrity. In modern times it is well recognized that insurance holds out peculiar temptations for the dishonest; this is largely because the normal course of business for a new insurance company involves the receipt of a considerable amount of premium income well before that income is matched by a corresponding volume of liabilities. Dishonest or even reckless modes of carrying on insurance business are, therefore, in nearly all countries today the subject of extensive regulation and control. What is surprising about eighteenth-century insurance business is that, without this framework of regulation and control, there seems in general to have been extraordinarily little fraud and dishonesty. English insurers very soon learnt the same lesson that the British Government had learnt—enlightened self-interest actually paid. The British insurance industry acquired a reputation for integrity and scrupulous honesty in the observance of its obligations. When, in the middle of the century, English insurers were temporarily prohibited from insuring the ships of nations at war with England, it was feared that much of the business might be permanently lost; but in fact the business 'was easily regained by the English insurers who dealt at a cheaper rate and more punctually than the insurers of other nations'.[63]

We must beware of exaggerating the increase of stability and order in commercial affairs. There *was* an increase, and it *was* significant and influential; but all things are relative. The stability of 1770 is not to be compared with the stability of 1970. Accounting skills were still scarce, and proper books and records all too rarely kept; frauds and swindles were commonplace; the mere failure to pay debts—despite the penalties involved—still a serious problem. Risks and uncertainty were still ever present in commercial affairs on a scale rarely known in modern times—

Commercial life was overshadowed by the fear of bankruptcy, ordinary life was profoundly affected by the threat of the debtor's prison. The risk of fire, which

[63] Or at least, so it was said by counsel (as though it were common knowledge) in argument in *Bristow v. Towers* (1794) 6 T.R. 35, 47; 101 E.R. 422, 428.

could cripple the most prosperous in a few hours ... was only just beginning to be limited by insurance ... Uncertainty stimulated fraud and brutality. Thus deceit in revenue dealings, documented by the committee on Customs frauds in 1733, was a constant preoccupation of the legislature.[64]

I have so far said much about trade and commerce and little about industry. In 1770 trade and commerce were still much more important than industry; indeed the very word 'industry' had not yet acquired its modern significance.[65] 'Industry was taken for granted by most people, as a comparatively static and undramatic part of the national life.'[66] That does not mean that industry made no significant overall contribution to the economy; in fact it is estimated that some 24 per cent of G.N.P. was derived from industry in 1770. But the idea of rapid and sustained growth in industry had not yet developed. Although modern historians date the beginnings of the Industrial Revolution around 1760, or even earlier, this merely means that there was at that period a noticeable quickening in the rate of growth in a number of key industries— noticeable, that is, to the modern historian with graphs and statistical tables in front of him. From these it is possible to see, for example, that coal shipped from Newcastle and Sunderland to other parts of England was in the 1760s almost twice what it had been in the 1740s; that imports of iron increased from an annual average of 26,000 tons in the 1740s to an annual average of 45,000 tons in the 1760s;[67] that exports of copper and brass nearly tripled between the 1740s and the 1760s;[68] that new industries, like paper-making, plate glass, pottery and earthenware, were slowly rising; and so on. These undramatic figures were part of the steady, silent, largely imperceptible process which was shortly to have such dramatic and very perceptible results on the economy and every other aspect of life in England. At the same time a large quantity of capital investment was being laid down in forms which would produce returns over a long period of time, and in particular in transport. Investment was going on in roads, canals, bridges, ports, quays, ships, and warehouses; even the great landowners were beginning to dig for coal and other minerals on their estates.[69] These developments have to be taken together with the now growing returns from the Agricultural Revolution, which not only provided surplus capital for industrial development, but also released agricultural labourers for industry by the increased productivity of the remainder; and with the trading and

---

[64] Dickson, *The Financial Revolution in England*, p. 155.

[65] Raymond Williams, *Culture and Society 1780–1950* (Harmondsworth, 1963), p. 13.

[66] J. Steven Watson, *The Reign of George III*, p. 26.

[67] Peter Mathias, *The First Industrial Nation* (London, 1969,) Appendix, Table 27, p. 479.

[68] Ibid., Table 30, p. 482.

[69] J. T. Ward, 'Landowners and Mining', in *Land and Industry*, ed. J. T. Ward and R. G. Wilson (Newton Abbot, 1971).

commercial developments which have been sketched out above. It was the combination of these factors, together with a variety of other circumstances, to which the origins of the Industrial Revolution are today generally attributed.

3

THE INTELLECTUAL BACKGROUND IN 1770—I

THE SCOPE OF CONTRACTUAL IDEAS

THE law of contract in the modern world, even the ideas which underlie it, seem to have no relationship to the ideas which underlay the Social Contract. The relationship between Government and governed appears to have no connection at all with the relationship between contracting parties. The former is largely perceived as an authoritarian and hierarchical relationship. The State somehow stands above and beyond the citizen, remote and impersonal, represented, in common speech, by the ubiquitous 'they' who decide things. A contractual relationship, by contrast, is seen as deriving from agreement; it is felt to be the creation of the parties, who give it life. Far from standing above, and beyond them, a contract is a thing under the control of the contracting parties, and subordinate to their will. It is true that, even today, phrases like 'government by consent' and 'the will of the people' are popular enough, and not only in what we would call democratic societies; and it is also true that at least in democratic societies (and perhaps, in some sense in all societies) there is some substance to these phrases. But this makes no difference to the chasm which is today normally perceived to lie between the governmental and the contractual type of relationship. The role of agreement or consent in the two relationships is perceived as utterly and fundamentally distinct. It was not always thus.

In the eighteenth century the notion of contract, and the role of contract in society, were a great deal broader than they are today. Men thought their relationships with each other, and their relationship with the State, to be of a similar character. And over and above that, there is a sense in which they perceived the role of choice or consent in the one relationship to be the precondition for the proper role of choice or consent in the other. They *chose* to create a society in which free choice was one of their principal goals; they *voluntarily* created a society in which the voluntary creation of relationships would be permitted and respected; they *freely* instituted a society for the protection of their property in order that they could be free to acquire, exploit, or dispose of property to their best advantage. At this stage it is enough to make three points, some of which will receive extensive elaboration later in this work. The first is that the idea of an *ordinary* contract as the creation of a voluntary agreement, irrespective of previously existing duties or rights, was itself a relatively modern, and indeed, a still emerging idea in the eighteenth century. The very concept of contract was, at this time, in a transitional state. Traditionally, a contract was primarily conceived as a relationship involving mutual rights and obligations; there was not necessarily an implication that the relationship was created by a conscious and deliberate act of will, still less that the rights and duties thereby generated were the creatures of the will. Some degree of consent may have been thought of as normally necessary, but consent is a complex idea itself, and there may well have been cases where no consent at all—as we would say—was a necessary part of the relationship. If this is right—and the reader is asked to take it on trust at the moment, for its full elaboration is deferred till Chapters 6 and 7—it will be seen that there was nothing very unreal in seeing a close relationship between 'ordinary' contract and the 'social' contract. Both involved relationships in which mutual rights and duties were created. The concept of contract was, in short, replacing custom as a source of law—that is, as the regulator of social and political obligations—and as the source of individual rights and duties— that is, as the regulator of private obligations. Unfortunately we have no word other than 'contract' to describe these individual relationships (for 'status' does not really serve the purpose); but it must be remembered that the word does not, in this pre-eighteenth-century era, necessarily carry the strong consensual connotations it later acquired.

The second point is to remind the reader that throughout the eighteenth century the actual events of 1688 were still central to all political theory. James II *had* been abandoned by the free choice of the great Whig families. Many of them had had to make their fateful and desperately difficult decision in the few days that James was in London while William moved slowly towards the capital. Each one who threw in his lot with William did so knowing that if he was wrong he would almost certainly pay for his mistake with his life. This was free choice with a vengeance indeed. And when, eventually, James fled and Parliament met in 1689 to decide the fate of the nation, the first act of the House of Commons was to resolve that the King had 'by breaking the original contract between King and people' attempted to subvert the constitution and violate its fundamental laws. This was not just idle rhetoric to justify the Revolution. By 1688 nobody, except perhaps James himself, had any doubt that the King owed obligations to his people, as they owed duties to him. That relationship could, without unreasonable stretching of terms, be called contractual. Did not the King promise to obey the laws in his coronation oath? True, of course, as modern political theorists point out, the obligation of a monarch to his people cannot entirely depend upon the oath, for that would mean that he was not bound prior to his coronation, which would be odd indeed. But the oath is the monarch's acknowledgement that there are indeed duties binding upon him which arise out of the relationship. It is evidence of those duties, if it does not create them. And perhaps that is not very different from the function of a promise, or agreement even in an ordinary contract; that too, it is hoped to justify later in this work.

We must not forget also the last stage in the process by which England acquired a new monarch. For after the throne had been declared vacant by the two Houses of Parliament there followed a somewhat delicate process of negotiation between Parliament and William as to the terms on which the Crown was to be placed upon his—and his wife's—head. Not to put too blunt a point on it, a process of bargaining ensued which culminated in an agreement. To us, these famous events are too far distant to raise emotion or even excitement, but in the eighteenth century there must have been many whose parents and grandparents had actually participated in them. The idea that political society was founded on the basis of a contract would surely not have seemed far-fetched to them, even if it was not a contract to which the mass of the people were parties. And though memories of these events must have been fading in 1770, the American Revolution a few years later may well have revived the ideas behind them.

Thirdly, we must remember again a point made in the previous chapter about the cohesiveness of the governing class in the eighteenth century. One of the factors which makes it difficult for us today to think of our role in a political institution as resembling a contractual role is the sheer size of the body politic. It is hard to think in terms of a contract either with millions of our fellow citizens, or even in terms of a contract with a Government whose remoteness and impersonality derives largely from the fact that there are so many millions to be governed. But there can be more than two parties even to an ordinary contract. A group of persons may quite voluntarily, and by using the procedures of modern contract law, create an institution for some commercial, social, or recreational purpose. If the group remains small enough, the members are still likely to think of it as 'their' institution—'their' tennis club, or family company, or debating society, or whatever—even if they have gone through the processes of formally incorporating the body in question. The fact that the views, or even rights, of individual members may be overridden by majority vote, or that many decisions will be taken by committees or executive officers, rather than by all the members, does not necessarily prevent this sense of identification continuing to exist. If the numbers are small enough, the views of the members are likely to coincide on most major issues, and on the primary objectives of the institution; and so long as this remains the case, most members will be prepared to go along with majority votes even though they may disagree with the decision. When the institution becomes larger, however, this sense of identity is apt to disappear; the members no longer feel that it is 'their' club or company; they do not necessarily accept—though they may have to submit to—adverse majority votes. They certainly do not feel that what is done is done with their consent, or by their agreement.

Now in eighteenth-century England political society and political institutions seem to have represented a small enough group of people for them to have had this close sense of identification. It may seem strange that a political society of several millions could ever have this character, but if the number of the propertied (and educated) members of the society is small enough, and the geographical size of the country is small enough, it is quite possible for this to happen. Indeed, it is possible to see a closely parallel phenomenon to this day in African countries where the number of influential persons is so small that 'everyone knows everyone'. In eighteenth-century England, too, 'everyone knew everyone'; amongst the aristocracy, intermarriage was the rule; and even as one went down the social scale to the gentry, there were few who did not have relatives or at least friends in 'high places'. This was fruitful ground for Social Contract theory to flourish. The governing classes did feel that it was 'their' government, 'their' Parliament, and in rather a special sense, 'their' country.

THE SOCIAL CONTRACTARIANS

This is not the place for an exhaustive account of eighteenth-century ideas about the Social Contract,[1] but, as we have seen, the relationship between social contract ideas and 'ordinary' contractual ideas was so close that any historical study of contractual theory requires some exploration of this theme.

There have always been two separate relationships which have, at various times, been treated under the general head of the Social Contract. On the one hand there is the relationship, in any political society, between the governors and the governed, and on the other hand there is the relationship between the people themselves. Some theorists held that the relationship between the people was contractual; that political society was—or was to be treated as if—it had been instituted by an agreement by which the people abandoned their 'natural' freedoms and constituted themselves into one body politic. Everybody submitted himself to this new constitutional and legal order, thereby gaining the

[1] See generally, J. W. Gough, *The Social Contract*, 2nd edn. (Oxford, 1963); Sir Ernest Barker, Introduction to *The Social Contract, Essays by Locke, Hume and Rousseau* (London, 1947).

right to the due protection of its laws. Other theorists fastened on the relationship between sovereigns and subjects. Nobody, of course, had any doubt that a subject owed obligations to his sovereign, but there was a great deal more difficulty over the question of reciprocal obligations. Did a sovereign owe 'duties' to his people? And if so, who was to be the judge of the due performance of those duties, and how were they to be enforced?

Many of these ideas, in various forms, had been in circulation since the Middle Ages. Medieval writers had generally stressed the subordination of rulers to God. Sovereigns were not, in their eyes, autocratic despots but Princes who owed duties to God and even to their subjects who were to be ruled according to law—not just the human law of the Prince himself, but the law of God. It was, especially in the sixteenth century, common enough to refer to these reciprocal obligations as constituting 'covenants' or 'pacts', though it is not always clear what these ideas conveyed to those who used them. Twentieth-century writers, themselves imbued with modern ideas about contractual obligation, take the making of a contract to imply 'a conscious and deliberate act of will';[2] as a result, they sometimes argue that the medievalists did not have a 'proper' contractual theory. I have already suggested that—whatever a 'proper' theory of contract may require—this type of contractual thinking may well have been common to all types of contract. In the seventeenth century the use of contractual language and ideas became closely involved with the religious controversies of the time. The word 'covenant' became particularly associated with the relationships created amongst the members of sectarian congregations, and between them and their minister. In Scotland adherents of the Reformation had been 'covenant-ing' with each other since the mid-sixteenth century, and the Solemn League and Covenant of 1643 created the 'covenanters' who subsequently played a major part in the Civil War. Puritan theology also had its contractarian ideas; at times Puritan thinkers seemed to be contending that a bargain could be made with God. Many have suggested that the more politically-oriented social contractarianism of the eighteenth century may have originated in, or at least been influenced by this 'all pervading contractarianism of seventeenth century thought'.[3]

For our purposes the significance of these early historical origins of eighteenth-century contractual thought lies principally in the light they throw on the growing importance of individual freedom and free choice; the right of the individual freely to choose (even within limits) the nature of his relationship with God, was from the beginning closely associated

---

[2] J. W. Allen, *History of Political Thought in the Sixteenth Century* (London, 1928, reprinted 1961), pp. 317–19; J. W. Gough, *The Social Contract*, pp. 56–7.

[3] Christopher Hill, *Intellectual Origins of the English Revolution* (Oxford, 1965, reprinted Panther Books, 1972), pp. 268–9.

with his right to choose the nature of his relationship with his fellow men and with his ruler. In short, what was new in contractual theory was not the idea of a relationship involving mutual rights and duties, but the idea that the relationship was created by, and depended on, the free choice of the individuals involved in it. The waning of the medieval Aristotelian concept of man as an essentially political and social being, necessarily involved (without his choosing) in a network of communal and social relationships, inevitably brought with it a need to explain how societies existed at all. As Tawney put it:

The difference between the England of Shakespeare, still visited by the ghosts of the Middle Ages, and the England which emerged in 1700 from the fierce polemics of the last two generations, was a difference of social and political theory even more than of constitutional and political arrangements. Not only the facts, but the minds which appraised them, were profoundly modified . . . The natural consequence of the abdication of authorities which had stood, however imperfectly, for a common purpose in social organization, was the gradual disappearance from social thought of the idea of purpose itself. Its place in the eighteenth century was taken by the idea of mechanism. The conception of men as united to each other, and of all mankind as united to God, by mutual obligations, arising from their relation to a common end, ceased to be impressed upon men's minds.[4]

In short, the new man of the eighteenth century, who was the true descendant of post-Reformation man, was an individualist; and one of the essential differences between the social and political theory of the pre- and post-Reformation eras concerned the way in which individuals made up a community. It was only through the free choice of these free individuals that societies and political communities existed at all.

In this work it will be enough to say something of the role played by the concept of free choice in the work of Hobbes and Locke, the two most celebrated social contract thinkers of seventeenth century England. It is, perhaps, necessary to disclaim again any pretence of giving a full account of the ideas of Hobbes and Locke, let alone a full survey of what others have had to say about them. The purpose of this discussion is merely to give some idea of the general nature of contractual theory as it stood around 1770.

Hobbes

Hobbes has often been seen as the failed prophet of the Civil War, just as Locke was the successful prophet of the Revolution of 1688; because much of what Hobbes said in *The Leviathan* in 1651 was unacceptable to the Parliamentarians, while Locke's ideas fitted supremely well the Whig

[4] R. H. Tawney, *The Acquisitive Society* (London, 1921), pp. 12–14.

philosophy, it is easy to write off Hobbes as one of the last supporters of autocratic monarchy in England. Certainly there is much in *The Leviathan* which gave comfort to the Royalists when it was published, especially in the idea that the only form of social contract was between the members of society, and not between them and their sovereign. The central idea that once the people had created their political commonwealth and transferred their power to it, they could no longer call the sovereign to book, and had no right of rebellion, had little appeal to Parliamentarians who had cut off the King's head two years before. But there is also much in Hobbes that was forward-looking, and foreshadowed the social and political ideals of bourgeois economic liberalism. One of the leading modern interpreters of Hobbes's thought protests that 'there ought not to be any question as to whether Hobbes was in the main stream of English political thought; it should rather be acknowledged that he dug the channel in which the main stream subsequently flowed.'[5]

But for our purposes, perhaps the most interesting part of Hobbes's thought consists in his treatment of the ideas of freedom, and free choice. Notwithstanding his views on the impermissibility of rebellion and the impossibility of subjecting the sovereign to duties, Hobbes was no enemy to freedom. He insists, indeed, that it is only by creating their sovereign and giving him total power that the people enjoy any real liberty at all. The institution of civil society requires each person to give up his 'natural' right 'to all things; and be contented with so much liberty against other men as he would allow other men against himself'. But this is no real loss. In civil society men retain freedom on all matters not prohibited by the sovereign, so that 'The Greatest Liberty of Subjects, dependeth on the silence of the Law'.[6] And this is no mean liberty 'For seeing there is no Common-wealth in the world, wherein there be rules enough set down, for the regulating of all the actions, and words of men, (as being a thing impossible): it followeth necessarily, that in all kinds of actions, by the laws praetermitted, men have the Liberty, of doing what their own reasons shall suggest, for the most profitable to themselves.'[7]

In the 'state of nature', on the other hand, where every man wars against every other man, where there is no law, and hence no justice or injustice, where force and fraud are the two cardinal virtues, the only liberty a man has is the liberty to make war. I need not pause to ask whether Hobbes really thought there had ever been 'such a state of nature', or whether, as has been argued, he was really warning his fellow countrymen of the dangers of allowing the country to fall into such a

[5] C. B. Macpherson, Introduction to *The Leviathan* (Harmondsworth, 1968), p. 24. Page references to *The Leviathan* are to this edition.

[6] *Leviathan*, marginal note, p. 271.

[7] Ibid., p. 264.

state. What concerns us more is Hobbes's understanding of the relationship between freedom and the idea of contract, or covenant as he more usually calls it. Hobbes saw civil society as having been instituted by men by agreement, or imposed on them by conquest. In both cases he was convinced that men would gain far more than they would lose by having a proper and authoritative sovereign who could enforce laws. This absolutely overriding requirement of any form of civilization was so dominant in Hobbes's mind that he felt convinced that all rational men would accept it; and if they were not sufficiently rational, or educated, to understand its necessity, then it must be taught to them; and they would learn it as they learnt the precepts of religion.[8] As to the better educated or more rational part of the people, Hobbes had no doubts. But he was not satisfied with saying that they ought rationally to agree to surrender their 'natural liberty' to a sovereign, whether by conquest or by institution. He wanted to go on to say that they did in fact assent to this surrender. It is here that we reach a critical point in Hobbes's ideas. Hobbes tended to equate free choice with what we would call free will. If a man did something otherwise than under actual physical compulsion he did it freely.

Hobbes is quite consistent on this point. 'Feare and Liberty' he insists, 'are consistent; as when a man throweth his goods into the Sea for feare the ship should sink, he doth it neverthelesse very willingly, and may refuse to doe it if he will: It is therefore the action, of one that was *free*; so a man sometimes pays his debt, only for *feare* of Imprisonment, which because no body hindered him from detaining, was the action of man at *liberty*.'[9] Indeed, he goes even further; '*Liberty* and *Necessity* are Consistent', he argues; all human actions are, in a sense, necessary since they ensue in a continual causal chain from the first link 'in the hand of God, the first of all causes'. Hence 'to him that could see the connexion of those causes, the *necessity* of all mens voluntary actions would appear manifest', but that in no way lessens man's freedom of will. What men do voluntarily, they choose to do, and do freely.[10] Hobbes realises, of course, that there must be certain exceptional cases where the civil law in a political society will treat a promise as extracted by duress or illegal threats, and will be disinclined to enforce it. But even in such a case he appears to have some notion, peculiar though it may seem to us, that the promise is somehow prima facie binding, and it is only by the grace of the positive laws of the State that the promisor is freed from his promise.[11]

[8] Ibid., Part II, Chapter 30, pp. 378 ff.

[9] Ibid., Part II, Chapter 21, pp. 262–3.

[10] Ibid., p. 263. Hobbes would hardly have accepted the plea of the Roman citizen that 'though we willingly consented to his banishment, yet it was against our will': *Coriolanus*, Act IV, scene vi.

[11] Ibid., Part I, Chapter 14, p. 198. Is it possible that Hobbes was assuming that such a contract would be valid at common law, and could only be set aside in equity?

But if that is the case with the positive laws of the commonwealth once established, Hobbes is quite clear that it is not so in the state of nature. 'Covenants entered into by fear in the condition of meer Nature, are obligatory. For example, if I Covenant to pay a ransome, or service for my life, to an enemy; I am bound by it. For it is a Contract, wherein one receiveth the benefit of life; the other is to receive money, or service for it; and consequently, where no other Law (as in the condition of meer Nature) forbiddeth the performance, the Covenant is valid.'[12] He then goes on to refer to promises by prisoners of war to pay ransoms, or to the case of a weak Prince making a disadvantageous peace with a stronger. In both these cases promises are made out of fear, but because they take place in the state of nature (for Hobbes treats countries at war with one another as examples of his state of nature) they are binding.

Having thus established what he conceives of as free choice, Hobbes has little difficulty in justifying his argument that societies are voluntarily created by men, acting freely. It makes little difference whether they create a sovereign by instituting him as such, or whether they submit to a conqueror. In the former case they contract with each other, in the latter, they contract with the conqueror; in the former case, they contract out of fear of each other, in the latter they contract out of fear of the conqueror.[13] It is not the mere right of conquest, which gives the conqueror 'rights of Dominion over the Vanquished'. It is their own covenant. And equally, the vanquished owes no duty to the conqueror merely because he is 'beaten, and taken, or put to flight; but because he cometh in, and submitteth to the Victor'.[14]

There seems to be some inconsistency here. On the one hand, there is no law in the state of nature, where nothing exists but perpetual war; on the other hand, it seems that promises extorted by violence or fear even in the state of nature are somehow binding. But for present purposes this is of less importance than Hobbes's willingness to take such a broad view of consent and free choice. For plainly enough, if everything that men do is to be treated as being done voluntarily, it becomes possible to argue that nearly all human relationships rest on free choice. The citizen who submits to the laws of the State because he is compelled to do so by force is to be deemed to contract because he voluntarily chooses to submit, rather than be imprisoned or perhaps even killed. For a people who valued their civil liberties this was an unattractive dogma.

Locke

The Whigs found John Locke's ideas as acceptable as they had found Hobbes's ideas unattractive. There is, of course, much in common in the

---

[12] Ibid.   [13] Ibid., Part II, Chapter 20, p. 252.   [14] Ibid., pp. 255–6.

two men's thought, but it was Locke who provided the answer to Tory Royalism. John Locke (1623–1704) was the son of a lawyer who had fought on the Parliamentary side in the Civil War; after the Restoration Locke was closely associated with some of the leading Whig figures and he thought it advisable to stay out of England after the Monmouth rebellion. He returned in 1689 and accepted a minor public post under William III. His most famous works are the *Second Treatise on Government* (1690), the *Essay Concerning Toleration*, written in 1667, published in 1690, and the *Essay Concerning Human Understanding* (1690), a philosophical work, often regarded as the foundation of the English empirical tradition. Aside from the more direct political aspects of his ideas, Locke was the great defender of property rights, and there is no question but that much of his immense influence in the eighteenth century was attributable to this defence. It was he who provided the moral justification needed to satisfy the consciences of the propertied classes of the eighteenth century.

I shall here, as with Hobbes, concentrate on those aspects of Locke's thought which are of primary relevance to the theme of this work. I shall also stress those aspects of Locke's thought which differed from those of Hobbes's. My discussion will focus around four principal questions: first, the role played by property; secondly, the Natural Law basis to Locke's ideas; thirdly, the part played by consent; and fourthly, the nascent idea of the trust owed by Government to the people.

Like Hobbes, Locke starts with a 'state of nature'. But in his state of nature men are not constantly at war with their fellows; they are, in fact, busy acquiring property. In this state of nature men are naturally free and equal. God has given to man the earth and all its fruits, and though in the first instance all things belong to mankind in common, 'there must of necessity be a means to appropriate them some way or other before they can be of any use, or at all beneficial, to any particular men'.[15] Moreover, each man in this state of nature owns at least one piece of private property, not held in common, and that is his own person. 'This nobody has any right to but himself.'[16] Consequently, Locke argues, the labour of a man's body, and the work of his hands, are properly his. From this he draws the simple conclusion that labour was to be the method by which the common property of mankind was to be appropriated to individual use. Not only did this follow from the necessity of the case— for how else would the Indian have title to the deer which he killed?— but it also had a strong ethical base. For if labour was the title to property, it would be the hardworking ('the industrious and rational') who obtained the most property.[17]

Had Locke stopped at this point, his *Treatise* would have provided

[15] *Second Treatise*, Sect. 25.   [16] Ibid., Sect. 26.   [17] Ibid., Sect. 33.

support for revolutionaries rather than the governing classes. Manifestly, he had to explain how it was that the greater part of the earth's surface was in fact owned by those who laboured least. This he did by invoking two undeniable economic facts and one very dubious assumption. The first of his economic facts was the concept of scarcity. Men had no right, in the state of nature, even by their labour, to appropriate a greater share of the earth's resources than they had use for, if, by those means, they injured others by depriving them of needed resources. So long as there was abundance of resources a man could appropriate what he wanted without injuring his fellows; but once there was scarcity a man who hoarded property so that it rotted or putrefied before he could use it, 'offended against the common law of Nature'.[18] The unequal division of property in the state of Nature was, therefore, originally subject to severe limits. These limits were removed by Locke's second economic factor—the invention of money. Money enabled people to store wealth without fear of it perishing and it therefore became possible for great inequalities of wealth to grow up. Since money was an artificial contrivance, invented by men, it followed that they had, in effect, agreed to the possibility of this new, and greater inequality of property. Finally, Locke makes the somewhat dubious assumption that the present inequalities of property ownership are the consequence of the differing degrees of industry which have enabled some to multiply their possessions many times over.[19]

If the descriptive side of all this is somewhat unconvincing, it must be stressed that there is a prescriptive side interwoven into it. Locke is not merely, or perhaps even primarily, trying to explain how property rights have come into existence, and why they are so unequally distributed; he is trying to justify this state of affairs. And this justification is, essentially, the economic liberal justification which is also to be found in Hobbes. How will men be induced to labour if not to feed themselves and their families? How, if there is no money, will it be possible for one man to acquire and preserve more property than he can physically keep under his guard? And how, when money does exist, will people be induced to labour to increase their possessions unless they can barter what they have for money which they can store, or exchange for other possessions?

Having thus justified the institution of property itself, Locke's next task is to explain the role of Government and its relationship to property. In his state of nature, men have the right to protect their own property (and here we encounter Locke's use of the extended concept of property to include 'life, liberty and estate') and also the right to deal with those who attempt to interfere with his rights of property. This seems an

---

[18] Ibid., Sect. 37.   [19] Ibid., Sect. 48.

unsatisfactory state of affairs (though Locke is perhaps not wholly clear on how unsatisfactory he would find it) since it would involve each man being 'judge for himself and executioner'.[20] Consequently civil societies are set up in which each person surrenders his right to act as his own judge and executioner. The principal function of Government is thus to provide impartial judges and penalties to deal with disputes over property and offences against property; incidental to that, it is necessary for the commonwealth to define these offences and penalties—hence the need for a legislature—and to enforce the judgments of the courts— hence the need for an executive power.[21] This then is the primary purpose of Government—to protect rights of property whose existence predates Government itself. It follows that the next task is to ensure that the Governmental machinery fulfils its task so as best to preserve these property rights. This, he argues, will best be achieved where the legislature consists of many persons subject to the same laws, since they will then all be concerned to protect their property. In legislatures, on the other hand, which consist of 'one lasting assembly, always in being', or 'in one man, as in absolute monarchies', there is a danger that the members may think their interests separate from those of the rest of the community.[22] Moreover, 'the supreme power cannot take from any man any part of his own property without his own consent'.[23] Property is not property if it is subject to the arbitrary will of another. 'Hence it is a mistake to think that the supreme or legislative power of any commonwealth can do what it will, and dispose of the estates of the subject arbitrarily, or take any part of them at pleasure.'[24]

If the descriptive aspect of this seems again somewhat coloured (though certainly not so much as the descriptive side of the origins of property) it is once again clear that there is a strong prescriptive element in the exercise. Locke is telling us, not merely what he thinks Government is for, and how it is constituted, but what it *ought* to be for, and how it *ought* to be constituted. If Government is constituted for the defence of property, then it follows that Governments ought not to interfere arbitrarily with property rights.[25] But what was prescriptive in England became descriptive in the United States, where the Federal Constitution embodies Locke's ideas concerning the relationship of Government to property.

Finally, Locke drew a most important conclusion from his ideas about the 'true end' of government, and here he differed fundamentally from Hobbes. If Government fails to perform its function, if, for example, the ruler abandons his charge so that the laws cannot be enforced; or if the rulers so far forget their primary task as to 'endeavour to take away and

[20] Ibid., Sect. 87. [21] Ibid., Sect. 88. [22] Ibid., Sect. 138.

[23] Ibid. [24] Ibid. [25] Ibid., Sect. 137.

destroy the property of the people, or to reduce them to slavery under arbitrary power', then it follows that rebellion is justifiable. Of course, it must not be assumed that revolutions are justified 'upon every little mismanagement in public affairs' but it is starkly clear that it is for the people to judge whether they are faced with a 'little mismanagement' or a fundamental breach of trust by the Government. Rebellion is an act of self-defence; and the defender plainly must decide when to resort to force in his defence. All this, of course, was sweet music in the ears of the successful rebels of 1688, and doubtless helped the acceptance of other aspects of Locke's ideas. Later, it was the defence of property which was chiefly remembered, and the talk of rebellion which was apt to be discarded. But when the quarrel with the American colonists broke out in the 1760s, it was naturally to Locke that they turned for support. And the colonists had their defenders among the Whigs in England who were also prepared to accept the logic of Locke's arguments. The Whig lawyer, Lord Camden, for example, argued vehemently that taxation without representation was illegal, and nothing short of robbery. A man could not be deprived of his property without his consent; he could sell it with his consent, or he could be taxed with his consent—either his own, or that of a representative—but to tax a man without such a consent was to deprive him of his property in defiance of the laws of nature.[26]

The second principal respect in which Locke's ideas differed from those of Hobbes concerned the use he made of Natural Law. As we have seen Locke's state of nature was a much more civilized affair than Hobbes's; it was subject to the rule of Natural Law. It is the Law of Nature—deduced from a few basic assumptions about human nature, and the scarcity of resources in the world—which explains the origin of private property, money, and inequalities of wealth; it is these same principles of Natural Law which explain why men constitute civil societies and which limit the powers of Government so constituted. Locke is none too specific about the source of Natural Law, but it is clearly associated closely with the laws of God. A transgressor against the law of Nature, says Locke, 'declares himself to live by another rule than that of reason and common equity, which is that measure God has set to the actions of men for their mutual security'.[27]

Natural Law ideas had, of course, been in circulation for many years when Locke was writing. Locke himself was particularly influenced by Richard Hooker, the sixteenth-century Anglican divine and author of a famous treatise, *The Laws of Ecclesiastical Politie*. Hooker had played a part in a celebrated theological controversy during the reign of Elizabeth in which he had defended the establishment of the Protestant Church of

England and in doing so had relied on ideas not to be found in the scriptures, for which he was much abused by the Puritans. Hooker had argued that the universe was ruled by Natural Laws, appointed by God, and that these laws governed both the physical universe and moral questions. These laws were to be discovered by use of man's reason and were not solely to be found in the scriptures or in the direct teachings of the Church. Indeed, the Church, like civil Government, and the rest of the universe, was subject to these Natural Laws. There are also passages in Hooker's work which clearly bore more directly on Locke's ideas, in which he argued that civil governments were instituted by consent. Apart from Hooker, Natural Law theories had been extensively canvassed in the seventeenth century by Hugo Grotius (1583–1645), the Dutch jurist, who had gone back to the Roman *jus gentium* in his famous work, *De jure belli et pacis*, first published in 1625; and by Samuel Pufendorf (1632–94), a German jurist who was certainly well acquainted with the works of Grotius and Hobbes. Locke does not acknowledge Grotius or Pufendorf as sources for any of his ideas; but he frequently relies on Hooker. There seems no doubt that through most of the eighteenth century Locke's Natural Law ideas helped to make his position more attractive to the English governing classes. They added a moral—vaguely religious—basis to Locke's premises and they added a sense of inexorability to his conclusions about property and civil government. But this should not be allowed to conceal the fact that, for all the talk of Natural Law, there was much plain good sense in Locke's premises and conclusions, given agreement about the ends to be sought. Later, when tastes changed, 'the façade of natural law could be removed by Hume and Bentham, without damage to the strong and well-built utilitarian structure that lay within'.[28]

The third major point on which Locke differs from Hobbes concerns the role of consent. Like Hobbes, Locke insists that civil society is created by the consent of the people, but unlike Hobbes, he rejects the idea that a consent extracted by fear is a true consent. A conqueror acquires no title by conquest, nor even by extracting submission from the vanquished. 'Should a robber break into my house, and with a dagger at my throat, make me seal deeds to convey my estate to him, would this give him any title?'[29] Clearly not. What difference does it make, then, if the attacker is a Prince? 'The injury and the crime is equal whether committed by the wearer of a crown or some petty villain.'[30] And again, promises extorted by force are not binding; they are taken from me in the same way my horse may be taken by a thief. In either case I am entitled to resume my

[28] C. B. Macpherson, *The Political Theory of Possessive Individualism* (Oxford, 1962), p. 270.
[29] *Second Treatise*, Sect. 176.
[30] Ibid.

own. 'For the law of Nature laying an obligation on me, only by the rules she prescribes, cannot oblige me by the violation of her rules; such as the extorting of anything from me by force.'[31]

This was an important point. The binding force of a promise or consent obtained by threats had been the subject of a long-standing controversy going back to the Natural Lawyers and before them the Schoolmen. And though the controversy was not wholly stilled by Locke (echoes of it are still to be found in Adam Smith's work)[32] the weight of his influence may well have proved of importance to the shape of legal thinking. By rejecting the validity of promises or contracts extracted by force or fear, Locke strengthened the moral appeal of his position, and gave substance to the moral basis of obligations rooted in consent. It was much easier to support the idea that by 'Natural Law' consent was a valid source of political or legal obligations when it was at the same time insisted that the consent must be genuine and freely given. It was this (for example) which enabled Locke to get away with such extravagances as the assertion that the obligations created by promises by Natural Law 'are so great and strong ... that Omnipotency itself can be tied by them. Grants, promises and oaths are bonds that hold the Almighty.' [33]

On this point Locke's position was evidently more attractive than that of Hobbes, but it involved Locke in inconsistencies which Hobbes had avoided, and which survived to plague juristic thought many years later. For Locke was compelled to resort to two somewhat artificial devices to reconcile his position on promises extracted by fear or threats with his views on the role of contract both as a political and an economic concept. On the one hand he refused to question the validity of the political consent underlying the continuing obligations owed by the citizen to the State; and on the other hand he was compelled to slur over the problem of pressures arising in the market place itself.

Having thus, even at the price of some inconsistency, established the morality of consent-based obligations, it remained for Locke to re-interpret many traditional obligations as resting upon consent. This he did, in the political sphere, with which he was of course primarily concerned, by invoking the notion of a tacit consent. In a famous passage he posed the question how far a person may be looked upon as though he has consented tacitly to submit himself to the laws of a country:

And to this I say, that every man that hath any possession or enjoyment of any part of the dominions of any government doth hereby give his tacit consent, and is as far forth obliged to obedience to the laws of that government, during such enjoyment, as any one under it, whether this his possession be of land to him and

[31] Ibid., Sect. 186.
[32] See *The Theory of Moral Sentiments*, ed. Raphael and Macfie (Oxford, 1976), pp. 330–1.
[33] *Second Treatise*, Sect. 195.

his heirs for ever, or a lodging only for a week; or whether it be barely travelling freely on the highway; and, in effect, it reaches as far as the very being of any one within the territories of that government.[34]

Here we see, despite a very different approach on the surface, close underlying similarities with the position taken by Hobbes. Both of them want to treat the institution of Government, or civil society, as having taken place by the consent of the people; Locke goes further and wants to argue that the consent of the people is a continuing requirement of the society's legitimacy. Both essentially agree that there are mutual rights and duties between the members of a society though only Locke is willing to impose duties on a sovereign once instituted. But even Hobbes cannot deny that there is a mutual relationship between ruler and ruled. What we are seeing in both Hobbes and Locke is the attempt to rewrite the source of mutual rights and duties in an age-old relationship. The old customary ideas have broken down, and a new legitimacy is required for the source of these obligations; in both cases it is found in consent. In Locke's case there is also explicit discussion of a further problem which has troubled many social contract philosophies. If consent, and continuing consent, is a necessary part of the ruler's title to legitimacy, how is one to explain the principle of majority rule? To Locke this is necessarily implicit in the initial compact. For to consent to be tied no further than a person agrees to at some future time is not to consent to anything at all. Every man, therefore, who consents to the institution of society necessarily, and implicitly, 'puts himself under an obligation to every one of that society to submit to the determination of the majority, and to be concluded by it; or else this original compact, whereby he, with others incorporates into one society, would signify nothing . . .'[35]

It does not seem an exaggeration to suggest that both Hobbes and Locke, with their belief in rationality and the self-interested motivation of human beings, convinced themselves that men in fact consented to those things that they ought to have consented to if they were to achieve the goals which they were assumed to desire. If one starts by assuming that all men are rational, if one then assumes that they desire certain goals, if one can demonstrate that these goals are best reached by a certain path, and if one then finds man on that path, it is a natural conclusion that man finds himself there as a result of a deliberate act of free choice. Today this form of reasoning is often treated as highly fictitious,[36] but the problems involved in the whole idea of a tacit consent are extraordinarily complex.

There is one further respect in which Locke's ideas differed markedly

[34] Ibid., Sect. 119.
[35] Ibid., Sect. 97.
[36] See, e.g., J. Plamenatz, *Consent, Freedom, and Political Obligation*, 2nd edn., (Oxford, 1968), p. 8.

from those of Hobbes, and which I have yet to mention. As we have seen, in Hobbes's society, the sovereign owes no duties to his people, while the people are, of course, under duties towards him; in Locke's world, the position is almost the other way round. The sovereign certainly owes duties to the people, for the very purpose of his authority is to protect the rights and property of the people. And the people certainly have an obligation to obey the laws of the sovereign; but Locke seems reluctant to say that the people actually owe duties to their sovereign. To meet this problem, Locke introduces the idea of a trust being imposed on the sovereign.[37] This seems to suit his purpose better than treating the relationships between people and sovereign as a sort of enduring contract which would involve mutual rights and duties. Thus, when he talks of the acts which justify rebellion he talks in terms of breach of trust rather than breach of contract.[38] The idea was not fully elaborated by Locke, and it did not play a major part in social contract theory in eighteenth-century thought until it was taken up again by Burke, towards the end of the century.

Hume

In 1739-40 the twenty-eight-year-old Scotsman David Hume[39] published his *Treatise of Human Nature*, the last Part of which contained a lengthy and incisive critique of the ideas of Locke and his supporters. The book had little impact at the time, and some years later Hume rewrote much of it; in 1748 he published an essay, *Of the Original Contract*, in which he again dissected Locke's theories. There is no question but that Hume was a far greater thinker than Hobbes or Locke or any of the other social contractarians of the time; nor is there any doubt that Hume's ideas on the social contract, on the role of law, consent, property, and contract are all of the greatest interest to legal theory, as well as to the historian of ideas. It is indeed curious how he has been neglected by legal philosophers.[40] What raises more difficulty is the attempt to assess the influence of Hume's ideas on later thinkers generally, and in particular, for our purposes, to attempt to assess his influence on contractual theory. On the whole, it seems probable that Hume's direct influence was small; his indirect influence, via Bentham, Adam Smith, and others, was probably much greater, though virtually impossible to measure.

[37] *Second Treatise*, Sect. 134.

[38] Ibid., Sects. 221, 222.

[39] David Hume (1711–76), philosopher and writer, was a Scotsman and close friend of Adam Smith. His most famous works are the *Treatise of Human Nature* (1739–40) (hereafter cited as *Treatise*), much of which was subsequently rewritten and published in the form of two *Enquiries*, one *Into the Human Understanding*, and the other, *Concerning the Principles of Morals*; and his *History of England* (1754–62).

[40] See F. A. Hayek, 'The Legal and Political Philosophy of David Hume', in his *Studies in Philosophy, Politics and Economics* (Chicago, London, Toronto, 1967), Chapter 7.

The failure of Hume's ideas to make any immediate impact is perhaps not surprising, for he was years ahead of his time. In his *Treatise*, for example, Hume discusses the source of promissory liability, and demolishes the will theory of promising many years before that theory had even appeared in English law. His analysis of the reasons for which promises are regarded as the source of obligations is highly utilitarian in character, as we shall see later. But after giving his own explanation of the source of promissory obligation he goes on to examine what he evidently takes to be the generally accepted explanation of the matter. Because people generally accept that the mere expression of an intention to do something creates no obligation, they have difficulty in understanding how the addition of a certain form of words can make any material difference. The conventional answer to this, says Hume, is that 'we *feign* a new act of the mind, which we call the *willing* an obligation; and on this we suppose the morality to depend'.[41] But this, he objects, is mere superstition, 'one of the most mysterious and incomprehensible operations that can possibly be imagin'd, and may even be compar'd to *transubstiation*, or *holy orders*, where a certain form of words, along with a certain intention, changes entirely the nature of an external object, and even of a human nature'.[42] There *is* no such act of the mind as *willing* something; and if there were, it is not the will alone which creates an obligation, but the expression of that will. Moreover, the expression of the will is sufficient for the creation of the obligation even though the promisor has a secret intention to deceive us. The reality, of course, is far simpler. Promises are binding for reasons of human convenience.

Hume totally rejected almost every aspect of the social contract ideas which were still so widely influential in his time. There was, first, no state of nature. It was a mere 'philosophical fiction which never had and never could have any reality'.[43] It resembles perhaps the Golden Age of the poets except that it is represented as full of war, violence, and injustice. And society was certainly never constituted by a social contract constituted by promises. For one thing societies evolve and form gradually, and anyhow even if there may, conceivably, have been some sort of agreement at the first institution of societies, the subsequent obligations of its citizens do not, and cannot, derive from any original agreement, to which they were not parties (and why should the promise of the father bind the son?), nor from any renewed agreement or promise of their own. In reality all rulers expect allegiance from those in their territories, and to argue that political obligations depend on voluntary consent or mutual promises would, in most countries, invite prosecution

---

[41] *Treatise*, Book III, Part III, Sect. V.
[42] Ibid.
[43] Book III, Part II, Sect. II.

for sedition.[44] Even at times of revolution, certainly in 1688, the mass of the people are not consulted although they may acquiesce. Nor is it possible to save the argument by invoking the notion of tacit consent. Even a tacit consent requires some element of choice; but in practice allegiance does not depend upon choice. Emigration is not usually a real alternative since most people have neither the money nor the ability to live in another country. On this, we can quote the words of Adam Smith, Hume's friend and follower in rejection of social contract theory:

> To say that by staying in a country a man agrees to a contract of obedience to government, is just the same with carrying a man into a ship and after he is at a distance from land, to tell him that by being in the ship he has contracted to obey the master.[45]

The truth is, says Hume, that the obligation to perform contracts, and the duty of allegiance owed to a state, are both based on self-interest of a similar kind, and neither derives from the other. It is as unreal to regard the duty of allegiance as based on a promise, as it would be so to treat the obligation to 'abstain from the possession of others'.[46] What is more, nobody doubts that allegiance is owed to absolute governments, as well as to governments based on consent. Such governments are as common as any, and yet experience shows that those who live under them feel the same sense of allegiance. Moreover, people commonly distinguish between the ordinary duty of allegiance and the superadded duty of fidelity which may arise where a person expressly promises loyalty or allegiance to a ruler.[47] It is also impossible, declares Hume, to suppose that society is founded to protect property rights. The concept of a property right is itself an artificial concept depending upon morality and justice; these are notions created and recognized by society and therefore cannot pre-date society.

The absence of anything resembling a contract between rulers and people does not mean that the ruler is under no obligations to the people, or that the people are never justified in rebellion. Hume simply argues that those writers who rest the duty of allegiance on the original contract have adopted an unnecessary and cumbersome mode of justifying a perfectly sound conclusion. Of course the people are justified in overturning their government, as soon as it ceases to answer to the purposes for which it exists. Its purpose is purely utilitarian, namely to provide the security and protection which can only be enjoyed in political society. It follows that 'whenever the civil magistrate carries his oppression so far as to render his authority perfectly intolerable, we are

---

[44] *Of the Original Contract*, in *The Social Contract*, ed. Sir Ernest Barker, p. 214.
[45] *Lectures on Jurisprudence*, ed. Meek, Raphael and Stein (Oxford, 1978), p. 403.
[46] *Treatise*, Book III, Part II, Sect. VIII.   [47] Ibid.

no longer bound to submit to it. The cause ceases; the effect must cease also.'[48] It is as simple as that, and the whole contractual edifice of political theory is unnecessary.

Before leaving Hume, I must say something further about a very interesting point concerning the relationship between his views on the social contract and his views on the foundations of promissory liability. After disposing of the will theory of promises, as we have seen above, Hume proceeds to treat the obligation to perform promises as deriving from pure convenience. A promise, he says, is in effect an expression of the promisor's resolution to do something, combined with a particular form of words which function as symbols or signs recognizable by others. If it were not for this additional significance attaching to a promise, 'promises wou'd only declare our former motives, and wou'd not create any new motive or obligation'.[49] In other words, Hume is saying that every one who declares that he is resolved to do something has a reason for making that declaration, and if a promise did not add anything of its own to the declaration, it would merely be restating that reason. (Or, as we might say, the promise would merely be evidence of the reason which led us to declare our resolve; indeed, the promise might be merely evidence of an existing obligation.)[50] If, then, the promise is to have any purpose, it must add some force to the existing reason or obligation and this it does by virtue of the fact that the words used are known to function as symbols or signs. These symbols or signs are known to involve a commitment on the part of the person who uses them so that a person who breaks his promise 'subjects himself to the penalty of never being trusted again in case of failure'.[51] There is nothing very sophisticated about the use of promises because 'There needs but a very little practice of the world, to make us perceive all these consequences and advantages'.[52] The interesting thing is that when Hume proceeds to explain how a promise acquires this particular signification, he seems to fall into precisely the contractarian language of which he is so critical when used of the concept of allegiance and political duty.

[W]hen each individual perceives the same sense of interest in all his fellows, he immediately performs his part of any contract, as being assur'd, that they will not be wanting in theirs. All of them by concert, enter into a scheme of actions, calculated for common benefit, and agree to be true to their word; nor is there anything requisite to form this concert or convention, but that every one have a sense of interest in the faithful fulfilling of engagements, and express that sense to other members of the society.[53]

The modern reader, especially perhaps the legal reader, is likely at this

---

[48] Book III, Part II, Sect. IX. [49] Ibid., Sect. V.
[50] See post, p. 143. [51] Treatise, Book III, Part II, Sect. V.
[52] Ibid. [53] Ibid.

point to accuse Hume of inconsistency. Is he here suggesting that promises acquire their significance by an agreement? Is he suggesting that men agree, in effect, to perform their agreements, or promise to perform their promises? The answer to this charge of inconsistency lies in the precise meaning of the words used by Hume, and in particular, the meaning of the word 'agreement'. Hume is using this word as synonymous with 'convention'. Both justice in general, and rights of property in particular, as well as the obligation to perform a promise, he has previously argued, derive from convention, in the same way that the use of money or language derive from convention. But,

This convention is not of the nature of a *promise*: For even promises themselves arise from human conventions. It is only a general sense of common interest; which sense all the members of the society express to one another, and which induces them to regulate their conduct by certain rules. I observe, that it will be for my interest to leave another in the possession of his goods, *provided* he will act in the same manner with regard to me. He is sensible of a like interest in the regulation of his conduct. When this common sense of interest is mutually express'd, and is known to both, it produces a suitable resolution and behaviour. And this may properly enough be call'd a convention or agreement betwixt us, tho' without the interposition of a promise; since the actions of each of us have a reference to those of the other, and are perform'd upon the supposition, that something is to be perform'd on the other part. Two men, who pull the oars of a boat, do it by an agreement or convention, tho' they have never given promises to each other.[54]

This passage is very revealing. Hume is here distinguishing between the act of agreeing or of making mutual promises on the one hand, and an 'agreement' which consists of merely doing something with a common purpose, and involving reciprocal obligations. This distinction is of central importance to the theme of this work, for it recognizes that *common action*, involving reciprocal obligations, though it may be called an agreement, nevertheless differs from *the making of an agreement* by an exchange of promises. It differs in two important but related ways; first, in that the reciprocal obligations in the first case arise out of the *common action*, that is, out of what is *done*, even though it is done in concert, while in the second case, the obligations arise out of what is *said*, that is, out of the expressed intentions, or promises, of the parties. And in the second place, it differs in that common action, although involving some measure of consent or agreement, does not rest entirely upon an act of consent or agreement, in the way that promissory liability may rest. The analogy as to the source of language is interesting. For Hume is clearly right in holding that communication through the medium of language would be impossible if people did not generally *agree* upon the meaning of the

[54] Book III, Part II, Sect. II; and see also the *Enquiry Concerning the Principles of Morals*, Appendix III.

words they used; but he is also clearly right in refusing to say that people *make an agreement* (even impliedly) to use words in any particular way.

It is, to the modern lawyer, almost irresistibly tempting to dispose of the distinction by saying that the case of common action is one of *implied* consent or agreement, while the case of express promises is one of *express* consent or agreement. Whether this approach will stand up to a full analysis will be the subject of discussion elsewhere.[55] Here I am concerned with history, and from the historical point of view the interesting, and indeed, extraordinary thing is, that in the area of social contractarianism Hume's ideas eventually came to be accepted by almost everybody, while in the wider, and legal, sphere of contractual thought, his ideas have never even been seriously developed, down to the present time.[56] The notion that social contract theory could be saved by invoking the idea of implied or tacit consent was, as we have seen, vigorously repudiated by Hume; and though he himself may not have been very successful in knocking Locke off his pedestal in the middle of the eighteenth century, his disciples eventually did so. Bentham, Adam Smith, and even Paley, succeeded in that exercise where Hume had failed. But in the wider area of contractual thought generally, and more especially in the legal field, the notion of an implied or tacit consent, became of enormous importance. Indeed, it is not too much to say that it was the notion of implied consent which, already in 1770, was coming to be the base to a completely new theory of obligation in the law. For, as the idea of free choice swept all before it, the paradigm of legal obligation came to be seen as that which was created by the deliberate and conscious choice of a man who made a promise; and by 1770 this was already beginning to lead to the conclusion that *all* legal obligations arose from free choice—which, if it was not expressed, must then be implied.

Rousseau

Jean-Jacques Rousseau (1712–78) published his little book *Du Contrat Social* in 1762. Rousseau was not a great thinker but his ideas subsequently had an influence out of all proportion to their intellectual value. He is famous in particular for one idea in this book which is of interest to us and that is the use he makes of the idea of a 'general will'.

This concept of the 'general will' seems to be not unrelated to those continental juristic ideas about contract in the late eighteenth and early nineteenth century, which have come to be known as 'will theory', and which eventually, if somewhat surprisingly, filtered into English law. It is hardly likely that Rousseau was influenced by the most famous of these

---

[55] In a forthcoming volume.

[56] It is worth noting that Hume had himself studied law in Scotland, though apparently he never took to the subject.

continental theories of contract, or at least the one which came to be best known in England, for that was contained in the *Traité des obligations* of the French jurist R. J. Pothier, which was published only the year before *Du Contrat Social*. But Rousseau was no stranger to the works of legal and political theorists. He was clearly acquainted with the works of Hobbes and Locke, of the seventeenth-century Natural Law jurists Grotius and Pufendorf, and also of a number of contemporary continental jurists.[57] Although Rousseau's ideas about the 'general will' influenced a number of later thinkers such as Hegel, and, in England the so-called 'Idealists' including T. H. Green and Bernard Bosanquet, there is certainly no evidence that, directly or indirectly, these ideas had any impact on English contractual theory.[58] But the close parallel between the political theory of the 'general will' and the contractual 'will theories' does at least justify a passing glance at the former.

Rousseau, like Hobbes and Locke, sees civil society being created by a social contract entered into by people in a state of nature. But the act of creation he sees in a very different fashion. It involves a somewhat mystical pooling of individual wills 'under the supreme direction of the general will'.[59] The people by this contract incorporate or create a sovereign, but at the same time sovereignty is itself 'nothing other than the exercise of the general will'. Although the general will is the creation of all the individual wills, it is in totality something over and above them. Thus, not only may each citizen find that his individual will differs from the general will, but the general will is not necessarily even the same as the will of all:

the general will studies only the common interest while the will of all studies private interest, and is indeed no more than the sum of individual desires. But if we take away from these same wills, the pluses and minuses which cancel each other out, the sum of the difference is the general will.[60]

It does not seem too fanciful to see some relationship between this idea and the somewhat more commonplace legal notion that a contract may have 'an intent' of its own which is separate from and distinct from the intent of either of the contracting parties, but is nevertheless the creation of their joint intent. Closely related to the whole concept of the general will is the problem which (as we have seen) troubled Locke, as it has troubled most social contract thinkers; namely, if society is based on the consent of its members, how does a person become bound by a majority

---

[57] Maurice Cranston, Introduction to the Penguin edition of Rousseau, *The Social Contract* (Harmondsworth, 1968), p. 26. Page references are to this edition.

[58] It is not impossible that T. H. Green had some impact on contractual thought in other respects, see *post*, p. 585.

[59] Book I, Chapter, 6, p. 61.

[60] Book II, Chapter 3, pp. 72-3.

decision to which he does not consent? Rousseau's answer to this is somewhat confused. In the first place it seems that the actual institution of the political society requires unanimous agreement; any dissenter remains outside it. But once society is instituted the position is different. Now, it seems that by voting at all I have consented to be bound by the general will; and if my vote is in the minority I have simply mistaken the general will. I therefore do, in effect, consent to everything done by the majority because that is the general will; at this point Rousseau appears to recollect that he has earlier said that the general will is not necessarily the will of the majority, and he therefore hastens to add that he has to presuppose that all the characteristics of the general will are to be found in the majority, for if these cease to be there, then there can be no freedom.[61]

Blackstone

It remains only to mention Blackstone as an important propagator of social contractarianism in the Locke tradition. If anybody was needed to convert Locke's ideas into an influential tool for lawyers—and perhaps none was needed for every educated lawyer must have read Locke—this part was played by Blackstone. Blackstone, of course, was no philosopher; he conceived his task in writing the *Commentaries* as that of trying to reduce the body of English law to a set of intelligible principles such as could be read with profit by all educated men. Despite the fierce onslaughts of Bentham, from which Blackstone's reputation has never wholly recovered, Blackstone says little about social contract ideas to which even Hume need have taken exception. The 'state of nature', he says, is 'too wild to be seriously admitted',[62] and is anyhow contrary to the revealed account of the origins of mankind (not that Hume would have agreed with that); 'the only true and natural foundations of society are the wants and fears of individuals'[63]—Hume virtually says the same. And although he goes on to say that the original contract 'in nature and reason must always be understood and implied, in the very act of associating together',[64] it seems clear that, at least at this point, he is also saying little that Hume would have disagreed with. For he is not here saying that men impliedly agree to observe the laws or to render allegiance to the State; what he says is very much what Hume says, namely that it is the sense of their own weakness that *keeps* men associated in political societies, and that the act of continuing so to associate implies the necessity for mutual rights and obligations. Thus the State must

---

[61] Book IV, Chapter 2, pp. 153–4.
[62] Blackstone's *Commentaries*, vol. i, Introduction, Sect. II, p. 47.
[63] Ibid.
[64] Ibid., pp. 47–8.

protect the individual, and the individual must obey the will of the whole. There are, it is true, other passages in the *Commentaries* (some of which will be referred to later) where Blackstone seems inclined to slip into the Lockean scheme of regarding every person as having impliedly promised to observe the laws, but these do not play a large part in his thinking.

Blackstone was the last major writer prior to 1770 to devote any attention—and it was, in the overall context, only a very minor attention—to social contract theory. And in many respects, the story of social contractarianism as an influential body of thought, at least in England, came to an end shortly after 1770 anyhow.[65] Only Burke, of major eighteenth-century political thinkers, could thereafter be said to be in the Lockean tradition, and Burke departed from Locke's ideas in many important respects. As Burke, and most of his fellow countrymen, shrank in horror from the excesses of the French Revolution in the 1790s, the virtues of rebellion began to seem less obvious than they had to Locke. On the other hand, one of Locke's less contractual ideas—that of regarding the sovereign as operating under a trust—appealed a good deal more to Burke, and came to have, in due course, much more significance. And by the time the Revolutionary and Napoleonic Wars had come to an end, the state of English political institutions did not lend themselves so readily to a contractarian approach. The Benthamite era was about to dawn, and the problem now was how to ensure that the interests of the governed and of their governors could be brought into harmony. That was not a task for contractual theory.

[65] But see *post*, p. 321, for Herbert Spencer. The work of John Rawls falls outside the scope of the present volume.

4

THE INTELLECTUAL BACKGROUND IN 1770—
II

THE RELICS OF MEDIEVAL THOUGHT

The Just Price

IT is now widely agreed that economic liberalism did not burst on the scene with the publication of *The Wealth of Nations* in 1776. For some two hundred years before that momentous event there had been a slow but not always steady movement towards an increase of economic freedoms. The change from the medieval to the market economy had been matched by, and was probably not uninfluenced by, a change in the intellectual climate. By 1770 these changes had gathered in momentum, and they were becoming more widely acceptable to the governing classes; but it is not pure antiquarianism that makes it worth beginning this story with a preliminary glance backwards at the older ideas. For the older ideas may well have had deeper roots than seemed the case in the nineteenth century. There is much in the modern world that suggests an affinity with some of the older traditions so that one may seriously pose the question whether we are not returning, in some respects, to those traditions, and whether they may not suggest that the great age of economic freedom represents an aberration rather than a norm in the development of English society.

A number of key ideas lay at the root of economic relationships in medieval societies in Western Europe. First, relationships were largely customary. A man had his place and role in a communal society; he inherited, usually, his father's trade or craft or status. He did what he did, not because he chose to, or agreed to, but because it was customary; in many cases the custom was backed by law, and anyhow law, custom, and morality were much less clearly distinguished at this time. His relationship with those with whom he dealt was also largely determined by customary patterns. If he was a labourer, the way he was paid, and how much he was paid (whether in money or in kind) was largely determined by custom. If he was a skilled artisan or craftsman, the work he did, the way he did it, and the amount he charged were likely to be largely customary. Secondly, economic ideas and ethical ideas were closely related. Some element of bargaining, and free choice, of course, must always have existed in man's relationships with his own kind, but the element of freedom was severely constrained by ethical ideas. Men were *not*, nor were they thought to be, free to do what they chose. Even their own property—as it came to be thought of in the seventeenth and eighteenth centuries—did not 'belong' to them. Land, the most important source of property, was not owned, but 'held'. The ancestors of the great landowners of the eighteenth century had been 'tenants' rather than owners in the fifteenth century. And if a man did not own his property to do what he chose with it, neither did he own his person absolutely. Medieval man was involved, whether he liked it or not, in an intricate network of relationships with his fellow men, and with the Church, which imposed duties on all men to each other, and to God. Thirdly, it was a natural corollary of these ideas that, in so far as freedom of choice did exist, that freedom must be exercised in a way which was consonant with a man's duty to his fellows and to God. The fundamental rules governing human relationships were designed to ensure that the relationship functioned in a way which was thought to be fair and just and in accordance with custom and tradition. In so far as free choice operated at all, it had to operate within these overall constraints.

From these medieval traditions there had sprung some firmly held convictions about contractual relationships. Justice was more important than freedom of choice. 'The essence of the medieval scheme of economic ethics had been its insistence on equity in bargaining—a contract is fair, St. Thomas had said, when both parties gain from it equally.'[1] Most, indeed, thought that strictly speaking it was not possible for both parties to an exchange to gain. 'That both sides to a bargain should be gainers sounds like a silly paradox.'[2] On this view an exchange either left both sides equally balanced, neither gaining nor losing, or it was imbalanced, one side gaining what the other lost. This way of thinking naturally led to the idea of the just price, the price at which a bargain, or an exchange, could be fairly carried through without gain or loss to either side. The notion of a just price (or just wage) and of its opposite—an extortionate price, or usury—was at the centre of medieval economic thought, and its influence was by no means dead in 1770. Customs and laws had grown up on the basis that it was the duty of those wielding authority—the Lord Chancellor, the Church, the local J.P.s—to see that prices and wages were just, and to stamp out the usurer. There were repeated attempts to impose price controls, especially on staple items such as bread and ale, as well as to regulate wages. Much scholasticism had gone into working out the implications of these ideas, and there were serious difficulties in

[1] R. H. Tawney, *Religion and the Rise of Capitalism* (first published 1926, reprinted Harmondsworth, 1972), p. 157.
[2] Leslie Stephen, *History of English Thought in the Eighteenth Century* (reprinted New York, 1962), ii. 253.

reconciling some of them with the very concept of trade. If everything had one just price, how was it possible for a person to buy at one price and sell at a higher? And yet how could any trade ever be done at all if a man could not sell for more than he bought? St. Thomas Aquinas and his followers had wrestled with these problems,[3] and modern historians have wrestled with the problem of what St. Thomas and his followers really meant. Perhaps, as has recently been argued, they were not so unworldly after all.[4] Perhaps they really did accept that, at least in trade, a just price was normally a market price, or a freely agreed price.[5] But if they accepted that, it seems clear that the bulk of their teaching was not concerned with the world of trade. It was directed to the largely closed medieval village community, and it is in relation to this kind of community that traces of the traditional ideas lingered on right up to 1770. Certainly the natural lawyers of the seventeenth century were still very much concerned with ideas about just prices and equality in contracting. Grotius, it is true, shows a tendency to dismiss the old learning where the parties have fully agreed upon a price of their own choosing,[6] but Pufendorf seems more doubtful on the point; at least he retains a considerable discussion on the question.[7]

In the relatively closed village community—still in the eighteenth century very much cut off from the outside world by poor communications—trade was not an important feature of life at all. Although subsistence farming was dying out, producers were still expected to sell their produce largely to consumers; people did not buy and resell for trade within these communities, although itinerant vendors might conduct a small amount of trade with neighbouring communities. But most buying and selling, even at the great fairs, still involved direct contact between producer and consumer. Indeed, the whole purpose of the fairs, in a sense, was to bring producers and buyers together at a time when the absence of middlemen made direct contact essential. This direct contact made the notion of a just price a much more real one, although it did not necessarily rule out any influence from the market situation. At a time when the principal commodities for sale were foodstuffs of various kinds, and the supply of food, especially wheat, varied so much from year to year, according to the harvest, prices did fluctuate very significantly.

But if in practice the market price of wheat fluctuated with the harvest,

---

[3] W. J. Ashley, *Introduction to English Economic History and Theory*, 4th ed. (London, 1909), pp. 132–48.

[4] De Roover, 'The Concept of the Just Price: Theory and Economic Policy', 18 *Journal of Economic Hist.* 481 (1958).

[5] Ibid.

[6] *De Jure Belli ac Pacis*, Book II, Chapter XII, Sects. VIII–XXVI.

[7] *De Jure Naturae at Gentium*, Book V, Chapter I, Sect. 8, Chapter III, Sects. 9, 10.

nobody doubted—neither rich nor poor, Church or laity—that every-body was entitled to a subsistence. A man's wage should be enough to enable him and his family to live, and if the price of wheat rose, not just temporarily as a result of one bad harvest, but steadily and over a period of any length, it was accepted that wages must rise too. Wages were, indeed, regulated or at least subject to regulation, at least in theory, from the fourteenth to the end of the eighteenth century. The earliest attempt to regulate wages, following the Black Death, was probably the result of the ensuing labour shortage, and was consequently an attempt to hold wages down, and in the fifteenth and early sixteenth centuries, there were again repeated attempts to impose maximum wage levels.[8] But the Regulations were so rarely revised, and after the Civil War, so ineffectively enforced, that there was a tendency for the levels to become minima rather than maxima. If employers had to pay more than the Regulation levels to get workmen, they were likely to do so. The medieval notion of a just wage had by the eighteenth century largely become transmuted into the idea of a subsistence wage. But if the governing classes of the seventeenth and eighteenth centuries were agreed that it was generally pointless to pay labourers more than a subsistence wage anyhow—for it would only lead them to work less[9]—they did at least still accept that the labourer had a right to subsist. By 1800 even that idea was beginning to succumb to the harsh new economic 'laws', but few would have challenged it in 1770.

It was not only goods which were still generally the subject of direct sale from producer to consumer. For services, especially those associated with food, were also largely supplied in the same way. In the cities a man might buy his bread, but in the villages the consumer would buy his wheat from the farmer, take it to the miller to grind it into flour, and then take the flour to the baker to have it made into bread. 'Millers and—to a greater degree—bakers were considered as servants of the community, working not for a profit but for a fair allowance.'[10] This type of distributive process, together with a considerable quantity of detailed regulations governing the operation of the local market, continued to reflect the older traditions about the nature of society and the role of contract well into the eighteenth century. It was not yet obsolete in 1770.

The paternalistic model existed in an eroded body of Statute law, as well as common law and custom. It was the model which, very often, informed the actions of Government in times of emergency until the 1770s; and to which

---

[8] E. Lipson, *Economic History of England*, iii. 275–6.
[9] Christopher Hill, *Reformation to Industrial Revolution*, p. 175.
[10] E. P. Thompson, 'The Moral Economy of the English Crowd in the Eighteenth Century', 50 *Past and Present* 76, p. 83 (1971).

many local magistrates continued to appeal. In this model, marketing should be, so far as possible, *direct*, from the farmer to the consumer. The farmers should bring their corn in bulk to the local pitching market; they should not sell it while standing in the field, nor should they withhold it in the hope of rising prices. The markets should be controlled; no sales should be made before stated times, when a bell would ring; the poor should have the opportunity to buy grain, flour, or meal first, in small parcels, with duly-supervised weights and measures. At a certain hour, when their needs were satisfied, a second bell would ring, and larger dealers (duly licensed) might make their purchases. Dealers were hedged around with many restrictions, inscribed upon the misty parchments of the laws against forestalling, regrating and engrossing, codified in the reign of Edward VI. They must not buy (and farmers must not sell) by sample. They must not buy standing crops, nor might they purchase to sell again (within three months) in the same market at a profit, or in neighbouring markets, and so on. Indeed, for most of the eighteenth century the middleman remained legally suspect, and his operations were, in theory, severely restricted.[11]

I will refer later to the old offences of forestalling, regrating, and engrossing. It is enough here to stress that if the older traditions about just prices were now (or perhaps even if they had always been) subject to market influences, it was quite clear that they did presuppose a certain type of market. They presupposed the absence of monopoly. They presupposed that the supply of foodstuffs, especially, should be open and above board; there should be no hoarding, no holding up the public to ransom in times of harvest failure. What was available for sale must indeed be made available, openly, and to consumers before dealers. It was thus not so much a free market as a regulated market, and the regulation was largely in the interests of the consumers.

Usury

If the just price was one side, usury was the opposite side of the coin, and throughout the Middle Ages usury was a burning question. It did not then have the same restricted sense which it normally bears today. To lawyers, perhaps, usury may have strictly meant payment for the use of money, rather than compensation for non-payment of money due (which was then the meaning of interest), but the word was also often used (even by lawyers) in a broader sense to mean any extortionate or grossly inequitable bargain.[12] 'The truth is, indeed, that any bargain, in which one party obviously gained more advantage than the other, and used his power to the full, was regarded as usurious.'[13] The social and religious

---

[11] Ibid. But Thompson is wrong in saying that the sale of standing crops was prohibited. This was only so where they were bought for resale. See *Slade's* case (1602) 4 Co. Rep. 91a, 76 E.R. 1072 and *Bristow* v. *Waddington* (1806) 2 B. & P. (N.R.) 354, 127 E.R. 664.

[12] R. H. Tawney, *Religion and the Rise of Capitalism*, p. 109.

[13] Ibid., p. 158.

background to usury are fully explored in Tawney's classical study, and more recently, Professor Simpson has traced the legal developments in some detail.[14] I can therefore deal with the subject briefly.

Till the end of the fifteenth century all lending at interest (in the modern sense) was, in theory at least, totally prohibited, although the common lawyers were willing to enforce penal bonds which could in practice provide a method of charging interest.[15] Even in 1571 an Act of the Elizabethan Parliament declared that 'all usurie being forbydden by the lawe of God is synne and detestable'. Nevertheless, usury was beginning to change its meaning, or at least its acceptability. For by this time it was coming to be confined to extortionate bargains, or extortionate rates of interest, and a reasonable return on a loan was coming to be given a grudging acquiescence. The Act of 1571 (repeating in this respect an earlier Act of 1545 which had been repealed in Edward VI's reign in 1551) in practice removed the prohibition on loans at interest not exceeding ten per cent. Even this Act did not permit the creditor to sue for such interest; it merely enabled him to recover payment of the loan, the actual interest remaining (in theory) forfeitable. But in practice the result of the Act was largely to legalize interest at rates of ten per cent or less, and when, in 1623, the rate was reduced to eight per cent, the enforceability of such interest was finally conceded.[16]

Ideas may, for once, have changed more slowly than the laws, or perhaps this is an example of the law's early attachment to economic liberalism. Certain it is that long after the legal enforceability of reasonable interest was effectively conceded, the debates among the Schoolmen as to what was usury, and when it was acceptable, continued to rage.[17] But in one sense all this was in practice becoming obsolete 'almost before it was produced'.[18] For the basic assumption that economic relations were subject to the broad disciplines of the Christian Church and Christian ethics was now unfounded. Secular morality had increasingly taken over in the commercial England of the seventeenth century. In 1622 it was being said by the judges that 'usury which is allowed by statute has obtained such strength by usage, that it would be a great impediment to traffic and commerce if it should be impeached'.[19]

But in another sense the ideas about usury lingered on, and indeed, have never wholly disappeared from English moral or legal thought,

---

[14] R. H. Tawney, *Religion and the Rise of Capitalism* and A. W. B. Simpson, *A History of the Common Law of Contract* (Oxford, 1975), especially at pp. 113–17, 510–18.
[15] A. W. B. Simpson, op. cit.
[16] Holdsworth, *H.E.L.*, viii. 110.
[17] R. H. Tawney, *Religion and the Rise of Capitalism*, pp. 186–7.
[18] Ibid., p. 186.
[19] *Sanderson v. Warner* (1622) Palmer 291, 2 Rolle Rep. 239, cited A. W. B. Simpson, *A History of the Common Law of Contract*, p. 514.

though the flame flickered very low in the middle of the nineteenth century. The idea that merely seeking a return for a loan was itself something usurious and sinful had largely disappeared by the seventeenth century; but the idea that an extortionate or unfair bargain was morally unacceptable did not disappear.[20] The forfeiture of a mortgage, or a penalty on a bond, even 'excessive' interest, continued to be repugnant to good conscience, and subject to the control of the Chancellors. Even in the eighteenth century, interest rates remained under statutory control although it was becoming increasingly clear that this control produced unsatisfactory distortions in the economy. For the usury laws did not apply to the Government, and when market rates of interest rose above the legal rate, all capital flowed to the Government, and private borrowers—landlords, farmers, merchants—were unable to obtain funds although they were willing to pay higher rates.[21] Even Adam Smith did not totally condemn the usury laws, and it was not until Bentham launched his attack on them in his *Defence of Usury*, first published in 1790, that intellectual opinion generally turned against them altogether.

THE ROLE OF GOVERNMENT AND OF THE INDIVIDUAL

The decline of the overall moral authority of the Church in the medieval economy was not immediately followed by a free for all; it was rather followed by two hundred years during which the state attempted to fulfil the role formerly played by the Church, with its secular laws substituting, somewhat half-heartedly perhaps, for the laws of God. Modern economic historians tend to discount the notion that the Governments of Elizabeth I's reign ever attempted an overall control of the national economy, but the fact remains that they pursued three goals which, taken together, involved a substantial measure of regulation.[22] These three goals had as their basic aims the regulation of the labour force, the encouragement of key industries, especially shipbuilding, and the advancement of agriculture. The labour force was, in many ways, the subject of the greatest degree of regulation. The Statute of Artificers (usually called the Statute of Apprentices) was passed in 1563 and remained on the Statute book until 1819; the Poor Law Act of 1601—which provided for much else besides poor relief—remained largely operative until the twentieth century. Between them, these Acts attempted 'to banish idleness, to advance husbandry and to yield to the hired person, both in times of scarcity and in times of plenty, a convenient proportion of wages'.[23]

---

[20] I think this point is insufficiently brought out in Professor Simpson's account which stresses the common law as opposed to the Chancery tradition.

[21] T. S. Ashton, *Economic History of England in the Eighteenth Century*, p. 29.

[22] Clark, *The Wealth of England*, p. 83.

[23] Ibid.

They controlled entry into the class of skilled workmen by providing for a compulsory seven years' apprenticeship; they reserved the superior trades for the sons of the better off; they assumed a universal duty to work on all the able-bodied; and empowered justices to require unemployed artificers to work in husbandry; they required permission for a workman to transfer from one employer to another; they severely restricted the freedom of movement of the poor by enabling a person without means to be removed by order of the justices to his original parish or last place of settlement; and they empowered justices to fix wage rates for virtually all classes of workmen. On the other hand, there was a *quid pro quo* for all this: the Poor Law recognized the right of the indigent to poor relief, to be provided at the charge of the parish, and there were also other provisions for the benefit of labourers and artisans such as attempts to ensure that they were employed under contracts of a year's duration.

The encouragement of industry and trade in Elizabethan England was attempted in a number of ways, but principally by the imposition of tariffs, or the granting of subsidies (then known as 'bounties'), on imports and exports. In the modern world restrictions on exports of ordinary trading commodities would seem an extraordinarily perverse policy; but throughout the whole of this period constant attempts were made to ban or regulate the export of one commodity or another. Sometimes this was done on grounds of supposed national interest—as with the restrictions on the export of wool; but frequently the restrictions seem to have been a simple response to pressure from the home purchasers of some product who realized that a prohibition of export would lower the demand and hence the price in England. There was also a constant background of ideas about international trade—those of the so-called 'mercantile' economists—which seem to have fluctuated in their influence on policy. These ideas were not unrelated to those governing ordinary exchanges or bargains. Here too it was widely assumed that an exchange might leave the position of the parties unchanged or that one might gain, while the other lost. The idea that both parties gained from trade seemed as paradoxical as the idea that both parties to an ordinary sale could gain. This—together, of course, with the new international rivalries developing in the seventeenth and eighteenth centuries—frequently led to the idea that a nation's trading policy should be calculated to benefit itself and beggar its neighbours. How this was to be achieved, needless to say, was usually a matter of acute controversy.

All these methods of regulating labour and international trade involved a loss of freedom for those who would and could have forged ahead independently. But there were other and even more direct infringements of commercial freedom. There were the monopolies granted by Elizabeth and later by the Stuarts. The restriction of a particular foreign trade to some society of merchant adventurers was, perhaps, obnoxious enough to those who would have liked to participate themselves; but it was as nothing to the resentments roused by the monopolies granted within the realm by James I, which were, in due course, declared illegal as granted without Parliamentary approval. There were also some extraordinary prohibitions on the manufacture or use of particular products, such as the Royal order to destroy the use of a needle-making machine in 1624, to prohibit the casting of brass buckles in 1633 and the use of sawmills for sawing wood in 1635.[24] This was protectionism run riot.

Throughout the late seventeenth century and the greater part of the eighteenth century these ideas had been coming increasingly under fire. But for every move in the direction of freedom of trade or freedom of contract, there was often a counter-move a year or two later. In 1721 Walpole had freed the export of many woollen and manufactured goods, and many import duties had been reduced. But in the same year a savage attempt was made to suppress altogether the new cotton industry.[25] And though writers, merchants, and economists (they were not called that then) may have called for the freeing of this or that trade, or the removal of this or that restriction, it was usually assumed that these were the call of the self-interested, and that it was the function of the Government to remain in overall charge. It was still widely assumed that the interests of men were in fundamental conflict amongst themselves, and that consequently public and private interests were likely to conflict. Naturally, therefore, it remained the function of Government to arbitrate over these conflicts of interest.

One idea that pervaded practically all thinking before 1750 was that the government had the right, even the duty, to regulate the economy in the national interest . . . Everyone shared these aims: the governed as well as the government, poor farmers clamouring for protection from exploitation by avaricious landlords and landlords seeking freedom to use their lands as they pleased. All proposals from pressure groups for particular policies emphasized that the suggested course of action would make the realm secure and prosperous.[26]

HARBINGERS OF THE NEW AGE

I have already discussed the social contract aspects of the work of Hobbes and Locke. Implicit in their ideas was a great deal about the nature of

---

[24] Christopher Hill, *Reformation to Industrial Revolution*, p. 95.
[25] Clark, *The Wealth of England*, p. 166.
[26] L. A. Clarkson, *The Pre-Industrial Economy in England 1500–1750* (London, 1971), p. 192.

society they envisaged in the future. Indeed, it is not too much to say that the seeds of bourgeois economic liberalism are well and truly sowed in the works of both Hobbes and Locke. This is not to say that Hobbes was in any sense a supporter of *laissez-faire*. In general he shared the mercantilist assumptions of the times regarding the role of the State in the encouragement of economic activity. Perhaps this is less true of Locke,[27] with his emphasis on the minimal role of the Sovereign as protector of property; but both Hobbes and Locke clearly envisaged the primary function of the State as being the maintenance and due enforcement of rights of property and the rules of a private market economy. In this new world of theirs,

Society becomes a lot of free and equal individuals related to each other as proprietors of their own capacities and of what they have acquired by their exercise. Society consists of relations of exchange between proprietors. Political society becomes a calculated device for the protection of this property and for the maintenance of an orderly relation of exchange.[28]

I need not spend much time on this aspect of Hobbes and Locke for the ground has already been thoroughly covered, notably in Professor Macpherson's *The Political Theory of Possessive Individualism*.[29] Professor Macpherson has identified a number of key assumptions in Hobbes's thought which all ultimately played their part in establishing the ideals of the market economy.[30] These assumptions which are also found in Locke, though not unalloyed by his Natural Law ideas, may be summarized as follows:

(1) Human beings are free from control by others; what men do, they do freely.

(2) Relationships with other human beings are voluntarily entered into out of motives of self-interest.

(3) The individual is essentially the proprietor of his own person and capacities; he can alienate his own labour by a contract which is perceived as a disposal of something belonging to the individual in much the same way as an alienation of his land or his goods. I have not said much about Hobbes's ideas about property; but on this point the ideas of Locke were immensely more influential.

(4) 'Human society consists of a series of market relations.' In this fourth assumption Professor Macpherson summarizes the central point of economic liberalism as it came to be preached so vigorously a hundred years after Hobbes's death. He argues that Hobbes's ideas were essentially

---

[27] According to Keynes, Locke stood 'with one foot in the mercantile world, and with one foot in the classical world': *The General Theory of Employment, Interest and Money* (London, 1936), p. 343.

[28] C. B. Macpherson, *The Political Theory of Possessive Individualism*, p. 3.

[29] See also his Introduction to the Pelican edition of *The Leviathan* (Harmondsworth, 1974).

[30] Macpherson lists seven; I have combined some of them in the interests of conciseness.

related to the emerging market society, and that Hobbes was, in effect, telling his fellow countrymen that in this new form of society a sovereign was essential to lay the ground rules, protect life and property, and define and enforce contracts.[31] The essential selfishness of man, together with his new-found freedom to act in his own interest, were what had made the need for a powerful sovereign so much greater than in the past:

A sovereign is needed to hold everyone within the limits of peaceful competition. The more nearly the market society approximates a possessive market society, subject to the centrifugal forces of opposed competitive self-interests, the more necessary a single centralized sovereign power becomes. In a customary society a network of conditional property rights may be maintained without a single central sovereign. But in a market society, where property becomes an unconditional right to use, to exclude others absolutely from the use of, and to transfer or alienate land and other goods, a sovereign is necessary to establish and maintain individual property rights. Without a sovereign power, Hobbes said, there can be no property . . .[32]

It may be added that this is why contract is such a central concept to Hobbes. Not only is it contract which creates civil society in the first place, but one of the primary purposes of that society, once created, is to enforce contracts. Moreover, as Professor Macpherson rightly insists, Hobbes sees contract very much in terms of a market relationship. It is, in the first place, all very rational. Men can see the point of the rule that contracts should be observed, but cannot always be trusted to abandon the short-term advantages of breaking a contract. In short (as a modern economist would say) contracts must be enforced to stop the freerider who will cheerfully accept the other party's performance if it is due first, but then neglect his own.[33] And in the second place, prices in the new market are set by what the buyer is willing to pay. In a celebrated passage Hobbes sweeps away all the old learning about Commutative Justice, about the just price and the equality of value of things contracted for. 'The value of all things contracted for', says Hobbes, 'is measured by the Appetite of the Contractors; and therefore the just value, is that which they be contented to give.'[34] Commutative justice, in short, is receiving what you are contractually entitled to receive.

(5) The fifth assumption which Professor Macpherson finds in Hobbes's thought is that political society is an artificial contrivance of human beings, designed to protect the individual's person, property, and goods, and to preserve orderly relationships of exchange between individuals.

[31] Macpherson, *The Political Theory of Possessive Individualism*, pp. 95–106.
[32] Ibid., pp. 95–6.
[33] Ibid., pp. 97–8.
[34] *Leviathan*, Part I, Chapter 15, p. 208.

We have seen enough of Hobbes's ideas to understand how central this idea was to his scheme.

If much of this is implicit rather than explicit in the ideas of Hobbes, and perhaps even less explicit in Locke, there were not lacking those who would quite explicitly make a case for economic liberalism. Even in the sixteenth century there had been those ready to argue in this way. Here, for instance, is an extract from Thomas Wilson's *Discourse upon Usury*, written in mid-century, though the views expressed are not those of Wilson himself:

For, I pray you, what trade or bargyning can there be among merchants, or what lending or borrowing among al men, if you take awaye the assurance and hope of gayne? What man is so madde to deliver his moneye out of his own possession for naughte? or where is he that will not make of his owne the best he can? or who is he that will lende to others and want himself? You see all men are now so wise, that none will lend for moonshine in the water; and therefore if you forbid gaine, you destroy entercourse of merchandize, you overthrowe bargainze.[35]

In the late seventeenth and early eighteenth centuries this kind of talk was becoming more common and more insistent, though it may still have been a minority view outside the mercantile community. Among this class, however, opinion seems to have hardened long before it spread through the country. In 1684, for example, Richard Steele in *The Tradesman's Calling* discusses the relationship between commercial enterprise and ethics for the benefit of the small shopkeeper.[36] Steele was well acquainted with the authorities about equity in bargaining, about just prices and fair dealings. But he suggests that in practice there are no ways in which just prices can be objectively determined, and the individual must judge for himself. 'Here, as in other cases, an upright conscience must be the clerk of the market.'[37]

A few years later Sir Dudley North published his *Discourses upon Trade*. North was a vigorous free trader who insisted that trade benefited both sides. Trade was 'a commutation of superfluities' in which each gave what he could spare in exchange for what he needed.[38] Since trade was voluntary on both sides it was absurd to assume that what was a gain to one side must be a loss to the other. Moreover, what was good for the individual was good for the nation. The trader profited from his trade but did the country not prosper too? Thus a hundred years before Adam

[35] See Thomas Wilson, *A Discourse Upon Usury*, ed. R. H. Tawney, p. 249.
[36] See R. H. Tawney, *Religion and the Rise of Capitalism*, pp. 242-4. Steele was not himself a tradesman, but a congregational minister, though he seems to have 'understood the spiritual needs of the City'. Ibid., p. 242.
[37] Cited R. H. Tawney, ibid., p. 243.
[38] E. Lipson, *Economic History of England*, iii. 15.

Smith, many of his ideas were already in the air, and even in print. Another work of a similar character was Sir Josiah Child's *A New Discourse on Trade*, published in 1693 though perhaps written as early as 1669. Child, as we shall see later, had something to say about the backwardness of the law.

Amongst the most remarkable precursors of Adam Smith there was also Sir William Petty, ancestor of the Lansdowne family, one of the great Whig families of the eighteenth century. Petty was scientist, industrialist, statistician, inventor, parliamentarian, and economist. Amongst other activities he found time to write a *Treatise on Taxes and Contributions* (1662) in which he argued (within limits) for free trade. With men like Petty becoming involved in Parliament and public affairs (and he was far from alone), it was inevitable that these ideas would gradually become more acceptable to those wielding political authority. By the middle of the eighteenth century Parliamentary committees on trading and commercial questions had begun, if not always consistently, to accept the case for economic freedom. In 1751, for instance, a Committee of the House of Commons on Trade and Manufactures commented adversely on recent prosecutions to enforce the regulations on apprenticeships. The Committee reported that:

Since the improvement of trade in general, it is found that all manufactures find their own value according to their goodness; and that scarce any prosecutions have been carried on upon these Statutes but against such as have excelled in their trades by force of their own genius and not against such as have been ignorant in their professions.[39]

Here in this one passage are to be found several of the themes which were to be elaborated by Adam Smith. Regulations as to quality are futile because manufactures 'will find their own value'. The Regulations are, anyhow, useless for the protection of the public since they are enforced not against the incompetent but (as a restrictive practice) to control those who would otherwise excel. And so on.

In 1756–7 there occurred the remarkable case of the Gloucestershire weavers which illustrates the fluctuations in opinion as well as any other event of the times.[40] In 1728 the local justices had revived the practice of fixing minimum wages for weavers in Gloucestershire but the clothiers had ignored these wage levels, and attempts at enforcement had been in vain. In 1756 the weavers petitioned Parliament and an Act was passed confirming the authority of the justices to fix wages. A full-scale hearing then took place before the local justices at which the clothiers presented a threefold case against wages fixing. They argued, first, that the fixing

[39] Ibid., iii. 290.
[40] For the whole of this episode, see E. Lipson, ibid., iii. 266–71.

of wages was largely impractical anyhow; there were so many types of cloth, and such a wide variety of skills involved, that it was not practicable to fix one, or even a handful of rates. Hundreds of different rates would be required, and even then it would be virtually impossible to prescribe different rates for work well done and work ill done. Secondly, they argued on fairly overt political grounds that the justices should not give aid and comfort to workers who were stirring up trouble. And thirdly, they argued openly and frankly for freedom of contract: 'We think it repugnant to the liberties of a free people and the interests of trade that any law should supersede a private contract honourably made between a master and his workman.'

The justices were, apparently convinced by these arguments, and declined to fix any wage rates. There followed a six-weeks' strike by the weavers as a result of which the justices went back on their previous decision and sanctioned a wage scale. However, few of the clothiers observed it, and in the following year they in turn petitioned Parliament with the same arguments that they had previously presented to the justices. Parliament was also convinced by these arguments and promptly repealed the confirmatory Act which it had passed only the previous year. But this was not the end of the story for Parliament itself did not proceed in a particularly rational manner at this time, perhaps for the very reason that opinion had not settled strongly enough for a consistent policy to be adopted. Thus even after the events of 1756–7 Parliament by no means abandoned the habit of legislating to fix prices or wages in some particular industry or region whenever a pressure group was sufficiently persuasive. But the fixing of wage rates by local justices (which had been going on since 1563) was, by this time, on the decline. From the mid-eighteenth century, wage assessments steadily became less frequent and their enforcement more sporadic.[41]

Over all, it is certain that slowly and inexorably, opinion was shifting. I have quoted above the remarks of L. A. Clarkson to the effect that before 1750 the role of Government in regulating and controlling the economy was still accepted by 'everyone'. It is clear that this was not literally true, and as time went on, it became less and less true. 'For more than a hundred years before the industrial revolution', says T. S. Ashton, 'the State was in retreat from the economic field.'[42] It may have been slow, and it may have been a retreat in good order; but it was a retreat none the less. 'In 1776 Adam Smith turned his batteries on a crumbling structure.'[43]

As opinion turned against a wide role for Government in the economic

---

[41] See W. E. Minchinton (ed.), *Wage Regulation in Pre-Industrial England* (Newton Abbot, 1972).
[42] *The Industrial Revolution 1760–1830* (London, 1947), p. 138.
[43] Ibid., p. 139.

sphere, so the place of the individual necessarily became more central, both in the world, and in men's ideas. Individualism had never been wholly absent in English society even in the Middle Ages. But during the seventeenth century, and increasingly thereafter, individualism was ceasing to play a subordinate role in human relationships and coming to be the dominant force of the times.[44] The older restrictions began to crumble on all sides. A market economy demanded freedom for men to work how they pleased, and the old regulatory framework of the Statute of Apprentices and the Poor Law was a serious obstacle to men's freedom to work as they chose. But the Acts were largely falling into obsolescence even though formal amendment was rare and complete repeal still a long way ahead. Still, there were changes. The Courts, for one thing, had long played a role in interpreting this legislation very narrowly.[45] And in 1694 Parliament itself had repealed the sections of the Apprentices Act excluding the sons of poorer freeholders from the clothing industry.

Similarly, monopolies and combinations had long imposed fetters on a man's right to work as he pleased. The old guilds, which had been largely responsible for enforcing the Statute of Apprentices, had been much weakened by the social dislocations of the Civil War. In addition, other factors had worked in the same direction. The Great Fire of London, for instance, had resulted in the building trade being thrown open to all comers; and at the end of William III's wars, all trades had been opened to the discharged soldiers.[46] The development of new industries based on coal, such as the Birmingham metal industries, also owed much to the fact that coal was being dug outside the towns controlled by the guilds, and was thus a free industry. The attack on monopolies in the seventeenth century had been sufficiently fierce to prevent the overt creation of new monopolies even by Parliamentary authority, though this had not prevented many combinations coming into existence amongst manufacturers in the eighteenth century. These combinations, it is true, often attempted to fix prices and other terms of trade.[47] By the end of the eighteenth century combinations on a national scale were not uncommon. But they were not powerful enough or exclusive enough to present a serious obstacle to the enterprising industrialist who wanted to go it alone when the opportunity occurred. They do not seem to have been a serious obstacle to freedom of enterprise.

In many areas of life the attack on monopolies and on the legal regulations of trade and business created a freer and more competitive market than there had ever been before or has ever existed since. The

---

[44] E. Lipson, *Economic History of England*, ii, p. viii; pp. cxv–cxvi, cxxv.
[45] See *post*, Chapter 5, pp. 127–8.
[46] Clark, *The Wealth of England*, p. 174.
[47] T. S. Ashton, *The Industrial Revolution*, pp. 122–24.

professions are a case in point. In the eighteenth century the medical profession was, for example, almost completely unregulated. Medicine was 'a free economic activity like any other'.[48] And the same was true of many other individualistic professions. 'In England it was', says G. M. Trevelyan, 'a great age for the energies of the private person—the adventurer, the merchant, the author—acting freely in a free community.'[49]

It is worth considering what was involved in this 'release of energy',[50] this new individualism, this new aggregation of freedoms; who wanted it; and why. The answer may be speculative but it seems reasonable to suppose that those who wanted it were the young, the energetic, the intelligent, the inventive, the enterprising. And it seems equally clear why they wanted these new freedoms. They surely wanted them because they wanted to be free of the burden of protecting, cosseting, carrying, the less able, the feeble, the inefficient, the unenergetic and unenterprising. In the medieval society, from which England had been slowly extricating itself for nearly three centuries, but traces of whose influence still lingered on, there had been an essential protective element in the communal spirit. The closed village communities had, to some degree, lived like the extended family of many African and Asian communities today. In these communities it is custom which rules, and as John Stuart Mill observed, 'Custom is the most powerful protector of the weak against the strong.'[51] In a custom-ruled society, work and rewards are allocated by some authoritative and traditional method which ensures that the strong labour for the weak as well as for themselves. In these communities people do not *compete* against each other, though they may compete against those outside the community. Naturally, when people do begin to compete, some will succeed and others will fall by the wayside. But in the long run, it may well be in the interest of all to allow the energetic and enterprising to detach themselves from the rest, to forge ahead on their own, even if in the meantime this means that some will be sorely pressed in the effort to keep up, and the stragglers will be left behind altogether. Before we condemn those who wanted to take part in this race, who wanted competition or freedom, rather than custom and

---

[48] Christopher Hill, *Reformation to Industrial Revolution*, p. 209, citing R. S. Roberts, *Medical History*, viii. 217–18 (1964).

[49] 'The Age of Johnson', p. 1, in *Johnson's England*, ed. Turberville.

[50] This phrase comes from a description of the parallel if somewhat later developments in America. See Willard Hurst, *Law and the Conditions of Freedom in the Nineteenth Century United States* (Madison, 1956), Chapter 1.

[51] *Principles of Political Economy* (various editions), Book II, Chapter 4. Mill here distinguishes between competition and custom as methods of social organization, a distinction which, it has been suggested, may have inspired Sir Henry Maine's more celebrated remarks concerning status and contract: Mark Blaug, *Economic Theory in Retrospect* (revised edn., Homewood, Ill., 1968), p. 175.

communalism, for their lack of compassion to their fellow men, there are some things to be said in their defence.

The first is that the demand for freedom carried with it a recognition of the right to equal freedom for all. The philosophy of the market economy, already implicit, as we have seen, in the ideas of Hobbes and Locke, assumed the equal freedom of everybody before the law and in the market place. We have also seen how, despite the political power and wealth of the aristocracy and the gentry in the eighteenth century, there was no fixed caste system. Compared with France, for instance, the class system was loose in the extreme. Not only was there a considerable degree of mobility, but the highest and lowest were equally subject to the law. It is, of course, easy to sneer at Locke for simply ignoring those—the great majority—who had no vote, when he wrote that 'every single person becomes subject equally, with other the meanest men, to those laws which he himself as part of the legislature, had established; nor could anyone, by his own authority, avoid the force of the law, when once made, nor by the pretence of superiority, plead exemption, thereby to licence his own, or the miscarriage of any of his dependents.'[52] But in the contemporary world, it was not a denial of political rights to the propertiless and poor which was in any way unusual, but rather the insistence on equality before the law, and in the market place, for all those who did have property as well as for those, where it was relevant, who had none.

The second point to be made in the defence of those who were seeking greater economic freedom is that they had first obtained and developed these freedoms amongst themselves, before seeking to extend them to the rest of the community. The merchants, in particular, had developed principles amongst themselves, and moral values in their wake, suitable for commercial and market dealings, long before these principles came to be applied to all social relationships. And while commercial men were striving after greater economic freedom in the eighteenth century, the paternal and protective tradition in the relationship between peer and domestic servant, landlord and tenant, farmer and labourer, gentry and poor, was still strong; aspects of it survived even in the more ruthless world of the nineteenth century. One of the more important practical consequences of the older values which survived throughout the whole of the eighteenth century was the recognition in the Poor Law of 1601 of a legal right to subsistence for the indigent. To those who have become accustomed to the ministration of the Welfare State this may seem little enough indeed; but in 1600 England must have been almost alone in the world in formally recognizing this legal right in its statute laws. Even in 1770 the new demands for freedom, competition, and the right to forge

[52] *Second Treatise*, Sect. 94.

on ahead, had not yet begun to challenge the rights of those who fell so far behind that their very subsistence become a responsibility for the property owners.

The third point to be made in defence of these early fighters for economic freedom is to stress, on the one hand, the nature of the restrictions they were trying to escape from, and on the other, the immensity of the opportunities they were trying to grasp. If it is true that many of the older traditions and customs had the result, and the not undesigned result, of protecting the old and the feeble and the less enterprising, the restrictions themselves must have come to seem maddeningly frustrating in the more scientific and rational age of the eighteenth century. The new generation of economic, commercial, and political writers and thinkers who came to the fore after the Restoration, and still more after 1688, saw what could be done with enterprise and hard work, if only men were allowed to get on with it.[53]

THE NEW MORALITY

By 1770 the process of secularizing morality had gone a long way. This may seem surprising to the modern reader who is apt to look back even to the nineteenth century as a time when Christian ethics were still professed, at least publicly, by almost everyone. And, of course, this was no less true of the eighteenth century. People still *believed* not only in God, and Christianity, but in hell fire; and a professed atheist, like Hume, was a subject of curiosity, not to say morbid fascination. But the point is that the morality of the Christian Church, except on matters of purely spiritual concern, was becoming more and more identified with the morality of the State and of those who ran it. By the eighteenth century, 'the very concept of the Church as an independent moral authority, whose standards may be in sharp antithesis to social conventions, has been abandoned.'[54] The traditional morality, suitable for the pre-commercial and industrial age, now seemed, and was even called, 'a Gothic superstition'.[55] If, for a moment, we move some fifteen years on, from 1770 to 1785 when Archdeacon Paley first published his *Principles of Moral and Political Philosophy*, we shall see how little that is peculiarly Christian is to be found in his ideas. What he offers is a sort of Divine-based utilitarianism, differing little from Bentham's more secular version except in being less subtle and inventive. Only in one place in his *Principles* does Paley say anything which might suggest the possibility of some serious conflict between Christian and secular ethics and even that

[53] P. G. M. Dickson, *The Financial Revolution in England*, p. 6; R. M. Hartwell, *The Industrial Revolution* (Oxford, 1970), pp. 114–15.
[54] R. H. Tawney, *Religion and the Rise of Capitalism*, p. 192.
[55] Ibid., p. 194.

passage he himself treated as something to be explained away. This was the famous parable of the pigeons which led to the nickname 'Pigeon Paley', and in which he appeared to be challenging the moral basis of the very institution of property.[56] Paley probably meant this as no more than one of those curious paradoxes with which eighteenth-century thinkers loved to tease each other. For in the next chapter he proceeds to offer the conventional justification for the inequality in the distribution of property; while extreme inequality is, he says, 'abstractly considered' an evil, it is nevertheless the result of the rules concerning the acquisition and disposal of property 'by which men are incited to industry, and by which the object of their industry is rendered secure and valuable'. The only respect in which his parable of the pigeons is to be taken as a criticism of society's rules lies in the principle that any 'great inequality' which is not justified by the need to encourage industry ought to be corrected. Yet even this explanation was apparently not enough to satisfy contemporary opinion. Despite the huge popularity of his *Principles* (which ran through sixteen editions in twenty years), Paley's parable was said to have cost him the chance of a bishopric.

The identification of the ethics of the established Protestant Church with those of the State meant, of course, that the former largely adopted those of the latter, and not the other way round. The growth of toleration was also a significant factor. The bigotry of anti-Catholic feeling throughout the eighteenth century must not blind us to the enormous change which came over the relation between Christian and State ethics as a result of the toleration of the non-Catholic dissenters. The established Church had ceased to be the sole interpreter of the Divine word. Implicit in that was that there was now a 'permanent public dubiety'[57] about many matters on which it would formerly have been an impiety to have had doubts at all.

With the withdrawal of the Church from the central role in the social order, a new source of morality had become necessary, and the eighteenth century had largely found this in the concepts of Natural Law. We have seen something of the long ancestry of Natural law ideas, but the Natural Law of the late seventeenth and eighteenth centuries was very different from that of the Middle Ages. By this time, '"Nature" had come to connote, not divine ordinance, but human appetites, and natural rights were invoked by the individualism of the age as a reason why self-interest should be given free play.'[58] This newly interpreted Natural Law brought all 'laws', human and divine, prescriptive and descriptive, within one broad framework, as in the work of Blackstone.[59] Although

[56] *Principles of Moral and Political Philosophy*, Book III, Part I, Chapter 1.
[57] Viscount Radcliffe, *The Law and its Compass* (Evanston, Ill., 1960), p. 7.
[58] R. H. Tawney, *Religion and the Rise of Capitalism*, p. 183.
[59] *Bl. Comm.*, i, Introduction, Sect. II.

Blackstone, as a lawyer, had no doubt that human laws differed from Divine laws in that they could be broken, it was an easy step to the comforting belief that it was futile to violate Natural laws. The analogy between economic laws, or the laws of the moral sciences generally, and the laws of the natural sciences, was also pressed home with the idea that prices (and perhaps people) would find their own level. Trade will have its own way, people will seek out their own self-interest, prices will find their proper level, all these ideas had been increasingly justified from the sixteenth century onward by invoking Natural Law.[60]

I have already referred to the individualist nature of the new society that had been growing up in the seventeenth and eighteenth centuries. And it is now clear that this individualism extended also to the moral foundations of the new society. But a further important step had to be taken before it was possible even to conceive of a moral system resting simply on individual choice and freedom. For if every individual was to be allowed free rein, and if Natural Law declared that it was futile to prevent men from seeking their own salvation and their own economic interests in their own way, what was to stop society from degenerating into the Hobbesian state of nature in which every man warred against everyone else? Eighteenth-century thinkers offered, in effect, two answers to this question. The first was the traditional answer of the Age of Enlightenment, namely that it was not unbridled licence which was contemplated, but enlightened self-interest. The second answer was to deny that the pursuit of self-interest would degenerate into a state of war anyhow. Provided that a proper framework of law and order and property rights was maintained, the pursuit of individual self-interest would anyhow further the national good. There was no conflict, but a natural harmony, between individual interests and the public interest.

Of these two answers, the first is spelled out most clearly perhaps in the works of David Hume, though it is also to be found in Adam Smith, despite the fact that Smith himself was to become largely responsible for the propagation of the second answer. Hume's position was simple enough.[61] He assumed that most educated men could be trusted to appreciate that it was in their own interests not to pursue short-term advantage at the expense of longer-term interests; those who could not, would be dealt with by the law and would soon learn their lesson. In the small world of the educated and the property owners, this optimism may have been largely justified. It is possible that their cohesiveness was enhanced by recognition of the fact that they *were* a small class, and that they had to observe the rules of enlightened self-interest for their own

---

[60] Chalk, 'Natural Law and the Rise of Economic Individualism in England', 59 *Journal of Political Economy* 332 (1951).

[61] This is most clearly set out in Hume's *Treatise*, Book III, Part II, Sect. I.

protection. They had, for example, learned how punctuality in servicing the public debt (that is, in effect, *their* debt) had reduced rates of interest. Hume took it for granted that only a very little understanding was necessary for men to appreciate the importance of long-term advantages in the matter of keeping promises. A man who failed to keep a promise, asserts Hume, would find himself never trusted again, a penalty which may have been real enough and severe enough amongst the small class of educated men at the time he was writing. Not long afterwards, Adam Smith analysed the nature of the self-interest which led men to observe their commercial engagements.[62] He comments on the fact that in commercial affairs the English had a greater reputation for probity and punctuality than the Scots but were thought much inferior to the Dutch. He rejects the idea that this is due to national characteristics, and he also rejects the notion that commerce first develops amongst those whose commercial integrity is highest. On the contrary, he urges, it is increased commercial dealings which lead to greater respect for commercial engagements. This is because it is self-interest which controls and regulates men's actions, and the more dealings they have, the more does self-interest demand that they honour their engagements:

When a person makes perhaps twenty contracts in a day, he cannot gain so much by endeavouring to impose on his neighbours, as the very appearance of a cheat would make him lose. When people seldom deal with one another, we find that they are somewhat disposed to cheat, because they can gain more by a smart trick than they can lose by the injury which it does their character.[63]

Adam Smith and Hume both seem to have seen enlightened self-interest as lying at the root, not merely of the legal obligation to perform contracts, but also of the moral obligation to observe promises. A man who makes a promise is *trusted* by the promisee and it is in his interest that he should be so trusted; the double meaning of the phrase 'to be given credit' clearly shows why it is in a man's interest that he should be so trusted. Of course, when the time for performance comes, the promisor may feel disinclined to carry out his promise; his immediate inclination may be not to perform; the cost or labour of performance may be high, the advantages remote and less obvious. This is why it is not immediate, but enlightened self-interest which dictates the advantages of performing a promise. The rational, intelligent, calculating man can see these advantages and resist the present temptation to consult his immediate interests.

[62] *Lectures on Jurisprudence*, pp. 538–9.
[63] Ibid., p. 254. Forty years earlier Defoe, in *The Complete English Tradesman*, pp. 56–7, had commented disparagingly on the fact that businessmen frequently broke promises to pay money 'without any scruple and without any reproach upon their integrity'. It seems probable that commercial morality had risen markedly during this period.

But even among the educated, and the property owners, self-interest was not always enlightened. A man did not always feel impelled to perform a contract which had turned out badly, especially perhaps where the element of risk was high. Very speculative contracts which turn out badly, involving substantial loss, nearly always *look* foolish and unfair in retrospect to the person who has lost. And his predicament will often attract the sympathy of third parties who may feel that the other party to the transaction has not really deserved his gains. There is some evidence that attitudes to risky and speculative transactions were changing significantly in the eighteenth century. I have already mentioned the firm stand which the Government took after the collapse of the South Sea bubble in 1721 when the former Government stockholders repented of the bargain whereby they had exchanged their stock for South Sea stock. We shall also see, when we come to examine legal developments during the eighteenth century, that there are marked signs of a change of attitude in the Court of Chancery to contracts which plainly involved some element of risk. As time went on Chancellors became increasingly unsympathetic with those who played with fire and then burned their fingers. They were thus playing their part in teaching that enlightened self-interest paid.

These thoughts suggest a point worth noting about the nature of promissory or contractual liability. If it is enlightened self-interest which lies at the root of these obligations, it is because promises and contracts invite trust, involve reliance and dependence by others on the word of the promisor. It is not, it seems, any inherent quality possessed by a promise, nor is it because promises are expressions of the will. It is more important not to disappoint another's trust, or reliance, than it is even to be truthful or sincere. This is spelled out with absolute clarity in Adam Smith's *Lectures on Jurisprudence* given in the 1760s. Smith in effect defines a promise as 'an open and plain declaration that he [the promisor] desires the person to whom he makes the declaration to have a dependence on what he promises'.[64] He then goes on to stress that it is not the will that makes a promise binding 'as some authors imagine'.[65] For, if that were the case, an insincere promise would not be binding. 'But such promises are and have universally been acknowledged to be as binding as any others, and the reason is plain: They produce the same degree of dependence and the breach of them the same disappointment as the others.'[66] He then goes on to suggest that reliance is even more important than sincerity, by offering the following interesting example:

If a man should engage to do me some considerable service, his failing in which would be a great disappointment to me, and should in this promise act sincerely, and really have an intention to perform, but should afterwards thro some

[64] *Lectures on Jurisprudence*, p. 87.   [65] Ibid., p. 93.   [66] Ibid.

inconvenience he found in the performance not fulfil his promise; if again another should thro levity or idleness promise me the same service tho he has no intention to perform it, but afterwards, from a sense of the great disappointment his failure should give me, should alter his former design and perform his promise: which of these two, I ask, would be the best man. The latter, without doubt, who tho he promised what he did not intend to perform, yet afterwards, reflecting on the disappointment I must suffer, became of a better mind.[67]

In another passage, indeed, Smith clearly declares that the foundation of contract is the reasonable expectation which the person who promises raises in the person to whom he binds himself.[68]

This fascinating discussion suggests that, to Adam Smith, it was the obligation not to disappoint dependence or expectations which was the source of promissory obligation. He does not, however, clearly distinguish dependence from pure expectations; he does not (as Grotius did)[69] pose the important question whether an *unrelied on* expectation creates an obligation to perform a promise. His answer to this would probably have been that it did, since it was the tendency of promises to be relied upon that gave them their binding quality, and not the precise effect of a particular promise in a particular case. This assuredly would have been Hume's answer to the problem which he too approaches without directly engaging. Hume stresses the importance of general *principles* in the law and in morality. 'For there is', he says, 'a principle of human nature, which we have frequently taken notice of, that men are mightily addicted to *general rules*, and that we often carry our maxims beyond those reasons which first induced us to establish them.'[70] Adding this predilection for general principles to the same self-interest that is the source of all obligations in the first instance, a 'sentiment of morals concurs with interest, and becomes a new obligation upon mankind'.[71] In other words, the obligation which originally comes from self-interest is generalized and built up by 'education and the artifice of politicians' until men are persuaded that the obligation is a general moral obligation, independent of the result in any particular case.

If it was enlightened self-interest which was at the root of the morality of 1770 so far as the property classes were concerned, it may well have had something, too, to do with the new work ethic which had been developing since the Reformation. It is now over seventy years since Weber first put forward the idea that the growth of capitalism had something to do with the work ethic which he associated specifically with Calvinism, and more broadly with Protestantism.[72] Weber argued that

---

[67] Ibid., pp. 93–94.   [68] Ibid., p. 89.   [69] *De Jure Belli ac Pacis*, Book II, Chapter XI.
[70] *Treatise*, Book III, Part II, Sect. IX.   [71] Ibid., Sect. V.
[72] Weber, *The Protestant Ethic and the Spirit of Capitalism* (first published 1904, English translation London, 1930, reprinted New York, 1958); see further, David Little, *Religion, Order and Law* (New York and Evanston, 1969).

Calvinism taught men that it was a duty to work and to seek an opportunity of making wealth; perhaps the underlying fear was of sloth and indolence which made men a natural prey for sin and the Devil. But whatever the underlying rationale, the result was the same. Money making became not only respectable, but a positive duty. Naturally, the associated virtues which won increasing recognition were those of diligence, thrift, sobriety, prudence, and careful calculation over the future. These were not very different from the virtues that Milton had admired, self-reliance, courage in adversity, and a restless, critical independence of mind.[73]

I have suggested that the second answer to the moral issue posed by the desire for increased economic freedoms was found in the doctrine of the harmony of interests. Nobody doubted, of course, that so far as concerned property, private rights were in harmony with the public good. Blackstone's pronouncement that 'the public good is in nothing more essentially interested than in the protection of every individual's property rights'[74] might have been taken straight out of Locke. But could this harmony between private interest and public interest be assumed also to exist in the commercial sphere? And what about the luxury expenditure of the rich? Could that also be of benefit to the nation? Throughout the eighteenth century much controversy raged on these questions. In 1723 Bernard Mandeville had published a revised edition of *The Fable of the Bees* in which he had playfully, but perhaps not without serious intent, argued that 'private vices' made for 'public virtues'. Many were taken in by this fallacious but not implausible reasoning, including Dr. Johnson who argued that luxury spending provided honest employment for the poor, while if the money were merely given to them it would support the idle rather than the industrious.[75] Others were scandalized by Mandeville's thesis, and yet others bemused by it.[76] It is not surprising if some were attracted by the simple solution of separating morality and ethics altogether from economic issues. If the market economy created new moral problems, '[o]ne solution was to let the market solve the problems it had created by giving free reign to economic forces'.[77] It may not have been so obvious then, as it became later, that this was not so much to separate morality and economics, as to adopt a particular type of morality in the interests of a particular type of economy.

[73] Christopher Hill, *Reformation to Industrial Revolution*, p. 202.

[74] *Bl. Comm.*, i: 139. This sentence was destined to be widely cited in American legal cases: Pound, 'Liberty of Contract', 48 *Yale Law J.* 454, 461 (1909).

[75] Boswell's *Life of Johnson*, 29 May 1776.

[76] See Phillip Harth, Introduction to Mandeville, *The Fable of the Bees* (Harmondsworth, 1970), pp. 21–6.

[77] Joyce Appleby, 'Locke, Liberalism and the Natural Law of Money', 71 *Past and Present* 43, 44 (1976).

In due course the doctrine of the harmony of interests was given much greater support and elaboration by Adam Smith in *The Wealth of Nations*. Although this doctrine never wholly superseded the idea of enlightened self-interest which continued to play an important role in the next century, it was Adam Smith's doctrine which henceforth settled the moral dilemmas concerning the pursuit of individual self-interest. As Locke had provided the moral justification for the property-based society of the eighteenth century, so Adam Smith in his turn provided the moral justification for the contract-based society of the nineteenth century. But further discussion of Smith must be postponed to Chapter 11.

FREEDOM OF PROPERTY

There is one final freedom of which something must be said before I turn to the law, and that, even though the law was part and parcel of that freedom. Perhaps surprisingly, the phrase 'freedom of property' never seems to have emerged in the eighteenth century as its successor, 'freedom of contract' took root in the nineteenth century.[78] Yet the ideal of freedom of property did take root and it was, in many respects, a necessary precursor of freedom of contract. Indeed, to a considerable degree, freedom of contract began by being freedom to deal with property by contract. I have already referred to the fact that the constitutional struggles of the seventeenth century were about the security of property as much as about political power; and I have also briefly referred to the changing conception of ownership itself. It is necessary now to elaborate slightly on these matters.

There is no question that since the sixteenth century, if not earlier, Englishmen had been seeking greater freedom to deal with land, nor that they had been coming to think of land ownership in a different way. We have seen how the abolition of the remaining vestiges of the system of feudal dues in the seventeenth century had completed the erosion of the rights of feudal lords at the expense of the freeholders. At the same time, or perhaps even earlier, the position of copyholders had largely become assimilated to that of freeholders also.[79] But the position of the freeholders was also changing in other respects, and these changes were closely related to the changes in ideas. A freeholder was nothing more than a free tenant in theory, and in strict law this remained the position in the seventeenth century, as indeed it does today. But this is a purely theoretical abstraction. The modern freeholder conceives of himself as an owner and this change dates from the seventeenth century.

[78] But we do find the phrase 'liberty of estate' used by Lilburne in 1645 (Macpherson, *The Political Theory of Possessive Individualism* p. 137), and similar phrases abound in Locke.

[79] Holdsworth, *H.E.L.*, iii. 180.

Moreover, the nature of this ownership was also tending to change, to become more 'absolute'; though again this change may have been more one of perception than of strict law, in due course these ideas began to influence the law. In medieval times the very concept of absolute ownership was scarcely recognized; it would have been repugnant to the nature of that society to admit that a man was absolutely free to do what he wanted with his property, as it was repugnant to think that a man was absolutely free to do anything at all. In that sort of world men were not absolutely free; they owed duties to their feudal lord, to their fellow men, to the Church, to God; and their 'tenure' of property was a transient thing. A man in possession of property was the temporary custodian of it rather than an owner; property was a 'responsible office'[80] carrying duties as well as rights. And before 1600 even legal restrictions on the extent of a man's possessions were not unknown. For example, a statute of the mid-sixteenth century restricted the number of sheep a man could keep and another limited country clothiers to one loom per person.[81] But all this had long passed away. So far as goods were concerned the new age was more clearly represented by the resolution of the House of Commons in 1628 that 'every free subject of this realm hath a fundamental property in goods'.[82]

However, it was land which was still far and away the most important form of property, and here too, from the fifteenth century onwards, men had been striving after freedom to acquire or sell, to mortgage or settle, to inherit or devise. By the late fifteenth century lawyers had discovered a way of barring entails, and in the next century, the Statute of Wills of 1540 had been one of the significant concessions made by Henry VIII to the country gentry after the attempted abolition of the old use in the Statute of Uses of 1535. It was clear that the power of testation, of devising land, was already greatly treasured. Evidently, men wanted the freedom to *deal* with their land; such freedom necessarily involved, and was closely related to, the growing desire of men to control their own destinies, to plan their own lives, and not to leave everything to Providence. They also wanted, as we have seen, greater *security* of ownership. From the sixteenth century we encounter the idea that 'every man's house is his castle'.[83] Men wanted to be free of arbitrary taxation or seizure of their property, of the danger of dying while their children were under age so that their lands might become a source of plunder to whoever held the wardship of their heirs. And, increasingly as time went on, they wanted to *use* their lands, to exploit them for agriculture or

[80] R. H. Tawney, *Religion and the Rise of Capitalism*, p. 153.

[81] Christopher Hill, *Reformation to Industrial Revolution*, p. 92.

[82] Ibid., p. 32.

[83] *Sendil's* case (1583) 7 Co. Rep. 6a, 77 E.R. 419; *Semayne's* case (1605) 5 Co. Rep. 91a, 91b, 77 E.R. 194, 195.

mining or any other economic purpose which suggested itself. It was no coincidence that one of the first Acts of the Parliament of 1688–9 surrendered the Royal claim to mineral rights on the subject's lands, except in respect of gold and silver.[84]

All these freedoms helped to create a climate of opinion in which property rights themselves came to seem more absolute, and the old grievances against feudal burdens and taxes helped to give this new attitude to property a sense of legitimacy:

The idea of the 'absolute' character of the domination over a thing was—in the history of human ideas—closely connected with that of its 'inviolability' and 'sanctity' which derived its political pathos from the fight against feudal burdens and restrictions.[85]

In the 1760s Whigs and Tories alike were seeing property in these absolute terms.[86] Thus Blackstone defines a right of property, at least in abstract, as 'that sole and despotic dominion which one man claims and exercises over the external things of the world, in total exclusion of the right of any other individual in the universe'.[87] And the Whig Lord Camden insisted, with no little vehemence, that 'whatever is a man's own is absolutely his own; no man hath a right to take it from him without his consent, either expressed by himself or representative; whoever attempts to do it, attempts an injury, who ever does it commits a robbery'.[88]

Nevertheless, there were in practice still important qualifications to the realization of this ideal of absolute ownership. The most essential freedom of property for a market economy is the freedom to sell. A market economy demands that property be freely transferable so that it can pass from hand to hand, coming to rest only in the possession of him who can most efficiently exploit it.[89] This freedom demands a very different outlook from that of the older customary type of society in which a man's right to property—so far as it is recognized at all— depends on his need to use it.[90] Now England in 1770 was a long way from that sort of customary society, but it was also still some way from the extreme individualism of the nineteenth century. In practice men frequently did not have the freedom to sell or otherwise dispose of or deal

[84] David Spring, 'English Landowners and Nineteenth Century Industrialism', in *Land and Industry*, ed. J. T. Ward and R. G. Wilson (Newton Abbot, 1971), p. 17.

[85] O. Kahn-Freund, Notes to K. Renner, *Institutions of Private Law* (English translation London and Boston, 1949, reprinted 1976), p. 66.

[86] E. P. Thompson, *Whigs and Hunters*, appears to treat this (at any rate in the early eighteenth century) as a Whig characteristic, but he concedes that this may have been because the Tories were excluded from power.

[87] *Bl. Comm.*, ii. 2.

[88] *Parliamentary History*, xvi, col. 178.

[89] See for a simple exposition of this point, R. Posner, *Economic Analysis of Law* (Boston, Toronto, 1972), p. 11.

[90] Hicks, *A Theory of Economic History* (Oxford, 1969), p. 34.

with 'their' land because of the presence of competing rights over the land. There were in principle two types of competing interest. In the first place there were the traditional customary rights, often enjoyed by the poorer residents on, or in the neighbourhood of, the land. These were use-rights such as rights of pasture, or rights to cut and remove turves or firewood. There is little doubt that the eighteenth century saw a prolonged and sustained campaign by the landed magnates to suppress these rights, with or without compensation. The Enclosures Acts are the best known of the more formal moves in this direction, but there were evidently other, less formal processes at work which may in practice have borne more harshly on the poor.[91] In these respects it can be said that the concept of land ownership and of the 'absolute' rights of the landowner became more dominant in the eighteenth century.

The second type of competing interests which restrained the 'absolute' rights of a landowner were also of a traditional character, but these concerned family rights. In particular, there was the traditional entail by which land was held by a tenant or holder without the power to sell, mortgage, or lease, the succession to the land being pre-determined usually in favour of eldest sons, one after another. The Whig aristocrats must have felt torn by their dynastic ambitions for their descendants, and on the other hand by their own desires to be free from the restrictions imposed upon them by the dead hand of the past.

The dynastic ideology was very important. Men desired property, and the freedom to deal with property, not just for its own sake, but to establish families, settled on, and associated with the land. The eighteenth century was the age of the strict settlement, that intricate piece of conveyancing designed to tie up property, provide for widows, younger sons, and daughters, and, above all, maintain the property intact—or preferably augmented—in the family.

These competing family rights necessarily meant that the freedom of the land 'owner'—who was often no more than a tenant for life, or tenant in tail, legally speaking—was limited. The freedom of one generation was limited by that of earlier and later generations. The freedom of a settlor to tie up an estate necessarily deprived his successors of their freedom to deal with it as they, in turn, thought right. The freedom of the present owner to control the income from the estates necessarily deprived his sons, while he was alive, of all freedom other than that of borrowing upon their expectations. Some of these conflicts of interest were the subject of legal compromises, of which the most famous was the Rule against Perpetuities.[92] Most of them were not settled by the law but by the social customs and conventions of the period, although these in turn not infrequently gave rise to legal problems. For example, the accepted

[91] See generally, E. P. Thompson, *Whigs and Hunters*.   [92] *Post*, p. 131.

practice of young heirs' living above their allowances, and borrowing on 'post-obit' bonds,[93] or selling reversionary rights, gave rise to a great deal of litigation; and so also did the delicate business by which great families joined together two of their members in elaborate marriage settlements.

These social, property-based, and family-oriented conventions, linked as they were to the peculiar moral code of the eighteenth century aristocracy, helped to perpetuate some residual notion of property as a source of duty, as well as a source of rights. To receive property from an ancestor, or even from a living person, placed a man under social and moral obligations to his family and posterity. In 1776 the young Scot, James Boswell, wrote to Dr. Johnson for advice, much troubled because his father sought his agreement in altering the terms of the settlement of their estates.[94] Young Boswell wrote that he felt 'under an implied obligation, in honour and good faith, to transmit the estate by the same tenure' under which he held, or expected to hold. The Doctor, with his robust good sense, persuaded Boswell to lay aside his scruples, which may anyhow have owed more to James's desire to annoy his father, the Laird of Auckinleck, than to respect the wishes of his ancestor. But the incident is none the less revealing. It suggests that men felt that the benefits they received under a devise or settlement carried, at least in the family, obligations resembling those we would call contractual; that the terms and conditions on which land was settled were morally binding on the present holder even though he merely accepted an estate, or the rights in question, without anything in the nature of an express promise to observe them. There is, in fact, much in eighteenth-century ideas about property to suggest that people saw a close connection between acquiring or disposing of property on death, and acquiring or disposing of it *inter vivos*. In Blackstone's *Commentaries*, volume ii is devoted to the Law of Property, in his quaint terminology, under the title 'Rights of Things'; and in this scheme contract and succession are both dealt with as means by which the title to property gets transferred. There is no doubt that freedom of contract and freedom of testation were then, and later, closely connected ideas.[95] Both ideas were steadily gaining strength in 1770; they reached their peak together in the next century; both have declined in the twentieth century.

---

[93] A post-obit bond was a bond payable after the death of a person whose life interest came before that of the party giving the bond. A good example of the social relationships which gave rise to these practices is furnished by that between Sarah, Duchess of Marlborough, the widow of the first Duke, and her grandson, Charles, who became third Duke. See A. L. Rowse, *The Later Churchills* (London, 1958), Chapters I and II. It was the third Duke's brother, John, who was responsible for the debts which led to the celebrated case of *Chesterfield* v. *Janssen* (1750) 1 Atk. 301, 26 E.R. 191, as to which see *post*, p. 124.

[94] *Life of Johnson*, vol. ii, Chapter 13.

[95] In *Townson* v. *Tickell* (1819) 3 B. & Ald. 31, 38, 106 E.R. 575, 577, it was held that a devise was 'nothing more than an offer which the devisee may accept or refuse'; and the Court relied upon

(continued)

There were also other respects in which property was still thought to create obligations, both of a social and a legal nature, and in these cases the duties were owed to the public. On the one hand there were the duties of a political nature. The idea of public and parliamentary service as a duty incumbent on the owners of property was no fiction in the eighteenth century, even if the duty ultimately rested on the fact that it was their government, instituted to protect their property. And more specifically, because legally exigible, there were duties related to taxation. In the seventeenth and eighteenth centuries it was still customary to see taxation as a burden borne largely by the propertied class in return for the protection which the State was created to afford them. Hobbes, for example, clearly saw taxation in this light and urged that taxes should be proportionate to the benefits received by the taxpayer, or property owner.[96] Similarly, Adam Smith says that 'The expense of government to the individuals of a great nation, is like the expense of management to the joint tenants of a great estate, who are all obliged to contribute in proportion to their respective interests in the estate'.[97] These ideas came the more naturally at the time no doubt, partly because two of the most onerous taxes were the Land Tax and the Poor Rate which were levied on the landowners. There are not wanting signs that even the Poor Laws were perceived as part of the price paid by the landowners for the acquiescence of the mass of the people in the eighteenth-century system of government.

What we see in 1770, thus, is a set of ideas still in process of transition. This is an Age of Property, and it is also an age of growing individualism. But we are not yet wholly extricated from the idea that property involves obligations as well as rights, particularly, though not yet exclusively, within the family. And though, as we see from Blackstone's rhetoric, absolute ownership as an abstract idea is well established, we are still a long way from a situation in which most property is in fact the subject of absolute ownership.

---

authorities dealing with *inter vivos* transfers. Compare also Montesquieu, *L'Esprit des lois*, Book V, Sect. 5, arguing that in democracies, restrictions are necessary with respect to dowries, gifts, succession, and 'all other forms of contracting' [*sic*]. 'For were we once allowed to dispose of our property to whom and how we pleased, the will of each individual would disturb the order of the fundamental law.'

[96] *Leviathan*, Part II, Chapter 30.
[97] *Wealth of Nations*, Book V, Part II.

5

THE LEGAL BACKGROUND IN 1770

PARLIAMENT, THE COURTS, AND LAW-MAKING

Parliament

SINCE the Reform Act of 1832 we have, in England, become used to the notion that the chief function of Parliament is to make laws, and that one of the chief functions of the Executive is to plan, prepare, and introduce legislation into Parliament, and then to see that Parliament passes it. But 1832 was as far from 1688 as it is from 1976 (when these words are being written). In the middle of the eighteenth century Parliament's principal function was not conceived as that of making law, nor was it regarded as an essential part of the responsibility of Governments to persuade Parliament to make new laws. The elder Pitt, although one of the leading statesmen of his time, is not (it was said by Lord John Russell in 1841) [1] credited with having carried a single legislative measure through Parliament; and his son, the younger Pitt, did not feel obliged to resign when he failed to carry a Bill through the House of Commons. It is, indeed, very doubtful if most people felt that law—real 'Law' with a capital 'L' (as distinct, say, from regulation)—was something to be 'made' at all. Law was 'there', somewhere in the background, to be deduced by judges from their books and Natural Reason. Given the Locke tradition, the belief in Reason, Natural Law, the unchanging stability of the natural order and rights of property, it is hard to see why men should or could have thought of law as something in need of constant and voluminous change.

I will begin with a cursory look at the Statute book around 1770, a year which may be taken as typical of the mid-century period. We shall find that general legislation was a rarity indeed at this time. The annual volumes of the Statutes are, it is true, as substantial as those of the nineteenth century, but external appearances are misleading. The Statutes inside the annual volumes are for the most part Private Acts, or, if not technically Private Acts, they are nevertheless mostly of a local or temporary nature. The typical Act of the period is an Act for repairing this bridge here, that road there, an Act for erecting a Workhouse in this city, or for paving a street in that. The annual volume for 1770, for instance, contains ninety-nine Acts passed during the course of the year.

[1] Walkland, *The Legislative Process in Great Britain* (London, 1968), p. 12.

Of these fifty-five were for specified road improvements and similar public works (including one for the repair of Magdalen Bridge, Oxford); nine for the improvement or regulation of specified canals, rivers, and harbours; nine concerned imports, exports, and excise duties; five related to other taxes, appropriation, and coinage; five concerned the armed forces; three were for the promotion of fisheries in specified areas; there were nine miscellaneous Acts all of a local or private nature (including three dealings with particular Crown lands); and finally four Acts which could be said to be of a public and general law-making character. These four concerned the keeping of gunpowder, the settlement of disputed elections, the regulation of hackney coaches, and the granting of leases by lunatics, none of them measures calculated to shake the social fabric of the nation. As Maitland says, 'In this "age of reason", as we are wont to think of it, the British Parliament seems rarely to rise to the dignity of a general proposition.'[2] There was, however, nothing contrary to reason in this method of proceeding, given the basic assumptions and preconceptions of the time.

Even when Parliament did try to use its legislative powers to stamp out some social evil it was, on the whole, extraordinarily incompetent. Over and over again, we find Parliament legislating by means of a temporary or local Act, frequently indeed by Acts which were both temporary and local, to deal with a problem which today would be dealt with by a public general Act. The Truck Acts may furnish a suitable example. Between 1465 and 1820 Parliament passed no fewer than twenty-eight Acts to regulate or prohibit the payment of wages by truck, that is, otherwise than in money.[3] Most of them were local and temporary, scarcely any of them were ever enforced for any length of time, and when in the nineteenth century some attempt was made to tackle the problem properly, the first thing that had to be done was to clear away all this clutter. Part of the difficulty was the absence of a proper bureaucracy to enforce and administer this sort of legislation; I have already discussed this aspect of the political machinery in the eighteenth century. But part of the problem was also due to other and perhaps deeper factors concerning the eighteenth-century conception of law, and the role of Parliament.

In the first place, the absence of a bureaucracy made the task of legislating in the modern style as difficult as the task of enforcing legislation. The modern Statute, though it is approved by Government and passed by Parliament, could not even be prepared without an army of civil servants. The collection of the preliminary data, statistics, and any necessary scientific or other professional advice, the consultation

---

[2] *Constitutional History of England* (Cambridge, 1908, reprinted 1955), pp. 382-4.
[3] G. W. Hilton, *The Truck System* (Cambridge, 1960), p. 7.

with those directly affected whose expertise often needs to be drawn upon for a proper understanding of the problem; the careful examination of a variety of methods by which the same ends may be achieved; and then the study of the existing legal and social framework into which the Act must be fitted; all this requires not merely skilled civil servants, lawyers, and draftsmen, but access to information, books, and advice, most of which was simply not available in the eighteenth century. The result was that general law-making by Parliament was very weak in preparation and amateurish in execution. Blackstone was not exaggerating when he protested about the appalling manner in which general legislation was prepared, and passed.[4] We cannot blame him if he thought the remedy lay in the legislators' learning some law, and in particular, studying 'the science of legislation, the noblest and most difficult of any'.[5]

The absence of an adequate bureaucracy could perhaps have been remedied, as it was—slowly and with difficulty—in the next century, if Parliament had felt that it wanted to make laws on a wider scale. But Parliament showed no inclination to do so. If there ever was a *laissez-faire* era in legislation it was in the first sixty years of the eighteenth century rather than in the nineteenth century where it is more commonly placed.[6] The local, private, and temporary legislation which occupied most of Parliament's time seems to have suited the age more than attempts at sweeping innovative law-making would have done. Fundamentally, this kind of legislation was a matter of 'making marginal adjustments to the reigning state of affairs' without any significant alteration of the social system.[7] The procedure adopted by Parliament for dealing with these Private Bills, was, in fact, more adjudicatory than legislative. Most of them were passed in response to petitions, which naturally tended to stress some particular local or temporary or private problem. Many of them involved some marginal adjustment to rights of property, which, indeed, was why they were needed at all. For instance, road widening schemes involved taking a piece of someone's land in return for appropriate compensation, and so on. The Private Bill procedure involved little more than a supervisory role to ensure that property rights were not unreasonably infringed. Anyone affected by such a Bill had the right to appear before a Parliamentary Committee, and be heard by counsel, much as in an ordinary Court. Naturally, this way of proceeding encouraged petitioners to get the prior approval or agreement of everyone affected before they presented their petition if they possibly could. If all parties agreed to the arrangement, the Bill's passage was likely to be correspondingly smooth. Only if agreement was

[4] *Bl. Comm.*, i. 9–10.   [5] Ibid.

[6] Basil Williams, *The Whig Supremacy*, p. 8. See also *post*, Chapter 16.

[7] Walkland, *The Legislative Process*, p. 14.

utterly impossible would petitioners be likely to proceed in its absence; and then Parliament would have to adjudicate on the reasonableness of the opposition.

But it was not only among the petitioners that contractual arrangements, or at least informal agreements, were thereby encouraged. The Parliamentary process itself sometimes represented a statutory bargain. Petitioners would want a Bill passed in order to enable them to do this or that—pave this street, light that one, clear a river to improve the navigation—and Parliament might, in effect, require a *quid pro quo* from the petitioners in return for the powers they sought. This might, for instance, consist in the petitioners accepting an obligation to keep in good repair the works they wanted to carry out, and keep them open to public use; or it might consist in some control over the right to charge for the use of the works, for example, tolls over bridges or highways. This vaguely contractual flavour to legislation was closely paralleled by a similar procedure which was applicable to the grant of Royal Charters. These too were usually granted in response to petitions; and here also the contents of the petition might well be the subject of some bargaining and negotiation between the Crown officials and the petitioners. It was natural and easy for both sides to see the resulting Charter as something in the nature of a contract. When Fox introduced the East India Bill in 1783 to alter the rights of the East India Company over the Government of India, the rights of the company were vigorously asserted to have been granted by a contract for which the company had given value. Even Burke accepted that there had been some sort of compact between Parliament and the company (though technically the Charter had been granted by the Crown alone), but he argued that the company had broken the contract.

I need not pursue this particular episode. My purpose is to stress the general contractual aura in which even legislation was prepared and carried. Government and Parliament did not so much *initiate* and *impose* policies and law changes on the people, as respond to outside initiatives and pressures. The absence of a powerful executive supported by an extensive bureaucracy necessarily leaves power in private and individual hands. And individuals, to get anything done, must needs combine, co-operate, and plan together. Inevitably agreement and contract figure prominently in such a society.

Even in spheres in which the central Government did formulate and execute policy, its own role often consisted of securing the agreement of those primarily concerned, and then putting such agreement forward for Parliamentary approval. In the mid-eighteenth century, for instance, it was becoming established practice for issues of Government stock to be authorized by Act of Parliament. The practice was for the Treasury to agree in advance with the proposed lenders as to the amounts they would subscribe, and then secure Parliamentary approval. The preliminary agreements were not legally binding, but, as a member of Parliament wrote in 1746, 'if it was not taken for granted that the House of Commons would always confirm these Agreements, no set of Men whatever would treat with the Treasury at all'.[8]

The Courts

We have already seen how society was thought to rest, and to a large extent did rest, on property rights; and how the function of the judges was, to a large degree, to protect those property rights, to enforce contracts arising out of property, and to punish crime most of which was seen as a threat to property rights.

At this point it is only necessary to emphasize the stability, orderliness, and predictability of the new legal order that grew up after 1688. The traditional Whig history books tended to stress the new political stability and the new civil liberties as the consequence of the elimination of the arbitrary power of the Crown. These were, of course, of paramount importance; but the element of stability and predictability in other respects was also of importance to the increasing commercial and industrial activity of the eighteenth century. The proper functioning of a market economy requires that individual entrepreneurs should be able to make rational investment decisions; they need to be able to plan ahead, to calculate the probable returns upon an investment, to assess and weigh up risks. Instability in the political system, instability in the financial system, and instability in the legal system are all enemies of this kind of rational and planned investment. We have already seen how, during the eighteenth century, the first two sources of instability were largely overcome. In this and the next Chapter, I shall be concerned with the increased stability of the legal order. Naturally, in this sphere the Courts played a central role. Even in the matter of law-making—a term which fits the times rather better than 'legislation'—the role of the Courts was in some respects more important than that of Parliament itself. Given that nobody who counted wanted to reform the whole social fabric, that changes in society were slow and usually made with the agreement of the governing classes, law-making was normally little different from much dispute-solving. The minor adjustments of property rights made by Parliament's Private Bill procedure differed little from the minor adjustments made by the Courts. Both responded to outside pressures rather than initiated solutions. In both types of decision-making process, the pressure to reach outside agreement before appealing to authority were great; both the cost and the dilatoriness of the judicial

[8] Dickson, *The Financial Revolution in England*, p. 221.

and parliamentary machines must have been enough to force people into compromises, agreements, arrangements which did not involve public arbitrament.

Even when the Courts did adapt and mould the old common law, the principal difference between their law-making function and that of Parliament was that the Courts were generally a good deal more efficient at it. This law-making generally took place in the basic areas of the law—the law of property, the law of contracts, commercial cases—so that naturally the expertise of the Courts was more evident than that of a Parliament and an executive unaided by a large staff of civil servants. Given that neither body had access to the social or statistical or scientific information so often required today for major legislation, there was good reason to assume that in general the Courts would make a better job of law-making than Parliament. The idea that the function of the Courts was simply to apply the existing law, and that change could be left to Parliament, was not one that dominated (though it sometimes influenced) eighteenth-century law. Lord Mansfield, in an unreported decision, was credited with having said, in answer to an argument that Parliament could be left to right an evil, 'What! pass a judgment to do mischief and then bring in a bill to cure it!'[9]

Morever, the appellate functions of the House of Lords—still exercised by all peers and not exclusively by the legal members of the House— meant that law-making as a judicial function and law-making as a legislative function were not so very distant. There was, of course, a technical difference, but it was not the difference which would come to mind today; it was not, that is, the difference between a decision given in a specific case, and an act of law-making of general application. The peers who had refused to convict Strafford of impeachable offences in 1641 voted for his conviction by a Bill of Attainder, as a legislative rather than a judicial act. The distinction centred round the necessity to act solely on the basis of publicly adduced evidence in judicial proceedings, while the legislative act could be more broadly justified. And the legislative act, of course, required the concurrence of all three branches of the legislature. When, therefore, Parliament did change the law by reversing judicial decisions—as it did occasionally, but rarely,[10]—its acts partook of the functions of an appellate court even when they were carried through by legislation. The distinction between 'reversing' a decision by legislation and 'overruling' it by the judicial act of a higher Court, was not nearly so clear cut then as it became later.

But although I have said that the Courts did not, at this time, acquiesce

---

[9] Cited by Best C.J. in *Fletcher* v. *Lord Sondes* (1826) 3 Bing. 501, 580, 130 E.R. 606, 637.

[10] Two well-known eighteenth-century examples are the Promissory Notes Act 1704, and Fox's Libel Act 1792.

in the notion that they could never modify or change the law, they certainly never conceived themselves free to do what they liked in the way that a modern Parliament sees itself. The law, to most people of the eighteenth century, including the lawyers, had, in its essentials, a sanctity and an unchangeability. Lawyers—or at least some of them—were willing to modify the law to bring it up to date with social and economic changes from time to time, but they certainly never contemplated the idea of using the law so as to create social and economic change. And in this they were not alone. Scarcely anybody—Bentham always excepted—conceived of law as having this potentiality in the eighteenth century. Parliamentarians and lawyers would have united in totally rejecting such a concept of law. If law could be used and manipulated to create social change in this way—as a piece of 'social engineering' in the modern phrase—why then there would have been no law at all. Law could not just be manipulated, and made out of nothing, as it were, to suit the passing fancies of a political party, a King, or even a Parliament; it was 'there', it had an objective existence of some sort; in its essentials it was unchanged and binding on everyone, including judges and Parliaments and Kings. It is true, of course, that if law was just 'there' still someone had to have the authority to say what it was; and it was also true, that with the gradual secularizing of society and of intellectual thought, the materials from which the judges had to 'find' the law were somewhat limited. The rejection of all forms of absolute authority which so characterized the Age of Enlightenment meant that neither the Divine scriptures nor the Year Books or Law Reports could any longer be taken to determine absolutely what the law was. The law had to be found in Reason and Principle, as Lord Mansfield insisted in 1774.[11]

Two hundred years after Bentham opened his campaign against this way of thinking, with his fierce polemic against Blackstone, it is difficult to sympathize with, or even to understand, the reality and sincerity with which it was pursued. We have learnt so much about unconscious motivations, about the role of law and power in society, about the way in which the law always reflects the interests of a governing class, that all this is apt to seem one more illustration of eighteenth-century hypocrisy. Of course the law was 'made', and of course it had no objective existence; it was made by and (largely) in the interests of, the governing class, as law is always made. Moreover, the impartiality and fairness, both of the law and of the judges in eighteenth-century England, have probably been much exaggerated by Whig historians. Where the interests of the landed classes clashed with those of other classes, the law as made by Parliament, and even the law as made by and applied by the judges, was not always as unbiased and upright as legal traditionalists have

[11] *Jones v. Randall* (1774) 1 Cowp. 37, 39, 98 E.R. 954, 955.

proclaimed.[12] But that does not mean that this law may not in general have been in the interests of the nation as a whole, still less does it mean that the governing class did not think that to be the case. In fact they clearly did think it was the case, and part of the function of the law, and of the judges, was to persuade the people that this was the case. Thus the notion, a commonplace in the twentieth century, that the proper and primary function of the Courts is to solve disputes as best they can, and to leave law-making to Parliament, fails to reflect the role of the Courts and the law in the eighteenth century. Doubtless, even then, the primary function of the individual decision was to settle a dispute, but the longer-term functions of Courts and judges and law were very much more obvious then than now.

Since 1688 the governing classes in England had made a conscious political decision to reject a powerful central executive government. In the absence of a proper administrative machine, of proper police, and of the many modern methods of maintaining law and order, two consequences inevitably followed. The first was that private initiative, private arrangements, and private incentives, became a necessary part of the process of maintaining law and order; and the second was that the people had to be persuaded to observe the law not only by threats, but also by educating them into a belief in, and respect for, the Law as something of transcendental value. I must say a little more about these two matters.

The judicial system was itself affected by the general hostility to extensive engines of authority, as well, doubtless, as the demand for economy in running the State. Throughout the eighteenth century there were only twelve common law judges, and two Chancery judges, one of whom (the Lord Chancellor) combined his judicial duties with substantial political and legislative duties. There was no organized system of local Courts at all, although a number of minor debt-collecting Courts of Requests were set up in some cities later in the century. There were well under three hundred barristers including serjeants-at-law and King's Counsel to serve these Courts, advise clients, and draw documents.[13] This, it will be remembered, was at a time when the population was some seven or eight million, perhaps a sixth or seventh of what it is today. Yet today there are at least ten times (perhaps twenty-five times) as many barristers and the total number of High Court judges, County Court judges, and other senior judges must be nearly twenty times what it was in 1770. Then again, the whole judicial process, both civil and criminal,

---

[12] See, in particular, E. P. Thompson, *Whigs and Hunters*.

[13] Mackinnon, 'Origins of Commercial Law', 52 *Law Q. Rev.* 30, 39 (1936). The figure of 300 barristers comes from a Law List of 1770 and probably includes many non-practising barristers, perhaps half.

depended throughout on private initiative to set it in operation and keep it going. The enforcement of the criminal law, at almost every stage of the proceedings—save for treason trials and a handful of political offences like sedition and some riots—was almost invariably left to private individuals or associations set up by property owners to protect themselves. The very detection of offenders, in the first instance, was left to private informers, and an extensive system of rewards existed in the eighteenth century to encourage such informers;[14] 'statutes, proclamations and private announcements held out to one and all financial rewards, which were often very considerable.'[15] Pardons were widely promised to accomplices who gave information or evidence; many statutes actually conferred a right to a pardon on those who turned King's evidence, subject to various conditions.[16] The system of common informers, whereby anyone could bring an action for a penalty (payable to him) for breach of some statute, had been widely used since Elizabethan times. In the 1730s it had been successfully used to stamp out the excesses of gin drinking when all earlier legislation had failed.[17] Common informers were generally very unpopular, but they could be exceedingly effective.

Judicial procedure itself, both civil and criminal, depended on the parties before it to take the initiative. The adversary procedure, so characteristic still of the common law Court throughout the whole common law world, fundamentally rests on the assumption that the parties—private parties—will always take the initiative in inviting the Court to do something. The Court never moves of its own motion; even to this day, English Court procedure still retains this basic feature. Naturally, this too fosters a tendency to encourage private arrangement and agreement. It is the parties, through their lawyers, who define the issues (in their pleadings)—and they may therefore agree upon them; it is the parties who select the witnesses, and though it is less easy to agree upon that, it is perfectly possible for them to agree upon other types of evidence—such as what documents should be placed before the Court. Even when a Court gives judgment, it is not the function of the Court or any other public body to enforce the judgment of its own motion. One of the parties must himself invite first the Court, and then the appropriate officials, to take suitable action for this purpose. These features of the English judicial process, so familiar today, fitted into the eighteenth-century background in some respects more easily than they do today, where some of them may look anachronistic in the framework of the

[14] Radzinowicz, *History of English Criminal Law* (London, 1956), ii. 33–6, 79–80.
[15] Ibid., p. 35.
[16] Ibid., p. 40.
[17] Ibid., Chapter 6. Some 12,000 informations were laid under this Act in the space of two years.

modern bureaucratic State. Probably some elements were very old; but in other respects the eighteenth century was the period when judicial procedure became more regularized. Mansfield is generally credited, for instance, with having settled the typical rules of civil procedure which govern the order of proceeding in an ordinary case.

Of course the judicial process was an inefficient one. The enforcement of the law by the common law Courts was clumsy in nearly every respect. Criminal prosecutions before the judges of Assize were all prosecutions by indictment, before juries, an incredibly cumbersome way of dealing with someone for letting a road get out of condition, or a bridge out of repair, or for infringing the Apprentices Act; a complicated enough process, indeed, for dealing with much petty crime. The methods of social control through the Courts in the eighteenth century were crude and lacked flexibility; they were unsuited to the needs of a mass production age, when those needs burst upon the scene around the end of the century. Much enforcement was in the hands of the justices of the peace, but this, though less cumbersome, was also inefficient because of the haphazard enforcement policies which depended so much on the energy and views of the particular justices. In these circumstances, it is not surprising that people rested their faith, not so much in the actual enforcement of the law, as in threats and persuasion.

It is well known that the criminal law became, at least on the surface, more and more barbaric as the eighteenth century wore on. The number of capital offences was hugely increased until even Blackstone lamented the readiness of the legislature to create such offences.[18] But it is simply not possible to see eighteenth-century England as a State in which the propertied class maintained power by a ruthless reign of bloody terror.[19] The reality is that without a proper and effective police force and other modern means of maintaining law and order, a great deal depended on the control which could be exercised over people's minds. This control was to a considerable degree achieved by a combination of threats of terror, tempered by mercy and a decent respect for public opinion.[20] A very small proportion of the capital sentences was ever carried out, and it is probable that even as Parliament created new ones, its members knew and approved of the way the law was actually administered in practice. In fact they could hardly help but know and approve, since many of the petitions for mercy which followed capital sentences were written by or supported by local squires, the gentry who sat in the Commons, and forwarded for further support to their social superiors

[18] *Bl. Comm.*, iv. 9–10.

[19] E. P. Thompson, *The Making of the English Working Class*, seems to want to offer such a version (e.g. at pp. 60–1), but cf. his *Whigs and Hunters* for a somewhat different emphasis.

[20] Douglas Hay, 'Property, Authority and the Criminal Law', in *Albion's Fatal Tree*, ed. Hay and others (London, 1975).

who sat in the Lords. 'The great majority of petitions for mercy were written by gentlemen on behalf of labourers. It was an important self-justification of the ruling class that once the poor had been chastised sufficiently to protect property, it was the duty of a gentleman to protect his people.'[21]

And if Parliament knew what was going on under the surface the Courts certainly knew it too. Eighteenth-century judges identified themselves as 'the Law' in the way the modern public identifies the police as 'the law'. But the judge did not use physical force himself as the modern policeman may have to; he used the law as an instrument of persuasion and education. Homilies to grand juries about the need for law and order were a common feature of eighteenth- and early nineteenth-century assizes. It was an important part of the function of the eighteenth-century judges to instil terror into the populace; not for them the principles of Beccaria who advocated the certainty of moderate justice and punishment as a more effective deterrent than ineffective and uncertain threats of greater severity. Romilly and Bentham were later to adopt Beccaria's message, but Blackstone explicitly rejects it,[22] and we may be sure that he reflects on this the point of view of his contemporaries on the bench. Eighteenth-century lawyers relied upon a combination of terror and mercy, harshness and equity, as a means of social control. 'The Courts dealt in terror, pain and death, but also in moral ideas, control of arbitrary power, mercy for the weak.'[23] Having sentenced a man to death, the judge was often the first person to write to the Secretary of State recommending a reprieve.

But if the law was to be generally respected and observed without the apparatus of a police state, it needed not only a combination of terror and mercy, but it also required an ideological strength. The law had to have something of mystery and majesty. These were provided by the ceremonial, formalistic, and ritualistic side of the law. Its technicalities, leading so often to unmeritorious acquittals, came to seem absurd to Bentham and later critics.

But it seems likely that the mass of Englishmen drew other conclusions from the practice. The punctilious attention to forms, the dispassionate and legalistic exchanges between counsel and the judge, argued that those administering and using the laws submitted to its rules. The law thereby became something more than the creature of a ruling class—it became a power with its own claims, higher than those of prosecutor, lawyers and even the great scarlet-robed assize judge himself. To them too, of course, the law was The Law. The fact that they reified it, that they shut their eyes to its daily enactment in Parliament by men

---

[21] Ibid., p. 47.

[22] *Bl. Comm.*, iv. 397.

[23] Douglas Hay, 'Property, Authority and the Criminal Law', p. 55.

of their own class, heightened the illusion. When the ruling class acquitted men on technicalities they helped instil a belief in the disembodied justice of the law in the minds of all who watched. In short, its very inefficiency, its absurd formalism, was part of its strength as ideology.[24]

It is probable that most of the judges themselves were believers in this ideology. Certainly, this conception of the supremacy of the law permeates Blackstone's *Commentaries*, and whatever his faults, Blackstone understood the legal mind.

All this may seem to have taken us far from my central themes. But this is surely not so. The picture that is emerging of England in 1770 is that of a society which largely ran itself, a society in which the machinery of law operated with a combination of threats, mercy, and ideology, in which the actual enforcement of laws was largely left to private initiative—as nearly everything else was—and was extremely inefficient. The inefficiency may have contributed to strengthening the ideology and the price may have been worth paying in the simple, rural, pre-industrial England of the early eighteenth century; but as the face of England began to change in the decades to come, the price became dreadfully high. In due course, a bureaucratic administrative machine had to be created to cope with these new problems. But that took time, and in the meantime, something else had to bolster up the inefficiencies of administration and law. Some new discipline was needed. It is part of the thesis of this work that that new discipline was found in Contract.

PROPERTY AND THE TRANSITION TO CONTRACT

In the eighteenth century a man's wealth was thought to consist largely of his 'possessions', of physical property, principally land; in the modern world, wealth has been said to consist largely of promises[25]—by companies to pay dividends on stocks and shares, by Government to pay interest on stock, by debtors to pay their debts, and so on. In and around the year 1770 this transition was in process of occurring. It was the process by which the law of property gave way in paramountcy to the law of contract. The process of change was slow; throughout the eighteenth century the greater number of legal cases on contract law themselves involved contracts relating to land. In Blackstone's world, or at least in Blackstone's *Commentaries*, contract not only played a very small part in the legal scheme, but its role was principally that of an appendage to the law of property. Blackstone deals with contract law very briefly, in two places in his *Commentaries*; in volume ii which is devoted to the law of property, he treats of contract (in Chapter XXX)

---

[24] Ibid., p. 33.

[25] Pound, *Introduction to the Philosophy of Law* (New Haven, 1922, reprinted 1954), p. 236.

as a means of acquiring title to property, and it is worth noting that this chapter immediately follows a discussion of the acquisition of title by succession in the preceding chapter. And in volume iii on 'Private Wrongs', Blackstone has another few sections on contract in the middle of Chapter IX entitled 'Of Injuries to Personal Property'.

Blackstone may well have been a rather conservative lawyer, even by the standards of his time, and perhaps inclined to underestimate the importance of contract law. But—if for the moment we advance some twenty years on—the same can hardly be said of John Joseph Powell who, in 1790, published his *Essay upon the Law of Contracts and Agreements*[26] in two volumes. For, as we shall see later, there are many respects in which Powell anticipates the nineteenth-century attitudes to contract law; but in other respects, his book is firmly planted in eighteenth-century property law. Powell's *Essay* is the first book which can claim to be something of a comprehensive treatise on the general principles of English contract law, and he cites a very large number of cases. The vast majority of these cases concern property transactions and marriage settlements, which were themselves an important type of property transaction. Powell, like Blackstone, may have underestimated the significance for contract law of the many new commercial cases coming before the courts, especially those concerning shipping and marine insurance. Nor does he have much to say about the law concerning bills of exchange and promissory notes which had, for at least a century when Powell wrote, been an important source of litigation; he probably would have regarded that as part of the Law Merchant rather than as part of the law of contract. But there is no doubt that, to Powell, contract law was fundamentally about property. In his Preface he had this to say :[27]

Contracts comprehend the whole business of human negotiations... They include every change and relation of private property ... But however different the objects, the contracts respecting them must uniformly be determined by the principles of natural or civil equity ... no treatise has hitherto appeared, written professedly to show the connexion between these general principles and the laws of property in England.

In one sense, this transition from a law of property to a law of contract relating to property merely reflects the now familiar process by which the significance of property rights changed from their use-value to their exchange-value. This change which is, of course, associated with the development of nineteenth-century capitalist economies, was already under way in 1770, although it is unlikely that the great landowners would have seen their family estates as having primarily exchange-value

---

[26] London, 1790.
[27] At pp. iii–iv.

at that time. Nevertheless, the process was under way. In the coming new world, property was to change its significance:

It does not matter what the thing is: it may be a block of flats, an agricultural estate, a factory, or so many South African gold shares. The property object has become "capital". But the law of property cannot by itself endow its object with the nature of capital. It must be assisted by complementary institutions most of which are to be found in the law of contract.[28]

But the connection between property and contract goes much deeper than this, and the transition from a property-based to a contract-based society was also a more complex process than this may suggest. The notion of a transition from use-value to exchange-value is sound, but it is apt to lead to a telescoping of several hundred years of history. Before property rights came to be seen primarily in terms of their exchange-value, the law of property and accepted ideas about property rights had grown far more sophisticated than the simple concept of use-value would suggest.

In the first place we must remember the invention and stabilization of money. When the value of money derived from, and was identical with, the value of the precious metal of which it was constituted, it may be said to have had a use-value, at least in an extended sense of 'use'. But long before the growth of anything resembling a capitalist economy the value of money often became detached from the value of the metal; it had an 'official' value deriving from the transmutation of raw metal into a minted coin. True it is that in 1770 the value of the metal in a coin still generally approximated the official value of the coin; the 'cartwheel pennies' of 1797 were heavy and cumbersome precisely because they contained one penny's worth of copper. And, of course, the official value could not long be allowed to fall below the market value of the metal for that would lead and did lead to the coins being illegally melted down and sold as metal. But it was not uncommon for the official value of the coin to be above the value of the metal contained in it. And when that was the case the full exchange-value of the coin lay in mere expectation—the expectation that the State would honour the value of its coinage, and the further expectation, that the public at large would also accept the coin as being of the official value which the State gave it. Thus, long before the eighteenth century, this form of property—coin of the realm—might derive its value in part from expectations rather than from the physical characteristics of the object itself.

With the beginnings of a paper currency this process obviously moved forward very substantially. For the value of paper notes rests entirely on expectations about the future willingness of other people to accept them

---

[28] O. Kahn-Freund, in Renner, *Institutions of Private Law*, pp. 27–8.

in exchange for articles of tangible utility. The modern origins of paper money in England date from the Goldsmiths' notes which began to be issued in the late seventeenth century. At first merely receipts for gold or valuables deposited for safe keeping, they soon became transferable notes. After the Revolution of 1688, when the political system stabilized, and still more after the creation of the Bank of England and the stabilizing of the monetary and financial system, banknotes began to be widely used, especially in trading circles. A banknote was originally nothing but a promissory note—it was a promise to pay money, real money, that is gold coin—but in due course when there was sufficient confidence in the expectation that the promise would be honoured, the notes became themselves accepted in most circles as the equivalent of actual money. They became property. Bank of England notes did not become legal tender until 1812; but this only gave formal recognition to a change which had long since been accepted in commercial circles.

The use of banknotes and more generally of bills of exchange and promissory notes had a major impact on modes of exchange for it meant that (for instance) a contract of sale could be completely carried through, executed on both sides in a legal sense, while yet, in another sense, the transaction was only half consummated. The seller who accepted Bank of England notes had been 'paid'; the contract was completely executed; the buyer had wholly performed his contractual obligations. And yet the seller held in his hand merely a few pieces of paper; at that time, it is true, he could expect to change those pieces of paper for gold at the Bank of England, but that was a mere expectation, and from time to time, the expectation was disappointed when payments of gold were suspended (as they were in the Napoleonic wars, for instance). But generally the expectations were not disappointed, and it was the stability in the political, the financial, and the legal system which tended to ensure that those expectations were not disappointed. Thus one of the principal types of property, even in this age of property, itself rested not on the physical properties of an object, not on the mere possession of something of utility; but on expectations.

But if that was true of money, it was, in fact, no less true of most other forms of property, though it required some percipience to see it. The Lockean tradition had encouraged people to see property rights as something which could exist before law or society, and although Locke himself had emphasized the importance of the invention of money, he did seem to think of property as a physical object, and a property right as in the nature of physical possession. It is, moreover, very probable that the Lockean tradition accorded in this respect with the legal tradition. English lawyers had for centuries been in the habit of conceiving of future rights and expectations as property rights. The medieval common lawyers had worked out a highly elaborate set of property rules which enabled all sorts of future arrangements to be made in advance by use of the appropriate legal concepts and language, but these arrangements were invariably treated as operating by means of property rights. In order to achieve this somewhat remarkable result, the early property lawyers had developed the doctrine of 'estates' which enabled them to conceive of a future interest as having a present existence. A man entitled, to take a simple example, to an interest in land after the death of a life tenant who was presently in occupation, was conceived of as *now* owning an estate in reversion or remainder. That estate was a present existing property right which could be bought and sold. There were, of course, infinitely more complex cases into which I need not delve here; the point to be made is simply that the medieval lawyers had used property law to regulate future arrangements concerning land in a wide variety of situations, many of which would seem to the modern lawyer to be primarily contractual. Instead of promising to do something in the future, a man would grant a right of property in the present.[29]

Now future rights of this kind, however they may have been treated as property rights by lawyers, rest ultimately on expectations. Indeed, the same analysis is equally true of the rights of a present owner, for his right of property—of ownership—necessarily stretches out into the future. If his right is more than that of merely retaining possession here and now, he must be protected in the future enjoyment of that right. At any given moment, these future rights also rest in mere expectation. All this, and much more, was clearly perceived by Hume whose analysis has rarely, if ever, been surpassed. He points out, in the first place, that the effect of custom and of long continued possession creates an expectation that the possessor will continue to enjoy the property he possesses, and that the starting point of all property laws is, in effect, that 'every one continue to enjoy what he is at present possess'd of'.[30] In due course laws, more and more complex, grow up, regulating the transfer by consent and succession of property so acquired; and other, less common methods of acquisition may also come to be recognized. But the relationship between a person and any piece of property of which he is not actually physically in possession is a relationship of the imagination; it is, that is to say, an artificial abstraction. Men have a powerful tendency to associate physical objects with people, and from this there arises the further tendency to see the abstract rights as though they were themselves physical objects. This, says Hume, is why we so often find that a physical

---

[29] A. W. B. Simpson, *Introduction to the History of the Land Law* (Oxford, 1961), p. 99; F. H. Lawson, *The Rational Strength of English Law* (London, 1951), pp. 87–8.
[30] *Treatise*, Book III, Part II, Sect. III.

delivery of property is necessary in law to transfer the right to it.[31] Of course, once rules develop and a proper system of justice and law is in operation, these expectations become more powerful partly because they are themselves protected by the law.[32] But Hume insists that expectations may be less worthy of protection if they are not conjoined to present or previous possession for the very good reason that 'Men generally fix their affections more on what they are possess'd of, than on what they never enjoy'd.' So that 'it would be greater cruelty to dispossess a man of any thing, than not to give it to him'.[33]

In this respect Adam Smith seems to have agreed with his friend Hume and he too emphasized the importance of expectations to property rights. In his *Lectures on Jurisprudence*[34] Smith rests property rights on 'reasonable expectations', which, in his moral philosophy, means expectations which would be shared by the sympathetic 'spectator'.[35] In his view the earliest ways of acquiring property are occupation, prescription, accession, and succession, all of which are based upon the expectation of being able to retain possession once acquired. As society becomes more complex, voluntary transfers are introduced, and later still, new expectations are generated in a variety of ways.[36]

Among these newer types of expectation were property rights concerning what is now sometimes called 'Intellectual Property'. Patent rights and copyright existed in eighteenth-century England. Both owed their origin to Statutes; patent rights originated in the Statute of Monopolies of 1623 which gave statutory confirmation to the judicially declared illegality of royal monopoly grants, but excepted the grant of a temporary exclusive right to manufacture 'a new invented art'. Copyright raised more interesting legal issues for it brought before the Courts some fundamental questions about the very nature of property rights. A Statute of Queen Anne's reign had created a form of statutory copyright, limited to twenty-eight years' duration, but for many years a controversy raged as to whether there might not co-exist with the Statute a common law copyright of perpetual duration. It was not often that the judges were forced to examine the very foundations of property law in the eighteenth century, but this issue compelled them to do precisely that. The question first came before the Court of King's Bench in *Millar*

[31] Ibid., Sect. IV. It is scarcely necessary to mention the old common law requirement of 'livery of seisin' as an illustration of Hume's point.

[32] *Enquiry into the Principles of Morals*, Appendix III, Sect. 260.

[33] *Treatise*, Book III, Part II, Sect. I.

[34] Ed. Meek, Raphael, and Stein (Oxford, 1978), p. 17.

[35] Smith's moral philosophy was much more extensively treated in *The Theory of Moral Sentiments* (first published in 1759, reprinted, ed. Raphael and Macfie, Oxford, 1976). See generally, Thomas Campbell, *Adam Smith's Science of Morals* (Glasgow, 1971).

[36] Campbell, op. cit., p. 197.

v. *Taylor*[37] when, for the first time in the history of the Mansfield Court, one of his colleagues was moved to dissent. The case concerned a book published forty-two years earlier which had not been registered, as was then required to secure statutory copyright, though that would anyhow have expired. Notwithstanding Mansfield's attempt to brush aside inferences 'from gathering acorns and seizing a vacant piece of ground'[38] the shadow of Locke lay heavy on the case. For Mansfield argued that the author's right to the actual physical copy of the book which he writes must rest on the same grounds as the claim to copyright itself. Why was it admitted on all hands that the author owned the former?

[B]ecause it is just that an author should reap the pecuniary profits of his own ingenuity and labour. It is just that another should not use his name without his consent. It is just that he should judge when to publish, or whether he will ever publish.[39]

And among his colleagues Willes J. and Aston J. were on his side. The notion that the author owned only the physical paper on which he first wrote was a primitive conception of property. After invoking Locke on property, Aston J. went on:

Since those supposed times, therefore, of universal communion, the objects of property have been much enlarged by discovery, invention and arts . . . The rules attending property must keep pace with its increase and improvement, and must be adapted to every case.[40]

But property in land was one thing; property in ideas was another. The celebrated dissent of Yates J. pointed out that the plaintiff (who was a bookseller and not himself the author) was seeking to monopolize control over the author's ideas. A man is, admitted Yates J., entitled to the fruits of his labour, but he must not expect these to be eternal, nor expect to 'monopolize them to infinity'.[41] Behind this argument about the nature of property rights there thus lurked a question about the right of the people to share in the marketplace of ideas. The fact that landownership was as much a monopoly as a claim to perpetual copyright did not seem to concern Yates J., nor did it concern Lord Camden who secured the final rejection of Lord Mansfield's views in the House of Lords in *Donaldson* v. *Becket*[42] some years later. The issue had, in a sense, become a political one. Lord Mansfield, politically a strong Tory, was for defending property rights to the utmost; Lord Camden, a Whig and champion of the people's rights (though, on other occasions also a staunch protector of property), wanted the public to enjoy the right to share in

---

[37] (1769) 4 Burr. 2303, 98 E.R. 201.
[39] 4 Burr. 2398, 98 E.R. 252.
[41] 4 Burr. 2359-60, 98 E.R. 231-2.

[38] 4 Burr. 2399, 98 E.R. 253.
[40] 4 Burr. 2339-40, 98 E.R. 221.
[42] (1774) 4 Burr. 2408, 98 E.R. 257.

ideas without having to pay for the privilege for ever.[43] The truth was laid bare for all who wanted to see it, though probably few did: property rights were not 'natural' but artificial creations of the law, and it was the law, based on values and policies, which determined the extent of those rights. Property had suffered its first major defeat.[44]

But if it is true that property rights are based on expectations, and if it is also true that they are artificial creations of the law and not themselves physical things which can be picked up in the state of nature, it is also true that property rights did seem more naturally based to eighteenth-century Englishmen. Expectations based on, and allied with, physical possession, seemed, in a stable society, to be the most natural type of expectation to be protected. Indeed, this is almost true by definition. For to protect the future extension of an existing possession is to maintain stability. And although there is a sense in which to compel a man to repay a debt also preserves stability—that is it restores the *status quo* to what it was before the debt existed—it nevertheless disturbs the *status quo* which exists immediately before the debt is in fact repaid. This is why even promises to return something which has been borrowed do not generate expectations as high as those generated by an extension of existing possession. The point was put long ago by Godwin, one of the anti-establishment thinkers of the late eighteenth century.

It is in vain that the whole multitude of moralists assure us, that the sum I owe to another man is as little to be infringed upon, as the wealth of which he is in possession. Everyone feels the fallacy of this maxim. The sum I owe to another may, in many cases be paid, at my pleasure, either today or tomorrow, either this week or next. The means of payment, particularly with a man of slender resources, must necessarily be fluctuating, and he must employ his discretion, as to the proportion between his necessary and his gratuitous disbursements. When he ultimately fails of payment, the mischief he produces is real, but is not so great, at least in ordinary cases, as that which attends upon robbery.[45]

Nor, we may add, is the legal sanction; for failing to repay a debt is not, and has never been, treated as an ordinary criminal offence.

Of course, the extent to which the law protects expectations, and the strength of those expectations which are generally held, naturally react, one upon the other. In the eighteenth century property rights in land had been protected, one way and another, for centuries; and since the

---

[43] The proceedings in the House of Lords are reported in full, not in Burrow's law report, but in the *Parliamentary History* xvii, at col. 954.

[44] Fifty years later the poet Robert Southey wrote to Brougham asking for the repeal of the Copyright Act 'which took from the families of literary men the only property they had to give them'. *The Greville Diary*, 12 February 1831 (ed. P. W. Wilson, London, 1927), i. 139.

[45] *Enquiry Concerning Political Justice* (first published, 1795, new edition, ed. K. C. Carter, Oxford, 1971), p. 109. Adam Smith says almost the same in his *Lectures on Jurisprudence*, ed. Meek, Raphael, and Stein, p. 87.

Revolution of 1688 they had become (as we have seen) more secure and more absolute. Naturally they gave rise to strong expectations which in turn reinforced the rigour with which they were protected by law. The protection of expectations deriving from promises or contracts, on the other hand, was still less sure; and the expectations themselves were also less strong, as the above quotation from Godwin shows. Naturally this too gave rise to action and reaction; low expectations were thought scarcely worth protecting, and the lack of protection kept the expectations low. But in 1770 the stability of the legal order was such that expectations of this nature were rising, and as they rose, the demand for their protection rose too. Eventually they were to burst through the barrier created by this process of action and interaction.

If it should be asked how these expectations came to be strong enough to justify greater legal protection, in the absence of adequate legal protection in the first place, the answer must be a complex one, and most of it falls within the scope of the next Chapter. But it can be said here that the dependence of contractual dealings on the legal protection of expectations is a good deal less than it is in the sphere of property. It is perfectly possible for contractual arrangements of a limited nature to work even in the absence of a proper law of contract.[46] It is a fallacy to suppose (as Hobbes did)[47] that men cannot make contracts 'in a state of nature', or (as Professor Hart appears to do)[48] that men cannot buy and sell without a law of contract. The Greeks appear to have managed without a law of contract,[49] and at all times men have been willing to enter into illegal and therefore unenforceable contracts such as those involving bribes, black market dealings, or prostitution. Even more legitimate exchanges are perfectly possible without a law of contract. Men may make simultaneous exchanges of property for money; men may give credit to carefully chosen and trustworthy friends, men may even give limited credit to those who are not known to be so trustworthy if they feel confident that the debtor will, for reasons of pure self-interest, find it necessary to pay the debt. And so on. But it is almost impossible to conceive of a society in which private property is recognized and permitted, but it is not protected by the law. This probably explains, at least in part, why, despite the fact that Hobbes and Locke lumped together the protection of property and the enforcement of contracts as the basic necessities of society, eighteenth-century law was a good deal more advanced in protecting property than contract.

Before closing this discussion of the transition from property to

---

[46] H. Havighurst, *The Nature of Private Contract* (Evanston, Ill., 1961), pp. 68–74.
[47] *Supra*, p. 42.
[48] *The Concept of Law* (Oxford, 1961), p. 32.
[49] J. W. Jones, *Law and Legal Theory of the Greeks* (Oxford, 1956), pp. 227–8.

contract, it is worth drawing attention to a number of more specific areas in the law in which the process of transition can be more clearly seen at work. Much the most fundamental of these concerns the extent of the freedoms which attached first to dealings in property, and later to all contractual dealings. So far as the land law was concerned, I have referred so far to the freedom of property in rather broad terms. But a narrower, though vitally important question for lawyers, concerned the extent to which landowners were free to tie up land, to create interests of a peculiar or idiosyncratic nature, to stamp their personal whims on a piece of land so as to bind it indefinitely. After the statutory changes created by the Statute of Uses and the Statute of Wills in the mid-sixteenth century the conveyancers discovered that they had been freed, as if by magic, from the old feudal restrictions on the kinds of interest that could be created, and the time during which land could be tied up. It soon became apparent that unlimited freedom could be used to destroy itself.[50] This problem was ultimately resolved by the Rule against Perpetuities which limited the freedom of landowners to tie up their property to a period of time extending no longer than twenty-one years after the death of any 'life in being'. As we shall see, a similar problem has long existed in contract law, though its relationship with the Rule against Perpetuities has rarely been remarked on.

A second area which helped the transition from property to contract concerned transfers or conveyances of interests in land which, for one reason or another, were ineffective in law. Because of the exceedingly technical nature of many of the rules governing the transfer of interests in land, this problem was a much more formidable one than it is today.[51] Moreover, in the eighteenth century the notion that it was the function of the law to give effect to men's intentions was gathering increased strength in every sphere, and when manifest intentions were defeated by old and technical requirements, the Courts increasingly sought a way round the technicalities. By the end of the seventeenth century it was well established that the Court of Chancery would construe an ineffective conveyance—subject to various conditions—as a promise or covenant to transfer,[52] and the rule was reaffirmed and extended in the middle of the eighteenth century.[53] Purported assignments of choses in action at law came to be treated in the same way in equity, and this rule remains in force to this day in certain classes of cases. It is often a sensible and just rule to compel a person to do effectively what he had purported to do, but in fact has done ineffectively.[54] But it is not at all obvious that an

---

[50] A. W. B. Simpson, *Introduction to the History of the Land Law*, p. 186.
[51] See Powell's *Essay*, i. 152–60.   [52] *Osmere* v. *Sheafe* (1694) Carth. 307, 90 E.R. 78.
[53] *Roe d. Wilkinson* v. *Tranmere* (1758) Willes 682, 125 E. R. 1383.
[54] But not, of course, always. For if the law prescribes formalities for good policy reasons, the evasion of these formalities simply defeats the purpose of the law.

ineffective transfer of property can rightly be called a *promise* to transfer the property; the reality seems rather that an ineffectual conveyance may generate expectations in the same way as a promise. The law thus protects expectations and then treats those expectations as the result of a promise.

A third area in which property rights and concepts gradually merge into contractual law concerns securities and mortgages.[55] Generally speaking, it seems true that in early law—specifically in early English Law—securities were designed to be transfers of property, which did not, therefore, require to be enforced by legal process on the part of the creditor. When property rights are protected by law, as an extension of rights of possession, the man in possession enjoys much greater protection than the person who seeks to enforce a contractual remedy by legal process, and that is true even when contractual rights are fully protected by law. To hang on to what you already have is so much simpler than to embark on litigation. Of course, if the possession is transferred as security only, it will have to be retransferred on discharge of the debt or other secured obligation; but that throws the onus on the debtor where it tends to fall in a free bargaining situation. Later, as the law came to protect property rights based on expectations not necessarily linked with prior possession, it became increasingly possible to grant security without a transfer of possession. A freeholder could mortgage his property without giving up possession. Even so, this was, at first, treated as a conveyance, though the mortgagor had a right to demand a reconveyance if he tendered the necessary sum to the mortgagee. Later still, the condition on which the mortgagor was entitled to recover his property tended to become the central element in the transaction, and was redefined or reconceptualized as a promise or undertaking.[56] The essential nature of the mortgage was by this time transformed. It had become a loan which the mortgagor promised or contracted to repay, on the terms that if he failed to do so, the mortgagee might forfeit the property (subject to any necessary procedures) or sue upon the contract to recover the loan, or take other appropriate remedial action.

THE LAW AND ECONOMIC LIBERALISM

Although the subject still awaits a full historical study, there has long been a belief, amongst both historians and economists, that there was a tradition of economic liberalism among the common lawyers, dating back to Sir Edward Coke, and perhaps even beyond. In this section I propose to offer some evidence in support of this tradition, though, it

---

[55] Llewellyn, 'What Price Contract?', 40 *Yale Law J.* 704, 726 (1931).

[56] See Ehrlich, *Fundamental Principles of the Sociology of Law* (English edn., 1936), p. 220, cited in H. Havighurst, *The Nature of Private Contract*, pp. 48–9.

must be repeated, the subject still requires a much fuller treatment than I am able to give it. We must not, of course, make the mistake of supposing that there was, before the time of Adam Smith, any coherent or well-thought-out body of ideas called 'economic liberalism' which was ready to hand for lawyers to read and digest. There plainly was not. But we have seen that from the sixteenth century onward ideas were gaining currency, especially among the commercial community, which can only be described in terms of economic liberalism. They were, in origin, ideas favouring freedom—freedom of property, freedom to trade and to work, freedom to lend money at interest, freedom from monopolies and combinations, freedom to make one's own decisions for good or ill, freedom from governmental and legal intervention. There is some ground for thinking that the common lawyers were peculiarly receptive to these ideas, and that they gained a ready acceptance among the lawyers before they spread through the community at large.

Why should this have been so? What was it about the work or nature or organization of the legal profession which made lawyers, or at least common lawyers, more receptive to ideas of commercial freedom? The traditional answer has been to trace the origins of this common law characteristic to Coke and to place it in the context of the legal and constitutional struggles in which he was involved. To Coke, freedom was political freedom from the arbitrary power of the Crown; and because the Tudors and the Stuarts after them tried to use the power of the Crown to restrict and regulate economic freedom as well as political freedom, the two became associated in the opposition of the common lawyers to the Crown. This may well be so, though it does not seem to be the whole story. I will return to Coke shortly, but it is worth suggesting— even if somewhat speculatively—that there may have been other factors at work in this process. The legal profession in England—the Bar and Bench—has changed very little over the centuries in some of its essential characteristics. It is a highly individualistic profession, a highly competitive profession. Barristers work on their own—not in anonymous firms—patronage and nepotism are not much use to the incompetent who will soon betray their incompetence; and although political views have, at times, been useful aids to getting on the Bench, it is rare that the really incompetent have made that transition. This is no place for a sociological study of the English legal profession, but there is little doubt that its traditions tend to foster a belief in the virtues of freedom and competition and enterprise. The judges, all appointed from the Bar, naturally tend to attribute their promotion to their own abilities, and to laud a system which has enabled them to rise. This was all the more so at a time when (as was well known) the law was one of the few paths by which the humblest and poorest could rise to the top.

Moreover, to the traditions of the profession itself, must be added something about the nature of their work, of their clients, and of the society in which they lived. In times of regulation and restriction, lawyers do not lack clients who wish to find a way round the regulations and restrictions. When, even in the fifteenth century, the lawyers found a way of barring an entail, it seems certain that they did so at the importuning of clients who wanted to be rid of the dead hand of the past. When, in the seventeenth and eighteenth century, lawyers attacked the monopolies, the guilds, the combinations which restricted free commerce and enterprise, we may be sure they did so because they had clients who wanted to be free. Of course, under the reign of the Stuarts (as in a modern totalitarian State) it was a dangerous activity to find ways of 'getting round' the laws. It is a characteristic of tyrants to treat an evasion of the law in the same way as a violation of the law. But the rule of law that prevailed in eighteenth-century England gave full scope to the skill of lawyers who could find 'ways round' the rules. Evasion and violation are different things in a society where the judges are independent and the rule of law prevails. Indeed, it is not too far-fetched to see a close and direct connection between economic liberal ideas and the rule of law as that came to be understood after 1688. The idea that the law should be regular, certain, and subject to interpretation by independent judges is itself an idea with a powerful value content; and the value behind it is the value of individual freedom, and free choice. The importance of predictability and regularity in law lies precisely in the fact that it enables individuals to appraise their position and choose how to act for their own purposes, their own good. It is for these reasons that we find it being said in modern times that the rule of law is (and was) a politically biased ideology. 'By promoting procedural justice it enables the shrewd, the calculating and the wealthy to manipulate its forms to their advantage.'[57] Historically, this may well have been true of eighteenth-century England; but if it had not been, perhaps England would not have been the first nation to have an Industrial Revolution.

A further factor may have had something to do with the social position of barristers, and hence of those who became judges. Barristers would often, in seventeenth- and eighteenth-century England, have been younger sons of the landed gentry for whom there was no landed estate to inherit. They were, in a sense, a species of *petite bourgeoisie*, as that term might be used today, although at that time they were perhaps more middle middle-class than lower middle-class. As such they were perhaps peculiarly liable to come into contact with other members of that class— commercial people, the new trading and mercantile class. It was from these classes that many of their clients must have increasingly been

[57] See Morton J. Horwitz, 86 *Yale Law J.* 561, 564 (1977) (review).

drawn. It is true that judges of the eighteenth century were often unfamiliar with commercial practice; but they were not unsympathetic to commercial practice, and where they did not know, they often made it their business to find out. Two of the greatest judges of the century, Holt and Mansfield, often resorted to commercial men both in and outside the courtroom for advice and information about the way they did business.[58] In some instances, family relationships must have helped feed the lawyers and judges with the nascent economic liberalism of the businessmen. For example, there were the Pollexfen brothers who flourished in the late seventeenth century.[59] Sir Henry (1632–91) was a lawyer and a leading Whig who took part in a famous case in 1684, in which the monopoly of the East India company was challenged as illegal.[60] He played a prominent part in the Revolution of 1688, became briefly Attorney-General, and thereafter Chief Justice of the Common Pleas. His brother, John (c. 1638–?) was a businessman, a free trader and writer on economic matters. He wrote in 1697 a free trade pamphlet entitled *A Discourse of Trade, Coyn and Paper Credit* to which Sir Henry contributed an Appendix. Another pair of brothers of an even more distinguished family, though Royalists and not Whigs, were members of the North family.[61] Sir Dudley North (1641–91) was a substantial and prosperous merchant who transacted much overseas business, especially with Turkey, where he resided for many years to manage his business. On returning to England he became a member of Parliament and, for a time, a Treasury Commissioner. In 1691 he published his *Discourses upon Trade*, a vigorous blast in favour of free trade, to which I have already referred. His brother, Francis North (1637–85), was a prominent lawyer who became Chief Justice of the Common Pleas in 1675 and Lord Keeper in 1682; he was raised to the peerage as Lord Guilford in 1683. Notwithstanding his Royalist inclinations, he sometimes showed signs of being an embryonic economic liberal at a time when such ideas were not expected of the presiding judge in the Court of Chancery.[62]

More generally, in the eighteenth century at least, prominent lawyers and judges were necessarily becoming more aware of, and more involved

[58] Holt consulted the goldsmiths about their usages, for instance, (see *Ford* v. *Hopkins* (1700) 1 Salk. 283, 91 E.R. 250); and Mansfield sometimes relied upon conversations 'with intelligent persons very conversant in the knowledge and practice of insurance' (see *Glover* v. *Black* (1763) 3 Burr. 1394, 1401, 97 E.R. 891, 895.) Hardwicke had also consulted the merchants occasionally (see *Kruger* v. *Wilcox* (1755) Amb. 252, 27 E.R. 168).

[59] The following information comes from the *DNB*.

[60] *East India Co.* v. *Sandys* (1684) Skin. 132, 90 E.R. 62. Holt had also been counsel for Sandys.

[61] For the North Family, see the *DNB*.

[62] See *post*, p. 176. The *Life of Francis North* (2nd edn., London, 1808) by his brother, Roger, unfortunately casts no light on the Lord Keeper's views on these questions. But we are told that when Dudley returned from Turkey, the brothers discoursed at length about 'trade and traffic in the world at large'; and that 'these new ideas did so possess his [the Lord Keeper's] thoughts ... that he could not be easy till he had laid them aside ...', ii. 12–13.

in, various types of commercial activity. They were, for instance, beginning to be significant investors in the Funds;[63] as lawyers, they were being asked to draft or advise on contracts for the sale of stock, often of a highly speculative nature.[64] A number of law suits (as we shall see) flowed from the bursting of the South Sea bubble. Sir Joseph Jekyll, Master of the Rolls from 1717–38, was a member of the House of Commons Committee appointed to investigate that disaster. And so on. I do not, of course, suggest, that every contact with commercial affairs turned a barrister or judge into an economic liberal; some of these contacts (such as the South Sea affair) may well have done the reverse. But, over all, this increased contact with the commercial community may have played a part in making the legal profession essentially sympathetic to the demands for economic freedom.

Before taking a closer look at some of the key figures and some of the key issues on this question, a reminder is in order about that part of the law which was not common law. If the common lawyers had a tradition of economic liberalism, there is no question but that the Chancery tradition was precisely the reverse. The Chancery tradition was one of regulation, protection, paternalism. It seems likely that the Chancery tradition was inherited from the activities of the Council in the Tudor period. In the reign of Elizabeth the Council was, as we saw earlier, exercising a considerable degree of control and regulation over the economy; but it also found time to deal with individual relationships and conduct. Nothing, it seems, was too big or too little for the Council to pry into.

Does a landowner take advantage of the ignorance of peasants and the uncertainty of the law to enclose commons or evict copyholders? The Council, while protesting that it does not intend to hinder him from asserting his rights at common law, will intervene to stop cases of gross oppression, to prevent poor men from being made the victims of legal chicanery and intimidation, to settle disputes by common sense and moral pressure, to remind the aggressor that he is bound 'rather to consider what is agreeable . . . to the use of the State and for the good of the common wealthe, than to seek the uttermost advantage that a landlord for his particular profit maie take amonge his tenants' . . .

The Council, which keeps sufficiently in touch with business conditions to know when the difficulties of borrowers threaten a crisis, endeavours to exercise a moderating influence, by making an example of persons guilty of flagrant extortion, or by inducing the parties to accept a compromise. A mortgagee accused of 'hard and unchristianly dealing' is ordered to restore the land which he has seized, or to appear before the Council. A creditor who has been similarly 'hard and unconscionable' is committed to the Fleet. The justices of Norfolk are

---

[63] Dickson, *The Financial Revolution in England*, pp. 297–8. In the early eighteenth century an otherwise unknown barrister, John Freke, published a price list of securities; ibid., p. 495.

[64] Ibid., p. 491.

instructed to put pressure on a money-lender who has taken 'very unjust and immoderate advantage by way of usury'[65]

Here, it seems, is the origin of the Chancery tradition, taken over by the Chancellors (who were prominent members of the Tudor Councils) and ultimately given greater importance by the abolition of the Council's executive and judicial powers.[66] The divergence between these two traditions was probably very old. Is it a concidence that in his *Discourse upon Usury* (published in 1572) Thomas Wilson, who is defending the older tradition, puts into the mouth of a lawyer the opposing view: 'Who I praye you would lende but to have some benefits of his money? And is that anye harm when bothe do gayne?'[67] Moreover, such is the force of tradition, especially among lawyers, that these divergent points of view, based on divergent values and moral systems, seem to have waxed strong right through the seventeenth and eighteenth century. By 1770, however, the economic liberalism of the common law was about to triumph over the protective paternalism of the Chancery; Equity was on the verge of a long period of decline. I shall have more to say about that later, but I propose now to say a little about some of the individual figures and the specific issues in which the common law attitudes manifested themselves.

Coke

We must begin with Coke if only because a substantial, if controversial, literature has grown up on the question of Coke's beliefs since the suggestion was first mooted some forty years ago that he could be ranked as an economic liberal.[68] On the whole, this suggestion has received the support of later writers,[69] though not without dissent.[70] My story really begins in 1770, but in 1770 legal ideas and the legal tradition owed a great deal to Coke, so something must be said about him.

It is possible to identify three particular respects in which Coke's ideas anticipated the economic liberalism of later years. First, he gave to the common law tradition that hatred of monopolies which it always thereafter professed (though sometimes with less than conviction). In 1600 England was still riddled with monopolies. The guilds and chartered corporations maintained a stranglehold on most forms of work

---

[65] R. H. Tawney, *Religion and the Rise of Capitalism*, pp. 171–3.

[66] R. H. Tawney, Introduction to Wilson's *Discourse upon Usury* (London, 1925), p. 12.

[67] Ibid., p. 202.

[68] Wagner, 'Coke and the Rise of Economic Liberalism', 6 *Economic History Review* 30 (1935–6). Earlier still, Roscoe Pound had argued for Coke's importance to the subsequent development of individualism, though not specifically in the economic sphere; 'Liberty of Contract', 18 *Yale Law J.* 454, 459–60 (1909).

[69] Christopher Hill, *Intellectual Origins of the English Revolution*, Chapter V; David Little, *Religion, Order and Law*, especially at pp. 238–46.

[70] Barbara Malament, 'The "Economic Liberalism" of Sir Edward Coke', 67 *Yale Law J.* 1321 (1967).

and enterprise within their spheres of interest; external trade was largely handed over by the Crown to great chartered companies who obtained exclusive rights to trade within the areas granted to them; and even within England itself the Crown had been in the habit of granting exclusive monopolies or patent rights in respect of particular commodities, both as a way of extracting taxes from the public and as a way of rewarding royal favourites. In 1602 in the famous *Case of Monopolies*[71] the Court of King's Bench held void and contrary to law an Elizabethan grant of a monopoly in respect of the making of playing cards. It is true that Coke was not on the Bench at this time, and indeed, as Attorney-General argued the case for the validity of the grant. But there are clear signs that he favoured the decision of the Court over his own argument. For Lord Ellesmere's Note, appended to the decision in the English Reports,[72] tells us that Coke's Report of the case (as was not indeed infrequent) was not wholly accurate. Coke's Report states that the Court decided not only that the monopoly within the country was void, but that the purported grant of the exclusive right to *import* playing cards was also void. Ellesmere tells us that the Court decided no such thing, and that those who observed the case know that the Court passed over that point in silence, and concentrated on the main issue. The question is not without significance because the prerogative powers of the Crown had always been recognized to be greater in relation to foreign affairs, and import and export regulation had long been thought supportable under the prerogative. Thus Coke's version of the decision was an extreme one, and must have represented his own views. And we know that Coke also did his best, in a variety of other cases, to limit the powers of the guilds and other monopolies.[73] The evidence on this fully supports Christopher Hill's verdict that Coke 'pursued with implacable hatred monopolists and patentees'.[74]

The second respect in which Coke displays early signs of economic liberalism is his general dislike of regulation and control, especially in the economic sphere. But political and economic liberties were anyhow not so easily disentangled. At a time when economic regulation was becoming so extensive that inspection into a man's private home might be necessary for enforcement purposes, a claim to freedom of property and freedom of the person could also be an effective demand for economic freedom. So that when Coke asserted that an Englishman's home was his castle, he was asserting a right which was bound to make economic regulation more difficult.[75] Similarly, Coke (like many of his fellow

[71] 11 Co. Rep. 84b, 77 E.R. 1262.
[72] At p. 1265.
[73] *Bonham's* case (1610) 8 Co. Rep. 107a, 77 E.R. 638; *City of London's* case (1610) 8 Co. Rep. 121b, 77 E.R. 658.
[74] Christopher Hill, *Intellectual Origins of the English Revolution*, p. 235.   [75] Ibid., p. 237.

countrymen) detested the common informers on whose services the Government largely relied for the enforcement of its detailed economic policies. So when Coke attacked the system of common informers, and required them to proceed in their local courts, where they would face the hostility of local jurors, he was also striking another blow at the means of economic regulation.[76] In the most recent and fullest study of Coke's ideas, David Little has concluded that, although there was evidently no full blown doctrine of economic liberalism in Coke's mind or anywhere else at that time, there are nevertheless signs of a marked difference of attitude to economic regulation.

Coke's legal decisions in the field of economic regulation do constitute a radical break with the past and do lay some legal foundation for what later amounts to modern rational capitalism.[77]

The third identifiable link between Coke and the later economic liberals is his belief in freedom to work, free trade, and (at least to some degree) faith in the workings of the market. He did not like the restrictions on the Englishman's freedom to work contained in the Statute of Apprentices, or in the controls exercised by the guilds over particular trades and professions. He did his best to outlaw the seventeenth-century equivalent of the closed shop in *Bonham*'s case,[78] and he argued that the market could be left to distinguish the competent from the incompetent workman. Nor was he blind to the interests of the common labourer, for he too was plainly motivated by economic incentives: 'make what statutes you please, if the plowman has not a competent profit for his excessive labour and great charge he will not employ his labour and charge without a reasonable gain to support himself and his poor family.'[79] On the other hand, if a man had a right to work, he also had a duty to work, for idleness was 'the root and cause of all mischiefs'.[80]

It has been said that Coke did not contribute much to the development of general contract law,[81] though even that is debatable. He certainly took part in the vitally important decision holding that contractual obligations could be enforced against executors in the new actions of *assumpsit*, unlike the old action of Debt.[82] We know also that Coke argued for the successful plaintiff in the celebrated *Slade*'s case in 1602,[83] and although one must not assume that what a man says as counsel necessarily

---

[76] M. W. Beresford, 'The Common Informer, the Penal Statutes and Economic Regulation', 10 *Economic History Review* 221 (1958).
[77] David Little, *Religion, Order and Law*, p. 244.
[78] (1610) 8 Co. Rep. 107a, 77 E.R. 638.
[79] *Tyrringham*'s case (1584) 4 Co. Rep. 36b, 39a, 76 E.R. 973, 982.
[80] Ibid.
[81] David Little, *Religion, Order and Law*, p. 205.
[82] *Pinchon*'s case (1612) 9 Co. Rep. 86b, 77 E.R. 859.
[83] 4 Co. Rep. 91a, 76 E.R. 1072.

(or at all) represents his own beliefs, when Coke reports his own arguments as fully as he did those in *Slade*'s case it is reasonable to assume that he believed in them. I do not have space for a detailed consideration of this much discussed case, and it must suffice to say that it was in many respects a critically important decision for the development of the law of contract. It represented the triumph of the new action of *assumpsit* over the old action of Debt, a triumph which involved the success of the more rational procedure of jury trial over that of compurgation.[84] But perhaps the decision can also be taken to symbolize the replacement of the idea of a legal obligation arising out of a relationship by the idea of a legal obligation created by the free choice and acts of the parties. For the action of Debt reflected the traditional view that even in a consensual transaction like a sale of goods, it was the law which created the liability. After *Slade*'s case it became easier to think of the liability itself (and not merely the relationship) as the creation of the parties.

Mansfield

I must move on a century and half to my next major figure. That is not to say that some of the intervening lawyers (Holt especially comes to mind) may not have been important in the growth of economic liberalism in the law, but considerations of space preclude a fuller account. In 1770 the towering figure of Mansfield dominated the legal scene. William Murray, as he was originally, was born in 1705, a member of an ancient Scottish family. Although educated in England his Scottish background probably played a part in his legal development because he was more familiar with civil law ideas than most of his contemporaries or predecessors had been. He was called to the Bar in 1730, and entered the House of Commons as Solicitor-General in 1742. By 1747 he was the acknowledged leader of the House of Commons on the Tory side and provided almost the only effective speaker against the elder Pitt. In 1754 he became Attorney-General in the Duke of Newcastle's administration. Two years later Sir Dudley Ryder, Chief Justice of the King's Bench, died in office, and Murray laid claim to the post. He is said to have resisted every blandishment from Newcastle who knew that his Government could not survive without Murray. Eventually Newcastle gave way, Murray was created Lord Mansfield and appointed Chief

---

[84] The literature on *Slade*'s case is enormous, though it mainly deals with doctrinal aspects of the case. See, in particular, A. W. B. Simpson, *A History of the Common Law of Contract*, pp. 295–313; J. H. Baker, 'New Light on Slade's Case', [1971] *Camb. L. J.* 51, 213; H. K. Lucke, 'Slade's Case and the Origin of the Common Counts', 81 *Law Q. Rev.* 422, 539 (1965), 82 *Law Q. Rev.* 81 (1966). One wonders whether Coke was not bringing a new attitude to bear in his argument (reported by Baker, op. cit., at p. 56) that there cannot be a contract without mutual promises or reciprocal agreement. The whole of this passage (which reads perfectly acceptably to a modern lawyer) may have been more innovative than it still seems to us.

Justice of the King's Bench, a post he was to hold altogether for thirty-two years. Politically Mansfield remained all his life a strong Tory—a Tory in the sense which the word came to bear later in the century. He had no taste for demagogues like Wilkes (though he quashed his outlawry on a legal technicality) ; he had no truck with sedition and crossed swords repeatedly with the Whig Lord Camden on the right of a jury to give a general verdict in a prosecution for seditious libel, an issue on which Mansfield prevailed in the Courts but Camden (and Fox) eventually prevailed in Parliament. Nor did Mansfield have any love for the rabble or the mob, which was probably why he was so bitterly attacked in the Letters of Junius, and which may also have been why the mob burnt his house to the ground in the Gordon riots in 1780. But, in many other respects, Mansfield was a vigorous reformer and a true harbinger of the new age. It seems impossible to deny him also the title of economic liberal.

Mansfield is best known for his work in the development and consolidation of much commercial law, especially the law of marine insurance and shipping, and the law of bills of exchange and promissory notes. Because this is the best documented side of his work[85] (though an adequate biography is still awaited), it is unnecessary to say much about it here. It is enough to stress a few points concerning Mansfield's underlying sympathies and objectives. It is quite plain that Mansfield had a considerable respect for the commercial community of his time. He knew a good deal about the already well established marine insurance industry before he went on the Bench, and what he knew had made him a free trader long before Adam Smith was heard of. In 1747, when a Bill was debated in Parliament to make it illegal for British insurers to insure French ships in time of war (for there was then no common law rule to this effect) Mansfield had opposed it. Both parties, he argued, gained from such trade and the British gained more than the French. 'To carry on trade for the mutual benefit of both nations', argued Mansfield, 'is not aiding and assisting the enemy.'[86] If this sentiment seems strange to an age which has grown accustomed to the idea that the objective of a war is the total destruction of an enemy, it must be remembered that what was strange in 1747 was the idea that trade benefited both sides. What Mansfield and the marine insurers wanted to combat was what they perceived to be the vulgar error that the sums paid to a French shipowner for an actual loss represented a net loss to Britain and a net gain to France. But there were wider principles at stake. The practice of controlling and regulating commercial affairs by law was too often mistaken, argued Mansfield. There were many examples where we had

[85] See C. H. S. Fifoot, *Lord Mansfield* (Oxford, 1936); Holdsworth, *H.E.L.*, xii. 464–78.
[86] *Parliamentary History*, xiv, col. 116.

'injured our own trade and promoted that of our most inveterate enemy by ill-judged regulation or mistaken polities'.[87] We ought, he said, to be cautious 'in making any new regulations or prohibitions with respect to trade, however plausible the pretences may be that are offered for inducing our approbation'.[88] This speech of Mansfield's must have been well known to the lawyers of the time. Later in the century, when the Napoleonic wars raised these questions for debate in the Courts, Mansfield's views were widely quoted though ultimately rejected.[89]

On the Bench, Mansfield's objective with regard to commercial law was to make the law more serviceable to the commercial community. That meant that it must become more rational, more intelligible, more predictable, and more just according to the standards of the mercantile world. Each one of these objectives Mansfield pursued. Rationality and intelligibility he tried to encourage by insisting, over and over again, that it was the *intention* of the parties that was to govern in commercial contracts.[90] Contracts had to be construed 'liberally' to give effect to probable intention. This may seem commonplace enough to us today, but in Mansfield's time most legal documents which came before the Courts concerned land; and the rules of interpretation for such documents dated from a period when giving effect to intentions was not the primary objective of the social order or of the law. The result was that many of these rules had ossified in ways which totally defeated normal intentions, and these rules were still being applied every day by the Courts. A man, for instance, who left 'my house Blackacre' to his wife in his will in all probability intended her to have the fee simple. But the law was clear: such words only passed a life estate. The land law was riddled with rules of interpretation of this kind, many of which seemed absurd and excessively technical to Mansfield.[91] But they seemed absurd and excessively technical, not just because many of them were obsolete or old-fashioned but because *values* had changed. These rules offended most those who believed in the new values of the enlightened age, those who believed that men had the ability to plan their affairs in an orderly, rational way, and were therefore entitled to the assistance of the law in giving effect to reasonable intentions. It may well be that there is a good case for stricter rules of interpretation for documents dealing with land (and even more, that there was such a case in the eighteenth century) and this may explain why Mansfield largely failed in his attempts to

---

[87] Ibid.   [88] Ibid., col. 112.

[89] See e.g. *Bristow* v. *Towers* (1794) 6 T. R. 35, 47, 101 E.R. 422, 428.

[90] *Hotham* v. *East India Co.* (1779), 1 Doug. 272, 99 E.R. 178; *Meres* v. *Ansell* (1771) 3 Wils. K.B. 275, 95 E.R. 1053 (where he went too far for his colleagues); *Rees* v. *Abbott* (1778) 2 Cowp. 832, 98 E.R. 1386.

[91] See e.g. *Loveacres d. Mudge* v. *Blight* (1775) 1 Cowp. 352, 98 E.R. 1125; *Perrin* v. *Blake* (1770) 4 Burr. 2579, 98 E.R. 355.

reform the land law;[92] but this must not obscure the measure of Mansfield's success in the contractual sphere. It was from his time and it was largely due to his efforts, that the law of contract came to attribute primacy to the intention of the parties.

Predictability of the law Mansfield also encouraged by his attempts to incorporate large areas of commercial practice into the law. This meant that questions which had formerly been left to the decision of a jury were now placed increasingly in the hands of the judge. Mansfield was not greatly enamoured of the ordinary jury (as we know from his attempts to keep general verdicts out of their hands in seditious libel cases) and in commercial cases he was convinced that the unpredictability of a jury's decision was a major source of dissatisfaction to businessmen.[93] It is true that Mansfield is famous for the use he made of special juries drawn from the City, but this was merely an intelligent process designed to pave the way for the ultimate withering away of the jury function in commercial cases. If the jury as general decision-maker on all issues was to be replaced by the judge, if jury mercy and popular equity were to give way to predictable and general principles of law, those principles of law must be properly made. We have seen how, in Mansfield's time, Parliament and Government had neither the staff nor the expertise to carry through intelligible and rational law-making themselves, and why therefore this task fell on the Courts. But in this new commercial age the Courts themselves—though better equipped than Parliament—often lacked the expert knowledge to develop principles of commercial law acceptable to the business community. It was to overcome this gap in their expertise that Mansfield called in aid the special juries. They were to decide the individual case in such a way that the judges would then be able to use that decision as a base for the erection of general rules of law. In this way the law could become at once more predictable, more regular, and more in accordance with commercial customs.

I shall be looking later at a number of Mansfield's decisions in particular areas; and I shall also have something to say about Mansfield's ideas on the doctrine of consideration. But before leaving Mansfield himself it is worth taking a closer look at one particular case, argued by him when he was Solicitor-General, which provides further evidence for his claims to be ranked as an economic liberal. This is the case of *Chesterfield* v. *Janssen*,[94] decided in 1750. The case involved the old

---

[92] Many of Mansfield's contemporaries disagreed vigorously with his emphasis on intention. See e.g. Fearne, *Essay on Contingent Remainders* (1772), cited Fifoot, *Lord Mansfield*, p. 178; 'Surely it is better that the intentions of twenty testators every week should fail of effect, than that those rules should be departed from upon which the general security of titles and quiet enjoyment of property so essentially depend.'

[93] See e.g. *Metcalf* v. *Hall* (1782) 3 Doug. 113, 115, 99 E.R. 566, 567.

[94] (1750) 1 Atk. 301, 26 E.R. 191.

equitable ideas concerning usury, unconscionable contracts, and expect-ant heirs about which I shall have something more to say later. John Spencer, grandson of the first Duke of Marlborough, and entitled to various reversions on the death of the Dowager Duchess, Sarah, borrowed £5,000 when he was thirty years old, and Sarah seventy-eight. As was customary, he gave a bond as security, and under the bond he bound himself to pay £10,000 on Sarah's death if he survived her; if he did not, nothing would be payable. He did survive her, though not by very long, and his executor, the Earl of Chesterfield, contested the liability to pay £10,000, offering instead to repay the borrowed sum plus reasonable interest. Had the facts stopped there it is likely that the Court, according to its old rules, would at least have examined the bargain to see whether it was a fair one. But in fact John Spencer had, after the death of the Duchess, confirmed the old bond by giving a new one 'in the freest and most voluntary manner imaginable', and the Court eventually decided that this confirmation of the transaction saved them the necessity of examining its fairness. The borrower may have had the right to repudiate the first bond on Sarah's death but he had by his free choice confirmed it. I will return to the significance of the decision. Here I am concerned with Mansfield's role in it. Counsel for Spencer's executor argued, in language which recalls the medieval conception of property rights, that the bonds were void as usurious and unconscionable: 'No man has a right in his own property beyond the limits of conscience; men are bound to use their own, so as not to hurt or prejudice another.'

In answer to this kind of talk, Mansfield proffered the language of Adam Smith and Bentham years before they produced it themselves:

A notion prevailed for many years [he says], that it was not lawful to take any hire for money; this was adopted from the canon law, and even prevails today in many catholic countries. It is astonishing how prejudice should have kept common sense so long out of the world! Why is not money a commodity, as well as anything else?[95]

And as for the argument that a man's freedom to borrow should be limited by the public good, this is his response:

Then what is this public good, this rule they so much insist on, that no man shall spend above his annual income? How can that be prevented? Is it in human nature? He will spend it; men of the best sense have done it; where will be the publick utility? Where the encouragement to industry? Will the court consider every man as a lunatick who exceeds his income? Another end, perhaps to lock up property for another age; is that desirable? Will it procure money on easier terms? It is directly to the contrary . . .[96]

---

[95] 1 Atk. 331, 26 E.R. 211. It is right to add that by this time Mansfield was arguing against a view which had few defenders; see *post*, p. 130 as to Blackstone's views.

[96] 1 Atk. 335, 26 E.R. 214. For other relevant Mansfield decisions upholding the right of free

I now turn to a brief survey of some of the particular areas in which the incipient economic liberalism of the common lawyers manifested itself in the seventeenth and eighteenth centuries.

Monopolies and Combination

I have already referred to Coke's hostility to all forms of monopoly, and it is unnecessary to traverse this ground again. But it must be stressed that the word 'monopoly' had a very wide connotation at that time, much wider than that which it generally bears in common parlance today. Any exclusive right to control or regulate a trade—even though it were only in one town—was a monopoly. The City and Trade Guilds of this period, bodies set up under Royal Charter, who claimed the right to make by-laws regulating a trade, either within the city in question, or a trade of a particular character, were often highly restrictive in their practices. They frequently operated rules designed to prevent new entrants to the trade, or new entrants of a particular type, such as foreigners. They also enforced the legal requirements of the Statute of Apprentices by which they tried to keep out those who had not served the statutory seven years in a trade. All these monopolies came increasingly under the hostile gaze of the common law. Whenever possible, the Courts appear to have construed their powers and privileges in the narrowest possible manner.

Combinations in Restraint of Trade

The hostility to monopolies also, quite naturally and logically, manifested itself in a general hostility to many forms of combination. Monopolies might be created by Royal grant—though that was now generally illegal—but they could also be created by groups of men forming a combination by which they tried to secure an entire trade or commodity to themselves. After the collapse of the South Sea scheme in 1721 there was, for a long time—indeed, until well into the next century—a general hostility to all corporations. At this time, corporations were still almost invariably created by Royal Charter, and they were closely associated in the public and the legal mind with monopolies. Throughout the eighteenth century, it was individual enterprise which was favoured, though there was no perceived objection to partnerships consisting of several individuals, freely united by contract. In 1761 the Attorney-General advised the Government against granting a charter to a proposed new insurance company, saying, 'A trade seldom requires the

choice, see *Hawkins* v. *Colclough* (1757) 1 Bur. 274, 277, 97 E.R. 311, 312 (arbitration awards are favoured because 'they are made by Judges of the parties own choosing'); and on individualism, see *Holman* v. *Johnson* (1775) 1 Cowp. 341, 98 E.R. 1120 (a man is not his brother's keeper when the latter chooses to violate a foreign law).

aid of such combinations, but thrives better when left open to the free speculations of private men; such measures are only expedient where trade is impracticable upon any other than a joint stock . . .'[97]

It was this general hostility to all combinations of a monopolistic character which underlay the notion that certain restrictive types of combination, or agreements in restraint of trade, as they were called, might be a conspiracy, and illegal. Agreements by sellers of goods to fix prices and not to undersell each other restrained the individual's freedom of enterprise which the new public policy required. It was not to be tolerated that the unfortunate buyer, faced with a combination of sellers, should have to agree their prices or do without. That was a form of monopoly. Moreover, it made no difference whether the combination was designed to fix the price of goods or the price of labour. In either case the result was a monopoly to the public prejudice. And in the eighteenth century there was no question of the illegality of conduct of this kind. In 1783, for instance, Lord Mansfield upheld an indictment against six workmen for a conspiracy to 'impoverish' a tailor in the exercise of his trade.[98] 'Persons in possession of any articles of trade may sell them at such prices as they individually may please, but if they confederate and agree not to sell them under certain prices, it is conspiracy; so every man may work at what price he pleases, but a combination not to work under certain prices is an indictable offence.'[99] It is clear, thus, that to Lord Mansfield, freedom of contract was not to be allowed to stultify the purposes for which it was created. The policy of the law was to encourage freedom of enterprise, freedom of trade, freedom to work; in so far as a person used this freedom to agree to deprive himself of that freedom, his agreement was not merely ineffective in law, but an offence, a conspiracy.

It would be wrong to think that this was some new doctrine designed to combat the activities of the new combinations of workers—the nascent trade unions—growing up in the late eighteenth century. It was all part of the traditional hostility to anything smacking of monopoly. In the early seventeenth century the Courts had first begun to *relax* the total ban on all agreements in restraint of trade, and had begun to uphold agreements whereby, for example, the seller of a business agreed not to compete with the buyer. One of the earliest such cases was *Rogers* v. *Parry* in 1614,[1] and it may not be without significance that Coke was involved in this case. Coke was not one to uphold a monopoly or a restraint of trade without good reason, yet he did uphold here an agreement by the defendant not to exercise his trade of joiner in certain premises leased to

[97] Cited Hunt, *The Development of the Business Corporation in England 1800–1867* (Cambridge, Mass., 1936), p. 11.

[98] *R.* v. *Eccles*(1783) 1 Leach 275, 168 E.R. 240.

[99] 1 Leach 276–7, 168 E.R. 241.

[1] (1614) 2 Bulst. 136, 80 E.R. 1012.

him for 21 years. It seems clear that both in this case, and also in the more seminal one of *Jollyfe* v. *Brode*[2] a few years later, the judges had come to realize that the encouragement of industry and enterprise might, within certain limits, actually favour reasonable restrictions of trade or work. A man who built up a business and then wished to retire in old age, and to sell the goodwill of the business, could not expect to realize its full value unless he could contract not to compete with the purchaser.[3] These derogations from the general opposition to monopolies and restraints of trade had been reviewed and confirmed, within limits, in *Mitchell* v. *Reynolds*[4] early in the eighteenth century, when the Courts had drawn a distinction between a *general* and a *partial* restraint, holding only the latter to be void as against the policy of the law. It seems clear that the judges here were still groping after something which they never wholly succeeded in recognizing, namely that they wanted to uphold freedom of contract in so far as that encouraged freedom of enterprise, but not in so far as it was used to destroy it.

The Statute of Apprentices

Closely associated with these anti-monopoly ideas was the attitude of the common lawyers to the Statute of Apprentices. Almost from its enactment this Statute, which compelled a man to serve a seven-year apprenticeship before he could legally exercise a trade, aroused the antagonism of the common lawyers. In the view of the common lawyers a man was entitled, and indeed, under a duty, to work, and anything which prevented him working at the trade of his choice was an unnecessary and evil restriction on his freedom. Had not Holt argued for the illegality of the East India monopoly by saying that 'there is a natural necessity laid upon a man to labour, and thereby it becomes a duty in him, which the King cannot prohibit, but ought to prevent and incourage'?[5] And if the lawyers could not challenge the supremacy of a Parliamentary Statute as they had the legality of Royal monopolies, they could certainly do their best to emasculate the statutory provisions. Almost from the beginning the Act was interpreted as only applying in towns and not in country areas; but when these country areas grew into large towns in the industrial revolution, the Act still did not apply to them. In 1670 Twisden J.

---

[2] (1620-1) Cro. Jac. 596, 79 E.R. 509.

[3] Traditional accounts of this case (e.g. Simpson, *A History of the Common Law of Contract*, pp. 523-4) appear to overlook this rationale, perhaps because they misinterpret the facts. These accounts assume that the defendant somehow swindled the plaintiff by selling his stock at an inflated figure, whereas in reality the defendant seems to have been deliberately selling the goodwill of his business, not merely the stock.

[4] (1711) 1 P. Wms. 181, 24 E.R. 347.

[5] *East India Co* v. *Sandys* (1684) 1 Skin. 132, 137, 90 E.R. 62, 64. Holt had been the Whigs' choice as Chief Justice of the King's Bench after the Revolution of 1688, and in this passage he seems to be echoing Locke.

declared that he had heard all the judges say that they would never extend the Act 'further than they needs must'.[6] By the time of Holt's Chief Justiceship, it was already well established that the Act only applied to trades existing at the time when it was first passed,[7] and shortly afterwards Holt's Court took the even stronger step of holding that the Act was satisfied when a man had served seven years in the trade even though he had never been bound apprentice, 'this being a hard law'.[8]

Fifty years later the tradition continued. In the first case which Lord Mansfield ever heard as Chief Justice he held that it was not contrary to the Statute for a man to be a sleeping partner of one who had served as apprentice in accordance with the Act.[9] The argument that the Statute was a protection to the public because it ensured that only competent and qualified men practised as tradesmen was rejected, as Adam Smith was later to reject all such arguments. 'Bad and unskilful workmen are rarely prosecuted.'[10] It was the market, and self-interest, which must determine with whom a man transacted business. A few years later the weavers of Oldham sought by means of a strike to enforce the apprenticeship regulations and made demands also for agreed and fixed prices for their cloth. When they were indicted for conspiracy they claimed that they were merely trying to enforce the existing law, but the argument was brushed aside by Foster J. who suggested that 'it might perhaps be of utility to have those Laws repealed as tending to cramp and ty down that knowledge it was at first necessary to obtain by rule'.[11] 'This remarkable judgment', says a modern historian, 'anticipated the actual repeal of the Statute of Artificers by more than half a century ... the laws of the land were set aside in favour of the as yet unstated doctrines of Adam Smith.'[12] He is probably wrong in saying that the laws of the land were set aside,[13] but certainly right in suggesting that the sentiments were those of Adam Smith.

The Marketing Offences

I have previously referred to the laws against regrating, forestalling, and engrossing, and it remains only to put them in their context in this chapter. These offences were designed to secure the operation of an

[6] *R.* v. *Turnith* (1670) 1 Mod. 26, 26, 86 E.R. 704, 705.

[7] *R.* v. *Harper* (1705) 2 Salk. 611, 91 E.R. 518.

[8] *R.* v. *Maddox* (1706) 2 Salk. 613, 91 E.R. 519.

[9] *Raynard* v. *Chase* (1756) 1 Burr. 2, 97 E.R. 155.

[10] 1 Burr. 6, 97 E.R. 157.

[11] Cited in A. P. Wadsworth and J. de L. Man, *The Cotton Trade and Industrial Lancashire* (Manchester, 1931), pp. 366–7.

[12] E. P. Thompson, *The Making of the English Working Class* (London, 1963), pp. 274–5.

[13] In all probability this was one of the areas where the Statute of Apprentices did not apply, having been outside the control of the city corporations in the sixteenth century.

essentially closed market, particularly in food supplies, and to ensure that such supplies were brought to the market by the producer and made available for purchase there by the consumer. The offence of 'regrating' was that of buying and then reselling in the same market. 'Forestalling'— as the name implies—was the offence of buying (or selling) prior to the holding of the market; it was designed to prevent a middleman from buying before the market and then reselling at the market, and also to prevent one buyer and one seller making a secret and private deal which might have had the effect of depriving other members of the public of the opportunity of obtaining supplies themselves. Forestalling also extended to conduct dissuading a producer from bringing his goods to market, that is, to attempt to hold back supplies in order to wait for a rise in prices. 'Engrossing' was the offence of cornering supplies, or buying up large quantities of corn or 'dead victuals', for the purpose of speculating, hoarding, or profiteering. These were all old common law offences, which had constantly been enforced, and as constantly evaded.

The constantly repeated rules against these practices and the endlessly recurring prosecutions mentioned in the records of all the larger towns prove that people did these things, that the desire to trade could not be suppressed, that there were always people ready to take a chance with the law to make a profit out of consumers less well informed and less sharp-witted than themselves.[14]

The laws and customs against these practices had been designed to support a market, but a market of a fundamentally different kind from that which was growing up in the seventeenth and eighteenth centuries. The paradox was that the old common law tradition against all forms of monopoly took the form of maintaining this older type of market structure, and when opinion turned against the enforcement of the old marketing offences, it was precisely because of the growth of the economic liberal ideas which elsewhere were embraced by the eighteenth-century common lawyers. Had the Mansfield tradition continued after his death it is possible that the Courts would have embraced economic liberalism here, as they did almost everywhere else, in advance of the legislature and of enlightened opinion. In fact this did not happen, partly because of the period of legal conservatism which set in after Mansfield under the influence of men such as Kenyon, Eldon, and Ellenborough. Under these judges, the common law marketing offences were briefly revived, as we shall see, around 1800, thirty years after Parliament had finally abolished the statutory offences. That was done by an Act of 1772[15] which declared that experience had shown that restraints on dealings in foodstuffs 'by preventing a free Trade in the said commodities

---

[14] Davis, *A History of Shopping* (London and Toronto, 1966), p. 6.
[15] 12 Geo. 3, c. 71.

have a tendency to discourage the growth and to enhance the price of the same'.

Usury

I have already written about changing attitudes to usury in society at large, and of the growing acceptance of the legitimacy of moderate interest on loans from the sixteenth century onwards. It remains only to suggest here that, once again, the common lawyers seem to have been in the van of change. Throughout the seventeenth and eighteenth centuries the common lawyers had constantly been faced with the problem of trying to find ways by which loans could legally be made at rates of interest exceeding those permitted by the law. When both intending parties, borrower and lender, were perfectly agreeable to a transaction of this nature, when they were both businessmen who knew their own interests, or even when (as in *Chesterfield* v. *Janssen*) [16] the borrower was an adult of full age and understanding, lawyers evidently felt the laws to be futile and tiresome. They had no compunction about finding ways of evading them, though they could never be wholly certain that the Court of Chancery would not ultimately be called on to examine the facts for signs of usury. Even the conservative Blackstone, for all the subsequent bitter and, on this point, unfair attack on him by Bentham, shows some vehemence in criticizing the outdated prejudices against usury.[17] The various ways in which the lawyers found it possible to evade the usury laws are described in standard works,[18] and it is unnecessary to go into them in detail. It is sufficient to make one point.

All the accepted methods of borrowing money at rates above the permitted maximum depended ultimately on the concept of risk. If the lender was certain to get his money back, and was certain to get, in addition, a return above the permitted maximum, then the transaction was usurious and illegal, no matter how it might be devised. Of course nobody is ever *certain* to get even his capital back, because debtors may default; but this risk was ignored by the law (hence its fundamental unreality, of course) and so it was always necessary to build in additional risks. One of the most common procedures, illustrated by the facts in *Chesterfield* v. *Janssen*,[19] was for the borrower to agree to repay a capital sum exceeding that which he borrowed, but only on the condition that he survived some other party, for instance, a life tenant keeping the borrower out of a valuable reversion. The lender thus took the risk of losing all if the borrower died first, and this risk generally justified a rate

[16] *Supra*, p. 124.
[17] *Bl. Comm.*, ii. 455.
[18]. Simpson, *A History of the Common Law of Contract*, pp. 113–17, 510–18.
[19] *Supra*.

of interest higher than that normally permitted. Throughout the eighteenth century, however, this type of transaction was always under attack. For it came to be possible and common for the lender to insure the borrower's life against the risk of his death prior to that of the life tenant, and as insurance became a regular and stable form of business, it became possible to put a fairly certain value on the element of risk involved. Borrowers would thus be tempted to go to the Court of Chancery and argue that the transaction was usurious because the cost of the insurance could be calculated and, when deducted from the lender's profit, still left an exorbitant rate of interest. A similar procedure, involving similar problems, was for the borrower to agree to pay an annuity terminable on his, the borrower's, death, in return for a capital sum. In form this transaction was thus a purchase of an annuity, but the underlying purpose was almost invariably a loan, for a man who really wanted to buy an annuity wanted it terminable on *his* death, not that of the other party to the transaction.

Perpetuities

I have referred briefly to this matter above. It seems probable that common law hostility to perpetuities was also a sign of nascent economic liberalism. The tying up of land by entails, or other legal methods designed to prevent the present occupier from dealing with the land, placing it on the market, mortgaging it, or devising it to whom he wishes, is bound to be a serious clog on the economic exploitation of land in a free market economy. There is at least one interesting judicial dictum dating from 1699 in which this common law policy is based on such economic ground. In *Scattergood* v. *Edge*[20] Treby C. J. is credited with the following remarks:

It was a great policy of the common law that alienation should be encouraged; for it is the greatest preserver and promoter of industry, trade, arms and study; and this was visible from the making of the Statute *De Donis*, until common recoveries were found out; and these executory devises had not been long countenanced when the judges repented them, and if it were to be done again, it would never prevail.

It is, of course, true that the period after 1688 did not see a satisfactory free market in land. The strict settlement was invented, and came to be the normal form of tying up property amongst the landed aristocracy for the next two centuries. In essence the strict settlement was simplicity itself, although an elaborate settlement acquired all sorts of complicated accretions. But the basic features were perfectly straightforward. Land was settled on the present occupier for life, with remainder to his eldest

[20] (1699) 12 Mod. 278, 287, 88 E.R. 1320, 1326.

son in tail, and on premature death of that son without further sons of his own, to the other sons of the occupier, also in tail. Now entails were no longer unbarrable, and if the eldest son in fact succeeded his father as tenant in tail, he could proceed to bar the entail forthwith, and the land then became freehold, at the disposal of the son. Even if this happened, there were likely to be encumbrances on the land which would prevent it being immediately alienable, however; for the land would probably be charged with (i.e. secured for) the former tenant for life's widow, not to mention possible portions for his daughters, if any. But there was, in fact, a far more serious problem, which in practice prevented the land from becoming alienable. It was only a tenant in tail in possession, and not a tenant for life, who could bar the entail. So long as the occupier remained alive, with a tenancy for life, he alone could not bar the entail, though he could do so with the aid of his eldest son once the son had come of age, so long as the son was entitled in tail. But in practice, these eighteenth-century aristocrats did not want to bar the entails, certainly not for the benefit of their eldest sons whom they so rarely trusted. When the eldest son came of age, therefore, the tenant for life would normally try to persuade him to join in 'resettling' the estate, that is to say, first barring the entail, then resettling the estate on the father for life (as before), on the eldest son for *his* life after the father's death, and then, in tail, on the eldest son of *that* eldest son, in due course to be born. It was not normally difficult to persuade the eldest son to join in such a resettlement, for eldest sons were naturally brought up to believe in the system of keeping the property in the family anyhow, and any resistance could easily be met by offering a little sweetener in the form of an allowance. Once the property had been resettled in this manner, it was effectively tied up for the whole of another generation; and perhaps even more, for in an age when sons often died before attaining their majority, it might often be a grandson or a younger son of a younger son who in fact succeeded to the property.

It has been suggested by Professor Simpson that it is unlikely that the rules worked out by the Courts on these matters can be explained in sociological terms, 'for example, in terms of a struggle between an entrenched and hereditary landed class, and a mercantile class eager to see land on the market so that they might become "squires by purchase" '.[21] On the other hand, the most recent historical research suggests that a struggle, if not quite of this kind, was in fact the source of the perpetuity rules as they ultimately developed.[21A] This research suggests that the common lawyers were moving, during the mid-

---

[21] A. W. B. Simpson, *Introduction to the History of the Land Law*, p. 195.

[21A] Haskins, 'Extending the Grasp of the Dead Hand: Reflections on the Origins of the Rule against Perpetuities', 126 *U. Penn. Law Rev.* 19 (1977).

seventeenth century, towards a much more restrictive perpetuity rule, and that this movement was not uninfluenced by the desire of the mercantile community for a freer market in land. By contrast, the *Duke of Norfolk's* case,[21B] which came to be the foundation of the modern rule was the reaction of the more conservative, aristocratic-minded judges of the Restoration period. Lord Nottingham, the Lord Chancellor who decided this case, was a royalist who sympathized with the desires of the landed magnates to tie up their land, and his decision in this famous case opened the door to the relatively extensive tying powers conferred by the modern Rule against Perpetuities. But even Lord Nottingham was well aware of the need to balance the desire of the landed magnates to tie their posterity, with their desire to be free of the like restrictions imposed on them by their ancestors. And the Rule against Perpetuities and the strict settlement which was built round that rule, do seem to have represented some sort of a compromise between these objectives. They did help to preserve the great landed estates and consequently the political position and power of the great families until late in the nineteenth century. And no doubt this did have severely restricting effects on the market in land, which began to be overwhelmingly important late in that century. But at the same time, things were not as bad in England as they were elsewhere. Adam Smith, while commenting adversely on the economic effect of entails, also noted that the position in England was not so bad as in Scotland or in most of Europe, where it was said that between one-third and one-fifth of all land was strictly entailed.[22] I do not, of course, suggest that the compromise struck between these two forces was necessarily the best or the wisest which hindsight might suggest; all I wish to do is to suggest that such a compromise was in fact being struck.

There is another respect in which the strict settlement necessarily involved some sort of compromise. Although its basic purpose was to tie up the land of a family from one generation to another—and therefore to restrict the freedom of future members of the family—some element of flexibility had to be built into the system. It was impossible to freeze, once and for all, the precise allocation of the income from landed estates for two generations, before the size (and sex) of the next generation could be known, and before prevailing conditions could be known. A well drawn settlement came, therefore, to embody some element of freedom for each generation, so far as this could be done without jeopardizing the main objective. For example, limited powers of dealing with the land, or part of it, by way of lease or mortgage might be granted to the tenant for life in such a way that his dealings would be binding even after his death and therefore after the termination of his life estate. And again, distribution of the shares of younger children by way (for example) of

[21B] (1681) 3 Ch. Cas. 1, 22 E.R. 931.   [22] *Wealth of Nations*, Book III, Chapter II.

'marriage portions' for daughters, could be allowed for by use of powers of appointment—a sort of limited delegated power of distribution vested in the tenant for life, or sometimes even in his widow. The conveyancers became adept at drawing highly elaborate settlements designed to cope with these problems, but the details are of less interest than the general picture.

The general nature of the problem, and of the solutions being worked out, are historically important for two reasons. First, because the strict settlement was in a sense the ancestor of the commercial companies which began to develop again, after a period of quiescence following the Bubble Act, late in the eighteenth century; and secondly, because the differing traditions of common law and of equity to the perpetuity question can perhaps be traced to this period, and to this source. As we shall see later, when the commercial companies began to develop again with the coming of the Industrial Revolution, they were at first created by deeds of partnership drawn up by conveyancers whose experience lay principally in land transactions and especially in settlements. These 'companies'—though called such, they were not strictly companies at all in the modern legal sense—like the settlements, had to reconcile the needs of present members with those of future members; and they also, like settlements, had to define the rights and duties of members *inter se* within each generation.

The company, like the family, was an institution, and the law was necessarily called upon to play a part in resolving potential conflicts of interest between its members, both those who were members at any given time, and those who were likely to be members over a span. In coping with these problems, equity, and the traditions of the equity conveyancers, turned out to have a larger role than the common law. Equity, unlike the common law, tended to look more favourably on the importance of the 'good of the institution', of preserving the institution, even at the expense of the freedom of action of the current generation. These equitable traditions eventually played an important role in the development of company law, and also in the development of ideas and attitudes to majority rule. Majority rule, which entails the power of a majority to coerce an unwilling minority, is totally contrary to the ethos of economic liberalism. Freedom of contract involves the freedom of the individual to choose, and majority rule deprives the individual of the right to choose in the interests of the group or institution as a whole. Now the strict settlement itself did not involve or require the principle of majority rule, for it was built around the position of the individual life tenant. But it did involve the idea of limiting the freedom of some members in the interests of the whole. When the new companies came to be created, and the similar problems of balancing the rights of some against others had to be solved in the context of an institution lacking a central tenant-for-life figure, it was natural for the conveyancers to settle for majority rule. And in other respects, too, as we shall see, it was the equitable paternalist traditions which tended to prevail in the new company law which grew up in the next century. This story is taken up again in Part II.

Negotiability and Assignment

A market economy requires an adequate system of credit at its base; and a sophisticated credit system requires that debts should be largely fungible. A debt grows out of a transaction (for example a sale on credit, or a loan of money) but a proper credit system requires that the debt should then be detachable from the transaction which gave it birth so that it can be used as a form of money for further transactions. Debts must, in other words be readily transferable, otherwise each credit transaction must be consummated before another can be undertaken.[23] Ideally, the debt must not only be transferable but it must be so detached from the transaction from which it arises that any counter claim against the creditor should not taint the debt itself. Thus if, for instance, a man sells goods on credit, but there is some fraud on his part, or some defect or deficiency in the goods which might enable the buyer to claim redress against the seller, a credit system requires in principle that the debt created by the transaction should nevertheless be transferable at least to one who takes it without notice of the circumstances which gave rise to it; the buyer, in other words, will still have to pay the full price eventually, when the debt has come to rest in the hands of he who demands payment. But the buyer may then pursue his remedy against the seller for the fraud or breach of contract. Between 1688 and 1770 the common law, with the aid of the Court of Chancery, created the legal principles necessary to support this credit system, though not without travail, and not wholly successfully.

The story falls into two part. There was first the ordinary common law which, from the earliest times, had refused to recognize the transferability, or assignment, of simple debts. It is widely thought that this rule originated with the dislike of 'maintenance', that is the process whereby one man would encourage another to bring and maintain some litigation in which he had no genuine interest. Whatever the origin of the common law tradition, there is no doubt that in the seventeenth century it was already firmly established and already much resented by the mercantile community as a hindrance to trade. The merchants were convinced that the prosperity of the Dutch was attributable in part to the system of

---

[23] J. Commons, *Legal Foundations of Capitalism*, p. 253; 'modern capitalism begins with the assignment and negotiability of contracts.'

transferable debts which existed in that country but not in England.[24]
After the Revolution of 1688 several attempts were made to legislate for
the transferability of certain debts, though without success.[25] But if the
common law remained obdurate, the Court of Chancery stepped into the
breach. Early in the eighteenth century, if not before, assignments came
to be recognizable in Equity,[26] though the only machinery whereby
Equity could achieve its objective was clumsy, and gave ample scope for
evasion and delay by an unscrupulous debtor. Since the common law
courts did not recognize the validity of an assignement of a debt, and
since the Chancellor did nor permit anyone to sue for a common law debt
in his Court, it followed that Equity could only enforce an assignment of
a common law debt by compelling the assignor (the original creditor) to
permit the assignee to sue for the debt in the common law courts in the
name of the assignor. Equity began to do this; but it was manifestly a
troublesome business if a creditor had first to sue in Chancery and then
at common law to obtain payment of his debt. The prospect of one law
suit is enough to deter most creditors, but two would normally suffice for
all except the hardiest or most obdurate.

In the second half of the eighteenth century there were signs that the
common law attitude to assignments might be changing. In 1762 an
assignment was, for instance, held a sufficient consideration for a
promise,[27] and there were signs that Mansfield might have been bracing
himself for total reversal of the common law rule. After Mansfield's
retirement, his disciple, Buller J., began dropping hints to the same
effect, and had the Mansfield reforming tradition continued the change
might have been carried through. But the tradition was not carried on.
Mansfield's successor as Chief Justice, Lord Kenyon, was a much more
conservative figure; and in 1800 he insisted that he would never subscribe
to the doctrine that a debt could be assigned at common law.[28] Thus the
door was finally slammed and it was not until the Judicature Acts that
assignments became recognized at law. The process of enforcement
through the assistance of Equity continued, but even apart from the
clumsy nature of the procedure involved in equitable enforcement,
assignment was never wholly satisfactory as a method of creating credit.
For the procedure of assignment did not sufficiently detach the debt from
the underlying transaction, the debtor was always entitled to raise
'equities' against the assignee, that is to say the assignee might, when he
came to enforce his claim, find that he was met by counter claims arising

---

[24] Lipson, *Economic History of England*, iii. 9–10.
[25] Holdsworth, *H. E. L.*, viii. 151.
[26] *Crouch* v. *Martin* (1707) 2 Vern. 595, 23 E.R. 987; *Row* v. *Dawson* (1749) 1 Ves. Sen. 331, 27 E.R.
1064.
[27] *Moulsdale* v. *Birchall* (1762) 2 W.Bl. 820, 96 E.R. 483.
[28] *Johnson* v. *Collings* (1800) 1 East 98, 104, 102 E.R. 40, 42.

out of the original transaction of which he had no knowledge. This is no way to establish and maintain confidence in credit, for a proper credit system requires that the transferee should be assured of ultimate payment. This rule was not very satisfactory for the transferor either, for it meant that when he 'paid' a debt by transferring a credit due to him from a third party, he did not absolutely discharge the liability. If it turned out that the third party ultimately refused to pay (or perhaps even if he simply failed to pay) the transferor might find that he was still liable.

These weaknesses and deficiencies in the law relating to the transferability of debts were largely met by a new process. Instead of openly modifying the common law rules, the judges attained their objective by 'incorporating' the law merchant into the common law. Mercantile practice had already conferred the characteristic of transferability and even negotiability (that is transferability free from counter claims, or 'equities') on various types of commercial document, the ancestors of the bill of exchange and the promissory note. In the fifteenth and sixteenth centuries some of these commercial customs had been enforced as 'law merchant' in special Courts like the Staple Courts and the Admiralty Courts. But these Courts had decayed by the seventeenth century, and as I have already observed, it was then that merchants began to complain loudly about the non-transferability of debts at common law. In the seventeenth century the common law judges began to say that the law merchant was 'part of' the common law,[29] though only with Holt did it cease to be necessary to plead and prove by evidence the nature of the commercial custom on which the plaintiff relied. This move (often wrongly attributed to Mansfield) meant that the law merchant ceased to be a law applicable only between merchants, or only applicable in particular places, or particular trades; it became part of the general law of the land governing all persons and all transactions. In the same way that moral ideas applicable to trade first spread through the community, so now the law relating to trade was adopted throughout the country.

There is no need to trace here the full story of this development which has been well told elsewhere.[30] Suffice it to say that the full negotiability of bills of exchange was established in the common law courts by a series of decisions, mostly of Holt C.J. in the last years of the seventeenth and the first years of the eighteenth century. The result was to create a kind of liability so easily enforced by the law that, as Adam Smith observed, 'money is more readily advanced upon [bills of exchange] than upon any other species of obligation.'[31]

---

[29] *Woodward* v. *Row* (1666) 2 Keb. 132, 84 E.R. 84; *Williams* v. *Williams* (1693) Carth. 269, 90 E. R. 759.

[30] J. Milnes Holden, *The History of Negotiable Instruments in English Law* (London, 1955).

[31] *Wealth of Nations*, Book II, Chapter II.

There was more difficulty over promissory notes, and the aid of an Act of Parliament was necessary to render these fully negotiable in the same way as bills of exchange, but that too was obtained in 1704. Shortly after that, the modern banknote evolved from the Bank of England's promissory notes and so successful was that species of 'credit' that very soon afterwards people began to treat Bank of England notes as a form of money rather than of credit. In *Miller* v. *Race*[32] Lord Mansfield set his seal upon this development by upholding the right of the bona fide purchaser of a stolen banknote to payment from the Bank of England: 'The whole fallacy of the [defendant's] argument', he said, 'turns upon comparing bank notes to what they do not resemble, and what they ought not to be compared to, viz., to goods, or to securities or documents for debts. Now they are not goods, nor securities, nor documents for debts, nor are so esteemed; but are treated as money, as cash, in the ordinary course and transaction of business, by the general consent of mankind; which gives them the credit and currency of money, to all intents and purposes.'[33] Thus there became apparent the immense value of separating a promise from the transaction to which it was attached, and treating it as a distinct and independent source of liability. It was also a signal victory for the growing importance of contractual expectations; the mere expectations of the bona fide holder of a banknote now served to defeat the property rights of the original owner. Promises and the expectations generated by them were thus becoming themselves an important form of property.

[32] (1758) 1 Burr. 452, 97 E.R. 398.
[33] 1 Burr. 457, 97 E.R. 401.

6

CONTRACT LAW AND THEORY IN 1770—I

PROMISES, CONSIDERATION, AND EVIDENCE

SINCE the developments in contract law and theory which began towards the end of the eighteenth century, and which led to the evolution of modern contract doctrine, a clear and relatively simple model of contract has dominated the thinking of common lawyers. I shall elaborate this model at a latter stage, but at this point it is enough to say that the essential core of the model is the idea that a contractual liability can be *created*—out of nothing as it were—by a promise, or at least an exchange of promises. Promises and contracts in the modern world are typically thought of as ways of creating wholly new obligations. Now this was nothing like so clear in the eighteenth century as it was to become later. Indeed, it seems evident that eighteenth-century lawyers lacked a general theory of contractual liability which could be reduced to the simple terms of modern contract doctrine. In so far as any general theories were implicit in the law, and in the ideas of lawyers and writers, they seem to have involved a confusing mixture of ideas. Some of these ideas are quite alien to those of modern contractual and promissory theory. Others may have been much closer to those of modern times. The more modern ideas were in process of development in the seventeenth and eighteenth centuries, but they co-existed for a long time with a much older tradition which may still have been influential around 1770, though it was then at the end of its long reign. Because of the ultimate triumph of the more modern theories, the older ideas have perhaps received less attention than is their due. On both historical and jurisprudential grounds, they are of the greatest interest.

In his *History of the Common Law of Contract*,[1] Professor Simpson has recently drawn attention to the fact that there are many signs, in the sixteenth- and seventeenth-century developments of the common law, of a theory of contractual liability very different from that of modern times. He argues that the word 'consideration' originally meant the reasons or motives inducing the giving of a promise. A promise given without any proper reason or motive was not binding, perhaps (as Simpson himself urges) because such a promise could not have been seriously intended, or perhaps more generally, because a promise given without any reason

[1] Especially at pp. 322-3, 391-4, 485-6.

would be a senseless act, not one capable of creating an obligation. In this scheme of things, it was not so much the promise which created the obligation, as the consideration itself:

> Granted this analysis it is plain that a promise to do something which one is already under an obligation to do, the promise being made in consideration of the circumstance giving rise to the obligation, is the paradigm or central case of a binding promise. For example, suppose A owes B a debt of £10, and because of this (in consideration ...) promises to pay £10. According to the theory the mere promise to pay £10 is not enough—it must be supported or bolstered up by an adequate motivating circumstance. What better circumstance than a pre-existing obligation to pay £10? Or again, take an illustration used by St. Germain. My father is cold and needs a gown to keep him warm—I ought, of course, as his son, to give him a gown, I have a natural duty to do so. If I now *promise* to give him a gown then the promise is binding. Hence in the early history of consideration it must be appreciated that what has come to be called pre-existing 'moral' obligation ... was not some curious aberration; it logically lay at the heart of the doctrine.[2]

It will be seen that, in this way of looking at things, the roles of promise and consideration were the reverse of what they are today. It was the consideration which was the principal ground for the creation of the obligation; the promise played a subordinate role. This may be a difficult idea to grasp for the modern reader who is apt to take as a starting point the 'naturally' binding nature of promises; moreover, this idea was itself one with an ancient history, for the concept of promissory liability was well known to Roman lawyers. But, as Pollock and Maitland wrote,[3] '[i]deas assumed as fundamental by this branch of the law in modern times and so familiar as apparently to need no explanation had perished in the general breaking up of the Roman system, and had to be painfully reconstructed in the middle ages.'

This particular idea was a long while being reconstructed. Apart from the evidence of the doctrinal developments in England which Professor Simpson has adduced, we know that the Natural Lawyers laboured hard to re-establish the idea that a promise had some natural and inherent binding force. The most celebrated of these writers were Hugo Grotius (1583–1645), the father of international law, and author of *De Jure Belli ac Pacis*, and Samuel Pufendorf (1632–94), author of *De Jure Naturae et Gentium*. Both writers drew heavily on Roman sources (and not exclusively legal sources)[4] and both argued against the consideration-

---

[2] Ibid, pp. 322–3.

[3] *History of English Law*, 2nd edn., (Cambridge, 1952), ii. 184–5.

[4] For example, they relied extensively on Cicero, *De Officiis*, which remained throughout the eighteenth century a most influential manual of prescriptive ethics. Cicero's ethics are significantly affected by his faith in the property basis of society, as to which his views resemble those of Locke.

based theory of promissory obligation which was still to be found in the common law in the sixteenth and seventeenth centuries. For instance, Grotius's main concern seems to have been to refute the views of the French jurist François de Connan (1508–51) who had argued that bare promises without cause or reason are not binding, and that promises are only binding when there is some exchange, or some pre-existing obligation, or when the promise has been relied upon. To Grotius the critical argument was that a man had a 'natural' right to dispose of his property; a promise, being in effect a disposition of a right (which he saw as somehow inferior to property), could not be less binding.[5]

Pufendorf's discussion is more illuminating, and not without interest even today. There are, it must be said, signs of confusion in Pufendorf's mind as to whether a bare promise can actually create a liability where none existed before, but he does emphatically come down on the affirmative side, 'since agreements, especially express agreements, lay upon us an obligation which nature did not otherwise enjoin, at least not so definitely'.[6] Like Grotius, Pufendorf criticizes the views of Connan, but unlike Grotius, Pufendorf is clearly aware that to treat a bare promise as binding is to recognize a right to a pure expectation. It is, he insists, 'a dangerous thing' to admit the argument that non-fulfilment of a promise leaves the promisee no worse off than he would have been without the promise.[7] But in explaining why this is a dangerous argument, Pufendorf ends rather lamely. Natural law, he insists, imposes a duty of humanity which requires a man to advance the interests of others, and not merely prohibits the causing of loss.

This slight digression may help us to see rather more clearly the nature of the rival theories that were still struggling for supremacy in eighteenth-century England. On the one hand, there were these newer notions about the inherently binding nature of promises, but at the same time there were still the traditional ideas in which promises were neither necessary nor sufficient conditions for the creation of obligations. In this older scheme, duties arose out of relationships or transactions; even where the relationship or transaction was itself a consensual one, such as a simple sale, the obligations that arose out of the transaction were, in a sense, the consequence of the law, not simply of the parties' intentions. A sale, for example, created a debt, but although it was the act of the parties which created the sale, it was the law which created the debt. Similarly, a contract of service might be created by the voluntary acts of the parties but most of its incidents were fixed by the law; it was for this reason (it

---

[5] *De Jure Belli ac Pacis*, Book III, Chapter XI, Sect. 1.3.

[6] Book III, Chapter IV, Sect. 3. Even in this sentence, the idea of a promise as having an evidentiary or clarificatory role is clear enough.

[7] Book III, Chapter V, Sect. 9.

has recently been argued) that Blackstone still tends to see service in terms of status rather than contract.[8] And then, of course, there were the cases concerning the common callings in which even the creation of the obligation was far from voluntary.

A second respect in which eighteenth-century contract theory differed fundamentally from that which grew up later, was in its treatment of the part executed contract, rather than the wholly executory contract, as its paradigm case. Ever since the nineteenth century the law has adopted the wholly executory contract as its typical case; contracts are assumed to be arrangements which are made for future performance. The separation of the making of the contract—the creation of the legal tie, or obligation—from the performance of the contract is an absolutely central feature of modern contract theory. It was barely present in eighteenth-century theory.

The third respect in which the eighteenth-century model of contract differed from that of the present day concerned the nature of the remedy which a plaintiff was given for a breach of contract. In modern English contract law a plaintiff is assumed to have—as a matter of course—a claim for damages for his 'loss' as a result of a breach of contract. This 'loss' is, in principle, defined by the *expectations* which the plaintiff was entitled to have as a result of the making of the contract. The fact that the plaintiff has or has not acted to his prejudice in reliance on the defendant is generally regarded as immaterial, except to the purely arithmetical calculations; the fact that the defendant has or has not received a benefit as a result of some act of performance by the plaintiff, is also treated as, in principle, immaterial in modern English law. In other words, it may be said that English lawyers today see no relationship between the three elements which together make up the grounds of contractual liability, that is, promise, detrimental reliance, and benefit, on the one hand, and the nature of the damages which may be awarded to an injured plaintiff on the other hand. But my concern at present is not with modern theory but with that of the eighteenth century; and my suggestion is that at that time there was a much closer relationship between the nature of the liability sought to be imposed on a defendant, and the ground of the plaintiff's claim. In particular, if liability was sought to be imposed—as could quite typically be imposed in any contractual action today—for breach of a wholly executory and unrelied-upon promise, the reaction of the courts was still fundamentally hostile. The notion that a promisee was entitled to have his *expectations* protected, purely and simply as such, as a result of a promise and nothing else, was not generally accepted in eighteenth-century law.

---

[8] O. Kahn-Freund, 'Blackstone's Neglected Child: The Contract of Employment', 93 *Law Q. Rev.* 508 (1977).

Promises as evidence

There is a sense in which the older, traditional ideas in which consideration was the primary source of the liability, can be explained by seeing the role of a promise as largely evidentiary rather than substantive. If, as I have suggested, promissory obligation was often perceived as depending on the existence of some prior obligation, then it is not difficult to rationalize this, in terms of modern concepts and categories, by suggesting that the promise evidenced but did not create the obligation.

The notion of a promise as being somehow evidentiary, as being invoked to support an independently existing duty, is likely to seem strange at first sight; and many objections to this way of looking at things will come to mind. It is hoped to answer these objections in due course; but perhaps the most obvious one which will come to the mind of a modern lawyer is to ask what purpose can be served by a promise if it merely reinforces a duty which has some independent existence.[9] The answer to this, it is suggested, is that a promise has considerable evidentiary value wherever there are areas of doubt concerning the existence or extent of the independent duty. A man who borrows money of another, for example, plainly owes him a legal duty to repay that money. A modern lawyer conceives of that duty as resting on an express or implied promise; but the medieval lender of money did not 'think of himself as relying upon a promise for its return',[10] nor, I suggest, had the eighteenth-century lawyer wholly departed from his ancestors' ways of thought in these respects. He thought the borrower's duty to repay the money was a legal duty, a duty created by morality, custom, and law; it arose out of the transaction, to be sure, and the transaction might involve some element of intentional conduct, some degree of voluntary participation, but that did not mean that the obligation was somehow thought to have been the creation of the parties. To take a modern analogy, a man who drives his car on the road is doing a voluntary act, but the legal duties he owes as to the manner of his driving are not conceived of by the modern lawyer as being voluntarily assumed by the driver. These duties are imposed on him by the law. If he injures someone by his negligence it is the law of torts and not the law of contracts that determine his liability. And every law student is taught from his earliest days that the law of contract is concerned with duties created by act of

[9] Much the same question (or complaint) was put by Godwin about the use of oaths. What, he asks, does an oath add to the duty to tell the truth? *Enquiry Concerning Political Justice*, ed. K. C. Carter (Oxford, 1971), p. 231. But compare Bentham, *Introduction to the Principles of Morals and Legislation* (Collected Works, London, 1970), p. 207, n. 2: 'It is indeed common enough to exact a promise, in order the more effectually to oblige a man to do that which he is made to promise he will do.'

[10] S. F. C. Milsom, 'Reason in the Development of the Common Law', 81 *Law Q. Rev.* 496, 501 (1965).

the parties, and the law of tort with duties imposed by the law. This dichotomy was not part of medieval thinking, and it was only slowly evolving in the seventeenth and eighteenth centuries.

To return to the immediate question: if the duty to repay borrowed money was created by law, what was the purpose of a promise to repay it? The answer plainly is that the promise was very good evidence of many matters. It was, first, evidence of the nature of the transaction; a promise to repay would plainly negative any suggestion of a gift.[11] Secondly, the promise could be evidence that the borrower had received the money, for he was hardly likely to promise to repay it unless he had done so. In this respect the promise was merely a form of acknowledgment of a liability. Thirdly, in the event of doubt or dispute, the promise might be evidence as to the amount received, for if the borrower promised to repay £100 it would be hard for the lender to argue that he had lent £200. Fourthly, there might be arguments or disputes about the parties to the transaction. There might, for instance, have been no doubt that someone had lent money to another, and that the debt did exist, and that there was a legal duty to pay it; but there might have been uncertainty about the parties. The lender might wish to claim that though he had put the money into the hands of A, it was really B who ought to repay, for A was merely B's servant, or B's wife, or B's son, or B's father. In these circumstances, too, a promise by B would be extremely valuable as evidence of the relevant relationships, and of other factors rendering it just that B should pay. For, obviously, a man was not always liable to repay money put into the hands of his servant, wife, son, or father, but there were some circumstances in which he was so liable; and if he acknowledged his liability by a promise, clearly that was good evidence of the liability.

Similarly, a promise might be very good evidence of a large number of ancillary or fringe matters about the transaction.[12] For instance, it might determine the rate of interest (within limits) which ought to be payable, which it was fair or just to pay; more broadly, in a very large number of transactions, a promise would be evidence of the fairness of the exchange which the parties had arranged. If a man promised to pay £1 for a parcel of cloth, this would be, even in the earliest times, good evidence that the cloth was in fact worth £1, and, therefore, a good starting point for determining what was a just price, or a fair price.

And if a promise can be good evidence of the nature or value of a

---

[11] Adam Smith refers to the value of promises in clearing up ambiguities with the use of language. *Lectures on Jurisprudence*, ed. Meek, Raphael, and Stein, p. 88.

[12] In the same way a testamentary direction to an executor to pay the deceased's debts may have some point, even though the executor must pay them anyway, because, e.g., it may indicate which assets the debts are to be paid out of. This was more important in the eighteenth century when land was not normally liable for debts.

benefit conferred, it can also be evidence of the nature of some relationship that justifies 'trust', dependence, or reliance. A man to whom (for instance) goods were entrusted for repair or carriage might be under a duty with respect to those goods, not because of any promise he had made, but because of who or what he was—because of his status. A common carrier or a common innkeeper, for example, would have been under various duties in medieval law, not because he promised, but because of the legal duties associated with his status. Now even in such a situation, a promise might be valuable as evidence. If a man promised to shoe another's horse for him, this would, in the Middle Ages, have been good evidence that the promisor was a common blacksmith—for who else would make such a promise? But in such a situation it seems clear that a promise might have a broader significance. For it might come to have, not merely an evidentiary, but a justificatory force as regards matters of trust or reliance. If a man relied upon another, trusted him, by delivering goods into his care, or delivering his own person into his care (for example, an innkeeper, or ferryman) a promise might come to be seen as justification for the act of reliance. It was, in short, a promise that made a reliance seem reasonable.

Both these possible uses of promises are illustrated by the liability of a surety to a creditor. If the surety has requested the creditor to grant credit to the debtor, his request (as we shall see) may itself have been a ground on which he could be held liable. But a request, standing alone, would have been weak. A creditor who acted on such a request (which might amount to little more than a commendation or a credit-reference) might be acting on his own initiative, at his own risk, 'of his own head' as the saying went. But when to the request was superadded an express promise to be answerable for any resultant loss, the action of the creditor in granting the credit could be more readily laid at the door of the surety. The promise did not create the obligation, the debt, for that already existed. But the promise provided a justification for the creditor's action in reliance on the surety; and that action in reliance could be seen as itself a ground upon which the debt could be laid at the surety's account. Similarly, the promise, coupled with the request, was strong evidence that the surety was benefited by the granting of credit.

Now the idea of treating a promise as strong, or even conclusive evidence of an obligation would obviously have been of considerable attraction to a pleader, especially if the facts themselves were doubtful or complex, and all the more so when rules of procedure were excessively technical. Indeed, we know that one of the principal reasons for the early use of *assumpsit* by pleaders in cases where Debt had been the traditional and correct remedy was precisely that in Debt, the facts alleged to create the obligation had to be set out in great detail, and with minute accuracy.

If the defendant had promised to meet this pre-existing obligation, he had in effect *admitted* his liability, so what more natural than that the pleader should try to persuade the Court to treat that admission as conclusive (or at least as strong prima facie evidence) and so dispense with the need for a detailed inquiry into the facts?

In suggesting that promises in the eighteenth century still often had this evidentiary character, I should enter a number of caveats. I do not suggest that this theory was consciously present to the minds of the lawyers of the time, nor that it was ever clearly articulated. It was not, in this respect, like the theory of the next century—the era of freedom of contract—which clearly was consciously held and very positively articulated. Nor would it be correct to say that an evidentiary theory is consistent with all legal doctrine of this time. One must beware of giving this theory a coherence and logical strength which it never possessed, or of imposing on the historical data a distinction between substance and evidence which is itself much more clearly grasped in modern times and was only in process of formulation in the seventeenth and eighteenth centuries. Nevertheless what I do suggest is that, to the modern lawyer, the idea of a promise as having an evidentiary role helps to convey some at least of the underlying contractual theory in this transitional period. The lawyers of this time were attempting to graft their newer ideas about freedom of choice onto the older ideas in which legal duties arose from status, from custom, from relationships and transactions: inevitably, the conclusiveness, the bindingness of promises and free choice was at first less strong, as well as less necessary.

Promises and Fair Exchanges

I have said above that a promise was, at this stage in our legal history, neither a necessary nor a sufficient condition for the existence of a legal duty. Cast into language with which the modern lawyer is perhaps more familiar, this means that a promise, though prima facie evidence of the existence or nature or scope of a legal duty, is not conclusive evidence, and that it is capable of being rebutted. And secondly, and conversely, it means that in many circumstances the duty will exist whether or not a promise was given, and that the absence of a promise is barely any evidence that there is no duty at all. In the eighteenth century, the way in which the law treated promises, as neither conclusive, nor necessary, is well illustrated by the equitable rules about fair exchanges, and that part of the law which came to be known as the law of quasi-contract.

It must, of course, be admitted at the outset that there has never been an overt principle of fairness in the common law of contract. At no stage in the long history of the action of *assumpsit*, to go back no further, is there any trace of any rules or doctrines requiring that an exchange be fair, that there should be an adequate return for a promise, or that a transaction with a grossly excessive consideration might be set aside. But it would be surprising if the common lawyers were indifferent to these matters in the seventeenth and eighteenth centuries, as they generally became indifferent to them in the nineteenth. For, as we shall see, when in the last century the Courts began to adhere, as a positive act of faith, to the principle that the fairness of a bargain was no concern of theirs, they did so under the influence of ideologies and circumstances which were notably absent in the preceding centuries. What we know of moral beliefs and principles in these earlier periods suggests that the fairness of exchanges would normally have been an important consideration to lawyers, and this was still a time when the law of contract was being profoundly influenced by moral ideals. The doctrine of consideration itself was a reflection of a moral ideal, not of some amoral commercial practices.[13] These facts must be borne in mind in assessing the significance of the absence of any recognized principles about fairness, or even of any reported arguments about such issues in the courts of common law. Any account of these matters must be somewhat speculative, but at least two possible or partial explanations can be given, each of which is discussed more fully later. The first is that if indeed promises were often enforced because of some pre-existing or otherwise independent duty, the fairness of an exchange could not be measured by examining the promise, but only by examining the duty itself. And since one of the principal purposes of relying upon promises was to dispense with that necessity, i.e., to treat the promise as (nearly) conclusive evidence of the duty, this possibility was often effectively ruled out. But the second point is that jury control over the damages (which included simple matters of price) may have rendered it unnecessary to strive for substantive fairness of exchange anyhow.

At any rate, it is, I suggest, clear enough that in and around 1770 it was at least the established tradition in Chancery that a contract must basically be fair; or perhaps, to be more strictly accurate, that a grossly unfair contract was liable to be upset. It must also be remembered that throughout most of the eighteenth century it was in Chancery that the greater part of contract litigation took place, as I have already suggested. And all those special equitable rules which came to seem so anomalous in the nineteenth century (and which still seem anomalous to the modern lawyer, with one foot planted in the nineteenth century) were the staple diet of contract law in 1770. Mortgages were regularly treated as secured loans at reasonable interest in the teeth of express contractual promises; absolute sales of reversions were simply converted into loans at security and discharged on payment of capital and interest as fixed by the Court;

[13] A. W. B. Simpson, *A History of the Common Law of Contract*, p. 488.

forfeiture of leases for breach of covenant was set aside if it seemed unfair, despite express contractual provision, penal bonds, despite the most absolute language customarily employed, were not enforced except to the extent of actual loss suffered; covenants in restraint of trade were set aside if unreasonable and unfair; unconscionable bargains of every kind, unfair transactions as seen by the chancellor, were set aside whenever any form of imposition was practised or the transaction appeared grossly unfair. Indeed, the very enforcement of a contract in Chancery was a matter of discretion, and was not uncommonly denied if the contract seemed excessively unfair.

The importance of these facts has been obscured for us because this body of equitable doctrine, on its way down to the twentieth century, had to pass through the nineteenth. And in the nineteenth century these rules came to seem increasingly anomalous, and many glosses were put on the older case law. It was always possible to find dicta here or there more in accordance with the views of nineteenth-century lawyers, and these dicta were given great prominence by those more concerned with the consistency of legal doctrine over the centuries than with authentic legal history. The nineteenth-century glossators laid stress on two features which they found, or thought they found, in the Chancery case law of the seventeenth and eighteenth centuries. First, they stressed cautionary words found here and there, such as those of Lord Nottingham in 1676 that 'Chancery mends no man's bargain',[14] while tending to discount actual decisions, not to mention dicta pointing in the opposite direction. The reality was quite otherwise, for any examination of the Chancery cases of this period will confirm that Chancellors regularly set aside transactions which they felt to be excessively harsh or unfair (and I shall be giving examples shortly) but they did not want to publicize this fact too widely.

The second point stressed by the nineteenth-century glossators was that Chancellors frequently refused to enforce a contract in their own Court while leaving a party to 'take his remedy at law'. The implication of this gloss on eighteenth-century law was that the Chancellors were not unwilling to see contracts strictly enforced, according to the letter of the law, even where they themselves would not stretch out the hand of mercy or equity. Now undoubtedly this came to happen in the nineteenth century, but it does not represent eighteenth-century law or attitudes. What this overlooks is the great change which came over the role and power of the jury between 1770 and (say) 1850. In 1770 the jury still retained a considerable measure of discretion over the application of legal rules, and judges were not unwilling to connive at, or even encourage, the doing of substantial justice by juries in many civil (as well

[14] *Maynard* v. *Moseley* (1676) 3 Swan. 651, 655, 36 E.R. 1009, 1011.

as criminal) cases. In contract matters, this meant, among other things, that the damages were almost entirely at the jury's discretion. The result was that if (for instance) a seller brought an action for the price of something sold to the buyer, and if the buyer could persuade the jury that the price he had agreed to pay was grossly excessive, the jury might well award damages representing a fair price, rather than the agreed price.[15] Moreover, it would be wrong to suggest even that in such a case the law 'in theory' was one thing, and the law 'in practice' was operating in disregard of its own rules. That, again, is to read later law back into the past. Throughout most of the eighteenth century Chancellors and judges knew that the common law jury had these discretionary powers 'to mitigate damages';[16] they even encouraged their use where appropriate; and they made their own decisions on the basis that juries would continue to operate in the future as they had operated in the past. But attitudes were changing. The element of discretion, of mercy, of equity in the law came increasingly under attack as the century wore on, and after 1770 both jury and Chancery discretions were significantly curtailed.

Contracts and Quasi-Contracts

If the equitable rules about fair exchanges support the notion that promises were not conclusively binding, were not sufficient grounds for the creation of legal duties, the law of quasi-contract (as it came to be called) illustrates the fact that promises were not thought necessary to create legal duties. I have suggested that one of the root ideas underlying contractual liabilities was the notion that a man who received a benefit from another normally had a duty to recompense the other or to repay the benefit in some form. This idea obviously straddled the areas of law known to later lawyers as 'contract' and 'quasi-contract', or in the more fashionable modern term, 'restitution'. If it is right to suggest that promises often played an evidentiary role in the law of obligations in the eighteenth century, then it should not be in the least surprising if lawyers of that time found a close affinity between all forms of obligations to pay for benefits received. A man had to pay for a benefit received, when it was his duty to pay, and whether or not that duty was acknowledged by a promise, was a secondary matter. The result is well known: contract and quasi-contract were both enforced by the same action of *assumpsit.* In the nineteenth century, when theories of liability changed, when lawyers (and others) came to see free choice and promise as very nearly a sufficient as well as almost a necessary ground for liability, the association

---

[15] Two early and well-known cases are *James* v. *Morgan* (1665) 1 Lev. 111, 83 E.R. 323; and *Thornborrow* v. *Whitacre* (1705) 2 Ld. Ray. 1164, 92 E.R. 270.

[16] See, e.g., Powell J. in *Mitchell* v. *Reynolds* (1711) in the less-known report in 10 Mod. 27, 29, 88 E.R. 610, 611; *Hicks* v. *Philips* (1721) 2 Eq. Cas. Abr. 688, 22 E.R. 579.

of contract and quasi-contract came to be seen as anomalous and even absurd. It was all put down to a procedural confusion, dictated by the forms of action. Lawyers began to say that quasi-contract had 'no relationship' with real contract. It was all a ridiculous confusion of eighteenth-century lawyers who could not see the distinction between a promise 'implied in fact' and a promise 'implied in law'. Promises 'implied in fact' were real promises, genuine inferences from conduct and speech, cases where the party consented to the liability; promises 'implied in law' were purely fictitious promises, inventions of the judges, created to impose a duty with no semblance of genuine promise or consent. There may be some truth in all this; but it would not be surprising if eighteenth-century lawyers still saw real substantive affinities between many forms of contractual and many forms of quasi-contractual obligation. Both often centred around the duty to pay for or restore benefits received; both were in a sense based on the notion of 'unjust enrichment'. Although the phrase is a modern invention, the concept itself must be as old as (because it is inherent in) private property.

Moreover, the distinction between a contract 'implied in fact' and a contract 'implied in law' may well have had a different connotation to the eighteenth-century lawyer from that which it acquired later. A contract 'implied in fact' at this time generally meant no more than a contract (or duty) found by a jury, while a contract 'implied in law' was a contract (or duty) found by the Court.[17] The general division of functions between judges and juries at this time normally left juries free to decide on matters such as whether a person had received a benefit, whether he should pay for it, and how much he should pay for it. But through the eighteenth century the judges were striving to find ways of controlling and limiting the jury's functions, and the imposition of contractual liability, based on the receipt of some benefit, came under increasing judical control in two respects. First, the judges, by deciding that there could be a contract 'implied in law' were, in effect, taking certain decisions out of the jury's hands altogether; they were thus taking upon themselves the right to determine that *some* benefits gave rise to duties, and one reason why they did this was precisely that they did not always trust the juries to behave sensibly.[18] These thus became a matter of law. And secondly, the judges limited the jury's right to find for a plaintiff by use of the 'request' principle. I must say a little about both of these.

If the receipt of a benefit is regarded as the primary basis of a legal

---

[17] Indeed, in the seventeenth century an implied-in-fact promise was itself thought of as largely fictional. A. W. B. Simpson, *A History of the Common Law of Contract*, p. 493.

[18] See Holt C.J. in *York* v. *Toun* (1701) 5 Mod. 444, 87 E.R. 754: 'It is hard that customs, bye-laws, rights to impose fines, charters and everything should be left to a jury.'

liability there are plainly going to be needed a number of legal rules to define somewhat more closely what benefits ought to be paid for, when the duty arises, and so on. Even the most property-dominated society cannot always find it just or expedient or even practical to compel a man to pay for a benefit he has received. For example, the person rendering the benefit may himself have been doing only what he ought to have done anyhow; and no contracts lawyer can fail to recognize that familiar argument, nowadays linked with the doctrine of consideration. And then again, what about the value of the benefit, and the balance of the relationship between the benefit and the corresponding burden of liability? Thus the benefit rationale was not necessarily a very simple one. It inevitably raised the question: when is it just, when is it a man's duty to pay for (or restore) a benefit conferred upon him by another? In the nineteenth century, of course, lawyers gave an unhesitating answer to that question which still dominates legal theory and legal thinking, namely that it is just if (and usually only if) he has agreed or promised to do so. But in earlier times a lawyer would have been much more doubtful about the reply. Indeed, in all probability his answer would have been that a man should be compelled to pay for a benefit when he had a *duty* to pay for it, when he *ought* to pay for it. Even a promise was only binding if the promisor ought, in some sense, to have done the act promised in any event.[19] This may seem somewhat unhelpful and circular to the modern lawyer, but it would hardly have seemed so at a time when legal and moral duty were so much more overtly entwined than they are today. In 1770 legal positivism had still to appear as a legal philosophy—1776 was the year of the publication of Bentham's *Fragment on Government* from which Austin later drew most of his ideas.

Now in this process of saying what a man ought to do, when he ought to pay for a benefit he had received, it had been traditional to rely on a jury. Most men knew well enough what their duty was, when they ought to pay for benefits received, but in case of doubt or dispute, the jury would determine what ought to be done. And of course everyone anyhow must be taken to have agreed to do his duty, for surely nobody would have the hardihood to deny that he willingly did his duty? The jury thus bridged the gap, both historically and analytically, between morality and law, between what a man promised to do and what he ought to do, between the individually self-imposed liability of the promisor and the objectively imposed liability of customary (or modern) legal rules. When the jury held that a man ought to pay for some benefit, they were in effect saying that a reasonable man, a moral man, would have been under a duty to pay for it. The contract implied in fact thus concerned a benefit which a jury felt ought to be paid for. And when a court implied a

[19] A. W. B. Simpson, *A History of the Common Law of Contract*, p. 457.

contract in law, the judges equally were in effect saying that the benefit was one which ought to be restored or paid for. Thus Blackstone, for all his fictions, may be telling us how lawyers perceived things when he says that 'implied contracts' 'though never perhaps actually made, yet constantly arise from this general implication and intendment of the courts of judicature, that everyman hath engaged to perform what his duty or justice requires'.[20]

There is another point to be made. It is easy to assume that—whatever may have been the position with respect to implied promises—at least an express promise had then precisely the same significance as it has today. Even this assumption would be unfounded, not because the meaning of the concept has changed, but because the rules of procedure have changed. In the eighteenth century a defendant who was faced with an allegation that he had made an express promise to do something was faced with a pleader's dilemma. Generally speaking he had to make up his mind either 'to plead' (that is, to deny that he had made the promise) or 'to demur' (that is, to argue that even if he had made the promise, he was not liable in law). He could not generally use both arguments, in the alternative. Now a defendant in this situation would often choose to demur, even if he had made no express promise, for at least his case would then turn on the law and be in the hands of the judge, while if he denied the allegation, the jury might find against him on the facts even though his denial were well founded. If the defendant demurred, the facts were taken as found against him, and thus he would be assumed to have made an express promise. If the court then found against him on the law, the defendant would thus be held liable on an ordinary, or express promise, even though he might not have made any such promise at all. This meant that the law provided a standing temptation to a plaintiff who felt that a defendant was under some duty to do something—to pay for some benefit, for instance, or to use due care in rendering a service; the plaintiff had only to bring an action alleging an express promise (even though there was none) and he might win.[21] This must have helped to blur the line between the contract implied in law and the contract implied in fact.

Requests

If the judicial willingness to find implied contracts 'in law' meant that judges would sometimes impose a liability where they feared the jury might not, the doctrine of 'request' seems to have performed the opposite

[20] *Bl. Comm.*, iii. 162.

[21] It is possible that this happened in *Atkins* v. *Hill* (1775) 1 Cowp. 284, 98 E.R. 1088, where defendant's counsel was refused permission to withdraw his demurrer and plead, after the demurrer had been overruled. One wonders too, if the defendant in *Coggs* v. *Barnard* (1703) 2 Ld. Ray. 909, 92 E.R. 107, really promised to move the casks 'safely', as the plaintiff alleged.

function. It was, that is to say, a method of preventing the jury from finding for a plaintiff where the Court felt that evidence of the receipt of a benefit was not satisfactory. Throughout the seventeenth and eighteenth centuries the idea of a 'request' was a fundamental feature of contract law; the cases on it were legion.

The doctrine of requests—if it can be called that—played an important role in the pleading requirements of *assumpsit*,[22] but it also had a major substantive role; and it is this latter role with which I am concerned. Broadly, the law was that a benefit (or a detriment) was only a 'good consideration'—that is, could only be used to justify action on a promise—if the consideration was supplied *after* the promise. In the terminology of the law it had to be either an executory consideration—that is something promised in return by the plaintiff and not yet performed at the time of trial, or an executed consideration—something already done by the plaintiff at the time of trial. But it could not be past consideration, that is, something done before the promise was given. There were, however, exceptions to this: if the past consideration was supplied *at the request* of the promisor, and he subsequently promised to pay for it, he could be held liable on the contract though the promise followed the consideration.[23] It seems reasonable to suppose that the original purpose of these rules (though they later became highly technical) was to ensure that the defendant was not made to pay for something which really had not benefited him. In the modern law, this problem is largely taken care of by the rules requiring an offer to be accepted; but there were no rules of offer and acceptance at this time. The 'request' principle was a part substitute for these rules. Generally speaking if a person actually accepted something—if he received goods or money which were delivered to him—it was possible to assume, without more, that this amounted to a benefit.[24] Similarly, if the existence of an independent duty was quite clear, no request was needed. But if the case was one in which mere services were rendered to the promisor, or if the promisee had supplied goods or money to some third party, then a request had to be shown.[25] The reason for this seems clear: a promise given *after* the rendering of some service, or the delivery of some goods to a third party, was not, in the view of the Courts, sufficient evidence, by itself, that the promisor had obtained any benefit out of it. Only if the promise was given before the consideration was supplied, or if the consideration was supplied at the request of the promisor, could the Court be reasonably sure that the promisor had indeed had his benefit. No doubt there were cases where

[22] A. W. B. Simpson, *A History of the Common Law of Contract*, pp. 576–8.

[23] See H. K. Lucke, *'Slade's* Case and the Origin of the Common Counts', 81 *Law Q. Rev.* 422, especially at pp. 437–40 (1965).

[24] *Wheatley* v. *Lowe* (1624) Cro. Jac. 667, 79 E.R. 578.

[25] *Hayes* v. *Warren* (1731) 2 Stra. 933, 93 E.R. 950; *Birkmyr* v. *Darnell* (1705) 1 Salk. 27, 91 E.R. 27.

other evidence of the benefit was clear enough, and in such circumstances the Courts may have encouraged juries to find an 'implied request'.[26] There were also cases in which even the Court would be willing to find a contract implied in law, and in those cases the fact that the promise was given subsequently was immaterial. For example, a man who acted the good neighbour in some emergency, as by burying another's child,[27] or calling in a doctor for the child,[28] was entitled to be repaid even in the absence of a request. A request could not be demanded in an emergency where the party now sued could not be contacted. And in those cases, there was (in effect) other evidence of the benefit—evidence acceptable to the Court as a matter of law—and it was therefore unnecessary to rely upon the promise as evidence of the benefit. Obviously a man who performed one of these emergency duties was rendering a benefit to his neighbour who would otherwise have had to bear the burden.

THE EVIDENTIARY ROLE OF PROMISES

It is now necessary to examine rather more closely some of the particular types of case which provide support for the idea that promises often played an evidentiary role in seventeenth- and eighteenth-century law.

Promissory Notes

The modern promissory note originated from the goldsmiths' notes of the seventeenth century, as we have previously seen. The earliest of these goldsmiths' notes were not in fact worded as promises at all, but as mere receipts.[29] They acknowledged the receipt of a certain sum of money. Nobody would ever have doubted that the acceptance of the money by the goldsmith created thereby a legal duty to restore or repay the money. The acknowledgement of its receipt was, of course, excellent evidence without any express promise to repay. But it soon became customary to word the receipt in the form of a promise to pay, rather than a mere acknowledgement. The reason for this may have been that the merchants who deposited their money with the goldsmiths wanted to be able to transfer these notes to others, to use them, that is, as currency. Now an acknowledgement, while perfectly adequate evidence so far as the original depositor was concerned, may have been felt less adequate if the note was to be transferred. Consequently, it became customary to word the receipt as a promissory note, that is to say, the goldsmith (either with or without a separate acknowledgement of receipt) promised to pay the depositor *or bearer* the amount deposited. In addition, by drawing the

[26] H. K. Lucke, 'Slade's Case', p. 440.
[27] Church v. Church (1665) T. Raym. 260, 83 E.R. 133.
[28] Style v. Smith (c. 1585) cited in A. W. B. Simpson, A History of the Common Law of Contract, p. 456.
[29] J. Milnes Holden, The History of Negotiable Instruments in English Law, p. 73, n.1.

note in this form, it became possible to clarify other matters, such as (for example) when the amount was payable, which a mere receipt might have left uncertain. It rapidly became customary to make these promissory notes payable on demand. Now in one sense the change in the wording of these documents—the change from a mere receipt to a promise to pay—did not alter the basic liability of the drawer of the note to the depositor of the money. He remained liable to pay because he had received a deposit of money, a benefit, from the depositor, and not because he had promised. If a man issued a promissory note to one who did not deposit anything with him (or give any other form of value) the note was not enforceable in the hands of the recipient. Nor is it today. The promise is prima facie evidence that value has been given for it (for is it not a reasonable presumption that men do not usually make promises to pay money without some return?) but that evidence is rebuttable. If the promisor can give some explanation as to why he should have given the other a promissory note without receiving any return (for example, that he was coerced, or swindled, or mistaken in thinking that he owed the money) the promise will not be enforceable.

But although one may argue today that the change in wording of a goldsmith's receipt did not change the nature of his liability, it is easy to see why men began to think that it did so, and why lawyers began to see promises as having a significance of their own. It was (as we saw previously) very important for the maintenace of credit that these promissory notes be treated as the equivalent of currency, and there was, therefore, a tendency to treat the promise with some stringency. The vital change occurred when the promissory note came into the hands of a third party—a bearer to whom (for example) it was sold for value by the original holder. In the hands of such a holder the promise was enforceable even if the promisor had never received any value, any benefit, himself. But even in the hands of a third party the promissory note was not enforceable unless the third party had himself given value for it. Now a third party who gave value for a promissory note could be said to be acting in reliance on the faith of the note, giving credit to the person who drew it and issued it.[30] This reliance could hardly be said to be unreasonable, for a person who issues a promissory note, payable to bearer, must anticipate that the note may be negotiated, and unless the third party is to be expected to verify with the drawer that he did indeed issue the note, and accepts his liability upon it, there is nothing unreasonable in relying on the note itself.

It is commonly said today that the law relating to promissory notes (and bills of exchange, which is similar) constitutes an exception to the

[30] See, e.g., the remarks of Lord Mansfield in *Walton* v. *Shelley* (1786) 1 T.R. 296, 300, 99 E.R. 1104, 1107.

doctrine of consideration, and it is true that there may be a number of marginal situations where differing rules apply. But in the light of what has been said above, it should now be apparent that there is nothing so exceptional about this law in its origins, or even now. In principle, the liability of the drawer of a promissory note or a bill of exchange can be seen as ultimately based either on some benefit which he has received or on the detrimental reliance of the holder of the note or bill. Of course, as has happened with the rest of the law of contract, that is not how things came to be seen in the nineteenth century, nor how modern lawyers see it. The promise came to be seen here, as elsewhere, as the centre of the picture.

Trusts and Promises

By contrast with the law of promissory notes and bills of exchange, let us turn to some equitable doctrines, normally thought to be as far removed from commercial law as it is possible to get. The Court of Chancery had been enforcing trusts since the seventeenth century, and before the Statute of Uses in 1535 it had been enforcing the medieval version of the trust, known as the 'use'. It is unnecessary here to explore the origins of the use, or even of the trust. It is enough to say that a trust is—and nearly always has been—a part executed arrangement under which one party hands over property to another, who is thereby trusted, or entrusted with it. There is (or there certainly would be if the trust were not enforced by the Courts) a benefit to the trustee arising from the receipt of property which was never intended to be his beneficially; we may say that he would be unjustly enriched, indeed, if he were not compelled to observe the terms of the trust. Moreover, there is not only an element of potential unjust enrichment in the trust situation, there is also an element of detrimental reliance. The former owner of the property, after all, has parted with it to the trustee. If the trustee now disregards the trust, not only will he be unjustly enriched, but the former owner will have suffered a loss, a detriment, through his reliance, his confidence, in the trustee. Frequently, of course, a trustee will expressly agree, or promise to observe the terms of a trust, but because the law of trusts antedated the Age of Promises, and because, being a part of the doctrines of the Chancery Court, it escaped contamination by the common law action of *assumpsit*, modern trust law is still largely rooted in (though not openly based on) the ideas of unjust enrichment and confidence (or reliance) which gave it birth. The law of trusts, in other words, never underwent the metamorphosis which the law of contract and the law of quasi-contract underwent. The promissory element remained always a relatively insignificant part of trust law.

It is only necessary to make two further points. The first is that there is one respect in which the origins of the law of trusts still have a bearing on modern law. From the earliest beginnings down to the present day there have been significant differences between fully constituted trusts and imperfectly constituted trusts. Very broadly, this distinction may be said to be the same as that between a part executed and a wholly executory contract. If the property is actually handed over, actually entrusted, to the trustee, the element of potential benefit and the element of reliance are already present, and the trust will be enforced. A promise, if expressly given, is evidence of the circumstances under which the trustee took the property, but does not create the source of the liability. If, on the other hand, the property has not yet been handed over, and the trustee has merely promised to carry out the trust in the future, then this is an 'imperfectly constituted' trust; in principle, such a trust is not enforceable unless there is some *other* consideration (i.e. some element of benefit or detriment, other than that involved in the delivery of the property to the trustee). Thus we see how, in the law of trusts, as in the law of contract, mere promises as to the future would not generally be enforced, whereas unjust enrichment would be prevented, detrimental reliance protected, even in the absence of a promise.

The second point is this: because trusts *were* enforced, and no unjust enrichment was permitted, it is easy to assume that there was no benefit in the transaction so far as the trustee was concerned. Indeed, trusts are today, and have long been, somewhat onerous offices which do not prima facie carry any reward or remuneration for the trustee. But when the validity of the trust is in dispute, when the trustee or alleged trustee asserts that he is entitled to the property beneficially, and is not bound by any trust, the element of benefit will be much more apparent. The aggrieved beneficiary will certainly feel that the trustee is getting an undeserved benefit in the form of the property he has received. Nevertheless, it is true that the element of benefit, and the desire to prevent an unjust enrichment, even if it does underlie the recognition and enforcement of a trust, is not of the same nature as the element of benefit which may be found in an ordinary commercial exchange, an ordinary contract. That is because there is no real *exchange* involved in most trusts. It is, therefore, somewhat easier for us today to see the reliance element than the benefit element in the law of trusts. But it is also somewhat unfortunate that this element of reliance has become so far separated from the law of contract for it might otherwise have helped the modern law of contract to return to more satisfactory foundations than it presently has. If modern lawyers were more aware of the extent to which the law has historically protected action in reasonable reliance on the conduct of another outside the field of contract law, they might be more willing to turn modern doctrine back onto more fruitful paths.

I need here only refer to a number of eighteenth-century Chancery cases—which have never been lost sight of in Equity—in which a person to whom property has been left by a deceased has been compelled to observe the terms on which it was committed to him.[31] Often, indeed, it has been possible to find an express promise in such cases, but they have rarely (in England) been enforced as contracts,[32] though they have equally never been denied enforcement as trusts. Nevertheless, the language used sometimes shows well enough the connection with contractual ideas. For example, Lord Hardwicke in *Drakeford* v. *Wilks*[33] says that the Court will always enforce a trust if the beneficiary declares or undertakes to do an act 'in consideration of the testator's devising [some land] to that legatee'. And modern textbooks use language similar to that of the contract books when discussing the 'acceptance' of the terms of a trust.[34]

The Liability of Executors

It is a natural transition from the equitable doctrine of the trust to the liability of executors for debts and legacies. The liability of an executor for the debts of the deceased had long been a problem as is illustrated by the large number of legal cases arising on this question in the seventeenth and eighteenth centuries. In Lord Mansfield's time, another similar question arose, which concerned the liability of an executor for a legacy left by the testator in his will. Now eighteenth-century law was, in theory, fairly clear. An executor was liable for the debts of the deceased but only to the extent of any assets which he received out of which they could properly be paid. Freehold land was not generally chargeable with debts—indeed land normally passed straight to the person entitled and did not go through the hands of the executor at all. If the executor promised to pay the debts of the deceased, a frequently recurring question was whether the promise rendered the executor liable to pay out of his own pocket if the assets from the estate were insufficient.

So far as the debts were concerned, the liability of the executor to pay out of assets received, was plainly imposed on him by the law; the liability arose out of his status as executor, and not because he himself had made a promise. Bentham, who on this point may well have

---

[31] *Drakeford* v. *Wilks* (1747) 3 Atk. 539, 26 E.R. 1111; *Barrow* v. *Greenough* (1796) 3 Ves. 152, 30 E.R. 943. These are the origin of the modern law of 'secret trusts'.

[32] In America promises of this character have sometimes been enforced as contracts, e.g. *Lawrence* v. *Oglesby* 52 N.E. 945 (1895). For an early English case of a similar kind, see *Starkey* v. *Mill* (1651) Style 296, 82 E.R. 723.

[33] 3 Atk. 540, 26 E.R. 1111.

[34] See, e.g., Halsbury's *Laws of England*, 3rd edn., xxxviii. 847. 'A person may accept a secret trust expressly or by silently acquiescing in it when committed to him.' Silent acquiescence does not normally constitute acceptance in contract law, but it could hardly do otherwise when accompanied by receipt of property.

represented an older tradition in a way that was not usual for him, poured scorn on the notion that an executor was liable on a covenant for the same reason as the deceased. 'A covenant', he says, (and here is the voice of the nineteenth century speaking) 'is an expression of will on the part of the person whose covenant it is said to be'.[35] But executors and heirs are not liable because of an expression of will; they are liable 'because their respective rights only extend to the net value of the goods of their principal'.[36]

As in the case of trusts, some element of benefit was obviously involved,[37] although, once again, if the executor was made to disgorge the whole of the assets he would ultimately receive no benefit. In practice, the problem was to get him to disgorge anything. There seems no doubt that it was very difficult to obtain payment of debts from executors, especially if there were no adequate written record of the debt. The notion of keeping the assets of the deceased separate from those of his family when he died, and of keeping proper accounts of sums due from and to the estate, was clearly a long time in becoming established. It was easy for an executor to fob off the creditors by saying there were no assets, or that the assets had already been disbursed in payment of other debts; it seems certain that it was to meet this difficulty that creditors (whether genuine or fraudulent) took to alleging that the executor had himself promised to pay the debts so that he could be sued upon that promise, irrespective of the sufficiency of the assets. Now we know that such actions must have been common even in the seventeenth century for in 1677 the Statute of Frauds contained provisions to discourage them by requiring written proof of such a promise.

The interesting thing about this episode is that the Courts seem to have assumed that a promise by an executor personally to pay the deceased's debts was evidence that he had in fact received adequate assets to pay them.[38] This assumption may have been reasonable but trouble may well have arisen from the over willingness of juries to find such express promises on somewhat meagre evidence. It is easy to imagine an executor fobbing off creditors with assurances of future payment, and a subsequent jury decision that this amounted to an express promise to pay out of his own assets. It was, presumably, to stop such over-ready inferences that the relevant section of the Statute of Frauds was passed; though that did not wholly dispose of the problem. But the important point is that the promise was, when enforced, a promise given in support of an independent duty, and it is not difficult to see its evidentiary force.

---

[35] Bentham, *Of Laws in General* (Collected Works, London, 1970), p. 65.
[36] Bentham, *Works* (ed. Bowring), iii. 191.
[37] See E. H. Bennett, 'The Nature of Consideration', 10 *Harvard Law Rev.* 35 (1897).
[38] *Cleverly* v. *Brett* (1773) 5 T.R. 7, 8n.; 101 E.R. 4; *Barry* v. *Rush* (1787) 1 T.R. 691, 99 E.R. 1324.

As so often was the case, however, the *extent* of the liability, once admitted, was determined by the promise and not by the preceding duty. The Statute of Frauds can be seen as an attempt to prevent, or hold back, this last consequence; to insist that it was the size of the benefit received by the executor—the extent of the assets—which should determine his liability, and not any promise, real, or found by an imaginative jury. And in 1778 the house of lords made a further attempt to hold back the dykes in *Rann* v. *Hughes*.[39] This decision is better known for its rejection of Lord Mansfield's boldest attempt to reform the law of contract; I shall return to that aspect of the decision later. Here it must be observed that in *Rann* v. *Hughes* the House of Lords tried to insist that a promise to perform an existing duty was invalid in so far as it extended beyond that duty. The promise, they insisted, 'must be co-extensive with the consideration'; that is to say, unless some additional element of benefit, or detrimental reliance, could be shown, a promise added nothing to an existing liability. A promise by an executor to pay the debts of the deceased was enforceable because the executor received the assets of the deceased, and was anyhow under a duty to use the assets to pay the debts. Therefore, the promise could not extend the executor's liability beyond the assets. Here again we see the way in which the promise is still fundamentally evidentiary. It is evidence of receipt of assets, but not conclusive evidence. The decision was, of course, a threat to the emergence of a promise-based law of contract. But it could not prevent the coming change. Despite the occasional reiteration of the idea that a promise had to be co-extensive with the consideration—indeed this is still found as late as 1842[40]—the development of a promise-based law of contract absolutely depended on the rejection of this idea. For if a promise had to be co-extensive with the consideration, and if, as I suggest, it was originally the consideration which was the source of the liability, then the promise would never have added anything to the liability. It was because promises often did add something different to the original liability—in the way of terms, parties, time, or in some other respect—that they were made.

The problem over legacies was rather a different one, for it concerned jurisdiction. The Courts of common law had no jurisdiction over the enforcement of legacies. In theory these were subject to the control of the ecclesiastical courts but in practice it had, in the eighteenth century, become more usual to try to enforce payment of a legacy by filing a bill in Chancery for an order for the administration of the estate. This was, however, a clumsy weapon when the claimant merely sought payment of a simple pecuniary legacy and did not want to get involved in any

---

[39] (1778) 7 T.R. 350, 101 E.R. 1014.
[40] *Roscorla* v. *Thomas* (1842) 3 Q.B. 234, 236–7; 114 E.R. 496, 497–8.

wider issues. Moreover, in the later years of the eighteenth century the creeping paralysis that later beset the Court of Chancery had begun to set in, and Chancery suits became famous for their dilatoriness. It was in these circumstances that the attempt was made in *Atkins* v. *Hill*[41] in 1775 to sue for a legacy in the King's Bench. Since it was universally recognized that the Court had no jurisdiction over legacies in the ordinary way, the plaintiff here claimed that the executor had expressly promised to pay the legacy, and so brought his action as on a contract. As the modern lawyer understands the doctrine of consideration, this action would raise a serious problem with that doctrine. The plaintiff gave nothing for the legacy, nor had he suffered any detriment as a result of the promise. But, after what has been said above, it should be apparent that this was not how the Court saw the problem. The executor had received assets from the deceased out of which to pay the legacy—that was a benefit; moreover, the real ground of liability was not the promise anyhow, but the fact that the assets received by the executor were already earmarked for the legacy, and that the executor was anyhow bound to pay the legacy. The promise was almost a technicality, necessary to give the Court some excuse for assuming jurisdiction; indeed, the promise may well have been fictitious altogether, for the defendant demurred to the plaintiff's claim and so never had an opportunity to dispute the giving of the promise. Under Lord Mansfield's guidance the Court assumed jurisdiction and gave judgment for the plaintiff.

A few years later Lord Mansfield and his brethren reaffirmed this decision in *Hawkes* v. *Saunders*,[42] but in this case Lord Mansfield dropped the broadest hints that he was about to extend the jurisdiction even further. For he now argued that an express promise to pay the legacy was unnecessary. The executor was, after all, under a 'legal'[43] obligation to pay the legacy if there were adequate assets; and that 'legal' obligation could be treated as a sufficient foundation for an implied promise. 'Where a man is under a legal or equitable obligation to pay, the law implies a promise, though none was ever actually made.'[44] This was the clearest possible indication that Mansfield was willing to enforce legacies outright through the medium of the action of *indebitatus assumpsit*, on the theory of an implied promise. Nothing could more clearly demonstrate that the Court was willing to enforce the payment of sums of money which it perceived to be legally due, in order to prevent a manifest unjust enrichment, or, that is to say, to compel a defendant to disgorge some benefit which he had no right to retain. There was no need for an express

[41] (1775) 1 Cowp. 284, 98 E.R. 1088. For some seventeenth-century attempts to sue for legacies at common law, see A. W. B. Simpson, *A History of the Common Law of Contract*, pp. 440–2.

[42] (1782) 1 Cowp. 289, 98 E.R. 1091.

[43] 'Legal' in the sense of being enforceable in a court of law, not a court of common law.

[44] 1 Cowp. 290, 98 E.R. 1091.

promise, no need for a jury finding that there was a benefit or request; if it was once proved there were sufficient assets the Court would say as a matter of law that there must have been a benefit to the defendant which he ought to account for.

As in the analogous problem of debts, there was the further difficulty over promises to pay legacies for which there were insufficient assets. Was the executor to be held liable personally on his promise to pay a legacy? In *Reech* v. *Kennegal*[45] in 1748 Lord Hardwicke, sitting in Chancery, held not. In this case the executor had promised the dying testator to pay a legacy of £100 to the plaintiff, and the testator had as a result left his will unaltered. After the testator's death the executor repeated the promise to the plaintiff, but he subsequently failed to pay it, and indeed denied that he had ever made the promise. Lord Hardwicke had no doubt that the executor ought to be held liable to pay the legacy if there were assets, for in that case, he declared, there would be liability even at common law; the receipt of the assets would constitute consideration or amount to evidence of a promise. But Lord Hardwicke was more dubious about holding that there was a personal liability beyond the extent of the assets: 'as to the promise after the testator's death,' he said, 'I at first doubted if it would not bind him personally; which I would do if I could: but fear it would be going too far upon so loose a thing as this promise is. It is no promise. Then there is no consideration arising ...'[46]

The implications are clear. Promissory liability has still not overtaken consideration-based liability. The executor is liable, not because he promised, but because he received assets earmarked for a legacy. The promise is evidence of that fact; but it is not the promise which creates the obligation.

The Moral Obligation Doctrine

During Lord Mansfield's time the birth pangs of the emerging promise-based law of contract gave rise to another set of cases which came to be known as the 'moral obligation doctrine'. According to these decisions a promise to discharge a duty which was morally but not legally binding on the promisor could be a valid consideration. For example, a promise by a man to pay debts incurred during infancy, or to pay debts from which he had been discharged by the Statute of Limitations, or by a discharge in bankruptcy, or a promise by a widow to pay debts incurred by her when she was married and therefore incapable of binding herself, and other analogous cases, were all treated by Mansfield as sufficient to found a legal liability.[47] These cases gave rise to much trouble and were eventually overruled in the nineteenth century.

---

[45] (1748) 1 Ves. Sen. 123, 27 E.R. 932.   [46] 1 Ves. Sen. 126, 27 E.R. 933–4.
[47] See especially *Trueman* v. *Fenton* (1777) 2 Cowp. 544, 98 E.R. 1232.

The decisions are traditionally seen as an unsound and radical piece of innovation by Lord Mansfield which received the quietus they deserved in the more stable conditions of the nineteenth century when judges returned to the path of righteousness. But as Professor Simpson has demonstrated, the moral obligation doctrine fitted very naturally into a system of law in which a promise was actionable because it reinforced (or as I have argued) evidenced an existing obligation of one kind or another. The key point about the moral obligation doctrine is that in the mid-eighteenth century the Courts were increasingly faced with a problem they had rarely encountered before, at least in this sphere—namely, a series of cases where there appeared to be a marked divergence between the law and morality. I have already referred to the fact that there was no legal positivism around in 1770. We have also seen how, in the cases concerning the liability of executors, jurisdictional problems amongst the various Courts tended to obstruct the idea of a 'law of the land'. There was, of course, also another obstruction about which I have said little, namely the writ system. A man who brought an action might find that the law was one thing if he used one writ, and something else again, if he used another writ. Moreover, Chancellors, sitting in Equity, still invented new rules and doctrines as occasion demanded to meet the manifest demands of justice; and even in Courts of common law moral ideas still very obviously led to the creation and development of legal rules in many instances. Naturally, all this tended to hinder the development of the idea that there was one set of rules—*the* law—different from moral rules.

If I am right in the suggestion that early contract law was often, or perhaps primarily, concerned with the enforcement of duties which existed independently of promises, with duties arising primarily from the rendering of benefits, or acts of reliance, which the Courts felt ought to be paid for; then it can be seen that, as the law developed along more modern lines, as the criteria for the validity of legal rules became clearer, law and morality would be bound to diverge, and the identification of the duties which deserved legal enforcement would necessarily become troublesome. It seems to have been to resolve this difficulty that Mansfield formulated the moral obligation doctrine. A promise to perform an independent *legal* duty was clearly good, and enforceable; similarly if the promise was to perform an *equitable* duty (in the technical sense, of a duty recognized by the Court of Chancery); it seemed natural to add the third case, a promise to perform a *moral* duty. In fact, all the cases which Mansfield generalized in this formula, were cases in which the promisor had plainly received some benefit at the hands of the promisee, and had not paid for it. The element of enrichment, or benefit, was thus present; the difficulty was to say that the enrichment was unjust when the law itself prescribed the result. Clearly, without a promise, there was no duty here, no legally enforceable duty at all events. And therefore, the enforcement of these promises was, in a sense, part of the movement towards a promise-based law. But it was nothing like so extreme a movement in Mansfield's time as it no doubt appears today. It involved, of course, rejection of the idea that a promise had to be co-extensive with the consideration—for here the promise actually created the legal duty, and was not merely adding to it, evidencing it, or modifying it. On the other hand, the promise did not create the moral duty which existed independently of it.

Accounts Stated and Statutes of Limitation

Where two persons have a large number of mutual dealings, with liabilities accruing sometimes from one, and sometimes from the other, it is natural for them to go through their accounts, strike a balance, and agree that the party who is a net debtor should pay the balance due to the other party. This is technically known as an 'account stated'. In modern law a distinction is drawn between an account stated which is a mere acknowledgement of a liability arising from the preceding debt; and an account stated which itself creates a wholly new liability based on a new promise and a new consideration for it.[48] The distinction is essential to modern contract theory which treats contractual liability as arising from the promise and not from the consideration.

But this distinction is of dubious validity, and it was much less clear in the eighteenth century. The truth is that the distinction is a mere matter of degree: all accounts stated are at bottom grounded in the original liability, and the process of striking a balance is evidentiary. But some pieces of evidence are more rebuttable than others, some accounts stated are more defeasible than others. They are all defeasible by fraud, or coercion, or a mistake of a sufficiently serious character; but others are even more defeasible, for example they might be put aside by evidence of any kind of mistake. So long as the main emphasis of the law of contract was on the consideration rather than the promise—so long as the promise was seen as primarily evidentiary—the distinction between the two types of account stated could hardly arise. In both situations, the liability arose from the original debt. But in the nineteenth century, as the law became more promise-based, accounts stated became less defeasible, and the modern distinction evolved.[49]

In the seventeenth and eighteenth centuries, the law relating to accounts stated became entangled with the Statutes of Limitation. The problem was that the limitation period prescribed by the Statute might

---

[48] *Camillo Tank S.S. Co.* v. *Alexandria Engineering Works* (1921) 38 T.L.R. 134.

[49] *Dawson* v. *Remnant* (1806) 6 Esp. 24, 170 E.R. 819; *Laycock* v. *Pickles* (1863) 4 B. & S. 497, 122 E.R. 546.

have expired since the date of the original debt, but not since the date when the account was taken and the balance struck. Was the Statute to apply or not in such circumstances? The eighteenth-century answer was that the mere acknowledgement of the debt which was involved in an account stated was sufficient to create a new liability and keep out the Statute of Limitations.[50] No express promise to pay was needed.[51] Indeed, the Statute was excluded not merely by an acknowledgement from which a promise could reasonably be implied, but even by an acknowledgement which was totally inconsistent with a new promise, as where the defendant agreed that he owed the money but stated that he could not or would not pay it.[52]

These cases, like those on the moral obligation doctrine with which they were linked by Lord Mansfield, show the law in the process of transition. It was still the original debt which was the primary ground for the liability as is shown by the fact that a mere acknowledgement was enough to exclude the Statute; but the change was foreshadowed by the fact that the acknowledgement was treated as an 'implied promise'. Later, as we shall see, these mere acknowledgements were held insufficient.[53]

Forbearances and Compromises

The notion that a creditor's forbearance to press a claim would be a good consideration for a promise to pay the debt appears very early in the law; certainly in the seventeenth century this is a common form of declaration in an action of *assumpsit*. Once again, it seems plain that in these cases the promise is originally treated as being evidentiary. Because the defendant has promised to pay, this is good prima facie evidence that there was originally a debt, but the action is nevertheless brought upon the later promise rather than the earlier debt. This is normally done, either because it fits the action of *assumpsit* better, or sometimes, because there are differences between the subsequent promise and the original debt. For instance, in *Hunt* v. *Swain*[54] the defendant promised to pay the plaintiff the amount due on a bond originally given by the defendant's father who was now dead. Prima facie the defendant was not liable on the bond without proof of assets; a hundred years later (as we have seen) Mansfield would have held the defendant liable without more. But at this time the plaintiff felt it necessary to argue that he had forborne from pressing his claim at the defendant's request, and that this request

[50] *Hyleing* v. *Hastings* (1698) 1 Ld. Ray. 389, 421, 91 E.R. 1157, 1179.

[51] *Quantock* v. *England* (1770) 5 Burr. 2628, 98 E.R. 382.

[52] *Bryan* v. *Horseman* (1804) 4 East 599, 102 E.R. 960; *Leaper* v. *Tatton* (1812) 16 East 420, 104 E.R. 1147.

[53] *Post*, p. 440.

[54] (1665) T. Raym. 127, 83 E.R. 69.

was, in effect, an admission by the defendant that he was liable on the bond.

But it seems quite clear that generally speaking a forbearance was only a good consideration if something of real value was forborne; hence it was open to the defendant to rebut the presumption that the promise was prima facie evidence that there really was an underlying liability which the plaintiff had refrained from pressing. If the defendant could show that there never had been an underlying liability, the forbearance to press it was no real benefit to the defendant, no real loss to the plaintiff, and hence there could be no liability.[55] It was not until the nineteenth century that the Courts uniformly adopted the modern attitude of holding bona fide forbearances and compromises to be binding even in the absence of any underlying liability.[56]

There seems no doubt that the basis of the old rules about waiver are traceable to the same source. It is, of course, well known that in the early common law a creditor could not validly waive part of a debt in return for payment of less than was due. This rule was originally recognized not in the context of a promise to waive part of a liability (for such a promise, being wholly executory, would not have been binding then for other reasons)[57] but in the context of actual acceptance of less than was due. But the essence of the matter was the same. For acceptance was a voluntary act, and the argument of the debtor in such cases was that the creditor, by such a voluntary acceptance, intends to waive part payment, and should be held to his intention. It is equally well known that the Courts would not accept this argument. In the famous *Pinnel*'s case[58] the Court resolved that payment of a lesser sum than was due could not be a satisfaction of a greater sum; 'it appears to the Judges that by no possibility a lesser sum can be a satisfaction to the plaintiff for a greater sum'.[59] Payment of a lesser sum earlier than the due date, or payment in some other form (as with 'a horse, hawk or robe') could suffice, for that might be more beneficial than full payment of the original sum on the due date. In the modern law this rule is treated as an abomination, and is evaded by the Courts wherever possible. But in the context of a legal system where promises and intentions were not regarded as such conclusive sources of legal duties, the rule seems more intelligible. If a man owes another £10 how can payment of £5 discharge the debt? The answer of the modern lawyer, namely that it should discharge the debt because the creditor has voluntarily accepted it, would have seemed unconvincing to the seventeenth-century lawyer. After all, if the creditor gave up the balance of the debt so willingly, why is he now suing for it

[55] *Tooley* v. *Windham* (1591) Cro. Eliz. 206, 78 E.R. 463; *Lloyd* v. *Lee* (1718) 1 Stra. 94, 93 E.R. 406.
[56] *Post*, p. 438.   [57] *Post*, p. 203.
[58] (1603) 5 Co. Rep. 117a, 77 E.R. 237.   [59] 5 Co. Rep. 117a, 77 E.R. 237.

before the Courts? The modern lawyer's answer to this would presumably be that this only shows that the creditor has changed his mind. To which the seventeenth-century lawyer might very well have responded: And why shouldn't he? The truth is that the rule in *Pinnel*'s case only seems an abomination when one starts with the idea that intentions and promises can be declared in such a way as to *bind* a man for the future. That idea, a commonplace since the nineteenth century, was simply not generally accepted in the early seventeenth century.

A hundred years after *Pinnel*'s case the Courts were still unwilling to depart from it. In *Cumber* v. *Wane*[60] the Court refused to hold that a note for £5 accepted in payment of a debt for £15 had effectively discharged the debt. 'We are all of opinion that the plea is not good', says Pratt C.J., 'as the plaintiff had a good cause of action it can only be extinguished by a satisfaction he agrees to accept, and it is not his agreement alone that is sufficient, but it must appear to the Court to be a reasonable satisfaction; or at least the contrary must not appear as it does in this case.'[61] In other words, the acceptance of the note might be prima facie evidence that it was beneficial to the plaintiff to accept it, but the presumption was rebutted when the facts were examined.

Later in the eighteenth century, there were characteristic signs from Lord Mansfield that the promise, or intention, of the creditor might be given greater weight. Although there is no reported decision to this effect, there is a dictum of Mansfield's disciple, Buller J., some years after his master's death, in which Buller J. attributed to Lord Mansfield the remark that 'if a party chose to take a smaller sum, why should he not do it?'[62] Later still, the Courts increasingly adopted this course, though they never went all the way with free choice in this particular instance.

THE FAIR EXCHANGE

It is important not to overlook the general background of the law and the legal system in a detailed study of the relationship between promises and consideration in the eighteenth century. The extreme individualism, the belief that all prices are a matter of subjective choice, the stress on will and intention, of the nineteenth century were not found in the law of the eighteenth century to any significant degree. There are growing signs of these attitudes here and there through the century, but only as we approach its end do they become dominant. Throughout the greater part of the century, 'law was conceived of as protective, regulative, paternalistic, and above all, a paramount expression of the moral sense

---

[60] (1721) 1 Stra. 426, 93 E.R. 613.
[61] 1 Stra. at 426–7, 93 E.R. at 614.
[62] *Stock* v. *Mawson* (1798) 1 B. & P. 286, 290, 126 E.R. 907, 910.

of the community'.[63] When we bear in mind the property orientation of this community in the eighteenth century it should not be a matter for surprise that the law was inevitably and fundamentally concerned about the fairness of an exchange. The subsequent idea that the adequacy of consideration is for the parties alone is only one of the nineteenth-century doctrines that would have been subjected to severe qualification by eighteenth-century lawyers, though I have also pointed out that they did not necessarily want to publicize these facts too loudly. In this section we must look at some of the specific areas of the law where efforts were bent to secure a fair exchange. These can all be seen, broadly speaking, as situations where the law was more concerned with the benefit a party received in a transaction than with the promises he had made. They can thus be said to be cases where the presumption of a fair bargain or a just price which might arise from a promise, or an agreement, was rebutted.

We should begin by noting that in the latter half of the eighteenth century there were signs of an emerging principle of good faith in contract law. The idea of good faith would, of course, have been completely congruent with the traditional morality, though it needed someone like Mansfield to enunciate and apply the principle in a wide variety of cases. Mansfield began this task, but it was never completed, for the economic liberalism which he also favoured and helped to develop, ultimately proved fatal to anything as paternalistic as a general principle of good faith. Nevertheless, some relics of this stillborn principle are even today to be found in the law, although the subsequent history of one of these relics, at least, illustrates how principles of good faith can be perverted to support the most inequitable decisions. I refer to the principle introduced by Mansfield in *Carter* v. *Boehm*[64] to the effect that a contracting party ought to disclose unusual facts known to him, but not known to the other party to the transaction. In later days, this principle was confined to insurance contracts, and was then altered out of all recognition so that it became a method by which an insurer could evade a liability even where he could have himself discovered the facts without difficulty.[65] But in *Carter* v. *Boehm* Lord Mansfield placed this decision on the broad principle of good faith, and made it quite clear that he envisaged this principle as one applicable to all transactions. 'The governing principle', he said, 'is applicable to all contracts and dealings. Good faith forbids either party, by concealing what he privately knows, to draw the other into a bargain, from his ignorance of that fact and his believing the contrary.'[66]

[63] Morton J. Horwitz, 'The Rise of Legal Formalism', 19 *American Journal of Legal History* 251, 257 (1975).
[64] (1766) 3 Burr. 1905, 97 E.R. 1162.
[65] Hasson, 'The Doctrine of *Uberrima Fides* in Insurance Law—A Critical Evaluation', 32 *Modern Law Review* 615 (1969).   [66] 3 Burr. at 1909-10, 97 E.R. at 1164.

A similar principle evidently underlies another of Mansfield's decisions, this time a principle which did survive, though its subsequent history has been quiescent. In *Bexwell* v. *Christie*[67] Mansfield held that a person who put up something for sale by auction and advertised that it would be sold to the highest bidder committed a gross fraud if he surreptitiously employed someone to bid himself. It will be seen that the highest bidder in such a situation nevertheless *bids*, that is promises to pay the price he chooses to offer; and subsequently much difficulty was felt with Mansfield's decision for this reason. Nevertheless, the next case along these lines came before the Common Pleas in 1825 when Best C.J. was presiding;[68] and Best C.J. was an old-fashioned judge with a strong moral sense somewhat in the eighteenth-century tradition. He agreed entirely with Mansfield's judgment and carried his Court with him. The result was that this rule survived the new nineteenth-century doctrines, and is still with us.[69]

Just Prices

It is still widely believed that, from the sixteenth century on, the common law Courts had committed themselves to the rule that the adequacy of consideration was immaterial to a bargain, and that this represented the triumph of the free choice ideal a hundred years before even Hobbes enunciated the principle that 'the value of all things contracted for is measured by the Appetite of the Contractors'.[70] It is manifest that something has gone badly wrong with this traditional version of the history of contract law. Hobbes himself was years ahead of his time and it seems inconceivable that in the reign of Elizabeth I the common law judges could have been uninterested in fair bargains, or the justice of an exchange. I have already said a good deal about the concept of the just price, and about the extent of regulatory statutes which continued to be passed, though with less frequency and less effectiveness as the eighteenth century wore on. But still it was common for prices and wages to be controlled at least in theory and often in practice right up to 1770 and beyond. It is not possible to believe that the doctrines of economic liberalism were already well established in the common law in the reign of Elizabeth I. Part of the trouble undoubtedly stems from overlooking the role of the jury in mitigating the damages in contractual claims throughout the whole of this period, a point to which I have previously referred.[71]

But part of the trouble also seems to stem from a group of very early

[67] (1776) 1 Cowp. 395, 98 E.R. 1150.
[68] *Crowder* v. *Austin* (1825) 2 C. & P. 208, 172 E.R. 95. See further as to Best C.J., *post*, p. 369.
[69] Now in section 58 of the Sale of Goods Act 1893.
[70] *Supra*, p. 71.
[71] *Supra*, p. 148.

cases in which it was said that (for example), 'the smallness of a consideration is not material, if there be any';[72] and again, 'when a thing is to be done by the plaintiff, be it never so small, this is a sufficient consideration to ground an action.'[73] It is, of course, easy to read these cases as support for the view that the parties were the sole judges of the fairness of their exchange—easy, but dangerous and wrong. For in all these cases, the promise being sued upon was given in support of a previously existing obligation or debt, and it is quite clear that it is that previous debt which is the substantive ground for the action. The promise is either being used as mere evidence, or as sufficient ground for invoking the new action of *assumpsit* at a time when it might still have been argued that the plaintiff should have sued in Debt. It will suffice to mention the facts of one of these cases. In *Sturlyn* v. *Albany*,[74] the plaintiff had leased a property to one J.S. who had assigned the lease to the defendant. The plaintiff demanded rent from the defendant which he was, of course, entitled to by virtue of the lease and the assignment. The defendant said that if the plaintiff showed him (the defendant) a deed evidencing the rent due, then he would pay it. The plaintiff duly showed the defendant the deed, but the defendant did not pay. The plaintiff now sued in *assumpsit*, and the Court held that the showing of the deed to the defendant was a sufficient consideration. Of course this was the barest technicality. The defendant was really liable for the rent because he had taken an assignment of the lease; the promise was only prayed in aid as an excuse to justify the bringing of *assumpsit*. After *Slade*'s case,[75] this sort of transparent device should have become largely unnecessary, but there remained some cases in which it was useful. Nevertheless, it is quite clear that these cases had nothing to do with the fairness of an exchange; but they were, of course, good material for those (like Powell), who, at the end of the eighteenth century, wanted to argue for the new doctrine of free choice.

If a promise or agreement was merely evidence of the fairness of an exchange, the force of its evidentiary value varied considerably with the circumstances, and there were a number of cases in which its evidentiary value was so slight as to be almost negligible. There were, for example, obvious cases like infants' contracts. In principle these were cases where the Courts would open the whole transaction and examine whether it was for the benefit of the infant or not.[76] The infant's agreement was of no evidentiary value at all. There was a considerable body of case law dealing with infant's contracts at this time and nearly all of it involved

---

[72] *Knight* v. *Rushworth* (1596) Cro. Eliz. 469, 78 E.R. 707.
[73] *Sturlyn* v. *Albany* (1587) Cro. Eliz. 67, 78 E.R. 327.
[74] *Supra*; see A. W. B. Simpson, *A History of the Common Law of Contract*, pp. 446–7.
[75] (1602) 4 Co. Rep. 91a, 76 E.R. 1072.
[76] See, e.g., *Gilbert* v. *Ruddeard* (1608) Dyer 272b, 73 E.R. 606.

a weighing up of the two sides of the transaction to ensure that the
infant's interests were properly protected.[77] Some of the most difficult
and important cases concerned marriage settlements entered into by
infants, and here the Courts were in general unwilling to upset the
settlements after the marriage had been celebrated and especially after
issue had been born. The Courts began increasingly to take the view that
the question of an infant's marriage had been entrusted to the parents,
but the notion that some sort of a fair exchange was involved even in a
marriage was strong. It was not, however, necessarily 'a strict equality of
fortune'[78] that must be looked to. Other things counted too, for example,
'the inclination of the parties, their rank and quality, the person superior
perhaps in this respect to whom the infant is to be married, and other
advantageous circumstances; the conveniences too and propriety of such
a match as to preserve the whole estate in the family'.[79] Naturally these
things were hard to weigh up and evaluate by the Court, but they 'are
matters proper for parents to judge of'.[80] Here again, therefore, the
notion of leaving the parties and their advisers to decide on the fairness
of an arrangement was gaining ground.

But there were other persons to be protected, and other cases, in which
the Courts still took seriously their function of weighing up the value of
a benefit, of the consideration supplied.[81] One of the forgotten episodes
of legal history concerns the law's extraordinary paternal attitude to
sailors. This protective attitude is to be found both in Equity and in
legislation throughout the eighteenth century, and right into the middle
of the nineteenth century. The cases nearly always concerned a sailor's
right to a share in prize money. Maritime law then, as now, provided
that in the event of a ship or her cargo being salvaged by the efforts of
another vessel, the salvors were entitled to a reward in the form of prize
money, the amount of which would be fixed, in the event of dispute, by
the Prize Court. It has always been the law that the owners and officers
and members of the crew are entitled to share in the prize money, in
proportions fixed by the Prize Court in the event of disagreement. It is
clear that many a common sailor who came ashore after taking part in
a salvage expedition which had earned him a right to prize money—yet
to be paid—was easy prey for unscrupulous speculators. The sailor could
readily be induced to sell his rights for a fraction of their value. Neither
Courts of Equity nor the legislature would tolerate this. The following

---

[77] See, e.g., Powell's *Essay*, i. 44–54.

[78] *Harvey* v. *Ashley* (1748) 3 Atk. 607, 612, 26 E.R. 1150, 1152 *per* Lord Hardwicke.

[79] Ibid.

[80] Ibid.

[81] In sale of goodwill cases the issues turned almost entirely on whether the party binding himself
not to compete received an adequate consideration, e.g. *Mitchel* v. *Reynolds* (1711) 1 P. Wms. 181, 24
E.R. 347.

passage from a judgment of Lord Hardwicke in a case in 1748[82] gives an entertaining side-light on the failure of sailors to live according to the principles of enlightened self-interest:

There cannot be a more useful set of men to the public, nor a more unthinking sort of people than common sailors who, as soon as ever they get on shore, for the sake of a little immediate pleasure are willing to part with their right to anything in expectation, for a very little in possession . . . I do not say that every contract with a sailor is void, or ought to be set aside, but every contract with them must be fair.

The contract in this case was set aside on repayment of the money advanced with interest at 5 per cent.

Another person who always obtained the very special protection of the Chancery was the 'expectant heir'. This was no new problem in the eighteenth century. It is clear that even in Elizabethan England the young heir who went to the big city was liable to fall into the clutches of moneylenders and other unscrupulous operators who would inveigle him into borrowing at high rates of interest, or selling his birth right for 'brown paper and old ginger'.[83] But in the eighteenth century the expectant heir was often the heir to landed estates, a member of the governing classes; and it was important that he should not dissipate his wealth before he obtained possession of his estates. There was, therefore, an element of class protection in the rules about expectant heirs. But there was more to it than that. Reversions and expectancies had acquired, for almost the first time in eighteenth-century England, a reasonably measurable and objective value. The stability of the legal system meant that expectancies and reversions could now confidently be expected to fall into possession in due course of law; the stability of the commercial and financial system meant that interest rates were low and that money was available at a measurable market price; the invention of life insurance meant that it had now become possible to discount the value of a reversion or an expectancy by the appropriate number of years. Dealings of this nature were, in short, no longer purely speculative forms of gambling. The proper method of discounting expectancies to arrive at a fair present value is now a commonplace among professional men, and all educated men know that this can be done, even if they do not know how to do it themselves. But the young expectant heirs of eighteenth-century England very often did not know about these things at all. Like

---

[82] *Baldwin and Alder* v. *Rochford* (1748) 1 Wils. K.B. 229, 230, 95 E.R. 589, 590. An Act of 1747 (20 Geo. 2, c. 24) gave the Courts statutory control over such contracts but did not apply to this case which occurred before the Act was passed. Still stronger decisions are *Taylour* v. *Rochfort* (1751) 2 Ves. Sen. 281, 28 E.R. 182—compromise of a legal suit to set aside sale of prize money itself set aside; and *How* v. *Weldon* (1754) 2 Ves. Sen. 516, 28 E.R. 330—sale set aside against sub-purchaser.

[83] *Measure for Measure*, Act IV, scene iii.

the common sailors, they had very little idea of the present value of a future right, and many of them did not even appreciate that they could apply for professional advice to discover what they did not know themselves. Inevitably, they fell a prey to those who understood how to value future rights, and frequently made dreadfully disadvantageous bargains.

Throughout the eighteenth century the Court of Chancery would not tolerate such unfair bargains. Whatever the form of the transaction might be—sale of a reversion, sale of an annuity, or straightforward loan on security—the Court of Chancery was always willing to open up the transaction and, if it was found excessively unfair, to set it aside, on repayment of the amount provided, together with interest fixed by the Court, usually at 5 per cent. In cases of this kind the Court often heard evidence from insurance experts about the fair value of the rights which were the subject of the contract. In the result many transactions which constituted, in form, outright sales of future expectations were in effect converted into mortgages, or secured loans, before or at the time when the property fell into possession. The notion which came to be widely adopted in the nineteenth century, that the Court would not make a contract for the parties, had no place in eighteenth-century Equity. The Court was constantly making contracts for the parties.[84] Nor was this practice confined to the rich and powerful heirs of the landed aristocracy. As the protection of the common sailor shows, Chancery's protective mantle was available for whoever could bring his case before the Court.

Now it is quite true that throughout the eighteenth century there were doubts as to whether the Court would set aside a transaction on the ground of *mere* inadequacy of consideration; as the century wore on, these doubts became more insistent, until eventually, towards the end of the century, the question was finally answered in the negative. But it is easy to be misled by this. Modern lawyers have relied on these old dicta as proof that fraud or misrepresentation or some serious form of imposition always had to be shown before a contract would be set aside in Equity. That may be the modern law, but it is misleading to think that that was the law of the eighteenth century. The reality seems otherwise. The references to 'mere inadequacy of consideration' can, it must first be stressed, be read in two ways. They may be references to the need to show some other invalidating cause such as fraud, and certainly they were so used in some cases. But they can also be read as meaning that it is not *any* inadequacy of consideration, but a *gross* inadequacy that must be shown in order to set aside a transaction. That too, seems to have been what the

---

[84] Another respect in which the Court of Chancery remade bargains was by enforcing contracts for the sale of land with an abatement for the price if the land was less in area or otherwise differed from what was stated. In 1790 Powell complained about this derogation from free choice: *Essay*, i. 149.

Court meant on some occasions. But that is not all. The Court's view of what was required, in addition to 'mere' inadequacy of consideration, to justify setting aside a contract was very wide indeed. It was not only fraud or misrepresentation in the modern sense that sufficed. It was also any unfair dealing, any form of imposition, any taking advantage of the ignorance or poverty or distress of another, any weakness of understanding, any mistake, which might suffice to set aside a contract. Now a moment's thought will show that if a contract is made on grossly unfair terms—if, that is, one party receives a grossly excessive return on the exchange—it must almost inevitably be due to one or more of these factors. It is hard to conceive of a man making a grossly unfair bargain unless it is due to mistake, ignorance, weakness of understanding, imposition, or fraud, or the like. Thus to understand what Chancery was doing at this time it is necessary to read the judgments and the decisions with great care. For instance, one could easily be misled by the remark in one of the common sailor cases,[85] that 'if men, who are free agents, will with open eyes, ratify unfair agreements, this court will not relieve fools'; for in fact the Court proceeded to set aside the contract on the ground of the ignorance and poverty of the plaintiff. Or again, we find Lord Thurlow in 1787 saying that he could not upset a transaction on the ground that the price paid was below the market price for if he did, 'every transaction of this kind would come into a court of equity'.[86] But he then goes on to say that if the inadequacy of consideration is so gross that it shows that the plaintiff did not really undertand the transaction, or was so oppressed that he was glad to make it, this will amount to fraud. But if that amounts to fraud, it is simply a roundabout way of saying that gross inadequacy of consideration justifies setting aside a contract, and Lord Thurlow's own judgment shows clearly enough why he preferred the roundabout way of saying it to the straightforward way of saying it. He did not want to be turned into a Court of Appeal to settle every price of every contract.

There was one further problem about inadequacy of consideration which needs mentioning because it illustrates a fundamental change of attitude as the century wore on. Adequacy of consideration is peculiarly difficult to measure in any sort of a speculative transaction. A person who indulges in a foolish speculation is apt to feel, after the speculation has failed, that it was an unfair arrangement. Of course, the same is true of any transaction which necessarily involves some element of risk, though that is not nearly so obvious to the parties involved. Throughout the eighteenth century, attitudes to risky or speculative transactions

[85] *Taylour* v. *Rochfort, supra,* 2 Ves. Sen. at 284, 28 E.R. at 184; see too *Willis* v. *Jernegan* (1741) 2 Atk. 251, 26 E.R. 555.

[86] *Heathcote* v. *Paignton* (1787) 2 Bro. C. C. 167, 29 E.R. 96.

constantly wavered.[87] The law did, indeed, seem to depend on the length of the Chancellor's foot—in fact, even the same Chancellor's foot seemed to vary from day to day. Sometimes the older, laxer, moralities seem to have prevailed. In *Stent* v. *Baillie*,[88] in 1724, the defendant agreed to sell eleven shares in a company at £58 a share; the inflated price was due to the speculative mania which gripped the country during the South Sea affair. Before the shares were transferred the bubble burst and the shares became worthless. The plaintiff brought a bill for relief in Equity and the Master of the Rolls set aside the transaction as 'against natural justice'. On appeal, the Lord Chancellor encouraged the parties to compromise the case, though seeming less favourably inclined to the buyer. In *Savile* v. *Savile*,[89] another case arising out of the South Sea mania, the defendant had agreed to buy a house at a price of £10,500 and paid a deposit of £1,000. After the collapse of the market, he refused to complete, offering to forfeit his deposit. Lord Macclesfield allowed the buyer to escape from his bargain arguing that if the seller could not get £9,500 from another buyer, 'it would appear dear sold and consequently a bargain not fit to be executed by this court'.[90] Yet another of the South Sea cases was *Keen* v. *Stuckeley*[91] where the plaintiff sought specific performance of a sale of land at a manifestly exorbitant price. The buyer argued that a Court of Equity would not enforce an unconscionable bargain, but the seller responded with the argument that (in effect) there could be no such thing as an unconscionable bargain. A man 'was obliged to perform a bargain, tho' it was a hard one; and where he was obliged in conscience, it was no hardship upon him to be compelled thereto.'[92] Perhaps the most significant thing about this case is that the House of Lords avoided pronouncing on this critical point, but nevertheless found some technical ground on which to reject the plaintiff's claim.

On the other hand, other contracts involving some element of speculative risk, such as the sale of an estate for two lives,[93] or a compromise which turned out to be based on a misunderstanding,[94] or a

---

[87] In fact these vacillations can be traced back at least to the late seventeenth century. See, e.g., John Selden's *Table Talk* (first published in 1689, reprinted London, 1869), pp. 40–1, 76, 78.

[88] 2 P. Wms. 217, 24 E.R. 705.

[89] (1721) 1 P. Wms. 745, 24 E.R. 596. The Reporter added a disapproving Note, saying, 'This is not the general law of this Court', but we must beware of assuming the Reporters were any more agreed than the judges on these issues. The Reporter to *Heathcote* v. *Paignton* (*supra*) added a Note to that case arguing that Lord Thurlow was wrong in treating mere inadequacy of consideration as insufficient to set aside a contract. Lord Macclesfield may have had more sympathy for the buyer in *Savile* v. *Savile* as the result of his own unsuccessful speculations in the South Sea affair, see J. Carswell, *The South Sea Bubble* (London, 1960), pp. 161, 223.   [90] 1 P. Wms. at 747, 24 E.R. at 597.

[91] (1721) Gilb. Rep. 155, 25 E.R. 109.   [92] Gilb. Rep. at 156, 25 E.R. at 109.

[93] *Nichols* v. *Gould* (1752) 2 Ves. Sen. 422, 28 E.R. 270.

[94] *Cann* v. *Cann* (1721) 1 P. Wms. 723, 24 E.R. 586, another decision of Lord Macclesfield's; *Stapilton* v. *Stapilton* (1739) 1 Atk. 2, 26 E.R. 1. Compare *Pusey* v. *Desbouverie* (1734) 3 P. Wms. 316, 24 E.R. 1081.

contract involving some commercial risk,[95] might be upheld. But there was simply no way of predicting how Chancellors would react to these cases. One day the Chancellor would stress that every contract involved some element of risk and that, 'As a beneficial bargain will be decreed in equity, so if it happens to be a losing bargain, for the same reason, it ought to be decreed.'[96] Another day the Chancellor would set aside a similar contract on the ground 'of it being a misapprehension in him'.[97] One day a Chancellor would set a contract aside because 'it seems hard'[98] or because the plaintiff had been driven to it out of necessity, another time this is brushed aside because 'One that is necessitous must sell cheaper than those who are not . . . where people are constrained to sell they must not look to have the fullest price.'[99] It is, of course, pointless to try to 'reconcile' these cases in the modern style. There was simply a clash of moralities between the older, laxer, more paternal, protective Equity; and the newer individualism, stressing risk-taking, free choice, rewards to the enterprising and sharp, and devil take the hindmost. Throughout the eighteenth century these two moralities co-existed uneasily; generally the older morality had the upper hand at first, but increasingly gave way as the century wore on.

Nor was it just a moral problem; there was perhaps too an economic issue tied up in all this. In modern times, lawyers and economists are accustomed to think of contracts—executory contracts for future performance—as devices for allocating the risks of future events. So prevalent is this viewpoint that it is commonly assumed that this is the sole function of contracts, and that every contract must necessarily allocate the risk of future events affecting its performance. Now in the eighteenth century it is probable that a contract expressly designed to allocate the risk of future events would have been thought to be akin to a wagering contract. Wagering contracts and litigation over such contracts were indeed quite common at this time, and the distinction between wagers and insurance contracts was only slowly being drawn. In the early eighteenth century there was also much hostility over the new dealings in stocks since many of them plainly partook of wagering. An Act of 1734 prohibited dealings in options and other semi-wagering transactions, and frequent attempts at regulating such dealings were

[95] *City of London* v. *Richmond* (1701) 2 Vern. 421, 23 E.R. 870.

[96] Ibid.; see also *White* v. *Nutts* (1702) 1 P. Wms. 62, 24 E.R. 294.

[97] *Gee* v. *Spencer* (1681) 1 Vern. 32, 23 E.R. 286.

[98] *Pusey* v. *Desbouverie, supra*, 3 P. Wms. at 320, 24 E.R. at 1082.

[99] *Batty* v. *Lloyd* (1682) 1 Vern. 141, 23 E.R. 374. This was a decision of Lord Keeper Guilford who was in advance of his age on such matters. If he had had his way the law's protection of 'expectant heirs' would have been scotched before the eighteenth century: see *Nott* v. *Hill* (1683) 1 Vern. 167, 23 E.R. 392, where he said, 'if it were to be declared a law in Chancery that no man must deal with an heir in his father's lifetime, that were something.' His decision here was reversed by Jeffreys who succeeded him as Lord Chancellor. See further as to Lord Guilford, *supra*, p. 115.

made during the first half of the century. By 1771 opinions were changing, and in a debate in the House of Commons it was argued that 'the trading of stock like every other thing ought to be free of interruption'.[1]

Thus the idea that it was an acceptable and useful function of contracts to allocate future risks was not at all an obvious one at this time. The Chancery cases referred to above show that the idea was, however, gaining ground.

Benefits and Corresponding Burdens

There are a few miscellaneous cases and situations worth referring to in which eighteenth-century lawyers groped after some idea of a correspondence between a benefit and a burden arising out of the ownership of property, or out of some transaction. It is not difficult to see these as cases in which the Courts were striving after the notion of a fair exchange, a fair bargain. There was, first, the law of bailments. The idea that the extent of a bailee's liability should correspond with the purposes of the bailment, and therefore, to some extent at least, with the extent of the benefit he took under it, is to be found both in Holt C.J.'s judgment in *Coggs* v. *Barnard*[2] and in Sir William Jones's *Essay on the Law of Bailments*, published in 1781. If goods are bailed for the benefit of the bailee alone, he is to have a greater duty of care than if the goods are bailed for the benefit of both parties, and *a fortiori* where the goods are bailed for the benefit of the bailor alone. So also there were cases of liability of an owner to a bailee with whom he had not personally contracted, as for instance the liability of a consignee to pay freight to a carrier. These cases were at first rested on a contract or promise 'implied in fact' but it seems clear that the benefit to the owner was the underlying rationale.[3] More generally, wherever a person is asked to render a service, and is not being paid for it, the burden on him (if any) is lower than where he is being paid, or professes some skill. So, for instance, even though a man may be liable for negligently rendering a gratuitous service, he is not to be held to the same standard of care and skill as if he were being paid.[4]

Then again, we find traces of the origins of the law of vicarious liability in tort, and also of the liability of a principal for the acts of an agent, in this same notion that benefits carry corresponding burdens. For example, in *Bush* v. *Steinman*[5] we seem to see the origins of some types of

---

[1] Dickson, *The Financial Revolution in England*, p. 520.
[2] (1703) 2 Ld. Ray. 909, 92 E.R. 107.
[3] See *post*, p. 483.
[4] *Shiells* v. *Blackburne* (1789) 1 H. Bl. 158, 126 E.R. 94.
[5] (1799) 1 B. & P. 404, 126 E.R. 978.

vicarious liability in tort. The defendant, the owner of a house adjoining the highway, is held liable for the negligence of a man employed by a sub-contractor working on the plaintiff's house. The plaintiff's main contention was that a person 'is liable for the consequences of every act done for his benefit, at least if the act takes place on his own premises'.[6] Property, after all, carries responsibilities as well as rights. The Court upholds the defendant's liability though Eyre C.J. has the greatest difficulty in expressing the reasons for the decision. Rooke J., however, adopts the plaintiff's arguments. Then also, there was *Waugh* v. *Carver*[7] in 1793. This case decided that a person who lent money to another for use in a business, and received a share of the profits in return, was to be liable as though he were a partner. As a recipient of a benefit from the enterprise, the defendant was held bound to share the corresponding burdens. The case was not unrelated to the usury problem, for one of the reasons which led investors to take a share of profits rather than a fixed return was their desire to obtain a return greater than permitted by the usury laws. But this does not alter the fact that the Court evidently thought it was *just* that a man who derived a benefit from an enterprise should also share in the liabilities.

Caveat Emptor

There were, of course, even in the earliest times, some things whose value was largely subjective. As early as 1617 we find it being argued that 'the value of a jewel consists in the estimation of him who will buy it';[8] but in the same case the Court made it clear that a jewel was one thing, silver (which was sold by weight and had a measurable value) something else. In all probability this also explains the famous case of *Chandelor* v. *Lopus*,[9] a case which had an extraordinary history. The defendant in this case was a goldsmith who sold a 'stone' to the plaintiff for £100, a considerable sum of money for the time, and 'affirmed' it to be a 'bezar stone'. The plaintiff complained that the stone was not a bezar stone, and sued for breach of warranty. However, he lost his case, the Court declaring that the defendant had only affirmed, and not warranted, the stone to be a bezar stone. This decision, which in the twentieth century was resuscitated as a leading authority on sales warranty law,[10] is often taken to be the origin of the doctrine of *caveat emptor*. And that doctrine is, in turn, taken to be evidence that the Courts were uninterested in the fairness of an exchange, which they regarded as a matter for the parties

[6] 1 B. & P. at 405, 126 E.R. at 978.
[7] (1793) 2 H. Bl. 235, 126 E.R. 525.
[8] *Southern* v. *How* (1617) Cro. Jac. 468, 469, 79 E.R. 400, 401.
[9] (1603) Cro. Jac. 4, 79 E.R. 3.
[10] By Lord Moulton in *Heilbut, Symons & Co.* v. *Buckleton* [1913] A.C. 30. See Williston, 'Representation and Warranty in Sales', 27 *Harvard Law Rev.* 1 (1913).

alone. If a buyer failed to obtain a warranty, and in consequence made a bad bargain, that was regarded as his affair.

But again, both the premises and the conclusion are highly suspect. The first thing to be noted is the peculiar nature of the stone in *Chandelor* v. *Lopus*; a 'bezar stone' apparently is a stone found in the stomach or intestines of certain animals, and was at one time believed to have magical antidotal or medicinal powers. Even at a time when the Courts still had some belief in just prices one can understand the reluctance of the Court to attempt to value such a strange object, and perhaps even greater reluctance to attempt to discover whether it was indeed what the goldsmith said it was. In all probability the plaintiff was complaining not that it was not a 'bezar stone' but that it did not have the magical qualities he had expected. It seems extraordinary that this case should have been regarded as laying the foundation of the later law of *caveat emptor*.[11] Nevertheless, with or without the aid of *Chandelor* v. *Lopus*, the doctrine seems to have gained a foothold in the law with the growing commercial freedom of enterprise in the seventeenth century. In 1693 the merchant Sir Josiah Child, in *A New Discourse on Trade*, says, evidently repeating what passed for common commercial talk: 'No man can be cheated except it be with his own consent, and we commonly say *caveat emptor*.'[12]

Had there been a strong common law tradition of actions for breach of warranty prior to the eighteenth century we might have expected to see here, as so often elsewhere, the protective paternalism of the eighteenth century gradually giving way before the emergent individualism of the new order. But in fact the protection of the buyer against shoddy or defective goods does not seem to have been a common law tradition, perhaps for the simple reason that few goods would have cost enough to justify a suit in the courts of common law, and perhaps also because buyers did generally examine the goods they bought with as much care as they could. Where such an examination would not avail, where for instance the seller used false weights or measures, or where he adulterated the food or milk he sold, he was in fact subjected to a battery of legal penalties. Indeed, throughout the fourteenth, fifteenth, and sixteenth centuries there had been a vast amount of detailed regulatory statutes, generally enforced locally, to protect the consumer against all rogueries and trickeries of this kind.[13] But when householders bought most of their commodities at local markets or fairs, when they were able to examine what they bought by look and feel, and haggle over the price,

---

[11] See on this famous case, Holdsworth, *H.E.L.*, viii. 68–9, a note in 8 *Harvard Law Rev.* 282 (1894) and A. W. B. Simpson, *A History of the Common Law of Contract*, p. 536.

[12] At p. 111. It was in this book that Child pressed for the assignability of common law debts.

[13] Warren A. Hamilton, 'The Ancient Maxim, *Caveat Emptor*', 40 *Yale Law Journal* 1133 (1931).

it may be that they 'would be more likely to feel ashamed of being outwitted than outraged at being swindled'.[14]

Whatever the cause, the amount of eighteenth-century case law on this question was very small. But it does not follow that a buyer who bought without an express warranty was thereby getting an unfair bargain. Given the great problems involved in litigating, or of returning defective goods, it seems more likely that—except in cases of actual fraud or trickery—prices were generally discounted to reflect the risk that the article might not be sound. Paley, writing in the late eighteenth century, certainly assumes that every person who buys a horse without a warranty—and horses were to eighteenth-century sales law what cars are today—knows of the risks involved and pays a smaller price because of it.[15] But that, of course, is to adopt the new definition of a fair bargain. The older tradition would have been inclined to think the bargain unfair, even if the buyer did pay a discounted price, if he later found that the article he bought was totally worthless, or even if it was worth less than he paid. This older tradition had its defenders right up to the end of the century. In 1793 Blackstone's successor in the Vinerian Chair, Professor Wooddeson, thought that *caveat emptor* was 'now exploded' and he invoked the contrary maxim which he enjoyed a fair vogue, that 'a fair price implied a warranty'.[16]

But it was, as usual, Mansfield's views which had the most influence. Mansfield was once again the harbinger of the new age. He believed that individuals should make their own decisions, exercise their own prudence and judgment,[17] and ask for a warranty if they wanted one. Only where an express warranty was given or the defendant was guilty of actual fraud would Mansfield allow the buyer a remedy.[18] 'Mansfield's rejection of the maxim that a sound price warrants a sound commodity met with general approval in England as well as in most of the United States.'[19] But that does not mean that Mansfield would have approved of all that was later done in the name of *caveat emptor* in England, still less in the United States. His belief in good faith would assuredly have led him to place some restrictions on the new doctrines. In fact, as we shall see, the doctrine of *caveat emptor* never seems to have been nearly as rigorously applied in England as is popularly believed,[20] and certainly not as rigorously as it was later applied in America.

[14] Davis, *A History of Shopping*, p. 9.

[15] *Principles of Moral and Political Philosophy*, Book III, Chapter 7.

[16] *A Systematical View of the Laws of England* (1793), ii. 415–16. But compare Fonblanque, *A Treatise of Equity* (1793), pp. 109–10, 373–4, where the opposite view is taken.

[17] See, e.g., *R.* v. *Wheatley* (1761) 3 Burr. 1125, 97 E.R. 746.

[18] *Stuart* v. *Wilkins* (1778) 1 Doug. 18, 99 E.R. 15.

[19] F. Kesseler, 'The Protection of the Consumer under Modern Sales Law', 74 *Yale Law Journal* 266–7 (1964).

[20] *Post*, pp. 471 *et seq.*

BENEFIT AND QUASI-CONTRACT

I have already suggested that the close affinity between contract and quasi-contract throughout the eighteenth century is partly explicable by the underlying benefit rationale of the law. Benefits, prima facie, were to be recompensed; whether a man promised to make a recompense or failed to promise when he still plainly ought to make a recompense was a secondary matter. In a sense both these bodies of law can be said to have been rooted in proprietary ideas.[21] If one's property came into the possession of another without explanation, or cause, or consideration, then prima facie that property must be returned or paid for. One possible explanation (or consideration) which would eliminate the need for a recompense, would be that this benefit was itself rendered in return for some previous benefit already conferred. Thus was born the doctrine, still known in modern law, of 'failure of consideration'. The principle was enunciated by Holt C.J. in 1691: 'The money was received without any consideration, and consequently was originally received to the plaintiff's use',[22] that is, it must be treated as having been received on trust for the plaintiff. And early in the next century it is stated more broadly that 'whenever a man receives money belonging to another without any reason, authority, or consideration, an action lies against the receiver as for money received to the other's use'.[23]

This way of looking at things shows quite clearly the early relationship between contract and quasi-contract, and it is extraordinary how, later, under the influence of the will theories of the nineteenth century, it came to be said that there was no connection between them. The use of the word 'consideration' in this branch of the law has continued unabated till the present day in the phrase, 'total failure of consideration'. And it is plain that the two sets of rules were mutually complementary. A man who paid money to another for some good reason (or consideration) naturally could not reclaim it; a man who paid money to another without good reason (or consideration) could reclaim it. A man who promised to do something without good reason (or consideration) was not bound by his promise; a man who promised to do something for a good reason (or consideration) was bound by his promise.

[21] S. J. Stoljar, *The Law of Quasi Contract* (Sydney, Melbourne, Brisbane, 1964), pp. 5–9. In 29 *Modern Law Review* 347 (1966) I reviewed Stoljar's book in terms which I now think failed to do justice to his perception of this point. See also Anson's *Principles of the Law of Contract*, 1st edn. (Oxford, 1879), Appendix A, p. 301: 'It is not improbable that the relation which we call quasi-contract, or "contract implied in law", and the genuine contract arising upon consideration executed, sprang alike from this notion of the adjustment of proprietary right.'

[22] *Martin* v. *Sitwell* (1691) Holt 25, 25, 90 E.R. 912, 913. It is strange that the common law phrase 'money had and received to the plaintiff's use' never seems to have been associated with the old equitable 'use'; those who argue for a modern law of Restitution, linking quasi-contract and the constructive trust, have at least this historical element on their side.

[23] *Attorney General* v. *Perry* (1733) 2 Com. Rep. 481, 92 E.R. 1169.

I have no space to explore the substantive law of this period at any length in relation to cases which today would be called quasi-contractual. I need only make three points. The first is that the action of *indebitatus assumpsit* which came to be widely used for the enforcement of these liabilities was sometimes put to broader uses still. In the time of Holt C.J. the action came to be available for the enforcement of all kinds of legal liabilities involving payment of a fixed or liquidated sum of money, such as sums due under by-laws, customary dues, and even fines. It was in relation to obligations of this kind that Holt C.J. made his famous remark that the concept of a promise was here a 'metaphysical notion'.[24] Clearly these kinds of legal duties were of a different order, and had no connection with other types of legal liability enforced either in *assumpsit* or *indebitatus assumpsit*. It does not follow, of course, that Holt C.J. would have regarded other forms of quasi-contractual liability—those resting on recompense for benefit—as depending on the 'metaphysical notion' of a promise. We do not know how far he would have regarded those liabilities as of the same generic kind as contractual liabilities enforceable by *assumpsit*, though there are signs that he, at least, did not, and would have resisted the development of *indebitatus assumpsit*;[25] but on this point Holt C.J. may have been ahead of his colleagues, and it was their view which prevailed.

The second point to be made concerns the importance of this type of liability in connection with family relationships. Throughout the eighteenth century a man was generally regarded as liable to pay, not only for benefits which he had received at the plaintiff's hands, but for benefits received by members of his family, and even his household. Goods or services supplied to his wife or minor children living with him, or even to his servants, were generally a sufficient basis for liability. It is hard to say—in modern terms—whether this was conceived of as contractual or quasi-contractual. The point simply did not arise. The man was liable because he plainly owed a duty to maintain his family and anyone who supplied goods or services to them was rendering a benefit to the head of the household. In such cases it was not difficult to find an 'implied promise' against the head of the household where liability had to be imposed upon him. So long as his wife or child was living under his roof, it was hardly likely that the head of the household would not know of the goods or services supplied, and such knowledge was usually treated as sufficient to 'imply' a promise. Where the wife or child lived separately, however, some further protection was needed against unreasonable liabilities being imposed on the head of the

---

[24] *Starke* v. *Cheesman* (1699) 1 Ld. Ray. 538, 538, 91 E.R. 1259, 1260.
[25] Holdsworth, *H.E.L.*, viii. 92–6.

household. In the case of a wife, he was generally[26] held liable for 'necessaries' supplied to her which was, of course, a way of ensuring that the goods or services supplied were in truth of some benefit to the husband. It was not his agreement which rendered him liable, but the Court's objective determination that the goods were necessaries. The extended meaning given to this term ensured that the Court had a reasonably free hand in these cases. In the case of minors living apart from their parents, the liability was placed directly on the minor rather than the parent, but here too the liability was confined to one for 'necessaries'. This may well have been perceived as a protection to the father as well as to the infant himself, for there must have been many cases in which in practice the father had to discharge his sons' debts.

There is no doubt that some of these old family and household cases arose from emergency situations. When communications were as difficult as in eighteenth-century England, it must often have been necessary for good neighbours to render acts of assistance to wives or children where the master of the house was temporarily absent. Certainly, in medieval times, the obligation to act as a good neighbour in such circumstances was, at least in Europe, a justification for the imposition of liability to recompense such acts of neighbourliness.[27] And even in the late eighteenth century there are signs that this source of liability had not yet wholly disappeared. In *Jenkins* v. *Tucker*,[28] for instance, the defendant's wife died in England while he was in Jamaica. The plaintiff, the wife's father, paid the funeral expenses and then reclaimed them from his son-in-law. The defendant was held liable even though he had neither assented nor requested. It is to be observed that the Court saw the problem in terms of 'consideration', that is, it perceived the problem as being whether the defendant had received a benefit which he should be made to pay for.[29] Of course, in most circumstances of this kind, the master or head of the household probably agreed to what had been done when he was communicated with, and it then became possible to sue him on the promise if he subsequently defaulted. The fact that the consideration was past would then have been no obstacle to the action, for a past consideration was sufficient when the original act of the plaintiff created a liability on its own. It was here that the law relating to past consideration and the law of quasi-contract intersected in a way

[26] But not for a wife who deserted her husband: *Manby* v. *Scott* (1660) 1 Lev. 4, 83 E.R. 268. Interestingly, the wife's company is here described as 'one consideration of [her] maintenance'. 1 Lev. 5, 83 E.R. 269.

[27] John P. Dawson, '*Negotiorum Gestio*: The Altruistic Intermeddler', 74 *Harvard Law Rev.* 817 (1961).

[28] (1788) 1 H. Bl. 90, 126 E.R. 55.

[29] 'I think there was sufficient consideration to support this action for the funeral expenses, though there was neither request not assent on the part of the defendant . . .' *per* Lord Loughborough 1 H. Bl. 93, 126 E.R. 57.

which again illustrates the absurdity of trying to separate these two branches of the law in the way that was later attempted.[30]

The third point I wish to make concerns the relative importance of the law of quasi-contract in the late eighteenth century, compared with the law of contract. To the modern lawyer, accustomed as he is to the very minor role of the law of quasi-contract in contemporary England, few things are more puzzling about the law of the late eighteenth century than the apparent dominance of this branch of the law. Throughout the Mansfield era, and indeed right up to the turn of the century, there seems to be more quasi-contractual law than contractual law in the courts. Cases involving issues of mistake, coercion, duress, fraud, failure of consideration, and other doctrines, all seem to have been litigated as though they raised quasi-contractual questions. Why was this so? The answer to this puzzle, it is suggested, has little to do with the conceptual distinctions between contract and quasi-contract which did not really exist at this time; it has far more to do with the distinction between the executory and the part-executed contract. Where the law of contract is built around part-executed contracts rather than wholly executory contracts, it is not surprising that claims arising out of the failure or misfire of some transaction were normally brought after the transaction had been partly performed, after the plaintiff had rendered some benefit to the defendant. Indeed, it is not too much to say that the idea of a failure of consideration, was, at this stage, far better grasped than the idea of damages for breach.[31] I have already observed that the law relating to damages was very late in being developed, and as we shall see, one of the reasons for this was that the whole notion of protecting expectations, that is of enforcing rights arising from purely executory contracts, was still very undeveloped around 1770. This is why we appear to find, in the late eighteenth-century case law, such a procession of quasi-contractual claims. Actually what we are seeing is a claim for the recovery of benefits, or money paid over, being used as a general contractual remedy at a time when contract law centred around the part-executed contract.

DETRIMENTAL RELIANCE

I have already made a number of scattered references to the fact that detrimental reliance, or injurious reliance, was a good consideration, and also that, as in the case of benefits, the role of a promise was originally not simply to create the liability but often to justify the act of reliance. I now

[30] See, e.g., *Sidenham and Worlington's* case (1585) 2 Lev. 224, 74 E.R. 497.

[31] There are, e.g., decisions upholding a right to recover for partial failure of consideration (*Stevenson* v. *Snow* (1761) 3 Burr. 1237, 97 E.R. 808), a flexibility clearly needed when this was a more general contractual remedy. Later this element of flexibility was lost as damages for breach became the general remedy.

need to say a little more about the concept of detrimental reliance as a source of liability. There is, of course, no question but that, from the very earliest time—that is the second half of the sixteenth century—when the doctrine of consideration was being formulated in connection with the new action of *assumpsit*, detriment and benefit were seen as alternative forms of consideration. There are scores of cases from the reign of Elizabeth I in which this is stated perfectly clearly.[32] In the late nineteenth century when historians and scholars turned their attention to the origins of the doctrine of consideration, some of them were puzzled about the way in which detrimental reliance came into the law as a valid consideration. It was widely thought that the notion owed something to the original delictual nature of the action of *assumpsit*; but the trouble with this explanation was that—to these same scholars and historians— it did not explain the thing they found most puzzling of all. In the nineteenth century it was assumed that, in so far as a detriment was a valid consideration, it had to be an act which induced the making of the promise. Detrimental reliance was only actionable (to put it crudely) if the party relying had *bought* the right to rely. The problem was to explain how *this* notion of detrimental reliance could have descended from the delictual type of case in which the reliance is the consequence but not the motivating cause of the promise.[33]

It is not surprising that scholars found this a puzzle for the truth seems to be that they were barking up the wrong tree altogether.[34] The whole of this problem seems to have arisen from the failure of nineteenth-century legal scholars and historians to perceive the changes which had occurred in contractual theory during their own century. These historians assumed that contractual theory in the seventeenth and eighteenth century had been based—as it came to be based in the nineteenth century—on the idea of mutually *binding* promises; the promises had to be binding at the time when they were exchanged for that was when a contract was thought to be 'formed'. Consequently, they did not understand how an act of detrimental reliance occurring *after* a promise was given could *ex post facto* invest the promise with a binding contractual character.[35] But in assuming that this was the law even of the nineteenth century they were off course (as we shall see) though undoubtedly the law tended increasingly in that direction; in assuming

---

[32] For one example, see *Manwood and Burston*'s case (1587) 2 Leo. 203, 74 E.R. 479. See generally, A. W. B. Simpson, *A History of the Common Law of Contract*, pp. 323–5, 391–2.

[33] See K. C. T. Sutton, *Consideration Reconsidered* (St. Lucia, Queensland, 1964) p. 5.

[34] See Ames, 'The History of Assumpsit', 2 *Harvard Law Rev.* 1 (1882); Salmond, 'The History of Contract', 3 *Law Q. Rev.* 166 (1887); Pollock, 'Afterthoughts on Consideration', 17 *Law Q. Rev.* 415 (1901).

[35] It was not perceived (nor indeed is generally perceived today) that the same retrospectivity is involved in substance when a 'binding' promise is broken and only thereafter does any actionable damage occur.

that this also was the law of pre-nineteenth-century England they made a catastrophic mistake. The truth is that the vaguely delictual idea, that an act of reasonable reliance on a promise can create a liability for subsequent loss, *never* disappeared.[36] Certainly it continued to play a major role in the law throughout the seventeenth and eighteenth centuries. And, as I have argued, this kind of liability was in a sense based on the very idea of reasonable reliance itself, rather than on the promise, the promise being primarily of justificatory force.

I have already pointed out how the law of trusts, and in some cases the law relating to the liability of executors, was in a sense based on some act of reasonable or justifiable reliance, combined also, in these cases, with ideas of unjust enrichment. It seems plain enough that similar ideas underlay the liability of persons to whom goods were entrusted by the owner for carriage or other services, as for example, the shoeing of horses; and equally with the liability of innkeepers, ferrymen, and other similar classes of person. To entrust your goods to someone who exercised one of the common callings was to act in reliance on him; by virtue of his status he owed duties to those who sought his services. He had no 'free choice' in the matter of selecting his customers for it is clear that in the fifteenth and sixteenth centuries he was bound to offer his services to whoever sought them and was willing to pay for them.[37] On the other hand to trust your goods to someone who did not exercise a common calling was not, in these early times, seen as justifiable at all unless the defendant had made some express promise to take care of them or do some act in relation to them; in the absence of such a promise, it was a man's 'own folly' to trust another.[38]

It was this old law which was affirmed and explained by Holt C.J. in *Coggs* v. *Barnard*.[39] In this famous case the defendant who, apparently gratuitously, undertook to carry some casks of wine for the plaintiff, damaged one of them by his carelessness, and was held liable. In modern times, the sort of liability upheld here is seen as a liability in tort, for two reasons. First, because modern lawyers do not understand how the doctrine of consideration can be said to be satisfied in such circumstances. Holt's explanation—that the owner's trusting the goods to the defendant was a sufficient consideration—has always puzzled lawyers brought up in the nineteenth-century tradition.[40] For the act of the owner in trusting

---

[36] For other cases based squarely on reliance see *Keyne* v. *Goulston* (1665) 1 Lev. 140, 83 E.R. 338 (defendant held liable on promise to pay education fees if plaintiff sent child to board); *Nurse* v. *Barns* (1664) Ray. 77, 83 E.R. 43 (jury award of £500 reliance damages on £10 contract upheld).

[37] Holdsworth, *H.E.L.*, iii. 385–6, 348; *Anon* (1502) Keilwey 50, 72 E.R. 208; *White's* case (1558) 2 Dyer 158b, 73 E.R. 343; *R.* v. —— (1623) 2 Rolle Rep. 345, 81 E.R. 842.

[38] Ames, 'The History of Assumpsit'.   [39] (1703) 2 Ld. Ray. 909, 92 E.R. 107.

[40] For example, Markby, *Elements of Law*, 5th edn. (Oxford, 1896), found this unintelligible: p. 316. Perhaps equally significant was that neither Pollock nor Anson so much as mentioned the case in their first editions.

his goods to the defendant was not exchanged for the defendant's promise, not did it induce the promise; on the contrary it was the promise which induced the trust, or the reliance. The case is thus the plainest illustration of liability based on subsequent, unbargained-for reliance. The second reason why modern lawyers tend to see this sort of liability as tortious is because Holt made it plain that there would have been no liability if the defendant had failed to move the casks at all. Because liability for total non-performance of an executory contract has been regarded as the hallmark of contract since the nineteenth century, the absence of such liability here seems to stamp the case, to the modern lawyer, as non-contractual. This is to misread history in the light of modern doctrine. In the first place, *Coggs* v. *Barnard* shows that the modern contract/tort distinction was still in process of evolving at this time; and in the second place (as I have previously argued) liability on wholly executory contracts was still imperfectly understood and enforced at this time. There was nothing odd to a lawyer of this time in a contractual liability which only protected the plaintiff after he had relied upon a promise.

The real difficulty in the case was whether the plaintiff's trust or reliance on the defendant was enough to support the action. For the plaintiff had entrusted his goods to the defendant voluntarily, and so prima facie might have been thought to be himself to blame for the consequences. Throughout the history of the law, until comparatively recent times, we find many signs of this theme. A man who trusts someone cannot, without more, impose obligations on that other. True, where some element of unjust enrichment threatens to arise as well, duties may be imposed, as with the liability of trustees or executors; but in cases involving carriers, bailees, innkeepers, and the like, there was not usually any question of unjust enrichment at all. The liability, if any, must arise squarely from the act of reliance itself. Throughout the eighteenth century, it was still necessary to place this liability on the basis of a promise, though the promise may often have been 'implied' or even fictitious; in due course, the need for a promise was discarded and the modern law of negligence came to apply to these cases.

At the end of the eighteenth century, as I have earlier briefly noticed, there was a series of other cases which continued this tradition, though with increasing difficulty. In *Wilkinson* v. *Coverdale*,[41] for instance, Lord Kenyon was prepared to hold, after initial doubts, that a person who had sold a property to the plaintiff and (gratuitously) promised to transfer the insurance into his name, would be liable for a breach of that promise; in *Shiells and Thorne* v. *Blackburne*[42] a man who gratuitously offered to

---

[41] (1793) 1 Esp. 75, 170 E.R. 284; see also *Whitehead* v. *Greetham* (1825) 2 Bing. 464, 130 E.R. 385, for a surprisingly late decision to the same effect.   [42] (1789) 1 H. Bl. 158, 126 E.R. 94.

enter a parcel of goods belonging to the plaintiff at the customs for export barely escaped liability for so negligently entering them that they were seized and forfeited by the authorities; he was held not liable only because some of his own goods had suffered the same fate, and the Court evidently thought that this demonstrated that the defendant had displayed that degree of care which he normally exhibited even in his own affairs. Consequently the plaintiff had to bear the blame for having relied upon him.[43] It was his own folly. Sir William Jones is quite explicit on this point with respect to bailments, holding that, 'where the bailor has not been deluded by any but himself, and voluntarily employs in one art a man, who openly exercises another, his folly has no claim to indulgence; and that unless the bailee makes false pretensions, or a special undertaking, no more can fairly be demanded of him than the best of his ability.'[44]

Similarly, the early beginnings of the law of fraud and warranty clearly rest on the idea of a justifiable reliance. The question always seems to be, did the plaintiff reasonably rely upon what the defendant said, or should the plaintiff have made his own inquiries, his own examination? Was it his own folly to trust the defendant, or was it a reasonable and sensible thing to do? Throughout the eighteenth century, from the time of Holt,[45] through Mansfield's decisions on the duty to disclose in insurance contracts,[46] and on to *Pasley* v. *Freeman*,[47] the origins of the modern law of fraudulent misrepresentation; from the common law rules to the statutory provisions concerning weights and measures; the underlying philosophy was the same, namely that a man who trusts another or relies upon him must show some justification for doing so. The justification might lie in the circumstances generally, or it might lie in the common practice of mankind; or it might lie in a promise. The one thing that changes as the century wears on is the growing number of situations in which the Courts treat reliance on a promise as justifiable and reasonable. It does not seem far-fetched to relate this change to the social and economic and even political changes we have previously discussed. In a period of greater stability, greater regularity of law, and greater predictability of behaviour of the Courts, and of businessmen, reliance became more natural and more justifiable. The concept was in a sense pulling itself up by its own bootstraps. As people grew to rely on

[43] Paley, *Principles of Moral and Political Philosophy*, Book II, Chapter XII, is clearly of this opinion, and was in fact cited in *Shiells and Thorne* v. *Blackburne, supra.*

[44] *Essay on Bailments*, p. 99.

[45] See, e.g., *Lysman* v. *Selby* (1704) 2 Ld. Ray 1118, 92 E.R. 240—seller of land held liable for falsely affirming rents more than they were. Note Powell J.'s doubts: 'the matter that sticks with me is that the vendee might have inquired into the rents.'

[46] *Carter* v. *Boehm* (1766) 3 Burr. 1905, 1909, 97 E.R. 1162, 1164: 'the underwriter trusts to his [the assured's] representation and proceeds upon that confidence.'

[47] (1789) 3 T.R. 51, 100 E.R. 450.

others so they grew to think it justifiable to do so; and as they found it more justifiable to do so, they expected the law to protect them when their confidence turned out to have been misplaced. It has proved a serious obstacle to the rational development of the modern law that many of these cases have been lost sight of, though never formally overruled. For the idea that an act of justifiable reliance on a gratuitous promise could create a legal liability almost completely (though never quite) disappeared from the law during the nineteenth century, and was not, indeed, 'rediscovered' until 1947; and even though this 'new' discovery has been somewhat developed since that date, we have still not quite returned to the position that was current in the seventeenth and eighteenth centuries.[48]

THE ENFORCEMENT OF CONTRACTUAL DUTIES

If the preservation of property and the enforcement of contracts were regarded as the chief functions of the law in eighteenth-century England, one might *a priori* have expected a fairly rigorous and severe enforcement process. But in fact, as we have already seen, even the machinery for the prevention of crime against property was extraordinarily inefficient; and it was widely agreed also (despite frequent assertions to the contrary) that to fail to pay a debt was not so serious as to steal.[49] It is therefore not surprising that the procedure for enforcing contractual duties was exceedingly inefficient. This procedure also shared many of the other characteristics of the criminal law of the eighteenth century.

In the first place, everything was left in the hands of creditors themselves. This did not mean only, as it means today, that it is for a creditor to initiate process and to take the necessary steps to enforce judgment. It meant that the whole business of trying to extract payment from a debtor, almost from beginning to end, fell upon the creditor. It was, first, his right and choice to imprison the debtor on *mesne* process, that is, without even having first obtained judgment against him. And if the debtor failed to pay the debt or to obtain bail, it remained entirely for the creditor whether to release him or not. In theory he could rot in jail for ever though in practice this did not happen. Similarly, the bankruptcy laws, which (like the law merchant, and perhaps like the new morality) originally applied only to traders, were administered entirely by creditors themselves. Under the Bankruptcy Act of 1732[50] which governed bankruptcy proceedings for the next century (though subject to numerous

---

[48] It is, e.g., not at all clear that *Keyne* v. *Goulston* (1665) 1 Lev. 140, 83 E.R. 338 (*supra*, p. 186, n. 36) would be decided the same way today; similarly many of the other reliance cases cited above appear to be in advance of modern case law, e.g., *Argy Trading Co.* v. *Lapid Developments Ltd.* [1977] 1 W.L.R. 444.

[49] *Supra*, p. 109.   [50] 5 Geo. 2, c. 30.

amendments) the appointment of assignees in bankruptcy (the equivalent of the modern trustee in bankruptcy), the administration of the estate, the payment of dividends, and the discharge of the debtor were entirely in the control of the creditors. Fraud and abuse were widespread, but as the only redress was an appeal to the Lord Chancellor, supervision of bankruptcy administration was totally inadequate.[51]

Even in modern law, the extent to which self-help remains a vitally important part of the enforcement procedures of civil law is probably greatly underestimated. In the eighteenth century it seemed natural to expect the machinery of law enforcement to be in the hands of those who wanted to enforce it. Outside the field of simple contractual debts, self-help was also widely used. One of the most important types of land contract was, of course, the lease; and the proper and sensible way to enforce the provisions of a lease against a tenant had for centuries been by distraining for rent, or in extreme circumstances, by treating the lease as forfeited under an appropriately drafted clause. Forfeiture of leases, like forfeitures of mortgages, had gradually been coming under Chancery control, but even here it will be observed that it was, in the first instance, for the tenant to appeal to Chancery for relief. Only after this form of relief had become well-established was the onus thrown onto the landlord to seek permission of the Court of Chancery before exercising his rights of self-help—by which means they ceased to be rights of self-help.

It was not very different to enforce contracts of employment by imprisonment. In the middle of the eighteenth century Statutes were passed giving justices power to jail workmen who absented themselves from their work in breach of contract 'to the great disappointment and loss of the persons with whom they so contract'.[52] In modern times labour lawyers naturally fulminate about the iniquities of such laws, but it must not be forgotten that any simple debtor was liable to be arrested at the suit of his creditor at this time without even the formality of a judicial hearing.

There was one important consequence of this extensive reliance on self-help, on non-judicial enforcement of debts and contracts. If contracts, especially commercial contracts, were to be readily enforced without recourse to the Courts, it was very important that they should be intelligible to commercial men without the aid of lawyers. It was for this reason that Mansfield so stressed the importance of interpreting contracts in accordance with the intention of the parties. In modern times, stress of this kind, insistence on looking for the actual intention of the parties in

---

[51] The following account is drawn from Ian P. H. Duffy, 'Bankruptcy and Insolvency in London in the late Eighteenth and Early Nineteenth Centuries', an unpublished D. Phil. thesis, Oxford, 1973. I am grateful to Professor Duffy for permission to draw on his thesis.

[52] 6 Geo. 3, c. 25, section 4.

the particular circumstances of the case, instead of reliance on fixed rules, is seen as a recipe for uncertainty in the law. But it was precisely the reverse to Mansfield who assumed that if only contracts were interpreted in accordance with the intention of businessmen, then businessmen would be able to perform their contracts and resolve their own disputes, whereas if contracts were subject to fixed and arbitrary rules of interpretation then only the Court would ever be able to say what they meant:

The daily negotiations and property of merchants ought not to depend upon subtleties and niceties, but upon rules easily learned and easily retained, because they are the dictates of common sense, drawn from the truth of the case. If the question is to depend upon the fact, every man can judge of the nature of the law before the money is paid: but if it is to depend upon speculative refinements from the law of nations or the Roman *Jus Posliminii* . . . no wonder merchants are in the dark, when doctors have differed upon the subject from the beginning and are not yet agreed.[53]

The law relating to the enforcement of debts shared another characteristic of the eighteenth-century criminal law, namely its reliance on threats tempered with mercy. I have suggested above that the absence of adequate administrative machinery at this time led to the use of threats of terror as a primary weapon of control against the masses, though the terror was in practice always greatly mitigated by reprieves and other forms of mercy. The enforcement of contractual liabilities, and especially debts, was the subject of very similar processes. The threat of perpetual imprisonment for non-payment of a debt which in theory was held over anyone who was not a trader (and so could not invoke the bankruptcy procedure) was in practice mitigated by the passing of special relief Acts from time to time releasing from jail debtors who had already been there for more than six months; in the result few debtors stayed in jail for periods in excess of a year.[54] There were, of course, other means of mitigating the severity of the laws in favour of the rich who were entitled, on payment of a fee, to live outside the jail so long as they remained within a defined area close to the Fleet or the King's Bench jail.[55]

It will be seen that there was a close association between the blend of threat and mercy relied upon by the insolvency laws and the same blend relied upon by many parts of the ordinary law of contract. In the first place, the normal type of written contract throughout the seventeenth and eighteenth centuries continued to be (as it had been from medieval

---

[53] *Hamilton* v. *Mendes* (1761) 2 Burr. 1199 at 1214, 97 E.R. 787 at 795.

[54] Duffy, 'Bankruptcy and Insolvency in London', pp. 81–2.

[55] On the other hand it should be noted that the special Acts for releasing debtors from jail usually excluded large debtors.

times) the penal bond.[56] The penal bond was a document under seal 'acknowledging' that the debtor was indebted to the creditor in a certain sum (normally twice the value of the real indebtedness) but providing that the bond was to be void if the debtor performed some specified act or acts by a certain date. The acts so specified were, of course, simply the contractual duties assumed by the debtor. If the bond was a security for a simple loan, for instance, of £100, to be repaid by 1 July next, it would acknowledge the debtor to be indebted to the plaintiff in the sum of £200, but the bond would be void if the debtor should pay £100 plus interest by 1 July next. The same form could be and was adapted for much more complicated contracts than loans. The early mortgage was, in its origins, probably a simple variant of the penal bond. The owner of the land conveyed the land to the creditor on the terms that it would be completely forfeited if he failed to repay the debt by the date specified. By the reign of Elizabeth I, the Court of Chancery was beginning to grant relief against the penal provisions of these bonds, as well as against the forfeiture of mortgages. By the seventeenth century it had become an established and regular part of the Chancery jurisdiction, and by the latter part of that century the courts of common law were following suit in the case of penal bonds. In the eighteenth century there was little substantive difference between a simple contract and a penal bond. Yet penal bonds continued to be used; and mortgages continued to be drafted so as to appear that they were liable to absolute forfeiture on non-payment at the due date. Why did lawyers go on using these forms so long after they had lost their legal validity? One answer might be that it was due to sheer legal conservatism. But it seems reasonable to suppose that that was not the whole story, and that lawyers and creditors found it useful to threaten debtors with penalties and forfeitures even though they knew that in the last resort relief might be available to the debtor in Chancery.[57] A Chancery suit, after all, was not a matter to be lightly undertaken; it was not an everyday event for a debtor to appeal to the Chancery though it must have been an everyday event for creditors to attempt to enforce debts. Equity, though far more regular and predictable than it had ever been before, still had some of the attributes of mercy. The whole process was not, after all, so very different from that by which sentences of death were passed but were subject to commutation on a very wide scale under the royal prerogative of pardon.

It does not seem far fetched to suggest that there was a sense in which the very idea of a promise-based law of contract fell naturally into the

---

[56] A. W. B. Simpson, 'The Penal Bond with Conditional Defeasance', 82 *Law Q. Rev.* 392 (1966).

[57] Even today it is not unknown for contracts to contain plainly invalid clauses (for example exemption clauses) whose sole value is that they may mislead contracting parties, and so act *in terrorem*. Use of some of these clauses is now prohibited.

same pattern as penalties, forfeitures, and other threats. If, as Mansfield wanted, the law should depend on 'rules easily learned and easily retained', what could be easier than to persuade people that promises were absolutely binding, and that they ought always to perform them? If they could only be persuaded of that, how much simpler everything would be. They could then pay for the benefits they received, or make good any loss resulting from another's reliance upon a promise without opening all sorts of troublesome questions (about the value of the benefit, or the extent of the reliance, for instance) and above all, without troubling the Courts who were quite busy enough as it was. Of course, in the last resort the lawyers and the educated classes knew that the notion of a promise being absolutely binding was not to be taken too literally; if nobody had acted on the promise, and if nothing had been paid for the promise, as a matter of fact, it was hardly binding at all. And besides, if the literal enforcement of the promise was liable to produce unfair results, a common law jury or the Lord Chancellor could be trusted to see that actual justice was done, and the letter of the law tempered with mercy. Promises might be binding in theory but in practice the bonds were not very strong, especially where the promise was still wholly executory.

Naturally this policy would not work if most people did not realize that the threats were not, in practice, very formidable. If it became generally known that, in reality, promises were not rigorously binding because the Chancellor would generally relieve against an unfair bargain; or that imprisonment for debt was not really perpetual because Parliament was sure to pass a relief Act; or that a penalty was quite invalid at common law, then the efficacy of the threat would obviously be undermined. It is, therefore, not surprising that attempts were made to conceal the likelihood of equitable relief or mercy being available, and rather to emphasize the threat itself. Chancellors nearly always relieved against excessively unfair bargains, but did not want to say so; Parliament always relieved against imprisonment for debt by special Acts, but would not make them a permanent part of the law; and lawyers continued to use penal bonds.

7

CONTRACT LAW AND THEORY IN 1770—II

THE EXECUTORY CONTRACT AND THE ROLE OF CONTRACT LAW

In the last chapter I referred to the fact that the eighteenth-century law of contract was fundamentally a law of executed and part-executed contract. It was principally in relation to such contracts that I argued that promises could still be seen as having primarily an evidentiary rather than a substantive role. There is obviously difficulty in seeing how the function of the promise in a wholly executory contract could have had such a limited role, but more of this later. In this chapter I must say something more about the nature and function of contract law in the eighteenth century, and about the process of change which it was undergoing. In brief, it will be suggested that wholly executory contracts were rarely sued upon, were imperfectly recognized and enforced, and did not constitute the paradigm case of contract theory at all. In saying this I am oversimplifying a very complex problem, for a great deal turns upon what is conceived of as 'enforcement' of a contract. It is not suggested that eighteenth-century lawyers had any conceptual difficulty with the specific enforcement of an executory contract; for specific enforcement ensured that, generally speaking, an exchange would be carried through. In the simplest type of case, if two parties contracted for the purchase and sale of an estate for an agreed price, there was not the least difficulty about decreeing the performance of such an executory contract. The vendor would receive his price and the purchaser would receive a conveyance of the land; the exchange would, albeit compulsorily, be carried through. Each party would receive value, or consideration, for his own performance. Each party had to perform because the other would also perform. The rights and duties of the parties still depended, at least in one sense, not on their intentions or promises, but on the exchange of benefits.

Nor do I suggest that eighteenth-century lawyers would have had any problem about enforcing a promise which had been relied upon to the detriment of the promisee even though no actual benefit had yet been received by the promisor, and even though the actual performance of the contract had not been begun. In my terminology, a transaction relied upon in this way would not have been conceived of as a wholly executory transaction, even though in modern law it might be so designated.

What I do suggest, however, is that enforcement by way of a claim for damages for loss of bargain, representing the difference between the value of the defendant's performance and the cost to the plaintiff of *his* performance, which is the typical mode of enforcing an executory contract today, was almost completely unknown. Although in modern law the requirement of the doctrine of consideration is said to be satisfied by an exchange of promises (and although that idea was in one sense known in the eighteenth century), this modern method of enforcement of an executory contract gives the plaintiff damages for his 'loss' without any performance being required from him. His own obligations are discharged by the defendant's breach, or refusal to perform, and yet he remains entitled to damages. This seems to modern English lawyers the most natural proceeding in the world (though, as we shall see, signs of change are appearing here) but it would not have seemed natural to eighteenth-century lawyers at all. To give the plaintiff what he 'expected' to make on the bargain, without requiring any performance from him, generally seemed on the contrary a very strange idea. Indeed, it might almost have smacked of usury. Was the plaintiff to get damages for doing nothing? Was he entitled to have his mere expectations protected? Was the defendant to be liable without any consideration passing? How could the plaintiff's promise be treated as a consideration if the plaintiff was discharged from performing it? What kind of alchemy was it by which the plaintiff's own promise was to be treated as a consideration one moment, and yet he was discharged from performing it the next? And, if no real consideration was to pass, if the defendant was to get nothing in return for the damages he was to pay, how could he be made liable at all? True he had promised, but the idea that a bare promise was 'naturally' binding was only slowly gaining ground. A promise to do one's duty, to be sure, might be binding, and a promise to make an agreed exchange might be enforced by insisting on the exchange being carried through, but if there was no consideration, no reason for a promise, how could it be binding? It is not a coincidence that the phrase, a 'gratuitous promise', means both a promise without return, and a promise without reason. This, it is suggested, is how eighteenth-century lawyers saw the problem of the wholly executory contract, though change was slowly going on all the time.

All this does not mean that there was no way of making future arrangements, binding oneself to some future performance, in eighteenth-century law. As we have already seen, ever since the medieval period it had been possible to make elaborate future dispositions of land, though these were not conceptualized as contractual arrangements. A man bound himself not by a promise to do something in the future, but by granting here and now an estate or interest which would only fall into possession in the future. It seems very probable that this was also how eighteenth-century lawyers conceptualized the process by which men bound themselves by deeds and other formal contracts, like bonds. A bond was often called 'an obligation', and a man who granted a bond to another, and delivered it into his hands, was thought somehow to be *granting* him there and then certain rights; the delivery of the bond was spoken of as the delivery of 'an obligation'. As we have already seen, the typical bond was not worded in the form of a promise at all; the obligor acknowledged his liability, he did not *promise* to do anything. In this way it was accepted that it was possible for a man to bind himself even by a gratuitous deed or bond; the delivery of the obligation was a grant, like a grant of property.[1] It was also perfectly possible to use contracts for regulating future relationships so long as it was not desired to make the contract 'binding' before some act of reliance, or some act of performance took place. It does not seem pure coincidence that in insurance practice (which became properly established in the eighteenth century) executory contracts are rarely made even to this day. Until the first premium is paid insurance contracts do not usually come into operation; of course today that is a result of express provision in the pre-contract documents, but the practice may well date from a time when insurers were none too confident of their ability (whether in law or in practice) to enforce payment of a premium after the period of the policy had expired without the occurrence of the insured event.[2]

Furthermore, this process of conceptualizing a future right as a present right was one which could be prayed in aid in other types of transaction. For example, in the law of sale of goods it seems to have been accepted as early as the fifteenth or perhaps even the fourteenth century that the mere making of the agreement was enough to vest the property in the goods in the buyer, and pass a right to the price to the seller; the buyer could have his writ of detinue, the seller his writ of debt, as soon as the contract was made, even before the goods were delivered. But it is absurd to conclude (as has sometimes been done)[3] that this shows the beginnings of the modern consensual contract. Substitute some unascertained goods—next year's crop of corn, for example—for some specific item such as a particular cow, or parcel of wheat, and it will be seen that here was no true consensual contract. Detinue plainly would not lie in such a case—property could not pass in unascertained goods—so nothing could bind the parties other than their bare wills in this event. And the fifteenth century knew nothing of will theory.

[1] Powell, *Essay*, i. 332.

[2] Corbin, 'Conditions in the Law of Contract', 28 *Yale Law J.* 739, 746 (1919) says: 'Before bilateral contracts became enforceable this was the only way for a promisor to secure his desired object'.

[3] C. H. S. Fifoot, *History and Sources of the Common Law* (London, 1949), pp. 227-8, 304.

The absence of any sophisticated law of wholly executory contracts at this time need not surprise us, for the reality is that—outside the land law—there was little call for making plans and arrangements for some long term future. Sales of goods were still mostly sales of specific goods; there was no national market in which future crops could be sold, and indeed, the marketing offences actively discouraged such future dealings. As the eighteenth century wore on, all this began to change, markets began to grow wider, and merchants began to want to plan ahead. 'In a market goods came to be thought of as fungibles; the function of contracts correspondingly shifted from that of simply transferring title to a specific item to that of ensuring an expected return. Executory contracts, rare during the eighteenth century became important as instruments for "futures" agreements.'[4]

This was also generally true of other types of contract. In the absence of substantial capital investment in industry, the need for long-term future planning and for binding arrangements and commitments had not yet significantly affected the law of contract. Most contracts were still generally more or less immediate exchanges. The use of money, and then the invention of the bill of exchange and promissory note, enabled some postponement of performance to take place without altering the conceptual character of an exchange. For payment by those means was (as we have seen) readily enough accepted as actual payment, and not just as a promise of future payment. There was, of course, a need for certain types of long-term arrangement, particulary those of a continuing character, for example leases, partnerships, contracts of employment, and in such transactions there is in a sense a series of continuing present exchanges combined with an executory element so far as the future is concerned. In the eighteenth century it was perfectly possible to make a long-term contract of this character for a fixed period, but what is perhaps more interesting is that in the absence of a fixed term, the contract was normally terminable on reasonable notice. This principle, which of course remains the modern rule, only binds the future conduct of the parties to a minimum degree; in fact, it could be said that it binds the parties to the degree necessary to safeguard the interests of each, in so far as he has relied on the arrangements continuing.

We have already seen, in the previous chapter, that much of the law around 1770 seems to have grown up around the part-executed transaction. Litigation over the doctrines which later made up much of the bulk of the law of contract was, in the eighteenth century, almost entirely conducted in part-executed cases. I have referred there to the fact that nascent doctrines of mistake, coercion, and fraud all arose at this

---

[4] Morton J. Horwitz, 'The Historical Foundations of Modern Contract Law', 87 *Harvard Law Rev.* 917, 918 (1974).

period in the context of part executed contracts, and were treated as grounds for the recovery of money paid; only in the nineteenth century do we find these doctrines reappearing in the guise of defences to actions on wholly executory contracts.

Another piece of evidence for the relative unimportance of the wholly executory contract is provided by the absence of any rules of offer and acceptance until the last few decades of the eighteenth century. This has been explained by saying that there was only a law of promises and not a law of contracts during this period[5] but the truer explanation surely lies in the absence of a law of executory contract. The 'request' rules, which I discussed earlier, served the purpose of many of the modern offer and acceptance rules, but in the context of part executed contracts.

Assumpsit and Promissory Liability

What I have been saying so far is so contrary to the traditional ideas about the history of English contract law that some further elaboration is necessary. It is well known that even in the reign of Elizabeth I the courts of common law were working out the basis of liability in the new action of *assumpsit*; and there is no doubt that during this period there were a large number of decisions in which the relationship between the new action and the older ideas about consideration were being reformulated. Amongst other things, it is quite clear that it was during this period that the judges began to lay down firmly the rule that a 'promise for a promise' could be an adequate consideration; and accordingly, that when a plaintiff sued upon such a contract he need only show that he had given a promise, and not that he had performed his promise. This has commonly been taken to represent the beginnings of the consensual contract in modern English law so there appears to be some difficulty in arguing that even in the eighteenth century the wholly executory contract was not fully recognized.

However, the more closely that we look at the possibility of purely executory liability, the more puzzling and confusing the picture becomes. Professor Simpson has recently suggested that the references to consideration being satisfied by 'promise for promise' do not mean that the sixteenth-century Courts enforced purely executory contracts.[6] To Professor Simpson, the notion of a 'binding' executory contract means a contract which is unilaterally irrevocable, and he has cited cases from the late seventeenth century which suggest that the Courts were even then not unwilling to envisage the possibility of unilateral revocation before reliance.[7] Thus, he says, 'all talk about the recognition of "wholly

[5] Simpson, 'Innovation in Nineteenth Century Contract Law', 91 *Law Q. Rev.* 247, 257–8 (1975).

[6] A. W. B. Simpson, *A History of the Common Law of Contract*, p. 467.

[7] *Mayor of Scarborough* v. *Butler* (1685) 3 Lev. 237, 83 E.R. 668; *Howe* v. *Beeche* (1685) 3 Lev. 244, 83 E.R. 671.

executory", "bilateral", or "consensual" contracts in that [the sixteenth] century is wholly misconceived.'[8] It is right to add that Professor Simpson's account stresses that sixteenth- and seventeenth-century lawyers simply did not see the problems in the way they are seen today. At that time, he insists, lawyers saw the principal issues as pleading points, and they also saw the law as centring around the idea of an actionable promise rather than a 'binding' contract.

There is no point in becoming entangled in a series of verbal issues about the meaning of a wholly executory contract. The truth seems to be that in modern English law the wholly executory contract has a number of characteristics, of which unilateral irrevocability is one, the ability of the plaintiff to sue prior to performance or reliance is another, and entitlement to a particular type of damages is a third. Although some of these characteristics may have emerged in the sixteenth and seventeenth centuries, I suggest they had not all done so. In particular, it is my thesis that the third of these characteristics was largely unknown prior to the end of the eighteenth century, and that in the absence of that characteristic it is misleading to speak of wholly executory contracts, or of consensual liability. It is true that the recognition of 'promise for promise' as constituting a ground of liability prior to performance or reliance must have contained the seeds of consensual liability. But this was not the consensual liability known to nineteenth-century lawyers. The truth seems to be that the transition to the wholly executory contract of modern times was a much longer process than has generally been thought; in fact I suggest that this transition lasted from the reign of Elizabeth I to the end of the eighteenth century.[9] It would also be wrong to think that lawyers throughout this period were anxious to hasten on the transition. In some respects (as I have argued) it may indeed be that common lawyers were generally anxious that contract law should develop along the lines more usually associated with the nineteenth century; but in other respects, as I shall suggest below, it may be that the lawyers actually tried to hold back these developments, and prevent a fully-blown consensual law from coming into existence.

As a result of Professor Simpson's very full account of the law of the sixteenth and seventeenth centuries, it is unnecessary to set out the position at this time in any detail. For my purposes it is sufficient to stress a number of central points. The first is that the plaintiff suing in *assumpsit* had to allege a consideration which had to be either present, continuous, or future. If he averred a future consideration, then he normally had to aver also that he had performed the consideration; if he averred a

---

[8] *A History of the Common Law of Contract*, p. 467.

[9] In this I follow Morton J. Horwitz, *The Transformation of American Law* (Cambridge, Mass. and London, 1977), pp. 162 *et seq*.

promise as a consideration, then he did not have to aver that he had performed the promise. Only where a promise was alleged as the consideration, therefore, could the claim be said (in modern terminology) to be a claim on an executory or consensual contract.

Now where the plaintiff pleaded a promise as the consideration, and therefore did not have to aver that he had performed his promise, it obviously might happen that the defendant would be held liable even though the whole transaction was still executory. In this sense it was possible for wholly executory contracts to be enforced at this time. But there was one vital difference between the enforcement of such contracts in the sixteenth and the twentieth centuries. Where the plaintiff had not yet performed his own promise at the date of the action, he was not generally discharged from performing himself, but remained liable to perform his own promise after the action against the defendant. It naturally followed that the mode of calculation of the damages was then very different from what it is today. In modern law, broadly speaking, the plaintiff recovers the *difference* between the value of the defendant's performance and the cost to him of his own performance, *which he will no longer have to render*. But in the sixteenth and seventeenth centuries, when the plaintiff generally remained liable to perform his own promise in the future, the damages he was entitled to claim represented the *full value* of the defendant's promise.[10] The plaintiff's claim was therefore much closer to what we would understand as an action for specific performance, rather than an action for damages for loss of bargain. Although it is possible to say that damages in such a case are given in compensation for the plaintiff's lost expectations (as Professor Simpson does)[11] these are *not* expectation damages in the modern sense. In modern law, such damages are called expectation damages because the only ground upon which the plaintiff appears to be entitled to damages at all is that he has suffered a disappointment of his expectations; in the absence of any performance by the plaintiff, or of the receipt of any benefit by the defendant, this is the only ground of liability. But in pre-eighteenth-century law, the reason for holding the defendant liable was not merely to satisfy the plaintiff's expectations; the plaintiff's own performance remained due. The plaintiff was thus entitled to sue, not just because he had reasonable expectations, but because he remained liable to be sued himself. It is misleading to refer to damages in this situation as expectation damages.

The key point, then, is that damages for the loss of a mere expectation, unpaid for and unrelied upon, were not generally awarded before the late eighteenth century, and that in the absence of such damages it is not really possible to talk of a proper law of executory contracts. It is worth considering further why such expectation damages are so rarely to be

---

[10] A. W. B. Simpson, *A History of the Common Law of Contract*, pp. 583-7.   [11] Ibid., p. 584.

found before the very last years of the century. Damages for the protection of a pure expectation (in the sense I have explained) presuppose one of two things; they presuppose either that the cost of the plaintiff's performance is, at the time the contract is made, less than the value to him of the defendant's performance; or, alternatively, that after the making of the contract and before its performance, a change has taken place in the relative values of the plaintiff's and the defendant's performance such that the defendant's performance is now worth more to the plaintiff than his own performance will cost him. If neither of these is the case, then there will be no award of expectation damages, for even on the most extended meaning of the term 'loss' there will be no loss at all. (I am assuming, it must be remembered, that there has been no benefit to the defendant, and no reliance by the plaintiff.) Now a plaintiff who wished to claim expectation damages on either of these two grounds in the eighteenth century was liable to be faced with a certain amount of traditional hostility. Let me take them in turn.

If the plaintiff claimed that, at the time he made the contract, his performance would cost him less than the defendant's was worth, the plaintiff would be in danger of seeming to have agreed to buy something for less than a just or fair price. It must be remembered that the idea of a middleman who buys at one price and sells at a higher was still barely acceptable till the very end of the century. People who bought were supposed to buy for use; and if they bought for use they ought to pay a proper price. If the buyer complained that he had agreed to buy something for less than its proper value, that, in other words, he had expected to make a profit out of the purchase, whether by resale, or simply by virtue of having bought at less than the market price, he was likely to face a hostile reception. His prima facie position, far from being that of an injured and innocent contracting party who had suffered a loss through the other's failure to perform—as it came to be seen later— would on the contrary have been that of an extortioner whose nefarious scheme had been foiled by the defendant's breach. Little sympathy would be due to him on this score. This attitude was, of course, already becoming obsolete by mid-eighteenth century, if not earlier, but it was far from dead.

The alternative possibility was that the plaintiff had agreed to pay a fair price at the time the contract was made, but owing to changes in the market situation, or other relevant factors, by the time performance was due, the price originally fixed was plainly less than the present value of the defendant's performance. Now here again, it later came to be felt that the plaintiff was manifestly entitled to expectation damages for the difference in the value of the two performances at the time performance was due. When the focus of attention shifted from the performance to the making of the contract, all contract formation came to be seen as a risk-allocation process. If performance was separated in time from formation, then plainly a risk existed that prices would change in the interim. Obviously, in *some* cases, the purpose of the contract was to shift this risk; therefore, it came to be deduced, with little logic, that in *all* cases, this risk must be treated as having been shifted. But, once again, this involved a frame of mind which was only slowly developing in the eighteenth century. For one thing, it involved recognition that *change* was the normal possibility; that contracts were entered into for future performance to fix the risks of such future changes. Again, this later came to be thought to be the case; but the eighteenth century was not an age of rapid and perpetual change in most of those things that men contracted about; the price of land, for instance, changed very slowly during this period. When contracts were made for future performance in the eighteenth century the purpose of postponing performance was usually a mere matter of practical convenience—perhaps to give time for legal formalitites. It was not normally thought to be an exercise in risk allocation. Only when markets came into existence, where prices fluctuated daily, as everyone came to observe, did it become reasonable to assume that contracts entered into for future performance were deliberately designed to shift risks of such future change. This happened during the eighteenth century with regard to the Funds, for which a market was (as we saw earlier) in existence from the very beginnings of the century. But it did not happen in most other produce or goods till late in the century; and it did not happen for land until the nineteenth century, and by then it was too late to introduce the expectation damages rule into contracts for the sale of land.

There is one further point to be made about awards of expectation damages. An award of such damages in either of the two situations envisaged above was, in a sense, a reward for diligence, skill, and foresight. The man who managed to buy at less than market price, the man who had the foresight to buy in advance of changes in market price, was a man who outsmarted his contracting partner. It was precisely this sort of diligence, skill, and foresight which, it was coming to be felt, ought to be rewarded and encouraged. In the next century, this indeed became the dominant philosophy of the age. But in the eighteenth century (as, perhaps, today) there were many who viewed these qualities with some distaste rather than with admiration. To make a contract to buy at less than the market price was to outwit your contracting partner, perhaps to take advantage of his ignorance or foolishness or necessitous circumstances. Was this to be encouraged? Or again, to make a contract for future performance, and then to insist on performance at the contract price when the market had changed, was hardly gentlemanly; it might indeed, be a pure form of gambling, in which case it was socially acceptable but not exactly morally justifiable; alternatively it might be to take advantage of a pure windfall which was morally unfair; or it might be to take advantage of superior foresight in anticipating change. That, as before, was a quality viewed with less than whole-hearted admiration by men in eighteenth-century England. The modern reader, who is likely on most of these matters to share the sympathies of the eighteenth-century Englishman, rather than his nineteenth-century successor, should have little difficulty in understanding why expectation damages were not widely awarded in the eighteenth century.

In one of the most common types of contract which could be made, such damages were actively discouraged.[12] In contracts for the sale of land, the famous decision in *Flureau* v. *Thornhill*[13] denied any damages, where the vendor was without fault unable to make a good title, for the 'fancied goodness of the bargain which he [the plaintiff] supposes he has lost'.[14] The disdainful way in which De Grey C. J. thus dismissed the plaintiff's claim for expectation damages is itself highly suggestive. To ask for expectation damages is to ask the Court to count the plaintiff's egg as a chicken before it is hatched. The Court evidently feels that this is going too far.

We may next observe that in one type of case the executory contract was quite positively denied validity altogether; where 'accord and satisfaction' was pleaded, that is to say, where it was alleged that a duty had been discharged, it was not enough to show an unfulfilled contract to discharge the duty. This rule was challenged in 1696, which suggests that the consensual contract was then gaining ground, but the challenge was rebutted by the Court;[15] and another hundred years later, the rule was reaffirmed in a particularly strong case.[16] Not until the nineteenth century did it become possible to discharge an existing duty by a wholly executory agreement to discharge it.

Apart from these two specific types of case, it is difficult to be sure how far expectation damages may have been awarded in the eighteenth century because damages were still largely a jury matter. The chief grounds for supposing that awards of expectation damages were rare are,

---

[12] Although not strictly concerned with expectation damages, the rules against the award of interest are also relevant. See George Washington, 'Damages in Contract at Common Law—I', 47 *Law Q. Rev.* 345, 366–8 (1931); and see *post*, p. 422.

[13] (1775) 2 W. Bl. 1078, 96 E.R. 635.

[14] 2 W. Bl. at 1078, 96 E.R. at 635. Compare the words of an American judge in 1785: 'Men do not make purchases, with a view of merely having interest for their money; but they contemplate the rise in value of the thing purchased'. See Morton J. Horwitz, *The Transformation of American Law*, p. 59. Needless to say, socially and economically, land played a very different role in America and England at this time.

[15] *Allen* v. *Harris* (1696) 1 Ld. Ray. 122, 91 E.R. 978.

[16] *Lynn* v. *Bruce* (1794) 2 H. Bl. 317, 126 E.R. 571.

first, the rule that the plaintiff generally remained liable to perform his own obligations (which I will deal with more fully below) and, secondly, the absence of reported cases in which wholly executory contracts (in the modern sense) were being sued upon. But there were two classes of cases in which such actions were not uncommon. Actions on wagers and actions for breach of promise of marriage were by far the most common types of action on wholly executory contracts, at least in the sixteenth and seventeenth centuries. Now these two classes of contract share one peculiar feature, namely that they cannot subsist at all except as wholly executory arrangements. It is not possible to have a part executed wager, or a part executed promise to marry. Moreover, marriage contracts had another peculiarity, namely that the distinction between a contract to marry and an actual marriage was very unclear. In the absence of any clear requirements as to the formalities needed for an actual marriage, many wholly informal exchanges of vows or promises could be (and for centuries had been) construed as themselves constituting a marriage. Thus a breach of promise of marriage closely resembled a repudiation of an actual marriage.

Actions on wagers may well have been more important in familiarizing lawyers with the idea of contracts as risk-allocation devices, but these too were (and are) a peculiar sort of contract. In particular, a wager consists of an exchange of promises, but it does not contemplate an exchange of performances. Unlike the ordinary contract of modern times where both parties are generally expected to do something, only the loser of a wager will normally have to do anything. Naturally, therefore, the concept of the 'damages' payable in a wager and an ordinary contract are different. The plaintiff suing on a wager (in so far as this is legally permissible) claims his winnings; he does not, in the normal sense, sue for 'damages' at all. But a claim for 'winnings' in a wager is much more like a claim to expectation damages in the modern sense where only the defendant is obliged to do anything. It may be that familiarity with actions on wagers influenced the changes in the common law whereby expectation damages came to be the normal remedy for breach of contract, and performance from the injured plaintiff ceased to be required.

Other instances of actions on wholly executory contracts appear to have been rare before the late eighteenth century, and it may be that the ordinary commercial agreement would not normally have been sued upon in this way. The rules of pleading and the attitude of juries may have inclined pleaders to sue on commercial engagements only after some element of performance or reliance by the plaintiff.[17] In other words, contracts which to the modern lawyer might appear to be wholly executory contracts were liable to be treated as consisting of a promise in

[17] I owe this suggestion to Professor Simpson.

return for a future act, or future consideration. A contract of this nature was conceptually similar to the modern unilateral contract. Such contracts were not then, nor indeed are today, thought to be generally actionable until the act has been performed.

There is another point which needs to be made about the enforcement of wholly executory arrangements. Agreements which lack any element of performance or reliance, and which therefore rest entirely in the intention of the parties, are plainly more difficult to *prove*. Even in modern times, it is a great deal easier to prove an agreement where the plaintiff has (for instance) delivered goods or rendered services to the defendant, or even relied upon a promise by changing his position in some way. Acts of this kind are usually objective facts, provable by disinterested witnesses, and they usually require some sort of explanation from the defendant if he denies the plaintiff's case. But a bare agreement, unless it is evidenced in writing, is clearly more difficult to prove, for it requires evidence of what the parties have said to one another. Now in the period of which I am writing, proof of parol agreements was a great deal more difficult than it is even today, as a result of the rules of procedure which excluded the parties and any other interested persons from giving evidence. To prove the making of a purely parol agreement which had not been performed or acted upon in any way must have been a practical impossibility in a great many cases because of these rules of procedure. Nor should we too readily assume that lawyers at this time saw the distinction between substantive law and modes of proof in the same way as modern lawyers. To them, one reason for making it more difficult to prove a parol contract may have been that they were less satisfied with parol contracts as a substantive ground of liability. This naturally leads us on to the Statute of Frauds.

The Statute of Frauds

This famous Statute, passed in 1677, required that a number of types of contract should be evidenced by some note or memorandum in writing, although in contracts for the sale of goods of the value of £10 or over, alternatives were provided, and it may well be that in sales of land, an alternative to writing was also envisaged. The contracts thus enumerated by the Statute have long puzzled historians for they seem to lack any rational coherence.[18] Among the contracts enumerated, apart from the contracts for the sale of goods of £10 or above and contracts for the sale of an interest in land, were promises by executors to be personally answerable for the debts of their testators, promises made in consideration of marriage, promises to answer for the 'debt default or mis-carriage' of another (that is contracts of suretyship), and contracts not to be

[18] A. W. B. Simpson, *A History of the Common Law of Contract*, pp. 615 *et seq.*

performed within a year. It does not seem difficult to see in this Statute an attempt to hold back the advance of the consensual contract and to require parol contracts to be part-executed before they were enforced.[19]

So far as contracts for the sale of goods are concerned, the Statute itself clearly provides for this; writing is only required if the goods have not been delivered and accepted, or if no part of the price has been paid. As Maitland observed many years ago, the requirements of the Statute were in substance the same as those stated several centuries previously by Glanvill for the *validity* of contracts of sale.[20] Later historians, without Maitland's perceptiveness, have dismissed this comment of his as a rare aberration, for how could there be any connection between the twelfth-century requirements for the *validity* of a contract of sale, and the seventeenth-century requirements for the mode of *proving* a contract of sale?[21] The answer to this may well be that there was indeed such a connection. If we assume that the law was, in 1677, already beginning to recognize wholly executory contracts in some cases, and if we further assume that lawyers were unhappy about the result, then it is not difficult to see the Statute as a compromise between the older view and the newer. The executory contract is not ruled out as a matter of principle, but more solid proof of its existence is required in the form of writing; naturally, if the contract is in fact part-executed, the requirement of writing does not apply. To the modern lawyer the Statute of Frauds seems only to show a concern with evidence rather than with substantive liability. Provided some written evidence could be produced, the law would recognize and enforce a wholly executory contract, in so far as such contracts were enforced at all at that time. And it is true that one of the motivating causes for the passing of the Statute was a belief in the unreliability of evidence of the spoken word, and a dread of perjury and fraud about the spoken word. The Popish Plot, a year or two later, demonstrated that these fears were only too well founded. But it does not follow that contemporary lawyers perceived the statutory requirement of writing as primarily an evidentiary requirement. I have already suggested that at this time bonds, covenants, and written 'obligations' were still seen as in the nature of grants rather than promises; if this was the analogy which lawyers of the time had in mind in drafting the Statute they would not necessarily have thought of writing as primarily evidentiary.

There is thus a sense in which the Statute can be seen as a conservative piece of law reform, an attempt to restrict the development of the

---

[19] See, e.g., the judgment of Holt C. J. in *Thorp* v. *Thorp* (1701) 12 Mod. 455, 464, 88 E.R. 1448, 1453.

[20] Pollock and Maitland, *History of English Law*, 2nd edn. (Cambridge, 1952), ii. 207-8.

[21] C. H. S. Fifoot, *History and Sources*, pp. 226-7, n. 54.

executory contract, and to use, as the means of restriction, the traditional grounds of liability. Either writing must be produced, or there must be some part performance. So far as contracts of sale of goods were concerned, the requirement of part performance was actually written into the Statute. The position with regard to contracts for the sale of land or an interest in land came ultimately to be very much the same. Although the Statute did not here contain an exception for the partly executed contract (as it did for contracts of sale) we know that very soon after it was passed Equity 'invented' the doctrine of part performance. In other words, Courts of Chancery enforced part executed contracts for the sale of land without insisting on written evidence. In later years it came to be said that the doctrine of part performance was imposed in the teeth of the statutory requirements, but Professor Simpson has recently argued that there is evidence for the view that the Statute was never intended to apply to suits for specific performance in Equity where it was known that part performance would suffice as a ground of enforcement.[22] And certainly it is difficult to believe that the property-minded lawyers who drafted this Statute would have been content to see a purchaser of an estate, who had entered into possession and was willing to pay the price, turned off the land merely because he had no written evidence of his contract. It is true that payment of the price never came to be dealt with as a form of part performance which justified a decree of specific performance; but that too is intelligible in the context of a property-dominated society. This property owner who has not yet given up possession will of course have to return any part of the price paid in advance, but he is not to be turned out of his estates on the strength of a parol contract which he has not yet begun to perform.

Whether this explanation holds good for some of the other provisions of the Statute of Frauds is less clear. Perhaps the provisions dealing with sureties arose from the fact that the surety derives no benefit from his transaction and although the principal creditor may act in reliance on the promise, it may have been thought hard then to hold a surety liable as a result of such reliance without any corresponding benefit. This reluctance is one which judges appear to have felt through the ages, for the surety has always been favourably treated in English law. As to promises by executors, I have already suggested that the statutory requirements may have been designed to prevent too ready a willingness by juries to infer the existence of such promises in the absence of real evidence; here, too, it will be observed that the requirement of writing may have served to protect an executor from paying out more in debts than he had received in assets, which is also suggestive of a desire to preserve the old benefit-based law in preference to the new promise-

[22] A. W. B. Simpson, *A History of the Common Law of Contract*, pp. 615 *et seq.*

based law. Then there is the peculiar provision directed against promises not to be performed within a year whose purpose has baffled lawyers and historians ever since. Although I have no evidence to support the suggestion, it seems (in the light of all that has been said) at least possible that this provision was simply designed to put an outer limit to the enforcing of executory contracts. A man might bind himself for the future if he pleased, but, at least in the absence of writing, he was not to be held bound to any performance due more than a year later.[23] As the Statute of Frauds failed to hold back the onward march of the executory contract, and as the executory contract became in due course the paradigm of contractual duty, the very idea that there could be anything wrong in binding oneself to a long-term future performance became so foreign to legal ways of thought that this explanation never seems to have occurred to anyone. I offer it as a speculation.

EXECUTORY CONTRACTS, DAMAGES, AND THE INDEPENDENT COVENANT RULE

I have suggested above that eighteenth-century lawyers would not have seen any problem about actions for specific performance because an exchange would still take place and consideration would therefore pass on both sides. I have also suggested that generally speaking the common-law rules up to the late eighteenth century tended to produce a result closely analagous to a decree of specific performance in all actions on wholly executory contracts. To understand the law as it still stood around 1770, it is necessary to grasp the relationship between two complex sets of rules concerning, on the one hand, the extent of the damages to which the plaintiff was entitled, and on the other hand, the rule that mutual promises were prima facie deemed to be independent of each other. As I have already said, the position was that a plaintiff who sued on a wholly executory contract was normally entitled to the full value of the defendant's performance *because* he remained liable to perform himself after the present proceedings were over. These two rules were inextricably interrelated. Prima facie, mutual promises were seen as independant obligations, that is to say, the failure of the plaintiff to perform his promise did not discharge the defendant from the performance of *his* promise. This rule, which seems so extraordinary to us today, was an absolutely key feature of seventeenth- and eighteenth-century contractual thought. Promises once given were, in a sense, conceived of as already granting a right to the promisee; the promisor was 'chargeable' on the promise as soon as it was given,[24] and prima facie

---

[23] This could be seen as a generalization of the provision requiring leases to be evidenced in writing if they were for a period exceeding three years.

[24] A. W. B. Simpson, *A History of the Common Law of Contract*, pp. 463-4.

he remained chargeable on it despite the failure of the promisee to perform his side of the bargain. The promisor's remedy for breach of the other's promise was, in turn, to sue him.

The reason why these two rules were so interrelated seems to have been this: if a plaintiff were to be defeated by proof that he had not himself performed, then there was a real danger that, in subsequent proceedings, the present defendant would be able to sue the present plaintiff and recover the full value of the present plaintiff's performance. That would clearly be unfair for the result would be to give the present defendant the full value of the present plaintiff's performance without having himself performed at all, he having already been sued and held not liable. Consequently, the failure of the plaintiff to have performed his own side of a wholly executory contract was generally thought to be immaterial in an action brought upon it. In short, if the plaintiff had not already performed before the trial, he was still bound to perform afterwards, and in this way even an action for damages on an executory contract envisaged an exchange being carried through. It is thus not absurd to suggest that even executory contracts were, in a sense, based on an exchange of benefits, and that the source of the defendant's liability was not a pure promise, but the very fact that he was entitled to the performance of the plaintiff's promise.

But although the normal rule was that mutual covenants or promises were independent, there were exceptions. There were some cases in which the Courts held that the promises were not independent, cases in which the wording of the contract made it clear that one promise was to be performed before the other. If the defendant's performance was due before the plaintiff's this gave rise to no problem; once again, the plaintiff would obtain judgment, and would himself remain bound to perform afterwards. But if it was the plaintiff's performance which was due first, then problems might indeed arise. Everything depended, of course, on *why* the plaintiff had not performed. If he had failed to perform because of his own neglect, he would plainly lose his action, and rightly; but if he had failed to perform only because the defendant had refused to allow him to perform, then real difficulty arose. Now a law of contract which is fundamentally a law of part executed contracts plainly has the greatest difficulty with this case. There *has* been no performance, no benefit conferred, perhaps even no reliance; yet it seems excessively hard that the plaintiff should have no remedy where he has been willing to perform, perhaps has even tried to perform but the defendant has refused to allow him to do so. It is precisely this type of case which we may expect to provide the bridge to the law of executory contracts, and it seems indeed to have proved so in eighteenth-century England. Two ways of trying to provide a remedy to the plaintiff were tried; the first eventually proved a blind alley, but the second provided a general transition to the enforcement of executory contracts.

The first method was to argue that if the defendant had refused to allow the plaintiff to perform, then the plaintiff must be deemed to have performed; a sort of fictitious or 'constructive' performance would be assumed. There are signs of this in *Peeters* v. *Opie*[25] in 1671, where the plaintiff, a builder, had agreed to pull down a wall for £8. The defendant, the owner of the premises, had changed his mind, and refused to allow the builder to do the work. When sued, the defendant argued that he could not be expected to pay the builder in advance of the work being done, and that the money was therefore only payable if and when the work was done; here it had never been done, so why should he pay at all? The argument was not, in 1671, nearly so unmeritorious as it may appear at first sight, for the defendant was, in effect, arguing for the right to change his mind prior to performance, a right which necessarily exists before the executory contract is wholly recognized; and a right, we may add, which is extensively claimed by, and conceded to, the modern consumer. But, nevertheless, the right was denied in this case; the defendant was held liable, because he 'ought not to take advantage of his own wrong'.[26] Now this obviously had disadvantages too. It might be hard if the plaintiff could recover nothing in this situation, but it would also be hard if the plaintiff could recover the full value of the defendant's performance without having to perform himself. We do not know what the jury actually awarded the builder, though legal theory would suggest that he should have recovered £8 in full.

But we have seen already that the jury's right to mitigate the damages was an established feature of seventeenth- and eighteenth-century law, and it seems probable that juries helped to solve this problem by giving appropriate damages in such circumstances and not the full value of the defendant's performance. We know very little about how juries behaved at this time, and what they normally did in computing damages in contractual actions, but here and there we find evidence that juries rebelled at the theory which required the plaintiff to recover the full value of the defendant's performance. For example, in *Kenrig* v. *Eggleston*,[27] though this was a case of malperformance rather than refusal to perform, the jury deducted the value of the one performance from the other, rather than leave the defendant to sue the plaintiff for his reward after the trial. And more generally it may be that in practice the rules about independent covenants were made tolerable by the common sense of juries. If the plaintiff sued without alleging performance, perhaps juries generally could be trusted to give him a verdict only where they

[25] (1671) 2 Wms. Saund. 350, 85 E.R. 1144.
[26] 2 Wms. Saund. at 351, 85 E.R. at 1145.   [27] (1662) Aleyn 93, 82 E.R. 932.

were confident that he had performed or would perform,[28] or to anticipate the later law and deduct the value of the plaintiff's non-performance from the damages.

The idea of treating the plaintiff as having fictitiously or constructively performed where the defendant refused to allow him to perform never wholly died out in the eighteenth century. It is, for instance, still stated in Powell's *Essay* in 1790,[29] although it did not last much longer. But at the same time a second rationale for enabling the plaintiff to obtain damages for breach of an executory contract where his own performance was due first, was gaining ground. This was the idea that the plaintiff *was discharged from performing* where the defendant refused to accept his proffered performance. For example, in contracts for the sale of goods or of Government stock, the idea was emerging that if the buyer refused to take or accept the proffered goods or stock, the 'property' revested in the plaintiff who thereby became free to dispose of it elsewhere. Two consequences followed from this. The first was that the revesting process necessarily brought to an end the plaintiff's own obligation to perform, and instead of being entitled to the full value of the defendant's performance he became entitled only to sue for the deficiency, the difference between the price which the buyer had agreed to pay and that which the seller was able to obtain on resale. The second consequence was that the 'offer' of performance by the plaintiff (tender, as it came to be technically known) became of crucial significance, for it was the acceptance of this offer which discharged the plaintiff's obligation to perform his own promise. This development was the key to the transition to the wholly executory contract for it was this which finally opened the door to the recovery of expectation damages by the plaintiff without any performance on his part.

The change can be seen occurring in a case in 1724.[30] In this case the plaintiff had sold Government stock to the defendant, and when the buyer refused to accept delivery, the plaintiff resold it elsewhere, and then claimed damages for his loss on the resale. The buyer argued, in effect, that he could not be liable because the seller had not formally offered him a transfer of the stock, nor had he formally declined it. No exchange had therefore taken place, nor was the plaintiff freed from performance. But as the plaintiff was no longer in a position to perform, the defendant should also be freed from liability. For if the defendant was made to pay damages, what consideration would he be receiving in return? The judges at first were divided on the issue, and Eyre J. argued

[28] See on this H. K. Lucke, '*Slade's* Case and the Origin of the Common Counts', 81 *Law Q. Rev.* 539, 541 (1965).

[29] i. 419–20.

[30] *Wyvil* v. *Stapleton* (1724) 1 Stra. 615, 93 E.R. 735, affirmed in the House of Lords, 3 Bro. Parl. Cas. 89.

that as the seller was suing for the deficiency only 'the mutual remedy is gone', that is to say, the buyer would not, after judgment, be able to claim the stock. But on reargument, judgment was given for the plaintiff. 'The money', says Pratt C. J., 'is not to be paid as the consideration of a transfer, but of the covenant to transfer; and the true consideration in this case is the remedy which the defendant has upon the covenant to transfer'.[31] The alchemy is here at work. The consideration for the defendant's liability is the plaintiff's promise; true, the plaintiff will never have to perform that promise, but that is the defendant's fault. The upshot is that the defendant can now be made to pay damages without actually receiving any consideration. This was a momentous change. Nearly two centuries after the judges had first begun to say that 'promise for promise' was good consideration, the Courts were now beginning to invest that idea with a new significance. The truly executory contract was being born.

But these changes did not happen overnight. In 1768 a seller of goods who had resold them after the buyer had refused to take them could still seriously argue that he was entitled to the full price from the buyer, not apparently realizing that if he was held entitled to the full price, the buyer would be entitled to the value of the goods.[32] He was, however, unsuccessful. The very fact that the question of damages was so largely in the hands of the juries probably helped to make this development slower than it might otherwise have been. For not until the Courts made it clear that prima facie a plaintiff could sue for loss of his bargain on breach of an executory contract, could it really be said that the wholly executory contract was fully recognized.[33] This change was well under way by 1770, but it is not the way of the common-law judges to advertise the fundamental nature of the changes they make; indeed, they often seem unaware of the changes themselves. It was not until the full implication of the changing rules about damages had begun to be grasped that it became somewhat clearer that the law of part executed contracts was giving way to an entirely different law of executory contract. And that change may be dated as taking place in the period between 1770 and 1830.

Promises, Intentions, and Will Theory

As executory contracts came to be more fully recognized, in the sense which I have explained—that is, without any element of exchange before or after trial—it necessarily followed that the basis of contractual liability came to change also. In this kind of executory contract a man cannot be

[31] 1 Stra. at 617, 93 E.R. at 736.
[32] *Smee* v. *Huddlestone*, apparently unreported, but noted in Sayer, *The Law of Damages* (London, 1770), pp. 49–52.
[33] Morton J. Horwitz, 'The Historical Foundations of Modern Contract Law', p. 936.

liable because of anything that is done; he must be liable because of his intention, his will, his promise. There is nothing else which can create the liability when a man is made to pay damages without any actual consideration passing, any element of benefit or detrimental reliance. And throughout the eighteenth century the idea that intention, will, promise, could be a sufficient ground of liability, had been gathering force, not only with lawyers but with thinkers generally.

As to lawyers, I have previously discussed Mansfield's emphasis on intention in the interpretation of contracts, and already in some of Mansfield's judgments we can see the beginnings of nineteenth-century will theory, as for example where he speaks of 'the intent' of a transaction,[34] as though a transaction itself could have an intent. And if the interpretation and effects of a contract depended entirely on intent, why should not the creation of a liability also arise from a man's intent? Similarly, Mansfield had to begin that process of reinterpreting duties arising out of customary ideas of morality and equity in the light of this new will theory, as for example where he argued that an unfair contract induced by coercion was really entered into against a person's will.[35] And we must not forget, too, *Chesterfield* v. *Janssen*[36] which surely owed as much to Mansfield as to the judges who decided it. This seminal decision had decided that an unfair bargain would become binding if freely and voluntarily confirmed by the losing party. This may seem obvious enough today, but at the time the decision was a vital breakthrough; for it meant that a subsequent assent could now put right a first defective assent, or that, in effect, assent could make an unfair bargain binding with two bites of the cherry. And that was a revolutionary change, for unfair bargains had, in the past, been upset by the Court of Chancery because they were unfair, not because they had not been properly assented to.[37] Evidently it would not be long before people began to ask why two bites of the cherry were needed to make an unfair bargain binding.

Not until late in the eighteenth century do we encounter serious suggestions that the causes of invalidity of unfair contracts are ultimately to be found in deficiencies of the will; but we do find increasing talk of the importance of the 'will' in the law generally. Blackstone, for instance, talks a good deal about the 'will' in connection with the criminal law, and discusses in that context acts of duress and coercion as constraints

[34] *Kingston* v. *Preston* (1773) 2 Doug. 689, 99 E.R. 437.

[35] 'It is absurd to say that any man transgresses a law made for his own advantage willingly'. *Smith* v. *Bromley* (1760) 2 Doug. 697, 698, 99 E.R. 441, 444.

[36] (1750) 1 Atk. 301, 26 E.R. 191; *supra*, p. 124.

[37] Even after this case, the Courts were still sometimes willing to upset a very unfair bargain despite subsequent confirmation if they could find some ground for saying that the losing party did not fully understand his rights: *Taylour* v. *Rochfort* (1751) 2 Ves. Sen. 281, 28 E.R. 182, a very strong decision.

upon the will.[38] Then too we must remember the Lockean tradition with its emphasis on contractarianism and its use of the idea of 'implied' contracts and 'implied assent.' If the reciprocal obligations of citizen and ruler rested not upon the fact of the relationship, or the benefits they derived under it, but upon some shadowy 'implied' assent, why should this not be true of private relationships?

We know also that the idea of a promise as having a 'naturally' binding force was gaining ground. The Natural Lawyers had deduced the idea that a man could bind himself by a mere act of will, and that a promise was the expression of such an act of will. A promise itself was, therefore, something inherently binding; it did not need to be supported by any element of exchange of benefits or detrimental reliance, though to be sure even the Natural Lawyers might hesitate over the validity of a promise given without any reason at all, without any 'cause'. Such a promise might simply be due to a mistake, and hence not binding. Now even English lawyers in the cultured world of the eighteenth century were not ignorant of the writings of men like Grotius and Pufendorf, and in Scotland their works were very well known indeed. Francis Hutcheson, Adam Smith's predecessor as Professor of Moral Philosophy in Glasgow, was only one of those who was greatly influenced by natural law theories. Hutcheson combined a sort of utilitarianism with his Natural Law learning, and to him the binding force of a promise followed not only 'from our immediate sense of its beauty' but also from 'the mischiefs which must ensue upon violating it.'[39]

We have already seen how both Hume and Adam Smith had a good deal to say about the source of promissory and contractual obligations. Both of them went out of their way to reject what they regarded as the fallacies of the will theories of the Natural Lawyers. But both would, as I suggested earlier, almost certainly have accepted without question that promises, even though unrelied upon, and unpaid for by any benefit, were and should be binding because of the general tendency of mankind to rely upon them. Hume added that the sense of obligation arising from these principles is strengthened by the 'artifice of politicians who, in order to govern men more easily, and preserve peace in human society, have endeavoured to produce an esteem for justice and an abhorrence for injustice'.[40] This seems to have been almost literally true of the inculcation of belief in the moral force of promises. Politicians had discovered the advantages of maintaining the public credit by scrupulous discharge of the nation's debts, and the preservation of faith became an increasingly important part of the moral code of the eighteenth century aristocracy.

[38] *Bl. Comm.*, iv. 20, 27, 31.

[39] Cited in Peter Stein, 'Law and Society in Eighteenth Century Scotland', in Phillipson and Mitchison (eds.), *Scotland in the Age of Improvement* (Edinburgh, 1970), p. 153.

[40] *Treatise*, Book II, Part II, Section II.

Judges, too, appear to have quite deliberately set about trying to intensify the strength of the principle that promises should be kept. 'Can a man be bound too fast not to break his word?' asked Pratt C. J. in 1711.[41]

There was, moreover, a very natural transition from the part executed contract to the wholly executory contract once the role of promises became more central. Although I have argued that promises were originally largely evidentiary in their function, we have also seen how often the promise added some new element to the independent duty which it was evidencing. It might be that a new party came to be liable; it might be that the precise amount of a liability otherwise existing was quantified; it might be that a moral duty became a legal duty; but above all, it seems always to have been accepted that the promise and not the benefit or the reliance measured the extent of the liability. Not until 1936 was any serious question raised as to why this should be so, why a man who is liable on a promise because of another's detrimental reliance should be liable to the full extent of the promise rather than the cost of the reliance.[42] Had lawyers stopped to think about it, they might have argued that many forms of reliance involved costs which were very difficult to measure. The new idea of opportunity cost must have been becoming more obvious to men with some acquaintance with mercantile dealings. If a buyer defaulted on a sale, for instance, how was the seller to prove what he had lost by failing to try to find another buyer all the while he regarded himself as bound? How much simpler to hold the buyer liable for making good the whole loss resulting from his breach of promise than to delve into these difficult factual issues.[43]

There was another very important result of the transition to promissory liability. As the law moved increasingly to a recognition of the generally binding nature of promises and contracts, it became possible to *generalize*. Law now began to be *about* promises, wills, intentions, contracts; and not about particular relationships and particular transactions. I have mentioned earlier the small role played by contract law in Blackstone's *Commentaries*. But I should now qualify this by saying that it was the *general* law of contract which played such a small role. For in Blackstone's *Commentaries* much law of contract was still discussed in terms of particular transactions or relations. His first volume, on the *Law of Persons*, for instance, contains chapters on Master and Servant, on Corporations, not to mention other chapters on Husband and Wife, Parent and Child, and so forth, which contained much law that would have been regarded

---

[41] *Mitchell* v. *Reynolds* (1711) 10 Mod. 130, 137, 88 E.R. 660, 663.

[42] Fuller and Perdue, 'The Reliance Interest in Contract Damages', 46 *Yale Law J.* 52 (1936).

[43] An interesting hypothetical case is discussed by Sir William Jones, *Essay on Bailment*, at pp. 56–7, anticipating closely the facts of *East Suffolk Catchment Board* v. *Kent* [1941] A.C. 74. Jones would have decided for the plaintiff on grounds (in effect) of opportunity cost reliance, though he does not of course use such terms.

as contractual in the eighteenth century. The difference between Blackstone's *Commentaries*, written in the mid-eighteenth century, and Powell's *Essay*, written forty years later, is highly revealing. By the end of the eighteenth century a general law of contract was for the first time coming into existence.

It is appropriate to conclude this Part of this work with a reference to *Pillans and Rose* v. *Van Mierop and Hopkins*,[44] a case known to all law students for Lord Mansfield's attempts to downgrade the doctrine of consideration. The case raised a point of some considerable difficulty. The defendants had promised to accept bills of exchange drawn by the plaintiffs but it was very hard to establish any real reliance. The plaintiffs had acted in anticipation of the promise, which was then forthcoming, but it was their misfortune that they had not waited for the promise before acting upon it. Nevertheless, it was not impossible to find some element of reliance in the case, for the plaintiffs might—if it had not been for the promise—have attempted to obtain some recourse against the man on whose behalf the bills had originally been drawn. However, the hunt for some element of detrimental reliance of this nature was clearly likely to prove complex and raise tricky factual issues. It was in these circumstances that Mansfield uttered those famous dicta about 'the ancient notion of consideration being for the sake of evidence only'. Every law student knows that this view was overruled by the House of Lords in *Rann* v. *Hughes*.[45] But it should by now be apparent that to say that Mansfield's views were 'overruled' is too simple an account of what was happening. When Mansfield talked of consideration being evidence only, he was in effect saying, or certainly implying, not one proposition, but three: first, that the primary basis of contractual liability is the intention of the parties, and not the consideration; secondly, that consideration is merely evidence of the parties' intentions; and thirdly, that other forms of evidence (such as, in a business case, writing) may be equally satisfactory. The first two of these propositions were not as revolutionary as the third, but they did nevertheless reflect the changed emphasis in the roles of promise and consideration which only reached its culmination around the end of the century. *Rann* v. *Hughes* rejected the third of Mansfield's propositions. But the second has been largely accepted, at any rate at the level of theory, and the first has without doubt, formed the very basis of contractual liability for nearly two hundred years. There is a sense, therefore, in which Mansfield's famous dictum in this case, far from suffering the ignominious fate universally ascribed to it, has triumphed beyond measure. It is ironical that I feel compelled, later in this work, to suggest that the idea is now obsolescent.

[44] (1765) 3 Burr. 1663, 97 E.R. 1035.
[45] (1778) 7 T.R. 350, 101 E.R. 1014.

Part II

The Age of Freedom of Contract: 1770–1870

8

THE CONDITION OF ENGLAND, 1770–1870

CHANGE

FEW societies have undergone a greater change in a shorter period than that which transformed the shape of England between 1770 and 1870. It was, indeed, in this period, and as a result of the events which occurred during this period, that change became the normal condition of most human societies. Societies which had hitherto changed, if at all, so slowly that a man might scarcely observe the differences in a life of sixty or seventy years, now began to change so fast that everyone who lived to adulthood died in a world manifestly different from that into which he was born. The era of change had arrived.

It was generally welcomed, too, for change was widely thought to be change for the better. It was a period when men first began to become supremely confident of their ability to shape the world in their own fashion. Modern technological wonders are today so much taken for granted that it is difficult to understand the immense pride which Englishmen took as they first saw science harnessed to the benefit of mankind. The exhilarating sense of power over natural conditions—the 'Conquest of Nature'—as many saw it, brought with it, as we know, immense problems; but looking at these events after the lapse of a further century, many people today seem to see the immensity of the problems without understanding the greatness of the achievement. To those who lived through this period the problems may have been great, but the achievements were immeasurably greater. Here for example, is the Victorian apostle of individual virtues like thrift and self-help, Samuel Smiles, writing in 1875 of the past century:

Certainly there is a very great contrast. England was not a manufacturing country a hundred years ago. We imported nearly everything except corn, wool and flax . . . Coal could scarcely be had, for the coal-pits could not be kept clear of water.

A hundred years ago, we could not build a steam-engine; we could scarcely build a bridge. Look at the churches built a hundred years ago, and behold the condition of our architecture. A hundred years ago we had fallen to almost the lowest condition as a nation. We had not a harbour, we had not a dock. The most extensive system of robbery prevailed on the River Thames. The roads, such as they were, swarmed with highwaymen . . . A hundred years ago our ships were rotten; they were manned by prisoners taken from the hulks, or by working men pressed in the streets in open day ... Less than a hundred years ago, the colliers and salters of Scotland were slaves. It is not forty years since women and children worked in coal-pits ...

Towns and cities swarmed with ruffians; and brutal sports and brutal language existed to a frightful degree ...

A hundred years ago, literature was at a very low ebb. The press was in a miserable state ... The upper classes were coarse, drunken, and ill-mannered. Bribery and corruption on the grossest scale were the principal means for getting into parliament ...

Though drunkenness is bad enough now, it was infinitely worse a hundred years ago ...

What were the popular amusements of the people a hundred years ago? They consisted principally of man-fighting, dog-fighting, cock-fighting, bull-baiting, badger-drawing, the pillory, public whipping and public executions.

But bull-baiting, cock-fighting and other ferocious amusements have now departed. Even the village stocks have rotted out. Drunkenness has become disreputable. The 'good old days' have departed we hope never to return.[1]

It is likely that most of Samuel Smiles's compatriots would have agreed with this verdict on the previous century's changes. As Englishmen surveyed the country and the world in the mid-nineteenth century, it was pride and confidence which they felt, not shame nor anxiety. Industrially, Britain was at the height of its prosperity compared with the rest of the world; imperially, it was at the zenith of its majesty and power; politically, it was one of the very few free societies in the ancient world, or (apart from countries whose founders had themselves come from England) the modern world. It is true that there were social problems aplenty, but there had always been problems. What was new was not the evils, but (as Macaulay said) 'the intelligence which discerns and the humanity which remedies them'.[2]

Two Versions of History

The changes wrought during the century between 1770 and 1870 took place in many fields. In this work I am primarily concerned with those which took place in the law, and in social and economic organization; but inextricably related to these changes were those which took place in the realm of ideas. Unfortunately, in both fields, we are faced with a preliminary difficulty. The 'popular' version of the history of this period is fundamentally opposed to that which is accepted by many (though not all) serious historians. The popular version spans both the realm of social and economic events, and the realm of ideas. In this version, greedy factory owners and capitalists exploited the working classes by over-working and under-paying them; they pursued profit-making single-

[1] Samuel Smiles, *Thrift*, first published 1875 (London, 1903), pp. 224–7.
[2] *History of England* (London, 1850), i. 417.

mindedly and with no concern for the public interest; they operated thus within the framework of a legal and political system which favoured the new industrialists and made them the dominant class (at any rate after 1832) enabling them to overthrow the old benevolent Tory paternalism as they trampled the workers underfoot. At the same time they found the philosophical and intellectual justifications for this class exploitation in the economics of Adam Smith and the philosophy of *laissez-faire*. Both of these provided the intellectual justification for the system of freedom of contract which was (of course) only freedom for the industrialists and capitalists. The working class had no real freedom for they had to submit to the exploitation imposed upon them or starve. Thus freedom of contract, like much else in Victorian England, was based on humbug and hypocrisy. At this point some variations appear in the 'popular' version. In the more traditional and moderate versions, the reaction against industrial exploitation arose from the manifest social evils thrown up by the new factory system. The insanitary conditions in the towns, the harsh working conditions in the factories, troubled the consciences of the old Tories and even some of the more humanitarian Whigs and the new Radicals. The utilitarian ideal—that Government should be carried on for the greatest good of the greatest number—began to grow in influence and led to a gradual widening of the electoral franchise. Individualism began to give way to more Collective or Socialist legislation and ideals.[3] Gradually, the working class began to be paid a more fair share of the wealth they produced though the process has, perhaps, still not gone far enough. There is, of course, a still more radical version of this popular history, namely the Marxist version which largely agrees with the version sketched out above as to the sources and origins of the social evils produced in the nineteenth century, but naturally differs about the extent to which they have been alleviated and the causes of that alleviation (if any). On this view, all the improvements in working-class conditions which occurred were concessions wrung from the industrialists to stave off the inevitable revolution.

This popular version of nineteenth-century history owes much to the literary tradition, the literature of protest, the writings of Dickens, Carlyle, and Ruskin, of Wordsworth, Shelley, Coleridge and Byron, and of many others besides. This was a great tradition of writing, but its very popularity even at the time it was written should warn us against assuming too readily that it was a literature of pure dissent. The immense popularity of Dickens, for instance, suggests that he was reflecting public opinion rather than leading it, or moulding it in a different direction.

---

[3] Even here there are many sub-varieties of this version of history, and there are also rival versions of the 'popular' history, e.g. in the works of Sir Arthur Bryant. The precise relationship between Benthamite utilitarianism and individualism is discussed in Chapter 12.

Moreover, even Dickens was often writing about past problems rather than present ones. Mr. Micawber, who went in perpetual fear of imprisonment by his creditors, could have walked the streets in peace at the time when *David Copperfield* was published in 1849–50. Arrest on *mesne* process, that is to say, imprisonment for debt without the judgment of a Court, had been abolished in 1838—perhaps in part as a result of *Pickwick Papers* which had begun to appear in 1836. And *Bleak House* which contained the famous Chancery suit of *Jarndyce* v. *Jarndyce* was not published until 1853 when at least some of the evils there depicted had become a distant memory.[4] The truth is that many, perhaps most, contemporaries of these literary figures would have agreed with much of what they said. There was not, of course, unanimity about social problems and how to deal with them in nineteenth-century England, any more than there is today, but the modern reader will get a very distorted image of how most people reacted to social conditions in the first half of the nineteenth century if he assumes that much of what was attacked by the literary figures of the day was not equally deplored on all hands. The major problem was not to secure agreement in deploring the social ills of the time; it was to discover how best to deal with them.

Towards the end of the nineteenth century this literary tradition began, it seems, to have a significant influence on historians, many of whom wrote with pronounced working-class sympathies, such as the Hammonds and the Webbs.[5] By the early twentieth century this version of the history of the Industrial Revolution had passed into common currency, perhaps with the aid of school history books. In a modified form, it is still supported by some modern historians who make no attempt to conceal their political sympathies.[6]

But there is a rival version of history which owes its origins perhaps chiefly to the works of Sir John Clapham[7] and T. S. Ashton.[8] These historians have stressed the vast new wealth created by the enterprise, skill, and resourcefulness of the entrepreneurs of the Industrial

[4] As pointed out in a review by Lord Denman. See further Chester New, *The Life of Henry Brougham to 1830* (Oxford, 1961), p. 217.

[5] See J. L. and Barbara Hammond, *The Village Labourer* (London, 1911, 4th edn., reprinted 1966), and *The Town Labourer* (London, 1917, reprinted 1949); S. and B. Webb, *History of Trade Unionism* (London, 1894, reprinted 1919). See also the Webbs monumental 11-volume *History of Local Government* (London, 1903–29). An earlier, but more balanced view, is contained in Arnold Toynbee's *The Industrial Revolution*, first published 1884 (reprinted Boston, Mass., 1956). See too M. J. Thomis, *The Town Labourer and the Industrial Revolution* (London, 1974).

[6] For example, E. P. Thompson, *The Making of the English Working Class* and E. J. Hobsbawm, *Industry and Empire*. For the different views of another well-known socialist, see R. H. S. Crossman, Introduction to Walter Bagehot, *The English Constitution* (first published 1867, London, 1963), p. 14: 'The capitalists and entrepreneurs who had become the new ruling class since 1832 were not—as anybody could see who looked at them objectively—the inhuman self-interested money-makers that Benthamite doctrine assumed [*sic*], and Charles Dickens portrayed in *Hard Times*.'

[7] See his *Economic History of Modern Britain*, vol. i (Cambridge, 1926).

[8] See especially, his *The Industrial Revolution, 1760–1830*.

Revolution. The creation of this wealth owed little to the State and nothing to Government planning. What was required was to release the entrepreneur from the old restrictions on industry and trade, together with conditions suited to the accumulation of capital. These conditions—which involved a substantial degree of inequality of wealth—existed in ever greater measure as the eighteenth century wore on, until the Industrial Revolution really began to take off around 1760 or 1770 in the form of self-sustained economic growth. At the same time, huge new increases took place in population; though it is not known whether these increases were caused by, or were a cause of the Industrial Revolution, it seems certain that without the wealth created by the new industries, this explosion of population could not have been sustained. In Ireland, where a comparable population increase took place without an industrial revolution, the result was famine and mass starvation when the people's staple crop failed disastrously in the 1840s. The same fate would, in all probability, have overtaken England had it not been for the Industrial Revolution. At the same time, this version rejects the idea that freedom of contract was merely freedom for the industrialists to exploit the workers. Freedom of contract existed in some measure even for the workers; they moved from the rural agricultural communities in which they had formerly lived and worked, to the new towns in search of work in the factories, and they did this voluntarily because the factories offered higher wages than farm labouring. Indeed, it is still bitterly and furiously controverted whether throughout most of the years of the Industrial Revolution, the workers were not, on average, generally financially better off than they had been before.[9] Of course, by modern standards the workers were extremely poor, but this poverty was the result not of exploitation but of the natural poverty of any well-populated country in the early stages of industrial development.

This version of history then goes on to suggest that the growth of industry and the social problems created by the rapid increase in urban population led to problems of social organization to which there was no immediate and ready answer. Social reform was held up not primarily by ideological adherence to *laissez-faire* principles, as by the absence of adequate Governmental machinery to cope with these new problems. The creation of this administrative machine itself involved another Revolution—a revolution in the modes of government—and was inevitably a slow and gradual process. The building up of a new bureaucratic machine itself depended on the growth of scientific, professional, and legal skills over a wide area, which in turn required yet

[9] See on this debate, Peter Mathias, *The First Industrial Nation*, pp. 213-23; E. P. Thompson, *The Making of the English Working Class*, pp. 207 *et seq.*; A. J. Taylor (ed.), *The Standard of Living in Britain in the Industrial Revolution* (London, 1975).

other social developments, such as changes in education. Roughly speaking, it may be said that this Revolution in Government occupied the period 1800 to 1870 by which time the foundations of the modern administrative machine were firmly laid. The growth of Government was, however, no more planned than the Industrial Revolution itself had been. It was built up by a process of slow accretion in response to particular problems. As will be seen, this book largely accepts the second of these two versions of nineteenth-century history, because in those areas with which I am chiefly concerned, that is with the legal framework of social and economic organization, there is little evidence to support the more popular version.

The Industrial Revolution

Somewhere around 1760 or 1770 England's Industrial Revolution began. It did not at first begin with a dramatic flourish, nor did it begin in a vacuum. In one sense the beginning of the Industrial Revolution was itself the culmination of many long-drawn-out developments, dating back to the Reformation. But towards the end of the eighteenth century it was increasingly apparent that a real Revolution was under way. Its first manifestation was in the production of cotton cloth. Between 1783 and 1820 (despite the fact that Britain had been fighting a bitter war for the greater part of this time) cotton exports increased in value from some £800,000 to over £21 million per annum.[10] By 1871 they were worth over £100 million per annum. Total manufactures increased in value from some £30 million in 1770 to over £348 million in 1871, from 24 per cent to 38 per cent of G.N.P.[11] By 1870 Britain was, without doubt, the greatest industrial nation in the world. 'Over half of the world's coal was raised from her pits, over half its pig-iron and forty per cent of its steel came from British furnaces, and almost half its cotton cloth was spun and woven in British mills. Britain produced well over a third of the world's output of manufactured goods. Her export trade was greater than that of France, Germany and Italy put together, and four times that of the United States'.[12]

The manifestations of these immense changes were visible on all sides. Factories had sprung up everywhere—the 'dark, satanic mills', whole new towns had sprung up—'Coke Towns', dominated by smoking chimneys, and hideous slums, bringing with them enormous problems of sanitation and public health. The changes in population were no less obvious. Even without the new censuses to tell people what was happening, the increasing size of the new industrial towns was visible to all. The population of Britain increased from some 10·69 million in 1801 to 14·21

[10] W. W. Rostow, *How It All Began* (London, 1975), Table 15, pp. 194-5.
[11] Ibid.   [12] Graham Turner, *Business in Britain* (Harmondsworth, 1971), p. 3.

million in 1821, an increase of nearly forty per cent in twenty years. In the next fifty years the increase was even more staggering, from 14·21 million, to 26·16 million.[13] What was worse, the rate of increase was far from even, being heavily concentrated in the new towns of the industrial North. In the ten years between 1821 and 1831 Manchester, Leeds, Bradford, Birmingham, Liverpool, and Sheffield each increased their population by at least forty per cent.[14] Transport too, had been changed out of all recognition. First the new turnpike roads, then the canals, and finally from around 1840, the railways, had changed the face of the country. Britain, and more especially England, had changed from a simple rural agricultural country, to a densely populated, urbanized, and industrial country.

The great new wealth created by these industrial changes did not, it is true, lead to much, if any improvement in the standard of living of the mass of the people until perhaps 1850 or thereabouts. But that is hardly surprising; these very rapid increases of population—though providing labour for the new industries—also led to huge social costs. The capital costs needed to provide any sort of urban housing, water supply, drainage, and sanitation facilities for an additional four million people in twenty years would tax the resources of a modern State. And yet Britain had to deal with this increase between 1801 and 1821 with the barest rudiments of a modern State—without a bureaucracy, without adequate statistics or knowledge of what was going on, without the scientific and professional expertise to cope with the existing problems, let alone to plan for the vastly increased ones.

Even from the beginning of industrialization some of the workers in the factories probably earned more than they had ever earned as agricultural labourers. And some historians believe that in the first twenty or thirty years of the nineteenth century the working classes were, on average, better off then they had been in the eighteenth century, despite—or rather because of—the 'dark, satanic mills' which were creating the new wealth on which the people lived. But averages can be misleading, and there were undoubtedly periods and localities of great hardship during this time. For example, the period 1795–1800 was one of poor harvests and high prices. The price of wheat in 1799 was nearly twice what it had been in 1770 at a time when the condition of the poorer classes still depended very largely on the cost of bread; in 1800 and 1801 the price reached near-famine levels. And as industrialization proceeded some groups of workers whose skills became redundant (like those of the ill-fated hand-loom weavers) sank into ever greater poverty. And then there were the sporadic and severe recessions which marked the early

---

[13] Peter Mathias, *The First Industrial Nation*, Table 1, p. 449.
[14] Asa Briggs, *Victorian Cities* (Harmondsworth, 1968), p. 86.

industrial period when, without a Welfare State to fall back upon, the industrial workers found themselves often unemployed, at a time when it was widely thought that unemployment was due only to idleness or insobriety. But by the middle of the century evidence of greater prosperity began to appear even amongst the working classes. And by 1870 signs began to emerge of the possibility of a really prosperous urban proletariat. For the first time it became possible to believe in the prospect of a society in which the large mass of the people did not live from birth to death in grinding and despairing poverty.

INDIVIDUALISM AND COLLECTIVISM

There is a sense in which the period 1770–1870 saw, first the emergence of a highly individualist society, and then the gradual creation of a collectivist society. But the story is much more complex than it seems at first sight, and there was certainly no moment of time when everything suddenly changed gear, when individualist values and laws were discarded in favour of collectivist values and laws. Both in matters of opinion, and in institutions and the law, the older traditions and the newer ones co-existed uneasily side by side for many years. Indeed, in the law there are marked signs that the still older eighteenth-century, paternalist traditions, handed on the torch to the later collectivist ideas in some areas, even while in other areas the individualism normally associated with the nineteenth century was holding full sway. The history of freedom of contract during this period is inextricably related to these great changes. I must first say a little about some of the background economic and social changes, and I shall then turn to an examination of some of the intellectual influences at work.

The Growth of the Free Market

Closely associated with the Industrial Revolution was the rise of the market economy. It has, indeed, been said, though with some exaggeration, that all the changes which took place 'were merely incidental to one basic change, the establishment of [a] market economy'.[15] Gradually, the old restrictions on the mobility of capital and labour, and to a lesser extent, of land, disappeared. The legal restrictions were (as we have seen) already being dismantled in the late eighteenth century. Freedom of labour was not, indeed, wholly achieved until 1834 when the New Poor Law was enacted, but at least the old Settlement Laws were relaxed in 1795 and this introduced some flexibility into the supply of labour. Middlemen were also springing up everywhere by the late eighteenth century, and though much of the traditional hostility

[15] Karl Polanyi, *The Great Transformation* (Boston, Mass., 1957), p. 40.

against them remained for many years, they were already contributing to the expansion of trade which necessarily accompanied the Industrial Revolution. Bankers facilitated the accumulation and use of capital; factors—paid by commission—speeded the volume of sales; merchants dealing in grain could enable the farmer to turn over his capital more quickly while they were also able to rationalize the distribution of food supplies; foreign currency brokers, insurance brokers, shipping brokers, were all on the scene and ready to play their role in the huge expansion of international trade which began later in the eighteenth century.[16]

Throughout the whole of this period the size of the market was being steadily increased by developments in transportation. I have already referred to the developments which, by mid-century, if not before, had rendered virtually the whole of Britain one market for the new industrial manufactures. Simultaneously, the growth and improvement in shipping services was tending to break down the physical barriers to international trade. For many years a prolonged and acrimonious political debate took place in Britain over the legal restrictions on international free trade, but the debate was virtually terminated by Peel's decision to repeal the Corn Laws in 1846. Although this split the Tory party, and for some years afterwards the new leaders, Derby and Disraeli, attempted to keep alive the protectionist cause, the issue was to all intents and purposes dead. Free trade had won the day, and for the next seventy-five years Britain remained firmly committed to the cause. Towards the end of our period, around 1860 to 1875, there was, fleetingly, something approaching close to a world free trade in capital, goods, and labour.[17] Customs barriers and tariffs almost everywhere came down, the gold standard ensured the free flow of capital—and after the railway boom in England in the 1840s was over, there was so much capital seeking investment that much of it did flow abroad—and restrictions on immigration scarcely existed anywhere. This period of a free world economy—or anyhow something approaching it—lasted scarcely a decade. It was shattered by the tide of protectionism in the 1870s when cheap American corn from the virgin fields of the mid-West began to pour into Europe at prices far below those which could be matched by European farmers. But even then England stubbornly, or tenaciously, according to opinion, clung to its belief in free trade and a free economy. Englishmen were convinced that a free market economy was the road to prosperity for themselves and for the rest of the world. And it was true that the vast increase in international trade had immeasurably increased the range and variety and cheapness of the goods available to the public both in England and elsewhere.

[16] T. S. Ashton, *Economic History of England in the Eighteenth Century*, pp. 66–7; R. B. Westerfield, *Middlemen in English Business* (Yale, 1915, reprinted, New York, 1968), pp. 369 *et seq.*

[17] Karl Polanyi, *The Great Transformation*, Chapter 1; E. J. Hobsbawm, *Industry and Empire*, p. 140.

This was, moreover, a period in which the market in England itself came as close as any market has ever done to operating as freely as economic theory suggested it should. Industry and business was highly and aggressively competitive. When Brunel was known to be building the first iron ship in 1837 designed to operate from Bristol across the Atlantic, two rival companies were rapidly formed to build competitors in order to maintain Liverpudlian supremacy in transatlantic shipping.[18] When the early railway companies were formed, and were laying down their lines—even though each company was largely a monopolist over its own lines—there was the most intense competition in the design of locomotives. Races and other experimental contests were held to test rival designs and often attracted considerable public interest.[19] Even patent stealing was not uncommon in this fiercely competitive period.[20]

Moreover, because this was the first Industrial Revolution, the speed of change, whether by technological innovation, or by organizational and administrative skills, was immense. The penalties for failure, and the rewards for success, both reflected the volatility of a free economy at a time of such rapid change. Supply and demand and competition did regulate prices. Manufacturers were compelled, time and again, to reduce the price of their products, by the pressures of competition. Those who, by skill, resourcefulness, or luck, or by a combination of all three, succeeded, could and did make immense fortunes. The first Sir Robert Peel, father of the Sir Robert who became Prime Minister in 1841, and one of the greatest of the early cotton manufacturers, left a fortune of over a million and a half pounds.[21] The economist and financier David Ricardo retired from business after about 25 years in the City with a fortune of some £700,000 made with an initial capital of £800.[22] Many of these early success stories concerned men who began life with no advantages of any kind. Some were even illiterate. A Mr. Horsfield, who could hardly write his name, and who began life with 'not five shillings in the world', was, in 1837, worth at least £300,000.[23] Samuel Smiles, besides preaching the gospel of self-help, recounted many of these success stories in his hugely successful books.[24] The prizes that could be won by success were so great that many were tempted to take immense risks. Entrepreneurs 'with exceedingly little technical knowledge were

[18] L. T. C. Rolt, *Isambard Kingdom Brunel* (Harmondsworth, 1974), p. 253.

[19] Ibid., pp. 200-1.

[20] Some examples are given in Samuel Smiles, *Self-Help* (first published 1859, centenary edn., London, 1958), pp. 78-9.

[21] E. J. Hobsbawm, *Industry and Empire*, pp. 62-3.

[22] R. M. Hartwell, Introduction to Ricardo, *Principles of Political Economy and Taxation* (Harmondsworth, 1971), pp. 34-43.

[23] M. W. Thomas, *The Early Factory Legislation* (Westport, Conn., 1970), p. 4.

[24] See especially *Self-Help*.

prepared to risk large sums of money in manufacturing ventures'.[25] By modern standards many of these risks were imprudent to the point of madness. In the railway age, for example, railway contracting was one way to make a rapid fortune, but estimating for railway work was unbelievably crude. Those whose tenders were low enough to be accepted, but high enough to cover the cost, stood to make immense fortunes; those whose tenders turned out too low could lose every penny they possessed.[26]

The speed with which everything was happening meant also that there was little time for research and experimentation with new ideas, new technologies, before they were tried out in earnest. Vast sums were risked on new engineering and scientific projects which, by modern standards, had been quite inadequately researched and tested. Once again, the rewards of success were high and the penalties for failure correspondingly severe. The threat of failure, of bankruptcy, of personal financial disaster, was ever present to the industrialists and financiers of the early nineteenth century. 'The major worry was "failure". In a period when hectic booms alternated with financial panics and there was no such thing as limited liability, the business magnate and the public investor were haunted by specters of bankruptcy and the debtor's jail'.[27] The intense activity in litigation and in bankruptcy proceedings testifies to the reality of these fears. Legal cases in the Law Reports from this period often show immense sums of money at stake which would have meant the total difference between prosperity and ruin to the parties involved. Risks were concentrated and not spread. Rarely does modern litigation have, for any given individual, the same measure of personal financial involvement as frequently occurred in the first half of the nineteenth century. And the bankruptcy laws at this period were far more important than they have ever been before or since, as the number of books written on the subject attests. For one man's failure often triggered off a whole series of other failures. Innocent partners, guarantors, and creditors could go down in the holocaust when a major business failure occurred.

This free market economy was, moreover, very much a market of individuals. It is true that here and there statutory companies— companies in the modern sense, with limited liability—had been brought into existence by Parliament. The canals, for instance, had been mostly built by such bodies because the amount of capital necessary normally required some contribution from large numbers of investors. And, again

[25] P. L. Payne, *British Entrepreneurship in the Nineteenth Century* (London and Basingstoke, 1974), p. 34.

[26] Terry Coleman, *The Railway Navvies* (Harmondsworth, 1968), pp. 62-3.

[27] Walter E. Houghton, *The Victorian Frame of Mind 1830-1870* (New Haven, Conn., and London, 1957), p. 60.

given the risks involved, it was not easy to create a company with a large number of investors without limited liability, for this required each investor to stake his whole personal fortune on the integrity and competence of those who joined in the enterprise with him. The more of them there were, the greater the risks, and the less the chance of knowing each partner in the business. And when the railway companies arrived on the scene, the same considerations applied to them too. But until 1855 limited liability was the exception, not the rule; and this meant that most businesses were in a very real sense run by individual entrepreneurs, or by small numbers of entrepreneurs, joined together in partnership by mutual selection and mutual agreement. The days of the remote, impersonal investor, interested in the dividends and not otherwise involved with the success or failure of the business, only arrived in a large way with the gradual growth of the modern public company, a development which hardly got under way before 1870.

The belief in individualism as a moral and economic ideal—about which I shall have more to say later—was, in the first half of the nineteenth century, not unmatched by the reality of social and economic organization. Society was not yet organized in institutions to any significant degree. Neither Government itself (at any rate, till the 1830s or 1840s) nor local government, possessed institutional bureaucracies. Business and industry were still, as I have just observed, largely in the hands of individuals, or groups of individuals, not yet united in institutional shape. Workers, it is true, were constantly striving to set up Unions, or Combinations as they were then called, and—as we shall see—this was a continual source of trouble both politically and in the law. But the whole thrust both of the ideology and of the reality of the market economy and the free society in the first half of the nineteenth century was towards an atomistic view of the individual's role. In one sense, indeed, this democratic-industrial society 'was not a society at all. Men and classes were no longer integral parts of a Christian-feudal organism where everyone has his recognised place and function and was united to Church and State by established rights and duties. In the new liberal theory all men were free, politically and economically, owing no one any service beyond the fulfilment of legal contracts; and society was simply a collection of individuals, each motivated—naturally and rightly—by self-interest'.[28]

Naturally this individualist society based on a free economy produced great inequalities of wealth. Such inequalities were, of course, not new. There had always been 'the rich' and 'the poor', and in some agricultural societies the gulf between them was larger than that in nineteenth-century England. But in the past the difference was that almost everyone

---

[28] Ibid., p. 76.

belonged to 'the poor'; in a poor society—and every agricultural society (unless it is very sparsely populated) must necessarily be poor—nearly all the population are poor. The rich, in the eighteenth century, consisted of no more than a few hundred large landowners, and perhaps a few thousand smaller ones. These inequalities had been due to birth and inheritance. In the great majority of cases the eighteenth-century rich had still been rich because of who they or their ancestors were, rather than because of anything they or their ancestors had done. In the industrial conditions of the early nineteenth century this was beginning to change. Side by side with the old landowners, there was growing up a new class of rich businessmen and industrialists. These people were rich not because of who they were, but because of what they did. Like the old rich they believed, naturally enough, in a society and an economic system which threw up inequalities. They did not believe in political equality for all, and they certainly did not believe in any ideal of economic equality. I shall return later to what they did believe in but I wish to emphasize here that the new industrial middle classes of England brought with them some very insistent desires and demands, and it was their gradual success in achieving these which in the end largely destroyed the individualist society and the free market economy which had brought them power and prosperity. They wanted law and order in the streets; they wanted an end to filth and slums and insanitary houses; they wanted regularity in life, in business, in the payment of debts and the observance of contracts; they wanted greater decency and refinement in life, an end to barbarities and cruelties, to the slave trade, to the pillory and public executions, to public drunkenness, to the employment of children as chimney sweeps and women in coal mines.[29]

They discovered that they could not achieve these ends by reliance on the individualist society and the free market although they often spoke and wrote as if they thought they could have the best of both worlds. In this age of Individualism, often still thought of as the age of *laissez-faire*, the new middle classes set about the creation of a wholly new kind of society in which administrative powers and processes replaced, as modes of social and economic control, the discipline of free choice and freedom of contract. Because this is so contrary to the received version of nineteenth-century history—or at least that version which is still generally current among modern English lawyers—I must say something about the source of this older version.

Dicey and Laissez-Faire

In his *Lectures on Law and Public Opinion in England During the Nineteenth*

[29] T. S. Ashton, *The Industrial Revolution*, p. 115. This verdict is emphatically confirmed by Francis Place in his *Autobiography* (Cambridge, 1962). Writing in 1833, he had no doubt that the laws and manners of fifty years before were infinitely 'more unfeeling and barbarous', p. 62.

Century, first published in 1905, A. V. Dicey[30] gave wide currency to the belief that social reform had been held up in the middle of the nineteenth century by an ideological belief in the doctrines of *laissez-faire*. Dicey saw the nineteenth century as falling into three phases; first the period of 'old Toryism', as he called it, from 1800 (perhaps earlier) to 1820 or 1825; second, the era of 'Benthamite liberalism', which he associated with the ideal of *laissez-faire*, and which lasted from 1820 or 1825 until around 1870; and finally, an era of collectivism which began around 1870 and was still flourishing with ever increasing vigour at the end of the century, by which time 'the doctrine of *laissez-faire*, in spite of the large elements of truth which it contains, had more or less lost its hold upon the English people'.[31]

Dicey was not the only person to think of the nineteenth century in this way. During the mid-nineteenth century many popularizers of the new political economy, such as Harriet Martineau (who wrote many simple tales in *Illustrations of Political Economy*)[32] and James Wilson, editor of the *Economist*, adopted the most extreme and uncompromising form of *laissez-faire* doctrines.[33] And if the popularizers were not influential enough on their own to convince history that this was the age of *laissez-faire*, their opponents helped the cause along. The thunderous onslaughts of Carlyle on the 'pig philosophy' of the political economists, as he called it,[34] were matched only by his denunciations of the 'do-nothingism' of *laissez-faire*. Robert Southey, poet and Radical turned Tory, was another who assumed that the new commercial morality which he detested had taken over: 'Throughout the trading part of the community everyone endeavours to purchase at the lowest price and sell at the highest, regardless of equity in either case'.[35] He too attacked *laissez-faire* as though it were the dominant philosophy of the age. Thomas Arnold was another. In the 1830s he criticized *laissez-faire* as 'one of the falsest maxims which ever pandered to human selfishness under the name of political wisdom ... We stand by and let this most unequal race take its course forgetting that the very name of society implies that it shall not be a mere race, but that its object is to provide for the common good of all'.[36]

But of course, the most influential writer of all was Charles Dickens. In *Hard Times* (first published in 1854) Dickens satirized unmercifully what he took to be the commercial morality of the age, and bitterly attacked

[30] London, 2nd edn., 1914, reprinted 1962.

[31] Ibid., p. xxxi.

[32] London, 1832-4, 9 volumes.

[33] Scott-Gordon, 'The London *Economist* and the High-Tide of Laissez Faire', 63 *Journal of Political Economy* 461 (1955). Herbert Spencer was assistant editor of the *Economist* from 1846 to 1853.

[34] 'Essay in Jesuitism' in the *Latter Day Pamphlets* (vol. xx, *Complete Works*, London, 1898), pp. 315-18 (first published, 1850).

[35] Cited, R. Williams, *Culture and Society*, p. 42.

[36] Ibid., pp. 123 4.

the resulting hideousness of Coketown. In this novel Dickens quite specifically took a side-swipe at the philosophy of *laissez-faire*, characteristically putting the attack into the mouth of the honest working man, Stephen Blackpool. When asked what was wrong with Coketown, he disclaimed knowledge of what would put things right, but he knew well enough what would not do so:

The strong hand will not do't. Vict'ry and triumph will never do't. Agreeing fer to mak' one side unnaturally and awlus and for ever right, and to other side unnat'rally alwus and for ever wrong, will never, never, do't. Nor yet lettin' alone will never do't. Let thousands upon thousands alone, aw leading the like lives and all faw'en into the like muddle, and they will be as one, and yo will be as another wi' a black unpassable world betwixt yo . . .

Opponents of a political or social philosophy are always prone to exaggerate its influence and importance as much as they over-emphasize its least attractive features; and we have been well reminded that 'the political concepts which are today out of fashion are known to most of our contemporaries only through the picture drawn of them by their enemies'.[37] The influence as well as the unattractiveness of the philosophy of *laissez-faire* were exaggerated to the point of caricature by its contemporary opponents, and it was their views which passed into later history.

There was, of course, just enough truth in it to make it plausible, and to explain why subsequent historians like Dicey found *laissez-faire* at the centre of nineteenth-century history. It is true that Englishmen had at this time a distrust for Government, especially central Government. They thought that Governments were bureaucratic, corrupt, inefficient, and a source of tyranny and oppression—as most Governments in the world were. It is also true that most Englishmen then, as now, disliked paying more taxes for Government expenditure even when they were satisfied that it was really needed. It is again true that (as we shall see) the classical economists, from Adam Smith on, had argued for the removal of many obsolete controls and restrictions on the free market which they believed, generally rightly, to be harmful to the prosperity of the nation. It is true that the legacy of Locke, with his belief in the minimal State, designed to protect life and property, was still not without force. It is true, also, that if there was no coherent and systematic philosophy of *laissez-faire*, except among its opponents, there was 'a well used set of *laissez-faire* clichés which possessed emotional appeal'.[38] It is true that on many specific issues politicians and publicists who opposed Government activity would use whatever arguments lay to hand and the principle of *laissez-faire* was often one of those arguments.

[37] F. A. Hayek, *Individualism and the Economic Order* (London, 1949), p. 3.
[38] W. L. Burn, *The Age of Equipoise* (London, 1968), p. 289.

But it is emphatically *not* true that any influential body of persons ever believed in *laissez-faire* as a *system*, that is, believed that Government should confine itself to the minimum role of securing the national defence and maintaining law and order. Nor is it true that there was any time in the nineteenth century when, on specific social problems, *laissez-faire* principles determined for any prolonged period the beliefs of the political economists or the policy of the Government, or the votes of the legislature. Almost every modern historian who has written on this question has come to the same conclusion[39]—the idea of an age of *laissez-faire* is a myth, 'one of the grander misunderstandings of intellectual history'.[40] The myth was propagated by Dicey who totally overlooked the extent of Parliamentary and Governmental interference, the vast mass of legislative intervention with freedom of contract and the free market, which can be traced back to the very beginnings of the nineteenth century, as well as the enormous growth of the Government bureaucratic machine which this legislation necessitated. *Law and Public Opinion*, says one of Dicey's modern critics,

is essentially the work of a lawyer and student of political ideas rather than that of an historian. Dicey marks change in terms of changes in the law. He does not ask how or whether a law was enforced, or how or whether it changed people's lives. And he finds reasons for legal changes almost exclusively in terms of abstractions . . . Simply, practical government did not exist for Dicey.[41]

Other modern critics have been even more outspoken: '*Law and Opinion* is a highly misleading book, and if we are misled about the nineteenth century revolution in government, it is largely because Dicey has misled us.'[42] And yet another dismisses *Law and Public Opinion* as a 'political pamphlet which has been unfortunately mistaken for good history for half a century.'[43]

I have reviewed at some length this crescendo of criticism for two reasons. First, because so many English lawyers have been brought up on Dicey's *Law and Public Opinion* and are likely to regard his ideas as an

[39] E. J. Hobsbawm, *Industry and Empire*, seems the only exception. He virtually repeats the old Diceyan myths: 'Few countries have ever been more totally dominated by an *a priori* doctrine than Britain was by *laissez faire* economics': p. 230. See also Calvin Woodard, 'Reality and Social Reform: The Transition from *Laissez Faire* to the Welfare State', 72 *Yale Law J.* 286 (1962).

[40] George Watson, *The English Ideology* (London, 1973), p. 69.

[41] O. MacDonagh, *A Pattern of Government Growth: The Passenger Acts 1800–1860* (London, 1961), p. 325. See also his 'The Nineteenth Century Revolution in Government: A Re-Appraisal', 1 *Historical Journal* 52 (1958).

[42] Henry Parris, 'The Nineteenth Century Revolution in Government: A Re-Appraisal Re-Appraised', 3 *Historical Journal* 17 (1960), p. 18. See also, for similar criticisms, G. Kitson Clark, *The Making of Victorian England* (Edinburgh, 1972), *passim*; W. L. Burn, *The Age of Equipoise*, pp. 132–3: W. C. Lubenow, *The Politics of Government Growth* (Newton Abbott and Hamden, Conn., 1971), p. 9.

[43] Flinn, Introduction to E. Chadwick, *The Sanitary Conditions of the Labouring Population of Great Britain* (reprinted, Edinburgh, 1965), p. 38.

illuminating contribution to the history of freedom of contract. The reality is, as we shall see, that in a great many areas, Dicey's contributions are so misleading that the modern reader will need to put aside any preconceptions he may have about the age of *laissez-faire* if he is to understand the history of freedom of contract. But there is another and more interesting question of particular concern to the lawyer. In thinking that *laissez-faire* was a more important and more influential philosophy than it had ever really been, was Dicey sharing a misconception common to the generality of the legal profession? Dicey clearly linked *laissez-faire* with freedom of contract in the legal sense. He thought that the belief in the extensions of freedom which marked mid-nineteenth century England (and which reached their apogee in Mill's *On Liberty* in 1859) naturally justified the idea of freedom of contract (even though Mill himself refused to draw this conclusion in *On Liberty*).

Once admit [says Dicey] that A, B or C can each, as a rule, judge more correctly than can anyone else of his own interest, and the conclusion naturally follows that, in the absence of force or fraud, A or B ought to be allowed to bind themselves to one another by any agreement which they choose to make—i.e. which in the view of each of them promotes his own interest, or in other words, is conducive to his own happiness.[44]

It seems quite likely that Dicey was, in 1905, reflecting a strong legal professional tradition. English lawyers are as a rule, very conservative people, not merely in their current beliefs, but also in their beliefs about history. Moreover, when lawyers encounter ideas from outside the law, as they do from time to time, they tend to absorb a smattering of these ideas which may then remain with them, handed down from generation to generation, until they emerge from their narrow professional interests to look at the same problem perhaps fifty or a hundred years later. I shall return to this theme when I come to examine the developments which took place in the common law of contract in the nineteenth century. We shall then see that there is some evidence to support the view that ideas based on *laissez-faire* principles may well have had more influence on the judges and on judge made law than they did on any other organ of the State. And English lawyers tend to look at the common law as the repository of principle, and Statute law as a series of modifications, exceptions, and anomalous cases not based on any coherent social philosophy. Indeed, it went further than that, for in the particular case of contract, the statutory changes were gradually expelled from the emergent conceptual scheme of a general law of contract based on free market principles. The common-law concept of contract retained its purity and its basis in the free market only by a process of definition.

[44] *Law and Public Opinion*, pp. 150-1.

Everything which did not fit the scheme of the free market, or of the general principles of contract law which were based on the free market, was simply defined as not being part of the law of contract, but of some other special and exceptional body of rules—company law, or factories legislation, or building regulations, or sanitary laws, or licensing requirements, or any one of a hundred other different branches of social or economic activity.[45] The law of contract became increasingly pure at the very same time that the volume of regulatory law was increasing. As we shall see, this had important results on the way in which the common law developed, and on the value system which the legal profession carried over into the twentieth century.

Why did this happen? Part of the answer is very simple. The modern historians, whose views I have quoted above, are unanimous on one point. England stumbled into the modern administrative State without design, and even contrary to the inclinations of most Englishmen. They dealt with social problems, one by one, as these were brought to their attention by the stream of investigations, Blue Books, inquiries, and by the simple process of accretion of knowledge. Without fully appreciating what they were doing Englishmen were busy laying the foundations of the modern bureaucratic State. 'Many men, even intelligent men in a position to know, such as journalists or Members of Parliament, did not realise what was happening, and when they came upon traces of it they were angry. They had sometimes willed the end but they had seldom willed the means by which alone it could be reached.'[46] So far as lawyers were concerned it may seem even more surprising that they did not realize what was happening as the legislation multiplied, but in fact the explanation for their ignorance is simple. This vast new body of law was not in general enforced by the lawyers at all. Its enforcement lay, in the first instance, in the hands of the new bureaucracy, the new administrative staff and their expert advisers who were multiplying so rapidly in the middle of the century. The earliest attempts to use the superior Courts as enforcement machinery—and there are signs of this in the 1830s—were rapidly abandoned in the light of experience. And when judicial enforcement was required as a last resort against recalcitrant men or institutions, the new administrators and their legislation turned increasingly to the local magistrates courts. Despite their inadequacies, despite the fact that they were so often chaired by Justices of the Peace more sympathetic to those accused of offences under the new type of legislation than to the victims, these courts had incomparable advantages over the superior Courts when it came to enforcing the legislation. Only

---

[45] This idea was first developed by Lawrence M. Friedman, *Contract Law in America* (Madison and Milwaukee, 1965).

[46] G. Kitson Clark, *The Making of Victorian England*, p. 109.

very rarely were cases brought before the superior Courts, on appeal from the local justices, in matters of this kind, and when they were the judges had very little perception of the fact that they were only seeing the tip of an immense iceberg. It is not true that they were generally unsympathetic to the legislation themselves—there are instances where they were clearly far more sympathetic to it, and enforced it far more impartially than the local justices—but they simply were inexperienced in handling problems of law concerning administrative matters in this new age. The result was that this revolution in Government to a substantial degree grew up silently, unnoticed by the lawyers as it was unnoticed by most Englishmen. Indeed, lawyers may well have been even slower to grasp the significance of what was happening than many other important sections of the community. It is hardly possible that Lord Hewart could have written his tirade against the new administrative state in 1929—*The New Despotism*, he called it—if he had had much understanding of this chapter of his country's history. Had the book been written eighty years earlier, its influence might have been incalculable, for it would have compelled Englishmen to face up to what they were doing to their cherished legal system. But Lord Hewart had been brought up on Dicey's *Law and Public Opinion* to believe that the State's administrative machine did not exist prior to the twentieth century, and like many other lawyers he only awoke to the reality in the 1920s almost a hundred years after the process had got substantially under way.

9

THE ROLE OF GOVERNMENT, 1770–1870

In Part I we reviewed the state of the machinery of Government up to 1770, and we saw how up to that time England was still an extraordinarily undergoverned country. Basically a rural society and an agricultural economy it simply ticked over with virtually no administrative processes, under the vaguely benevolent eye of the Whig-dominated Parliament and the somewhat sterner eye of the judges. But what was possible in this simple and relatively sparsely populated period became manifestly impossible under the pressure of industrialization, urbanization, and the seemingly endless and explosive increase in the sheer number of human beings. Between 1770 and 1870 the whole machinery of Government had to be overhauled, indeed, it had to be created virtually out of nothing. I cannot tell the whole of this story here, but it has an important and direct bearing on the theme of this work. For it will be appreciated that, as the role of Government increases, the role of the individual decreases. As Governments make more decisions and undertake more activities, what the individual citizen *must* do if society is to function at all is necessarily reduced, and what he *may* do is also likely to be reduced. In this chapter I propose merely to sketch some of the principal problems which arose in the creation of this new administrative machine, and the significance of what was happening for its bearing upon the role of individual decision-making in society. In Chapter 16 I shall examine in some detail a number of key areas in which legislative interference with freedom of contract played a particularly prominent role in nineteenth-century development.

The Obstacles to Government Growth

I must begin by indicating briefly some of the immense difficulties which were encountered in the creation of the new administrative State. These difficulties were quite enough—without dragging in the supposed ideological commitment to *laissez-faire*—to explain why it took seventy years to build the modern State. Indeed, as one looks at some of these difficulties, what seems surprising is not that the pace of reform was so slow, but that the change was very largely accomplished within three-quarters of a century, and accomplished without any loss of civil freedoms, and without any of the internal political upheavals and the accompanying bloodshed which affected virtually every other major nation in the world at some time during this period.

It is not necessary to assume reactionary political views, or class hatred, or lack of compassion for the poor, to understand the sense of helplessness with which many people viewed some of the appalling social problems of, say, the 1820s, 1830s, or 1840s. To many of them, the problems must have seemed as baffling and insoluble as do those of a modern Asian country whose population expands as fast, if not faster, than its G.N.P. In one respect, the problems were less severe, for at least G.N.P. was rising so fast that eventually it provided the wealth which enabled these social problems to be overcome without any sacrifice of political freedoms. But in some respects the problems were even worse, for they were all new, and the remedies for them were unknown and had to be discovered.

Indeed, many doubted whether there were any remedies. To many, the country was in the grip of a Malthusian situation of over-population which could take years to right itself, and would never right itself at all if the poor continued to reproduce at the same rate. And the idea that the economic and social conditions of the country were largely the outcome of 'Laws of Nature' over which man had little if any control, was still extremely powerful, even among those who would have counted as radical reformers. In the Report of the Poor Law Commissioners in 1834 (a Report largely drafted by Edwin Chadwick, perhaps the greatest social reformer of the day),[1] for example, we find it insisted that the existing Poor Laws were doomed to failure because they 'attempt to repeal *pro tanto* that law of nature by which the effects of each man's improvidence or misconduct are borne by himself and his family'.[2]

Even among those who rationalized less consciously about Natural Laws, or the threat of over-population, this sense of helplessness was strong. George Greville, writing in his Diary in 1832, described Bethnal Green in these terms:

The district is in a complete state of insolvency and hopeless poverty, yet they multiply, and while the people look squalid and dejected as if borne down by their wretchedness and destitution, the children thrive and are healthy. Government is ready to interpose with assistance, but what can Government do?[3]

This sense of helplessness in face of the facts, this acknowledgement of the limits to which men can remedy the ills they find around them, was,

---

[1] The economist Nassau Senior was the other person principally responsible for the Report. A new edition of the Report, ed. S. G. and E. O. A. Checkland, is now available in a Pelican edition (Harmondsworth, 1974). Page references are to this edition.

[2] Ibid., p. 156.

[3] *The Greville Diary*, ed. P. W. Wilson (London, 1927), i. 303-4, 17 February 1832.

of course, very old. In all previous ages the governing classes had comforted themselves with the reflection that there had always been rich and poor, and that it could not be otherwise. Had not Pitt himself commented on the limits which natural events placed on Ministerial power? Had not Addington written, in 1812, that 'Man cannot create abundance where Providence has inflicted scarcity?'[4] Before we dismiss such thoughts and remarks as the comfortable rationalizations of those who sought to maintain a privileged status there are two points that should be borne in mind. The first is that it is probably psychologically impossible for human beings to believe themselves—for any sustained period of time—to be responsible for, or for changing, a state of affairs which they do not have the power to change. Indeed, our very notion of responsibility (and cause, which is allied to it) is, without doubt, closely related to questions of capacity. He who does not have the capacity to control or change a situation is not normally regarded as responsible for it. The second point which needs to be borne in mind is that the great confidence—the over-confidence—which society has today in its ability to change the circumstances in which people live, is the result of three great revolutions directly traceable to the early nineteenth century. The first was the scientific and technological developments which underlay the innovations of the Industrial Revolution, and which led men to dream of the total control of their physical environment; the second was the gradual accretion of detailed knowledge of the social problems; and the third was the Benthamite message which taught men that the legislative machine could be used to control the social and institutional environment.[5]

The first of these developments falls far outside the scope of this work; the second I deal with below; the third I shall return to in Chapter 12. Here I merely emphasize that until these developments had done their work—perhaps by 1850 it was largely done—many men still felt a sense of helplessness in the face of the immense social problems they saw around them. And it was this which led so many to place their trust in individualism. If the State simply could not cope, if mankind collectively was unable to deal with social problems, then individuals must look to their own salvation. If poverty itself could not be abolished—and in 1800, even in 1850, the abolition of poverty was simply a Utopian dream—then the only hope was for some individuals to climb out of the class of the poor by their own exertions, skill, and enterprise.

[4] R. J. White, *From Waterloo to Peterloo* (Harmondsworth, 1957), p. 111.

[5] The origins of the nineteenth-century revolution in Government are still traced by different protagonists to one or other of these key developments (or some other alternative such as Tory paternalism), though it is difficult to understand why it so often seems assumed that they are mutually exclusive alternatives. For a survey, see Aydelotte, 'The Conservative and Radical Interpretation of Early Victorian Social Legislation', 11 *Victorian Studies* 225 (1967).

The feeling of helplessness about most of the social problems of the day, especially, of course, the one overriding problem of the poverty of the mass of the people, was not, in (say) 1800, or even 1820, by any means an unfounded one. Let us consider some of the problems faced by Government at that time, even by those who would not have been unwilling to do what they could. The first problem was, perhaps, that of the Government's own ignorance of the nature and scope of the problems themselves. Twentieth-century historians know far more about the social problems of 1800 or 1830 than the Government itself knew about the problems at the time. Until 1800 there had never been a census in England; nobody knew how many people there were in the country, nor even whether the number was increasing or decreasing; estimates on these questions varied wildly. The first census, held in 1801, is today generally thought to have been very inaccurate, and even that did not tell Government for sure that the population was increasing until the next census ten years later. And a third census was really necessary before it was possible to become reasonably confident that a significant trend was in operation, from which future prognostications could be made.

And how were these prognostications to be made anyhow? Who was to make them? The science of statistics was still in its infancy, and the Government itself did not collect any statistics. Not till 1832 was a statistical division set up in the Board of Trade followed a year later by the founding of the Royal Statistical Society.[6] And in these early days the Government figures were often wildly unreliable; in the census of 1831 there are two separate figures given for the total acreage of England, with a discrepancy between them as large as Berkshire.[7]

Population figures alone did not tell much, nor even did changes in population figures reveal vitally important information about trends in (for example) birth rates and death rates. Not until 1838, when registration of births, marriages, and deaths was first instituted, did it become possible to ascertain variations in death rates, for instance, which revealed that some areas of the country were so much more dangerous to live in than others.

And the collection of statistics was only the beginning. When it became known (for example) that this town had a far higher death rate than that one, the next question was to ascertain the cause. This was no easy task either. Medical science was still in an extremely rudimentary state by modern standards. Not until the twentieth century did doctors discover what was the cause of typhus; and the most violent controversies raged

[6] G. M. Young, *Victorian England, Portrait of an Age*, 2nd edn. (London, Oxford, New York, reprinted 1973), p. 32.
[7] Ibid.

about the causes and the mode of the spread of the dreaded cholera. Many people, especially those who (like Chadwick) studied the statistics, did believe that it had something vaguely to do with filth and lack of sanitation, but how, and how to prevent it, were matters of the greatest scientific controversy.[8] And suppose then that people could be persuaded that sanitation was the way to cope with the medical and public health problem, the next stage was to learn how to improve the sanitary facilities. The answer to these problems, too, did not simply lie at hand, waiting for indolent Government ministers to propose the necessary legislation. The answers had first to be found. For a start, water supplies were grossly inadequate for the vastly swollen towns of the mid-nineteenth century. In 1845 only 5,000 of Bristol's 130,000 inhabitants, less than a quarter of Manchester's, and about a fifth of Birmingham's population, had piped water. Much of this water was insanitary and even dangerous.[9] In 1854 it was finally discovered that water was one of the prime sources of the spread of cholera epidemics, but already by then the most vigorous efforts were being made to improve the water supplies by installing many miles of new pipe, building new reservoirs, and imposing standards of purification. And as to the development of proper sanitation, drainage, and sewage disposal, here again, the first necessities were to ascertain the nature of the problem and then to devise the basic methods of dealing with them. Everything was new and had to be tackled from first principles. Even when the basic decisions were taken, the scientific and engineering controversies as to the methods were endless. What kind of drain pipes, how to manufacture them, how to lay them, what fall was required to dispose of the sewage, and hundreds of similar questions remained to be answered. 'It is impossible to overstate the primitiveness of sanitary science in 1847.'[10] Even the use of spirit levels to measure the levels of drains and sewers was new.[11] The very pipes needed to service the sewers and drains had to be designed, and manufactured. 'To talk as though there was a vast supply of these materials piled up somewhere, approved by all the eminent civil engineers and public health "experts", and only prevented from being used by the selfishness of "vested interest", is to talk nonsense. There had to be trial and error in the technological as well as in the administrative field; and, embarrassingly, these two processes had to go on at the same time.'[12]

What was true of sanitary problems was true of virtually every social

[8] See S. E. Finer, *The Life and Times of Sir Edwin Chadwick* (London, 1952), pp. 341-2, for some of the fantastic theories current about the causes of cholera.

[9] Brian Harrison, *Drink and the Victorians* (London, 1971), pp. 298-9.

[10] S. E. Finer, *Life and Times of Sir Edwin Chadwick*, p. 298.

[11] Ibid., p. 216.

[12] W. L. Burn, *The Age of Equipoise*, p. 137.

evil. In the modern world, when the Government collects vast quantities of information and statistics on every subject under the sun, when newsmen and television cameras and photographers bring pictures of this or that event into every home in the land almost as soon as it occurs, it is difficult to conceive of a state of society in which only the vaguest and most shadowy knowledge of social problems was diffused through the public. In case after case the first serious investigation of the facts, and the first publication of a Report, made a tremendous impact on Parliament and public alike, and the demands for immediate action were no less insistent then than they would be today.

The first of the long series of Passenger Acts—of which I shall have more to say later—was passed in 1803, early in Dicey's period of 'Old Toryism', and it was passed as a result of a violent wave of indignation sparked off by the mere discovery of some very shocking facts about the emigrant passenger trade which had not hitherto been public knowledge. The facts were brought to light almost by accident, as a result of a Commons Committee investigation into a totally different topic, and instantly a comprehensive Bill was prepared and passed without a single dissenting voice being raised against it.[13] Professor MacDonagh, who has written at length about the history of the Passenger Acts, regards this first Act as introducing 'a revolutionary principle to English law', an unprecedented interference with freedom of contract. 'The innovation was the interference of the legislation with freedom of contract—for buying a passage was after all to make a contract—upon the ground that the free, sane and adult citizens concerned required a peculiar statutory protection in these transactions.'[14] Professor MacDonagh is a historian, and not a lawyer, or he might have appreciated that in 1803 the principle of freedom of contract, in the sense in which he uses it, was barely established. We have already seen something of the paternalism of eighteenth-century Equity, and of the extent of the protection afforded by the law to poor and ignorant persons who were led into unfair, oppressive, or extortionate bargains.

I will return to the Passenger Acts later. My present concern is to show that one of the principal factors holding up social reform at this period was not a belief in *laissez-faire* or freedom of contract, but ignorance of the evils and of how to remedy them. Other examples are not hard to find. The appalling conditions of work in the coal mines, especially the use of children and women in hard manual labour underground, made a deeply disturbing impression on the nation when the facts came out—once again largely by accident—as a result of a voluntary investigation and Report made in 1836 by one of the Commissioners studying the state of

[13] O. MacDonagh, *A Pattern of Government Growth*, pp. 58–9.
[14] Ibid., p. 59.

the handloom weavers. When Ashley—later Lord Shaftesbury, the most famous of the Tory social reformers—told the Commons of this Report the outcry was so great that a Royal Commission was at once set up to investigate the facts fully. Legislation was introduced as soon as the Report was received and passed overwhelmingly.

Poverty itself, the one great social question which oppressed all thinkers and politicians, was extremely difficult to measure. I have already spoken of the increase in population, but there was no less difficulty in knowing the levels of wages and prices in the different parts of the country. In 1839 Carlyle, in his work on *Chartism*, refers to the lack of adequate knowledge of wages in any part of the country, what were the levels of unemployment, how they fluctuated from year to year and season to season, whether labourers were able to save, and if so, whether their position was improving or worsening. 'The simple fundamental question,' he complained, 'Can the labouring man in this England of ours, who is willing to labour, find work, and subsistence by his work? is matter of mere conjecture and assertion hitherto, not ascertained by authentic evidence.'[15]

Even when the information was finally becoming more available, and even when scientific opinion began to harden as to the best ways of dealing with various questions, the public still had to be educated to understand the necessity for the remedies. In a free society, the Government had patiently to educate the public to a willingness to pay the taxes for the measures even after they themselves became aware of their necessity. Here too, it is hard for the modern reader to appreciate the ignorance of educated men of the early nineteenth century on (for instance) such matters as the relationship between filth and disease. In 1854 Palmerston lamented that his fellow countrymen were still so parsimonious about spending on public health measures, commenting that at Newcastle, where cholera had struck in 1849, they had waited to 'see their neighbours perish around them and risk the lives of their wives and children and their own, rather than ward off the dangers by arrangements which might involve a sixpenny rate forgetting or not knowing that in the end such measures would be a real economy of money'.[16]

The patient gathering of knowledge on the social problems thrown up by the industrialization and urbanization of England began in a serious and reasonably systematic way with the return to power of the Whigs in 1830. Behind this desire to search out the facts one can discern two powerful influences at work. One was the Benthamite influence,

---

[15] *Critical and Miscellaneous Essays*, reprinted in the *Works of Carlyle* (London, 1898), iv. 127–8.
[16] David Roberts, *Victorian Origins of the British Welfare State* (New Haven, Conn., 1960), pp. 282–3.

beginning to be felt through his friends and disciples amongst the Whigs and Radicals, men who believed, as Bentham had so vigorously preached, that society could be ordered by legislation, but that it was first necessary to gather the facts. And secondly, one can discern the gradual growth of professionalism, as the Radical politicians and the middle-class professional men—the new doctors, engineers, scientists, accountants, businessmen, and even the maligned lawyers, began to turn away from the casual amateurism of eighteenth-century Whiggism. From the 1830s onwards a vast number of serious investigations began by Royal Commissions, individual Commissioners, and Parliamentary Select Committees, and the resulting information was widely published in the Press and discussed among the public and in Parliament. The process began with the Royal Commission into the Poor Laws in 1832, and it proceeded apace after that. 'In a few years the public mind had been flooded with facts and figures bearing on every branch of the national life . . . No community in history had ever been submitted to so searching an examination. Copied or summarized in the Press, the Blue Books created a new attitude to affairs; they provided fresh topics for moralists and fresh themes for poets.'[17] They also provided an endless supply of subjects for legislation.

As the legislation got under way, one of its principal features was the creation of official Commissioners and Inspectors, also one of Bentham's favourite ideas. This proved a secondary, and in the end, an even more valuable source of information. The new inspectors of factories, of mines, of prisons, of schools, the new Poor Law Commissioners (and their indefatigable secretary, Chadwick), had to go out into the field, to study at first hand the problems they were trying to cope with, and the efficacy of the early legislative attempts. Many of these men started by being firm believers in individualism and self-reliance, and had the then conventional belief in the political economy of Adam Smith and Ricardo. Their experiences in the field soon converted them into zealous public servants who demanded more legislation, better enforcement procedures, and more administrative staff.[18] Their demands were backed by a steady stream of detailed reports and information much of it supplied beyond the strict call of duty, and much of it too powerful and too well documented to be gainsaid. They also learnt lessons about the unreality in application of some of the theories they had started out with. Two young barristers, for example, fresh from Oxford and the Inns of Court, who had both begun their work imbued with the idea that men could always find work at the proper price for their labour, soon discovered

[17] G. M. Young, *Victorian England*, p. 33.
[18] David Roberts, *Victorian Origins of the British Welfare State*, pp. 180–1.

that in times of depression work was not to be had at any price.[19] And another reported in the slump of 1842 that 'there can be no such thing as freedom of labour when there is such a competition for employment.'[20]

Of course there *was* opposition to the growth of the government administrative machine, there was hostility to the need to vote the taxes for it, even if this was not generally based on rigid adherence to *laissez-faire* principles, or devoted respect for freedom of contract. Generally speaking this opposition was based on three dislikes which many Englishmen shared. They disliked paying more taxes. They disliked the corruption and jobbery which they associated with the growth of a bureaucracy. And they disliked the increase of powers of central Government at the expense of local government, for they assumed that local government was more democratic—it was the self-government of the local community—while central Government was likely to be more remote and dictatorial; and in the distant background, there was the constant belief that strong central Governments were the road to tyranny, as (Englishmen generally assumed) had been demonstrated by the European experience, while weak central Government was the explanation for the civil liberties traditionally enjoyed by Englishmen. These three dislikes, and the fears that lay behind them, never disappeared in nineteenth-century England. Even when the reformers had the upper hand, even as the new legislation poured out of Parliament in the wake of the Blue Books and the Parliamentary investigations, there were always those who, on this or that specific issue, were ready, Cassandra-like, to warn of corruption, jobbery, and the threat of tyranny. Sydney Smith, no enemy to reform, objected to the appointment of Inspectors of Prisons in 1821 because he took it for granted that the posts would be treated as sinecures and filled with place holders who 'would never look at a prison'. Even while he was busy setting up the Metropolitan Police in 1829, Peel expressed his anxiety to Wellington that the police force might become 'a job, if gentlemen's servants and so forth are placed in the higher offices'.[21]

Joseph Hume, Radical M.P., and friend and associate of Bentham and James Mill, nevertheless spent years in and out of Parliament attacking every increase in public expenditure, and adding the idea of 'Retrenchment' to the Radical programme of Peace and Reform. The belief that all Government activity was hopelessly bumbling and incompetent received a considerable fillip during the Crimean War. The revelations of appalling incompetence on the military side, the dreadful administrative failures to provide adequate medical and hospital facilities,

[19] Ibid.
[20] Ibid., p. 226.
[21] Sir Llewellyn Woodward, *The Age of Reform*, 2nd edn. (Oxford, 1962), p. 466.

contrasted, in the eyes of most Englishmen, with the ebullient successes of its manufacturing and engineering industry.[22] To many, it confirmed what they always suspected about the inevitable incompetence and inefficiency of all Government activity. But despite this, the demands for more Government activity did not abate. It was with some exasperation that Herbert Spencer wrote in 1857 that events had proved 'the Government to be the worst owner, the worst manufacturer, the worst trader; in fact, the worst manager, be the thing managed what it may'.[23]

But Herbert Spencer was wrong about the efficiency of the new Government machine, as he was wrong in a great many other things. The difficulties under which it laboured were immense, 'new problems were constantly being added to the back-log of half-solved problems which existed'.[24] The parsimony of Parliament which refused to appoint and pay adequate numbers of administrators, and the sheer lack of professional people with the necessary skills, and not the inefficiency of the central Government machine, were the realities of the time. It was local government where the real inefficiencies, corruption, and bungling amateurism were to be found. Ministers and officials of the central Government were aware of it, thinkers and writers like Bentham, Mill, and the jurist John Austin, were aware of it, and fought against what they regarded as unreasoning prejudice,[25] but the prejudice of most Englishmen and many M.P.s remained very stubbornly in favour of local and against central Government. The wild and unreasoning hostility which was aroused by all proposals to establish a police force, is well known. As late as 1816 a House of Commons Committee reported against the creation of a preventive police force as 'odious and repulsive', and, although Peel succeeded in carrying his proposals in 1829, many Englishmen were quite convinced that this was the end of all liberty. The popular hostility to Peel's Bill was immense.

It was not only public hostility, nor even the need to discover the facts which were obstacles to the ability of Government to cope with the problems of the age. Other difficulties arose from the necessity of creating and building up proper professional skills in a wide variety of fields. The new Radicals and professional middle classes who came to the fore after the Reform Act of 1832 distrusted the old amateur tradition which was so closely associated with jobbery and incompetence. 'I would as soon trust an amateur to shoe my horse', declared the economist Nassau Senior, 'as to inspect my school.'[26] In almost every field, the huge

---

[22] Asa Briggs, *Victorian People* (first published 1954, revised edn., Harmondsworth, 1975), p. 72.
[23] 'Representative Government—What is it Good For?' reproduced in *The Man Versus the State,* 1884 (reprinted Harmondsworth, 1969), pp. 256–7.
[24] W. L. Burn, *The Age of Equipoise,* p. 138.
[25] David Roberts, *Victorian Origins of the British Welfare State,* Chapter 3.
[26] Cited in S. L. Levy, *Nassau W. Senior* (Newton Abbott, 1970), p. 184.

population growth and the new social problems, created a demand for professional skills which simply could not be met for many years. There were not enough doctors, for example, and their training was inadequate. When demands were made that passenger ships carrying emigrants to the new world should have a qualified physician on board, they simply were not available.[27] Indeed, when the first reforms were being imposed on the passenger emigrant business the Government lacked any adviser 'with a technical knowledge of ships and sailing, a first-hand knowledge of the trade and a professional interest in its amendment'.[28]

Architects, and engineers of every description, were needed in ever-increasing numbers, but only the 1830s saw the founding of the Royal Institute of British Architects, and the 1840s the Institutes of Civil and, later, of Mechanical Engineering. The growth of commerce, and the modern corporation brought a demand for greater order and regularity in accountancy procedures, but in 1822 a British Professional Directory listed only 73 accountants in the entire country. Even in mid-nineteenth century, accounting was still a much neglected profession, a constant source of trouble for insurance companies, friendly societies, and trustees in bankruptcy.[29] When the first railway companies were created, the accounting requirements were rudimentary in the extreme, and the Government rejected demands for public auditing to protect the shareholders. It is easy to misinterpret this as yet another example of *laissez-faire* principles, a philosophy of letting the shareholders look after themselves. But in fact, as we shall see, the Government and the law were very far from adopting any such general policy in railway affairs, and it is much more likely that this particular episode was due to an awareness of the lack of the necessary skilled accountants.

Not only were these professional and skilled men not available in sufficient numbers; even the means of educating them barely existed. England's universities in the eighteenth century (in contrast to Scotland's) had fallen into an appalling state, and things were no better in the early nineteenth century. England had, at this time, 'the worst educated middle class in Europe'.[30] Oxford and Cambridge were still dominated by the Classical and mathematical traditions, and even in these subjects serious scholarship was rare. The Benthamites had founded London University in the 1820s to provide a new type of education, more in tune with the professional ideals of the utilitarian age, but it was a long while getting off the ground. When Faraday gave evidence on scientific

[27] O. MacDonagh, *A Pattern of Government Growth*, p. 144.

[28] Ibid., p. 98.

[29] See Report of the Select Committee on Assurance Companies (1852–3) *H.C. Parliamentary Papers*, XXI, iii; Yamey, 'Scientific Bookkeeping and the Rise of Capitalism', 1 *Economic History Rev.* (N.S.) 99 (1949).

[30] G. M. Young, *Victorian England*, p. 89.

education to a Royal Commission he told them that before science could be taught science teachers had to be created.[31] The civil service itself, often the very source of many of these new developments, had to be cleansed and purged by the Northcote Trevelyan reforms in 1854, which threw most of the important positions open to competitive examination. A new cadre of professional administrators had to be built up requiring a great increase both in quality and in quantity. In 1832 the Home Office employed 29 men, and all the Home departments of the central Government employed only 101.[32]

If the machinery of central Government required such drastic overhauling and rebuilding during this period, the same was no less true of local government. I have written in a previous chapter of the extent to which lack of communications left the local officials—such as they were—with a considerable degree of independence of central Government throughout the eighteenth century. Little had happened to alter this situation till the Reform Act of 1832 although the huge growth of the new industrial towns had created problems there on a new scale, akin to those which had long been known in London itself. Basically the unit of local government was still the parish, and there were 15,000 parishes in England and Wales. In addition there were some 200 of the older Chartered corporations, almost everyone of them a corrupt and self-perpetuating body. None of these bodies had any sort of a proper administrative staff, most of the work falling either on the 5,000 Justices of the Peace or on a handful of generally inefficient and corrupt officials. Apart from administering the Poor Law, these local government units provided few services of any value to their residents, and certainly none commensurate with the costs they imposed in the form of corruption and restrictive practices. There were, for instance, still no proper police forces either in the country areas or even in the great new industrial cities. In 1815 there were still no municipal fire-fighting services; it was left to the private initiative of the insurance companies to supply the deficiency in some measure—but naturally only for those properties which were insured.[33] But in addition to the older local government bodies there were an increasing number of those new special bodies, set up by Private Acts, such as the Turnpike Trustees, the new Paving, Lighting, and Sewer Commissioners who were ultimately to provide the nucleus of modern local authorities. But in the 1830s this was still a long way off.

However, reform was at hand in some form, even here. The new Municipal Corporations Act of 1836 followed hard on another of those

---

[31] Ibid., p. 97.
[32] W. C. Lubenow, *The Politics of Government Growth*, pp. 15, 18.
[33] Sir Llewellyn Woodward, *The Age of Reform*, p. 367.

new Parliamentary inquiries and though this gave very narrow powers to the local government authorities it did at least begin the process of reforming the old oligarchic, privately controlled, corporations of the previous century. In the 1840s and 1850s a new spirit became evident in these cities, and many improvements began to take place.[34] At first much of this was done on a voluntary or semi-voluntary basis. All sorts of societies began to spring up, professional, statistical, charitable, public health improvement; they were run by energetic, active, middle-class men, determined to take a pride in their towns, and to clear up the mess and the slums. New roads, paving, lighting, parks, sanitary measures, were provided, often with the help of still further private Acts obtained by public-spirited citizens, and not infrequently with the aid of private benefactions as well. A healthy rivalry between the cities developed and completely new types of municipal activity began to flourish. Municipally owned waterworks, kitchens, baths, wash houses, and markets sprang up; magnificent new Town Halls were built. By 1870 there were forty-nine municipal gas undertakings in England and Wales, the earliest (in Manchester) dating from 1817, and sixty-nine locally owned waterworks. All this in the period generally thought of as the very heyday of *laissez-faire*!

LAWYERS AND THE LEGISLATIVE PROCESS

One of the professions which changed and modernized its techniques was the legal profession; and one of the most important aspects of the change in legal methodology was the change in legislation itself. The characteristics of the Bar and the higher judiciary, those parts of the legal profession most visible to the public eye, may have changed little between 1770 and 1830 or even 1870. The changes in this side of the profession were important enough, but they were not changes which met the eye; the changes lay principally in the attitudes and values of the profession, and in the sort of fields in which they worked. Here there were changes enough; barristers began, in the 1820s and 1830s, if not earlier, to handle an increasing volume of commercial work; and the judges of the 1840s and 1850s were men of a different stamp, with different backgrounds from those of the first quarter of the nineteenth century. I shall return to these changes later. The other side of the legal profession changed far more visibly. 'From the mass of pettifogging attorneys of the eighteenth century there developed the respectable profession of solicitors effectively organized by a succession of Solicitors Acts, a profession in whose hands an immense amount of confidential business was placed.'[35] The mid- to

---

[34] See generally, Asa Briggs, *Victorian Cities*, and especially at pp. 217–24.
[35] G. Kitson Clark, *The Making of Victorian England*, p. 261.

late-nineteenth-century solicitor was another member of this new breed of middle-class professionals. They were men of integrity, of repute, men who believed in property and in freedom of contract. Their clients knew their interests and these solicitors knew how to advise them. Like old Soames Forsyte, they were men of honour and punctilious in the discharge of their obligations, as they expected their wives and their architects to be punctilious in the discharge, in turn, of their duties.[36]

Like the other professions, the lawyers had, at this time, no proper system of professional education. In 1817 a student reading for the Bar was recommended to start with Blackstone, and to proceed thence to Selwyn's *Nisi Prius Cases* (a mere Digest of cases of little importance), Peake's *Law of Evidence*, and Tidd's *Practice*; he was then expected to pass on to Littleton's *Tenures* (a work some centuries out of date), Coke *On Littleton*, Cruise's *Digest of Conveyancing*, and Fonblanque's *Treatise on Equity*, a work which owed its reputation only to the absence of a rival.[37] As Fifoot says, 'Blackstone was inevitable, Littleton lucid; a sustained attack upon the rest would drive the student to the madhouse.'[38] Thirty years later, things had hardly improved. A House of Commons Select Committee on Legal Education received some devastating comments from Lord Brougham, who, despite all his faults, was one of the first of the nineteenth-century professional lawyers, a professional in the modern sense of the term.[39] He did not mince his words in telling the Commons Committee what he thought of the state of 'legal science' in 1846. Not only was there no education to speak of, he protested, but there were scarcely any legal books of worth. 'At present we are indebted both in our public institutions and in the profession for whatever works of eminence we use, either to the schools of the Continent or to those of America.'[40]

Nevertheless, despite these unsatisfactory if characteristic signs of legal conservatism, some very fundamental changes took place between 1770 and 1840 or 1850 in the most important legal branch of the day, that is, in the legislative process. It is not too much to say that the shape and form of the Statute Book were revolutionized during this period, nor is it too much to say that without this revolution, the substantive statutory changes would scarcely have been possible. We have already seen, in an earlier chapter, something of the general nature of Acts of Parliament

---

[36] It will be recalled that Soames sued his architect 'as a matter of principle' for exceeding his authority in relation to the cost of his house: John Galsworthy, *The Forsyte Saga*, Part III, Chapter V.

[37] C. H. S. Fifoot, *English Law and Its Background* (London, 1932), p. 183.

[38] Ibid.

[39] Brougham disliked amateurism, and was once shocked beyond measure when Lord Grey told him that he could not ask a colleague to move to another Ministry for reasons of delicacy: Frances Hawes, *Lord Brougham* (London, 1957), p. 239.

[40] Report of the Select Committee on Legal Education (1846), *H.C. Parliamentary Papers*, X, 1, p. xl.

around 1770—amateurish, casual, frequently the work of Parliamentary back-benchers, usually of local or temporary significance only, constantly amended and barely intelligible even to lawyers. By the mid-nineteenth century all this was changing rapidly, and by 1870 the legislative process had reached what is very nearly its present form. I need only sketch the most important of these changes. In 1796 Charles Abbott, later Lord Chief Justice Tenterden, persuaded the Commons to appoint a Committee of Inquiry into the publication of the Statutes. Shortly after this the Commons began to distinguish more clearly between Private and Public Legislation and separate provision was made for publishing the Public General Acts.[41] In the nineteenth century attempts began to be made to improve the legibility of the Statute Book, first by consolidating great masses of Statutes with their amendments, and secondly, by simplifying drafting techniques. In 1825 the mass of Customs legislation—consisting of no fewer than 442 earlier Acts—was consolidated into one Act, a huge number of criminal law statutes were simplified and consolidated into six principal Acts in 1828, and in 1850 Brougham secured the passing of the first Interpretation Act which greatly shortened the length of statutes by eliminating much unnecessary verbiage. The serious process of Statute Law Revision, that is of combing through older legislation to clear away spent and obsolete enactments, began in 1868. But the most significant change of all may well have been the selection of Henry Thring to draft the great Merchant Shipping Act of 1854. Thring was a barrister who had written a pamphlet advocating a number of measures for simplifying the style of legislation, and at this time most legislation was drafted by barristers in private practice, just as most Government work was done by private contractors. In drafting the Merchant Shipping Bill, Thring put into practice what he had preached.[42] The Act was divided on a rational pattern into Parts, sub-divisions, and Schedules. The sections were broken up into sub-sections and paragraphs. This massive Act of over 500 sections has been said to be 'a masterful blending of exacting detail and sound principle . . . [which] illustrated that new talent for minute planning which the Victorian middle class brought to the central administration'.[43] There is no doubt that it owed as much to the draftsman as to its political originators. In 1860 Thring was appointed Counsel to the Home Office, and in 1869 the new Office of Parliamentary Counsel to the Treasury was established with Thring at its head. In due course this Office became—as it remains today—responsible for the drafting of all Government Bills. Today there are many who think that the present style of Parliamentary drafting leaves much to be desired,

[41] See Erskine May's *Parliamentary Practice*, 18th edn. (London, 1971), p. 980.
[42] See H. Thring, *Practical Legislation* (London, 1902), pp. 1–4.
[43] David Roberts, *Victorian Origins of the British Welfare State*, p. 147.

and it may well be that new thinking is required about the future of the Statute Book in the 1970s. But there can be no doubt that the changes made by Thring in the 1850s onwards represented a great advance at the time.

Other significant changes in the legislative process involved the gradual elimination of many of the *ad hoc* or individualized Acts which had formerly been typical of legislation. The Railway Acts of the early 1840s were the last set of Statutes which embodied large numbers of standard clauses all drafted according to precedent. In 1845 a series of standardized 'Clauses Acts' were passed—the Companies Clauses Act, the Lands Clauses Act, and the Railways Clauses Consolidation Act— each of which contained a set of general provisions which were in future to apply, in the absence of contrary stipulation, in any Act which attracted their provisions. Another similar change was the development of an alternative to the Private Bill legislation which had formerly been required for the establishment of local Commissioners for road building, paving, drainage, and similar urban improvements. This was the Provisional Order procedure invented by Chadwick (who was 'inordinately proud of it')[44] and was the precursor of a vast mass of delegated legislation. Originally adopted in the Public Health Act 1848, this procedure looks cumbersome enough today, but it was a great advance on the previous process of Private Bill legislation.

The effect of all these changes, together with changes in the character of the substantive legislation going through Parliament, can be seen by a comparison of an annual volume of the Statute Book from the 1840s onwards, with an annual volume of the eighteenth century. In an earlier chapter[45] I analysed the public Acts for 1770. By comparison I have performed a similar exercise for 1844, a year chosen entirely at random. In this year Parliament passed 113 Public General Acts. Of these, some 58 could be characterized as of local or temporary significance (such as Road Acts, Crown Lands Acts, financial statutes, and so forth) while the remainder were all of a general law-making character. And among these general Acts were at least half-a-dozen of major importance, including the Factories Act, the Merchant Shipping Act, the Companies Act, the Copyright Act, and several important Acts dealing with the Courts and the administration of justice.

Closely paralleled to this change in the style and substance of legislation was the change in responsibility for its production. In 1770, as we saw previously, Government did not regard itself as under any particular responsibility for the preparation and introduction of legislation. Even in 1836 Melbourne could declare that 'the duty of a

---

[44] S. E. Finer, *Life and Times of Sir Edwin Chadwick*, p. 432.
[45] *Supra*, pp. 91–2.

Government is not to pass legislation but to rule.'[46] But this was already an out-dated view. In 1847 Sir George Lewis told the Prime Minister that 'the business of legislation is now more exclusively in the hands of the government than at any previous time.'[47] As this happened, another, more subtle change, was also occurring. In the 1820s and 1830s many private members of Parliament had secured the appointment of Select Committees with the hope and intention of persuading the Committee to adopt some particular proposal that the member wished to see enacted. In the 1840s and 1850s many members who continued to adopt the same tactics found that the Committee hearings were changing in character. The principal witnesses were now the officials, the inspectors, the Commissioners, well briefed and armed with facts; the honourable members of the House of Commons found themselves being educated by these new public servants as to the precise details of the problems.[48] This too tended to change the character of the legislation which was ultimately enacted. The earlier reforms—those of the 1820s and 1830s, for example—had often been based on a somewhat simple understanding of the problems and a naïve belief in how they could be dealt with. Supported, to some extent, by some of the simplistic slogans which Members of Parliament derived from the political economists, and the popularizers of the time, some of these early attempts at legislative reform had been over-confident. It was still an age when people believed that social problems could be definitively solved with a dose of legislation based on simple liberal principles. Far from being reluctant to reform, to legislate, to act, they were often too confident of their ability to solve a problem once for all by some simple legislative stroke: 'It was tempting to pass an Act, to create a sort of dramatic *dénouement*, to end an "evil", or an "abuse"; it was embarrassing to learn, a little later, that it had done nothing of the sort or had only created a second "abuse" to replace the first.'[49] As the 1840s passed into the 1850s this naïvety began to wane. Parliamentarians discovered that their Bills rarely solved problems definitively, that they were setting up an administrative machine which would require constant patching, renewal, and repair; and that it was the new public servants who would brief them and advise them, through the Government and through their Select Committees on what was needed. Professionalism was winning the day.

These immense changes in the character, nature, and quantity of legislation are of greater relevance and importance to the theme of this work than may at first sight appear. Quite apart from the fact that much

---

[46] Cited in O. MacDonagh, *Early Victorian Government 1830–1870* (London, 1977), p. 5.
[47] David Roberts, *Victorian Origins of the British Welfare State*, p. 253.
[48] Ibid., pp. 255–6.
[49] W. L. Burn, *The Age of Equipoise*, p. 50.

of this legislation involved manifold and direct interference with freedom of contract—the details I shall look at later—it had other and more subtle implications for the whole ideal of a contract-based society. First, legislation was becoming steadily more positivist in character, and ceasing to have any significant resemblance to an act of contractual self-government. Secondly, the relationship between Parliament and the Courts was profoundly affected by these changes, and this in turn had long-run effects on private law, and in particular on Contract law. This relationship was altered in two quite different but equally important ways. First, the relationship between Parliament and Courts as *law-makers* was greatly affected, for as Parliament wielded the legislative power more and more massively and more and more efficiently, the Courts abandoned the overt exercise of law-making powers. And secondly, because as the *enforcement* of this great new mass of legislation passed largely into the hands of the bureaucracy and of the local magistrates' Courts, the role of the superior Courts as the principal organs of law-enforcement of the State also began to decline.

10

THE ROLE OF THE INDIVIDUAL, 1770-1870

INDIVIDUALISM

THE concept of 'Individualism' is a complex one, which has meant different things at different times and still often means different things to different people.[1] The century about which I am now writing, that is the period 1770-1870, is often thought to have been a century of individualism in England. But for my purposes it is important to distinguish between two different (though not unrelated) ideas involved in the concept of an age of individualism. The first concerns individualism as a social mechanism, and the second concerns individualism as a value-based ideal, an aspiration. Historically the two concepts of individualism were closely connected in this period for a number of reasons. Individualism as a value had traditionally been held in the highest respect by Englishmen since 1688 and continued to be so held throughout the nineteenth century. But individualism as a social mechanism had very largely broken down by 1870, and had been replaced by a different order of society in which control, regulation, licensing, and institutional arrangements had become the dominant modes of social organization. As we saw in the previous chapter, many of those who lived through this period did not appreciate what was happening, and would have protested at the totality had they grasped its significance. They thought that the erosion of individualism as a social mechanism would necessarily erode individualism as a value; in this they may have been wrong, though even today it may be premature to give a final answer to that question.

Individualism as a Social Mechanism

There are, in any institution, whether it is a State, or a smaller and less sovereign body, two modes of exercising control over the members. The first mode is basically that associated with individualism, free choice, and free market economies, and the second is basically that of administration. The first mode largely leaves people free to make their own arrangements, but it recognizes and enforces those arrangements once made. It requires that people control themselves, by making their own decisions, and then

---

[1] See generally, Steven Lukes, *Individualism* (Oxford, 1973); Duncan Kennedy, 'Form and Substance in Private Law Adjudication', 89 *Harvard Law Rev.* 1685, 1713-16 (1976).

compels the observance of the course of action thereby decided upon. It naturally stresses the desirability of self-reliance, and individual free choice. It also stresses both the need for education, and the importance of a proper system of rewards and penalties for virtuous and anti-social behaviour. If people are to make their own decisions, they must be taught how to make those decisions, both by direct instruction, and by ensuring that they receive their just deserts whether they make the right or wrong decisions. The alternative mode of social control is the administrative process. This is fundamentally a process which involves a hierarchy of decision-makers, each of whom exercises a delegated authority. In the administrative process the decisions are avowedly based on some collective values; they are decisions made, not in the interest of the decision-maker, but of some other group, such as the public as a whole, where the administrative authority represents the State. It is widely believed that the administrative process is a more authoritarian one, which, in the political arena, is usually associated with dictatorship, and which leaves less room for free choice than the first.

Individualism as a social mechanism in fact proved a relatively short-lived transitional form of social organization in nineteenth-century England. It simply filled the gap—for lack of anything else—between the collapse of one form of social organization and the growth of another, infinitely more complex one. At the beginning of this period, around 1770, many features of the old eighteenth-century, simple rural society still prevailed. Social organization was itself simple. Over most of the country, village communities existed in which landowners, tenant farmers, and agricultural workers shared a common interest, and each occupied a defined role in the social hierarchy. They were, of course, separated by differences of status and of wealth, but they also shared certain bonds. Indeed, in one sense, this remained true of rural England until the late nineteenth century; the difference between 1800 and 1870 lay not in the rural areas themselves, so much as in the fact that they had ceased to represent the most important, populous, and prosperous parts of England.

As the Industrial Revolution got under way, and people moved into the towns, they found themselves taken out of this older social environment. And at the same time, the townsmen themselves, who had known their older customary social position, as craftsmen, as artisans, working in a defined social hierarchy, found their world turned upside down by the influx of population and the springing up of the new factories. Most forms of institutional organization—such as the Guilds or the City Corporations—were corrupt, unpopular, and under ever-increasing attack as monopolies. They were also increasingly weakened by the competition from the new towns not subject to their stranglehold.

The old relationship between the cottage-worker, who worked at home, with his family, on materials brought round to his house by a small employer, declined and then disappeared in the holocaust. In this new world, individualism operated as a social mechanism, simply because there was nothing else. It was every man for himself. The new relationship between the mill hand and the factory owner was far more impersonal, by dint of sheer numbers and by the lack of any geographical relationship. Even amongst those who were decent employers, with a due share of humanity and compassion, the new relationship tended inevitably to be a more impersonal, financial one, the 'cash-nexus' relationship which Carlyle so furiously attacked. Robert Owen tried in his New Lanarkshire mills to run a modern factory on the old paternalist traditions, but the experiment failed, perhaps inevitably.

It was not just the employment relationship which was new and impersonal. It was the whole way of life which the industrial worker found in the swollen Northern towns. He no longer lived, as his forebears had done, in the country, near his place of work, in a cottage, perhaps owned by his employer. He was forced to find and rent housing on the open market, and so new impersonal relationships evolved between urban landlords and tenants. Similarly, the new industrial worker no longer took his flour to the village baker to be baked, nor could he buy provisions from his employer or some nearby farmer, nor could he grow his own food on some small allotment. He now had to buy his provisions at some urban shop, and worse still, he was now enabled to buy far more drink than was good for him at the vast number of new beer shops and gin shops. It would be misleading to idealize over some 'golden age' of honest rural peasants in the manner of William Cobbett, or many of his later successors. Eighteenth-century rural life was often harder than nineteenth-century urban life for an honest, industrious, and sober working man—at least when he was in work. And, as I have previously said, the men who moved into the new industrial towns, seeking work in the factories, frequently did so because the wages offered were higher than anything they were used to earning. The point I am making here is that the older relationships which had characterized eighteenth-century life had largely disappeared in the urbanized industrial towns by the 1820s or 1830s. And until a new set of relationships came into existence, until a new set of institutions could be created, individualism was the only social mechanism there was.

Moreover, considerable efforts were directed to prevent, or at least restrict, the creation of new institutions by the industrialized workers. For the most natural type of relationship for them to form in the new towns was a relationship amongst themselves—combinations or unions. Not only were these likely to be a natural focus for social relationships between men of the same type thrown together in large numbers, but they also offered, of course, the possibility of increasing the bargaining power of the factory hand. I shall have to say something about the history of the Combination Acts later; but it is enough to say here that until 1824 virtually all workers' combinations were illegal, not primarily because the mill owners wanted to suppress potentially powerful bargaining unions, but because the governing classes were frightened of all urban combinations. Before the establishment of the London police force, a crowd of even a few hundred men could easily degenerate into a mob capable of causing the most devastating damage. And the fear of actual revolution was never very far away.

I have referred earlier to the increasing use of middlemen in industrial and commercial organizations. The division of labour, so stressed by Adam Smith in *The Wealth of Nations* as one of the great sources of increasing prosperity, involved subdividing a task, and then contracting out part of it to someone else. The Industrial Revolution brought a tremendous increase in specialization in the manufacture of a vastly increased number of manufactured components for engineering plant and equipment of every variety. Towards the end of the century Alfred Marshall described this process as it had affected the printing industry.[2] Originally the printer had done everything himself; as specializations developed, the type-founder separated off, then printers delegated the making of the presses to others; in due course the ink and the rollers were made by specialist contractors. This sort of process was repeating itself in every activity in society, and not merely in industry. For example, there was, through the nineteenth century, an increasing tendency for teachers to become employees of, rather than owners and managers of, the schools in which they taught. These changes in organization necessarily brought a great increase in the sheer number of contractual relationships. Relationships which had formerly taken place within some kind of institutional framework were now taking place on an individualized basis through the medium of contract.

The general picture of England around 1770 and 1800, then, is that of a society rapidly becoming highly atomistic in its social organization. The individual stood or fell alone as the unit of organization. His relationships with his fellow men were increasingly of a bilateral rather than a multilateral nature, increasingly voluntarily chosen rather than imposed upon him. In 1861 Sir Henry Maine gave famous expression to this change by observing that the progress of societies had in general been marked by the movement 'from status to contract'.[3] But it is commonly the case that even the most percipient of men only observe a

---

[2] *Principles of Economics*, first published 1890, 8th edn. (London, 1961), p. 228.
[3] Sir Henry Maine, *Ancient Law* (first published 1861), Chapter IX.

movement when it has virtually run its course, and Maine failed to observe that during the preceding fifty years many new forms of social, commercial, and legal organization had been coming into existence. The extreme individualism of England's social organizations in 1800 had been very greatly modified by 1860, though individualism as a value— as a social and intellectual force—perhaps only reached its apogee with the publication of Mill's classic, *On Liberty*, in 1859.

Individualism as a Value

Individualism as a value was, of course, not new in the nineteenth century. Its roots lay deep in the eighteenth century and still earlier periods. Some of the early strands I have already reviewed in Part I when I looked, for example, at the beginnings of economic liberalism, of the social contractarianism of Hobbes and Locke, and of the Natural Law ideas which were so popular in the Age of Enlightenment. Between 1776 and 1830 or thereabouts, two important bodies of ideas grew up which gave an enormous impetus to individualism, namely the political economy of the classical economists, and the utilitarianism of Bentham and his disciples. I reserve these for fuller treatment in the next two chapters. Here I merely give some indication of how these bodies of thought related to individualism, and what were the practical conclusions which men drew from individualism as a value.

It is important first to stress that individualism as a value was, in the nineteenth century, asserted most emphatically as a moral principle, and as a highly desirable principle to be observed in social and political reform. Nothing could be a greater mistake than to equate individualism with selfishness or egoism. The individualist was not a person without ideals, but a person with different ideals.[4] The fact that the classical economists and the utilitarians wanted to free people to follow their interests, their wills, did not mean that they were indifferent to what people did with these new-found freedoms. Still less did it mean that they advocated or approved a society in which everybody selfishly pursued his own interests in total disregard of the interests of every one else. On the contrary, they were intensely concerned with the way men exercised their freedom. They wanted men to have free choice, but they also had a good deal to say about how they should choose. They had, too, a great faith in education, not to say propaganda, for they wanted to teach people how to choose wisely, while leaving the ultimate choices to them.

---

[4] H. M. Robertson, *Aspects of the Rise of Economic Liberalism* (Cambridge, 1933), p. 34. See also, T. S. Ashton, *The Industrial Revolution*, at p. 127: 'The idea that somehow or other, men had become self-centred, avaricious and anti-social is the strangest of all the legends by which the story of the industrial revolution has been obscured.'

In the economic sphere, the emphasis was, of course, on the role of the individual at the centre of the free market. As consumer, as buyer, the individual chooses what he will buy, and how much he is prepared to pay; as earner, or worker, he chooses what work he will do, where he will work, and how much he is prepared to work for; as investor, he chooses how much he will save, and where he will invest his money, and what rate of interest he will demand. In the more personal sphere, the individual is to have the right, if not indeed the duty, to realize his highest potential; the variety of aptitudes and talents among different men means again that each must be left to choose the appropriate mode of self-fulfilment. The State's right to interfere with the individual stops short at that point where his activities affect only himself or others who give 'their free, voluntary and undeceived consent and participation'.[5] In the political sphere, a similar role for the individual was found by James Mill and Bentham.[6] Their acceptance of the democratic ideal was explicitly based on the belief that only through democracy could a harmony of interests be ensured between governed and governors. A market place of ideas would develop in which the individual voter would exercise the same sovereign choice as he exercised in the commercial market place. Politicians would seek the votes of the electors and would have to respond to their desires. In this way the people would be able to seek political self-fulfilment through the democratic process. Moreover, this process would result in the breaking of the paternalist aristocratic traditions, and the social bonds associated with them. In a democracy, as Tocqueville observed of early nineteenth-century America, the chain which links the people in social hierarchical relationships is severed, and its members 'become indifferent and as if strangers to one another'.[7]

There was thus a pleasing symmetry between the role of the individual in the political process and his role in the market economy. So far as the propertied classes were concerned this symmetry had already been an important part of eighteenth-century thought. For it was a part of the Locke tradition that a man could only be deprived of his property by his consent, that is, in the market place by contract, or politically by taxation to which he or his representative consented. But the new radicals were trying to extend the role of the sovereign consumer and voter from the propertied classes to the whole populace, and although they were eventually successful in both spheres, they were not successful in the two at the same time. The transformation of England into a free market economy was accomplished long before its transformation into a

---

[5] *On Liberty* (Penguin edn., Harmondsworth, 1974), p. 71. Page references are to this edition.

[6] In particular, in Mill's *Essay on Government*, as to which see *post*, pp. 310-11.

[7] Cited in Steven Lukes, *Individualism*, p. 13. The very word 'individualism' is first found in English in Henry Reeve's translation of Tocqueville's *De La Démocratie en Amerique* in 1840.

democracy. The vote was still (in broad terms) confined to the upper and middle classes even after the 1832 Reform Act, and by the time something approaching real democracy had arrived in England, belief in the free market economy was already waning, especially among the intellectuals. The result was that this attractive theory which linked the sovereign role of the individual in the political process and in the market place never really took root in England; and, indeed, today (as we shall see later)[8] the paradoxical situation has arrived in which the greater the sovereignty which the individual exercises in the political process, the faster does he assist in the destruction of his sovereign role in the market place.

But if this particular idea did not prove very fruitful in England, there was a broader sense in which individualism was felt by many to be closely associated with liberties generally, and political liberties in particular. So, too, freedom of expression was not unlinked with the other freedoms. If a man was to choose for himself, if he was to be sovereign in the economic market, if he was to decide how best to realize his aptitudes, he needed the fullest opportunity for deciding what was true or false himself. The individual had to be free to question every form of authority and to make his own decisions; others were free to persuade but not to coerce. And even the basic liberties of which Englishmen were so inordinately proud, were not unrelated to this individualism. The influential *Edinburgh Review* argued in 1843 that all freedoms were part of one fundamental freedom, and that 'all must be maintained or all risked'.[9] Even the working man who in some ways distrusted talk of individualism, if it meant that he could not join with his fellows in a combination or union, was an individualist in the sense that there were limits beyond which 'he was not prepared to be "pushed around"'.[10] His stance may have been anti-absolutist rather than democratic, but, at least, he 'felt himself to be an individualist, with few affirmative rights but protected by the laws against the intrusion of arbitrary power'.[11]

In studying these broad changes of trend, extending over a whole nation and over many decades, stretching out into centuries, we must guard against two great dangers of over-simplification. The first of these dangers is to assume that the people of nineteenth-century England were any more monolithic in their ideas, values, moral and intellectual beliefs, than the people of twentieth-century England. They were not. One has only to read a newspaper or a copy of *Hansard* from this period to see that the diversity of views was as great on most of their issues as it is now on

---

[8] See *post*, p. 590.
[9] Cited, A. W. Coats (ed.), *The Classical Economists and Economic Policy* (London, 1971), p. 30, n. 2.
[10] E. P. Thompson, *The Making of the English Working Class*, p. 79.
[11] Ibid.

most of our issues. Of course, the issues have changed, so that on some things about which there was virtual unanimity then, there is a greater diversity of views today; but the converse is also true. The other danger of over-simplification is to assume that changes in intellectual or moral movements occurred cleanly at given moments of time.

There are clear signs, for instance, that the waning of the older pre-nineteenth-century type of paternalism, was a much more protracted affair than has sometimes been appreciated, and certainly in the law, there are signs of eighteenth-century morality in legal cases right up to 1850 or longer. What we thus seem to find is a long drawn out and messy end to the paternalism and traditional customary moralities of the eighteenth century, pretty well stretching out towards the beginnings of the modern collectivist or quasi-socialist period. The famous period of Victorian individualism and *laissez-faire* seems virtually to disappear at both ends.

Individualism and the Working Class

As the nineteenth century wore on, individualism began to lose some of its appeal, and it lost its appeal particularly amongst the working class. There is a sense, indeed, in which the working-class ethos had from the beginning been one of solidarity rather than individualism. Individualism, like economic liberalism, is a creed which attracts minorities, and eccentrics, and men of unusual ability. Those who differ from their fellow men, whether in having greater aptitudes, ability, energy, or even eccentricity, are likely to be individualists. Given an adequate protective framework of law and order—and I shall have more to say about that important proviso later—they are likely to do better for themselves in a society in which individualism flourishes. In the early part of the nineteenth century this was often the case even amongst working class men. Throughout the first sixty or seventy years of the nineteenth century there was a significant gulf between the skilled artisan and the common labourer. The former could by dint of hard work, thrift, sobriety (and, perhaps one should add, the luck of a not over-fertile wife) aspire to a modest standard of comfort, a decent home, and membership of a friendly society to guard against periods of sickness and even to provide some sort of living for old age. To the working man who saw this as a sufficiently satisfying life, individualism was not an unwelcome philosophy. These were basically the working-class élite of the mid-nineteenth century. This somewhat superior working man, it has been said,

shared many middle-class attitudes; a distaste for mobs, a repudiation of the whole complex of behaviour associated with race courses, fairs, wakes, brothels, beer houses and brutal sports. He was more likely than his inferiors to vote liberal, if only because his work situation frequently fostered individualism, self-education and social ambition. If he drank at all, he drank soberly . . . He was probably interested in religious matters—often a chapelgoer or a secularist. He was strongly attracted by the ideology of thrift, with its stress on individual self-respect, personal moral effort, and prudence. He joined craft unions in their elitist mid-Victorian phase, read widely and often joined a mechanics' institute.[12]

In the modern world many of these men would probably have passed on to higher education and into professional or at least middle-class life. Indeed, even in the first half of the nineteenth century some (such as Francis Place)[13] succeeded in making this transition. But to the mass of the working class at this period, to those who had neither the ability, nor the self-discipline, nor the sobriety, to improve their lot in life, individualism held out little hope. While the middle classes preached individualism at them as the only way to improve themselves, most knew in their hearts that this was only the path for the few. For the many, for the great mass of the working classes, individualism became a dead-end philosophy. They came increasingly to believe that they would only help themselves by solidarity, by standing firmly together, by creating unions which would represent the weak and strong alike, and by securing the enactment of laws which would help the less able even at the expense of the more able.

Working-class solidarity, in some of its less attractive forms, was, indeed, probably much older than the nineteeenth century. It is, of course, perfectly natural for the weak to unite against the strong, and the strength of that union depends on the extent to which it holds together under pressure. The greater the pressure, the greater is the tendency for any form of association to split apart, for each man to seek his own safety or salvation. When that happens, the strong survive, and the weak go to the wall; but if the association can be held together, the weak will benefit from their association with the strong. By the beginning of the nineteeenth century many working-class men knew this very well, and already at that time the virulent hatred of the strike breaker and the 'scab' or 'blackleg' was an established tradition.[14] This solidarity extended also to those involved in riots, Luddism, or worse. Two Nottingham Luddites who turned informer begged the Government to send them to Canada to escape the vengeance of their former colleagues; and another refused to live with his wife after she had betrayed, even by

---

[12] Brian Harrison, *Drink and the Victorians*, pp. 25-6.

[13] Francis Place (1771-1854) illustrates so many of these themes that he deserves a footnote to himself. A working man, trained in making leather breeches, he organized a strike in 1793 which failed and resulted in his being 'blacklisted' by the employers. He suffered extreme privation for some months as a result, but later built up a highly successful tailor's business in Charing Cross which at one time brought him in £3,000 *per annum*. He later became active in politics as a self-educated and self-made man, and was closely associated with Bentham, James Mill, and others of that circle. His *Autobiography* was first published (ed. Mary Thale) in 1972 (Cambridge).

[14] E. P. Thompson, *The Making of the English Working Class*, p. 262.

chance, a member of a gang of Luddites who had actually committed murder.[15]

This working-class collectivism or solidarity had thus, from the earliest times, a strong coercive streak to it. Within the group, the majority will prevailed, and dissenting minorities were liable to be coerced and even intimidated into falling into line. This attitude was by no means confined to trade union activities or industrial relations. It was found in all sorts of associations, including, for example, those involved in the Temperance movement. In 1839 a tremendous schism rent this movement: the extremists wanted members to take the 'long pledge', that is, not merely to abstain themselves, but also to cut themselves off from friends who drank, to dismiss servants who drank, and to refuse to serve drinks in their homes, while the more moderate members merely undertook to abstain themselves. Those who supported the 'long pledge' were generally the working-class members of the movement, while it was the middle-class members who wanted to leave each person to make his own individual decision, free from the coercion of others. 'The correlation between extremist standpoint and lower social grade is repeated in all subsequent temperance schisms... It can also be seen in the feminist, anti-slavery and secularist movements.'[16]

But it was, inevitably, in the industrial relations sphere that working-class collectivism was most important, and had its greatest impact. The legal developments in this area I shall look at later; here I can do no more than draw attention to an important change which took place in the role of trade unionism, and its relationship to individualism, as the nineteenth century wore on. In the middle of the nineteenth century, there is certainly some evidence to support the view that the trade unions were substantially dominated by the more élitist members of the working class. The Webbs on the whole rejected the idea that there was any real working-class collectivism at this period, though they also suggested that 'the insistence upon the Englishmen's right to freedom of contract was, in fact, in the mouths of staunch Trade Unionists, perilously near cant.'[17] But it is not easy to see why this was cant in the mouths of those who did accept middle-class values, political economy, and the individualist role which went with it. The working man who really believed in these ideals may well have resented interference with his freedom of contract since it may have cut his potential earning power (for example by reducing hours of labour) while it increased that of his neighbour. However, there is now widespread acceptance of the view that the Webbs underestimated the extent to which a working-class collectivism did exist, even in mid-

[15] Ibid., p. 583.
[16] Brian Harrison, *Drink and the Victorians*, p. 143.
[17] *History of Trade Unionism*, p. 280.

century, though not necessarily amongst the more influential trade unionists.[18]

Towards the end of this period, that is around the 1860s, it seems clear that the attitude of trade unionists began to change. The unions themselves fell increasingly into the hands of the unskilled labourers, the broader mass of working men who despised the individualist aspirations of the élitist worker. Robert Applegarth, himself one of the 'respectable' union leaders of the mid-nineteenth century, was pressed on some of these issues by the Royal Commission on Trade Unions to which he gave evidence in 1867. At this time the unions were already opposing piece work, which (of course) has always enabled the hard worker to earn more than his less able or energetic colleague. Was everybody then to be paid the same, he was asked, no matter how industrious or idle? Was Praxiteles, the sculptor credited with the statue of Venus, to be paid at the same rate as other sculptors? Applegarth rejected the comparison:

I do not admit that is a fair application of principle. We are not all Arkwrights, Brunels, or Stephensons. Men of such extraordinary talent soon become other than working men. We have to make rules and regulations which will apply to workmen generally.[19]

And in the following year, in the Annual Report of his union, Applegarth said that his union was 'tired of the individualism' which gave full scope for extraordinary skills, 'but leaves the thousands less skilful to scramble through a selfish world as best they can'.[20]

The impact of working-class collectivism, however, had its greatest successes after 1870, and though we shall see something of these ideas at work when we look at the Factories legislation in Chapter 16, the greater part of this development lies in Part III of this work.

INDIVIDUALISM AND EDUCATION

The role assigned to individualism by the economists, by the utilitarians, by the Radical politicians, and by middle-class morality, depended to a substantial degree on the educability of the public. At the beginning of the nineteenth century education was seen as a profoundly important way of inculcating social disciplines, but it was also seen—and not necessarily by mutually exclusive groups—as potentially the greatest of all forces for the improvement of society. To understand how people felt about these questions we must bear in mind that almost to the end of this period, certainly to the middle of the nineteenth century, a very large

[18] W. L. Burn, *The Age of Equipoise*, pp. 108 *et seq.*; E. P. Thompson, *The Making of the English Working Class*, p. 424.
[19] Asa Briggs, *Victorian People*, p. 193.
[20] Ibid.

part of the population were not merely illiterate—which was almost a minor matter—but simply did not know how to lead responsible social lives in the kind of society which was growing up in England. Many of them spent enormously on drink; many of them drank most of their wages away in two or three days after receiving them. In large areas of the country few people turned up for work on Mondays—which was jocularly named 'St. Monday'—because they had not yet recovered from a weekend of drink. Frequently, they spent so much on drink that they had not enough to buy food. 'Drinking places on pay days were besieged by wives desperately anxious to feed and clothe the family; many married couples fought over the wage packet, and many wives were kept ignorant of its contents ... To make matters worse drunken husbands were often stung by the wife's silent or open reproach into the wife-beating for which Englishmen were notorious abroad.'[21] The number of drink sellers in England was prodigious: in 1850 there were more drink shops than fishmongers, dairy-keepers, cheesemongers, greengrocers, butchers, bakers, and grocers combined.[22]

Even when in good employment, earning a reasonable wage—and many men did earn perfectly adequate wages by the standards of the day—large numbers never thought of putting anything away for emergencies or periods of sickness or unemployment. That this was perfectly possible is shown by the fact that many working men—the more thrifty, sober, and industrious, did so—but millions did not. Violence was still endemic. In his Sanitary Report in 1842 Chadwick estimated that some 12,000 deaths in England and Wales were every year due to various forms of violence.[23] Popular amusements for the mass of the people still tended to consist of barbaric cruelties like prize fighting, bear-baiting, and cock fighting, the last two of which were made illegal in 1833 and 1835. Jews were maltreated and assaulted in the streets as a form of 'good sport' in Francis Place's childhood.[24] Till 1870 and even beyond, it was almost impossible for a crowd of people to gather in public without the strong probability of drunken violence and hooliganism breaking out on a scale exceeding that associated even with a 'bad' football match today. In some localities, private warfare could be conducted between gangs of toughs who disappeared long before the forces of law—such as they were—could be called upon.

To many of the optimistic reformers of the early nineteenth century the only real hope for the future, the only prospect of eliminating many of these social conditions, lay in education. If the people could only be

[21] Brian Harrison, *Drink and the Victorians*, pp. 46–7.

[22] Ibid., p. 58.

[23] Edwin Chadwick, *The Sanitary Conditions of the Labouring Population of Great Britain*, originally published in 1842, reprinted, ed. Flinn (Edinburgh, 1965), p. 270.

[24] *Autobiography of Francis Place*, Introduction by Mary Thale, pp. xxiv–xxv.

taught to understand their own interests, if they could be taught self-reliance and self-discipline, if they could be taught that enlightened self-interest paid, the prospects for the future improvement of mankind were incalculable.

The early utilitarians had an unbounded faith in the possibility of educating the masses to understand their own interests; they were to be taught how to choose intelligently in their own interests, they were to be taught enlightened self-interest. It was a remarkable coincidence that when James Mill and Bentham came to these optimistic conclusions about the possibilities of education they should have thought of trying the experiment on the young John Stuart. The result of this extraordinary experiment in education, described by the younger Mill in his *Autobiography*,[25] must have seemed successful beyond the wildest dreams of James Mill and Bentham. Clearly, one only had to be rigorous enough, start the process young enough, and everybody could be educated to the same standard as the young John Stuart. We do not know whether James Mill ever really believed that, but the astonishing precocity of his son must have helped confirm his belief in the possibilities of education. These beliefs were, of course, passed on to other members of the Benthamite circle, such as Brougham, who for many years took a keen interest in the subject, and who was influential in helping to secure the first Government grant for educational purposes in 1833.[26]

But education was required not only to help the people help themselves; it was also, as I have suggested, required as an important social discipline. The relationship between education on the one hand, and morality and legal rules on the other, was much more closely perceived around 1800 than it is today. People had to be taught to be moral; they had to be taught the word of God; and they had to be taught enough about the law to make them more inclined to observe the law without compulsion. Even in Paley's *Principles of Moral and Political Philosophy* it is clear that ethics is seen as an intensely practical subject; his book had the fundamental purpose of exploring 'the science which teaches men their duty and the reasons for it'. And although Paley was hardly writing for the common man, he was writing for the clergymen whose business it was to guide the common man. To Paley, as to most Englishmen between 1770 and 1870, Christianity was important not only for its own sake, not only for the salvation of souls and the worship of God, but for much more mundane reasons as well. Paley was appalled by Hume's secular ethics which depended entirely on the prudential

[25] *Autobiography*, ed. Jack Stillinger (Oxford, 1971), especially at pp. 64 7; and for Mill's (and his companions') later disillusionment with the efficacy of education, see p. 68.

[26] On Brougham's interest in education, see Chester New, *Life of Henry Brougham to 1830*, Chapter XII.

standards of mutual self-preservation. It was all very well for Hume to argue that everyone could see the value of property laws because each property owner respected the other's rights in return for respect for his own; it was all very well to argue that the virtues of truth and respect for promises depended on this same mutual understanding that what is good for the other party today will prove beneficial to oneself tomorrow. But what of those who had no property, what of those who had no care for the morrow? When people have read over Hume's ideas, said Paley, 'let them consider whether any motives there proposed are likely to be found sufficient to withhold men for gratification of lust, revenge, envy, ambition, avarice, or to prevent the existence of these passions.'[27] Belief in hell fire was thus necessary for the security of the State, and for the preservation of property.

Fifty years later, in the Victorian era, the links between religion, morality, and the precepts by which the lower classes were to be kept in order were still very strong.[28] Sir James Fitzjames Stephen, the judge, who himself became an agnostic, wrote in 1879 that though he did not doubt the truth of his own beliefs, he greatly doubted the capacity of people in general to bear them, and was 'much alarmed' at the possible spread of agnosticism.[29] All this may seem like nauseating hypocrisy to the modern reader, but two pleas in mitigation should be entered. The first is, at least until the end of the period I am now dealing with, that is up to 1870, agnosticism and disbelief were not very widespread. By and large the educated classes believed in hell fire themselves, and their Christian beliefs were not unconnected with their own sense of duty and their own belief in the virtues of discipline, hard work, and self-denial. The second plea in mitigation that needs to be made is to remind the reader once again that belief in the social order and in property, and in anything which helped to preserve that order, was not in early nineteenth-century England based purely on the selfish desires of a privileged class to preserve their own position. To these people all civilization, everything of value in their country (both then and in the past), depended on the preservation of the social order and on rights of property. They were convinced that if the country fell into the hands of the mass of the people, all industry and science, all art and culture, would disappear, the forces of law and order themselves would collapse as property was plundered by the propertiless, and in the end even the poor would pay the penalty of destroying the social order. Nothing was too high a price to pay to avoid this ultimate disaster. Even the religious intolerance against which John Stuart Mill protested,[30] the prison

[27] *Principles of Moral and Political Philosophy*, Book II, Chapter IV.

[28] See, e.g., Walter E. Houghton, *The Victorian Frame of Mind*, p. 59, citing E. Belfort Bax, *Reminiscences* (New York, 1920), p. 189.

[29] W. L. Burn, *The Age of Equipoise*, p. 275.   [30] *On Liberty*, pp. 90–4.

sentences for blasphemy, the refusal to allow atheists to take an oath or give evidence in Courts, had some long-run justification when things were seen from this angle.

But it was not enough for the middle classes to hold to these beliefs and virtues. It was essential to educate the mass of the people to share the same values. And the new belief in education was designed to achieve precisely that. While it would be wrong to think that the desire for the spread of education was never based on more disinterested or compassionate motives (for example, with men like Brougham), when it came to persuading men to vote money for public education, it was these broader motives that seemed to count most. The matter was summed up by Macaulay in a debate in the House of Commons, in 1847, on a motion for the grant of £100,000 for public education. To him, the duty of the Government to provide for the education of the people followed from its duty to ensure the safety of the public and the preservation of property. An uneducated people could not be trusted to abstain from riot and pillage. The Gordon riots of 1780, for example, would not have occurred if the labourers had been taught to respect legitimate authority, and to seek the redress of real wrongs by peaceful means. 'And what', went on Macaulay, 'is the alternative? It is universally allowed that, by some means, Government must protect our persons and property. If you take away education, what means do you leave? You leave means which only necessity can justify ... You leave guns and bayonets, stocks and whipping-posts, treadmills, solitary cells, penal colonies, gibbets.'[31]

The message could hardly have been spelled out more clearly. Law and order, the protection of person and property, could only be ensured by educating the mass of the people, or by sheer brute force. Given the traditional freedoms of England, the latter was an unthinkable alternative. The money was voted. When the new school inspectors (who were first appointed in 1840) began to report on the State-aided schools, it is clear that they regarded the inculcation of moral beliefs as an important part of the education they were supervising. They combined a strange mixture of individualism and paternalism in their attitudes; paternalism in that they wanted to instil habits of order, virtue, kindness, and obedience, but individualism in that they wanted the children to learn the 'truths' of political economy, to learn to make their own free choices, to stand on their own feet.[32]

[31] Citation from Macaulay, *Miscellaneous Writings and Speeches* (London, 1889), p. 737 where the text was revised by Macaulay himself. The published version differs somewhat from that in *Parliamentary Debates*, 3rd series, vol. 91, col. 1007.

[32] David Roberts, *Victorian Origins of the British Welfare State*, p. 199. J. Symons, one of these Inspectors, himself wrote a book entitled *Popular Economy* (1840) to popularize the 'great truths' of political economy. Many of the early inspectors started out as individualists, but 'as bureaucrats their experiences made them more collectivist, and they vigorously urged governmental intervention to remove the physical, moral and social evils that afflicted the lower classes.' Ibid., pp. 320-1.

There were, of course, the inevitable paradoxes here, as there were in so many other spheres of potential Government activity. Men could and did demand that the Government should keep its hands off education in the name of individualism. Was it not the duty of each parent to educate his own children? If parents exploited their children by sending them to work in the mills and then spending their earnings on drink or by renting them out to professional beggars (as, it must be said, many did), was the State to relieve the parent of his proper responsibility for educating the children? Individualism meant to many, if it meant anything, the fundamental responsibility of a man for maintaining himself and his family; and naturally, maintenance included education. Nor was it true that all those who failed to educate their children were too poor to do so; many who could afford to do so, simply would not. Naturally, if the State took over the burden, there would be even less incentive for these parents to accept their responsibility. Worse, those who were already making sacrifices to educate their children might begin to neglect the burden and pass it onto the State. If the arguments have a familiar ring it is because the fundamental nature of the issues have changed so little. But in this area, the principle of Government assistance was gained at an early date, for it was after all the children who were to be educated, and even in the 1830s the paternalist role of the Government to children was well-recognized. By mid-century, at least, the case put by Macaulay for a more socially based education was clearly won. If people were to be left, in this individual world, to make their own decisions, then they *must* be given adequate guidance about the implications of their decisions.

The drink problem also produced vigorous demands for Governmental action in the educational field. Some, indeed, began to talk of prohibition, but that degree of coercion was too strong to be contemplated by most of the temperance reformers till very late in the century. Nothing could more clearly illustrate the way in which individualism could pull both ways in matters of social reform than the drink question. I have already referred to the truly appalling dimensions of the problem in the first half of the nineteenth century, but the individualism of the times made it hard to propose vigorous measures of control and regulation. The attitude of the middle classes to the drink problem combined paternalism and individualism in a way which seems utterly foreign to the modern world, so used to the coercive and heavy hand of the State. Middle-class men felt to the working classes as they may have felt to their own wayward children; they had to learn self-discipline, they had to be left to make their own decisions for good or for ill. It was an inevitable 'law of nature' that the self-indulgent would sink into degradation and poverty, while the self-disciplined would better themselves by their own efforts. Each man's salvation must come from within, and not be imposed from without. It was not, after all, very different from the attitude which Christians imputed to their own God in his dealings with his creatures; He had endowed them with free will to use for good or ill, but He was not indifferent to the way they used it. On the other hand, precisely the same intellectual ideals could be used to preach almost precisely the opposite message. In 1857 F. R. Lees, in an essay[33] on the drink problem which was awarded a Prize by the Temperance Alliance, argued for the total prohibition of the liquor trade, though he would have left people free to make their own drinks. Taking his stand on Benthamite principles, he vigorously repudiated the *laissez-faire* philosophy of the minimum State preached by Herbert Spencer, particularly with regard to the education of the people:

Government is for the defence of *all* rights, whether natural or civil; and comprizes everything necessary to a just and efficient defence of them. It comprehends Instruction—whether through Parliamentary discussion, the promulgation of laws, Judicial decisions, or the common Schoolmaster. Government *must* teach—even if it be only so far as to announce its own decrees. Government *must* discipline—if it be only its criminals, or expect its subjects to be plundered again. Government *must* educate—for acts of punishment and discipline are true educational influences; and the Society which has a right to teach by facts has an equal right to do so by formulas. Government *must* feed and clothe, as well as train and educate its Juvenile delinquents, and its pauper orphans, or become *particeps criminis* in the harvest of crime that will inevitably follow the neglect to do so.[34]

Not the least interesting part of this passage is that which suggests that Government, by inaction, is responsible for the evils existing in its midst. Bentham's message had done its work. It was now clear that everything *could* be regulated by the State; and the result was that notions of social responsibility were changing. The evils could no longer be laid solely at the door of those who created them. They were also the responsibility of those who failed to eliminate them. Thus what began as an argument derived from individualism passed, by an easy process of transition, into a fundamentally anti-individualist position.

INDIVIDUALISM AND DISCIPLINE

In the industrialized and over-populated England which was coming into existence in the early nineteenth century, a considerable increase was required in the forms of social discipline. Factory life required a different approach from agricultural life; wages paid in cash to the mill hand at regular (or, still worse, irregular) intervals, needed stricter

---

[33] *An Argument for the Legislative Prohibition of the Liquor Traffic* (London and Manchester, 3rd edn., 1857).   [34] Ibid., p. 30.

husbanding than might have been necessary for the farm labourer; the behaviour of large crowds in urban areas created new problems of public order, even if they were not of a revolutionary character; and, above all, the rapid increase of population itself required (as many thought) a different attitude to early marriage and child rearing. The reconciliation of the need for discipline in these and many other respects with the traditional civil liberties of the Englishmen was one of the fundamental problems of the first half of the nineteenth century. While the bureaucratic State was in process of being built, the answer to this problem was largely found in that form of individualism which is reflected in self-discipline and self-reliance. Englishmen were taught self-discipline by every possible means. This too, fitted well with the new political economy and with Benthamite utilitarianism. If people could learn to discipline themselves, it would obviate the need for costly and probably corrupt State officials to do the disciplining for them. The basic principle was that the Englishman was free to do what he chose, but if he chose wrongly, or illegally, he paid the penalty. The penalty was not necessarily a legal one—it might be loss of employment, for example, eviction for non-payment of rent, or a refusal of credit to someone who had shown himself untrustworthy. Penalties of this nature were not imposed by the Courts, the conduct involved was not necessarily prohibited or punishable; indeed, individualism meant that a man might go on making the same mistake, choosing wrongly again and again. 'The strange medley of licentiousness and legal restraint,' wrote a foreigner, 'of freedom and confinement—of punishment for what is done and liberty to do the same thing again is very curious.' But he concluded that it was more nearly in accordance with Natural Law than the artificial processes adopted by other countries.[35] The whole essence of this form of individualism was that a man was left free to choose, but he paid the 'natural' penalty if he chose wrongly. It was a splendid, simple and cheap way of imposing social discipline, or rather of encouraging the people to discipline themselves. It sometimes worked, especially in the long run. But it frequently did not work in the short run, and it occasionally did not work at all.

Let us consider some of the particular respects in which discipline was required in this new world. Inevitably, the first was the discipline of the factory, and the discipline of time, of the clock. Factories involved substantial capital investment, and if this investment was to pay an adequate return, the machinery had to be worked for long hours. Moreover, bringing together large numbers of persons in the factories meant that they had to work regular hours, and that they had to start and finish at the same time. All this involved a completely different

[35] Arthur Bryant, *The Age of Elegance* (reprinted, London, 1975), p. 263.

work-rhythm from that which had prevailed in eighteenth-century agriculture. In the eighteenth century, it was not uncommon for periods of intensive activity to be followed by periods of almost complete idleness for the farm labourer. A day off here or there made little difference, so long as all hands turned out at the essential times. And this rural work-rhythm had, in the eighteenth century, affected the city workers too. The number of public holidays and feast days—legitimately or illegitimately taken—was enormous. In 1761 the Bank of England closed for 47 days in the year, and the number had only come down to 40 in 1825.[36] Thereafter, modern industrial working habits began to be imposed; the number of Bank holidays dropped to 18 in 1830 and four in 1834.[37]

Then there was punctuality. Here too men had to be taught new standards of regularity in behaviour and in life. Men who had never owned a watch, who had perhaps been used to tell the time by the sun (when it shone!) had to learn that time mattered. Attitudes to time-keeping in early nineteenth-century England differed little from those that can still be observed in many African countries today where the same process of transition is taking place.[38] In many of the early cotton mills time-keeping was enforced by stringent methods. Workmen were often severely 'fined' for unpunctuality, and in some mills it was the practice to lock the gates excluding those who were only a minute or two late. Regular attendance was often as difficult to secure as punctual attendance. 'Cotton spinners would stay away without notice and send for their wages at the end of the week.'[39] The habit of simply taking 'St. Monday' off, despite the fact that failure to attend for work was a criminal offence, has already been noted.

Within the factory itself, discipline also had to be maintained. What was good enough for agricultural labourers, out in the fields, was simply not good enough in a crowded factory, with expensive machinery running at full blast. New standards of sobriety at work were required, new standards even of cleanliness in many of the better mills. And the work itself required a steady, methodical application and new, though rarely stringent, standards of care and skill. In many factories a strict disciplinary regime operated in which rules and regulations were simply posted up on doors or notice boards, and enforced by the owner, or foreman. Severe 'fines' were imposed by deduction from the wages due. The fines might, for example, be as much as a quarter of an hour's earnings for three minutes' lateness, or a quarter of a day's earnings for

[36] Perkin, *The Age of the Railway* (London, 1970), p. 206.
[37] Ibid., p. 211.
[38] E. P. Thompson, 'Time, Work-Discipline and Individual Capitalism', 38 *Past and Present* 56 (1967); E. J. Hobsbawm, *Industry and Empire*, pp. 95–6.
[39] S. Pollard, 'Factory Discipline in the Industrial Revolution', 16 *Economic History Rev.* 254, 255–6 (1963).

twenty minutes' lateness.[40] In the case of apprentices and children, even beatings were not unknown, though in many of the better mills this was strictly forbidden. Dismissal, and even blacklists maintained by groups of employers, were naturally the ultimate and readily available sanctions. These codes of discipline were, of course, unilaterally imposed by the employers, and doubtless in most cases they were never challenged in the Courts. But even if they were, the workman stood little chance of sympathy in the local magistrates' courts where such disputes were litigated under the Master and Servant Acts; they were generally better off in the superior Courts (as even Engels grudgingly acknowledged),[41] despite the common belief that the judges were always hostile to working-class litigants. But in the magistrates' courts, where the justices were, as like as not, themselves mill owners, or friends of mill owners, the working man generally got short shrift. Engels, though not the most temperate commentator on social conditions in mid-nineteenth-century England, was probably perfectly accurate in his account of this question. Inside the factory, he wrote, 'the employer is absolute law-giver; he makes regulations at will, changes and adds to his code at pleasure, and even if he inserts the craziest stuff, the courts say to the working man: "You were your own master; no one forced you to agree to such a contract if you did not want to, but now, when you have freely entered into it, you must be bound by it."'[42]

It was not, by any means, only amongst the mill hands that new disciplines, new order and regularity in life were needed. The general task of disciplining and professionalizing work which had formerly been undertaken in a casual and amateurish fashion was one which affected a wide variety of activities. The creation of the new police force, for example, a process of turning 'half-literate labourers into reasonably reliable policemen',[43] was at first marked by serious problems of drunkenness and a high dismissal rate. New disciplines also had to be learned in the slowly professionalizing civil service. In the 1820s Lord Palmerston tightened up the discipline of the War Office 'clerks' in a variety of ways, and in particular he insisted that they should stop receiving private visitors during office hours.[44] Even a small contractor doing a minor piece of work for a middle-class client might find himself

[40] F. Engels, *The Condition of the Working Class in England*, first published (in German) in 1845 (Panther edn., Frogmore, St. Albans, Herts., 1969), p. 207. Page references are to this edition.

[41] For example, Engels relates how in the 1840s the miners' union secured the services of W. P. Roberts, an energetic solicitor (and Chartist) who took many appeals from the justices to the Court of Queen's Bench, where he was regularly successful: pp. 278–80.

[42] Ibid., p. 206.

[43] W. L. Burn, *The Age of Equipoise*, p. 173.

[44] Jasper Ridley, *Lord Palmerston* (Panther edn., London, 1970), p. 87. Anybody acquainted with the workings of a modern African public service will appreciate the nature and importance of this kind of problem.

subjected to a dose of discipline, as happened to the contractor who botched a job for Edwin Chadwick in 1839. 'I quite see', Chadwick wrote to him, 'that to pass over these things from the inconvenience to oneself in having them altered is to give a bounty on indolence and bad workmanship.'[45]

Little by little these new disciplines were learnt, and had their effect. The process was long and doubtless hard, but it was an indispensable requirement of the modern social world in which millions lived together in crowded cities, and were necessarily dependent on each other. In 1835 Dr. Kay (later Sir James Kay-Shuttleworth) recorded that, in comparison with the Irish, who were known for their unreliability, the English 'are more steady, cleanly, skilful labourers, and are more faithful in the fulfilment of contracts made between master and servant'.[46]

But it was self-discipline which was really the most important lesson. Coercion was necessary, no doubt, but in the long run self-discipline was more effective, as well as being simpler. Self-discipline, the self-imposed restraint on the urge to immediate pleasures, enlightened self-interest, all these had been lessons learnt by the commercial men and industrialists of the preceding century; now the same lessons had to be taught to the mass of the people. They did not lack teachers, either. By far the best known of them was Samuel Smiles (1812–1904), the greatest popularizer of mid-Victorian individualism. His books on the simple virtues of *Self-Help* (1859), *Thrift* (1875), and many others of a like character, sold by the million. Self-discipline, self-denial, and order, were some of the messages preached by Smiles. Just as the Whig landowners of the early eighteenth century had discovered that prompt payment of debts was the secret to creditworthiness and low interest rates, so Smiles and his kind preached a similar message to the working-class men of nineteenth-century England. It was not, indeed, precisely the same message, for Smiles preached saving and thrift, not borrowing; but, *mutatis mutandis*, the underlying idea was the same. It is necessary to deny oneself in the present for the sake of the future; it is necessary to think ahead, to take store for difficult times, to postpone consumption. It is also necessary to pay one's debts, to perform one's contracts, to render one's neighbour his due. To be fair to them, the Victorian middle classes in general practised what they preached. They themselves indulged in self-denial on a truly massive scale, and they often required the same self-denial of their children.[47] Even the prosperous and successful industrialists of the new age were more noted for the profits they invested in the businesses they

[45] S. E. Finer, *The Life and Times of Sir Edwin Chadwick*, p. 5.

[46] E. P. Thompson, *The Making of the English Working Class*, p. 433. Kay-Shuttleworth, a doctor and educational reformer, was a brother of Kay L. J. who sat in the Court of Appeal later in the century.

[47] For some extreme examples of this, see Walter E. Houghton, *The Victorian Frame of Mind*, pp. 233–7.

had created, than for those they spent.[48] They saw no reason why the same gospel of self-restraint should not be learnt by the working classes.

Promise-keeping was one of the most important forms of self-discipline and self-denial preached by Smiles. A man who kept his promises, and paid his debts, became known as a trustworthy person. This was to his advantage because it meant that when he required the co-operation of another which involved that other's reliance upon him, it would be more likely to be forthcoming. Smiles quoted the words of the Duke of Wellington about prisoners on parole: 'When English officers have given their parole of honour not to escape, be sure they will not break it. Believe me—trust to their word. The word of an English officer is a surer guarantee than the vigilance of a sentinel.'[49]

Of course, long before Smiles began to preach his message, some working men had discovered it for themselves. Francis Place, for instance, without a shilling to his name had established a highly prosperous business as a tailor in Charing Cross around the turn of the century. Without any capital he knew he would have to establish his business by skilful use of credit, buying on credit, and reselling in good time to enable him to meet his obligations. By taking care to pay for what he had bought before the term for credit had expired he established a reputation for punctuality within such a short time that he was able to have credit to any amount whatever.[50] It was not always easy; sometimes he and his wife wanted for food while they had money put by which they dared not touch lest it might lead to irregularity in payment of his suppliers, and so ruin the credit on which he utterly depended.[51] But in the end he succeeded, and was soon making three thousand pounds a year.

If there was one sphere in which self-denial was more important than another, it was with regard to early marriage and child rearing. The Malthusian spectre haunted most thinking Englishmen of the first few decades of the nineteenth century. By this time the censuses had confirmed what they could see with their own eyes, that population was growing faster than the social machinery of the State could cope with. To Malthus himself, it was all a matter of simple arithmetic. The population grew by geometric progression, while food supplies could only be increased by arithmetic progression. In this Malthus was wrong, but his message was deeply disturbing to contemporary Englishmen. The idea at one time entertained (for example) by Paley in his *Principles*, that the contentment of a nation, like that of a happy family, increases with its numbers, was replaced for Paley himself, as well as for many others, with

[48] T. S. Ashton, *The Industrial Revolution*, p. 97.
[49] *Self-Help*, p. 376.
[50] *Autobiography of Francis Place*, pp. 137–8.
[51] Ibid., p. 174.

the conviction that the rapid increase of numbers was potentially a disaster of the first magnitude. To Malthus himself, and some of his early converts, the message he preached was chiefly one of gloom, unrelieved by hope. Population *would* continue to increase at rates which would inevitably outstrip food supplies; and the result would be that wage rates, responding to surplus labour conditions, would inevitably hover around the level of bare subsistence, sometimes even falling below it in times of actual famine.[52] But to some of the more optimistic of the new Radicals and Benthamites, as John Stuart Mill relates in his *Autobiography*, the Malthusian message was turned upside down into a message of hope.[53] If only the mass of the people could be taught self-restraint in marriage and sex, population increases could be brought under control; and as the increase was controlled, wages would inevitably rise. Labour would become scarcer, and the fund of capital available for the maintenance of the workers would be shared out among smaller and smaller numbers. They began to see, in the distant future, hope of a time when the working people of England could, for the first time in history, become a reasonably prosperous, educated, and civilized class of society. But once again, the key to it all, the salvation of the working class, lay in their own individual hands. Self-denial, late marriages, fewer children, were the indispensable condition for this golden age of the future. It is a measure of their unbounded optimism in the potentialities of education, and of the power of the human will, that so many of the classical economists and the Benthamites really believed that all this could be achieved by individual effort.[54]

INDIVIDUALISM AND SELF-RELIANCE

Self-denial is not the same thing as self-reliance, but the two were closely related in the individualist creed of early nineteenth-century England. Both could be treated as prudential virtues, perhaps both were originally based on prudential considerations. In the social and commercial conditions which prevailed in early nineteenth-century England it was prudent to deny oneself today in order to have a care for the morrow; and it was also prudent to rely upon oneself, for reliance upon others was, in a competitive, volatile world, fraught with dangers. Too many men had seen bankruptcy and business failure affect innocent partners and guarantors who had trusted too much, had relied too much, on the

---

[52] In later editions of his work, Malthus himself seems to have become less gloomy, holding out some hope that 'moral restraint' might check population increases sufficiently to stave off indefinitely the otherwise certain famine. See *post*, Chapter 11.

[53] *Autobiography*, p. 64.

[54] Although Francis Place (who had fifteen children) once wrote to James Mill (who had nine) commenting sardonically that they were fine men to preach moral restraint!

integrity or competence of others. A writer in 1833 commented that few rich men who entered the cotton industry had made a success of their business. 'They trusted too much to others—too little to themselves.'[55]

Virtually every class in early nineteenth-century England had learnt the lessons of self-reliance at some stage in their lives. Even the aristocrats, sheltered from the harshness of a competitive society by their inherited wealth, sent their sons to public schools. And in the public schools at that time—as for many years after—the emphasis on character building depended, by design or by lack of it, on something very close to the law of the jungle. Sir James Stephen, at Eton in the 1840s, learnt 'that to be weak is to be wretched, that the state of nature is a state of war and *Vae Victis* the great law of Nature'.[56] Rober Lowe at Winchester in the 1820s had learnt the same lesson, and later told Stephen that he had there discovered that a man could count on nothing in this world except what lay between his hat and his boots.[57]

Amongst the commercial and industrial middle classes much the same lessons were learnt, from the greatest to the smallest. The successful industrialists of this period, almost without exception, took the greatest pains to keep themselves informed of every detail of what went on in their enterprises. Frequently the gap in ability, integrity, and energy between the men at the top and their assistants was so great that the former had perforce to rely on themselves, and supervise every detail of their businesses themselves. When Josiah Wedgwood pored over his accounts trying to cut costs and adopt a more rationalizing pricing policy, he soon discovered that his accountants had been cheating him.[58] When Sir James Graham took over the management of his vast estates in Netherby he discovered that the family's agent kept the estate accounts in his head and not on paper.[59] The engineer Brunel, who built the Great Western Railway from London to Bristol, surveyed almost every inch of the line himself.[60] These men practised self-reliance because it was the only way they could do what they wanted; to them self-reliance was not so much a moral principle, as a plain necessity of circumstances. It was not very different with the great mass of smaller businessmen, small manufacturers, contractors, retailers. Reliance on others carried enormous potential dangers. The law itself imposed the direst penalties on those who relied unwisely. A man who trusted his agent with too much

[55] Cited by M. W. Thomas, *The Early Factory Legislation*, p. 5.

[56] Introduction by R. J. White, to J. F. Stephen, *Liberty, Equality, Fraternity* (reprinted, Cambridge, 1967), p. 4.

[57] Ibid. A contemporary of Lowe's at Eton was Roundell Palmer, later Lord Chancellor Selborne; there is no evidence whether he learnt the same lesson.

[58] Neil McKendrick, 'Josiah Wedgwood and Cost Accounting in the Industrial Revolution', 22 *Economic History Rev.* 45 (1970).

[59] J. T. Ward, *Sir James Graham* (London, Melbourne, Toronto, 1967), p. 56.

[60] L. C. T. Rolt, *Isambard Kingdom Brunel* (Harmondsworth, 1974), Chapter 4.

responsibility might find himself liable on a disastrous contract entered into without his consent; a man who did not keep a close watch on his partner might find himself ruined from a careless transaction, again perhaps made without his knowledge. And partnerships, or unlimited liability companies, were still the normal form of commercial enterprise until the middle of the nineteenth century.

And if the upper and middle classes learned self-reliance the hard way, the poor learnt it even harder. With no Welfare State to fall back upon, with the new Poor Law after 1834 denying assistance to the able-bodied unemployed unless they went into the work-house, with the virtual inaccessibility of the Courts to the poor to assist them secure redress from those they trusted too wisely, most grew up learning not to trust to anyone but themselves. Among the real dregs of society, in the slums and underworld of the large cities, a man could not survive at all except by trusting to himself. Here, 'there was a fully competitive society without disguise, where all could see that strength, cunning, quick response to opportunity and danger, courage and freedom from scruple, were the keys to survival.'[61]

Once again, Samuel Smiles was to the fore preaching the virtues of self-reliance, or as he usually called it, self-help. Much of his preaching took an intensely practical form. Smiles insisted that everybody knew that some working men, even then, were earning more than some of the poorer clergymen or teachers, and yet they failed to measure up to their social and family responsibilities.[62] If working men failed to help themselves, he insisted, it was their own fault. 'We often hear the cry raised, "Will nobody help us?" It is', he protested, 'a spiritless, hopeless cry. It is sometimes a cry of revolting meanness, especially when it issues from those who with a little self-denial, sobriety and thrift, might easily help themselves.'[63]

It was precisely this belief in self-reliance which led the Victorians to lay so much stress on charity. Charity for those who could not help themselves was an absolutely indispensable part of the Victorian social order, and there is no doubt that vast sums were regularly disbursed in charity throughout the nineteenth century; in 1870 the economist, W. S. Jevons, estimated that the total amounts paid out in charity greatly exceeded the total cost of Poor Law relief.[64] But he also argued, as nearly all the Victorians did, that charitable aid could not be converted into a right without seriously weakening the force of self-reliance. For the early Victorians the case against this had been thoroughly argued in the Poor Law Report of 1834.

[61] Kellow Chesney, *The Victorian Underworld* (Harmondsworth, 1972), p. 143.
[62] *Thrift*, 1903 edn., p. 4.   [63] Ibid., p. 25.
[64] 'Economic Policy' in *Essays in Economic Method*, ed. Smyth (London, 1962).

If self-reliance was to be taught, it was easy to slip into the way of treating it as a moral, and not just a prudential virtue, and this too happened in the Victorian period. To rely on oneself came to be seen, not just as a piece of sound practical common-sense, but as an inherent moral good. One of Samuel Smiles' precepts was the familiar idea that Heaven helps those who help themselves.

Similarly, the transition by which self-reliance became a moral virtue had an important and long lasting effect on ideas about credit. For many people, to be in debt became something akin to a sin, even where the debtor was perfectly capable of paying a proper rate of interest, and even where the repayment of the capital was adequately secured. Years before, Bentham had argued that hiring money was no different from hiring a horse, and his views came ultimately to prevail to the extent that the legal control of interest rates was eventually abolished. But no sooner had Bentham's ideas prevailed on this point than they came up against the new Victorian middle-class morality about indebtedness. And from their point of view, the Victorians were right and Bentham was wrong. For the difference between hiring money and hiring a horse is that the hirer can use the money for any purpose he pleases—including wasting it—while a horse can only be used for those purposes for which a horse is suited, and will normally still be available to be returned to the owner when the hirer has finished with it. Since this new morality was fundamentally designed for the education of the working classes, this difference was a very important one. After all, if working people did not often hire horses, they did rent houses, and nobody wanted to discourage them from that; but nobody wanted to encourage the Victorian worker to hire money, not at any rate until later in the nineteenth century when modern consumer credit first appeared.

If self-reliance was to be a moral virtue, it is not surprising that some Victorians preferred individualism as a social mechanism, as well as a value. Although I have previously suggested that these are two distinct concepts, they are plainly related at this point. For when decisions are taken collectively, nobody feels quite the same sense of responsibility for the outcome as when they are taken by individuals acting alone. One of Herbert Spencer's complaints about the corporate form, and especially about the railway companies, was based on his belief that the corporate conscience was inferior to the individual conscience. A body of men will jointly commit an act, he argued, from which each would individually shrink.[65]

The belief in the virtues of self-reliance had an impact on the law during this period which I shall examine in some depth later. But it is

[65] 'Railway Morals and Railway Policy' (1854) reprinted in Essays, iii (London and Edinburgh, 1891), p. 60.

worth observing here that it also had a great impact on ideas about responsibility and cause which themselves underlie many ideas about justice, and are ultimately influential on the law.

When a person is thought to be morally responsible for a state of affairs, it is likely that there will be pressures to make him legally responsible for it too. When people believed that a man ought morally to rely upon himself, and not upon others, it was natural to conclude that what happened to him was his own responsibility, his own fault. And if it was his fault, plainly there was no case for imposing legal liability on anybody else for what had happened. This also had considerable implications for the concept of responsibility for omissions. Basically, a person is not usually thought of as either morally or legally responsible for omitting to do something, unless he has a duty to do it in the first place. And if a person has no duty to help his neighbours because they are regarded as fundamentally responsible for their own fate, because they have no right to rely on anyone else for his assistance, then legal liability for omissions is likely to be extremely curtailed. An illustration of the lengths to which this moral attitude could be taken is provided by the events surrounding a celebrated prize fight in 1860. Prize fights were at this time regarded as illegal in themselves, but many people saw nothing wrong in merely *watching* a prize fight. In this particular case the South Eastern Railway Company laid on special trains to carry the spectators to watch this event, and one of the spectators was none other than Lord Palmerston, Prime Minister of Great Britain.[66] Although Palmerston was criticized for his conduct, he defended himself in the House of Commons arguing that merely watching an illegal prize fight was not itself illegal.[67] He was right, too.[68] In this individualist nineteenth-century world a man was not his brother's keeper.

There were, as always, countervailing beliefs, opposing attitudes. Society was a complex institution, and people had perforce to rely upon others in a thousand different ways. Was such a reliance to be always regarded as morally wrong, and as legally unprotected? This simply could not be so. If it were, even the laws for the protection of property and for the enforcement of contracts could not be justified. After all, the thief is 'a very paragon of self-reliance',[69] and the man who lends money to another is undoubtedly relying on the other's honesty and credit-worthiness, as well as his own judgment. The fact that the ethos of the times was one of self-reliance did not and could not mean that reliance on others was never justifiable, never legally protected. But what it did

---

[66] W. L. Burn, *The Age of Equipoise*, p. 284.

[67] *Parliamentary Debates*, 3rd Series, vol. 158, cols. 1319–25.

[68] So held by the Court for Crown Cases Reserved by a majority of 8 judges to 3 in *R. v. Coney* (1882) 8 Q.B.D. 534.

[69] Duncan Kennedy, 'Form and Substance in Private Law Adjudication', p. 1719.

mean was that the onus was, as it were, thrown on he who relied to show that his reliance was reasonable; and in an individualist era, reasonableness in reliance was evidently less easy to establish. The extent of the impact of this ethos on the law I shall examine in Chapter 15. Here it is enough to draw attention to the fact that even in moral and social attitudes, there were respects in which Victorian individualism gave way to other aspects of Victorian morality. Indeed, it could be said that it was precisely the problems which arose out of the ethos of self-reliance which gave rise to some other facets of the Victorian moral code.

The powerful moral force which came to be attached to truthfulness, honesty, promise-keeping, the whole code of honour associated with the concept of the 'gentleman', the extremely stringent ethical and legal standards required of a trustee, all attest to the great importance which the Victorians did place on circumstances in which reliance on others was a necessary feature of life. One had to rely on another when he gave his word, when he was a gentleman, when he accepted the burdens of a trustee. These were circumstances in which reliance was inescapable, and therefore all the more stringently protected.

THE COMPETITIVE SYSTEM OF REWARDS AND PENALTIES

Belief in individualism and self-reliance, both as a value and as a social mechanism, carried with it a belief in the virtues of a competitive society, and in a proper system of rewards and penalties. It also carried with it a corresponding rejection of the ideal of equality which, indeed, seemed the very negation of the principles on which a just society must be founded. For did not justice require that every man receive his due? And if the dues were different, as unquestionably they were, did it not follow that to give equally to every one was inherently unjust?

Throughout the whole period 1770–1870, the belief in competition, both in commercial and industrial affairs, and in life generally, was powerful and itself largely paralleled what was going on in the world. As we have already seen, this was an intensely active and competitive period in industrial affairs, and the penalties of failure were as severe as the rewards for success were high. Fortunes could be made and were made by humble, even illiterate people, with skill, ingenuity, and enterprise.

To many of the thinkers of the early part of this period, all this was, in fact, simply in accord with the Laws of Nature, or—if less grandiose appellations were in order—with the natural order of things. Those who worked hard naturally received their due reward, all the more naturally perhaps to those who still lived so close to a time when the whole country largely subsisted on farming. And these 'Laws of Nature' were, of course, not merely moral or legal rules. They extended far beyond that. Every type of activity had its own reward or penalty according as to whether it was desirable or not. Legal rules and penalties naturally awaited those who violated the laws; but frequently these were backed up by moral penalties or rewards, and still others of a purely natural kind. For example, the ill-repute of the idle and dissolute was a 'natural' penalty paid by such people; the drunkard's humiliation (not to say his hangover) was 'nature's warning against self-indulgence'.[70] And the supreme crime of poverty, or at least indigence, obviously also carried with it the 'natural' penalty of actual want or hunger. It was a simple and perfectly obvious Law of Nature that if a man had more children than he could afford to feed, then they would want. One of the chief objections to the old Poor Law as administered under the Speenhamland system from 1795 to 1834—whereby workers' wages were supplemented by the Poor Law authorities on a scale related to the size of their family—was that it attempted to repeal this law of nature.[71] For if a man could always be assured of enough to eat, no matter how many children he had, and no matter how idly he lived, the 'natural' system of rewards and penalties would be abolished.

All this presupposed a competitive society in which men desire to improve their lot, to make more money, not necessarily for its own sake, but for what went with it, as well as to improve their opportunities for education, self-respect, and a more comfortable way of life. In fact it is not at all clear that most English labourers shared this desire in the 1770s, though some undoubtedly did so. Max Weber argued that 'A man does not "by nature" wish to earn more and more, but simply to live as he is accustomed to live, and to earn as much as is necessary for that purpose.' He went on to say that, 'Wherever modern capitalism has begun its work of increasing the productivity of human labour by increasing its intensity, it has encountered the immensely stubborn resistance of this leading trait of pre-capitalistic labour.'[72] If Weber is right, then it becomes necessary to say that the labouring classes had to be propagandized, or 'educated', into accepting this new competitive work-ethic. Perhaps he was right, and certainly there is something faintly absurd in this educative process by which the poor were vigorously taught what they were supposed to want 'by nature'. But it must also be remembered that, before the time of universal education, Government grants to university students, and so on, there must have been many exceptionally gifted children born every year into the labouring families whose only way out lay in their own

---

[70] Brian Harrison, *Drink and the Victorians*, p. 208, attributing this opinion to J. S. Mill.

[71] *The Poor Law Report of 1834*, p. 156.

[72] *The Protestant Ethic and the Spirit of Capitalism*, p. 60; see also Pollard, 'Factory Discipline in the Industrial Revolution', at p. 254 who says that the factory men 'were non-accumulative, non-acquisitive, accustomed to work for subsistence, not for maximization of income . . .'

hands. To these children, many of whom must have been aware of their unusual abilities from an early age, the older, customary way of life may well have seemed quite unnatural. To them, the ability to rise above the common herd, to get on by natural ability, hard work, and enterprising skill may have seemed as natural as it did to the middle-class economists and utilitarians who were generally responsible for preaching the message.

In the mid-nineteenth century, the idea that competition was a 'Natural Law' received a powerful impetus from the writings of Charles Darwin, and the use to which they were put by Herbert Spencer. Darwin's *Origin of Species* was first published in 1859, and it was (as he himself acknowledged) much influenced by Malthus and also by Spencer. Applying the ideas of Malthus to the whole animal and vegetable kingdom and combining them with the concept of the social struggle for survival propagated by Herbert Spencer, Darwin had hit upon the theory of natural selection. In the animal and vegetable kingdom, unlike that controlled by humans, increase in the food supply was not possible and it was evident, therefore, that there were far more individuals of each species than could possibly survive. In the recurring struggle for survival that necessarily followed, the process of 'natural selection' operated—that is those survived who were best adapted to survive in the given conditions; the others perished. The phrase, 'the survival of the fittest' which was used by Darwin was, in fact, borrowed by him from Herbert Spencer, who had previously used it in a description of the social struggle which takes place among mankind.

Naturally, Spencer seized avidly upon the new theory of evolution. Here it seemed was further proof of the scientific nature of these 'Natural Laws' by which the social as well as the physical universe was governed. Competition thus became justifiable on these pseudo-scientific grounds. Life was a constant struggle for survival. Those who were fittest, that is, toughest, most able, most enterprising, would survive; the weak would, if not physically perish, assuredly fail. This was an inexorable scientific process. Nothing the Government or anyone else could do would arrest it in the long run; but for the Government to interfere with the process would be disastrous in the short run for it would ensure a longer period of survival of the unfit. As we shall see later, Herbert Spencer was the great apostle of freedom of contract in the later half of the nineteenth century, and he naturally linked his beliefs in freedom of contract with this new theory of natural selection. The resultant body of ideas, which have come to be called 'Social Darwinism', never had a great following in England, perhaps because of the onslaughts of the great biologist, T. H. Huxley. Already in 1871 Huxley was arguing that Spencer's analogy between the social and the physical organism was absurd, and he returned even more vigorously to the attack in the 1890s. Social Darwinism died a quiet death in England, although it flourished for many years in the United States.

INDIVIDUALISM AND EGALITARIANISM

Mid-Victorian individualism was plainly antagonistic to egalitarian ideals. But ever since the French Revolution egalitarianism had had its supporters, few though they were, and oddly enough both individualism and egalitarianism drew support from similar sources, and in particular from the ideas of Natural Law. Belief in individualism and competition descended to a large degree from Locke and the seventeenth-century Natural Law thinkers of whom I have spoken briefly before. After the French Revolution broke out and brought with it new connotations to Natural Rights (as with Tom Paine and his *Rights of Man*), an uneasy conflict existed between the traditionalists like Locke's descendants, the political economists from Adam Smith onwards, and the new egalitarians, or even revolutionaries. They both laid claim to the support of Natural Law. Equality of treatment—not just equality before the Law, a long and well established Whig concept—but new, financial equality, redistributive equality, appeared as a political ideal and claimed a legitimate descent from Natural Law. The new idealists like Tom Paine had, of course, little influence on more orthodox thinkers, and still less on Government policies or Parliamentary opinion right up to the end of this period, that is up to 1870. Throughout this period, belief in equality, in economic equality—or as it is now more euphemistically called, Social Justice—really had very little support in public or political opinion. That is not to say that a working-class tradition did not exist, a tradition of Utopians like Godwin, of radical politicians like Paine himself and perhaps Cobbett, of dreamers and visionaries among whom might be counted Robert Owen, all of whom had their followers. But so far as events, politics, the law, were concerned, these ideals would generally have been dismissed as Utopian, and even something more harmful.

Generally speaking, mid-nineteenth-century England had little belief in equality as an ideal. Men simply were not equal, as anybody with eyes in his head could see. Some were educated, others illiterate; some were hard-working, others idle; some were self-controlled, others dissipated; some drunk, others sober; some wastrels, others thrifty; some good and others bad. The idea that all these people could and should be treated as equal was simply preposterous. The great majority of middle-class Englishmen, for example, totally rejected political democracy up to the middle of the nineteenth century. Political democracy, if it meant giving the vote to everyone was, in the views of many, simply to hand over political power to the mob, the uneducated and ignorant majority. Since these people could not normally be trusted even to manage their own affairs so as to ensure (for example) that their wages lasted the week through, it was simply madness to think of handing over the nation to their power. This rejection of equality in the political and economic sphere naturally carried over into the social sphere to produce the Victorian snobbery, so much despised today. But the Victorians saw nothing wrong with looking down on their inferiors, and looking up to their betters. It was all part of the system of penalties and rewards which ruled every inch of society. Indeed, they revelled in these inequalities for reasons which seemed highly moral to them. 'It is a gross understatement to describe mid-Victorian society as undemocratic; it prided itself not on its equality, but on its balance, on its nuances of social status, on its varied but converging ideals.'[73]

To be defensible, even to be self-consistent, these beliefs demanded a high degree of social mobility. If a man was to be judged as what he was because he was responsible for what he made himself, then there had to be plenty of opportunity for moving up and down in the scale. This too was one of the facets of this competitive society, though it cannot be denied that social mobility was not so easy as economic mobility. It was (as I have emphasized) easy to make a fortune one day, and lose it the next if you were a member of the new industrial and commercial classes. The older aristocracy did not move up and down quite so easily as this. Indeed, there were not wanting complaints that the strict settlement and family trusts made it very difficult for aristocratic wastrels or drunkards to pay the same penalties as would men of the same disposition who were lower down the social scale. And this, no doubt partly explains why the aristocracy tended to look down socially at the *nouveaux riches*. But even in this, most snobbish of eras, and most snobbish of attitudes, we must remember that things were not pressed too far. The *nouveaux riches* themselves passed easily enough into the ranks of high society. If the age was one which stressed inequalities, they were, in Bagehot's phrase, 'removable inequalities'.[74]

In stressing that mid-nineteenth-century Englishmen generally rejected the ideal of equality or social justice, we must beware of convicting them of having embraced a materialist and unjust philosophy. To them, their competitive society was of the very essence of justice. It was through competition that men struggled to improve their lot and themselves, and in doing so (as the political economists were credited with having proved), improved the collective lot of society as a whole. Competition was thus a moral virtue, good for the individual and good for society.

[73] Asa Briggs, *Victorian People*, p. 20.
[74] W. L. Burn, *The Age of Equipoise*, p. 104; Asa Briggs, *Victorian People*, p. 106.

Justice consisted in ensuring the rules of fair play, setting the framework within which the competition was to take place, and then enforcing the results. The fact that all the competitors in the struggle did not start equally was, no doubt, unfortunate, but it could not be helped. Basically, those who succeeded, owed their success (it was thought) to their own virtues, while those who failed had only themselves to blame. The blind Goddess distributed her favours and penalties indifferently to those who deserved them. What was unjust about this process?

Nevertheless, as the nineteenth century wore on, an increasing number did see the process as unjust. Competition began to be seen, at least in some eyes, as a degrading, constant social struggle which set man against man instead of encouraging social co-operation. The fact that those born to wealth and position had such an immense advantage in the competitive struggle began to receive greater emphasis; the fact that many of those who succeeded or failed seemed to owe their success or failure more to good or ill luck than to their own merits, came to be increasingly observed upon. And the ideal of equality itself began to have a greater weight in human affairs.

To take the last point first, the campaign in the early nineteenth century for the abolition first of the slave trade, and then of slavery itself, owed a good deal to the religious fervour of the evangelists, and especially to the Quakers, who had insisted on the equality of all men in the eyes of God.[75] And though it was a far cry from freeing slaves to any idea of economic equality, it is clear that even before the end of the eighteenth century, moralists were beginning to wonder whether the existing extremes of wealth and poverty could be justified for the sake of encouraging industry and enterprise. Paley, for instance, was at pains to justify the moral basis of the existing inequalities in society.[76]

By the mid-nineteenth century, a minority of thinkers and writers were beginning to take some of these doubts about the competitive society a great deal further, and perhaps a more broadly-based set of opinions was already in process of formation. Many strands entered into this transition. Perhaps the first and most important was the challenge to inequalities of wealth on the very terms now being argued by its defenders. If, as Paley argued, the inequalities were only justified in so far as they provided the incentives and industry needed to keep society going, then it was time to take a closer look at the inequalities to see whether this justification was always maintainable. It was no longer enough to justify inequality by a broad appeal to the need for incentives. The case must be proved in each instance. This was an important change, for it meant that the onus of proof was reversed. Those who defended

[75] Asa Briggs, *Victorian People*, p. 210.
[76] *Principles of Moral and Political Philosophy*, Book II, Chapter VI.

inequalities of wealth were going onto the defensive, where they have remained ever since. By 1861 John Stuart Mill was plainly on the defensive in discussing inequalities in *Utilitarianism*. He concedes there that to many people equality is seen as constituting the very essence of justice, though he also insists that 'Each person maintains that equality is the dictate of justice, except where he thinks that expediency requires inequality.'[77] Thus inequality was now reduced (at least by Mill) to being defended on grounds of mere 'expediency'. Here was another important concession, for although Mill himself offered a sophisticated version of the relationship between justice and expediency, it is likely that most of his contemporaries still saw a vast gulf between the two. If justice demanded that wealth be equally distributed, or at least, more equally distributed than hitherto, and it was only expediency that stood in the way, how long would the public tolerate this injustice?

It seems no coincidence that the upholders of inequality went onto the defensive at about the same time as increasing political power was coming into the hands of the propertiless. In the eighteenth century, when political debate was still conducted largely among the Whig aristocrats themselves, and egalitarians could be dismissed as eccentrics, there was little need to argue in defence of inequalities of wealth. Locke had provided the Whigs with their fundamental defence of property rights and he sufficed for most of them, partly at least because most of them were on the same side of the debate. By 1850 or thereabouts, the debate was being conducted before a much wider audience. The working class had still to acquire the vote, it is true, but they were now far more politically conscious and articulate. The popular Press had given them a forum for ultra-Radical, or even socialist opinions, the Chartist movement, and to some extent the trade unions, had provided some institutional strength, and some of the more fiery Radical politicians had, on this or that issue, espoused their cause.

There were many other forces at work in the same direction. For one thing, education and the popular press were beginning to spread more and more widely, and it was no longer so easy to preach a hypocritical message to the working class while practising something quite different. Paternalism might still be a force, but it was becoming more difficult to maintain the extreme forms of paternalism whereby the working classes might be fobbed off, for 'their own good' with messages no longer really believed in by the governing classes. The difficulty appears from an *Essay* of John Stuart Mill's in 1845 in which he said that it was one thing to tell the rich that they ought to take care of the poor, and another thing to tell the poor that the rich ought to take care of them.[78] The trouble was that

[77] *Utilitarianism*, Chapter 5.
[78] Cited by L. Robbins, *Evolution of Modern Economic Theory* (London, 1970), p. 145.

by 1860, if not earlier, it was very difficult to tell the rich they owed a duty to take care of the poor without the poor coming to learn of the fact, and draw their own conclusions.

Mill was also responsible for another weapon which came ultimately to have a greater significance in the case against inequality. In his *Principles of Political Economy*[79] Mill drew attention to the fact that those who earn very large rewards (for example in the professions) by reason of exceptional skills and aptitudes are, in a sense, receiving their rewards not because of competition, but because of its absence. It is precisely because there are so few people who possess these rare skills and natural talents that they are able to command so high a price; it is in effect, a monopoly price, the effect not of a legal, but of a 'natural' monopoly. Mill himself did not develop this theme at great length, though (when taken with some of his other doubts about competitive earnings) it has sometimes earned him the surely unmerited title of the father of English socialism. But the idea proved important at a later period, and it opened up a still wider gap between the idea of competition and moral virtue. If a man's earnings in a competitive society depended less on his own hard work and enterprise, and more on the natural endowment of talents, then the really successful could no longer claim any moral virtue in their success. They were, in fact, little better than monopolists.

There were also other factors tending to iron out differences in earnings based on market conditions. As factories got larger, as commercial organizations employed more workmen, as Government itself grew bigger and employed more public servants, it became more difficult for employers to match the wage to the man. Calculating the marginal productivity of a single member of a large team is difficult enough on its own; if the workers in the interests of solidarity try to cover up for the weaker and less efficient members of their team, it may become virtually impossible. But anyhow, not everybody was paid a wage fixed on market principles. Mill also observed, for instance, that the fees charged by professional men such as doctors, and barristers, were largely fixed by custom, and not by the market. The same was true of many other classes of workers, such as domestic servants and business clerks. But belief in the very principle of equality as an ideal was having its influence too. By the middle of the nineteenth century the Government was generally paying the same wages to labourers employed in different parts of the country even though the market wage for labour differed significantly from place to place. When challenged, the Government defended its action as a modern Government would—by blandly asserting that equality of treatment was more important than responding

---

[79] Book II, Chapter 14, Sect. 2.

to market conditions. 'If varying rates were adopted by the Government they would create a good deal of heartburning.'[80]

There was, finally, the problem of the imprecision of the effects of the competitive system. The energetic might succeed in general, and the idle might fail in general. But many others were swept along in the net with them. We may leave the last words to Ruskin:

[I]n a community regulated only by the laws of demand and supply, but protected from open violence, the persons who become rich are generally speaking, industrious, resolute, proud, covetous, prompt, methodical, sensible, unimaginative, insensitive and ignorant. The persons who remain poor are the entirely foolish, the entirely wise, the idle, the reckless, the humble, the thoughtful, the dull, the imaginative, the sensitive, the well-informed, the improvident, the irregularly and impulsively wicked, the clumsy knave, the open thief and the entirely merciful, just and godly person.[81]

[80] *Parliamentary Debates*, 3rd Series, vol. 149, col. 1248 (1858).
[81] *Unto this Last* (1862) reprinted in *Works*, vol. xvii (London, 1903–8), p. 90.

11

THE INTELLECTUAL BACKGROUND,
1770-1870—I

POLITICAL ECONOMY

THE intellectual background to the legal developments during the century between 1770 and 1870 was dominated by two bodies of thought. The first, associated with Adam Smith and his successors, were the economic theories which have come to be called 'classical economics', known in their time as 'political economy'. And the second was the body of thought, known then and now, as utilitarianism, associated, inevitably with Jeremy Bentham, and his coterie. We must beware of assuming that these bodies comprised two solid phalanxes of thinkers and writers who agreed with each other on all or even on most major issues. The political economists disagreed amongst themselves on almost every issue of importance; and the utilitarians disagreed almost as much, though there was anyhow less of a coherent body of ideas associated with utilitarianism. But in their methodology, and, to some degree in their substance, as well as in the *dramatis personae* of the period, political economy and utilitarianism were closely associated. Bentham is treated by some as entitled to rank as one of the classical economists, and certainly some of his economic writings are quite in the classical tradition. James Mill, Bentham's greatest disciple and propagandist, was certainly one of the classical economists, and also one of the most vigorous and active of the utilitarians. His son, John Stuart Mill, is often regarded as the last of the classical economists, and was one of the most articulate defenders of utilitarianism. Indeed, in one sense all the classical economists were utilitarians at heart. But apart from the high priests of these two religions, there was a much larger number of men associated, more or less closely, with one or both of the inner circles. Among these men on the periphery were some who held, or came to hold, positions of power and responsibility in the State, such as Henry Brougham who was virtually leader of the Whig opposition in the House of Commons for over ten years before 1830, and Lord Chancellor from 1830 to 1834. Moreover, political economy and utilitarianism shared a common evangelical streak. Their founders and supporters were not cloistered academics, writing in professional journals for a narrow circle of like-minded men. They were men convinced of the importance of their messages, and of the desirability of their practical application. They preached their lessons at every opportunity; in Parliament,[1] in new widely read journals like the *Edinburgh Review*, the *Quarterly Review*, and the *Westminster Review*; in pamphlets and in books, in speeches and by personal contact. And below this level of still relatively sophisticated discussion, there were the popularizers, the journalists and pamphleteers, who simplified the message or messages, in an attempt to make them intelligible to the man in the street, even to make them suitable subjects for governesses to teach young ladies.

It is scarcely possible that any educated man growing to maturity between (say) 1800 and 1850 would not have read a good deal of the new political economy and radical political utilitarianism. Many were profoundly influenced by it, and many more were influenced by simplified versions of these bodies of thought. Amongst those there were certainly a number of the most important legal figures of the nineteenth century, including many leading judges. Moreover, the compartmentalization of knowledge, against which Universities are today reacting, had not then seriously begun at all. Apart from the division between the physical or natural sciences (comprising what we tend today to call simply 'science') and the 'moral sciences' (which we would today tend to call the arts and the social sciences) there was little sub-division or specialization of knowledge. Political economy, law, philosophy, political theory, and history were all expected to be within the grasp of a properly educated man. Many of the classical economists wrote extensively in areas outside economics; some of them were actually trained as lawyers, or had acquired a legal qualification; and conversely, a man going into the learned profession of the law was expected to cultivate some knowledge of the moral sciences.

The close relationship between law, economics, and the social sciences generally was particularly strong in the first forty years of the nineteenth century; thereafter it waned and by 1870 was largely at an end. After that, political economy became a good deal more professionalized and distinct as a branch of learning—this was marked by the change in name to 'economics'—the language which economists wrote became less intelligible to men of other disciplines, and new economics departments grew up in the Universities, with salaried Chairs attached to them. The separation of the disciplines had begun in earnest, and, in England at least, there was little contact between lawyers and economists from about 1870 to the 1950s. One of the consequences of this, it will be suggested, was that such economic ideas as influenced the lawyers and judges and therefore the development of the common law, from the beginning of the

[1] Fetter, 'The Influence of Economists in Parliament on British Legislation from Ricardo to John Stuart Mill', 83 *Journal of Political Economy* 1051 (1975).

nineteenth century, were on the whole the ideas of the classical economists who flourished between 1776 and 1870. The influence of the post-1870 economists on the common law and legal thought was virtually negligible until after the Second World War.

In a work of this kind, it is impossible to give a full account of the development of classical economic thought;[2] but it is equally impossible to dismiss it with airy references to 'economic liberalism', *laissez-faire*, and Adam Smith. The fact is that the concept of freedom of contract was at the very heart of classical economics, and there is good ground for thinking that the common lawyers may have taken over the concept from the economists in the early part of the nineteenth century. The lawyers were, indeed, receptive to the message—I have already suggested that the common lawyers were in the van of the movement to economic liberalism throughout the seventeenth and eighteenth centuries—and there may have been other influences at work in the same direction which owed nothing to economics, but it is impossible to doubt the influence of political economy on the law of contract during this period. A great deal of further research still needs to be done to document the full extent of this influence, but at least the evidence assembled in this book will, it is hoped, put the connection itself beyond doubt. The evidence is examined mainly in Chapters 13 and 16. In this chapter I must say something about the political economists, and some of their ideas, and in particular, their views on freedom of contract.

Adam Smith

It is necessary to begin with a few remarks about the sources of much of this new economic theory, about the methodology of the political economists, and about their general role in the context of the times. We have already seen, in an earlier chapter, something of the growing strength of ideas in favour of economic freedom throughout the seventeenth and eighteenth centuries. The almost instant success of *The Wealth of Nations* when it was published in 1776, itself says something of the general state of opinion at the time. Smith was not the first man to say many of the things which he said in *The Wealth of Nations* and the message was not itself wholly new. What was new was the attempt to bring it all together, to offer a systematic account of economic affairs and of the effect of laws and regulations on a nation's prosperity; and to do all this in a manner which made it appear that political economy was simply a matter of common sense, with a dash of history and philosophy.

[2] The literature is, of course, immense. For the reader without economic background, the following may be recommended: L. Robbins, *Theory of Economic Policy in English Classical Political Economy* (London, 1952); A. W. Coats (ed.) *The Classical Economists and Economic Policy.* Somewhat more advanced are D. P. O'Brien, *The Classical Economists* (Oxford, 1975), and Mark Blaug, *Economic Theory in Retrospect* (London, 1964).

In one respect *The Wealth of Nations* appears to differ significantly from the mass of classical economic literature to which it gave rise, that is, it appears to contain a great deal more factual data, and to be more of an empirical work than those of the later classical economists. Adam Smith was not a pure theorist; he was also a most acute observer, and he put many of his observations to good use in his great work. But there is a sense in which this is misleading. Smith himself may have been less of a pure theorist than Ricardo, but in fact much of the main thrust of *The Wealth of Nations* did not derive from the empirical data in it. The chief lessons which Smith drew and which he endeavoured to propagate were based to a considerable degree on the same handful of Natural Law principles as those of Locke had been, and as those of his successors were. These principles were few and simple, and part of the appeal of the classical system undoubtedly rested on this fact. To a large degree, the principles were also those on which Bentham in turn built his ideas, even though Natural Law ideas were, as such, anathema to Bentham.

There were four basic ideas to these principles of Natural Law.[3] First, there was an underlying order in all material phenomena as there was in the social order. In the material world, the physical world, the laws were those of 'science', the inexorable laws of the natural sciences. In the social sphere, the underlying order was no less, but the laws were of a different kind. However, these too were, in a sense 'Natural Laws' and although it might be possible to violate them (some would have disputed even that), in the long run such violation would be useless. The Natural Laws governing the social arrangements of man were, in the long run, no less inexorable than those governing the physical universe. These laws, secondly, could be discovered by use of man's innate reasoning and moral sense. Thirdly, it was possible from such material to deduce laws of general application, which, if observed in practice, would lead to the most desirable results. And fourthly, it was socially desirable for man's positive laws to reflect these Natural Laws as closely as possible. To these ideas, of course, we must add the Lockean social contract designed for the protection of property.

In their search for the Natural Law principles governing political economy, the classical economists, from Adam Smith on, began with a number of assumptions about man's 'nature'. They were, in essence, absurdly simple ideas. In the first place they assumed man to be a rational being who preferred pleasure to pain. They next assumed, or deduced, that men would, if left to their own devices, choose to maximize their pleasures or their happiness. What made one man happy, or gave

---

[3] D. P. O'Brien, *The Classical Economists*, Chapter 2; O. H. Taylor, 'Economics and the Idea of Natural Law', 44 *Quarterly Journal of Economics* 205 (1929); Joyce Appleby, 'Locke, Liberalism and the Natural Law of Money', 71 *Past and Present* 43 (1976).

him pleasure, was not necessarily the same as what made another happy, or gave *him* pleasure; but each was by far the best judge of this for himself. They next assumed that each man would, if left to himself, choose to do what would bring him most pleasure. It was, of course, only too obvious that a great many of the uneducated labourers did not, in fact, choose what would give them the greatest pleasure in life—for example, they spent far too much money on making themselves drunk—but the answer to such difficulties was twofold. First, the education of the working classes to understand their own interests better, and to train them to exercise self-restraint so as to dispense with a lesser pleasure at the present moment in order to enjoy a greater one at a later date; and secondly, even if it were true that some men did not rationally calculate what was in their best interests, the great mass of mankind did so. Any attempt to protect the former, small, class from their own folly, would, therefore, inevitably deprive the great majority of their natural freedom to look after their own affairs as best they could.

This utility-maximizing man lived, of course, in society, and nobody doubted that it was an essential part of society's job to protect property. It was simply taken for granted that the incentive to work necessitated a system of property laws which constituted the framework within which man would seek his own happiness. Into this framework Adam Smith next injected the crucial idea of Exchange. Man, he asserted, had a 'natural propensity' to 'truck, barter and exchange' one thing for another.[4] If he has more of one thing than he wants, he will exchange the surplus for another of which he has insufficient supplies and thus 'every man lives by exchanging, or becomes in some measure a merchant'.[5] From this propensity arises contract, trade, and the division of labour. And from these there arise a whole series of inexorable Natural Laws about political economy. The law of supply and demand which—at least in the short run—regulated the price of commodities, was by far the most important of these Natural Laws. For it was this law which brought into harmony the myriad activities of all the individuals acting in society, each acting in such a way as to maximize his own happiness. Each person, it is assumed, is bent on maximizing his own happiness by obtaining the greatest quantity of those things which give him happiness. But to obtain these things, he knows that he will have to be willing to part with things which others want, and which they are prepared to take from him in an exchange which satisfies both parties. The self-interest of each person therefore compels him to consult the interests of others. 'It is not from the benevolence of the butcher, the brewer, or the baker that we expect our dinner, but from their regard to their own interest. We

---

4 *Wealth of Nations*, Book I, Chapter II.
5 Ibid., Book I, Chapter IV.

address ourselves, not to their humanity, but to their self-love, and never talk to them of our own necessities but of their advantages'.[6]

It is this never-ceasing search after self-interest which provides the motivation to exchange and production. When commodities are in short supply, their price rises in the market. This is, though it may seem otherwise, in fact a good thing even for consumers. In the short run consumers will be inclined to reduce their consumption so that demand will fall to the levels supply can meet. In the long run shortages and consequential price rises will lead to an increase in supply because it is this rise which leads producers to think that they can make greater profits by supplying the demand. Producers therefore will move their energies and resources to manufacturing this commodity; because prices are high, they will be able to borrow capital at higher rates of interest— the capitalist also seeking his self-interest—and obtain labourers at higher wages—they in turn moving to employment where they can expect to earn more. Conversely, if the public tastes alter, or the availability of goods changes, so that public demand requires less of this commodity and a greater quantity of something different, the reverse process will take place. Demand falls, prices drop, and producers pull out some of the resources devoted to this commodity. Capital and labour will flow away to the production of other commodities now in greater demand. In this way, the public demand for commodities is always met. Every person in the market, producers, capitalists, and labourers, consult only their own interest, but the result, as if by magic, is to produce what the public wants. In one of his most famous passages Adam Smith attributed a vaguely Divine source to the working of the market. Writing in particular of the provider of capital—though it is clear that his arguments apply equally to the provider of labour or other resources— Smith says:

He generally, indeed, neither intends to promote the public interest, nor knows how much he is promoting it . . . He intends only his own gain, and he is in this, as in other cases, led by an invisible hand to promote an end which was no part of his intention.[7]

Short-term fluctuations of market price are, in Smith's view, oscillations around the 'natural price' of commodities. There is always a *tendency* for market prices to move towards their 'natural price' in the long run if the market works freely as described by Smith. Quite what this 'natural price' is remains a much more difficult question. Smith, like the later classical economists, devoted a great deal of effort to trying to establish a 'theory of value', but for my purposes it is enough to make one or two brief comments. First, Smith distinguished quite clearly between the

⁶ Ibid., Book I, Chapter II.   ⁷ Ibid., Book IV, Chapter II.

value-in-use and the value-in-exchange of a commodity. The price of a commodity is the exchange-value of that commodity—what it can be sold for. Clearly a thing must have *some* use-value if it is to have any exchange-value at all; but use-value is not proportionate to exchange-value. The famous paradox of the varying use-values and exchange-values of diamonds and water illustrated this point in the manner so pleasing to eighteenth-century readers. Water is infinitely more useful than a diamond, but is vastly cheaper in price. The explanation of this paradox had to wait until the discovery of 'marginal utility theory' a hundred years later, and I need not pursue it here. The point is that use-value, at any rate, did not determine exchange-value, or price. If not, then what did? Smith's answer to this is, roughly, that the natural price is determined by the cost of production.

It will be seen that Smith's views about prices are a great advance on the scholastic ideas about 'just prices' in that he allows for fluctuations in market prices, and does not assume that everything always has one fixed just price. At the same time Smith by no means adopted Hobbes's sweeping argument that a price agreed to by the parties is always a just price merely by virtue of the agreement. Nevertheless, he did give substantial support to those who wished to argue like Hobbes; for Smith provided a rational and scientific explanation of why it was in general desirable that prices should rise and fall in the market. If prices did not rise when commodities were scarce, consumers would have no incentive to reduce their consumption and producers would have no incentive to step up their production to meet the manifest public demand. Whether these high prices were or were not to be condemned as 'unjust' was a point which did not seem sensible to ask. Quite clearly, it was expedient, it was in the public interest, that prices should be allowed to rise in this fashion. There were, however, important qualifications to be made to this. It was only in the public interest for market prices to rise and fall with public demand so long as there was a free and competitive market, so long as there was no combination or monopoly involved. It was the competition of buyers and sellers which drove prices up and down when demand rose or fell, and if there was no competition but a monopoly supplier, or purchaser, then the movement in prices would not necessarily be in the public interest at all.

Smith's concept of 'monopoly' was a very wide one. In effect, he tended to include most interferences with the free market as creating forms of monopoly. A prohibition on imports, for example, gave a monopoly to the home supplier; a prohibition on exports, gave a monopoly to the home buyer; the Apprenticeship Laws gave a monopoly in the type of work in question to those who had served their apprenticeship. These were all monopolies created by law and Smith railed against them. He also had a good deal to say about private monopolies, or what we would today call restrictive practices. Agreement by suppliers not to sell below a certain price, or agreement by employers not to pay above a certain wage, was also, in Smith's understanding, something akin to monopoly. Agreements of this kind prevented prices rising and falling in accordance with demand, and therefore were harmful to the public interest.

One of the chief attractions of this market mechanism was that it was, in Smith's view, self-regulating. One only had to leave it alone, allow self-interest to operate, and the result would favour the public interest. Moreover, changes in the conditions of the market, for example, changes in public tastes or changes in the availability of certain commodities, or changes in costs of production, would automatically be taken care of by the market's own self-regulation. Not only was it unnecessary to interfere, but interference was likely to be positively harmful in the short run, and futile in the long run. If, for example, a particular commodity became scarce, and attempts were made to hold the price down, the result would be harmful in the short run because producers would not have the incentive to step up their supply of the commodity, and neither would consumers have the incentive to reduce their consumption. In the long run, however, such regulation was likely to prove futile, because suppliers, observing the scarcity, would be unwilling to sell at regulated prices, and would withhold their supplies from the market altogether; alternatively a 'black market' would develop in which illegal prices would be paid and charged, since it would be in the interests of both buyers and sellers to exchange at such illegal prices.

It is, moreover, clear that to Smith himself, interference with the free market was nearly always designed to further the interests of particular classes or groups at the expense of consumers, or the public generally. Much later, it came to be widely thought that a policy of non-interference (or *laissez-faire*) was itself a policy favouring the industrial and commercial classes, but nothing could have been more contrary to Smith's own ideas. To him there was a natural harmony between private and public interests in 'the system of natural freedom' as he was apt to call it; interference with this system distorted the natural harmony in the interests of selected groups. Much of the *ad hoc* economic regulation of the past was thus, as Smith argued, introduced simply to further the interests of producers or purchasers of this or that particular commodity. Generally these favoured groups were commercial interests in a particular trade or region who had persuaded Parliament to pass laws which in effect subsidized their activities by means of tariffs or the creation of legal monopolies (in the extended Smithian sense). Because the cost of such subsidies did not visibly fall on the Treasury, Governments and Parliaments had been misled into thinking that they involved no real public cost. In this they were mistaken because even where there was no visible subsidy payable by taxpayers, there was usually some additional cost payable by consumers in the form of higher prices. The only solution, urged Smith, was generally to sweep away these obsolete regulations and laws, and allow the market to work naturally.

The market mechanism as described by Adam Smith came to be the central point of all classical economic theory. It was not, in fact, deduced very rigorously from first principles, even in the much more abstract methodology employed by Ricardo. Much later, economists devoted much time and effort trying to *prove* that the free market produced an optimal allocation of resources, but what they in fact proved was that this was only the case under conditions of the most inconceivable stringency. In ordinary life, there are many reasons why a free market may fail to produce optimal results. But all this still lay a long while in the future when Adam Smith and his successors were writing. They were, in truth, largely content with some pretty rough reasoning on behalf of the free market, which often consisted of 'nothing more complex and penetrating than the simple reason that where there was free exchange there could be no robbery, but rather there must be some advantage to both sides'.[8] Similarly, competition was a virtue for Adam Smith for the same reason that it appeals to many laymen, that is because he thought it had a dynamic effect on individual incentives. Only much later was the theory of 'perfect competition' worked out in which, given certain totally unrealistic conditions, a perfect allocation of resources would result.

Nevertheless, the comprehensive sweep of the economic vision presented by Adam Smith struck a responsive chord in his contrymen (and, remembering that he was a Scotsman) still more among Englishmen. The notion of Exchange, and of Free Exchange, now became of overriding significance in the whole system of political economy, both internally, and also internationally. Free trade—that is the right to import and export without restriction—became the overseas equivalent of freedom of contract. All restrictions on free trade or freedom of contract simply protected (or exploited) some groups at the expense of others. Prohibitions on export were, in effect, a subsidy to the internal purchaser of the commodity in question at the expense of the producer, for the price would be lowered in the absence of competing foreign buyers. Restrictions on imports were a tax on the purchasers of similar home-produced goods who would pay a price higher than that which they would pay if there were no such restrictions—and what was more the tax would not go to the Treasury, but to the home producer. Even import duties (tariffs) were not much better because, so long as the

[8] T. W. Hutchison, *A Review of Economic Doctrines 1870–1929* (Oxford, 1953), pp. 282–3.

English supplier kept his price below that of the imported, taxed product (but higher than it would have been in free competition with untaxed imports) he was still effectively being subsidized by the consumer.

Restrictions on the movement of labourers under the Settlement Laws also prevented them from moving to areas where work was to be had at higher wages instead of remaining where they were, and receiving lower wages, or even poor relief. Apart from being 'contrary to natural liberty and justice'.[9] Adam Smith therefore condemned these laws on grounds of economic efficiency. The same was true of all other restrictions on employment. Even the old Apprenticeship Laws, he argued, were unnecessary, for if a man were willing to employ an unqualified person to do a piece of work for him, could he not trust his own judgment as to whether the work would be well enough done? Adam Smith was one of the first, though not the last person to look with extremely suspicious eyes on claims that restrictive practices of this kind were in the public interest. To prevent a man from using his 'most sacred and inviolable property', that is the strength and dexterity of his hands, merely because he had not served a seven-year apprenticeship, is, argues Smith, 'a manifest encroachment upon the just liberty both of the workman and of those who might be disposed to employ him'.[10] And what was it for anyhow? 'To judge whether he is fit to be employed may surely be trusted to the discretion of the employers whose interest it so much concerns.'[11] The truth is that the long seven-year apprenticeship gives no adequate protection to the public against incompetence. Fraud is one thing, and the laws must provide protection against that, but incompetence is something else—let the employer take care who he employs.

So also, if labour were to be free, in the sense that the apprenticeship restrictions were to be lifted, it also followed that wage fixing was obsolete and should be abolished. Who knew better than the parties to the exchange itself what value to place on the labourer's services? Nor does this mean that Smith was unaware that the labourer was at a disadvantage in bargaining with employers. He knew this was so, he knew that employers could easily combine and agree not to pay wages above a certain amount, while it was illegal for workers to combine for a similar purpose. He was not unsympathetic to the worker on these scores, but allowing the workmen to combine in order to bargain the better with the employer would have been righting one wrong with another. The only right course was to try to stop the employers from combining even though this could never be wholly successful.

[9] *Wealth of Nations*, Book I, Chapter X.
[10] Ibid.
[11] Ibid. Smith was even prepared to do without licensing of doctors. He did not think consumers needed any great skill to detect good from bad doctors, see E. G. West, 'Private versus Public Education', in A. W. Coats (ed.), *The Classical Economists and Economic Policy* (London, 1971), p. 128.

Thus labour was to operate in a free market, and international trade should be permitted freely across State boundaries. Rents, of course, were free and totally uncontrolled at this time, and it was another century before anybody began to talk seriously about interfering in the contract between a landlord and a tenant. It only remained to free capital and allow money to be lent at whatever interest rates might be agreed between the parties. Oddly, Adam Smith did not himself take this final step of advocating repeal of the Usury Laws. He did have a good deal to say about the accumulation of capital which he attributed to the thrift and foresight of private frugality, and he contrasted this with the profligacy of Governments who wasted capital in war and in opulent monarchical courts; but he did not totally oppose all control of interest rates. It was left to Bentham to out-do the Master on this issue. Applying Smith's own arguments Bentham produced a devastating case for the abolition of the Usury Laws in 1790 and sent a copy to Smith hoping for his approbation. But Smith was dying when he received it and Bentham never obtained his answer. However, public opinion on this question thought that Bentham had largely made out his case, and in due course, the Usury Laws were first modified and then repealed, though not until 1854 was that consummation finally achieved.

Adam Smith never doubted that he was describing, and making policy recommendations, for the economic activity of nations. His individual, guided though he might be by an 'invisible hand', was not operating in a Lockean State of Nature, but in a modern State. And even if Smith argued so vigorously that intervention with the natural market mechanism would generally do more harm than good, he did not have a purely negative view of the function of the State. In fact he devoted a good portion of *The Wealth of Nations* to stating what precisely were the functions of the State. In his view, the State or Sovereign, had three principal purposes; first, there was the duty to protect the society from external enemies; secondly, there was a duty to protect the citizens from oppression, force, and fraud, and to make provision for administering a system of justice to that end; and third, there was a duty to erect public works and institutions which were for the public interest but too large or substantial in cost to be carried out by individuals. Each of these purposes was capable of being viewed quite broadly. External defence, for example, was sufficiently important to justify the Navigation Acts, which interfered substantially with the total freedom of overseas trade. And under his third head it was possible to justify a considerable extension of governmental functions, for example, in relation to such matters as the construction of highways, bridges, canals, docks, and harbours. But it was the second of his three heads which is of most interest to us and here too, it is clear that Smith took no minimal view of the functions of

Government. Oddly enough he says little directly about the duty of Government to enforce contracts, though it is clear from isolated passages in *The Wealth of Nations*, as well as from the *Lectures on Jurisprudence*, that Smith assumed this was one of the primary functions of any civilized country. He also makes it clear that the regulation of certain types of contract is far from being inconsistent with his overall views, for example (as we have seen) he did not altogether reject the idea of regulating interest rates, nor did he see anything wrong with the Truck Acts.[12] And he also advocated laws for the control of monopolies. He was, too, very concerned at the power of banks to issue notes without limit, and his discussion of this point shows perhaps better than anything else in *The Wealth of Nations* that Smith rejected any absolute dogmatic prohibition on all State interference with contracts:

> To restrain private people, it may be said, from receiving in payment the promissory notes of a banker, for any sum whether great or small, when they themselves are willing to receive them; or to restrain a banker from issuing such notes, when all his neighbours are willing to accept of them, is a manifest violation of that natural liberty which it is the proper business of law, not to infringe but to support. Such regulations may, no doubt, be considered as in some respect a violation of natural liberty. But those exertions of the natural liberty of a few individuals, which might endanger the security of the whole society, are, and ought to be restrained by the laws of all governments . . . The obligation of building party walls, in order to prevent the communication of fire, is a violation of natural liberty, exactly of the same kind with the regulations of the banking trade here proposed.[13]

The general notion, therefore, that Adam Smith was advocating a regime of total *laissez-faire* is somewhat misleading. But it is true that, compared with those who preceded him, Smith's emphasis on a general presumption against interference in the workings of the market, was sufficiently novel to place him in a class of his own as the founder of a new theory of economics which advocated the general principle of maximum economic freedom.[14] If he was no doctrinaire advocate of *laissez-faire* as a cure for all economic problems, it remains the case that 'the central theme that inspires *The Wealth of Nations* is the workings of the "invisible hand"'.[15] It was his fundamental belief in a natural harmony between individual self-interest and the public interest which was seen as the principal message of the work. It is true that there are parts of the book which suggest that Smith knew perfectly well that private economic interests are not always in natural harmony with the public interest but

[12] D. P. O'Brien, *The Classical Economists*, p. 32.

[13] *Wealth of Nations*, Book II, Chapter II, cited, D. P. O'Brien, *The Classical Economists*, pp. 274-5.

[14] Jacob Viner, 'The Intellectual History of Laissez Faire', 3 *Journal of Law and Economics* 45 (1960); also his *The Long View and the Short* (Glencoe, Ill., 1958).

[15] Mark Blaug, *Economic Theory in Retrospect*, p. 57.

the overall message that came through was that if only Governments would leave business alone, the public interest would generally be served.

Before we leave Adam Smith and his work, something should be said of one of the most popular misconceptions about his ideas, and indeed, those of the classical economists generally. It was widely thought, then and perhaps is even now, that Adam Smith was essentially advocating a society based on selfishness and greed. The motive of self-interest which Smith took for granted as the mainspring of all work, saving, and improvement both for the individual and for society as a whole, can be and often is misrepresented for this purpose. It is, however, the misrepresentation of the ignorant. Nobody who has read *The Wealth of Nations* can possibly believe that Smith *advocated* a materialist, selfish, greed. And Smith had, anyhow, set forth his moral philosophy years earlier in *The Theory of Moral Sentiments* (first published in 1759) which was well known throughout Europe, and on which, indeed, Smith's early reputation had rested. In this book Smith discusses the whole basis of moral feelings or sentiments and their relationship with justice. There is one passage in particular from this work which should be a sufficient answer to those who accuse Smith of advocating a moral system based on greed and self-interest. In this passage[16] Smith argues that though men have natural sympathy for each other, and are even moved by this sympathy to acts of benevolence, these motives are insufficient to curb men's natural propensity to act in their own interests rather than in that of their fellows. It is to counteract this natural selfishness that Justice exists, and Justice is to him the supreme virtue:

Justice . . . is the main pillar that upholds the whole edifice. If it is removed, the great, the immense fabric of human society, that fabric which to raise and support seems in this world, if I may say so, to have been the peculiar and darling care of Nature, must in a moment crumble into atoms. In order to enforce the observation of justice, therefore, Nature had implanted in the human breast that consciousness of ill-desert, those terrors of merited punishment which attend upon its violation as the great safeguards of the association of mankind, to protect the weak, to curb the violent, and to chastise the guilty.

THE LATER CLASSICAL ECONOMISTS

The publication of *The Wealth of Nations* in 1776 had a major impact on public and political thought about economic matters. The book became widely known and within a few years Adam Smith's ideas were being relied upon by politicians, and he himself was consulted on various issues in the 1770s and 1780s by a number of leading Ministers of the Crown.

[16] *The Theory of Moral Sentiments*, ed. Raphael and Macfie (Oxford, 1976), p. 86.

By the end of the century a whole new line of economists was beginning to produce a new body of literature, much of which became equally well known to the educated public and equally influential on policy making. Something must be said here of a few of the most famous of these classical economists, focusing on aspects of their work of particular relevance to freedom of contract.

But it is as well to add first a few words on the popularizers of political economy during this period. In the 1820s, 1830s, and 1840s, in particular, a great deal was done to propagate some simplified versions of political economy by a number of most influential writers. Two of the most significant of these were James Wilson, editor of *The Economist*,[17] and Harriet Martineau, author of a series of simple *Tales* in *Illustrations of Political Economy*.[18] The version of political economy preached by these writers tended to be of a very simplistic character, and generally amounted to a rigid advocacy of the doctrine of *laissez-faire*. Basing themselves on what they took to be the teachings of Adam Smith (and, later, of Ricardo), the popularizers preached the simplest of messages. A smattering of traditional ideas, drawn from Locke, Rousseau, and Paley, together with a dash of Benthamism, was added to the message of the economists to produce a simple synthesis. All interference with the 'natural order' was and must be wrong. 'To the philosophical doctrine that Government has no right to interfere, and the divine miracle that it has no need to interfere, there is added a scientific proof that its interference is inexpedient.'[19]

Absolute freedom of contract was no less obvious a message to be drawn from these simple premises. At the conclusion of volume vi of her *Tales*, Miss Martineau summarized what she took to be the principle of freedom of contract as follows:

The countries of the world differ in their facilities for producing the comforts and luxuries of life.

The inhabitants of the world agree in wanting or desiring all the comforts and luxuries which the world produces.

These wants and desires can be in no degree gratified but by means of mutual exchanges. They can be fully satisfied only by means of absolutely universal and free exchanges.

By universal and free exchange,—that is by each person being permitted to exchange what he wants least for what he wants most,—an absolutely perfect system of economy of resources is established; the whole world being included in this arrangement.

---

[17] See Scott-Gordon, 'The London *Economist* and the High-Tide of Laissez Faire', 63 *Journal of Political Economy* 461 (1955).

[18] London, 1832-4, 9 volumes.

[19] J. M. Keynes, *The End of Laissez Faire* (London, 1926), p. 11.

Malthus

One of the first and most significant of the later generation of classical economists was Thomas Malthus, the celebrated author of the *Essay on the Principles of Population* which was first published in 1798. This *Essay* which immediately became well known to the public, and also added a major new dimension to economic theory, needs to be seen in the context of its times to be properly appreciated. The particular problem which was causing anxiety to many politicians and economists at the time when Malthus wrote was the terrifying increase in the cost of the Poor Rate since Adam Smith's day. Although actual knowledge of the fact of the population increase itself was still awaited with the first census of 1801, everyone knew that the Poor Rate had increased with frightening speed. In 1760 the cost of the Poor Rate to the whole of England had been some £1·25 million; by 1784 it has risen to £2 million, and less than twenty years later, in 1803, it was over £4 million. These figures represented a substantial proportion of public expenditure, swollen though it was by the needs of the war with France, amounting to between ten and fifteen per cent of total expenditure, and a good deal more if military expenditure were left out of account. The causes of this increase were many, but the one which gave rise to the greatest concern was the new Speenhamland system, introduced in 1795, of supplementing the wages of workers with allowances which varied according to the number of their dependents.

Shortly before Malthus wrote his *Essay*, William Godwin had published his *Inquiry Concerning Political Justice*. Godwin was a Utopian who had argued for an egalitarian society and had urged that poverty was caused by the mal-distribution of society's wealth. Like many others, before and after him, Godwin had looked on the wealth of the rich and had convinced himself that there was enough for all, if only it were shared around more evenly. It was against this background, and in response to Godwin's book, that Malthus first wrote his *Essay*. His main purpose was to destroy the Utopian beliefs of men like Godwin by showing that in fact it was quite impossible for society to adopt a purely egalitarian system of rewards for labour. A man with a larger family would always need to earn more in order to feed more mouths, and any interference with his right to do this would be (echoing the words of Adam Smith) 'a violation of the first and most sacred property that a man possesses'.[20] More important was the fact that Malthus tried to emphasize, both in the *Essay* and in later works, that it was impossible to increase the well being of the mass of the people simply by paying them more, whether in wages or in

---

[20] *Essay on the Principle of Population* (ed. Flew), Pelican edn. (Harmondsworth, 1970), p. 181. Page references are to this edition.

poor relief, if the supply of food was not increased also. At the time when he was writing—the last few years of the eighteenth century—the possibility of increasing food supplies had been greatly diminished, first by a succession of poor harvests, and secondly by the Napoleonic blockade. The result had inevitably been to drive up the price of wheat and bread to levels which undoubtedly caused real deprivation, but Malthus was, of course, quite right in insisting that this state of affairs could not be remedied by simply paying the poor more money. For, if the supply of food remained stationary, the only result would be to raise the price still further, and 'if we interfere to prevent the commodity from rising out of the reach of the poorest . . ., whoever they may be, we must toss up, draw lots, raffle or fight, to determine who are to be excluded'.[21]

All this, of course, was merely the introduction to the main theme of the *Essay*, but it set the stage by insisting that the prosperity of the mass of the people necessarily depended upon the proportion between their number and the quantity of the available supplies of food. And this was the point at which Malthus enunciated his famous principle to the effect that population would always increase more quickly than food supplies, and that it was impossible to envisage any future Utopia in which the labouring class could ever really enjoy any prosperity. For present purposes the most important part of Malthus's theme was that he took it for granted, as indeed most writers of his time, that population increased in response to demand like any other commodity; there is in fact much evidence to suggest that in the eighteenth century and earlier times, population did respond quite regularly to economic factors.[22] When times were good, and labour was scarce, wages naturally were higher; and when wages were higher, labourers were encouraged to marry earlier, with the result that the women spent more of their child-bearing years in the marital state. In the social conditions of the time, this led to increased population. Conversely, when times were bad, wages were poor, marriages were postponed, and population declined, or at least rose much more slowly.

Malthus linked his principle of population with these traditional ideas, arguing that there was a constant tendency for population increase to outstrip food supplies, and that only if this tendency were checked by some means would the labourers avoid a steady decline in their standard of living. In the *Essay* as first published Malthus saw little sign of hope at all; the only checks to the tendency of population to increase seemed to him to be famine on the one hand or 'vice' on the other. Later he became somewhat less gloomy about the future prospects and accepted that

---

[21] From *An Investigation of the Cause of the Present High Prices of Provisions*, cited by Keynes, *Essays in Biography* (revised edn., London, 1951), p. 105.

[22] E. J. Hobsbawm, *Industry and Empire*, pp. 42–4.

'moral restraint' might provide an alternative check to the working of his law. In fact, of course, a great deal of what Malthus wrote was really nonsense from the start. The contrast between the geometric rate of increase in population and the arithmetic rate of increase in food supplies was quite bogus. Moreover, his thesis was totally unhistorical, because he seemed to assume that his principle would start operating in his own times, and he never adequately explained why, if this law had operated in earlier times, England had become (as Adam Smith had clearly demonstrated) steadily richer and richer through the centuries.[23] And the possibility of artificial contraception, already advocated by Francis Place, ultimately provided, at least for developed countries, a complete answer to the Malthusian fears—though these remain even today serious enough for the undeveloped world, and therefore inevitably for the rest of the world too.

But for present purposes what proved of most importance in Malthus's work was his criticism of the Poor Laws. The existing Poor Laws, says Malthus in the first *Essay*, tend to worsen the condition of the poor in several respects.[24] Although instituted for the most benevolent purposes, they have, he argues, only made things worse. A labourer is encouraged to marry and have children without pausing to consider whether he can afford it. They have also contributed 'to generate that carelessness and want of frugality among the poor'[25] which leads them to live from hand to mouth. Even those who can save for the future never feel the need to do so because they know the Poor Laws are always there to fall back upon in case of need. Although Malthus is afraid that the evil has gone too far to be remedied he nevertheless argues that the only palliative which exists for it is the abolition of the existing Poor Laws, and the total opening of the labour market.

This would at any rate give liberty and freedom of action to the peasantry of England, which they can hardly be said to possess at present. They would then be able to settle without interruption, wherever there was a prospect of a greater plenty of work and a higher price of labour. The market of labour would then be free, and those obstacles removed which, as things are now, often for a considerable time prevent the price from rising according to the demand.[26]

Some form of relief, in the shape of County Workhouses, would need to be provided for cases of extreme distress. These 'should not be considered as comfortable asylums in all difficulties, but merely as places where severe distress might find some alleviation'.[27] Passages like this,

[23] For the controversy between Malthus and Nassau Senior on this, see B. Inglis, *Poverty and the Industrial Revolution* (London, 1972), pp. 280-3.

[24] See Chapter V of the *Essay on Population*.

[25] Ibid., p. 98.

[26] Ibid., Chapter V, p. 101.

[27] Ibid., Chapter V, p. 102.

and there are others even more terrible elsewhere, such as the famous passage in which Malthus refers to the poor having no place at Nature's table, can easily give the wrong impression to the modern reader. It is easy to see Malthus as a severe disciplinarian, lacking in compassion for the poor, but nothing could be more mistaken. Malthus was simply making the point that there were severe limits to what could in fact be done by mankind to assist the poor. I referred in an earlier chapter[28] to the sense of helplessness felt by many in the early nineteenth century as the poor seemed to multiply so visibly around them. It is clear that Malthus keenly felt this sense of helplessness, too: 'To prevent the recurrence of misery, is, alas! beyond the power of man.'[29] Unfortunately, in their benevolent attempts to alleviate the distress of the poor, Englishmen had simply made things worse. Nobody could read the first *Essay* without sensing the strong sympathy with the poor which pervades the whole work. The Poor Laws as they then stood, Malthus seemed to say, were a swindle:

We tell the common people that if they will submit to a code of tyrannical regulations, they shall never be in want. They do submit to these regulations. They perform their part of the contract, but we do not, nay cannot, perform ours, and thus the poor sacrifice the valuable blessing of liberty and receive nothing that can be called an equivalent in return.[30]

The only remedy was to abandon the pretence that the common people could be assured of a decent subsistence, no matter how much they multiplied. They must be made to see that this was a sheer impossibility, and that their future lay in their own hands. Freedom of contract must be restored to the labourer, the Settlement Laws abolished, the Speenhamland Poor Laws removed so that wages would rise to their natural level. Freedom of contract between employer and labourer, though it might sometimes lead to the evil of oppressive labour, was better than dependence:

The man who does a day's work for me confers full as great an obligation upon me as I do upon him. I possess what he wants, he possesses what I want. We make an amicable exchange. The poor man walks erect in conscious independence; and the mind of his employer is not vitiated by a sense of power.[31]

These criticisms of the Poor Law had a great impact. They deflected Pitt from his intention to introduce a Bill which would have given statutory effect to the Speenhamland system, and ultimately they played a part in creating the opinion needed to carry through the Poor Law Amendment Act of 1834. They also had a more general impact both on public opinion, and on the trend of classical economic theory. For one

---

[28] *Supra*, p. 234.   [29] *Essay on Population*, Chapter V, p. 102.
[30] Ibid., Chapter V, p. 103.   [31] Ibid., Chapter XV, p. 179.

widely held (though far from unanimous) view resulting from Malthus's work was the belief that he had proved the 'Iron Law of Wages'. This was supposed to be a 'law' stating that the standard of living of the poor could never effectively rise above subsistence level for any prolonged period of time, because any such rise would merely lead to an increase in population which would, in due course, produce a surplus of labour and a fall in wage rates. In fact, apart from Malthus himself, and Ricardo, and perhaps James Mill, it is not at all clear that the other classical economists really believed in this so-called 'law'.[32] I have already referred to the views of the younger Mill who, with many of his utilitarian and Radical friends, turned Malthus's message upside down into a message of hope for the future. And as the nineteenth century wore on, and the productive power of the country began manifestly to outstrip the increases of population, the 'iron law of wages' faded into the background, together with the general spectre of over-population. Only in recent years has the Malthusian ghost returned to haunt modern man, but this time there is no Poor Law to be blamed or reformed.

James Mill

I pass from Malthus to say something of James Mill and David Ricardo. Of the elder Mill I need to say but little. As an original thinker he contributed little of value to economic theory. Indeed, his main claim to fame is that he is credited with having persuaded Ricardo to write his *Principles*, and with having taken a leading role in the founding of the Political Economy Club to which all the leading theorists and many practical men of affairs also belonged. But James Mill is nevertheless a person of some interest to this story. He was, perhaps, the central figure who brought together the classical economists and the utilitarians. He was a close friend of Bentham's and of Ricardo's; his *Essay on Government* (1819) is said to have converted Bentham to a belief in democracy, and the methodology to be found in that *Essay* bears a close similarity to that which was employed by Ricardo in his *Principles* and elsewhere.

It is clear that both James Mill and Ricardo were greatly attracted to the highly abstract *a priori* modes of reasoning which are to be found in these two works. This type of abstract deductive thinking may well have played an important role in the popularization of both utilitarianism and of Ricardian economics. And James Mill was himself the supreme propagandist. He regarded it as his mission to spread the Benthamite message, and since he took Ricardo to be a disciple of Bentham's, he extended his mission to include the propagation of political economy as well. From the point of view of the propagandist, this abstract

[32] A. W. Coats, 'The Classical Economists and the Labourer', in A. W. Coats (ed.), *The Classical Economists and Economic Policy*, pp. 169–70.

methodology had certain advantages. It enabled the argument to proceed, in the first place, in total isolation from any empirical data. At a time when the data of the social sciences were (as we have already seen) in a most rudimentary state, this was no mean advantage. Both in Ricardo's *Principles*, and in James Mill's *Essay*, there is an almost total lack of any factual propositions. It was for this reason that Mill's *Essay* suffered severely at the hands of Macaulay who wrote a brilliant and scathing review of it in the *Edinburgh Review* in 1829. 'We have here', wrote Macaulay, 'an elaborate treatise on Government, from which, but for two or three passing allusions, it would not appear that the author was aware that any governments actually existed among men. Certain propensities of human nature are assumed; and from these premises the whole science of politics is synthetically deduced!'[33] The whole of this review was, in effect, an appeal for an empirical methodology in the social sciences,—the method of Induction, 'by observing the present state of the world,—by assiduously studying the history of past ages,—by sifting the evidence of facts,—by carefully combining and contrasting those which are authentic,—by generalizing with judgment and diffidence,—by perpetually bringing the theory which we have constructed to the test of new facts,—by correcting or altogether abandoning it, according as these new facts prove it to be partially or fundamentally unsound.'[34] But that was not Mill's method and it was not Ricardo's either.

Their methodology also had advantages in enabling simplifications to take place in presenting a message. Because the facts themselves could be put aside, awkward modifications, exceptions, and counter-propositions could be ignored, and the message could be preached loud and clear in its pristine simplicity. Although it cannot be said that all of Ricardo's works had this simplicity—indeed, they are often abstruse and difficult reading for those without previous knowledge of the subject—it does seem that this characteristic helped their propagation, if not directly, then at second hand. And as we shall see in due course, the very simplicity of this message in regard to freedom of contract, may well have been influential on the development of the law.

As to James Mill's writings on political economy, I need only refer to one or two passages which bring out the simplistic effect of his approach on some key issues. Here, for instance, is a typical specimen of Mill on the self-evident fact that both parties to an Exchange must be gainers by it:

When a man possesses a certain commodity, he cannot benefit himself by giving it away. It seems to be implied, therefore, in the very fact of his parting with it for another commodity, that he is benefited by what he receives. His own

[33] Macaulay, *Miscellaneous Writings and Speeches* (London, 1889), p. 161.
[34] Ibid., p. 182.

commodity he might have kept, if it had been valued by him more than that for which he exchanges it. The fact of his choosing to have the other commodity rather than his own, is a proof that the other is to him more valuable than his own.[35]

What might be a reasonable prima facie inference is here stated as a piece of revealed truth—no qualifications or doubts are thought necessary, nothing about the possibility of mistake, misinformation, change of mind, fraud, or any of those other possibilities known to lawyers which lead to unprofitable exchanges being made.

Similarly, when he comes to discuss the principle of non-interference, where Adam Smith had introduced qualifications or exceptions based on observed facts, and past experience, all is simplicity itself to Mill. It is, he asserts, 'fully established that the business of production and exchange, if left to choose its own channels, is sure to choose those which are most advantageous to the community. It is sure to choose those channels, in which the commodities, which the community desires to obtain, are obtained with the smallest cost.'[36] Obviously, therefore, all interference is bound to make matters worse. It is not surprising that many people came to the conclusion that the economists believed in the principle of *laissez-faire*, come hell or high water.

Ricardo

With Ricardo, we are clearly on a different level, for although much of the reasoning is of this same *a priori* kind, it is not nearly so simplistic. Ricardo was clearly a far greater thinker than Mill, and the rigorous nature of his deductions are apparent, even where the premises are themselves no more complex. Ricardo was a financier with a taste for economic theorizing. He had, in 1819, retired from the Stock Exchange where he had made a fortune, but he was well known as an economist at least from 1810 until his death in 1823. His *Principles of Political Economy and Taxation* appeared in 1817, and he became a Member of Parliament through the good offices of Brougham in 1819. His reputation as an economist and financier was immensely high, and the publication of his *Principles* 'invested him with almost oracular authority'.[37] As a rigorous analytical thinker Ricardo still retains the highest reputation among modern economists.[38] And in Parliament he was always listened to with the greatest respect,[39] particularly by the lawyers.[40] But his theoretical

[35] *Elements of Political Economy*, 3rd edn., 1844 (reprinted, New York, 1965), pp. 125–6.

[36] Ibid., Sect. XVII.

[37] B. Inglis, *Poverty and the Industrial Revolution*, p. 189.

[38] See, e.g., Mark Blaug, *Economic Theory in Retrospect*, pp. 126–7.

[39] See generally Barry Gordon, *Political Economy in Parliament, 1819–1823* (London and Basingstoke, 1976).

[40] Ibid., p. 3.

approach to all problems sometimes proved too much for the pragmatic members of the House of Commons, and Brougham was once moved to protest that Ricardo 'had argued as if he had dropped from another planet'.[41]

Ricardo's methodology resembled (as I have said) that of James Mill except that it was far more rigorous. He began with a few simple axioms of the Natural Law variety and proceeded to deduce from them, link by link, a long and frequently tortuous chain of conclusions. The resultant conclusions, if they correctly followed from the premises, were treated as 'laws' of political economy—and it has been said that Ricardo was the first economist to use the word 'law' to describe economic phenomena.[42] If the deductions were made in accordance with the strict principles of logic, then they must, of course, be sound, provided the premises were sound. Unfortunately, his premises were as abstract and frequently as unreal, indeed, they were often the same premises, as those adopted in Mill's *Essay on Government*. Ricardo himself seemed unconcerned about the reality of his premises for he was evidently much more interested in the analytical model-building itself. On one occasion he even wrote to Malthus, that 'It would be no answer to me to say that men were ignorant of the best and cheapest mode of conducting their business, and paying their debts, because that is a question of fact, not of science, and might be argued against almost every proposition in Political Economy.'[43] But of course, if his facts and his premises were unsound, then the conclusions, however logically they might follow from the premises, were of no value in the real world. And to make practical policy recommendations on the basis of logical conclusions drawn from unsound premises has been said to be the Ricardian vice.[44]

I propose to limit myself here to commenting on a few points on which Ricardo's ideas may have been influential in the practical world of politics and the law, bearing in mind, of course, that I am here concerned with the possible influence of economic ideas on freedom of contract. On this point Ricardo seems to have been more dogmatic and general than Adam Smith or any of the other economists. He not only believed that all contracts should be left to the freedom of the market, but he also argued strongly for the need for the law to *facilitate* exchange. He criticized, for example, taxes on the transference of property in the following terms:

For the general prosperity, there cannot be too much facility given to the

[41] See Ricardo, *Works*, ed. Sraffa (Cambridge, 1962), v. 56; see also Brougham's 'Sketch of Ricardo in Parliament', reprinted, ibid., pp. xxxii–xxxiv. For a detailed assessment of Ricardo's influence in Parliament, see Barry Gordon, *Political Economy in Parliament*.

[42] R. M. Hartwell, Introduction to Ricardo, *Principles of Political Economy and Taxation*, Pelican edn. (Harmondsworth, 1971), pp. 23–4.

[43] Cited, F. A. Hayek, *Individualism and the Economic Order*, p. 48.

[44] By J. Schumpeter, cited D. P. O'Brien, *The Classical Economists*, p. 3.

conveyance and exchange of all kinds of property, as it is by such means that capital of every species is likely to find its way into the hands of those, who will employ it in increasing the production of the country. 'Why', asks M. Say, 'does an individual wish to sell his land? It is because he has another employment in view in which his funds will be more productive. Why does another wish to purchase this same land? It is to employ a capital which brings him in too little, which was unemployed, or the use of which he thinks susceptible of improvement. The exchange will increase the general income, since it increases the income of these parties. But if the charges are so exorbitant as to prevent the exchange, they are an obstacle to this increase of the general income.'[45]

It is, perhaps, surprising that Ricardo (who had been investing in land for some years when he wrote this) did not comment on the extraordinarily heavy *legal* charges attending conveyancing and the transfer of land at this time—for this was still in the unreformed era of fines and recoveries, and other monstrous remnants of the Middle Ages. Not until 1828 was an Inquiry instituted, as a result of Brougham's great law reform speech, into the system of conveyancing, and not until 1833 was any serious reform in fact undertaken. But it is, all the same, noteworthy that the complaints against the law of property at this time were nearly all to do with the process of transfer, with the conveyancing system. It was cheaper and simpler (and quicker) methods of exchange which were being demanded.

On the Poor Law, Ricardo agreed almost completely with Malthus. The Speenhamland system became every year more discredited with the weight of the attack on it by the political economists, especially after the census of 1810 confirmed that population was increasing.[46] The law as then administered deprived labourers of all incentive, since they were paid the same whether they worked or were idle; it shifted a substantial part of the cost of farm labourers from the farmers to the ratepayers for farmers paid lower wages in the knowledge that any deficiency would be made up out of the Poor Rate. Ricardo also agreed with Malthus that the 'natural price' of labour was a subsistence wage, and that the market price would, in the long run, tend towards the natural price. He did, however, recognize the possibility that what was a subsistence wage was itself a matter of custom and could alter over time, so that he held out some hope of a slow and gradual betterment of the condition of the labouring classes. Nevertheless, as to the policy of freedom of contract, he had no doubts:

Like all other contracts, wages should be left to the fair and free competition of the market, and should never be controlled by the interference of the legislature.[47]

[45] *Principles*, p. 172. The quotation comes from J. B. Say (1767–1832), the French economist.
[46] Brian Inglis, *Poverty and the Industrial Revolution*, pp. 185–9.
[47] *Principles*, p. 126.

Like Malthus, he also wanted the labourers to be educated to understand that the improvement of their condition lay fundamentally with themselves. 'Gentlemen ought', he once told the House of Commons, '. . . to inculcate this truth on the minds of the working class—that the value of labour, like the value of other things, depended on the relative proportion of supply and demand. If the supply of labour was greater than could be employed, then the people must be miserable.'[48]

He even opposed the renewal of the Truck Act in 1822 as an 'obnoxious' interference with the free market, although it is possible that he was motivated by the knowledge that Robert Owen was supplying goods in his Truck Shops to his workers at the New Lanark Mills, and that Ricardo did not want to prevent this.[49] His opposition, anyhow, seems to have helped prevent the Act being renewed, though it did not prevent the more effective and comprehensive measure of 1830 about which I shall say something later.

As might be expected, Ricardo also opposed all control over interest rates. He gave evidence before a Select Committee of the House of Commons on this subject in 1818, arguing that the Usury Laws were in practice evaded by all manner of legal stratagems (such as the granting of annuities) and that the only effect of the laws was to drive up the cost of borrowing money. The lender, he said, 'exacts a premium for his risk in breaking the law'.[50] It is, of course, perfectly clear from his evidence to the Select Committee that Ricardo was thinking entirely of transactions between merchants, businessmen, and landowners, and that he was resting on his familiar assumption that people generally knew their own interests best in such matters.

On international free trade, Ricardo threw his weight behind the principles of Adam Smith, and against the Corn Laws, though he was willing to see them repealed gradually. It has sometimes been argued that the movement for international free trade and the repeal of the Corn Laws had little to do with the movement for internal freedom of contract and the application of principles of *laissez-faire*. But if this was so politically, it was because the landed interest stood to lose from repeal of the Corn Laws while it was the new mercantile and industrial class that opposed interference with freedom of contract and the operation of their own businesses. In economic theory, the case for freedom of contract seems to have been precisely the same as the case for free trade. Here, for instance, is Ricardo's case for free trade, made in language every bit as applicable to internal freedom of contract:

Under a system of perfectly free commerce, each country naturally devotes its

[48] Ricardo, *Works*, ed. Sraffa, v. 302–3 (1823).
[49] Ibid., p. 218.
[50] Ibid., pp. 335–6; see also his *Principles*, pp. 358–9.

capital and labour to such employments as are most beneficial to each. This pursuit of individual advantage is admirably connected with the universal good of the whole. By stimulating industry, by rewarding ingenuity, and by using most efficaciously the peculiar powers bestowed by nature, it distributes labour most effectively and most economically: while, by increasing the general mass of productions, it diffuses general benefit, and binds together by one common tie of interest and intercourse, the universal society of nations throughout the civilized world.[51]

But despite this apparent acceptance here, and elsewhere, of Adam Smith's idea of the harmony of private and public interests, Ricardo often seemed to argue as if the interests of the landed classes were fundamentally opposed to the interests of the public at large; and he also often spoke as if he agreed that the interests of labour conflicted with the interests of employers. There is clearly something of a logical difficulty in seeing how the interests of the landowners on the one hand and the farmers and labourers on the other could diverge if there was an identity of interest between these classes and the public as a whole. Whose interest in fact coincided with that of the public? And yet, if there was not a natural harmony of interests, the fundamental argument for non-interference, the argument for leaving parties always to the freedom of the market, seemed to break down. If Ricardo did not really believe in the fundamental doctrine of the natural harmony of interest why did he none the less so vigorously preach freedom of contract? The answer to this puzzle is of less interest than the fact that Ricardo's influence was generally seen by others as supporting the principle of freedom of contract, but one possible explanation has been offered by Halevy:

The theory of economic freedom, in Ricardo, is on occasions less like an act of faith in nature than a recognition of man's powerlessness to correct the calamities which assail him. It is a fatalism rather than an optimism. The government must not try to interfere in economic relations, for possibly the remedies it tried would be worse than the evils to be cured.[52]

Ricardo is famous in the history of economic thought for two important theories—the theory of value and the theory of rent. I have little space to devote to either of these two theories, the first of which, in any case, has little bearing on the theme of this work. Ricardo's theory of value was, in essence, based on the idea that the exchangeable value of commodities depended on the amount of labour embodied in them, and in any plant or machinery used in their manufacture. Later in the nineteenth century this Labour Theory of Value, as it came to be called, was taken up by Marx who developed from it the theory that the surplus wealth created out of manufactured products belonged entirely to the labourers who produced it, and that the capitalists (and landlords) whose investment

[51] *Principles*, p. 152.
[52] E. Halevy, *Growth of Philosophic Radicalism* (reprinted, Boston, Mass., 1955), p. 340.

contributed to the production had no rights to any part of it. This extreme view never had any significant influence on lawyers or policymakers in England, and I can disregard it as irrelevant to this work.

The theory of rent, however, did ultimately have a greater importance on the concept of freedom of contract. Prior to Ricardo, rent had been regarded as a sort of payment for the bounty of Nature. Agricultural produce was regarded as created by the combined efforts of labour, capital, and the beneficence of Nature in providing the land and the rainfall. Rent was a sort of bonus which accrued to some form of capital investment but not to others. All this rather woolly thinking was already tottering before Ricardo wrote, as other economists had begun to point out that rent was merely a payment by one class of the community to another, and did not itself add anything to national wealth. Ricardo himself developed, with his usual analytical precision, the idea that rent derived from the scarcity of land, and the varying fertility of differing parcels of land. Rent is, in effect, the surplus produce arising from better quality land, compared with the produce derived from land which is just profitable enough to cultivate. As population grew (and it must be remembered that this was a time when population growth was giving rise to great anxiety) more and more land had to be taken into cultivation which formerly had been left to waste, as too unprofitable to cultivate. This inevitably created higher rents, since it enlarged the gap between the productivity of the more fertile land and that which it now became profitable to cultivate. This new theory threw into much sharper relief the nature of rent as a sort of tax paid by the major section of the community to the landowners; it also stressed the inevitability of this tax being increased as population increased. As the supply of land could not be increased, the landowners were, in effect, monopolists. One result of this was to cast a good deal more doubt on the morality of the old Lockean concept of property. Far from being the natural reward for labour and enterprise, property now seemed a way of obtaining increased returns by the mere growth of population. In the later nineteenth century this began to have economic and political consequences of the highest order; it also began to have an impact on ideas about freedom of contract, particularly in the landlord and tenant relationship. I shall return to this important topic in Part III.

Nassau Senior

Nassau Senior (1790–1864) was one of the most influential of the classical economists in a practical sense, for he was a constantly sought adviser to the Whig politicians of the 1830s and 1840s. Trained as a lawyer, he began life as a conveyancer and Chancery barrister, and for many years held a semi-sinecure as Chancery Master. One of his earliest publications concerned the law, rather than political economy, and was an attack on Lord Eldon's decisions in the field of copyright. Because of the readiness with which Eldon would hold publications to be blasphemous or seditious, and in consequence (as he also held) not protected by copyright, Senior argued that much uncertainty had been introduced into the law.[53]

Senior gave evidence before the Real Property Commissioners of 1828 on the law concerning conveyancing and the transfer of land; and in 1832 he was asked by Melbourne for a Report on Strikes and Trade Unions.[54] In 1834 he was a member of the Commissioners on the Poor Law, and, together with Chadwick, was largely responsible for the Report and the subsequent legislation. As his views on the Poor Laws largely coincided with those of Malthus and Ricardo, it is unnecessary to add more than a brief word on this subject. But it is, perhaps, worth recording that Senior, like Malthus and Ricardo, wanted to see the total abolition of the Settlement Laws which restricted the freedom of labourers to move around the country, although on this point the Report of the Commissioners was not fully implemented.[55]

In 1837-41 Senior was Chairman of a Commission to inquire into the condition of the handloom weavers, and the Report of the Commission, presented in 1841, illustrates, once again, the views of the classical economists on freedom of contract and the principle of non-interference. The handloom weavers were in a dreadfully depressed state since they had been totally overwhelmed by the cheaper products of the new power-looms, and though many of them clung to their trade for many years, they nearly all suffered steadily falling incomes as a result. The Commission reported that the main cause of the distress was the excess supply of handlooms but they recommended very little by way of positive action. They rejected the idea of minimum wage legislation on the ground that it would only make matters worse by tending to increase the supply of handloom weavers when the real remedy was for their numbers to be reduced. They also rejected various schemes for restricting the use of power looms. 'Each of them proposes', said the Commission, 'to benefit a single portion of the community at the expense of the rest. Each of them proposes to sacrifice the permanent interest of the whole body of consumers to the temporary interest of a single class of producers.'[56] The

[53] S. L. Levy, *Nassau W. Senior* (Newton Abbott, 1970), p. 49. Amongst the authors so deprived of copyright protection were Byron and Robert Southey. See *Walcot* v. *Walker* (1802) 7 Ves. 1, 32 E.R. 1; *Southey* v. *Sherwood* (1817) 2 Mer. 435, 35 E.R. 1006.

[54] Most of this Report is reprinted in S. L. Levy, *Nassau Senior*, Appendix VIII.

[55] Ibid., pp. 89-90.

[56] Ibid., p. 149. It is noteworthy that a carefully picked Select Committee had previously proposed a scheme of statutory wage regulation: Duncan Bythell, 'The Handloom Weavers in the English Cotton Industry during the Industrial Revolution: Some Problems', 17 *Economic History Rev.* 339, 351 (1964-5).

Report ended rather bleakly by telling the handloom weavers that their fate lay in their own hands in finding other employment, and ensuring that their children were trained for other work. The whole report illustrates one of the constant weaknesses of the classical economists, namely that though they were often correct in their analysis of the problems facing them, and also in their diagnosis of the long-run solutions, they failed to consider adequate short-term palliatives.

John Stuart Mill

The younger Mill is usually treated as the last of the classical economists. His *Principles of Political Economy* first appeared in 1848 and are regarded as firmly based on Ricardian principles, brought up to date to take account of the repeal of the Corn Laws in 1846. Mill was, of course, much less abstract as a thinker than Ricardo, and his *Principles* are very much fuller on empirical questions. Between 1848 and 1870 Mill's *Principles* went through a number of editions and completely dominated orthodox political economy. I have space here to refer only to a very few points of interest, especially as I have already made several references to Mill's ideas on the Malthusian question and a number of other issues.

The broad liberalism represented by Mill is to be found, of course, in his classic *On Liberty*, but it is worth noting that he sharply distinguished between civil and commercial matters when it came to Governmental interferences with liberty. In *On Liberty* Mill quite specifically refused to place freedom of contract on the same grounds that he insisted upon for freedom of thought and expression. The distinction between purely self-regarding acts, and acts which affect other people, Mill regarded as irrelevant to freedom of contract because trade always did affect the public at large.[57] Consequently he insisted that Society was always entitled to regulate trade or commercial matters.

The same point is made quite plainly in the *Principles*. Mill refused to accept that there was somehow no *right* for the State to interfere in commercial or business matters. Although he agreed with the other classical economists that the State would be wise to refrain from interference as a general rule, he was willing to envisage far wider limits to the proper extent of intervention. Moreover, the grounds on which he supported non-interference in commercial matters were somewhat different. He does not seem to have seen any fundamental objections of principle to Government interference with freedom of contract. Indeed, (and I shall return to this point) Mill was the only one of the classical economists to point out that the enforcement of contracts was itself a form of Governmental activity, and that this necessarily imposed on the

[57] *On Liberty*, Pelican edn. (Harmondsworth, 1974), p. 164. Page references are to this edition.

State a duty to determine which contracts should be enforced. 'Every question which can possibly arise as to the policy of contracts, and of the relations which they establish among human beings, is a question for the legislator; and one which he cannot escape from considering, and in some way or other deciding.'[58]

It is true that on a great many of the traditional issues, however, Mill was unwilling to depart from the general views of the classics. He had little faith in the competence of Governments, and (at least in his younger days) enormous faith in the possibilities of educating the people so that they really would learn to judge better of their own interests. On usury, for example, he was convinced by Bentham's 'triumphal onslaught' into believing that the restrictive laws could not be justified either in the interests of the public, or of the borrower. The general faith in the judgment of individuals as to matters involving their own interests appears with Mill as it does with the other classics,[59] but there are passages in his *Principles* in which he admits to doubts about the proposition that the consumer is a competent judge of the commodities he buys—especially 'commodities' other than goods, those for example 'which are chiefly useful as tending to raise the character of human beings'.[60] Then again, Mill was unconvinced that people were generally far-sighted enough to know what would be in their long-run interests many years in the future; though he was thinking here especially of marriage, his arguments would equally tell against recognition of the permanent binding force of many long-term contracts.[61]

There were also moments when Mill seemed to despair at the possibility of really teaching the working class how to manage their own affairs, commenting that the extent to which the poor were 'insensible to their own direct personal interests' would not be credible without experience[62]—a scarcely concealed rebuke to the naïvety of his own youthful beliefs.

Nevertheless, Mill had the same belief as the other classics in the fundamental motive of self-interest as the generator of all economic activity. Indeed, it was really on this ground only that he believed in the general principle of freedom of contract and non-interference. It was on this ground, for example, that he supported the reform of the Poor Laws in 1834. But unlike many of the other political economists Mill did not think that competition was itself a particularly admirable way of life. There are too, especially in his later days, signs of a greater sophistication

[58] *Principles of Political Economy*, Book V, Chapter 1, Sect. 2.
[59] Ibid., Book V, Chapter X, Sect. 2.
[60] Ibid., Book V, Chapter XI, Sect. 8.
[61] Ibid., Sect. 10.
[62] From an Essay in the *Edinburgh Review*, vol. 164, p. 511 (1845), cited A. W. Coats (ed.), *The Classical Economists and Economic Policy*, pp. 152, 153.

about Mill's ideas on these matters; he seems, as he got older, as well he might, to have grown to distrust some of the ready answers, the facile assumptions, the oversimplifications of classical economics, as well as of utilitarianism. He sometimes wrote, for example, as though he wanted to convince himself that the coming democracy would not show the people to be wanting in their new responsibilities, while in his heart he was yet afraid that this might prove to be the case. One of the major differences between modern man and the classical economists lies in the scepticism with which we have grown used to look at panaceas for social problems. Mill shows marked signs of having acquired some of this scepticism in the course of his own lifetime.

Herbert Spencer

Herbert Spencer (1820–1903) cannot be ranked as a classical economist, and indeed, scarcely deserves to rank as an economist at all. He was, however, a political and social thinker who wrote a vast number of semi-popular books and articles many of which touched on important economic themes. I refer to him here mainly in order to put the classics in true perspective with regard to their beliefs in freedom of contract and *laissez-faire*. In the necessarily simplified account that I have so far given of the classical economists, it may seem that I have, in fact, done little to dispel the idea that they were vigorous propagators of *laissez-faire* in every corner of the economy.[63] As we have seen, they nearly all agreed on the utter failure of the State's regulatory efforts in the Poor Law, in the laws regulating apprenticeships and other restrictions on labour, and in the Usury Laws, and they nearly all supported free trade on the same general principles. In these matters they were generally following in Adam Smith's footsteps in demanding the clearing away of the accumulated lumber of older regulations and restrictions. But when newer issues arose in the nineteenth century, concerning new problems, the question of public education, the regulation of hours and conditions of work, the problems of sanitation and public health, limited liability, the control of the railways, the passenger emigration trade, and kindred matters, then (as we shall see) opinion was far from uniform or simplistic. The economists differed amongst themselves on many of these issues as the politicians and the public did. Very few people of any note then persisted in defending *laissez-faire* and freedom of contract to the utmost. One of these was Spencer, and a comparison between his views and those of the classical economists shows them to have been a good deal more moderate in their views than has often been thought.

[63] See generally, H. Scott-Gordon, 'The Ideology of Laissez-Faire', in A. W. Coats (ed.), *The Classical Economists and Economic policy*, pp. 180 *et seq.*

In his *Social Statics*, first published in 1851 Herbert Spencer idealized freedom of contract as the supreme mechanism for maintaining the social order with the absolute minimum of compulsion or coercion. He argued that freedom of contract was the ideal middle road between total anarchy on the one hand, and total tyranny on the other. He deduced freedom of contract from the same Natural Laws as the classical economists, except that he modified it by treating it as 'the law of equal freedom'. Freedom to buy or sell was part of a man's ordinary freedom; so was freedom to refuse to deal.

Evidently [he says] each is free to offer; each is free to accept; each is free to refuse; for each may do these to any extent without preventing his neighbours from doing the like to the same extent, and at the same time. But no one may do more; no one may force another to part with his goods; no one may force another to take a specified price; for no one can do so without assuming more liberty of action than the man whom he thus treats.[64]

His belief in equality, of course, was extremely limited; it was a belief in the right to the equal pursuit of happiness, not a right to equal happiness. It is not equality to reward men equally for unequal endeavour, for the natural diversity of talents, energies, and skills must be appropriately rewarded in the natural state of equal liberty. Moreover, he believed quite literally in the doctrine of the struggle for survival and the survival of the fittest. All restrictions on freedom of contract interfere with this natural order of things and enable the unfit to survive longer than they would otherwise do.

We have seen that generally speaking the classics argued that men must be left to their own judgment in their dealings with each other. But most of the classics supported the principle of State-aided education when it was introduced in 1833, and the younger Mill justified it on the ground that 'the interest and judgment of the consumer are not sufficient security for the goodness of the commodity'.[65] This called forth an absolute torrent from Herbert Spencer who protested that this excuse was always given for every interference with individual freedom of choice. 'Plenty of trickeries, plenty of difficulties in the detection of fraud, plenty of instances showing the inability of purchasers to protect themselves are quoted by the advocates of each proposed recourse to official regulation.'[66] But in fact, he went on, experience always shows that 'the choice of the commodity may be safely left to the discretion of the buyers'.[67] In the result he objected to the Poor Laws—*all* poor laws— he objected to State-aided education, he objected to colonization and emigration programmes, he even objected to the sanitary and public health laws, and the licensing of doctors. He saw no reason why drains

[64] *Social Statics* (London, 1851), pp. 146–7.   [65] Ibid., pp. 336–7.
[66] Ibid., p. 337.   [67] Ibid.

and sewers should not be commercially owned and their services offered to consumers for private payment.[68]

In his more philosophical moments he went further still. He believed that man was still in process of evolution into a higher form of life. In this new shape man would, it seems, be a more complete social being in which all his relationships were conducted on a free and voluntary basis. When this consummation came about, all ·coercion would finally disappear, as all crime would disappear.[69] Presumably, Spencer assumed that in this new shape man would make, but never break, contracts, an idea which at first sight seems somewhat puzzling, for if nobody ever broke a contract it is a little difficult to see why anybody would need to make contracts for future performance, as opposed to present exchanges. It is precisely because men are unwilling to rely wholly on the present expectation of another's future performance that contracts are made which bind the other to future performance. Unexecuted contracts thus necessarily imply that a party (or both parties) will be *bound* to some performance which they may not wish to carry out when the time comes, and they therefore usually involve the existence of coercion to compel that performance. It is, therefore, likely that in Spencer's Utopia where all coercion has disappeared, executory contract will disappear too, and be replaced entirely by simultaneous exchanges.

But it is not worth devoting any more attention to Herbert Spencer. Probably few modern English lawyers have even heard of him,[70] and he may be allowed to remain in the obscurity into which he has deservedly fallen.[71]

[68] Ibid., pp. 393–4.

[69] Ibid., pp. 202–3.

[70] Probably some will recall Holmes J.'s famous remark that 'the Fourteenth Amendment does not enact Mr. Herbert Spencer's *Social Statics*': *Lochner* v. *New York* 198 U.S. 45, 75 (1905). Surprisingly, though, Holmes J. wrote to Pollock in 1895, saying that he thought Spencer had done more than anyone except Darwin to 'affect our whole way of thinking about the universe': *Pollock-Holmes Letters* (Cambridge, 1942), i. 58. This must have reflected the influence of Spencer on American thinking and law which, despite Holmes's efforts, was formidable, and certainly far greater than in England.

[71] For those who wish to enlarge their acquaintance with Spencer's ideas, reference may be made to J. D. Y. Peel, *Herbert Spencer: The Evolution of a Sociologist* (London, 1971); David Miller, *Social Justice* (Oxford, 1976), especially Chapter VI.

12

THE INTELLECTUAL BACKGROUND,
1770–1870—II

BENTHAM, UTILITARIANISM, AND FREEDOM OF CONTRACT

IN the course of his long life Bentham wrote and said so many things on so many topics that it is not surprising that difficulty has been found in summarizing his ideas on any one theme, or finding him an appropriate place in the history of ideas. There is no doubt that Benthamite utilitarianism was (as I have already said) closely related to classical political economy. Throughout the period 1770–1870 the utilitarians and the classical economists were 'complementary and mutually reinforcing elements in the liberal-individualistic stream of thought and action'.[1] The two sets of ideas had much in common. They both shared a belief in individualism, as a value and as a social mechanism; they believed in freedom of contract as a general principle; they accepted as their starting-point that individuals generally knew their own interests best; both were concerned primarily with maximizing—the one wealth and the other happiness—without unduly worrying about how the resulting wealth or happiness was distributed. But on other points there has been a good deal of difficulty and disagreement in interpreting both their relationship in the realm of ideas, and their influence on the course of events. The greatest puzzle of all, perhaps, has been that of trying to reconcile the image of Bentham as a warm disciple of Adam Smith, urging freedom of contract and *laissez-faire*, with that of Bentham the father of law reform and the modern administrative state machine. I will endeavour to give some answer to this and other difficult questions, though the limited scope of my theme, in relation to Bentham's wide interests, must be stressed.

Certainly in some of his early works Bentham shows all the signs of being in agreement with Adam Smith's general philosophy in economic matters. His essay in *Defence of Usury* was entirely in the Adam Smith tradition. Although Smith himself had not totally condemned the Usury Laws, it was Smith's own arguments that were deployed by Bentham; the *Defence of Usury* was a criticism of Smith 'from a more-Smithian—than Smith point of view'.[2] The standard genuflections in the direction of freedom of contract are found here, as elsewhere: 'No man of ripe

[1] A. W. Coats, Introduction to *The Classical Economists and Economic Policy* (London, 1971), p. 24.
[2] T. W. Hutchison, 'Bentham as an Economist', 66 *Economic Journal* 288, 292 (1956).

years and of sound mind, acting freely, and with his eyes open, ought to be hindered, with a view to his advantage, from making such bargain, in the way of obtaining money as he thinks fit; nor (what is a necessary consequence) anybody hindered from supplying him, upon any terms he thinks proper to accede to.'[3] And it is not only unjustifiable to do this in the interests of the parties themselves, there can also be no real objections from a public point of view. What does it concern others how the borrower and the lender arrange their affairs?

Then there are, in addition, the usual confident assertions that, 'Generally speaking, there is no one who knows what is for your interest so well as yourself—no one who is disposed with so much ardour and constancy to pursue it.'[4] Restrictions on freedom of contract are restraints on liberty, and, prima facie, all restraint on liberty is an evil and needs to be justified. And there are again, the usual admonitions to Government not to interfere too readily with things it does not understand. 'The motto or watchword of Government ... ought to be—Be Quiet.'[5] Like the classical economists, Bentham also criticized the 'mania for regulation' which still left so many controls over labour in the form of Settlement Laws, Apprenticeship Laws, wage fixing, and so on.

So far as ordinary contract law was concerned, Bentham was one of the few utilitarians or classical economists to devote even a very brief attention to the question. His object in doing so was simply to establish that the general enforceability of contracts was a rational matter, and could be derived from his principle of utility.[6] One of the four great principles of legislation which he enunciated was the importance of respecting security. It was this which justified property rights. But similarly contractual rights could be derived from the fact that all contracts involved mutual advantages for the parties. Contracts and dispositions of property both rest upon 'the same fundamental axiom, that every alienation imports an advantage'. There is nothing very new or very interesting here; much of it comes straight out of Hume or Adam Smith.

But nevertheless, there are also profound differences between Bentham's views and those of the classical economists on a wide variety of topics, but still more, in his whole methodology and in some of his most fundamental ideas. When Bentham talked of Governmental non-interference being a general principle only, and insisted that it could be outweighed by any countervailing considerations, he really meant what he said. In 1801, when there was a severe shortage of wheat and bread,

[3] *Jeremy Bentham's Economic Writings*, ed. Stark (London, 1952), i. 129, hereafter cited as Stark.
[4] Bentham, *Works*, ed. Bowring, iii. 33.
[5] Ibid., p. 35.
[6] *Theory of Legislation* (London, 1911), p. 193; see also, *View of a Complete Code of Laws*, *Works*, ed. Bowring, iii. 190.

Bentham argued for a maximum price for bread in language which suggested that he was very far from being a dogmatic advocate of *laissez-faire*:

I have not, I never had, nor ever shall have, any horror, sentimental or anarchical, of the hand of government. I leave it to Adam Smith, and the champions of the rights of man . . . to talk of invasions of natural liberty, and to give as a specific argument against this or that law, an argument the effect of which would be to put a negative upon all laws. The interference of government, as often as in my humble view of the matter the smallest balance on the side of advantage is the result, is an event I witness with altogether as much satisfaction as I should its forbearance, and with much more than I should its negligence.[7]

It is hard to imagine any of the classical economists, except perhaps John Stuart Mill, agreeing quite so enthusiastically with the possibility of Government intervention.

And we know, too, that as Bentham got older, and his inventive mind poured out endless schemes for the improvement of the people, their laws, their social conditions, their education and health, he envisaged a vast legislative programme, and a substantial increase of Governmental power, in order to give effect to it. If there is one thing which the modern world owes to Bentham, it is the belief that the social order can be manipulated by the mere act of legislation. In this ' demystification'[8] of the law, in this demonstration that the law was a purely human and social creation, which could be made and unmade at man's mere pleasure, Bentham succeeded perhaps only too well. This is, however, something of a digression from our theme. The relevant point is that Bentham could and did combine his belief in non-interference in certain areas, with a belief in the potential power of interference for the public good by the legislative process. Well might it be wondered how Dicey convinced himself that Benthamite utilitarianism was synonymous with individualism and *laissez-faire*.[9]

The answer to this puzzle, as well as the true explanation of the relationship between Bentham's ideas and those of Adam Smith, surely lies in Bentham's rejection of Natural Law. To Adam Smith, and those who believed with him broadly in the natural harmony of interests (whether they thought the 'invisible hand' was the hand of God or some less deistic benevolence), a background of Law and Justice was always taken for granted. Adam Smith himself (as I have previously said) certainly never for a moment contemplated that the free interplay of

[7] Stark, iii. 257–8.
[8] See H. L. A. Hart, 'Bentham and the Demystification of the Law', 36 *Modern Law Review* 2 (1973).
[9] See Brebner, 'Laissez Faire and State Intervention in Nineteenth Century Britain', *Journal of Ec. Hist. Supplement* 59 (1948).

competition could take place in a State of Nature. He assumed a framework of laws enforced by a State, invested with the appropriate powers of legislation, execution, and judging. He took it for granted, indeed, he makes it explicit, that there would be a framework of laws in which, at a minimum, property would be protected and contracts enforced. 'It is', he insists in *The Wealth of Nations*, 'only under the shelter of the civil magistrate that the owner of that valuable property which is acquired by the labour of many years or perhaps of many successive generations, can sleep a single night in security.'[10] And it is also clear that Smith believed that his framework of laws would provide for the enforcement of contracts, and for protection against force and fraud. The idea of free competition as a race or contest was based on the very civilized concept of a race under proper rules. In *The Theory of Moral Sentiments*, for instance, Smith says that the individual, 'in the race for wealth and honours and preferments . . . may run as hard as he can, and strain every nerve and muscle, in order to outstrip his competitors. But if he should jostle or throw down any of them, the indulgence of the spectators is entirely at an end. It is a violation of fair-play, which they cannot admit of.'[11]

Now it has been deduced from this that to Adam Smith, the 'invisible hand' is 'not the hand of some God or some natural agency independent of human effort; [but] it is the hand of the law-giver, the hand which withdraws from the sphere of the pursuit of self-interest those possibilities which do not harmonize with the public good.'[12] The difficulty with this explanation is that in effect it eliminates the distinction between the outer framework of laws, which are largely given and immutable, and the inner sphere of human activity, within which the competitive pursuit of self-interest is to have free reign. For if, in some respect, the result is deemed not to harmonize with the public good, the framework of laws can be altered and expanded, and the inner circle can be diminished. It is doubtful whether Adam Smith would have agreed with this if only because he does seem to accept that part of the outer framework of the State and its laws is dictated by immutable principles of Natural Law. To Bentham on the other hand, Natural Law was pure nonsense, and it is therefore quite clear that, in Bentham's eyes, there was no essential difference at all between the framework of the laws and the inner circle where individual self-interest could operate. The job of the law-maker, in Bentham's world, was to create, manipulate, and constantly adjust the laws so that there would be in the result an artificial harmony of interests

[10] Book V, Chapter 1.

[11] *Theory of Moral Sentiments*, ed. Raphael and Macfie, p. 83.

[12] L. Robbins, *Theory of Economic Policy in English Classical Political Economy*, p. 56; see also, 'Bentham in the Twentieth Century' in the same author's *The Evolution of Modern Economic Theory*, p. 76; J. Viner, *The Long View and the Short*; D. Lyons, *In the Interests of the Governed* (Oxford, 1973), pp. 55–9.

between the individual action and the public good. Bentham's theory of punishment shows this clearly enough. In the absence of any law at all, there would be no property rights, and everybody could simply take what he was strong enough to seize from his neighbour. There was no Natural Law to prohibit this, but such a state of anarchy would be contrary to the principle of utility, the principle that society should be so arranged as to lead to the greatest happiness of the greatest number of people. It was therefore necessary to make laws to protect property and to punish theft in order that the interests of the thief and those of the public should be brought into harmony. To achieve this end the thief must be made to understand that what he stood to gain from his theft would certainly be less than he would lose by the subsequent punishment imposed on him by the State. If the thief could be made to understand the certainty of this, he would perceive that it could not be in his interests to steal, and all theft would cease. His interests and those of the public would then be in total harmony.

Thus, so far as Bentham was concerned, there was no difference of principle, no line dictated by Natural Law, which separated off the outer framework of laws from the inner circle of freedom. The point where the line was to be drawn depended entirely on the principle of utility—the greatest happiness principle. But few of the classical economists (except perhaps John Stuart Mill)[13] would have wanted to follow Bentham thus far. Whether or not they really believed in Natural Law and Lockean rights of property, whether or not they believed in a Divine source to rights of property, they would have been most unhappy to see these matters openly discussed. For to adopt a Benthamite position threw open to question the very rights of property on which most middle- and upper-class Englishmen assumed the whole fabric of society depended. Consequently, except for Bentham himself, and to a lesser extent, the younger Mill, and some of Bentham's other followers (such as Chadwick), nearly all the other thinkers and writers, not to mention the politicians, lawyers, and practical men of affairs, assumed the existence of some outer framework of laws within which competition and the pursuit of self-interest could be left alone.

But in practice, as well as in logic, this was an extremely difficult position to maintain. When government interference with this or that type of contract was in question, for example, the legitimacy of the intervention would depend on precisely where the line was drawn between this outer framework and the inner circle. And that depended largely on the perception of what was 'natural' and immutable. It was

---

[13] In *Utilitarianism*, Mill argues very clearly that there is no natural harmony of interests but that it is the law-maker's task to create an artificial harmony: see pp. 268–9 of the Fontana edition, ed. Mary Warnock (London, 1962).

not just a matter of belief in Natural Law; it was rather that whatever seemed a more 'natural' state of laws to one person, inevitably meant that, to him, interference with it was wrong, an encroachment on the inner circle of free competitive individual action. If, to someone else, the existing law seemed less 'natural' and more artificial, and therefore open to change, he would be more inclined to see that law as part of an incorrect outer framework, even though the resultant change might be to encroach somewhat upon the inner circle. Now people's perception of what was 'natural' was at this time (as it still commonly is today) highly variable, and the result was that one man's *laissez-faire* tended to be another man's intervention.[14] The point can be illustrated with a few simple examples.

When the issue was raised of repealing the Combination Acts in 1824–5, the existing Acts were thought of by some as part of the 'natural' framework of the laws—they had after all been in operation for a quarter of a century—so that to repeal them was, in a sense, a form of intervention by the law-maker. On the other hand, to those who assumed that a 'natural' state of the law was one in which total freedom of combination prevailed, the Acts themselves were interventionist and to repeal them was to follow the principle of *laissez-faire*. A more difficult question concerned the various ways in which contractual liability could be limited by law—for instance by bankruptcy legislation or by recognizing the principle of incorporation with limited liability. We today are so used to laws of this character that they seem 'natural' to us, a part of the outer framework of laws whose basic principle we take for granted. Thus to abolish limited liability today (to take a fanciful illustration) would seem an extraordinary act of 'interference'. But to some of those who had been brought up in a legal system where limited liability was unknown, and where the 'natural' way of enforcing a debt was by incarcerating the debtor in jail, the introduction of bankruptcy legislation and corporate limited liability seemed a radical interference with the natural order of things. The very constitution of Parliament itself raised precisely the same issue. To the traditionalists, it was perfectly natural that Parliament should represent the landed aristocracy in the House of Lords, and that the Commons should be full of representatives of rotten and even corrupt boroughs. To establish a democratic system of representation (which, of course, is the 'natural' system to us) would have seemed, and did seem, to most Englishmen of the early nineteenth century totally unnatural, and a wild interference with the basic framework of the Constitution.

The Enforcement of Contracts—Laissez-faire or Intervention

We now come to a curious point in the history of these various intellectual

[14] A. J. Taylor, *Laissez Faire and State Intervention in Nineteenth Century Britain* (London, 1972), p. 12.

movements. Despite the constant association of freedom of contract with the ideals of classical political economy and of utilitarianism, no real thought was ever devoted to the law of contract and its relationship with the outer framework of law. All the classical economists took it for granted that the laws must provide for the enforcement of contracts just as much as they provided for the protection of property. But, with the partial exception of the younger Mill, none of them ever stopped to enquire what was involved in the enforcement of contracts, and why such enforcement was not itself a form of Government intervention. There is nothing 'natural' about laws for the enforcement of contracts.[15] Aristotle tells us that the Greeks generally did not recognize actions for the enforcement of contracts 'on the grounds that if A has given credit to B he should settle with him in the spirit of their bargain'.[16] It is true that the law does not need to *enforce* simultaneous exchanges of property (or exchanges or property for services) and that therefore it may seem somehow more 'natural' to grant recognition to such exchanges. But the law of contract, and in particular the law developing in this very period, was not primarily concerned with simultaneous exchanges but with executory contracts. And in the case of the executory contract the law's role cannot by any possibility be classified as a passive one. It is the law, set in motion indeed by the aggrieved individual, which authorizes the State to exert its coercive power on the defendant, either to perform his contract or to compensate the plaintiff for the loss. Most of the arguments profferred by the classical economists for freedom of contract were concerned with laws which *prohibited* certain contracts being made. Their arguments were fundamentally directed to ensuring that exchanges should be *permitted*. But to the lawyer freedom of contract meant, or was coming to mean, not merely that exchanges should be *permitted*, but also that executory exchanges should be *enforced*. An immense gulf separates these two things, and it is possible that the earlier classical economists were still thinking in terms of a law of executed contracts, rather than of the enforcement of executory contracts. It was very difficult, as John Stuart Mill pointed out, to see how this form of enforcement could be brought within the minimum role envisaged for the State by those who would confine its activities to the prevention of force and fraud:

The legitimacy is conceded of repressing violence or treachery; but under which of these heads are we to place the obligation on people to perform their contracts? Non-performance does not necessarily imply fraud; the person who entered into the contract may have sincerely intended to fulfil it; and the term

---

[15] But in the United States Marshall C. J. in 1827 extended the Lockean concept of property in the State of Nature to include contractual rights: R. L. Hale, 'The Supreme Court and the Contract Clause', 57 *Harvard Law Rev.* 512, 526–7 (1944).

[16] *Nic. Ethics* 1164b; also 1162b.

fraud, which can scarcely admit of being extended even to cases of voluntary breach of contract when no deception was practised, is certainly not appropriate when the omission to perform is a case of negligence. Is it not part of the duty of governments to enforce contracts? Here the doctrine of non-interference would no doubt be stretched a little, and it would be said that enforcing contracts is not regulating the affairs of individuals at the pleasure of government but giving effect to their own expressed desire. Let us acquiesce in this enlargement of the restrictive theory, and take it for what it is worth. But governments do not limit their concern with contracts to a simple enforcement. They take upon themselves to determine what contracts are fit to be enforced ... But when once it is admitted that there are any engagements which for reasons of expediency, the law ought not to enforce, the same question is necessarily opened with respect to all engagements. Whether, for example, the law should enforce a contract to labour, when the wages are too low or the hours of work too severe ...[17]

With the exception of a brief passage on the bankruptcy legislation by J. R. McCulloch in his *Principles of Political Economy* this is virtually the sum total of classical discussion on the actual enforcement of contracts. McCulloch's discussion is also worth a mention if only because it shows how simple and, indeed, circular, much classical thinking was on these issues. McCulloch argued in favour of the abolition of imprisonment for debt, saying that it encouraged easy credit.

If a tradesman trusts an individual with money or goods which he is unable to repay, he has made a bad speculation. But why, because he has done so, should he be allowed to arrest the debtor's person? If he wished to have perfect security, he should not have dealt with him, or dealt only for ready money: such transactions are, on the part of the tradesman, perfectly voluntary; and, if they place undue confidence in a debtor who has not misled them by erroneous representations of his affairs, or misconducted himself, they have themselves only to blame.[18]

This passage reveals all too clearly the impossibility of justifying the law of contract on any grounds of a natural framework of outer laws. McCulloch argues that the transaction is perfectly voluntary on the part of the tradesman, and that on that account he should have no right to imprison the debtor. But the voluntariness of the transaction is something which must be measured against the background of the law (and perhaps also of people's expectations). For if the tradesman knows that the law allows him to imprison the debtor after judgment (as it did when McCulloch wrote) the tradesman has only voluntarily parted with his goods on the basis that he has that legal right. Only if the tradesman foresaw (or should have foreseen) the possibility of the law being changed will the price exacted by the tradesman fairly recompense him for loss of

[17] *Principles*, Book V, Chapter 1, Sect. 2.
[18] *Principles of Political Economy*, 5th edn. (London, 1864), p. 212.

the right. One cannot, therefore, deduce what rights the tradesman should have by some 'natural' process, and then enforce those rights. The point is too complex to pursue at length here, but the essence of the matter is that the bargain struck between the parties, if they both know the law, and both act as rationally as economic men are supposed to act, will reflect that law as it stands, together with appropriately discounted probabilities of its being changed. Since the bargain struck, and the price to be paid, will thus reflect the legal remedies which are (or are expected to be) available, it is quite impossible to deduce what those legal remedies should be from the bargain itself. The voluntariness of the transaction is neither here nor there.

The result of this great weakness in classical economic theory was that when specific issues were raised by legislative proposals which would involve interference with freedom of contract, the arguments on the *principle* of interference were totally valueless, and indeed rather meaningless, from an economic viewpoint.

Externalities

The other great weakness of the classical economists on this question is that they almost totally failed to grasp the problem known today as that of externalities. If A and B make a contract which benefits both parties it still cannot be deduced that the performance of the contract will be in the public interest unless it is clear that the contract will not impose any costs on third parties; or, more accurately, that it will not impose costs on third parties in excess of any benefits conferred on third parties. The only prominent public figure who seems to have shown any understanding of this question in the first half of the nineteenth century was Edwin Chadwick.

Chadwick had served Bentham in the last years of his life as his secretary, but his training was in the law and not in economics. Nevertheless, he showed himself in many respects more able than any of the classical economists on the question of externalities.[19] And recognizing, or at least groping after, the problem, Chadwick's solution was right in the Benthamite tradition, that is to say, it was to provide for an adjustment of the law so as to internalize the cost, and so to ensure as far as possible that private interests harmonized with the public interest. As a member of the Royal Commission on the Poor Laws in 1834, as secretary of the resulting Poor Law Commission from 1834 to 1841, as author of the famous *Sanitary Report* published in 1842, and as author of innumerable schemes of social reform, Chadwick played a significant role in the establishment of the modern bureaucratic machine. Yet he was himself no collectivist; he fought against Ashley's Ten Hours Bill in

[19] See S. E. Finer, *The Life and Times of Sir Edwin Chadwick*, pp. 24–5.

1833, bitterly arguing for freedom of contract for adult workers, and he even showed some spirit as an entrepreneur when in 1842 he collected some friends and founded a private company to carry out some of the sanitary reforms that he had vainly urged upon the government.

But it remains his ideas on externalities, and his ingenuity in trying to modify the law to ensure harmony between public and private interests, that are so remarkable, and deserve further amplification. It was his work on the Poor Law Commission that first drew Chadwick's attention to the problem of externalities. For he discovered that a considerable part of the costs borne by the Poor Law authorities arose from the private activities of third parties who were not called upon to meet the burden. When, therefore, he was also appointed to the Commission on the Factories in 1833 (while the Poor Law Commission was still at work) he took the opportunity to slip in a number of recommendations towards the end of the Report on the problem of workers' compensation. Chadwick had become convinced that the rate of industrial accidents would not be seriously reduced until the victims had to be compensated by the parties responsible. It is plain that he was moved not so much by compassion for the victims, nor by the desire to see them properly compensated, for in fact it was largely a question of shifting the cost of the compensation from the Poor Law authorities to the employers. What motivated Chadwick was the belief that the employers would only be induced to take precautions to avoid accidents if they bore part of the cost.[20] The Factories Report had been produced in tremendous haste and the subsequent Bill was rushed through Parliament in 1833 with little discussion of these questions. Poulett Thomson, President of the Board of Trade, told the House of Commons that there were adequate common law remedies for injured workmen[21] (this was before *Priestley* v. *Fowler*[22] was decided), and the clauses on workmen's compensation were dropped.

But Chadwick returned to the attack in 1846[23] when he secured the appointment of a House of Commons Select Committee to inquire into the conditions of the railway labourers. The great boom in railway building had recently got under way, and the railway navvy was appearing on the scene all over the country, and bringing many new social problems with him. The idea that the contracts of employment between the navvies and their immediate employers, or that the contracts between the railway companies and the chief contractors, were of no public concern, was here revealed as an utter absurdity, for all the talk

[20] R. E. Lewis, 'Edwin Chadwick and the Railway Labourers', 3 *Economic History Rev.* 107, 117–18 (1950).

[21] S. E. Finer, *The Life and Times of Sir Edwin Chadwick*, p. 61.

[22] (1837) 3 M. & W. 1, 150 E. R. 1030, *post* p. 502.

[23] He also slipped in a reminder on the point in his *Sanitary Report* in 1842 at p. 271 of the 1965 edition, ed. Flinn.

of freedom of contract. For the railway companies let the work to contractors, who engaged sub-contractors, and they in turn either engaged still further sub-contractors or employed gangs of navvies for the hard manual labour. Each party attempted to clear himself of all responsibility for the social costs that the railway work threw on the surrounding districts. Yet these costs were heavy and visible to all. The navvies had no proper quarters in which to live while working on the lines; they were expected to build their own shanty towns, and simply move them along every few miles. They naturally drank far too much, involved the local people in riots and disorders, accosting the women and taunting the men,[24] and spread disease (many were seen with 'smallpox thick upon them wandering into the lanes');[25] the injured were sent to local hospitals to be treated at the public expense, and at the end of the job, many of the navvies were thrown on poor relief themselves. Chadwick focused specially on his scheme for compensating the injured workmen; he wanted to throw onto the railway companies themselves (not the immediate employers of the navvies) the responsibility for paying such compensation, and he wanted this to be done whether the accident was avoidable or not. He was convinced that if the railway companies bore this liability, they would have the power and the ability to compel the contractors, the sub-contractors, and the men themselves, to take much greater care to reduce the accident rate. It was a scheme years ahead of its time—fifty years before Workmen's Compensation legislation was introduced in England, and over a century before the economic arguments surfaced again in the works of Professor Calabresi of Yale[26]—but it was a typical Benthamite scheme. By imposing the costs on the railway companies, the legislator would bring self-interest into play on the side of accident prevention. 'It dispenses with agencies of inspection,— and *a priori* regulations; it reaches where they would not reach, and renders arbitrary and troublesome interferences unnecessary—it is awake and active when authority and public attention, and benevolence and humanity are asleep or powerless.'[27] The Committee took up the proposals enthusiastically, but they were never implemented. The only result of all this effort was the passage of Lord Campbell's Act of 1846 which gave a remedy to the dependants of someone killed by an accident, or in other circumstances in which legal liability would have arisen if death had not occurred.[28]

---

[24] Kellow Chesney, *The Victorian Underworld*, p. 95.

[25] Terry Coleman, *The Railway Navvies*, p. 140.

[26] See *The Costs of Accidents* (Yale, 1969).

[27] Cited, R. E. Lewis, 'Edwin Chadwick and the Railway Labourers', p. 112.

[28] Chadwick also discusses another example of market failure in a pamphlet *On the Jurisprudence of Chargeability for Sanitary Works, etc.* (London, 1873).

Distributive Questions

The classical economists had little to say about the distribution of the national product. From Adam Smith onwards, they had broadly been content to describe the way in which 'the annual produce' of the nation (still thought of largely in agricultural terms) was divided among the three classes of producers, that is, rent to the landowners, profits to stock owners, and wages to labourers. There was little sophistication about the analysis of the way in which the relative shares of these three groups were made up. Perhaps unconsciously thinking in terms of the landowners as the governing class, both Smith and Ricardo tended to see rent as a residual income, representing what was left after the necessary disbursements had been made by way of interest (or profit) to the provider of capital, and by way of wages to the labourers.[29] They did not envisage a society in which the capitalists had the upper hand, and in which payment of rents and of wages were seen as necessary charges on capital, leaving the residue as the fairly earned income of the capitalist— a point of view which might have seemed a lot more natural between (say) 1850 and 1900; and they certainly did not envisage a society in which rent and profits are seen as necessary (or even largely unnecessary) charges on the produce of the country, the residue of which belongs by rights to the labourers or working classes, which would seem to many a more natural point of view today. Least of all did they share the modern economists' viewpoint that there is no residue at all, and that all three factors of production simply share in the total produce according to their marginal value.

The weakness of classic theory on distributional questions led to a number of results of varying importance. The first was that many people tended to assume that the conditions of free competition which the classics assured them would lead to the greatest total production of wealth, also necessarily led to a fair distribution of that wealth so produced. We have already seen how easy it was for the prudential considerations about individualism and competition to be treated as though they were moral considerations. It was equally easy to deduce that what a man succeeded in obtaining in the competitive struggle was his moral desert. He either made, or produced, the wealth itself, or he exchanged what he produced for other things which he wanted. Exchange itself, therefore, came to be vested with some semi-moral flavour, as for example, with Paley who argued that there was only one principle that could ever become universal with regard to the distribution of wealth and that was the principle of Exchange.[30] Paley, moreover,

---

[29] See generally, G. J. Stigler, *Production and Distribution Theories* (New York, 1941).
[30] *Principles of Moral and Political Philosophy*, Book III, Part I, Chapter III.

explicitly stated that where there was no monopoly a market price was always a fair price.[31] In so interpreting the economists, it may well be that people attributed ideas to them which they did not entertain. It may, perhaps, be that to Adam Smith, and Ricardo, and the other economists of the first half of the nineteenth century, some of these questions were so unreal that they were not even considered. The distribution of the national produce was simply not a moral question; market arrangements were not, *per se*, moral arrangements, market prices were not in themselves just prices.[32] Perhaps so; but it was easy to interpret the economists in the opposite sense. Certainly, if they thought the existing distributional system was unjust, they said little to invite its correction. Only John Stuart Mill, last of the classics, insisted upon separating questions of production from questions of distribution.[33] By the time he wrote his *Principles*, in 1848, it is clear that redistribution in various ways was already well begun; and Mill insisted that, while the principles or 'laws' governing production were well settled, and inexorable, the principles governing distribution were man-made and could be altered. Although Mill's views on distribution were very advanced by current standards (for example, he pressed for substantial redistribution through the laws of inheritance) there was still, by modern economic standards, little sign of any sophistication in the analysis of problems of distribution and the relationship between distribution and production.

Modern economic theory insists that even in the highly theoretical conditions of 'perfect competition' a market system will only produce optimal results for a given distribution of income and wealth. If there are few rich people in a society, for example, the market economy will produce very few Rolls-Royces; if there are vast numbers of wage earners not rich enough to afford cars at all, the market economy will produce plenty of bicycles and buses. Equally, if there are no rich people, a free market economy is unlikely to produce things which require large concentrations of capital to produce. In a more equal society, it is widely assumed that savings and investment would be low, for there is a tendency for people of poor or modest means to consume a higher proportion of their earnings. There is little sign that much of this was perceived during the classical period. The agglomeration of wealth in the hands of the large landowners was still largely seen (by those who approved it) as contributing to social and political stability, rather than as having any major economic significance. And the huge gap between the rich and the poor was often seen as an inevitable (and perhaps just) outcome of the laws of political economy.

[31] Ibid., Book III, Chapter VII.

[32] So argued in 1886 by H. Sidgwick: 'The Scope and Method of Economic Science', in *Essays in Economic Method*, ed. Smyth (London, 1962).

[33] See Alan Ryan, *J. S. Mill* (London, 1974), pp. 163–8.

Now it is clear that the principle of freedom of contract tended to perpetuate this state of affairs, if it did not even aggravate it. For the price at which a bargain is struck necessarily depends to some degree on the distribution of income and wealth in society. The price of more expensive commodities tends to fall as the rich become poorer, and the price of cheaper things tends to rise as the poor become richer. The result is that the justice of a bargain struck in the open market—the fairness of a market price—is itself dependent on the distribution of wealth and income. So long as some kind of moral sanctity was given to market prices, the result was, consciously or unconsciously, to give a similar moral blessing to the inequalities of wealth. And conversely, as the inequalities themselves came under challenge, the principle of freedom of contract itself came to be increasingly eroded. Although little of this may have been consciously perceived or articulated before 1870 the facts themselves often thrust the issue before the public's eyes. For example, public grants of money for educational purposes which were often opposed or attacked as a form of 'interference' were defended by the younger Mill as a palpable redistribution device. Since the wages of some unskilled labourers were inadequate to cover the cost of educating their children someone else simply had to pay.[34] Then again, much of the legislative interference with freedom of contract—dealt with in greater detail below—which took place before 1870, was greatly weakened in effect by the social inequalities of wealth which prevailed in the country at the time. One instance of this should suffice to make clear the great importance of this point.

The Passenger Acts provide an example of how limited all efforts at interference with freedom of contract can be, until the purchasers of the product in question have sufficient money to buy a more expensive article. These Acts were concerned with the appalling condition in which emigrant passengers to Canada and the United States were carried during the first fifty or sixty years of the nineteenth century. In the early days they were carried in conditions somewhat worse than slaves or cattle, and inch by inch, legislative improvement in the conditions was imposed on the shipowners. But the important point for present purposes is that most of these emigrants were exceedingly poor—many were Irish—who could barely save up the necessary £5 for a transatlantic fare even after months of hard work. Now it may well be that the shipowners made a significant profit from this trade, even at £5 per head. But it is clear that if legislative efforts at improving the conditions on the ships moved too far or too fast, the trade would simply have dried up overnight—for nobody would have been able to afford an economic fare. What the legislation might have done, however, was to redress the

[34] Mill, *Principles of Political Economy*, Book V, Chapter XI, Sect. 8.

bargaining power between shipowners and emigrants somewhat, so that the services supplied by the shipowners, while still low enough to provide them with a profit, were not so high as they might have been in open market conditions. It is, of course, very hard to know what the result of the legislation was in terms of the prices paid and the shipowners' profit margins. If the only result of the legislation was to drive up the price slowly, as the services supplied by the shipowners were also being driven up, then the shipowners' profit margins might have remained unaffected, and the effect of the legislation in economic terms would have been very small; its only real effect would have been to deprive the consumer of the choice of buying a very cheap service. (Even that would have been quite a reasonable thing to do when this very cheap service was potentially lethal and the purchaser was too ignorant to appreciate the fact). But it is also possible that the legislation affected the precise point at which the bargain was struck, thus, in effect, providing some small redistributive element to the transaction. If, for instance, the result of the legislation was to drive up the minimum cost of providing the service from (say) £4 to £4 10s., and the price remained at £5, then obviously an element of redistribution would have taken place. Economic theorists perhaps too readily assume that no such redistribution would normally take place, but it is easy to posit circumstances in which, at least in the short-run, there would have been redistributive results from legislative intervention of this character.

And where market failures led to statutory intervention, as they did in many situations discussed more fully in Chapter 16, the intervention might well contain more substantial redistributive elements even in the middle of the nineteenth century. Open redistribution of wealth might still be politically impossible, but when, for example, the Public Health Acts set about the problem of clearing up the filthy conditions of the cities, it was impossible to ensure that the cost fell precisely and proportionately on those who benefited. An interesting example of the redistributive effects of such legislation is to be found in the case of *Darling* v. *Epsom Local Board of Health*[35] in 1855. In this case the local Board of Health levied a special rate on the whole district to pay for improvements in the supply of proper sewer, water, and lighting facilities. The area covered by the Order included the town of Epsom, which was in a deplorable state, having no sewage or drainage or water facilities to speak of, and the surrounding area where the more prosperous middle-class citizens lived in salubrious comfort with the benefit of private drains and wells. Moreover, the surrounding areas were too low to benefit from the proposed new sewers which were evidently designed for the benefit of the townsfolk. Nevertheless it was held by the Queen's

[35] (1855) 5 E. & B. 471, 119 E. R. 556.

Bench that the rate was validly levied on the occupiers of the surrounding areas as well as those in the town. It was, said the Court, impossible to insist on proof of direct benefit to each householder subjected to the rate; indeed it was unjust. For though there might be no direct benefit to the inhabitants of the outlying areas there would be indirect benefits. The values of the properties would be enhanced by the improved sanitation of the town, and their owners and occupiers would, on their visits to the town, have the advantage of walking through clean and well-lit streets, instead of dark and stinking ones. Plainly, this sort of compulsory rating had redistributive effects; indeed, this was one of its primary purposes since if there was no redistribution involved the legislative intervention might have been unnecessary—the market might have provided the necessary facilities to those willing to pay. Nevertheless, these interferences with the free market were obviously of limited scope. The rates had to be paid by the townsfolk as well as the suburban middle class. The size of the rates to be levied had to reflect the public's capacity to pay.

The same position basically held true of the labour market. There appears today to be a widespread but simplistic belief that wages were very low in the early part of the Industrial Revolution because the workmen were exploited by the employers, and that wages have risen to their present heights because the power of the trade unions has brought this exploitation to an end. In fact, of course, this is very nearly a complete myth. The reason why the wage of the worker of (say) 1850 was only a fraction of his wage today is because the national product in 1850 was only a fraction of the national product today. The difference made by the shift in the relative bargaining power of employers and workmen only affects the additional, relatively small proportion of the wage which the employer can pay without bankrupting himself on the one hand, and the worker can forgo without serious loss to himself on the other hand. In a free and competitive market (which, of course, modern Britain is not) wages cannot rise above that point at which the employer can still make sufficient profit on his investment, and they cannot fall below that point at which the workmen would find it not worth his while to work for that employer, or to work at all. The bargaining power of the parties only affects the sum which lies between these extremes, and equally, therefore, any legislative interference with freedom of contract can only affect this amount. It follows that no amount of legislative interference with freedom of contract in the early nineteenth century could have improved the standard of living of the working classes to any substantial extent.

Because the classics were so little concerned with questions of distribution, and because they had so much faith in competition, they said very little about inequalities of bargaining power. In modern times, it is this inequality of bargaining power which is usually treated as the principal reason for rejecting complete freedom of contract, but there has been an unfortunate tendency to assume that differences of bargaining power have a much greater role in the free market than they in fact have. Apart from the fact that (as I have just said) they can only affect a small part of the range of possible prices for a product or service, there has also been a tendency to equate bargaining power with size and sophistication. This too is potentially misleading; although these things can affect bargaining power, the classics tended to pay little attention to them because they assumed the existence of a highly competitive market. And in highly competitive conditions, even the relatively ignorant and weak consumer has a considerable degree of bargaining power—he can transfer his custom.

If the classical economists lacked a theory of distribution in economic matters, the Benthamite utilitarians provided what proved, at least in the long run, an immensely important ideal for distribution in social and political matters. For the most important facet of Bentham's greatest happiness principle proved in the end to be the corollary which he attached to it, rather than the principle itself. The corollary was, that each individual was to count as one, and nobody for more than one, in the computation of the aggregate happiness of the community. Bentham did not, of course, mean that everyone was entitled to an equal quantity of happiness but only that the ordinary people were to count equally with everyone else in computing the total happiness to be aimed at. It was this egalitarian aspect of Bentham's principles which was so novel when he first pronounced them. Few people even in 1776 would have rejected the idea that legislation should be for the 'public good' or in the 'public interest' or for the greatest happiness of the greatest number. Most politicians regularly used such language then, as they do now. But what was very much more dubious, if not downright shocking, was the notion that every one should count equally for this purpose. That *was* new, and originally, it was entirely subversive if taken in a political sense. Of course Bentham did not at first put his principle forward as a political or constitutional principle, but as a moral and legislative one. But early in the nineteenth century he came to the conclusion that political equality—with each man counting for one, and no more than one—was an essential precondition of all his other reforms, and he threw in his lot with the Parliamentary Reformers. Bentham accepted James Mill's *Essay on Government* as stating the Radical case for representative government.

In thus embracing democracy, Bentham was not alone. Most of the political economists were believers in democracy, at least as an ultimate aspiration. To the modern reader, one of the strange things about the intellectual movements of this period was the compatability of belief in democracy (an advanced 'left' political stance) with general adherence to the ideal of freedom of contract (today an extreme 'right' political stance). The explanation of this puzzle lies in the fact that both these beliefs grew out of the rejection of traditional Whig paternalism. Both arose out of the idea that the people could be trusted.

I suggested in an earlier chapter that social contractarian ideas were greatly forwarded because the small group of great landowners who largely ran the country in the eighteenth century identified themselves and their interests with the country as a whole. They treated the country and its institutions as theirs, as set up for the protection of their property. But the fundamental political changes which transformed England from an aristocracy in 1770 to something passably resembling a democracy in 1870 brought with them a number of profoundly important changes in the way in which men thought about the relationship of the individual to the State.

The fact that politics was now played out on a stage before a much wider audience, combined, of course, with the growth of population itself, and the waning power of the aristocracy, meant that people began to see the law-maker as somebody remote and detached from themselves. Where the eighteenth-century Whigs had seen themselves banded together in the Social Contract for the protection of their property and rights, the nineteenth-century middle classes began to see Parliament as a remote and abstract law-maker, above and beyond the people but (they hoped and insisted) responsive to their interests and desires. The changing attitude to legislation is well illustrated by comparing two views, as set out in the following citations. The first comes from a work of Sir John Byles, later a judge of the Court of Common Pleas, in 1845. Byles was (as we shall see) very hostile to the philosophy of *laissez-faire* and he said of social legislation that it amounted to 'the concentrated action of the wisdom and power of the whole society on a given point. A mutual agreement by all that certain things shall be done.'[36] Much of this social legislation was passed by overwhelming majorities in both the Houses of Parliament, and frequently those who disagreed with it were eccentrics or die-hards. To secure unanimity in such circumstances would have seemed absurd to the Government as it would to the people. But that did not prevent such legislation from being seen by Byles as 'a mutual agreement', a self-imposed act passed by the people in Parliament assembled.

The newer attitude, by contrast, is to be found quite explicitly stated by Bagehot in *The English Constitution* in 1867: 'We look on State action', he wrote, 'not as our own action but as an alien action; as an imposed

[36] *Sophisms of Free Trade* (reprinted, London, 1904) Chapter VIII; see *post* as to this book, p. 380.

tyranny from without, not as the consummated result of our own organised wishes.'[37] The change in attitude was, of course, mirrored in the growth of legal positivism. Bentham's *Fragment on Government* had provided the first clear alternative legal philosophy to social contractarianism in modern English legal thought. In 1832 these ideas were developed at length by John Austin in his *Province of Jurisprudence Determined*; together with the later jurist, T. E. Holland, Austin (it has been said) 'set up an abstract analysis of the legal equilibrium of a social system just as Ricardo, Mill and Jevons propounded an equilibrium analysis of the economic order'.[38] Law was no longer the outcome of a social contract, but of a command. Instead of a contract, there was a hierarchical relationship of power, stretching up from the citizen to those who wielded authority over him. The source of the authority was none other than customary obedience. Laws were commands of this Sovereign addressed from on high, to his subjects.

The change from social contractarianism to legal positivism may not, at first, have carried much practical significance.[39] But these changing ways of thinking about the relationship between the individual and the State were ultimately to be of profound importance. In the contractual model, Government operated by the consent of the governing class; laws of any practical significance were expected to be changed only when the whole, or substantially the whole, of the landowning classes accepted the changes. Contracts could not be changed by the mere whim of one of the contracting parties. But after the Reform Act of 1832—and still more after the Reform Act of 1867—the electorate had become so large that these contractual ideas became inappropriate. Inevitably, the command theory carried with it implications about majority rule. If the Sovereign could command, he could coerce; indeed, the whole essence of a law was that it was a command backed by a sanction. There was no longer any question about assuming that the fundamental principles of the State could not be altered without the broad consent of the landowning, or any other class. Every class was now at the mercy of a Parliamentary majority.

In a sense the change which began to come over England in 1832 was rather like that which comes over a family company when it 'goes

---

[37] Reprinted, London, 1963, p. 262.

[38] C. A. Cooke, 'Adam Smith and Jurisprudence', 51 *Law Q. Rev.* 326, 330–1 (1935).

[39] But it must not be assumed that there was never any interrelationship between practical men and academic argument at this time. For one example, see Sir George Cornewall Lewis, *The Use and Abuse of Some Political Terms* (Oxford, 1832, revised edn., 1877) in which the author discourses very learnedly about the meaning of 'implied' contract and quasi-contract in connection with Social Contract theory. Lewis had been trained as a barrister and attended Austin's lectures; he later went into Parliament and served as a Member of the Poor Law Board (1839–47) and Chancellor of the Exchequer (1855–8).

public'. A family company may originally have been created by the most individualist of entrepreneurs; even when (perhaps on the death of the founder) it passes into the control of a handful of children or grandchildren, the sense that they are bound together by consent is strong. A majority in a family company will usually be reluctant to overbear the minority on a major matter on which the minority feel strongly. Although on minor matters, everyday routine questions may be decided by majority vote, in practice most questions are likely to be decided by general agreement. If the company was originally created by several parties rather than one, the result is still very similar. Their original partnership will have been based on mutual agreement; a majority would not (or not necessarily) have the power to bind the minority on fundamental matters. Certainly, whatever the strict legal position may be, a partnership is unlikely to prosper if the majority has to coerce the minority on matters of fundamental importance. But when a company 'goes public', all this may change. Shares are now issued to the public at large. The new electorate has, in theory, complete control over the Board, assuming that a majority of the total voting shares are issued to the public. The shareholders can now dismiss the Board and elect a new one. It can change the policy of the company out of all recognition. The agreement of the former family shareholders is no longer required for changes of policy. Changes can be imposed upon them whether they agree or no. The principle of majority rule is ultimately the negation of contractarianism, individualism, and consensualism. Of course, when the family company goes public, the family do not expect all these things to happen at first, if at all. They hope to retain control; they hope the electorate will not want to change the policy of the company in any fundamental matters; their *de facto* position remains strong out of all proportion to their numbers. And so it was in England which 'went public' in 1832. Contrary to the views of the pessimists who thought the Act of 1832 was the first step to turning England into a Republic,[40] the results of the change were slow in manifesting themselves. The consequence was that the *fact* of majority rule slipped quietly into English political life, so quietly, indeed, that it can be argued precisely when it really happened.[41] And few thinkers or writers saw anything wrong with it, except Herbert Spencer who naturally attacked it bitterly. In the absence of agreement to be bound by a majority, he argued, with

[40] Greville recorded in his Diary in 1838 a conversation in which Brougham had prophesied that the (secret) ballot would follow the Reform Act and Parke B. had responded that Britain would, in that case, be a Republic within five years: *The Greville Diary*, ed. P. W. Wilson (London, 1927), ii. 222.

[41] In strictly numerical terms, not even half the adult population was eligible to vote until 1918 when (some) women were first enfranchised.

considerable logic, but little perception of the changing consensus on these matters, a majority has no right to coerce a minority at all.[42]

Once this change had occurred, however, and in an important though not a strictly numerical sense it did occur in 1832, attitudes began slowly to change. Law-making was no longer based on an agreement amongst a small number of people to make some minor adjustment in their relationships. Law-making now could be frankly redistributive. Openly to take the property of some members of the State by taxation, and use it for the benefit of other members of the State, became, for the first time, morally and politically acceptable. Conversely, the idea that taxation was a form of contractual payment, made by the property owner to his Association, in return for the protection of his person and property, began to wane. The difference on this point between John Stuart Mill's *Principles*, and *The Wealth of Nations* is very marked. Except for one or two items (such as the cost of defence), Adam Smith would have liked to place the burden of taxation as closely as possible on those benefited by the various services provided by the State.[43] Mill, on the other hand, totally rejects the contractual idea of taxation.[44] To him, those who gain most from the laws and services of the State are the weak in mind or body; if they had to pay in proportion to the benefits they received, this would be the very reverse of the true idea of distributive justice which redresses the inequalities of nature. The true and sufficient principle is that all are interested in the maintenance of Government, and that each should contribute to its cost according to his means.

But in other respects, the change of power in 1832 merely meant that the new legislation was designed primarily to serve the interests of the new middle class. Since they believed in the free market, much of the legislation was at first designed to create the conditions for the market to operate. Some of this was simply the negative task of clearing away the restrictive legislation which obstructed the growth of the free market— indeed, in this respect there was nothing very new or dramatic about the events after 1832 because this had been going on for sixty or seventy years. But in other respects, the new legislation took on a more positive form, in assisting the conditions needed for the operation of the free market. Modern economists, especially those of the Chicago school who believe that the State should adopt the minimal role laid down (for example) by Milton Friedman, frequently argue that if there is a sufficient demand for something in a free market economy, the market will supply it; entrepreneurs will spring forth, having divined what is wanted, and will supply it in hot competition with each other, at the

---

[42] *The Man Versus the State* (first published 1884, reprinted, Harmondsworth, 1969), pp. 155–61.

[43] *Wealth of Nations*, Book V, Chapter I, Conclusion.

[44] *Principles*, Book V, Chapter II, Sect. 2.

lowest feasible cost. But as a matter of historical fact, this is not what happened in England during the nineteenth century. It was precisely because the market manifestly failed to satisfy so many middle-class demands that they turned to Parliament instead. They found it very much simpler and quicker to use the machinery of Parliament to create the conditions, and supply the essentials of the modern State, rather than to leave their supply to entrepreneurs. They did not, of course, do this in every field, nor even in most fields where ordinary commercial goods and services were concerned. But they did begin to do it in a great many fields where private entrepreneurs had been doing it, but not very effectively (as, for example, with the police), or where the State had traditionally played a role (as with the Post Office),[45] or where externalities led to market failures (as with public health measures), or where consumers were unable to judge their own interest best (as with education or the adulteration of food), or where monopolies were in question (as with the railways and later water, gas, and electricity supplies).

Much of this legislation was lumped together as 'Collectivism' by Dicey, at least in the post-1870 period. But in origins, very little of the nineteenth-century legislation began as collectivist. Once the legislation was passed, and conditions changed, some of the legislation itself changed in character. It changed, sometimes because of the internal momentum of Governmental bureaucracy, sometimes because conditions themselves changed; sometimes because, once Government had embarked on the activity, it was not easy for private entrepreneurs to compete, even if they were permitted to. Gradually, much social legislation which had originally owed its inception to Parliaments devoted to the ideal of the free market changed into truly collectivist legislation. By and large that did not happen until the twentieth century, and remains for Part III of this work.

AN AGE OF PRINCIPLES

Behind much that I have already written about political economy, utilitarianism, and individualism, there lay an idea of sufficient intellectual importance to deserve brief examination of its own—the idea of Principles. The period 1770–1870 seems to have been dominated by the idea of Principles. There were principles of political economy, principles of ethics and morality, principles of jurisprudence, principles of political behaviour, principles of commercial behaviour; there were

[45] See Hemmeon, *History of the British Post Office* (Cambridge, Mass., 1912), esp. at p. 61. Business was severely hampered by the inefficiencies of the postal service, according to the evidence given to the Committee which adopted the Rowland Hill penny postage scheme in 1840.

also Men of Principle; and there was the contrast between Principle and Expediency. Because of the importance of principles in the law, because freedom of contract was itself regarded by many as an important principle, and because fidelity to promises was also a profoundly important principle in Victorian morality, it seems worth devoting a few words to the very concept of Principle.

In part, it seems clear that this concept was one of the products of Natural Law theories. A principle was a generalization which helped to explain the way the world worked. In the physical sciences, the 'laws' of the universe were not now called 'principles', but in the moral or social sciences, the word 'principle' was often interchangeable with the word 'law'. They both involved a generalization about social or human phenomena. But this was clearly not the whole story, for the concept of a principle was also highly prescriptive. Principles were not merely generalizations about how social phenomena operated, but were also important guides about how people should behave. They were, therefore, essential educational tools. It is, perhaps, difficult for us today to appreciate how important many felt the search for proper principles of behaviour to be at this period. Already in the eighteenth century the role of the priest which still prevails in many Catholic communities, as the general guide and adviser on all kinds of moral or other issues, had quite disappeared in England. The village parson did not have the authority that his Catholic colleagues had; the bare word of authority was not enough. Reasons had to be given for advice or recommendations as to a course of behaviour. The old scholastic science, known as Casuistry, which had attempted to think up an appropriate course of action in every conceivable kind of situation, had long since fallen into disrepute in England. In their search for an alternative men fastened upon the idea of principle.

The idea is to be found in a well-developed form in Hume who observed that in ordinary daily life men tend to act, not according to rules, but according to the demands of the particular circumstances.[46] And even if men do sometimes lay down rules for their own conduct, the rules tend not to be inflexible but to allow of many exceptions. This would not be a tolerable way of settling disputes among men in society, however, for too much uncertainty would tend to arise (for example with regard to rights of property) and men are compelled to agree upon more settled and less flexible principles of law and jurisprudence. Even these principles rest on self-interest in the long run, but because of their generality we find cases in which a single act of justice is actually contrary to the public interest. 'When a man of merit, of a beneficent disposition, restores a great fortune to a miser, or a seditious bigot, he has acted justly

[46] *Treatise*, Book III, Part II, Sect. VI.

and laudably, but the public is a real sufferer.'[47] We cannot, however, permit single instances to upset the rules governing men's relationships amongst themselves, for men cannot be trusted to act impartially contrary to their own interests; and there would, therefore, be a tendency for men to seek for exceptions or reasons why they should not comply with the general rules, whenever such compliance would run counter to their immediate interests. If everybody did this, society would dissolve, and men, perceiving this to be an ultimate danger, in fact accept compliance with the rules even contrary to their own immediate desires or interests.

What emerges from this is the importance of generality in principles, and the fact that, if the conduct of the agent is being focused on, he is not an appropriate person to weigh up with any niceness the question whether his case falls within the rules, or whether some exception to them might not be found. Both Hume and Adam Smith at this point agree that though men may fail to perceive that it is in their own interest to comply with a rule, they never fail to see the injustice of someone else omitting to comply with a rule; and this produces a sense of sympathy with the person wronged.

This stress on rule or principle is an important element in eighteenth- and nineteenth-century intellectual ideals. It is plainly related closely to the idea of self-government in the most literal sense. If Englishmen were to be free, and to be allowed to choose for themselves how to behave, without having a despotic police state imposed upon them, then they had to learn how to behave in a social manner. And to do this, it was necessary to learn principles of behaviour of some generality for it was impossible to have guidance on the proper mode of behaviour in every set of circumstances which might arise. Thus we find Paley, for instance, stressing over and over again the importance of general principles of behaviour, principles whose effect must be judged by their general tendency.[48] We find Burke stressing the importance of men following principle in political affairs, and more generally, Burke argued in classic fashion for what he termed 'prejudices' but what might today be termed long-standing custom, or even principles. Even where the reason for the 'prejudice' is not obvious, even where it may appear to be some obsolete anachronism, Burke argued that it might contain latent wisdom, and that we should hesitate long before throwing it aside. To cast it out would leave every man the right to decide on his conduct for himself, which, of course, was precisely what the Revolutionaries were claiming. Burke was among many who feared this result intensely; he did not believe that the mass, the public, the 'swinish multitude' as he referred to them in one

[47] Ibid., Part II, Sect. II.
[48] *Principles of Moral and Political Philosophy*, Book I, Chapter VI.

unfortunate moment, were responsible enough to decide for themselves on the vast number of questions which arose in life. People must learn to behave in an orderly, predictable fashion, and they would only do so if they followed 'prejudices' or principles without too close an inquiry into their applicability in the instant case.[49]

It was not only in political affairs that Burke stressed the need for principles. He—in common with many others—also argued strongly for commercial principles. In his indictment of the East India Company on Fox's Bill to vest their powers in Commissioners, Burke set forth six principles of commercial conduct, some of which may look surprising to the modern reader.[50] First, he said, came the principle of 'buying cheap and selling dear'—the 'great fountain of mercantile dealing'. Second, 'A great deal of strictness in driving bargains for whatever we contract is another of the principles of mercantile policy.' The third was to see that employees or agents made no secret dealings on their own account; the fourth to be 'exact' in one's accounts; the fifth was the necessity of calculating the probable profit to be made before seeking money to invest in business; and the sixth was the need to retain sufficient cash to meet bills drawn upon one.

And if political and commercial principles were important, surely moral principles could not be far behind. Yet in fact, there had been (as we have already seen) a tendency, illustrated best, perhaps, by Paley, to separate moral principles from the teachings of the Christian church. Victorian Christianity had little to say about a man's duty to his fellow men, or his duty to the public; and, according to Mill, many of the principles of private morality most valued in the Victorian period came not from Christianity, but from the Greeks and Romans.[51] Of course some Christians protested against this attempt to minimize the role of the Church in moral matters, this separation of Church and State. Professor F. W. Newman, for example (brother of the Cardinal), argued that the laws of the State were immensely influential on the moral principles of the nation, and that the Church could not therefore stand aside from these matters of State, affecting to treat them as purely concerns of Caesar.[52] But more influential, perhaps, on actual social behaviour, was the moral content in the ideal of the 'gentleman' which became so important in the Victorian era. The gentleman was, above all, a man of principles. He

was expected to treat his fellow creatures of all ranks openly and frankly, even

[49] Reflections on the French Revolution in Burke on Government, Politics, and Society, ed. Hill (Glasgow, 1975), p. 354.
[50] Ibid., pp. 226–7.
[51] On Liberty (Harmondsworth, 1974), pp. 112–13.
[52] 'Moral Influence of Law' (1860) reprinted in Miscellanies, vol. ii (London, 1887).

when it meant sacrificing his interests to do so. A gentleman did not tell a lie, for that was cowardice, he did not cheat, go back on his word, or flinch from the consequences of his actions . . . A man's reputation as a gentleman was looked on as his most valuable possession.[53]

Throughout most of this period moralists were apt to draw a pointed, if not always wholly clear, contrast, between Principle and Expediency, the latter usually being somewhat tendentiously given the adjective, 'mere'. There seem to have been several different senses which this contrast was designed to serve. In one sense, to follow Principle, to act on Principle, to be a Man of Principle, was to act without regard to consequences. The morality of an act was derived from the intrinsic nature of the act itself. An act was right or wrong in itself without regard to anything that might flow from it. The most extreme version of this morality is, of course, to be found in the maxim, *Fiat Justitia Ruat Cælum*. In this morality, an expedient act was one which was morally wrong, but which might seem right because it led (apparently or even really) to more satisfactory consequences. It was against this type of morality that the utilitarians had rebelled. To them, the morality of an act was not some inherent quality, different from its consequences. It was the consequences of an act which determined whether it was right or wrong. But they too contrasted Principle with Expediency. However, to the utilitarians, expediency was not something necessarily wrong—after all, in a sense, 'expedient' is almost a synonym for 'right'—but an expedient act was an 'easy way out', a short-run solution that was likely to store up trouble for the future, the solution that swept the problem temporarily out of sight, but did not really solve it.

A good illustration of the point is the contrast between the expediency of exercising mercy on someone guilty of an apparently trivial, but potentially serious offence, and, on the other hand, the principle of sternly (but wisely) insisting upon the full penalty for the act. Adam Smith, for example, discussed this problem in connection with the case of a sentry who falls asleep at his post in time of war, and who thereby becomes liable to be sentenced to death.[54] The punishment, he says, seems excessively severe, and it is hard to reconcile one's heart to it. But, he insists, 'a man of humanity' (or, he might say, a man of principle) 'must recollect himself, must make an effort, and exert his whole firmness and resolution'[55] in order that the long-term interests of the many be preserved. Although Smith does not specifically discuss this case in terms of principles, it is clear that it is precisely this point that he has in mind. The adherence to principles, for their long-term benefit to the many, is

[53] Sir Arthur Bryant, *The Age of Elegance*, p. 290.
[54] In *The Theory of Moral Sentiments*, ed. Raphael and Macfie, p. 90.
[55] Ibid.

what he is insisting upon, as opposed to the expediency of giving way to the compassion of the moment for one individual.

But the contrast between principle and expediency was also used in yet another sense. For example there was much debate in the nineteenth century about the policy of non-interference with freedom of contract: was that a matter of principle or of mere expediency? In this debate the result of holding non-interference to be a matter of principle seems generally to have meant that the consequences were to be ignored in deciding whether to interfere in any particular case. But those (including many of the political economists and the utilitarians) who insisted that it was a matter of mere expediency did not thereby mean that they preferred a short-run to a long-run perspective. In this sort of context they appear to have meant that non-interference could not be treated as an absolute rule, and that each case should be examined on its merits.

In the nineteenth century many people, especially those who were hostile to its basic premises, were inclined to treat utilitarianism as a philosophy which set up 'mere expediency' as the criterion of right and wrong. To them there were more fundamental principles which were incompatible with 'mere expediency'—especially, for example, the principles of Justice. In his *Utilitarianism*, John Stuart Mill took great trouble to reconcile the common notion of Justice as resting on fundamental long-term principles, with the basic philosophy of utilitarianism.[56] The gist of his solution was that principles of justice are themselves principles of long-term expediency, or principles depending on the long-run utility of the actions in question. There is no real difference between principles of justice and other principles of utility or expediency, although the former may be a sub-class of the latter. Not everything which is right or expedient is something to which the concept of justice would be applied, but everything which is a matter of justice is also a part of the general utility. If principles of justice seem stronger, and arouse greater emotional strength than do cases of mere expediency, or mere utility, it is only because principles of justice are of more fundamental importance to the security of human beings.

If Mill did not convince the majority of his contemporaries, he was, nevertheless, representing a viewpoint commonly held at least by those to whom all morality could not be based on Divine origins. Moreover, this viewpoint would almost certainly have been held by many lawyers of the mid-nineteenth century, for although they were fond enough of the old maxim, *Fiat Justitia Ruat Cælum*, they did not generally act as though they believed in it too seriously. Legal arguments in cases before the Courts continued as they had always done, to be based partly at least on ideas of general convenience and utility; and judges, used to thinking

[56] *Utilitarianism*, Chapter V.

out the consequences of their own decisions, were not inclined to judge of the morality or legality of actions without regard to their consequences. Lawyers liked the concept of Principle as much as any other class, but to most of them a legal principle was itself something to be derived from its expediency or utility. Over twenty years before Mill's *Utilitarianism* appeared Baron Alderson of the Exchequer Court wrote to the Home Secretary, Sir James Graham, criticizing Peel for seeking the immediately rather than the ultimately expedient. 'Principle', he wrote, 'not expediency must ultimately prevail and govern the people of this kingdom ... [but] That which is *ultimately* expedient is only another word for an adherence to fixed and good principles.'[57]

With political, commercial, economic, and moral principles so much in the air, it is not surprising that law itself was being similarly treated. We have seen in an earlier chapter how Mansfield had begun to insist that the law was based on principles, and not merely on precedent. Among Mansfield's contemporaries was Sir William Jones, the celebrated orientalist, who wrote a treatise on the *Law of Bailments* in 1781. To him, also, law had to be based on principles if it was to have any pretensions to being a 'science':

If law be a science, and really deserve so sublime a name, it must be founded on principle, and claim an exalted rank in the empire of reason; but if it be merely an unconnected series of decrees and ordinances, its use may remain, though its dignity be lessened, and he will become the greatest lawyer who has the strongest habitual or artificial memory.[58]

A related idea was that of minimizing discretion in legal decisions. The law was to become more certain, more predictable, more intelligible. In 1818 Lord Eldon expressed his desire to make Equity 'almost' as settled and uniform as the common law.[59] When Pothier's *Law of Obligations* appeared in English translation in 1806 it was avidly seized upon by English lawyers and judges, partly because they lacked anything comparable of their own, but partly also because, in this age of principles, lawyers were beginning to think in terms of general principles of jurisprudence. They knew, of course, that on this or that point, the laws of different countries would differ, but they began to expect that in their fundamental principles the laws of all countries—or at least all 'civilized', or all Christian, countries—would be similar. Renewed study of Roman

[57] J. T. Ward, *Sir James Graham*, p. 167.
[58] At pp. 123-4. Jones (1746-94), best remembered today as an Oriental scholar, practised at the Bar in England for some years before taking up an Indian judgeship. He was a great believer in principles, and once contemplated writing a work on the whole body of English law, which would 'reduce all the intricate cases that have occurred, to their first principles or maxims'. See *The Letters of Sir William Jones*, ed. Garland Cannon (Oxford, 1970), i. 130.
[59] *Gee* v. *Pritchard* (1818) 2 Swanst. 402, 414, 36 E.R. 670, 674.

law, which also dated from the last quarter of the eighteenth century (inspired to some extent by the appearance of Gibbon's great *History*) had also made English lawyers familiar once again with the concept of the *ius gentium*—those laws which the Romans had assumed to be common to the whole civilized world. And the legacy of the Natural Lawyers was still strong in the early nineteenth century.

But in addition to these influences, there may well have been another factor of some importance. With the growth of population, and the huge increase in commerce and industry, there must have come a great increase in the number of situations in which people other than lawyers had some contact with the law. The new bureaucrats, for a start, found themselves entangled with the law increasingly from the 1830s onwards. Commercial men must also have come more frequently into contact with the law when they sought to enforce their rights, or when others proceeded against them. The old Justices of the Peace, of course, had long been used to deciding cases in very informal procedures but as cities grew and communications improved, they no longer operated in quite the isolation they had in the eighteenth century, and this may have made them more aware of the need to take seriously their duties as lawyers. All this occurred at a time when the number of common law judges remained stationary (they were only increased after 1830) and when there was still virtually no forum for civil disputes outside the superior courts: not until 1846 were the County Courts set up. There had, too, been a great change in the length of contested cases. Where Buller, Kenyon or Ellenborough could dispose of twenty or twenty-five cases in a day, the average in 1840 had dropped to around six.[60] The result of all these developments must have been to strengthen the desire to make the laws more intelligible; and when to this we add the professional pride of men like Brougham who wanted to see the law earn its due place among the sciences, the demand for principle in the law is readily intelligible.

The result was of profound importance for the intellectual tradition of the common law. From the 1830s or thereabouts until far into the twentieth century, lawyers increasingly saw their subject as one based on principles. Like the other moral sciences, law began to seem like a set of principles, deduced from basic ideas of natural law; a vast set of self-consistent rules, each deriving some authority from a principle. The power of the Judges to make and adapt the law began to diminish partly, at least, because they themselves, or at least some of them, became convinced that law was largely a matter of deductive logic.

The principle that promises should be observed was one which fell very naturally into place in this world. As we have seen, it is by no means

---

[60] P. C. Scarlett, *A Memoir of James, First Lord Abinger* (London, 1877), p. 62.

clear that in the sixteenth and seventeenth centuries common lawyers would have regarded the obligation to perform a promise as a basic principle of Natural Law; indeed, there are many signs that they thought a man was not bound to perform a promise to do something if he was not already, in some sense, bound to do it, if there was no reason or cause why he should do it.[61] But Grotius and Pufendorf had rediscovered the principle that promises were binding as a matter of natural reason, and in the Age of Enlightenment, everybody agreed that the obligation to perform a promise was a perfectly natural and necessary principle of human intercourse. Hume explained it on grounds of mutual self-interest; Paley, on the ground that the promisor is urged on to perform by fear of punishment in the afterlife;[62] Bentham, on the ground that it complies with the principle of utility; Adam Smith, both on grounds of self-interest and also on the ground that men have a tendency to rely upon promises which would be defeated by their non-fulfilment. Even the anti-utilitarians (who judged the morality of an act without regard to consequences) never doubted that fidelity to promises was an intrinsically binding principle of justice. But if many writers and moralists gave different explanations for the enforcement of promises, there was, at this time, very little opposition[63] to the importance of the principle that promises should be performed, and (what was thought of as following almost inexorably) that the performance of promises should therefore be enforced by law. It was an important principle of social life amongst 'gentlemen'; it was an important commercial principle, for businessmen had to rely on the promises of others; it was an important principle of social behaviour and discipline for the public, who had to learn that once arrangements had been made, they must be observed; it was an important principle of justice too, for justice required that every man be given his due, and what was more obviously due than what had been promised? It is not surprising that, during the period 1770–1870, the principle of the due observance of promises became the pivotal key around which the modern law of contract was built.

At this point I wish to confine my remarks to a few general propositions about the applicability of the concept of a principle to the case of promising. The first is that there was, as we have seen, a strong movement at this time, for 'deducing' principles from simple premises, for rejecting the empirical method and proceeding by broad *a priori* generalizations. Both the classical economists and the utilitarians had suffered somewhat

---

[61] *Supra*, p. 140.

[62] Though he also added a more mundane explanation in Book III, Part I, Chapter V.

[63] William Godwin, in his *Enquiry Concerning Political Justice*, is virtually the only writer of the times to challenge the conventional belief in the importance of promising; perhaps there was some vague inkling in his mind that the enforcement of promises was likely to be in the interests of the better educated and better off classes.

from this tendency, perhaps a rather un-English tendency, for the English generally pride themselves on their pragmatic rather than logical approach to problems.[64] And the principle that promises should be observed, though perhaps based more on empirical observation (of the results of unperformed promises) than many other principles of the period, was in part at least supportable by reference to the *a priori* assumptions of the economists and the utilitarians. For if everyone had to be presumed to know his own interest best, if the butcher, the brewer, and the baker supplied their customers, not from benevolence, but from self-interest, did it not also follow that if they *promised* to supply their customers, the promises must be presumed to have been made in their best interests? And if that were so, why then, of course, it must be sound policy to enforce all promises, for the promise was obviously in the interests of both parties, and not just one.

The second point to be made, and this may to some extent follow from the first, is that the principle of the due observance of promises fitted in very well with the ethic of self-discipline and self-reliance. To perform a promise was usually like doing labour—to the classical economists and the utilitarians this was a painful exertion, a 'dis-utility'—but in the long run, good would come of it to the promisor. If the promisor had not yet received any benefit from his promise—if some counter-performance was due afterwards—the reward for performing the promise would be direct and immediate. But even if the promisor had already received his due, he would still gain in the long run from performing his own promise. His credit would be maintained, he would be trustworthy in future; he would find others willing to deal with him, to trust his word. This belief in the importance of long-run consequences as opposed to immediate or short-term consequences, was one of the most pervasive ideas throughout our period of 1770–1870. In morality, in economics, in politics, in law, it was the same. Indeed, for some it was part of the concept of a principle that it should aim at long-run consequences rather than short-term ones. And for those who did not want to look to consequences at all, the result was not very different. Fidelity to promises was a binding moral principle which the true man of principle observed with scrupulous exactness.

The stress on the long-run consequences of behaviour (or of disregarding consequences altogether) was closely linked with another characteristic of principles, namely the tendency of such principles to become absolute and to admit of no exceptions. If principles are seen primarily as educational tools, as methods of inculcating self-discipline, it is clear that they must not admit of being too readily evaded by exceptions. This explains why the utilitarianism of Paley, Bentham, and Mill was—in the modern jargon—almost certainly of the 'rule-utilitarian'

[64] See J. Plamenatz, *The English Utilitarians* (Oxford, 1966), pp. 147–8.

variety. They believed in principles of behaviour which, taken over all, would produce the greatest happiness; but they did not believe that each individual act should be weighed in the balance (at least by the common herd) to decide whether it would promote the greatest happiness or not. In modern times, philosophers have argued with great subtlety and sophistication over the distinction between 'act-utilitarianism' and 'rule-utilitarianism',[65] though there have also been arguments that the latter tends to collapse into the former. This has produced a prolonged debate on the question whether utilitarianism can provide any sort of an explanation of why there should be any obligation to perform a promise. If the promised act is the one which is likely, all things considered, to produce the greatest happiness in the world, then it ought to be performed, on a utilitarian view of morality, even though it was not previously promised. And if it was previously promised, the promise itself adds nothing to the obligation to perform the act, which still derives from the fact that it will produce the greatest happiness. Conversely, if the performance of a promise will not produce the greatest happiness but some other act will, then the promise ought to be broken.[66]

I do not have space, in this historical volume, to discuss these issues fully (though I hope to do so in a later volume). But it is difficult to understand how anybody could ever have interpreted the early utilitarians as being supporters of anything other than rules, or principles, the general tendency of which is to create the greatest happiness. I have already said enough of Hume's opinions to show that he must be classed as a rule-utilitarian. Bentham himself constantly used the language of 'tendency'—what result does this class of act tend to produce?[67] So also did Paley who insisted both on the importance of the tendencies of the kind of act in question, and also on the long-run tendencies as opposed to the immediate result. For instance, he says, speaking of sexual licence, that 'malignity and moral quality of each crime is not to be estimated by the particular effect of one offence, or of one person's offending, but by the general tendency and consequence of crimes of the same nature'.[68] Similarly, John Austin insists on the absoluteness of moral principles. Even if in the tenth or hundredth case, violation of the rule would do

---

[65] This debate was sparked off by R. Harrod's article, 'Utilitarianism Revised', 45 *Mind* 137 (1936). It seems to have been generally assumed before this article that the early utilitarians were 'act-utilitarians' who believed that the utility of each individual human action had to be judged in light of its consequences.

[66] Godwin, *Enquiry Concerning Political Justice*, did very largely take this position. He assumed that most promises concerned duties which ought to be performed anyhow (reflecting a state of the law then becoming obsolete, *supra*, p. 134), and if there was no such duty, then the promise ought not to be binding. His position is close to that of an extreme act-utilitarian who ignores the effect of the promise itself, e.g., in creating an expectation.

[67] See Mary Warnock, Introduction to Mill's *Utilitarianism*, Fontana edn., p. 22.

[68] *Principles of Moral and Political Philosophy*, Book II, Chapter II.

more harm than good, it must not be violated. For this would weaken the force of the general rule. 'In the hurry and tumult of action it is hard to distinguish justly. To grasp at present enjoyment, and to turn from present uneasiness, is the habitual inclination of us all. And thus, through the weakness of our judgments and the more dangerous infirmity of our wills, we should frequently stretch the exception to cases embraced by the rule.'[69] Indeed, Austin spelt out with stark clarity the implications of utilitarian ethics.[70] The 'multitude', he admitted, would never be able to study the tendencies of actions in order to judge their effect. For them, the only precept was to follow the principles of utility without attempting to judge the consequences of an act. It was for the moral élite to propound the principles themselves through study of the tendencies of actions.[71]

There has been more controversy over John Stuart Mill's position, and no doubt there are ambiguities in the texts,[72] but if the problem had been put to Mill as it is put by modern philosophers, it is hard to believe he would not have sided with the rule-utilitarians. Even Herbert Spencer, who adhered to his own idiosyncratic form of utilitarianism, did not believe that the morality of each single action should be judged by its expediency. And interestingly for present purposes, he selects the illustration of contracts to make the point:

The doctrine of expediency [which is Spencer's name for utilitarianism] is not a doctrine implying that each particular act is to be determined by the particular consequences that may be expected to flow from it; but that the general consequences of entire classes of acts having been ascertained by induction from experience, rules shall be framed for the regulation of such classes of acts, and each rule shall be uniformly applied to every act coming under it. Our whole administration of justice proceeds on this principle of invariably enforcing an ordained course, regardless of special results. Were immediate consequences to be considered, the verdict gained by the rich creditor against the poor debtor would generally be reversed, for the starvation of the last is a much greater evil than the inconvenience of the first . . . Now the binding nature of agreements is one of the commonest and most important principles of civil law. A large part of the causes daily heard in our courts, involve the question, whether in virtue of some expressed or understood contract, some of those concerned are, or are not, bound to certain contracts or certain payments. And when it has been decided what the contract implies, the matter is settled. The contract itself is held sacred.[73]

[69] *Province of Jurisprudence Determined* (London, 1861), p. 35.

[70] Ibid., Lecture III.

[71] See R. J. Halliday 'Some Recent Interpretations of John Stuart Mill', 43 *Philosophy* 1 (1968).

[72] See J. Urmson, 'The Interpretation of the Moral Philosophy of J. S. Mill', 3 *Phil. Quarterly* 33 (1953). Compare J. D. Mabbott, 'Interpretations of Mill's Utilitarianism', 6 *Phil. Quarterly* 115 (1956); Mandelbaum, 'Two Moot Issues in Mill's *Utilitarianism*', in *Mill: A Collection of Critical Essays*, ed. J. B. Schneewind (London, Melbourne, 1968), p. 206.

[73] 'Railway Morals and Railway Policy' (1854), reprinted in *Essays*, vol. iii (Edinburgh, 1891), pp. 95–6.

It has been argued that the rule-utilitarian position is untenable in strict logic. It has been urged, for example, that if in a particular instance, following a rule does not produce the best result, then the rule ought to be modified to provide an exception to cover that particular type of situation; for if the situation recurred exactly, then it would once again be clear that following the rule would not produce the best results. Consequently, in the last resort, rule-utilitarianism would simply lead to more and more exceptions, sub-rules, and individualization of rules, until it totally collapsed into act-utilitarianism.[74] Whatever the logic of this may be, it must be clear in this historical study, that this argument would have been totally rejected by the early nineteenth-century utilitarians. For the argument overlooks the *educational* purpose behind their rules and principles.[75] People can be taught to behave only by giving them rules of some generality. The more complex the rules become, the greater the number of exceptions and sub-rules, the less valuable the rules are for this purpose. If the only object of a rule is to enable a Judge to decide *after the event* whether the right act was done or not, rules would be largely unnecessary and could be replaced by giving a discretion to the Judge to decide what he thinks fair in all the circumstances. Modern law tends increasingly in that direction, as we shall see. But in the period of which I am writing, the function of law was not seen as merely that of deciding, after some event, whether a person had acted wisely or morally. The function of law, as the function of morality, and of social or commercial principles, was to give people guidance on their behaviour in advance of the necessity for action.

It is the same historical explanation which must be pleaded against the modern philosopher who argues that the rule-utilitarian is encouraging rule-worship.[76] On this view rule-utilitarianism is a hypocritical and pharasaical doctrine. It involves the adoption of principles and rules which must be blindly observed by all without pausing to inquire into the reason for the rule, or whether, in the case in question, the rule ought not to be modified or departed from. It means that the person who adopts the rule regards himself as wise enough to frame general principles of behaviour, but does not trust the public, or even himself, to have the sense to know when to depart from the principle. The rule-utilitarian thus does not really believe that people can be trusted to act in such a manner as to produce the greatest happiness, and he is compelled, in effect to say: 'I don't want to preach utilitarianism to the masses because

[74] See Wasserstrom, *The Judicial Decision* (Stanford, London, 1961); D. Lyons, *Forms and Limits of Utilitarianism* (Oxford, 1965).

[75] This point is made, in the modern rather than the historical context, by R. M. Hare, 'Principles', 73 *Proc. Arist. Soc. Supplement*, 1 (N.S.) (1972-3).

[76] George C. Kerner, 'The Immorality of Utilitarianism and the Escapism of Rule-Utilitarianism', 21 *Phil. Quarterly* 36 (1971).

they may lack the ability to calculate the utility of particular actions and even misuse my doctrine as an excuse and rationalization for their selfish behaviour. As a rule-utilitarian bent on realizing my total goal, I will try to induce rule-worship in people. And, as a utilitarian, I may not even trust myself. I too may be stupid, biased and often lack the necessary time to take all the precautions . . .'[77]

One can only reiterate, in response to this argument, that that does seem to be what the early utilitarians thought; and if we today still had to face the same problem of teaching social discipline to millions of rough, tough, largely uneducated, urbanized men and women we might well feel the same. It must be conceded, of course, that such rigid adherence to principle assumes that people cannot be trusted to understand the difference between the case where the principle should operate, and the circumstances in which it should be departed from. For there is no harm in weakening a principle if the only result is that the principle comes to be departed from where it should be departed from. But again, nineteenth-century moralists and lawyers would have had no doubt of the dangers of this course. They thought that the weakening of a principle by refusing to apply it even where there was a good case for not applying it, would inevitably tend to lessen its force even in those cases where it should be applied. Even today it is hard to believe that they were wrong. Indeed, the century and a half which has elapsed since these questions were being disputed seems to prove that they were right. This period has witnessed a great decline in the strength of many principles of morality or law, such as the principle that promises must be kept. And this decline appears plainly to have originated with the tendency to allow exceptions to the principle in genuinely mitigating circumstances, but to have spread from such cases to many others where there are less or no mitigating circumstances.

We can, perhaps, leave the last word on this point with Paley. In discussing the binding force or promises given under some misapprehension, Paley concedes that the problem is attended with some difficulty, 'for to allow every mistake, or change of circumstances to dissolve the obligation of a promise, would be to allow a latitude, which might evacuate the force of almost all promises: and on the other had, to gird the obligation so tight, as to make no allowances for manifest and fundamental errors would, in many instances be productive of great hardship and absurdity.'[78] Paley was not himself a lawyer, but in this passage he put his finger on a fundamental dilemma of the law: how absolute is the principle that promises must be performed?

[77] Ibid., pp. 36–7.
[78] *Principles of Moral and Political Philosophy*, Book II, Part I, Chapter V.

13

THE LEGAL BACKGROUND, 1770–1870

LAWYERS AND THE COURTS

THE century between 1770 and 1870 saw profound changes in the law, in the organization of the Courts, and in the attitudes and values of the legal profession. In broad terms it cannot be doubted that these changes were the result of the economic and social revolutions which took place during this time, and of the intellectual revolution, no less profound, which owed so much to the political economists and to Benthamite utilitarianism. It is not part of my task to trace in any detail the institutional and statutory changes which, especially after 1832, gradually reformed the character of the Courts and paved the way for the Judicature Acts in 1873–5. This story is well known and is fully told in many standard works to which reference can be made.[1] My purposes require a somewhat closer look at a number of themes in this era of change; in particular, I am concerned with the legal profession and the ideas and attitudes influencing the judiciary, and secondly, with the general change in the relationship between Parliament and the Courts. I shall then examine some of the general characteristics of the law during this period which proved of particular significance in connection with freedom of contract.

It is, in a broad sort of way, possible to divide the period 1770–1870 into three phases, corresponding roughly with changes in the political situation. The first phase, which was largely a continuation of the traditional eighteenth-century period, lasted until around 1793 when the Revolutionary wars began, and when a period of intense conservatism set in generally in England. The second period runs from around 1793 to 1830 when the Whigs finally returned to power, and the era of great reforms began. The third period runs then from 1830 to 1870 and is the period during which the law, and much else in England, was undergoing the fundamental changes described broadly in earlier chapters. Nevertheless, this division into three periods needs to be treated with great caution. In the first place, the very concepts of 'conservative' or 'radical' changed and changed again during this century, so that one finds the most conservative of politicians or judges sometimes adopting attitudes that would appear to be radical to the lawyer of today. And secondly, it

---

[1] See, e.g., Holdsworth, *H.E.L.*, vol. i.

has to be remembered that judges are human beings like all other human beings. They differed greatly in age and in outlook. Because judges tend to be appointed in middle age, and perhaps also because once barristers get caught up in the hurly-burly of practice they have little time for other activities, it often happens (as Dicey suggested)[2] that judges tend to reflect opinions of an earlier time. But one must not carry this too far. At any given time the gap in age between the oldest and the youngest judges on the Bench may be twenty or thirty years. Furthermore, judges are not monolithic in their opinions any more than any other group, though it may be that they tend to be somewhat more homogeneous than other groups as a result of their early training, and the pressures to conformity in the English legal profession. On the other hand it should also be appreciated that until the present century, most judges received a broad liberal education before embarking on legal practice. Many of them would certainly have been familiar with the works of Hobbes, Locke, Paley, and Adam Smith, as well as those of Grotius, Rousseau and Pothier.[3]

1770–1793

I need say little here about the judges of the first period 1770–1793. Throughout most of this period the legal system was still dominated by Lord Mansfield who only retired in 1788 though he had not then sat for some years. The work of the Courts during this period, and the relationship between Parliament and the Courts, continued to be very much as it had been throughout the eighteenth century. The land law still dominated the ideas of most lawyers although commercial cases were beginning to come before the Courts in increasing numbers. Contract law, though gaining in importance, only acquired its first textbook with Powell's *Essay* in 1790, and that was still devoted principally to cases involving land transactions and marriage settlements. We have seen already something of the work of Mansfield and his influence as a reformer, albeit a Tory reformer, in the work of the common law during his tenure of office. This willingness to experiment with modest reform in the Courts was not unmatched by minor political and institutional reforms which took place in the years immediately before the outbreak of the Revolutionary wars. On the other hand, the problems of the Court of Chancery were already beginning to show up, and these problems stemmed at first from the sheer lack of adequate judicial personnel. All through the eighteenth century there were only two judges in the

---

[2] A. V. Dicey, *Law and Public Opinion in the Nineteenth Century*, 2nd edn., p. 369.
[3] To cite one example for whom evidence survives, Abinger C.B. was in his youth familiar with the works of Rousseau, Locke, Paley, Montesquieu, and Grotius. P. C. Scarlett, *A Memoir of James, First Lord Abinger*, p. 37, 44, 53.

Chancery Court—the Lord Chancellor himself and the Master of the Rolls—and neither of these was a full-time judicial office. The Lord Chancellor was, of course, an active politician, although his political duties then were much lighter than they later became; and even the Master of the Rolls was, at this time, permitted to, and often did, retain a seat in the House of Commons.

Of course, the whole machinery of the law and the judicial system was beginning to creak even when Blackstone was delivering his encomiums in 1765. The encrustations of centuries were evident especially in the documentary side of the law. Conveyancing and pleading were excessively technical and full of fictions. These may not have been so troublesome in practice as they appear to a more rational age looking back from today's vantage point; and even the extra expense that they added to legal procedures probably did not seem a major problem when so many clients of the legal profession were drawn from the landed aristocracy or gentry. But the lack of an adequate system of minor Courts was a growing and serious problem, as population expanded and commercial men began to demand more efficient ways of collecting their debts. Despite these warning shadows, the general opinion on the state of English law and the Courts was highly favourable. Blackstone was voicing the opinions of the common man when he treated the law as a virtually perfect instrument. Indeed, this 'veneration, superstitious to the verge of idolatry'[4] lasted well into the nineteenth century when there was very little ground for it. John Stuart Mill tells us in his *Autobiography* that before the 1820s when his father and Bentham had been pounding away at the law's idiocies for many years, the general opinion was still that English law was a model of excellence.[5] And, indeed, by the standards of the time, this may well have been true. English law, with all its imperfections, was probably still the best system of law in the world in the early nineteenth century.[6]

1793–1830

The period which ran from around 1793 till 1830 was, however, a disastrous period for the law and legal institutions in England. At the very time when population was increasing with explosive force, and when the Industrial Revolution was (despite the Revolutionary wars) gathering ever-increasing momentum, the governing classes in England were swept by the most intense sentiments of Conservatism. In the law,

[4] J. Forrest Dillon, 'Bentham's Influence in the Reforms of the Nineteenth Century', in *Select Essays in Anglo-American Legal History* (Cambridge, 1907–9, hereafter cited as *Select Essays*), i. 494.

[5] Oxford, 1971, p. 55.

[6] J. H. Beale, 'The Development of Jurisprudence during the Nineteenth Century', in *Select Essays*, i. 558.

this period was dominated by Lord Eldon who was Lord Chancellor for some twenty-five years, by Lord Kenyon, who was Chief Justice of the King's Bench from 1788 until 1802, and then by Lord Ellenborough who succeeded Kenyon and remained Chief Justice till 1818. It is well known that these three men opposed practically all legal reform for nearly thirty years.

Eldon's conservatism is notorious and was so even in his own lifetime. Politically, he was an influential figure who dominated the House of Lords for many years at the beginning of the nineteenth century. On legal questions it was difficult to persuade the Lords to vote against him, and long after he retired Greville recorded in his Diary that 'he had offered a determined and uniform opposition to every measure of a Liberal description . . . [and] was certainly a contemptible statesman', though he 'was still venerated by the dregs of that party to whom consistent bigotry and intolerance are dear'.[7] On commercial matters Eldon was so old-fashioned that he once had to be reminded by Heath J. that a jobber or dealer in the funds performed a useful public function and was not 'always to be considered as a culpable person'.[8]

Lord Kenyon had been a Member of Parliament from 1780, Attorney-General from 1782–3, and Master of the Rolls from 1784 before he was appointed to succeed Mansfield as Chief Justice of the King's Bench. Less politically influential than Eldon, he was nevertheless a very conservative figure in the law compared with his great predecessor. Many of Mansfield's decisions in the field of land law were reversed during Kenyon's period of office, and many other possible developments (such, for example, as the recognition of assignments of debts) were stifled. Nevertheless, there were aspects of eighteenth-century conservatism which may appear to be of a radical and reforming character even today. There was, for example, the old tradition of benevolent paternalism, particularly evident in Equity but also known in the common law throughout the eighteenth century. At the time when Kenyon was sitting, this paternalism was already going out of fashion among the new generation who were growing up under the influence of Adam Smith. To them, the modern and fashionable notions were those of self-reliance, freedom of contract, and each man for himself. But Kenyon was totally out of sympathy with these new ideas. As late as 1792 we find him echoing one of Mansfield's less characteristic but more advanced notions which ultimately withered on the vine—namely the idea of a general duty of good faith in contract.[9]

[7] *The Greville Diary*, 23 Jan. 1838, i. 182. In 1845 (ibid., p. 183) Greville noted that Parke and Rolfe BB. rated Eldon as a lawyer 'astonishingly low'.

[8] *Morris v. Langdale* (1800) 2 B. & P. 284, 288, 126 E.R. 1284, 1286.

[9] *Mellish v. Motteaux* (1792) Peake, 115, 117, 170 E.R. 113, 113.

But more interesting were the attitudes of Kenyon and Eldon to restrictive agreements and monopolies. Both had been brought up in the old tradition of extreme hostility to all kinds of restrictive agreements and monopolies, and both persisted in these attitudes even though they may well have involved certain inconsistencies. Lord Campbell (though he has a reputation as an execrable biographer) was almost certainly accurate when he wrote that Eldon had a horror of forestalling and regrating, though it is not clear on what authority Campbell added that Eldon 'had heard his grandmother at Newcastle and afterwards his tutor at Oxford' say that these practices 'cruelly enhanced' the price of provisions for the poor.[10] Certainly, there are a number of judicial decisions in which these attitudes were revealed all too clearly. For example, in *Cousins* v. *Smith*,[11] in 1807, a group of traders had formed a sort of embryo trade association called The Fruit Club which attempted to get control over the English import trade in fruit by refusing to deal with importers unless they were offered the whole of the importer's consignment. Eldon held that this was an illegal association, even though it might not technically amount to forestalling, regrating, or monopolizing the trade. In commenting on this case, Campbell, writing in 1847, ridiculed the decision, saying that the purchaser was deprived of his right to sue 'because the partnership he dealt with was called The Fruit Club, instead of "Smith, Tomkins & Co." ' It will be seen that Eldon's attitude is much nearer that which would be generally adopted today than Campbell's. As we shall see later, by the middle of the nineteenth century the common lawyers had generally interpreted the teachings of political economy to mean that freedom of contract should be protected even where this involved some deprivation of freedom to trade; Adam Smith's warnings against monopolies and restrictive practices were forgotten, and only the arguments in favour of freedom of contract were apparently taken seriously.

Equally illustrative of the same theme, though more difficult to interpret from an economic viewpoint, are two famous cases which came before the King's Bench in 1800, at a time of acute shortage and high prices of basic provisions, including bread and ale. In these two cases the King's bench, under Kenyon, upheld prosecutions for regrating and engrossing at common law. The statutory offences had been abolished in 1772, and Adam Smith, in *The Wealth of Nations* had approved of their abolition. Even the forestaller, he argued, does not really harm the public interest, for if he buys up the provisions, anticipating a shortage, and a shortage does result, the forestaller will then gradually release his supplies onto the market while the shortage lasts. If he had not bought up

[10] Campbell, *Lives of the Lord Chancellors* (London, 1847), vii. 653–4.
[11] (1807) 13 Ves. 542, 33 E.R. 397.

the supplies they would have been consumed more rapidly as people would not have realized that a shortage was coming later.[12] More generally, Smith had compared the public fears of forestalling, regrating, and engrossing with 'the popular terrors and suspicions of witchcraft'.[13] These laws, he argued, prevented a natural division of labour from arising, for they compelled the farmer to act also as merchant, selling his supplies direct to the public, whereas it was more efficient to allow middlemen to act as merchants if they in fact found it profitable to do so. It will, of course, be remembered that Smith was most emphatically not arguing for *carte blanche* in favour of monopolists and restrictive agreements (which he would have called monopolies too). It is, therefore, necessary to examine the facts of a case with some precision before one can be sure that Adam Smith himself would have approved of what was being done. In fact, when these cases came before the Courts, this was not done at all. Adam Smith was invoked in defence of total freedom of contract, and these arguments were rejected in favour of the traditional old laws.

In *R. v. Rusby*[14] the defendant was indicted for regrating, that is for buying and immediately reselling 30 quarters of oats at the same corn market; he bought for 41s. and resold for 43s. a quarter. The Court was pressed with Adam Smith's ideas, but Kenyon resisted them, and his language is worth quoting if only because it so clearly illustrates the benevolent paternalism of eighteenth-century judges:

Though in a state of society some must have greater luxuries and comforts than others, yet all should have the necessaries of life; and if the poor cannot exist, in vain may the rich look for happiness or prosperity. The Legislature is never so well employed as when they look to the interests of those who are at a distance from them in the ranks of society. It is their duty to do so; religion calls for it; humanity calls for it; and if there are hearts who are not awake to either of those feelings, their own interests would dictate it. The law has not been disputed, for though in an evil hour all the statutes which had been existing above a century were at one blow repealed, yet thank God, the common laws were not destroyed . . . Speculation has said that the fear of such an offence is ridiculous, and a very learned man, a good writer, has said you might as well fear witchcraft. I wish Dr. Adam Smith had lived to hear the evidence today, and then he would have seen whether such an offence exists, and whether it is to be dreaded. If he had been told that cattle and corn were to be brought to market and then bought by a man whose purse happened to be longer than his neighbours, so that the poor man who walks the street, and earns his daily bread by his daily labour could get none but through his hands, and at the price he chose to demand; that it had been raised 3d., 6d., 9d., 1s., 2s. and more a quarter on the same day; would he have said that there was no danger from such an offence?[15]

[12] Book IV, Chapter 5.   [13] Ibid.
[14] Peake Add. Cas. 189, 170 E.R. 241.   [15] Peake Add. Cas. at 192-3, 170 E.R. at 242.

The answer to this question is almost certainly, Yes, for Adam Smith would surely have said that if the corn was insufficient to supply the poor's needs in full, it were still better that the price should rise so that consumers would cut their consumption and importers be stimulated to bring in the necessary supplies. But the second case is much less clear for it appears that the defendant in this case may have been guilty of attempting to influence the market by spreading false rumours. This was the case of *R. v. Waddington*[16] which was evidently something of a *cause célèbre* at the time. The defendant, who was a prosperous merchant of some standing, was indicted for engrossing hops. It appears that he had been buying up enormous quantities of hops and had travelled around the hop-growers trying to discourage them from selling to the brewers by spreading rumours of impending price rises. It seems probable that the prosecution was brought by the brewers, who by 1800 were a powerful and well-organized group used to combining in their trade interests.[17] No fewer than twelve counsel were engaged in the case, eight for the prosecution and four for the defence. The defence was a major challenge to the older common law traditions, undertaken in the name of Adam Smith and political economy. The Court was pressed with the case for freedom of trade, and counsel argued that the defendant had done no more than businessmen did every day of the week. Lord Kenyon once again rejected the argument, saying, on this occasion that he had endeavoured to inform himself on these questions by reading Adam Smith's work, 'and various other publications upon the same subject, though with different views of it'.[18] Once again, Kenyon invoked the need to protect the poor's right to buy their basic necessities (and he plainly took ale to be one of these) and the importance of preventing the rich from speculating with such basic provisions. Waddington was convicted and fined £500, and sentenced to one month's imprisonment. Shortly afterwards he was indicted again for similar offences committed before the previous trial, and on this occasion he was sent to prison for three months. As I have suggested, it is is not clear whether Adam Smith would have sympathized with Waddington or condemned him as a monopolist. The important point, however, is that the new generation of lawyers who lost in this case thought that Adam Smith's doctrines were on the side of complete freedom of trade.

Thus was Adam Smith (at least as so interpreted) worsted on his first encounter with the common law. It seems probable that Kenyon and his brethren were very much in tune with the opinion of the labouring classes themselves who still believed in 'just' prices long after Adam

[16] (1800) 1 East 143, 102 E.R. 56.

[17] See Mathias, 'The Brewing Industry, Temperance and Politics', 1 *Historical Journal*, 97, 102 (1958).

[18] 1 East at 157, 102 E.R. at 62.

Smith's time.[19] They may also have been in tune with many local magistrates and gentry folk who had not yet learnt the new political economy. These were the magistrates who, in 1795, had introduced the Speenhamland system to protect the poor against the high price of provisions which prevailed in those last few years of the century. But the new doctrines were gaining ground in London if not in the provinces. When the Town Clerk of Oxford wrote to the Duke of Portland, then Secretary of State at War, and told him that the city was very active in suppressing the principal causes of the dearness of provisions by prosecutions for forestalling, he received in reply a lordly reproof commending the policy of *laissez-faire*.[20] And when, a few years later, Waddington had another brush with the law of forestalling he found the judges a good deal more sympathetic to his activities.[21]

But, once again, it must be observed how paradoxical is all talk of 'conservative' and 'radical' in connection with these times and these issues. As I have indicated, to many people, Kenyon was old-fashioned in failing to keep up with the times. William Cobbett, for example, the Radical firebrand, who was the working man's champion, roundly condemned Kenyon's decision in *Waddington*'s case.[22] Another paradox concerned the attitude of these 'conservative' judges to the modern industrial company. In the early years of the new century Eldon was to make a thorough nuisance of himself on the subject of companies. As the Industrial Revolution got under way, and projects requiring larger and larger capital were dreamt up, new 'companies' began to be formed with many members and transferable shares. Technically these were partnerships because there was no way by which they could become incorporated except by the grant of a Royal Charter. Eldon's first reaction was to treat all these new companies as illegal monopolies contrary to the Bubble Act. And when the Bubble Act was eventually repealed, Eldon threatened for many years to hold them still illegal at common law—and this at a time when a considerable number of large companies had been formed and were doing business on a substantial scale. The trouble was caused by the association between companies and monopolies. The old eighteenth-century tradition had been that people traded either alone, or in small firms, with non-transferable membership. Anything else was a company, requiring a royal charter, and usually including some monopoly element. It was some time before the argument began to be more widely accepted that incorporation was different from

[19] E. P. Thompson, *The Making of the English Working Class*, pp. 63–7.
[20] E. P. Thompson, 'The Moral Economy of the English Crowd in the Eighteenth Century', 50 *Past and Present* 76, 130–1 (1971).
[21] *Bristow* v. *Waddington* (1806) 2 B. & P. (N.R.) 354, 127 E.R. 664.
[22] See *Rural Rides*, first published 1830 (Penguin edn., Harmondsworth, 1975), p. 179.

monopoly, since there could still be competition between companies as much as between individuals.[23]

But despite Eldon's extreme conservatism on most issues, there were some questions on which he seemed more in tune with the coming age. Although he does not seem to have been greatly enamoured of the role of the new executory contract—in one case he rather lamented that the Courts had ever sanctioned the making of a contract by correspondence[24]—there were other respects in which his views were clearly in accord with nineteenth-century thought. He wanted (as we have seen) to introduce greater certainty and to reduce the discretionary element in equitable principles.[25] He also wanted to cut down the traditional Chancery willingness to protect parties from their own folly, by restricting the jurisdiction of Equity on penalties and forfeitures. As counsel, Eldon had once tried (unsuccessfully) to enforce a penalty clause arguing that 'It was impossible a jury . . . could assess any other damages than those already assessed by the parties themselves.'[26] And as Chancellor he only accepted with great reluctance the jurisdiction to refuse enforcement of penalty clauses, saying that he could see nothing irrational in the parties choosing to incorporate a penalty in their contract, and that it was 'extremely difficult to apply with propriety the word "excessive" to the terms in which the parties choose to contract with each other'.[27] And in another very important decision—*Hill* v. *Barclay*[28]—Eldon held that the rule enabling Equity to relieve against the forfeiture of a lease for breach of a covenant to pay rent could not be extended to breach of a covenant to repair. In all these respects Eldon was acting very much in the spirit of the new age—full freedom of contract for the parties, and reduction in every judicial power to mitigate the effects of a harsh contract.

In assessing the influence of the older traditions on the law, it is necessary to bear in mind the point previously made about the tendency of judges to represent an older generation. Between 1816 and 1824 all the judges of the King's Bench were men born in the 1750s or 1760s, and three of them were still there in 1830. Even in 1840 when three members of the Court, including the Chief Justice, were representatives of the new age, the fourth member was still Littledale J. who had been born in 1767 and made a judge in 1824. And Littledale J., though a judge with a high reputation as a pure lawyer, seems to have entertained some extraordinary eighteenth-century notions about the land law. In one case, for example, he expressed the view that it was 'contrary to the policy of the

[23] See *post*, pp. 563-4.   [24] *Kennedy* v. *Lee* (1817) 3 Mer. 441, 36 E.R. 170.
[25] *Supra*, p. 351.   [26] *Sloman* v. *Walker* (1783) 1 Bro. C. C. 418, 28 E. R. 1213.
[27] *Astley* v. *Weldon* (1801) 2 B. & P. 346, 351, 126 E. R. 1318, 1321.
[28] (1811) 18 Ves. 56, 34 E.R. 238.

law that a man should offer an estate for sale before he has obtained possession of it'.[29] Clearly, to Littledale J., men bought land for use or occupation, and not for resale.

There were many issues on which it seems that some of the early nineteenth-century judges were still sufficiently in the eighteenth-century tradition to bring a strong 'moral' flavour into the law. This flavour contrasted with that of the newer generation of judges who seem generally to have been much more under the influence of the political economists and the Benthamites. And these traditional-minded judges in some cases, at least, carried this moral attitude sufficiently far forward for it to survive the new generation of judges, and to be picked up, eventually by yet another generation of judges, those who were influential after 1870. This seems to have largely happened in the law relating to implied warranties in sale of goods. I shall explore this in some detail later; here I am concerned with the influence of particular judges, and with the influences operating on those judges. Early in the nineteenth century, the three Common Law Courts were operating on very divergent lines with regard to implied warranties and the principle of *caveat emptor*.[30] In general, it was the Court of Exchequer, with Abinger C.B. and more especially Parke B. in the van, which was most favourably inclined to the stern severity of *caveat emptor*. Of these two judges, Abinger C.B. had certainly been exposed to the views of the political economists, and may well have embraced them himself. As Sir James Scarlett he had sat in the Commons from 1819 to 1834, first as a Whig but later as a Tory. In 1821 he had introduced a Bill to amend the Poor Law along the lines advocated by the political economists, and for similar reasons.[31] He wanted to reform the settlement laws as well, on the grounds that they restricted 'the free circulation of labour'.[32] His Bill was supported by Ricardo who spoke immediately Scarlett had sat down.[33] Apart from the decisions on *caveat emptor*, Abinger C.B.'s Court was responsible for at least two important decisions which might possibly have been influenced by his views on political economy, viz., *Priestley* v. *Fowler*[34] and *Winterbottom* v. *Wright*.[35] I shall return to these cases later.

On the other hand, the Court of King's Bench decided a large number of cases under the influence of Ellenborough C.J. which tended to

---

[29] *Walker* v. *Moore* (1829) 10 B. & C. 416, 422, 109 E. R. 504, 507. Yet already in 1806 Cobbett was complaining that the new order had 'made land and agriculture objects of speculation'. R. Williams, *Culture and Society 1780–1950*, p. 32.

[30] See Llewellyn, 'On Warranty of Quality and Society', 36 *Columbia Law Rev.* 699 (1936).

[31] *Parliamentary Debates*, N.S. (1821), vol. v, cols. 573–82, 987–99, 1228–30, 1479–83.

[32] Ibid., col. 579.

[33] Ibid., col. 587. See further as to this Bill, and Abinger's second Bill in 1822, J. R. Poynter, *Society and Pauperism* (London and Toronto, 1969), p. 296.

[34] (1837) 3 M. & W. 1, 150 E.R. 1030; see *post*, p. 502.

[35] (1842) 10 M. & W. 109, 152 E.R. 402; see *post*, p. 502.

fluctuate between the *caveat emptor* principle, and appreciation that commercial men expected a decent standard of quality in the goods they bought. Ellenborough C.J. was, as I said earlier, one of the strong conservative influences in English law and politics in the early part of the century. He had begun his political career as a Whig, but had followed Burke in breaking with the Whigs over their attitude to the French Revolution. Later he became steadily more conservative though never so obsessive as Eldon. On the whole, his decisions in the implied warranty area represent the older eighteenth-century paternalism, rather than the new political economy. And if that was true of Ellenborough C.J. it was far more true of Best C.J. who presided in the Court of Common Pleas from 1824 to 1829. Best was quite clearly a judge in the eighteenth-century mould, with a strong moral sense. Politically, he was a strong Tory, and after he was raised to the peerage (as Lord Wynford) he fought against the Reform Bill and nearly all the Whig measures of the 1830s.[36] It seems unlikely that he would have had any time for the political economy of the new age which placed the individual at the centre of law and society, and assumed he was capable of protecting his own interests in all his contractual dealings. That was not Best's view of the functions of the law at all. 'The first object of the law', he once said, 'is to promote the public interest; the second to preserve the rights of individuals.'[37] And in dealing with implied warranty cases, Best C.J. from the very beginning refused to have any real truck with *caveat emptor* which he plainly regarded as a highly immoral principle. A man who reasonably relied on the commercial integrity of a seller from whom he bought some commodity was, in his view, plainly entitled to an article corresponding to the price he paid.

1830–1870

By the 1830s, a new generation of lawyers and judges was beginning to come to the fore in England. Abinger C.B. in the Exchequer Court was one of them, and so was Parke B. For some twenty years, between 1834 and 1856, Parke B. exercised a dominating influence in the Court of Exchequer. The evidence of his judgments alone suggests that he was very much in sympathy with the ideas of the political economists and the interests of commercial enterprises.[38] Another member of that Court through the years of the mid-century was Alderson B. Although he does not seem to have had any great interest in, or contact with, political economy—he had no political career—he was plainly not unacquainted

[36] See Foss, *The Judges of England* (London, 1864), ix. 11–12. His political views may possibly have influenced Denman's judgment of him as the worst judge he had ever known. See J. Arnould, *Memoir of Lord Denman* (London, 1873), i. 211–12.

[37] *Homer* v. *Ashford* (1825) 3 Bing. 322, 326, 130 E.R. 537, 539.

[38] Many of Parke B.'s judgments are referred to in Chapters 14 and 15.

with some of the current ideas on the subject. In his Charge to the Grand Jury of Dorset in 1831, for example, he referred, in connection with the local disorders and Luddite riots, to the unfortunate effects of the Poor Law which gave encouragement 'to early and improvident marriages and the consequent forced increase of the population'.[39] And in the same Charge he referred to the machinery which was being attacked by the Luddites as being for the good of the labourers themselves in the long run. 'The cheapness of production which is caused by machines increases the demand for manufactured articles; that increased demand causes a further demand for labour; and thus machinery in the end increases labour.'[40]

In the King's Bench also, a new generation was taking charge, though, on the whole not until the 1840s did this Court fall into the hands of judges born after 1770. Their leading representative was Thomas Denman who was Chief Justice from 1832 to 1850. Denman had been an active politician on the Whig side, having served as Attorney-General and been responsible for the drafting of the great Reform Bill. He had also been closely associated with Brougham who was principally responsible for his appointment as Chief Justice, and later for his elevation to the peerage. Although he may not have been a great lawyer, he played an active role in the campaign against the slave trade and in matters of law reform, even after his appointment to the Bench. Altogether he was a courageous and much respected judge,[41] and hardly deserved the strictures of Greville who described him as 'a second rate Whig adherent' and the Court of Queen's Bench as in a 'lamentable state' under his Chief Justiceship.[42]

But by far the most influential of the new judges was Brougham. For more than ten years before 1830 Brougham had been leading the Whig opposition in the House of Commons; though nominally independent of the party, he had been a member of its inner councils for over twenty years. His judgment had always been erratic but his ability as well as his oratory commanded enormous respect, and his defence of Queen Caroline had made him one of the most popular men in England. When the Whigs finally returned to power in 1830 everyone knew that Brougham must command high office, and it was a matter of general surprise that he chose to leave the Commons for the Woolsack. He

[39] Charles Alderson, *Selections from the Charges and Other Detached Papers of Baron Alderson* (London, 1858), p. 172.

[40] Ibid., p. 177. It is not clear if Alderson knew anything of Ricardo's highly controversial views on this question, or of his dispute with McCulloch. See Blaug, *Economic Theory in Retrospect*, pp. 172–3.

[41] See generally J. Arnould, *Memoir of Lord Denman*.

[42] *The Greville Diary*, 27 Nov. 1842, i. 483: 'Denman has just law enough to lead him almost always wrong, John Williams has no law at all, Wightman is idle, and Coleridge weak.'

occupied it for only four years before his personality made him intolerable to his colleagues and when the Whigs were briefly turned out of office in 1834 Brougham himself went out never to return. But despite his brief tenure of office it seems certain that Brougham brought new life to the law. He had for many years been closely associated with the political economists and also with Bentham. It was (as we have seen) due to his influence that Ricardo entered Parliament,[43] and Brougham also played an important role in the founding of the *Edinburgh Review* which for many years gave wide publicity to the new political economy. Brougham himself wrote a great deal for it, especially in its early years.[44] His great speech on Law Reform in the House of Commons in 1828 (despite Bentham's condemnation of it) was highly influential in a number of specific areas, and led directly to the setting up of a number of Commissions of Inquiry which produced, in due course, reform in the Land Law Acts of 1833. And more generally, Brougham remained a force to be reckoned with in politics and the law for thirty years. Generally a Whig and a free trader, he supported the repeal of the Corn Laws in 1846; but on the other hand he was no friend to the idea of limited liability for companies, and on one occasion he persuaded the Lords to throw out a Bill to enable such companies to be created. But, as we shall see later, limited liability was one of those subjects on which the advocates of freedom of contract could be found on both sides.

It is hard to measure the influence of a man like Brougham, especially on so amorphous a subject as the law, and particularly, the common law, which grows by accretion rather than by acts of sudden creation. But it seems probable that his influence has been underestimated in the past.[45] In particular, there is a case for saying that Brougham was the man who made Benthamism respectable to English lawyers. There has, in recent years, been a considerable controversy raging over the influence of Bentham himself on the development of the English governmental machine in the mid-nineteenth century,[46] but his influence on the common law and on the judges is if anything even more difficult to measure. Bentham's own language, his violent abuse and contempt for so much which lawyers held dear, his derision of Blackstone, still revered among the common lawyers, his tendency to sweeping condemnation,

[43] In 1809 Brougham also introduced Malthus to Lord Grey, later Prime Minister. See Brougham's own *Life and Times of Lord Brougham* (London, 1871), i. 436, 438.

[44] F. W. Fetter, 'The Authorship of Economic Articles in the Edinburgh Review 1802-1847', 61 *Journal of Political Economy* 232 (1953). In the first twelve issues all but one of the articles on economic issues whose authorship is identifiable were written by Brougham or Francis Horner.

[45] See generally Chester New, *Life of Henry Brougham to 1830.*

[46] See Roberts, 'Jeremy Bentham and the Victorian Administrative State', 2 *Victorian Studies* 193 (1959); Parris, 'The Nineteenth Century Revolution in Government: A Reappraisal Reappraised', 3 *Historical Journal* 17 (1960); J. Hart, 'Nineteenth Century Social Reform: A Tory Interpretation of History', 31 *Past and Present* 39 (1965).

could hardly have endeared him to the practising profession. And yet we have the testimony of John Stuart Mill in 1838 that there were already men 'in the highest seats of justice' who would acknowledge the justice of Mill's own assessment of Bentham's great contribution to law reform.[47] So also Dicey wrote that the 'best and wisest of the judges who administered the law of England during the fifty years which followed 1825 were thoroughly imbued with Benthamite liberalism'.[48] And even if we must treat this remark with some caution because of Dicey's extraordinary association of Benthamite liberalism with *laissez-faire*, there is plainly substance in the remark. But if this is all true, part of the credit surely belongs to Brougham who reinterpreted many of Bentham's ideas into a form acceptable to the legal profession. As a commanding figure in Parliament, as a member of the inner circle of the Whig party, as a leading member of the Bar, then as Chancellor, and finally as a former Chancellor, Brougham was a man to be listened to with respect. And for a period of some twenty years or more (from 1828 to the 1850s) Brougham placed himself at the helm of the law reform movement which translated into practice so many of Bentham's specifically legal proposals.

There can be no doubt, also, that among many of the secondary figures in the Law there was, in the 1830s and 1840s, a considerable degree of personal contact between lawyers on the one hand, and the political economists and the Benthamite utilitarians on the other. I have already referred to some of these figures, a few of whom (like Nassau Senior and Chadwick) had actually been trained in the law. In addition there were many other figures who were more or less influential in bridging the gap between the lawyers, the political economists, and the Benthamites. There were, for example, the two Austin brothers, one of whom was the famous Professor of Jurisprudence,[49] and generally credited with founding the Positivist school of legal philosophy. There was J. A. Roebuck, a Queen's Counsel and for many years an influential member of Parliament. There was Thomas Denman who (as we have seen) later became Chief Justice of the Queen's Bench. There was Henry Bickersteth, M.P. from 1834 to 41 and Master of the Rolls as Lord Langdale from 1841 to 1851. And even among those who were not really members of either circle, there is no doubt that the influence of the political economists and the utilitarians did penetrate with many

---

[47] In an 'Essay' in the *London and Westminster Review*, cited in Mill, *Utilitarianism*, ed. Mary Warnock, p. 111. Mill must have had Denman particularly in mind.

[48] Dicey, *Law and Public Opinion*, p. 199.

[49] According to Mill, *Autobiography*, p. 107, John Austin professed 'great disrespect for what he called the universal principles of human nature of the political economists and insisted on the evidence which history and daily experience afford of the "extraordinary pliability of human nature"'.

influential lawyers. Edward Sugden, later Lord St. Leonards and Lord Chancellor, for example, was converted to the cause of usury law repeal by Bentham's arguments and himself wrote a pamphlet in 1812 which, as he acknowledged, owed much to Bentham.[50] In 1818 he gave evidence, together with Ricardo, before a House of Commons Select Committee appointed to examine the question.

One of the great changes which came over the judicial scene with the arrival of the newer generation of judges in the 1830s and even more in the 1840s was that many of these judges had had substantial commercial experience at the Bar, unlike their predecessors. For example, Bosanquet J. who sat in Common Pleas from 1830 to 1842 had been standing counsel to the Bank of England from 1819 to 1830. Maule J. who also sat in the Common Pleas from 1840 to 1855 (after a year in the Exchequer) had had an extensive commercial and insurance practice and also been Counsel to the Bank of England from 1835 to 1839. In 1834 the formidable public servant, Sir James Stephen, wrote somewhat rudely to the Attorney-General, Sir John Campbell, saying that it was 'a mere matter of form and etiquette to attribute to the Attorney-General and Solicitor-General for the time being any better notions on Topics of this kind [Corporations] or any more general knowledge than belongs to their neighbours.'[51] He added, 'The fact is that a man may pass a long life in Westminster Hall, without having half a dozen times to turn his mind to the Question of the proper constitution of corporate charters or commercial partnerships. The Merchants on the Royal Exchange would be tenfold better authorities than all the four Courts united.'[52] If this was still true in 1834 (and it may even then have been an exaggeration), it was rapidly ceasing to be true. The new judges had been brought up in the England of the Industrial Revolution.[53] It may, however, have been another twenty years or so before these changes became more pronounced in the holders of the most influential office of all—that of Lord Chancellor. 'A change of generation and outlook which in general politics started with Peel', it has been said, 'affected the highest legal offices only in the 1860s. Lord Chancellors Campbell, St. Leonards, Chelmsford, Cranworth, Westbury and Hatherley were of the pre-1832

---

[50] Stark, *Jeremy Bentham's Economic Writings*, ii. 31. Yet he is referred to as an 'archetypal diehard' by Thompson, 'Land and Politics in England in the Nineteenth Century', 15 *Trans. Roy. Hist. Soc.*, 5th series, 23, 33 (1965).

[51] Cited, Hunt, *The Development of the Business Corporation in England*, p. 59.

[52] Ibid.

[53] Though, according to Laski, no judge appointed between 1832 and 1906 had received any formal training in economics: *Studies in Law and Politics* (Yale, 1932), p. 172. But Laski may have overlooked H. H. Cozens-Hardy (appointed as a judge in 1899, and later Master of the Rolls) who obtained first prize in an examination in political economy in 1860, ahead of W. S. Jevons who was placed third; see Keynes, *Essays in Biography*, p. 293.

generation, and lived in the almost purely legal world of the *ancien régime* lawyer.'[54] But Brougham must be exempted from these remarks.

A great deal of biographical research is still needed in order to fill in the details in this picture; we do not know nearly enough about the judges, their training, their beliefs and attitudes, in order to give a proper assessment of the influence on the detailed rules of law in any particular area of (say) the ideas of the political economists. The tradition of the neutral, value-free judgment, based on legal doctrine rather than on any sense of justice or any particular policy, often makes it hard to detect the underlying, and perhaps unconscious influences at work. Nevertheless, judges sometimes give themselves away, almost unconsciously displaying their beliefs or values in judgments which appear to be based on pure legal doctrine, and we shall see a number of specific examples of this kind of thing in the case law which remains to be examined. Indeed, we have already seen examples of this sort of thing as where, for instance, Mansfield or Eldon expressed their conviction that contracting parties should be left free to judge their own interests. But there are two judges whom I propose to look at in greater detail because in these particular instances, extra-judicial writings and activities make it easy to identify the values at work, and both of them had a good deal to say about freedom of contract.

Bramwell

George William Wilshere Bramwell[55] was born in 1808 in the first decade, and died in 1892, in the last decade of the nineteenth century. Called to the Bar in 1838, he was a member of the Common Law Procedure Commission whose labours led to the Common Law Procedure Act of 1852, and later, of the Mercantile Law Commission which reported (among other things) on limited liability for companies. He was appointed Baron of the Exchequer Court in 1856, Lord Justice of Appeal in 1876, and created a peer in 1882. Although he was not appointed a Lord of Appeal, Bramwell sat for many years hearing appeals in the House of Lords, until his death in 1892. Bramwell is of great interest to the historian of nineteenth-century law because he made no secret of his political convictions and because it is not difficult to trace the influence of these convictions on his legal judgments in a wide variety of cases.

In his youth Bramwell had absorbed the orthodox political economy of the time, and he had taken Adam Smith and Ricardo to his heart. Later he came to think of Herbert Spencer as '[t]he profoundest thinker of the age'.[56] On at least one occasion, he cited Ricardo in a judgment.[57] In 1855 he became a member of the Political Economy Club, and for the whole of his life he adhered to the simple principle of *laissez-faire*. Although there is no evidence that he ever really mastered Ricardian economics, he remained convinced throughout his life that the political economists had proved that the principle of freedom of contract was a necessary part of the laws of a civilized state. In 1888 he gave the Presidential Address to the Economics section of the British Association on 'Economics and Socialism'[58] in which he said that there was only one really important principle of political economy and that was the principle of *laissez-faire*. In 1882 he joined the newly formed Liberty and Property Defence League which was largely set up to combat the ideas of Henry George on the nationalization of land. The details of this controversy will have to wait till Part III of this work, and it is enough to say here that Bramwell gave devoted support to the League to the end of his days. He wrote a number of short pamphlets which were published by the League, amongst which there was one on *Laissez Faire* (1884) and another on *Drink* (1885) the latter of which sold 100,000 copies. Bramwell denied being a doctrinaire adherent of *laissez-faire* in the sense that he acknowledged the necessity of some State interference, as he insisted his masters Adam Smith and Ricardo had done. But in practice his belief in interference was largely limited to a belief in the necessity for the State to create rights of property, and he opposed virtually every proposed interference with freedom of contract. In the last twenty years of his life he frequently wrote letters to *The Times* protesting at proposed legislation interfering with freedom of contract (usually signed 'B.'), and he often addressed public meetings on similar themes.[59] His pamphlet on *Drink* perhaps contains the arguments with which modern readers would be in most sympathy. If it is true, he says, that over £100 millions are spent annually on drink, then that 'shows the amount of enjoyment that must be derived from it'. He goes on to concede that society has a right to prohibit the sale of drink, but asks, 'is it fair, is it just, is it reasonably expedient, because some take it to excess, that it is to be denied to millions to whom it is a daily pleasure and enjoyment with no attendant harm?'

I will be discussing later many of the issues to which Bramwell addressed his attention. Here it is enough to draw attention to some of the topics on which Bramwell's somewhat simplistic faith in *laissez-faire* and

---

[56] In his pamphlet on *Laissez Faire*, cited Fairfield, op. cit., p. 140.

[57] In *Archer* v. *James* (1859) 2 B. & S. 62, 95-6, 121 E.R. 998, 1006. He also cited *The Wealth of Nations* in the same case.

[58] Published as a pamphlet by the Liberty and Property Defence League.

[59] See, e.g., *Report of the Industrial Remuneration Conference* (London, Paris, New York, and Melbourne, 1885) which contains an address by Bramwell at pp. 419 *et seq*.

freedom of contract affected his judgment on what the law ought to be, and in many cases, on what the law actually was.

On the law of contract itself, Bramwell adhered firmly to the general notion that a man should only be bound by a contract to which he gave a clear assent. Thus he dissented from the decision in *British and American Telegraph Co. Ltd.* v. *Colson*[60] in which his colleagues held that an offeror might be bound by a posted letter of acceptance which went astray. He also disliked the whole law of quasi-contract, for he could not understand how a man could be forced to pay for a benefit which he had received but which he had not agreed to pay for. While many people would accept the justice of this as a general rule, Bramwell carried it so far that it is difficult to see any room at all for quasi-contractual liabilities in his philosophy. In 1854 Bramwell expressed his views on this point in the *First Report of the Mercantile Law Commission*:

I ask, why should a man who buys goods pay for them? Either he has undertaken to do so, or he has not. If he has, make him liable to the extent of his undertaking; to his last shilling and acres if he has pledged them. But if he has not, if he has not undertaken at all, or if he has limited his liability, I do not only see no reason why he should be called on to do that which he has not engaged to do, but I think it a positive dishonesty to attempt to make him.[61]

In 1857 Bramwell largely gave judicial effect to these views in *Boulton* v. *Jones*[62] in which he seems to have been quite willing to contemplate a person being free of all liability to pay for goods he had consumed, simply because they were supplied to him in error.

Bramwell was one of the strong supporters of the introduction of limited liability for companies. He argued that this naturally followed from the principle of freedom of contract, since a man dealing with a company which had limited liability would know that fact, and would, therefore, take account of it in his dealings with the company. This is a good illustration of Bramwell's simple faith in the idea that if the facts were well known to contracting parties, or even if they were capable of being ascertained, the parties would automatically take account of them in their bargain. He never seems to have had any doubts—except perhaps in the case of the Truck Acts, to which he was almost willing to give a grudging acquiescence in recognition of Adam Smith's blessing[63]— that parties would in fact take account of all the circumstances in striking their bargain. Nor does he seem to have recognized that this approach failed even to begin to answer the question, where should the liability be placed by the law. A modern economist would say, in regard to limited

[60] (1871) L.R. 6 Ex. 108.
[61] H.C. *Parliamentary Papers* xxvii. 445, 471.
[62] (1857) 2 H. & N. 564, 157 E.R. 232. See also *Brice* v. *Bannister* (1878) 3 Q.B.D. 569, 580–1.
[63] *Archer* v. *James, supra*, n.57, 2 B. & S. at 88–9, 121 E.R. at 1006.

liability, that the bargain struck by the parties would take account of the law, whatever it might be; if it provided for limited liability, the bargain might compel the company to pay some trifling additional price as a premium for the extra risk, while conversely if the law did not provide for limited liability, no such payment would be needed. In either case, the result would be economically efficient. Economic arguments along these lines are only relevant if transaction costs are taken into account, for example, if it should be more troublesome for a company to expressly contract without limited liability (where the general law provided *for* limited liability) than it would be for the company expressly to contract *with* limited liability (where the general law provided otherwise). There may, of course, be other economic arguments in favour of the principle of limited liability, but these were all far beyond Bramwell's simple and rather naïve faith in freedom of contract ideas.

Exactly the same simplicity is to be found in Bramwell's ideas on employer's liability for injury to his workmen. We have already seen how Chadwick's ingenious and fertile mind had grasped the essential economic issues on this question, but Bramwell's was a simpler faith. He believed that the bargain struck by the employer and the workman for the workman's wages excluded any right to compensation for injury. The workman was paid for taking the risk of injury because he did take the risk of injury. Hence, if he was allowed to claim damages for the injury, he would, in effect be paid twice over. He expressed this view in his dissenting judgment in *Smith* v. *Charles Baker & Sons*[64] in which the majority of the House of Lords held that a workman was not debarred from claiming damages as a result of a danger arising from his employment merely because he knew of it.

It is [says Bramwell] a rule of good sense that if a man voluntarily undertakes a risk for a reward which is adequate to induce him, he shall not, if he suffers from the risk, have a compensation for which he did not stipulate . . . But drop the maxim [i.e., *volenti not fit injuria*]. Treat it as a question of bargain. The plaintiff here thought the pay worth the risk, and did not bargain for a compensation if hurt; in effect, he undertook the work, with its risks, for his wages and no more. He says so. Suppose he had said, 'If I am to run this risk, you must give me 6s. a day and not 5s.,' and the master agreed, would he in reason have a claim if he got hurt? Clearly not. What difference is there if the master says, 'No; I will only give the 5s.?' None. I am ashamed to argue it.[65]

What Bramwell failed to perceive here as in numerous other instances, was that he was always assuming what he set out to prove. If the workman knew, when he took the job at the wage fixed, that he had no right to

---

[64] [1891] A.C. 325.

[65] At p. 344. Bramwell had already given this example in almost the same words in his pamphlet on *Laissez Faire*, p. 20.

claim compensation, then, at least in economic theory, it might be argued that the resulting wage was a fair bargain which reflected the risk. But if the workman assumed, or thought, that he might have a right to compensation for injury, then Bramwell's whole argument simply begged the question. When Bramwell gave evidence to a House of Commons Select Committee on Employers' Liability in 1876,[66] he was asked why a passenger who was injured through the negligence of the railway company was entitled to damages when the injured workman was not. His reply was to the effect that the passenger was entitled to compensation by virtue of his contractual right to be carried safely. When the committee members then pressed him to explain why the workman did not have a right to be safely employed, Bramwell could only reiterate his original argument, that the workman was paid to take the risk. He was, in truth, rather obtuse on this point, his mind having evidently been made up at an early stage, and he never understood the circularity of his reasoning.

Nor did Bramwell ever grasp the fact that if the law were changed so as to create new contractual liabilities or rights, future contracting parties would be bargaining against the new legal background and would, of course, take that into account as much (or as little) as they did the existing legal background. Thus there was little substance in Bramwell's constant complaint that interference with freedom of contract encouraged a sort of fraud, because it enabled a man to make a contract on certain terms, and then go back on the terms in reliance on new statutory rights.

Among other areas of the law where Bramwell's views seem to have coloured his legal judgments are those dealing with fraud and with vicarious liability in tort. On the first question, Bramwell seems to have been influenced by his political economy into believing that there was some sort of a 'natural' meaning to the concept of fraud, and that it was merely the judge's duty to apply that natural sense of the word. This meant that he was able to take to an extreme the idea that the law did not 'interfere' with freedom of contract, even in cases of fraud. 'I do not', he said in *Weir* v. *Bell*,[67] 'understand legal fraud. To my mind, it has no more meaning than legal heat or legal cold, legal light or legal shade.' Bramwell was in effect arguing that the law merely identified, but did not define, the concept of fraud.

On the law relating to vicarious liability in tort, Bramwell's individualism seems to have been largely responsible for his idiosyncratic opinions. For many years in the second half of the nineteenth century Bramwell dissented in case after case in which his colleagues expanded

---

[66] (1876) H.C. *Parliamentary Papers*, ix. 669 and (1877) x. 551, 628 *et seq.*
[67] (1878) 3 Ex. D. 238, 243. See also *Derry* v. *Peek* (1889) 14 App. Cas. 337 discussed *post*, p. 673.

the extent of vicarious liability.[68] It is clear that he felt that a man should be responsible for his own misdeeds and for nobody else's. It was not only that he felt the employer should not be liable, but also that he felt the employee should be liable to pay for his carelessness; and although these decisions did not technically exonerate the employee from his own liability, Bramwell was plainly aware that in practice the employee would never be made to pay if the employer was held liable. In modern times, vicarious liability has been justified on economic grounds as a means of making firms pay for the costs they impose. But in the early nineteenth century when the individual was seen as the unit of social organization, it is easy to see why vicarious liability may have seemed contrary to the teachings of political economy. But Bramwell never seems to have appreciated the possible inconsistencies in his views on vicarious liability and limited liability.

Finally, I should refer to one of Bramwell's most interesting judgments which shows strong traces of Benthamite influence as well as the usual economic arguments. This is *Bamford* v. *Turnley*[69] in which the defendant was sued for nuisance caused by pollution, and he set up the public interest by way of defence. Bramwell's answer at first was to say that 'that law is a bad one which, for the public benefit, inflicts loss on an individual without compensation'. He then went on,

But further, with great respect, I think this consideration misapplied in this and in many other cases. The public consists of all the individuals of it; and a thing is only for the public benefit when it is productive of good to all those individuals on the balance of loss and gain to all. So that if all the loss and all the gain were borne and received by one individual he, on the whole, would be a gainer. But whenever this is the case—whenever a thing is for the public benefit, properly understood—the loss to the individuals of the public who lose will bear compensation out of the gains of those who gain. It is for the public benefit that there should be railways; but it would not be unless the gain of having the railway was sufficient to compensate the loss occasioned by the use of the land required for its site; and accordingly, no one thinks it would be right to take an individual's land without compensation, to make a railway. It is for the public benefit that trains should run; but not unless they pay their expenses. If one of those expenses is the burning down a wood of such value that the railway owners would not run the train and burn down the wood if it were their own, neither is it for the public benefit that they should if the wood is not their own. If, though the wood were their own, they still would find it compensated them to run trains at the cost of burning the wood, then they obviously ought to compensate the

[68] See, e.g., *Collett* v. *Foster* (1857) 2 H. & N. 356, 157 E.R. 147; *Waite* v. *North Eastern Rly. Co.* (1859) E. B. & E. 728, 120 E.R. 682; *Weir* v. *Bell, supra* n. 67.; *The Apollo* [1891] A.C. 499; he recanted his judgment in the *Waite* case, but very half-heartedly in *The Bernina* (1888) 13 App. Cas. 1, 13.
[69] (1862) 3 B. & S. 67, 122 E.R. 27.

owner of such wood, not being themselves, if they burn it down in making their gains.[70]

On this point Bramwell's economics seems to have been somewhat sounder, and indeed, not unsophisticated, for he was taking into account externalities. It is difficult to understand why he never saw the need to do this when discussing freedom of contract.

We shall see more of Bramwell's influence and work in relation to some of the specific legal issues which remain to be examined in the next two Chapters, and again, in relation to some of the questions which arose after 1870. But before we leave Bramwell for the moment, it is well to make it plain that he seems to have been far from representative of judicial opinion during the period when he was sitting. Certainly, towards the end of his life, his adherence to *laissez-faire* and freedom of contract was tending to make him an isolated figure on the Bench; but even in his prime, in the 1860s and 1870s, he was more often in dissent than would be expected in the normal course of judicial disagreement. The truth is that in his pursuit of individualism and freedom of contract, he always seems to have been something of a fanatic.

Byles

My next judge, Sir John Byles, was a much less known figure than Bramwell. Byles was born in 1801 and died in 1884. From 1858 until 1873 he sat as a judge of the Court of Common Pleas. He is known to modern lawyers almost exclusively through his authorship of a treatise on the law of bills of exchange, known to successive generations of lawyers as *Byles on Bills*. But there was another, less well known side to Byles. He was interested in political economy. In his youth, he entertained the popular opinions of political economy, and he even wrote for his own use an abridgment of Ricardo's *Principles*. But 'more mature reflection' led him, later in life, to the conclusion that much political economy was fallacious. He left behind him two works in which he expressed these views with considerable cogency. In 1845 he published a little book entitled *Observations on the Usury Laws*,[71] and a few years later he published (anonymously) a more general work, whose contents may be divined from its title, *Sophisms of Free Trade*.[72] The book was a huge success, and ran through eight editions in two years. It was reprinted in 1870 when Byles allowed his name to appear for the first time on the title-page, and again in 1904 when it was rediscovered by a couple of academics.[73] It is interesting to note that (according to the *D.N.B.*) Byles had in his lifetime a reputation as being 'always a strong and old fashioned conservative'.

[70] 3 B. & S. at 84–5, 122 E.R. at 33.   [71] London, 1845, hereafter cited as *Usury*.
[72] London, 1849.
[73] London, 1904, ed. Lilly and Deves. This is the edition cited throughout.

Yet his views on political economy which may have seemed old-fashioned in his own day would now appear far in advance of his times. The temptation to quote at some length from these two books is irresistible. The first, that on the Usury Laws, was written because Byles sensed a growing demand for the total repeal of the laws, and wanted to warn the public of the dangers of this course. He began this book with some general reflections on political economy, observing that this branch of human knowledge was 'in its very infancy'. He went on:

[N]o one can peruse the writings of Say, Ricardo, Malthus, Mill, Torrens, Senior, McCulloch, without admitting two things; first, that whatever additional light they may throw on many topics, there is scarce a single doctrine on which the disciples are fully agreed, except that some of the views of their master, Adam Smith are erroneous; and next, that the disciples are far more disposed than their master to indulge in abstract reasoning, and to acquiesce in its conclusions as truths, which may be safely made the basis of legislation.[74]

He goes on to urge that these theories need testing against experience and that knowledge of the facts is still inadequate for conclusions to be firmly reached in many cases. Interestingly, Byles suggests that around 1830 'it was generally considered as settled' that *laissez-faire* was to be the maxim of statesmen, but that public opinion was then (that is, in 1845) rapidly undergoing a reaction, and that a distrust of the 'let alone system' was becoming more apparent among enlightened men.

Turning to the Usury Laws themselves, Byles attacks the fundamental premise of the political economists which lies behind the demands for freedom of contract, namely that men are the best judges of their own interests, and can safely be left to make their own contracts in their own way:

The rule proposed [he says], that is to say, perfect freedom in contracts and an uniform application of the law to them all, is specious and seducing, from its simplicity. It is easily understood and easily applied. Men congratulate themselves on their superior wisdom, and look down with a smile of contempt on the antiquated and barbarous rubbish of public regulations. The painful duty of investigating details, and judging by experience of the applicability of the principle to particular classes of case, is superseded.[75]

He goes on to urge that this is too simple a view, and that actual experience has taught that regulation of many contracts is, in fact, desirable. He refers to the equitable rules governing penalties, mortgages, the Truck Acts, and a variety of other legislative interferences with freedom of contract such as the Weights and Measures Acts, the Passenger Acts, the Factories Acts, laws relating to compulsory registration of medical practitioners, and so on. He concludes by emphasizing that

[74] *Usury*, pp. 1–3.   [75] Ibid., p. 54.

where contracting parties are not bargaining as equals, but one of them has an extraordinary or unusual advantage, 'the laws of all nations frequently recognise the claims of the weaker party to extraordinary legislative protection'.[76]

In his second book, *Sophisms of Free Trade*, Byles launched a more general attack on *laissez-faire*. The whole of society, he insists, rests upon rejection of this principle:

Man without artificial culture, without intellectual, moral, religious education, is a stupid, sensual, ferocious and disgusting savage . . . Nor is artificial regulation less necessary to man in the aggregate than to man individually. Life, personal liberty and inviolability, family, property, reputation, are guarded by laws, complex and artificial in proportion to the advanced state of society . . . Withdraw the interference of the law, leave things alone and families no longer exist, society relapses into barbarism. The institution of property, the spring of all industry and improvement leans entirely on an artificial system of laws, civil and criminal, defining its limits, protecting its enjoyment and securing its peaceable and certain transmission . . .

But a still deeper and steadier insight into the constitution of society, will disclose not only artificial political arrangements, but commercial and fiscal ones, tending to the virtue, the happiness, the wealth, the power, the grandeur and the duration of states. The possibility of such artificial regulations is agreeable to analogy and conformable to experience. But both analogy and experience forbid the expectation, that the increase of wealth and equitable distribution by the full, various and permanent employment of the people, will flow from the *let alone* system.[77]

In a later chapter he returns to the theme and lists the great number of instances in which the law already interferes with freedom of contract. Amongst these examples, he mentions the rule against the enforcement of penal bonds, the law of mortgages, the requirement of writing for many contracts, assay marks on gold and silver, legislation against falsely packed hops, the Passenger Acts, the control of the medical and legal professions. Challenging head-on the philosophy of the classical economists, he insists that 'Competition for practice on the one hand, and the ordinary prudence of mankind on the other' have not been found by experience sufficient to protect the public against dishonesty and incompetence. Elsewhere, he argues—years ahead of his time—that tenants should be compensated for improvements carried out even against the will of the landlord and that the strict settlement system should be brought to an end. Altogether, this book is a valuable corrective for those who think that all nineteenth-century judges believed wholeheartedly in freedom of contract and *laissez-faire*.

It is, however, not nearly so easy in the case of Byles, as it is in that of

[76] Ibid., p. 73.   [77] Chapter III.

Bramwell, to trace the influence of his views on specific legal judgments. In one case, indeed, where a crucial point on the interpretation of the Truck Act was in question, and the Court of Exchequer Chamber split three judges to three, Byles found himself on the same side as Bramwell, deciding against the application of the Act.[78] Nevertheless, he made it clear in his judgment in this case that he had no doubt as to the soundness of the policy of the Act, and he insisted that it ought to be liberally construed despite the penal clauses.[79] In another case on the restraint of trade doctrine, Byles J. went out of his way to reject the argument that prima facie all agreements should be enforced on the assumption that they are in the interests of both parties:[80]

It is a popular, but in my judgment a mistaken notion, that parties ought to be at liberty to enter into contracts after their own fashion. The legislature has not thought this expedient; for it has, in numerous instances, interfered in the way of limitation or prohibition—as for instance in the disposition of property by will. There are many cases in which it is expedient for the law to interpose for the protection of the ignorant or of those who would otherwise be subjected to undue influence or pressure.

It seems probable that Byles was even less representative of judicial opinion in the mid-nineteenth century than was Bramwell. Probably, at least in the middle third of the century, the majority of the judges would have inclined more to Bramwell's position, though in the latter half of the century, opinion may have begun to moderate slightly. But so far as the influence of these attitudes on the law of contract is concerned, it does seem (as will appear in greater detail later) that once the basic tenets of political economy had been translated into law by the judges in the form of adoption of the principle of freedom of contract, they remained there. Judicial attitudes showed little sign of movement away from total adherence to the principle of freedom of contract until the twentieth century, long after the political economists had abandoned *laissez-faire* even to the extent that they had ever embraced it.[81]

PARLIAMENT AND THE COURTS

I must next say a little about the change which came over the relationship between Parliament and the Courts during this period. As we saw

[78] *Archer* v. *James, supra,* n. 57.

[79] 2 B. & S. 83, 121 E.R. 1004.

[80] *Mumford* v. *Gething* (1859) 7 C. B. (N. S.) 305, 325–6, 141 E.R. 834, 842. For another case in which Byles's values seem to have influenced his judgment, see *post,* p. 486.

[81] This perhaps illustrates the applicability to lawyers of Keynes's famous dictum that 'in the field of economic and political philosophy there are not many who are influenced by new theories, after they are twenty-five or thirty years of age, so that the ideas which civil servants and politicians and agitators apply are not likely to be of the newest'. *General Theory of Employment, Interest and Money* (London, 1936), pp. 383–4.

previously, in and around 1770 the Courts were, in the field of private law, more efficient as law-makers than Parliament. And Parliament generally recognized this fact, confining itself to relatively minor adjustments to the general rules of the common law. But during the course of the nineteenth century, and especially after 1830, all this began to change. I have already said something about the improvements in the actual law-making process itself, and about the growth of the Government bureaucratic machine which also led to such an increase in the amount of information available to Parliament. No comparable change took place in the work of the Courts, so that when issues of major public concern arose for decision in the Courts after 1830, the judges often began to show a greater deference to Parliament than they had shown before. There is a sense in which the great Parliamentary Blue Books, with their stream of data, statistics, and evidence of expert and professional witnesses, performed for the English legal system the sort of function which in the twentieth century was performed for the United States by the 'Brandeis brief'. But these were parliamentary briefs and the Courts had no access to the information now being accumulated in the growing Government departments. Judges began to feel that they were less informed than Parliament, and they began to be reluctant to tread in political fields. The extremely controversial nature of many of the new domestic issues was also not without effect. The broad consensus of eighteenth-century political opinion (at least on domestic affairs) had gone for good. Some of the judges began to be aware that (for example) the political economists were bitterly divided amongst themselves on numerous questions. For example, Denman C.J. in *Hitchcock* v. *Coker* remarked that it was difficult to say what was in the public interest on account of the variety of opinions that existed on so many questions.[82] And it is unlikely that a judge in 1830 or 1840 would so blithely have insisted on his own views over those of Parliament's on questions of economic policy as Lord Kenyon did in *R.* v. *Waddington*,[83] or Lord Eldon did on the legality of companies.[84]

One result of all this was that the judges were encouraged in their tendency to withdraw into the realm of abstract general principle. There was, between 1800 and 1850, for example, a marked shift of opinion on the extent to which the Courts should hold contracts contrary to public policy, and so refuse to enforce them. Around the turn of the century Lord Kenyon had had no hesitation in overturning some of Mansfield's decision on the permissibility of insurance by English insurers on foreign ships in time of war.[85] And similarly, the Courts were inclined, in general,

---

[82] (1838) 6 Ad. & E. 438, 445, 112 E.R. 167, 170.
[83] *Supra*, p. 365.   [84] See *post*, p. 564.
[85] *Brandon* v. *Nesbitt* (1794) 6 T.R. 23, 101 E.R. 415; *Potts* v. *Bell* (1800) 8 T.R. 548, 101 E.R. 1540.

to lend their aid to Statutes creating criminal offences, by refusing to countenance contracts in breach of their provisions.[86] As late as 1826 an old-fashioned judge like Best C.J. could discuss an issue in terms of the broadest policy considerations, justifying himself with the remark that 'if there be any doubts what is the law, Judges solve such doubts by considering what would be the good or bad effects of their decision'.[87] But opinion on these questions was undoubtedly changing. Even Best C.J. himself had only two years earlier argued strongly that the Courts must confine themselves on policy issues,[88] and in the same case Burrough J. made his famous remark about public policy being an unruly horse— 'when once you get astride it you never know where it will carry you.'[89]

The decisive case, which settled the judicial attitude to questions of public policy was *Egerton* v. *Brownlow*.[90] This case in fact concerned a will and not a contract, but the principles of public policy with regard to freedom of testation were generally the same as the principles with regard to freedom of contract. The case was a very unusual one on its facts, for it concerned a devise of an estate on the condition that if the devisee failed to secure the title of Marquis or Duke within a certain time, the estate would pass to another party. The case is also unusual for another reason, for the House of Lords decided against the validity of the condition attached to the devise (by a majority of four to one) after summoning the judges to give their views, and after the judges had almost unanimously decided in favour of the condition. And finally, the case is still more unusual in that it was the principles expressed by the majority of the judges, and not by the House of Lords, which came to be regarded as correctly stating the proper judicial attitude to issues of public policy.[91] There is a sense in which this was the case which finally decided that prima facie all contracts (and wills) were entitled to the protection of the law, and that they were only to be held void on the clearest grounds of illegality. The leading judgment, on behalf of the judges, was given by Parke B. with whom Erle and Wightman JJ. concurred. This is what he said:[92]

Prima facie, all persons are free to dispose of their property according to their will and pleasure, and are free to make such contracts as they please, and are morally and legally bound by them, provided in both cases, they adopt the formalities required by the common and statute law.

The argument that the condition was contrary to public policy was

[86] *Bensley* v. *Bignold* (1822) 5 B. & Ald. 335, 106 E.R. 1214.
[87] *Fletcher* v. *Lord Sondes* (1826) 3 Bing. 501, 590, 130 E.R. 606, 641, a dissenting judgment.
[88] *Richardson* v. *Mellish* (1824) 2 Bing. 229, 242–3, 130 E.R. 294, 299.
[89] 2 Bing. 252, 130 E.R. 303.   [90] (1853) 4 H.L.C. 1, 10 E.R. 359.
[91] See as to this, Viscount Radcliffe, *Law and its Compass* (Evanston, Ill., 1960), p. 48.
[92] 4 H.L.C. 123–4, 10 E.R. 408–9.

dismissed, because public policy 'is a vague and unsatisfactory term, and calculated to lead to uncertainty and error when applied to the decision of legal rights.' The term might mean political expediency, or that which was best for the common good of the community, and 'in that case there may be every variety of opinion, according to education, habits, talents and dispositions of each person.' Public policy was a matter for statesmen, not lawyers. Alderson B. argued to much the same effect.

To all this a most spirited rejoinder came from Pollock, C.B. Public policy, he insisted, was the very foundation of the law, and he proceeded to cite cases in which contracts had been held void in a variety of circumstances. He then went on:[93]

> My Lords, after all these authorities, am I not justified in saying that, were I to discard the public welfare from my consideration, I should abdicate the functions of my office—I should shrink from the discharge of my duty? . . . My Lords it may be that Judges are no better able to discern what is for the public good than other experienced and enlightened members of the community, but that is no reason for refusing to entertain the question, and declining to decide upon it.

I have quoted at length from these judgments because this discussion, despite all its peculiarities, is so very central to the whole theme of freedom of contract. The majority of the judges whose views prevailed, if not in this particular instance, were in effect arguing as the political economists had argued. Freedom of contract was a starting-point, a part of the natural background, and it was 'interference' which had to be justified. Only Pollock C.B. in effect insisted that it was public policy which determined that prima facie contracts should be enforced, and therefore there was no reason for public policy being prayed in aid against a contract in particular circumstances. To the majority, the function of the law was to give effect to principles and precedents which were firm and settled, unlike public policy which was something on which opinions differed with every change of the wind. This attitude came to dominate the whole common law of contracts, and indeed, it came to dominate the judicial function altogether. Judges began to talk more in terms of precedent and principles, and less in terms of policy than they had ever done before.

Of course, what the judges said was one thing; what was necessarily implied or involved in their decisions was something else again. The reality is that many policy issues simply cannot be spirited away by refusing to discuss them in terms of policy. A refusal to face them is itself a policy—a policy in favour of freedom of contract, which might very well mean, and sometimes did mean, a policy favouring the strong, the energetic, the enterprising, and disadvantageous to the weak, the

---

[93] 4 H.L.C. 144, 10 E.R. 417.

ignorant, and the foolish. It also meant, especially when combined with an unwillingness to look too closely into the reality of the mutual assent that founded a contract, a policy favouring companies and organizations whose contracts were made on printed forms. The standard form contract received, in effect, a judicial blessing. And that result was not long in becoming apparent. In *Scott* v. *Avery*,[94] only three years later, the House of Lords was called upon to decide on the validity of an arbitration clause in an insurance policy. It had previously been held that an arbitration clause did not preclude an action upon a contract, on the ground that the jurisdiction of the Courts could not be ousted by the mere agreement of private parties. It was the law which gave a right of action, and in the eighteenth century, an attempt to oust the jurisdiction of the Courts would have seemed as absurd as an attempt to oust the jurisdiction of Parliament. But in *Scott* v. *Avery* the contract had adopted a slightly different form of wording—it had provided that an arbitration award was to be a condition precedent to a right of action on the policy—and the House of Lords seized upon this technicality to overrule or, technically, to distinguish the previous decisions. Martin B., dissenting, argued that this distinction was the barest evasion, since all arbitration clauses, however worded, were intended to replace the Courts as the forum for solving disputes. But these objections were brushed aside, and in so far as policy was discussed at all, it was made quite clear that the policy was now in favour of the widest liberty of contracting. The older cases were 'directly contrary to the spirit of later times, which leaves parties at full liberty to refer their disputes at pleasure to public or private tribunals'.[95]

By 1870 the Courts had not only adopted the principle of freedom of contract but had extended it to its highest point. The remarks of Jessel M.R. in a case in 1875 are so often quoted, even in modern textbooks, that it is worth remembering that the opinions of the political economists on which freedom of contract had been so firmly established, were already beginning to change significantly by this time. So, too, was much political opinion, as we shall see later. But in the Courts, opinion was still firm in favour of freedom of contract. This is what Jessel M.R. said:

If there is one thing which more than another public policy requires, it is that men of full and competent understanding shall have the utmost liberty of contracting, and that their contracts when entered into freely and voluntarily shall be held sacred and shall be enforced by courts of justice. Therefore you have this paramount public policy to consider in that you are not lightly to interfere with this freedom of contract.[96]

[94] (1856) 5 H.L.C. 810, 10 E.R. 1121.   [95] Coleridge J., 5 H.L.C. 843, 10 E.R. 1134.

[96] *Printing and Numerical Co.* v. *Sampson* (1875) L.R. 19 Eq. at 465. Jessel was born in 1824, the son of a substantial Jewish merchant. It would not be surprising if he was brought up on Ricardo's *Principles*.

It is not often recalled that Jessel said very much the same thing in another decision, concerning moneylending—a decision which shocks the modern conscience, and indeed, probably shocked the conscience of many at the time. In this case Jessel M.R. upheld a moneylending transaction entered into at rates of 60 per cent by a man who had ample assets, but who was plainly an alcoholic.

I will assume him to have been a drunkard [said Jessel], a man who has had delirium tremens may recover and take a very strong dose [i.e., an antidote] and be able to write very firmly. A man may agree to pay 100 per cent if he chooses. There is no reason why a man should not be a fool. A man is allowed by law to be a fool if he likes. Suppose [the deceased] had gambled on the Stock Exchange, or at a gaming table, or had spent his substance in debauchery. A man may be a foolish man to do that, but still the law does not prevent him from being a fool.[97]

Thus far had the idea of freedom of contract reached in 1876. However, this has carried us beyond our immediate period to which we must now return.

THE RISE OF FORMALISM AND THE DECLINE OF EQUITY

As the Courts increasingly eschewed overt dicussion of policy questions, a number of closely allied developments occurred. One of the most significant of these was the rise of 'formalism'. This concept is well known in American legal literature, where it is relatively easy to explain its significance by contrasting it with the concept of 'realism' which eventually supplanted it. But English law has never had a realist revolution, and it is less easy to explain to an English reader precisely what was involved in the idea of formalism. Formalism really represents an attitude of mind rather than anything else; the attitude is that of the judge who believes that all law is based on legal doctrine and principles which can be deduced from precedents; that there is only one 'correct' way of deciding a case; that it is not the function of the judge to invoke policy considerations, or even arguments about the relative justice of the parties' claims; that the reasons behind principles and rules are irrelevant; that the role of the judge is purely passive and interpretive; that law is a science of principles, and so on. So far as contract law in particular was concerned, this concept of the judicial role played a vital part in the development of the law during the period 1770–1870, especially the latter part. It is, for example, possible to see formalism as affecting the following ideas, all of which came to be of importance in this period.

[97] *Bennet* v. *Bennet* (1876) 43 L.T. 246n., 247. Observe how Jessel completely equates the executory promise to pay interest with the actual loss incurred by gambling transactions.

First, the idea that it is for the parties to make their own contract, and to select their own terms, and not for the Courts to interfere in this process. Secondly, the idea that the effect of a contract once made is, again, not for the Courts to determine in any active sense. The Court's function is purely passive and interpretive; the Court must determine what the contract means, to be sure, but in doing so it is only giving effect to the intentions of the parties. Thirdly, generally speaking the process of formalism was combined with a tendency to 'literalism', that is, a refusal to read into the contract anything which the parties had not expressly provided for, and an insistence that implications could only be made when absolutely necessary to make the contract workable. Fourthly, formalism meant that the Courts basically disclaimed any power or right to 'interfere' in order to achieve a just result. The justice of the contract, the fairness of a bargain, was, indeed, not a matter which concerned the Court at all. It was for the parties to choose their own terms and make their own bargains, and if one chose skilfully while the other chose foolishly, this was merely the working of the free market system. A fifth identifiable feature of formalism was the tendency to construe rights in absolute terms. The Courts were unwilling to examine what motivated a contracting party to act in any particular manner. If a buyer of goods, for example, had a right to reject the goods because the seller delivered them one day late, the buyer's rights would be scrupulously insisted upon without pausing to inquire into why he had chosen to reject the goods. It was not for the Court to judge why a man exercised his rights in a particular manner, for that was the prerogative of the right-holder alone.

I shall shortly be examining these and other developments more closely in relation to the case law which developed during the period 1770 to 1870. Here I wish merely to draw attention to the close relationship between these developments, and the background to the law which I have already described. Plainly, the growth of formalism was closely related to the ideas of the political economists and to the rise of the market economy.

The Courts began to take for granted a certain 'natural' background of law (which they did not conceive of as interference at all) and this background was virtually the same as that assumed by the political economists. It was the background in which property rights were secured, and contracts were enforced. Rules designed for these purposes were not thought of as policy-oriented rules, but as 'purely legal'. And as Horwitz has said, 'What came to be certified as purely "legal", of course were those rules of law that had been established . . . to implement a market regime.'[98] It is, of course, possible to see a sinister, or even Marxist

[98] Morton Horwitz, 'The Rise of Legal Formalism', 19 *American J. of Legal Hist.* 251, 256–7.

interpretation to all this. The new formalism gave the impression that the laws of contract, like the laws of political economy, were inexorable deductions drawn from neutral principles, while in reality they were no doubt broadly in the interests of the new commercial and industrial classes. Nevertheless, it is too simplistic to see this whole process in class terms. English judges almost certainly believed their own dogmas. Moreover, they were never wholly successful in creating this new body of value-free law, for they were engaged upon an impossible exercise. Questions of justice and questions of policy would keep arising; and when they did so, the actual decisions of the Courts by no means betrayed a uniform class bias. There are, moreover, good reasons for believing that the growth of formalism was linked with a number of other developments which cannot be simply explained in class terms.

One of the other developments, whose importance has never yet been adequately evaluated, was undoubtedly the growing pressure on the Courts arising from the vast increases in population and commercial activity.[99] Until the creation of the County Courts in 1846 there were (it must be remembered) only fifteen common law judges in the entire country; and even though the County Courts did relieve the superior Courts of a substantial quantity of minor debt-collecting business, their jurisdiction was, for many years, limited to the very smallest sums. Combined with this pressure on the Courts was the growing distrust of the jury system. The Common Law Commissioners of 1852–3 expressed a good deal of disquiet with the jury as a mode of civil trial. Juries were slow, and in some cases, simply inadequate to cope with (for instance) complex accounting issues

[W]e are not at all blind to the fact [said the Commissioners, with a refreshing bluntness which would be unthinkable today] that in many instances juries are not so constituted as to ensure such an average amount of intelligence as might be desired; . . . in the agricultural districts the common juries are sometimes composed of a class of persons whose intelligence by no means qualifies them for the due discharge of judicial functions. Such persons, unaccustomed to severe intellectual exercise or to protracted thought . . . sometimes pronounce verdicts which bring the institution of juries into disrepect.[1]

Of course the unreliability of juries can also be interpreted as a nuisance to the needs of the new industrial and commercial classes. Unreliability meant unpredictability, and predictability was an important requirement of the rational, calculating world of commercial men. But there was another side to this. Juries were not only unpredictable;

---

[99] In 1837, at the beginning of Victoria's reign, 300 cases awaited argument in *banc* before the Queen's Bench and 859 in Chancery: Bowen, 'Progress in the Administration of Justice during the Victorian Period' in *Select Essays*, i. 523, 528.

[1] (1852–3) H.C. *Parliamentary Papers*, xl. 701, 708.

they were slow, and the more factual issues which were submitted to them for trial, the more the judicial system would have been congested and unable to cope with the rising tide of cases. It is against this background that one must also see the rise of formalism and literalism. These new approaches gave the Courts much greater control of cases by emphasizing the legal issues and ignoring, or treating as irrelevant, many factual issues. When, for instance, judges held contractual rights to be absolute, to be exercisable at the sole whim of the holder, they were eliminating from relevance highly difficult factual questions. To take the example given above, the refusal to inquire into the motives of a buyer who rejected goods delivered fractionally too late, eliminated all inquiry into the factual issues which would otherwise have arisen into the buyer's motives. The issues became purely legal questions for the judges to settle: did the buyer have the right or did he not? A very large number of rules of nineteenth-century origin which are of this general character appear unjust to the modern lawyer, who wants to inquire into the facts in more detail. The very emphasis, in nineteenth-century contract law, on the pre-eminence of free choice, frequently ruled out factual issues which to the modern lawyer (or even layman) may seem of great importance, for example, why did one party insist on this clause in the contract? Why did this or that party refuse to perform? What did the parties actually intend by what they said? Why did this party refuse to accept the other party's offer? Did this party actually rely on the other party's promise? Did that party receive any actual benefit from the other party's performance? And so on. If all these important factual issues had been litigated out in the nineteenth century, they would have been decisions for the jury; moreover, many of them would have been factual issues as to motives for action, which are issues that often require a great deal of difficult evidence for their resolution. Given the pressures on the Courts, it is not surprising if the judges often seemed to go out of their way to turn potentially factual issues into legal ones. 'At the height of the classical period', says Grant Gilmore, with pardonable exaggeration, 'it seemed that it was hardly possible to phrase any contract issue other than as a question of law.'[2]

One particular area in which the Courts tended not to inquire too closely into the facts aroused the wrath of Bentham. This was the area of bankruptcy and insolvency law. As we have seen, the law relating to the enforcement of debts was in an appalling state in 1770, and it was no better in 1830. Part of the problem, as Bentham insisted, was undoubtedly

---

[2] *The Death of Contract* (Colombus, Ohio, 1974), p. 99. Even in Equity where there was no jury problem, there is evidence of this same tendency to eliminate factual inquiry in some cases, e.g. where a trustee purchased or otherwise profited from use of trust property, no inquiry was permitted into the fairness of the transaction. Here again modern judges have felt unhappy at this approach. See, e.g., *Boardman* v. *Phipps* [1967] 2 A.C. 46.

due to the lack of inquiry into the facts. *Why* had the debtor failed to pay his debt? Was it because he was unable to pay or merely because he was unwilling to pay? How did he become indebted in the first place? Was it a case of fraud or a case of misadventure? Did the debtor deserve to be punished, or was it a case where he had become indebted through no real fault of his own? 'To all these distinctions', protested Bentham, 'under the guidance of Judge & Co., existing law inexorably shuts her eyes. Why? Because . . . to make these distinctions it would be necessary for the judge to hear evidence—to hear evidence from the best source, in the best shape, and at the properest time;—against all of which he sits resolved.'[3] In this particular instance, the failure to inquire into the facts was of long standing, and cannot be put down to nineteenth-century ideas, or to the role of juries. But the same story occurs again and again long after the reform of the law of bankruptcy and debt.

Closely allied with this development was the importance (as we have seen previously) of the concept of principle at this time. The rule-utilitarianism which (if not by that name) largely pervaded the legal system after the 1830s, made the civil law of this period profoundly different from that which preceded it, as well as from that which succeeded it, and which is in operation today. The difference is reflected in two closely connected points. The first was the tendency to search for fixed principles which would govern large numbers of cases without too close an inquiry into the facts, and with the danger, therefore, that the individual decision might be (or anyhow, might seem) hard and perhaps even unjust. And the second was the tendency for the Courts to regard the deterrent or hortatory functions of the law as much more important than the dispute-settlement function. Both these aspects of mid-nineteenth century law tended to stress the long-term effects, the educational and precedential value, of legal decisions. If an action was brought, for instance, on an executory contract, judges were less likely to ask whether the plaintiff had actually relied on the promise, and more likely to ask about the general tendency of promises to be relied upon, and about the effect their decision would be likely to have as a precedent in the future. To insist that promises were binding in principle because of the tendency of people to rely upon them (even though no actual reliance might have occurred in the instant case) was thus doubly desirable. It turned the question at issue into one of law for the judges, and it spelled out a clear educational message both for the populace and for future judges.

The growth of formalism coincided with the decline of Equity—in both senses of the term. The Court of Chancery itself went into a period of decline towards the beginning of this period from which it never wholly recovered. Partly, if not chiefly, this decline was due to the purely

---

[3] *Introductory View to the Rationale of Evidence*, Appendix B, in *Works*, ed. Bowring, vi. 182.

fortuitous nature of Lord Eldon's disposition. Eldon's unwillingness to come to a final decision, his tendency to procrastinate endlessly, had, during his twenty-five year tenure of the Great Seal, combined with the growth of business in the Courts generally, to bring the work of the Chancery almost to a grinding halt. But even after Eldon quitted the scene, the situation did not greatly improve. A Vice-Chancellor was created to join the Master of the Rolls and the Lord Chancellor as regular judges of the Court, and Brougham in his four years' tenure of office did much to clear off the arrears. But (as we have noted already) in 1837 there were no fewer than 859 cases set down for hearing, and many of these had been waiting for several years. In 1839, Mr. George Spence, a leading writer and practitioner in the Chancery Court, declared with all seriousness that 'No man, as things now stand can enter into a Chancery suit with any reasonable hope of being alive at its termination if he has a determined adversary.'[4] A decade later things had not improved very much. A House of Commons Select Committee on the Law of Partnership in 1851 was told by Mr. Commissioner Fane of the Bankruptcy Court that it was, in practice, almost impossible to get a decision from the Chancery Court on a disputed question concerning partnership accounts. When a member of the Committee asked if this meant that one partner could be robbed by another without any possibility of obtaining redress, the Commissioner agreed that that was so.[5]

Eventually things did improve, a second Vice-Chancellor was created, the bankruptcy jurisdiction was transferred to a new Court, a separate Court of Appeal for Chancery cases was established, the administrative procedure of the Court was improved. On the other hand the relative status of Equity and common law was affected by the virtual withdrawal of the Lord Chancellors from the Court of Chancery in mid-century. Thus by the time the first Judicature Act was passed in 1873 Equity had been severely crippled by nearly a hundred years of decline.

But it was not only the Court of Chancery which had declined. It was the very concept of equity itself—equity as a form of mercy, to be applied in a vaguely discretionary manner to temper the strict letter of the law, but co-existing with, rather than replacing the law in the generality of cases. We saw earlier how this notion of equity was still of great importance throughout most of the eighteenth century, influencing not only the civil law, but also the criminal law. By mid-nineteenth century, these ideas had all undergone the most profound change. In the criminal law, Beccaria's ideas, taken over and propagated in England by

---

[4] Cited in Bowen, 'Progress in the Administration of Justice during the Victorian Period', p. 529.
[5] *Report* of the Select Committee on Partnership Law, (1851) H.C. *Parliamentary Papers*, xviii. 1, 85-7.

Romilly and Bentham, had finally triumphed. The idea of passing capital sentences for every trivial offence, and then mitigating the results by widespread use of the prerogative of pardon, had disappeared. The number of capital crimes was enormously reduced, and the use of the pardon correspondingly diminished. Indeed, although the prerogative of pardon continued to be used in the remaining capital cases, the very idea of interference with the due course of law came to be seen as somewhat undesirable.[6]

Similarly, the civil law was profoundly affected by these ideas, as Equity hardened into a set of principles as rigid as those of the common law. In the law of contract, as we shall see, all the old equitable rules about penalties, forfeitures, mortgages, and unconscionable contrasts were whittled away, and some of them were almost entirely forgotten. In the first edition of his *Principles of Contract* in 1876, Pollock lamented that writers on the law of contract had been confining themselves (save for very brief allusions) to the common law, leaving the rest to be sought in books on Equity.

So, too, the decline of the jury in common law actions tended to eliminate a source of vaguely discretionary mercy. Even where the jury remained as the tribunal of fact, the common law Courts began increasingly to direct the juries on the proper performance of their duties. Questions concerning damages, for example, which had previously been almost entirely within the province of the jury, began to come increasingly under judicial control.

I must now return to the point made above about the importance of the long-term effects of judicial decisions. It is scarcely possible to exaggerate the difference of attitude on this point between that of a judge of the mid-nineteenth century, and that of the judge of today. The judge of 1850 was much more concerned, even in civil law, with the influence of his decision on the behaviour of people in the future. The long-run effects of all law, the civil law as well as the criminal law, were regarded as more important than the task of doing justice in the individual case. It was not possible to examine every individual case with the necessary detail to see that perfect justice was done. Principles were what mattered; if the right principles were selected, they had to be applied in the belief that their general tendency would be to produce justice overall, even though in the case in hand, the result might seem harsh. Legal decisions could not be looked at in isolation to determine the fairest or most just solution in the particular circumstances; every decision had to be looked

[6] In 1822, concerning a petition for mercy on behalf of a poacher sentenced to death for wounding a gamekeeper, Lord Palmerston wrote that 'The capricious remission of punishment out of regard to private favor and personal affection was one of the great abuses of prerogative complained of at the period of the Revolution and provided against by the Bill of Rights.' Jasper Ridley, *Lord Palmerston*, pp. 109–10.

at in the overall social context. From this perspective, even harsh decisions had a role to play in educating people how to behave. Those who took a long view, and who had great confidence in the 'laws' of political economy or radical utilitarianism, could always reconcile themselves to the harshness of a particular decision by reflecting that in the long run the good results might outweigh the bad. Parke B., it was often said, was a great stickler for the procedural technicalities of the time, and seemed to take a positive delight in nonsuiting a plaintiff for a badly drawn declaration. If there is truth in this, it is reasonable to suppose (given what we know of Parke B.'s predilections) that he thought that by these means lawyers would be taught to draw their pleadings more carefully. True, the immediate penalty was inflicted on the unfortunate client and not the barrister; but the lesson would not go unobserved. This client would be unlikely to use the same barrister again; and his professional reputation might suffer a general decline. Thus the apparent hardness of the decision could be justified by these long-run advantages, in the same way that high prices in times of shortages were justified by the need to encourage suppliers to increase their production. Even a relatively sophisticated theory of justice, like that offered by John Stuart Mill in his *Utilitarianism*, rested upon an identification of long-term utility with justice.

In modern times this long-term deterrent or hortatory aspect of the law has almost entirely disappeared from the civil law and has greatly waned even in the criminal law. It is a very widely held point of view that in civil cases, the principal function of the Court is to do justice in the circumstances of the case, and that the civil law is not concerned to influence the behaviour of the public in future cases. The whole spectrum of civil law—from the law of contract to tort, to matrimonial law, to company law—has been most profoundly affected by this change in attitude. In matrimonial law, it used to be widely believed that the law was an important influence on the behaviour of spouses, so that, for instance, if divorce was difficult, spouses would make a greater effort to live together in mutual harmony; or that if a man could not marry his deceased wife's sister, he and the sister would be less likely to have an illicit love affair, or that, if a woman who committed adultery was not allowed to have the custody of her children, she would be less likely to commit adultery. Similarly, in tort actions, it used to be thought that liability for negligence would encourage people to behave more carefully, that the rules of contributory negligence would encourage people to take greater care for their own safety, and so on.

Now in the mid-nineteenth century, the belief in the long-term, deterrent, or hortatory effects of the law of contract, were still very important. It was widely believed that the chief functions of the law of contract were to encourage people to keep their promises and pay their debts. Even a forward-looking person like John Stuart Mill protested against the idea that the task of the law was merely to pick up the pieces after a dispute. Discussing the reform of the insolvency laws, he said that:

[T]he doctrine, that the law has done all that ought to be expected from it, when it has put the creditors in possession of the property of an insolvent, is in itself a totally inadmissible piece of spurious humanity. It is the business of law to prevent wrong-doing and not simply to patch up the consequences of it, when it has been committed.[7]

There were, moreover, good reasons for the belief that the law needed to use every weapon in its arsenal to encourage compliance, though perhaps there was less reason for the confidence that these weapons actually worked. The need for them arose, in part, from the general lack of order and social discipline in commercial affairs, from the simple matter of payment of debts to the more complex business of the keeping of proper accounts by large corporations. In a modern, ordered, and reasonably disciplined society we take it for granted that responsible organizations, such as public authorities, large and even small commercial concerns, professional people and their firms, and probably also a substantial majority of ordinary individuals, will comply with their civil obligations, payment of debts, and performance of contracts, as a matter of course. There are, of course, genuine disputes as to the existence or extent of obligations in particular cases, and there are also genuine mistakes, oversights, and unexpected events which result in performance being overlooked, or neglected or deferred, though these too are less frequent the more orderly and disciplined the society is. But in less orderly societies (such as England in say, 1830, or most African countries today) things are very different. First, the oversights and mistakes are far more frequent, because records are not well kept, clerical staff are less well trained, and often more hard-pressed, and interrupted by personal importunities of 'favoured' or 'privileged' clients who must be given priority. And secondly, deliberate prevarication leads readily enough to deliberate non-performance. Indeed, the difference between these is very slim where the consequences of non-performance are not severe and prompt. If people hope that a problem will 'go away' it may do just that if the judicial remedies are not adequate.

It is against this sort of background that the law of the mid-nineteenth century must be understood. Adherence to principle was the important thing, even though, here and there, the results might seem harsh, or unjust. After all, the competitive system of society itself rested on this belief. Bramwell once gave voice very bluntly to this point, stressing the

---

[7] *Principles*, Book V, Chapter IX, Sect. 8.

sheer incapacity of the law to cope with every individual case. In an address to the British Association in 1888,[8] he argued in his usual manner, that society would prosper best if every one was left alone to pursue his own interests as skilfully and energetically as he could. He then added this:

If it is said that poverty and misery may exist without fault in the sufferer, it is true. But it is but rarely that they do, and the law cannot discriminate such cases.[9]

Probably by 1888, Bramwell was expressing a minority viewpoint, for more and more people were demanding that the law *should* discriminate, and that if it could not, the whole system must be reformed. But in the period 1770–1870, this view of Bramwell's would surely have commanded general assent.

[8] *Economics and Socialism*, published by the Liberty and Property Defence League, 1888.
[9] Ibid., p. 13.

14

FREEDOM OF CONTRACT IN THE COURTS, 1770–1870—I

CONTRACT LAW AND THE FREE MARKET

THE period 1770–1870 saw the emergence of general principles of contract law closely associated with the development of the free market and the ideals of the political economists. The period saw the shift in emphasis from property law to contract; and within the realm of contract it saw the shift from particular relationships, or particular types of contract, to general principles of contract, and the shift from executed to executory contracts. The first requirement of the lawyers in this new age was for a new kind of literature. They needed books which treated contract law as a whole, which enunciated general principles of contract law, and illustrated the application of these general principles to the solution of particular problems. The existing literature lacked the necessary generality, it emphasized procedure rather than substance, and it also lacked simple clarity let alone any literary grace.[1]

I have already mentioned J. J. Powell's *Essay upon the Law of Contracts and Agreements* which was first published in 1790, and which attempted to fill this gap. There was no doubt of Powell's liking for principles. He saw his book as a search for principle. Contracts were about a variety of relationships (mostly, in his view, dealing with property) but still, 'however different the objects, the contracts respecting them must uniformly be determined by the principles of natural or civil equity'.[2] He goes on to stress, in the manner of the age, that 'All reasoning must be founded on first principles. The science of the law derives its principles either from that artificial system which was incidental to the introduction of feuds [that is, the feudal system] or from the science of morals.'[3] Here, too, we see the beginnings of the new hostility to Equity. True, he admits, the law may need minor changes to adapt it and keep it up to date. 'But', he continues, 'it is absolutely necessary for the advantage of the public at large, that the rights should, when agitated in a Court of Law, depend upon certain and fixed principles of law and not upon rules and constructions of equity, which when applied there, must be arbitrary and

---

[1] See A. B. W. Simpson, 'Innovation in Nineteenth Century Contract Law', 91 *Law Q. Rev.* 247, 251–2 (1975).

[2] Preface, p. iii.

[3] Ibid., p. v.

uncertain, depending in the extent of their application upon the will and caprice of the judge.'[4]

We shall see later how Powell's *Essay*, coming so early in this period of change, still does not reflect the full maturity of the new contract law with its focus on executory contract, intention, and will theory. But Powell was only the first of a long line. His book was followed by the works of Chitty (1826), Addison (1847), and later Leake (1867), Pollock (1875), and Anson (1879). The last two fall into the next period of this study, and Leake's book, coming almost at the end of the present period, was hardly able to exert much influence before 1870. It was, nevertheless, as we shall see, particularly influential on one point—that is, in helping to establish the distinction between implied and quasi-contracts. But in some ways, more influential than the early English authors (partly because they drew upon it) was the English translation of Pothier's *Law of Obligations* which appeared in two volumes in 1806.[5] One of the reasons for Pothier's great influence in English law was that he had written his book for the express purpose of providing those general principles of Contract law which modern English lawyers were particularly looking for. Pothier had written especially to provide a uniform body of general principles which could be applied across France and could replace the mass of local, customary law, which still hindered the institutional and cultural unity of France. In his *Éloge* in the first volume, the King's Advocate had lamented that French law was almost entirely positive and arbitrary, and that 'reason has scarcely any influence in the establishment of principles'.[6] These words were echoed by the translator, an English barrister named Evans, who stressed the importance of general jurisprudence, and welcomed the signs of renewed interest in Roman law. There is no doubt that the influence of Pothier's book was considerable.[7] It was welcomed as being of the highest authority by English lawyers and both Byles J. (in his book on *Bills of Exchange*) and Best C.J. went out of their way to pay tribute to Pothier's learning as well as to emphasize that his book could be treated as authoritative in England.[8] In 1887 Kekewich J. noted in *Foster* v. *Wheeler*[9] that the definitions of contract in the textbooks were all founded on Pothier's own definition.

Pothier, far more than Powell, was the person who first gave expression to the notion that a contract is primarily an agreement based on the intention of the parties, and that it is their will which creates the legal

[4] Ibid., p. x.

[5] First published in French in 1761–4.　　　[6] i. 17.

[7] Sir William Jones in his *Essay on Bailments* (London, 1781) at p. 9 had first drawn the attention of English lawyers to Pothier's works, and exhorted them to 'read them again and again'.

[8] See *Cox* v. *Troy* (1822) 5 B. & A. 474, 481, 106 E. R. 1264, 1266.

[9] (1887) 36 Ch. D. 695, 698.

obligation—essentially the theory of contractual liability which passed into English law, and has remained there ever since. The subsequent English authors were all more or less influenced by Pothier's approach, as well, of course, as by the growing signs of its acceptance in the English Courts. The central idea that characterized all these writings was the *generality* of contract law, the fact that it could be stated at a high level of abstraction, and that the law applied indifferently to all kinds of contracts irrespective of the subject-matter. Addison, for instance, in the Preface to the first edition of his *Treatise*, published in 1847, protests that contract law is not 'a mere collection of positive rules', but is founded upon 'the broad and general principles of universal law.' Indeed, he goes further, and insists that it is not only English law which can be generalized. 'The law of contracts may justly indeed be said to be a universal law adapted to all times and races, and all places and circumstances, being founded upon those great and fundamental principles of right and wrong deduced from natural reason which are immutable and eternal.' Here, indeed, was a set of principles to match the principles of Political Economy! By the time of Leake's book, published in 1867, it was possible for a book to be written exclusively on the general principles of contract law, and without discussion of particular types of contract. Leake claimed that as a virtue for his book; it was, he wrote in his Preface, concerned only with 'the law of contracts in its general and abstract form apart from its specific practical applications'.

There seems no doubt that all this generality, this attempt to state the law in terms of abstract principle, fitted well with the new political economy. It was a law suited to the free market, in which the subject matter of the contract was immaterial. During the course of this century, that is between 1770 and 1870, this general law of contract did very largely create a body of rules applicable to all contracts alike. To take two extremes, on the one hand, there was the law concerning land— land, which in the eighteenth century had been the foundation of social position and political power, became in the nineteenth century a commodity, just like any other. The notion which Littledale J. expressed in 1829, that it was contrary to public policy for a buyer of land to resell it before he gained possession, largely gave way, for example, to the notion that land could be bought and sold like any other commodity. In 1877 this new philosophy was expressed by Bacon V.C. in *Noble* v. *Edwards*[10] in which the plaintiff contracted to buy some land for £21,000 and then resold it, before obtaining a conveyance, for £33,000: 'A man', he said, 'who speculates in land means always to get as much profit from it as he can. If, by his superior skill, he foresees that he can make an advantageous profit by working, cultivating, and improving a farm,

[10] (1877) 5 Ch.D. 378.

certainly if it is worth his while he can do that, and it would be quite worth the while of anybody buying from him to pay him whatever in their respective judgments, the land is worth, without considering what the then vendor gave for it himself. What is more common? It is everyday practice in this court.'[11] The Court of Appeal reversed this decision on technical grounds, but nobody doubted the new commercial attitude to land.

At the other extreme, we may take a matrimonial agreement as an example of a contract of an entirely different social character. Yet here, too, the abstract law of the market place came to be applied by the Courts, although some of the judges had qualms at the result. In *Hall* v. *Wright*,[12] the plaintiff brought an action for breach of promise of marriage against the defendant who admitted that he had promised to marry her, but pleaded that he had since become severely ill, so that he was (he claimed) incapable of marriage. The Court of Queen's Bench and the Exchequer Chamber were divided but the majority found in the end for the plaintiff. The Appeal Court's decision turned quite plainly on the argument of the defendant's counsel that a contract of marriage was a peculiar sort of contract which deserved to be treated differently from other contracts. The majority rejected this argument: the defendant had contracted to marry, and the risk of being unable to carry out that promise was on him. Pollock C.B.'s argument that a contract to marry could not be placed on the same footing as a bargain for a horse or a bale of goods was brushed aside. It was this same Pollock C.B., it will be remembered, who had argued for a different view of public policy in *Egerton* v. *Brownlow*,[13] and there are grounds for thinking that he may have been closer to public and parliamentary opinion than his colleagues both on that and on this issue. By 1879 the House of Commons expressed approval of a proposal to abolish actions for breach of promise of marriage (except where actual pecuniary loss was proved)[14] though in fact no such reform was carried out until 1970. But in the Courts, matrimonial contracts were now, and remained for many years, subject to the general law of the market. As late as 1929 Lord Atkin, generally considered a forward looking judge in his day, said, in relation to a separation deed, that 'there is no caste in contracts. Agreements for separation are formed, construed and dissolved and to be enforced on

---

[11] At p. 390. See also *Smith* v. *Hughes* (1867) L.R. 6 Q.B. 597, 604.

[12] (1858) E.Bl. & E. 746, 120 E.R. 688; (1860) E.Bl. & E. 765, 120 E.R. 695. See too *Beachey* v. *Brown* (1860) E.Bl. & E. 796, 120 E.R. 706, where it was held that a woman who accepted a man's proposal of marriage was not bound to disclose that she was then engaged to be married to another man.

[13] (1853) 4 H.L.C. 1, 10 E.R. 359; *supra*, p. 385.

[14] See White, 'Breach of Promise of Marriage', 10 *Law Q. Rev.* 125 (1894).

precisely the same principles as any respectable commercial agreement, of whose nature indeed, they sometimes partake.'[15]

This emphasis on contract law as the law of the market was, in England at least, well established by 1870, although in America it may have been a later development.[16] One of its principle characteristics was its abstractness, its lack of particularity, its attempt to treat all contracts as being of the same general character. 'This abstraction', it has been said by an American scholar of the parallel development in the United States,

is not what people think of when they criticise the law as being too abstract, implying that the law is hypertechnical or unrealistic (though often it is). The abstraction of classical contract law is not unrealistic; it is a deliberate renunciation of the particular, a deliberate relinquishment of the temptation to restrict untrammeled individual autonomy or the completely free market in the name of social policy.[17]

Some have, indeed, seen a positive virtue, a sign of judicial impartiality, in this abstract application of the law of the market place. The emphasis on the fixed rules of contract law, the emphasis on the abstract nature of these rules and of their applicability to all people and all subject-matter alike, has been treated as part of the very nature of certain and predictable rules as opposed to more flexible, but more unpredictable discretionary justice.[18] The rule of the market place is thus equated with the Rule of Law itself. Whatever may be thought of the value-judgments implicit in such an equation in the modern world, there seems little doubt that historically the equation is correct. I have previously referred to the importance of the Rule of Law in the eighteenth century as providing that necessary framework of predictability for the operation of a market economy.

In general terms, this equation of general principles of contract law with the free market economy led to an emphasis on the framework within which individuals bargained with each other, and a retreat from interest in substantive justice or fairness. The model of contract theory which implicitly underlay the classical law of contract—for such we may now call it—was thus the model of the market. Essentially this model is based on the following principal features. First, the parties deal with each other 'at arm's length' in the legal phrase;[19] this carries the notion

[15] *Hyman* v. *Hyman* [1929] A.C. 601, 625–6. Yet all separation agreements are necessarily bilateral monopolies.

[16] Grant Gilmore, in *The Death of Contract*, treats this development as dating from the publication of Langdell's *Casebook on Contract* in 1871. But despite his references to some English authorities it is clear that Gilmore is thinking primarily of American law.

[17] L. Friedman, *Contract Law in America* (Madison and Milwaukee, 1965), pp. 20–1.

[18] See, e.g., F. A. Hayek, *The Road to Serfdom* (Chicago, 1944), pp. 73, 101.

[19] The *O.E.D.* gives the earliest usage of this phrase as 1858 in Lord St Leonards' *Handy Book of Property Law*; but it is used by Lord Eldon in *Turner* v. *Harvey* (1821) Jacob 168, 178, 37 E.R. 814, 817–18.

that each relies on his own skill and judgment, and that neither owes any
fiduciary obligation to the other. In the market place, no man is his
brother's keeper. Secondly, the parties bargain or negotiate, they higgle
over the price and terms of the deal. Offers are made, accepted, rejected,
or met by counter-offers. Prior to acceptance, offers can be revoked, even
though relied upon. Neither party owes any duty to the other until a deal
is struck, hence silence is not binding even where a reply might be
expected. Third, neither party owes any duty to volunteer information
to the other, nor is he entitled to rely on the other except within the
narrowest possible limits. Each party must study the situation, examine
the subject-matter of the contract, and the general market situation,
assess the future probabilities, and rely on his own sources of information.
He may take advice, consult experts, buy information from third parties;
but if he does not do so, he relies on his own judgment and acts at his peril.
The only limitation to this market bargaining is that there must be no
fraud or misrepresentation, but even these concepts are narrowly
construed. Prima facie a man must rely on his own judgment, and not on
what the other party says in the normal process of negotiation. Only if
categorical statements of fact are made by one party is the other entitled
to rely upon them, and even then, his remedies may be limited if the
statement is not made fraudulently. Fourthly, the deal is finally struck
when the parties agree, or indicate their agreement. Mistakes and
subjective intentions are irrelevant unless they can be said to affect the
'free' and voluntary consent needed to reach agreement. The agreement
must be made 'freely' and without 'pressure' but these concepts are very
narrowly interpreted, for they must not conflict with the rule of the
market place; and in the market place pressures are themselves a normal
part of the scene. It is not these pressures, but only abnormal pressures,
wholly exceptional pressures, which can be said to affect a party's free
consent or free will and hence relieve him of his obligations. Fifthly, the
content of the contract, the terms and the price and the subject-matter,
are entirely for the parties to settle. It is assumed that the parties know
their own minds, that they are the best judges of their own needs and
circumstances, that they will calculate the risks and future contingencies
that are relevant, and that all these enter into the bargain. It follows that
unfairness of the bargain—gross inadequacy or excess of price—is
irrelevant, and that once made, the contract is binding. 'The common
lawyers hardly recognised the principle of fair dealing as one that needed
independent support. For them free dealing was fair dealing.'[20] Finally,
this bindingness is, in principle, a matter of pecuniary calculation. Each
party is bound; he must therefore perform, or pay damages for his failure
to perform.

[20] Devlin, *The Enforcement of Morals* (Oxford, 1965), p. 47.

The Court's function in all this is to ensure procedural fair play: the Court is the umpire to be appealed to when a foul is alleged, but the Court has no substantive function beyond this. It is not the Court's business to ensure that the bargain is fair, or to see that one party does not take undue advantage of another, or impose unreasonable terms by virtue of superior bargaining position. Any superiority in bargaining power is itself a matter for the market to rectify. If there is free competition in the market, mere size or skill should not in any case confer an undue advantage, since the forces of competition will ensure fairness in terms and prices. Nor is it the Court's business to create or impose obligations on anybody from its own sense of justice. It is the task of the parties to fix their liabilities themselves. A person is not to be liable for example, for a benefit received at the hands of another unless he has agreed to pay for it; there is scarcely any room for a law of quasi-contract in the market place. Nor, conversely, is there much room for the protection of reliance unless it has been expressly bargained for. If a party buys advice, for example, from a paid agent, then he is entitled to rely on that advice; or if he buys a warranty from a seller, he is entitled to rely upon the warranty. But unbargained-for reliance is at a man's own risk in the market place. The only justifiable way to protect such reliance is to bring it under the head of tort or Equity; but tort law and Equity, like quasi-contract, have a very limited role in the market place. Their task is the simple one of preventing force and violence and outright fraud.

This theoretical model of contract ideals came to underlie the general principles of contract law during the classical period. But three important qualifications need to be made to this if an accurate picture of the period is to be obtained. The first is that English judges have always been stronger in doing justice in a pragmatic fashion, than they have been in theoretical justifications for what they are doing. While the English judge's sense of justice had been to some degree conditioned by his acceptance of the ideals of a free market economy, there were occasions when it revolted and refused to abide by those ideals. Wherever the rule of the market place seemed to lead to results which outraged the judicial conscience, there was even in the classical period, always the chance that somehow substantive justice would be achieved, for example, by invoking Equity or by implying suitable terms in a contract, or by finding the facts in an appropriate way. The second qualification that needs to be made is to bear in mind the sheer force, at times, of precedent and legal doctrine. Occasions arose, even in the heyday of classical law, when older eighteenth-century principles were adhered to simply because of legal inertia, or the weight of precedent or the conservatism of the particular judges who happened to be hearing an important case. For example, the older rules with regard to the refusal of expectation damages in an action for the sale of land, and again the older rules as to the award of interest on overdue debts, were adhered to throughout the classical period, even though they accorded ill with the law of the market. And thirdly, we must bear in mind the statutory changes which were going on throughout the whole of this period. These changes I shall consider in detail in Chapter 16, but it must be appreciated that even while the common law of contract was gradually being converted into the law of the market place, statutory erosions of the freedom of the market were taking place. How were these new statutes to be reconciled with the principles of a contract law based on the free market? The answer was largely found in a semantic trick. Statutory changes were excluded from the emerging general law of contract by the simple process of definition. If a statute made particular provision for companies, or for passengers, or for factories, or for prohibiting the payment of wages in truck, or for the protection of the consumer, then these statutory changes were not part of the general law of contract. They were special rules, exceptional, anomalous, possibly justifiable (though the judges sometimes showed some scepticism even of that), but in any event, they were on no account to be allowed to influence cases to which they were not quite explicitly applied by Parliament. The parallel development in America has been well described by Friedman:

'Pure' contract is blind to details of subject matter and person. It does not ask who buys and who sells, and what is bought and sold. In the law of contract, it does not matter whether the subject of the contract is a goat, a horse, a carload of lumber, a stock certificate or a share. As soon as it matters—e.g., if the sale is of heroin, or of votes for governor, or of an 'E' Bond [non transferable U.S. Governments Bonds], or labor for twenty-five cents an hour—we are in one sense no longer talking pure contract. In the law of contract it does not matter if either party is a woman, a man, an Armenian-American, a corporation, the government, or a church. Again, as soon as it does matter—if one party is a minor, or if the transaction is one in which a small auto company sells out to General Motors, or if a seller of legal services happens to be a corporation instead of a partnership or individual—we are no longer talking pure contract. When the relationship of parties to land is treated as creating distinctive legal issues, simply because land is involved, this is land law or property law, but not contract.[21]

WILL THEORY AND THE AUTONOMY OF PRIVATE CONTRACT

One of the principal characteristics of classical contract theory was the tendency to attribute all the consequences of a contract to the will of those who made it. As I have already suggested, this was in a sense a

[21] L. Friedman, *Contract Law in America*, p. 20.

necessary consequence of the shift in emphasis from the part executed to the wholly executory contract. If liabilities were now to arise from the mere fact of the agreement, or an exchange of promises, and not as a result of anything that the parties actually did, it was easy to deduce that it was the mere will of the parties which created the obligations. This idea has proved so tenacious in English law that even the modern lawyer, accustomed as he is to the many derogations from freedom of contract today, still takes it for granted that contractual obligations are created by the will or the intention of the parties. The modern lawyer, still under the influence of the nineteenth-century heritage, sees little or no difference between saying that parties voluntarily enter into a transaction to which the law attributes certain consequences, and saying that the consequences themselves are the creation of the will of the parties. But in the early nineteenth century these ideas still had the attraction of novelty in English legal theory.

I need do no more now to trace the history of this theme than to recall that these ideas had been vigorously propagated by the Natural Lawyers, especially Grotius and Pufendorf, whose views were not unknown in eighteenth-century England, even though they did not find favour with Hume, Bentham, or (on this point) Adam Smith. Pothier, by contrast, was very much influenced by these ideas, and it seems probable that his book was one of the most important sources of their introduction into English law. From the time when the translation of Pothier's book first appeared, the 'will theory' of contractual obligation gained ground fast. The influence of Pothier's book can be gauged to some extent by a comparison between the state of contract theory to be found in Powell's *Essay* (which appeared in 1790) and the later books and cases of the nineteenth century.

In Powell's *Essay* there are marked signs of the growing influence of will theory, but it is also clear that the older eighteenth-century ideas have not yet been superseded. Powell talks, for example, a great deal about 'tacit agreements', a sure sign of will theory. He even attributes at one point the obligation to pay damages for breach of contract to 'one species of tacit agreement which runs through and is annexed to all contracts, conditions and covenants'.[22] Similarly, the attribution of a husband's liability for necessaries supplied to a deserted wife to the husband's tacit assent, as well as the idea that an illegal contract is void because 'it may be presumed that' the parties have not given their full and free assent [23] are extreme versions of will theory, even more extreme, in the case of illegal contracts, than nineteenth-century doctrine. On the other hand, Powell was still inclined to place invalidity resulting from

[22] *Essay*, i. 136–7.
[23] Ibid., p. 139.

duress on grounds of unfairness rather than defective assent.[24] Then we have the idea that fraud may render a contract not binding because 'the assent is yielded under an idea that the facts are strictly stated'.[25] Similarly, insanity and infancy are grounds for impeaching a contract because they are examples of lack of proper assent,[26] though Powell has a good deal of difficulty explaining why the dispositions of a lunatic are only voidable and not void.[27] We even get the argument that if the performance of a contract is rendered impossible by reason of subsequent Act of Parliament, the parties must be supposed to have consented under the tacit condition that the contract would continue to be legally performable[28]—a clear precursor to the 'implied term' theory of the doctrine of frustration which eventually emerged in the nineteenth century.

By the middle of the nineteenth century, will theory had taken root in English law. The somewhat mystical idea had gained acceptance that an obligation could be created by a communion of wills, an act of joint, if purely mental procreation. Even pragmatic English judges who have usually been strong on experience and weak on theory, began to talk in these terms.[29] In 1861 Kindersley V.C. referred to the creation of a contract in language strikingly similar to that found in Savigny's treatise on contracts (*Das Obligationenrecht*) published in 1853: 'When both parties will the same thing, and each communicates his will to the other, with a mutual agreement to carry it into effect, then an engagement or contract between the two is constituted.'[30]

By 1870 this sort of language was quite common, and in the first edition of his *Principles* in 1876, Pollock (who acknowledged his debt to Savigny) treated it as the basis of contractual liability. But it was too theoretical to last long, or to be taken too literally while it did last. The Courts continued indeed, to talk of contracts as created by, and depending on, the intention of the parties, but at the same time (as we shall see) they were busy objectivizing the methods of proving intent.[31] Intent was a verbal formula; the reality was external signs and manifestations of

<hr>

[24] Ibid., p. 165.

[25] Ibid., p. 140.

[26] Ibid., pp. 10–11.

[27] Ibid., pp. 14–20.

[28] Ibid., pp. 444–5. The argument can also be found in Paley, *Principles of Moral and Political Philosophy*, Book III, Chapter V.

[29] See, e.g., *Pole* v. *Leask* (1863) 33 L.J.Ch. 155, *post*, p. 497; *Dickinson* v. *Dodds* (1876) 2 Ch.D. 463, 472; *Cundy* v. *Lindsay* (1878) 3 App. Cas. 459, 465.

[30] *Haynes* v. *Haynes* (1869) 1 Dr. & Sm. 426, 433, 62 E.R. 442, 445. Compare the Rousseau-like language of Savigny (cited in Holland, *Jurisprudence* (Oxford, 1880), p. 190) who says there must be 'a union of several wills to a single whole and undivided will'.

[31] Of course there was nothing very new in this objective approach to intention in the law. Hume, in his *Enquiry into the Principles of Morals* (1751), Sect. III, Part II, treats this as well-established law, and suggests that giving effect to 'secret reservations' was a 'Jesuitical' or Catholic notion.

assent. Judges who took the talk of a meeting of the minds—a *consenus ad idem*—too seriously were put in their place by their colleagues.[32] In his third edition, Pollock relegated Savigny to an Appendix, and stressed the element of reliance, rather than 'the artificial equation of wills or intentions'. Even in an executory contract, where there was no actual reliance (or actual benefit), the basis of liability, Pollock now said, was that he who gives a promise 'has so expressed himself as to entitle the other party to rely on his acting in a certain way'.[33] Forty years later Pollock claimed to have treated the protection of reasonable expectations as the foundation of contractual liability, but the passage itself stresses reliance rather than mere expectation.[34]

The autonomy of the free choice of private parties to make their own contracts on their own terms was the central feature of classical contract law. Its influence is to be found in every corner of contract law, but I shall limit myself here to a number of key areas. It is necessary to stress at the outset that the importance attached to free choice, and to the idea that a contract was a vehicle for giving effect to the will of the parties, had a profound effect on the very functions of contract law, as it was perceived by the Courts. The primary function of the law came to be seen as purely facultative, and the function of the Court was merely to resolve a dispute by working out the implications of what the parties had already chosen to do. The idea that the Court had an independent role to play as a forum for the adjustment of rights, or the settlement of disputes, was plainly inconsistent with this new approach. The result was to mark off contract law more clearly from (say) the law of torts or the law of constructive trusts where the function of the law, and its agent, the Courts, was seen more clearly to be that of resolving a conflict, or adjusting mutual claims. The law of contract became like the law of wills, a device for enabling private individuals to make their own arrangements, and to summon the State to their aid to see that those arrangements were adhered to.

Freedom of Contract and Freedom of Trade

One area in which there was always difficulty concerned contracts in restraint of trade, agreements by employees or sellers of a business not to compete, or rings by which several businesses carved up a market, or agreed to fix prices. In all these cases the Courts were faced with the

---

[32] For example, Brett J. in *Brogden* v. *Metropolitan Rly. Co.* (1877) 2 App. Cas. 666; Bramwell B. in *British and American Telegraph Co.* v. *Colson* (1871) L.R. 6 Ex. 108. See too *Rumsey* v. *N.E. Rly. Co.* (1863) 14 C.B. (N.S.) 596 where it was held that a railway passenger who had intended to evade payment of a charge for his luggage, was bound to pay it on the ground of an 'implied assent'.

[33] *Principles of Contract*, 3rd edn. (1881) p. 1.

[34] *Pollock-Holmes Letters* (Cambridge, 1942), ii. 48. When pressed by Holmes, Pollock was inclined to give the credit for discovering the importance of reasonable expectations in contract law to Archbishop Whately (who had been Professor of Political Economy at Oxford, 1829–31): ibid., p. 54. Pollock seems to have quite overlooked the claims of Hume, Bentham, and Adam Smith.

fundamental dilemma that freedom of contract could be used to destroy freedom of trade, though it is not clear whether they really understood the nature of the problem. Throughout this period the Courts generally upheld partial and 'reasonable' restraints, while continuing to declare that they would not uphold general restraints. In practice, general restraints were rare, and the result was that in most of the cases to come before the Courts during this period, restrictive agreements were upheld. Apart from a case in 1808 where Lord Ellenborough protested about the 'tied house' leases, binding lessees to sell only beer supplied by the lessor,[35] the Courts generally appear to have looked with favour on restrictive agreements, so long as the restraints were not excessively or outrageously wide. An agreement between two coach operators to operate on different days of the week was held to be 'merely a convenient mode of arranging two concerns which might otherwise ruin each other';[36] an agreement by three manufacturers to divide the whole of the English market between them was held a mere partial restraint and enforceable;[37] an agreement publicly advertised, by a number of dyers, bleachers, and dressers that they would only accept goods on a general lien was upheld mainly (it seems) because the Court felt that it was perfectly reasonable for such parties to have a general lien anyhow;[38] and in general the Courts also inclined more favourably to covenants not to compete entered into by employees or vendors of business. This partly followed from the Court's newly declared unwillingness to investigate the adequacy of the consideration in such cases,[39] but probably also owed something to the greater belief in freedom of contract.[40]

In modern times restrictive agreements of all kinds are generally thought to give rise to possible conflicts between public and private interests; and we have seen too that this was an important feature of eighteenth-century law. The marketing offences, and the hostility to monopolies and conspiracies all involved recognition of this potential conflict, and eighteenth-century judges had not hesitated to invoke the public interest in order to condemn private agreeements of this character. But in the nineteenth century, and in particular after 1830 or thereabouts, a number of new factors entered upon the scene. The first perhaps was the growing acceptance of the *popular* version of political economy which was so widely thought to demonstrate that there was always a natural harmony between public and private interests. Now (as we have seen)

[35] *Cooper* v. *Twilbill* (1808) 3 Camp. 287n., 170 E.R. 1384.
[36] *Hearn* v. *Griffin* (1815) 2 Chit. 407.
[37] *Wickens* v. *Evans* (1829) 3 Y. & J. 318, 148 E.R. 1201.
[38] *Kirman* v. *Shawcross* (1794) 6 T.R. 14, 101 E.R. 410.
[39] *Post*, p. 451.
[40] See, e.g., *Homer* v. *Ashford* (1825) 3 Bing. 322, 130 E.R. 537; *Mumford* v. *Gething* (1859) 7 C.B. (N.S.) 305, 141 E.R. 834; *Leather Cloth Co.* v. *Lorsort* (1869) L.R. 9 Eq. 345.

this was a serious misconception. Adam Smith himself had never had the slightest doubt that monopolies and restrictive agreements were contrary to the public interest, and if his successors said less about this subject, it was probably because the question had become of less practical importance rather than because they disagreed with the master.

This period, especially the years from around 1800 to 1870, was a time when (as we have already seen) the most intense competition flourished in England. Businesses were still, generally speaking, very small. Few enterprises could hope to acquire a monopoly for any length of time, even by joining forces with others. The market was too large, entry into it too easy, and the competitive spirit too strong for rings or restrictive agreements to stand much chance of survival. It was widely believed, and generally with justification, that monopolistic rings were unstable and would collapse from pressure of competition. In *Wickens* v. *Evans*,[41] the case referred to above in which three manufacturers of trunks and boxes entered into a market-sharing agreement, it was argued that the brewers or distillers might create a monopoly over the whole of London by a similar agreement if this were permissible, but the answer of the Court was to point to the forces of outside competition. 'If the brewers or distillers of London were to come to the agreement suggested, many other persons would soon be found to prevent the result anticipated; and the consequences would, perhaps, be that the public would obtain the articles they dealt in at a cheaper rate.'[42] After the Corn Laws were repealed in 1846 and England embarked on a policy of complete free trade for imports, this argument naturally became all the stronger. For even if the whole of the British market could, perchance, be monopolized by a handful of enterprises there was nothing to stop external competitors from breaking up the ring by selling imported goods at lower prices.

If, then, the judges generally upheld contracts in restraint of trade during the classical period, it was not necessarily because they were any less hostile to monopoly, but because in the state of the economy at the time, the problem simply was not, in general, a serious one. But there was one important area in which it *was* a serious problem, and that was in the area of Workmens' Combinations, or Unions. Because this area of the law was mainly statutory, I shall deal with it in Chapter 16, but I need to refer to it here because of one important decision of the Courts on a point of common law. In *Hilton* v. *Eckersley*[43] the Court was faced with a very far-ranging agreement entered into by eighteen cotton spinners; the agreement was, in effect, an embryonic Trade Association of the kind that became dominant in British Industry after the First World War.

[41] *Supra*, p. 409, n. 37.
[42] *Per* Hullock B., 3 Y. & J. 330, 148 E.R. 1206.
[43] (1855) 6 El. & Bl. 45, 119 E.R. 781, affirmed, 6 El. & Bl. 66, 119 E.R. 789.

The agreement required all the members to abide by majority decisions as to the wages they would pay, and the hours of work they would require, even to the extent of requiring a member to accept a decision to shut down his whole works if necessary. The agreement was, of course, an attempt by the employers to combine for the purpose of fighting the new powers of the Workers' Combinations. Its only redeeming feature was that it was limited in duration to twelve months. Now at this time combinations of workers were, in general, permitted under the Act of 1825, in the sense that they were not indictable or punishable offences. But, not surprisingly, nobody had ever thought to enforce by civil action, an agreement by a workman to abide by the terms of a strike call, or other restrictive arrangement. In the instant case, it seems to have been agreed on all hands that what was law for the employers must also be law for the workmen. Lord Campbell in the Queen's Bench insisted that 'there must be entire reciprocity between liberty to the masters and liberty to the men'.[44] If the agreement had been held legally enforceable, therefore, the Courts would have been committed to the enforceability of an agreement between workmen which required them (for example) to abide by a majority decision to strike. This the Courts were not prepared to do. A majority of the Queen's Bench,[45] and the unanimous Exchequer Chamber, decided that the agreement between the employers was unenforceable as an unreasonable restraint of trade. Freedom to trade was plainly more important than freedom of contract. Thus spoke Alderson B. for the Exchequer Chamber;

Prima facie, it is the privilege of a trader in a free country, in all matters not contrary to law, to regulate his own mode of carrying it on according to his discretion and choice. If the law has in any matter regulated or restrained his mode of doing this, the law must be obeyed. But no power short of general law ought to restrain his free discretion. Now here the obligors to this bond have already clearly put themselves into a situation of restraint.[46]

It is clear from this that the judges, like the political economists, had an atomistic view of the nature of the market economy. They expected individuals to be free to make their own decisions, whether to work, or not to work, whether to employ a workman or not to employ him. This freedom was the freedom of workmen and employers alike. Men were free to argue and to try to persuade their colleagues to work or not, but coercion or intimidation was not to be tolerated. While it was not a criminal offence to enter into restrictive agreements of this nature, that

[44] 6 El. & Bl. 65–6, 119 E.R. 788–9.

[45] Erle J. dissenting. In the light of subsequent history, his reasons make interesting reading. Erle J. argued that if the law refused recognition to such agreements, extra-legal and less desirable ways would be found of enforcing them. Erle J. was appointed Chairman of the Royal Commission on Trade Unions in 1867, and was more sympathetic to union aspirations than most of his colleagues.

[46] 6 El. & Bl. 74–5, 119 E.R. 792.

did not mean that they could be enforced by the Courts, whether against a workman or against an employer. In practice, no doubt, things did not always work out in the same way. It was easy, and not uncommon, for employers to make these agreements and others (such as those to blacklist 'troublemakers'), and generally speaking to abide by them.[47] It is always easier to hold fast to a restrictive ring when the parties are few in number. Workers' combinations, on the other hand, must have been difficult to uphold. In the absence of legal sanction (though it is doubtful whether workers would have had much joy from such sanctions in practice anyhow) the temptation for an individual workman to break ranks, and accept employment at lower pay, or on worse terms, must have been strong. It was precisely because workmen did tend to break ranks in this way, that strikes and other restrictive labour practices were not so effective at this time as they are today. But this does not mean that the judges, any more than the political economists, were 'biased' towards employers and against employees. In a sense the judges were trying to do precisely what Adam Smith had urged. While it was then thought impossible in practice to prevent employers' restrictive agreements, the courts would at least 'do nothing to facilitate them, much less to render them necessary'.[48] Modern labour lawyers who are very free with accusations of class prejudice against nineteenth-century judges, rarely observe that the arguments which are often relied upon in modern times for not imposing legal controls on workers' restrictive agreements are the same as those offered by Adam Smith for not imposing such controls on employers, namely that 'it is impossible to prevent [them] by any law which either could be executed or would be consistent with liberty and justice'.[49] But unlike the nineteenth-century judges, the modern labour lawyer does not then deduce that nothing should be done to facilitate or render necessary these restrictive agreements.

The Effects of Contracts on Third Parties

One respect in which classical contract law, like classical economics, went somewhat astray, was in its failure to assess adequately the effects of certain types of contract on third parties. Where contracts related directly to property rights, the Courts were aware of the importance of limiting freedom of contract so as not to allow unreasonable fetters to be placed on subsequent property owners. Lord Brougham, for instance, showed sharp awareness of these problems in *Keppel* v. *Bailey*[50] where he declined to recognize the power of contracting parties to create rights

---

[47] E. P. Thompson, *The Making of the English Working Class*, p. 200.
[48] *Wealth of Nations*, Book I, Chapter X.
[49] Ibid.
[50] (1834) 2 My. & K. 517, 39 E.R. 1042.

over land which would be binding on subsequent owners. Some inroads on this were made in the famous case of *Tulk* v. *Moxhay*[51] which created the law of restrictive covenants, in the sense that it enabled a vendor of property to take a covenant from the purchaser which would be binding on subsequent purchasers with notice. Up to a point the results of this case may have been beneficial, in that it opened the door to a sort of limited private town-planning system; but these beneficial results may well have been fortuitous, and due to the skill of subsequent conveyancers and judges. The decision itself shows no appreciation of the important public issues which arose when contracts were held enforceable against property owners as such. A similar reproach could be made against the freedom of settlors to create special protective interests, such as life interests, terminable upon bankruptcy.[52] Here too the Courts seemed quite unwilling to recognize the fact that the validity of the arrangements had important consequences for third parties—creditors of the life tenant—who were not parties to them. Later in the nineteenth century, lawyers were to become very adept at manipulating some of the rules of contract law (such as rules about passing of property in contracts of sale) very much to the prejudice of third parties. But the Courts never appeared to be concerned by these results, or even aware that freedom of contract in such circumstances had significant effects on those who were not party to them.

The modern doctrine of privity, known to the modern law as a set of rules whereby a contract cannot confer rights or impose liabilities on third parties, was not really known as such until very late in the nineteenth century. The decision in *Tweddle* v. *Atkinson*[53] in 1861 was, in a sense, a very late example of a refusal to recognize the autonomy of private contracts, and a reversion to the idea of a fair exchange. The case involved an agreement between the fathers of an engaged couple whereby the bridegroom's father undertook to pay £100, and the bride's father £200, to the groom. Unusually, the agreement specifically declared that it was to be enforceable in any court of law or Equity by the bridegroom. Yet when he came to sue upon it, the Court declined to assist him, chiefly because they seem to have thought it would be unfair if the groom could sue his father-in-law, and yet be free from liability if his own father failed to make his contribution. 'It would be a monstrous proposition to say that a person was a party to the contract for the purpose of suing upon it for his own advantage, and not a party to it for the purpose of being sued.'[54]

[51] (1848) 2 Ph. 774, 41 E.R. 1143.
[52] See, e.g., *Rochford* v. *Hackman* (1852) 9 Hare 475, 68 E.R. 597.
[53] (1861) 1 B. & S. 393, 121 E.R. 762.
[54] 1 B. & S. 398, 121 E.R. 764.

This case was, of course, the starting-point of the modern doctrine of privity, but that doctrine seems to owe very little to the actual reasoning of the Court in *Tweddle* v. *Atkinson*. As has often happened in the law, the case became important, not for what the judges said, but for what the legal profession came to believe the case stood for. And what they believed that *Tweddle* v. *Atkinson* stood for was the proposition that it is somehow contrary to the inherent nature of a contract that it should be capable of conferring enforceable rights upon third parties.

There is a sense in which the new doctrine of privity was an important development in the law at a time of increasing complexity in multilateral commercial relationships. The appearance of middlemen in all sorts of commercial situations served to separate the parties at either end of the transaction, and it was generally accepted that no privity existed between them. Economically, this may have served a useful purpose, in that it encouraged the development of a more market-based concept of enterprise liability. But on some occasions the results were not only economically dubious but socially disastrous. In the passenger legislation, for example, much trouble was caused because the passengers who paid for and bought shipping passages on the transatlantic emigrant ships frequently dealt with middlemen and not the owners of the ships.[55] The result was that when they did not receive fair value it was not possible to hold the shipowners responsible for what had happened.

Penalties and Forfeitures

The new attitude to the autonomy of private contracts was, inevitably, difficult to reconcile with the old equitable doctrines about penalties and forfeitures. For centuries Courts of Chancery had been overriding the express terms of bonds and contracts on the ground that they were penal in their effect, and that in the result, they gave one party an unfair advantage in the exchange. In 1801 Lord Eldon lamented this jurisdiction, although in fact concurring in the extension to the Courts of Common Law of the power to refuse enforcement to a penal clause.[56] During Lord Erskine's brief tenure of the Great Seal, the older attitudes were reasserted,[57] but shortly after Eldon resumed the Woolsack he decided in *Hill* v. *Barclay*[58] that the old rules about relief against forfeiture of a lease for failure to pay rent could not be extended to breaches of other covenants, such as covenants to repair. After stating the extent of

[55] O. MacDonagh, *A Pattern of Government Growth: The Passenger Acts 1800–1860* (London, 1961), pp. 89, 140.

[56] *Astley* v. *Weldon* (1801) 2 B. & P. 346, 126 E.R. 1318.

[57] *Sanders* v. *Pope* (1806) 12 Ves. Jun. 282, 33 E.R. 108. Erskine was, of course, a Whig who had fought for the people's rights as the most famous advocate of his day. At this time paternalism was still a feature of Whig policy.

[58] (1811) 18 Ves. 56, 34 E.R. 238.

the old decisions, Eldon went on to say that the Court was 'surely not authorised so to deal with contracts . . . [I]t is taking a prodigious liberty with a contract,'[59] he added, to relieve the tenant against the consequences of a clear breach of his covenant.

These remarks of Eldon's cannot be put down to his conservatism; in fact they represented the spirit of the new age, not the older attitudes of the eighteenth century.[60] For many years after Eldon relinquished the Great Seal, this newer attitude prevailed[61] and only in the most extreme cases were penalty clauses refused enforcement.[62] By mid-century the House of Lords was regretting its inability to overrule the cases giving the Courts power to relieve against penalties.[63] In fact there are not lacking signs to suggest that the Courts actually approved of the imposition of penalties on parties guilty of breaches of contract, at least in some cases, for example, of wilful breach. The doctrine of 'entire contracts' whereby a party who had failed to perform precisely and fully in accord with the contract was held not entitled to recover anything at all, grew up in the first half of the nineteenth century; and this doctrine was certainly penal in result, and possibly in intent also.[64] It appears to have been one way of disciplining servants and contractors, and certainly the first half of the nineteeenth century saw much emphasis on the need for social and commercial discipline.[65]

The law of mortgages was, of course, far too well settled to be affected by these changing views on freedom of contract. In any event, the rules here were so well known that the intention of the parties in an ordinary case could not be supposed to be in accordance with the literal terms of the mortgage instrument, but in accordance with the doctrines of Equity. It was still customary to draft a mortgage in the form of a conveyance with a right to redeem within six months' and with provision for forfeiture of the land if payment was not made at the end of that period. Since everybody knew that in Chancery this provision was void, and an equitable right to redeem was retained by the mortgagor after the expiry of the specified period, it was not in reality a violation of the intention of the parties to continue to maintain the equitable doctrines. Even Lord

[59] 18 Ves. 62, 34 E.R. 240.

[60] It was Mansfield who had first shown a desire to restrict the jury's right to give relief against penalties, see *Lowe v. Peers* (1768) 4 Burr. 2225, 98 E.R. 160.

[61] See, e.g., *Green v. Price* (1845) 16 M. & W. 346, 153 E.R. 1222; *Sainter v. Ferguson* (1849) 7 C.B. 716, 137 E.R. 283.

[62] See, e.g., *Kemble v. Farren* (1829) 6 Bing. 141, 130 E.R. 1234.

[63] *Ranger v. G.W. Rly. Co.* (1854) 5 H.L.C. 72, 10 E.R. 824.

[64] See, e.g., *Spain v. Arnott* (1817) 2 Sta. N.P.C. 256, 171 E.R. 638. *Sinclair v. Bowles* (1829) 9 B. & C. 92, 109 E.R. 35; *Munro v. Batt* (1858) 8 E. & B. 738, 120 E.R. 275. See Glanville Williams, 'Partial Performance of Entire Contracts', 57 *Law Q. Rev.* 373, 490 (1941), an interesting article but somewhat flawed by the author's totally unhistorical approach.

[65] See for another example of a quasi-penal decision, *Sterne v. Beck* (1863) 1 De G. J. & Sm. 595, 46 E.R. 236.

Bramwell, towards the end of his life, while lamenting that Courts of Equity had ever interfered with the literal terms of mortgage agreements, was constrained to admit that it was now impossible to go back on the equitable rules.[66]

The Supersession of Status Relationships

It will be remembered that, in the older law, contractual liabilities were often held to arise out of a status relationship. The classic example of these relationships in English law were the 'common callings'. The common innkeeper, the common carrier, the ferryman, the farrier, and various others, had, from medieval times, been under legal obligations arising out of his status. He did not have the freedom to pick and choose his customers, because he was obliged to serve the public. It followed, too, that he had little freedom in choice of terms, because such a freedom would inevitably enable him to offer prohibitive terms to some clients and in effect give him the power to refuse to do business with them. He was, of course, protected against abuse by the Courts, but the fact remained that he was not thought to have the right to deal as he pleased. Indeed, in some cases the public likewise had no right to go elsewhere.[67] Free choice was first conceded to the public in *Richardson* v. *Walker*[68] in 1824, narrowing down a long line of precedents.

Inevitably, in the nineteenth century, these status relationships came to seem more anomalous. And, inevitably too, they were eventually largely swallowed by the expansive concept of contract which the Courts were now developing. In *Boorman* v. *Brown*[69] it was laid down that a plaintiff might sue a professional man, or a commercial agent, either in contract or in tort, when he alleged a negligent breach of duty. The idea was thus sanctioned that a duty to take care could arise from a contractual relationship as well as from the general law. The absence of anything resembling an express promise to exercise due care gave the Courts no trouble, for this was, of course, one of the easiest things to imply. In the process, an important change occurred in the nature of the duty, for it began to be seen as a duty to exercise 'reasonable care', an objective standard naturally being used. In the previous century, by contrast, duties of care arising between parties to such relationships had often been said to be duties to exercise only one's best endeavours. A man who trusted another (for example, as bailee) was thought to be entitled only to that degree of care and skill which the bailee actually possessed.

A few years later, the Courts took the next step of holding that the

[66] *Salt* v. *Marquis of Northampton* [1892] A.C. 1, 18–19.

[67] For example, they might be compelled to use the local miller to grind their corn. See *Bl. Comm.*, iii. 235; *Cort* v. *Birbeck* (1779) 1 Doug. 218, 99 E.R. 143.

[68] (1824) 2 B. & C. 827, 107 E.R. 590.

[69] (1844) 3 Q.B. 516, 11 Cl. & F. 1, 8 E.R. 1003.

liability of a common innkeeper (as that of others in the common callings) was of an essentially contractual and not tortious nature.[70] It was now said that, 'where a relation exists between two parties, which involves the performance of certain duties by one of them, and the payment of reward by the other, the law will imply, or the jury may infer, a promise by each party to do what is to be done by him.'[71] Thus the mere existence of reciprocal obligations was now thought enough to justify the classification of the case as contractual. The Courts had blurred the line, drawn by Hume a century before,[72] between two parties doing an act *in agreement* with each other, and their *making an agreement*.

The Absoluteness of Contractual Rights

Yet another consequence of the growing importance of the autonomy of private contract was the tendency of the Courts to treat the free choice of the contracting parties as beyond challenge. Both under the rules of the common law which the Courts were themselves developing, and under the express terms of contractual provision, the tendency was to hold that a man was not accountable to the Courts for the reasons for his decisions. A man, for example, had a right to decide with whom he was to deal. That right was generally treated as absolute, so that even the most unreasonable caprice could not be challenged.[73] A person who had agreed to hire a coach from a firm consisting of S and R was thus entitled to give up the contract when S retired and the business was transferred to R alone.[74] Lord Tenterden C.J. asserted that the 'defendant may have been induced to enter into this contract by reason of the personal confidence which he reposed in S',[75] but this was posited as a possibility, not as a fact to be inquired into. Similarly, when a man ordered goods from a shopkeeper with whom he had been used to deal, and the goods were supplied by the shopkeeper's successor, it was held that the buyer did not have to pay for the goods, even though he had consumed them.[76] The buyer was entitled to choose with whom to deal. The old rules holding that a man who exercised a common calling was obliged to serve anyone who wanted to deal with him, came to seem more and more anomalous.

Then again, there were some highly technical decisions holding that

[70] *Morgan* v. *Ravey* (1861) 6 H. & N. 265, 158 E.R. 109.

[71] 6 H. & N. 276, 158 E.R. 113.

[72] *Supra*, p. 56.

[73] Cf. Emerson's *Esssay* on Self-Reliance (first English edn. 1841, reprinted, London, 1903), p. 38. 'Expect me not to show cause why I seek or why I exclude company.'

[74] *Robson & Sharpe* v. *Drummond* (1831) 2 B. & Ad. 303, 109 E.R. 1156.

[75] 2 B. & Ad. 307, 109 E.R. 1158. See also *Humble* v. *Hunter* (1848) 12 Q.B. 310, 317, 116 E.R. 885, 887; 'You have a right to the benefit you contemplate from the character, credit and substance of the party with whom you contract.' (Lord Denman.)

[76] *Boulton* v. *Jones* (1857) 2 H. & N. 564, 157 E.R. 232; see *post*, p. 485.

a surety could be discharged by the minutest variation in the contract entered into between the creditor and the principal debtor. The reason given was always that the surety was entitled to choose himself for what he was to be answerable, and it was for him, and not the Courts, to judge of the materiality of the variation.[77] Similarly, the right of a buyer to reject goods because of some trifling breach by the seller—shipment a day too late, or even too soon, for example—was held to be absolute. The Court would not pause to ask the buyer *why* he wanted to reject the goods; it was enough that he *might* have had good reason for inserting the contractual requirement broken by the seller.[78]

In general, the Courts took a similar line when faced with express contractual provisions. For example, where parties agreed on the sale of an estate at a price to be fixed by two persons, or in default of an agreement, by an umpire named by them, it was held that the contract could not be enforced where no umpire could be agreed upon. How was it possible, demanded the judge, for the Court to require someone to sell at a price to be fixed by one man when the party had shown that he only reposed confidence in another?[79] Again, when a company's articles of association gave the directors power to refuse to register a transfer of shares, it was held that the directors were sole judges of the reasons for such a refusal, and the Court could not examine into them at all, at any rate in the absence of something like corruption.[80]

A more controversial question concerned conclusive evidence clauses. In *Dallman* v. *King*[81] an agreement provided that a tenant should spend £200 on some premises let to him, and that the work should be done in a substantial manner to be approved by the lessor. Here the Court refused the lessor an untrammelled right to declare his dissatisfaction with the work done. Emphasizing that the agreement was in two parts, requiring the work to be done in a substantial manner, as well as requiring the approval of the lessor, the Court declared that 'It never could have been intended that he [the lessor] should be allowed capriciously to withhold his approval.'[82] Perhaps the spirit of Best C.J. still lived on in the Common Pleas where this case was decided, for it is hard to see Parke B. giving it approval. In 1863 the case was almost distinguished away by the Queen's Bench in a case where a builder contracted to lay down some drainage work 'as rapidly and satisfactorily as required' by the clients.[83] Where it appears, says Cockburn C.J., that

[77] See, e.g., *Holmes* v. *Brunskill* (1877) 3 Q.B.D. 495.
[78] *Bowes* v. *Shand* (1877) 2 App. Cas. 455.
[79] *Milnes* v. *Gery* (1807) 14 Ves. Jun. 400, 33 E.R. 574.
[80] *Re Gresham Life Assurance Society* (1872) L.R. 8 Ch. App. 446.
[81] (1837) 4 Bing. N.C. 105, 132 E.R. 729.
[82] 4 Bing. N.C. 109, 132 E.R. 730.
[83] *Stadhard* v. *Lee* (1863) 4 B. & S. 364, 122 E.R. 138; see also *Andrews* v. *Belfield* (1857) 2 C.B. (N.S.) 779, 140 E.R. 622.

'however unreasonable and oppressive a stipulation or condition may be, the one party intended to insist upon and the other to submit to it, a Court of Justice cannot do otherwise than give full effect to the terms which have been agreed upon between the parties.'[84]

THE RISE OF THE EXECUTORY CONTRACT

As I endeavoured to show in Part I of this work, contract theory until the late eighteenth century was still largely based on the idea that obligations were created by the acceptance of benefits, or by acts of reasonable reliance; obligations, in other words, were created by what men did, rather than by their pure intentions. I also attempted to demonstrate how this had naturally resulted in the law, up to the late eighteenth century, being largely a law of executed contracts, and not a law of executory contracts. Now Powell's *Essay* in 1790 shows the law in a state of transition. In some places he gives a definition of a contract indistinguishable from that which later became commonplace, as an agreement binding on both parties, or as a transaction involving reciprocal promises.[85] But in other cases he distinguishes between an agreement which is an executory contract, and an *executed* contract which to him seems to be a transaction differing from an agreement.[86] In one particular passage Powell appears, to the modern reader, to confuse the question of the enforceability of a contract under the Statute of Frauds, with the question whether an executory contract is binding at all. This is what he says:

So, if one buy of me an house, or other thing for money, and no money be paid, nor earnest given, nor day set for payment, nor the thing delivered; here no action lies for the money or the thing sold, but the owner may sell it to another if he will; for such promises or contracts are deemed *nuda pacta* there being no consideration or cause for them, but the covenants themselves which will not yield an action.[87]

This passage, it may be thought, confirms the suggestions I have made about the changing role of consideration and the transition from executed to executory contracts at this period. For Powell here is saying that mutual covenants are not consideration until one of them is performed; the whole passage appears to rule out purely executory contracts altogether. On the other hand, the examples given suggest that Powell was thinking of the contracts governed by the Statute of Frauds, though he does not mention the statute in this passage. This may also reinforce

---

[84] 3 B. & S. 372, 122 E.R. 141.
[85] Vol. i, Introduction, pp. vi, vi–vii.
[86] Ibid., i. 234–5.
[87] Ibid., p. 331. There is a similar passage in *Bl. Comm.*, ii. 447.

the suggestion made earlier that until the end of the eighteenth century the Statute of Frauds was conceived as fitting into a general law of executed contracts, rather than as somehow limiting, in exceptional cases, the enforceability of executory contracts.

Now there can be little doubt that shortly after 1800 the very concept of contract in English law and theory changed its character, and the executory contract became the paradigm of contract theory. All contracts came to be seen as consensual; even wholly executed contracts, even those consisting of an immediate and simultaneous exchange, such as the sale of an object in a shop, came to be perceived as depending on an agreement, or an exchange of promises. Similarly loans of money, or other one-sided contracts which might previously have been treated as not binding until there had been performance on one side, now began to be seen as binding in their inception. The focal point of contract law shifted from the performance back in time to the 'making' of the contract. Indeed, the very concept of a contract as a 'thing' which is 'made' was itself new and not uninfluential on the way lawyers began to think about contracts. These momentous changes had a profound influence on the approach to practically every branch of contract law. The rules about expectation damages and independent covenants first required modification. This, in turn, brought into existence rules about the mitigation of damages. The new theory also required a new role for the doctrine of consideration, for now that it began to be possible for a party to be sued on a wholly executory contract, it was necessary to square this result with the doctrine of consideration. So also, the new emphasis on executory contracts brought new rules about anticipatory repudiation as well as a new doctrine of frustration. In the following pages I will attempt to sketch out some of the most important of these changes, but it is not my intention to trace the changes in every branch and doctrine of the law of contract. This work is not a general history of contract law, but of those parts which are concerned with the concept of freedom of contract.

The basic shift from executed to executory contracts seems to have been closely linked with the very idea of freedom of contract, and with the emergence of the free market economy. From the conceptual or doctrinal viewpoint that result seems to have followed because the movement back in time from the actions of the parties—the receipt of benefits or acts of reliance—to the moment of the making of an agreement, necessarily shifted the emphasis from the judicial imposition of liabilities to the idea that the parties created their own liabilities.

But apart from these doctrinal changes, it does not seem unduly speculative to suggest that the same shift to the executory contract was closely bound up with the growing commercial and economic changes themselves. An executory contract is, in a sense, an instrument of private planning. When such contracts become fully protected by the law, mere expectations can be counted on, and planning is facilitated. Now in the highly volatile commercial and industrial activity I have described in previous chapters, it does not seem surprising that businessmen came to demand a greater degree of legal protection for careful planning. Vast sums of money depended on the skill with which men could now plan; the mill owner needed to buy his supplies of cotton in advance, so that it would be available in a continuous flow; he needed to be assured of his labour supply in advance for the same reasons. Or again, the landowner thinking of investing in the mining of coal on his lands, might need the safety of forward contracts relating to the carriage of coal, when it was dug. Merchants exporting and importing the hugely increased flow of commodities had to plan future shipments with some regularity with the aid of the new brokers who were springing up everywhere in the second half of the eighteenth century.

One particular sphere in which there is evidence of the growing importance of planning, of the executory contract, and of the elimination of 'just' or customary prices in favour of agreed prices, concerns Government building contracts. Until the 1830s it had been common practice for the Government to employ contractors on large building projects without agreeing prices in advance.[88] The practice was for the contractor's surveyor to demand the 'customary price' for each item of the works, and, if the Government surveyor did not accept this figure, for the dispute to be taken before the Courts or an arbitrator where professional witnesses gave varying valuations and the judge or arbitrator took some sort of average. Plainly, this was a procedure which had great disadvantages, and from the 1830s onwards it became common for the Government to let its projects at fixed prices. Larger contractors were now coming into existence, better able to calculate prices and to take the risk of error; they, as well as the Government, preferred to deal on the basis of fixed prices. 'To the Victorian middle class patron, the idea of knowing in advance how much one would have to lay out must have appealed strongly.'[89] It is easy to see how the transition to fixed prices also tended to encourage the transition to binding executory contracts. When the prices were calculated on some customary basis after the work was done, there would have been less call for any binding contract prior to the execution of the work. Now that prices were being fixed by agreement, this had to be done in advance. And even though the primary purpose of the advance agreement may have been to obviate arguments about customary or fair prices, rather than to create a binding

[88] See Port, 'The Office of Works and Building Contracts in Early Nineteenth Century England', 20 *Economic History Rev.* 94 (1967).
[89] Ibid., p. 109.

commitment prior to the actual commencement of the work, it would have been natural for this latter result to follow from the former.

Another area in which one can see the growing importance of planning, and, therefore, the need for greater protection for the executory contract, concerns the attitude of the Courts to timely performance of contracts. In the eighteenth century, for example, both common law and Equity illustrated, in their different ways, a very cavalier attitude to unpunctuality of performance of contracts. At common law, for instance, it had long been the rule that no interest was recoverable for the delayed payment of a debt or other legal obligation,[90] except where the payment was due on a bill of exchange.[91] Lord Mansfield,[92] and his disciple Buller J.,[93] had dropped hints suggesting that this rule might be modified, and in the early nineteenth century repeated attempts were made by litigants to persuade the Courts to follow up these hints. It is clear that the new commercial men must have felt outraged by the courts' refusal to award interest on overdue payments in simple commercial contracts, where the result might be to turn a profitable contract into an unprofitable one. For example, in *Gordon* v. *Swan*[94] the plaintiff sold 150 tons of copper at £84 per ton, payable after six months. Merely because he had failed to take a bill of exchange, the plaintiff was held not entitled to claim interest from the date of default to the date of trial, a sum of about £300. In one or two cases Best C.J. showed a willingness to sanction the fiction of an 'implied agreement' to pay interest,[95] and it is interesting to observe how the older morality represented by Best C.J. was, in these respects, more in tune with the commercial needs of the time, than the sterner morality of the nineteenth century. In this new morality, the making of the contract was the duty of the parties. A man who failed to stipulate for interest in the event of default had only himself to blame.

The person who barred the way repeatedly to attempts to modernize the law here was Ellenborough C.J. In case after case he insisted on the very narrow class of cases in which interest could be awarded,[96] sternly rebuking those judges who would have taken a more liberal view. The final blow was delivered by the King's bench after Ellenborough had left it, when his successor, Lord Tenterden, declined to follow Best C.J. of the

---

[90] See, e.g., *Tappenden* v. *Randall* (1801) 2 B. & P. 467, 126 E.R. 1388.

[91] *Robinson* v. *Bland* (1762) 2 Bur. 1077, 97 E.R. 717, another of Mansfield's innovations.

[92] *Eddowes* v. *Hopkins* (1780) 1 Doug. 376, 99 E.R. 242.

[93] See *Walker* v. *Constable* (1798) 1 B. & P. 306, 126 E.R. 99.

[94] (1810) 12 East 419, 104 E.R. 164.

[95] *Carr* v. *Edwards* (1822) 3 Sta. 132, 171 E.R. 798; *Arnott* v. *Redfern* (1826) 3 Bing. 353, 130 E.R. 549.

[96] *Chalie* v. *Duke of York* (1806) 6 Esp. 45, 170 E.R. 826; *Gordon* v. *Swan, supra*, n. 94; *Carlton* v. *Bragg* (1812) 15 East 223, 104 E.R. 828; *De Havilland* v. *Bowerbank* (1807) 1 Camp. 50, 170 E.R. 872.

Common Pleas in 1829.[97] This state of the law was held to be too firmly
fixed for judicial alteration when the opinion of the House of Lords was
finally taken in 1893.[98] This rigid position was so inconsistent with
commercial needs that some modification was necessitated and in some
measure this was duly achieved by the Civil Procedure Act of 1833 and
the Judgments Act 1838.

Courts of Equity had similarly shown a tendency to treat punctuality
as something of trivial importance in the performance of contracts. Even
express conditions providing for penalties or forfeitures for the
unpunctual performance of contracts or payment of debts were treated
as not binding in Equity. However, Equity showed a greater flexibility
to change than the common law in the early years of the nineteenth
century, though in a sense both bodies of doctrine were moving towards
the elimination of discretion and unpredictability. Thus the newer
attitudes in Equity manifested themselves, for example, in cases where a
vendor of land was unable to make a good title within a reasonable, or
set period. The new commercial flavour of such cases is shown by a
number of cases in the early nineteenth century. In *Wright* v. *Howard*,[99]
the vendor had failed to make a good title for fourteen years, and now
sought an order for specific performance against the buyer. The
defendant's counsel protested that his client had wanted the land to build
a commercial establishment on it, and that it was now far too late. 'If', he
said,

> the defendant, desiring to embark all his property in this undertaking was
> induced to enter into this engagement, and then found that the vendor could not
> put him in possession, would the court act on a principle which must suppose
> that the defendant, thus contracting, was to give over all thoughts of employing
> his money in trade? Was he to keep his capital unemployed all the while,
> because at the end of twelve years the vendor, by some acts done in the interval,
> was able at that distance of time to make a title?[1]

Not long after this, the Court began to insist that a vendor must bring his
suit for specific performance almost at once if he was not to be accused of
undue delay. In *Watson* v. *Reid*[2] a vendor waited almost a year before
bringing his suit, and yet this was held too long. His counsel, doubtless
accustomed to the more leisurely ways of the Court in earlier periods,
when Eldon rather than Brougham sat on the Woolsack, protested, but
in vain, that, 'Never till now was it suggested that a vendor who, instead
of rushing instantly into a suit, waited for nine or ten months before he

---

[97] *Page* v. *Newman* (1829) 9 B. & C. 378, 109 E.R. 140.
[98] *London Chatham & Dover Rly. Co.* v. *S.E. Rly. Co.* [1893] A.C. 429.
[99] (1823) 1 Sim. & St. 190, 57 E.R. 76.
[1] 1 Sim. & St. 200, 57 E.R. 80-1.
[2] (1830) 1 Russ. & M. 236, 39 E.R. 91.

took that step, thereby lost his right to the assistance of a Court of Equity.'[3]

Not the least interesting aspect of some of these decisions is the growing awareness they show of the idea of an opportunity cost. Before the political economists themselves had formulated any theory on this subject, commercial men, and lawyers, were becoming aware that capital lying idle was a cost, an opportunity foregone. The failure of a debtor to pay was a cost to the creditor since it deprived him of the chance to make use of that money; the failure of a vendor to sue at once on a purchaser's refusal to take a conveyance of land was a cost to the purchaser since it might compel him to keep his money liquid or uninvested.

Expectation Damages and the Independent Covenant Rule

We have seen how, until late in the eighteenth century, expectation damages for breach of a wholly executory contract were rarely awarded, and indeed, in the case of contracts for sale of land, were specifically denied. I have also argued that the early rules which treated mutual promises as independent of each other were closely related to the denial of relief for an executory contract. Now these rules underwent a complete reversal in the last thirty years of the eighteenth century. The change in the rules about dependent and independent promises (or covenants) is well known and can be traced through a number of cases beginning with *Kingston* v. *Preston*[4] in 1773. In this case Lord Mansfield first enunciated the principle that it was the intention of the parties which determined whether mutual promises were independent or dependent. Where it was clear that the whole purpose of the contract would be defeated if the promises were treated as independent, then they would necessarily be dependent. In a sequence of cases at the end of the century Lord Kenyon adopted and extended this principle, in effect reversing the prima facie position and holding that generally promises were to be construed as mutually dependent unless one of them was clearly to be performed first.[5]

It seems certain that this change in doctrine was accompanied by, and perhaps caused by, a parallel change in the rules about damages. Instead of a plaintiff now claiming the full value of the defendant's performance which seems to have been the original common law rule (as we saw in Part I), the courts began increasingly to insist that the plaintiff was only entitled to sue for the difference in value between the two promises. This

---

[3] See also *Walker* v. *Jeffreys* (1842) 1 Hare 341, 66 E.R. 1064 and compare *Shepherd* v. *Johnson* (1802) 2 East 211, 102 E.R. 349 where it was held that the defendant could not complain of the plaintiff's delay in bringing his action.

[4] 2 Doug. 691, 99 E.R. 437.

[5] *Goodisson* v. *Nunn* (1792) 4 T.R. 761, 100 E.R. 1288; *Glazebrook* v. *Woodrow* (1799) 8 T.R. 366, 101 E.R. 1436; *Morton* v. *Lamb* (1797) 7 T.R. 125, 101 E.R. 890.

change must have been related to the growing significance of rules about the mitigation of damages.

Because questions of damages were still almost entirely a matter for the jury until late in the eighteenth century, little is known for certain about the origin of the mitigation rule. But it seems possible that there were several different stages in the early development of the principle. In the earliest period, when the plaintiff was still generally understood to be entitled to sue for the full value of the defendant's promise, the question of mitigation could not have arisen at all. In this situation, the plaintiff was still bound to perform his own promise, and could have been under no obligation to mitigate. Indeed, if he attempted to mitigate (as, for instance, by reselling elsewhere goods which the defendant now refused to accept) he would have disabled himself from performing, and may have lost any right to recover damages at all. The first stage in the development of the mitigation principle was that which *permitted* the plaintiff to seek performance elsewhere and then sue for the deficiency. As I have previously explained, it was this development which first opened the door to the award of expectation damages in the modern sense. The next stage (though this is wholly speculative) may possibly have been to recognize the right of the jury to award damages on a similar basis even where the plaintiff had not mitigated his loss but the jury felt that he ought to have done so. The final stage was the development of the rule that, as a matter of law, the plaintiff *must* mitigate his loss, and the jury *must* only award damages representing the loss which the plaintiff would have suffered if he had done so. These rules were very late in being settled, but it is at least clear that early in the nineteenth century expectation damages were being awarded in actions for non- or late delivery of stock.[6]

The next breakthrough, and the first recognition of the market price rule in contracts of sale of goods, was made in 1824 in *Gainsford* v. *Carroll*[7] where it was held that on default by the seller in delivering a quantity of bacon the buyer ought to have gone into the market at once and bought the necessary quantities; and since he had failed to do this, he could not recover damages in respect of the increase in the market price after that time. He was limited to recovering the difference between the price of the goods at the date of the contract and the market price at the date of breach. It was, however, a long time before the principle that the plaintiff must mitigate his damage was generalized through the law. In shipping contracts, for example, the rule was very late in being adopted. There was for long, as noted in McGregor on *Damages*,[8] a tendency to hold that

---

[6] *Shepherd* v. *Johnson* (1802) 2 East 211, 102 E.R. 349; *McArthur* v. *Seaforth* (1810) 2 Taunt. 257, 127 E.R. 1076.

[7] (1824) 2 B. & C. 624, 107 E.R. 516.

[8] London, 1972, 13th edn., Sect. 25, n. 13.

the normal measure of damages against a defaulting shipper was the full freight less only any sums which had *actually* been earned by the shipowner as a result of the defendant's default, and not the full freight less all sums which the plaintiff *ought* reasonably to have earned by looking for alternative cargoes in the market. As late as 1858 Martin B. doubted whether a party who breaks a contract has a right to say, 'I will not pay you the damage arising from my breach of contract, because you ought to have done something for the purpose of relieving me.'[9]

I suggest that this was still a residual hangover from the original common law idea that damages for breach of contract represented the full value of the defendant's performance, the plaintiff himself remaining liable to perform, although it is not at all obvious how the plaintiff could remain liable to perform a shipping contract if the shipper failed to load a cargo at the right time. However, by the mid-nineteenth century the mitigation rule was generally established throughout most of contract law. For example, in 1849 it was established that a dismissed employee was under an obligation to mitigate his loss by obtaining work elsewhere, and could only recover damages for the difference in wage or salary.[10] Shortly after mid-century, two further decisions settled the modern doctrine on two other important points. First, it was held in *Cort* v. *Ambergate Rly. Co.*[11] that when a party makes it clear that he will not perform his obligations, the other party may be discharged without formally tendering a performance. In this case the buyer of goods to be manufactured by the seller—a wholly executory contract—made it clear that he would not accept the goods and the seller therefore sued him without manufacturing the goods at all. It was held that the seller was entitled to damages; the decision, it will be seen, involves the protection of the purest expectation. The plaintiff is entitled to damages for the loss of the profit he expected to make on work which he has not, and now will not, undertake at all. He may, of course, have incurred expenditure in reliance on the contract, but his right to recover damages is not dependent on proof of any such reliance. The buyer, for his part, has to pay damages without receiving any actual benefit.

The second decision was that in *Hochster* v. *De la Tour*,[12] in which it was held for the first time that a plaintiff can sue for damages at once in the event of a repudiation of the contract by the defendant, even though the repudiation and the action both occur prior to the time fixed for performance. There are arguments of a policy nature both for and against any such rule,[13] but for present purposes the interesting thing

---

[9] *Smith* v. *M'Guire* (1858) 3 H. & N. 554, 567, 157 E.R. 589, 595.

[10] *Beckham* v. *Drake* (1849) 2 H.L.C. 579, 9 E.R. 1213, especially at pp. 607-8 and 1223 of the respective reports (Erle J.).

[11] (1851) 17 Q.B. 127, 117 E.R. 1229.   [12] (1853) 2 E. & B. 678, 118 E.R. 922.

[13] See G. H. Treitel, *Law of Contract*, 4th edn. (London, 1975), pp. 580-1.

about the decision is the light it throws on the judicial perception of a contract in 1853. This decision, in a sense, represents the apotheosis of the executory contract. Not only does the contract create a right prior to any performance, but it is even possible to sue and recover damages prior to the date set for performance. What has happened here is that the Court has conceptualized the contract as a thing that is 'made'—'there is a relation constituted between the parties' says Campbell C.J.[14]—and if the thing can be 'made' prior to performance, there is no reason why it should not also be 'broken' prior to performance. The executory contract has been reified, as though it were a box which is first made and then broken.[15] However defensible the decision may be on policy grounds, it is not easy to reconcile it with a promissory theory of liability. As Kelly C.B. said in *Frost* v. *Knight*,[16] it is 'clear and incontrovertible in fact, that a promise by a man to marry a woman after his father's death is not and cannot be broken while his father is yet alive'.

The increasing protection accorded to the executory contract, and the increasing willingness to award expectation damages which necessarily went with it, accorded ill with the old rule in *Flureau* v. *Thornhill*[17] in which, it will be recalled, expectation damages were denied for breach of a contract for the sale of land. During the nineteenth century, it is not surprising to see that this rule came increasingly under attack. In *Hopkins* v. *Grazebrook*[18] the earlier case was distinguished on the ground that the defendant, having contracted to buy the land, had then resold it before he had had a chance to examine the title. For this negligence, it was held, he must pay damages for the buyer's loss of bargain. In *Walker* v. *Moore*,[19] on the other hand, the plaintiff who had himself contracted to resell land before investigating the title, was held unable to claim damages for his loss of bargain. This seems to have been a clear example of the older traditions holding sway in the newer context, for the whole transaction here was plainly of a commercial character, the plaintiff having bought a piece of land and having proceeded at once to resell a part of it at a substantial profit. It was in this case that Littledale J. made his remark (to which I referred earlier) about it being contrary to the policy of the law for a man to resell land before he had obtained a conveyance, a sentiment somewhat out of tune with the treatment of land as an ordinary article of commerce.

[14] In *Hochster* v. *De La Tour* 2 E. & B. 689, 118 E.R. 926.

[15] For another example of the reification of contract, see *Lumley* v. *Guy* (1853) 2 E. & B. 216, 118 E.R. 749 where the Court extended to *executory* contracts the tort of unlawfully persuading an employee to break his contract.

[16] (1870) L.R. 5 Ex. 322, 326-7; but the decision was nevertheless reversed and the defendant held liable: (1872) L.R. 7 Ex. 111.

[17] (1776) 2 W. Bl. 1078, 98 E.R. 635.

[18] (1826) 6 B. & C. 31, 108 E.R. 364.

[19] (1829) 10 B. & C. 416, 109 E.R. 504.

By the mid-nineteenth century, as the general rules for the award of expectation damages had become fairly well settled, the anomalous nature of the rule in *Flureau* v. *Thornhill* became more than ever apparent. It was challenged head on in *Pounsett* v. *Taylor*,[20] and again in *Engel* v. *Fitch*,[21] but in both cases the Courts felt the rule too well established to be upset. Finally, the rule was affirmed by the House of Lords in *Bain* v. *Fothergill*[22] where some attempt was made to find a rational basis for it, but at the same time it was held that the rule applied whether or not the seller had already obtained a conveyance when he resold. Thus *Hopkins* v. *Grazebrook* was largely overruled.

It is clear that most of these developments represented a great increase in the protection of mere expectations. As Hume, Adam Smith, and Bentham had all argued, the binding nature of promises was coming to depend on the idea that the expectations thereby created were entitled to protection. Bentham, indeed, had belaboured the lawyers after his usual fashion because they refused to acknowledge the principle itself. '[T]he word expectation', he had protested, 'is scarcely to be found in their vocabulary; an argument can scarcely be found in their works, founded upon this principle. They have followed it, no doubt, in many instances, but it has been from instinct, and not from reason. If they had known its extreme importance, they would not have omitted to name it.'[23] But although Hume, Adam Smith, and Bentham were all agreed on the importance of expectations in justifying the binding nature of promises, they all agreed also that bare expectations were less important than expectations allied to present rights, especially rights of property. Hume and Adam Smith, for example, both said that expectations arising out of rights of property deserved greater protection than expectations to something which had never been possessed.[24] To deprive somebody of something which he merely expects to receive is a less serious wrong, deserving less protection, than to deprive somebody of the expectation of continuing to hold something which he already possesses.

The extraordinary thing which happened to contract theory in the mid-nineteenth century was that contracts came to be protected as expectation-rights in all circumstances, and not merely where purely executory contracts were concerned. Executory contract theory—or will theory—came to swallow the part executed and even the wholly executed

---

[20] (1856) 17 C.B. 660. 139 E.R. 1235.

[21] (1868) L.R. 3 Q.B. 314, affirmed, (1869) L.R. 4 Q.B. 659.

[22] (1874) L.R. 7 H.L. 158.

[23] *Principles of the Civil Code, Works*, Bowring ed., i. 308.

[24] Hume, *Treatise*, Book III, Part II, Sect. I; Adam Smith, *Lectures on Jurisprudence*, ed. Meek, Raphael, and Stein, pp. 87-8; Bentham, *Principles of the Civil Code*. Bentham did, however protest at the way in which lawyers tended to confuse contracts with dispositions, see *Works*, ed. Bowring, iii. 191-2, and also *Collected Works, Of Laws in General* (London, 1970), pp. 23-5.

contract in one of the strangest developments in legal theory that has ever occurred. Lawyers began to say that a man was liable, even on a part executed contract, not because he had received any benefit, nor because the plaintiff had relied upon him, but because he had promised. A man who borrowed money was thus liable to repay it, not because he had had the benefit of it, nor because the lender had lost the benefit of it, but because of the borrower's promise to repay. This development was taken still further when the very idea of a wholly executed contract—a simultaneous exchange of goods for money—came to be treated as an *agreement*, or as an exchange of promises. To this day the common lawyer thinks of a cash sale in a shop, for instance, as an exchange of *promises*, and not as an exchange of money for goods. The remarkable aspect of this extreme extension of will theory was that it treated mere expectations as entitled to the same protection as actual property. The 'loss' of an expectation, which is only a loss in an extended sense of the term, came to be seen as a real loss, a present loss. A plaintiff with an egg was, in short, entitled to be treated as though he had a chicken. It is easy to see now why the notion of a contract as 'binding' in its inception began to seem so important and also so real.

But at the same time there was a joker in the pack. Because, even though an executory contract might be treated as 'binding,' even though mere expectations were protected, the new rules about expectation damages only protected the plaintiff's expectation of net profit. Since a promisee was not now generally entitled to demand full performance by the defendant, even on tendering his own performance, there was, and remains today, an important sense in which an executory contract is only contingently binding. It is only binding if, and to the extent that, the promisee expects to make a profit on the transaction which he is unable to make elsewhere as a result of the breach. In practice this rule means that large numbers of contracts are regularly made which, so long as they remain wholly executory, are not in any meaningful sense 'binding' at all. An agreement for the sale of goods at market prices is not effectively binding so long as the market price remains unchanged, and so long as there is adequate supply and demand for both parties to the transaction. For while this remains the situation, default by one party leaves the other free to go into the market and buy or sell there. So long as there are no additional and identifiable costs of making the second sale (and English judges on the whole discourage too minute a search for such costs) the first contract can be broken with impunity, or subject only to a liability for nominal damages. The same is true of all other contracts, and not just those for sale of goods. An executory contract of employment is not effectively binding so long as an adequate market exists (at comparable wages) in which the employer can find alternative employees, and the employee can find alternative work. An executory contract of carriage is not effectively binding so long as the shipowner and the consignor can find alternative cargoes, or ships, at comparable rates of freight. For some years now common lawyers have become used to the idea that the 'duty of care' in the tort of negligence is a fiction with little meaning unless and until actionable damage occurs; but it has not been generally perceived that the same is largely true of the duty to perform an executory contract.

Thus the reality is that the bindingness of executory contracts protects not the expectation of performance, but the expectation of profit; and even that is only protected so long as the promisee cannot secure it elsewhere. Towards the end of the nineteenth century Holmes J. gave expression to a similar idea by saying that a contract was merely a conditional obligation, either to perform or to pay damages.[25] This approach did not win much support, either at the time or subsequently. It was, for example, pointed out by Pollock that Holmes's formulation did not explain the possibility of specific performance being decreed, nor did it explain a variety of other legal rules such as those recognizing the tort of procuring a breach of contract.[26] What was overlooked by Pollock and most lawyers, however, was the distinction between theoretical conceptualizations, and the facts of a particular case. In reality, many executory contracts are not binding *in the sense that* in the particular circumstances of the case, there is no real likelihood of specific performance being decreed, and there is no question of interference by a third party. If the matter is looked at, as Holmes J. suggested, as the 'bad man' would look at it, we can envisage such a man (who need not necessarily be 'bad' so much as pragmatic) asking his lawyer what his position is as a result of an executory contract. His lawyer may respond, that 'of course, the contract you have made is binding, and you must perform it.' If the 'bad man' or the 'pragmatic man' then asks, 'But what happens if I don't?' the lawyer may reply, 'Well, it depends.' He will then explain, that when he told his client that he 'must' perform, he did not mean to suggest that the client would be subject to any criminal penalties if he did not; the worst that can happen is that the client may be held liable to damages. If the client then goes on to ask, 'How much?', the lawyer will have to explain that this depends on whether the contract is still wholly executory, and if so, what the market position is, or was at the date of breach. If there has been no change in the market price, and if the supply and demand is adequate on both sides, the client will soon appreciate that he is in fact free not to perform without risk of penalty.

[25] See *The Common Law* (Boston, 1881, reprinted, 1949), pp. 299–300; see also 'The Path of the Law', 10 *Harvard Law Rev.* 457 (1897).

[26] *Pollock-Homes Letters*, i. 79 80, ii. 201, 233.

The lawyer may insist that he is legally 'bound' and morally ought to perform; but the pragmatic client will understand the reality.

Now I do not wish here to become further involved in the philosophical or theoretical question about the meaning of 'bindingness' in the circumstances I have described. What I am more concerned to do is to suggest that there were good historical reasons for the development of the law along these lines. These reasons lay, essentially, in the educative functions of the law, at a time when law and morality were both seen as laying down rules of behaviour for the private citizen. Few lawyers today regard the law of contract as having much, if any, function in instructing people how to behave; but in the nineteenth century things were very different. The rule that a person ought to keep his promises, observe his contracts, be faithful to his engagements, was a most important rule of behaviour in nineteenth-century life. It is obvious that the message would have been greatly weakened, if it had been qualified as the reality might have required. This does not necessarily mean that the lawyers and judges were hypocritical in enunciating these rules of behaviour while suppressing the important qualifications. For in fact the lawyers and judges came to believe in the rules themselves. While they must have been aware of the practical limitations on the rules, their own conceptual processes led them to adopt the simplistic versions of the rules which they were preaching to the populace. The idea that an executory contract was 'binding' came to be accepted by almost everyone; the fact that it was only contingently binding came to be forgotten.

I proceed now to examine some of the results of the shift in emphasis from executed to executory contracts in the nineteenth century.

Further Developments in the Law of Damages

Throughout the second part of this period, that is from around 1820 to 1870, the Courts were busy evolving the new law of damages for breach of contract. I have no space to review this story in any detail here, and it is enough to observe that even in cases of executed or part executed contracts, there was a tendency to treat the rules as to damages as following from the parties' own intentions. The leading case of *Hadley* v. *Baxendale*[27] introduced the idea that the damages were to be such as were in the 'contemplation of the parties' at the time the contract was made. The importance of the decision may well have lain primarily in the *limits* that this placed on the liability of a contract-breaker,[28] as well as in the

---

[27] (1854) 9 Ex. 341, 156 E.R. 145. See the excellent historical study of this case and its background by Richard A. Danzig, '*Hadley* v. *Baxendale*: A Study in the Industrialization of the Law', 4 *J. Legal Studies* 249 (1975). One of the delicious ironies of this case was that Baxendale, the defendant, was in the habit of posting up notices at his places of business about the importance of punctuality. For the text of one of these notices, see Samuel Smiles, *Thrift* (London, 1903), pp. 172-3.

[28] See Charles T. McCormick, *Law of Damages* (St. Paul, Minnesota, 1935), pp. 564-5.

fact that the limits were now to be laid down by the Courts and not handed over to juries. But there was nothing very strange in the importation of the notion of foreseeability as the key factor in determining the extent of the contract-breaker's liability. For one thing, a similar idea had already been put forward in Pothier's *Law of Obligations*, and a comparison between his language and that used by the Court in *Hadley* v. *Baxendale*, suggests the possibility of borrowing.[29] But more generally, the notion that a man was responsible for the foreseeable consequences of his actions was an important, and perhaps an essential, part of utilitarian philosophy. If the morality of an act was to depend upon its consequences for increasing or decreasing human happiness, it was obviously necessary to have regard to the foreseeable consequences of an action in determining its desirability. In 1835 John Stuart Mill had insisted upon the fact that the consequences of many actions are foreseeable, and that 'the whole course of human life is founded upon the fact.' He went on to say that 'The commonest person lives according to maxims of prudence founded on foresight of consequences.'[30]

But there is another point which has been generally somewhat forgotten in English jurisprudence, despite the considerable literature on *Hadley* v. *Baxendale*. When a contract or exchange misfires in some way, many losses may result to one or other of the parties, some or all of which may have been more or less foreseeable. If they were in fact foreseen as possibilities, then it is likely, or even probable, that the risk of their occurrence would have been taken account of by the parties in fixing the terms of the bargain. Certainly, classical economic theory would readily have assumed that this would be the normal course of events. Indeed, the classical economists would probably have gone further and insisted that this *must* be the case without factual inquiry into the question whether the consequences were in fact foreseen or not, and whether they entered into the fixing of the terms of the bargain or not. But in practice there are many situations in which these consequences are unlikely to affect the bargain. For example, in cases like *Hadley* v. *Baxendale* where damages are claimed for a consequential loss resulting from a delay in performance, the possible consequences of a delay are not likely to be known by the carrier, and are most unlikely to enter into the computation of the charge for carriage. Even where the consignor informs the carrier's agent or employee of the importance of speed, or otherwise gives some indication of the loss he may suffer from delay, the reality of commercial organization is such that this information is unlikely to affect the terms of the bargain. The information may be given to a mere clerk, or

[29] See A. W. B. Simpson, 'Innovation in Nineteenth Century Contract Law', 91 *Law Q. Rev.* 247, 274–7 (1975).

[30] See Mill's review of Sedgwick's *Discourse*, first published in 1835, reprinted in the Toronto edn. of *Collected Works of John Stuart Mill*, x. 33, at pp. 63–6.

employee, who plays no part in negotiating the terms; and indeed, the terms are likely to be fixed by the carrier on the basis of some general rate applicable to the weight or volume or quantity of the goods to be carried. It is normally impracticable to fix a separate rate for every contract.

It seems to be for these reasons that the Courts were inclined to limit the damages so severely in cases of delay in carriage throughout most of this period. In *British Columbia Saw Mill Co. Ltd.* v. *Nettleship*[31] and again in *Horne* v. *Midland Rly. Co.*[32] these seem to have been precisely the grounds on which the Courts denied liability even though in both cases some information was available to the carrier about the possible consequences of delay. In the former case, for example, Willes J. said that he was disposed to take the narrow view that 'one of two contracting parties ought not to be allowed to obtain an advantage which he has not paid for'.[33] Mere knowledge of certain facts suggesting that a particularly serious consequence might result from delay was not enough, he urged. 'The knowledge must be brought home to the party sought to be charged under such circumstances that he must know that the person he contracts with reasonably believes that he accepts the contract with the special condition attached.'[34] And similarly, in the second case, Blackburn J. insisted that 'the defendant shall not be bound to pay more than he received a reasonable consideration for undertaking the risk of at the time of making the contract'.[35]

What is most significant about these decisions is that they represent the first major departures from the theory that parties *must be assumed* to have contracted on the basis of the facts and information available to them. A few years previously there had been some suggestion that this normal presumption would operate, for in another case involving a railway company Pollock C.B. had argued that if the company knew of the consequences of the delay they would probably have charged a higher rate.[36] But by the end of this period the Courts appear to have recognized that this was too theoretical an approach. They must have come to see that railway companies and shipowners found it impractical to charge special rates to consignors for whom delay was likely to have particularly serious consequences. And with this appreciation, they began to abandon the convictions which had been at the foundation of classical contract law for the past half-century or more. It was no longer enough to *assume* that parties always took account of the facts and information available to them; some inquiry by the Courts into the facts was needed. But if this

[31] (1868) L.R. 3 C.P. 499.
[32] (1873) L.R. 8 C.P. 131.
[33] L.R. 3 C.P. 508.
[34] Ibid., 509. This judgment was 'highly approved' by Holmes J. See *Pollock-Holmes Letters*, i. 119.
[35] L.R. 8 C.P. 132-3, in argument.
[36] *Gee* v. *Lancs. & Yorks. Rly. Co.* (1860) 6 H. & N. 211, 158 E.R. 87.

were so with regard to damages, why was it not also true of other matters? How could the Courts continue to insist that the parties always took account of the relevant factors in weighing up risks, and in determining all the other terms of a contract? Plainly, a dangerous Pandora's box was liable to be opened if this new approach was pressed too far. In fact it was a long time before the traditional assumptions began to be questioned in other spheres.

The true significance of these cases was obscured by subsequent developments in the law relating to damages. For the *British Columbia Saw Mill* case and the *Horne* case represented the high-water mark of the bargain approach which placed such severe limits on the damages recoverable. In later years the Courts began to relax these rules, and damages were awarded more readily for consequences which might be, in one sense, 'foreseeable' but which plainly had not affected the terms of the bargain. The culmination of this process was not reached until recent years; indeed, it was only with the decision of the House of Lords in *Czarnikow* v. *Koufos Ltd.*[37] in 1969 that it was reached, and that (in effect) these two leading nineteenth-century cases were discarded. The explanation for these later developments lies in the growth of modern tort law, and tort ideas. For (as we shall see later) the development of tort law after 1870 began to cast doubt on the idea that a man should only be liable for a result for which he had received a reasonable consideration. A man might now become liable for a result for which he had not received any consideration at all; naturally, as tort law became the dominant sector of private law, the older rules about contract damages began to seem less justifiable. The modern rules, though nominally rules of contract law, cannot really be understood except in the wider context of the changes in private law since 1870.[37A]

The Application to Executory Contracts of Rules for Executed Contracts

We must next observe that many of the rules and doctrines of contract law which had been largely worked out in the eighteenth century in connection with executed contracts, now came to be applied to executory contracts. In eighteenth- and early nineteenth-century law, for example, duress and mistake appear almost always in connection with claims to recover money paid;[38] in the mid-nineteenth century, they begin to appear as defences to actions brought upon executory contracts. Moreover, in the process of transition, some peculiar things happened to these two doctrines. The first was that they came to be explained as being

[37] [1969] 1 A.C. 350.

[37A] In effect, modern contract law has largely adopted the tort damages principles of *Smith* v. *L. & S. W. Rly. Co.* (1870) L.R. 6 C.P. 14 in preference to the contract cases of that time.

[38] See, e.g., *Cartwright* v. *Rowley* (1799) 2 Esp. 723, 170 E.R. 509; *Morgan* v. *Palmer* (1824) 2 B. & C. 729, 107 E.R. 554.

illustrations of defective assent, or an unfree will. In the eighteenth century these doctrines had appeared generally to be based on simple ideas of fairness.[39] A man who was coerced or paid under a mistake was not likely to obtain a fair return for his payment. But now that the fairness of an exchange was itself coming to be treated as not a matter for the Courts anyhow, some other ground for invoking such doctrines had to be found. The second change which occurred as a result of the shift to the executory contract was a great restriction on the availability of the doctrines. Duress and mistake were whittled away in the nineteenth century as defences to actions on executory contracts till virtually nothing was left of them.

In a sense, the severe limitations now imposed on the concept of duress were a natural corollary of will theory. If a man willingly made a contract, if a contract was essentially the product of the will, how could it be argued that a contract was entered into against a man's will? As we have seen, this view had already been pushed to its very limit by Hobbes, while Locke had, less logically, if more acceptably, opted for a somewhat more moderate position. It was Locke's position which was essentially adopted by the Courts in the nineteenth century.

The decisive case in the law of duress was *Skeate* v. *Beale*[40] in which the Courts, in effect, refused to countenance the idea of economic duress, or (as it was there referred to) duress of goods. To apply force or threats to the person was the only coercive act which could be treated as vitiating a contract. To threaten the person takes away 'the free agency', and besides leaves no time for appeal to the law; but to threaten a man with purely economic coercion, e.g. by threatening to deprive him of some goods, does not deprive a man 'of his free agency', at least if he 'possesses that ordinary degree of firmness which the law requires all to exert'.[41] Moreover, in this case, there is time for redress to be available from the Courts. This, in the fashion characteristic of the time, was stated as an assertion of law—no inquiry was contemplated into the possibility that there might not be time for appeal to the forces of law and order. One of the peculiarities of the decision, frequently noted by subsequent commentators, was that it seemed to impose more stringent conditions for invoking the doctrine of duress as a defence to an executory contract, than had previously been held to exist for the application of the doctrine to claims for the recovery of money paid. The absurd result might be, at least in theory, that a person might be held bound under an executory

---

[39] Powell, *Essay*, ii. 110 *et seq*.

[40] (1841) 11 Ad. & E. 983, 113 E.R. 688. For a forerunner, see *Essex* v. *Atkins* (1808) 14 Ves. 542, 33 E.R. 629.

[41] Lord Denman, 11 Ad. & E. 990, 113 E.R. 690. Cf. *Morgan* v. *Palmer* (1824) (*supra*, p. 434, n. 38) where the Court was still willing to talk about unequal bargaining power in relation to the illegal exaction of a fee.

contract entered into as a result of some economic coercion, while if he performed the contract, and paid the money demanded, he might be able to recover the sum so paid. The explanation for the absurdity, of course, is simply historical. The rules relating to the recovery of money paid were eighteenth-century rules; the rules relating to executory contracts were nineteenth-century rules. And the nineteenth-century rules were made in the context of a market-based law of contract. In the market, economic pressures are commonplace, and a market-based law of contract cannot treat them as a vitiating ground. Only pressures of a different character, personal pressures, could be available as a defence in this new law of contract.[42]

Nevertheless, the result of this decision, and of the tendency to treat coercion as something affecting the free will, was unfortunate. The idea that a man's will is 'overborne' by certain types of pressure and not by others is, both in logic indefensible, and in practice impossible of application. The reality is that some forms of pressure are in conformity with the social and economic system and the moral ideas of the community, and others are not. The line can only be drawn by distinguishing between different *kinds* of pressure, not by attempting to analyse the effect of the pressures on a man's mind. The result was to make it virtually impossible for a sensible law of duress to develop at all during this period. In practice, however, it mattered little, for duress almost disappeared from the law of contract altogether during the nineteenth century.

A somewhat similar fate befell the law of mistake, although there were other important factors at work here. Throughout the classical period, mistake as a defence to an executory contract rarely makes an appearance in the Law Reports, though it was not until 1867 that any serious attempt was made to lay down a general principle as to the effect of mistake in contracts.[43] To some extent the whittling down of mistake doctrines was a reflection of the law of the market, and the principle of *caveat emptor*. To allow a person to escape the consequences of a mistake as to the quality of something he had contracted to buy would have been an easy evasion of *caveat emptor*, and although that principle had itself largely disappeared by 1870 in contracts of sale of goods, it still held general sway in other contractual cases.

But there is a broader sense in which classical contract theory was inimical to any wide doctrine of mistake, as also to its sister-doctrine, frustration. As I have already stressed, classical theory emphasized the executory contract as a risk-allocation mechanism. In the market, parties were expected to calculate rationally the various risks, whether of past or

---

[42] See *Williams* v. *Bayley* (1866) L.R. 1 H.L. 200.
[43] *Kennedy* v. *Panama Royal Mail Co.* (1867) L.R. 2 Q.B. 580.

of future events, which might affect the value of the contract. Provided that there was no fraud, and provided that the bargaining process was itself fair, the result must be deemed to be fair. Unexpected events, unknown factors, whether occurring before or after the contract was made, were not to be allowed to upset the resultant bargains. In principle all such risks were capable of being perceived and evaluated; in practice, not everybody succeeded in doing so, or doing it very well. But that was naturally irrelevant. The whole point of the free market bargaining process was to give full rein to the greater skill and knowledge of those who calculated risks better. There was, too, a disciplining and an educational function involved in it. He who failed to calculate a risk properly when making a contract would lose by it, and next time would calculate more efficiently.

It is therefore not surprising that classical contract doctrine found little room for a law of mistake or frustration, though eighteenth-century doctrine generally continued to govern claims for the recovery of money paid, as opposed to claims on executory contracts. Once again, as with the law of duress, this led to problems in reconciling the strictness of the doctrines applicable to executory contracts with the greater laxity permitted in executed contracts. Moreover, in this instance, the nineteenth century itself saw examples of the older rules being affirmed in executed transactions. For instance, in *Kelly* v. *Solari*[44] the Court of Exchequer affirmed the simple rule that money paid under a mistake of fact may be recovered from the payee without adverting to the distinction between an executed and an executory transaction. The decision was based on the simple idea that if money was paid to a person which he was not entitled to receive, he was receiving possession of property which did not belong to him. The difference in approach to a plea of mistake in an excuted as opposed to an executory transaction has remained in the law to this day; the common lawyer still feels intuitively more favourably inclined to a claim for recovery of money paid under mistake, than he feels to a defence of mistake in an executory transaction. Yet obviously the two types of case raise, at least in some cases, virtually identical issues. If A enters into a contract with B as a result of a mistake, and then pays him money in pursuance of that contract, is A's claim to recover the money to be based on the quasi-contractual principles or the contractual principles? In the twentieth century this was to give rise to a somewhat arid academic controversy as a result of the decision in *Bell* v. *Lever Bros.*[45]

---

[44] (1841) 9 M. &. W. 54; 152 E.R. 24. The Court brushed aside the defendant's argument that she ought not to be made to repay the money because she had (or might have) spent it (i.e. had relied on the plaintiff's acts as evidence of entitlement).

[45] [1932] A.C. 161. See P. A. Landon, 51 *Law Q. Rev.* 650 (1935); T. H. Tylor, 52 *Law Q. Rev.* 27 (1936); P. A. Landon, 52 *Law Q. Rev.* 478 (1936); C. J. Hamson, 53 *Law Q. Rev.* 118 (1937).

Nobody, however, seemed to appreciate that the cause of the controversy, if not its solution, lay in history.

The defence of mistake attracted, like that of duress, its fair share of will theory. Already in Leake's work in 1867, there was an attempt to bring together, under the heading of Mistake, a variety of cases, not always openly dealt with as such by the Courts (for example, *Couturier* v. *Hastie*)[46] and to treat them as based on defects in the party's assent. This approach was pursued, shortly after the end of the present period, by Pollock and Anson.

Forbearances and Compromises

In Chapter 6 I suggested that, in general, the law relating to forbearances and compromises in the eighteenth century was centred around the executed form of the transaction. The Courts were, at that time, still more interested in seeing that parties to a contract made a fair exchange, than they were in enforcing bare promises. Here too we see the influence of changing theory in the nineteenth century. First, there was the problem of getting rid of the old rule that it was not possible to discharge an existing obligation by a new agreement but only by an actual performance of the new agreement—the old insistence on accord and satisfaction. In the 1830s the Courts wavered, sometimes insisting on the old rule,[47] and sometimes evading it, or distinguishing it.[48] In 1850 the Court of Queen's Bench seemed willing to treat the issue as one of construction of the new agreement, that is, if the new agreement was intended to discharge the old obligation forthwith, then it would have this effect, while if the intention was to discharge the old obligation only on some new performance, then that would be the result.[49] This approach, of course, gave the Courts the freedom to do virtually what they wanted, since any actual intention in these cases would usually have been absent. In the same year the Court of Exchequer—throughout this period almost always ahead of the other Courts in adherence to market principles—virtually settled the issue in *Henderson* v. *Stobart*.[50] From now on, an agreement to discharge an obligation was generally treated as binding in its inception like any other executory contract.

The second line of cases involved compromise agreements. In the eighteenth century, as we saw in Chapter 6, the Courts were apt to be very unsure in deciding these questions. Sometimes they held that money paid under a compromise was recoverable, if it turned out that nothing

---

[46] (1856) 5 H.L.C. 673, 10 E.R. 1065.

[47] See, e.g., *Bayley* v. *Homan* (1837) 3 Bing. N.C. 915, 132 E.R. 663.

[48] See, e.g., *Good* v. *Cheesman* (1831) 2 B. & Ad. 328, 109 E.R. 1165; *Cartwright* v. *Cooke* (1832) 3 B. & Ad. 701, 110 E.R. 256.

[49] *Crowther* v. *Farrer* (1850) 15 Q.B. 677, 117 E.R. 615.

[50] (1850) 5 Ex. 99, 155 E.R. 43.

was in fact due; sometimes, they applied the more modern idea that such payments necessarily involved an acceptance of the risk of mistakes by the payer. Later in the eighteenth century, opinion was hardening on these cases where the money had actually been paid. In 1795 Eyre C.J. criticized *Moses* v. *Macferlan*[51] in which Mansfield had allowed a party even to re-open a judgment of an inferior Court as a result of which he had been forced to pay money not due.[52] This was closely followed by a number of decisions which virtually settled the rule for executed transactions. Money paid, under pressure of threats of legal action, or by way of settling a legal claim, or by way of compromising a suit, was held to be irrecoverable, even on proof that nothing was due, or that less was due than had been paid.[53] In this instance, there was an appreciable time lag before these doctrines came to be applied to executory contracts. As late as 1843 even Abinger C.B. in the Exchequer insisted that a compromise was not binding if there was no underlying debt at all, but only if there was a debt, and its amount was uncertain.[54] But here too change was at hand. In the mid-nineteenth century, a number of cases decisively settled the law and upheld executory compromises of legal claims.[55]

These cases were justified by the assumption that an agreement to compromise a legal claim was necessarily a device for allocating all risks arising out of the uncertainty which led to the compromise. No inquiry was permitted into the facts, such as might (for example) have shown that the compromise had proceeded, on both sides, on the assumption that there was some debt, and only a dispute as to its amount, the view for which Abinger had argued in 1843. Similarly, there was a tendency to assume, as a matter of law, that a payment made as a result of a mistake as to the law was necessarily made in response to threats of legal action.[56] A bona fide compromise of a claim in such circumstances is, in point of fact, obviously a very different thing from a payment casually assumed to be due because of a mistake as to the law, where there has been nothing in the nature of a threat of legal action. But this factual distinction was shut out by the approach of the Courts.

The final group of cases to be mentioned here concerns the rule in

[51] (1760) 2 Bur. 1005, 97 E.R. 676.

[52] *Phillips* v. *Hunter* (1795) 2 H. Bl. 402, 414–16, 126 E.R. 618, 624–5.

[53] *Knibbs* v. *Hall* (1794) 1 Esp. 84, 170 E.R. 287; *Brown* v. *M'Kinally* (1795) 1 Esp. 279, 170 E.R. 356; *Mariott* v. *Hampton* (1797) 7 T.R. 269, 101 E.R. 969. Cf. *Cobden* v. *Kendrick* (1791) 4 T.R. 431, 100 E.R. 1102, somewhat against the trend.

[54] *Edwards* v. *Baugh* (1843) 11 M. & W. 641, 152 E.R. 962; *Wade* v. *Simeon* (1846) 2 C.B. 548, 564, 135 E.R. 1061, 1067.

[55] *Cook* v. *Wright* (1861) 1 B. & S. 559, 121 E.R. 822; *Callisher* v. *Bischoffsheim* (1870) L.R. 5 Q.B. 449. The earliest case along these lines seems to be *Longridge* v. *Donville* (1821) 5 B. & Ald. 117, 106 E.R. 1136.

[56] *Brisbane* v. *Dacres* (1813) 5 Taunt. 143, 128 E.R. 641.

Pinnel's case. It will be remembered that in the seventeenth and eighteenth centuries it was not possible to discharge an obligation by payment of less than was due, even though such payment was accepted by the creditor. In the mid-nineteenth century the Courts went close to overruling these old doctrines. In *Sibree* v. *Tripp*[57] the Court of Exchequer held that an agreement to pay a debt of £500 by two notes of £125 each and one for £50 was binding in its inception. *Cumber* v. *Wane*[58] (referred to in Chapter 6) was overruled, on the ground that if a note was agreed to be given in discharge of a debt, the Court could not inquire into the reasonableness of the satisfaction. To complete this particular story, by 1882 the Courts were prepared to hold that a simple acceptance of a cheque for £100 in payment of a debt of £125, was a binding discharge.[59] But two years later the House of Lords recoiled in *Foakes* v. *Beer*[60] from the decisive step of holding that an executory agreement to accept less than is due can bind the creditor. This decision represented, in a sense, the ebbing of the tide from the high-water mark of freedom of contract. The insistence of the Lords that there must be some consideration, even for an agreement to discharge a debt, was a return to the idea of a fair exchange, and a movement away from the idea that a bare agreement was always binding. Perhaps it is significant that the main judgment was delivered by Lord Selborne, a leading Equity judge and Lord Chancellor, and that the common lawyer, Lord Blackburn, was nearly moved to dissent.[61]

The Statutes of Limitation

I referred in Chapter 6 to the way in which the eighteenth-century judges had held that an acknowledgment of a debt took a case out of the Statute of Limitations and prevented time running against the debtor. These cases had pushed this doctrine to the extreme lengths of upholding the liability of the debtor even when the acknowledgement was coupled with a refusal to pay the debt. Although, technically speaking, the decisions rested on the implication of a new promise the judges do not seem to have been troubled by the fact that the implication was manifestly a fiction. The explanation for this, I suggested, may well have been that the Courts saw the primary liability as still arising from the previous debt, and that the promise was merely evidence of that debt.

[57] (1846) 15 M. & W. 22, 153 E.R. 745.

[58] (1721) 1 Stra. 426, 93 E.R. 613, *supra*, p. 167.

[59] *Goddard* v. *O'Brien* (1882) 9 Q.B.D. 37.

[60] (1884) 9 App. Cas. 605.

[61] Lord Blackburn had been responsible for many of the leading decisions in the 1860s and 1870s generally upholding the market-based law of contract, e.g. *Cook* v. *Wright*, *supra*, p. 439, n. 55, *Kennedy* v. *Panama Royal Mail Co.*, *supra*, p. 436, n. 43. His judgment in *Foakes* v. *Beer* is, in substance, a dissenting judgment, since the reasons given are those he had prepared in favour of allowing the appeal.

But in the nineteenth century, these rules began to seem more anomalous. The idea that a promise could be implied in the teeth of an express refusal to pay was finally rejected in *Tanner* v. *Smart*,[62] and in 1844 it was insisted that the 'new promise and not the old debt, is the measure of the creditor's right'.[63] The basis of the liability had thus shifted from the old debt to the new promise, from the consideration to the promise.

The Rise of the Bilateral Contract

A further consequence flowing from the increasing emphasis on the executory contract was, not surprisingly, that transactions capable of being interpreted in their inception as bilateral or unilateral, in the modern terminology, tended to be seen as bilateral. Simultaneous exchanges and even unilateral contracts, transactions which are only binding after one party has performed, scarcely deserved to be called contracts at all. Freedom of contract meant freedom to make an enforceable executory contract, not merely freedom to make a present exchange.[64] It came to be assumed, as the classical economists had assumed, that if parties are to have freedom to make a present exchange, then logically it follows that they must also have freedom to bind themselves to make a future exchange. It was not observed what a gulf separates these two freedoms, that the first involves only the passive recognition by the State of what parties themselves choose to do, while the second involves the active intervention of the State to compel one party to do something which he no longer wants to do.

The unilateral contract is a species of part executed contract, and it did not figure prominently in nineteenth-century law. In fact, it was something of an embarrassment to the classical law of contract since many such contracts did not appear to rest on an *agreement* at all. This was one reason why classical contract theory found such difficulty with some of the problems to which unilateral contracts gave rise, such as the revocability of a promise after there has been part performance of an executed consideration. We begin to encounter the famous problem of the promise to give £10 to a man if he walks to York, and of its revocability after he has walked half-way there.[65] One answer to this problem was to interpret virtually every transaction as though it were bilateral, as though there were an exchange of promises. Indeed, towards the end of this period, there are signs that the unilateral contract was about to disappear from the books altogether. The great common lawyer,

---

[62] (1827) 6 B. & C. 603, 108 E.R. 573.

[63] *Philips* v. *Philips* (1844) 3 Hare 281, 300, 67 E.R. 388, 396.

[64] See for example, Bramwell's pamphlet on *Laissez Faire* cited in Fairfield, *Some Account of Lord Bramwell*, p. 141. On this point Bramwell's view seems to have been the general opinion; see also, *supra*, p. 330.

[65] See Addison on *Contracts* (London, 1842), pp. 34–6, for some of these difficulties.

Lord Blackburn, spoke in *Maddison* v. *Alderson*[66] as though there was no such thing as a unilateral contract.

In some areas, it is possible to observe a type of commercial relationship which has been interpreted in different ways during three different periods of the common law's development, that is first in the pre-will theory stages, secondly in the mid-nineteenth century phase, and thirdly in more modern times when (as we shall later see) there have been marked signs of a return to eighteenth-century values. One particularly good example of this type of relationship concerns the commission agency. Suppose A invites B to sell some property for him, and agrees to pay him a commission on the sale. Suppose, then that A later revokes this arrangement prior to a sale. Has B any cause for complaint in law? The answer depends on how the initial arrangement is interpreted. Have the parties made a binding agreement? Are there mutual promises in this arrangement? In the earliest cases to raise such questions (mostly concerning ship brokers) there seems to have been a clear tendency to treat the arrangement as not binding unless and until a sale took place.[67] Indeed, this view generally prevailed until 1830 or thereabouts. After that, the attitude of the Courts appears to have veered right round, and they began to interpret such arrangements as 'agreements' which, of course, in one sense they clearly are.[68] It began to be said that an arrangement of this kind was a binding executory contract, involving mutual promises. The commission agent undertook to do his best to sell the property; the owner undertook to pay him commission on sale. But the conclusion which the Courts then deduced from this intepretation was that once the arrangement was made the contract could not be revoked. The property owner now became liable to pay damages to the commission agent if he changed his mind and withdrew the property from sale; thus will theory prevailed to the extent that the property owner became liable to pay damages even though he received no benefit from the arrangement at all. If it were argued that the owner ought to have the right to change his mind, the answer would be that the whole point of a contract was to create binding mutual obligations which did not permit a change of mind.[69] This interpretation prevailed until 1942 when it was overruled by the House of Lords in *Luxor Ltd.* v. *Cooper*,[70] a

---

[66] (1883) 8 App. Cas. 467, 487.

[67] *Haines* v. *Bush* (1814) 5 Taunt. 521, 128 E.R. 793; *Hamond* v. *Holiday* (1824) 1 C. & P. 384, 171 E.R. 1241; *Read* v. *Rann* (1830) 10 B. & C. 438, 109 E.R. 523; *Dalton* v. *Irwin* (1830) 4 C. & P. 289, 172 E.R. 708; *Broad* v. *Thomas* (1830) 4 C. & P. 338, 172 E.R. 730.

[68] *Simpson* v. *Lamb* (1856) 17 C.B. 603, 139 E.R. 1213; *Campanari* v. *Woodburn* (1854) 15 C.B. 400, 139 E.R. 480; *Prickett* v. *Badger* (1856) 1 C.B. (N.S.) 296, 140 E.R. 125; *Green* v. *Mules* (1861) 30 L.J.C.P. 343; *Green* v. *Read* (1862) 3 F. & F. 226, 176 E.R. 101. The cyclical movements of the law are traced in Ash, *Willing to Purchase* (London, 1963) though he does not see them in any historical perspective.

[69] The clearest and most extreme case was *Inchbald* v. *Western Neilghery Coffee, Tea etc. Plantation Co.* (1864) 17 C.B. (N.S.) 733, 144 E.R. 293.   [70] [1941] A.C. 108.

case to which I shall return later. The House of Lords here repudiated the mid-nineteenth century cases and reinterpreted the transaction as a unilateral arrangement which was not binding on the owner. The whole of this sequence of cases illustrates the influence of changing theories and values. In the mid-nineteenth century, when will theory was at its height, any arrangement was apt to be interpreted as a binding agreement, subjecting a party to liability to pay damages for the protection of the mere expectations of the other party. To appoint a man as a commission agent was, in effect, to give him an entitlement to have his expectations protected. On the other hand, in the earlier period, and again in the modern period, there is a greater tendency (whatever theory may say today) to restrict the protection of bare expectations.

Continuing Contracts

A second illustration of changes in the law which flowed from the growing emphasis on the executory contract, was the development of new rules regarding contracts of a continuous nature such as contracts of employment, leases, licenses, partnerships, and so forth. Prior to the development of will theory, indeterminate arrangements of this kind were generally treated as binding in relation to the future, only to the minimum degree necessary to protect each party's reliance on the probable continuance of the contract.[71] Thus, in principle, these continuing contracts were generally terminable at will in the early law, provided that sufficient notice was given to enable the other party to make alternative arrangements. Similarly, relationships entered into for a fixed term but continued after the expiry of the term were held to be terminable only on reasonable notice, and were not regarded as continued merely from day to day.

So far as contracts of employment were concerned, it is not even clear that a wholly executory contract was recognized at all prior to the nineteenth century. Generally speaking, the remedy of the employee in pre- and early nineteenth-century law seems to have been confined to an action for the value of any work actually done. Indeed, even an agreement for a fixed time was (very surprisingly to modern eyes) capable of being interpreted as a unilateral arrangement under which the servant was not bound to remain in the employer's service for the whole period because the employer had made no express promise to employ the servant for the whole period.[72] Not until 1853 was it finally established that a contract of employment could actually be binding as

[71] See, e.g., *Right* v. *Darby* (1786) 1 T.R. 159, 99 E.R. 1029, for a clear instance of a reliance-based liability masquerading as a consent-based liability.

[72] *Lees* v. *Whitcomb* (1828) 5 Bing. 34, 130 E.R. 972; *Bayley* v. *Rimmell* (1836) 1 M. & W. 506, 150 E.R. 534; *Aspdin* v. *Austin* (1844) 5 Q.B. 671, 114 E.R. 1402; *Dunn* v. *Sayles* (1844) 5 Q.B. 685, 114 E.R. 1408.

to the future, so that a dismissed servant could sue, not only for money already earned, but for damages for wrongful dismissal, and thus obtain damages for his expectations of continuance in the employment.[73]

Interestingly enough, it is possible to trace the development of the executory contract of employment in statute law as well as in the common law cases. For in the eighteenth century the first Master and Servant Act of 1747[74] made it an offence for a workman to commit 'any misdemeanour, miscarriage or ill-behaviour' in his employment, but said nothing about failing to turn up for work at all. The next Act, that of 1765,[75] recited that 'it frequently happens that artificers, callico printers, handicraftsmen, miners, colliers, keelmen, pitmen, glassmen, potters, labourers and others, who contract with persons for certain terms do leave their respective services before the terms of their contracts are fulfilled; to the great disappointment and loss of the persons with whom they so contract', and proceeded to make it an offence for a workman so to absent himself. This obviously involved a recognition that such contracts were binding for the future, at least where they were entered into for a fixed term, and where the service had actually commenced. In this respect the Courts seem to have been much slower than Parliament to recognize the binding nature of such contracts. The final statutory development on this point, is to be found in the Act of 1823[76] where it was made an offence for a servant who had entered into a written contract to refuse even to commence work; where there was no written contract, it remained an offence for the servant to absent himself only after the employment had commenced. Thus here (as with the Statute of Frauds) we see some indication that only written executory contracts were to be enforceable.

As the nineteenth century wore on, there was a marked change of attitude to continuing contracts, especially those entered into by the new commercial corporations. Indeed, by 1875 the House of Lords was prepared to lay down the astonishing rule that prima facie a contract of indefinite duration was to be construed as lasting for ever.[77] '[A]n agreement *de futuro* extending over a tract of time which, on the face of the instrument, is indefinite and unlimited must (in general) throw upon anyone alleging that it is not perpetual, the burden of proving that allegation.'[78] The facts in this case were, admittedly, of an extreme

---

[73] *Emmens* v. *Elderton* (1853) 4 H.L.C. 624, 10 E.R. 606; *Whittle* v. *Frankland* (1862) 2 B. & S. 49, 121 E.R. 992. See M. R. Freedland, *The Contract of Employment* (Oxford, 1976), pp. 19–23.

[74] 20 Geo. 2, c. 19 s. 2.

[75] 6 Geo. 3, c. 25 s. 4.

[76] 4 Geo. 4, c. 34 s. 3.

[77] *Llanelly Rly. & Dock Co.* v. *London & N.W. Rly. Co.* (1875) L.R. 7 H.L. 550. Compare Mill's views on long-term contracts, referred to *supra*, p. 320.

[78] *Per* Lord Selborne at p. 567.

nature, involving an agreement between two railway companies by which one company gave the other 'running powers' over its lines; but it was nevertheless a remarkable prima facie rule which the House of Lords here laid down. This was a binding executory contract indeed! The analogy of partnerships, leases, and other similar contracts was rejected on the somewhat circular ground that the law being well settled in those cases, 'the parties ... must be supposed to have intended' the results prescribed by the law.[79] Needless to say, this new concept of a perpetual contract caused a good deal of trouble, and that rule is now little more than a rule of construction which is inapplicable to most 'commercial' contracts, and is hardly likely to be applied to any other.[80]

Corporate Contracts

Yet another illustration of the changing attitudes to the executory contract is to be found in the law relating to the contractual capacity of corporations. In early law a great deal of trouble was caused by the common law rule requiring corporate contracts to be in writing and sealed with the corporation seal. This rule was relaxed in a variety of cases and in particular, it was relaxed where two conditions were satisfied: first, where the contract was a routine contract falling within the everyday business of the corporation, and secondly, where the contract had been executed on one side, so that one party had actually received the benefit of the other's performance.[81] Manifestly, the injustice of refusing to enforce a part executed contract is so great that only in the most extreme cases is it likely to be countenanced by the Courts. But in 1839 the Queen's Bench swept away the old distinction, and held that it was impossible to distinguish between an executed and an executory contract.[82] In a somewhat remarkable judgment, Denman C.J. said this:

Now the same contract which is executory today may become executed tomorrow; if the breach of it in its latter state may be sued for, it can only be on the supposition that the party was competent to enter into it in its former, and, if the party were so competent, on what ground can it be said that the peculiar remedy which the law gives for the enforcement of such a contract may not be used for the purpose? It appears to us to be a legal solecism to say that parties are competent by law to enter into a valid contract in a particular form, and that the appropriate legal remedies for the enforcement or on breach of such a contract are not available between them... [W]e do not see how to support any

[79] Lord Cairns at p. 560.

[80] See *Martin Baker Aircraft Co. Ltd.* v. *Canadian Flight Equipment Ltd.* [1955] 2 Q.B. 556; Carnegie, 'Terminability of Contracts of Unspecified Duration', 85 *Law Q. Rev.* 192 (1969).

[81] See *Beverley* v. *Lincoln Gas Light & Coke Co.* (1837) 6 Ad. & E. 829, 112 E.R. 318; *East London Water Works Co.* v. *Bailey* (1827) 4 Bing. 283, 130 E.R. 776. A somewhat similar distinction between executed and executory contracts had previously been adopted in the case of goods or services supplied to a lunatic: *Baxter* v. *Earl of Portsmouth* (1826) 5 B. & C. 170, 172, 108 E.R. 63, 64.

[82] *Church* v. *Imperial Gas Light & Coke Co.* (1838) 6 Ad. & E. 846, 112 E.R. 324.

distinction between express executory and executed contracts of the description now under consideration.[83]

In effect the Court has here subsumed executed contracts under the generic class of contracts, and it has argued that a rule applying to executed contracts must equally apply to an executory contract. And all this is said without a single reference to the fact that the refusal to enforce an executed contract gives rise to the extreme injustice of allowing an unjust enrichment to one party, and an unjust loss to the other, while refusal to enforce an executory contract is merely refusal to protect a bare expectation. Of course, it is natural enough for the Court to wish to limit this old technical and highly inconvenient rule about the requirement of a seal for corporate contracts, and doubtless any arguments will do in a good cause; nevertheless, it is symptomatic of the conceptual processes of the period that the Court is here able to argue in this fashion.

The Formation of Contract—Rules of Offer and Acceptance

I said earlier that one of the consequences of the rise of the executory contract was the growing tendency to reify contracts—to treat a contract as a thing which was intentionally made by the parties. The earlier idea that a contractual liability was a creation of the law, that contract was thus a remedial concept, like (say) tort or the constructive trust, was naturally more easily applicable to a law of executed contracts. When the legal results of an arrangment or transaction only had to be considered after something had happened, after benefits had been accepted, or acts of reliance undertaken, it was unnecessary and would have been difficult to conceive of a contract as a thing. But now that contracts came to be thought of as relationships intentionally entered into for future performance, a different perspective became necessary. And so also, it became necessary to formulate rules to determine *how* a contract was made. The rules of offer and acceptance became a necessary part of contract law.

These rules were of very late origin in the common law, for they cannot really be traced back before the last decade of the eighteenth century. There is virtually nothing about formation of contract in Powell's *Essay*. The first traceable cases on the rules of offer and acceptance are *Payne* v. *Cave* (1789),[84] *Cooke* v. *Oxley* (1790),[85] *Kennedy* v. *Lee* (1817),[86] *Adams* v. *Lindsell* (1818),[87] and *Routledge* v. *Grant* (1828).[88]

---

[83] 6 Ad. & E. 859, 112 E.R. 324. See too *Hunt* v. *Wimbledon Local Board* (1878) 4 C.P.D. 48, 55, where Bramwell L.J. argued likewise.

[84] 3 T.R. 148, 100 E.R. 502.   [85] 3 T.R. 653, 100 E.R. 785.

[86] 3 Mer. 441, 36 E.R. 170.   [87] 1 B. & Ald. 681, 106 E.R. 250.

[88] 3 C. & P. 267, 172 E.R. 415, and 4 Bing. 653, 130 E.R. 920.

These, with a handful of later decisions, and some assistance from the textbook writers, helped to create virtually a wholly new chapter in the law of contract. By the time that Pothier's book appeared in England, interest was obviously aroused in this topic, for his translator, Evans, discusses the significance of *Cooke* v. *Oxley* at some length in the light of Pothier's views.[89] By 1834, when the second edition of Chitty's book on *Contract* was published, we find a statement under the heading of 'Assent' of a few rules on offer and acceptance, largely based on Pothier's treatment, and a reference to a handful of cases.[90] Austin also gave the subject some attention in his *Province of Jurisprudence Determined*, and his treatment again follows that of Pothier, as well as owing some influence to the Roman lawyers.

There is no need in a work of this nature to go through these early cases in any detail. But there is one point that must be made. The early cases all insist, from *Payne* v. *Cave* on, that one party cannot be bound while the other is not. Either both parties must be bound, or neither can be bound. This requirement came to be called 'mutuality' and it was insisted upon in scores of cases in the late eighteenth and early nineteenth centuries. Best C.J. was particularly prone to rest his decisions on this ground.[91] It is quite clear that this requirement was imported into the early cases simply to give effect to the judges' sense of justice, for no authority or principle was stated to justify it. It was simply assumed, as a matter of natural justice and equity, that contracts must be two-sided exchanges, and not one-sided promises. As these decisions were analysed and restated it came to be said that an executory contract depended upon an exchange of promises. Now the question of consideration was not raised in any of the early cases, and one can understand the difficulty that the Courts must have felt under when they tried to square the new decisions, recognizing the idea of an executory contract, with the old ideas about consideration. As I have already explained what happened was almost a piece of sleight of hand, probably not even consciously perceived or understood by the Courts. The idea of benefit or detriment was transferred from the performances to the promise; if there was no exchange of performances, there was at least an exchange of promises. Each promise was necessarily a consideration for the other promise, even if it were never performed at all. The law, as it is known today, was stated by Pothier's translater:

Where a contract is entered into, which is not executed on the one side at the

---

[89] ii. 24 *et seq.*

[90] p. 8 *et seq.*

[91] See, e.g., *Routledge* v. *Grant, supra; Thomas Smith* v. *F. & R. Sparrow* (1827) 4 Bing. 44, 130 E.R. 700; *Beverley* v. *Lincoln Gas Light* (1837) 6 Ad. & E. 839, 112 E.R. 322; *Mayor of Stafford* v. *Till* (1827) 4 Bing. 75, 77, 130 E.R. 697, 697.

time, but there is a mutual engagement to be performed at a future period, the promise of the one party is a consideration for the promise of the other, and the engagement must become obligatory on both parties at the same time.[92]

CONSIDERATION IN SEARCH OF A NEW ROLE

The profound changes in the conceptual structure of contractual theory which I have sketched above naturally had a great influence on the function of the doctrine of consideration. In this new world of the executory contract, what purpose did it serve? 'It [was] now generally assumed that so far as consideration [was] concerned the executory bilateral contract [was] on a complete parity with the situation where the plaintiff [had] already paid the price of the defendant's promised performance.'[93] If there were mutual promises, then by definition, consideration was normally present. If there were no mutual promises, then, prima facie, there was no contract at all. Where did consideration fit into all this? What was to happen to benefits and detriments?

The difficulty was reinforced by the fact that the Courts now finally repudiated the eighteenth-century ideas about the fairness of an exchange, and emphatically decided that the value of the consideration was a matter for the parties alone. It will be remembered that until 1770 there was still a considerable degree of flexibility in the attitude of Equity to hard and unconscionable bargains, and that even in the Courts of common law jury discretions served to prevent any serious injustice arising from excessive, or grossly inadequate consideration. Moreover, in some cases at least, for example those involving an infant or a restrictive agreement entered into by a servant or seller of a business, the Courts had quite explicitly insisted that the contracts would only be upheld if there was a fair consideration.

Towards the end of the eighteenth century the attitude of the Court of Chancery began to shift significantly on the question of adequacy of consideration. Lord Thurlow, as Lord Chancellor in the 1780s, insisted on the difference between a bargain that turned out unfortunately for one party and a bargain that was unfair at the outset. The notion of an executory contract as a device for allocating risks began to be stressed. In *Mortimer* v. *Capper*[94] a man sold land for £200 and an annuity of £5 per annum on his own life. The seller was found drowned two days after making the contract so that the annuity was lost, but Lord Thurlow refused to set the contract aside at the suit of the seller's executors. Two years later he decreed specific performance of a contract for the sale of a

---

[92] ii. 24.
[93] Fuller, 'Consideration and Form', 41 *Columbia Law Rev.* 799, 816 (1941).
[94] (1782) Bro. C.C. 156, 28 E.R. 1051.

piece of land at an exorbitantly high price, despite the fact that the buyer had failed to get permission from the Bristol Corporation to build a mill on the site. The buyer had known that such permission was needed, but the seller had refused to make the sale conditional on their consent. 'I am not very anxious', said the Lord Chancellor,

to discuss the point, what bargains the Court will execute or not ... [R]ules ought to be fixed, and it would be calamitous that the matter should rest upon such loose expressions as hard and'unconscionable—which expressions, unless they are properly applied, mean little or nothing. The bargain, if impeached, must be so at the time of commencement; for nothing has happened since to impeach it, unless that the party has failed in his speculation in respect to a bargain which he made with his eyes perfectly open.'[95]

The decisive case in Equity may well have been *Griffith* v. *Spratley*[96] though this was actually a decision on the Equity side of the Exchequer Court rather than in Chancery itself. The plaintiff, a sailor in distressed circumstances, sold various reversionary interests to a broker for an annuity which (he alleged) was worth far less than the interests sold. The plaintiff now sought to set the sale aside, contending that the mere inadequacy of the consideration was, on its own, sufficient to justify the Court acting thus. The Lord Chief Baron rejected the contention, saying that the consideration, though probably inadequate, was not grossly so. But he also insisted that mere inadequacy of consideration was not a ground for setting aside a contract:

I know of no such principle: the common law knows of no such. The consideration more or less supports the contract. Common sense knows no such principle. The value of a thing is what it will produce, and admits of no precise standard. It must be in its nature fluctuating, and will depend upon ten thousand different circumstances. One man in the disposal of his property may sell it for less than another would; he may sell it under pressure of circumstances, which may induce him to sell it at a particular time. Now if Courts of Equity are to unravel all these transactions, they would throw everything into confusion and set afloat all the contracts of mankind. Therefore I never can agree that inadequacy of consideration is in itself a principle upon which a party may be relieved from a contract which he wittingly and willingly entered into.[97]

A few years after this decision Powell's *Essay* was published. Although he does not seem to have been too confident that the new doctrine was firmly settled, he certainly gave it his full support and condemned the earlier laxity.[98] He also insisted that there was no difference between common law and equity on this point, saying that 'it is the consent of the

[95] *Adams* v. *Weare* (1784) 1 Bro. C.C. 567, 28 E.R. 1301.
[96] (1787) 1 Cox Ch.C. 383, 29 E.R. 1213.
[97] 1 Cox. Ch.C. 388–9, 29 E.R. 1215.
[98] ii. 72, 78, 144, 152, 158–9.

parties alone that fixes the just price of anything, without reference to the nature of things themselves, or to their intrinsic value.'[99] Thus were the views of Hobbes, reinforced, now, by those which were being attributed to Adam Smith, at last being imported into English law.[1]

There remained some tidying up to be done. In Equity it was not possible wholly to get rid of the basic Chancery attitude that harsh and unconscionable contracts should not be enforced. But by the mid-nineteenth century it was being said that if the equitable jurisdiction was exclusive, so that the rejected litigant had nowhere else to go, then even the Court of Chancery would enforce a harsh or unreasonable contract.[2] The discretion to refuse specific performance was said to apply only where equitable relief was concurrent with some legal remedy. But in fact the discretionary element was declining in importance all the time. By now, if Equity refused to enforce an unfair or harsh bargain, and left the plaintiff 'to take his remedy at law', the plaintiff was, indeed, likely to do just that, for the old jury discretions were also being eliminated.[3] And as time went on the tendency grew to insist on the plaintiff's right to specific performance even in cases of concurrent jurisdiction.[4] By 1880 the element of discretion in cases of hardship had almost entirely vanished.[5] For some time an idea lingered on that there might be a distinction between executed contracts (where hardship was pleaded by the plaintiff as a ground for setting aside a contract) and executory contracts (where hardship was pleaded as a defence). But gradually this distinction disappeared too.

The old rules about 'expectant heirs' and dealings in reversions also fell into disrepute. In 1840 the House of Lords held that in transactions of this kind, the market price *was* a fair price.[5A] In 1867 the Sale of Reversions Act declared that a mere undervalue on a sale of a reversionary interest was no longer to invalidate the contract. Lord Selborne, the last strong Equity Chancellor for half a century, insisted shortly afterwards that this Statute in no way restricted Equity's jurisdiction to deal with contracts made with expectant heirs where something more than mere undervalue was shown,[6] but by this time

---

[99] ii. 229.

[1] In fact, in so far as the lawyers attributed these ideas to the political economists, they were largely anticipating the views of the next generation rather than drawing on Adam Smith or Ricardo. The classics by no means subscribed to a purely subjective theory of value, a theory which only came with Jevons in the 1870s. See L. Robbins, *Evolution of Modern Economic Theory* (London, 1970), pp. 173–6; D. P. O'Brien, *The Classical Economists* (Oxford, 1976), Chapter 4.

[2] See E. Batten, *The Law Relating to the Specific Performance of Contracts* (London, 1849), p. 248.

[3] See, e.g., *Mortlock* v. *Buller* (1804) 10 Ves. 292, 32 E.R. 857, where specific performance was refused, but the plaintiff then sued at law and obtained an advantageous settlement. For this sequel see *Burrow* v. *Scammell* (1881) 19 Ch.D. 183.

[4] *Borell* v. *Dann* (1843) 2 Hare 440, 67 E.R. 181.   [5] *Tamplin* v. *James* (1880) 15 Ch.D. 215.

[5A] *Earl of Aldborough* v. *Trye* (1840) 7 Cl. & F. 436, 7 E.R. 1136.

[6] *Earl of Aylesford* v. *Morris* (1873) L.R. 8 Ch. App. 484.

equitable intervention of this kind was becoming to seem more and more anomalous.

There remained also some troublesome old cases at common law concerning restraints of trade. As late as *Horner* v. *Graves*[7] in 1831 the Court of Common Pleas examined the fairness of the consideration in a case in which the defendant had been employed as an assistant to the plaintiff, a dentist, at a salary of £120 per annum. The defendant had covenanted not to compete within a hundred miles of York on penalty of a liability of £1,000. The Court held this covenant to be bad because the defendant was liable to be dismissed on three months' notice, and this was 'a very slender and inadequate consideration for such a sacrifice'.[8] This was not, of course, anything in the nature of a general principle concerning adequacy of consideration because the restraint of trade cases had always been subject to special rules. But even this degree of intervention was too much for the common law Courts in the new age, and in *Hitchcock* v. *Croker*[9] the Exchequer Chamber repudiated the doctrine that required it to weigh the adequacy of consideration; the King's Bench immediately fell into line.[10]

It was not long before the Courts were prepared to say that the mere receipt of a promise in exchange for another was proof that it was beneficial. If a person gave his promise in exchange for another, that was in itself proof that the latter promise was of some value. In *Haigh* v. *Brooks*[11] the defendant had promised to meet bills to the value of £9,000 in consideration of the plaintiff returning to the defendant a guarantee under which the defendant appeared to be liable for sums of up to £10,000. There was, however some doubt about the validity of the guarantee and the defendant refused to meet the bills, and when sued, argued that there was no consideration for his promise. The Court held that even if the guarantee had been void, and had been known to be such, the mere handing to the defendant, at his request, of a piece of paper (or the promise to do so) was a sufficient consideration. The defendant, after all, had assessed its value by promising to pay £9,000 for it. It was not for the Court to say that the defendant had valued it wrongly. So, at last, the principles of Political Economy had (it seemed) triumphed. Parties must be free to make their own bargains and to fix their own prices. The law might still require a consideration, but the value of that consideration was entirely a matter for the parties.

The doctrine of consideration was, by now, well on the way to

[7] (1831) 1 Bing. 735, 131 E.R. 284.   [8] 1 Bing. 743, 131 E.R. 287.

[9] (1838) 6 Ad. & E. 438, 112 E.R. 167.

[10] *Archer* v. *Marsh* (1837–8) 6 Ad. & E. 959, 112 E.R. 367.

[11] (1839) 10 Ad. & E. 309, 113 E.R. 119, affirmed (1840) 10 Ad. & E. 323, 113 E.R. 124. For another remarkable example of a promise being enforced without any real benefit to the promisor, see *Hamilton* v. *Watson* (1845) 12 Cl. & F. 10, 98 E.R. 1339, a decision which shocks the conscience today.

becoming a bare technicality.[12] The only purpose which it continued to serve was to exclude liability on a unilateral, gratuitous promise, not made by deed. In this respect, English law continued to differ from that stated by Pothier who, of course, discussed the concept of *cause* rather than consideration. The two concepts seem, without doubt, to have been the same in their essentials, especially when applied to executed contracts.[13] For the only significant difference between *cause* and consideration was that beneficence or liberality could be a sufficient *cause* while it could not (as it is usually stated) be a sufficient consideration. But this distinction only existed, or certainly only came into prominence, with the rise of the executory contract. For, so long as executed transactions alone were under discussion, beneficence or liberality was just as good in English law as it was in French.[14] To make a gift by delivery of something, or by signing a deed of gift, has always been valid in English law, and what is this other than an executed transaction, supported by a good *cause*? Both *cause* and consideration performed the function of insisting that a person was not to be made liable under an obligation without some good reason. A promise prima facie *was* a good reason, but if the promise could be shown to have been made without good reason, for example, because the promisor was under no obligation to do what he promised, then, certainly in the eighteenth century, the promise might well have been held not binding. But in the classical age, as the executory contract became the focal point of contract law, promises came to be treated as generating their own ground of liability. They were no longer evidence of some pre-existing, independent duty, as they had so often been in the past; they were themselves the sources of contractual duties. Consequently it now became difficult to see why a gratuitous promise was not binding. Such a promise, if made from motives of liberality, had a good *cause*, but it did not have a good consideration. It was, therefore, at this point that the two concepts diverged.

But for many in the classical period, it was English law which was out of step, not French. There are signs in the mid-nineteenth century that the doctrine of consideration, in so far as it prevented enforcement of gratuitous promises, was about to wither away altogether. In 1854 the Mercantile Law Commission appear to have contemplated total abolition of the doctrine,[15] and two years later Pollock C.B. made some highly

---

[12] See, e.g., *Thomas* v. *Thomas* (1842) 2 Q.B. 851, 114 E.R. 330.

[13] Cf. A. T. Von Mehren, 'Civil Law Analogues to Consideration: An Exercise in Comparative Analysis', 72 *Harvard Law Rev.* 1009 (1959).

[14] There is an interesting passage on the distinction between a present and a future will in *The Leviathan*, Chapter 14, p. 67 of the Pelican edn.

[15] Second Report, (1854–5) H.C. *Parliamentary Papers*, xviii. 664, 678. There is, however, some obscurity in the Report, and it is not entirely clear whether the Commissioners were talking about the whole doctrine of consideration, or its applicability in specific cases.

critical remarks about the doctrine in directing a jury.[16] By the end of the classical period, jurists and writers like Markby[17] and Leake[18] could find nothing to say for the doctrine as a substantive ground of liability. Markby argued that it was a matter of form, like writing, while Leake treated it as evidence of the serious intention of the parties. This latter idea, which has been repeated by many later writers, indicates the extent to which the executory contract has triumphed over the executed contract. If A lends B £100, is B's promise to repay the money the sole ground of liability, the fact of the money having been received by him merely evidence of the seriousness of his promise? If X sells *and delivers* goods to Y is Y's promise to pay for them the only ground of his liability? Is the receipt of the goods merely evidence of the seriousness of his intent? These grotesque distortions are still the heritage of the modern common lawyer who has, for over a hundred years, learned to think of contract theory exclusively in terms of executory contracts.

Now that the doctrine of consideration had ceased to have very much to do with the idea of benefit or detriment, the way was open for it to acquire some new content. And early in the nineteenth century we do, indeed, find the idea of consideration being prayed in aid in a variety of cases which, to later generations, seemed to have more to do with public policy than with consideration. For example, there were the cases in which the consideration was said to consist of something that a party was already bound to do, such as a seaman being promised extra pay for working a short-manned ship, or a witness answering to a subpoena.[19] A large number of nineteenth- and twentieth-century cases involved problems of this kind and many of them were dealt with as raising questions about consideration. I do not suggest that the concepts of benefit and detriment are totally irrelevant in these cases. Indeed, it is clear that they still did raise issues of this kind; if a seaman did extra work because his ship was short-handed, was the shipowner getting any 'real' benefit from this, since the seaman obviously 'ought' in one sense to do it anyhow? But what I do suggest is that the doctrine of consideration tended, from now on, to become fragmented into a number of sub-doctrines concerned with specific issues of this nature. Once the basic notion had been conceded that a bare unperformed promise was good consideration simply because the promisee chose to buy it, there was little room for any systematic development of the doctrine of consideration in terms of benefits and detriments. These had become matters solely for the parties. It followed that unless there was some public policy involved,

---

[16] *Hulse* v. *Hulse* (1856) 17 C.B. 711, 717, 139 E.R. 1256, 1258.

[17] *Elements of Jurisprudence*, first published 1871, 3rd edn. (Oxford, 1885), pp. 308 *et seq.*

[18] *Contracts* (London, 1867), p. 10.

[19] *Stilk* v. *Myrick* (1809) 2 Camp. 317, 170 E.R. 1168; *Hartley* v. *Ponsonby* (1857) 7 E. & B. 872, 119 E.R. 1471; *Collins* v. *Godefroy* (1831) 1 B. & Ad. 950, 109 E.R. 1040.

some element of public interest, there was virtually no further room for discussion about benefit and detriment. The substantive core of the doctrine of consideration had been eliminated by the move to the executory contract.

15

FREEDOM OF CONTRACT IN THE COURTS, 1770-1870—II

THE DECLINE OF RELIANCE AND BENEFIT

IN the previous chapter I described the rise of consensualism, the increasing importance attached to promise, agreement, and intention as the basis of legal liabilities. Inevitably, the counterpart of this was the decline in the importance attached to other sources of liability, and in particular, the concepts of Reliance and Benefit. It is important that we should be clear in what sense these concepts declined in this period. In one sense, the decline was primarily verbal or conceptual. Courts, judges, and lawyers came to perceive nearly all liabilities as arising from contract, and from the consensualism that they now took to underlie contract. They tended, therefore, to base liability, even where there was an important element of reliance or benefit in the case, not on that element, but on some consensual element. If they found a consensual element coinciding with an element of reliance or benefit, then they tended to emphasize the former at the expense of the latter. If there was no apparent consensual element in the case, but the Courts still felt moved to impose liability, either as a result of their own sense of justice, or as a result of the weight of tradition and precedent, then they were inclined to find some 'implied' contract, consent, promise, or agreement. There was, of course, nothing new in the notion of an 'implied' promise; indeed, there was nothing very new even in the fictitious implication of intentions or promises. Locke's social contract theories were full of 'implied' agreements; and Bentham had already railed at the lawyers for the irrationality of their use of such fictions.[1] But there certainly was a great increase in the extent to which the Courts came to rely on such implications in the period 1770–1870.

Now the decline of reliance and benefit in this conceptual sense was, in some respects, a very paradoxical development. Because as the Courts began to impose liabilities on a consensual ground, they came to protect expectations; and whenever they did that, they tended to increase the liability they were imposing. If a person is entitled to have his full expectations protected, he will generally be given more extensive rights than if he is merely protected against the costs of any reliance he may have incurred; and similarly, if a man who has received some benefit has to pay, not the value of that benefit, but the expectations derived by the

[1] *Works*, ed. Bowring, iii. pp. 190–1.

other party from the transaction, he may well have to pay more. The strange result, therefore, was that, in so far as the Courts came to protect expectations based on a consensual theory of liability, they actually created greater liabilities than had previously existed when only reliance or benefit interests may have been protected. It must be borne in mind, throughout this chapter, that the decline of the importance directly attached to reliance and benefit, often had this result.

But there was another sense in which reliance and benefit declined in importance, and in this sense the result was not even primarily conceptual, but of substantive importance. For the judicial sense of justice was itself affected, to some degree and in some cases, by the increasing importance attached to consensualism, and all that went with it. The idea that a man might be held liable, without his consent, merely because he had received a benefit at the hands of another, or merely because the other had relied upon him to his loss, began to lose its hold on the sense of justice. After all that I have said in previous chapters, it should be apparent that this was no peculiarity of the judicial mind, but was part of the general atmosphere of the times. Inevitably, as men became convinced of the importance of the free market, as they became more attached to the social ideals of individualism and self-reliance, as they came to accept (more or less) the atomistic view of society in which all relationships depended on free choice, they tended also to feel that it was unjust that a man should have liabilities thrust upon him which he had not agreed to bear.

The result of these developments in the theoretical basis of the law was that, to a substantial extent, both the benefit and the reliance concepts were split down the middle. The cases in which benefits and reliance interests were regarded as worthy of protection came to be reinterpreted as depending on expectations. The executed contract was swallowed by the executory contract, and the benefit or reliance was incidentally protected as part of the broader protection now accorded to mere expectations. On the other hand, where this was not possible, where there had been some benefit conferred or some act of reasonable reliance, which was impossible to support as part of a broader expectation, where the circumstances made it hard or impossible to spell out a contract from the transaction or the events which had occurred, the benefit and the reliance tended to go unprotected. Thus benefits came to be increasingly compensated as part of contract law, while quasi-contract declined in importance; and similarly, reliance interests were increasingly protected as part of a general protection of expectations in contract cases, while reliance which was not attributable to a contract, tended to become less well protected. Nevertheless, here as elsewhere, the new theory never quite attained its logical goals. The law of quasi-contract obstinately refused to die; there remained a residue of cases in which the Courts were obliged to protect restitution interests, were obliged to compel a man to pay or repay for a benefit received, even where no contract could possibly be spelled out of the circumstances. And there also remained a hard core of cases in which reliance interests were protected because the Courts felt that some act of reasonable reliance simply could not be left unprotected even though it was hard or impossible to spell out a contract. Moreover, the decline was short-lived. At least in some areas there are clear signs of a resurgence of benefit-based and reliance-based obligations by 1870.

RELIANCE

As I have said above, reliance cases, like benefit cases, tended to be split down the middle by the new conceptual structure. Where reliance was to be protected at all, it was now increasingly protected as a part and parcel of the protection of expectations. Where it could not be protected in this fashion, it tended to go unprotected altogether, but there remained a residue of cases which simply could not be accommodated within the confines of the new theory.

In the first group of cases, reliance interests came to be protected increasingly as part of the general protection of expectations which was accorded by recognition of the executory contract. In a sense, this was a logical and inevitable part of the switch to the executory contract. Courts no longer asked whether the plaintiff *had* relied upon a promise, or on some act of the defendant; it was enough that the plaintiff *might* have so acted. So long as a contract could be spelled out of the circumstances, the bare possibility of reliance was thus enough. There are a great many cases which illustrate this first change. To take one example, in *Shadwell* v. *Shadwell*[2] the defendant promised to pay the plaintiff, his nephew, an annual allowance on hearing of the plaintiff's engagement to be married. The nephew duly got married, the uncle duly paid the allowance; but eventually the uncle died, and his executors refused to continue its payment. The Court upheld the plaintiff's claim, mainly on the ground that the nephew *might* have acted in reliance on the promise so as materially to change his position.[3] It is, of course, clear enough that there was no bargain, no commercial exchange contemplated here. The plaintiff's case was that he had been led to expect payment of the allowance and had changed his position in reliance on that expectation. This ground of liability was, however, subsumed under the more extensive liability implied by the holding that there was actually an executory contract made which gave full protection to the plaintiff's

[2] (1860) 9 C.B.(N.S.) 159, 142 E.R. 62.
[3] 9 C.B.(N.S.) 174, 142 E.R. 68 (Erle C.J.).

mere expectations. It was thus unnecessary to inquire whether he *had* in fact changed his position in reliance on the promise. The fact that he *might* have done so was sufficient.[4] In modern times, the holding that there was a binding executory contract in this case is, with some reason, considered very odd—did the nephew promise his uncle to marry the lady of his choice? But rejection of this holding should not carry the conclusion that the plaintiff was not entitled to any remedy at all; the possibility of inquiring into the facts to see if the plaintiff actually had made his financial position worse (and if so to what extent), and of compensating him for that reliance, remains open.

This case was not untypical of a large class of difficult nineteenth-century decisions; they all involved promises or agreements to settle property or money, or to make some similar arrangement, in the event of a marriage taking place. Frequently (though not always) the promise was made by the father of the prospective bride to the prospective groom; of course, the proper procedure was to have an elaborate marriage settlement prepared and executed prior to the marriage, though making its operation conditional upon the marriage taking place. But, for one reason or another, this procedure was not always followed, and litigation was not an uncommon result. Throughout the whole of this period, that is from 1770 to 1870, cases of this kind gave the Courts much trouble. At first there was a tendency to protect the party who had relied on the promise, though nearly always to the full extent of the expectations generated.[5] But in 1854 the House of Lords in *Jorden* v. *Money*[6] refused protection in a case of this kind, though the true explanation of this case is much controverted.[7] But however difficult it is to explain this decision, one point seems clear enough: the majority of the House of Lords rejected the notion that a promise or a representation as to future conduct which was acted or relied upon by the promisee or representee could be binding unless it was binding as a contract. A promise or statement of intent is either binding as a contract or it is not binding at all: there is no *tertium quid*, no possibility of protecting the reliance interest, compensating the plaintiff to the extent that he has actually worsened his position but no further.

----

[4] It was argued that the plaintiff, being already engaged to be married when the uncle made the promise, did not in fact act in reliance on the promise. But a careful reading of the case suggests the possibility that the uncle first made an oral promise on the strength of which the nephew became engaged; and that this oral promise (not being enforceable because of the Statute of Frauds) was then confirmed in writing. The nephew, who was a barrister, must have known that the oral promise would be unenforceable.

[5] See, e.g., *Luders* v. *Anstey* (1799) 4 Ves. 501, 31 E.R. 263; *Crosbie* v. *M'Doual* (1806) 13 Ves. 148, 33 E.R. 251; *Hammersley* v. *De Biel* (1845) 12 Cl. & F. 45, 8 E.R. 1312; *Bold* v. *Hutchinson* (1855) 5 De G. M. & G. 558, 43 E.R. 986.

[6] *Jorden* v. *Money* (1854) 5 H.L.C. 185, 10 E.R. 868.

[7] See my *Consideration in Contracts* (Canberra, 1971), pp. 53–8.

Another type of case in which the possibility of reliance seems to have been treated by the Courts as a ground for protection of the expectation interest concerns those circumstances in which a defendant misled the plaintiff as to his intentions. If the defendant gave the plaintiff cause to think that he meant to accept an offer, or that he accepted some proposed term, or if the defendant simply conducted himself in such a way as to give a misleading impression of his own intentions, it was the external signs which counted. This 'objective' approach to the formation and interpretation of contracts was clearly established throughout this period—it is already stated in Powell's *Essay*[8]—even at the time during which the 'will theory' of contractual obligation was at its strongest. It has, indeed, been said that one of the greatest puzzles of contract law is to understand why the Courts should have wished to couple a bargain theory of contracts with this hard objectivism.[9] At the very same time that the Courts were insisting that contracts should be construed so as to give effect to the intention of the parties, they were also adopting rules which often precluded a search for any real intent. So far as the classical period is concerned, the explanation of this puzzle seems to lie in two factors. First there was a determination to keep factual questions down to a bare minimum. A man who behaved in such a way as to lead another to suppose that he meant one thing was to be treated as though he did mean that thing. The other *may* have relied upon these external signs of intent; no inquiry was to be permitted into whether he actually did so, or not; no inquiry was to be permitted into what actual loss might have been sustained by reliance on the external appearances of intent so conveyed. The apparent intent was to be deemed a real intent; the expectations so generated were entitled to the full protection of the law precisely as though there had been a real intent behind them.

The second reason behind the extreme objective approach is to be found in the importance of principle. The classical contract lawyers assumed that if it was open to a man to deny that his apparent intent was his real intent, many cases might occur in which the Courts would *wrongly* accept such a defence. In order to exclude the possibility of such erroneous decisions being made, therefore, it was desirable to exclude the question from consideration altogether. This line of reasoning is seen perhaps most clearly in those cases in which the Courts laid down the parol evidence rule. Under this rule a written contract was not to be varied by oral evidence that it did not correctly represent the intention of the parties.[10] This rule which probably originated with wills, rather than

---

[8] i. 372 3.

[9] R. Bronaugh, 'Contracting: An Essay in Legal Philosophy', unpublished B. Litt. thesis (Oxford, 1976), p. 156.

[10] *Goss* v. *Lord Nugent* (1833), 5 B. & Ad. 58, 110 E.R. 713.

contracts, was emphatically affirmed in a case in 1842.[11] This case concerned a deed made in 1704 where a great deal of trouble was caused at the trial by attempts to ascertain the actual intention of the grantor of the deed, and the judges called on to advise the Lords, castigated these attempts at a search for the actual intent. Erskine J. expressed clearly the anxiety that opening the door to such evidence might simply lead to more erroneous than correct decisions. If the parol evidence rule were once weakened, he insisted, 'every man's will and intention, however expressed, would be liable to be defeated, not, as now sometimes the case, by his own defective expression of that will, but contrary to his own plainly declared intention.'[12]

The judicial willingness to protect reasonable reliance by finding implied contracts in the mid-nineteenth century is illustrated by a number of cases from this period which have looked dubious to modern lawyers, even though the results may sometimes be thought desirable. These cases include, in particular, *Hammersely* v. *De Biel*,[13] where it was held that a father's statements to his prospective son-in-law about his daughter's inheritance could be a binding commitment; *Denton* v. *Great Northern Rly. Co.*,[14] where it was held that publication of a railway timetable was a promise to run the trains there shown, capable of acceptance by a passenger tendering the money for a ticket; *Warlow* v. *Harrison*,[15] where it was held that an auctioneer's announcement that a sale will be held without reserve is a promise accepted by the highest bona fide bidder; and *Collen* v. *Wright*,[16] where it was held that a person who relied upon an agent's representation that he had authority to conclude a lease, was entitled to sue him on an implied contract whereby the agent warranted his authority. In the first three of these cases the protection of the party who had acted in reasonable reliance was achieved by giving him a full contractual right, and thereby protecting his expectations. *Collen* v. *Wright* is as unusual as it is interesting on this point, for the case does in fact distinguish between protection of the reliance interest and protection of the expectation interest. The plaintiff, having negotiated a lease of a property with the agent, moved into the premises, only to discover that the landlord repudiated his agent's conduct and demanded that the plaintiff quit the premises. The plaintiff declined, was sued, and lost, whereupon he sued the agent. In upholding his claim to damages the lower Court suggested to the plaintiff's counsel

---

[11] *Shore* v. *Wilson* (1842) 9 Cl. & F. 355, 8 E.R. 450.
[12] 9 Cl. & F. 514, 8 E.R. 513.
[13] (1845) 12 Cl. & F. 45, 8 E.R. 1312.
[14] (1856) 5 E. & B. 860, 119 E.R. 701.
[15] (1859) 1 E. & E. 309, 120 E.R. 925.
[16] (1857) 8 E. & B. 647, 120 E.R. 241.

that he might rest content with recovering the damages representing the money actually thrown away, and not pursue a further claim for loss of bargain; and the plaintiff accepted this invitation.[17] Nevertheless, it seems clear enough today that the plaintiff in such a case is entitled to protection of his expectation interest, precisely as though the agent had expressly contracted to see that the plaintiff received the full value of the bargain.

All of these cases seem to the modern lawyer to rest upon somewhat dubious foundations. The first three were roughly handled by Pollock in his *Principles of Contract* first published in 1876;[18] the second is almost certainly no longer law, and the third continues to attract criticism.[19] The fourth is generally accepted on account of the manifest injustice which (it is generally felt) would be suffered by a party relying upon an agent's implied representation of authority, if he was held without remedy against either principal or agent himself. The decision has, in any event, been approved by the House of Lords.[20] Nevertheless, all four decisions seem difficult to reconcile with modern contractual ideas, and the reason is surely plain enough. In all these cases the Courts wanted to protect a party who had reasonably relied (as was thought) on some statement or promise or conduct, and thereby suffered loss, but such protection was afforded by the extreme step of giving the plaintiff full contractual expectation rights. I need not pursue here the policy issues arising in modern conditions in such cases. My point is that at the height of the classical period the Courts seem to have thought that they could only protect reliance interests by protecting expectation interests.[21] That was then, and has generally continued to seem, a somewhat extreme protection. What was evidently missing in the mid-nineteenth century was the idea that reliance could be protected on its own, without also protecting expectations. To the modern lawyer, that may seem like a suggestion that reliance might have been protected by an expansion of tort liability rather than by stretching contractual concepts. There is truth in this way of putting the matter, but there is also distortion, for it implies that the Contract–Tort distinction is based on some natural or immutable foundation. This is, of course, only so by process of definition; and the definitions of contract which we generally use today are the result of the very developments I am describing. As we saw in Part I, there was nothing strange to eighteenth-century lawyers in protecting

[17] See 7 E. & B. 311, 119 E.R. 1262.
[18] pp. 176–9.
[19] Slade, 'Auction Sales of Goods without Reserve', 68 *Law Q. Rev.* 238 (1952) cf. Gower, ibid., 457; and see Slade's reply, 69 *Law Q. Rev.* 21 (1953).
[20] *Starkey* v. *Bank of England* [1903] A.C. 114.
[21] This is indeed stated almost in terms by Lord Cranworth in *Maunsell* v. *Hedges* (1854) 4 H.L.C. 1039, 1055–6, 10 E.R. 769, 775–6.

reliance interests through the medium of contract law, as is shown by *Coggs* v. *Barnard*.[22] In that case, it will be remembered, the plaintiff was suing for reliance damages—for the damage to one of his casks of wine— not for his loss of bargain, not for the protection of his bare expectations. By mid-nineteenth century *Coggs* v. *Barnard* was beginning to look anomalous and difficult to understand, although this did not actually prevent the decisions mentioned above.

Another important line of authority in which reliance came to be protected by the creation of full contractual expectation rights concerns those cases in which an owner of land stood by and allowed another to spend money by building on the land in the belief that it was his land, or that the owner had consented to his actions. This line of cases, which like the ones referred to above, later came to seem anomalous, has in fact a long ancestry. Like the previous cases, these authorities can be traced back to eighteenth-century decisions upholding the right of the party who has relied to his detriment.[23] Interestingly, in this instance, it is possible to find traces of the shift from protection of the reliance interest, to the protection of the expectation interest. In *Winter* v. *Brockwell*,[24] in 1807, the defendant gave the plaintiff oral permission to erect a skylight in his house which obstructed the light and air to the defendant's house but apparently the result was worse than the defendant had expected. In an action before Lord Ellenborough, the Chief Justice held that the plaintiff had reasonably relied upon the defendant's consent; at first Lord Ellenborough was inclined to allow the defendant to revoke his oral permission provided he paid the cost of erection of the skylight; but eventually he held that the defendant could not revoke his permission at all. Thus the plaintiff's expectations were protected. Subsequently, a long line of cases applied these principles in Equity, though there does not seem to have been any significant difference between the rules of law and those of Equity on this point.[25]

In all these cases, it came to be felt, somewhat after the end of this period, that the decisions were anomalous. Contracts were being enforced without consideration, it was said. The idea gained ground that it was not possible to treat action in reliance on a promise or a representation or other conduct as a good consideration. The reason for this seems to have been due almost entirely to the growing idea that a contract was a

---

[22] (1703) 2 Ld. Ray. 909, 92 E.R. 107.

[23] In *R.* v. *Butterton* (1796) 6 T.R. 554, 101 E.R. 699, Lawrence J. recalled such a case before Lord Mansfield.

[24] 8 East 308, 103 E.R. 351.

[25] *Dillwyn* v. *Llewellyn* (1862) 4 De G. F. & J. 517, 45 E.R. 1285, a decision in Equity holding that the expenditure of money in building on the faith of an invalid memorandum itself 'supplied a valuable consideration': pp. 522–3 and 1287 of the respective reports. See also *Ramsden* v. *Dyson* (1866) L.R. 1 H.L. 129.

'thing' which was intentionally made, and that it was made with a view to future performance. To treat *subsequent* action in reliance on a promise as a ground for enforcing that promise meant that it might not be possible to say whether the promise was binding or not when it was first made. No contract was then 'made'. How was it possible that such action subsequently could have the restrospective effect of 'making' a contract? And did this not go too far anyhow? For if such action made a promise binding, did this not mean that a wholly gratuitous promise could become binding by action in reliance on the promise? Some years later Holmes J. expressed these fears in an American case, saying that 'It would cut up the doctrine of consideration by the roots if a promisee could make a gratuitous promise binding by subsequently acting in reliance on it.'[26] This was, of course, part and parcel of Holmes's 'bargain theory of consideration'.[27] According to this theory, detriments and benefits were not to be treated as consideration unless they were intended by the parties to be consideration, unless that is, the parties had contemplated a real exchange of promises. Subsequent action in reliance could then only be treated as a good consideration where that action was demanded by the original bargain. A person only had the right to rely upon another party if he had *bought* the right to rely. This evidently fitted well the new market ideologies, and there are certainly traces of the theory in some English cases.[28] Nevertheless, in general, English classical theory, perhaps surprisingly, failed to evolve this bargain theory in any explicit fashion.

On the other hand, as we have seen, there were many cases in which the Courts did uphold the actionability of a promise on grounds of subsequent reliance. The sense of justice was simply too strong to be bowed down by these rather abstract and theoretical forms of reasoning. The result was a tendency to try to explain the decisions away. The decisions could only be supported on some Equitable ground, or possibly, as an extention of the doctrine of estoppel. That doctrine was, of course, itself one of the ways invented for the protection of reasonable reliance in the nineteenth century, perhaps precisely because of difficulty in treating some cases as contractual. There is some ground for thinking that it was the Statute of Frauds which first led the Courts to invent the separate doctrine of estoppel as a way of protecting action in reliance on a representation.[29]

[26] *Commonwealth* v. *Scituate Savings Bank*, 137 Mass. 301, 302 (1883). In practice U.S. Courts never adhered rigidly to this any more than English Courts, see, e.g., *Devecmon* v. *Shaw* 14 Atl. 464 (1888); *Hamer* v. *Sidway* 27 N.E. 256 (1891).

[27] More fully elaborated in *The Common Law*, Lecture VIII. See further, Grant Gilmore, *The Death of Contract*, pp. 19–21.

[28] See, e.g., *Oldershaw* v. *King* (1857) 2 H. & N. 517, 157 E.R. 213.

[29] See my *Consideration in Contracts*, p. 57.

The growing emphasis on the executory contract throughout the nineteenth century may also have played a role in some of the difficulties felt about representations of fact. An executory contract is something which looks forward to a future performance. A contract becomes, necessarily, a contract *to do* something; hence the easy transition from the idea of the parties *being in agreement* to the idea of the parties *making* an agreement,[30] from the idea of agreement to the idea of mutual promises. But promises are not the only form of behaviour on which others may reasonably rely. People often rely on statements of fact, representations of various kinds, and they may even rely on mere behaviour. Now the old common law, in which reliance had been more of a substantive ground of liability, had long recognized the concept of a warranty, that is, a contractual statement of fact, and it was not impossible to 'find' a contract by implying a warranty, even though there was no other promise to which it could be attached. The cases referred to above, like *Collen* v. *Wright*, had proceeded on this basis. Nevertheless, one reason for the increasing dubiousness of these decisions seems to have been the growing doubts about the propriety of treating representations as contractual concepts. A warranty which was part of a wider contract was one thing; but to treat a representation standing alone as a contractual statement did involve conceptual problems. Throughout the nineteenth century the Courts generally adhered to the position that representations were not actionable unless they were made fraudulently (that at least had been settled in *Pasley* v. *Freeman*)[31] or were of a contractual character, like warranties. But some measure of protection for other representations was provided by the doctrine of estoppel, though it was generally insisted upon in this period (and later) that estoppel provided no ground of action, but was only available by way of defence.

Caveat Emptor

The doctrine of *caveat emptor* can be said to represent the apotheosis of nineteenth-century individualism. The classical model of contract law, as we saw earlier, left each party to a contract to rely on his own judgment, and not that of the other party. Neither party owed duties to the other to volunteer information, or even to undeceive him when he plainly laboured under some misapprehension. Further, there was no presumption that the terms of the contract bore any particular relationship to the price agreed upon; in a contract of sale, for example, classical contract theory did not assume, because the buyer paid a price

---

[30] Cf. Hume's ideas, *supra*, p. 56.
[31] (1789) 3 T. R. 51, 100 E.R. 450.

which was fair or normal for sound goods, that therefore he was entitled to a warranty that the goods were sound. Whether there was such a warranty depended upon the actual terms of the sale. Prima facie, the formalist attitude of the Courts meant that only expressed undertakings were to be considered as warranties. Implications were not to be read into the contract. A party who wanted a warranty ought to specifically ask for one. Moreover, all this was, in theory anyhow, normative; that is to say, the Courts did not inquire whether one party *had* in fact relied upon the other, but whether he *ought* to have done so, and similarly, the Courts did not ask what expectations a man might in fact have acquired as a result of his dealings with the other party, but what expectations he was *entitled* to have acquired.

In one sense, all this appeared to follow from the principles of political economy. In earlier ages there had been a vast amount of regulation concerning the quality and fitness of various commodities, in particular bread, ale, cloths, and other common articles, not to mention special articles such as gold and silver or fire-arms, chain cables, and anchors. In the early nineteenth century, much of this fell into disrepute as a result of what the political economists were believed to have demonstrated. In a broad sort of way, the equation of *caveat emptor* with the ideas of the political economists was not wholly unjustified. If Adam Smith or Ricardo had been asked how best to prevent the manufacture and sale of shoddy goods, for example, they would unquestionably have recommended the principle of *caveat emptor*. If the responsibility for ensuring that a man acquired a reasonable purchase at a fair price were thrown upon the purchaser, they argued, then the purchaser would assuredly take the trouble to examine what he was buying with due care. Shoddy goods would disappear from the market, or if buyers in fact were willing to buy them at prices reflecting their poor quality, then the goods would find a market at that price and deservedly so. All this would follow from throwing the responsibility upon the purchaser, without any legislation or litigation.[32] It was, in theory, a simple and self-operating mechanism. By contrast, to give the buyer statutory rights, by way of exception to *caveat emptor*, involved, first the trouble of legislating, and then that of litigating. It was assumed that the buyer would have to sue the seller for redress in the event of his having purchased shoddy goods, and inevitably, such litigation would only be costly and wasteful both for the parties and from the public point of view. It was, moreover, widely assumed that

---

[32] This is quite plainly spelt out in the Second Report of the Mercantile Law Commission (1854–55) H.C. *Parliamentary Papers*, xviii. 653, 662, in comparing Scots and English law. Similarly when California was debating in 1850 whether to adopt common law or civil law a preference was shown for the common law because of the principle *caveat emptor* which did not assume a man was 'incapable of judging for himself'. L. Friedman, *Contract Law in America* (Madison, Milwaukee, 1965), p. 103.

prices were set in accordance with the principle of *caveat emptor*, that it is to say, it was assumed that buyers discounted the prices they were prepared to pay to allow for the risk that the commodity they were buying might prove defective. Consequently, if the buyer were given statutory redress against the seller, the result would be to give him a bonus for which he had not really paid. And although, no doubt, some buyers were too careless or foolish to pay adequate attention to the quality of the goods they were buying, the general principle was more important than doing justice in each particular case. Moreover, these individual cases of hardship would become less frequent as buyers learnt their responsibilities.

This theory, or set of ideas, grew up with the new political economy. It differed without doubt from the paternalist traditions of the eighteenth-century judges who felt that a man was entitled to receive fair value from a sale. At the end of the eighteenth century, there was a transitional period in which the newer ideas struggled for supremacy with the older ones. In the law, we see men like Lord Kenyon in *Mellish* v *Motteaux*,[33] still invoking a general idea of good faith in a contract of sale and imposing liability on a seller who had sold 'with all faults' a brig which turned out, on examination, to be utterly unseaworthy. And as late as 1792 the Vinerian Professor at Oxford was lecturing to the effect that the doctrine of *caveat emptor* was 'now exploded'.[34] Around the same time, moralists like Paley were searching their consciences to see how far *caveat emptor* was reconcilable with the duty of an honest man. Paley's ideas on the subject are an interesting and curious mixture of the older paternalist traditions and the newer individualist morality. On the one hand, Paley thought it dishonourable to sell anything without revealing any defects known to the seller, but he made an exception for the sale of horses. The custom of demanding a warranty of soundness in the sale of horses was so well established, he asserted, that anybody who bought without a warranty (for example, at an auction) must be assumed to know that he was thereby taking on himself the risk of unsoundness, with a consequent discount in the price.[35] Then again, Paley argues that a tradesman who sells goods for above a fair price is, morally speaking, imposing on the buyer in an unacceptable fashion. But he had some difficulty with this case, for 'as the man's goods were his own, and he had a right to prescribe the terms upon which he would consent to part with them, it may be questioned what dishonesty there can be in the case.'[36] His answer to this

---

[33] (1792) Peake 115, 170 E.R. 113. Cf. Lord Ellenborough, dissenting from this case in *Baglehole* v. *Walters* (1811) 3 Camp. 154, 170 E.R.1338. See also *Pickering* v. *Dowson* (1813), 4 Taunt. 779, 128 E.R. 537.

[34] *Supra*, p. 180.

[35] *Principles of Moral and Political Philosophy*, Book III, Part I, Chapter VII.

[36] Ibid.

is that a tradesman who sells in the market impliedly engages to sell at market prices, and so imposes upon the buyer if he charges more. By contrast, a man who sells outside the market (in a rather narrow sense of the term), for example, a man who sells an estate, can name a price double what it cost him without any imputation of injustice or extortion, for he makes no such implied engagement.[37]

But in the heyday of the new political economy, in the 1820s and 1830s, most of these older moralistic ideas were thought by many to be outmoded. In his *Principles of Political Economy*, for example, J. R. McCulloch gave expression to the newer views as follows:

It is perhaps hardly necessary to advert to the regulations intended to secure the quality of manufactured goods that were formerly so very general. These are now almost everywhere abolished; and it appears to be universally conceded that in this, as in most other things, the free competition of the producers is the only principle on which reliance can ordinarily be placed for securing superiority of fabric as well as cheapness. Wherever industry is emancipated from all sorts of restraints, those who carry it on endeavour, by lessening the cost, or improving the fabric of their goods, or both, to extend their business; and the intercourse that subsists among the different classes of society is so very intimate that an individual who should attempt to undersell his neighbours by substituting a showy and flimsy for a substantial article, would be very soon exposed, and be obliged to reduce its price to its proper level.[38]

It must not be thought that the principle *caveat emptor* was only applicable to contracts of sale of goods. Although it was in that field that the most extensive litigation took place, the principle was, in one sense, of general application throughout the law. It was part and parcel of the process by which actual reliance became downgraded as a ground of liability in classical contract law. Wherever parties entered into contractual relations, no matter what the nature of the contract, the responsibility lay on each party to rely upon his own judgment, and to demand an express warranty where he was uncertain of his judgment. Thus unbargained-for reliance, actual reliance which was not protected by express warranties, was prima facie not legally justifiable and not legally protected. A man who entered into a contract to marry a woman took the risk that a fine head of hair was in reality a wig,[39] a man who rented a field for grazing his cattle took the risk of the field being contaminated with some poison which killed his cattle,[40] a man who rented an unfurnished house took the risk that it was infested with

---

[37] Ibid.

[38] 5th edn. (London, 1864), p. 215. But McCulloch approved legal protection for the buyer of fire-arms, chain cables, and anchors: p. 216.

[39] *Beachey* v. *Brown* (1860) E.B. & E. 796, 799, 120 E.R. 706, 708.

[40] *Sutton* v. *Palmer* (1843) 12 M. & W. 52, 152 E.R. 1108.

bugs,[41] a man who consulted a doctor took the risk that the doctor might be medically unqualified, a man who bought a business took the risk that the seller might open a new one next door, and so on. But it was, all the same, in the law of sale of goods, that the principle received most discussion. The clearest formulation of the basic model of classical contract law is to be found in *Smith* v *Hughes* in 1871.[42] Although this case is known to most students as an authority on the law of mistake, it includes a number of passages in the judgments which represent to perfection the classical ideas about contract formation. The buyer in this case had bought some oats after being given a sample by the seller; he then refused to accept the oats, complaining that he thought they were old oats (which he wanted for race horses) whereas they were in fact new oats. The Court sent the case back for a new trial on grounds of misdirection, but in the course of his judgment Cockburn C.J. gave expression to the basic principles of the time:

Now in this case, there was plainly no legal obligation in the plaintiff in the first instance to state whether the oats were new or old. He offered them for sale according to the sample, as he had a perfect right to do, and gave the buyer the fullest opportunity of inspecting the sample, which, practically was equivalent to an inspection of the oats themselves . . . If, indeed, the buyer, instead of acting on his own opinion, had asked the question, whether the oats were old or new, if he had said anything which intimated his understanding that the seller was selling the oats as old oats, the case would have been wholly different . . . Here, however, nothing of the sort occurs. The buyer in no way refers to the seller, but acts entirely on his own judgment.[43]

Apart from the case of express warranty, the only protection accorded to contracting parties in derogation of the principle of *caveat emptor* was the case of actual fraud. In case of downright fraud, the Courts had given a legal remedy in damages, not only to contracting parties, but even in tort to a person who entered into a contract with a third party in reliance on a fraudulent misrepresentation of the defendant. This had been recognized in *Pasley* v. *Freeman* in 1789.[44] But even the concept of fraud was whittled down a good deal during the classical period. First, there was an insistence that fraud only covered statements of fact, and not mere matters of opinion. In *Pasley* v. *Freeman*, even though fraud was proved, Grose J. dissenting would have discharged the defendants from liability on this ground. The case involved a simple recommendation of one F as creditworthy, with the result that the plaintiffs entrusted goods to F to the value of £2,600. Whether a man deserves credit, said Grose

---

[41] *Hart* v. *Windsor* (1843) 12 M. & W. 68, 152 E.R. 1114.
[42] (1871) L.R. 6 Q.B. 597.
[43] At pp. 604–5.
[44] (1789) 3 T.R. 51, 100 E.R. 450.

J., depends on opinion; and the plaintiffs might have inquired of others as to F's creditworthiness. '[I]t was their fault that they did not, and they have suffered damage by their own laches. It was owing to their own gross negligence that they gave credence to the assertion of the defendant.'[45] One must also observe that the changing ideas about causation (which I have previously referred to)[46] may well have been relevant here. To suffer loss by reliance upon another would often be seen as solely due to the actions of the party relying; even a fraudulent misrepresentation would never cause any loss by itself, since only if the representee acted upon it, would there be any ill-consequences. In the conditions of mid-nineteenth-century England, when self-reliance and individualism were so highly rated, it was easy to see a person who suffered loss through relying upon another as the author of his own misfortune. Indeed, in *Pasley* v. *Freeman* itself, there was much to be said for Grose J.'s argument, for to entrust goods to the value of £2,600 (probably more than twenty times as much in today's money) to a stranger on the strength of one reference seems to have been the height of folly. Although the principle of *Pasley* v. *Freeman* was never challenged[47]—and indeed, could be supported as a deterrent against fraud[48]—the actual decision might well have been different if the case had arisen in (say) 1850.

The second limitation on the concept of fraud, which became more firmly established in the classical period, was that it did not cover mere non-disclosure. In a sense, this was logically implicit in the very concept of *caveat emptor* which required each party to act on his own judgment. By 1821 Lord Eldon (who, despite his extreme conservatism, was sometimes in tune with the morality of the new age) accepted the idea that, 'if an estate is offered for sale, and I treat for it, knowing that there is a mine under it, and the other party makes no inquiry, I am not bound to give him any information of it; he acts for himself and exercises his own sense and knowledge.'[49]

However, it is now necessary to observe that much of what has been said was somewhat theoretical, and at no time did this austere and amoral market law ever wholly represent the practice of the Courts. Indeed, there is also ground for thinking that it never wholly represented

[45] 3 T.R. 56, 100 E.R. 453.
[46] *Supra*, p. 282.
[47] Lord Eldon animadverted against it, but mainly (it seems) because he thought it an encroachment on equitable jurisdiction: *Evans* v. *Bicknell* (1801) 6 Ves. 174, 186, 31 E.R. 998, 1003–4.
[48] The problem of false character references seems to have been a well known social evil at the time of *Pasley* v. *Freeman*. It is commented on by Paley, *Principles of Moral and Political Philosophy*, Book II, Chapter XI; and the giving of false and fraudulent references was made an offence by statute in 1792 (23 Geo. 3, c. 56).
[49] *Turner* v. *Harvey* (1821) Jacob 168, 178, 37, E.R. 814, 817–18.

the views of the political economists either. It was all very well, in theory, to assert that the consumer was always the best judge of his own interests, and could always detect the sound from the shoddy in the way of goods, or the sound from the unsound horse, or the fine estate from the tumbledown house. But in practice, the infinite variety of circumstances constantly threw up cases in which the consumer simply could not judge of these matters. Adam Smith might argue that even the licensing of doctors was unnecessary because the consumer could soon learn to distinguish the competent from the incompetent, but his successors were by no means so sure of the consumer's ability to make such distinctions. J. R. McCulloch argued that the consumer might be able to distinguish the competent from the incompetent tailor, but the patient who went to an incompetent doctor might pay for his mistake with his life, and the mistake might even remain undetected.[50] Similarly, John Stuart Mill argued that the proposition that the consumer is a competent judge of what he buys can only be admitted with numerous abatements and exceptions.[51] Even Herbert Spencer complained in 1871 that the law was seriously deficient in not affording a quick and cheap remedy for the consumer who was supplied with something which was not precisely what he had asked for.[52] We have also seen something[53] of the views of Byles J. who, in a slightly different context, argued that many consumers would never learn their lesson if they were not given adequate protection by the law against their own mistakes and misjudgments; he also added the very convincing argument that such learning was, anyhow, not inherited. Consequently, each generation of consumers had to learn the lessons afresh, and in the process much hardship would be caused if the law stood aside. A writer in *Fraser's Magazine* in 1870 made the same point arguing that *caveat emptor* would work well if we all lived for some two or three hundred years.[54]

There was another point which does not seem to have been adequately grasped by the proponents of *caveat emptor*, whether they were economists or lawyers. The refusal of any redress to a consumer who has entered into an unsatisfactory contract may be characterized as 'non-intervention' and so in accord with principles of *laissez-faire* only if the contract is already executed. If defective goods are actually delivered to, and accepted by, a buyer, the onus will be on him if he wishes to seek redress, and he will need to satisfy the Courts that there are grounds for intervention in his favour. But when executory contracts come to be

---

[50] *Principles of Political Economy*, 5th edn., p. 228.
[51] *Principles of Political Economy*, Book V, Chapter XI, Sect. 8.
[52] *The Man Versus the State* (reprinted, Harmondsworth, 1969), p. 294.
[53] *Supra*, p. 382.
[54] Jan. 1870, p. 76.

readily enforced the position is different. A buyer who refuses to accept delivery of some defective article does not need the 'intervention' of the law for his protection. It is the seller who seeks the legal enforcement of the contract, and the buyer who may set up the defective nature of the goods by way of defence. That, however, was not generally how things were perceived either by lawyers or by economists. The enforcement even of an executory contract was somehow regarded as the 'natural' state of affairs, and the buyer who wished to escape liability for defective goods was seen as demanding the law's 'intervention'.

Nevertheless, despite all this, the principle of *caveat emptor*, both in contracts of sale of goods, and in contract law generally, was never enforced to the utmost rigour. Indeed, as one surveys the nineteenth-century case law (let alone the statute law which is reserved for Chapter 16), the reality seems to be that the principle was honoured far more in the breach than in the observance. What is puzzling is to understand why the principle was (and is) so widely thought to have represented the law when it so manifestly did not in a very wide variety of circumstances. There is a curious and close parallel here with the principle of *laissez-faire* which (as we have seen) was also believed to represent parliamentary and governmental policy to a much greater extent than was ever warranted by the facts. What seems to have happened is that commentators and the legal profession came to attribute a much wider significance to one or two particular cases than was justified by the case law generally; there was also, it must be observed, a marked divergence of policy between the different Courts for much of the period centring around the middle thirty or forty years of the nineteenth century.[55] In the Court of Exchequer, the dominating figure of Parke B., generally supported, but sometimes restrained by Abinger C.B., nearly always argued for *caveat emptor*. In the Common Pleas, so long as Best C.J. sat, precisely the reverse policy was followed. In the King's Bench, there was much wavering, first under Ellenbrough C.J. and later under Denman C.J., before the doctrine of *caveat emptor* was seriously cut down.

I do not have space for a full survey of the case law here, and I must rest content with a selection, spread over a number of areas. In contracts of sale of goods which gave rise to much the greatest litigation, the principle of *caveat emptor* arose in connection with title and also with matters of quality and fitness. In the former class of case, the question at issue is whether a seller who sells without title is liable to the buyer if the true owner should subsequently demand and recover the goods from him. In 1844, in a decision in which Parke B. appears to have had no part, the Court of Exchequer had rejected the idea that *caveat emptor*

---

[55] See on this Llewellyn, 'Across Sales on Horse Back', 52 *Harvard Law Rev.* 725 (1939).

applied to matters of title.[56] It was preposterous that a seller should be able to sue the buyer for the price when the buyer had already had to surrender the goods to the true owner. Five years later, under Parke B.'s influence, the same Court repudiated (or rather ignored) these heresies, and insisted on the application of *caveat emptor* to questions of title, at any rate on a sale of specific goods.[57] Fifteen years later, the same issue came before the Court of Common Pleas where the doctrine of *caveat emptor* had received but scant respect since the days of Best C.J. The Court emphatically insisted that a seller of goods must be taken implicitly to warrant his title as a general rule.[58] The contrary proposition 'must shock the understanding of any ordinary person'.[59] The older cases were explained away as depending on an implicit assumption of the risk by the buyer, in certain particular circumstances, that the seller may not have title. For example, where the seller is known to be a pledgee or a sheriff selling goods under a writ of execution, the buyer might be held to have assumed the risk that the seller had no title.

In matters of quality and fitness, the volume of litigation was huge, and the variety of factual situations was equally diverse. The cases fell into two main groups, those concerned with an express warranty, and those in which the buyer claimed on an implied warranty. In the first group of cases, the main problem was usually that of distinguishing definite assertions of fact from statements about matters of opinion, or vague assertions ('mere representations'). Generally speaking, these cases turned on the Court's view as to the reasonableness of the buyer in relying on the seller's words. Prima facie, it might be true that a buyer should rely on his own judgment, but a categorical assertion of fact by the seller served naturally to 'lull [the buyer] into security as to the goodness of the commodity'.[60] There was, at this time, no magic in the words 'representation' or 'warranty'. Especially in Best C.J.'s court, a man could not escape responsibility for a statement of fact by saying it was a mere representation on which the buyer should not have relied. 'If a man says, this horse is sound, that is a warranty',[61] was the doctrine of the Common Pleas.

But there were more difficult cases. What if the buyer and seller were higgling over a quantity of barley which was visible in front of them, for

---

[56] *Allen v. Hopkins* (1844) 13 M. & W. 94, 153 E.R. 39. There is no record of Parke B. having sat in this case.
[57] *Morley v. Attenborough* (1849) 3 Ex. 500, 154 E.R. 943.
[58] *Eichholz v. Bannister* (1864) 17 C.B.(N.S.) 708, 144 E.R. 284.
[59] *Per* Erle C.J., 17 C.B.(N.S.) 722, 144 E.R. 289.
[60] *Per* Lord Ellenborough C.J. in *Williamson v. Allison* (1802) 2 East 446, 102 E.R. 479.
[61] *Per* Best C.J. in *Salmon v. Ward* (1825) 2 C. & P. 211, 212, 172, E.R. 96, 96; see also *Wood v. Smith* (1829) 4 C. & P. 45, 172 E.R. 600, where the statement, 'I never warrant, but he is sound as far as I know', was held to be a warranty that so far as the seller knew, the horse was sound.

both to see and examine? In such a case the fact that the seller called it (wrongly) 'seed barley' was not a warranty, for the buyer did the same, and each was mistakenly relying on his own judgment.[62] What if the buyer did examine the goods, or appointed an agent to do so, and yet some defect remained undiscovered, perhaps undiscoverable? Was the buyer in such a case entitled to rely on the seller's statements or were the statements deemed to be overtaken by the buyer's examination? The answer might well depend on the Court before which the question arose. If if came before the Exchequer, either when Parke B. or Bramwell B. was sitting, the buyer was liable to lose.[63] In the King's Bench,[64] or the Common Pleas, the buyer was more likely to get a verdict. Then there were cases in which both parties had proceeded upon the same assumption, dealing, for example, over a ship thought to be at sea but (unknown to the parties) wrecked before the contract was made, or dealing over a bar of silver wrongly certified by an assayer to contain so many ounces. Here again, attitudes varied in the different Courts. In *Barr* v. *Gibson*[65] the Exchequer Court compelled a buyer to pay the agreed price of £4,000 for a ship which had been wrecked before the contract and was only worth £10. On the other hand in *Cox* v. *Prentice*[66] the King's Bench held *caveat emptor* inapplicable to the sale of a silver bar in which the quantity had been wrongly certified because it was plain that neither party was relying on his own judgment, but both relied on the certificate.

For some reason which is difficult to understand, here as elsewhere with the doctrine of *caveat emptor*, one decision came to be regarded as a leading case even though it was decided on very special facts, and even though there was clearly a great deal of contrary authority. The case in question was *Hopkins* v. *Tanqueray*[67] where the buyer bought a horse at an auction at Tattersalls, having been given a private assurance earlier that the horse was sound. This was held not to be a warranty, mainly because it was widely known that auctions at Tattersalls were invariably held without warranty. But the decision came to be thought to be authority for the proposition that even express statements made at the time of sale could be disregarded as 'mere representations' and not warranties. It is extraordinary that such a notion should ever have prevailed for there is nothing in the case itself to support it.

[62] *Carter* v. *Crick* (1859) 4 H. & N. 410, 157, E.R. 899.
[63] *Taylor* v. *Bullen* (1850) 5 Ex. 779, 155 E.R. 341 (Parke B. sitting); *Stuckey* v. *Bailey* (1862) 1 H. & C. 404, 158 E.R. 943 (Bramwell B. sitting).
[64] See, e.g., *Tye* v. *Fynmore* (1813) 3 Camp. 462, 170 E.R. 1446; *Shepherd* v. *Kain* (1821) 5 B. & Ald. 240, 106 E.R. 1180.
[65] (1838) 3 M. & W. 391, 150 E.R. 1196.
[66] (1815) 3 M. & S. 344, 105 E.R. 641.
[67] (1854) 15 C.B. 130, 139 E.R.369.

The second group of cases, which concerned implied warranties, involved much greater difficulty with *caveat emptor*, for inevitably to hold that there was an *implied* warranty on a sale was a direct contradiction of the principle itself. If a buyer was entitled to assume from the mere fact of the sale (or perhaps from the mere fact of paying a fair price) that the goods were sound, it is hard to see what would be left of the principle at all. Nevertheless, even here, the Common Pleas from the earliest times was willing to follow Best C.J. in holding that a sound price implied a sound commodity, at least where the fault in the goods was not something readily discoverable. In this new era of manufactured goods, the quality of commodities could not be so readily determined as had been the case with simple foodstuffs sold by the sack, or cloths and fabrics, which could be tested by the eye and the hand. In *Jones* v. *Bright*[68] the Court was concerned with copper sheathing bought for a ship, which should have lasted from four to five years, but corroded and fell to pieces in four months. To allow the seller to retain the full purchase price on the ground of *caveat emptor* was too much for Best C.J.'s moral sense. 'It is', he insisted, 'the duty of the Court, in administering the law, to lay down rules calculated to prevent fraud; to protect persons who are necessarily ignorant of the qualities of a commodity they purchase; and make it the interest of manufacturers and those who sell, to furnish the best article than can be supplied.'[69]

But the battle for implied warranties of quality was not to be so easily won. In the King's Bench, *Parkinson* v. *Lee*[70] was thought for many years to lay down the contrary doctrine at least where the buyer had some opportunity to examine the goods or a sample, even though, in fact, the defect was so hidden that it could not easily be discovered by such an examination. And for many years the Exchequer Court fought against these implied warranties.[71] As late as 1862 that Court declined to hold that there was an implied warranty of fitness even on a sale of meat for human consumption.[72] But, in the end, the judicial sense of justice proved too strong. It was all very well to assert that a man who relied on his own judgment took the risk of goods being defective, but the reality of the matter was that buyers frequently did not rely on their own judgment, but on the integrity and responsibility of sellers, or on the general course of business. A person who paid a price which was fair for a sound commodity was, by that fact alone, demonstrating that he expected to

[68] (1829) 5 Bing. 533, 130 E.R. 1167.

[69] 5 Bing. 542-3, 130 E.R. 1171. But Best C.J. (like Paley) agreed that there was no implied warranty on the sale of a horse because on such a sale, 'the buyer puts no question, and perhaps gets the animal cheaper'.

[70] (1802) 2 East 314, 102 E.R. 389.

[71] See, e.g., *Burnby* v. *Bollett* (1847) 16 M. & W. 644.

[72] *Emmerton* v. *Mathews* (1862) 7 H. & N. 586, 158 E.R. 604.

get a sound commodity, and if he did not, the contract was simply an unfair exchange. Although the Courts did not revert to the old language of just prices or fair exchanges, the effect of their decisions in the 1860s was to do precisely this. In two important cases in that decade, first the Exchequer Chamber [73] and then the Queen's Bench,[74] laid down the new rules. *Caveat emptor* was in future to apply only to cases where specific goods were sold which the buyer had examined and upon which he had exercised his own judgment. Where the buyer had had no opportunity for any examination, and where the goods were generic goods, sold by description, rather than specific goods, it was the seller's responsibility (at least if he was a merchant) to supply merchantable goods. The result of these decisions, which still broadly represent the modern law, was in large part to expel the normative element from the question of reliance. It was now, not merely a question of whether the buyer had reasonably relied on the seller, or whether he ought not to have relied on his own judgment, but also of whether he had in fact done so.

Very much the same development occurred with those cases which concerned, not so much the quality of the goods, but their fitness for a particular purpose. If the buyer relied upon his own judgment he could not complain, but if he relied upon the seller's judgment or assurance that the goods were suitable for a specific purpose, then a warranty to that effect would be implied.[75]

Outside the sphere of contracts of sale of goods, very similar developments were occurring, but because of the variety of differing contracts and relationships encountered, the new rules were never crystallized so clearly as in contracts of sale. Indeed, there is a sense in which even today the rule of *caveat emptor* at least prima facie applies to many contracts because there are no standard implications which can be read into them as in the case of sales; but in practice the result is not so very different for implications will still frequently be made where necessary to achieve justice. And one of the principal grounds on which such terms can be implied into a contract is that one party has relied upon the other in relation to the matter in question. But perhaps in these cases the normative element in the reliance is still somewhat stronger. For example, a person who buys a house is expected to examine it before he buys it, and it is almost impossible to persuade a Court that any term is to be implied in such a contract. Similarly, at common law, no term as

---

[73] *Bigge* v. *Parkinson* (1862) 7 H. & N. 955, 158 E.R. 758.

[74] *Jones* v. *Just* (1868) L.R. 3 Q.B. 197.

[75] Cf. *Ollivant* v. *Bailey* (1843) 5 Q.B. 288, 114 E.R. 1257 (Queen's Bench) with *Chanter* v. *Hopkins* (1838) 4 M. & W. 399, 150 E.R. 1484 (Court of Exchequer). See too *Brown* v. *Edington* (1841) 2 M. & G. 279, 133 E.R. 751; *Shepherd* v. *Pybus* (1842) 3 M. & G. 868, 133 E.R. 1390—both decisions of the Common Pleas.

to fitness can be implied in a lease of an unfurnished house,[76] although it was held in 1843 that there was a term of reasonable fitness attached to the renting of a furnished house.[77] Perhaps this was because it was not uncommon for people to take furnished houses for short periods (a 'season') without personally examining them, and consequently it was thought that the tenant could not be said to be relying on his own judgment in such cases.

Throughout the years 1770-1870 there seems also to have been a very similar process going on in the Court of Chancery. In that Court the issue usually presented itself in a somewhat different form—namely a defence of misrepresentation to a suit for specific performance—but in substance the issues were often the same. The question was whether the buyer (or tenant) did or should have relied on his own judgment, or whether he did (and was entitled to) rely on the words of the seller or lessor. In the first few decades of the nineteenth century, the tendency was to allow the seller a good deal of latitude in advertising or commending his property, and to assume that only a very foolish buyer would rely upon such statements.[78] In 1838 the House of Lords, in a complex case concerning the sale of some mines, insisted that the 'question is ... whether the parties have used that ordinary degree of vigilance and circumspection in order to protect themselves, which the law has a right to expect from those who apply for its aid'.[79] In this case, where some mines were sold for £550,000 and it was found that they would only yield a net profit of some £6,000 to £8,000 per annum (that is about 1 to 1¼ per cent) the buyer was held disentitled to relief on the ground that he had made his own examination and relied on his expert's reports, despite the misrepresentations of the seller. Lord Brougham, giving judgment against the buyer in language which Ricardo would surely have approved, said: 'If a mere general intention to overreach were enough, I hardly know a contract, even between persons of very strict morality, that could stand; we generally find the case to be that there has been an attempt of the one party to overreach the other, and of the other to overreach the first; but that does not make void the contract. It must be shown that the attempt was made and made with some success.'[80] A somewhat similar attitude was shown in some early nineteenth-century cases concerning the sale of a business with its goodwill, where Courts of Equity held that, absent an

---

[76] As was said in *Robbins* v. *Jones* (1863) 15 C.B.(N.S.) 221, 240, 143 E.R. 768, 776, 'there is no law against letting a tumbledown house.' How could there have been when perhaps half the houses in the country were 'tumbledown houses'?

[77] *Smith* v. *Marrable* (1843) 11 M. & W. 5, 152 E.R. 693.

[78] See, e.g., *Trower* v. *Newcome* (1813) 3 Mer. 704, 36 E.R. 270; *Scott* v. *Hamson* (1826) 1 Sim. 13, 57 E.R. 483, affirmed (1829) 1 Russ. & My. 128, 39 E.R. 49.

[79] *Attwood* v. *Small* (1838) 6 Cl. & F. 232, 344, 7 E.R. 684, 727.

[80] 6 Cl. & F. 448, 7 E.R. 765.

express covenant, the vendor could not be restrained from opening a new business in competition with the old.[81] It was a case of *caveat emptor*; the buyer ought to demand an express covenant not to compete.

But this sort of cut-throat competition, in which all business was conducted in an attempt to cheat the other party, ill accorded with traditional attitudes of Equity; and it is very doubtful if it even accorded with commercial morality. For the fact is that the standard of commercial morality in England in the nineteenth century was generally very high. Especially in the latter half of the century, British businessmen acquired the highest reputation among overseas merchants for the exactness and scrupulousness with which they carried out their engagements, and indeed, for the fairness of the bargains which they expected to strike.[82]

Besides, there were certain traditional attitudes of Equity which were completely at odds with the principles of the competitive market. The law relating to trustees, and other fiduciary relationships, had long proceeded on the basis that—in the appropriate circumstances—one man was entitled to rely on another, entitled to place full confidence in him. The rules about undue influence, for example, had been reaffirmed in the early nineteenth century in a case famous for Romilly's argument;[83] they continued to be regularly applied to established cases such as the relationship between solicitor and client;[84] and towards the end of this period, in 1866, the Courts once again insisted on not confining this equitable jurisdiction within any rigid limits.[85] There is a sense in which these cases illustrate an interesting contrast between Victorian business morality and Victorian personal morality. In business, the rule of self-reliance, each man for himself, and devil take the hindmost, might prevail. But in personal relationships, in those of a more intimate or confidential character, the rules of Equity reflected a totally different set of moral principles. Here the stress was on the high morality of men of honour, men of integrity, and the strictest codes of conduct prevailed.

All these cases, of course depended on the existence of some special relationship of trust or confidence, but by mid-century Courts of Equity were beginning to re-establish their belief in good faith and fair dealing in contracts in a more general way. A striking example of this is to be found in *Piggott* v. *Stratton*[86] in 1859, a case which in itself should refute the belief that this was the heyday of *caveat emptor*. The defendant in this

---

[81] *Cruttwell* v. *Lye* (1810) 17 Ves. Jun. 335, 34 E.R. 129; *Harrison* v. *Gardner* (1817) 2 Madd. 198, 219, 56 E.R. 308, 316.

[82] Sir Arthur Bryant, *The Age of Elegance* (reprinted London, 1975), p. 270. See also Welbourne, 'Bankruptcy Before the Era of Reform', 4 *Camb. Hist. J.* 50, 62 (1932).

[83] *Huguenin* v. *Baseley* (1807) 14 Ves. 273, 33 E.R. 526.

[84] See, e.g., *Goddard* v. *Carlisle* (1821) 9 Price 169, 147 E.R. 57.

[85] *Tate* v. *Williamson* (1866) L.R. 2 Ch. App. 55.

[86] (1859) 1 De G.F. & J. 33, 45 E.R. 271.

case was a lessee of two building plots, A and B, it being a condition of the lease that he should not build on plot A closer than thirty feet to plot B, in order that the sea view from the latter plot should not be obstructed. The defendant offered a sub-lease of plot B to the plaintiff who inquired about the possibility of building on plot A. The defendant referred him to the covenant in the head lease, and the plaintiff, in reliance on this, took the sub-lease and built on the land. The defendant then proceeded to surrender his lease to the head landlord and took from him a new lease without the restrictive covenant. When he started to build on plot A so as to obstruct the plaintiff's view, the plaintiff sought an injunction. Lord Campbell and the Lords Justices of Appeal granted the injunction, and strong comments were made about the defendant's conduct. Yet it will be seen that the plaintiff had not protected himself against this conduct by taking an express covenant which, of course, he could have demanded. He had simply relied on the defendant's good faith, and on the expectation that the defendant would not obtain a release of his covenant from the landlord. The plaintiff was thus seeking protection for an unbargained-for reliance or even expectation. The Court's answer to this argument, however, was that 'the business of life could not be conducted if it were required that men should anticipate and expressly guard against the wily devices to which the deceitful may resort'.[87] The Court was, thus, protecting reasonable reliance and reasonable expectations even though the letter of the contract did not extend to them.

Now it may well be that during the course of the nineteenth century, changes took place in men's expectations of those with whom they did business. Perhaps, in the late eighteenth or early nineteenth century, the 'natural' state of affairs was simply to hold to the status quo after a contract had been executed. The difficulty of getting redress in law is always great; during the period 1770–1830 or thereabouts the difficulty was probably greater than it has ever been since. The Courts of Common Law were seriously overburdened; the Court of Chancery was well nigh choked to death; and there were no inferior Courts where minor suits could be brought. A man who bought some commodity and paid for it probably thought of the 'natural' order of things as one in which things were left undisturbed. If he had made an unfortunate bargain, if the goods turned out defective, he may have shrugged his shoulders and determined to learn his lesson for the next deal. By mid-nineteenth century, things may have begun to change. First, there was an increasing likelihood that the plaintiff might be suing on an executory contract. It is surely not unduly speculative to suggest that a man who has made a bad bargain, even been cheated, may put up with the situation if the transaction is executed, and his only recourse is to go to law; where the

[87] 1 De G.F. & J. 50, 45 E.R. 278.

same man might fight vigorously against an attempt to enforce an executory transaction against him. In this situation, the onus is not on him to go to law, but on the other party; and if the defendant is to be dragged into Court, he may well attempt to defend himself. But apart from this, changes may have been developing in people's expectations as a result of changing commercial customs and practices. As greater regularity and order came into business, as records began to be better kept, as manufactured products began to become more reliable and less risky, as the volatility of the early years of the industrial revolution passed away, contracting parties may well have grown used to having their expectations fulfilled. Prices would naturally have tended to be adjusted upwards as buyers (for example) began to expect goods to be more reliable, or to expect manufacturers to replace defective goods without further charge. This in turn may have reacted on the law; higher expectations deserved higher protection, partly at least because they were likely to be paid for in higher prices.

But we must not overstress these somewhat speculative suggestions if only because they suggest that the law underwent a greater change than in reality it did. The truth is, as we have seen, that the early nineteenth century saw little more than a brief flirtation with the doctrine *caveat emptor*; from the beginning this flirtation had to contend with serious opposition from judges who still believed that it was part of the job of the Courts to see that contracts were fair; and by the 1860s, at least in contracts of sale of goods, these judges had won out, and the flirtation was over. The common law had, in large part, returned to the traditions of eighteenth-century Equity when the fairness of a contractual exchange was still an all-important part of contract law. The strange thing is that nobody wanted to recognize the facts; nobody wanted to recognize that *caveat emptor* had about as much (or as little) influence as *laissez-faire*, and that it was pretty well dead and buried by 1870. It is not easy to understand why this happened, but the answer may lie partly in the new textbooks which appeared in the 1870s and which did not adequately reflect the return to the common law's earlier ideals. Anson may have had as much to do with perpetuating the myth of *caveat emptor* as his contemporary, Dicey, had to do with the myth of *laissez-faire*.[87A]

BENEFIT

The notion that a person ought generally to pay a fair recompense for a benefit received, suffered, during the classical period, very much the

---

[87A] Anson states the law as though *caveat emptor* was still the general rule in his 2nd edn. at p. 231. Perhaps Benjamin on *Sale* (first published, 1868) was also influential on this point. Benjamin gives *caveat emptor* as the general rule in his first edition (p. 479) and, less justifiably, in his second in 1873 (p. 525).

same fate as the parallel doctrines concerning reliance. There was, that is to say, a tendency for the concept of be split down the middle. So long as some agreement to pay for the benefit could be found, or at least implied, the interests of the party conferring the benefit (restitution interests in the American terminology) were well protected. Indeed, as in the case of reliance, they were, in a sense, sometimes overprotected. Because they were protected not overtly, not by simply requiring the recipient of the benefit to pay for the value he had received from it, but by protecting the expectations of the other party to the transaction, it would often happen that the recipient would be required to pay *more* than the value of the benefit he had received. On the other hand, where no expectations could be protected, where there was no semblance of an agreement to pay for the benefit conferred (and no possibility of implying one), there was a tendency to allow the restitution interest to go unprotected. The parallel with reliance is also to be found in the fact that the logic of this approach never entirely won out. Had it done so, the entire body of law, now known as the law of quasi-contract, or the law of restitution, must have withered on the vine. In fact this never happened, although this branch of the law was certainly much suppressed during and after the classical period. The notion that a man ought to be compelled to pay for a benefit he had received but which he had not agreed to pay for, was, in general, contrary to the ethos of the times.

Quasi-Contract

It will be remembered that in and around 1770, the Courts had not yet made any serious attempt to mark off the law of contract from the law of quasi-contract. At this time the classification universally adopted for purposes of pleading and argument divided contracts into two groups, express contracts and 'implied contracts'. What seems so confusing to the modern lawyer, brought up in the shadow of classical contract theory, is that the category of 'implied contracts' included what were later called genuine implied contracts on the one hand, and quasi-contracts on the other hand. In the former class of case, it came gradually to be said that the implication was a 'genuine inference', while in the latter class the implication was a fiction. I suggested previously[88] that this was not how matters seemed to eighteenth-century lawyers at all. To them, I suggested, implied contracts were all cases in which some benefit had been conferred by one party on another in circumstances in which it was felt that payment ought to be made—if it was for the jury to make that decision, the case was called one of a contract 'implied in fact', while if the Court was to make the decision, then the contract was 'implied in law'. Now the

---

[88] *Supra*, p. 181.

older terminology survived, in the Courts and among academic writers, almost throughout the classical period. In Powell's *Essay*,[89] for instance, we find it stated that implied contracts do not arise from the 'special agreement' of the parties, but by implication of law; but Powell then goes on to give as examples, first the case of money paid under compulsion which is not really due, and secondly, the cases of goods or services supplied on request—'if an hostler gives my horse meat, or a taylor make my cloaths'. The modern lawyer would find this a confusing mixture, as he would wish to say that in the first case there is no 'real' agreement at all, while in the second case there is a 'genuine' implication because the party receiving these benefits would, in practice, have known that he was liable to pay, and would have intended to pay.

The same usage of 'implied contract' is still to be found in the second edition of Chitty in 1834,[90] and in the first edition of Addison on *Contracts* in 1842.[90A] But here, as elsewhere, the new terminology was at hand, though in this particular instance, it was slow in making headway in the Courts. In Pothier we find the Roman law distinction between contracts and quasi-contracts: 'In contracts, it is the consent of the contracting parties which produces the obligations: in quasi-contracts there is not any consent. The law alone, or natural equity, produces the obligation, by rendering obligatory the fact from which it results.'[91] Similarly in Austin's *Lectures on Jurisprudence* which were first published in 1863, the Roman law distinctions replaced those used by English lawyers,[92] and the use of the concept of 'implied' contracts was castigated as a confusion of two quite different species of obligation. Sir Henry Maine's famous work on *Ancient Law*, published in 1861, also drew attention to the distinctions drawn by Roman lawyers between genuine contracts and quasi-contracts, and stressed that quasi-contracts were not genuine contracts at all.[93] The first serious practitioners' work on English contract law to adopt this new terminology and classification was Leake's book, first published in 1867. Leake was (as he acknowledged) heavily indebted to Austin, and thus the Roman-inspired distinction between contract and quasi-contract replaced (at least in textbook formulations) the old English distinction between express and implied contracts. After Leake's book was published, all subsequent English writers on contract law adopted the new approach. Pollock, indeed, excluded quasi-contracts altogether from his *Principles of Contract*, first published in 1876, and Anson relegated the subject to an Appendix in his *Principles*, first published in 1879.[94] Thus the next generation of English lawyers, those

---

[89] i. 245-6.   [90] pp. 16 *et seq.*   [90A] Chapter 7.
[91] *Law of Obligations*, i. 69.   [92] iii. 127-35.   [93] Chapter IX.
[94] See generally on this, R. M. Jackson, 'The Scope of the Term Contract', 53 *Law Q. Rev.* 526 (1937).

who received their first instruction from textbooks, in particular those taking the new Oxford law course, were all brought up on the Roman law distinction, and turned their backs on the older English classification. However, it was a long time before the judges were converted to this new way of thinking.

Lord Mansfield had briefly flirted with the new terminology, referring to liabilities *ex contractu* and liabilities *quasi ex contractu* in *Moses* v. *Macferlan*,[95] but after his retirement the older terminology and the older classification reasserted themselves. The category of 'implied contracts' continued to be used by the Courts to include both the so-called 'genuine inferences' and the so-called 'fictitious implications'. Indeed, it was not until the 1930s that this new textbook learning came to be adopted on the Bench,[96] and when it did, the academic controversies flowed fast and furious.[97]

It is surprising that the judges resisted the terminology of quasi-contract for so long, because the Roman law distinction accorded well with the new will theory which was generally being so enthusiastically adopted by English Courts. If contracts were based on will, promise, agreement, then they could not be based on any notion that a benefit ought to be paid for. The new will theory of contract found no place for the age-old factor of benefit—notwithstanding the manifest connection which this established between contract (where benefit had always been an important part of consideration, and hence the basis of liability) and quasi-contract (where, of course restitution of benefit was the very essence of the liability). Now I suggest that, by and large, these ideas were in substance adopted by English Courts. As we shall see, there were many particular areas of law in which the notion of recompense for benefit declined in importance, or was superseded by promise-based liability, so that, in substance, the judges were in tune with the new terminology and its basis. But they were very reluctant to adopt the new terminology itself, and continued to use the generic term 'implied contract' to cover both cases of non-express genuine contracts, and the cases of a legally imposed liability not dependent on promise at all.

The confusion between the older and the newer approach is well illustrated by the muddle into which the Courts placed themselves in *Sanders* v. *Vanzellar*[98] in 1843, a case concerning the liability of an endorsee of a bill of lading to pay for the freight if the consignor failed to pay. It had earlier been established[99] that the endorsee normally was

---

[95] (1760) 2 Burr. 1005, 1008, 97 E.R. 676.
[96] By Lord Wright in *Brooks Wharf and Bull Wharf Ltd.* v. *Goodman Bros.* [1937] 1 K.B. 534; and again in the *Fibrosa* case [1943] A.C. 32.
[97] P. A. Landon, 53 *Law Q. Rev.* 302–4 (1937); Winfield, ibid., 447–9.
[98] (1843) 4 Q.B. 260, 114 E.R. 897.
[99] *Cock* v. *Taylor* (1811) 13 East 399, 104 E.R. 424.

so liable on an 'implied contract'. The basis of this 'implied contract' was not very clearly spelt out by the Courts but it seemed to arise from the fact that the endorsee received the benefit of a delivery of the goods, while the carrier suffered the detriment of abandoning his lien by the delivery. Thus the presence of benefit to one party and detriment to the other was treated as sufficient 'evidence' of an agreement. But in *Sanders* v. *Vanzellar*, the endorsee challenged this implication, and the jury found a special case in which they found the delivery of the goods as in the earlier cases, but also negatived any express promise by the endorsee to pay for the goods. As a result the Court of Queen's bench felt obliged to give judgment for the endorsee. The 'implication' of a promise was held to be an implication of fact for the jury, and therefore had to be found as a fact by the jury. Counsel for the shipowners was clearly outraged by this result since it appeared plainly enough, on the authorities, that the endorsee was liable for the freight in such circumstances, and he appealed to the Exchequer Chamber. But that Court also decided against him. They admitted that 'it had been so much the practice for the indorsee of such a bill of lading to pay the specified freight, if he accepts the goods under it, that there is little or no doubt that the jury would, on such a question, have found in favour of the shipowner if the indorsee received the goods without a disclaimer of his liability to pay the freight'.[1] But, like the lower Court, they insisted that the promise must actually be found by the jury before judgment could be given for the shipowner. The case illustrates the increasing unwillingness of the Courts to impose a liability on a party who had received some benefit unless a promise could be found by a jury.

It is worth pointing out (contrary to received modern doctrine) that there were certain inconsistencies in the new distinction between contract and quasi-contract, although there is no real evidence that the Courts were much influenced by these inconsistencies. The newer ideas did not then, nor do they today, satisfactorily explain how a 'genuine' implication can be made of a promise to pay where there is clear evidence that the alleged promisor never intended to pay at all. If a person gets on a train, with intent to avoid payment of his fare, or orders a meal in a restaurant, without any intention of paying for it, the newer classification requires us to say that there is a 'genuine' implication of an express promise to pay. Now the Courts never had any real trouble with these cases, partly at least because they could always justify liability by praying in aid 'implied contract'.[2] But if they had had to explain whether they were invoking 'genuine' implied contract, or quasi-contract, as the ground for their decisions, they might well have had problems on their hands.

[1] 4 Q.B. 295, 114 E.R. 911.
[2] See, e.g., *Rumsey* v. *N.E. Rly. Co.* (1863) 14 C.B.(N.S.) 640, 650, 143 E.R. 596, 600 *per* Erle C.J.

I propose now to adduce some evidence for the view that, notwithstanding their adherence to the old terminology, the judges were on the whole inclined throughout the classical period to reduce the importance attached to the mere receipt of a benefit, and to stress the need to find some promise to pay for that benefit. General dicta in support of this approach can be found as early as 1799, even with judges like Lord Kenyon, who were on the whole more in the eighteenth-century tradition. In *Exall* v. *Partridge*,[3] for example, he, and indeed the whole Court, denied that, as a general proposition, a man who was benefited by the payment of money by another, was liable to pay for that benefit. One of the main arguments used by the Court here was that such a general proposition would make all debts assignable, for if the assignee paid the debt, he was plainly benefiting the debtor, and could then claim against him on an implied contract. This, of course, was not then the law, and Kenyon had several times rejected any attempt to change the old rule against assignments. There is thus the somewhat paradoxical spectacle of the Court using an old and outdated rule to justify a more modern approach. Surprisingly, it continued to be asserted, years after assignments became generally permissible, that one man could not force a benefit on another behind his back, so as to give himself rights against the other.[4] Indeed, this kind of proposition is still occasionally to be found in modern cases,[5] despite its manifest inconsistency with the free assignability of debts. It is, at least, clear that in the nineteenth century this sort of language reflected the new emphasis on free choice and voluntarily created rights. Only where the plaintiff had paid money to the defendant,[6] or where he had been compelled by law to make a payment which the defendant was legally bound to make, was the quasi-contractual remedy still generally available.[7] And it is easy to see why the Courts generally drew the line at this point, for in these cases the defendant's liability turned largely on questions of law. In the first case it could be assumed that an actual payment by the plaintiff to the defendant had benefited the defendant, and the only issue was therefore whether the payment was legally due or had been made (for example) by mistake. In the second case, similarly, the Court was only bound to ask first whether the defendant was legally liable for the payment, and secondly, whether the plaintiff had been compelled by law to make it. The conclusion followed as a matter of law that the plaintiff had

---

[3] (1799) 8 T.R. 308, 101 E.R. 1405. Cf. the differing attitude shown only a dozen years earlier in *Deering* v. *Winchelsea* (1787) 2 B. & P. 270, 126 E.R. 1276.

[4] *Falcke* v. *Scottish Imperial Insurance Co.* (1886) 34 Ch. D. 234.

[5] *Owen* v. *Tate* [1975] 2 All E.R. 129.

[6] *Kelly* v. *Solari* (1841) 9 M. & W. 54, 152 E.R. 24.

[7] *Bleaden* v. *Charles* (1831) 7 Bing. 246, 131 E.R. 95; *Moule* v. *Garrett* (1872) L.R. 7 Ex. 101.

conferred a benefit upon the defendant. No factual inquiry was necessary. The difficult problem of deciding whether the plaintiff's actions had benefited the defendant in point of fact was entirely avoided.

I have already referred, in Chapter 13, to some of Bramwell's extreme views on freedom of contract, and here I need only remind the reader that Bramwell quite explicitly argued in the Report of the Mercantile Law Commission in 1854, that he could see no 'natural justice in, or connexion between, buying goods and paying for them'.[8] To him, the liability to pay even for goods delivered and consumed, depended not on the benefit received by the party to whom the goods were delivered, but on his agreement or promise to pay. In the absence of such an agreement, there could be no liability.[9]

It is obvious that if this sort of approach had been widely adopted by the Courts in the nineteenth century, there would have been many cases in which liability would have had to be denied although it had been regularly imposed in the eighteenth century. For example, there were the cases in which a tradesman sued a head of household for goods or services supplied to members of his family, or even his domestic servants, in which liability had been freely imposed in the eighteenth century. Generally, in the older law, it had been held that the head of the household was liable, either if the goods or services were necessaries, or if his assent could be presumed. Now it came to be said that all these cases rested on an implied assent,[10] and a considerable tightening-up took place as to the circumstances from which such an assent could be implied.[11] As to children, the rule was firmly laid down in *Mortimore* v. *Wright*,[12] that a father was only to be liable if he had authorized his child to pledge his credit as his agent. 'In point of law', said Lord Abinger, 'a father who gives no authority, and enters into no contract, is no more liable for goods supplied to his son, than a brother, or an uncle, or a mere stranger would be ... In order to bind a father in point of law for a debt

---

[8] (1854) H.C. *Parliamentary Papers*, xxviii. 445, 467, 471; *supra*, p. 376.

[9] *Boulton* v. *Jones* (1857) 2 H. & N. 564, 157 E.R. 232; the case may have turned on a set-off which the defendant had against the former owner, but in the report in 27 L.J. Ex. 117, it seems to be implied that the set-off was immaterial.

[10] *Montague* v. *Benedict* (1825) 3 B. & C. 631, 107 E.R. 867; *Seaton* v. *Benedict* (1828) 5 Bing. 28, 130 E.R. 969.

[11] The older attitude can still be seen up to the 1820s. See *Cooper* v. *Martin* (1803) 4 East 76, 102 E.R. 759 (a strong decision in a rather different factual situation); *Blackburn* v. *Mackey* (1823) 1 C. & P. 1, 171 E.R. 1076; *Fluck* v. *Tollemache* (1823) 1 C. & P. 5, 171 E.R. 1078; *Cameron* v. *Baker* (1824) 1 C. & P. 268, 171 E.R. 1190; *Nichole* v. *Allen* (1827) 3 C. & P. 38, 172 E.R. 312. In *Law* v. *Wilkin* (1837) 6 Ad. & E. 718, 112 E.R. 276, Parke J. (later B.) directed a nonsuit, but was overruled by the Court of King's Bench *in banco*.

[12] (1840) 6 M. & W. 482, 151 E.R. 502. See also *Urmston* v. *Newcomen* (1836) 4 Ad. & E. 899, 111 E.R. 1022, where defendant's counsel boldly protested that a father had no common law duty to maintain his children. If this was a result of the individualism preached by the political economists, they would have been horrified at it.

incurred by his son, you must prove that he has contracted to be bound, just in the same manner as you would prove such a contract against any other person.'[13] And in the same case Parke B. insisted that juries must not be allowed to find presumed consent without proper evidence.

As to the liability of a husband for goods supplied to his wife, the new doctrines were clearly laid down in *Jolly* v. *Rees*.[14] The wife had here been supplied with drapery and clothing suitable to her station in life (as the formula went) and it was also found that the defendant, her husband, did not give his wife an adequate allowance for such purchases. But the husband had told his wife that she must not buy goods on credit in his name, and on this ground (though it was not known to the tradesman) it was held that the defendant was not liable. Erle C.J. used the language of will theory to reject the plaintiff's claim: '[I]t is a solecism in reasoning to say that she derives her authority from his will, and at the same time to say that the relation of wife creates the authority against his will, by a presumption juris et de jure from marriage.'[15] Thus the implied or presumed authority of the husband was now liable to be rebutted as a question of fact. Byles J. dissented from the majority, holding that the apparent authority of the wife was a legal matter which could not be rebutted. In view of Byles's antipathy to the then popular version of freedom of contract, his dissent here is of particular interest. But it was to no avail. In 1880 the House of Lords approved the decision in *Jolly* v. *Rees*.[16] Will theory had triumphed over the idea that a husband ought to pay for his wife's clothes. All that remained of the old law was the husband's liability for his wife's funeral expenses.[17]

A similar trend is observable in connection with cases where one person was under some social or even legal obligation to another who was not a member of his family. For example, in 1795 Lord Kenyon held that an apothecary could recover against a defendant for medicine and attendance on the defendant's servant.[18] The decision was not based on any notion of implied authority, but on the plain ground that a master was obliged to provide for his servant in sickness and in health.[19] But in

---

[13] 6 M. & W. 486, 151 E.R. 504.

[14] (1864) 15 C.B.(N.S.) 628, 143 E.R. 931.

[15] 15 C.B.(N.S.) 641, 143 E.R. 936.

[16] *Debenham* v. *Mellon* (1880) 6 App. Cas. 24. It is clear that the temptation held out to wives to purchase clothes on credit was regarded at this time as a serious social problem for which the tradesmen were largely to blame. See Samuel Smiles, *Thrift* (first published 1875, London, 1903), p. 241.

[17] *Rogers* v. *Price* (1829) 3 Y. & J. 28, 148 E.R. 1080; *Ambrose* v. *Kerrison* (1851) 10 C.B. 776, 138 E.R. 307.

[18] *Scarman* v. *Castell* (1795) 1 Esp. 270, 170 E.R. 353.

[19] In *Dalton's* Justice (1742 edition) this was stated quite categorically at p. 141. This work was much relied on by local justices.

the new century Lord Kenyon's decision was overruled,[20] and it was also held that a parish could not be liable for the cost of medical attendance on a pauper in their care without evidence that they had authorized the attendance.[21] The parish was, indeed, still thought to be bound to provide medical attention to paupers in its care, but it was now insisted that it was the right of the parish to choose who they were to employ.[22]

It is worth observing that these trends against the imposition of quasi-contractual liability (as it would be known today) were not unrelated to the new emphasis on the long-term, hortatory, or deterrent effects of the law. Tradesmen who supplied goods to wives or children were, in effect, being disciplined by the Courts; they were being warned that if they did not take care to secure the authority of the husband or father, or other head of household, before they supplied the goods, they might be deprived of payment. In earlier times (and perhaps again today, as we shall see later) where the law was less concerned with these longer-term disciplinary results, the moral appeal of compelling the recipient of a benefit to make due recompense was (and is) greater. If the law tends to be more backward-looking, less concerned with deterrence and discipline, it is more likely to condone the fault of the party rendering the benefit in overlooking the need to obtain a clear prior sanction, and more likely to stress the element of hardship imposed if he is not recompensed, and the element of unjust enrichment if the other party does not have to pay.

The point may be illustrated by referring to a not unamusing incident in the life of David Hume.[22A] In 1774 Hume was sued by a small contractor in Edinburgh for some work done to Hume's house at a time when it was let (to James Boswell) and sub-let to a sub-tenant. Apparently with the authority of the sub-tenant, but without Hume's own authority, various works of repair and improvement had been done by the contractor for which Hume declined to pay. He was held liable in the first Court and evidently in some exasperation drafted his own grounds of appeal. The pursuer, he protested, had never even alleged that the works had been carried out with his (Hume's) authority. 'The only answer he could make to this was, that the work was necessary to be done, but this your Petitioner apprehends is no good answer, because by the same Rule he may go through every house in Edinburgh, & do what he thinks proper to be done, without the Landlords consent or approbation and give the same reason for what he did, That the work was necessary and that the house was the better of it, a Doctrine quite new, and as your petitioner apprehends, altogether untenable.' The

---

[20] *Wennall* v. *Adney* (1802) 3 B. & P. 247, 127 E.R. 137.
[21] *Atkins* v. *Banwell* (1802) 2 East 505, 102 E.R. 462.
[22] *Paynter* v. *Williams* (1833) 1 C. & M. 810, 149 E.R. 626.
[22A] See E. C. Mossner, *Life of David Hume* (Edinburgh, 1954), p. 564.

interesting thing is that (on whatever grounds) this defence failed and Hume was compelled to pay. But it is difficult to believe that his defence would have failed in any of the superior Courts at Westminster in the mid-nineteenth century. If it was not felt necessary to discipline the tradesmen of Edinburgh in the 1770s, it certainly was (or was thought to be) necessary to discipline the tradesmen of London and England in 1850.

Another series of decisions, which are perhaps more closely related to what is today thought to be the law of quasi-contract, concerned the right of a party to recover when he had performed his obligations in part, but not in full. For some years at the beginning of this period, that is, between around 1770 and the early nineteenth century, two principles were warring in the Courts. On the one hand, there was the old idea that if the plaintiff had conferred some benefit on the defendant, even by a partial performance, he ought to be entitled to recover something for his pains.[23] And on the other hand, there was the newer feeling that to allow recovery for partial performance was, in effect to rewrite the contract.[24] Already in 1797 we find expression being given by the judges to the idea that 'we do not sit here to make, but to enforce contracts'.[25] It was the newer ideas which prevailed, leading to the doctrine of 'entire contracts', that is, to the idea that a plaintiff in default could not recover anything for any benefits conferred.[26]

Rather similar to these are the cases about the recovery of money paid on the ground of failure of consideration. In the eighteenth century recovery had been permitted for partial failure of consideration, that is, the Courts had permitted this remedy to be used in order to remake the contract, to adjust the parties' rights to the performance which had actually occurred. Towards the end of the eighteenth century, this came to seem anomalous, and the Courts eventually repudiated the idea that there could be recovery in such circumstances.[27] The plaintiff was obliged to sue for damages for breach of contract. One highly abstract doctrinal oddity resulted from these cases. It came to be said[28] that, in order to recover money paid as on a total failure of consideration, the plaintiff had to show that the contract had been 'rescinded', and thus, in some sense, 'got rid of'. If he could show this, there would then be no ground on which the defendant could retain any money paid in

---

[23] *Luke* v. *Lyde* (1759) 2 Burr. 882, 97 E.R. 614; *Farnsworth* v. *Garrard* (1807) 1 Camp. 38, 170 E.R. 867.

[24] *Ellis* v. *Hamlen* (1810) 3 Taunt. 52, 126 E.R. 21.

[25] Per Lord Kenyon in *Cook* v. *Jennings* (1797) 7 T.R. 381, 384, 101 E.R. 1032, 1033.

[26] *Sinclair* v. *Bowles* (1829) 9 B. & C. 92, 109 E.R. 35; *Munro* v. *Batt* (1858) 8 E. & B. 738, 120 E.R. 275.

[27] *Towers* v. *Barrett* (1786) 1 T.R. 133, 99 E.R. 1014.

[28] *Towers* v. *Barrett, supra*; *Beed* v. *Blandford* (1828) 2 Y. & J. 278, 148 E.R. 924; *Planche* v. *Colburn* (1831) 8 Bing. 14, 131 E.R. 305.

pursuance of the contract. But, conversely, if the contract remained 'open' and was not 'rescinded' the plaintiff could not recover his money in this form of action, but had to sue for damages for breach of contract. This passed firmly into the law and remains today a part of English contract doctrine. It seems to have represented the attempt of the judges to distinguish, in terms of the new contract theories, between cases in which the plaintiff received some benefit under the contract and cases where he received none. In modern times it has also helped to justify the idea that the right to recover payments in such circumstances is quasi-contractual in contrast to the right to recover damages which, falling somehow 'under' the contract, is seen to be contractual. It is scarcely necessary to add that this distinction does not seem to rest on very sound foundations. It is hard to see why the right to recover payment on a total failure of consideration is any less contractual than the right to recover damages for breach.[29] Neither right arises, in any realistic sense, from the intention of the parties; but on the other hand, both rights arise out of a misfire or failure in an arrangement, usually of a consensual character, and both are the creation of the law.

One further example of the shift in quasi-contractual ideas which developed during the classical period concerns the early privity cases. I have previously drawn attention to the large number of cases in the early nineteenth century which were discussed in terms of the doctrine of privity. These cases nearly always involved a payment of money by one party (A) to a second party (B) with instructions to pay the money over to a third party (C). The question which then arose was whether A or C was the right party to sue B if he should make default. It was never doubted that B was liable to someone; if A was the appropriate plaintiff he would sue as on a failure of consideration; if B was the plaintiff he would sue for money had and received to his use. It was also possible that C might have the right to claim the money as a beneficiary of a trust. There were a very large number of cases of this type in the late eighteenth and early nineteenth century, probably because in the absence of wider banking facilities, the middle party, B, was often acting as a sort of banker to A. The tendency at first was for the Courts to ask whether B was 'accountable' to A or to C, and to answer this by inquiring whether B had dealings primarily with A or with C.[30] But in the nineteenth century, the Courts moved away from this idea towards that of a more promise-based liability. It came to be said that B was liable to A unless and until he promised C that he would pay the money to him.[31] But then

---

[29] See Perillo, 'Restitution in a Contractual Context', 73 *Columbia Law Rev.* 1208 (1973).

[30] *Israel* v. *Douglas* (1789) 1 H. Bl. 239, 126 E.R. 139.

[31] *Williams* v. *Everett* (1811) 14 East 589, 104 E.R. 725; *Wedlake* v. *Hurley* (1830) 1 C. & J. 83, 148 E.R. 1344.

could C sue on that promise? Was there any consideration? In *Liversidge* v. *Broadbent*[32] it was held that C could not sue in such circumstances because he provided no consideration. But in *Griffin* v. *Weatherby*[33] Blackburn J. brushed aside the consideration problem, echoing, probably unconsciously, Lord Mansfield's decision, and almost his very words in *Hawkes* v *Saunders*.[34] The payment of the money by A to B creates an equitable right in C, and when B promises to pay the money to C, 'then that which was merely an equitable right becomes a legal right in the transferee, founded on the promise'.[35] As in *Hawkes* v. *Saunders*, which involved the liability of an executor to pay a legacy, which he had promised to pay, the requirement of consideration was to be found in the very transfer of the money to the party who subsequently promised the third party to pay it to him. That transfer was both a benefit to the transferee (or at least would be a benefit if he was allowed to keep the money) and an act of detrimental reliance on the part of the transferor. But by 1868 this way of looking at the doctrine of consideration had largely faded into history, and Blackburn J's arguments were destined to be misunderstood. The whole of this area of the law was now about to fall into desuetude, partly as a result of the growth of modern banking facilities, but partly because of changes in legal doctrine. After the Judicature Acts, the problem which had previously been dealt with in these cases tended to be treated as a question in the law of assignments. That did not of course dispose of the substantive issues which remained troublesome, because there is still a valid distinction between a revocable mandate by a creditor to his debtor to pay money to a third party, and an equitable assignment which actually transfers that right.[36] But it did at least remove this body of law from the action for money had and received to the sphere of equitable assignment. When in 1958, the subject was resuscitated in *Shamia* v. *Joorey*,[37] the old law seems to have been totally misunderstood. By this time there seemed nothing odd in holding that a liability based *on an express promise to pay* was quasi-contractual rather than contractual. This baffling reinterpretation of old law need not detain us here. My concern is merely to point out how, during the classical period, rights which had formerly been treated as arising from payments of money, by operation of law, tended to be recast into the language of contract.

[32] (1859) 4 H. & N. 603, 157 E.R. 978.
[33] (1868) L.R. 3 Q.B. 753.
[34] (1782) 1 Cowp. 289, 98 E.R. 1091; *supra*, p. 161.
[35] At p. 758.
[36] *Percival* v. *Dunn* (1885) 29 Ch. D. 128; *Rekstin* v. *Severo, etc. and Bank for Russian Trade* [1933] 1 K.B. 47; *Curran* v. *Newpark Cinemas Ltd.* [1951] 1 All E.R. 295.
[37] [1958] 1 Q.B. 448; see Davies, *'Shamia* v. *Joorey*: A Forgotten Chapter in Quasi-Contract', 75 *Law Q. Rev.* 220 (1959).

The Moral Obligation Doctrine

I referred in Chapter 6 to Lord Mansfield's decisions holding that, in some circumstances, a moral obligation might be a sufficient consideration for a subsequent promise.[38] I suggested there that these decisions are more readily intelligible if it is remembered that in the eighteenth century contractual obligations still largely arose from promises to perform an independent obligation. But as contract theory changed, as promissory liability came to be seen to be at the basis of contract law, the notion of a promise to perform an independent obligation ceased to make much sense to lawyers. In 1802 the Law Reporters Bosanquet and Puller appended a Note to the decision in *Wennall* v. *Adney*[39] which was destined to become better known than the decision itself. In this Note, the Reporters argued that the cases in which a moral obligation could be a sufficient consideration were all cases in which a benefit had been conferred which would normally have created an actionable right in itself, but which, by reason of some special rule of law (such as infancy, or the Statute of Limitations), did not create such an obligation. In these cases the subsequent promise could be held to be actionable. But they argued strongly against the idea that any moral obligation could be a sufficient consideration for a promise. In *Lee* v. *Muggeridge*,[40] however, Mansfield's opinions were still taken to be the law, and were even extended to cover the case of a subsequent promise by a widow to pay debts originally incurred while she was married (and therefore without any legal capacity to contract). But professional opinion was hardening against the whole moral obligation doctrine[41] and it was eventually rejected in *Eastwood* v. *Kenyon*.[42]

In this case the plaintiff had been executor to one Sutcliffe who had died leaving a daughter, Sarah, and a number of cottages. The plaintiff alleged that he had laid out some money (borrowed from one Blackburn) in expenditure on the cottages, and in maintaining Sarah. When she came of age Sarah promised to repay the plaintiff for this expenditure, and when she married, her husband, the defendant, did likewise. But the husband's promise was held unenforceable on the ground of lack of consideration. There is no doubt that this is one of the most puzzling of all nineteenth-century decisions on contract law.[43] Why did the Court go

---

[38] *Supra*, p. 162.

[39] (1802) 3 B. & P. 247, 249, 127 E.R. 137, 138.

[40] (1813) 5 Taunt. 36, 128 E.R. 599; see also the prior equitable decision in (1812) 1 V. & B. 118, 35 E.R. 46.

[41] See, e.g., Chitty on *Contract*, 2nd edn. (1834), pp. 42–3, where the moral obligation doctrine is criticized for its vagueness.

[42] (1840) 11 Ad. & E. 438, 113 E.R. 482.

[43] See my *Consideration in Contracts*, pp. 37–8 where I offered an explanation that does not now satisfy me; Holdsworth, 'The New Rules of Pleading of Hilary Term 1834', *Camb. L.J.* 261 (1923),

(continued)

out of its way to overrule decisions representing the law of some seventy years' standing, when the result seemed so unjust? Further, if, as I have argued, the whole trend of contract law had been to stress the importance of the promissory basis, is it not passing strange that the Court here should have invoked the doctrine of consideration (which elsewhere had been reduced by this time to a bare technicality) to defeat a clear and express promise? Moreover, the idea that this was a conservative decision, a return to the old, true, pre-Mansfield law, does not square with what we know of Denman. For though Denman may not have had any great reputation as a lawyer, he was by no means a conservative figure. He had spent many years as a fairly radical Whig in Parliament, was a close associate of Brougham's, and even while on the Bench, took an active part in many law reform proposals.

I suggest that three factors may have been responsible for the decision. First, there was the growing strength of positivism which stressed the line between law and morality far more than had ever been the case in Mansfield's time. Positivism owed its origins to Bentham's *Fragment on Government*, but was given much greater elaboration and force in Austin's *Province of Jurisprudence Determined*, first published in 1832. Austin, it must be remembered was a member of the Benthamite circle, on the outer fringes of which had been Denman himself before he became Chief Justice. Denman may have been acquainted with Austin, and, more likely, with his work. It does not seem unduly speculative to suggest that the Court was unhappy at the idea of having openly to convert moral obligations into legal ones.

The second factor is less obvious, and more dubious, but I suggest that there is a sense in which the decision was part of the process of downgrading quasi-contractual duties, liabilities not based on consent, which was such a pronounced feature of the times. The fact that in the case itself there was an express promise is no doubt paradoxical, but the point is that the original benefit received by Sarah was not at that time the subject of any promise to pay, either by Sarah or by her husband. If there had been any quasi-contractual duty on Sarah to reimburse the plaintiff for his expenditure, then there is no doubt that she at least would have been subsequently liable on her promise. The Court stressed the rule that where a benefit is rendered in circumstances which create a legal liability to pay without any promise, then a subsequent promise is itself binding and the past consideration is treated as good.[44] In a sense,

argues at pp. 273–5 that the case was somehow a result of the new pleading rules, in a way which also fails to convince. See also, A. W. B. Simpson, 'Innovation in Nineteenth Century Contract Law', 91 *Law Q. Rev.* 247 (1975).

[44] Other cases in this period also stress that subsequent promises based on a pre-existing duty cannot bind further than the duty itself: *Hopkins* v. *Logan* (1839) 5 M. & W. 241, 151 E. R. 103; *Roscorla* v. *Thomas* (1842) 3 Q.B. 234, 114 E.R. 496.

therefore, the importance of the decision may lie not so much in the denial of liability on the express promise, but in the denial of any pre-existing quasi-contractual duty. Certainly, the Note by Bosanquet and Puller previously referred to, can be interpreted as being concerned with this point. The Reporters seem to have been concerned not so much with the liability on an express promise, but with the notion that a quasi-contractual duty might arise out of the mere receipt of a benefit conferred on oneself or on some close relation. Now we have seen how, around 1840, the Courts were cutting down on such liabilities. A man was not to be held liable for some benefit conferred upon his wife or his child, unless authorized by him. And in *Eastwood* v. *Kenyon* the Court appears to be insisting that the authority must be contemporaneous with the conferring of the benefit. Benefits are not to be thrust upon people behind their backs, and then promises afterwards extracted from them.

The third possible factor which may have contributed to the decision in *Eastwood* v. *Kenyon* was the disappearance of the idea that the binding nature of a promise rested upon some pre-existing obligation. This is shown by the fact that Lord Denman rejects the argument that a moral obligation can amount to a consideration by arguing that all promises anyhow give rise to moral obligations, and the doctrine, literally applied, would eliminate the need for consideration altogether.

The Statute of Frauds

In Chapter 7 I suggested that the Statute of Frauds could be seen as an attempt to hold back the gradual rise of the executory contract. Because the Statute did not generally apply, or was held not to apply, where there had been part performance of the contract, the result was, in effect, to require written confirmation of a large class of purely executory contracts, while not affecting the enforcement of the same contracts when they had been part executed. Whether such acts of part performance are seen as involving the conferring of benefits or as acts of reliance is not material for present purposes.

In the early years of the nineteenth century there is little sign of the judicial hostility to the Statute of Frauds which later became so apparent.[45] As late as 1828 Parliament passed an Act, generally called Lord Tenterden's Act, which actually extended some of the provisions of the Act so as to overrule a number of previous decisions. For example, the Act required acknowledgements in bar of the Statute of Limitations to be in writing, and it also extended the requirements in contracts of guarantee to the somewhat analogous case of credit references. But it

---

[45] See, e.g., *Wain* v. *Warlters* (1804) 5 East 10, 102 E.R. 974; cf. *Egerton* v. *Mathews* (1804) 6 East 307, 102 E.R. 1304.

seems clear that the day of the Act was necessarily doomed as the emphasis of the law shifted to the enforcement of executory contracts. If contractual liability was essentially to be based on the promise or will of the parties, the requirement of writing or of part performance was bound to seem increasingly anomalous.

The first reaction of the Courts was to pursue the somewhat extraordinary idea that section 17 of the Statute of Frauds did not apply at all to executory contracts of sale of goods. But this plainly would not do, for the Statute scarcely ever applied to an executed contract, and this early line of decisions was soon disposed of.[46] The next thing that had to be sorted out was the juristic status of the written note or memorandum required by the Statute. So long as the Courts thought primarily in terms of executed transactions it is understandable that the written document required by the Act should have been thought of as the equivalent of the act of part performance, that is, as the very basis or essence of the liability somewhat similar to a bond. And it is, therefore, not surprising that originally the Courts appear to have thought that the absence of writing made an executory contract wholly void.[48] But this view was clearly incompatible with the new will theory of contractual liability. The source of the liability could not be a mere piece of paper—it was necessarily the will of the parties, or the agreement, which created the liabilities. Pothier had already argued, in discussing a French statute analogous to the Statute of Frauds, that the requirement of writing was a mere matter of proof, and that 'it is not intended that the writing shall be considered as the substance of the agreement, which is valid without writing'.[49] This pronouncement (in the original French text) had been drawn to the attention of the Courts in 1800,[50] and by 1852 they were ready to adopt it. In *Leroux* v. *Brown*[51] the Court accepted counsel's argument that the agreements affected by the statute could not be wholly void if there were no writing. 'It is everyday practice in the courts of equity', argued counsel, 'to enforce the performance of contracts not in writing where there has been a part performance. That could not be, if the contract were wholly void.'[52] Thus, it was now argued that enforcement of a contract on the grounds of part performance—on the ground that a benefit had been conferred—necessarily demonstrated the existence of a valid agreement. The idea could no longer be understood that Courts of Equity might be trying to remedy an injustice arising from

---

[46] *Rondeau* v. *White* (1792) 2 H. Bl. 63, 126 E.R. 430.
[48] See *Carrington* v. *Roots* (1837) 2 M. & W. 248, 255, 257, 150 E.R. 748, 751, 752.
[49] *Law of Obligations*, i. 11.
[50] *Cooth* v. *Jackson* (1800) 6 Ves. 12, 23, 31 E.R. 913, 919.
[51] 12 C.B. 801, 138 E.R. 1119.
[52] 12 C.B. 821, 138 E.R. 1128.

an unjust enrichment rather than trying to enforce an agreement. As late as 1883 Lord Selborne, an Equity judge, insisted in *Maddison* v. *Alderson*[53] that Courts of Equity, in enforcing part executed contracts, were charging the defendant on the equities arising from the part performance and not from the agreement itself; but this kind of language was no longer intelligible to a generation of lawyers brought up on the executory contract. Lord Selborne's language came to be treated as a specious attempt to explain away Equity's evasion of the statute.

The next requirement was to work out the nature of the part performance required. There were several attempts to hold that even at common law part performance would suffice on the ground that the Statute of Frauds did not apply at all to part executed contracts. This was emphatically stated by Tindal C.J. in 1846,[54] and was acted on up to 1875,[55] but the idea eventually proved too difficult to reconcile with the common law view that liability in contract was now basically consensual.[56] It came to be left to Equity to enforce the doctrine of part performance in most cases (although the Statute itself, of course, provided for certain types of part performance in contracts of sale of goods) and the equitable doctrine came to be increasingly technical.[57] The original idea that it was more unfair to refuse protection to restitutionary or reliance interests, than to refuse enforcement of an executory contract, was quite lost sight of in a morass of technicalities. Only in the last few years has some attempt been made to go back to this central notion.[58]

By mid-century, opinion seems to have been hardening against the Statute altogether. The Mercantile Law Commission recommended repeal of section 17 in so far as it related to contracts of sale of goods[59] although (as we have seen) they recommended strengthening its provisions in relation to contracts of guarantee. The second, but not the first, of these recommendations was carried out at once. The first had to wait for a hundred years, by which time the values and policies on which contract law were based had to a large extent retreated from the high-water mark of Victorian consensualism and will theory. There was, in truth, more to be said in defence of these provisions of the Statute of Frauds in 1954 when they were repealed, than in 1854 when such repeal was first recommended.[59A]

---

[53] (1883) 8 App. Cas. 467.

[54] *Souch* v. *Strawbridge* (1846) 2 C.B. 808, 814, 135 E.R. 1161, 1164.

[55] *Scarisbrick* v. *Parkinson* (1869) 20 L.T.R. 174; *Knowlman* v. *Bluett* (1874) L.R. 9 Ex. 307.

[56] *Sanderson* v. *Graves* (1875) L.R. 10 Ex 234; *Jorden* v. *Money* (1854) 5 H.L.C. 185, 10 E.R. 868; see too the analogous case of *Hunt* v. *Wimbledon Local Board* (1878) 4 C.P.D. 48.

[57] *Maddison* v. *Alderson, supra* was the turning point.

[58] *Steadman* v. *Steadman* [1976] A.C. 536.

[59] *Second Report* (1854–5) H.C. *Parliamentary Papers*, xviii. 653, 658.

[59A] See *post*, p. 691.

Agency

The law of agency was very undeveloped prior to the end of the eighteenth century. I have previously referred[60] to a number of cases in the late eighteenth century, in particular, *Waugh* v. *Carver*[61] and *Bush* v. *Steinman*[62] which show the beginnings of the law relating to the liability of a principal, both in contract and in tort, being based on the somewhat vague notion that a man who received some benefit from an enterprise ought to bear his share of any losses arising from it. In the nineteenth century these cases were found unsatisfactory. So far as contract law was concerned, it was necessary to reconcile the liability of a principal with the new will theory. There was no problem, of course, where the agent acted within the scope of his authority, but serious difficulty arose in trying to explain away the liability of a principal for unauthorized acts. The practical bent of English judges, and their growing understanding of commercial realities, ensured that they continued to uphold the liability of a principal on contracts made by an agent within the apparent scope of his authority, though actually contrary to his instructions, but they were hard pressed to explain the basis of this liability. It was, of course, and is, based ultimately on the idea of reasonable reliance; there is, indeed, a close analogy between the objective interpretation of a contracting party's intentions (however contrary these may be to his 'secret intentions') and the questions arising in the agency cases, where the principal might be liable on the basis of the external manifestation of assent by his agent (despite 'secret instructions' from the principal). In both situations the Courts took a strong objective line. Even Pothier was wholeheartedly in favour of this objective approach in the agency cases, and his views were cited to the Court in *Smith* v. *M'Guire* in 1858.[63] The basis of the liability of the principal was here explained in very clear terms by Pollock C.B. as resting upon the reasonable reliance of the third party. The whole issue, in his view, turned on the question whether the third party was entitled to rely upon the agent's apparent authority, and upon whom lay the burden of making further inquiry. If it was the third party's duty to make inquiry of the principal, then he obviously could not rely upon the apparent authority. But if it was the principal's duty to make inquiry as to what his agent was doing in his name, then the third party might reasonably rely on the apparent authority of the agent, and so hold the principal liable. If it was then asked, how the

---

[60] *Supra*, pp. 177–8.

[61] (1793) 2 H. Bl. 235, 126 E.R. 525. Bramwell B. had expressed his total inability to understand this case as a member of the Mercantile Law Commission. See the *First Report* (1854) H.C. *Parliamentary Papers*, xxvii. 445, 471.

[62] (1799) 1 B. & P. 404, 126 E.R. 978.

[63] (1858) 3 H. & N. 554, 157 E.R. 589.

Court was to decide which party was under the duty to make inquiry, the Court was ready with its answer: persons are expected to carry on their business 'according to the ordinary arrangement of mankind generally'.[64] Commercial custom and practice was thus to dictate the answer to the question.

In general the Courts adhered to this approach, although efforts were made by some of the judges to reconcile the practical necessities with the new contractual theories. In *Pole* v. *Leask*[65] Lord Cranworth found the objective approach of his colleagues too much, and he felt it necessary, in a dissenting judgment, to remind them of the basis of all contractual liability:

No one can become the agent of another person except by the will of that other person. His will may be manifested in writing, or orally, or simply by placing the person said to be an agent in a situation in which, according to ordinary rules of law, or perhaps it would be more correct to say, according to the ordinary usages of mankind, that person is understood to represent and act for the person who has so placed him, but in every case it is only by the will of the employer that an agency can be created.[66]

While he went on to admit that there could be an agency by estoppel, he seems to have treated this as slender foundation for liability. The fact that an agent had acted on fifty occasions with the authority of his principal, does not, says Lord Cranworth, justify the third party in assuming that the agent is authorized on the fifty-first occasion. It is difficult to reconcile this with the idea of reasonable reliance at all, and it is not surprising that his lordship was in a minority on this occasion.

A more important decision was *Cox* v. *Hickman*[67] in the House of Lords in 1860. The defendants were two creditors of a firm in liquidation whose business has been assigned to trustees. The business had been carried on by the trustees, on behalf of all the creditors, but the defendants had only been nominal trustees, not taking any part in the business. The business, even in the hands of the creditors, failed, and the plaintiffs were holders of bills signed by trustees on behalf of the firm. They sought to hold all the creditors and trustees liable on the ground that the business was being carried on for their benefit, and that in accordance with *Waugh* v. *Carver* they were to be deemed to be partners of the active trustees. But this argument was rejected by the House of Lords and *Waugh* v. *Carver* was effectively overruled. The decision must be seen in its context. First, the Usury Laws had now been repealed, and the old justification no longer held, that a man who took a share in the profits of a business was attempting to obtain an illicit return on his investment. Secondly, the

---

[64] 3 H. & N. 561-2, 157 E.R. 593.
[66] At pp. 161-2.

[65] (1862) 33 L.J. Ch. 155.
[67] 8 H.L.C. 268, 11 E.R. 431.

principle of limited liability had recently been recognized by Parliament, and it was becoming more apparent every day that corporate activity was a very different thing from individual activity. The idea that a man who shared in the profits of a business ought to be liable for all the debts of the business might have been acceptable when the business was run by a small number of individuals; but applied to great new corporations, such as the railway companies, this would create liabilities wholly disproportionate to the benefits received. Some of the creditors in this case were owed very small sums of money, and the House could not accept the idea that it was just to make them liable for the whole of the debts of the business.

As to the precise formulation of the new legal principles being adopted, the case probably illustrates, better than any other single decision, the shift in the basis of liability from benefit to will. The House, consisting of Lords Campbell, Brougham, Wensleydale (formerly Parke B.), and Cranworth, unanimously held that the defendants could not be liable unless they had themselves accepted the bills, or authorized the active trustees, as their agents, to accept them, or held them out as having an apparent authority to accept them. Receipt of a benefit in the form of a share of the profits was not itself enough to make a man liable as a partner; it was merely evidence that he had authorized the other to act as his agent. Lord Wensleydale, after citing Story and Pothier, proceeded to lay down the 'true' principles:

A man who allows another to carry on trade, whether in his own name or not, to buy and sell, and to pay over all the profits to him, is undoubtedly the principal, and the person so employed is the agent, and the principal is liable for the agent's contracts in the course of his employment. So if two or more agree that they should carry on a trade, and share the profits of it, each is a principal, and each is an agent for the other, and each is bound by the other's contract in carrying on the trade, as much as a single principal would be by the act of an agent, who was to give the whole of the profits to his employer. Hence it becomes a test of the liability of one for the contract of another, that he is to receive the whole or a part of the profits arising from that contract by virtue of the agreement made at the time of the employment. I believe this is the true principle of partnership liability. Perhaps the maxim that he who undertakes the advantage ought to bear the loss, often stated in the earlier cases on this subject, is only the consequence, not the cause, why a man is made liable as a partner.[68]

Similarly, Lord Cranworth said that it was a fallacy to suppose that a man who obtained a benefit by sharing in the profits of a business was, on that ground alone, liable for its losses. No doubt, in a general way, he went on, this was a sufficiently accurate way of putting the matter. 'But

[68] 8 H.L.C. 313, 11 E.R. 449.

the real ground of the liability is, that the trade has been carried on by persons acting on his behalf.'[69] If it is correct (as I have suggested) that, prior to the classical period, contractual obligations arose primarily from receipt of benefits (or acts of reliance) and that promises had a merely evidentiary force, then this decision must mark the point at which the House of Lords set its seal on the reversed roles of benefit and promise. It is now the will, the agreement, the authority conferred by the principal, which makes him liable; his receipt of a benefit in the shape of a share of profits is not the ground of liability, but evidence of the principal's will, agreement, or authority.

Inevitably, these changes in the ideas underlying agency law led to a shift in legal doctrines in various respects. One concerned the doctrine of the undisclosed principal. Given the generally accepted objective approach to all questions of contract formation, lawyers and jurists began to see the rights and liabilities of an undisclosed principal as increasingly anomalous. In 1887 Pollock argued that the whole doctrine was an anomaly, and he put its origins down to a sort of 'common law equity' which had led to 'the feeling that a person who had got the advantage of a purchase ought to pay for it if the agent to whom the seller really trusted was not able to do so'.[70] Another result was an increasing tendency to treat as totally anomalous the cases in which a person could be treated as 'an agent of necessity'. In eighteenth-century law there had been a number of decisions, mostly concerned with shipping and salvage matters, holding that a ship's master could bind the owners by acts done for their benefit, even without any actual authority. As late as 1801 the Admiralty Court was prepared to extend these doctrines so that the ship's master was held to have power to bind the cargo owners, as well as the shipowners, by acts done for the purpose of repairing the ship.[71] The whole doctrine was justified by Sir William Scott as resting on the benefit to the cargo owners. 'In all cases, it is the prospect of benefit to the proprietor that is the foundation of the authority of the master. It is therefore, true that if the repairs of the ship produce no benefit or prospect of benefit to the cargo, the master cannot bind the cargo for such repairs.'[72] But he went on to add that even an indirect benefit to the cargo owners from the repair of the ship was sufficient to make them liable.

But this was virtually the last extension of the law along these lines. As early as 1775 it had been held that the finder of a lost dog, who had kept it for 12 months, was not entitled to demand payment of the cost as a

[69] 8 H.L.C. 306, 11 E.R. 446.
[70] 3 *Law Q. Rev.* 358, 359 (1887).
[71] *The Gratitudine* (1801) 3 C. Rob. 240, 165 E.R. 450.
[72] 3 C. Rob. 260–1, 165 E.R. 457.

condition of returning the dog.[73] Indeed, counsel simply declined to argue the case for the finder. In 1793 it was again held that a finder of lost property who salvages it, is not entitled to a lien on it for his costs, when the owner demands its return.[74] This decision did not wholly rule out the possibility of the finder having some claim for his costs, for the actual decision was concerned only with the possibility of the finder having a lien. In practice, however, to refuse a lien meant that the finder would have to give up the goods on demand, and the onus would then be on him to sue for a reward, or for some return for his expenses, if the owner proved recalcitrant. This probably proved a sufficient discouragement to the making of such claims, especially during the early years of this period when the Courts were so heavily burdened. Courts of Equity, however, were sufficiently flexible to protect the occupier of land in somewhat analogous circumstances. For example, it was often held that a person in bona fide possession who had spent money on improving the land, or building on it, could demand to be repaid for the increased value of the land if the owner sued to recover it.[75] The conceptual ground on which such cases rested was never fully explained by the Courts, it generally being assumed that the owner could be compelled to pay for the enhanced value of his land, as a condition of the granting of the discretionary relief which he sought. In practice, of course, these were simply cases in which the sense of justice demanded repayment for a benefit conferred, and this sense of justice did not wholly disappear even during the period of classical contract law.

One other offshoot of the early benefit ideas in agency cases needs to be mentioned. This line of development led to the growth of the law of vicarious liability in tort. In the earliest cases, vicarious liability seems to have been treated very much as *Waugh* v. *Carver* had treated the liability of a partner. A man was liable for acts done on his behalf, or for his benefit, if they should in fact cause loss to another.[76] Although this idea was still influential as late as 1839,[77] it is clear that the benefit basis of liability was too wide. As with the case of partners, some further limit had to be placed on the extent of this liability. The limitation was slow in coming; it was canvassed in 1826, when all twelve judges tried to settle it, but failed.[78] It was only resolved in 1840 when the Court of Exchequer with Parke B. at the helm, decided the case of *Quarman* v. *Burnett*.[79] This decision recognized for the first time the distinction between a servant

---

[73] *Binstead* v. *Buck* (1775) 2 W. Bl. 117, 96 E.R. 660.
[74] *Nicholson* v. *Chapman* (1793) 2 H. Bl. 254, 126 E.R. 536.
[75] *Mill* v. *Hill* (1852) 3 H.L.C. 828, 10 E.R. 330; *Cooper* v. *Phibbs* (1867) L.R. 2 H.L. 149.
[76] *Bush* v. *Steinman* (1799) 1 B. & P. 404, 126 E.R. 978.
[77] See *Duncan* v. *Findlater* (1839) 6 Cl. & F. 894, 910, 7 E.R. 934, 940.
[78] *Laugher* v. *Pointer* (1826) 5 B. & C. 547, 108 E.R. 204.
[79] (1840) 7 M. & W. 499, 151 E.R. 509.

and an independent contractor, confining liability to the acts of the former. Like the decision in *Cox* v. *Hickman*,[80] the case can be seen as part of the evolution of an important economic principle, namely the principle that an enterprise should bear the costs of its activities. The very concept of an enterprise was, at this time, in the course of development. The modern registered company did not yet exist, most business was still carried on by individuals or partners (as we have seen), and the separation of an individual's personal assets and liabilities from those of his business was still often incomplete both in law and in fact. In *Quarman* v. *Burnett* the Court recognized plainly enough that a master was liable for the acts of his servant; but they rejected as impossibly wide the idea that a man could be liable for the acts of anyone else merely because he derived a benefit from them. That was 'too large a position' which would produce results shocking 'to the common sense of all men'. It would render liable the hirer of a post-chaise, hackney coach, or wherry on the Thames, and might even render liable the buyer of an article in a shop if the shopkeeper's carelessness injured someone while he was on the way to deliver it. The examples are drawn from the personal experiences of judges and men of the upper class of Victorian England, but it would be surprising if Parke B. did not have commercial considerations in mind also.

THE EMERGING LAW OF NEGLIGENCE

The period 1770–1870 was not a time when there was dramatic change or development in the law of torts, and that need hardly occasion much surprise. If this was, as I suggest, the heyday of classical contract theory, when nearly all liabilities were thought to depend on some element of free choice, or consent, there was naturally little scope for the development of legally imposed duties. In the earliest part of this period, tort law was still fundamentally concerned with protecting property rights, and with rights directed against infringement of a man's personal integrity—assaults, false imprisonment, libel, and so on. The modern law of negligence was still almost wholly undeveloped. And it is not difficult to see why, for negligence as a tort presupposes that a man has a right to the due care of his neighbours as a matter of plain law. Now in the period of classical contract law, a right to due care was still largely seen as something for which a man had to pay. There were, it is true, the older reliance-based decisions like *Coggs* v. *Barnard*[81] and cases stemming from that idea, but we have already seen that these came to seem anomalous in Victorian England. There were also reliance-based cases

[80] 8 H.L.C. 268, 11 E.R. 431, *supra*, p. 497.
[81] (1703) 2 Ld. Ray. 909, 92 E.R. 107.

like *Pasley* v. *Freeman*[82] imposing liability for fraud, but such cases could be seen indifferently as contractual or tortious, resembling as they did the warranty cases. And we must also remember that prior to the mass production of the motor car, most personal injury accidents occurred in some kind of relational setting. A man might be injured at work, or he might be injured while on some dangerous premises, or he might be injured while travelling on a railway, but all these sorts of accidents presented a contractual flavour to the nineteenth-century lawyer.

So far as work-connected injuries was concerned, it was the invention of the doctrine of common employment which first tended to bar liability; and that doctrine was, once again, the work of the Exchequer Court during Parke B'.s tenure of office. It took its origin, as is well known, with the decision in *Priestley* v. *Fowler*[83] in 1837, and was pretty well settled by the decision in *Hutchinson* v. *York, Newcastle and Berwick Rly. Co.*[84] Abinger C.B. delivered judgment in the former case, and Alderson B. in the second, but Parke B. sat in both and it is difficult not to see his hand at work.

In *Winterbottom* v. *Wright*[85] the same Court (though this time without Parke B.) denied the liability of a manufacturer of a carriage to the servant of the purchaser who was injured by a defective wheel. It was this case which introduced into the law what later came to be known as the 'privity of contract fallacy'. It came to be said that the decision was based on the ground that the plaintiff could not sue on the contract because he was no party to it, and that it was 'deduced' that he therefore could not sue in tort either. This 'fallacy' which escaped the perspicuity of judges like Abinger C.B. was, of course, brilliantly exposed in the twentieth century in *Donoghue* v. *Stevenson*.[86] But what passes for legal reasoning in students' textbooks cannot satisfy us as sound history. The story is almost complete nonsense. First, the action in *Winterbottom* v. *Wright* was fully argued in tort by Byles, not a man to overlook a non-contractual argument. Secondly, the privity of contract rule was not clearly established at this time anyhow. And thirdly, it was no logical 'fallacy' but policy arguments which swayed the Court. One argument was the familiar one, but by no means as unfounded as later lawyers have thought, that to allow the action would be to open the door to vast numbers of potential lawsuits. But another argument did rest on the background existence of the contract between the manufacturer and the

---

[82] (1789) 3 T.R. 51, 100 E.R. 450.

[83] (1837) 3 M. & W. 1, 150 E.R. 1030.

[84] (1850) 5 Ex. 343, 155 E.R. 150. The idea that the workman was paid wages to cover the risk of being injured seems to have originated with Blackburn J. in *Morgan* v. *Vale of Neath Rly. Co.* (1864) 5 B. & S. 570, 580, 122 E.R. 944, 948, affirmed (1865) L.R. 1 Q.B. 149.

[85] (1842) 10 M. & W. 109, 152 E.R. 402.

[86] [1932] A.C. 562.

plaintiff's employer: the arrangements between these parties should not be 'ripped open by this action of tort', said Lord Abinger.[87] What he meant by this somewhat cryptic remark seems to have been this: that the manufacturer sold the carriage to the plaintiff at a price based upon the manufacturer's expectations as to his potential liabilities. These expectations (it seems to have been assumed) did not cover possible liability to servants such as the plaintiff, because such actions were unheard of. Therefore, if the action was now allowed, the manufacturer's expectations and calculations would be upset; the basis of the contract of sale would thus be 'ripped open'. This was not so much a privity of contract fallacy, as the Bramwellian fallacy.[88] And it was only a fallacy in a limited sense, anyhow. If and in so far as the Court may have correctly judged the expectations of the manufacturer, the decision was in one sense correct. But it was wrong in other respects; it was wrong in assuming that the manufacturer's expectations were the only relevant factors, and it was also wrong in failing to perceive that, if liability were once declared against manufacturers in such circumstances, the potential liability would in future enter into their calculations, and their prices would (or should) take account of the fact.

But before the end of this period, a number of new cases were beginning to foreshadow the extensive developments in tort liability which lay ahead. In *Indermaur* v. *Dames*[89] the plaintiff, a workman employed by a third party, was injured by falling down an unfenced shaft, while working on the defendants' premises.[90] It was held that the defendants were liable for 'unusual dangers' to persons in the position of the plaintiff who could not be treated as a 'mere volunteer'. The case later fell into the classification of 'Occupiers' Liability', but it is clear that at the time, the main problem was very similar to that in *Winterbottom* v. *Wright*. The plaintiff was a mere servant of the third party; he had no contract with the occupiers. Was he entitled to warning of dangers when he had no contract himself? The decision in the Court of Common Pleas rested on the analogy of the rules as to voluntary gifts and liens, cases themselves drawn from the principle in *Coggs* v. *Barnard*. On appeal, the decision was affirmed on the ground that the plaintiff was not a 'mere volunteer' but was on the premises on business, with the occupier's consent and for his benefit. With the advantage of hindsight, the

---

[87] 10 M. & W. 115, 152 E.R. 405.

[88] *Supra*, pp. 376–8.

[89] (1866) L.R. 1 C.P. 274 (1867) L.R. 2 C.P. 371.

[90] At this time industrial accidents due to unfenced shafts were a constant source of concern, both to workmen and the Factory Inspectorate. In 1853 Palmerston, as Home Secretary, had made a Regulation requiring all shafts over seven feet high to be fenced. This Regulation became quite notorious; it was bitterly attacked by Harriet Martineau as 'worse than shipmoney'. See David Roberts, *Victorian Origins of the British Welfare State* (New Haven, Conn., 1960), pp. 248, 270.

twentieth-century lawyer insists that this was a species of tortious liability. But at the time the boundaries of contract and tort were not nearly so clearly drawn as they became later, and it will be seen that there were elements of consent and benefit in the case—two of the three bases of contractual liability. In the same year the Queen's Bench held that an infant child who had been taken on a train by its mother, without payment of any fare (although half fare should have been paid), was entitled to sue the railway company for injuries incurred in an accident caused by their negligence.[91] The ground of the decision seems puzzling to modern lawyers for at least two of the judges clearly thought that the plaintiff was suing on his mother's contract, based on *her* fare. Only Blackburn J. adopted the modern view of treating the case as lying in tort.

A whole series of further cases against railway companies paved the way for a more general recognition of tort liabilities in negligence. These cases involved difficulties because of the arrangements between the railway companies which were extensively adopted in the 1850s and 1860s, whereby the companies obtained running powers over each others' lines. The result was that a plaintiff might buy a ticket from one company, and be injured at a station, or by the negligence of a servant, of another company. Attempts were made to overcome the difficulty of an apparent lack of contract, by implying agencies of various kinds, but constant trouble arose because plaintiffs were held to have sued the wrong railway company.[92] This was clearly an intolerable situation, and it was only finally ended by two decisions in 1880 holding firmly that tort liability existed against a negligent railway company, without any necessity of proving a contract.[93] But this victory of the infant tort law still showed its origins in a number of contractual type arguments. First, there was the point (specifically taken by Thesiger L.J. in the decisive case) [94] that the defendant railway company derived a benefit ('more or less directly or indirectly') from the carriage of the passenger, and therefore should 'come under some corresponding obligation towards him'. But then there is another, wider, idea which may be thought to lie behind these extensions of tort liability. It must be remembered that there had always been a vague idea that a person was not entitled to treat as a consideration that which he was obliged to do anyhow.[95] And there

[91] *Austin* v. *Great Western Rly. Co.* (1867) L.R. 2 Q.B. 442.

[92] *Scotthorn* v. *South Staffs. Rly. Co.* (1853) 8 Ex. 341; *Mytton* v. *Midland Rly.* (1859) 4 H. & N. 615; *Coxon* v. *Great Western Rly. Co.* (1860) 5 H. & N. 274; *Bristol & Exeter Rly. Co.* v. *Collins* (1859) 7 H.L.C. 194, 11 E.R. 78.

[93] *Foulkes* v. *Metropolitan District Rly. Co.* (1880) 5 C.P.D. 157 (personal injury); *Hooper* v. *Great Western Rly. Co.* (1880) 50 L.J.Q.B. 103 (property damage).

[94] In *Foulkes* v. *Metropolitan District Rly. Co.* (1880) 5 C.P.D. at 170-1.

[95] This idea was never a purely contractual one anyhow. It underlies, e.g., the old rule that a pilot obliged to offer his services is not entitled to reward for salvage, as he would be if he acted quite

is a sense in which, as the Courts began to extend tort liability, they did so because they came to think that due care was something which a person was generally obliged to show, anyhow.[96] A person could not complain that he was not being paid to exercise due care, because that was something he was bound to do in any case.

It is, therefore, not unreal to see liability in the tort of negligence as growing out of contractual ideas;[97] there was nothing inherently different between a contractual obligation, and the new tortious duty to show due care. In fact, most early tort cases in negligence, involved situations of a contractual or closely analogous character. The road accident between two strangers was not the paradigm of nineteenth-century tort law. And in both cases consent, benefit, and reliance were frequently the key concepts of liability. The later idea that tort liabilities are wholly different from contractual liabilities because the latter arise from consensual obligations is not soundly based, either in logic or in history. In both cases, the law was frequently concerned with the untoward consequences of human activity; in both cases that activity might itself have originally been largely intentional, and if more than one person was involved, consensual. In both cases the imposition of the legal liability at the end of the day was the work of the law.

voluntarily: *The General Palmer* (1828) 2 Hagg. Adm. 176, 166 E.R. 209. And in modern times, the same idea has surfaced again in cases concerning matrimonial property law, see *post*, p. 770.

[96] See, e.g. *Marshall* v. *York, Newcastle & Berwick Rly. Co.* (1851) 11 C.B. 655, 664, 138 E.R. 632, 636.

[97] Thus Addison, who published volumes on *Contracts* (1847) and *Wrongs* (1860), treated negligence in the former volume.

16

FREEDOM OF CONTRACT
IN PARLIAMENT, 1770–1870

THE PARLIAMENTARY BACKGROUND

IN this chapter I shall concentrate on the Statute Law of the century under review, but we need first to take a preliminary look at some of the influences operating on Parliament. It will be suggested that, in the earlier part of this period, from 1770 to perhaps 1830, Parliamentary policy was generally very similar to that of the judges, but that significant differences were evident as early as the beginning of the new century, and that these differences became more marked as time went on. By 1840 or 1850, a marked divergence existed between the attitude of Parliamentarians and the attitude of the judges to the principle of freedom of contract. By 1870, when the principle had, at any rate in some respects, reached its apogee in the Courts, it had already been in practice departed from by Parliament in a very wide variety of situations. Parliamentarians were, however, slow to recognize what they were doing, and lip service continued to be paid to the principle long after it had ceased to count for much in practice.

There is no doubt that in the century commencing in 1770 the principles of political economy, as taught by Adam Smith and his successors, were most influential in the development of Parliamentary policies.[1] The younger Pitt, it is well known, almost instantly accepted many of the ideas advocated in *The Wealth of Nations*, and allowed his policies to be significantly affected by them. On several occasions he paid tribute to Adam Smith in Parliament; it has been said that he made the political economy of Adam Smith the official doctrine of the Tory party,[2] though later, in the 1820s and 1830s, the new political economy came to be adopted more by the Whigs and Radicals. In 1795 Pitt withdrew his proposals for regulating wages and giving family allowances in deference to the teaching of the political economists, and in 1800, at a time of severe shortage of provisions in England, he refused for similar reasons to buy corn overseas, leaving this to the freedom of the market. In this, he may have been influenced by a memorandum prepared for him by Burke in 1795 which also drew heavily upon Adam Smith.[3] Among Pitt's

---

[1] See A. W. Coats (ed.), *The Classical Economists and Economic Policy* (London, 1971), pp. 23–32.

[2] R. J. White, *From Waterloo to Peterloo* (Harmondsworth, 1957), pp. 59–60.

[3] Bonar, 'Old Lights and New in Economic Study', in *Essays in Economic Method*, ed. Smyth (London, 1962).

undistinguished successors as leaders of the Tory party in the reactionary period which followed the French Revolution, Lord Sidmouth and Lord Liverpool were both great believers in leaving things alone. Lord Liverpool who presided over the Cabinet as Prime Minister for fifteen years, from 1812 to 1827, believed that Government interference in economic matters was nearly always disastrous, and he was generally unwilling to do anything which infringed 'the sacred principle of "freedom of contract"'.[4]

From 1817, when Ricardo's *Principles* were published, it seems that the influence of political economists, at any rate in the realm of theory, became stronger than ever. In 1817 Canning admitted in a Commons debate to a growing conviction in favour of the theory of 'non-interference in contracts between man and man'.[5] For a few years, perhaps a decade, many politicians deferred to Ricardo's ideals, and embraced freedom of contract as a practical legislative policy as well as in theory.[6] They were, during these years, exposed more than ever to the teachings of the political economists. In 1824 and 1825 J. R. McCulloch gave the Ricardo Memorial Lecture on political economy before a wide audience of politicians, cabinet ministers, and other public figures.[7] In 1826-7 a House of Commons Select Committee was so far convinced that all interference was harmful that it recommended total repeal of the Passenger Acts, and indeed succeeded in carrying this policy through.[8]

Similarly, around the same period, there was a growing revulsion against the remnants of the old statutory wage regulation and price fixing in many industries. In 1825 a Commons Committee looked into the statutory authority which magistrates had to fix rates for the land carriage of goods by common carriers, and came to the conclusion that 'the public on the one side, and the proprietors of public carriages on the other, were so much alive to their mutual interests, that legislative checks were no more necessary in their dealings than in transactions carried on by persons in any other business or trade'. The next year, the old statutes were repealed. And again, the repeal of the old Combination Acts in 1824 and their partial replacement in 1825, is a familiar story. The repeal in 1824 was largely due to the work of Francis Place who convinced Parliament partly by drawing on the political economists.

Among the next generation of politicians, especially after the return to power of the Whigs in 1830, there was, if anything, even greater sign of the influence of the orthodoxies of political economy. Brougham and

---

[4] R. J. White, *From Waterloo to Peterloo*, p. 98.
[5] Cited, B. Inglis, *Poverty and the Industrial Revolution* (London, 1962), p. 197.
[6] See Barry Gordon, *Political Economy in Parliament, 1819-1823* (London and Basingstoke, 1976).
[7] D. P. O'Brien, *J. R. McCulloch* (London, 1976), pp. 50-51.
[8] O. MacDonagh, *A Pattern of Government Growth: The Passenger Acts 1800-1860* (London, 1961), p. 66.

Althorp, both influential figures in Grey's ministry from 1830 to 1834, were also members of the Political Economy Club, and the former at least (as we have seen) was an associate of Ricardo and of many of the classical economists, having been also a founder member of their propaganda sheet, the *Edinburgh Review*. For many years, in and out of Parliament, Brougham expressed great respect for the principles of political economy and for the political economists themselves.[9] In particular, he was much influenced by the Malthusian theory of population, and was one of the moving forces behind the Poor Law Reform of 1834. Melbourne, who became Prime Minister in 1834, and remained in office with one brief interval for the next seven years, thought that the Benthamites were fools, but was convinced that 'the whole duty of government is to prevent crime and to preserve contract'.[10] The problem of poverty, he felt sure, could only be solved by reliance on the law of supply and demand. Trade unions, he thought, were 'inconsistent, impossible and contrary to the law of nature' because, of course, they attempted to fix wages at an artificially high level.[11] Among Melbourne's colleagues was Poulett Thomson, Lord Sydenham, who was President of the Board of Trade during Melbourne's premiership. He was another convert to political economy and the ideals of *laissez-faire*, and gathered round him a collection of like-minded disciples. 'For years they rigged select committees, managed witnesses, trimmed evidence, as they steered England steadily toward free trade.'[12] Throughout the whole of Melbourne's premiership one of the principal advisers of the Whig Government on economic affairs was Nassau Senior, himself one of the classical economists, and joint draftsman with Chadwick of the Poor Law Report of 1834.[13] Also in Melbourne's Government was Lord Palmerston, who served as Foreign Secretary for the whole period, 1834–41, and later went on to be Foreign Secretary again under Russell (1846–51), Home Secretary in Aberdeen's Government (1852–5), and Prime Minister with one short intermission from 1855 to 1865. Palmerston had been brought up from his earliest days on the orthodoxies of political economy. As a boy of sixteen, he had been sent to Edinburgh in 1800 to study under Dugald Stewart, one-time colleague of Adam Smith. From him, Palmerston imbibed ideas of Natural Law and political economy which he never forgot. In his maiden speech in the Commons, he invoked Natural Law as authority for the right of international self-defence, and he never lost an opportunity to preach free trade and freedom of contract in his diplomatic Notes.[14]

[9] See, e.g., *Hansard* (2nd. series), vol. 41, col. 1196 (1819).

[10] David Cecil, *Lord Melbourne* (London, 1954), p. 124. Yet according to Dicey, these two ideologies were one and the same!   [11] Ibid.

[12] C. H. Wilson, *Economic History and the Historian* (London, 1969), p. 152.

[13] See *supra*, p. 317 as to Nassau Senior, and *post*, p. 525 as to the Poor Law Report.

[14] J. Ridley, *Lord Palmerston* (London, 1972), pp. 32, 54, 90, 290–1, 645.

On the Conservative side of the Commons, Sir Robert Peel, Prime Minister from 1841 to 1846, finally went over to the cause of free trade with his decision to repeal the Corn Laws, even though the result was to split his party. But it is now generally agreed that the repeal of the Corn Laws had little to do with *laissez-faire*, though a great deal to do with the political and economic demands of the new industrialist classes.[15] Among Peel's colleagues was Gladstone who gradually moved England towards free trade in a series of budgets as Chancellor of the Exchequer, and went on to found, and to dominate, the Liberal party which emerged from the Parliamentary chaos of the mid-nineteenth century. And if there was one principle which seems today to have characterized nineteenth-century liberals, it was a belief in free enterprise, free trade, and *laissez-faire*. Another of Peel's colleagues was Sir James Graham who occupied the Home Office from 1841 to 1846 and who also 'gave a general approval of the theoretic laws of the political economists'.[16]

On the back benches, too, throughout the half-century from 1820 a small group of men who had devoted serious thought to political economy, exercised an influence out of all proportion to their numbers. '[F]rom Ricardo to Mill economists as back-benchers had an impact on legislation, by voting, by speeches, by sponsoring of legislation, and by activities on Committees, that is unmatched at any other time or in any other country.'[17]

Nevertheless, detailed examination of what the politicians were actually engaged in doing, rather than saying, during this period, has shown that general adherence to the principles of political economy was, time after time, thought to be compatible with policies of direct interference with the economy, or with the principle of freedom of contract. This became, as we shall see, more and more pronounced after 1830, but even in the first thirty years of the century there were many occasions on which the principles of political economy or of freedom of contract were openly confronted and defeated in Parliament. It is true that from 1770 on, Parliament was busy repealing many of the old regulatory Acts. The statutory marketing offences were abolished in 1772, the Poor Law was amended in 1795 to permit greater mobility of labour, the Statute of Apprentices went in 1809, and scores of Acts regulating particular trades or places were repealed or allowed to expire unextended. But almost at the same time, a new type of regulation was coming to be imposed. The first Factories Act, and the first Passenger

[15] It is symptomatic that repeal was combined with an offer of cheap Government loans to farmers to help in drainage projects—hardly signs of a *laissez-faire* policy. See J. D. Chambers and E. G. Mingay, *The Agricultural Revolution 1750-1880* (London, 1966), p. 176.

[16] J. T. Ward, *Sir James Graham* (London, Melbourne, Toronto, 1967), p. 309.

[17] Fetter, 'The Influence of Economists in Parliament on British Legislation from Ricardo to John Stuart Mill', 83 *Journal of Political Economy* 1051, 1060 (1975).

Act, both date from the first years of the new century. And in other respects too, Parliament frequently refused to be bludgeoned into a universal acceptance of political economy. In 1817, the year Ricardo's *Principles* were published, an attempt was made to abolish the privilege of Oxford and Cambridge of receiving free copies of every book published in the country; the Universities should pay for their books, was the message of political economy. But the attempt failed.[18] In the same year the Government actually secured the passage through Parliament of a Keynes-like measure to provide cheap Government loans to industry with a view to reducing the level of unemployment.[19] And, in practice, the actions of many a politician belied his own words on this matter of freedom of contract and free trade (the terms were often used indiscriminately at this time). Melbourne, whose views I have cited above, was in fact responsible for setting up the Factories Commission of Inquiry in 1833 (he gave them six weeks to produce a Report) and for insisting on the inclusion of the clauses limiting the hours of work of young persons between 14 and 18 years of age.[20] Gladstone, for all his views on free trade, took a strong line over the monopolistic railways, and was even persuaded that investors in railway company shares were entitled to protection against their own folly. Graham, though in principle a supporter of *laissez-faire*, never used it as an excuse for inaction when he felt an abuse needed remedying. It was he who first sought to legislate for the registration (and hence control) of medical practitioners in 1846, although in fact another twelve years passed before such legislation was carried.

And Graham's chief, Peel, was himself a pragmatic and cautious reformer, rather than a slavish adherent to political economy. His views on these questions are well illustrated by a curious incident which occurred in 1846. In the debate on the Ten Hours Bill of that year, Macaulay, from the Whig benches, attempted to raise the important question of principle. In a celebrated speech Macaulay argued that the principle of free trade, or freedom of contract, only extended to commercial matters. In other matters, such as concerned public health, or public morality, there was no principle against legislative interference with freedom of contract. He pointed out that any such principle was quite inconsistent with the then proposed public health legislation which would prohibit any one from letting insanitary dwellings or building houses without adequate drains.[21] But although this speech became famous as a statement of the case for interference with freedom of

---

[18] *Hansard* (2nd. series), vol. 36, col. 1063–70 (1817).
[19] 57 Geo. 3, c. 34.
[20] S. E. Finer, *The Life and Times of Sir Edwin Chadwick* (London, 1952), pp. 63, 71.
[21] *Hansard* (3rd series), vol. 86, col. 1027 (1846).

contract,[22] Macaulay seems to have misjudged the temper of the House. Far from being in the van of the reformers, he seems, on this occasion, to have been behind the general opinion. The honourable member who immediately followed Macaulay in the debate, though unknown to history, deserves to be remembered for his remarks. The whole system of social policy in this country, he said, was founded upon interference. What was a Legislature for if it was not to protect the weak against the strong? It was an abrogation of the functions of legislation to decide they should not interfere. Everything was interfered with in fact. But Macaulay's speech also stung the Prime Minister, Sir Robert Peel, into a last-minute intervention. What, he asked, was Macaulay trying to prove? That the principles of free trade ought not to control our legislation provided that we can promote the health or morality of our community by doing so? But if that were all that Macaulay were saying, his remarks were only addressed to about ten members of the House, for there were no more who believed that the pure principles of non-interference should govern all legislation.[23]

It is true, that, from time to time, especially perhaps in the early 1820s, Parliament did seem to be almost completely under the influence of Ricardo's principles. Undoubtedly, there were occasions on which a majority of the members of a Select Committee (usually hand-picked) were wholly in favour of the principle of non-interference, and sometimes the House could be persuaded by such a Committee into hasty action. This may explain the recommendation of the Committee on the Passenger Acts in 1826-7. But it is important not to overlook the sequel to such events as these. The Passenger Acts had no sooner been repealed in response to this Committee's recommendations, than the results became so much worse that the Government was moved to action. In 1828 new legislation was pressed through the House by the Government, and the free trader Huskisson insisted that it was the duty of the State to stop the enormities which had been revealed 'even in the teeth of science and philosophy [i.e., political economy]'.[24]

And there were other occasions when Select Committees' Reports were simply not implemented, or were greatly watered down. The Committee on the Usury Laws in 1818, for instance, addressed by Ricardo and the future Lord St. Leonards, dutifully recommended complete repeal. But complete repeal did not come until 1854.

There were also many occasions when debates seemed to be not so much about the principle of non-interference, or about any principles at all, but about the self-interest of a number of particular groups, whether

---

[22] See Alan Bullock and M. Shock (eds.) *The Liberal Tradition* (Oxford, 1956), pp. 55 *et seq.*
[23] *Hansard* (3rd series), vol. 86, col. 1062 (1846).
[24] O. MacDonagh, *A Pattern of Government Growth*, p. 69.

employers or employees, in a particular trade. A striking illustration of this took place in 1823 with the presentation to Parliament of a petition by the Spitalfields Silk Manufacturers. They asked Parliament to repeal a number of Acts regulating the manufacture and sale of silk, but only applying to the Spitalfields manufacturers. They protested that the rest of the country was not subject to this legislation, and that they were greatly disadvantaged in competing with rival industries as a result. The price of labour, they complained, had been fixed so high by the justices under these Acts, that they could not compete, and all the work went elsewhere. Ricardo expressed astonishment that the Acts were still on the statute book, and Huskisson, President of the Board of Trade, promised a Bill to repeal them.[25] A confusing scene then took place in the Commons when someone remembered that the House had made a standing order not to proceed on a Bill imposing restrictions on trade without first sending it to a Committee for Report. Did this Order apply to Bills proposing to lift restrictions? Nobody knew because nobody remembered the Standing Order.[26] It is symptomatic of the influence of the political economists both that such an order was made, and that it was apparently never acted upon. The next thing that happened was that the Spitalfields' workers petitioned *against* the proposed repeal, and members were not wanting in the House of Commons to support this rival petition. One member complained that the existing Acts might be a deviation from general principles but where it suited particular interests, the House frequently deviated from such principles. When the repeal Bill was duly presented, a lively debate ensued.[27] Another member, supporting the interests of the workers employed by the Spitalfields' manufacturers, argued that 'it was rather hard to say to these poor people, that they should lose their bread by principles of political economy'. He went on to point out that the original legislation had presumably been framed on what were then considered sound principles; that Adam Smith had overturned the previous principles of political economy, and in turn had had his principles overturned by Ricardo. Ultimately, the repeal Bill was carried, but only by 68 votes to 60.

The Equitable Adjustment of Contracts

During the years 1819–23 there occurred a series of debates in Parliament which illustrate a movement parallel to the rise of formalism and the decline of Equity in the law of contract applied by the Courts. In 1819 the Government had adopted the policy known as 'resuming cash payments', or as it came to be known in later years, of returning to the

[25] *Hansard* (3rd series), vol. 9, cols. 143–50 (1823).
[26] Ibid., cols. 377–87.
[27] Ibid., col. 811.

gold standard. Since 1793 the Bank of England had been relieved of its legal obligation to honour its banknotes by tendering gold coin to those who demanded it, and in the war years inflation had resulted in these banknotes falling well below their nominal value in terms of gold. The resumption of cash payments (which was in effect a revaluation of the currency) was followed, partly for these reasons, but partly for other reasons, by a severe fall in agricultural prices which by 1821 was a cause of much concern. The increase in the national debt during the war (which by this time was one of the main burdens on taxation) meant that the cost of paying interest to the Government fundholders now fell with redoubled effect on the landed interest. Landowners (and therefore farmers and even labourers) found their share of the national income greatly reduced while the fundholders found their interest payments correspondingly enhanced in value. A similar redistribution of income had taken place between private debtors and creditors. Landowners burdened with mortgages found that the income from the land was, in some cases, inadequate even to pay the interest charges. Just as in modern times, inflation robs creditors at the expense of debtors, so during this period, deflation had redistributed much of the national income from debtors to creditors.

In 1821 demands began to be made for some 'equitable adjustment of contracts' to remedy this state of affairs.[28] Although some openly advocated a devaluation of the currency, this was not generally what was being sought. What was demanded was nothing less than a reduction of interest rates payable to the fundholders without their consent, something which had not been contemplated for over a hundred years. There were also some suggestions for some sort of judicial—or equitable—tribunal to look into private contracts and make similar adjustments to interest rates here too. Naturally enough, these proposals were denounced as a 'breach of the public faith' by the Government, as well as by Ricardo and many others.[29] But not everyone was so sure that adhering to the strict letter of the fundholders' contracts was a requirement of the public faith in the changed circumstances which had occurred. Even Earl Grey, the most honourable of Whig aristocrats, felt that perhaps the nation had contracted to do the impossible, and could plead the maxim, *Nemo tenetur ad impossibile.*[30] Lord Erskine, former Whig Lord Chancellor, agreed that the fundholders' contracts were sacred, but somewhat disingenuously argued that they should be taxed more heavily so as to relieve the burden on the landed interest.[31] Lord Stanhope, in 1823, protested that the public faith 'did not and could not pledge the nation to pay the public

[28] See Barry Gordon, *Political Economy in Parliament.*
[29] *Hansard* (3rd series), vol. 4, cols. 833-4 (1821).　　　　[30] Ibid., cols. 835-6.
[31] *A Letter to the Proprietors and Occupiers of Land* (London, 1823), p. 40.

creditors twice as much as they ought to receive'. He went on to suggest that if the question was argued in the Chancery as a point of conscience, the Chancellor would be bound to decide 'upon the principles of equity, that if you increase, by a legislative measure the value of the currency, you ought in the same proportion to diminish the amount of the payment, whether public or private'.[32] Lord Stanhope was no lawyer, however, and it is unlikely that in 1823 the Court of Chancery would have behaved in this fashion, which was, no doubt, why Parliamentary action was demanded. Nevertheless, it was (as I pointed out in connection with the South Sea affair) part of the established Chancery doctrine that a mortgagor-debtor could always pay off a mortgagee-creditor, notwithstanding any agreement to the contrary, and this doctrine naturally could be invoked when interest rates fell. In effect Lord Stanhope was pleading that the nation should revert to this equitable doctrine, and turn its back on the principle which it had adopted at the time of the South Sea affair, and adhered to ever since, the principle that a debtor could not pay off his creditor contrary to the terms of their agreement merely because interest rates had fallen, or the currency had risen.

The debate continued on and off for some years, but each time the subject was raised in Parliament, the proponents of 'equitable adjustment' faced a more difficult task than on the previous occasion. Inevitably, as time went on, new contracts were being made on the basis of the new value of the currency, and there was plainly little justification for adjusting these contracts at least. Indeed, in an important debate in 1823, Peel, for the Government, insisted that it had all along been intended and declared that cash payments would be resumed after the war, so that contracting parties would have made their arrangements on that footing ever since the suspension of cash payments.[33] This was, in effect, the sort of argument about fair contracting which had been gathering force in eighteenth-century Equity and which the political economists had been propagating. Changed circumstances, on this view, did not render contracts unfair because the parties must be assumed, as rational men, to have made their bargain with a view to the possibility of such changes. Peel went on to point out that equitable adjustment could not be confined to debtors who had not settled their obligations but would in fairness have to extend to those who had discharged their debts at any time since 1793.[34] Were all contracts entered into since then to be subject to 'equitable adjustment'? As Huskisson said, that would necessitate 'more Courts of Chancery . . . than public houses'.[35]

[32] *Hansard* (3rd series), vol. 8, cols. 18–19 (1823).
[33] Ibid., cols. 262–3.
[34] Ibid., cols. 932–3.
[35] Ibid., col. 943.

This debate largely killed off the campaign for equitable adjustment, and with the stabilization of prices, and increasing prosperity, no more was heard about it for many years. It came to be accepted on all hands that fluctuations in the value of goods or the currency were matters which contracting parties could allow for in making their contracts. As with all other risks, contract prices could, and in theory would, be adjusted to reflect the risks. Those who calculated badly would, naturally, lose; those who calculated well would prosper. Much later in the century, the economist Alfred Marshall began to throw doubts on these assumptions and argued for some form of indexation for long-term contracts,[36] but nothing ever came of it. The debate continues today.

The Failure of Private Law Enforcement

In general, as we shall see later, the process of statutory interference with freedom of contract was determined by pragmatic considerations which varied from case to case. But one general characteristic which is to be found in much of this legislative interference, was that it resulted from the failure of the atomistic view of society to work properly. And one reason why it failed to work properly was the failure of the law enforcement processes of private law, and especially, of contract law. If it had been as easy in practice, as it seemed in theory, for individual rights to be vindicated whenever they were infringed; if the system of rewards and penalties had worked with even a modicum of efficiency; if the frauds and dishonesties could have been dealt with as easily as economic theory seemed to suggest, it is possible that a free market economy could have flourished in fact, as it did in theory. But in practice, enforcement was the Achilles' heel of private law. Leaving individuals to sue in order to enforce their private rights, simply did not work in a large number of cases. The problem of protection for the consumer was then, as it is today, difficult to regulate through private litigation. And much that occurred in the period 1800–70 was in the nature of an experiment to discover how laws could be made enforceable, once it was appreciated that they were not generally self-enforcing.

The very enforcement of the criminal law, the whole foundation of law and order, the protection of the lives and property of the people, was, it will be remembered, still a matter of private initiative in 1770, and even in 1820. The eighteenth-century processes had assumed that laws would be enforced as a result of the self-interest of the persons protected by them, and to some extent this had, indeed, occurred, as property owners set up associations for the prosecution of felons. And the system of rewards—'blood money' as it was called—for information leading to arrest and conviction of offenders relied extensively on private contract

[36] See *post*, p. 624.

for the enforcement of the law. As late as 1815 the Government paid out £80,000 in 'blood money'.[37] Unfortunately, the system worked badly in practice. Conditions in London at the beginning of the nineteenth century almost defy description.[38] Every corrupting influence, every kind of crime, flourished as if unchecked. Large numbers of urchin children lived by their wits in the streets, selling their pickings to one of London's 8,000 receivers. Violence and murder were commonplace. Forged notes and coins deluged the country. Drivers of hackney cabs conspired with thieves to steal baggage from their roofs. Robberies from banks were often followed by offers to pay a reward if the property was restored, with no questions asked. A Committee of the House of Commons found in 1828 that 16 banks had been blackmailed into paying £200,000 'protection money' in a short time. The system of private contract led to a number of professional informers who were only interested in obtaining rewards, whether by fair means or foul. Trumped-up cases and perjured evidence for this purpose were commonplace. Nobody attempted to *prevent* crime before it occurred. Even the famous Bow Street runners were paid fees for criminals caught, and not for crimes prevented.

The maintenance of order in public places, the prevention of riots, even the detection of treason or sedition, was also very imperfectly managed in the first half of the nineteenth century. Not until the middle of the century could it be said that the whole country was effectively under the control of the civil force. Not until the defeat of the Chartists in 1848, or perhaps indeed, for some years after that, did people feel that they were generally secure from violent riots or even revolution. And though controversy still exists over whether there were any serious revolutionary activities in the first two decades of the century,[39] there is no doubt that many people, and not only Eldon, were convinced that sedition and blasphemy were serious threats to the safety of the State. This failure to maintain order, or to keep adequately under supervision any revolutionary elements in the country, was largely due to the absence of an adequate police force. Another way of looking at the problem would be to say that the Government relied too much on private contract, and too little on its own employed staff, for the maintenance of law and order. Even the spy known as 'Oliver' who fomented the Pentrich rising of 1817 was casually employed on a payment-by-result basis.[40] This reliance on private contract had simply not worked. The free market, as it then existed, failed to deliver the goods.

The creation of the Metropolitan Police Force in 1829 by Sir Robert

---

[37] W. L. Melville Lee, *History of Police in England* (London, 1901), p. 212.
[38] Ibid., pp. 197–201.
[39] E. P. Thompson, *The Making of the English Working Class*, argues that there were, pp. 650 *et seq.*
[40] R. J. White, *From Waterloo to Peterloo*, p. 173.

Peel was one of the earliest examples of the use by Government of methods of direct administration and control for the purposes of enforcing the law. The new police were employed by the Crown and paid salaries so that they were expected to be impartial and independent in carrying out their duties. Their primary task was to prevent crime, rather than to catch criminals, or to prosecute for crime, but at least in performing these latter duties they would not be subject to the temptations of perjury for reasons of self-interest—or so it was hoped. And there is no doubt that the new police force was a great success from the start. Even so, it was a long while before the whole country had a proper police force. In the boroughs outside London little was done before 1839, and many country areas remained without proper police until they were compelled to create a force by an Act of 1856.

But law and order was only the beginning. There were other laws to enforce too. In the eighteenth century the enforcement of *all* laws was thought of as primarily a private matter; in the nineteenth century this idea gradually gave way, first in the matter of crime, and then in many other areas. But here the solutions were different and, in a sense, the problems were different too. As Parliament began to legislate for the protection of workers and consumers in factories, mines, passenger ships, for the improvement of public health and education, and in a hundred other areas, it became gradually clear that here, too, self-enforcement generally did not work. Many years later it came to be widely thought that much of the early legislation was merely window-dressing, not designed to have real teeth, because no proper enforcement machinery was provided. But it is plain that the very idea that laws had to be enforced and that some administrative machinery had to be created for that purpose, was a lesson only slowly and painfully learnt.

Similarly, when the Passenger Acts were being reviewed in 1833, the Agent-General for Immigration wrote to his superiors in London to explain that it was quite out of the question to think that the emigrants could remain where they disembarked in Canada 'to abide the issue of a lawsuit for non-fulfilment of a contract on the part of the captain'. The process of the law, he explained, was 'so exceedingly expensive and tedious that it is better to submit to any loss than to have anything to do with it'.[41] Evidently, matters were not very different in Canada from what they were in England.

Paradoxically, there were also cases in which the enforcement procedures had been too effective. The most notable of these was, of course, the law providing for imprisonment for debt. At the end of the eighteenth century, this was still being defended even by moralists like Paley.[42] Certainly the judges still regarded it as an essential means of

[41] O. MacDonagh, *A Pattern of Government Growth*, p. 82.
[42] *Principles of Moral and Political Philosophy*, Book III, Chapter VIII.

law-enforcement. Lord Kenyon, for instance, is recorded as having told Parliament in 1797 that 'the law of arrest as it at present prevailed, had conduced in an essential degree to the increase of commerce and the extent of trade'.[43] But despite the harshness of this method of self-help in the enforcement of debts, there is also evidence that irregularity in the payment of debts was still a very widespread and troublesome problem in the early nineteenth century. To some extent the harshness of the laws may have been counter-productive because, though imprisonment for debt was often imposed on small and ignorant debtors, the more clever and unscrupulous escaped all the ferocity of the law.[44] The trouble with the remedy of imprisonment was that the law depended on it too heavily, and where it was evaded or defied, a wealthy debtor might simply avoid payment of debts for years. There was, too, still a somewhat cavalier social attitude to minor debts, especially tradesman's debts, up to the beginning of the Victorian era, which may have been partly the result of the lack of credibility of the threat of imprisonment. This attitude is illustrated by the career of Lord Palmerston who was sued no fewer than twenty times in thirty years for minor tradesmen's debts.[45] Similarly, the irregularity in the public's debt-paying habits, and the difficulties in the way of enforcing payment by legal process, is shown by the fact that so many of the Commissioners, Boards, and early rating authorities of this period were given power to distrain.

Something was, of course, done to improve things with the reform of the 1830s. Land of judgment debtors was made liable to process for the payment of debts in 1833. Imprisonment before judgment was abolished except in rare cases by the Civil Procedure Act 1838.[46] Interest also was made payable on judgment debts by the same Act. Other relevant reforms came with the Common Law Procedure Acts which for the first time provided for the speedy enforcement of claims for liquidated sums, such as simple debts, or money due on a bill of exchange, on which there was frequently no possible defence. These procedural reforms were an indispensable result of the abolition of imprisonment for debt on *mesne* process. The enforcement of ordinary debts became a relatively simple and cheap matter; this was virtually the only instance of judicial procedure becoming simple and prompt, and it was, in a sense, achieved

---

[43] *Parliamentary History* (1797), xxxiii. 181.

[44] Even the reformer Romilly complained that not 5 out of 5,000 debtors who deserved prosecution were prosecuted between 1732 and 1818: Ian P. H. Duffy, 'Bankruptcy and Insolvency in London in the Late Eighteenth and Early Nineteenth Centuries', unpublished D. Phil. thesis, Oxford, 1973, p. 39.

[45] J. Ridley, *Lord Palmerston*, p. 94. Three of these actions were brought in 1840–1 when Palmerston was Foreign Secretary and one of the best known men in England.

[46] 1 & 2 Vict., c. 110. This Act also contained a remarkable piece of paternalism in sects. 9 and 10 which prohibited the use of a warrant of attorney to confess judgment unless it was witnessed by an attorney who declared that he had informed the debtor of the nature and effect of the instrument.

by providing for a semi-administrative process under the general supervision of the Court. By 1857, indeed, complaints were being made that the new County Court judges were using their powers to enforce payment of debts in a 'summary and vindictive' manner and that 'well meaning and honest customers' were becoming reluctant to buy on credit unless they had the immediate power of payment.[47] Thus the discipline of contract was working.

Nevertheless, it is clear that the commercial community remained very largely dissatisfied with the enforcement processes of the Courts (much more so than with the substantive law) and complaints in Parliament were very common.[48] Above all, the laws relating to bankruptcy and insolvency were the subjects of repeated complaints, particularly in the first thirty or forty years of the nineteenth century. And it is, perhaps, worth drawing attention to the point that one of the principal grounds of complaint was that, when a debtor defaulted, some of his creditors seemed to secure full payment while others received nothing. Even in this competitive age, men did not take kindly to the idea that the energetic and skilful creditor who stepped in first, should be entitled to such an advantage over more dilatory or less grasping creditors. Nor did men take kindly to the idea that one creditor should, by obstinacy, or through the hope of stealing a march on the other creditors, be entitled to hold up a reasonable settlement of the debtor's affairs. The Bankruptcy Act of 1844 first introduced the principle of majority decision-making among the creditors of an insolvent debtor, although the proposals were extremely cautious, and only permitted the coercion of a minority of creditors under safeguards of great stringency. Under this Act it was provided that a composition proposal could be drawn up by creditors representing a third in value and in number of all the creditors. The proposals were then to be put before all the creditors, not once, but *twice*. If the statutory majorities could be obtained at both meetings, the composition could be approved by the Court; and on such approval it would be binding on every creditor. What strikes one today is the very great care taken to ensure that a creditor's rights were not unreasonably overridden by a majority; but at the time what was, perhaps, more significant, was the principle itself. Majority rule was, in the long run, to prevail. A contractual right might be cut down against the wishes of the creditor, by a majority of other creditors. The rights of the individual were subjected to those of the majority. Individualism gave way to collectivism.

But we must return to the general problem concerning the enforcement of the law. These difficulties in the enforcement process ran through the

---

[47] W. L. Burn, *The Age of Equipoise*, p. 139.

[48] See, for one of many debates on these issues, *Hansard* (3rd series), vol. 149, cols. 1142–61 (1858).

length and breadth of the legal system, and it seems no exaggeration to suggest that this was the point at which the theoretical models of the philosophical radicals tended to break down in practice.[49] The difficulties affected tort law as much as contract law. For example, had the law of public and private nuisance been a more efficient instrument in practice, it might have been extensively used as a method of public health control. It is by no means apparent that the judges would have been unsympathetic to such attempts.[50]

It would thus be over-simple to suggest the common law failed to meet the needs of the time because the judges were too wedded to freedom of contract, or were heedless of the problem of externalities. This was doubtless sometimes the case, but it was the slowness, the cumbersomeness, of common law procedures, and the lack of sufficient judges and Courts, which largely prevented the common law being used as a routine administrative machine. The sheer force of numbers was one of the most crucial elements of all. In 1833 there were still only fifteen common law judges in England; there were then 15,500 parishes, 5,000 justices, and innumerable local commissioners attempting to administer the country. The judges could offer little more than the barest oversight of this vast mass of petty authorities.[51]

The problem of enforcement of the new protective legislation exercised many people during the 1830s and 1840s. Bentham and Chadwick, each in their different ways, both played a major role in the solution of the problem. Bentham had for years advocated the principle of central administration with inspection of local administration. That method was first tried out with the new Poor Law in 1834 and was afterwards adopted in many other spheres, including the factories, mines, schools, and prisons. But even inspection and supervision was scarcely enough to control the local administrators at first. They had been so used to their independence, so free from control, both in law and in practice, and they were generally served by such incompetent and corrupt officers, that it was not possible to assume that they would generally observe the law, even when they were advised or admonished to do so from Whitehall. In modern times, defiance by a local authority of the law, or of legal directions issued from the central Government, is so rare as to make the headlines when it occurs. But in the early years of the nineteenth century, this tradition of due observance of the law simply did not exist in the old local authorities.

[49] As late as 1851 it was possible for a reputable businessman like Brunel to take the law into his own hands (ejecting a railway contractor with the aid of a private army) in a way unthinkable in modern times: Terry Coleman, *The Railway Navvies* (Harmondsworth, 1968), pp. 110-14.

[50] For decisions showing judicial sympathy with public health legislation, see *R.* v. *Pedley* (1834) 1 Ad. & E. 822, 100 E.R. 1422; *Soady* v. *Wilson* (1835) 3 Ad. & E. 248, 111 E.R. 407; and *Darling* v. *Epsom Local Board of Health* (1855) 5 E. & B. 47, 119 E.R. 556.

[51] David Roberts, *Victorian Origins of the British Welfare State*, p. 17.

Chadwick had studied this problem from the first time that he became involved with proposals for new administrative machinery as a member of the Poor Law Commission. His initial reaction was to make the draconian proposal that the new Poor Law Board should have the powers of a Court of Record, including the power to commit for contempt.[52] Chadwick evidently used the only available analogy in trying to solve the problem of compelling observance of the law, thinking in terms of the King's Bench powers to issue prerogative writs, and to enforce compliance with them by the threat of contempt proceedings. But this proposal was too much for the politicians and it was quietly dropped when the Bill was in Committee.[53] Chadwick may have regretted this, because he later had many years of frustration trying to persuade local officials to observe the law, and the legal directions of the central government, both in relation to the Poor Law, and later, public health. The problem reached its climax in the cholera epidemics of 1848–9, when local Boards of Guardians repeatedly defied the legal and imperative directions emanating from the General Board of Health, while people were dying all around them. The Nuisance Removal Act of 1848 was, as its title shows, still very much influenced by common law concepts. It had given the General Board of Health power to make regulations for the removal of nuisances, and dangers to health, but had left enforcement entirely to the ordinary legal processes.[54] But time and tide waits for no man, and cholera did not wait for the Court of King's Bench. At the height of the epidemic, when there were 5,000 deaths a month, an amending Act was rushed through Parliament giving the General Board power to do itself what was necessary, and to prosecute for wilful neglect of its orders.[55] Nothing had more clearly demonstrated that the enforcement of the law could not be left to the ordinary processes of the common law and the procedures of the superior Courts. As the lessons went home, the enforcement of the law came more and more to be a matter for administrators rather than for the superior Courts.

What in fact largely happened—though the process was slow and long drawn out—was that both central Government and local authorities came to rely increasingly on their own staff, the new bureaucrats, men of efficiency and integrity, instead of contracting out work to be paid for by fees. Chadwick himself was convinced that this was the key to the new administrative methods that were needed.[56] All this, of course, presaged the growth of the bureaucracy, and this was much resented and constantly criticized by those who wanted to keep the cost of Government down, as well as by those who saw in it a threat to their traditional

[52] S. E. Finer, *The Life and Times of Sir Edwin Chadwick*, p. 80.
[53] Ibid., p. 90. [54] Ibid., pp. 324–5, 366–7.
[55] Ibid., pp. 348–9. [56] Ibid., pp. 384–5.

liberties. Their protests may have slowed the process down, but they did not prevent it. In every sphere of activity—factories, mines, public health, education, prisons, poor law—inch by inch, year by year, the law came to be more steadily and generally enforced. First defiance, and then, more subtle and more difficult to cope with, evasion and prevarication, held things up. But the steamroller ground remorselessly on.

The part played by the Courts in this process faded into the background. The superior Courts were rarely called upon to interfere, or to order compliance with the law. What was left was a general oversight, a power of review, and in a limited sense, a power of control through appeal. This was a task for which they were much better suited, because it meant that they could be reserved for special cases of unusual importance or difficulty. The routine enforcement of the law was not a job for which the common law Courts had ever been suited, and in the new administrative fields, it left their hands never to return.

The day to day judicial enforcement of the new laws was largely placed in the hands of the local justices. This left a great deal to be desired. The justices were often incompetent, and frequently biased in dealing with legislation designed for the control of mill owners, or the protection of workmen. And some very peculiar things (by modern standards) sometimes happened as justices began to learn how to handle the new laws.[57] The partiality of the justices to mill owners was a common source of trouble in the enforcement of the factories legislation. The Home Office and the Law Officers were well aware of it, but there was little they could do about it in practice. The independence of the judiciary, even the magistracy, had to be respected, and it was the middle classes who had demanded the inclusion of commercial men on the local Bench. In the last resort cases could be taken to the King's Bench, but that was a desperate expedient, to be resorted to as rarely as possible. Some people thought the judges were apt to be biased too, inclined to interpret the new legislation so as to protect rights of property and traditional freedoms wherever possible, and with little insight into the problems of the new administrators. Even the Attorney-General in 1847 told Ashley, before a crucial decision on the effect of the Ten Hours Act, that the judges would give judgment, 'not according to law, but on policy'.[58] According to Ashley, the Attorney went on to attribute to Parke B. the remark that the Act would be interpreted contrary to the intention of the framers, because it was a law to restrain the exercise of capital and property, and therefore had to be construed strictly.[59] It may

[57] See, e.g., M. W. Thomas, *The Early Factory Legislation* (Westport, Conn., 1970), p. 244.
[58] Ibid., p. 311.
[59] Ibid., pp. 422–5. This was the decision in *Ryder v. Mills* in the Court of Exchequer, (1850) 3 Ex. 853, 154 E.R. 1090.

be that there was some substance in this criticism.[60] And if there was, it is not unintelligible. Since almost everyone, in and out of Parliament, paid lip service at least to the general principles of the political economists, it is not surprising if the judges also reacted in this way. Confronted with one of the new statutory provisions which flew in the face of those principles, the judges may well have seen the Acts as exceptional derogations from principles accepted by the whole country and therefore naturally to be construed narrowly.

THE LAW OF EMPLOYMENT

It is plain that I cannot survey the whole law of employment in this work, and that I am concerned with the much narrower question involving the extent of statutory intervention with freedom of contract in this period. I must begin with the process by which freedom of contract came to apply to contracts of employment in the first place, and we shall then observe the curious fact that this process was never wholly completed at all. As the new political economy began to call for a free market in labour, as the changes in social conditions led to a decline in the old paternalism involved in the master and servant relationship, so new statutory protections were forthcoming. There was no gap but an overlap between the completion of the one process and the commencement of the other. Here, as elsewhere, the dismantling of the old law and the creation of the new went on side by side.

I have already said something about the changes in the social nature of the master-servant relationship, and about how these changes led to changes in the common law. The disappearance of the master's liability to provide medical attention, and to pay wages to a servant who was sick, were examples of these changes. The impersonality of the new employment relationship, the 'cash-nexus' which was the sole connecting factor between industrial employers and factory hands, was commented on and lamented by many writers in the early nineteenth century, such as Cobbett, Carlyle, and Walter Scott.[61] These changes, of course, took place under the influence of circumstances, especially the great growth in the factory system, and not merely as a result of changes in ideas. But the change in ideas also led to demands for a free market in labour. In the eighteenth century (as we have seen) the market remained very much a controlled market, although the use of the controls was steadily waning throughout that century, and they themselves were becoming obsolete. But in 1770 the Statute of Apprentices was still in force at least in theory,

[60] But allowance must also be made for the inefficiency of the legislative process, and the incompetence of the draftsman, *supra*, p. 92.

[61] See, e.g., R. Williams, *Culture and Society, 1780–1950*, p. 33; Dicey, *Law and Public Opinion*, 2nd edn. (London, 1914), p. 120.

and so was the Act of Settlement of 1662, and a variety of other regulatory Acts. The former was finally repealed in 1809. The Act of Settlement which was bitterly attacked by Adam Smith in *The Wealth of Nations*, both as an infringement of civil liberties, and as a serious hindrance to the mobility of labour, was greatly modified in 1795. Under the amending Act of that year [62] a labourer was only liable to be removed to his parish of settlement if he actually became chargeable to the parish, and not if he merely was a potential charge. Other restrictive statutes (such as those prohibiting the emigration of skilled artisans) were repealed in 1824. The improvement in communications and roads in the latter part of the eighteenth century had also greatly assisted mobility of labour, so that regional variations in wages had tended to become ironed out as the century went on. Even so, mobility must have been greatly hindered by sheer ignorance. In his lectures on *The Industrial Revolution* Toynbee said that in 1872 there were labourers in Devon who had never heard of Lancashire where they might have earned double their own wages. [63]

The Poor Law

By far the greatest obstacle to the freedom of the labour market was the Speenhamland system of administering the Poor Law, which was adopted in 1795, the same year in which the amendment of the Act of Settlement had removed the principal statutory obstacle to a free labour market. The Speenhamland system was the name given to the administrative practice, first sanctioned by the Berkshire Justices meeting at Speenhamland, of giving poor aid relief to labourers *in employment* in the form of family allowances. The amount paid varied somewhat from place to place, but it was, in principle, fixed by the number of dependents which the labourer had. The practice had been adopted as a result of the hardship and deprivation which the labouring classes suffered in the 1790s through the high price of provisions, as 'a last inefficient, ill-considered and unsuccessful attempt to maintain traditional rural order in the face of the market economy'. [64] The practice had spread throughout the country, and it survived the Napoleonic Wars. By then the amounts paid out in poor rates had soared and were a major source of anxiety. But it was not principally on account of the size of the poor rate (which had anyhow declined somewhat by 1834) that the economists demanded reform of the Poor Law. What they objected to most was the elimination (as they believed) of all incentive. The amount of the Poor Law allowances given always depended on the actual earnings of the labourer, with the result, it was claimed, that labourers had no incentive to work

---

[62] 35 Geo. 3, c. 101.   [63] Reprinted (Boston, 1956), p. 43.

[64] E. J. Hobsbawm, *Industry and Empire* (Harmondsworth, 1974), p. 105.

well, to save, or to restrain themselves from early marriage or large families. However the labourer chose to live, he would receive the same total income at the end of the week. The result was not merely to remove all incentive from the labourers, but also to encourage the employers, the farmers, to pay less than a fair wage. Since the farmers knew that the labourers would have their wages made up by the Poor Law allowance, they did not compete for labour among themselves, and wages fell below their proper rate. In the result a significant part of the total costs of agriculture were being borne by the poor rates and not by the farmers. In economic terms this obviously led to a serious misallocation of resources.

And if that was only the overall position, there were many details which made things worse still. For example, many parishes adopted the 'labour-rate' principle under an enabling Act which permitted those liable to the poor rate to discharge some of their liabilities by employing persons on the parish. The farmers, therefore, took to employing men who received poor relief, in preference to those who were independent or who had no dependents, because by doing so they paid off part of their own liability to rates. Inevitably, this created a vicious circle in which the most able and efficient workers were left unemployed, while the least able or efficient were employed. So too workers had no incentive to save, for those with savings were denied poor relief until their savings were spent; and since they were denied poor relief they were often also denied employment. Then the Poor Law interfered with the market in land as well as with the labour market. The poor rate was a significant charge on land, often equalling or even exceeding the rent for agricultural land. Those in receipt of poor relief were themselves exempt from the poor rate, and their rent was paid by the parish; the result was that the rent payable by a farmer might depend on the proportion of his labour force which was on poor relief, and this in turn affected the value of the land itself.

But the major fear was probably that of over-population. By the 1830s three successive censuses had shown the huge rate of population increase; and although the increasing wealth created by the Industrial Revolution and the abundance of capital for investment, was visible on all sides, there was no sign of any increase in the prosperity of the labouring poor. The only explanation of this puzzle, it seemed, was in the tendency of the poor to marry too early and to breed too fast. And the explanation of that, in turn, was the Speenhamland system which sought to repeal the fundamental laws of nature by which a man was liable to maintain his own dependents.

The Poor Law Report was largely written by Nassau Senior and Edwin Chadwick. Although subsequent historians have often suggested that the evidence contained in the Report was selected to justify the conclusions that the Government wanted it to arrive at, few now quarrel with the general nature of the Commission's diagnosis.[65] The Speenhamland system had led to disastrous results; the paternalism of the country justices, seeking to protect their labourers from high prices, had made things worse. There was a serious misallocation of resources in allowing a large part of agricultural costs to be borne by ratepayers instead of farmers; and the lack of incentive had bitten deep into the ways of life of the labourers. All this was true enough, and the Commissioners sought the remedy in establishing the principle of freedom of contract between master and men. 'We deplore the misconception of the labourers', said the Report, 'in thinking that wages are not a matter of contract, but of right; that any diminution of their comforts occasioned by an increase in their numbers without an equal increase of the fund for their subsistence, is an evil to be remedied, not by themselves but by the magistrates; not an error, or even a misfortune, but an injustice.'[66] The remedy was obviously to restore the contractual tie, to remove the element of poor relief from the labourer's wages, and the wage element from the poor relief. What a man received by way of wage was a contractual right, something which was his due, and which bore some proper relationship to the value of his services, the extent of his skill and exertions. Poor relief, paid out of taxes, was essentially different. It was not a matter of justice at all, but of charity. It bore no relation to what a man earned, or what his services were worth.

But if the diagnosis was accurate enough, the remedy was less successful. The Committee wanted to distinguish between the able-bodied poor who were too idle to work and the old, sick, or infirm poor who could not work because of their personal disabilities. But given the incompetence and crudity of the administrative machine with whose aid these distinctions had to be drawn in thousands upon thousands of cases in every village and hamlet, the Commissioners sought ways of making the new law largely self-executing. Chadwick's fertile mind came up with the answers, part at least borrowed from Bentham.[67] First there was the principle of less eligibility: the poor who were given relief must not have their condition made better than it would be if they were at work. And secondly, there was the new workhouse principle. The able-bodied poor were only to be relieved if they entered the workhouse where life was deliberately designed to be spartan and severe. By means of these two simple principles, the new Poor Law would be largely self-enforcing.

[65] See generally, Hobsbawm, op. cit., and K. Polanyi, *The Great Transformation* (reprinted Boston, 1957).

[66] *Poor Law Report*, ed. S. G. and E. O. A. Checkland (Harmondsworth, 1974), p. 325.

[67] See on this O. MacDonagh, *Early Victorian Government, 1830–1870* (London, 1977), pp. 99–104.

The able-bodied who were genuinely unemployed would be distinguished from those who were merely work shy; those who could work would have every incentive to go out and find work if it was at all possible. Like much else which emanated from the political economists, and the other social theorists of the early nineteenth century, the chief problem with these recommendations lay in their over-simplicity. The problems were more complex than the theories allowed for. In particular, the Commissioners had not grasped the problem of industrial unemployment caused by recessions, during which work was not to be had even to the most enterprising and hard-working of men. Nor did the Report adequately allow for the transitional problems of introducing the new system; nor again did it pay sufficient regard to other influences on human behaviour besides the carrot and the stick. Nevertheless, it would be wrong to think of the new Poor Law as something emanating solely from the political economists and thrust upon an unwilling Parliament by a Government dominated by theorists. The new Poor Law was in fact carried by huge majorities in Parliament in 1834, and on subsequent renewals. It was not a party issue, and the main opposition came from those who did not like the new centralized powers conferred on the Poor Law Board at the expense of the parish authorities.[68]

In practice the new Poor Law came to be regarded as an instrument of oppression by the poor, and the workhouses with detestation and loathing. It was never possible to implement the proposals in full with regard to the prohibition on outdoor relief to the able-bodied, especially in the industrial North. However, for present purposes what is important is not so much the success or failure of the new Poor Law, but rather the attitude of mind which it reveals. Fundamentally, the ideals behind the new law were all of a piece with the belief in self-reliance, individualism, and freedom of contract. The old Poor Law had been (as Malthus argued) something of a confidence trick. The poor had been assured that, if they would surrender some of their freedom (such as the freedom to move in search of new work) they would never suffer deprivation. That promise the State had never been in a position to honour. To supply bounty for all in an overpopulated world was simply not possible. The old bargain must be repealed: the workman was given freedom of contract, freedom of movement, in return for the loss of his right to subsistence from the State, except in case of extreme deprivation.

The reality or unreality of these freedoms was then, as it has tended to remain, a source of controversy. Freedom to starve was no freedom; freedom to move in search of work was no real freedom for the man with a wife and several small children; freedom of contract for the labourers was no real freedom since most had to submit to the terms offered by the

[68] W. C. Lubenow, *The Politics of Government Growth* (Newton Abbott, 1971), pp. 41–6.

farmers or industrial employers. There is no need to labour these points which are today well recognized by everyone; indeed, what perhaps ought to be stressed is that these freedoms were not totally imaginary. Men did become more mobile; there was a shift in population from the countryside to the Northern cities (although the first waves of this movement were already over by 1834); it is not true that labourers never had the choice between different employers or even between agricultural labour and industrial employment. But of course these freedoms tended, then as now, to be of most value and to have most reality for a small minority; the energetic, able, and enterprising rarely form a majority of any group of human beings. And in a country and an age where the majoritarian tradition holds sway, it is not surprising if these freedoms have seemed, in retrospect, to be of little value. They may have seemed of more value to those who were able to take advantage of them.

Combinations and Unions

The relationship between ideas about freedom of contract, and the right of workmen freely to combine in combinations or unions inevitably raised problems and conflict throughout almost the whole of the period 1770–1870. Did freedom of contract mean that workers were to be free to combine on what terms they pleased? Did a majority of workmen in a Combination or Union have the right to bind a minority to observe a strike call, or to picket, or to indulge in other restrictive practices? On the whole, the attitudes, both of the political economists and the lawyers, to these and similar questions were consistent with their general beliefs in freedom of contract and freedom of trade.

The early years of this period saw the Courts and Parliament still hostile to all monopolies and restrictive practices, as they had traditionally been. There was nothing peculiar, or anything especially partaking of class bias, in their hostility to workers' combinations. They believed in the freedom of individual workers to make their own bargains with individual employers, though (as we have seen) in the agricultural labour market this principle had been largely destroyed between 1795 and 1834. They did not, in principle, object to workers binding themselves by contract in friendly societies or other associations designed for mutual self-help, but they did object to restrictive associations or agreements. An agreement by a workman to abide a majority decision not to work, for example, was still a common law criminal conspiracy and indictable as such. In theory this was also true of corresponding agreements between employers, although in practice it was very difficult to mount an indictment against employers.[69] But the decision in *R. v. Waddington*,[70]

---

[69] See M. I. Thomis, *The Town Labourer and the Industrial Revolution* (London, 1974), p. 46.
[70] *Supra*, p. 365.

misguided though it may have been in the particular circumstances of the case, shows that the superior Courts, at least, were perfectly willing to enforce the law, even to the extent of imposing jail sentences on businessmen whom they took to be indulging in restrictive practices hostile to the interests of the poor, or the public.

After the outbreak of the Revolutionary Wars, however, the authorities began to take a different view of combinations, principally because they saw any association of workmen as a possible source of subversive or revolutionary ideas. At a time when new concentrations of population were appearing in great new cities, and there was still no proper police force to control them or maintain some surveillance over them, all combinations inspired fear and dread in the authorities. The result was the Combination Acts of 1799 and 1800 which made virtually all combinations, whether of employees or even employers, a crime. After the end of the Napoleonic Wars, opinion began to swing against these draconian laws. In 1818 the radical firebrand William Cobbett began to preach Adam Smith's principles in defence of worker's combinations. Like Adam Smith himself, he argued that the worker's labour was his property, and like all forms of property it ought to be free to be disposed of as the owner pleased. If labour was a man's property, then he had a right to sell it, a right to refuse to sell it if he chose, and a right to demand his own price if he sold it.[71] Unfortunately, this was a bad time for such radical views. The Cato Street Conspiracy, the Peterloo massacre, and the six Acts of 1819 added to the repression rather than relaxed it. But within a few years there was once again a change in the climate of opinion, and there is no doubt that this time the political economists were influential in the change, although there were also other forces at work.

The economists argued a twofold case.[72] On the one hand, they insisted that freedom of contract ought to be extended to permit workers to combine on any terms they thought fit, and on the other hand they argued that combinations in restraint of trade, restrictive agreements to demand higher wages or shorter hours, were bound to be ineffective anyhow. They believed then, as they generally continued to believe throughout most of the nineteenth century, that the competitive market conditions which existed at that time were too strong to be controlled by any restrictive agreements. Workers who attempted to go on strike would, if they were trying to push their wages above the 'natural' or prevailing rate, merely stultify themselves. For one thing, other workers seeking employment might be recruited by the employers, and the strikers dismissed, but even if that did not happen and the strike

[71] Cited, R. Williams, *Culture and Society*, p. 35.
[72] L. Robbins, *Theory of Economic Policy in English Classical Political Economy* (London, 1952), pp. 105 10.

succeeded in its objectives, its success would be short-lived. For the higher wages would mean higher prices, this in turn would cause demand to fall, and the employer would then have to reduce wages, or dismiss part of his work-force. And there was indeed much truth in this so long as the size of the unions was not co-extensive with the size of the market in which the employers sold their products. For a strike in one factory or plant could hardly succeed in the long run if lower wages were paid by a rival manufacturer in the next town. Until the unions began to grow to national strength towards the end of the century their power was inevitably limited.

All this was backed by the 'wage fund' theory of the economists, the belief that the aggregate wages available for workers in the whole country depended upon the aggregate capital invested, and could not be arbitrarily increased by the actions of trade unions.[73] If one union succeeded in obtaining higher wages, therefore, this must inevitably be at the expense of other workers since it would involve extracting additional sums of money from a limited pool, or fund. This theory was not discredited till about 1870; it seems then to have been discredited rather too successfully and people forgot the element of truth in the theory—namely, that the real value of wages in any period cannot be increased beyond the real value of the goods and services produced, which in turn is limited by the amount of past investment. But in the early nineteenth century all the economists believed in the theory as an economic truth, and did their best to convince politicians (and the workers themselves) of this economic truth.[74]

In 1824, when the influence of the political economists seems to have been at its highest point, Francis Place pulled off something of a Parliamentary coup and engineered the repeal of the Combination Acts. In all probability, this was not due solely to the theorists. Employers themselves knew that the Acts were largely ineffective in preventing combinations which often continued to flourish underground or in the guise of Friendly Societies. They also knew that labour relations were not helped by reliance on the law which was therefore invoked but rarely, and then only in times of great disturbance.[75] Place himself apparently believed, with the political economists, that the repeal of the Combination Acts would not lead to an increase in the strength of combinations; he believed in the atomistic view of society and thought that men would make their own individual bargains once they saw that the combinations

[73] M. Blaug, *Economic Theory in Retrospect* (revised edn., Homewood, Ill., 1968), pp. 168-72.
[74] The lesson was rammed home in one of Harriet Martineau's *Illustrations of Political Economy* (London, 1832-4), Tale VII, vol. 3, pp. 121-2, 188-9.
[75] W. S. Jevons, *The State in Relation to Labour*, 3rd edn. (London 1894), p. 115: P. Mathias, *The First Industrial Nation* (London, 1974), p. 367.

could not do much to help them. They would, therefore, tend to wither away once they were legalized. This withering-away process, however, proved as realistic as the withering-away of the Marxist Soviet State after the Russian Revolution. The immediate result of the repealing Act of 1824 was a wave of strikes and violent disturbances, and streams of complaints poured into Peel at the Home Office from all over the country. The result was a speedy Select Committee and a new Bill was hastily drafted and passed as the Combination Act 1825.

The new Act preserved the basic legality of trade unions which had been conceded by the Act of 1824, but it considerably tightened up on the ways by which a union could enforce its decision on its members. Workmen were now permitted to agree among themselves about the wages and hours of work which they would seek from their employers, but each worker was still left free to make his own bargain. The majority of a union was not entitled to impose its views on a minority by threats, or coercion, or molestation. To the modern labour lawyer the Act of 1825 was an absurdity. It recognized the legality of unions but refused to permit them the weapons with which they could effectively work. For workmen knew well enough that their strength lay entirely in their solidarity. Strikes were never effective unless the men all downed tools and stood together. One or two 'strike-breakers' who insisted on their freedom of contract, their right to work, would soon destroy any strike. And it was hard to secure unanimity for any length of time. Men with large families to feed, and with little or nothing in the way of strike pay to maintain them, would always be tempted to break ranks, and return to work. But, to the political economists and parliamentarians, there was nothing absurd or inconsistent in their policy towards unions at this time. It was, indeed, precisely because they thought the strike weapon would be largely ineffective and also unobjectionable if every workman was entitled freely to decide whether to work or not, that they were willing to concede the legality of unions.

It is instructive to observe how the attitudes of the differing groups tended to favour freedom of contract when it operated in their interests, and to oppose it when it operated against them. The nineteenth-century radicals, not to mention extremists like Engels, denied that there was any real freedom of contract in the employment relationship, much as their modern sympathizers have done. But within the new unions, the working-class leaders had no great liking for freedom of contract themselves. They fought hard to make freedom of contract within the unions as unreal as they complained that it was within the factories. They did not appreciate—indeed they bitterly opposed—the law's insistence that individual workmen should be left free to decide whether to work or not, whether to strike or not; they wanted to impose the principle of majority rule, whereby the minority would be bound to observe the decision of the majority of the union. By contrast, of course, the economists, lawyers, and parliamentarians, who glossed over much of the unreality of freedom of contract in the employment situation, worked strenuously for that reality within the unions.

In the middle of the nineteenth century a series of indictments for conspiracy made it clear that the Courts were not prepared to allow the majority of workmen in a union to coerce or intimidate a minority. All must be left to choose freely. The judges echoed the views of the economists. In a charge to a grand jury in 1842, for example, Abinger C.B. protested at the 'intolerable tyranny' involved in attempts to force others to stop work. 'What right has any man to dictate to another at what price he should labour?'[76] In *R. v. Selby*,[77] Rolfe B.[78] directed a jury that workmen were free to agree with each other at what wages and conditions they would work, and they were free to try to persuade each other, even by pickets, to work or not to work. But intimidation, obstruction, and molestation were illegal. The market price of labour, he added, in a homily to the jury, would find its own level according to the supply and demand of labour, and 'that is the policy of the law'. A few years later this decision was approved by the Court of Queen's Bench in *R. v. Rowlands*.[79] As late as 1867 Bramwell B. gave expression to similar sentiments in binding over some tailors convicted of conspiracy to molest other workmen.[80] The men convicted of these offences have, of course, long since acquired the martyrdom accorded those deemed to have suffered in the cause of labour, but the ideals which the judges were trying to uphold do not seem to have been so reprehensible. No doubt there was vagueness in concepts such as 'molestation' and 'intimidation', and no doubt it was often difficult to know where the judges would draw the line, but the ideal that each workman should be free to choose for himself, free to persuade, but free also from coercion, naturally fitted the times. Some slight relaxation in the law was made by the Molestation of Workmen Act 1859, but apart from that, the uneasy balance between legality and illegality was maintained until almost the close of this period.

In 1867 this balance was disturbed by the decision in *Hornby* v. *Close*.[81] At this time there was no provision for the incorporation or even registration of trade unions as such, and many of them had registered under the Friendly Societies Acts—indeed many of them either were friendly societies or performed some of the functions of friendly

---

[76] P. C. Scarlett, *A Memoir of James, First Lord Abinger* (London, 1877), pp. 179–80. Brougham seems to have had similar views: *Autobiography* (London, 1871), iii. 322.

[77] (1847) 5 Cox 495, 497.

[78] Lord Cranworth, Lord Chancellor, 1852–5 and again 1865–8.

[79] (1851) 5 Cox 466.

[80] W. L. Burn, *The Age of Equipoise*, p. 68.   [81] (1867) L.R. 2 Q.B. 153.

societies.[82] But in *Hornby* v. *Close* it was held that a trade union with objects in restraint of trade, that is, objects which included restrictive agreements on the freedom of the members to agree their own terms of employment, could not validly register under the Friendly Societies Act. The decision itself concerned the attempt of a union to use a provision of the Friendly Societies Act containing a summary remedy against its own Treasurer who withheld the society's funds. The action was dismissed because the union's registration was invalid. The decision was widely interpreted as meaning that a trade union's funds could be stolen with impunity by treasurers or other officials. This was probably a misunderstanding because the illegality of the union did not itself prevent an indictment for larceny or embezzlement being laid, but the resultant uproar led to the Royal Commission of 1868–9 and eventually to the Trade Union Act of 1871. This Act expressly provided that a union could be registered and that its objects were not to be deemed illegal or void merely because they were in restraint of trade.

From this time onwards, trade unions really pass out of this story. The agreement by which unions were created, and by which its members associated themselves together, ceased to have any close contact with contract law and theory. Unions acquired an increasing *de facto* personality which was, in due course, given some sort of legal recognition in the *Taff Vale* case.[83] The relationship between a union and its members, while retaining some of the characteristics of a contract or agreement, like the relationship between a corporation and its members, tended increasingly to be treated as *sui generis*. If it was in some respects still treated like an ordinary contract, in other respects it acquired some very peculiar characteristics. In particular it was a contract, the terms of which could be altered by some parties without the consent of the others. The removal of the taint of illegality from unions in restraint of trade meant that majority rule had replaced freedom of contract as the governing principle. By joining a union a man now bound himself in advance to surrender his freedom of action and subordinate himself to the majority.[84] So long as workers had real freedom to choose whether to join a union or not, this consequence could still, in a limited sense, be attributed to the workman's free choice.

The Truck Acts

Payment of workmen was a very irregular business in the late eighteenth and early nineteenth centuries. Payment by a regular weekly pay packet

---

[82] On the friendly societies themselves, see P. H. Gosden, *The Friendly Societies in England 1815 to 875*, (Manchester, 1961), p. 173.

[83] [1901] A.C. 426.

[84] See *post*, p. 740.

was the exception rather than the rule. Men were usually paid at irregular intervals, often at irregular places (payment in public houses was a not uncommon phenomenon),[85] and not always in cash. Many employers operated 'tommy shops' at which the workmen were able to buy on credit while they waited for their wages. Because of the irregularity in payment, resort to the tommy shop (which might be the only source of credit available) was often a necessity for the workers. In some cases, too, the tommy shop might have an effective monopoly because of the isolation of the workmen. This occurred in particular in some mining villages, and similar arrangements were widely practised among the railway navvies who might be working and living several miles from the nearest village. The tommy shops tended to overcharge the workers, and this was much resented even though the overcharging has been estimated to represent no more than 7 to 10 per cent of profits.[86]

The truck system was closely associated with the tommy shops because payment of wages otherwise than in money usually consisted of payment by tickets cashable at a tommy shop, or even by a simple allowance of credit at the shop. However, the truck system was not always operated for these reasons. There were at least three other reasons why some employers resorted to truck, two of which had no sinister basis at all. Sometimes truck was adopted because of the shortage of small coins[87] and sometimes it was adopted as a way of restricting the temptation to spend the pay packet on drink.[88] But by far the commonest reason for the use of truck was that it enabled employers to undercut their competitors or to evade fixed or union-agreed wage rates. Frequently, it was the smaller and less reputable employers who resorted to these tactics, and it was their competitors who sought anti-truck legislation, or the enforcement of the existing legislation, as a means of restricting competition.

Anti-truck legislation went back to 1465, but in the early years of the nineteenth century the political economists began to question its desirability. As early as 1812 Joseph Hume addressed the House of Commons with classic freedom-of-contract arguments: 'If it should be more convenient or profitable for a workman to receive payment for his labour partly or wholly in goods why should he be prevented from doing so?' After all, he went on, if the workman did not like this method of payment, he could choose to work elsewhere.[89] But the larger and more influential nail-masters (the employers of nail-makers, largely a domestic

---

[85] For miners, this was prohibited by a section inserted in the Mines Act 1842 when it was before the House of Lords, but the practice was not totally prohibited for all workmen until 1883.

[86] See G. W. Hilton, *The Truck System* (Cambridge, 1960) p. 40.

[87] T. S. Ashton, *Economic History of England in the Eighteenth Century*, reprinted (London, 1972), p. 207.

[88] G. W. Hilton, *The Truck System*, pp. 44–8.   [89] Ibid., p. 92.

industry) were not particularly impressed by these arguments. In a depressed industry, hit by the competition of the new factory-made product, there was a constant pressure from the smaller employers to cut their costs by using the truck system. The nail-masters secured the passage of an Anti-Truck Act in 1818, and another in 1820, though the opponents of this Act succeeded in making it a temporary measure, to last two years only.[90] When this Act came up for renewal in 1822, the opposition was greater, and Ricardo threw his weight against the Act as an 'obnoxious measure'.[91] He pointed out that Robert Owen in his New Lanarkshire Mills operated shops for the benefit of his workmen at which he sold better commodities more cheaply than they could be bought elsewhere. Other members argued that if workers were overcharged, the forces of competition could be relied upon to solve the problem. There was also scepticism, not unjustified, as all experience showed, of the effectiveness of such legislation. The result was that the Act was not renewed.

In 1830 the issue erupted again. A strike was organized by the Gloucester weavers against a clothier who was claimed to be a hard truckmaster. The other leading clothiers refused to help him, and indeed petitioned the Home Office for renewed legislation. The result was the introduction of a new Bill in 1831.[92] This Bill, drafted by Sir James Stephen and Sir James Scarlett, cleared away the accumulated debris of centuries, and attempted to state the law in a more intelligible manner. The Bill was designed to be of general application (though it did not apply to all trades) and of unlimited duration. It aroused a great deal of interest and wide public support. Only the economists and their supporters among the radicals, such as Hume, opposed it. But the Bill passed easily enough though, once again, it was not very effective.[93] Despite a spate of prosecutions when the Act came into force, it was extensively violated and by 1838 it was said to be a dead letter though this was certainly an exaggeration.

As with nearly all the early reforming legislation of the nineteenth century, the problem was the difficulty of effective enforcement; but the problem was probably also aggravated by the fact that the principal supporters of the legislation were not so much the exploited workmen as the employers' competitors. Consequently there may have been many cases in which truck was used where the alternative would have been dismissal of the workman, or an overtly lower rate of pay. In such circumstances it may have been the lesser of two evils from the workman's

---

[90] Ibid., p. 17.
[91] *Hansard* (2nd series), vol. 7, col. 1123 (1822).
[92] G. W. Hilton, 'The Truck Act of 1831', 10 *Economic History Rev.* 470 (1958).
[93] G. W. Hilton, *The Truck System*, pp. 116–17.

point of view to accept the truck system, and attempts to enforce the legislation might have led to the combined opposition of those who practised it and those who were its nominal victims. Certainly there is no evidence to suggest that Parliament or Government did not want to see the legislation enforced,[94] and from time to time, especially in periods of depression, there was a serious attempt to enforce the law. Anti-truck societies were formed 'for the protection of fair trade and the working man'; one recalls that the expression 'fair trade' came in the twentieth century to be an American euphemism for the highly restrictive practice of resale price maintenance. These anti-truck societies were an anti-competitive device in much the same way, for their primary purpose was to prevent concealed wage reductions in the form of truck, usually when depressions were forcing down prices. But they could be extremely active. In 1844 Engels noted that the Act was effectively enforced in the towns, if not in the countryside, and he records a dozen convictions referred to in the press between November 1843 and June 1844.[95] In 1850 one anti-truck association secured no less than 250 convictions under the Act,[96] but the task seems to have been like trying to block up the holes of a sieve. Truck went on being used, particularly in depressions.

In 1846 a Parliamentary Select Committee looking into the working conditions of railway navvies observed that the Truck Acts did not apply to such workmen. They examined the question with some care, and their Report shows a much greater awareness of the practical aspect of the matter than the political economists had shown in 1831. They pointed out that there was nothing in the Truck Acts to prevent an employer trying to sell goods to his workmen in his own shops, but they insisted that the workmen should be given a choice between the employer's shop and any competitors:

If the employer can provide what his men want cheaper or better or more readily than other dealers, his labourers will have recourse to that source of supply in preference to others; if he cannot do so, it is a hardship on the men to force them to buy in a dear and bad market.[97]

They added that the objection to the truck system was that it opened a door to fraud, because the men were in practice unable to keep an adequate record of their purchases in the tommy shops. It was this same Committee which, instigated by Chadwick, reported in favour of some workmen's compensation provision for the railway labourers.[98] And they deliberately went out of their way to challenge *laissez-faire*

---

[94] See, e.g., J. T. Ward, *Sir James Graham*, p. 191, for Graham's attitude.

[95] F. Engels, *The Condition of the Working Class in England* (reprinted St. Albans, Herts., 1974), p. 209.

[96] G. W. Hilton, *The Truck System*, p. 123.

[97] (1846) H.C. *Parliamentary Papers*, xiii. 425, 430.   [98] *Supra*, p. 333.

sentiments, saying that 'whatever can be affected within the legitimate province of the legislature should not be left unattempted in order to turn the scale in favour of amelioration'.[99]

Nothing was, however, done to implement this Report. In 1854 Sir Samuel Peto, one of the largest and most reputable of the great railway contractors, who had employed over 30,000 men, and never used truck, pressed for new legislation.[1] But again, nothing was done. In 1870, however, a two-man Commission of Inquiry was appointed under Charles Bowen, a barrister who later became a Lord of Appeal. This Commission made a more thorough study of the truck problem than had ever been attempted before.[2] They argued with a convincing display of evidence that the principal source of the trouble lay in the lengthy intervals at which workmen were paid in certain employments, particularly in the Welsh and Scottish collieries. The result of these delays in payment meant that the workmen were forced to buy many supplies on credit and the employers' tommy shops were often the only source of credit. They thus established an effective monopoly, particularly for those workmen who were unable to budget carefully so as to ensure that one pay packet lasted until the next one was due. The result of this monopoly was, as usual, that the workmen paid higher prices for their supplies. The Report made two principal recommendations, first that employers should be legally compelled to pay wages weekly, and secondly that there should be public inspection and enforcement of the Truck Acts. In fact the problem was evidently dying, and although the Commission's main recommendations were not carried out, a number of minor legislative amendments were made in 1874 and 1887. The T.U.C. decided in 1877 that further control of truck was unimportant and it is clear that the problem was by then largely dead.

The Factories Acts

The story of the early Factories legislation has often been told,[3] and I have no space here for a full review. But enough must be said to show how unreliable is the widely held popular version of the story. The popular version is, of course, the story of how the dogmas of *laissez-faire*

---

[99] At p. 428.

[1] Terry Coleman, *The Railway Navvies*, pp. 88–92.

[2] 1871 C. 325. See G. W. Hilton, *The Truck System*, pp. 13–15. The Report contains a useful Appendix summarizing the reported decision on the Truck Acts. These do not appear to show any signs of bias against the Acts, except possibly for *Archer* v. *James* (1859) 2 B. & S. 61, 121 E.R. 998, where the judges split three-three. By contrast a strong decision upholding the Act is *Wilson* v. *Cookson* (1863) 32 L.J.M.C. 177 where it was held that the Act was violated even by the supply of goods to a workman with his own consent.

[3] J. T. Ward, *The Factory Movement* (London, 1962); M. W. Thomas, *The Early Factory Legislation*; W. C. Lubenow, *The Politics of Government Growth*; O. MacDonagh, *Early Victorian Government 1830–1870* (London, 1977).

were invoked to protect the workers' 'freedom of contract' while in reality the result was to give the factory owners complete freedom to exploit and ill-treat the workers. This version is to be found as early as Engels's book on the *Condition of the Working Class in England*, published in 1844, while the Ten Hours debate was reaching its climax. It was given broad support by most historians, and even by Dicey, whose sympathies were not generally with the workers. In comparatively recent times historical research has begun to uncover many inconsistencies in this version of the facts.

The bare bones of the legislative story in the crucial years, from 1800 to 1850, can be quickly told. The first legislative intervention occurred in 1802 when Parliament passed the Health and Morals of Apprentices Act. At this time steam was not yet widely used in factories which were still mostly built in rural areas where natural water power was utilized. The consequent lack of suitable available labour had led the early mill owners to recruit orphan children as 'apprentices' from the Workhouses which were only too glad to be rid of a costly burden. As these children had no parents whose rights might have been said to be infringed by interference, Parliament readily accepted its right to protect them.

The next important milestone was the Act of 1819 introduced by Sir Robert Peel, himself the son of one of the greatest of the mill owners. By this time, the nature of the problem had somewhat shifted. Steam power was now being widely used, and in consequence, the mills were being built in the cities, were labour was already available, and to which flocked many new workers in search of the wages paid in the mills. The Act of 1819 was still concerned only with children, but it was not now dealing with orphan children for whom the State was *in loco parentis*. It was dealing with children under the control of their own parents. This gave rise to some opposition in the House of Lords in the name of 'that great principle of political economy that labour ought to be free',[4] but the Bill passed easily enough. There was little opposition to Peel's argument that children were not free agents, and were entitled to the protection of Parliament. However, it was then, and for many years afterwards, often thought that such legislative protection of children was not so much an interference with the freedom of the mill owners to employ the children, as an interference with the rights of the parents who were thought to be primarily responsible for ensuring the welfare of their children.[5] But it was a hundred years since Lord Chancellors had asserted their jurisdiction to protect children even against their own

---

[4] M. Blaug, 'The Classical Economists and the Factory Acts—a Re-examination', in A. W. Coats (ed.) *The Classical Economists and Economic Policy*, p. 106.

[5] See Sir James Graham in the debate on the Coal Mines Bill, 1842, *Hansard* (3rd series), vol. 63, col. 1358.

parents,[6] and Parliament now adopted the same principle. So far as the interests of the children themselves were concerned few would have disagreed with Mill's assessment that 'freedom of contract in the case of children, is but another word for freedom of coercion'.[7]

A slight advance was made in two further Acts of 1825 and 1831, but a more decisive battle took place in 1832-3. Shortly after the return of the Whigs to office in 1830, a Commons Committee, carefully chosen, and exposed only to evidence which its organizer (Michael Sadler) wanted it to hear, stirred up much support for the Ten Hours' Day movement, a movement designed to reduce the hours of work of adults as well as children. This Committee heard no evidence at all from the mill owners, and its report was therefore a simple *ex parte* document which condemned the excessive hours worked in the mills and demanded legislative control. It was to meet the Parliamentary demand for legislation following this Committee that the Whigs appointed the Royal Commission to inquire into Child Labour in the Factories. This Commission (which included Chadwick among its three members) was at first given only six weeks in which to produce a Report as the Government was desperately anxious to introduce its own Bill before Ashley (who had taken over Sadler's Bill) could marshal support for the Ten Hour Day Bill. The Report of the Royal Commission was hastily produced, and a Bill was at once drafted and introduced by Althorp. This was the Bill which became the Factories Act, 1833, and it was more protective towards children and young persons than Ashley's Bill. The supporters of the Ten Hours' Day movement had been agitating for a limitation on the hours of work of all factory hands, adults and children equally. They had not distinguished between them. Althorp's Bill, however, following the recommendations of the Royal Commission, did distinguish very sharply between adults and children.[8] Children under 9 were henceforth barred from factory employment altogether; children from 9 to 13 were limited to nine hours daily, and young persons from 14 to 18 were limited to twelve hours daily.

The debates on the Bill were long and bitter, but the Government stuck to its guns. The Ten Hours supporters seem to have been more interested in limiting the hours of adults to ten hours a day, than they were in limiting the hours of children to nine. Indeed, they actually moved an amendment to *increase* the permitted hours for children, in the

---

[6] See *Eyre* v. *Countess of Shaftesbury* (1722) 2 P. Wms. 118, 24 E.R. 659, said to have been the first case in which this had been done, see W. Welsby, *Lives of Eminent English Judges* (London, 1846), p. 217.

[7] *Principles*, Book V, Chapter XI, sect. 9. Even in the House of Lords, the opposition to this principle was very muted. See, e.g., *Hansard* (2nd series), vol. 39, cols. 339-48, 652-4 (1819).

[8] The Royal Commission noted that at fourteen children usually made their own contracts: (1833) H.C. *Parliamentary Papers* xx. 56.

interests of the adults, and were voted down by the Government's supporters.[9] The adult workmen were angry at the resulting Act which did little for them, and they condemned it as the work of the mill owners. But some of the mill owners attacked it as bitterly as the adult workers when they realized the implications. For in practice the work of adults and children was closely integrated in the mills, and the mill owners did not at first see how they were to keep the mills open twelve or fourteen hours a day if the children could only work nine hours. The answer was, in fact, found in the 'relay' system whereby two shifts of children were employed for one adult shift.

The battle over the 1833 Act was, of course, the beginning, rather than the end of the story. The agitation for a ten hour day continued, and year after year, resolutions were brought before the House of Commons in favour of the principle, though regularly defeated. In 1844 another major Act was passed by Peel's Government which brought the hours of children down further, and extended protection to children under 21. Still, the principle of not legislating for adults was adhered to, though this time the House of Commons first voted in favour of an amendment embodying the Ten Hours principle. The Government absolutely refused to accept it, however, and Peel made it a matter of confidence with the result that the amendment was once again defeated.[10] In 1846 Ashley was only just defeated in his attempt to get a new Ten Hours Bill through the Commons,[11] but the following year the Bill was finally carried. Unfortunately the campaigners for the Bill had defeated themselves by their own over-subtle ingenuity. For the Bill they drafted did not openly require the mills actually to be closed down after 12 hours (ten hours for work, plus two hours for meal breaks). What they did was to try to restrict the hours of children (without whose work the mills could not function) in such a way, as they thought, to prevent the use of the relay system. Here, however, they bungled, and the Court of Exchequer held in 1850 that the Act did not have this effect.[12] The struggle had to be renewed, and not until 1853 was success finally attained.

It must not be thought that the Factories legislation was solely concerned with hours of work. The Acts (especially that of 1844) were also concerned with a variety of other matters, such as safety and accident prevention, hygiene and sanitation, and the education of children.[13]

---

[9] M. W. Thomas, *The Early Factory Legislation*, pp. 63–4.

[10] Ibid., pp. 203 *et seq.*

[11] This was the occasion referred to *supra*, p. 511, when Peel told Macaulay that there were no more than ten members of the House who supported a pure policy of *laissez-faire*.

[12] *Ryder* v. *Mills* (1850) 3 Ex. 853, 154 E.R. 1090.

[13] On the education of the factory children, see Sanderson, 'Education and the Factory in Industrial Lancashire, 1780–1840', 20 *Economic History Rev.* 266 (1967). Many of the better employers provided educational facilities for their child employees before it was made compulsory in 1833.

Moreover, all these requirements brought in their wake a battery of ancillary provisions needed to ensure proper enforcement. Above all, the 1833 Act contained provision for the appointment of the first factory inspectors, an idea originally propounded by Bentham and taken up by Chadwick in the Royal Commission Report which led to the Act.

What concerns us most here is the nature of the debate that occurred during the crucial years 1833 to 1847 over the control of hours and conditions of work. Is it true that the opposition to interference with the hours of work of adults was based on the *laissez-faire* ideology, the belief in freedom of contract? In one sense, it is true. There is no doubt that the political economists were generally hostile to such legislative interference. In 1844 the Political Economy Club voted almost unanimously, on a motion by Chadwick, that interference with the hours of work of adult workmen was not justifiable.[14] And in Parliament, too, those who opposed such legislation often relied on this principle of non-interference. But it is too simple to write off the whole struggle as one fought between pragmatic reformers and adherents to an abstract principle. In fact, there are some indications that it was the reformers who were less pragmatic and more idealist, while the opponents were often influenced by practical arguments. The chief practical argument was that a reduction of the hours of work from twelve to ten would significantly reduce the earnings of the mills and hence would necessarily reduce the wages that could be paid. Not everyone argued quite so dogmatically as Nassau Senior to the effect that the total profit made in the mills was made in the last hour of the day, so that the elimination of that hour would drive the mills to lower wages or bankruptcy;[15] but many argued, with a good deal of rationality, that it would be impossible to cut hours of work by a sixth and yet expect wages to remain the same.[16] The supporters of the Ten Hours movement, in so far as they were willing to consider the question at all, argued that a cut in production, with no cut in demand, would raise prices; this increase, they thought, would be sufficient to maintain wages at their existing level.

Many of these arguments seem naïve and over-simplistic today, but there is little sign that the debate in the 1830s and 1840s was more concerned with abstract principle than with the purely practical question of what was generally in the best interests of the labourers. If it were true

[14] M. Blaug, 'The Classical Economists and the Factory Acts', in A. W. Coats (ed.), *The Classical Economists and Economic Policy*, p. 112.

[15] Though even Senior insisted it was a matter of expediency rather than of principle. S. L. Levy, *Nassau W. Senior* (Newton Abbott, 1970), pp. 109–10. Perhaps significantly, it seems to have been lawyers like Brougham who stood out for non-interference on principle: J. T. Ward, *The Factory Movement*, p. 150.

[16] In fact wages did fall after the Ten Hours Day was introduced, though it is difficult to measure the amount, and buoyant production soon made up the loss: ibid., p. 116.

that a reduction in the hours of work would necessarily lower wages, then it is at least easier to understand why many thought it would be wrong to *coerce* labourers into reduced hours of work. Peel, for example, argued that it was constantly being said how little many of the workers earned anyhow, and how close to the bare margin of subsistence they lived. Any cut in their wages, he argued, would be a very serious loss to them; was this to be imposed on them by Act of Parliament?[17] Then also there was the point that some workers had larger families and hence greater needs than others. These men might well be willing to work longer hours if they could thereby earn more. Sir James Graham argued that, left to themselves, the mill hands nearly always chose to work in factories where the hours were longest because they wanted to earn more.[18]

Another point of some importance is that, as in the case of the Truck Acts, much of the legislative interference with factories was designed to bring the worst employers up to the level of the best. Frequently the better employers were not opposed to limitations of hours of work, provided only that everyone observed the same limitation. They could not afford to cut their own hours of work when other employers were running their mills for longer hours and thereby undercutting them in the market. This attitude affected not merely hours of labour but virtually every other aspect of the conditions of work. Those who exploited their workers most, who took least care for their health, safety, and comfort, who neglected the educational requirements for children, were able to cut their costs to the bone in this fiercely competitive age. The more decent employers were not sorry to see such competitors brought under statutory control. This divergence between the practice of the better employers and the less scrupulous mill owners runs like a thread through this story from the Act of 1802 on.[19] One of the first of the new inspectors commented later that if all the factories had been as well conducted as those of the Gregs, the Ashworths, or Ashtons, or many others, there would probably have been no need for legislative interference at all.[20]

Moreover, it must be stressed again that many of the early Acts did impose much 'interference' on the mill owners in matters not concerned with the hours of work. General complaint by the mill owners against interference, and arguments that they were being compelled to regulate their factories in 'impracticable' or even 'impossible' ways, received short

[17] *Hansard* (3rd series), vol. 86, col. 1062.

[18] M. W. Thomas, *The Early Factory Legislation*, p. 203.

[19] Ibid., p. 9; Marvel, 'Factory Regulation: A Re-Interpretation of Early English Experience', 20 *Journal of Law & Economics* 379 (1977).

[20] W. G. Carson, 'Symbolic and Instrumental Dimensions of Early Factory Legislation', in R. Hood, ed., *Crime, Criminology, and Public Policy* (London, 1974), p. 118.

shrift from the Royal Commission of 1833. These words, they said, were 'commonly attached by many of the manufacturers to any regulation which may subject them to expense or to temporary inconvenience'.[21] The Commission also noted that many employers were not unwilling that there should be a statutory limit on hours, but it was invariably found that each mill owner wanted to restrict labour 'to the exact time which he works his own mill'.[22] I may also draw attention again to the safety provisions of the Factories Acts. I referred previously to the fact that Chadwick slipped in some recommendations in the 1833 Royal Commission Report about making employers, or mill owners, civilly liable to workmen for injuries suffered in the course of their employment without regard to fault. And although this proposal was not enacted it is worth noting another proposal which was. In the 1844 Act provision was made for the Secretary of State to bring civil actions in the name of any person injured by machinery in a factory.[23] This highly paternalist provision (whatever became of it in practice)[24] should be noted by those who still think of the 1840s as the high noon of *laissez-faire* and freedom of contract.

Other Employees

I do not have space here to review all the legislative interference enacted in the interests of employees of different classes, such as the chimney-sweep boys, and those who worked in coal mines. But I cannot forbear from reference to the position of merchant seamen. For the paternalist legislation enacted for seamen, first in the Merchant Shipping Act of 1844 and then in that of 1854, bears out the suggestion that interference with freedom of contract was generally seen in Parliament as a matter of expediency rather than of principle. Where the provisions were unlikely to deprive the worker of some really valuable freedom (such as the freedom to work longer hours if he wished) there seems to have been little opposition to interference with freedom of contract.

The Merchant Shipping Act of 1844 contains a whole string of paternalist provisions for seamen. By Section 2 it was made an offence for a master of a ship to take a seaman to sea without a written contract specifying what wages were to be paid, the capacity in which he was to serve, and the nature of the voyage 'so that such seaman may have some means of judging of the period for which he is likely to be engaged'.[25] The agreement was to be 'read over and explained' to the seaman in the

[21] Cited, M. W. Thomas, *The Early Factory Legislation*, p. 157.
[22] Report of the Royal Commission, (1833) H.C. *Parliamentary Papers*, xx. 54.
[23] Sects. 24, 25.
[24] I have been unable to trace any evidence that this provision was ever used.
[25] For a sympathetic common law decision on this question, see *The Cambridge* (1829) 2 Hagg. Ad. 423, 166 E.R. 233.

presence of a witness. By Section 5, any agreement by which a seaman abandoned his lien on the ship for wages or other sums due, was rendered void; and so also, with an agreement to surrender a right to salvage, or to forego wages if the ship was lost. By Section 11 the ship's master was, with some exceptions, obliged to pay wages within two days of the end of the agreement. By Section 12, no attachment of wages was to be permitted, and assignment of a seaman's wage was prohibited. By the time of the Merchant Shipping Act of 1854, the protective provisions of the Act had swollen to sixty-eight sections (146 to 213, inclusive). Amongst the new provisions of this Act was one making it an offence for any person to solicit a seaman, within twenty-four hours of the arrival of a ship, to become a lodger.

These two Acts had been carried through Parliament with scarcely a voice raised in opposition to these provisions. Apart from one member who bleated that the 1844 Bill was 'an improper interference' between masters and men,[26] the Bills were generally welcomed and overwhelmingly passed. The Minister in charge of the earlier Bill said that the proposals were long overdue but that formerly there had been 'the greatest prejudice' against such interference. Both he and the House generally seemed to take it for granted that this 'prejudice' was a matter of past history.

One final example of legislative protection of employees in the mid-nineteenth century is worth referring to, because it illustrates the point that it was often the difficulty of enforcing civil rights, rather than substantive failures of the common law, which led to the demand for legislation. In 1850 two scandalous cases of ill-treatment of young domestic servant girls received wide publicity, and shocked the conscience of the nation. In one case convictions were secured by the normal process of criminal prosecution.[27] In the second case it was held that there was no criminal offence involved in failing to provide food or medical attention (even in breach of contract) to a servant unless the servant was of such tender years as to be unable to help himself or herself.[28] These cases immediately led to the Apprentice and Servant Act 1851 which converted a breach of contract of this nature into an offence punishable with up to three years' imprisonment.

CONSUMER PROTECTION

There is a widespread belief that until comparatively recent times (usually placed well into the twentieth century) freedom of contract was

[26] *Hansard* (3rd series), vol. 76, cols. 1510–11 (1844).

[27] *R. v. Bird* (1850) 5 Cox C.C. 1.

[28] *Sloane's* case does not seem to have been reported, but the facts are given in *Hansard* (3rd series), vol. 114, cols. 1297 *et seq.*

so stringently enforced that consumers were left to take care of themselves. Only in modern times does consumer protection appear as a recognized legislative principle, and even today, the Courts are reluctant to recognize that the consumer is entitled to any protection over and above that accorded by the general law of contract. Even with those who are aware that there were medieval examples of statutes directed to this end, it is widely thought that these statutes were all repealed in the nineteenth century, leaving a gap which was only filled in the twentieth. It is, of course, recognized that fraud had to be prevented—even the political economists insisted on that—but that (it is thought) was as far as the law went in the last century. In fact, this, like much else in the popular version of nineteenth-century legal history, is very largely mythical. Consumer protection was a major legislative preoccupation throughout the nineteenth century, and it was not by any means confined purely to the prevention of fraud. But in any event the attempt to distinguish sharply between the prevention of fraud and broader protection of the consumer is and was virtually impossible. Since fraud was often difficult to prove, it was very common for Parliament to legislate on the principle of preventing modes of commercial behaviour which *facilitated* fraud, whether or not fraud was actually committed. The weights and measures legislation, for example, made it an offence to sell many commodities except by imperial weight; thus sale by volume, or by the piece (for example, a loaf of bread) was often prohibited by such legislation, and a seller who violated it was guilty of an offence, whether or not any fraud was committed or intended. In one sense, such legislation was a direct interference with freedom of contract. Buyers no less than sellers could not (for instance) contract for bread by the loaf, even though they were both perfectly willing to make such a contract, unless the loaf was of the statutory weight. It is not possible to justify such legislation simply by arguing that it prevents fraud: the ambit of the legislation is much broader than fraud. But it was designed to prevent the facilitation of fraud, and it was generally assumed that the freedom which the consumer was required to give up was one of very little value to him and was more than outweighed by the benefit of the statutory protections. Arguments about the sacred principle of freedom of contract only rarely appeared in debates on this legislation. I have space only to sketch out some of the main legislative areas, but it is worth observing that a simple principle generally underlay most of the legislation. Statutory protection was generally afforded to buyers where personal visual inspection was not likely to reveal defects of quality or short measure. Nobody doubted that buyers should generally be responsible for exercising due vigilance as to their purchases, but where no vigilance was adequate, the buyer had to rely on the seller and was entitled to protection in that reliance.

Adulteration of Food and Drink

The adulteration of articles of food and drink has a very long history, going back at least as far as the Middle Ages, and attempts to stamp it out are equally old.[29] The problems became very much worse with urbanization,[30] and in the nineteenth century, it has been said, adulteration was an exceedingly widespread and highly remunerative commercial fraud.[31] It was sometimes a danger to health, but more commonly it was only a pecuniary fraud. Throughout the eighteenth century (to venture no further back) statutory attempts to prevent adulteration of this or that item were frequent. Statutes of 1730 and 1777 were passed to prevent adulteration of tea, statutes of 1718, 1724, and 1803 similarly tried to stop the inclusion of burned vegetable matter with coffee beans, statutes of 1758, 1822, and 1836 were passed to suppress the use of alum in bread, and statutes of 1761, 1816, and 1819 were passed to prevent the adulteration of beer.[32] Unfortunately much of this legislation was largely ineffective, but the reason for this was not the usual ineptitude of Parliament, but the lack of the necessary scientific skills. Until the arrival of adequate analytical chemistry, allied with methods of microscopic examination, the detection and proof of adulteration were frequently impossible.

The tide turned in the early 1850s when a series of articles was published in the *Lancet* by a Dr. Hassell who made more than 2,400 analyses with a new microscope.[33] The result of this was the appointment of a Parliamentary Select Committee in 1855 which heard evidence from Dr. Hassell and other scientific witnesses. The Committee's Report[34] concluded that adulteration was a widespread social evil which not only endangered the public health but also constituted a serious pecuniary fraud on the whole public. Moreover, the Report went on, 'the public morality is tainted and the high commercial character of this country seriously lowered both at home and to the eyes of foreign countries'.[35] They went on to add that it was usually the poor who suffered most from this evil, because the poor were unable to protect themselves so well as the rich. Their sources of supply might be more limited, and so many of the poor lived perpetually on credit that they were often effectively bound to one supplier. It has been suggested that even in this field the philosophy of *laissez-faire* had a retarding influence on legislative

---

[29] See Bell and O'Keefe's *Sale of Food and Drugs*, 14th edn., (London, 1968), pp. 1–3.

[30] J. Burnett, 'The History of Food Adulteration in Great Britain in the Nineteenth Century with Special Reference to Bread, Tea and Beer', 32 *Bulletin Inst. of Hist. Res.* 104 (1959).

[31] Ibid., p. 105.

[32] Bell and O'Keefe, *Sale of Food and Drugs*, 14th edn., pp. 1–3.

[33] J. Burnett, 'The History of Food Adulteration in Great Britain', p. 106.

[34] (1856) H.C. *Parliamentary Papers*, viii. 1.

[35] Ibid., p. 3.

reform,[36] but this idea is hard to reconcile with the language of the Parliamentary Select Committee: 'It has been objected', said the Committee,[37] 'that the best course will be to leave the buyer to take care of himself. But there are many adulterations which it is impossible for the buyer to detect ... It is said, too, that there are many frauds which legislation cannot reach or punish. But, on the other hand, it would be difficult to tell the numberless frauds which legislation may prevent. The great difficulty of legislating on this subject lies in putting an end to the liberty of fraud without affecting the freedom of commerce'. The Committee went on to point out that the existing common law remedies by way of indictment for public nuisance or a civil action for damages were 'too costly and too cumbersome for general adoption'. In the result they recommended that local authorities be given power to appoint official analysts to take samples of food and drink, and bring prosecutions before justices if adulteration could be shown.

The result of this Report was the enactment in 1860 of the Adulteration of Food and Drink Act which adopted most of the principal recommendations. As commonly occurred, when Parliament began a new type of legislative control over some social problem, the Act required frequent amendment but it is clear that this Act foreshadowed the end of adulteration as a serious social problem. Once the chemical skills were there, Parliament was not slow to use them.

Weights and Measures

A similar problem was presented by the methods of sale of many commodities in nineteenth-century England. The problem here was purely pecuniary of course, but here again, it cannot be said that the sole effect of the legislation was to prevent fraud, even if that was its chief purpose. Part of the difficulty arose from the fact that customary measures had been used in many parts of the country, all differing from each other, right up to the beginning of the nineteenth century. As England tended to become a single national market this bewildering variety of weights and measures became an obstacle to fair commercial dealings, and Parliament bent many efforts to provide a simple uniform set of weights and measures and gradually, to require their use in a great many ordinary transactions. During the century under review, there were significant Acts in 1795, 1796, 1797, 1815, 1824, 1835, 1859, and 1867, not to mention a number of minor and subsidiary enactments.

The Act of 1795 first provided for the appointment of local Inspectors by the Justices, with power to enter shops, to examine weights and measures in use, and to certify them if found accurate. The 1824 Act

[36] J. Burnett, 'The History of Food Adulteration in Great Britain', p. 106.
[37] Report (*supra*, p. 546, n. 34), pp. 4-5.

(which cleared a lot of old debris off the statute book) attempted to standardize measurements of length and volume as well as weights, and largely outlawed the 'heaped measure' still commonly used for measuring dry goods by volume. Except in certain limited cases, this Act required measurement to be by weight for dry goods, and 'all contracts, bargains, sales and dealings' were to be regulated accordingly. All contracts made otherwise than in the standard weights and measures were to be null and void. The next major Act was that of 1835 which tightened up many of the requirements of the previous Act and finally abolished altogether the old 'heaped measure'. Coal was now to be sold only by weight; and all approved weights were to have the weight stamped on them. The next year, an amending Act required all bread to be sold by weight, and not by the loaf. This story was a continuous one and at no point in the nineteenth century does there appear to have been a change of policy as a result of *laissez-faire* opinions.

Hallmarking and Assay

Legislation on the hallmarking and assaying (that is, testing) of gold and silver goes back to the Middle Ages.[38] Gold and silver are too soft to be used without the addition of alloys, but excessive alloys can easily be added to debase the metals, and this is virtually impossible to detect except by technical testing. This explains why some method of officially certifying the quantity of the precious metal in alloys has always been used. Between 1770 and 1870 Acts were passed on this subject in 1772, 1784, 1788, 1790, 1798, 1807, 1819, 1824, 1842, 1844, 1854, and 1867. At no time does it ever appear to have been seriously suggested that this legislation interfered with the principle of freedom of contract and ought therefore to be repealed. In 1856 a Parliamentary Select Committee made a (very brief) report on the statutes then in force.[39] They stated that the 'practice of assaying is calculated to afford protection to the public against fraud, and ought to be maintained'. They went on to recommend consolidation and simplification of the statutes. Another Select Committee in 1879 did make a brief allusion to the principle involved in such legislation, only to brush it aside: 'To the principle of compulsorily assaying and marking articles of gold and silver manufactures there are no doubt some objections. It is possible that if the matter were new, and it were for the first time in contemplation to establish an assay under the control of Government, these objections might prevail'. But, the Committee went on, the practice had existed in England since the time of Edward I, and had resulted in the maintenance of a 'high

---

[38] See *Report of the Departmental Committee on Hallmarking*, 1959, Cmnd. 163, Part II, for a review of the history of legislation on this subject.

[39] Set out in Appendix A to the *Report* of the 1959 Departmental Committee.

standard of excellence for all British assayed wares which has not only raised the reputation of British workmanship at home and abroad, but has also created a large amount of private wealth readily convertible by reason of the guarantees of value which the hall-marks afford'.[40]

Their recommendations were not implemented, but the Acts were not repealed either.

Merchandise Marks

The first of a long line of general Acts on the marking and description of goods was the Merchandise Marks Act 1842. In general the Act was designed to prevent fraudulent misdescription, but some surprising provisions amending the civil law are to be found in Sections 19 and 20. By Section 19, any person selling goods with any 'trade mark' warranted it to be genuine; by Section 20, any statement, description, or other information on the wrapping or cover of any goods being sold, and relating to the quantity, measure, or weight, or country of origin of the goods, was deemed to be a warranty, 'unless the contrary shall be expressed in some writing signed by or on behalf of the vendor and delivered to and accepted by the vendee'. This section goes far beyond the prevention of fraud, and is a striking example of consumer protection of a kind normally associated with twentieth-century legislation. Somewhat surprisingly, there is little trace of any litigation on these provisions.

A similar line of legislation, though confined to one particular trade, is to be found in the Hop Trade Acts. These Acts are of particular interest in view of the case of *Parkinson* v. *Lee*[41] which was for many years taken to be a leading decision in support of the *caveat emptor* principle. This case involved a fraud in the sale of hops (though not committed by the vendor himself) and it is clear that it was precisely against this sort of fraud that the Hop Trade Acts were designed. It seems, therefore, that Parliament was less enamoured of *caveat emptor* than the Courts. The first Act, that of 1800,[42] required hop growers to put their names and addresses in legible letters or characters 'with durable ink or paint' on all hop bags. The bags were also controlled as to weight by this Act. In 1808[43] and in 1814[44] new Acts were passed, and there are signs of an increasing note of desperation in these Acts. The 1814 Act required the bags to be marked with the owner's name and address in letters four inches long and half an inch in breadth. It also prohibited the use of bags with any other names besides that of the owner, a provision which suggests that an entertaining mode of evasion of the earlier Act had been

---

[40] See Appendix B to the *Report* of the 1959 Departmental Committee.
[41] (1802) 2 East 314, 102 E.R. 389, *supra*, p. 474.
[42] 39 Geo. 3, c. 81. [43] 48 Geo. 3, c. 134. [44] 54 Geo. 3, c. 123.

discovered. But it was all to little avail. In 1866 yet another Act[45] recited that the previous Acts had been ineffectual in preventing frauds and abuses in the hop trade, and set out a new system of detailed regulations and control. This Act specifically prohibited the fraud that had been encountered in *Parkinson* v. *Lee*, namely the mixing of different qualities so that a sample might not truly represent the bulk, and altogether the Act has generally a more professional tone to it.

Statutory protection was also afforded to purchasers of other particular commodities whose qualities were not always evident to simple inspection, such as chain cables and anchors,[46] and firearms.[47]

Usury

Throughout the whole period of the Industrial Revolution, the legal maximum rate of interest remained fixed by statute at 5 per cent. We have seen that methods of evasion were common although it was also widely believed that these evasions drove up the rate of interest; the lender, as Ricardo said, exacted a premium for the additional risk arising from the dubious legality of the transaction. Borrowers were thus being compelled to pay higher interest rates as a result of this paternalism. We have seen that opinion had turned against the Acts among the political economists and the lawyers by the end of the eighteenth century. Bentham's *Defence of Usury*, first published in 1790, had been very influential, and he was followed by nearly all the classical economists.[48] In 1816 the question of repealing the Usury Laws was raised by Brougham, but whatever the views of the economists and the lawyers[49] might have been, it seems that public opinion was not yet ready for this step.[50] It was evidently necessary to educate the public into a proper understanding of their own interests. Accordingly, a Parliamentary Select Committee was established in 1818.[51] This was a good example of the techniques used at this time by the philosophical radicals. The Committee was in no sense set up to conduct an impartial inquiry, but as a propaganda exercise, to convert public opinion.[52] Ricardo and Lord

---

[45] 29 & 30 Vict., c. 39.

[46] See Chain Cable and Anchor Acts 1864, 1871, 1874, and 1899.

[47] See Gun Barrel Proof Acts 1855 and 1868.

[48] See, e.g., J. R. McCulloch's *Interest made Equity* (1826).

[49] For other signs of the attitudes of contemporary lawyers towards usury, see Evans's note on usury in his edition of Pothier, *Law of Obligations*, i. 101–2; see too *Barnes Dowding and Bartley* v. *Hedley and Conway* (1809) 2 Taunt. 184, 127 E.R. 1047.

[50] See *Hansard* (N.S.), vol. 5, cols. 175–180 (1821), where Serjeant Onslow said that in 1816 the Chancellor of the Exchequer had argued that 'the state of the public mind was at that time such as to render the agitation of the question dangerous'.

[51] (1818) H.C. *Parliamentary Papers* vi. 139.

[52] Note the comment of Byles (in his *Observations on the Usury Laws*, p. 27): 'It is perfectly clear from the form of their leading questions that the greater part of the committee had already made up their minds on the subject, and expected the evidence to justify their preconceptions'.

St. Leonards gave evidence before the Committee which duly reported in favour of repeal. The laws served no useful purpose, they asserted, but merely compelled borrowers to pay higher rates of interest than they would otherwise have done. Nevertheless, when a Bill was introduced in 1821 to repeal the laws, there was still much opposition, and the Bill had to be dropped. An important concession was, however, made in 1837 when bills of exchange payable in under twelve months were freed from the Usury Laws, thus enabling much short-term commercial lending to take place at appropriate market rates.

It seems that the public must have been more attached to the Usury Laws than the economists and the lawyers, for they remained in force until past the middle of the century. They survived the Committee of 1818, and the Bill of 1821, and numerous other attempts at repeal.[53] Surprisingly, the articulated case against repeal, if it was ever coherently argued or expressed, has not come down to us from this period. A good case against repeal was, however, argued with much rationality by Byles J. in his *Observations on the Usury Laws*, published in 1845, to which I have previously referred. Byles argued that the problem arose from the difficulty of calculating the risk of default where the borrower could not provide good security. This is not something which has a market price (unlike the cost of borrowing by a man with good security); it differs in every case, and can only be guessed at. Moreover, the small borrower, 'the inferior tradesman' for example, is not a free agent when he needs to borrow. He is at the mercy of the moneylender, and has to borrow under duress. While the borrower with good security borrows in a competitive market, the borrower without security has no open market to deal in. He dares not disclose his circumstances or want of money for fear his business may be destroyed by the resulting loss of credit. The result is a gross inequality in the position of the parties.

But it was all to no avail. In the end the theorists had their way. The Usury Laws were completely repealed in 1854, and by this time there was scarcely any opposition. Although some of the judges may have agreed with Byles[54] there was little they could do. But within twenty years the problem of the small needy borrower was beginning to raise acute social problems. Rapacious moneylenders, backed to the hilt by the law, began to appear up and down the country, advertising freely in the journals and newspapers. New legislative controls became imperative. But that side of the story falls into our next period.

[53] Note also that control of interest rates was provided for by the Pawnbrokers Act 1800.

[54] Pollock C.B. writing to Bramwell in 1857 (after repeal) said it was the duty of decent judges to denounce usury when they came across it: Fairfield, *Some Account of Baron Bramwell* (London, 1898), p. 33. But in *Flight* v. *Reed* (1863) H. & C. 703, 715, 158 E.R. 1067, 1071, Pollock C.B. said that the repeal of the Usury Laws showed a new policy which the Courts should faithfully follow.

The Licensing of Doctors

One of the most widely used methods of protecting consumers in the modern world is by controlling the sort of person who is allowed to make a certain type of contract, rather than by directly controlling the terms of the contract. In mid-nineteenth century this process had hardly begun, and a vigorous public debate occurred over the proposals for the licensing of doctors. The medical profession had itself been divided on this issue, the Royal Colleges, with an élitist tradition on the one hand, and the general practitioners, then usually known as apothecaries, on the other. The Medical Act of 1858 attempted to solve this problem by a series of compromises. The Act did not ban anyone from practising medicine, even those without any qualifications at all. What it did, however, was to give the consumer some guidance in the exercise of his rights of free choice. The preamble to the Act states that it is expedient that persons requiring medical aid should be able to distinguish qualified from unqualified practitioners, and the whole Act was conceived in this spirit. It created a register of practitioners, to be maintained by the profession itself, entry upon which was to be dependent on obtaining suitable qualifications to the satisfaction of the professional bodies. Unqualified practitioners could continue to practise and could charge for fees, but they were disqualified from obtaining certain public and quasi-public positions, they were not permitted to represent themselves as qualified practitioners and they were not allowed to sue for fees. The Act, of course, recognized the right of existing practitioners to be placed on the register, whether they were qualified or not.

This is one of the more interesting and idiosyncratic of the Victorian compromises on the freedom of contract issue, all the more remarkable for having survived to the present day. Unlike many later regulatory Acts which did not hesitate to confine the carrying on of a profession to persons qualified in some appropriate manner, it still left it permissible for an unqualified person to carry on the profession of a medical practitioner provided that he did not describe himself as such. At least this Act shows clearly enough on its face that its purposes are for the benefit of the public, whereas many modern licensing Acts are purely restrictive devices to limit the number of persons who can carry on a particular type of business. But it also shows how difficult it is to classify much Victorian legislation as individual or collective. 'Who was the most "individualistic"—the layman who cherished his right to seek medical assistance where it could be found, the unqualified practitioner (the herbalist, perhaps, or the bonesetter), the apothecary who sought to elevate his status at the expense of those above him and those below him, the Fellow of the Royal College of Medicine who clung jealously to his prerogatives?'[55]

The Passenger Acts

The story of the Passenger Acts has been well and fully told elsewhere,[56] and I need only refer to some of the more salient points in the history of this legislation. Between 1803 and 1860 a large number of emigrants from England, and more especially, Ireland, took their lives in their hands and boarded an emigrant passenger vessel, usually at Liverpool. In the 1840s as a result of failure of the Irish potato crop, the numbers rose hugely, and between 1844 and 1852 some one and a half million persons sought to cross the Atlantic in search of a better life. Most of the emigrants were very poor, many had worked for months to save up the fare—little as it was—many were illiterate, and nearly all were imposed upon. The conditions on these ships were, at the beginning of the century, appalling. The emigrants were crammed into the ships, sometimes with barely room to stand up, let alone lie down, there were no sanitary facilities of any kind, no privacy, no segregation of the sexes, and no food was provided: the passengers were expected to bring their own. When it ran out, as it might do if the voyage was prolonged, they either starved or bought supplies from the ship's master at enormously inflated prices. Disease was rife, and many ships arrived in America or Canada with rotting corpses littering the decks.

The facts first came to light almost by accident, in 1803, when a Select Committee inquiring into the Scottish highlands was fed a great deal of information about the emigrant trade. They were told, for example, of a ship in which three-fifths of the passengers had died, and thirty corpses were found when it arrived. The reaction was instantaneous. A Bill was hastily drafted and passed without a single voice being raised against it. But the Act did more credit to the heart than to the head of its sponsors. It threw away, indeed, any notion of freedom of contract and constituted what Professor MacDonagh has called a revolutionary breach of this principle. But as I have previously pointed out, in 1803 the principle had barely been formulated, for the equitable jurisdiction at that time provided many forms of redress for poor and ignorant contracting parties who were imposed upon by others. In any event the Act did not work. It was too burdensome on the shipowners, and if it had been enforced, the cost of a passage on an emigrant ship would have been priced beyond the reach of the passengers.

We have also seen how in 1826-7 a Parliamentary Select Committee suddenly woke up to the fact that the Act represented an infringement

---

[55] W. L. Burn, *The Age of Equipoise*, p. 211.
[56] O. MacDonagh, *A Pattern of Government Growth: The Passenger Acts 1800-1860.*

of the important principle of freedom of contract and secured its repeal and how, almost immediately, new revelations about the appalling conditions in the trade led to more legislation. In 1828 a new Act was passed, more modest in its requirements, and this time, though (it seems) largely by accident, the Act was enforced. This came about because the draftsman of the Act, A. C. Buchanan, was appointed Agent-General for Emigration to Canada; in that capacity he took it on himself to prosecute for breaches of the Act and to present annual reports on his efforts to Parliament. An amending Act of 1835 required the shipowners to pay 1s. per day detention money to passengers waiting for their vessel in Liverpool. This Act also required the ships to carry 'sufficient' medicines for the voyage and to post up price lists for the food on sale to the passengers. As usual it was enforcement which remained the principal problem. The Acts conferred all manner of contractual rights on the passengers, but once aboard the ships there was nothing that anyone could do to enforce his rights. Complaints were often made at the other end, but the survivors were generally only too eager to disembark and get away as fast as they could. It was unthinkable for any of them to wait around at the place of disembarkation in order to bring a civil action for damages. Sir James Stephen, Under-Secretary in the Colonial Office, commented somewhat fatalistically, that 'These Irishmen are not the first, nor will they be the last, to make the discovery that a man may starve and yet have the best right of action that a special pleader could wish for'.[57] But this fatalism did not satisfy everybody, and demands for more rigorous enforcement by the Government were frequent. By 1836–40 even the political economists had quite abandoned their opposition to the legislation and were as keen as anyone to suggest tightening-up of the requirements. A Report on the Acts in 1842 paid lip service to the principle of *laissez-faire*, arguing that Acts of Parliament could not 'supply the want of proper discretion in individuals',[58] but generally speaking these cautionary words had little effect.

An important Act was drafted and carried in 1842, based on the detailed proposals of the new emigration officers. This Act was quite destructive of what remained of freedom of contract. It required a written contract in a prescribed form to be given to the passengers, it required the licensing of brokers and agents, compulsory provision of food for the passengers both on board, and even prior to embarkation, from the day appointed for departure. The Act was drafted with a view to its enforceability and it was enforced. The new Commissioner for Emigration was given power to sue the shipowners in the name, and on behalf of, the passengers, and for some years after the Act was passed the Commissioner was recovering some £1,500 annually on their behalf.[59]

[57] Cited, ibid., p. 106.   [58] Ibid., p. 146.   [59] Ibid., p. 163.

And so the story continued. Gradually, inch by inch, the standards of space, hygiene, and food, were driven up by the legislation. Further Acts of 1847 and 1848 and a host of statutory regulations laid down new requirements, somewhat over-optimistically, in an attempt to meet the problems arising from the vast increase in the number of Irish emigrants. In 1854 a Select Committee looked into the operation of the Acts and came up with yet more regulatory proposals. In their report the centre of the debate shifted altogether, it has been said, from 'the proper limits of state intervention to the most effective means of state control'.[60] With the passing of the Act of 1855, the passage contract had been almost completely rewritten by Parliament. After this the story begins to change. Treasury parsimony, and Gladstonian Liberalism, combined to prevent the new bureaucracy from making the best use of the scientific and professional expertise becoming available. But anyhow, the need for tighter control was beginning to pass. After the 1840s the size of the trade declined dramatically, and by the 1860s the long series of early scandals was just about over.

In summarizing this episode Professor MacDonagh has argued that little thought was given, except perhaps in the earliest stages, to the philosophical principles involved in this legislation. The legislation was largely dictated by the sheer force of events, and the perfectly natural reaction of members of Parliament, and the civil servants, to the conditions that were revealed as the story unfolded. Once the initial step to legislate had been taken, or at least, once it had been reaffirmed in 1828, the control acquired a momentum of its own. The legislation created bureaucrats, and the bureaucrats fed the legislature with information about the still existing abuses, and the best way of dealing with them.

It is perhaps worth again drawing attention to a point which was made earlier about the severe limits on the power of legislation to correct 'abuses' without the more fundamental social changes involved in a redistribution of income. It was no use Parliament attempting to impose requirements on the shipping companies which would have led fares to be priced out of the reach of the emigrants. So long as the existing social structure remained basically untouched the redistributive effect of the legislation was very small, and the pace of change and reform inevitably slow.

Hackney Carriages

It is curious to observe the extent of legislative control over the ordinary hackney cabs and stage coaches in the first half of the nineteenth century. Parliamentarians, lawyers, and political economists alike must have been

[60] Ibid., p. 273.

regular users of hackney cabs at this time. But notwithstanding their many and repeated appeals to the principles of non-interference with contracts, to the ability of the consumer to judge for himself as to the value or safety of the commodity offered to him, and to the unwisdom of legislative attempts at price control, legislation continued to be passed on this subject.

The earliest Acts, which required the licensing of hackney carriages and stagecoaches appear to have been mainly concerned with revenue raising. But the Act of 1831, for the regulation of London hackney carriages, went well beyond that. This Act[61] contained fixed schedules for hire rates, calculated by time or distance at the driver's option, and went on to render void any agreement to pay more than the statutory rate, even going so far as to confer a right to recover any sums overpaid (Section 43). It penalized drivers for refusing to accept, or for overcharging, a passenger.

Further legislation on the subject of stage coaches and hackney carriages took place in 1837,[62] 1843,[63] and 1853.[64] This last Act had a number of provisions designed for the safety of passengers, giving the police power to inspect carriages and to declare them unfit for use. It also required the fare rates to be posted up inside and outside a hackney carriage, and the number of persons permitted to be carried was to be painted on the outside. Section 10 of this Act required the driver to carry a reasonable quantity of luggage without additional charge. A further, more modern piece of legislation is to be found in an Act of 1869[65] which gave the Secretary of State power to make regulations for the control of fares and a number of other matters.

Carriers and the Railways

Before 1830 the protection of the consumer against land carriers was almost entirely a matter for the common law. Common carriers were subject to legal control in a variety of traditional ways. They were obliged to carry goods offered to them at a proper and reasonable charge, and any unjustified refusal was indictable as a common law misdemeanour. They were, moreover, strictly liable for any loss of the goods entrusted to them. These old common law rules were probably not uninfluenced by the fact that many carriers would have had a monopoly of a particular route, and also by the ease with which goods could disappear or be lost through the collusion of the carrier with highwaymen

---

[61] 1 & 2 Will. 4, c. 22.

[62] 1 & 2 Vict., c. 79.

[63] 6 & 7 Vict., c. 86. This Act provided that the owner of the cab could not recover payment from the cab driver except under a written, witnessed agreement (sect. 23).

[64] 16 & 17 Vict., c. 33.

[65] 32 & 33 Vict., c. 115.

and thieves. However, towards the end of the eighteenth century carriers had begun the practice of posting up notices excluding their liability for loss or theft. Because of the very large value of some of the items they were being required to carry (including for instance, packages containing a number of bills of exchange), these exclusion clauses were by no means unreasonable. In *Riley* v. *Horne*[66] their validity was considered by the Common Pleas under Best C.J., a Court largely dedicated to ideas about fairness in contracts which were rapidly becoming obsolete. The Court ruled that the carrier was entitled to charge an appropriate premium against the risk of loss, as well as for the actual carriage, but they went on to hold, in the paternalist spirit favoured by Best C.J., that it was the carrier's duty to inform the consignor properly of the desirability of insuring the goods. 'This is a convenient rule'; said the Chief Justice, 'it imposes no difficulty on the carrier. He knows his own business, and the laws relative to it. Many persons who have occasion to send their goods by carriers, are entirely ignorant of what they ought to do to insure their goods. Justice and policy require that the carriers should be obliged to tell them what they should do.'[67] It would have been interesting to see how later judges would have reacted to this paternalism had the development of the law been left to them. But it was not.

In 1830 Parliament took the hint dropped by Best C.J. in *Riley* v. *Horne* and passed the Carriers Act. Under this Act a carrier was entitled to an increased charge for carrying goods of the value of £10 or over, but was only to be liable for loss provided the true value of the goods was declared. In other cases, that is where the goods were worth less than £10, the carrier was no longer to be allowed to rely on public notices posted up at his office, but was still entitled to rely on any 'special contract'. The subsequent history of these provisions is largely tied up with the railways which had scarcely been thought of in 1830.

There had been a long tradition of imposing controlled rates on monopoly carriers, going back to the earliest canals, as well as affecting the turnpike trusts. When the first railways were constructed it was originally thought that the company owning the lines would have to permit other owners of rolling stock to use their lines; the railways were, in effect, envisaged as roads open to all comers. Perhaps for this reason no control of rates was imposed, although there was power to do this under the Railways Act of 1844 and this Act also gave the State power to take over the railways after twenty-one years, a power which obviously constituted a powerful intimidating threat in the background. The

---

[66] (1828) 5 Bing. 217, 130 E.R. 144. Contrast with this paternalism the views of the Parliamentary Committee in 1825, cited above, p. 507.

[67] 5 Bing. 223, 130 E.R. 1046. See also the previous case in the Report, *Macklin* v. *Waterhouse, Clench and Weeks* (1828) 5 Bing. 212, 130 E.R. 1042.

failure to impose rate control on the railways cannot be put down to any belief in freedom of contract, or *laissez-faire*, because it is quite plain that from the 1840s onwards almost everybody agreed on the necessity for State control over the railways.[68] Even the Political Economy Club unanimously agreed in 1842 that the monopoly power of the railways required them to be placed under the control of the State.[69] And in fact the Board of Trade exercised a degree of supervision and control over many aspects of the railways' business which seems quite startling even today.[70] The 1844 Act also imposed on the railway companies the requirement to run cheap trains for third class passengers.[71]

But if there was no control over general freight rates on the railways, the provisions of the Carriers Act 1830 still applied to them. However, the railways exploited the loophole referring to 'special contracts' by handing printed tickets or notices to consignors on which were printed wide exclusion clauses. These led to much complaint from the public and eventually new provisions were made in the Railway and Canal Traffic Act of 1854. This Act was, unfortunately, very obscurely drafted and it was not until 1863 that the House of Lords finally settled its effect. Basically, the Act permitted the railway companies to contract out of their liability as common carriers (that is, their no-fault liability) by means of a simple printed notice. But control was more stringent over clauses which sought to protect the companies even from liability for negligence. As subsequently interpreted by the House of Lords in *Peek* v. *North Staffordshire Rly. Co.*,[72] such conditions were only valid if they were contained in a document signed by the consignor, and also if they were *just and reasonable*.[73] This case involved something of a clash between parliamentary and judicial attitudes to freedom of contract. As I have sought to demonstrate in this and the previous two chapters, by 1860 the Courts had moved a long way towards acceptance of freedom of contract and all its consequences while Parliament, notwithstanding frequent lip service to the principle, had abandoned it time and again in relation to

---

[68] T. S. Ashton, *Economic History of England in the Eighteenth Century*, pp. 82–3. Again, the Courts seem to have lagged behind parliamentary opinion in upholding 'pooling' agreements which eliminated competition, see, e.g., *Hare* v. *London & N. W. Rly. Co.* (1861) 2 J. & H. 80, 70 E.R. 978.

[69] W. C. Lubenow, *The Politics of Government Growth*, p. 23.

[70] In 1842 a complaint about a late train led to Gladstone asking a railway company for a return of *all* its late trains! W. C. Lubenow, op. cit., p. 36. In 1853 the Board of Trade insisted on a company altering the departure time of a train to enable passengers to make a connection: ibid., p. 142. See generally, Parris, *Government and the Railways in Nineteenth Century Britain* (London, Toronto, 1965), especially Chapter 7.

[71] These came to be known as 'parliamentary trains', a phrase remembered today by virtue of some famous lines in *The Mikado*.

[72] (1862–3) 10 H.L.C. 473, 11 E.R. 1109.

[73] See O. Kahn-Freund, *The Law of Carriage by Inland Transport*, 4th edn. (London, 1965), pp. 218–27.

specific legislation.[74] Among the judges summoned to advise the House of Lords in the *Peek* case it is clear that some of them could scarcely believe it possible that they were required to pronounce on the reasonableness of contractual charges.[75] For years the judges had been accustomed to take the view that a freely made contract was *ex necessitate* just and reasonable, and they had also tended increasingly to disregard monopoly conditions or other factors which rendered the voluntariness of a contract unreal in many circumstances. But there was another problem. Reasonableness was normally a question of fact for a jury, yet this Act made it into a question of law for the judges; and questions of law had to be determined without evidence. How were the judges to decide what was a reasonable charge when no evidence was permitted to be given? In another appeal to the Lords raising the same question some years later Bramwell gave forcible expression to this difficulty: 'Here is a contract made by a fishmonger and a carrier of fish who know their business, and whether it is just or reasonable is to be settled by me who am neither fishmonger nor carrier, nor with any knowledge of their business'.[76]

But the problem had to be solved, and an ingenious solution was found under the guidance of Lord Blackburn. Since no evidence could be given as to the reasonableness of the conditions offered by the railway company, the Courts would insist that a proper choice was offered to the consignor. If the railway company wished to exclude its liability for negligence, it was incumbent upon it to offer the consignor two different sets of terms, one with liability and one without. Provided the additional cost of the former was not exorbitant (though it is not easy to see how the Courts would have judged that) this choice would, in principle, make the contract just and reasonable. In effect the Lords shifted the requirement of reasonableness from a substantive role to a procedural role. So long as the contract was made in a just and reasonable way, the result would be deemed just and reasonable. A just and reasonable way of making a contract was normally to make it in the market where there was a choice between different terms available; since the railways were often a monopoly that possibility did not exist, and therefore a choice had to be offered by the railway company itself.[77] In this way the legislation was interpreted so as to conform with the general tendency of the law to

[74] Section 7 of the Act had been added in Parliament over the objections of Lord Campbell who had said that judges were not competent to judge of the reasonableness of fares: Cleveland-Stevens, *English Railways* (London, 1915), p. 204, n. 1.

[75] See, e.g., the judgments of Willes and Crompton JJ.

[76] *Manchester, Sheffield & Lincolnshire Rly. Co.* v. *Brown* (1883) 8 App. Cas. 703, 716.

[77] For some other legislative controls over quasi-public monopolies in mid-nineteenth century, see W. L. Burn, *The Age of Equipoise*, p. 153, referring to the Gasworks Clauses Act, 1847, and the Waterworks Clauses Act, 1847. The Gas Act of 1860 gave the Home Secretary power to limit price rises on appeal by consumers.

confine its interest to procedural rather than substantive fairness in contracting.

Drink

In *The Wealth of Nations* Adam Smith had argued for free trade in ale as in everything else.[78] He agreed that this freedom was liable to be abused by some people spending too much money on drink, but then, so could many other freedoms. A glutton or a beau (a dandy) might equally spend too much on food or clothes, but that was no reason to control their sale. Moreover, it would generally be to the advantage of the working man to buy his beer as he needed it, a little at a time, instead of brewing it himself or buying in large quantities from the brewer. He should therefore be allowed to buy it from a retailer in the same way as anything else. For many years nobody seems to have taken much notice of these remarks, but after the end of the Napoleonic wars, there was something of a campaign for free trade in drink. This was by no means launched on pure grounds of abstract principle for there were a number of abuses associated with the licensing system then in force. The high taxes on drink were thought by many to encourage smuggling and adulteration, and a Government inquiry in 1821 was sufficiently impressed with these arguments to recommend a reduction of the duty on spirits.[79] The campaign then switched to beer, and it was argued that if the rich were to have free (or anyhow freer) trade in spirits, so the poor should have free trade in beer. Brougham took up the cause and in 1824 even *The Times* argued that the sale of drink should be controlled by the laws of supply and demand and not by licensing laws. In 1830 the (Tory) Government, in the last year of its life, introduced a Bill which had the effect of greatly reducing the duty on beer and allowed any householder to obtain a licence to sell beer on payment of a fee of two guineas. This Bill led to a revolt on the Tory backbenches and it was only carried with the support of the Whigs. There seems little doubt that part of the motivation behind the Bill was the belief in freedom of trade for all commodities, although it has been argued that there were many other factors involved.[80]

If the Beer Act was the result of the belief in freedom of contract it was almost the last time that this belief had much influence on the drink problem. In 1834 a Commons Committee on Drunkenness insisted that '[t]he right to exercise legislative interference [*sic*] for the correction of any evil which affects the public weal, cannot be questioned'.[81] And if this Committee was not wholly representative of Parliamentary opinion,

---

[78] Book IV, Chapter III.
[79] B. Harrison, *Drink and the Victorians* (London, 1971), p. 65.
[80] Ibid., pp. 81-2.   [81] Ibid., pp. 110-12.

the fact remains that many of the Whig M.P.s who had voted for free trade in drink in the heady days when they scented power just ahead of them in 1830, subsequently lived to modify their ideas in the light of experience. Among them was M. D. Hill, a barrister and subsequently Recorder of Birmingham, M.P. from 1832 to 1835. In 1855 he wrote that in his youth he had, in common with many other supporters of *laissez-faire*, believed 'its dominion to be almost unbounded', but that he had later come to modify his opinions. So far as the drink question was concerned, he was now convinced that the State had a complete right to regulate the trade because of the huge expense incurred by society in dealing with the consequences of drunkenness.[82]

The usual result gradually unfolded. Statutory regulation of the sale of drinks and the opening hours of drink shops, was steadily tightened up, and the duties were increased throughout the 1830s. In 1872 the virtually free licensing of beer shops was brought to an end, and they were placed firmly under the control of the justices once again. And apart from legislation, there was, throughout the Victorian era, a most vigorous temperance movement which, at least from 1853, openly campaigned for legislative prohibition. Lord Brougham who, like M. D. Hill, seems to have changed his views as he got older, gave strong support to the U. K. Alliance, the prohibition movement, though he was not himself an abstainer. Bramwell, by contrast, reacted strongly against them, and even wrote a pamphlet on the subject in which he defended the Englishman's right to decide for himself if he wanted to drink.[83] Although the prohibition movement never made much headway in Parliament, its support throughout the country even in the 1850s and 1860s suggests that coercive laws designed for a man's own good would not have been condemned by the people at large nearly so enthusiastically as they were condemned by John Stuart Mill in *On Liberty*. F. R. Lees, who wrote in 1857 the Prize Essay for the U. K. Alliance on the subject of prohibition,[84] totally rejected *laissez-faire* ideas and the minimal role of the State. Unlike Dicey who thought that Benthamism was synonymous with *laissez-faire* liberalism, this author took his stand with Bentham's principles of legislation in order to make a sustained plea for Government suppression of the drink trade. 'The activity of the State', he insisted, 'if it be a wise activity, is no more objectionable than the activity of an Individual'.[85]

[82] W. L. Burn, *The Age of Equipoise*, p. 283.

[83] Lord Palmerston seems to have agreed. He defended his policy over the sale of opium to China by saying that it was not the duty of the British to protect the morals of the Chinese 'who were disposed to buy what other people were disposed to sell'. When accused of forcing the Chinese to buy opium he said that that was as if a man were accused of forcing an Englishman to drink beer: J. Ridley, *Lord Palmerston*, p. 350.

[84] *An Argument for the Legislative Prohibition of the Liquor Traffic*, 3rd edn. (London and Manchester, 1857).   [85] Ibid., p. 30.

COMPANY LAW

The century after 1770 saw the rise and development of modern company law, and a brief reference is necessary to this important chapter in legal history because it was, in its origins, closely linked to the concept of freedom of contract in various respects. From the last third of the eighteenth century two quite distinct types of commercial organization had been coming into existence. On the one hand there were the statutory companies, incorporated under Acts of Parliament, and usually involving works of some magnitude. In particular most of the canal companies were established in this way between 1766 and 1800; in fact 81 were created in three 'mania years' between 1791 and 1794.[86] Subsequently, the railway companies were created in similar fashion, and again there were a series of boom years, the first just after 1825, the second in and after 1836, and the third, and easily the largest and wildest, in 1845–7. In the 46 years between 1801 and 1847 nearly one thousand Railway Acts were passed.[87] These statutory corporations possessed most of the attributes which later came to be associated with the modern public company; they were given corporate personality, with the right to sue and be sued, their capital was subscribed partly by shareholders who were given freely transferable shares, and partly by secured debenture holders who likewise had freely transferable debentures; and the investors had the benefit of limited liability. All these benefits were sanctioned by Parliament in some sort of a statutory bargain, in which the rights of third parties were protected and the public interest was not overlooked. For example, as we have seen, there was control of freight rates in many of the Canal Acts, and the railway companies had to accept a considerable measure of govermental supervision as the price of their Statutes.

Towards the end of the eighteenth century, the upsurge in commercial and industrial activity associated with the industrial revolution, led also to the growth of non-statutory 'companies'. Legally speaking these bodies were partnerships, with elaborate 'Deeds of Settlement' drawn up so as to confer as many as possible of the advantages of corporate status. In the absence of any legal provision for the creation of corporations by mere registration, and in the absence too of a Royal Charter or an Act of Parliament, these companies could not strictly speaking be treated as bodies corporate. They could not sue or be sued in their own names, and they could not be invested with the benefit of limited liability. The 'shareholders' were, in law, partners, and as such, liable for the whole debts of the business. In fact many of these Deeds of Settlement tried to

---

[86] Hunt, *The Development of the Business Corporation in England 1800 to 1867* (Cambridge, Mass., 1936), p. 10.
[87] W. C. Lubenow, *The Politics of Government Growth*, Chapter 4.

overcome these problems by including contractual clauses whereby the shareholders were entitled to limited liability *inter se*; and they often advertised for shareholders to whom they offered 'limited liability'. They also attempted, so far as practicable, to make their shares freely transferable. By 1800 there was a considerable number of such companies in existence, and by 1820 or thereabouts, very large quantities of capital had been subscribed in them, and many larger scale businesses were operating in this fashion.

There was, lurking in the background, a serious legal difficulty in the form of the so-called Bubble Act of 1720 which had never been invoked, but which cast some doubt on the legality of the new unincorporated companies. But it was not only their legality which was in question, for many people were dubious of their desirability. Companies had traditionally been associated with monopolies in England; the old Chartered corporation had usually been given a monopoly of a particular trade, or area of activity, and many of the canal and railway companies, although not necessarily monopolies, were in practice likely to have some monopoly element. And there were many who saw dangers in any corporate activity which was not subject to parliamentary approval. On the other hand, there were those who urged that freedom of contract necessarily conferred the right to join together with others in a business enterprise. By modern standards, some of those who took part in these debates are to be found on what appears to be the 'wrong' side. For example, when in 1810 a Committee on Insurance advocated the repeal of the Bubble Act, and cited Adam Smith on the need for more competition in the insurance industry, they were met by a furious onslaught from Lloyds underwriters in defence of individualism in business. 'Was not Britain's unexampled prosperity', they demanded, 'due to the competition of individual exertions?' The very concept of a joint-stock company, they declared in a somewhat inaccurate prophecy, was an 'exploded system'.[88]

But early in the nineteenth century, opinion was beginning to shift in favour of the new joint-stock companies, particularly for enterprises requiring large scale capital, beyond the resources of individuals. In 1806 Sir Frederick Eden (known to history chiefly for his work on *The State of the Poor*) made a spirited argument for incorporation at least for insurance companies in a tract, *On the Policy and Expediency of Granting Insurance Charters*. Because of the long term nature of many insurance contracts, especially life insurance, and because of the nature of the risks involved, he argued that the insured was more likely to be protected by a company with a joint-stock than by the liability of any individual, however prosperous. He also argued that incorporation and monopoly

[88] Hunt, *The Development of the Business Corporation in England*, pp. 23–4.

were two distinct things, for there was no reason why companies should not compete against each other as much as individuals. In the state of business and commercial enterprises at the time he was writing, and indeed, for many years afterwards, Eden was probably accurate in drawing this distinction. Most corporations, except those created by Act of Parliament, remained relatively small businesses until late in the nineteenth century; and their existence did not prevent competition. In the mid-1820s when freedom of contract arguments appear to have been at their highest point, one 'Leguleius' in the *Morning Chronicle* called for a hands-off policy in the name of 'that sacred and golden principle of political economy—not to interfere with the mode in which individuals employ, or even squander their money . . .'[89]

Nevertheless, the Bubble Act was still on the statute book (though nobody knew what it meant) and, what was more, Lord Eldon was still on the woolsack. Eldon was at his most reactionary, and it may be added, at his most irresponsible, in dealing with the new companies. Even after the Act was repealed in 1825,[90] he continued to threaten to treat unincorporated companies as illegal associations at common law.[91] In one case,[92] where a bona fide dispute between members of a company was brought before the Chancery for resolution, and where both counsel unhesitatingly accepted the legality of the company, Eldon nevertheless threatened to hold it illegal; though in the end he did decide the dispute on its merits. He was, however, supported by Best C.J. whose old-fashioned views had (as we have seen) led him to oppose the *caveat emptor* principle, but who, on this subject, sided against history.[93] Clearly, this could not go on in the new age. In 1833 Lord Brougham repudiated the idea that these unincorporated companies could be *per se* illegal,[94] and a decade later the issue was put beyond doubt by the Courts of Common Law.[95] These decisions were closely followed by Gladstone's Companies Act of 1844 which provided for the registration and incorporation of companies along modern lines. Their legality was thus settled.

But legality was one thing, limited liability was another. And on this issue, both the opponents and the proponents relied on freedom of contract arguments. Those who favoured the principle of limited liability

[89] Ibid., p. 40.

[90] As a result of *Josephs* v. *Pebrer* (1825) 3 B. & C. 639, 107 E.R. 870, where the Act was invoked to hold a company illegal, though in this case, not without some cause.

[91] Ellenborough was much less hysterical on this question, see *R.* v. *Dodd* (1808) 9 East 516, 103 E.R. 670; *R.* v. *Webb* (1814) 14 East 406, 104 E.R. 658.

[92] *Kinder* v. *Taylor* (1825) 3 L.J. Ch. 68; see also *Van Sandau* v. *Moore* (1825) 1 Russ. 441, 38 E.R. 171.

[93] *Duvergier* v. *Fellowes* (1828) 5 Bing. 267, 130 E.R. 1056.

[94] *Walburn* v. *Ingelby* (1833) 1 My. & K. 61, 39 E.R. 604.

[95] *Garrard* v. *Hardey* (1843) 5 M. & G. 471, 134 E.R. 648; *Harrison* v. *Heathorn* (1843) 6 M. & G. 81, 134 E.R. 817.

argued that a person who made a contract with a company would know that its shareholders had limited liability, and must, therefore, be deemed to contract on that basis. Those who did not favour the principle argued that the existing law, which rendered a man liable in full for his (and his partner's) debts, was the 'natural' state of things, and any change in this law would be an unwarranted 'interference' with freedom of contract. Among those in favour of limited liability were John Stuart Mill and Baron Bramwell. Among those against were Huskisson, Brougham, and J. R. McCulloch. For some thirty years the debate raged furiously. In 1824, even before the repeal of the Bubble Act, Huskisson objected to limited liability as an 'interference with private contracts',[96] but in the same year the mathematician and actuary, Charles Babbage, wrote that, '[i]t will scarcely be credited some years hence that well informed persons seriously questioned whether, if two parties entered into a written agreement ... the one to purchase ... the other to contract a certain limited responsibility ... the law ought not to interfere and compel the one to incur a greater responsibility than the other has paid for'.[97]

Nearly thirty years later, the disagreements were still as profound as ever. The Mercantile Law Commissioners were unable to reach any satisfactory conclusion on the question in their first Report,[98] though one of its members, Bramwell, had no doubt about the proper answer.[99] In his usual, rather simplistic fashion, Bramwell said the question was whether it was desirable to prohibit, by law, persons from dealing together 'on the terms that the liability of one or more or all' should be limited? He insisted that limited liability would impose no compulsion but would merely remove a restriction in the law. He then went on to examine the objections to the proposal which had been put forward. These objections, he asserted, contended that limited liability might be against the interests of, first, the partners (or members of a company), secondly, those who dealt with them, and thirdly, the public. He protested vigorously against the first two objections having a hearing at all.

I will not say the State has no right, because to that expression no determinate idea is annexed; but I do say that it ought not to interfere to prevent, for their own sakes, any persons from entering into any agreement they may be willing to form. There may be real or apparent exceptions to this rule, as where the thing agreed to be done is malum in se; but for the purpose of protecting the parties themselves, I say the State ought not to interfere, but to leave every man to the most zealous and best informed of all protectors, himself.[1]

---

[96] *Hansard* (N.S.), vol. 11, col. 1088 (1824).
[97] Hunt, *The Development of the Business Corporation in England*, p. 33.
[98] (1854) H.C. *Parliamentary Papers*, xxvii. 445 *et seq.*   [99] At pp. 467–72.
[1] At p. 468. J. S. Mill says much the same in his *Principles*, Book V, Chapter IX, sect. 6, and this has been said to be 'the classic formulation of the principle'. L. Robbins, *Evolution of Modern Economic Theory* (London, 1970), p. 152.

On the other side, J. R. McCulloch was equally dogmatic, and equally appealed to first principles:

In the scheme laid down by Providence for the government of the world there is no shifting or narrowing of responsibilities, every man being personally answerable for all his actions. But the advocates of limited responsibility proclaim in their superior wisdom that the scheme of Providence may be advantageously modified, and that duties and obligations may be contracted which the debtors, though they have the means, shall not be bound to discharge.[2]

Perhaps the most surprising thing about this whole debate is the somewhat low level of sophistication of the arguments. Virtually the only practical issues discussed were whether limited liability would encourage additional capital to be invested in industry, and whether there was any shortage of capital such that an encouragement was needed; and, secondly, whether limited liability would not unduly encourage risky and speculative enterprises embarked upon by those who knew that they themselves had little or nothing to lose.[3] Nor was there much appreciation of another important result of limited liability, namely that it enabled large losses to be widely spread, because the failure of a business would lead to small losses amongst all the creditors of a business, instead of large losses amongst a small number of shareholders.[4]

But the outcome of the debate appears today to have had an air of inevitability about it. For it is apparent from the perspective of the twentieth century that limited liability was only part of a broad process which was taking place at the middle of the nineteenth century, to limit the responsibility of contracting parties.[5] There were, for example, the bankruptcy laws which had been reformed and modernized in the 1830s, with the abolition of imprisonment on *mesne* process, and generally facilitating the discharge of bankrupt creditors. So too, common law decisions like *Hadley* v. *Baxendale*[6] and *Cox* v. *Hickman*[7] can be seen as part of the same process. Indeed, it is possible that, if Parliament had not passed the Limited Liability Act in 1855, the Courts would have 'implied'

---

[2] Cited Hunt, *The Development of the Business Corporation in England*, p. 117. Elsewhere McCulloch wrote in a less lofty vein that the question was not one of abstract principle, but of practical results: D. P. O'Brien, *J. R. McCulloch* (London, 1976), p. 291.

[3] A. J. Saville, 'Sleeping Partnership and Limited Liability 1850–1856', 7 *Economic History Rev.* (N.S.) 418 (1956).

[4] See Pigou, *The Economics of Welfare*, 4th edn. (London, 1960), Appendix, sects. 10–11.

[5] Perhaps this movement was indeed part of a still broader process of limiting the liability of enterprises and activities generally and thereby subsidizing them. It has been argued that in America the parallel process was a more or less conscious policy of favouring commercial and industrial activity: Morton J. Horwitz, *The Transformation of American Law* (Cambridge, Mass. and London, 1977).

[6] (1854) 9 Ex. 341, 156 E.R. 145.

[7] (1860) 8 H.L.C. 268, 11 E.R. 431.

contractual terms limiting liability at common law. The Courts had in 1852 upheld the validity of an express limited liability clause in an insurance contract,[8] though two years later it was held that such clauses could not be implied as against creditors.[9] But it was becoming common practice at this time for many companies to contract subject to an express provision for limited liability, and if it had not been for the Act of 1855 it is not unlikely that the Courts would have gradually shown willingness to 'imply' such a clause, perhaps from constructive notice of the provisions of the Deed of Settlement.[10]

Nobody, in the course of this debate, seems to have raised the question of tort liabilities. Was the victim of a tort also to be deemed to have 'dealt' with the company on the terms that its members were to have limited liability?[11]

There was one other issue in the emerging company law which involved arguments about freedom of contract, and that concerned the extent of the liability of investing shareholders for the acts of their directors. Were the investors to be deemed to buy shares subject to the old principle *caveat emptor*? Were they to be deemed capable of understanding balance sheets and other such documents published by directors? Were they (or the company itself, come to that) to be liable on all contracts entered into by the directors, no matter how remote they might be from the original purposes of the company? The answer to these and similar questions was an emphatic No from virtually everyone. Economists, lawyers, the press and parliamentarians were at one on these questions, and that is perhaps not surprising. Those who made public opinion were on the whole investors and potential investors, and they saw too many signs of fraudulent directors to feel any responsibility for the acts of their directors. On the contrary, they demanded protection from them. In 1825 the *Morning Chronicle*, normally a staunch supporter of *laissez-faire*, utterly rejected the applicability of *caveat emptor* to the investing public.[12] Ten years later J. R. McCulloch, writing in the *Edinburgh Review*, declared that he was astonished that anyone should think that the publication of balance sheets or profit and loss accounts was an adequate protection to investors.[13] Most of them, he said, were quite unable to understand them at all. And at the height of the railway mania in 1845, even Gladstone wrote to the Chancellor of the Exchequer urging that

[8] *Hallett* v. *Dowdall* (1852) 21 L.J. Q.B. 98.

[9] *Re Sea Fire and Life Assurance Co.* (1854) 3 De G. M. & G. 459, 43 E.R. 180.

[10] See *Ridley* v. *Plymouth Grinding & Baking Co.* (1848) 2 Ex. 711, 154 E.R. 676; *Kingsbridge Flour Mill Co.* v. *Plymouth Grinding & Baking Co.* (1848) 2 Ex. 718, 154 E.R. 679. See too Maitland, 'Trust and Corporation', *Collected Papers* (Cambridge, 1911), iii. 392.

[11] Berle and Means, *The Modern Corporation and Private Property*, revised edn. (New York, 1967), p. 120, n. 2.

[12] Hunt, *The Development of the Business Corporation in England*, p. 54.

[13] Ibid., p. 70.

'there is little force in the popular argument that private parties are the best judges as to the expenditure of their own capital to these companies under present circumstances'.[14] And in the following year he wrote, that 'with regard to joint-stock speculation we are a nation of children who will not allow our nursery maids to govern us'.[15]

One result of the numerous frauds and scandals affecting companies at this time was the serious discussion of the possibility of subjecting railway company accounts to a Government audit. A Select Committee reported in favour of this proposal in 1849,[16] but a subsequent Bill was defeated in Parliament.[17] The principal reasons for the rejection of the Bill seem to have been the shortage of qualified accountants and also the fear that Government audited accounts would be regarded by the public as carrying a State guarantee of their accuracy.

It is against this background that the case law relating to the *ultra vires* doctrine must be understood. In a series of cases culminating in *Ashbury Rly. Co. v. Riche*[18] the Courts insisted that a company had no power to make contracts beyond the authority conferred in the memorandum of association. In later years, this decision came to be seen as unfair to third parties who contracted with a company in reliance on the apparent control of the company exercised by its directors. Sympathy was switched from the shareholders to the commercial third parties who were thought to be entitled to rely on the apparent authority of the directors. But in the middle of the nineteenth century, everyone sympathized a great deal more with the unfortunate investors. It was widely felt that they had perforce to rely on the directors who ran the companies, and that third parties who dealt with the company were in a much better position to make due inquiry concerning the authority of the directors. This point of view is to be found in the works of such widely differing writers as John Stuart Mill[19] and Herbert Spencer.[20] It is also to be found in nearly all the relevant cases in the third quarter of the century.[21]

---

[14] Ibid., p. 104.

[15] F. E. Hyde, *Mr. Gladstone at the Board of Trade* (London, 1934), p. 190.

[16] (1849) H.C. *Parliamentary Papers*, x, p. xvii.

[17] Hunt op. cit., p. 113.

[18] (1875) L.R. 7 H.L. 653.

[19] *Principles*, Book V, Chapter XI, sect. 11, mainly concerned with monopoly companies.

[20] Herbert Spencer, *Essay on Railway Morals* (1854), p. 89. This Essay states the layman's case for the *Ashbury* decision with great clarity. See too Jhering, *Law as a Means to an End* (English translation, Boston, 1913), p. 167, arguing that self-interest did not work well where property owners delegated its management to administrators such as company directors.

[21] Even in *Royal British Bank* v. *Turquand* (1859) 3 De G. & J. 387, 44 E.R. 1317, where the directors were held to have had authority to bind the company, Lord Chelmsford plainly shows his sympathy with the shareholders at pp. 428–9, 1333–4 of the respective reports.

Part III

The Decline and Fall of Freedom of Contract: 1870–1970

17

THE CONDITION OF ENGLAND, 1870–1970

In the century which has elapsed since 1870 a number of landmarks stand out in what seems, in restrospect, to have been a period of continuous decline for England. The two world wars, the Great Depression between them, the disintegration of the British Empire, and the economic difficulties of the past thirty years, all seem to have been facets of this decline. But for present purposes this is a misleading perspective. In relative terms, both politically and economically, there is of course no doubt that England has slipped steadily down the league table during this past century. But it is also true that England has become an immeasurably richer country during this period. England now has, in common with the industrialized Western world, what no country had in 1870—a working class educated enough and prosperous enough to share in many of the good things of life. The consumer society has arrived. And, among the other changes which have taken place during this past century, so also the democratic society has arrived. England was a free country in 1870 but it was barely a democratic country. Only in 1867 was the vote conferred on the mass of industrial workmen, not until 1884 was the like right conceded to the agricultural labourer, and only after the First World War, was the principle adopted of one man (and one woman), one vote. Two other changes have taken place which make modern England a vastly different country from what it was in 1870. The first of these is the growth of the corporate society. The increase in the number and power of the institutions in which men are organized for economic and other purposes has created centres of collective power undreamed of in 1870. First corporations and then trade unions have acquired immense powers over individuals and even over Government itself. And fourthly, there has been a huge and very visible change in the activities of Government in all its forms. Central Government has become a vast bureaucracy, perhaps tottering on the brink of that self-defeating strangulation which seems to affect all bureaucracies once they advance beyond a certain size. And, apart from central Government, this century has seen a great proliferation in the variety of Government's manifestations in society. Local Government, organized, and reorganized, nationalized industries, boards, commissions, authorities, and agencies, all are brought into existence, and given powers of control and regulation over the lives of the citizen. Such is the extent of the interference in the regulation and management of the economic system that we have become accustomed to the idea that we live today under a 'mixed economy', a union of private enterprise and public control, and even management of large sectors of the economy. In this chapter I shall look briefly at these four major themes of change in the past century, each of which has had profound repercussions on the concept of contract.

THE CONSUMER SOCIETY

The additional wealth created by the Industrial Revolution had (as we have previously observed) little impact in improving the standard of living of the English working class before the middle of the nineteenth century. But from then on the improvement in general standards of living became more and more pronounced. Between 1850 and 1880 national income nearly doubled, and income per head increased by some 25 to 30 per cent.[1] After 1870 there was for some twenty or thirty years a period which became known as the Great Depression, during which agriculture in particular, was much affected by the flood of cheap imported food from the United States. But not everyone suffered from these changes in the economic scene. Corn growing farmers certainly suffered, and the acres under wheat fell by fifty per cent between 1870 and 1910, but dairy farmers actually benefited from the cheaper grain prices. And the working classes had no cause for complaint as the prices of many foodstuffs dropped steadily.[2] It was true that, for those who could see them, there were ominous writings on the wall. Britain's industrial leadership had already largely come to an end as the productive capacity of American and German industry began to surge forward and as tariff barriers were erected by many countries trying to keep out English exports in order to protect their own nascent industries. Between perhaps 1870 and 1940 the Empire helped to provide the markets that were beginning to disappear elsewhere, but already by 1900 it was clear that Britain's undisputed position as the workshop of the world was at an end. Increasingly Britain was relying for her exports on capital plant and equipment which, once installed and productive overseas, would inevitably cut still more deeply into exports of manufactured goods. By 1900 British industrial growth had slowed down so much that it was barely keeping pace with expanding population. Between 1900 and 1914 *per capita* income scarcely increased at all.[3]

The overseas countries who were thus protecting themselves from

---

[1] W. L. Burn, *The Age of Equipoise*, p. 16.
[2] C. H. Wilson, *Economic History and the Historian*, Chapter 11.
[3] R. S. Sayers, *A History of Economic Change in England 1880–1939* (Oxford, 1967, reprinted 1973), p. 11.

British competition, and competing with Britain for markets elsewhere, had none of them developed along the same lines as Britain herself. In every case these countries had seen a much closer degree of partnership or co-operation between industry and Government. The need for protective tariffs had inevitably led their industries to seek the help of their Governments, and both in Germany and the United States, Government had in fact been called upon in a large variety of ways, for assistance in the development of their economies. Inevitably, British businessmen, watching these events from afar, began to look on Government activity at home with a less hostile gaze. 'Increasingly, business, in one way or another, called on the state not only to give it a free hand, but to save it.'[4] And, as the new century opened, some politicians, like Joseph Chamberlain, were prepared to respond. For the first time for half a century, Englishmen began to talk seriously of turning their backs on the free trade policy, and introducing protective and retaliatory tariff barriers themselves.

But despite these ominous trends, the period between 1870 and 1914 saw a great increase in working-class prosperity. Real wages of urban workers increased perhaps sixty per cent between 1860 and 1900.[5] For the first time in English history the working classes were themselves becoming a substantial market for manufactured goods. A great variety of new goods was becoming available to meet this demand, and so were new methods of retailing them. Towards the end of the nineteenth century new shops, new advertising, much of it in the new penny newspapers, and prepared consumer goods such as ready-made clothes, shoes, patent medicines, and some pre-cooked or pre-packaged foodstuffs were becoming widely available. Where such goods had previously been supplied, if at all, from the village craftsman, they were now pouring out of the factories. 'From machine to shop there flowed the branded, packaged, standardized, advertised products newly characteristic of this urbanized, industrialized society that was setting itself new patterns and standards of social life.'[6] The only consumer item whose consumption began to drop, at any rate after 1900, was beer, and that was a gain, rather than anything else, for it signalled the beginning of the emancipation of the English working class from the excesses of alcohol.

Between 1875 and 1914 a revolution occurred in the distributive trades to meet these new mass consumer demands. New techniques, new wholesale and retail organizations, new flamboyant window displays, and above all new methods of advertising gradually spread through the economy. Great new department stores grew up, like Debenhams, Swan

[4] E. J. Hobsbawn, *Industry and Empire*, p. 131.
[5] P. Mathias, *The First Industrial Nation*, p. 378.
[6] C. H. Wilson, *Economic History and the Historian*, p. 181.

and Edgar, and the Army and Navy in London, and David Lewis in the provinces, stores which set out 'to make retailing "democratic" in an increasingly democratic age'.[7] And so too did the multiples like Boots chemists' shops and the new style co-operative stores. Durables, too, made a modest appearance. Bicycles, sewing machines, furniture, and other household goods began to be bought by the working class, ready to take advantage of their increased leisure hours, or to furnish and equip the better housing now becoming available.

In a hundred different ways the new range of goods and the new methods of retailing them differed from the older pattern, and (in due course) raised new social and legal problems. First, there was the disappearance of the old casual credit selling of groceries and household necessities. Many of the new stores were able to cut their prices vigorously by refusing credit altogether. Some, like Boots, even made a virtue of it by incorporating the word 'Cash' into their trade names. But as the older style of credit selling disappeared, new demands for credit arose. Items like furniture, bicycles, and sewing machines had sufficient durability and sufficient value to constitute an acceptable security, and new moneylending techniques grew up to assist the working class to buy such items on credit. First, bills of sale were widely used as security for such credit, and later, after the first legislative protection for the users of this credit had been passed, there was a switch to the new hire-purchase. This blossomed rapidly, and by the end of the nineteenth century was the established way of selling goods on credit, while retaining some security right over the goods.

A second major change which came with the new stores was the disappearance of higgling over prices. Fixed prices became the rule everywhere, and, slowly at first, resale price maintenance made its appearance. Many of the larger stores fought against resale price maintenance because their profitability lay largely in the ability to undercut the smaller older style shopkeepers by more efficient organization and bulk buying. But the mass of small tradesmen protested bitterly against these low prices with which they could not compete, and it was they who in the first instance brought pressure to bear on manufacturers to impose minimum resale prices. Another change was the gradual elimination of the producer-cum-seller, and the rise of the branded, pre-packaged products.

The big jars of loose syrup and treacle, the open sacks of flour and sugar and oatmeal, the barrels of currants, the cannisters of coffee-beans, the chests of tea, disappeared one by one, from the sawdusted floor of the traditional grocer and were replaced by shelves upon shelves of branded pre-packaged articles that neither mouse or dust could corrupt nor dogs walk in and defile.[8]

[7] Asa Briggs, *Friends of the People* (London, 1956), p. 39.
[8] D. Davis, *A History of Shopping* (London and Toronto, 1966), p. 284.

Of course, as every lawyer knows, the pre-packaged articles might not be open to mice on the grocer's shelves, but they were not immune from contamination by mice or snails or other foreign matter while still in the manufacturer's hands. That too gave rise to legal issues over the responsibility of the manufacturer to the ultimate consumer in the 1930s. But meantime the large department stores and the multiples had themselves initiated a new policy by offering to take back and replace defective or unsatisfactory goods without question. This policy was important because it meant that the consumer did not have to examine the particular article he was buying—indeed, where it was, as now so often the case, pre-packaged, he could not easily do this anyhow. 'The willing exchange of unsatisfactory goods established links of confidence between buyer and seller, even though they might not know each other personally as traditional retailers and their customers had done.'[9] It also made it more reasonable for the consumer-buyer to rely on the integrity of the seller.

The new signs of working-class prosperity were not to be found solely in the goods they bought. Other aspects of their lives were also changing for the better during these years. Better housing, for example, drained and sewered as required by the Public Health Acts, was becoming the norm. Municipal housing, under the Artisans Dwelling Acts, despite the old-fashioned name of the enactments, was, for many, a substantial improvement, and other municipal facilities, such as baths and wash rooms were also becoming available. Then there was a great increase in leisure. The appallingly long hours of the early Industrial Revolution were over at last, for adults as well as children. In 1871 the August Bank Holiday was sanctified by Parliament, Saturday had become a half-day for many workers, and paid summer holidays began to become widespread in the 1880s. Entertainments and sports grew up as the working class began to have the leisure to turn to them. The musical-hall, the Saturday afternoon football match in the winter, the seaside excursion train in the summer, had arrived.[10] And, of course, there was also the spread of literacy with the introduction, first of the national Education Act of 1870, and eventually, of compulsory elementary schooling.

Another change which made its appearance during these years was the great expansion in advertising, the beginnings of the use of advertising to create wants, or to persuade the consumer by 'vigorous assertion', rather than by merely giving him information.[11] Much of this advertising seems, by modern standards, to have descended readily to downright fraud and dishonesty. In 1884 David Lewis affronted the Manchester coal dealers by advertising coal which he claimed would

[9] Asa Briggs, *Friends of the People*, pp. 28–9.
[10] G. Kitson Clark, *The Making of Victorian England* (reprinted, Edinburgh, 1970), pp. 145–6.
[11] J. B. Jeffreys, *Retail Trading in Britain 1850–1950* (Cambridge, 1954), p. 38.

burn for twice as long as any other coal merchant's fuel.[12] Not surprisingly he declined to submit his claim to empirical verification. The patent medicine and drug trade was also a fruitful field for wild and extravagant claims, such as 'the dubious claims of curative syrups and "electric" belts to disperse all human ills from heart disease to indigestion'.[13] And no lawyer will overlook the immortal claim to fame of the Carbolic Smoke Ball Company which offered £100 reward to any person who used their smoke ball as prescribed and still had the misfortune to fall a victim to 'flu, a cold, or any other disease caused by taking cold.[14] These advertisements were being widely disseminated in the new popular press whose respect for the truth was little greater than that of its advertisers. The new *Daily Mail*, which first appeared in 1896, was deliberately designed to cater for the literate working classes. It differed from the traditional newspapers in that it did not simply print the news leaving the reader to draw his own conclusions; the *Daily Mail* not only gave its readers the facts, it also told them what they ought to think. Its advertisements did much the same.

As the working man began to settle into his new style of life towards the end of the nineteenth and the beginning of the twentieth century, his demands for greater security became more insistent. As his life-style became more orderly, more regular, so his expectations rose, and when, therefore, he suffered a temporary, or even more, a permanent loss of income, through injury, sickness, unemployment, or old age, his need for something to fall back upon became more pressing. Working men began to feel (as Hume and Adam Smith had argued many years earlier) that to be deprived of what you have is to suffer a greater wrong than not to be given what you have never had. As Galbraith has put it:

In the grim world of Ricardo and Malthus, the ordinary citizen could have no interest in social security in the modern sense. If a man's wage is barely sufficient for existence, he does not worry much about the greater suffering of unemployment. Life is a heavy burden in either case. Men who are engaged in a daily struggle for survival do not think of old age for they do not expect to see it. When the normal expectation of life is very low, sickness and death are normal hazards . . . With increasing well-being all people become aware, sooner or later, that they have something to protect.[15]

These rising expectations ultimately had important repercussions on the law, both private, judge-made law, and public, statutory law. Just as possession of property had given rise to expectations which had led to the recognition of property rights; just as contractual arrangements had

[12] Asa Briggs, *Friends of the People*, pp. 75-6.
[13] C. H. Wilson, *Economic History and the Historian*, p. 190.
[14] [1893] 1 Q.B. 256, *post*, p. 677.
[15] *The Affluent Society*, 2nd edn. (London, 1969), p. 104.

created expectations which had led to the recognition of the executory contract and the right to damages in protection of those expectations, so now working people, becoming used to a regular weekly or monthly pay packet, began to develop new expectations which required protection. The development of tort rights to damages to compensate for a lost income, and the recognition of Workmen's Compensation rights, and later of social security rights for sickness and unemployment, were the result of these rising expectations. I shall, later, have to say something further about the particular form which these developments took.

The two world wars, and even the great depression between them, did little more than interrupt the increasing affluence of the working class and a continuation of the trends begun around 1870. Although these events were, inevitably, a searing experience for those who lived through them, although the First World War destroyed the old social order perhaps more than any other event, and although the two wars greatly impoverished the nation, the setbacks, in purely economic terms, were merely temporary. National income rose by 37·5 per cent between 1913 and 1937, and income per head by some 23 per cent, a considerably higher growth rate than had prevailed just before the First World War.[16] Part of this increase in (real) income was due, as in the period 1870 to 1890, to falling world prices for food. As a major importer of foodstuffs, Britain benefited from the low prices caused by the Depression. A basket of food which cost £8 in 1927 could be had for £6 11s. in 1931 and only £6 in 1933.[17] And even the great slump between 1929 and 1938, surprising though it may seem, did not prevent a considerable increase in national income.[18] During this decade Britain was near the top of the league in growth rates, and only two countries recorded higher increases in the rates of productivity per man. Total output grew at 2·3 per cent per annum between 1929 and 1938, an average growth rate which was actually higher than the rate between 1870 and 1913, and much more than the rate between 1913 and 1929.[19] Despite the dreadful unemployment, the appallingly depressed state of many traditional industries such as Manchester textiles, coal mining, shipbuilding, and agriculture, the fact remains that most English people were substantially better off on the eve of the Second World War than they had ever been before. There were two million unemployed, but 'for the four out of five who were still in work there was a sizeable and growing margin for new forms of consumption'.[20] For all the depressed state of some industries, there were a number of new industries where vigorous growth was taking place.

[16] P. Mathias, *The First Industrial Nation*, p. 432.

[17] R. S. Sayers, *A History of Economic Change in England*, p. 57.

[18] Aldcroft, 'Economic Growth in Britain in the Inter-War Years: a Re-appraisal', 20 *Economic History Rev.* 311 (1967).

[19] Ibid., p. 312.   [20] R. S. Sayers, *A History of Economic Change in England*, p. 57.

The motor industry and a whole string of related industries, such as those in rubber, oil refining, metals and mechanical engineering, electrical goods, with their associated capital investment in the generation of power, radios and telephones, were all booming in the inter-war period. Standards of living continued to rise, and the consumer society was increasingly taking shape.

After the Second World War Britain's economy had suffered severe dislocation, and the gradual disintegration of the old Empire and the markets which it had provided for British goods, added to the problems. The long story of economic crises from 1945 until the present day, the succession of booms and recessions, the recurring balance of payments difficulties and the slow, apparently inexorable, fall in the value of the pound are a story all too familiar to those who have lived through it. But, at any rate until the 1970s, national income was still rising, and so were average earnings. The factories poured out a stream of radios and television sets, vacuum cleaners, washing machines, refrigerators, and motor vehicles. The consumer society had arrived. The demand for more and more consumer goods and services, together, perhaps, with the ready promises of the politicians, gradually created a situation in which public expectations were raised to higher and still higher levels. People began to take for granted an annual increase of earning power, and the more they got, the more they expected. Inevitably, the crash had to come when public expectations could no longer be met, a position reached perhaps in 1974 or 1975. For present purposes the important point concerns the role of the individual as a consumer, and his rights in relation to the economic system of which he used to be the theoretical sovereign. In one sense it seems true that in this modern world the consumer is more firmly than ever enthroned at the centre of the economic picture, in the sense, that is, that almost everyone agrees that the fundamental purpose of society and the economic system is to provide him with more and more of the good things of life. But there is another sense in which the position of the individual consumer has been eroded by the decline of the free market, and a number of other developments which have deprived the consumer of much of his freedom of choice in the controlled and regulated market which still exists. The consumer does, of course, still have a considerable degree of choice, even in the regulated economy of modern England. The Englishman thinks of himself as a free man living in a free country. He can still choose where he is to live, what work he is to do, and how he will spend his income. Or can he? In fact these three simple propositions need a great deal of qualification if the reality of the present day is to be understood.

Many consumers have little choice as to where they will live. Millions of them live in council accommodation which is so heavily subsidized that it is unthinkable for the tenant to throw away the subsidy and move elsewhere. The modern working-class council tenant has in practice little more freedom of movement than the agricultural labourer in the days of Adam Smith. The position of those who live in private rented accommodation is hardly better. The destruction of the free market in housing by the policies of successive Governments since 1914 has deprived Englishmen of the right enjoyed by the people of most other countries, to rent reasonable accommodation, furnished or unfurnished, in the open market. The consequence has been that the supply of private rented accommodation has not been adequate to meet the demand for a great many years, and, indeed, the supply of unfurnished accommodation for private rent is almost non-existent outside a few major cities. The owner-occupier is rather better placed in these respects. He can still buy and sell within the limits of his resources and his borrowing ability, and the house-purchase market is a relatively free market in which freedom of contract still prevails to a considerable degree. But even in this market the Government's general control over the economy means that market movements, both of house prices and of interest rates, are to a large degree affected by external influences operating on the market, rather than by the free choice of individuals dealing in the market.

The Englishman's freedom to choose what work he is to do is likewise restricted in practice in a great many respects. Large numbers of employments are only open to those who acquire professional or other specialist qualifications. There is today a vast mass of regulatory legislation which restricts the individual's freedom to enter into various types of business without the approval of some licensing authority, and consequently restricts his freedom of contract, and (what is frequently overlooked) the freedom of contract of the public who are deprived of the opportunity of doing business with such persons.[21] And this does not take account of the increasing control of a non-statutory kind, over particular trades and businesses exercised by closed-shop arrangements, which restrict the freedom of employers to choose what employees they will engage. Much of this legislation is, doubtless in a broad sense, in 'the public interest'. Most of it has been passed with a view to protecting the public from sharp practice, fraud, imposition, and the like. I shall have more to say about the nature and effect of this legislation later, but it is necessary to stress here that all this legislation has a cost in the limitations of freedom which it imposes. While it may protect many members of the public who are not able to take care of themselves, it also has the effect of restricting the freedom of those members of the public who are able to take care of themselves.

[21] A rough count has revealed twenty-two Acts passed between 1967 and 1975 which contain (or re-enact) such restrictions.

Freedom of choice with respect to employment is also greatly influenced by the erosion of the market wage. While the influence of the market has not been wholly eradicated, concepts of equity on the one hand and the monopoly power of trade unions on the other increasingly determine what the public is to earn. And in so far as earnings influence choice of occupation, these factors inevitably limit the role of free choice still more.

The third broad freedom of the individual which I referred to, that of deciding how to spend his own income, has of course, also been increasingly eroded in a variety of ways, but most of all by taxation. The concept of a money income naturally entails the idea that the recipient has the right to choose what he will buy with it from the range of goods and services which are available to him, and the restrictions on the individual's freedom of choice are here less obvious than they may be in other respects. But they exist nevertheless. Total public expenditure in Britain (even excluding transfer payments) approaches fifty per cent of the national income. Much of this money is spent on public goods (such as education, health, and municipal services) which are thereupon supplied to the consumer, not by way of contract, but by way of free grant. Inevitably, if consumers do not freely contract for these public goods, the demand is likely to be virtually insatiable, and other non-market methods must therefore be found of deciding who is to receive them. For example, academic merit and potential is used for the selection of those members of the public who will receive a share of the State's expenditure on tertiary education. It is no longer possible to buy higher education in this country even for those who have the money to spare and would choose to spend it on their children if they were permitted to. It may well be that other similar restrictions on the freedom of the individual to spend his money as he wishes will eventually be imposed, for example, his right to buy private medical services, or perhaps even his right to buy private schooling for his children.

Such losses of freedom do not apply only to the rich. The tendency of the modern welfare system to provide many free or subsidized benefits in kind has precisely similar results for the poor. Those who benefit from subsidized housing, free school meals, half-price bus fares, concessionary electricity, and the like, are equally deprived of their freedom of choice as to how they will spend their subsidies. The State provides but does not allow the individual to choose the form of the provision, or to sell his benefits.

But apart from these positive restrictions on the freedom of the individual to spend his income how he chooses, it must also be recognized that the market in which he does spend his money is, in England, scarcely deserving of the name of a free market. The prices of, and therefore the demand for, an immense range of goods and services is today influenced by a variety of economic controls, ranging from Government taxation and subsidy policies to trade union monopoly control of the supply of labour and therefore of the price of labour. I have already referred briefly to the cost of housing which has been kept artificially low by a policy of subsidizing council-house tenants, granting tax relief on interest repayments to owner-occupiers, and regulating the rents payable in the private sector. But what is true of housing is, to a lesser degree, true of almost every commodity or service available to the consumer.

The nationalized industries, which today account for a substantial section of the total economy, are nearly all, to a greater or lesser degree, monopolists, and the trade unions which control their labour supply are as much monopolists as they are themselves. The pricing policy adopted by the nationalized industries is in practice largely free from public or market controls, and may well involve significant subsidies to some consumers at the expense of others. Moreover, the levels of taxation are today such that tax reliefs, or adjustments to the taxation of profits, no longer have a merely minor effect on prices. The result of all this— without even taking account of the reappearance of actual legal price controls in the past decade—is that the consumer today no longer spends his income in a free market. The prices of many, even of most of, he things he buys are not set by the free play of competition, and his apparently 'free choices' are therefore constrained choices. Who can doubt, for instance, that if the taxes on wine, whisky, beer, cigarettes, petrol, or cars were at the same level as taxes on (say) housing, clothes, furniture, or foodstuffs, there would be an enormous shift in the pattern of consumer expenditure?

All this may seem to have taken us far from our theme, but it has been necessary to stress these questions in order that the nature of our 'consumer society' should be clearly perceived. It is true that the consumer's needs and wants are still at the centre of our economic system; but it is also true that these needs and wants are not those which the consumer would choose unaided in a free market economy, or even something passably resembling such an economy.

DEMOCRACY AND MAJORITY RULE

We must return now to 1870 and the developments since then which have led to this changing role of the individual consumer, for there is no doubt that part of the explanation for these changes lies in the growth of democracy and the concept of majority rule. Although democracy and political or civil freedoms are usually associated, England was both a free society and yet an undemocratic one throughout the first two-thirds of the nineteenth century. The Reform Act of 1832 had, in a sense, brought the middle classes, the new industrial and commercial and professional classes, a share of the political power in the State, though it by no means signalled the end to the power of the landed aristocracy. But the working classes were still fundamentally without a vote until the Reform Act of 1867. And we have seen, too, something of the fears of the politicians and the intellectuals about the dangers of extending the franchise. Even many humanitarian liberals were, at heart, afraid of the working-class masses, and there is no doubt of the reason for this fear. It was the fear of the property owners in the State for what might happen if political power was handed over to those who had no property. 'Behind the argument for and against democracy, from the start, stood a spectre vaster and darker than the suffrage—the issue of equality itself.'[22]

There is no need here to look for the possible unconscious motivation of these middle- and upper-class Victorians who possessed the lion's share of the nation's wealth and had no wish to see it spread around equally among the populace. For we have already seen enough of intellectual opinion to provide a more than adequate explanation of their distrust of equality as an ideal. Their belief in competition, in the need for incentives for men to strive and struggle to improve themselves, and incidentally, the society in which they lived, their conviction that men were simply *not* equal, in ability or moral virtue, and, on the other hand, their fervent belief in freedom of the individual, all led them to reject economic egalitarianism without hesitation. Many were convinced (like Bagehot and Stephen)[23] that freedom and equality could not co-exist. Since men were in fact unequal, anything resembling economic equality could only be imposed by coercion of the minority by the majority. The mid-Victorian liberals had already seen enough of trade union activities to make them very mistrustful of the way in which working men might try to coerce minorities, minorities who were (they thought) usually the more able, the more individualistic, the more enterprising. Already in the 1850s and 1860s the coercive and majoritarian streak in working-class (and not only in trade union)[24] habits was perceived with dismay, perhaps most of all by those, like John Stuart Mill, who were at the same time sympathizers with working-class aspirations and yet fervent believers in the right of every individual to his own self-fulfilment. And there was the simple ignorance and lack of education which were still widespread among the mass of the people. Much of the paternalist legislation interfering with freedom of contract, which was discussed in Chapter 16, had been justified then, as it would be today, by stressing the

[22] G. Watson, *The English Ideology* (London, 1973), p. 164.
[23] Ibid., p. 166; J. F. Stephen, *Liberty, Equality and Fraternity*, 2nd edn. (Cambridge, 1967), pp. 174–175.   [24] *Supra*, p. 265.

sheer ignorance, incredulity, and simplicity of many of those whom it was designed to protect. Were these people to be given the ultimate political power in the State?

The answer, of course, was yes. The movement towards democracy was too strong to be denied. Some, like Robert Lowe, Sir James Fitzjames Stephen, Sir Henry Maine, and, later A. V. Dicey, never wholly reconciled themselves to the movement; but the leap into democracy had been made with the 1867 Reform Act, and from then on there was no turning back. The middle and upper classes took comfort in the belief that the workers would realize that they were not competent to exercise their own judgement in political affairs, and would rely on the advice and guidance of those who were. The politics of deference, as it came to be called, was the hope of those who took their courage in their hands, and supported the cause of Parliamentary Reform even with the gravest of misgivings. And for a while, they seemed to be proved right. Neither the Act of 1867, nor the Act of 1884 which conferred the right to vote on most agricultural labourers, appeared to make much difference to the electoral process or the composition of the House of Commons. Indeed, partly as a result of the Irish problem, the electorate swung decisively to the right after 1885 and for the next twenty years the Conservatives held office for all but three. And yet there is a sense in which, despite this long period of Conservative dominance, the underlying changes in the democratic process were beginning to have a significant effect on politics, and were laying the foundations for even greater changes in the future. For one thing the political parties were undergoing a great transformation, even before the arrival of Labour on the scene.[25] Changes in party organization strengthened the power of Governments over the House of Commons, and the power of the party collectively over the individual member.

And as party organization changed, so too did their policies, and their relationship to the electorate. Gladstonian liberalism gave way to Asquithian liberalism, and with it there came an increasing concern for the under-privileged and the poor, an increasing willingness to enact paternalist legislation, an increasing acceptance of the redistributive nature of much social legislation. On the other side, Joseph Chamberlain took with his band of Liberal Unionists, a radical reforming streak into the Conservative party. As Mayor of Birmingham where he had presided over a local authority dedicated to the improvement of the City, Chamberlain had already displayed his belief in public enterprise, and his election campaign in 1885, before the split over Home Rule, represented a new style of politics, a frank appeal to the mass of people. It was Chamberlain who, during this campaign, brought into the centre

[25] G. Kitson Clark, *The Making of Victorian England*, pp. 231–8.

of the political stage the fundamental issue of economic inequality which has dominated British politics ever since.

And, less visible at the time, but perhaps more important in retrospect even than the grafting of Chamberlain's radical stock onto the Conservative party, the 1880s also saw the serious beginnings of socialist activity in British politics. There were a number of separate strands in these early stirrings. There was, first, the genuinely working-class movement, the trade union movement, broadening out to represent the mass of the working class, and not merely the skilled worker, the élite of the class who had founded and dominated the early unions. Then there were the intellectual influences which mixed in with the trade union movement, the Fabians and the Marxists. The importance of these groups, especially perhaps the former, was that they brought some middle-class respectability to the political, but more especially the economic, arguments, which some of the workers' leaders had always believed in, but which had previously been regarded as suspect. Bernard Shaw, one of the most influential of the Fabians, observed with percipience that the extension of the franchise had changed the whole meaning of legislative 'interference' with the free economy. In an essay on *The New Radicalism* written in 1887 and unpublished at the time, though typical of much that Shaw was saying and publishing, he wrote:

Nothing indeed is more stimulating to the ironic sense than the preposterous appeals to free contract, free competition, free trade and laisser-faire in support of this outrageous protection allowed to the monopoly of industrial organization by private proprietors against the people organized as the State. Of course the secret of it has been that the State has not hitherto been the people organized for economic production and just distribution, but the proprietors organized to keep up rent, interest, and profit, and keep down wages. But the extension of the franchise has changed that; and there are plenty of propagandists on foot making the people conscious of the power the change has given them.[26]

While much of the economics which Shaw talked was nonsense, his political judgment was right. Freedom of contract and *laissez-faire* were no longer the slogans of Liberals and Radicals, supporting the demands of the commercial and industrial classes to be freed from State regulation; they were becoming the slogans of Conservatives, not the radical conservatism represented by Chamberlain, but a more old-fashioned conservatism, associated with the landed aristocracy and traditional individualism. In or around 1880 *laissez-faire* and freedom of contract crossed the floor of the House of Commons. Where in the 1830s and 1840s the old Tory benevolent paternalism had resisted the new fashionable radicalism and political economy and argued for the right of the State to intervene to protect those who could not take care of themselves, now in

[26] G. B. Shaw, *The Road to Equality*, ed. Louis Crompton (Boston, Mass., 1971), p. 33.

the 1880s and 1890s it was the Conservatives who demanded to be left alone, and the new Radicals who called for more State interference. Perhaps the increasing size and impersonality of industries (of which more later) was partly responsible for the changes. The Liberals and Radicals found it less easy to identify with large corporations than they had with individual entrepreneurs. And the Conservatives, for their part, had been selling their landed patrimony and investing in company securities on an increasing scale since the Settled Land Act of 1882; so perhaps they were now readier to identify with industry, as they certainly became in the twentieth century. On a whole series of political issues, and most strikingly in connection with reform of the Land Laws (as we shall see), Liberal legislation in and after the 1880s quite deliberately set out to upset the terms of contracts and leases between (for example) landlord and tenant in a way which would hardly have been possible thirty years earlier.

In a well-known lecture on *Liberal Legislation and Freedom of Contract*[27] in 1881, T. H. Green, the Oxford philosopher and political thinker, set out to challenge the primacy of the principle of freedom of contract. Green was unwilling to concede even a prima facie case against State activity or legislative interference with freedom of contract. Although there had been no shortage of legislative interference with free contract in the period 1800–70, the nature of the debate was now changing. No longer was it even necessary to adopt the apologetic tone of one who concedes that he is making an exception to an important principle. The right of the State to intervene to protect the weak, the poor, the underprivileged, was now being placed on an equal footing with the general desirability of maintaining the rule of free contract. There was no longer any presumption against interference. 'To uphold the sanctity of contracts', said Green, 'is doubtless a prime business of government, but it is no less its business to provide against contracts being made, which from the helplessness of one of the parties to them, instead of being a security for freedom become an instrument of disguised oppression.'

The change in attitudes went much deeper than merely to adjust by a few degrees the extent to which State interference now became legitimate. In the work of Green and others, there came for the first time into English political thought some of the Continental, and specifically Hegelian, influences about the meaning of liberty and the role of the State.[28] It came to be said that liberty was not merely a negative concept,

[27] *Works of T. H. Green*, ed. R. L. Nettleship (London, 1888), iii. 365. As a Fellow of Balliol T. H. Green tutored a succession of Liberal statesmen from the 1860s till his death in 1882. The Liberal Cabinet of 1906 contained six of his former pupils including Asquith. See M. Richter, *The Politics of Conscience: T. H. Green and his Age* (London, 1964).

[28] Sir Earnest Barker, *Political Thought in England 1848 to 1914*, 2nd edn. (London, New York, Toronto, 1947), p. 24.

but had also a positive side to it. Traditional freedoms, like freedom of contract, had over-stressed the negative side; but for those who could not benefit from these freedoms, freedom of contract was no better than freedom to starve. Positive freedom, by contrast, was not freedom from restraint, or indeed, freedom *from* anything; it was the freedom to do something worth doing, to achieve the self-fulfilment of which the individual was capable.[29] After all, argued Green, even savages are quite free from legal restraint, but their positive power to achieve satisfying lives is infinitely less than that of the humblest citizen of a civilized State. Many of the legislative measures which were, in 1880, being attacked as infringements of freedom of contract, were, said Green, interferences with negative liberty, in the interest of expanding positive liberty. Legislation to improve public health, for example, might restrict freedom of contract in various respects; but its object was to improve the health and prolong the lives of the people.

Moreover, once the emphasis shifted to positive freedoms in this way, the role of the individual and the State underwent important modification. For positive freedom was the freedom to achieve ends which derived most of their meaning and value from being social ends. Liberals like Green did not, of course, press this too far. Individuals were still central to his way of thought. 'The life of the nation', he insisted, 'has no real existence except as the life of the individuals composing the nation.'[30] Nevertheless, there was a significant shift in political thinking of this kind. Individual rights were not seen as emerging from, or operating in, a Lockean State of Nature. They were the rights of individuals who inevitably formed a social group, and many of the rights themselves had no meaning except within the framework of a social group. Naturally the State came to seem a more benevolent institution when things were seen in this light. Even where the State was exercising authority to coerce individuals, it could be said that '[t]he function of State coercion is to override individual coercion'.[31]

The more abstruse and somewhat metaphysical speculations about the relationship of the social order to the individual, and the nature of the State and other social groups and corporations, may not have had much influence in England outside the select band of thinkers who were acquainted with German philosophy;[32] but there was a sense in which these newer ideas were a natural outgrowth of the spread of democracy. As the mass of the people came to wield the political power of the State,

[29] *Liberal Legislation and Freedom of Contract*, in *Works of T. H. Green*, ed. Nettleship, iii. 371.

[30] Cited, Sir Earnest Barker, *Political Thoughts in England*, p. 47.

[31] L. T. Hobhouse, *Liberalism* (1911) cited in Alan Bullock and M. Shock, *The Liberal Tradition* (Oxford, 1967), p. 194.

[32] Compare F. A. Hayek, *The Road to Serfdom* (Chicago, 1944), pp. 21–3, where it is argued that after 1870 Western Liberal thinking was profoundly affected by German intellectual influences.

and as they came to use that political power to combat what they took to be the old privileges and inequalities surviving from the pre-democratic era, they, at least, began to have good reason to look on the State and on State coercion with a more benevolent eye. When Liberal legislation overrode the rights of landlords in the interests of tenants in the 1880s, when money was taken from the rich in taxes to pay old age pensions in 1908, the beneficiaries of the legislation were unlikely to see anything evil or sinister in this form of State activity.

In any event it is plain that the late 1880s virtually saw the end of freedom of contract as a political slogan, capable of swaying opinion to any great degree. There is much evidence to suggest that this was clearly perceived on all hands by politicians, political theorists, and philosophers, and social reformers of all kinds.[33] Winston Churchill, in his biography of his father, published in 1906, wrote that by the 1880s *laissez-faire* had lost its hold on the public because it was perceived that the lot of the mass of the people had scarcely improved. 'Trade was free. But hunger and squalor and cold were also free and the people demanded something more than liberty.'[34] Joseph Chamberlain, in the election campaign of 1885, sounded the death knell of freedom of contract as a political ideal by placing it in the scales against the interests of the masses:

The great problem of our civilisation is still unresolved. We have to account for and to grapple with the mass of misery and destitution in our midst, co-existent as it is with the evidence of abundant wealth and teeming prosperity. It is a problem which some men would put aside by reference to the eternal laws of supply and demand, to the necessity of freedom of contract, and to the sanctity of every private right of property. But gentlemen, these phrases are the convenient cant of selfish wealth.[35]

In the same year, a Conference on Industrial Remuneration was held in London at which the poverty of the working classes was the principal theme for discussion.[36] Lord Bramwell was there to offer his usual platitudes in defence of freedom of contract,[37] but a spirited attack from Frederic Harrison, barrister and professor at the Council of Legal Education, illustrates how each interference with freedom of contract tended to add to the weight of the precedents for the next intervention:[38]

---

[33] See, e.g., Ritchie, *The Principles of State Interference* (London, 1891); H. Sidgwick, *Methods of Ethics*, 7th edn. (London, 1907), p. 275. In 1884 Herbert Spencer mournfully complained in *The Man Versus the State* that the press daily spoke of *laissez-faire* as an exploded doctrine: Pelican edn. (Harmondsworth, 1969), p. 98.

[34] *Lord Randolph Churchill* (London, 1906), pp. 265–9.

[35] Cited, H. Schultz, *English Liberalism and the State* (Lexington, Mass., 1972), p. 57.

[36] *Report of the Conference* (London, Paris, New York, Melbourne, 1885).

[37] Ibid., pp. 419 *et seq.*

[38] Ibid., pp. 428 *et seq.* Harrison had been a member of the Royal Commission on Trade Unions in 1867 and it was largely due to him that the Unions secured most of what they wanted.

The sticklers for absolute respect for Liberty and Property have not the courage of their doctrines. If they are logical they should ask for the abolition of all legislation against truck, dangerous structures or practices, unhealthy buildings, oppressive regulations and fraudulent devices of any kind. They ought even to call for the abolition of all inspection, all compulsion, all monopolies, and the State manufactures or even regulation of industry in any form. Cab-drivers would be free to charge the unwary what they pleased; girls and boys would be ill-used in any way short of violence. The population would grow up a prey to small-pox and all infectious diseases; the children would be untaught; salesmen would be free to falsify their weights and measures, and to adulterate their goods without check; sailors would be drowned, pitmen blown to cinders and trains wrecked entirely at the mercy of certain owners; and we should have to forward our own letters and (why not?) protect our own houses ourselves ... Once show a few cases where State control has certainly made industrial life a little more humane and checked some forms of misery, the abstract doctrine of non-interference is blown to the winds. But cases of successful State control abound in all societies, and noteably in ours. The rule of *caveat emptor* is perfectly observed only by savages.

Also in the same year the indefatigable Chadwick, still pouring out a stream of pamphlets and suggestions for social reform, published an essay bitterly attacking George Goschen for some ill-chosen remarks on the excesses of State interference. Goschen was one of those whose life reflected the changing political attitudes to State interference, for he had begun his career as an old-fashioned Liberal, but had gradually lost sympathy with the increasing radicalism of the Liberal party, and was eventually to take office in the Conservative Government in 1886. In this pamphlet,[39] Chadwick attacked Goschen's complaints of undue interference affecting the merchant marine, and referred to one of his favourite examples of State interference with contracts, namely the adjustment of the terms on which pauper emigrants to Australia had been carried so that payment was only made for each passenger who disembarked alive at the other end. This move, as Chadwick triumphantly insisted, had greatly cut the death rate, and 'the contract secured for every live passenger who died at least one sincere mourner'.[40]

By the end of the century, freedom of contract was scarcely worth raising in debates in parliament. The last rites were performed by Sir Matthew Ridley, the Home Secretary, in 1897 when, on the debates on the Workmen's Compensation Bill, he replied to a member who had raised the traditional argument:

The right honourable gentleman opposite says we have abandoned freedom of contract. There is no such thing as freedom of contract in this country or any

[39] 'On Unity as against Laissez Faire in Legislation', published in *On the Evils of Disunity in Central and Local Administration* (London, 1885).
[40] Ibid., pp. 96-7.

other. We make our own arrangements as regards houses or farms, under the conditions of the law, which lays down certain conditions with which you must comply; and this Bill lays down conditions with which employers and workmen must comply.[41]

There is little doubt that, as Shaw perceived, it was the arrival of democracy which had finally spelled the doom of arguments based on *laissez-faire* and freedom of contract. For freedom of contract in general presupposed a faith in the existing distribution of wealth, and a belief in the virtues of individual effort and competition, both of which were fundamentally rejected by the newly enfranchised majority. They believed, on the contrary, that the existing inequalities of wealth were fundamentally unacceptable, and naturally this meant that they saw freedom of contract simply as a means of preserving the existing inequalities. Conversely, to interfere with freedom of contract, might enable some redistribution of wealth to take place on the limited and modest scale which was, at first, all they could hope to achieve. For example, they clearly thought that to compel employers to pay workmen's compensation benefits to those injured in industrial accidents would improve the bargains made by workmen with employers. In addition to their wages, workmen would now receive these new benefits, to be paid for by employers. Modern economists may argue that this belief was naïve, that the cost of any statutory benefits which the employer has to pay will inevitably be taken into account in the fixing of wages, and that, in the long run, the benefits will be paid by the workmen so that no redistribution will result. In a totally free market this might be so, but in practice, it seems unlikely that such an adjustment was ever completely made, so that some permanent element of redistribution between employers and employees may have resulted from measures of this kind.[42] But even if this was not so, there was another type of redistribution, which the new majoritarian tradition of the electorate also espoused, and that was redistribution, through insurance, even among the workers themselves. If (for example) workmen's compensation benefits were paid for by employees rather than employers, they would at least be paid by all employees, and not merely by those injured in accidents.

In the case of workmen's compensation benefits, this form of redistribution may have been wholly justifiable, even though the insurance was, in effect, a compulsory levy on the workmen. But some of the other paternalist legislation which also dates from the 1880s and

[41] *Hansard* (4th series) H.C., vol. 49, col. 699.

[42] Moreover, the cost and number of accidents may well have been reduced because employers were better able to take the necessary accident prevention measures, as Chadwick had always argued.

1890s (such as the consumer protection legislation dealing with moneylending and bills of sale which I discuss later) involved different issues. For in these cases interference with freedom of contract involved redistribution, not among the victims of accidents, but to those who were foolish, ignorant, irresponsible, feckless, or even dishonest, from those who were capable, knowledgeable, responsible, conscientious, and honest. Much of the paternalist, protective legislation of the 1880s and 1890s was of this character, and it is difficult not to conclude that it derived from the increasing majoritarianism of British political life. Such paternalist legislation may have been necessary or justifiable; but it is important to remember that there is always a social cost involved in intervention of this character.

The arrival of democracy and majoritarianism in English life has produced a strange paradox in the differing treatment of the political and the economic fields. We saw earlier how, in mid-nineteenth-century utilitarian and economic thinking, a close association was perceived between the role of the individual in the political sphere and his role as a consumer in the economic sphere. In both areas, it was thought by many that the best results would be obtained from the sovereignty of the individual. The paradox is that after a hundred years of democratic political rule, the sovereignty of the consumer in the economic sphere has been, at least in England, almost entirely eroded. And with this paradox have come many others. Politically, the firm belief in democracy is not seriously undermined by the limited abilities of the mass of the public to understand the complex issues which they are called upon to decide with their votes. It is still assumed in the political sphere, that the public are the best judges of what they want. Indeed, so much has this become the case that politics largely consists, not so much in offering the public a set of policies which the politicians themselves believe to be right, but in searching for those policies which the public is thought to favour. But, while this tendency has become ever more pronounced in the political sphere, it has proved ever less acceptable in the economic sphere. Few people accept that the public as consumers (rather than as voters) know their own interests best, and can, therefore, be safely left to judge (for example) of the quality of the products offered them for sale. The seducing advertising of the manufacturer or businessmen is condemned, controlled, or even made downright illegal (for example, in the case of cigarettes), while in the market place of ideas, politicians are free to deceive and defraud the public.[43] The temptations to make a contract whose immediate attractions may be so great as to displace the thought of the future burdens (such as, for example, buying heavily on credit) are carefully controlled and regulated by law to protect the consumer from

[43] J. Schumpeter, *Capitalism, Socialism and Democracy*, 4th edn. (London, 1966), pp. 256 *et seq.*

his own folly and misjudgment. But the temptation to vote for a policy or party which offers immediate short-term advantages at the price of heavy future burdens remains as strong as ever. Enormous tensions are being created by this disparity in the role of the individual as economic consumer (and earner) and as political voter.

Two further comments are worth making about the growth of the majoritarian tradition in England. The first is that it has, for various reasons, developed along peculiarly authoritarian lines. Both in politics and in other spheres (for instance, trade unionism) the English tradition has, in recent years, paid little attention to the rights of minorities. Majorities, however narrow, and however they have been arrived at, are nearly always deemed an adequate justification for action, even over the protests of a considerable minority, and even though the issues may appear to be fundamental ones. Only minorities too strong to be coerced constitute an exception to this in modern Britain. It will be seen how antithetical this majoritarian tradition is to the concepts of individualism and freedom of contract. For, as soon as bilateral contractual relationships give way to multilateral relationships, whether contractual or of any other character, the individual is largely at the mercy of the majority. His agreement to the original arrangements is deemed to be an agreement to those arrangements, subject to such change as is made from time to time. His consent is not required to any changes which are made by the majority. Although this tradition is more important in politics than in law, we shall see later some examples of the influence of these ideas on the law itself.

One of the powerful influences behind this majoritarian tradition has surely been the consciousness that minorities derive many benefits from the activities, and even from the mere existence of the social group as a whole. This belief is very widespread in modern England. English people today have a strong sense that, with regard to national prosperity, or national decline, 'we are all in this together'. The idea that some put in more and are thereafter entitled to take out more has waned as the majoritarian tradition has strengthened. The idea that the majority has no more *right* to coerce the minority or to tax away their wealth, than the minority would have to do these things to the majority,[44] is one which most English people would find unintelligible. The idea that the majority, even without such coercion or taxation, already derives benefits equal to, or greater than, those derived by the minority from the existence of the social group, or the State itself,[45] is, likewise, one which would have difficulty in obtaining even a serious hearing in modern England.

All this is not to say that the liberal tradition is quite dead, that these

[44] See R. Nozick, *Anarchy, State and Utopia* (New York, 1974).
[45] Ibid., p. 195.

developments have taken place without protest and opposition. We hear, for instance, rather less today about the ideas of positive freedom, and the benevolent role of the State, than were fashionable with liberals in 1880.[46] And short-term fluctuations of opinion, even electoral opinion, may seem to contradict these suggestions. But, in general, the long-term trend seems unmistakable, and the reason is plain enough. Majorities always have the votes; intellectuals and liberals may win debates, but it is votes which decide issues. Majoritarianism, once firmly entrenched, can scarcely be dislodged short of revolution.

The second point to be made is that the majoritarian tradition also appears to be surprisingly unconcerned at the way in which the majority has been arrived at. Parliamentary majorities are absolute, irrespective of the fairness or acceptability of the electoral system itself; votes in the House of Commons may be decided by a majority by the accidental chance that members of one side or the other are absent on urgent matters or due to sickness. Decisions of bodies like the T.U.C. and the Labour Party are made by the wielding of huge block votes, which themselves may represent the narrowest of majority decisions. As Berle and Means pointed out in the 1930s, with respect to the new corporate giants, it was becoming increasingly possible for power to rest not so much in the hands of an absolute majority, but in a majority of a majority. In the 1970s it was becoming only too clear that the same was true of England's political system. In 1976, for example, the Prime Minister was elected by a majority of the members of the House of Commons, themselves elected by a majority of votes and, indeed, in many cases by a minority of votes in a majority of constituencies. Yet few people thought there was anything odd or unreasonable about the process.

If this cavalier attitude to the method of arriving at majorities is added to the absolute power so often wielded by majorities, it will be seen that the rights of the individual, and the role of freedom of contract, are necessarily downgraded even further. Indeed, it is easy to see how the role of the individual, once on this slippery slope, can rapidly disappear over the edge into the abyss.

THE ARRIVAL OF THE MIXED ECONOMY

The changing role of the individual in the economy and in the political sphere has been matched, during the past hundred years, by the changing role of Government in the economic system. As we have seen, there was no shortage of legislative intervention even before 1870, but after that

---

[46] See, e.g., Sir Isaiah Berlin's essay, 'Two Concepts of Liberty', reprinted in *Four Essays on Liberty* (Oxford, 1975).

date Government itself, both central and local, began to play a steadily increasing role as owner and manager of quasi-commercial activities. The central Government had in 1868 acquired the privately owned telegraph services in an attempt to create the sixpenny telegraph to match the success of the penny postage on the mails. This first attempt at nationalization was, at least in terms of these aspirations, a total failure, though that did not discourage those who sought a larger role for Government in the economy. Meanwhile local authorities too were embarking on a variety of new services to add to the municipally-owned waterworks and gasworks. Electricity undertakings, public transport, public baths, wash rooms, and laundry services all appeared before the nineteenth century was out. So too did municipal housing.

These developments were but the beginning. The twentieth century was to see an immense increase in the role of Government in the economy, an increase which brought with it a vast change in the way in which resources were allocated, and income distributed. For these changes brought a huge expansion in the range of services provided by the Government, not on a contractual basis, but as public goods. The Liberal Government of 1906–14 created the first social security system in Britain, making provision for compulsory sickness and health and unemployment insurance, and also for old age pensions paid for directly out of taxation. And there were also many other services which first began to be regularly supplied by Government or local government on a free basis around this time. Public libraries, museums, and art galleries, for example, sprang up all over the country. Expenditure on free education was mounting steadily, and leapt upwards spectacularly after the First War when secondary and tertiary education began to be publicly financed.

The First World War brought with it the first attempt by the Government to take over and manage the control of the entire economic system. For some three or four years the normal economic system substantially ceased to exist as the nation's resources were channelled into the war effort by the Government. Raw materials were purchased by the Government and allocated to industry, prices were controlled, rents were controlled, even employment was controlled. All this was accompanied by a phenomenal increase in Governmental expenditure, which mounted sevenfold between 1914 and 1918. Rates of taxation soared—though they were never as high then as they are today. Much of this Government activity ceased as soon as the war was over, but in other respects the increase in Governmental activity left a permanent mark on the economy. For one thing the Government had greatly encouraged the growth of the corporate giants in the war. It was impossible for Government to deal with thousands of small individual firms while attempting to regulate the entire national economy, and the movement (which had begun long before the war) to larger industrial units, as well as to more powerful trade associations, was given immense impetus by the war. When the depressions came, first in 1921, and then again in 1929, the defensive reaction of industry, in the way of controlling output and minimizing competition, was assisted by the centralization which had come into existence in the war and never been entirely dismantled. Then again, the attitude of the Government to agriculture never reverted wholly to one of basic indifference after the war. The need for an adequate home farming industry had been brought home to the public and the Government by the war, and in the following decades the free market in agriculture was almost completely dismantled. Regulation of the contractual arrangements between farmers and landlords, which had begun in the 1880s, was increased; a series of Agricultural Marketing Acts created a number of Boards to control the supply and price of agricultural produce, and in the 1930s Britain finally abandoned international free trade and went over to the system of imperial preference.

Industry went steadily in the same direction. Governments felt forced increasingly to intervene in the inter-war period, as the depression deepened and unemployment grew. The price fixing and other 'rationalization' schemes for controlling production, to which industrialists increasingly resorted, were generally given every encouragement and assistance by the Government. On the eve of the Second World War, even statutory price controls were being brought back, as defence needs were once again making their influence felt. Then there were the quasi-public monopolies, such as the electricity supply industry, which was brought increasingly under public ownership, partly because of the obvious efficiencies flowing from the establishment of the National Grid. Similarly with the railways, which remained privately owned, but were increasingly regulated by the State, a regulation emphasized by the Government-imposed merger which reduced the number of companies to four. By the late 1920s the old liberal world-free trading economy was totally destroyed. By the 1930s the huge numbers of unemployed workers in England and throughout the world led many to believe that the capitalist system itself was doomed. And in a sense this was true; certainly the free enterprise economies which had existed in the nineteenth centuries, and limped on, in an increasingly regulated world, into the 1930s, died in the Second World War and have never come to life again.

When the Labour Party swept into power with a huge majority in 1945, it brought with it a determination that the events of the 1930s should never be repeated. Supported by the new Keynesian economic theory, the Government embarked on the management of the economy in a totally new way. The avoidance of unemployment became the chief priority of Government economic policy, but the depletion of the nation's gold reserves during the war also meant that home demand had to be restrained for many years while industrial effort went into the export trade. This too brought a battery of controls; exchange control regulations were tighter than they had ever been before, and virtually all industry was subject to regulations which restrained what they were permitted to supply to the home market. Food rationing, which had been imperative during the war, was retained for more than five years afterwards principally because the Government continued to believe in itself acting as bulk purchaser of food supplies instead of re-opening the free market. At the same time, the Government embarked on its nationalization programme in an attempt to build the new socialist State. Coal mines, the railways, electricity and gas supplies, the iron and steel industry, and the airlines all became publicly owned and managed in the first few years after the end of the Second World War.

In the following thirty years this process continued, but as time went on, there developed an increasing doubt as to the precise direction in which all this was heading. In the early heady days of the first post-war Labour Government, nobody in the Government doubted that it was about to embark on the building of the new socialist State, but few paused to ask what this involved for the market system or the role of the consumer in that system. Was the Government to plan everything, to allocate all resources, to decide v/hat was to be produced, or was there still some sense in which consumer sovereignty was to prevail? How was planning to be reconciled with the role of the sovereign consumer in a free society? Were the nationalized industries to be run on ordinary commercial lines, or were they to be run, as many socialists demanded, as a 'social service'? Government policy and thinking on these questions showed a confusing mixture of socialist and market ideas,[47] and it was evident that the issues had simply not been coherently thought out. But it was at least clear that the role of freedom of contract as any kind of a regulating mechanism in the British economy had been so emasculated that it was surely not too early to speak of its demise.

There is one other factor which must be mentioned, and that is the increasing menace of inflation. The period since the end of the Second World War has been in England (and generally elsewhere also) marked by persistent, and latterly increasing, rates of inflation. By 1974–5 the rates in England had soared to such heights as to threaten the foundations of the national economy, and desperate attempts are now being made to bring them under control. All these events, like those referred to in the

[47] See for an early critique of the ambivalence of Labour policy on these issues, Jewkes and Devons, *Lloyds Bank Rev.* 1 (April 1947). See also D. H. Robertson, *Utility and All That* (London, 1952), pp. 49–50.

previous paragraph, are only too familiar as part of the current politico-economic scene and my purpose is not to dilate on the facts themselves. But inflation has repercussions on all forms of planning, private as well as public. When nobody can count on the value of money retaining its stability even over a period of months, let alone years, the making of rational forward arrangements becomes more difficult, and in many cases, impossible. The problem affects everyone. Government economic planning is itself dependent on the movements in the inflation rate; businesses find it harder to calculate the probable returns on an investment, and may therefore cease to invest; and consumers, too, find it difficult to make long-term commitments without knowing how their own earnings will alter in comparison with the general alteration in costs. And the balance between lenders and borrowers of money is upset to such a ludicrous degree that it not infrequently happens at the time of writing that lenders are actually paying borrowers for the privilege of borrowing their money. Naturally these uncertainties have implications for contract law as an instrument of planning, that is for *executory* contract law. I do not suggest that there may not be some means of mitigating these difficulties within the accepted framework of contract law; such mitigations are possible, but they only result in shifting the uncertainties from inflation from one party to the other. And in many cases such mitigation simply does not occur through the normal medium of contract arrangements. One result of all this has been to encourage the shift away from executory contract law as a way of *binding* both parties to a particular set of arrangements, and a corresponding shift towards a more flexible type of quasi-administrative arrangement which enables adjustments to be made to the arrangements from time to time. In short, the risk-allocation function of contract has increasingly been splitting off from the exchange function. This is, of course, particularly true of contracts which envisage a continuing relationship rather than a discrete transaction, or even a series of discrete transactions. I shall return to this theme in Chapter 22.

THE RISE OF THE CORPORATE STATE

The last of the four leading characteristics of the past century of English history is the phenomenon of institutional growth. In 1870 British industry was still widely fragmented and highly competitive. Most businesses were still in the hands of individual entrepreneurs; although some of them had taken advantage of the Companies Acts to incorporate with limited liability, the majority had not, and even those which had, still generally resembled the modern family company or partnership. In the last thirty or perhaps forty years of the nineteenth century this scene changed rapidly, and it was a change which had 'deep, silent effects on the whole tone and fabric of English life'.[48] Where in earlier decades the railways, insurance, mining, and banking industries had been chiefly prominent in corporate form, manufacturing industry itself now began to join in the conversion. In the first four years after the new Companies Act of 1862 over 3,500 new companies were registered, and in 1865 *The Times* was lamenting that the whole country was growing everyday into 'one vast mass of impersonalities'.[49] Among the older-established, more traditional businesses, the change was more protracted. In 1884 there were 1,642 firms engaged in the spinning and weaving business, of which less than a fifth were joint-stock companies.[50] Nevertheless, virtually all major businesses had converted to the corporate form by 1900, and by then even the one-man companies had begun to make their appearance.

From the 1880s and rather more so, from the 1890s another, less welcome trend, became visible to those with eyes to observe it.[51] A wave of mergers and amalgamations began which led gradually to larger and yet larger corporations. In the United States, a contemporaneous movement, triggered off by ruthless, aggressive, competition, sent many smaller businesses spiralling into bankruptcy and left the successful ones with larger and larger shares of the market. The resulting loss of competition led there to the Sherman Anti-Trust Act in 1890. But in Britain the movement was less ruthless and less competitive, and in some respects it took a form which actually militated against mergers for some years. For many of the smaller businesses in Britain responded to the threats of international competition by creating more or less powerful Trade Associations. These Associations were essentially instruments for maintaining the status quo and for suppressing any tendency to severe competition; they appealed particularly to the smaller and less efficient enterprises, and actually held up the process of rationalization and merger.[52] In this respect they were probably more insidious and more dangerous to the public interest even than overt mergers leading to a monopoly trader, for a monopolist could be controlled or regulated, and was at least likely to be more efficient within its own organization if so controlled. But the Trade Associations, at least as they developed in Britain, especially after the turn of the century, were every bit as anti-competitive as a single, uncontrolled monopolist, while yet lacking all incentive to internal rationalization.

Nevertheless, until the First World War at least, the Trade Associations

[48] R. C. K. Ensor, *England 1870–1914* (reprinted, Oxford, 1949), p. 112.
[49] Hunt, *The Development of the Business Corporation in England 1800–1867*, pp. 145–6.
[50] R. S. Sayers, *A History of Economic Change*, p. 101.
[51] P. L. Payne, 'The Emergence of the Large Scale Company in Great Britain 1870–1914', 20 *Economic History Rev.* 519 (1967).
[52] G. Turner, *Business in Britain* (Harmondsworth, 1971), p. 27.

gave rise to little public concern or comment. From time to time there was anxiety about particular combines, such as the Salt Trust which gave rise to much concern in 1888,[53] and the economist Alfred Marshall noted with some alarm the growth of the shipping conferences, as well as the House of Lords' decision in the *Mogul* case[54] which established their legality. But in general, Englishmen were confident that these associations were unstable, and would be destroyed by the forces of competition. This faith was largely the product of the free trade policy which England still pursued, as well as the experience of a hundred years of intensely competitive activity. It was true that restrictive associations and combinations had tended to prove unstable during the nineteenth century, and even in 1900 Britain was still generally a much more competitive country than the United States.[55] But the stability and power of the Trade Associations increased steadily, and were given a substantial additional fillip by the use made of them by the Government in the First War to help in the regulation of the economy for war purposes.

By 1919 the Government was sufficiently concerned to appoint a Committee to examine the situation. This Committee found that there was 'in every important branch of industry in the U.K. an increasing tendency to the formation of Trade Associations and Combinations, having for their purpose the restriction of competition, and the control of prices'.[56] Indeed, it was evident from the Committee's findings that the general belief in the virtues of competition which had largely characterized British industry in the previous century, had all but evaporated. Competition was now seen as 'vicious' or 'cut-throat' or 'unfair'. The mere fact that one manufacturer sold his products at a lower price than another was likely to be seen by the latter as 'unfair' competition. Prices were being driven down so low, it was said, that there was no profit left for investment. In fact the Committee took much of this with a pinch of salt, and observed that there was a tendency for prices to be fixed by Trade Associations at levels which would permit the least efficient member to make an adequate profit. All incentive to increase efficiency and a consequent share of the market was suppressed by Trade Association rules requiring the more efficient firms to pay part of their profit into a pool for the compensation of those whose profits declined. The Committee ended up by recommending the Government to establish proper machinery for the investigation of the Associations and Trusts. Two members (Ernest Bevin and Sydney Webb), while signing the

[53] Sir John Clapham, *Economic History of Modern Britain* (Cambridge, 1938), iii. 215. This combination eventually came before the Courts in *North Western Salt Co.* v. *Electrolytic Alkali Co.* [1914] A.C. 461, *post* p. 700.

[54] [1892] A.C. 25, *post* p. 697.

[55] Alex Hunter, *Competition and the Law* (London, 1966), p. 73.

[56] *Report of the Committee on Trusts*, Cd. 9236 (1919), p. 2.

Report, added a Note of their own designed to suggest a greater urgency about the situation: 'The fact is', they said, 'that Free Competition no longer governs the world. The common assumption that the rivalry of traders affords a guarantee that the price of commodities will oscillate closely about the necessary cost of production—whatever may have been its degree of truth in the past—is now, in this country nowhere to be implicitly relied on. It is nowadays open to doubt whether we ever buy anything at the cost of production . . . Such a conclusion has momentous implications.'[57] But the 'momentous implications' for the socialist authors of this Minority Note were not so much that competition had to be restored to industry by legislation, but that, if there was to be no competition, industry might as well be owned by the State.[58]

The Government took no action on the Report, and things went from bad to worse, with the assistance (as we shall see) of the Courts whose belief in freedom of contract extended to its use in the destruction of freedom to trade, and free competition. In the 1920s and 1930s, the Trade Associations extended their control over the whole of British industry, and they also perfected the system of resale price maintenance by refusing supply to those who tried to compete effectively, thereby establishing an iron grip on minimum prices. But in addition, real mergers on a massive scale were now beginning to take place. In 1926 I.C.I. was created, in 1929, Unilever; the railway mergers were carried through by the Government itself in 1921; the banks had already consolidated themselves into the Big Five who were reduced to the Big Four in the 1970s. The motor industry, somewhat later, went through the same rationalizing process of mergers and amalgamations. Some twenty prosperous companies in the inter-war period were gradually reduced to three in the 1970s. Other large mergers took place in grain milling, rayon, and the electrical industry. A further investigation by a Government Committee in the late 1920s brought to light some more detailed information on the extent of growth of mergers and restrictive arrangements, but the stress in these years of depression was on the elimination of surplus capacity, and again nothing very dramatic emerged in the way of recommendations.[59]

After the Second World War, there were (as we shall see later) a number of developments which tried to restore some competitiveness to British industry. Many restrictive practices were outlawed; and monopolies and mergers became subject to examination and regulation by the Government. But at the same time, the trend towards size and

[57] Ibid., p. 13.
[58] See E. V. Rostow, 'British and American Experience with Legislation against Restraints of Competition', 23 *Modern Law Review* 477 (1960).
[59] See Final Report of the Committee on Industry and Trade, Cmd. 3282 (1929).

concentration of industrial units greatly increased. The nationalized industries arrived on the scene as gigantic monopolists, albeit public monopolies. And the growth of industrial companies continued, if anything, on a larger scale than ever before.

Parallel with the trend towards larger industrial units has been, over the past hundred years, the trend towards national and more powerful trade unions. As we have seen, the trade unions largely secured the legality and power which they needed in 1871 and 1875. Since then, they have, on several occasions, felt the need for, and secured, further protective legislation to offset the results of judicial decisions which they have thought to constitute a threat to their position. This legislation has, in every case, increased the bargaining power of trade unions by widening the scope of the pressure they are legally entitled to exert. But in many ways, more important than these additional legal protections has been the trend to larger, national unions, who bargain nationwide with employers, also in many cases representing a whole industry. This trend, like the trend to industrial mergers and combinations, can largely be traced back to the 1880s and 1890s.[60] With the change in size came a change in philosophy. The unions of the 1890s had begun to represent the majority of the working classes, and they were now turning their backs firmly on the old middle-class values which they had often accepted in mid-century. By 1890 'only a small segment of the established union leadership still clung stubbornly to a belief in laissez faire and the virtue of self-help'.[61] The new unions, far from fearing the State's intervention, were anxious to capture its power and recruit its assistance on their behalf. In this, they were, of course successful when their political wing, the Labour Party, came to dominate British politics, first after 1945 and then again in the 1960s.

But their very success has brought problems to the unions as it has to the Labour Party. They have been forced, perhaps for the first time in the 1970s, to face the question as to their relationship to Government, and indeed, as to their fundamental political beliefs. These questions, like those discussed above, are the controversies of the moment, and I cannot develop them here. It is enough to observe on the paradox of a trade union movement, most members of which, at the time of writing, continue to proclaim their belief in 'free collective bargaining' (which is nothing else than a particular form of freedom of contract), while the Liberal party supports the continuance of firm controls on wage bargaining. The sight of those few conservatives who still believe in the principles of the free market uniting with the trade unions to demand, in

---

[60] A. E. P. Duffy, 'New Unionism in Britain, 1889–1890: A Re-appraisal', 14 *Economic History Rev.* 306 (1962); E. J. Hobsbawm, 'Trade Union History', 20 *Economic History Rev.* 358 (1967).

[61] A. E. P. Duffy, 'New Unionism in Britain', p. 319.

the 1970s, a return to freedom of contract, must be enough to set Adam Smith chuckling in his grave.

I need not pursue these issues further. The important point for present purposes is to stress the sheer growth in the size of the institutions that are now dominating the economy. As we shall see, this had, and still has, many implications for the role of free contract in our society. To mention merely one point at this stage, the fewer the number of institutions there are, the fewer are the contractual relationships that they will need to make *inter se*; and the larger are the units, the greater is the extent of the administrative organization within the units themselves. One division of Government does not contract with another division; one section of a company does not contract with another section. Relations within an institution are maintained by administrative methods and not by contractual ones. This was first observed by Berle and Means in their classic study of the modern corporation, originally published in 1932:

The idea that an army operates on the basis of 'rugged individualism' would be ludicrous. Equally so is the same idea with respect to the modern corporation. Group activity, the co-ordinating of the different steps in production, the extreme division of labour on large scale production, necessarily imply not individualism but co-operation and the acceptance of authority almost to the point of autocracy.[62]

I shall develop this theme, together with a number of other consequences flowing from the growing size of corporations and other institutions, at a later point.

[62] *The Modern Corporation and Private Property*, revised edn. (New York, 1967), pp. 306–7.

18

THE INTELLECTUAL BACKGROUND,
1870–1970—I

THE NEW ECONOMICS

IT is widely agreed among economic historians that classical economics largely died with Mill in or around 1873. In England a new generation of economic thinkers was taking over, in particular, W. S. Jevons and Alfred Marshall, who between them largely dominated the subject between 1870 and 1914. These neo-classics, as they have been called, were professional economic thinkers in a way that the classics had not been. They were, for a start, academics, teaching and researching in Universities. And they were also specialists in their discipline in a way that none of the classics had been. It was still possible for a man like Henry Sidgwick, Professor of Philosophy at Cambridge between 1883 and 1900, to write both a leading work on moral philosophy and an elementary work on the *Principles of Political Economy*, but generally speaking the new generation of economists were among that breed of academics which knows more and more about less and less. They advanced the theoretical basis of their discipline in a number of most important respects, many of which remain essential keystones of modern economic theory, but in doing so they helped to make their subject less intelligible to the non-specialist. Almost deliberately they turned their subject slowly away from ethics, law, and politics, and in the process rechristened it, purely 'economics' rather than political economy.[1] And as they did so, the other social scientists were also, for their part, drawing away from the economists. The lawyers, in particular, ceased to have any significant contact with, or understanding of, the new economics. The personal relationships which had made law and political economy closely connected bodies of ideas centring around Benthamite utilitarianism were not renewed. From our point of view, these developments are not without their advantages, for they relieve us of the necessity of attempting to review the new economic theories in any depth. It is plain

---

[1] Though there were sometimes regrets (and warnings) about the separation of the disciplines. In 1904 Alfred Marshall wrote to F. W. Maitland about the importance of teaching law to economists in connection with monopolies and restrictive practices, and though he was too polite to say so, he evidently thought that lawyers ought to learn some economics: *Memorials of Alfred Marshall*, ed. Pigou (London, 1925, reprinted New York, 1966) p. 452.

that the history of freedom of contract in the legal sense was little influenced by economic theories after 1870, though in the long run these changes had profound (if not always clearly understood) influences on legal change. In this chapter I shall be more concerned with the general changes in the nature of economic theory, though we shall also look briefly at a number of the key advances in theory which may have been influential on the general intellectual climate of the times.

As I have said, one of the most marked, though at first gradual, changes was the process by which economics extricated itself from its association with ethics and politics, and in particular, from its relationship with utilitarianism. In Jevons's book, *The Theory of Political Economy*,[2] which is often taken to mark the beginning of neo-classical economics, there is indeed, no attempt to separate economics from utilitarianism at all. On the contrary, Jevons appears to be building on many of the Benthamite ideas, and he certainly uses the Benthamite terminology. In the Preface to the first edition he actually wrote that he had attempted to treat economics as a calculus of pleasure and pain, and there are passages in which he writes as if utility (and disutility) could be measured and compared.[3] In these respects the analysis appears to lie along Benthamite lines. But in other respects there were certainly changes. It was, for a start, the beginning of *analytical* economic theory. Jevons was interested in *how* the economic system worked, even if this made him concerned with how people maximize their utilities. But unlike the classics, the new economists were less interested in the normative questions of the subject; in particular, there is less emphasis on policy recommendations, and indeed, little interest in the question of how the national product should, in practice, be maximized or distributed. Economic theory seemed to have become largely concerned with explaining how things worked. There was also something of a paradox involved here, because the new economists like Jevons were, in many respects, more empirically minded than the classics. Jevons himself was one of the first economists to display a serious interest in the study of statistics and other data, from which he attempted to draw explanations of the phenomena. But at the same time, there was, in another sense, an increasing concern with pure theory. Where the classics had assumed in a rough and ready sort of way that free competition was the surest way to maximize production, some of the newer economists began to try to prove this as a mathematical proposition. And so, too, where the classics had been interested in a *changing* economy, in an economic system which was continually growing, post-1870 economists became more and more

---

[2] First published 1871, reprinted, Pelican edn., Harmondsworth, 1970, ed. R. D. Collison Black. Page references are to this edition.
[3] See Collison Black's *Introduction* to the Pelican edn., pp. 18–21.

concerned with the model of a static economic system, something which was necessarily a theoretical concept. Economics came to be concerned with the study of the efficient allocation of a fixed quantity of resources.

With Alfred Marshall (said by Keynes to have been the greatest economist for a hundred years)[4] this process was taken a good deal further. Marshall, too, began with some of the Benthamite ideas, or at least, their terminology; he had originally talked of 'pleasure' and 'pain' in his discussions of utility, but gradually he dropped this sort of language and used the more neutral language of 'satisfaction' and 'gratification'. On the substantive questions, he was from the beginning more rigorous than Jevons, whom he criticized severely on the very ground that Jevons had written as though utility and pleasure were the same thing. Marshall was at pains to point out that pleasure and pain were fundamentally subjective and unmeasurable, and that in any event, they often bore little relationship to the wants which motivated men to action. What a man wanted most might often turn out to give him little pleasure, or even pain; and what gave most pleasure was often something not sought after at all. It was, insisted Marshall, better to drop all talk of pleasure and pain. But to many of Marshall's contemporaries, even he was too ready to make normative assessments or assumptions: when his book on *Industry and Trade* was published in 1919 reviewers attacked it for its moral tone because 'in a scientific treatise a moral tone, however elevated, seems altogether out of place'.[5]

In a broader way, too, economics was tending to becoming less normative. Economists claimed that their subject was value-free and therefore a real science. They professed merely to describe the ways in which certain phenomena worked, and even if they did not all eschew the making of policy recommendations, these could (it was said) be understood as showing how certain objectives could best be achieved *if they were thought to be desirable*. But on the question of their desirability, the economists offered no opinion. By no means everyone accepted this somewhat eunuch-like stance. A. C. Pigou, for example, who published the first edition of his *Economics of Welfare* in 1912, and continued to have an important influence in the inter-war period, was perfectly prepared to make policy recommendations on the common-sense assumption that everybody would agree that an increase in economic welfare was desirable. The problem, however, which many economists, especially in the inter-war period, found to be an insuperable obstacle to this sort of approach was that which was known as the inter-personal comparison of utilities. It came to be argued that it was not possible, on any scientific or

---

[4] *Essays in Biography*, revised edn. (London, 1951), p. 140.
[5] Ibid., p. 191.

mathematical basis, to *prove* that one person's 'utility curve' was the same as another's, or that is, in plain English, that one person would derive the same satisfaction as another from the same good.[6] The whole matter is unprovable because it rests on knowledge of other people's actual feelings. Consequently, it followed that there was no way of proving what distribution of resources would give the maximum possible utility, and therefore no way even of proving what would be the best way of allocating the productive resources of the State.

At this point, it may be said that economic theory split into two. On the one hand there were those who rejected this somewhat arid attempt to develop a value-free science. Pigou himself continued to justify his assumption that utilities were broadly comparable. 'In all practical affairs we act on that supposition', he said,[7] and he might have added that so do Government, Parliament, and the Courts. And a number of other leading economists, such as D. H. Robertson, were willing to go along with him. But in the inter-war period a majority of economic theorists were unwilling to abandon the attempt to maintain their scientific objectivity, and a long struggle began to find ways of rescuing welfare economics from the problem of interpersonal comparison of utilities. In the end some sort of consensus began to emerge around the concept of 'Pareto-optimality', which consisted essentially in arguing that one situation could be proved to be superior to another, without making inter-personal comparisons of utility, if at least one person in the second state was better off than in the first state and if nobody was worse off. This approach, somewhat refined, is still used by many economists as the basis of welfare economics, but on the whole it can be said that, in England at least, economics has, in the post-Second World War era, tended to accept the challenge of making normative assumptions and basing policy recommendations upon them.

I have referred to these movements in economic thought mainly because there appears to have been a curious parallel between them and much legal thinking during the same period, even though (as I have suggested) direct influence of the one field on the other, in any substantive sense, seems to have been conspicuously absent. The resemblances are those of methodology. For (as we shall see) law, like economics, though surely somewhat less plausibly, tried to establish itself as a value-free science; and, again, as with economics, it was in the inter-war period that this movement reached its height. And if the economic theorists were more rigorous and more successful in maintaining contact with

---

[6] This argument was first put forward by Lionel Robbins in his *Essay on the Nature and Significance of Economic Science* (London, 1935).

[7] Appendix XI to *Economics of Welfare*, 4th edn. (London, 1960).

mathematical truths and the strict laws of logic, the lawyers may, perhaps, have remained more in contact with reality. There is even a parallel between the concept of Pareto-optimality and some legal thinking, because the Pareto requirement that nobody should be any worse off, if a changed situation is to be capable of being proved superior to the previous situation, naturally brings to mind the concept of freedom of contract. For the Pareto requirement is that nobody must be made worse off *in his own estimation*, if the second state is to be deemed superior to the first, and a lawyer would naturally translate this into the language of consent. In at least one version of the Pareto concept, this would mean, in effect, giving a power of veto over any change to any person affected by the change, and refusing to allow the majority to override that one person's dissent.

Moreover, the Pareto concept looked suspiciously as though it were itself value-loaded. For if no situation could be deemed an improvement on another so long as one single person claimed to be worse off in his own estimation, was this not simply re-erecting the value of free choice into the ultimate good? And was this not resurrecting classical economic value structures even at their most extreme? Herbert Spencer himself would have welcomed the new critique of welfare economics. Modern liberalism (not to mention socialism) is plainly incompatible with a restrictive concept of Pareto-optimality.[8] It would be virtually impossible to introduce any social reforms if Governments adhered to the rule of not making a single person worse off (in his own estimation) by the change. On the other hand it is possible to argue that the judgment that individuals are sometimes wrong in their estimation of what will bring them the most satisfaction has a greater value-content than the converse. Looking back on these debates today from the perspective, not of an economist, but of a lawyer, it is hard to understand how much heat they generated at the time. It seems extraordinary that well into the twentieth century, when Parliament and the law were constantly being used to override the values of individual free choice in the interests of some supposed national good, so many economists were prepared to insist that they had nothing to contribute in the attempt to evaluate these claims to improve the national good.

The parallel between economic and legal theory has continued for there has been a marked movement in the past decade or two away from the search for value-free law. Although it cannot be said that all English lawyers have yet fully accepted this change, there are now few who

[8] See Sen, 'The Impossibility of a Paretian Liberal', 78 *Journal of Political Economy* 152 (1970); 79 *Journal of Political Economy* 1406 (1971); Peacock and Rowley, 'Pareto Optimality and the Political Economy of Liberalism', 80 *Journal of Political Economy* 476 (1972); Hillinger and Lapham, 'The Impossibility of a Paretian Liberal: Comment by Two Who Are Unreconstructed', 79 *Journal of Political Economy* 1403 (1971).

continue to defend the idea that legal rules can be deduced by a logical process of reasoning without any reference to values.

The Theory of Marginal Utility

The greatest theoretical advance made by the neo-classical economists was to work out the theory of marginal utility. The theory was groped at by Jevons, though never wholly stated by him, at least in a form satisfying to a modern economist. But by the 1890s the work of Marshall and others had established this vital element in modern economic theory. The key to the theory was the 'law' of diminishing marginal utility, the assumption (or fact) that as an individual acquires more and more quantities of any good, each additional increment is of less utility to him than the previous one. The old paradox of the diamonds and the water was now satisfactorily explained at last. Diamonds are normally more valuable than water only because most consumers have ample access to water anyhow; but to a man dying of thirst, a cupful of water would not only have more utility than a diamond, but it would (in his estimation) be worth a great deal more. Thus it is not really true that water is more useful but less valuable than diamonds. The paradox arises from the failure to distinguish between an aggregate quantity of the goods, and each additional marginal increment.

Developed marginal utility theory came to be applied in a number of different cases, and to signify several different things. First, it came to mean that a consumer could optimize his satisfactions by so distributing his income that, at any given moment, the marginal utility of an additional pound spent, should give him equal satisfaction no matter that there is a whole range of goods that he might choose to spend it upon. If he could obtain twice as much utility by spending it on one commodity than another, this would be a sign that he had previously spent too little of his income on the first and too much on the second commodity. Secondly, it came to signify that a producer would optimize his profits by ensuring that the marginal product of each pound's worth of expenditure, whether on any form of capital or labour, would be equalized. The law of diminishing marginal productivity played the same role here as the law of diminishing marginal utility in the theory of demand.[9] But the third, and for present purposes, much the most important conclusion that could be drawn from marginal utility theory, was that society's total aggregate of utility could be substantially increased by a greater equalization of wealth. If the law of diminishing marginal utility had any validity, then it must equally apply to money and wealth generally, as to everything else. The millionth pound earned or possessed by the millionaire would give him less satisfaction than the hundredth pound

[9] Mark Blaug, *Economic Theory in Retrospect*, revised edn. (Homewood, Ill., 1968), p. 276.

earned or possessed by the more modestly-off citizen. In one sense there was nothing new in this. It had been stated by Bentham himself many years earlier when he had insisted that ten times the wealth does not produce ten times the quantity of happiness, and had therefore concluded, that '[t]he more nearly the actual proportion approaches to equality, the greater will be the total mass of happiness'.[10] But the difference in emphasis that arrived with the neo-classical economists was great. Bentham had been no egalitarian, and most of the classical economists were so imbued with the importance of preserving property rights as the political and economic foundation of society that redistributive ideas had not been taken seriously before the 1870s. Mill, it is true, had argued for some element of redistribution but on these matters his ideas were very advanced and probably had more influence after his death than during his life.

In the period after 1870, what was new was the use being made of the law of diminishing marginal utility as a deliberate weapon with which to campaign for greater equality of wealth and earnings. Indeed, it was precisely against this use of economic theory that Robbins and others rebelled in the inter-war period, for they wanted to demonstrate that the move to egalitarianism was a political or ethical movement, not justified on 'pure' economic grounds. But in the early years of this period, between perhaps 1870 and 1914, these voices of protest had not yet been raised, and there was, for the first time, a strongly felt, and a strongly voiced, conviction that the distribution of wealth was too unequal to be tolerable. It is paradoxical that these voices were being raised so loudly at the very moment that the working class began to climb so strongly out of the bare subsistence level of life to which they had been condemned from time immemorial. But in a sense it was this very increase in working-class affluence which was itself part of the cause of changing attitudes. Working-class wages were no longer seen as a mere irreducible 'cost' of production, but themselves a source of utility. As soon as working-class welfare began to be seriously taken into account by economists it was seen that 'the utility of goods consumed by workers was no different from any others'.[11] No doubt there were other influences at work in the rise of egalitarianism. Perhaps it was partly due to the growing political power of the working class; perhaps it was due to the fact that conspicuous consumption was becoming a more marked feature of upper-class life during this period when social standards were largely set by the Prince of Wales, later Edward VII; perhaps it was due to the growing conviction that the wealth of the aristocracy was based on its monopoly control of most the nation's land;[12] perhaps it was due to the passing away of the

---

[10] *Principles of the Civil Code, Works*, ed. Bowring, i. 305.
[11] Joan Robinson, *Economic Philosophy* (London, 1963), p. 51.   [12] See *post*, p. 633.

Malthusian fears, and to the growing acceptance that the condition of the poor was an economic rather than a moral problem.[13]

But whatever the causes, it is clear that from the 1870s onwards the economists began to take redistribution much more seriously. Jevons, for example, argued for the development of public goods and services like free public libraries on the ground of 'the enormous increase of utility which is thereby acquired for the community at a trifling cost'.[14] Similarly, paintings in the possession of private individuals could only be seen and enjoyed by a handful of people, whereas paintings in a public art gallery could be enjoyed by thousands and could therefore be justified by 'the principle of the multiplication of utility, a principle which lies at the base of some of the most important processes of political economy ...'.[15] So too Marshall quite openly accepted that the law of diminishing marginal utility applied to money, with all that that implied: 'A shilling is the measure of less pleasure, or satisfaction of any kind, to a rich man than to a poor one ... The clerk with £100 a year will walk to business in a much heavier rain than the clerk with £300 a year; for the cost of a ride by tram or omnibus measures a greater benefit to the poorer man than the richer. If the poorer man spends the money, he will suffer more from the want of it afterwards than the richer would.'[16] By the time of Pigou's book on the *Economics of Welfare* the arguments were beginning to assume a more dogmatic form. So long as the national income as a whole is not decreased, asserted Pigou, 'any increase within wide limits in the real income enjoyed by the poorer classes, at the expense of an equal decrease in that enjoyed by the richer classes, is practically certain to involve an addition to economic welfare.'[17]

Moreover, together with these overt arguments in favour of a greater measure of economic equality, there was increasing faith in the probability of long-term improvement of working-class conditions. The old 'iron law' of wages was discredited. It was no longer true that whenever wages rose, population correspondingly increased to force them down again. Population was, indeed, still increasing, but so was the national income. Increased numbers of workmen no longer forced wages down. So, too, the final discrediting of the 'wage fund' theory opened the door to recognition that trade unions and wage bargaining could actually increase working-class wages without corresponding decreases elsewhere

---

[13] Serious social studies of working-class poverty began in the 1890s with Charles Booth's work in London, and Seebohm Rowntree's in York; this was advanced by the Webbs' Minority Report in the Committee on the Poor Laws in 1905 and Beveridge's classic study of unemployment in 1909.

[14] 'Rationale of Free Public Libraries', first published in 1881, reprinted in *Methods of Social Reform* (London, 1883), pp. 28-9.

[15] Ibid.

[16] *Principles of Economics*, 8th edn. (London, reprinted, 1961), p. 16.

[17] *Economics of Welfare*, 4th edn., p. 96.

in industry; it was unfortunate, perhaps, that in the excitement of this discovery, the limitations on its truth were overlooked. Only in the 1970s did English trade unions leaders once again acknowledge that wage increases for some workers, without a corresponding increase in production, may still cause loss of earnings and even unemployment to other workers. But in the 1870s and the ensuing decades, few were worried by the limits on the extent to which redistribution could go. The facts themselves were, anyhow, there for all to observe. It was plain that workers were gradually rising off the floor of bare subsistence levels. Even the concern roused by the alarming findings of the new poverty studies, such as those of Seebohm Rowntree and Charles Booth, were in a sense a testimony to the general increase in working-class living standards. A generation earlier the facts revealed by Booth and Rowntree would have surprised nobody; now they appeared shocking.

And then, again, there was increasing doubt about the workings of the system of rewards and penalties in the now not quite so competitive society that England was becoming. For one thing, the divergence of economics from ethics now led economists to insist that an efficient distribution of rewards and penalties was not a matter of justice at all. They made no claim that a free market economy 'rewards moral excellence, but only that it rewards economic service'.[18] But there were even doubts about the system's efficiency in doing this too. As we have seen, Mill had expressed some of these views somewhat in advance of his times. But towards the end of the century they were becoming a good deal more commonplace. Were the rich and prosperous in fact enjoying the proceeds of skill and hard work? Were the poor also the idle and foolish? It seemed increasingly implausible as the nineteenth century drew to its close that these equations could still be made. Alfred Marshall, for example, in his quiet academic manner, suggested that:

there is some interest in the inquiry how much of the income of successful men is due to chance, to opportunity, to the conjuncture, how much to the good start they have had in life; how much is profits on the capital invested in their special training, how much in the reward of exceptionally hard work; and how much remains as a producer's surplus or rent resulting from the possession of rare natural gifts.[19]

Elsewhere Marshall warned against the over-sanguine belief that if only the existing national income was distributed more equally there would be more than enough to go round. This comfortable belief, which has supported egalitarians throughout the ages, was, as Marshall insisted, disproved by statistics.[20] There were too many poor and too few rich, but

[18] Cannan 'The Practical Usefulness of Economic Theory', in *Essays in Economic Method*, ed. Smyth (London, 1962), p. 190.
[19] *Principles*, p. 480.   [20] *Memorials of Alfred Marshall*, ed. Pigou, p. 162.

nevertheless, it is clear that, over all, Marshall was convinced that the existing inequalities were too great. The only justification for them was the necessity to provide the incentive to enterprise, saving, and progress, and '[a]ny diminution of them which [could] be attained by means that would not sap the springs of free initiative and strength of character, and would not therefore, materially check the growth of the national dividend, would seem to be a clear social gain'.[21]

The Growth of Empiricism

There is one further general characteristic of economic theory in the period 1870 to 1970 which is worth noting. As we saw in Part II of this work, one of the most striking characteristics of classical economic theory was its powerful tendency to *a priori* arguments, based on a minimum of factual premises. And even these premises were mostly assumed, rather than the result of empirical observation and measurement. One of the results of this had been that classical economic theory had abounded in broad and sweeping generalizations on which policy recommendations were based. In the period after 1870 this tendency was reversed. Economists began to eschew the broad statement of principle; they began to observe the data—which were themselves becoming increasingly available in Government statistics and the fruits of academic research-ers—and the data tended too often to disprove those broad and comfortable generalizations. And as they moved away from *a priori* argument they also tended to move away from the long-term view towards a short-term one. Instead of making policy recommendations based on what they took to be long-run tendencies, they were apt to make recommendations on the immediate short-term results of what they observed.

This movement, like many others of the neo-classical economists, had some roots with the classics themselves; and to a considerable degree it was probably due to the sheer accumulation of knowledge which had been going on, particularly since 1830. But by the time of Jevons, the change in approach had become more marked, and Jevons can claim to be the first serious empirical economic thinker of the new school. To take one or two instances, of particular relevance to our theme, Jevons rejected Ricardo's argument that wages always tended to fall to a subsistence rate. It simply was not true, he asserted; wages in England varied from ten to forty shillings per week in different parts of the country and there was no sign of any tendency for them to converge.[22] Perhaps Ricardo would have brushed this aside and retorted that he was talking of long-run tendencies, but it seemed that this long run would have to be measured in decades if not centuries, if the argument was to be

---

[21] *Principles*, p. 594.   [22] *The Theory of Political Economy*, p. 256.

revalidated. Then again, Jevons was a keen advocate of experimentation in the social sciences, and was even anxious to see this extended to legislation. Since the results of legislative changes were so often hard to predict, he urged, argument could in practice only be settled on the basis of experience, and that demanded a willingness to experiment. In a lecture in 1867, for example, he argued (at a time when the Post Office was widely thought to be an example of efficient state enterprise) that both State monopolies and private enterprise had great advantages, but that the choice between the two could not be settled by anything except experience,[23] and in another paper in 1880 he pleaded for social reforms to be tried out on a small experimental basis rather than by massive changes which, if unsuccessful, took years to undo.[24]

Similarly, Alfred Marshall, in his inaugural lecture at Cambridge in 1885, argued that the chief deficiency of the classics was not so much their tendency to abstract argument, but that they generalized too widely about how men would behave and react to given circumstances: 'The same bent of mind that led our lawyers to impose English civil law on the Hindoos, led our economists to work out their theories on the tacit supposition that the world was made up of city men.'[25] This, he said had led them to attribute a much more powerful effect than was in fact justified to the laws of supply and demand, for they overlooked man's 'human passions, his instincts, his class jealousies and class adhesiveness, his want of knowledge, and of the opportunities for free and vigorous action'.[26] And in 1897 he insisted that it was now patent 'even to those who are in a hurry, that no practical problems can be settled offhand by appeal to general doctrines'.[27]

One of the more interesting of the new empirical economists was Cliffe Leslie, an economist and also a member of the Bar, who held for many years a combined Chair of Jurisprudence and Political Economy at the Queen's University of Belfast. Cliffe Leslie (though known today to economic historians rather than lawyers) had studied under Sir Henry Maine and had evidently been deeply influenced by the rising 'historical school' of social science. This new historicism, especially when taken with the comparative dimension that Maine gave to it, helped to make social thinkers generally more sceptical of the sweeping *a priori* generalizations so beloved of the classical economists. It was no longer possible to rely on Natural Law to demonstrate this or that proposition when, in the pages of Maine, examples could be found of some Indian people whose customs and traditions flew in the face of Natural Law. One of Cliffe Leslie's more interesting writings for the lawyer is a paper

---

[23] *Methods of Social Reform*, p. 278.   [24] Ibid., p. 253–76.
[25] *Memorials of Alfred Marshall*, ed. Pigou, p. 155.
[26] Ibid., p. 154.   [27] Ibid., 266-7.

entitled 'The Known and the Unknown in the Economic World', in which he attacked the economic theorists' assumption of full knowledge on the part of those who deal in the market. 'Instead of the world of light, order, equality, and perfect organization, which the orthodox political economy postulates, the commercial world is thus one of obscurity, confusion, haphazard, in which amid much destruction and waste, there is by no means a survival of the fittest even though cunning be counted among the conditions of fitness.'[28]

In the twentieth century, this trend has, if anything, been accentuated. Perhaps Keynes added the final touch when he demolished the traditional belief in the self-righting mechanism which was thought to control the economic order. The comforting belief that, when unemployment was high, wages would fall, and employers would respond by hiring more men, was now shown to be an illusion. This result might, or might not follow: it depended on the circumstances. The generalization would no longer work. There was (and perhaps still is) even doubt about whether the most fundamental premises of the classics were right at all. In 1944 when many assumed that the post war world would turn away altogether from the capitalist system, Karl Polanyi asserted that even 'the alleged propensity of man to barter, truck and exchange is almost entirely apocryphal'.[29] Perhaps this view has not yet become widely accepted', but there is no doubting the move away from sweeping generalizations and long-run principles. Since the end of the Second World War the trend has been more marked than ever. The close relationship between economic policy and political government in these past thirty years has greatly shortened the time-scale of decision making. Governments want their economic policies to produce tangible benefits before the next election, not in the next decade, still less in the next century. This result of the modern democratic political machine has tended to sweep much economics along with it. Pragmatism is the respected approach to policy making, and principle is nowhere to be seen. Every problem is treated on its own merits, every case is entitled to a separate solution, and inevitably, in the process, long-run considerations tend to be forgotten.[30] As we shall see, here too, developments in the law have closely paralleled those in economics.

LAISSEZ-FAIRE AND FREEDOM OF CONTRACT

Whether or not the classical economists were rightly interpreted by contemporary opinion as being doctrinaire supporters of *laissez-faire* and

[28] *Essays in Political Economy* (2nd edn., Dublin, 1888, reprinted, New York), p. 235.

[29] *The Great Transformation* (Boston, Mass., 1944), p. 44.

[30] See L. Robbins, *Evolution of Modern Economic Theory* (London, 1970), p. 188; J. Viner, *The Long View and the Short* (Glencoe, Ill., 1958), p. 112.

freedom of contract, it is quite clear that the economists of the post-1870 period were determined not to be tarred with the same brush. In a lecture in 1870 J. E. Cairnes hit the nail firmly on the head, protesting that political economy was 'very generally regarded as a sort of scientific rendering of this maxim—a vindication of freedom of enterprise and of contract as the one sufficient solution of all industrial problems'.[31] The new economists felt it necessary to dissociate themselves from the idea that these were scientific truths of economic theory.

Of course, it remained true that freedom of contract, or freedom of exchange, at least, was a freedom, and like other freedoms was prima facie of value. In his *Theory of Political Economy* Jevons was still treating freedom of exchange as a most important and valuable part of the process by which resources are distributed through the community:

[S]o far as is consistent with the inequality of wealth in every community, all commodities are distributed by exchange so as to produce the maximum of benefit. Every person whose wish for a certain thing exceeds his wish for other things, acquires what he wants provided he can make a sufficient sacrifice in other respects. No one is ever required to give what he more desires for what he less desires, so that perfect freedom of exchange must be to the advantage of all.[32]

But the truth is that to Jevons this was little more than a ritual genuflection in favour of freedom. As he himself limits his remarks in this quotation, it is, for one thing, quite clear now that freedom of contract only produces the maximum of benefit, given the existing distribution of wealth. If that distribution is unjust, or unsatisfactory, then any resultant contractual exchanges will reflect that injustice or unsatisfactoriness. This vitally important qualification to the efficacy of freedom of contract to produce a satisfactory distribution had been almost totally neglected by the classics who had rarely questioned the existing inequalities. Now the position was being more clearly spelled out. To those (like Bramwell) who argued for protection of property *and* freedom of contract, the answer could be given, that freedom of contract had to follow and be based upon a just distribution of wealth; the sanctity of free contract could be no greater than that of the underlying distribution of wealth.

Then there was the greater empiricism, the greater awareness of the reality of much that went on in the name of freedom of contract. In a little book on *The State in Relation to Labour*, published in 1882, some twelve years after his *Theory*, Jevons insisted upon looking at the reality of things:

It is all very well [he protested] for theorists and 'cabinet philosophers' to argue

---

[31] Cited, T. W. Hutchison, *A Review of Economic Doctrines 1870–1929* (Oxford, 1953), p. 10.

[32] p. 171. Note that Jevons, like the classics, writes as though freedom of contract was freedom to make a present exchange, rather than freedom to bind oneself to the future.

about what people ought to do; but if we learn from unquestionable statistical returns that thousands of hapless persons do, as a matter of fact, get crushed to death, or variously maimed, by unfenced machinery, these are calamities which no theory can mitigate.[33]

And then again:

If an employer offers a man work in a very unhealthy workshop, and the man accepts the work and its conditions, are the employer and the workman at perfect liberty to carry out such a contract? . . . [E]ven in the extreme case of the adult man, experience shows that men from mere thoughtlessness or ignorance incur grave injuries to health or limb which very little pressure from the legislature would avert with benefit to all parties . . . [T]he first step must be to rid our minds of the ideas that there are any such things in social matters as abstract rights, absolute principles, indefeasible laws, inalterable rules, or anything whatever of an eternal and inflexible nature.[34]

And to ram home the lesson that matters of this kind were no longer to be settled by an appeal to principle, he went on:

I conceive that the State is justified in passing any law, or even in doing any single act which without ulterior consequences adds to the sum total of happiness. Good done is sufficient justification of any act, in the absence of evidence that equal or greater evil will subsequently follow.[35]

These words did not fall on deaf ears. They were read (for example) by Joseph Chamberlain, and subsequently quoted by him in a debate in the House of Commons in 1892.[36]

But this was not all, for Alfred Marshall, and following him, his Cambridge successor A. C. Pigou, were to devote much attention to actual demonstration, real mathematical proof, that there were a variety of circumstances in which *laissez-faire* and freedom of contract did not actually produce the maximum public advantage. These were cases, both where the law needed to prevent or prohibit contracts that would otherwise be entered into, and where, without State interference, contracts which would be beneficial to society would not be entered into by the parties. The cases of market failure, and those involving monopolies or restrictive practices, were all giving anxiety to Marshall who was much more aware than many of his contemporaries of the extent to which British industry had turned its back increasingly on the competitive model from the 1890s onwards. It is an interesting commentary on the nature of an academic discipline that it was the theoretical demonstration by Marshall that *laissez-faire* sometimes breaks

[33] 3rd edn. (London, 1894), p. 2.
[34] Ibid., pp. 5 6.
[35] Ibid., p. 13.
[36] David C. Hanes, *The First British Workmen's Compensation Act 1897* (New Haven, Conn., and London, 1968), pp. 98 100.

down, rather than any practical observations, which appeared to have had the greatest impact, at least on his fellow economists.[37] And what was true of internal policies was also true of free trade. Marshall was unwilling to accept the sacred dogma of free trade as it had become during the latter part of the nineteenth century. To him free trade was a pragmatic question. For an economy in a certain state of development, protection might well be justifiable, for example, for the nurturing of nascent industries through the difficult early periods when they might otherwise be stifled at birth by cheap imports. To Henry Sidgwick, one of Marshall's Cambridge contemporaries, free trade had been a policy peculiarly convenient to Britain when adopted in the mid-nineteenth century. It had amounted to '[t]he proclamation of a free race for all, just when England had a start which she might probably keep "for centuries" '.[38] If Sidgwick was somewhat out in his time-scale, the basic idea was clearly right.

There are three particular areas on which the economists of this period focused in their arguments against *laissez-faire* and freedom of contract, first, the monopoly problem, second, the market failure cases, and thirdly, the problem of (what may for short be called) consumer ignorance. I can deal, at this point, with each of these three matters fairly briefly.

Monopolies

As we have seen, it was in the last decade or two of the nineteenth century that the movement began towards industrial concentration in England. Trade Associations and actual mergers, as well as bilateral restrictive arrangements of various kinds, were becoming more observable in the 1880s and 1890s. The economists at first looked on this phenomenon with some surprise. In a paper to the British Association in 1888, H. F. Foxwell, a Cambridge economist who later held a Chair at London University, remarked that '[a]fter a century of the keenest and most unbridled competition the world [had] ever known, economists [were] finding some of their greatest problems in the consideration of the growth and future of monopolies'.[39] It was a surprise because economists had generally assumed that once the older forms of monopoly (the Royal and Guild monopolies) had been swept away, monopolies would disappear and be kept out by competition. Perhaps, mused Foxwell, this had all been a great mistake. Perhaps competition was not a natural state for an economy but a transient phenomenon. As world-wide markets had developed for many commodities, the size of businesses had tended to develop too, and this meant that monopolists now could be world-wide

---

[37] Keynes, *Essays in Biography*, revised edn., pp. 185 6.

[38] 'The Scope and Method of Economic Science', in *Essays in Economic Method*, ed. Smyth, p. 80.

[39] 'The Growth of Monopoly and its Bearing on the Functions of the State', in *Essays in the Economics of Socialism and Capitalism*, ed. Smyth (London, 1964), pp. 77 89.

as well. Once they reached a certain size, these giant corporations could squeeze out competitors almost anywhere; this was a new development, because in the past monopolists had tended to be limited to one particular market, and this had always meant that as markets expanded, producers from other markets could come in and challenge the local monopolists. This was no longer so with the new world-wide monopolists. And although there were yet few of these, the munitions business was already largely in the hands of one firm, commented Foxwell.[40] Still, Foxwell was not willing to write off competition. Where monopoly took the form of combinations, or agreements not to compete, they tended to be unstable. Speaking with prophetic insight he noted that the 'difficulties in the way of making and maintaining such agreements are so formidable that they are not likely to make much headway in general, until industry is much more highly organized'. He went on to observe that really effective competition was a much rarer phenomenon than people sometimes assumed, and that 'nothing [had] been more favourable to the growth of practical monopolies than the regime of *laissez faire*'.

Marshall, too, had observed the growing trend with some disquiet. In a letter to a colleague in 1914 he had criticized the legal members of the House of Lords for their lack of common sense and knowledge of business, and he added, apparently in a reference to the *Mogul*[41] decision, that 'Halsbury went out of his way to preach an enormous sermon in favour of unlimited freedom to grant rebates: and had no idea that American economists—who are the highest authority on this particular subject— are convinced that those rebates strengthen the destructive and antisocial effects of unscrupulous trade combinations more than almost anything else . . .'[42] But in the 1890s Marshall himself seems to have been less sure of the nature of the problem and of the right way to deal with it. In a lecture in 1890[43] he had argued that perhaps public opinion was the best way to deal with the problem, for the law at best must be 'slow, cumbrous and therefore ineffective'.[44] He had also pointed to the paradox that English law had, at that time, a restraint of trade doctrine, but no anti-monopoly doctrine. Thus, actual mergers of businesses were not subject to any legal control whatever, whereas restrictive agreements might, at least in theory, be declared unenforceable as in restraint of trade. Even Parliament and the Government appeared to have adopted the same inconsistent policy, for example, prohibiting the restrictive pooling agreements between railways and then allowing them to merge.

[40] The reference to the munitions industry is especially interesting in light of the *Nordenfelt* case [1894] A.C. 535.

[41] [1892] A.C. 25, *post*, p. 697.

[42] *Memorials of Alfred Marshall*, ed. Pigou, pp. 452–3.

[43] 'Some Aspects of Competition', reprinted in *Essays in the Economics of Socialism and Capitalism*, ed. Smyth, pp. 90–122.   [44] At p. 116.

Perhaps it was these developments which made economists less hostile to the trade unions and their restrictive practices. But it was not that they did not perceive the monopolistic nature of trade unions. Jevons, for instance, insisted that the trade unions acted in the same way as all monopolists, trying to restrict entry, to prevent others from working, to stamp out piece work or other forms of payment by results, and make their labour as scarce and hence as valuable as possible.[45] In effect unionism was a form of protectionism in which the well-organized gained at the expense of others, rather than at the expense of the employers, who simply passed on all price increases.[46] Much of this was sound enough, and still rings true and relevant to the present day scene. But its message was lost somewhere along the line. As we shall see later, one of the marked developments of competition law during the twentieth century was the process by which workmen acquired, first parity with industrialists, and then an incomparably superior legal position.

By the inter-war period, when British business had largely ceased to have any belief in competition at all, economists were still basically puzzled as to what to make of the new form of the economy. On the one hand, there was in some quarters a distrust of the Trade Associations and their anti-competitive stance. But on the other hand there was also doubt—which had existed from the time of Adam Smith onwards—about the effectiveness of anti-monopoly or anti-Trust legislation. How were businessmen to be prevented from meeting together and discussing prices, Adam Smith had asked a hundred and fifty years earlier? And the economists of the 1920s and 1930s were still not at all sure that they knew the answer.[47] Then there was the undoubted fact that economies of scale were themselves demanding larger and larger industrial units anyhow. To prevent combinations in these circumstances would plainly be injurious to the public interest. Nevertheless, Pigou, for one, was in favour of some cautious control over price cutting designed solely to keep out new entrants to a business.

More broadly, it may be said that economic theory did not really catch up with economic developments during this inter-war period. The reality of the economy was that oligopoly and monopoly and anti-competitive Trade Associations existed in almost every industry throughout the length and breadth of the country. New entrants were ruthlessly kept out wherever possible by boycotts and, if necessary, secondary boycotts. In the newspaper retail trade, to take just one instance, it became the practice for local newsagents to establish a committee which had the power to vet all applicants who desired to open

[45] *The State in Relation to Labour*, 3rd edn., pp. 106-7.
[46] *Methods of Social Reform*, pp. 111-14.
[47] See, e.g., Pigou, *The Economics of Welfare*, Part II, Chapter XXI.

up a newsagent's shop in the district in question. If the Committee refused their sanction the applicant could not get supplies from the newspaper suppliers; for if the suppliers did supply him in defiance of the local Committee, the other newsagents—representing the whole of the trade outlets—would, in turn, boycott the proprietors. In 1925 a boycott of this nature, followed by a counter-boycott by the newspaper suppliers themselves, finished up in the Courts; but the Courts in effect washed their hands of the whole business telling the parties that they were all entitled to boycott as much as they pleased so long as no overt acts of illegality were committed.[48] For present purposes the more important aspect of the case is the factual situation revealed by it. The idea of a Committee of those who are already in a business exercising a right of veto over those who wish to enter into it, with no kind of public control or accountability, or (frequently) even knowledge of what was going on at all, would have been enough to make Adam Smith turn in his grave. The public, of course, were ultimately the losers from these, as from all restrictive agreements of this nature.

Similarly, the huge growth of resale price maintenance was backed, during the inter-war period, by the same pressure of boycotts and counter-boycotts. A retailer who sold below manufacturers' fixed prices would be placed on a stop-list, and refused supplies by all wholesalers. Any wholesaler who supplied him would similarly be placed on the stop-list. Sometimes, industries established 'Courts' at which 'offenders' who sold goods below the manufacturer's prices could be 'charged' and 'tried'. They could be 'fined', too, as an alternative to being placed on the stop-list. Once again, these activities came before the Courts and again, the Courts washed their hands of them, insisting that the parties were free to trade or not to trade as they pleased.[49]

And if prices were not set by the free play of competition, the same was now largely true of wages. They too were fixed by agreement of some sort arrived at between the employers' trade associations and the national trade unions in very many industries. In others, statutory intervention was already taking place in the form of establishing minimum wage levels.

The result of all these developments was that the textbook version of the free market economy simply failed to mirror the realities. The model of the competitive society, with large numbers of small businesses, each alone unable to influence the market price, with free entry to the business, not to mention unrestricted entry to imports, and all employing labour equally competing with others in a free labour market, was simply non-existent. Eventually some of this began to filter into the economic

---

[48] See *Sorrell* v. *Smith* [1925] A.C. 700; *post*, p. 700.
[49] See *Thorne* v. *Motor Trade Association* [1937] A.C. 797; *post* p. 700.

textbooks. In England Joan Robinson's *The Economics of Imperfect Competition* in 1933 made the first real attempt to analyse how this new model of the economy actually worked, how prices and wages were determined. But curiously, books like this seem to have had little overall impact on economic theory.[50] They certainly had no impact whatever on the common law, the Courts or the Judges. Throughout these years the arguments in favour of freedom of contract, which had all sprung from a belief in a free market economy, were still being proclaimed (at any rate by lawyers) at a time when the basis of the competitive economy had quite disappeared.

Market Failures

The second major challenge to the effectiveness of market theory during this period centred around a variety of areas in which it came to be seen that the market might fail to produce optimal results. I have referred previously to the problem of externalities, which is one large area of concern to the market theorist. Strictly, an externality is a cost imposed on others, which does not have to be paid for, or a benefit conferred on others for which recompense cannot be obtained. In broad terms the concept of an externality was not grasped by the classical economists (although we have seen that Chadwick had a fair perception of it) and its elucidation was left to Marshall, and more fully to Pigou. Pigou's solution to the problem was basically to tax those who impose costs on others and to offer subsidies to those who would, if they acted, confer benefits on others.[51] But in some cases Pigou envisaged (or supported) simple interferences with freedom of contract designed, for example, to make one party pay for a benefit conferred upon him without his consent. For instance, Pigou argued that a tenant of a short lease, or the fag-end of a long lease, would invest in the land only if an adequate return on his investment were assured by some provision for compensation at the end of the lease. In the absence of such a provision, an investment which might socially be a desirable economic investment would not be made. Then there are cases where a cost of movement of resources would lead to a loss to the owner of the resources and hence would not be made, and yet, if it were made, there would be a net social gain. In such a case, a subsidy of some sort would be justified as, indeed, is now available, for example to industries establishing themselves in new areas of high unemployment. Then there are public goods for which charges cannot be made to those who use their services, of which the classic example has always been the lighthouse. This may easily save its cost in social terms but the owner of the lighthouse is unable to send a bill to every ship

[50] See J. K. Galbraith, *Economics and the Public Purpose* (Harmondsworth 1975), Chapter 2.
[51] *Economics of Welfare*, pp. 175–83.

which benefits from seeing it, and it will only be built, therefore, by the State, which can calculate a social benefit sufficient to offset the social cost.

But the problems were seen by some as much broader than this. In a modern industrialized and urbanized society, it is rare that any important decisions by individuals do not have some effects on third parties, and so far as third parties are concerned, the contracts or arrangements between those immediately concerned are not free arrangements at all; their consent is neither sought nor obtained. They may be benefited or harmed by such exchanges, but they are not normally charged for the benefit, or compensated for the harm.[52] And if the answer to these market failures was more action by the Government or the State, the problem could be aggravated, for public action also creates benefits and losses, frequently on a substantial scale. A Government decision to build a road here or a school there will benefit some and harm others; even decisions of a purely financial character, a decision to grant a subsidy here or impose a tariff there, to increase this tax or decrease that one, may have significant effects on individuals. As we shall see later, the legal analogue of these economic ideas comprises not merely the decline of contract, but also the rise, once again, of unjust enrichment ideas, stressing the need for benefits to be paid for, even where there has been no contract, and also the rise of tort and reliance-based ideas, stressing the need to compensate for harm caused.

Consumer Ignorance

As economists began to investigate the empirical basis of the competitive society one problem which became more and more obvious was the gulf between the way many consumers in fact behaved and how they needed to behave for the market system to have optimal results. This problem had many ramifications. There was, for instance, the time-stream problem, which had never been adequately perceived by the classical economists. Economists now began to argue that all pleasures or consumer satisfactions ought, in a wholly rational world, to be weighed at the same moment. There is no rational ground on which a consumer may prefer a present pleasure to a future one, unless it is merely to take account of the possibility that he may die before the future pleasure is obtained.[53] But in fact all people prefer the satisfaction of present wants to future wants, and it is scarcely possible to conceive of a human society which does not have this characteristic. However, people discount future satisfactions at very different rates. One man may measure the value of

[52] See, e.g., Knight, *The Ethics of Competition* (London, 1935), p. 53.
[53] Pigou, *Economics of Welfare*, p. 25. See also H. Sidgwick, *The Methods of Ethics*, 7th edn., pp. 381–4, where the same point emerges in a philosophical context.

present wants so highly over future wants that he is prepared, in effect, to sacrifice a very large proportion of future satisfactions in order to obtain them sooner. He has, as economists would say, a high discount rate for future wants. Another man, by contrast, may discount future satisfactions at a very low rate; he reckons even distant satisfactions as nearly as great as those he can have at present. The latter may be said to be a more rational choice, since it approaches close to the perfectly rational choice of having no discount rate at all, or only the minimum necessary to cover the risk of dying before the want can be satisfied. Not everybody would accept this concept of rationality with its implication that there are no wholly rational people at all, but it is plausible enough to argue that a person who discounts the future so highly that he always lives to regret his earlier choices is behaving irrationally.

In Britain in the 1970s the relevance of this apparently rather theoretical problem to practical economic realities is acute. For if the economic system is permitted to respond to the freely selected choices of individual consumers, and if, on aggregate, those consumers have a high discount preference rate, the result may be that they will over-consume today, and have, inevitably, less to consume tomorrow. In a nutshell, consumers with high discount preferences may be tempted to eat the seed corn with which they ought to be growing next year's corn, or to consume so much of the productive capacity of the nation that there is nothing left to invest for the future. If they do this, the national income will decline progressively, and, in a sense, this is precisely what began to happen in Britain during the mid-1970s. Any responsible Government must, in this situation, take the investment decisions out of the hands of consumers, and must itself decide what is the appropriate discount rate of future want satisfaction.

Now all this is by no means irrelevant to matters of private law. For if consumers in aggregate cannot be trusted to behave rationally with regard to the discounting of future preferences, then the market justification for permitting individual consumers to make decisions of this kind is removed. It thus no longer becomes defensible, on this ground anyhow, to uphold a contract, for instance, by which a consumer borrows at very high interest rates. Other justifications may remain open, but it is no longer possible to argue that consumers should be allowed to make these decisions for themselves on the assumption that they know their own interests best and that their interests will harmonize with that of the nation as a whole.

We saw earlier how, in the eighteenth century, Equity came to the protection of those who dealt with future expectations, such as expectant heirs or seamen with a right to a share in some prize money. I there suggested that many of these decisions appear to have been made to protect parties who had inadequate knowledge about measuring the present value of a future property right, but they might, of course, equally have been cases of highly irrational choices made about the discounting of future satisfactions. In the nineteenth century, one of the most frequent complaints voiced about working-class habits, among economists and others, was the general failure of working men to save for their future, or for contingencies like sickness and unemployment. Even the skilled artisans who earned substantially more than the unskilled labourers, and therefore could have saved something, however modest, were constantly being upbraided for their failure to do so.[54] And similarly, as the century wore on, consumer credit transactions of various kinds began to raise in an acute form problems of a parallel nature. Consumers who entered into credit transactions on highly disadvantageous terms might have done so because of ignorance, but might equally have done so because of irrational discount rates about future wants. In such circumstances, it could now be argued that the general presumption in favour of a harmony between social interests and the private interests of contracting parties was displaced. And although this justification for much of the legislation of the period was not articulated in this form, the basic idea does seem to have had a significant effect on legislative policy. As we shall see, for instance, the consumer protection legislation against money-lenders, and later, hire purchase finance companies, was in part influenced by the discovery that the terms of many such consumer contracts were so harsh that no rational man would have knowingly entered into them.[55] And although there could be no precisely comparable justification for social legislation such as the compulsory National Insurance Act of 1911, it was at least possible to argue that many (or most) workmen, if they behaved rationally on these matters, would find it advantageous to insure themselves against the risks covered by the Act on the terms provided by the Act. There is thus a sense in which much of this social legislation was designed to overcome the problem of the irrational discounting of future wants, either by reducing the binding force of contracts in fact entered into, or by compelling the workers to enter into compulsory contracts.

But the problem of consumer irrationality was only part of a much broader problem of consumer ignorance. The theory of perfect competition assumed that consumers were possessed of 'perfect knowledge' of the products or services bought (and also of those which they did not buy) as well as having perfect knowledge of what their future wants

[54] Jevons, *Methods of Social Reform*, pp. 145–6; Marshall, *Principles*, p. 187.

[55] See, e.g., *Samuel* v. *Newbold* [1906] A.C. 461, where a wealthy man, not short of liquid assets, borrowed £2,000 at interest exceeding 100 per cent. Lord Loreburn in the House of Lords said (at p. 465) the transaction was 'inexplicable except on the footing that [the deceased] was unfit to manage business'.

would be, and of how relevant factors might change in the future. As economists began, from the 1870s on, to take an increasing interest in working-class consumption, as the variety of goods and services within the financial reach of consumers began to expand, so there was a gradual emphasis on the more practical side of consumer ignorance. Both Parliament and Courts, for example, became less inclined to assume that consumers could judge of the veracity of advertising or of representations made by those with whom they dealt. As more and complex technological products became available for consumer purchase, these tendencies became more evident. Consumers who, in the days of Adam Smith, might have been trusted to judge of the quality of simple foodstuffs, or cloths, available for inspection, were now faced with a great array of electrical and mechanical gadgets, of man-made cloths and pre-packaged foodstuffs, whose qualities could not be perceived by simple inspection. Even the sale of commodities whose value was, in a sense, inherently speculative, such as company shares, had already by 1870 been subjected to substantial legal control, and here too, the tread towards greater control became evident as people of more modest means found themselves the victims of sharepushers and tricksters.

These developments affected primarily consumer transactions. Those transactions entered into solely by businesses, for instance, were less affected by changes in the law. But even commercial enterprises found the changing markets in which they dealt raising some of these questions in a form which affected them, as well as consumers. Business people buy as well as sell goods, and for them, too, the problems of identifying quality by inspection and sampling were greatly magnified by the increase in the variety of goods. And even if many felt (as they still do) that market principles should generally be left to operate in transactions between business enterprises, on the ground that at least in their case, rationality may be assumed, and that the market can still perform a useful function in assisting the skilful and efficient, and weeding out the less skilful and less efficient, there were less easy problems to overcome. Some of the future risks that businessmen have to take account of are barely susceptible of rational judgment, and may partake of the nature of a lottery, rather than a method for distinguishing the efficient from the inefficient. The problem of variations in currency values was already troubling economists before the end of the nineteenth century, though it was depression rather than inflation which was the cause for concern. In the 1880s Alfred Marshall proposed a scheme for indexing the currency unit in which many contracts should be made, arguing that uncertainty about the future value of money was a major cause of discontinuity in industrial development.[56] But despite the much greater problems of

[56] Keynes, *Essays in Biography*, revised edn., p. 168.

changing currency values today, no progress has yet been made along these lines. It is left to contracting parties to calculate the future probabilities as best they can (or to negotiate suitable contractual clauses if they can agree), even though it is manifest that, over anything other than the very short term, currency movements cannot be predicted, but only guessed at.

Two further comments may be added on the problems of consumer ignorance. The classical economists and the early utilitarians were not unaware of some of these difficulties, but they tended to understress them for two related reasons. The first was that they had such confidence in the potentialities of mass education that they assumed that the public could be taught to pursue their long-term interests so as to maximize their satisfactions. And secondly, they were willing to treat the cost of failure as itself a part of the educative process. The consumer who (for example) foolishly bought some defective article would learn from his mistakes to be more careful next time. But since 1870, and still more since 1970, these arguments have seemed less persuasive. A century of universal education has not eliminated the problems of consumer ignorance, and it has certainly not taught people always to pursue their long-term interests at the expense of short-term gain. And as faith in the educational process has waned, so too has the willingness to accept the cost of failure. The consumer who makes an unsatisfactory purchase is no longer seen as learning a salutary lesson, but as the victim of something akin to fraud or sharp practice.

The End of Laissez-Faire

The developments sketched above had largely destroyed any lingering faith in *laissez-faire* by the end of the First World War. And there were surfacing also, still wider themes which have received much greater discussion since the end of the Second World War. For example, voices began to be raised to suggest that one of the most fundamental premises of the market economy was itself false, namely the idea that consumer wants are given. It came to be argued that consumer wants are not given, but created and stimulated by the nature of the society in which we live.[57] And it was also argued that consumers do not anyhow just want material things in life, things with a measurable economic value. There were increasing doubts, too, about the nature of the competitive system. If it is true that 'some of the criticisms brought against existing society amount to condemning a foot race as unfair because someone has come out ahead',[58] it was also true that life was not a race or a game.

[57] Knight, *The Ethics of Competition*, in two essays first published in 1922 3; since then this theme has been much developed in the works of Galbraith.

[58] Knight, *The Ethics of Competition*, p. 61.

So far as economic theory was concerned, it was Keynes who pronounced the funeral oration. In a little work entitled *The End of Laissez Faire*,[59] published in 1926, he said:

It is *not* true that individuals possess a prescriptive 'natural liberty' in their economic activities. There is *no* 'compact' conferring perpetual rights on those who have or on those who acquire. The world is *not* so governed from above that private and social interest always coincide. It is *not* so managed here below that in practice they always coincide. It is *not* a correct deduction from the Principles of Economics that enlightened self-interest always operates in the public interest. Nor is it true that self-interest generally *is* enlightened; more often individuals acting separately to promote their own ends are too ignorant or too weak to attain even these. Experience does *not* show that individuals, when they make up a social unit are always less clear-sighted than when they act separately.

And if this were not quite the end, it was, appropriately enough, Keynes himself who delivered the *coup de grâce*, with his *General Theory* offered to the world in 1936. For it was the acceptance of Keynesian economics after the Second World War by virtually all Governments in the industrialized world—and much of the rest as well—that gave any needed justification to the idea that economies should and could be managed, rather than left to reach their own equilibrium in their own way. There was, Keynes demonstrated, no self-righting mechanism. High unemployment might depress demand, which in turn prevented the decline of unemployment. Only Governments, by spending their way out of depressions, could bring unemployment down. And for many years it seemed to work. The wealth of the industrial nations increased at rates of growth undreamt of in history and the benefits of this new prosperity were shared by all classes. Only with the 1960s and 1970s did elements of doubt begin to creep in again as inflation threatened to become an even greater menace than the pre-war depression. But, at least in England, there are, even now, few voices calling for a return to *laissez-faire*.

But if most economists are agreed that there can be no return to *laissez-faire*, there is still a fundamental ambivalence over the role of the free market in modern England. On some issues, on some occasions, there seems still to be a firm belief in the virtues of competition and in the role of the market as an efficient instrument for the allocation of resources;[60] on other issues and other occasions, these beliefs are replaced by an equally firm conviction in the virtues of planning, State monopoly, or the allocation of resources by Government fiat.

[59] London, 1926.
[60] See, e.g., The *Report* of the Crowther Committee on Consumer Credit (London, Cmnd. 4596, 1971).

19

THE INTELLECTUAL BACKGROUND,
1870-1970—II

INDIVIDUALISM AND THE NEW SOCIAL ORDER

I HAVE suggested that the individualism of the early nineteenth century was partly based on the need to impose social disciplines on the new industrial and urban millions, while the State was building its administrative machine. By 1870 the basic groundwork of this machine had been firmly laid. Law and order reigned throughout the land.The modern police organization was gradually extended, first to the provincial cities and eventually to the rural areas. In due course, the arrival of the telephone, the radio, and the motor vehicle enabled the new authorities to strengthen their grip over the country so that breakdowns of order occurred less frequently, and could be coped with more swiftly when they did occur. And with this basic control over the forces of violence and crime, there came also greater control exercised by administrative and institutional organizations. The arrival of the modern commercial world, as well as the modern administrative world, brought, in a sense, new forms of disciplines. The whole country became subject to bureaucratic control, as it became subject to police control. The commercial life of a modern industrialized society depends to a substantial degree on order and regularity in the flow of business and of money. Firms and corporations learnt to keep their accounts properly, to maintain proper records; consumers learnt to pay their debts as a matter of course. The citizen's relations with the State became a matter of routine, of the proper filling-in of forms, and the daily processing of thousands of like cases. Taxes, like debts, came to be normally paid, as a matter of course. Business concerns learnt to make proper provision for the payment of taxes; consumers were assisted to do so by the development of P.A.Y.E. The due discharge of pecuniary obligations, long before legal or other sanctions are brought to bear, is, in the great majority of cases, an accepted and indispensable feature of a modern society. In this sense government by consent is no empty phrase. If nobody ever paid his debts or his taxes until compelled to do so by the arrival of the bailiff at the door a modern society would quickly descend into chaos.[1]

By the last third of the nineteenth century, it seems safe to say, these

[1] See *Sunday Times*, 17 Oct. 1976, for an account of the trouble caused in Belfast by the increasing failure of householders to pay their rates.

characteristics of the modern State were firmly established. Discipline and self-discipline had been at work; habits of punctuality, regularity, reliability, had become established among the mass of the population. It is, of course, difficult to say whether this was in any way due to the middle-class preachers who had urged self-reliance, self-discipline, thrift, and sobriety on the poor, or whether it was simply the discipline of circumstances, of poverty itself, and of the conditions of industrial employment. But nobody acquainted with modern industrial societies and also with the undeveloped societies of Africa or Asia can have any doubt of the extent and importance of the disciplining process which exists so much more formidably in the former. In 1900, however, this was far from obvious. The younger generation who surveyed the country on the opening of the new century, took for granted the orderly regulation of society. Men like Keynes, in Cambridge at the turn of the century, 'were not aware that civilisation was a thin and precarious crust erected by the personality and the will of a very few, and only maintained by the rules and conventions skilfully put across and guilefully preserved . . . It did not occur to [them] to respect the extraordinary accomplishment of [their] predecessors in the ordering of life [as it later seemed to Keynes] or the elaborate framework which they had devised to protect this order'.[2]

In the twentieth century, and more particularly at the present day, there are many who would share the views of the young Keynes and his friends. One cannot doubt the trend away from the Victorian belief in individualism, self-reliance, and self-discipline. This trend has been influenced by many factors but one of the most important has been the changing attitudes to social problems and their causes. Victorian morality was, as I have suggested, strongly purposeful, but by the end of the nineteenth century, it began to be discovered that it was often easier to solve social problems by changing the laws and the physical environment in which people lived and worked, than it was to change the people themselves. It had been discovered that people lived cleaner and healthier lives when public health, sanitation, and water facilities were forced upon them, than when they were merely exhorted to live more salubriously or to rent better accommodation. It was discovered that it was easier to cut down drunkenness by limiting licensing hours, than by moral persuasion. Poverty itself was more easily controlled when many of its causes—sickness, unemployment, old age—were directly tackled by the State, than when thrift and friendly societies were encouraged with moral exhortation or even supportive legislation.

[2] *Two Memoirs* (London, 1949), pp. 99–100. But his biographer argues that Keynes himself was always aware of these facts: Roy Harrod, *The Life of John Maynard Keynes*, Pelican ed. (Harmondsworth, 1972), p. 114.

The nature, and theoretical foundations, of much social research greatly strengthened these tendencies. Researchers saw human beings tabulated in statistical tables which enabled them to predict, with some accuracy, that in given social conditions many people would respond in a particular way. The very concepts of causation and responsibility began to change. The responsibility of the individual was displaced by the responsibility of those who controlled his environment. Drunkenness was no longer the responsibility, or the fault, of the drunkard, but of those who supplied him with drink, or who made his life such a misery that he was driven to it.[3] Poverty was not the responsibility of the feckless who failed to save, or insure against known risks, but of the nature of a society which encouraged people to spend.[4] Easy credit, likewise, was not the responsibility of the debtor who borrowed more money than he could hope to repay, but of the creditor who lent it too readily. Even shoplifting has come to be seen by some as not the 'fault' of those who steal but of those who 'tempt' them by attractive displays of consumer commodities.

Part of the reason for these changes is also to be found in the greater scepticism which modern social research has induced in matters of social causation. No longer, for the modern social scientist, or even the cynical man in the street, is there the same naïve confidence in motivation and causation shared by the classical economists and the utilitarians. We have learnt about the unconscious motivations of the human mind, about the subtle influences of education, advertising, and social pressures; we have learnt, too, that education is not the universal panacea which it was thought to be early in the nineteenth century. After a century of universal elementary education, there are still many social illiterates in modern societies, the misfits, the inadequates, the sub-normal, whose behaviour cannot be expected to follow any 'rational' pattern, however the word is defined. As Keynes said in the remarks cited above,[5] it cannot be assumed that self-interest is always enlightened. We know too much about social behaviour to believe that people in general can calculate future chances and maximize their satisfactions over any period of time. And with this scepticism about social causation there has naturally been a weakening of belief in the system of penalties and rewards, a weakening that has affected the whole body of law and indeed the whole fabric of society.

As the power of the State has expanded, and as public belief in the power of the State has expanded even further, there has been an increasing tendency to call on the State to remedy social ills of one sort

---

[3] See, for an early example of this attitude, E. Parry, *The Law and the Poor* (London, 1914), p. 261. The author was a County Court judge.

[4] Ibid., pp. 60-2.

[5] *Supra*, p. 626.

of another. Where the State tries and fails, or tries, only to succeed partially, or even where the State refuses to take on the task at all, the mere awareness that the State might, or could, solve the problems by a sufficient expenditure of money and effort, has often resulted in a shift in people's ideas about cause and responsibility. If the State can do something and does not do it, then the ills which remain may be seen as the responsibility of the State, and even as having been caused by the State. In the law, these results have often led to an expansion of legal liability for omissions, both on the part of the State[6] and of other institutional bodies.[7] But more broadly, as the belief in individual responsibility in this sense has declined, the role of contract in modern society has declined along with it. If individuals are not seen as responsible for their own fate, as entitled by natural right to the rewards or penalties which they reap under the economic and social system, then it is plain that the notion of leaving them to make their own arrangements is likely to weaken.

It is not too much to say that the very concept of competition, with its system of rewards and penalties, has lost much of its attraction in modern England, both in the social and in the economic sphere. I have referred previously to the ambivalent attitudes existing in England today towards socialist-type planning on the one hand, and a belief in commercial competition on the other. In this chapter my concern is with the system of rewards and penalties outside the economic system, and it cannot be doubted that here too (for example, in education) there has been a trend away from the idea of individual responsibility, with individuals goaded on by the spur of competition, eager for success and fearful of failure. From John Stuart Mill on, there has been a tradition of social thought which totally rejects the competitive spirit, as the 'law of the jungle', a process in which the strong and vigorous are encouraged to trample underfoot the weak and the underprivileged.

The waning of the force of individualism as a social belief has gone hand in hand with legal and institutional change. While Gladstone could, in 1889, still urge caution in extending the powers of the State, could still argue that 'the spirit of self-reliance, the spirit of true and genuine manly independence, should be preserved in the minds of the people';[8] the new Fabians like Shaw could point to the great mass of legislative activity which made a mockery of this kind of talk. In a lecture in 1887 Shaw made fun of politicians, 'coming upon the platform to talk of thrift, self-help, co-operation, temperance, and steady industry, and then going into the Cabinet to pass Factory Acts, Truck Acts, Mines

---

[6] See, e.g., *Home Office* v. *Dorset Yacht Co.* [1970] A.C. 1004.

[7] See, e.g., *Dutton* v. *Bognor Regis U.C.* [1972] 1 Q.B. 373; P. S. Atiyah, *Accidents, Compensation and the Law*, 2nd edn. (London, 1976), pp. 92–108.

[8] *Speeches of W. E. Gladstone* (London, 1892), x. 132.

Regulation Acts, Education Acts, Employers' Liability Acts, every one of which would be monstrous violations of political principle and individual liberty if the workers whom they shield were really in the free and independent position implied by the speeches about thrift, industry and so on'.[9]

And the process has been gathering momentum since 1870. From writers and publicists like John Ruskin to Liberal politicians of the Asquithian era, a new anti-individualism was being preached. Ruskin, in particular, had vigorously attacked the so-called orthodoxies of political economy from the 1850s onwards, and had spread far and wide a distrust of the old individualism.[10] Though no socialist himself, he was very widely read among the working classes and certainly helped pave the way for newer collective ideas, both socially and economically. The growth of the new institutions, which I have previously discussed, naturally led opinion along the same paths. Workers increasingly saw their strength in the trade unions, and even businessmen who had traditionally argued for the virtues of competition and individualism, tended to see matters from a different perspective within their corporate organizations. Even in the 1930s it was possible for Berle and Means (perhaps with exaggeration) to argue that 'the corporation director who would subordinate the interests of the individual stockholder to those of the group more nearly resembles the communist in mode of thought than he does the protagonist of private property'.[11]

THE RISING TIDE OF EGALITARIANISM

After 1870 one of the most significant influences on society and law was, without doubt, the growing strength of the egalitarian ideal. Not only was there an increasing belief that simple fairness or justice required a greater degree of equality in treatment, but there was also a growing conviction that the social arrangements of the day did not produce a fair competitive result. The dice were too heavily loaded in favour of the upper classes. Not only did they own by far the greatest portion of the nation's land, but they also had all the advantages of better education and opportunities for advancement. The spread of the national educational system had not yet seriously begun to even out the chances of each new generation. And anyhow, it was coming to be increasingly recognized that education did not level out natural advantages, but merely enabled their possessors to use them with greater effect.[12] There

[9] 'The New Radicalism', in *The Road to Equality*, ed. Louis Crompton (Boston, Mass., 1971), p. 20.

[10] Sir Ernest Barker, *Political Thought in England, 1848–1914*, 2nd edn. (London, New York, Toronto, 1947), p. 171.

[11] *The Modern Corporation and Private Property*, revised edn. (New York, 1967), p. 245.

[12] See H. Foxwell, 'The Growth of Monopoly', in *Essays in the Economics of Socialism and Capitalism*, ed. Smyth (London, 1964), p. 79.

was now, too, a novel factor in the formation of opinion. The increasingly democratic electorate was able to mobilize opinion, through the press and by other means, to bring much greater pressure to bear on Members of Parliament. And the pressure they brought naturally was the pressure of the majority hungry for a share of what they took to be the illegitimate spoils of the minority. It was not merely a matter of the poor seeking a greater degree of the national wealth. The egalitarian spirit went far beyond that. It extended to a general desire to iron out many of the natural advantages and disadvantages enjoyed or suffered by varying social groups. The pressure to introduce increasing controls on the sale of alcoholic drinks, for example, was an attempt to even out the chances of life which made some people naturally more able to resist temptation than others. The self-disciplined were, in the interests of the undisciplined, to forego some of the benefits which they would have in an uncontrolled system. Writing in 1887, R. B. Haldane noted how considerations 'of expediency' might lead to regulation of all, with inconvenience to some, and benefit to others. But, he said, '[i]t may be that the considerations are so strong as to justify, in the general interest, the subjection of the sober section to some inconvenience for the sake of those whose motives are not enduring enough to save them from intemperance'.[13]

Similarly, the growth of insurance as a consumer, rather than as a commercial device, was much influenced by the desire to even out the chance distribution of misfortune. Samuel Smiles, always ready to praise any form of thrift or saving, argued for the benefits of life insurance by saying that it 'may be regarded in the light of a contract, by which the inequalities of life are to a certain extent averaged and compensated, so that those who die soon—or rather their families—become sharers in the good fortune of those who live beyond the average term of life'.[14] And this ideal was given much practical recognition with the beginnings of the State social insurance system in 1911, and its subsequent extension in the post-Second World War era, following the Beveridge Report. Social insurance from the beginning rested to some degree on compulsory and flat rate premiums which were essentially redistributive devices. The strong and healthy paid the same contribution premiums as the old and chronically sick. But in other respects the early Acts followed normal commercial practice in adjusting premiums to risk. By the time of the Beveridge Report, opinion had hardened in favour of flat rate contributions for all forms of social insurance. Beveridge's own words convey the ideal of social solidarity which lay behind his recommendation:

In the thirty years since 1912, there has been an unmistakeable movement of

---

[13] *Life of Adam Smith* (London, 1887), p. 156.
[14] *Thrift*, first published 1875 (London, 1903), p. 113.

public opinion away from these original ideas, that is to say away from the principle of adjusting premiums to risks in compulsory insurance and in favour of pooling of risks ... The term 'social insurance' to describe this institution implies both that it is *compulsory* and that men *stand together* with their fellows. The term implies a pooling of risks except so far as separation of risks serves a social policy.[15]

The irony in this passage, suggesting that men will only stand together when compelled to do so was, of course, unintentional. Beveridge was writing in the midst of the war, when egalitarian ideals were strengthened by the overwhelming sense that the whole nation was involved in one joint struggle. In the post-1945 period, the gathering strength of the egalitarian ideal has been phenomenal. As we shall see later, this movement to greater equality has necessarily interfered with freedom of contract, for it has involved the overriding of the free choice of contracting parties in the interests of socially proclaimed values. It is, too, a redistributive device. If (for example) all women receive equal pay it is inevitable that men will earn less (in terms of real earning power) as women earn more. The 'levelling up' process for some inevitably means a 'levelling down' for others.

It is impossible to do full justice to this massive theme in a work of this nature, and I propose therefore to concentrate here on two particular issues relevant to the question of freedom of contract. In Chapters 21 and 22 I shall also touch upon a number of other areas in which the growing force of egalitarianism has had an effect on national life.

The Land Question

In 1870 land still occupied the central position in much of the nation's social, political, and economic life which it had occupied from time immemorial. The great landowners still owned a huge proportion of the nation's surface. A semi-official nineteenth-century 'Domesday Book' in 1876 revealed that out of a total of 37 million acres in England and Wales, some two million were owned by 66 persons, more than a quarter of the whole was owned by 710 persons, and more than a half was owned by 4,500 persons.[16] This land was still—despite the growth of manufacturing industry—the chief source of the wealth of the rich, as well as the chief source of their political power which had by no means disappeared in 1870. A large proportion of it was still held on strict settlement which restricted its development and marketability, and much of it was let on agricultural tenancies to farmers, many of whom

---

[15] *Social Insurance and Allied Services* (The Beveridge Report), Cmnd. 6404 (1942), para. 25.
[16] This survey was full of inaccuracies, e.g., in treating 99-year leaseholders as freeholders. Attempts were made to correct these inaccuracies by various writers, some of whom came up with even more startling figures: W. L. Burn, *The Age of Equipoise*, pp. 305–6.

had no security of tenure beyond an annual lease. But most important of all was the fact that, with rising pressure of population, and the increasing affluence of the working classes, the demand for building land in the towns was raising the value of land year by year. With no effort on their part, and by virtue of the increase of the population and the improvement of civic amenities and facilities, the rich were able to grow richer every year.

There were at least three particular and identifiable grievances in this situation. The first was that of the farmers who rented the agricultural land from the landowners. These agricultural leases were usually annual leases so that the tenant had no security of tenure, nor had he any adequate incentive to invest in his farm. As an annual tenant he had no right, on termination of the lease, to compensation for improvements or fixtures, except in some places where certain customary rights were preserved. The tenant's legal position derived from the basic ideas of freedom of contract which had, by this time, became so firmly established. The landlord could not be made to pay compensation for improvements because he was under no obligation to pay for benefits conferred upon him without his consent. If the tenant chose to invest in the land, knowing of his limited security of tenure, it had to be 'assumed' that he knew what he was doing, and that he expected to derive an adequate return from the investment, even allowing for his limited tenure. There seems no doubt that during the last thirty years of the nineteenth century these factors were a serious inhibition on adequate investment in agriculture, although perhaps not so much as was once thought. In the seventeenth and eighteenth centuries, the system had, on the whole, encouraged investment and enterprise, rather than the reverse, because most of the investment capital had come from the owners, and not the farmers. But in the late nineteenth century, the owners were becoming more reluctant to invest in agricultural improvements, and they were themselves gradually losing their social and political roots in the landed estates themselves. Land was, increasingly, an investment, and one in which the greater part of their wealth was already invested. Far from investing more in land, the landowners were now about to start switching their wealth massively away from farms and into company securities. In 1870 only about ten per cent of the nation's farmers were owner-occupiers; by 1927 this figure had risen to 36 per cent,[17] itself a sufficient indication of the extent of this change. But there were also other problems. The strict settlement system still, in 1870, limited the landlord's incentive, or even ability, to invest in agriculture, as the short lease system limited the tenant's incentive. The landlord's powers to grant leases, to mortgage in order to raise capital, or to sell off part of an estate in order to develop the

[17] E. J. Hobsbawm, *Industry and Empire* (Harmondsworth, 1974), p. 202.

rest, were often circumscribed by the terms of the settlement under which he was, usually, a mere life tenant.

But the farmers had other grievances, too. There was, for a start, the question of shooting rights. Argicultural leases almost invariably preserved shooting rights to landlords, and even went so far as to restrict the tenant's right to put down the game in the interests of good farming. In many cases, no doubt, the tenant farmers were accustomed to these restrictions as part of a social order which had existed for centuries, and they may perhaps have derived corresponding advantages from these same social relationships with their landlords which compelled them to accept the game rights. But times were changing, the social order was changing, 'the politics of deference' was coming to the end of its long reign, and there were doubtless farmers who resented the social superiority of their landlords and the whole way of life of the 'idle rich' as they were coming to be called. Certainly to the radical politicians who took up their cause, these grievances began to seem intolerable, and the traditional defence of freedom of contract was wearing extremely thin. Even a relatively conservative lawyer, like Sir Frederick Pollock, writing in the early 1880s, argued that it was absurd to speak of freedom of contract in relation to the landlord and tenant relationship. For one thing, a large part of the legal content of the relationship was not expressed in a lease, but was 'implied' by the law anyhow:

The truth is . . . that the law of landlord and tenant has never, at least under any usual conditions, been a law of free contract. It is a law of contract partly express, partly supplied by judicial interpretation, and partly controlled by legislation and sometimes by local custom.[18]

Of course, lurking beneath the freedom of contract argument were yet more fundamental issues about the very right of property itself. A landlord was thought of as the *owner* of his rights in the land. The rights of ownership included, inevitably, the right to let the land at its full market price. To interfere in a freely negotiated contract between landlord and tenant was to deprive the landlord of part of his rights of ownership; it was, in effect, confiscation of property rights without compensation. Or so at least it had seemed to many Liberal politicians only one generation earlier. Lord Palmerston, for example, had repeatedly protested against legislation (at that time, generally proposed only with regard to Ireland, or the Colonies) which interfered in the contractual relation between landlord and tenant. In 1855, for example, when the rights of absentee landlords in Prince Edward Island were under attack by the local legislature, Palmerston had insisted that these landlords were owners of the land and that 'it would be as unjust and of

---

[18] *The Land Laws*, first edn. 1883, 3rd edn. (London, 1896), p. 150.

as bad example to *extinguish* the Rights of these owners as it would be to *extinguish* our Rights and to fix the conditions on which we shall be compelled to make over our farms to the tenants to whom we have let them. The legitimate and only honest way in which one man can become possessed of what belongs to another', he went on, 'is by Bargain and Purchase giving him the value which the owner is willing to take for it'.[19] And in 1863, when a proposal in relation to Ireland was under debate, he told the Commons that it was 'Communistic doctrine' to talk of the way in which landowners should be compelled to receive only such rents as other people might adjudge them entitled to receive.[20]

But in the 1870s Palmerston was dead and a new generation was in power. And the new generation was not afraid of some redistribution of wealth from landlords to tenants, if that was what was involved in interference with tenancy arrangements. To Joseph Chamberlain, for example, the rich already owned far too much of the nation's wealth, and any minor redistributive effect which legislation might have, would not, for that reason, have made it unwelcome. Not that such redistribution was openly advocated, or indeed, perhaps generally understood to be the result of legislative intervention. To many, legislation to give the tenant farmer security of tenure, or compensation for improvements, was simply a matter of fairness. Even if the landlord did not consent to the improvements, what did that matter so long as the improvement was real enough and genuine enough to raise the rental value of the land to an incoming tenant? As the nature of the agricultural lease was tending anyhow to become more of an investment than a social relationship, improvements to the land without the landlord's consent seemed no less justifiable than (say) ploughing back a proportion of company profits into further investments without the shareholders' consent.

As to the economists, they were not, on the whole, unsympathetic to legislative interference with freedom of contract between landlord and tenant. The lack of security of tenure to the tenant farmer, on the one hand, and the strict settlements restricting the powers of the landlord, on the other, were seen by many as creating a classic situation of market failure.[21] Investment which would be favourable from a social point of view was not being made because it was not sufficiently profitable either to the landlord or to the tenant. In economic theory, it can be argued that such market failures should not occur.[22] Landlords and tenants ought to perceive their interests, and if security of tenure is necessary to enable them both to benefit from profitable investment, it ought to follow that

---

[19] J. Ridley, *Lord Palmerston* (London, 1972), p. 690.

[20] Ibid., p. 688.

[21] Sir James Caird, *The Landed Interest and the Supply of Food*, first published 1877, 5th edn. by G. E. Mingay (London, 1967). See too, Marshall, *Principles of Economics*, 8th edn., p. 547.

[22] R. Turvey, *The Economics of Real Property* (London, 1957), Chapter VIII.

they would freely negotiate a lease with sufficient security of tenure to enable the investment to take place. In practice, however, this just did not happen.[23] Modern historians argue that this was by no means entirely the responsibility of the landlords.[24] In many cases, there was no security of tenure, not because the landlords refused to grant leases, but because the tenant farmers refused to take them. And the reason for this was that a fixed lease in those days was treated as involving a fixed rent, and tenants found that they were often better off without a fixed lease or a fixed rent. This was because, in good years, the landlord in practice found it impossible to raise the rent (except perhaps to a new incoming tenant) while in bad years, the landlord was often expected to, and virtually compelled to, forgo part of the rent. As Pollock observed at the time, 'in bad years it is the constant practice for the landlord to remit such a percentage of the rent as to leave the tenant answerable only for so much as the farm seems fairly capable of paying under the circumstances'.[25] Ideas of just prices, it seems, were not confined to the working classes.

But it was not only agricultural leases which raised social and economic issues in England in the last quarter of the nineteenth century. There was also the effect of the strict settlement on the marketability and availability of land for urban and even industrial development. For example, the fact that a life tenant could not usually grant leases for longer than 21 years began to be a serious obstacle to the grant of mining leases where large capital investment was required which could not easily be recouped within such a period.[26] But far more important, socially and politically, was the extent to which the great landowners still controlled urban development. They frequently regarded such development as primarily an investment, granting building leases for 99 years, but controlling the use to which the land could be put. Again, it began to be argued that freedom of contract in relation to such matters was unreal, if only because the landowners were frequently monopoly owners of huge tracts of urban land. Pollock, for instance, wrote in 1883:

It is evidently absurd to speak of freedom of contract in relation to such a system. Desirable building ground near towns, and still more the ground of towns and cities already long occupied, and eminently those districts and sites which are favoured by business or fashion, are a monopoly in the hands of the landowner.

---

[23] See Joseph Kay, *Free Trade in Land*, 3rd edn. (London, 1879), p. 69: 'As every lawyer knows ... not one man in ten thousand knows anything about this law [of fixtures]'. Kay was a Q.C. and an M.P., a brother of Sir James Kay-Shuttleworth and of Kay L.J.

[24] See J. D. Chambers and G. E. Mingay, *The Agricultural Revolution 1750–1880* (London, 1966), pp. 160–6.

[25] *The Land Laws*, 3rd edn., p. 155.

[26] J. T. Ward and R. G. Wilson (eds.) *Land and Industry* (Newton Abbott, 1971) p. 66.

The landowner dictates his terms to the building lessee, who in turn dictates them to an occupier, making the occupier's obligations, for his own protection, exactly follow those of the original lease. In this way the population of whole cities may be said to live at the will of a few great landlords. Over whole square miles of what is commonly called London, the Duke of Westminster or the Duke of Bedford may without appeal or control forbid any given kind of business to be carried on.[27]

There was also much complaint that the land in the hands of the old aristocracy did not come adequately onto the market, and since the time of John Bright, there had been Liberal demands for 'free trade in land'.[28] Much of the complaint against the system was misdirected, through ignorance, against the law of primogeniture, when in reality it was the strict settlement which was to blame.[29] The strict settlement, as we saw above, was a serious obstacle to investment and development of land. Conveyancers had, for many years, been writing in powers of leasing and management, to enable the tenant for life to develop the land in certain respects, but these common form powers too often proved inadequate in the late nineteenth century. There were complaints too, that the strict settlements protected the rich families from the follies and extravagances of life tenants. Because each life tenant had only a limited interest, the land could not be seized and sold to pay his debts, nor was it available for distribution in the event of his bankruptcy. There was, too, another problem arising from the practice of granting very long leases. These frequently contained all manner of restrictive provisions which could become totally out of date after the passage of a century, and yet could remain in force, hampering development, and adding to legal costs and obscurities of title.   There were also, by this time, protests being voiced against the practice of securing the resettlement of an estate as soon as the eldest son reached twenty-one years of age. It was rash to assume that, at such an age, and subject to family pressures, the eldest son could make a rational and dispassionate judgment as to his own best interests in the long-term future. The easy assumptions about the ability of each man to judge his own interests best were now being challenged here as elsewhere. The lawyer-economist Cliffe Leslie wrote:

Before the owner of the land has come into possession; before he has any experience of his property, or what is best to do, or what he can do in regard to it; before the exigencies of the future or his own real position are known to him; before the character, number and wants of his children are learned or the claims of parental affection or duty can make themselves felt, and while still very much at the mercy of a predecessor desirous of posthumous greatness and power, he

[27] *The Land Laws*, 3rd edn., pp. 157-8.
[28] Asa Briggs, *Victorian People* (Harmondsworth, 1965), p. 217.
[29] Joseph Kay, *Free Trade in Land*.

enters into an irrevocable disposition, by which he parts with the rights of a proprietor for ever and settles its devolution, burdened with charges, upon an unborn heir.[30]

It seems from the researches of modern historians, that many of these complaints (like those over agricultural tenancies) were much exaggerated at the time for political purposes. In the years before 1880, for example, there was an annual turnover estimated at between 300,000 and 600,000 acres, so the land market could hardly have been as stagnant as contemporary arguments might suggest.[31] Indeed, in the agricultural market, it was buyers (and tenants) who were in short supply in the depressed 1880s. Nevertheless, the political pressures did not abate, and in the 1880s there was a considerable debate over leasehold enfranchisement, that is to say, over the possibility of giving long leaseholders rights of compulsory purchase over the freehold. The Royal Commission on Working Class Housing in 1884–5 discussed these questions, and by a majority voted in favour of leasehold enfranchisement. 'The prevailing system of building leases', they said, 'is conducive to bad building, to deterioration of property towards the close of the lease, and to a want of interest on the part of the occupier in the house he inhabits'.[32] The diagnosis was correct, but the recommendations were a dubious remedy. Lord Salisbury, who was a member of this Committee, pointed out in his dissent from this recommendation, that very few occupiers actually held the long leases under discussion. Usually the long lease was retained by the middleman, often a mere builder or developer who built on the land, and then let the housing on short-term tenancies. Leasehold enfranchisement would simply enable the middleman to buy the long lease from the head landlord, and let, rather than sub-let, the housing. Subsequently, after Lord Salisbury had become Prime Minister, this recommendation was rejected by a Parliamentary Select Committee on Town Holdings. But for present purposes, more important than the precise fate of this recommendation, was that it was by this time possible to contemplate such a violation of freedom of contract. Even Salisbury had argued against the recommendation on the ground that it would not achieve the Committee's objective, rather than on any ground of principle. It was, thus, quite acceptable to contemplate giving a tenant power to compulsorily acquire the freehold of property held on long lease. The consent of the owner would simply be overriden, and a compulsory contract of sale imposed upon him. Of course, nobody doubted that it

[30] T. E. Cliffe Leslie, *Land Systems of Ireland, England and the Continent* (London, 1870), p. 199.

[31] See F. M. L. Thompson, 'The Land Market in the Nineteenth Century', 9 *Oxford Ec. Papers*, 285, 300 (1957).

[32] See *Final Report of the Leaseholds Committee* (Cmnd. 7982, 1950), paras. 32–52, discussing the historical background to leasehold enfranchisement.

would be necessary to ensure a fair price, for although there were by now calls (as we shall see below) for dispossessing landowners without compensation, they had scant chance of being carried in the House of Commons, and still less in the Lords.

But these interferences, or projected interferences, with freedom of contract were mild indeed compared with the more drastic proposals which began to be canvassed in all earnestness in the 1880s, for the nationalization of the land, with, or even without, compensation. We have seen something of the background against which these proposals came to be made, and to attract so much public support. With so much land still held by the descendants of the great landowners, and with the rising pressures of population in the cities, land was constantly increasing in value. Writing in 1877 Sir James Caird estimated that in the 1860s and 1870s land values had increased by some £330 millions at a cost to the landed interest not exceeding £60 millions.[33] These increases were widely coming to be thought to be the undeserved increment of monopolist owners. It was the work of the people, in developing the country, driving railways across it, building industries and towns, which had created this great new wealth. What right did the landed aristocracy have to retain it all for themselves? What did they do, what consideration did they provide, for this massive benefit, conferred upon them by the activity of the rest of the people?

Controversy on such issues went back to the classical economists. Ricardo's theory of rent had first directed attention to the monopoly nature of land ownership, and to the fact that, as population expanded, land values would go up. And James Mill had, in consequence, argued the case for a tax to syphon off this unearned increment, on the ground that the landowner did not make 'his arrangements' in the expectation of such increases, and 'could therefore have no reason to complain should a new source of income, which cost him nothing, be appropriated to the service of the state'.[34] McCulloch had disagreed, on the ground that the owner's property right 'extends to the whole of what the land can ever yield'.[35] James Mill's reply was that the real question turned upon what increase in values could be 'rationally anticipated'.[36] Unfortunately, neither of them appreciated the circular nature of this form of reasoning, which was precisely parallel with much of their reasoning on freedom of contract. What they overlooked was that if the law conferred upon the landowner the right to all incremental increases in value, then land would be dealt in on that basis; while if, conversely, the law provided for some tax to remove increments in the value of the land, then equally that

[33] *The Landed Interest and the Supply of Food*, ed. Mingay, p. 98.
[34] *Elements of Political Economy* 3rd edn., 1844 (reprinted, New York, 1965), pp. 252–5.
[35] Cited, ibid.   [36] Ibid., p. 254.

would become the basis on which land would be dealt with. If the law is changed, then expectations which were formerly reasonable will have to be adjusted to the new law, and the process of adjustment will entail some disappointment of existing expectations. But once the adjustment is made, expectations will settle down again, at a lower level for some (though perhaps at a higher level for others), and no further disappointment of expectations will result from that particular change. But only if society and its laws remain stagnant for ever is it possible to avoid disappointing some expectations, for all change leads to the disappointment of expectations. Only if everybody was able to foresee all future change would this cease to be so, a condition so remote from reality that it is needless to pursue it. The younger Mill saw many of the problems which his father had not seen, but he was willing to give a rough and ready answer to them.[37] If and in so far as the legislature had encouraged the expectation that increases in land values would not be taxed away, there might, indeed, be some injustice if that expectation were now disappointed; but in fact the legislature had been under the dominance of the landowning class for many years, during which great increases in land values had accrued to them. So far as the future was concerned, argued Mill, there would be no injustice in taxing away the whole of this unearned increment, so long as the effect was not to reduce the value of land below its then market value. As to the injustice of allowing the rich to retain this increment, apart altogether from any expectations that may have been aroused, there could be no question:

The ordinary progress of a society which increases in wealth, is at all times tending to augment the incomes of landlords; to give them both a greater amount and a greater proportion of the wealth of the community, independently of any trouble or outlay incurred by themselves. They grow richer, as it were, in their sleep, without working, risking or economising. What claim have they, on the general principle of social justice, to this accession of riches?[38]

Economically, this argument may have been weak,[39] but as an argument about social justice, it was more plausible. And in the 1880s there arrived in England the American prophet Henry George, to preach to the public the simple message which he had already published in his *Progress and Poverty*.[40] In this book, and in a series of speeches up and down the country, George took his stand on the Ricardian theory of rent, and

[37] *Principles of Political Economy*, Book V, Chapter II, sect. 5.

[38] Ibid.

[39] Mark Blaug, *Economic Theory in Retrospect*, revised ed. (Homewood, Ill., 1968), at p. 99 points out that (1) in the long run, even pure 'rents' are incentive payments justifiable as property itself is justifiable, and (2) in the short run, all agents (including labour and capital) can earn rents, and not just land.

[40] Everyman edn., London, 1911. See Elwood P. Laurence, *Henry George in the British Isles* (East Lansing, Mich., 1957).

on the arguments which the younger Mill had expounded in his *Principles*. As a remedy for this state of affairs George proposed a 'single tax', that is, he proposed that the whole rental value of the land should be taxed away, without affording any compensation to the landowners. In effect, all tenants would, in future, pay their rent to the State, and the landlords would simply be dispossessed. If this were done, argued George, the proceeds of the tax would be so great that all other taxation could be abolished; only this one single tax was needed for the whole servicing of the State—hence the name by which he became known, 'single tax George'. Henry George made a considerable stir in England, and his ideas were propagated far and wide.[41] Although there could not, in the 1880s, have been any likelihood of the actual confiscation of rents, as he proposed, being passed by Parliament, there was considerable support at least for taxing away the surplus rents arising from increased population and other factors not attributable to the activities or investments of the landlords. A Land Nationalisation Society was set up to propagate George's ideas,[42] and from 1889, at least, a Land Tax became a serious objective of all radical and socialist opinion. Chamberlain, while totally rejecting the nationalization of land, was not uninfluenced by George in other respects. In his famous speech in 1883 in which he attacked the landowners as 'a class who toil not, neither do they spin', he specifically referred to the added wealth they acquired 'by levying an increased share on all that other men have done by toil and labour to add to the general wealth and prosperity of the country'.[43] Similarly, the Fabians took George's proposals very seriously, and by 1900 even moderate Liberal opinion was moving towards a Land Tax. Lord Haldane, later Lord Chancellor, and one of the few judges of his time to have any acquaintance with economics, joined the movement, saying that every twenty years, Londoners paid an increased ground rent of nearly £6 millions, and that 'if we had proper laws, that £6 millions would belong to the people of London as a whole'.[44]

George did not have everything his own way, of course. The Liberty and Property Defence League, of which I spoke earlier, in connection with Bramwell's semi-political activities, was founded in 1882 to combat the Land Tax movement. Bramwell was on one occasion invited to debate the land issue with Henry George, but declined on the ground that he would be sorry to do anything which showed that there was

---

[41] It has been said that *Progress and Poverty* was 'without exaggeration . . . one of the dozen most influential books written in the Nineteenth Century': R. Douglas, 'God Gave the Land to the People', in *Edwardian Radicalism 1900–1914*, ed. A. J. A. Morris (London, 1974), pp. 148–9.

[42] J. Hyder, *The Case for Land Nationalisation* (London, 1914). Hyder was secretary to the Society for 25 years.

[43] J. L. Garvin, *Life of Joseph Chamberlain* (London, 1932), i. 392.

[44] Cited in Hyder, *The Case for Land Nationalisation*, p. 130.

something worth discussing.[45] And on another occasion he went so far as to say that landlords would actually fight if they were threatened with nationalization of the land.[46] But Bramwell could not stem the tide. Everything was moving in the same direction—the growing egalitarianism, the growing political strength of the mass of the people, and the pressures of population on land values.

In the 1909 Budget Lloyd George at last tried to introduce the Land Tax, proposing (modestly enough by comparison with what had been suggested by George) a 20 per cent tax on the unearned increment of land values after 1909. The frenzied response of the Lords, which created the most serious constitutional crisis since 1832, and ultimately led to the Parliament Act 1911, was without doubt, partly due to the fear that this was the thin end of the wedge of land nationalization. But they need not have feared. Lloyd George's was the first of a long line of proposals designed to tax away the unearned increments in land values, none of which has yet succeeded in working. Lloyd George's tax required all land to be valued, an immense task, which had to be postponed during the First World War, and was finally abandoned altogether in 1920. The Labour Government of 1929–31 tried again, with a new Land Tax in 1931, but that too had to be postponed as a result of the financial crisis which drove Labour from office in 1931, and it was in turn repealed in 1934. After the return to power of Labour in 1945, an attempt was made to nationalize all land 'development value' in return for compensation of £300 millions in a new attempt to tackle the old problem. This attempt not only failed, but in a sense aggravated the problem, for the nationalization of all development value was not followed by the use or sale of that value by the State. It was followed by the return of development value, in dribs and drabs, as planning permission was given to landowners for the development of particular sites. Thus the monopoly value of the right to develop land was greatly enhanced, while at the same time, the 'unearned increment' from such development was made to appear more than ever the work of the community rather than the landowner. The mere grant of planning permission to build a few houses on a piece of agricultural land, for example, could now multiply the value of the land tenfold overnight. The 1964 Labour Government made yet another attempt to lay hold of these unearned increments by the creation of the Land Commission which went the same way as all previous attempts when the Act was repealed by the following Conservative Parliament in 1971. And so to modern times, when the Community Land Act of 1975 has recently come into force, the last of

[45] Elwood P. Laurence, *Henry George in the British Isles*, p. 31.

[46] In an address to the British Association in 1888, reprinted in *Essays in the Economics of Socialism and Capitalism*, ed. Smyth, p. 57.

this line of attempts to secure for the State the unearned increment in land values. It is too early to predict how successful this Act is going to be, but there are not wanting warnings that it may go the same way as all the others.

When I come to deal more directly with the legal developments in the century 1870–1970 it will become evident enough why I have devoted so much attention to this piece of history. But it is worth saying at this stage that if there is one thing which this episode illustrates it is the opinion that it is unfair that a benefit should be received by A as a result of the labours of B. The fact that A has not agreed or contracted to pay for this benefit has generally been thought of as irrelevant in this context. In economic terms, this could be seen as a classic case of market failure. The efforts of the community, not to mention the mere increase in population, create an increase in values, yet the increase, in a *laissez-faire* situation, accrues to the landowner. In terms of the law, and of ideas about freedom of contract, it could be said that this episode illustrates the decline in the importance attached to consent and an increase in the importance attached to a non-consensual conferment of benefits. If we were compelled to see this in terms of existing legal categories, we could say that this represents a movement away from contractual and back to quasi-contractual ideas. It also represents, in some sense, a return to the values more prominent before 1770 when (it was argued) the mere conferment of benefits was widely thought sufficient grounds for recompense.

Just Wages

Inevitably, the movement to greater equality has had a profound impact on ideas about earnings and prices. We saw earlier how, even in the mid-nineteenth century, there were some factors tending against the use of the free market to regulate all wages and prices. For example, Government was already paying the same daily wage rates to labourers in different parts of the country, even where market rates differed. And so too, the growth of corporations and public bodies had already been making it difficult to match the wage to the man. Piece rates and payment by results had often given way already to hourly or daily rates of pay. After 1870 this process gathered increasing momentum. For one thing there was increasing scepticism over the idea that men with different abilities, or aptitudes, were somehow deserving of greater financial rewards. We have observed how the economists, from this time on, had tended to discard talk of moral worth, and to concentrate instead on the idea of economic service; and even that idea had taken some knocks from John Stuart Mill who had suggested that men of exceptional abilities were highly paid because of the scarcity of such abilities. Even the cautious Alfred Marshall had agreed that 'the greater part of the incomes earned by exceptionally successful barristers, and writers, and painters, and singers and jockeys may be classed as the rent of natural abilities'.[47]

And if the economists were cautious about raising such issues and warned about the need to preserve incentives, there were not lacking others, to argue more openly for a greater equality of income on grounds of social justice. Amongst the Fabians, for example, Bernard Shaw was prepared in 1910 to argue for absolute equality of incomes among the whole population. While few would have been prepared to go as far as this at that time, he made some telling points about the tendency of Government to pay the same wage or salary to men in the same positions: '[W]e pay judges more than policemen and majors more than privates; but we do not pay one judge more than another, one policeman more than another, one soldier more than another, though no two judges are alike, no two policemen alike and so forth'.[48] And a few years later he returned to the same theme, arguing that '[t]he dramatic effect of these contrasts [between the earnings of different classes of employees] blinds us to the vast plateaux of equality above which they tower'.[49]

And amongst the working classes themselves, it is not surprising that ideas about fair earnings began to surface again at this time; indeed, with this class they had probably never wholly disappeared, though when the Webbs brought many of these beliefs and practices to light, their researches 'had the air of archaeology'.[50] But by the end of the nineteenth century, the older ideas were taking on a new lease of life, and '[t]he scholastic tradition itself... was remodelled to fit an industrial society'.[51] Symptomatic of the change was the passing of the first 'Fair Wages Resolution' by the House of Commons in 1891, as a result of which Governments in future required all contractors employed by them to pay not less than 'standard wages' to their work people. Standard wages were defined as meaning wages agreed with the relevant trade unions, or, if there were none, wages such as were paid by 'good' employers. This was only the first of many such Resolutions, whose scope was gradually extended to cover the whole public service, including local authorities. The idea that it was the Government's business to secure its work at the lowest cost to the taxpayer, and that it was the business of contractors to secure labour at the lowest price at which labourers could be induced to work for them, gave way before the notion that workers ought to be paid a just or fair wage.

[47] *Principles of Economics*, 8th edn. (London, 1961), p. 518. See too H. Sidgwick, *Methods of Ethics*, 7th edn. (London, 1907), pp. 248-9.

[48] 'The Simple Truth about Socialism', in *The Road to Equality*, ed. Louis Crompton, pp. 155, 161.

[49] 'Redistribution of Income', ibid., p. 197.

[50] M. Fogarty, *The Just Wage* (London, 1961), pp. 19-20.

[51] Ibid.

The growth of collective bargaining in the twentieth century, and still more, the increasing frequency of 'pay policies' imposed by the Government in the period since the last World War, have strengthened this trend. Wage bargaining, though it may resemble contractual negotiations between the representives of employers and employees, has been said, in England today, to have little resemblance to the higgling of the market. It has, for instance, been suggested that trade unions do not behave like monopoly sellers of labour, for they will not seek to maximize the total earnings of their members without reference to the distributional pattern. It has also been suggested that wage bargaining involves *argument*, not just higgling, and argument requires a case to be made, some rational justification for what is sought. 'A collective agreement demands a degree of social justification which a private bargain can ignore'.[52] Similarly, the frequent arbitration of pay disputes by independent bodies or Tribunals has required them to act in a quasi-judicial manner (in appearance if not in the technical legal sense) hearing argument from both sides, and then giving a reasoned decision.

Nevertheless, it must be admitted that despite the constant appeals to fairness and equity in these matters, it has not been easy to agree on the criteria which ought to be used. Clearly, market forces are not wholly irrelevant, since the employer must be able to recruit an adequate staff, in competition with other employers, and if the evidence is that significant numbers of vacancies remain unfilled despite all endeavours, this is likely to be a good rational, as well as market, case for increased pay. Not long ago, it would also have been widely agreed that employers could not be expected to pay earnings beyond their capacity for this would simply be a recipe for bankruptcy. However, in the past few years, doubts have been cast even on this proposition, for at least in the nationalized monopoly industries, there is, in practice, little to prevent the employers and the employees agreeing to push earnings, and consequently prices, up as high as they please. If the earnings are out of line with international rates, the result may be to harm Britain's export industries and lead to greater unemployment, but the benefit of higher earnings will go to one group and the burden of unemployment to another. Even in private industry, there are signs that market forces operate as a constraint on the level of wages only in the long run, and then only if trade union leaders and the workmen themselves act on the basis of enlightened self-interest. For where the bargaining power is so greatly in the hands of powerful unions as it is today, wages can be pushed up higher and higher in the short run; only after the lapse of months or perhaps years, will this affect the rates of profits, investment, and exports, and hence the eventual levels of employment and real

[52] Barbara Wootton, *The Social Foundations of Wages Policy*, 2nd edn. (London, 1962), pp. 68-87.

earnings. So, too, in the 1970s at least, many of the most important wage settlements appeared to be supported with less in the way of justified argument, and more by sheer power combined with a frightening independence from ordinary legal control.[53]

But whatever may be the extent of the influence of market forces on earnings, there is no doubt that today many other factors are also treated as relevant. Levels of productivity, the nature of the work itself, the skills needed for the work, and the length of time needed to acquire those skills, whether 'unsocial hours' are worked, and above all comparability with other earnings, are all taken into account, one way or another, in the settlement of wage claims. Comparability with other levels of earnings is perhaps the single most influential factor in determining the sense of fairness on these matters, but it naturally leads to a perpetual leapfrogging process with results which the country knows only too well. The Prices and Incomes Board which operated between 1966 and 1970 made a determined effort to reduce the significance attached to comparisons with pay levels in other industries, and to fasten on the relationship between internal pay and internal performance in particular plants or industries.[54] In a sense this could be said to have been an attempt to return to market criteria, at least, in that pay was to be equated with marginal net productivity, and a movement away from egalitarianism. But the success of this move was anyhow short-lived. The Government itself constantly fell back on comparability criteria, and the unions also were unwilling to abandon their principal argument in pay negotiations. It can, of course, be argued that comparability (as indeed, many of the other factors referred to above, such as the nature of the work, unsocial hours, and so on) are all factors which would be taken into account in a free market situation. But it seems clear that comparability considerations have a distinct effect on the bargaining behaviour of employers and unions and affect pay claims independently of market considerations,[55] as for instance where workers in industries which are making losses expect to secure the same wage increases as workers in industries which remain profitable.

Throughout this period, another shift in emphasis has taken place in wage settlements, which also reflects the constantly growing strength of the ideal of economic equality. There has been a repeated tendency for differentials to be narrowed, so that the lower paid, the unskilled, and even the retired, have been capturing an increasing proportion of the national income. For one thing, payment by results has become less and less used. Despite its superficial attraction to the market-oriented

---

[53] Ralf Dahrendorf, *The New Liberty* (London, 1975), p. 27.
[54] Allan Fels, *The British Prices and Incomes Board* (Cambridge, 1972).
[55] Ibid., p. 122.

economist, or indeed to anyone else who believes in justice according to desert, all systems of payment by results are very troublesome in practice. They frequently involve insuperable difficulties in measuring normal working rates, and of comparison between one task and another. In 1961 only about one-third of the workforce received any payment in this form,[56] and since then the movement in the same direction has been unmistakeable. Indeed, it seems probable that the standard of living of the great mass of the English people now depends less on their own individual exertions and more on the performance of everybody else (as well as of Government taxation policies) than at any time since the new Poor Law of 1834.

The narrowing gap between higher and lower incomes (a process much enhanced by taxation) is not, of course, solely due to growing egalitarian sentiments. It is partly due to the majoritarian traditions of English life which I discussed previously. 'In any area, whether it be carpentry or plumbing or teaching, the majority of workers favour standard salary scales and oppose merit differentials for the obvious reason that the specially talented are always few'.[57]

The narrowing of earnings differentials has been accentuated by the various attempts to impose pay policies during the past two decades. There is little doubt that it is growing awareness of this fact that tends to lead to increasing opposition to such policies after two or three years, and to the growing demands for a return to 'free collective bargaining'. It is almost needless to point out that these demands come loudest from those who have the most bargaining power, and that they bear a strong resemblance to the arguments of industrialists and employers for the abolition of statutory wage rates in the early nineteenth century. Freedom of contract naturally suits the strong, and is disadvantageous to the weak. When there is a return to free collective bargaining, then the result will usually be an increase in earnings differentials, although not necessarily in the differentials most desirable in the public interest.

But whatever the future may hold in store on this question, it is hard to believe that earnings differentials can rise significantly so long as the public is so wedded to its egalitarian beliefs. Once market forces are left behind, there is little left except egalitarianism as a principle with which earnings can be regulated. Unlike prices (where the cost of production can always serve as a base for controls) there is no obvious base for earnings once subsistence levels are left behind. And though American political thinkers may argue that greater economic equality cannot be merely assumed to be a principle of justice, but needs to be justified,[58]

[56] Ibid., p. 142.

[57] M. Friedman, *Capitalism and Freedom* (Chicago, 1962), pp. 95–6.

[58] R. Nozick, *Anarchy, State and Utopia* (New York, 1974), pp. 232–3. Cf. I. Berlin in *Justice and Social Policy*, ed. F. A. Olafson (Englewood Cliffs, N.J., 1961), p. 131.

there is little sign that this is an acceptable position in England. This does not mean that there is yet much real public support for complete equality of earnings, but there certainly appears to be a demand for a greater equality than still exists. The movement towards greater economic equality appears to proceed in England with an overpowering weight of public opinion behind it.

Inevitably, these movements of opinion have had a profound influence on ideas about freedom of contract, free choice, and the importance of consent in exchange relationships. Few employees are today paid a wage or salary which they have, in any real sense, agreed with their employer; and conversely, the fact that an employee (or his union) has accepted a particular wage or salary, is scarcely ever regarded as precluding him from challenging it on the ground that it is unfair. The private law of contract has barely begun to recognize these developments, largely because the private law of contract does not in practice regulate these issues. Some statutory changes are only now beginning to impinge on contract law, such as those which outlaw racial or sex discrimination in employment. Here the free choice of employers and employees is overriden, because it is thought that equal treatment is a more important social objective than the exercise of free choice. And there have been other statutory changes of much importance to the employment relationship which emphasize the community's sense of fairness. The provisions against unfair dismissal, for example, like the anti-discrimination laws, stress objective fairness at the expense of free choice. And the Redundancy Payments Acts recognize the community's sense that a long-standing employment must not be terminated without some compensation. These developments are part and parcel of a much wider movement in the law which recognizes the importance of a fair exchange in contractual relationships, and rejects the idea that market-based terms necessarily represent a fair exchange.

THE DECLINE OF PRINCIPLES

I suggested in Chapter 12 that the period 1770–1870 could be characterized as an Age of Principles; by contrast the succeeding century has been an Age of Pragmatism. There has, without doubt, been a decline in the importance attached to principles, in economics, in moral issues, in law, and indeed in life generally. The very concept of a principle has become almost disreputable. Flexibility, as opposed to rigidity, compromise as opposed to single-mindedness, and pragmatism as opposed to principle, have become the virtues of the modern world.

In certain respects, this movement in ideas can be traced back to the 1870s; in economics, indeed, it is clearly associated with the demise of the classical tradition and the arrival of the neo-classics. It was, at least in England, Jevons who began the move to what is now known as 'ad hockery', the deliberate turning away from general solutions, general ideas based on abstract principles. It was he who insisted on looking at every case on its own merits to see if there was (for example) adequate justification for interfering with market forces. No doubt this was partly a reaction to the misuse to which so many economic principles had previously been put. Economists, by 1870, were growing tired of the way in which politicians or newspaper writers, with no real understanding of the issues, appealed to *laissez-faire* or freedom of contract as though they settled all policy questions.[59]

But this was not the only factor behind the decline of principle. Another, equally important factor, was the gradual shortening of the time scale within which economists were prepared to discuss the causative influence of economic policies, or to forecast the movement of events. As we saw previously, the classical economists tended to take a very long view of the questions to which they addressed themselves. After 1870 there was a pronounced move in the reverse direction, a move which was not unrelated to the growing empiricism of economic method. For the short-term results of events or policies are usually much more easy to discern in the social sciences; as the time scale becomes longer it becomes harder to say with any assurance that a particular result is the consequence of a particular policy or a particular decision. But there were other influences at work, too. The new democratic electorate was in more of a hurry than its predecessors. They wanted results and they usually wanted them quickly. As Bryce had observed in America, 'Men live fast and are impatient of the slow working of natural laws'.[60] The point of view of modern man, when told that things would right themselves in the long run, was well expressed by Keynes, in his celebrated observation that '[i]n the long run we are all dead'.

It was Keynes too, and his generation, who did much to destroy people's faith in moral principles, not because they were any less moral than their predecessors or successors, but because they had less faith in principles of any kind. Speaking of his early years at Cambridge around the turn of the century, Keynes said:

We entirely repudiated a personal liability on us to obey general rules. We claimed the right to judge every individual case on its merits, and the wisdom, experience and self-control to do so successfully. This was a very important part of our faith, violently and aggressively held, and for the outer world it was our

---

[59] L. Robbins, *Evolution of Modern Economic Theory* (London, 1970), p. 186; see too, F. A. Hayek, *Law, Legislation and Liberty* (London, 1973) i. 57-9.

[60] *The American Commonwealth* (New York and London, 1889), cited in J. W. Hurst, *Law and the Conditions of Freedom in the Nineteenth Century United States* (Madison, 1956), p. 73. Bryce was a Professor of Law 1870-93, and Ambassador to the U.S., 1907-13.

most obvious and dangerous characteristic. We repudiated entirely customary morals, conventions and traditional wisdom ... [W]e recognised no moral obligation on us, no inner sanction, to conform or to obey. Before heaven we claimed to be our own judge in our own case.[61]

This attitude, which has been said to have been widely shared by most active and independent spirits before 1914,[62] obviously raised new difficulties in this increasingly democratic age. I have suggested that the early utilitarians combined a degree of practical élitism with their belief in utility. While they accepted (I have argued) that someone, presumably themselves, would have to draw up the principles which would have to be generally observed if utilitarian goals were to be reached, they also insisted that the generality of the people would have to observe these principles without pausing to inquire in each case whether the principle ought to be followed or not. Even as to themselves, they certainly did not envisage the degree of freedom to inquire into every case on its merits which Keynes and his contemporaries were claiming. They had some fairly shrewd notions of the dangers of judging in one's own case, and they evidently thought, too, that many decisions would involve too long an inquiry if one had to decide them on their merits without appeal to rules. But now in the twentieth century, the younger intellectuals were more self-confident in their ability to make their decisions in this fashion, though they seem to have been surprisingly naïve about the extent to which they could maintain a privileged position on such issues.

No doubt, to some extent, ideas of this kind were influenced, at least among intellectuals, by the waning support for utilitarianism. The publication of G. E. Moore's *Principia Ethica* in 1903 had dealt a severe blow to the influence of utilitarianism (at least among philosophers), although perhaps not quite for the reasons which Moore had advanced. Moral philosophy after Moore came to be increasingly devoid of any faith in principles, and indeed, of any substantive content at all. To Moore himself, a moral obligation was a duty to perform that act which would produce the greatest amount of good in the world, but what *was* good was not definable. 'If I am asked, "What is good?" my answer is that good is good, and that is the end of the matter. Or if I am asked, "How is good to be defined?" my answer is that it cannot be defined, and that is all I have to say about it'.[63]

This sort of intuitionist ethics attracted a good deal of sympathy among moral philosophers, but it is evident that a morality of this kind

---

[61] *Two Memoirs*, p. 97.

[62] F. A. Hayek, *Law, Legislation and Liberty*, i. 26.

[63] *Principia Ethica* (Cambridge, 1903), p. 6. In 1903 Pollock wrote to Holmes 'the question—what *ought* we to judge good?—seems on this [Moore's] view to be rational only in the sense: By preferring what sort of "goods" do men and nations succeed? Not much catching the tail of the Cosmos there.' *Pollock-Holmes Letters* (Cambridge, 1942), i. 116-17.

can have no *social* purpose. It cannot teach others what they ought to believe, nor how they ought to behave, matters which had been of central importance to moral philosophy in the early nineteenth century. A similar movement could be discerned even among philosophers and thinkers who retained some faith in utilitarianism. For not all utilitarians accepted the role of rules or principles, even after it had been suggested that the early utilitarians were generally rule-utilitarians. Some remained wedded to 'extreme' or 'act'-utilitarianism as opposed to 'rule-utilitarianism'. The act-utilitarian was unwilling to accept an obligation to abide by a rule without examining the facts of the particular case to see whether, indeed, abiding by the rule would produce the best results in the particular circumstances of the case. If it would, he would act accordingly, in compliance with the rule; if it would not, he would act against the rule.[64] On this view rules ceased to have any purpose at all. For if acting in accord with the rule produced the right result, one was morally obliged so to act, but one would, of course, have been so obliged even in the absence of the rule. Philosophers surprisingly seem to have been untroubled by the fact that it is commonly difficult or impossible to say what action is likely to produce the best result, and that even a rule which only operated as a burden of proof, or a prima facie ground for action, would be far from valueless. In the law there can be no doubt that prima facie rules of this kind are often of real value; in some Australian States, to take one example, breach of a speed limit on a road is only prima facie evidence of a failure to drive with sufficient care having regard to all the circumstances of the case, but this certainly does not make the speed limit valueless or meaningless. But among philosophers, only one appears to have made any serious use of the concept of a prima facie duty.[65]

The Sanctity of Promises

It may be appropriate to add that the move away from moral principles of general, still more of universal, validity, has not generally shaken the belief of most philosophers in the sanctity of promises. Even the intuitionists seem ready to intuit a powerful principle to the effect that promises should be observed and the rule-utilitarians certainly accept, as their historical predecessors did, at least the prima facie likelihood that observing a promise is likely to be the act best calculated to forward utilitarian goals. The act-utilitarian naturally has more difficulty; he is accused readily enough by other philosophers, of wanting to examine the circumstances of each case to see if keeping a promise will produce the

---

[64] J. J. C. Smart, 'Extreme and Restricted Utilitarianism', 6 *Phil. Q.* 344 (1956).
[65] Sir David Ross, *The Right and the Good* (Oxford, 1930), pp. 21 *et seq.*; *Foundations of Ethics* (Oxford, 1939).

best result.[66] And such an attitude, it is objected, leads to the view that the promise is wholly irrelevant, adding nothing to pre-existing duties, and affording no reason in itself for performing an act if there are no pre-existing duties. In answer the act-utilitarian insists that even he is willing to treat rules as at least rules of thumb, to be applied where there is no time for further inquiry, or where he may be too self-interested to trust himself to produce an objective answer. 'But', continues one of the most articulate of the act-utilitarians, 'is it not monstrous to suppose that if we *have* worked out the consequences and if we have perfect faith in the impartiality of our calculations, and if we *know* that in this instance to break [a rule] R will have better results than to keep it, we should nevertheless, obey the rule? Is it not to erect R into a sort of idol if we keep it when breaking it will prevent, say, some avoidable misery? Is this not a form of superstitious rule-worship (easily explicable psychologically) and not the rational thought of a philosopher?'[67]

Much of this controversial philosophical debate has centred around the very example of promise-keeping, which makes it relevant for present purposes, particularly in the historical context. Since the decline of utilitarianism in the early twentieth century there has been a considerable literature about the basis of the obligation to perform a promise, and this literature has some illumination for the present context, even though much of it appears to the lawyer to be seriously misconceived. It appears misconceived because nearly all philosophers start with the assumption that there is some prima facie rule making promises 'binding', but few of them pause to inquire into what this means. To a lawyer acquainted with the difference between expectation, reliance, and restitution damages, it is not very meaningful to say that a promise is binding unless some further explanation is given of what sort of remedy is offered for its breach. If a promise is only binding in the sense that reliance or restitution interests are protected, then we need not treat the promise as adding much (if anything) to the nature of the obligation, which can be said to be primarily reliance-based or benefit-based. Only if an unrelied-upon and unpaid-for promise is to be treated as binding—only if expectation interests are to be protected—are we compelled to find the principal ground for liability as lying in the very promise itself. Now the philosophers who have debated these issues at such length have usually failed to draw these important distinctions.

The result has inevitably been a substantial degree of puzzlement as to the source of the moral obligation to perform promises. By eliminating the obvious cases where there are good rational or utilitarian grounds for

---

[66] See, e.g., Pickard-Cambridge, 'Two Problems about Duty', 41 *Mind* 145 (1932); J. Rawls, 'Two Concepts of Rules', 64 *Phil. Rev.* 1 (1955).

[67] J. J. C. Smart, 'Extreme and Restricted Utilitarianism', pp. 348-9.

holding promises binding (that is, where the promise is paid for or relied upon) and treating an executory gratuitous promise as the paradigm case for discussion, the philosophers naturally created a considerable difficulty for themselves. Where, they began to ask, did the obligation to perform a promise come from at all? It seemed almost as though one had to presume or imagine some sort of implied promise to keep promises.[68] That, however, seemed too fictitious, and suspiciously like a resurrection of social contract ideas. An alternative explanation, which found more support, was formulated, largely by H. L. A. Hart[69] and John Rawls.[70] This explanation posited the existence of a 'practice', whereby promises could be made, and if made, had to be performed. To make a promise was to take part in this practice, and to take part in a practice, like taking part in a game, was to enjoy its benefits and hence to subject oneself to its rules. To promise was to join a club; one got the benefit of membership, and it was therefore reasonable, and moral, to accept the burdens of membership as well.

It is worth pointing out a curious feature of this debate. There is a sense in which the search for a moral basis to promissory liability has paralleled the search for grounds for holding particular promises to be binding. At the higher level of generality—the search for a basis to the whole nature of promissory liability—there was first a half-hearted suggestion that perhaps the origin was to be found in some sort of (implied) promise to keep promises; that the whole basis of the liability on promises was, in other words, consensual, or arose from the will. The Hart-Rawls theory then shifted the emphasis away from this on to the theory of reciprocal benefits. Because a man who promises joins in the practice or institution of promising, and expects to obtain the benefits of it, he therefore becomes bound by its burdens. It may not be wholly coincidental that—as I shall suggest—the basis of liability for particular promises, at least in the context of the law, has similarly shifted. Whereas the key to liability was seen in the nineteenth century as consensual agreement, or an act of will, the trend today is to place liability once again on the receipt of actual benefits (or, of course, acts of reliance).

If I am correct in my historical thesis, then it would seem that most modern philosophers, who still cling to the idea that bare promises *per se* are morally binding, have fallen victims to the propaganda of the nineteenth-century lawyers, economists, and utilitarians. My thesis, it will be recalled, was that the absolutely binding force of bare promises

[68] H. A. Prichard, 'The Obligation to Keep a Promise', in *Moral Obligation* (Oxford, 1949), pp. 168 et seq.
[69] H. L. A. Hart, 'Are there any Natural Rights?', 64 *Phil. Rev.* 175 (1955); 'Legal and Moral Obligation', reprinted in *Essays in Moral Philosophy*, ed. Melden (Seattle and London, 1958).
[70] J. Rawls, 'Two Concepts of Rules'; *A Theory of Justice* (Oxford, 1972) pp. 342–50. See too, J. R. Searle, *Speech Acts* (Cambridge, 1969).

was deliberately inculcated as an important guide to social behaviour in the period between (perhaps) 1750 and 1870. It was adopted as part of the code of honour of gentlemen, and taught by them and lawyers and economists to the mass of the people, and they did so, if I am correct, because it was a much simpler rule of social (and legal) discipline than the more complex rules which would have been needed if the problem had been broken down by asking *why* promises should be obeyed. The irony of it all is that the early utilitarians, lawyers, and economists were addressing the masses, not philosophers whom they would have been willing to trust as part of the élite, the élite who could distinguish when promises were to be observed, and when there was adequate justification for not doing so.

Now that we have, in so many respects, passed out of the Age of Principle into the Age of Pragmatism, it would not be surprising to discover that the idea of a principle which holds bare promises to be binding, even prima facie binding, is beginning to break down. If, as I shall also argue, there has, at least in the law, been a movement away from abstract legal propositions to more detailed factual inquiries, it would be no surprise to find a tendency today to ask *why*, in any given circumstances, a promise should be treated as binding. Is it because mere expectations have been roused, because there has been reliance, or payment for the promise? It is perhaps, no coincidence that one of the most recent contributions to the philosophical literature, by a philosopher with a legal background, indicates some move in this direction.[71] This may perhaps represent the beginning of the dissolution of the consensual glue, linking reliance concepts and benefit concepts, which has lasted for so long, and in that sense, there are (as I shall suggest) marked parallels with what is happening in the law.

Outside the somewhat closed philosopher's world, it is hard not to discern a massive weakening in respect for, or at least belief in, the moral force of promissory obligations. Cloistered Oxford dons may still write and speak with the high moral tones of the Victorian gentleman,[72] but few people today appear to have the same respect for the sanctity of bare promises, without regard to whether they have been paid for or relied upon, that was commonly expressed a century ago. In the law, I shall argue in Chapters 21 and 22, there has been a gradual decline in the role of the bare executory contract during the past century, matching its gradual rise in the century before that. Partly, no doubt, this is due to the

[71] Neil MacCormick, 'Voluntary Obligations and Normative Powers', *Proc. Arist. Soc. Supplement* 59 (1972).

[72] See Michael Bernick, *Sunday Times*, 9 Nov. 1975. Bernick, an American postgraduate student at Oxford, remarked on the 'high sense of decency: an adherence to moral principles which forbid such actions as breaking promises . . .'

changing pace of life, which makes binding future commitments very much harder to make and adhere to. Few people today (except perhaps politicians) see much wrong in admitting to a change of mind, and the law indeed goes out of its way to recognize a man's right to change his mind and extricate himself from certain contracts. Marriage, for example, has ceased to be a life-long union for a significant portion of the population, and actions for breach of promise of marriage have been abolished altogether. Partly, the changes owe something to the rise of the Corporate State. Institutions do not feel the same sense of personal moral obligation as individuals. A company director, for example, may feel that his primary responsibility is (as the law directs) to the shareholders as a whole; such a responsibility may, on occasion, even require him to break a contract previously entered into by the company on the ground that the interests of the company will be served better by breaking than by performing the contract. Moreover, the unity and continuity of corporate personality in the law cannot disguise the fact that changes occur in the personnel responsible for acting on behalf of a corporation; and the moral strength of a commitment entered into by a previous director or agent acting on behalf of a corporate body is probably weaker than the sense of obligation which an individual has in respect of his own previous promises. It is perhaps, this more than any other factor which has, for upwards of a century, led to criticisms of companies as the owners of 'irresponsible wealth'; from Herbert Spencer on, people have complained that companies will.do things from which individuals would shrink.[73]

The weakening impact of the moral force of promises in such circumstances can be particularly observed in the case of elected bodies. A new City Council, for example, may feel totally uncommitted by a contract entered into by their predecessors, especially where the contract was made in pursuance of a policy which has constituted an electoral issue. In 1974 a new Manchester City Council openly repudiated binding contractual commitments made by their predecessors to sell council houses to sitting tenants. Although these tenants plainly had uncontestable legal entitlements, the new Council bitterly resisted their claims, and fought them all the way through the Courts. They lost in the County Court, appealed to the Court of Appeal, where they lost again, and then sought leave, unsuccessfully, to appeal to the House of Lords.[74] Again, in 1975 the Inner London Education Authority repudiated the most solemn written assurances to continue an annual grant to London University for

---

[73] *Supra*, p. 281; see too Sir John Macdonnell's *Notes on the Law Relating to Combinations* prepared for the Committee on Trusts and appendixed to their *Report*, Cd. 9236 (1919), p. 31.

[74] See *Storer* v. *Manchester City Council* [1974] 1 W.L.R. 1403; *Gibson* v. *Manchester City Council* [1978] 2 All E.R. 583.

a five-year period, from 1972 to 1977.[75] In this case, no legal proceedings ensued.

And what is true of local elected bodies is even more true of Governments and Ministers. As Keynes remarked, '[t]he commonest virtues of the individual are often lacking in the spokesmen of nations',[76] and a belief in the sanctity of promises and contracts is one of those virtues which are least likely to be found in those wielding authority on behalf of a nation. In Britain, the civil service has enunciated the principle that a 'pledge by a senior Minister must be regarded as valid only for the duration of the Minister's retention of a particular office'.[77] The pound sterling (not to mention other currencies) has been devalued so often that a change even in fixed rates is no longer regarded as a breach of faith, but as a normal risk of those who deal in the foreign currency market. And in 1975 the Labour Government of Mr. Wilson refused to regard itself as bound by the adherence of the previous Government to a solemn international treaty, and even submitted to the electorate for decision the question whether the country should violate its treaty commitment.

And if public authorities, Ministers, and Governments behave like this, it is not surprising if individuals also have to come to feel much less moved by the moral force of a bare promise. There seems little doubt that many people do in fact behave as though they were act-utilitarians, and as though a promise, of itself, added little or nothing to the other reasons for action; or perhaps it would be more accurate to say that they act as though a promise was merely one relevant factor to be considered along with others. Working men, considering industrial action, for instance, do not appear to be significantly influenced, if they are influenced at all, by any commitments they, or their representatives, may have made to observe grievance procedures. Newspapers (or some newspapers) appear increasingly willing to disregard undertakings to observe 'embargoes', that is, not to publish an item of news before a specified date.[78] More generally, there seems to be a significant tendency in moral attitudes and moral discourse, to examine the reasons in favour of action, apart altogether from any promise to act in a particular way. The overall fairness of the situation seems far more important than the bare fact of a promise. The point may, perhaps, be illustrated by comparing attitudes

---

[75] See letter to *The Times*, 15 Feb. 1975, by the Chairman of the University Court, to which no reply was ever made.

[76] *Economic Consequences of the Peace* (London, 1919), p. 59.

[77] See *Guardian*, 9 June 1975, citing the official reply to protests that V.A.T. on boats had been increased after a public pledge by the Chancellor of the Exchequer that no additional taxes would be placed on that industry.

[78] See *The Times*, 16 Oct. 1976, report of the findings of the Press Council. The complainants in this case were the I.L.E.A., themselves the guilty parties in the matter referred to, *supra*.

to a set of facts discussed by Stephen J. in the opening number of the *Law Quarterly Review* in 1885:[79]

A wanted to take a furnished house, expecting to have to pass the summer in London. He made a verbal agreement to take the house of B, a friend and a man in his own position in life, who was going out of town. The day after that agreement was made, A was ordered to return to his appointment in India instantly. A, being thus prevented from occupying the house, asked B to release him from his agreement, which I think most men in B's position would have done, as nothing had been done under it, and B had been put to no expense or inconvenience. B, however, refused. A reminded B of the Statute of Frauds, but added, that having given his word, he would if required, fulfil his agreement, whatever he might think of B's conduct. In this case [Stephen concludes] I think A did his duty as a man of honour . . .

But what to a Victorian gentleman were the demands of a sense of honour seem to the modern reader to have been an excess of delicacy—or perhaps, a result of pressing principles to extremes without adequate inquiry into the facts. There was, in this case, no reliance and no benefit. The enforcement of the promise could only be justified on the ground of the bare expectation created by it. No doubt B would have been disappointed if A had withdrawn, but this disappointment seems a minor matter to set against the loss or inconvenience to A of having to abide by the agreement. It is difficult to believe that today most people in A's position would have scrupled to rely on the Statute of Frauds to escape the legal liability, or that many would have condemned his conduct in doing so.

Now it is easy to see such changes as signs of a 'decline of moral standards' and as symptomatic of 'the degenerate age in which we live'. And there may be truth in the belief that there has been such a decline, and that (for example) people are readier to break promises and contracts (or at least to justify doing so) when their short-term interests seem to demand this, than was the case a century ago. If this is so, it could be the result of unwillingness or inability to give sufficient weight to the long-term consequences of actions, as compared with the short-term consequences. Or it could be that the extension of literacy and democracy have led most people to demand the right, as Keynes and his friends,[80] to be their own judge in their own case. But this is by no means the whole explanation of the change in attitudes. For it is possible to defend the weakening in the moral force of promises on the act-utilitarian's ground that what may be a good prima facie rule should not be erected into a case of rule-worship.

[79] 'Section 17 of the Statute of Frauds', 1 *Law Q. Rev.* 1 (1885).
[80] *Supra*, pp. 650–51.

As my purposes are primarily historical, I do not propose in this volume to engage in a full discussion of the weight of these arguments; nor can I here enter into the vitally important issues concerning economic efficiency which may be relevant to the extent to which promises and contracts ought to be enforced. All that I wish to emphasize here is that the declining strength of moral principles, and especially of the sanctity of promises and contracts, over the past century, cannot just be explained away as part of a general decline in moral standards.[81] The pendulum may, indeed, have swung too far; but it is also arguable that there was a rational case for a significant swing. It is not impossible that, even in a purely moral sense, the sanctity of promises was rated too highly in Victorian times; that principles were too rigidly adhered to without adequate discrimination between diverse factual situations; and that too little attention was paid to the ground on which promises were felt to be deserving of enforcement.

[81] See further my paper, 'From Principles to Pragmatism: Changes in the Function of the Judicial Process and the Law' (Oxford, 1978).

20

THE LEGAL BACKGROUND, 1870–1970

THE SEPARATION OF LAW AND POLICY

I SUGGESTED in Part II that until the middle of the nineteenth century English law and lawyers were receptive to influences from outside the law, and in particular were much influenced by utilitarianism and by political economy. But I suggested, too, that by the middle of the century, the influence of new external ideas was coming to an end, at least in the sense that the judges were less willing to discuss such policy issues openly in their judgments. From 1850 or thereabouts, the phenomenon of formalism took an increasing hold upon English legal thought. I have sketched above the principal characteristics of formalism as it affected English law; in particular, it involved rejection of the law-making power of the judge, rejection of the relevance of policy issues to legal questions, belief that law was a deductive science of principles, and that the one 'true' answer to legal questions could be found by a strictly logical process. It involved also a belief in the objective reality of legal concepts, so that, for example, lawyers came to see the answer to legal issues as depending on the 'true' delineation of concepts such as offer, acceptance, consideration, estoppel, and a variety of others. The notion that legal concepts and categories were merely tools by which the lawyer could arrive at a range of justifiable decisions was not so much rejected, as simply not entertained by most English lawyers. And inextricably involved in this development was the gradual decline of the influence of external factors or bodies of thought on the law. It was, indeed, partly because lawyers could no longer find their answers in broad theories about society, or political economy, or moral principles, that they increasingly turned inwards to the law itself.

It would, however, be wrong to suggest that the rise of formalism was a simple or clear-cut process, especially as the traditional style of the English judgment has changed little over the centuries. This means that the differences between the formalist and the realist judges are not always easy to draw merely by looking at the cold printed page of the Law Reports. Both formalists and realists tend to justify their decisions by a similar judicial process; both generally accept the conventions of the judicial style. And if the realist is more willing on some occasions to declare his open allegiance to some policy, the formalist is just as likely to be influenced by the same policy in an unconscious manner. Then, too, the realist judge may often use the formalist approach in order to make his conclusions more palatable to his colleagues in an appellate court. And even with the formalist, appeals to 'justice', 'equity' and notions of 'fairness' are perfectly in order, although overt discussion of policy or moral principles is avoided. The result is to make it exceedingly difficult to assess the influence of formalism, so much so that even today it is not possible to assert with any confidence that formalism is dead or that a majority of the English judiciary subscribe to a more realist vision of the legal process. All this means that the true history of formalism in English law requires a great deal of research about the non-judicial utterances and beliefs of the judges, and such a history remains to be written. In this work 1 must be content with a few general comments, supported by a limited body of evidence. But the topic cannot be altogether neglected because the development of contractual ideas was significantly influenced by judicial methodologies.

There is some evidence to suggest that the full flowering of formalism did not take place until after the First World War. For though judges and lawyers had for at least half a century before then been confining their attention more narrowly to the law proper, and ignoring outside ideas in economics or political and social thought, it is also true that these judges had been less fearful of appeals to policy, fairness and the sense of justice. In the law of contract, leading decisions from the 1870s, the 1880s, and 1890s, for instance, appear on the whole to accord with the general sense of justice even today, and although generalization in such matters is difficult, few of these cases bear the marks of mechanical jurisprudence.[1] Even in the opening years of the twentieth century the changes were slow in coming. In 1921 Sir Frederick Pollock, in the Preface to the ninth edition of his *Principles of Contract*, chided American academics for their excessive adherence to formalism in language which implied that this was no problem in England:

Learned Americans are still engaged from time to time in valiant efforts to reduce the common-law rules of contract, and the doctrine of consideration in particular, to strict logical consistency. That quest is, in my humble judgement, misconceived. Legal rules exist not for their own sake, but to further justice and convenience in the business of human life; dialectic is the servant of their purpose, not their master. Reasonableness, no doubt, is the ideal of the common

[1] See, e.g., *Carlill* v. *Carbolic Smoke Ball Co.* [1893] 1 Q.B. 256; *Byrne* v. *Van Tienhoven* (1880) 5 C.P.D. 344; *Henthorn* v. *Fraser* [1892] 2 Ch. 27; *Dickinson* v. *Dodds* (1876) 2 Ch.D. 463; *Stewart* v. *Casey* [1892] 1 Ch. 104; *Hughes* v. *Metropolitan Rly. Co.* (1877) 2 App. Cas. 439; *Lloyd's* v. *Harper* (1880) 16 Ch.D. 290; *Redgrave* v. *Hurd* (1881) 20 Ch.D. 1, though cf. *Turner* v. *Green* [1895] 2 Ch. 205 which does show signs of unthinking application of market principles to a non-market situation; *Cundy* v. *Lindsay* (1878) 3 App. Cas. 459 is more debateable.

law . . . ; nevertheless the field of reason as we understand it in English, includes many things outside the strict logical deduction. One could say more of this, but it would be superfluous for the greater part of English readers.[2]

It is with some astonishment that one reads these remarks today, for in 1921 American lawyers were on the verge of their realist revolution, and English lawyers were about to plunge more deeply than ever into the marshy waters of formalism. But Pollock himself illustrates the curious schizophrenic approach of many English lawyers which helped the development of formalism. For though he himself was far too intelligent, and far too learned, to believe in mechanical jurisprudence, he often wrote in a style which made him appear to favour a formalist approach. But if Pollock could still write in 1921 that the greater part of English lawyers were in no need of a lecture on realism, things were about to change drastically.[3] After three-quarters of a century in which English lawyers had been accustomed to argue and decide cases as if the law were an autonomous body of scientific principles, 'it was inevitable that a mechanistic theory, so regularly articulated, should ultimately influence the practical operation of the final appeal system',[4] and we may add, of much else besides.

The inter-war period, which saw some of the most exciting intellectual developments in the history of the common law, in the American realist revolution,[5] also saw English law descend to its lowest ebb. Judges now not only spoke the language of formalism, but they acted as though they believed in it, and many undoubtedly did so. Possibly influenced by their consciousness of the destruction of the old social order, with its roots in a private enterprise economy, and its shared moral preconceptions, the judges of this period (like the economists) appear to have turned inwards on their discipline to a greater degree than ever before. Legal reasoning in common law cases appeared to have become a mechanistic process in which the legal solution was drawn from neutral value-free legal principles. Law and policy became totally divorced, at least in conscious formulations of legal argument and legal justification. Even in cases involving the most important economic issues, such as the legality of the growing restrictive practices in industry, and the legitimacy of boycotts and stop-lists, a series of decisions were made during this period in which

---

[2] pp. x–xi.

[3] In 1930, for instance, it was Corbin who gently chided English lawyers for their belief in 'certainty' and the objective reality of legal concepts: 'Contracts for the Benefit of Third Parties', 46 *Law Q. Rev.* 12 (1930). See too the less gentle irony of Thurman Arnold, one of the new Yale realists, at the expense of A. L. Goodhart in a review of his *Essays in Jurisprudence and the Common Law* (Cambridge, 1930), in 41 *Yale Law Journal* 318 (1931).

[4] B. Abel-Smith and R. Stevens, *Lawyers and the Courts* (London, 1967) p. 124.

[5] See generally William Twining, *Karl Llewellyn and the Realist Movement* (London, 1973).

all the arguments floundered in a conceptual morass.[6] And what was true of cases involving public issues of this nature was even more true of purely private law adjudication. A long series of low quality decisions, in the civil and in the criminal law, marks the inter-war period.[7] It was, indeed, an age of mediocrity, in the law, as in politics.

The very quality of the judiciary seemed markedly lower than it had been in the Victorian age. There were, perhaps, no appointments to the Bench so bad as some of those made by Halsbury, such as that of Ridley J. in 1897. But there was a serious lack of able judges in the topmost positions. For much of the inter-war period Lord Hewart presided over the Queen's Bench Division as Lord Chief Justice, and he was, by common consent, the worst Lord Chief Justice England had had for generations. He was a bad judge and poor lawyer. His contemporary, Sir Ernest Pollock, who became Master of the Rolls as Lord Hanworth in 1923 and so presided over the Court of Appeal during much of this period, was (according to the *D.N.B.*) 'deemed fortunate in being nominated a Law Officer' when he first became Solicitor-General in 1919, and his appointment as Master of the Rolls 'was unexpected and the subject of considerable criticism in the press and at the Bar . . . [H]e was not legally or intellectually of the same calibre as the eminent holders of that office during the previous twenty years'. And, it must be recorded also, that (despite the fulsome praise traditionally lavished on some of them) the inter-war Chancellors were, on the whole, an undistinguished collection of mediocrities. The only outstanding occupant of the Woolsack during this period (with the possible exception of Lord Sankey) was Lord Haldane, and as so often has been the case with the best English judges in this century, he never devoted himself more than half-heartedly to the law.

There were, of course, able and even distinguished judges. Scrutton L.J., in the Court of Appeal, had a high reputation as a commercial lawyer,[8] although as a judge of first instance he had been rude and unpopular with the Bar. But more relevantly for present purposes,

---

[6] See, e.g., *Sorrell* v. *Smith* [1925] A.C. 700; *Thorne* v. *Motor Trade Association* [1937] A.C. 797; the *Crofter* case [1942] A.C. 435.

[7] For example, in contract: *Re Engelbach* [1924] 2 Ch. 348, an unbelievably perverse decision; *Upton on Severn U.D.C.* v. *Powell* [1942] 1 All E.R. 220; *Wyatt* v. *Kreglinger & Fernau* [1933] 1 K.B. 793 (perhaps influenced by the merits of the case which were not what they appear on a casual reading); *Re Mahmoud* [1921] 2 K.B. 716; *Anderson* v. *Daniels* [1924] 1 K.B. 138; *Thompson* v. *L.M.S. Rly.* [1930] 1 K.B. 41 (again, the merits are more debatable than may seem); *Vandepitte's* case [1933] A.C. 70; *Kreditbank Cassel* v. *Schenkers* [1926] 2 K.B. 450; *Houghton & Co.* v. *Nothard, Lowe & Wills* [1927] 1 K.B. 246; *Newsholme* v. *Road Transport Insurance Co.* [1929] 2 K.B. 356. In the criminal law: *R.* v. *Wheat & Stocks* [1921] 2 K.B. 119; *Duncan* v. *Jones* [1936] 1 K.B. 218; *Thomas* v. *Sawkins* [1935] 2 K.B. 249, and many others.

[8] Though he hardly deserves the exaggerated eulogies of Llewellyn who described him as a 'greater commercial judge than Mansfield', and 'the greatest English speaking judge of a century': 'On Warranty of Quality and Society', 36 *Columbia Law Rev.* 699, 699–702 (1936).

Scrutton was unable to see the point of view of the consumer in contractual relationships.[9] His long experience as a commercial barrister, almost invariably acting on behalf of commercial clients, combined with the general traditions of English contract law, made him see all consumers in the same light as the classical economists had done a hundred years previously. He was certainly not the kind of man who would have signed a document without reading it, and he had no sympathy with the consumer who did so.

In the House of Lords in the 1930s Lord Atkin, Lord Wright, and Lord Macmillan had high reputations, and did help to prevent the common law becoming totally bogged down in unchanging conservatism. Nevertheless, the general intellectual level of their work suffers by comparison with what was happening in the United States during the same period. It is painful, even for an admirer of Lord Wright, to compare the level of sophistication displayed (for example) in an article he wrote in the *Harvard Law Review*[10] in 1936, with that to be found in the article by Fuller and Perdue in the *Yale Law Journal* of the same year.[11] Even some of those judges who had considerable intellectual gifts, of whom the outstanding example was Lord Greene, seem, from the perspective of the 1970s, to have misused those gifts by an extraordinary over-devotion to the conceptual dogmatism of the common law. Lord Greene was one of those brilliant judges who was so devoted to the positivist ideal of law that he appears to have been unable to distinguish between justice and injustice. He personified the tradition that the judge was to have no truck with policy, morality, or justice, but to apply the law as he saw it with perfect impartiality.[12]

Nor, as I have said above, is it possible to be certain that the age of formalism is over. Certainly, in their public utterances, and even in their extra-judicial utterances, judges are still prone to stress that law and policy are two entirely separate matters. As late as 1951 Lord Jowitt, the Lord Chancellor, shocked the sophisticated Australian legal fraternity, by publicly insisting that for judges to look at social and political issues, was 'to confuse the task of the lawyer with the task of the legislator'.[13]

---

[9] See, e.g., *Newsholme* v. *Road Transport Insurance Co.*, *supra*, where the defendant insurance company's canvasser had filled in an application form and the Court held that he had done so as agent for the insured.

[10] 'Ought the Doctrine of Consideration to be Abolished from the Common Law?', 49 *Harvard Law Rev.* 1225 (1936).

[11] 'The Reliance Interest in Contract Damages', 46 *Yale Law Journal* 52 and 373 (1936). And see too the sophisticated symposium on consideration in 41 *Columbia Law Rev.* 777 (1941).

[12] Consider his dictum in *Re Legh's Settlement* [1938] Ch. 39, 44, that 'the temptation to construe words in such a way as to evade the [Rule against Perpetuities] is one which must be firmly resisted', to which the only possible, and sufficient answer, is Why? See also the *Upton on Severn U.D.C.* case, *supra*, p. 633, n. 7, and *A.G. of British Columbia* v. *Esquimault & Nanaimo Rly. Co.* [1950] 1 D.L.R. 305, 311.

[13] See 25 *Australian Law J.* 296 (1951).

Fifteen years later, Lord Evershed repeated that the separation of law and policy was 'the essential meaning of accepted parliamentary supremacy in twentieth century England'.[14] When the Restrictive Practices Court was set up in 1956, and given the power to adjudicate on whether various business practices were in the public interest or not, the presiding judge, Devlin J. (as he then was) went out of his way to insist in the first case before the Court that its function was no different from that of any other Court, namely 'to take the words of the Act according to their proper construction and see if, on the facts proved, the case falls within them'.[15] Even when sitting as members of the Law Reform Committee, a number of leading judges and barristers declined, in 1957, to make any recommendations that might interfere with freedom of contract because '[t]he desirability or otherwise of such legislation [seemed to them] a broad question of social policy outside [their] competence'.[16]

But in the past decade or two, at least there has been a significant movement away from this extreme viewpoint. Lord Denning has made no secret, both off and on the Bench, of his belief that cases should be decided in accord with the judge's views on policy, and indeed, that cases *are* so decided, and that judgments are written to justify decisions previously reached on policy grounds. And although Lord Denning's early judicial career often caused legal eyebrows to be raised at what was considered his unorthodox approach, he has lived to see many of the newer judges in sympathy with his outlook. Other judges, while agreeing in substance that Courts can and must take account of policy issues, have suggested that it is politic not to proclaim the fact too widely or too loudly.[17] Unfortunately, the difficulty with this last approach is that it encourages not only a bland judicial hypocrisy, but (what is much worse) the presentation of legal arguments in a form and substance which are not directed to the real issues in the case. If judges are to take account of policy matters in their judgments the argument of counsel must likewise be directed to the policy issues. If this does not happen—and it has not yet begun to happen on a significant scale—policy matters are likely to be decided in an uninformed and unsophisticated manner.

But, in any case, as I have previously suggested, the refusal to discuss policy issues is itself almost always a decision which consciously or unconsciously forwards certain policies. In the sphere of contract, the

---

[14] 'The Judicial Process in Twentieth Century England', 61 *Columbia Law Rev.* p. 761, n. 1 (1961).

[15] *Re Chemists' Federation* case (1958) L.R. 1 R.P. 75, 103. But in fact Devlin J. was not a formalist and these words may have been written deliberately to allay possible apprehension over the role of the judiciary.

[16] Report of the Law Reform Committee on *Exceptions and Conditions in Insurance Policies*, Cmnd. 62 (1957), para 12. The Committee included Lords Jenkins, Parker, Diplock, Gardiner, Sir Robert Megarry, and Professor A. L. Goodhart (not all then bearing these titles).

[17] Lord Radcliffe, *Not in Feather Beds* (London, 1968), p. 273.

refusal of the Courts to entertain questions of fairness, or questions of economic policy, did result quite demonstrably, in giving various biases to the law. For example, there was, first, the general bias in favour of freedom of contract which, by 1850, had become the starting point for all contractual issues.[18] But in addition, there were other biases which became especially noticeable in the inter-war period, for example, an anti-consumer bias, a bias favouring those who used written forms for their contracts, a bias in favour of institutions like companies and against individuals, like shareholders, a bias in favour of freedom of contract over freedom of trade, and a bias in favour of penalizing contract-breakers and against any use of discretionary equitable mitigation of penalties. In all these respects the 1960s and still more the 1970s have seen a marked swing away from the trends of the inter-war period. As we shall see, whether or not the judges consciously avow the policies they are pursuing, the change of attitude in so many areas of contract law is too pronounced to be explained away.

The Separation of Law and Economics

As we have seen, in the early formative years of general contract law, there is good ground to think that lawyers and economists were familiar with each other's basic ideas, and that the development of classical contract law marched in step with the development of classical political economy. But by the 1870s this association of lawyers and economists was rapidly disappearing. So far as the practising legal profession was concerned, the two disciplines went in very different directions as classical political economy gave way to neo-classical economics. For some seventy or eighty years after 1870 economic thought was largely a closed book to the bar and the Bench in England. The result was that lawyers, in so far as they ever thought about economic issues, tended to hark back to what their predecessors had learnt in the first half of the nineteenth century. An extraordinary illustration of this tendency can be found in the judgment of Younger L.J. (by no means an undistinguished judge) in *Attwood* v. *Lamont*,[19] in 1920, where he referred to the law relating to restrictive agreements as having been influenced by economic theories, and added that '[i]ts modern developments have grown up under the shadow of the "laissez faire" school of economics'. Fifty years after Jevons had renounced *laissez-faire*, lawyers were thus still thinking of it as a relatively modern development.

But the judges of the twentieth century were not expected to read

---

[18] In 1962 it was still possible for lawyers (and others) to argue the case for freedom of contract in relation to the issue of non-voting corporate shares on the assumption that no public interest was involved in such questions. See the (Jenkins) Committee Report on *Company Law Reform*, Cmnd. 1742 (1962), para. 128–34. But cf. the *Minority Report*, ibid., p. 207.

[19] [1920] 3 K.B. 571, 581.

economics, at least in England, and few did so. It is true that R. B. Haldane, who was to become Lord Chancellor in the twentieth century, wrote a short *Life of Adam Smith*[20] when he was a rising young barrister and Member of Parliament, but even he observed in this book that economics had tended to become a specialized discipline, and that 'every specialist, if he is to do well, has to know everything that has been done in his own department [so that] the attempt to blend the abstract investigation of human affairs with their management has certainly not proved a conspicuous success'.[21] Among Haldane's contemporaries, was J. A. Hamilton, later Lord Sumner. Hamilton was appointed a judge in 1909, a Lord Justice of Appeal in 1912, and became Lord Sumner, a Lord of Appeal in 1913. He had a high reputation as a judge, though it was probably higher then than it is now, but his ignorance of economics had calamitous results for Britain, because he was appointed by the Government to the three-man Reparations Committee after the First World War. It was Sumner and Cunliffe, the Governor of the Bank of England, who were christened by Keynes as the 'Heavenly twins' and who were responsible for the demand that the Germans should pay reparations amounting to £24,000 millions, a fantastic sum which, as Keynes explained, could not possibly be paid except by such an expansion of German exports as would ensure the total destruction of the British and French export industries.[22] It was largely the intransigence of Sumner and his two colleagues which was responsible for the eventual disastrous settlement, with such incalculable consequences for the future.[23] Judges of the 1930s and afterwards, and more particularly of the period after the Second World War, began to display a greater interest in economics. Lord Macmillan, a prominent Law Lord in the 1930s and 1940s, was Chairman of the Committee on Finance and Industry (on which Keynes was a leading member) in the late 1920s; Lord Radcliffe was Chairman of the Committee on the Monetary System in the 1950s; and the experiences of a number of judges on the Restrictive Practices Court after 1956 brought them into contact with economic thinking in some very practical matters.

Amongst academic lawyers, there has been a similar movement during the past century. In 1870 an academic legal profession scarcely existed, though there were a number of (usually part-time) Chairs in Law. At the Queen's University of Belfast there was, for some years, a combined Chair of Jurisprudence and Political Economy, but its institution owed more to the fact that there were not enough law students to justify a

[20] London, 1887.
[21] p. 96.
[22] See generally, J. M. Keynes, *The Economic Consequences of the Peace*.
[23] Roy Harrod, *Life of John Maynard Keynes* (Pelican edn.), pp. 283–5. Sumner was one of the judges who sat in *Roberts* v. *Hopwood* [1925] A.C. 578, see *post*, p. 668.

Professor of Law alone, and less to any belief that a multi-disciplinary Chair was desirable in itself. The combined Chair was abolished in 1909 when separate Chairs were created.[24] In other Law Faculties, no serious attempt was made to combine legal and economic work. One distinguished academic lawyer with a good understanding of economics was Sir John Macdonnell, sometime Quain Professor of Comparative Law in London, member of several Royal Commissions, Secretary to the Committee on Trusts in 1919, and leader writer in *The Times*. But it is, perhaps, illustrative of the lack of real contact between the two disciplines that Macdonnell left no memorial in the form of any literature devoted to the relationship between law and economics. Apart from Macdonnell, one of the very few lawyers to write on legal-economic issues in the inter-war period was C. A. Cooke, who spent many years as a Bursar of an Oxford College, rather than as a law don.[25] He referred in one of his publications to the fact that the economic ideas used by lawyers in England tended to be 'inconsistent and even incoherent',[26] but like Macdonnell, he made no impact on legal education or on the legal literature on which law students were brought up.

Not everybody regretted the separation of law and economics. Sir Frederick Pollock, the doyen of academics, though himself somewhat aloof from the generality of the academic profession, wrote in 1911 that, 'our lady the common law is not a professed economist';[27] but on the whole he thought this was no bad thing. If economic theories were studied by lawyers, he argued, they were as likely as not to be misunderstood; in any event, economic theories varied with the fashion, and if lawyers got things wrong, it would be necessary to resort to Parliament for corrective legislation, which would probably make matters worse. But the trouble with this attitude, like the whole attempt to adopt value-free legal principles, was that there was just enough residuary handing down of economic ideas in the law to give a decided bias towards the old principles of classical political economy. This bias revealed itself (for example) in the case of *Roberts* v. *Hopwood*[28] in which the House of Lords had to consider the legality of the actions of the Poplar Borough Council in paying its labourers wages far above the market rate. The Borough Council was controlled by the Labour Party (which had, after all, formed its first Government only the previous

---

[24] There were only three holders of this Chair, of whom much the most distinguished was T. E. Cliffe Leslie; see *supra*, pp. 612 and 638.

[25] See 'The Legal Content of the Profit Concept', 46 *Yale Law Journal* 436 (1937); 'Legal Rule and Economic Function', 46 *Economic Journal* 21 (1936).

[26] 'The Legal Content of the Profit Concept', p. 437.

[27] *The Genius of the Common Law* (New York, 1904), p. 194. But Pollock himself admitted to reading Marshall's *Principles*, whom he recommended to Holmes as a 'good deal more sociological than some economists', though some of it was 'stiffish reading': *Pollock–Holmes Letters*, i. 184.

[28] [1925] A.C. 578.

year) and the Council decided to implement the principle of paying what it regarded as a minimum living wage, irrespective of market considerations, trade union rates, or payments by other local or national authorities. It was held that the Council had no power to make such payments which were misguided philanthropism at the expense of the ratepayers. The decision is more defensible than it has often been made to appear when it is used as an illustration of class bias on the part of the judges. But the point to be made here is that the judges took it for granted that a power to pay wages presupposed a free market system, in which wages would be generally set by the market. The possibility of an alternative system of fixing wages does not seem to have occurred to their lordships.

On the other hand, if judges and lawyers often continued to think in terms of a classical market system, there have not been lacking allegations that modern lawyers have gone along too readily with economic departures from the classic system. F. A. Hayek, for example, has said that most contemporary works on legal philosophy 'are full of outdated clichés about the alleged self-destructive tendency of competition, or the need for "planning" created by the increased complexity of the modern world, clichés deriving from the high enthusiasm for "planning" thirty or forty years ago'.[29] He goes on to say:

It is, indeed, doubtful whether as much false economics has been spread during the last hundred years by any other means as by the teaching of the young lawyers by their elders that 'it was necessary this or that should be done', or that such and such circumstances 'made it inevitable' that certain measures should be taken.[30]

There is force in these remarks, and they suggest the somewhat depressing conclusion that the attempt by lawyers to extend their understanding of economic theory may often make matters worse, because most lawyers will only succeed in understanding what was orthodox a generation or two back.

The Separation of Law and Ethics

If law and economics have drifted steadily apart since 1870, notwithstanding some recent attempts to bring them together again, a similar, though not identical development has occurred in the relationship between law and ethics. What has largely happened here is that lawyers have abandoned the attempt to place the law in the framework of some overall and coherent moral philosophy. The disappearance, first, of belief in Natural Law and secondly, the decline in the importance of religion, both played a part in the increasing fluidity of moral ideas. By the late

---

[29] *Law, Legislation and Liberty*, i, pp. 68–9.   [30] Ibid.

nineteenth century, the second wave of religious toleration had paved the way for the secularization of thought and morality; and as it did so, there emerged in its wake not one, but a variety of secular moralities.

All this was given a new impetus by the destruction of the old social order in the First World War. In the inter-war period, and perhaps until the 1960s, this moral pluralism caused most difficulty to lawyers in connection with marriage and divorce, abortion, and obscenity, prostitution, and homosexuality. The change was not merely one of growing permissiveness, but of a growing variety of morally acceptable viewpoints. The lawyers resisted this movement for many years. In the inter-war period there was a growing gulf between the official, establishment morality of the legal profession and the judges, on the one side, and much liberal public opinion on the other. This gulf lingered on into the post-Second World War era until it was largely destroyed by the verdict of the jury in the case concerning *Lady Chatterley's Lover* in 1960.

On other matters the gulf between official morality and public morality may have been less marked, but what nevertheless was clearly marked was the extraordinary desire of lawyers to avoid discussing issues in moral terms. Just as economic and political issues were said to be irrelevant to the law, so it came to be more and more vigorously asserted that law and morality were distinct questions. The teaching of legal theory in the new Law Schools that began to grow up after 1870 was heavily dominated by Austinian positivism, a tradition which led to the belief that moral issues were irrelevant (*irrelevant!*) to legal issues. Many legal academics in the inter-war period carried this to the length of refusing to discuss policy issues in connection with the law. To do this, it was argued, was to lose 'objectivity'. Students must be firmly kept to the belief that 'the law is the law is the law', and not what it ought to be or what it was morally desirable for it to be. Even in 1963 it was possible for a legal work to state baldly: 'That morals are irrelevant to legal issues is perhaps too elementary a proposition to need reiteration, but it is strange how often the rule seems to be neglected in practice'.[31]

The difficulties facing lawyers in this world of moral pluralism may help to explain one of the most striking phenomena of modern law, namely the revival of casuistry, the increasing disinclination to lay down general principles, the growth of discretions, and of the practice of disposing of legal cases by findings of fact rather than decisions of law. Even the moral sanctity attaching to promises has, as we have seen, greatly waned in the past century. As far back as the 1930s, percipient American scholars were observing the effect on the law of changing moral ideas about the sanctity of promises. Morris Cohen, for example, commented on the difficulty facing lawyers once public opinion had

[31] Ash, *Willing to Purchase* (London, 1963), p. 104.

moved away from the idea that *all* promises should be enforced, and that situation, he asserted, already existed:

It is indeed very doubtful whether there are many who would prefer to live in an entirely rigid world in which one would be obliged to keep *all* one's promises instead of the present more variable system in which a vaguely fair proportion is sufficient. Many of us indeed would shudder at the idea of being bound by every promise, no matter how foolish, without any chance of letting increased wisdom undo past foolishness. Certainly, some freedom to change one's mind is necessary for free intercourse between those who lack omniscience.[32]

Similarly, Corbin in 1937 detected in very recent times, 'a serious decline in respect for the obligation of contract and a growing conviction that the breaking of promises is socially just and right, when their performance or enforcement involves hardship or a substantially greater effort and sacrifice than was anticipated by the promisor when the contract was made'.[33]

By contrast, English lawyers, like English philosophers, tended to shut their eyes to these developments. It was not true, they asserted, that promises were no longer absolutely binding. A promise only ceased to bind when it was implicit in the promise that it was not intended to bind in the circumstances in question.[34]

THE DECLINE OF EQUITY AND THE RISE OF DISCRETION

These changing moral values have coincided with the general legal movement away from principle and towards the pragmatic which has taken place in the century since 1870, though perhaps most of the movement has been confined to the past fifty years or so. It may be, as Sir Otto Kahn-Freund has suggested,[35] that the case-oriented methodology has traditionally tended to make English law intensely casuistical, but if so, the period from 1770 to 1870 was one which ran counter to this tradition. As I have suggested, it was during this period that English judges abandoned the short-term for the long-term considerations, the ideals of mercy and equity in favour of the application of firm principles, the conflict-adjustment function for the hortatory or deterrent functions of the law. The culmination of this process took place with the Judicature Acts of 1873-5 which marked the virtual demise of Equity as a separate

---

[32] 'The Basis of Contract', 46 *Harvard Law Rev.* 553, 573 (1933). This calls to mind a very similar passage in G. E. Moore's *Ethics* (reprinted Oxford, 1955), p. 111.

[33] 'Recent Developments in Contract', 50 *Harvard Law Rev.* 449, 473 (1937).

[34] Among lawyers the 'implied term' theory of the doctrine of frustration was still in the ascendant. Among philosophers, a precisely similar theory was developed by Sir David Ross, *Foundations of Ethics* (Oxford, 1939), pp. 94-9.

[35] Introduction to Renner, *The Institutions of Private Law* (English translation, 1949, reprinted London and Boston, 1976), pp. 13-16.

source of discretionary justice. Modern lawyers and historians have too often tended to see the Judicature Acts as representing a rationalization of civil procedure, or even as representing the final triumph of Equity over the common law. This is a great mistake. In fact the merger of Law and Equity (it has been said of the United States where it generally occurred rather earlier) marked 'the final and complete emasculation of Equity as an independent source of legal standards'.[36] This was nearly true of England as well, though the emasculation has, after all, not proved final.

At the time when the Acts were under debate, this fundamental subordination of Equity to the Common Law was perceived as one of the main objections to the proposed merger. Four Equity judges were to be merged with fifteen common law judges, protested Lord Cairns. Would this not result in the preponderance of the common law over equitable ideals?[37] In fact, for a decade or two after the Acts were passed, it seemed that Lord Cairns's fears were only too justified. Many of the common law judges had, as a contemporary observer noted, 'an intellectual antipathy' to the doctrines of Equity, and 'did not scruple to characterize some of the equitable rules as iniquitous'.[38] What was more, their ignorance of Equity was astonishing. In 1882, the same observer noted, the senior common law judge avowed 'his total ignorance of such things as equitable assignments'.[39] Lord Esher, who was Master of the Rolls from 1883 to 1897, and as such presided over the Court of Appeal which then usually sat in one division only, was a pure common lawyer and 'like most of his colleagues, he was not above an occasional sneer at equity'.[40] But more important was the changing role of the Lord Chancellor and the changing composition of the House of Lords as an appellate Court. Until the Judicature Acts, the Lord Chancellor was nearly always an Equity lawyer, and until the middle of the nineteenth century, Chancellors had regularly sat at first instance. Moreover, as a peer, the Chancellor also sat in the House of Lords to hear appeals from Common Law Courts, and it was by no means uncommon for such appeals to be heard by a tribunal comprising only ex-Chancellors. But after the passing of the Judicature Act, all this changed fast. The Chancellor now ceased altogether to sit at first instance, and the House of Lords ceased to be dominated by ex-Chancellors. The fact that the new House of Lords was the ultimate

---

[36] Morton M. Horwitz, *The Transformation of American Law* (Cambridge, Mass., and London, 1977), p. 265.

[37] *Hansard* (3rd series), vol. 215, col. 1266 (1873).

[38] *A Generation of Judges* (London, 1886), by W. D. I. Foulkes, published anonymously as by 'Their Reporter', p. 130.

[39] Ibid., p. 131. The senior puisne at this time was Grove J.

[40] Veeder, 'A Century of English Jurisprudence 1800-1900' in *Select Essays in Anglo-American Legal History* (Cambridge, 1907-9), i. 815.

appeal Court for Scotland and Ireland as well as for England, necessitated the presence of one Law Lord from each of these two jurisdictions, and the other positions were, at least in the early years, filled largely by common lawyers. Indeed, it was now no longer necessary for the Lord Chancellor himself to have any knowledge of Equity, and Lord Halsbury, who held the great seal for nearly twenty years at the turn of the century, had no experience of Chancery practice at all. He was once guilty of the elementary blunder of saying that if it was 'intended' to have a resulting trust, 'the ordinary and familiar mode [should be followed] that is, by saying so on the face of the instrument'.[41]

In contractual matters, the differing approaches of common law and Chancery judges had given rise, in the first half of the nineteenth century, to differences of attitude, which were reflected in particular in their approach to market principles. It was the common lawyers who had stressed the market ideal of the free bargaining, arms' length transaction, the principle (for instance) that parties should rely on themselves, and not on what they were told. Chancery lawyers, on the other hand, had been brought up to believe in principles of good faith, in the right of a man to rely upon someone in whom he had confided, or upon whose statements he had trusted. These varying attitudes had given rise to differing approaches in the law relating to misrepresentation, and it had originally been intended in the Judicature Act to include a clause giving precedence to the rules of Equity on this matter. But the clause was dropped from the Bill, and when the issue was litigated after the Act, in the famous case of *Derry* v. *Peek*,[42] it came ultimately before a House of Lords which did not include a single Chancery law lord.[43] It was no wonder that, according to Pollock, all of Lincoln's Inn thought the decision wrong.[44] The decision in *Derry* v. *Peek* was not only the final triumph of common law over Equity; it was the final triumph of market principles in the law of contract. By confining the definition of fraud within the narrowest grounds possible, the law lords here insisted upon the obligations of those who bought and sold in the market, to rely upon their own judgment, and not upon opinions proffered by the other party. The decision also represented the triumph of general principle over 'the desire to effect what is or what is thought to be, justice in a particular instance'.[45]

---

[41] *Smith* v. *Cooke* [1891] A.C. 297, 299.

[42] (1889) 14 App. Cas. 337.

[43] Lords Halsbury, Herschell, Bramwell, Fitzgerald, and Watson.

[44] *Pollock–Holmes Letters*, i. 215.

[45] Lord Bramwell, 14 App. Cas. at p. 352. For another instance of the influence of common law attitudes on Chancery doctrines, see *Speight* v. *Gaunt* (1883) L.R. 9 App. Cas. 1, where Lord Blackburn seems to have had difficulty grasping the idea that an unremunerated trustee could be liable for breach of trust.

There were, as we shall see later, other differences in attitude which appeared to survive the Judicature Acts for many years, even though some barristers began to practice in both divisions of the High Court. But at this stage I need only observe that by the 1890s or thereabouts, the long period of domination by the Common Law over Equity was drawing to its close. So far as the personnel of the House of Lords was concerned, the representation of Chancery practitioners was much strengthened by the appointments of Lord Macnaghten (in 1887) and Lord Davey (in 1894), though not until Lord Haldane became Lord Chancellor in 1912 was another Chancery lawyer to sit on the Woolsack. But a succession of other judges, like Jessel, Cotton, Fry, and Lindley also helped to keep equitable principles alive in the Court of Appeal, and by the close of the century there were some signs that the danger which the Judicature Acts had posed to Equity had been averted.

Nevertheless, the equitable rules which were in conflict with the principles of freedom of contract continued to receive a considerable battering at the hands of the Courts for many years. As late as 1891, for example, the equitable discretion to relieve against the effects of a forfeiture was cut down in a particularly hard case, in which a tenant underlet without seeking the landlord's consent.[46] There was no suggestion that the underlessee was not a perfectly acceptable tenant, nor that the landlord would have declined to give his consent if sought; but the Court upheld the forfeiture of the lease on the ground that there was here no 'mistake' but only forgetfulness. The law of mortgages too, was reconsidered in a series of important cases in the early years of the twentieth century. The upshot of these cases was a significant move towards upholding freedom of contract at the expense of the traditional equitable jurisdiction to interfere between mortgagor and mortgagee.[47] The modern view—or the view which would have seemed modern if adopted in 1850—was stated by Lord Parker in 1914: 'That the Court should be asked in the exercise of its equitable jurisdiction to assist in so inequitable a proceeding as the repudiation of a fair and reasonable bargain is somewhat startling'.[48] Of course, everything depended on the extent to which the Courts were willing to examine the fairness and reasonableness of the bargain; if indeed, it was, on the facts, shown to be fair and reasonable, then there could be no ground for interfering, and Equity never would have interfered. But these cases reflected the common law attitude that a contract was to be deemed fair and reasonable merely because it had been agreed; that at least was the conclusion drawn from them by the Court of Appeal in 1939, when it upheld a commercial

---

[46] *Barrow* v. *Isaac & Son* [1891] 1 Q.B. 417; see too *Wallis* v. *Smith* (1882) 21 Ch.D. 243.

[47] *Bradley* v. *Carritt* [1903] A.C. 253; *Kreglinger* v. *New Patagonia Meat Co.* [1914] A.C. 25.

[48] *Kreglinger* case [1914] A.C. 47.

contract which took the form of a mortgage irredeemable for forty years.[49] Lord Greene's language in this case would have been applauded by Parke B. a hundred years earlier:

A [contrary] decision . . . would, in our view, involve an unjustified interference with the freedom of businessmen to enter into agreements best suited to their own interests, and would impose upon them a test of "reasonableness" laid down by the Courts without reference to the business realities of the case.[50]

It is not clear why a test of reasonableness should have been contrary to the business realities of the case; such a test should necessarily have involved reference to the business realities, and if the bargain was in fact a reasonable one by the relevant business standards (which seems to have been the case) then plainly the decision was itself sound enough.

I do not suggest that these decisions, all of which involved mortgages between commercial organizations, were unreasonable, or that in such cases an equitable jurisdiction to intervene to ensure a fair result is necessarily desirable. Much obviously depends on the extent of the jurisdiction which it is sought to invoke—a jurisdiction to control harsh and unconscionable transactions is one thing, while a jurisdiction to override the express terms of a bargain merely to make a minor adjustment to the consideration being paid, is another. But I do, nevertheless, suggest that these decisions reflect the continuing decline of equitable discretions which lasted throughout the first half of the twentieth century, and perhaps have only been reversed in the present decade. Only with *Shiloh Spinners Ltd.* v. *Harding*[51] in 1973 was the equitable jurisdiction to prevent forfeitures emphatically reasserted in the House of Lords, even if in language which also insisted on due regard for contractual rights. Lord Simon of Glaisdale pointed out here that *Barrow* v. *Issac & Son*[52] was a natural consequence of the insistence on strict freedom of contract in *Hill* v. *Barclay*.[53]

I am bound to say [he went on] that it seems to me to demonstrate an abnegation of equity, and to show that the trail from *Hill* v. *Barclay* leads into a juristic desert . . . The last hundred years have seen many examples of relaxation of the stance of regarding contractual rights and obligations as sacrosanct and exclusive of other considerations: though these examples do *not* compel equity to follow— certainly not to the extent of overturning established authorities—they do at least invite a more liberal and extensively based attitude on the part of the courts which are not bound by those authorities. I would therefore myself hold that

[49] *Knightsbridge Estates Trust* v. *Byrne* [1939] Ch. 441, affirmed on different grounds, [1940] A.C. 613.
[50] [1939] Ch. at 454.
[51] [1973] A.C. 691; see too *Ebrahimi* v. *Westbourne Galleries Ltd.* [1973] A.C. 360.
[52] *Supra*, p. 674, n. 46.
[53] (1811) 18 Ves. Jun. 56, 34 E.R. 238; *supra*, p. 414.

equity has an unlimited and unfettered jurisdiction to relieve against forfeiture and penalties.[54]

I do not here cite the development of promissory or equitable estoppel in the years since the *High Trees*[55] case as evidence of a resurgence of equitable principles. These developments are an illustration of the ordinary movements of the common law, and there is nothing peculiarly equitable about them. Except perhaps for some dicta of Lord Denning's in one or two of these cases,[56] there has not been in this line of authorities any suggestion that the results should be dictated by discretion rather than fixed rule, nor has there been any suggestion that the Courts are arrogating to themselves a jurisdiction to override express contractual intentions. Indeed, there is some ground for thinking that the modern developments here are in truth more in line with common law thinking—which gave complete precedence to contractual intent—and less with equitable principles which were more concerned with the fairness of an exchange.[57] That does not mean that I am not in sympathy with the substance of this development although I could wish that it had taken a simpler form.

But apart from the revival of old equitable principles, there was, in any event, another important development which can be traced to the last years of the nineteenth century, and which (perhaps with a pause in the inter-war period) has gathered ever-increasing strength in the past few decades. For if Equity, at least as a source of independent legal rules and ideals, largely died with the Judicature Acts, it was eventually replaced by the phenomenon of the judicial discretion. The past century as a whole, and the period since the end of the Second World War in particular, have seen a formidable growth in the nature and extent of judicial discretions. The power to decide what is just and equitable in all the circumstances of the case, has become a familiar part of the judicial process. Inevitably, as discretions have risen in importance, rules and principles have waned. In some areas, it is barely an exaggeration to say that there are no rules left at all, only discretions. For instance, the modern law of succession gives power to judges to do virtually whatever they think is just in the distribution of a person's estate. The claims of a man's wife, *de jure*, or *de facto* (or both), of his children, and of other parties, are left to be weighed up by a judicial discretion which requires a most minute examination of the facts. The length of time for which a marriage has subsisted, the contribution made to it, and to the family

[54] At p. 726.
[55] [1947] K.B. 130.
[56] See, e.g., *D & C Builders* v. *Rees* [1966] 2 Q.B. 617, 625; *W. J. Alan & Co.* v. *El Nasr Export and Import Co.* [1972] 2 Q.B. 189, 213.
[57] See *supra*, p. 440.

property by the spouses, the relationship between a parent and child, the particular need of particular children, all these and many more factors are taken into account in such decisions. It is plain that Parliament has, in effect, decided that the variety of factual situations is too great to be encompassed within general rules and principles.

But this is only one field among many. The growth of discretions has been pronounced in other areas also. In contract law in particular, this trend towards discretions, 'ad hockery', and ex post facto decisions, can be observed at work in a variety of ways. For example, there has been an increasing tendency away from penal damages or results, and a like tendency to insist that the function of the Court is purely to compensate for actual losses. The gradual elimination of imprisonment for debt, beginning with the Debtors Act in 1869 and culminating in the Administration of Justice Act 1970, has been matched by a general whittling away of penal damages in contractual cases. In 1909, indeed, the House of Lords, decided that contractual damages should not generally include any penal element,[58] so that it may be said that the law of contract is now concerned primarily to patch up disputes, or pick up the pieces after a conflict, rather than to guide behaviour in the future. Similarly, the whittling away of the 'entire contracts rule' which often has penal results, is an indication of the same tendency. And businessmen too, are unlikely today to sue for breach of contract merely to teach someone a lesson, as commonly happened before 1890.[59] A trend of course, is not a monolithic force, and cases still occur, from time to time, in which the Courts award damages which (though not nominally penal) do appear to be intended to influence the behaviour of future contracting parties. For example, in *Jarvis* v. *Swan Tours*[60] the award of damages to a disappointed tourist for his 'loss of happiness' appears to have been motivated by a desire to penalize the careless production of over fulsome holiday brochures, much as *Carlill* v. *Carbolic Smoke Ball Co.*[61] may have been inspired by a desire to discourage reckless or fraudulent advertising. Similarly, the decision in *Bolton* v. *Mahadeva*,[62] where the entire contracts rule was invoked in modern times, may have been influenced by the desire to penalize contractors who fail to do a reasonable job for a consumer. But the overall trend is, nevertheless, plainly against the use of contract law for these purposes.

The same trend is observable in a variety of other respects. For example, there has been the movement away from the condition/

---

[58] *Addis* v. *Gramophone Co.* [1909] A.C. 488.
[59] See Lord Alverstone, *Recollections of Bar and Bench* (London, 1914), pp. 20–1.
[60] [1973] 2 Q.B. 233.
[61] [1893] 1 Q.B. 256.
[62] [1972] 1 W.L.R. 1009.

warranty dichotomy towards an ex post facto determination of whether a breach of contract has had sufficiently serious results to justify repudiation;[63] there has been, in public policy cases, a movement away from having regard to long-term 'tendencies';[64] there has even been a suggestion that the rule governing postal acceptances may be held inapplicable if it would produce 'manifest inconvenience and absurdity';[65] there has been a pronounced tendency for the Courts to retreat from solving contractual problems such as mistake or frustration by invoking fixed rules of laws, and instead a move towards relying on 'the construction of the contract' as the preferred procedure.[66] The new statutory definition of 'merchantable quality' which dates from the Supply of Goods (Implied Terms) Act 1973 is little more than an invitation to the Court to determine ex post facto, what standard of quality the buyer was entitled to expect. And the statutory discretions continue to multiply. The Hire-Purchase Act of 1938, now replaced by the Consumer Credit Act 1974, first gave powers to judges to rewrite hire-purchase contracts almost as they pleased, on a default by the hirer; since then similar, though not always such wide, discretions have been conferred by Acts dealing with the frustration of contracts, with liability for misrepresentation, and with the effect of exemption clauses in contracts for supply of goods or services.[67] Discretion in the award of interest and costs, of course, has long been part of the judicial process.

After what I have said in previous chapters about the decline of principle and the move towards pragmatism, it is unnecessary to add much by way of explanation of these trends in the law. It is only too evident that in most contract litigation today, the Courts see their function much as they do in accident litigation. A situation has misfired, something has, more or less unexpectedly, gone wrong in the performance of a contract. An unexpected event has occurred, perhaps, or performance has turned out more onerous than expected. The Court's function is then to adjust this conflict, to pick up the pieces, to achieve a just solution in all the circumstances of the case; the Court is not much concerned about the influence of the decision on future behaviour; it does not see its primary function as being that of laying down rules of good conduct for the citizenry, of encouraging the public to pay their debts or keep their promises.

---

[63] See, e.g., *Hong Kong Fir Shipping Line* v. *Kawasaki Kisen Kaisha* [1962] 2 Q.B. 26; *Reardon Smith Line Ltd.* v. *Hansen Tangen* [1976] 3 All E.R. 570.

[64] *Fender* v. *Mildmay* [1938] A.C. 1, 12-16.

[65] *Holwell Securities* v. *Hughes* [1974] 1 All E.R. 161, 166.

[66] See further, P. S. Atiyah, 'Judicial Techniques in the English Law of Contract', 2 *Ottowa Law Rev.* 337 (1969).

[67] Law Reform (Frustrated Contracts) Act 1943; Misrepresentation Act 1967; Supply of Goods (Implied Terms) Act 1973; Unfair Contract Terms Act 1977.

One must beware of overstating the case. It is precisely because much ordinary debt-collection or contract-enforcing raises no arguable issues, that routine cases go through the semi-administrative procedures of uncontested claims. And it is because these cases are not the ones which take up most judicial time, or space in the Law Reports or in students' examinations and textbooks, that their importance can be overlooked. It is, for example, still the case, that if a debtor does not pay until a summons is issued he will have to pay the costs of the summons, and any subsequent legal costs; and whatever the intention may be behind such procedures, their effect is still penal. The result, it may be, is no bad thing; for if there were no penalty of any kind attached to non-payment of debts, it is hard to see why anybody should pay his debts before the bailiff arrived at the door. But there are signs that even penalties of this nature are coming increasingly under fire. While (it may be) nobody has yet suggested that debtors should be relieved of the cost of a summons, there are not lacking suggestions that other types of penal sanction deployed to enforce payment of debts should be eliminated. For example, university students are pressing for the elimination of the power of a university to refuse to grant a degree until all debts due to it are paid; and steps have been taken (by administrative means) to reduce the power of Gas and Electricity Boards to discontinue supplies to customers who refuse to pay their bills.

My purpose here has been to describe a trend rather than to evaluate it; but once the extent of the trend is perceived, it is hard not to have doubts about its consequences. Few people today wish to argue for the application of firm rules, as opposed to varying standards of discretion. University teachers may bear a good share of the responsibility for this trend in the law, for they have, for thirty or forty years, nearly always thrown their weight behind judicial attempts to do justice in the circumstances of the case, rather than to lay down rules or principles of general application. But they are, probably, reflecting public opinion in these matters, and the media show a most powerful adherence to 'act-utilitarianism'. Newspapers and television or radio commentators, discussing an issue of this kind, never ask whether the rules are just, but whether a particular result is just. And, so far as the judges are concerned, the changing relationship between Parliament and Courts has continued to give a powerful impetus to this trend. For it is the responsibility of Parliament, as generally perceived, to lay down rules of conduct for the public; the judges' responsibility is to decide particular cases. But Parliament itself has shared in the movement away from principles towards discretionary decisions. Much legislation has been responsible for replacing fixed rule by discretions, both administrative and judicial.

Ultimately, the time must surely come when more harm than good results from the attempt to do justice in every particular case.[68] In contract law, for example, sympathy for debtors, when translated into the shape of fewer sanctions, or more lenient penalties, must drive up the cost of credit, or even render it unobtainable altogether. 'People will miss fewer trains . . . if they know the engineer will leave without them rather than delay even by a few seconds'.[69]

[68] See P. S. Atiyah, 'From Principles to Pragmatism: Changes in the Function of the Judicial Process and the Law' (Oxford, 1978).

[69] Duncan Kennedy, 'Form and Substance in Private Law Adjudication', 89 *Harvard Law Rev.* 1685, 1698.

21

THE DECLINE OF FREEDOM OF CONTRACT, 1870–1970

THE SETTLING OF CLASSICAL CONTRACT THEORY

By 1870, as we have seen, classical law had arrived at its mature form. A model of contractual theory had been largely worked out by the Courts which had been superimposed on the specific relationships and rules applicable to particular transactions. A general law of contract had come into existence with two principal characteristics. The first was that the model of contract was based on the economic model of the free market transaction; and the second was that contract was seen primarily as an instrument of market *planning*, that is to say, the model was that of the wholly executory contract. The model of the executory contract was so powerful that, even where the actual formation of the contract had not proceeded in accordance with the model, lawyers tended to conceptualize the process as though it had. Thus, partly executed, and even wholly executed, transactions were still seen by lawyers as corresponding to this model. The source of the legal obligation was still seen as located in mutual acts of will which created the contract, even where actual benefits had been rendered and accepted, or acts of reliance had been performed. Moreover, the contract once made was 'binding' without more. It is true that in certain circumstances (e.g., where market prices did not change) no substantive results flowed from a breach of such a binding contract, if it was still wholly executory, but that was a part of the law of damages, and not relevant to the formation or nature of the contract. Above all, of course, the model was suffused with the notion that the consequences of the contract depended entirely on the intention of the parties, and were not imposed by the Courts. The Courts did not make contracts for the parties, nor did they adjust or alter the terms agreed by the parties. The fairness and justice of the exchange was irrelevant.

But if this was all largely implicit in the case law which had grown up during the century from 1770 to 1870, it was necessary, if it was to survive in the changing world of the next century, that it should be made explicit. The model had to be written down and given some canonical form. And that was the important function of the textbook writers whose works (I suggest) were to have an important role in preserving the shadow of the classical model long after the substance had largely vanished. In and around the 1870s the classical version of contract theory was translated into a series of important books which continued to exercise a dominating influence on English contractual thought through the next hundred years, and indeed, may be said to still rule us from their graves. These writers had had their predecessors, like Powell, Chitty, and Addison, who had all been writing while the great transformation was taking place. And some of these books, suitably edited, continued to do service for many years; in some cases the names survive to this day. But with the first edition of Martin Leake's book in 1867 a significant change came over the new contract works. Leake was the first author to write purely on the general principles of contract law, excluding the law relating to particular contracts, and he was also the first author to write when the classical contract model was virtually established. He was, as we have seen, the first writer to incorporate into English law the Roman law distinction between 'genuine' implied-in-fact contracts, and quasi-contracts, in place of the indigenous common law distinction between express and implied contracts.

More influential than Leake, however, were the new works by Pollock (1875) and Anson (1879). These writers were academics, unlike all their predecessors. They were learned men, and men given to theorizing, not in the pejorative sense which the word still bears among legal practitioners, but theorizing in a more acceptable tradition; they were theorists in the sense that they sought to construct a theoretical and systematic framework of legal principle into which specific legal decisions could be fitted. They were also deeply versed in Roman law, and Pollock, at least, was well acquainted with modern civil law countries such as France and Germany, as well as with some of the developments in the United States. When these men came to write about the law of contract, they were not content to follow the traditional English practitioner's method of jumbling cases around without any sort of rational order or classification, or at best following a classification deriving from the forms of action. They found 'no literary tradition of expounding the law of contract in a form which invites the reader to proceed in the solution of problems by applying general principles of substantive law, principles under which the messy business of life is subsumed under ideal aseptic types of transaction, the types themselves being analysed and their legal consequences presented in a systematic form'.[1] They found it necessary to set about creating a new shape to the law of contract. In one sense, it was they who actually created the general law of contract which we still know today, for it was they who formulated it and made explicit much of which had been implicit in the cases. In doing this, they borrowed

[1] A. W. B. Simpson, 'Innovation in Nineteenth Century Contract Law', 91 *Law Q. Rev.* 247, 251 (1975).

heavily (as the Courts had been doing) from Roman lawyers, from Pothier, and in Pollock's case at least, from modern continental jurists, in particular Savigny. It is to these writers that we still owe our general conception of the shape of contract law; that is to say, that it is a body of rules concerned with the formation, performance, and discharge of contractual obligations by the acts of the parties themselves. It is to them that we owe the arrangements of modern English textbooks, with the Formation of the Contract at the beginning of the book, and the Law of Damages at the end—with no apparent connection between them. It is to them that we owe much of the still living tendency to formulate rules and doctrines in terms of will theory. And it is to them that we owe much of the power of the concepts of the law of contract; the belief in the objective reality of these concepts—offer, acceptance, consideration, and so forth—if it was not created, was certainly significantly assisted by these writers.

The most influential of all was probably Sir William Anson. Anson was one of the new Oxford academics, brought up in the classical tradition, with only a brief career at the Bar. His *Principles of the Law of Contract* was published in 1879 and it was expressly designed to meet the needs of the students reading for the new Oxford law degree first established in 1872. In the Preface to the first edition, Anson wrote that the book sets out 'general principles which govern the contractual relation from its beginning to its end. I have tried to show', he added, 'how a contract is made, what are its effects, how its terms are interpreted, and how it is discharged and comes to an end.' The modern textbook treatment of the subject is here quite recognizable in the Table of Contents. After a brief introduction, Part II of the book contains chapters on Proposals and Acceptance, Form and Consideration, Capacity and the Reality of Consent (under which are dealt mistake, misrepresentation, fraud, duress, and undue influence). Part III deals with Privity and Assignment, Part IV with Interpretation, and Part V with Discharge. In the Preface to his fifth edition (in 1885), Anson explained more fully the nature and purposes of his work, and contrasted the rival styles of Leake and Pollock, the two leading works in the field when his book was first written:

Mr Leake regards the contract from the point of view of the pleader's Chambers when it comes there as a subject of litigation. He seems to ask, 'What are the kinds of contract of which this may be one? Then—What have I got to prove? By what defences may I be met?' Mr Pollock deals rather with the mode of bringing about that legal relation which we call contract. He watches from the point of view of an outsider the parties coming to terms, and tells us how the contract can be made and by what flaws in its construction it can be invalidated.[2]

[2] 5th edn. (Oxford, 1885), p. vi.

He goes on to add, perhaps not insignificantly, that while he got most information from Leake, it was Pollock who 'started [him] on [his] way'.

There was no doubting the success of Anson's book. For university students it had no real rival, and it sold around a thousand copies a year for over twenty years. By the end of the century it had run through nine editions and sold over twenty thousand copies.[3] According to Professor Brierly's notice of Anson in the *D.N.B.* its success arose from 'directing the students' attention to general principles avoiding doubtful or exceptional cases, and the peculiarities of the special contracts'.

Pollock's book was more difficult for beginners than Anson's, and it was probably less used by university students. But it too was a very successful book by any standards. In sixty years (throughout the whole of which it was edited by Pollock himself) it ran through ten editions. It was the first Contracts book to be published after the Judicature Acts and which therefore attempted to give an account of both Law and Equity, but nevertheless the story told by the book, for all its wealth of learning, was essentially the story of the classical model. Certainly, one can see in it, from the first edition, the triumph of the executory contract. Contract is now virtually synonymous with Agreement, or at least is a sub-species of it. 'Every conveyance', says Pollock, 'includes an agreement . . . This is at first sight startling . . . But to say that a conveyance by way of gift imports an agreement is only to say that ownership cannot be thrust on a man against his will, and in this form there is nothing strange.'[4] This was the view which prevailed in English contract theory, and still prevails, to the extent that the English lawyer sees a conveyance as a species of contract, or an executed transaction as a species of agreement.

There were other, more jurisprudential works, dating from the same period which also contributed their support to the classical form of contractual theory. Markby's *Elements of Law*, first published in 1871, contains a discussion of contract which is entirely taken from Savigny, and is dominated by will theory. He adopts and approves Savigny's definition of a contract as 'the concurrence of several persons in a declaration of intention whereby their legal relations are determined'.[5] He then tries to fit into this definition the simultaneous exchange transaction, and says, with some justification, that 'English writers are not very clear upon this point.'[6] Despite some misgivings, he generally seems to accept the executed transaction as a species of contract. Holland's *Jurisprudence*, which dates from 1880, adopted a similar formulation, and

---

[3] I am indebted to Mr. P. H. Sutcliffe of the Oxford University Press for this information.

[4] 1st edn. (London, 1875), p. 3.

[5] 1st edn. (Oxford, 1871), p. 79.

[6] Ibid., p. 80.

was also plainly influenced by Savigny. He began by defining a juristic act as a manifestation of the will of a private individual',[7] and then went on to say that such a juristic act may be one-sided or two-sided, 'where there is a concurrence of two or more wills to produce the effect of a contract'.[8] It is also worth observing that in his Preface Holland had noted recent signs of change in the mental habits of English lawyers. 'Distaste for comprehensive views, and indifference to foreign modes of thought, can no longer be said to be national characteristics.'

Despite the disdain, not to say contempt, with which English practitioners and judges have often looked down upon academics, it seems probable that these writers exercised a very considerable influence on subsequent developments in contractual thought. By the 1920s there were a large number of barristers and even judges whose first acquaintance with the law of contract had been obtained through the pages of Anson and Pollock; and there is a tradition that 'taught law is tough law'. Nobody with any experience of legal teaching can doubt the power which legal concepts exercise over the minds of law students. Once a set of concepts falling into some overall pattern is grasped, the student often becomes incapable of seeing the physical facts themselves except through the conceptual process. Facts and events cease to be seen as physical occurrences and come to be seen as falling naturally into conceptual pigeon-holes. Indeed, the common English viewpoint that the function of legal education is to teach a student 'to think like a lawyer' is largely an expression of the desirability of this form of training. The student learns to characterize and classify almost intuitively, and without conscious appreciation of the mental processes involved; yet it is the initial act of classification which often determines the result of a case, while making it seem that the conclusion is deduced by inexorable logic from the facts. It was precisely this form of training and education which was initiated by the new textbooks, and which has continued to be the educational tradition of most English law schools to the present day. Markby, in his *Elements of Law*[9], explicitly declares that in a university, law must be taught as a science, or at least 'as a collection of principles capable of being systematically arranged, and resting, not on bare authority, but on sound logical deduction'. There were paradoxes here, for as we have seen, Pollock himself (and this may also have been true of Anson) was far from being a pure formalist. But the next generation of legal academics, those who dominated the scene between the wars, and for some years after the end of the Second World War, do seem to have been largely formalists. They were, on the whole, an undistinguished

---

[7] 2nd edn. (Oxford, 1882), p. 86.
[8] Ibid., p. 88.
[9] Preface to the 1st edn., p. x.

collection.[10] Sir Percy Winfield, for instance, had a high reputation, as was demonstrated by the knighthood he acquired for his services to legal education, but he was largely wedded to the formalist approach. He seems to have thought that there was a 'true' basis to the distinction between contract and tort and his little work on *The Law of Quasi-Contract* (published in 1952) shows an extraordinary adherence to the idea that there is such a thing as a 'true' quasi-contract, which he distinguishes from a pseudo-quasi-contract. After the Second World War, Cheshire and Fifoot's *Law of Contract* largely replaced Anson as the leading students' work, while strengthening the formalist approach.

It is, of course, difficult to measure the influence of law teachers and law textbooks on judges and legal decisions. But there are good grounds for thinking that, in this particular area, the influences were considerable. The evidence for this consists chiefly in the fact that the Courts continued to use the model of classical contract theory enshrined in the textbooks long after it had been weakened and departed from in a wide variety of particular situations. The tendency to believe in general principles of contract law was not seriously affected by the growing evidence that no such general body of contractual principles continued to have any extensive practical application. I have already drawn attention to the substantial encroachments made upon freedom of contract by legislative activity up to 1870; and these encroachments have continued on an ever increasing scale since then. The result is that special statutory rules now apply to virtually every type of ordinary contract, for instance, contracts of sale of goods, of hire-purchase, and now of all forms of consumer credit, contracts of employment, leases, shareholding contracts, contracts of carriage, whether of persons or goods, and whether by land, sea or air, and so on. Moreover, modern statutory provisions frequently themselves have a general application which is quite contrary to the classical model of contract theory. For example, the extensive use of price controls in the past decade (as well as in various other periods, as during the wars) makes nonsense of some of the most basic assumptions of the classical model. Then, also, there has been the growth of new types of relationships, which are quasi-administrative rather than contractual, such as the relationship between the consumer and the suppliers of gas, electricity, and telephone services, which are also impossible to square with the classical model. And even where traditional doctrines still appear to control legal decisions, the practices of lawyers (and others) have frequently made the traditional model obsolete. For example, the

---

[10] See F. H. Lawson, *The Oxford Law School 1850–1965* (Oxford, 1968), Chapter V, for some muted criticism of Oxford Law teachers in the inter-war period. The only English academic to display any understanding of the nature of American legal realism during this period was not a lawyer but Harold Laski.

widespread practice by which preliminary agreements for the purchase and sale of houses are today made 'subject to contract' has made a substantial change in the enforceability of wholly executory agreements of this kind. The result of all these developments has been to leave classical contract law still standing, but as a residuary body of rules, of little application in practice. What began by being the *general law* of contract has (it seems) become 'the law of left-overs, of miscellaneous transactions, the rag-bag and bob-tail which do not get treated elsewhere'.[11] Even in the case of straightforward commercial transactions between commercial organizations, the development of standard business forms, and of extra-judicial methods of enforcement, has left the classical law much shaken. Freedom of contract remains in theory the fundamental basis of the law, while in practice it has been eroded, and as a value it has been rejected.

There are some areas in which it is possible to be more specific about these developments. We have seen above how, during the course of the last century, ideas about just prices and just wages have once again become of great importance in the value systems of the community; and I shall suggest later that in practice these ideas have also come to have a significant impact on the actual decisions of the Courts. But these ideas are foreign to the classical model of contract which still constitutes the orthodox formulation of the law.

Towards the end of the nineteenth century, legal academics (especially in America) began to worry about the relationship between the classical model of contract and the doctrine of consideration. First, there was a controversy between those who argued that either benefit or detriment could be a sufficient consideration, and those who claimed that only detriment would suffice. By the beginning of the twentieth century, opinion had swung in favour of those who favoured detriment as the exclusive test.[12] But American lawyers were insistent that only a bargained-for detriment could be a consideration; subsequent, unrequested or unpurchased action-in-reliance on a promise could not make it actionable. That, anyhow, was the view of most academics and it required all the powers of Corbin in the 1920s and 1930s to convince them that the judicial decisions were not so limited.[13] Then there was a debate about the problem of the pre-existing duty. Was it a sufficient consideration for a person to promise to do what he was already bound to do?[14] But all this was merely preliminary skirmishing for the great

[11] R. S. Summers, 'Collective Agreements and the Law of Contracts', 78 *Yale Law Journal* 525, 565 (1969).

[12] K. C. T. Sutton, *Consideration Reconsidered* (St. Lucia, Queensland 1974), p. 18.

[13] See Corbin, 'Some Recent Developments in Contracts', 50 *Harvard Law Rev.* 449 (1937).

[14] See Williston, 'Successive Promises of the Same Performance', 8 *Harvard Law Rev.* (1894); Ames, 'Two Theories of Consideration—I', 12 *Harvard Law Rev.* 515 (1899).

academic battles which raged around the bilateral executory contract. For, in the midst of these skirmishes, the thought appears to have occurred to some of the learned academics that a bilateral executory contract was difficult to square with the traditional definitions of consideration. How was a promise to be treated as benefit or detriment until it was known if it was binding or not?[15] The firmament began to tremble. Was it possible that the whole law of executory contracts rested on a fallacy? Could it be contended that such contracts were not 'truly' binding because the reciprocal promises did not, in fact, constitute a benefit or detriment? Even Pollock, who (as we have seen) did not take all this formalism too seriously, referred to the binding nature of executory contracts as 'one of the secret paradoxes of the common law'.[16]

To those who have followed the historical account presented in this volume, there will be no secret paradox. The explanation of the problem lay buried deep in history. Benefit-based and reliance-based liability had existed long before the modern bilateral executory contract had been recognized. And when it was recognized the process was a confused, messy changeover involving the newer ideas about intention, consideration, and the damages rules in the manner I have previously explained. If there is a paradox in all this, it is that not until the end of the nineteenth century did lawyers begin to realize that the conventional accounts of the doctrine of consideration could no longer be squared with the fundamental basis of classical contract law, the bilateral executory contract.

But now that it was being recognized, lawyers were asking more seriously whether consideration was necessary at all. If the paradigm case of contract, the bilateral executory contract, was being regularly enforced without any actual benefit or detrimental reliance, surely the whole of the doctrine could be dispensed with. By the 1930s lawyers in England were prepared to talk openly of 'abolition' of the doctrine.[17] It is true that the Law Revision Committee, when offered the opportunity of actually proposing such abolition, balked at the hurdle and limited its support to the case of written promises.[18] But 'radical' opinion—still, it seems, under the influence of ideas which were radical in the 1830s—was not satisfied, and as late as the 1960s and into the 1970s the English Law Commission was prepared seriously to envisage abolition of the whole

[15] See Ames, 'Two Theories of Consideration—II', 13 *Harvard Law Rev.* 29 (1899); Langdell, 'Mutual Promises as Consideration for Each Other', 14 *Harvard Law Rev.* 496 (1901); Williston, 'Consideration in Bilateral Contracts', 27 *Harvard Law Rev.* 503 (1914); Ballantine, 'Mutuality and Consideration', 28 *Harvard Law Rev.* 121 (1914).

[16] 30 *Law Q. Rev.* 129 (1914), book review.

[17] See Lord Wright, 'Ought the Doctrine of Consideration to be Abolished from the Common Law?', 49 *Harvard Law Rev.* 1225 (1936).

[18] *Sixth Interim Report*, Cmnd. 5449 (1937).

doctrine. What I have to suggest here is that this proposal derived from the traditional power of the classical model, which still influenced much legal thinking. English lawyers, in their theoretical moments (as when drafting a new Contract Code) are still apt to embrace the values of the classical model of contract, freedom of contract and all. In this model, an act of will is sufficient to create a legal liability, and it is therefore argued that there is no reason to retain the doctrine of consideration at all. Yet in practice, abolition of the doctrine would be a move totally against the actual trend of events. As I shall suggest in Chapter 22, the past hundred years has seen a resurgence in the importance of benefit-based and reliance-based liabilities, while at the same time, liability on a wholly executory contract has been weakened in a variety of legal situations and by a variety of legal and practical methods. To abolish the doctrine of consideration today—to make a person liable on his bare word alone—would be an extraordinary reversal of an evolutionary process. And it would, furthermore, be based on an outdated dogma, and not on a belief that the community's moral values indicate the need for such a change. If Victorian England could not bring itself to recognize the sanctity of promises to the extent of making a gratuitous promise a binding contract, what a paradox it would be if we were to carry this change through today, after the weakening of the belief in the sanctity of promises which this past century has witnessed.

I do not have space here for a full review of the conceptual confusions involved in the proposed 'abolition' of the doctrine of consideration, but one point at least must be made. We have seen that the very notion of a binding contract is meaningless in the abstract, because there are degrees of bindingness. Wholly executory contracts are only binding to a limited extent, so that (for example) where revocation is communicated prior to any reliance or performance, the damages may be limited, or even non-existent if market prices have not changed. What then are we to make of a proposed abolition of the doctrine which does not indicate how binding a gratuitous executory promise would become? To 'abolish' the doctrine presumably means to recognize a right to full expectation damages for breach of a gratuitous promise, for it would hardly be 'abolition' if only reliance or restitutionary remedies were granted. But to grant such a right, to recognize expectation rights of this magnitude for a gratuitious promise, would be to enforce gratuitous promises more stringently than many presently enforceable promises. It should also be added that many of the arguments deployed by those who stated the case for abolition took for granted the model of classical contract law in which unbargained-for reliance interests were not *per se* protected.[19] As we saw previously, one

[19] Thus Lord Wright, 'Ought the Doctrine of Consideration to be Abolished from the Common Law?' at pp. 1253-4 gives examples of promises which have been relied upon as unenforceable by virtue of the doctrine of consideration.

of the characteristics of the classical period was the belief (not uniformly acted on by the Courts) that only bargained-for exchanges could constitute valid consideration. Now that the Courts have begun, albeit tentatively and cautiously, to recognize a need for a greater protection of reliance interests, the case for 'abolition' of consideration has become weaker.

A second, and not unrelated illustration of the influence of legal academics on modern contract theory, has been the invention of the 'doctrine' of the 'intent to create legal relations'. In modern times it is an accepted part of the law that an agreement is not a binding contract if the parties 'did not intend' to create or affect legal relationships. Now this notion was largely unknown in the nineteenth century. Generally speaking nineteenth-century judges, faced with the issues discussed under this rubric today, would have invoked the doctrine of consideration, or alternatively would have held that no promise, no commitment, was intended. If a person did not mean to bind himself, then he could not have *promised*. But Pollock borrowed this notion of intent to create legal relations from Savigny, and used it to explain why (for example) a social engagement is not a binding legal contract. Williston objected to Pollock's invention, saying that consideration was a perfectly adequate test of liability in contract and that there was no need for another. He went on to say that the only proof that the doctrine existed would be 'the production of cases holding that though consideration was asked and given for a promise, it is nevertheless, not enforceable because a legal relation was not contemplated'.[20] The English judges duly responded to Williston's challenge. In 1919 Lord Atkin borrowed Pollock's ideas and gave them judicial support in *Balfour* v. *Balfour*.[21] From there the doctrine passed slowly into the law, though instances of it being successfully invoked to deny validity to a contract are rare.

A third example of the power of the classical model to influence thinking, and even policy decisions, is to be found in the fate of the Statute of Frauds. As we have seen, the Statute of Frauds is readily understood in its historical context as a device for holding back the development of the executory contract. Only where writing was available could a purely executory contract be enforced if it fell within the scope of sections 4 or 17 of the Statute; but part performance (or, in contracts of sale of goods, other comparable acts) which rendered the transaction partly executed, was a sufficient alternative. At the height of the classical period, the Statute was evidently an anachronism. It conflicted with will theory, and with political economy, that a man should be able to escape liability on a purely executory contract merely

[20] 'Consideration in Bilateral Contracts', 27 *Harvard Law Rev.* 503, 507 (1914).
[21] [1919] 2 K.B. 571.

because of the absence of writing. It also conflicted with the sense of honour of the Victorian gentleman, and we have seen how, in 1885, Stephen J. called for a repeal of these provisions.[22] But repeal did not come in 1885; the Law Revision Committee repeated the call for repeal in 1937, again without result. Only in 1954 when the Law Reform Committee had endorsed the recommendation was the Law Reform (Enforcement of Contracts) Act finally passed. If I am correct in my historical analysis, this was a perverse development. Seventy-five years after the close of the classical period, at least a hundred years after Parliament had begun the practice of requiring written evidence as a form of consumer protection[23] (even if we ignore the Statute of Frauds itself), it now became the law that a person could be made liable on a bare executory contract for the sale of goods of an unlimited amount. And this happened (as we shall see) at a time when reliance-based and benefit-based liabilities were, generally speaking, being given greater protection at the expense of purely promise-based liabilities. The explanation is surely to be found in the continued power of the classical model of contract, and in the failure of lawyers openly to recognize the trend towards the enforcement of reliance-based (and benefit-based) liabilities. Indeed, one of the last cases to be litigated under these statutory provisions relating to contracts for the sale of goods, *Marcel (Furriers)* v. *Tapper*,[24] was not a case of a bare executory promise, but of actual reliance, though not of a kind to take the case outside the Act. It is symptomatic of the strength of the classical model that lawyers still seem to have seen the creation of a promise-based liability as the best (or only) way in which reliance interests could be protected.

One final example may be offered of the continued vitality of the classical model, even while its basis is crumbling on all sides. The classical model of contract, especially when made more explicit in textbook formulations than it had ever been in the case law, drew a much firmer line between contractual and non-consensual duties than had previously existed. In Part II, I referred to a variety of cases and fact-situations which showed that, even in the mid-nineteenth century, the actual case law was only slowly separating off consensual and non-consensual duties.[25] Nor should this be a cause for any surprise. The nature and extent of a person's consent to an arrangement vary so much from case to case, that a clean line between a duty arising from consent and a duty imposed by law is, and must be, an artificial line. But the textbook

---

[22] *Supra*, p. 658.

[23] See the many cases of interference with freedom of contract discussed in Chapter 16 where writing was required as a form of consumer protection.

[24] [1953] 1 W.L.R. 49.

[25] *Supra*, pp. 416–17, 460–2, 501 *et seq.*

formulations on this question adopted a much more black and white approach. Liabilities were either consensual, arising from the will of the parties, or non-consensual, and imposed by law. Winfield's well-known definition of tort liability in his *Textbook of the Law of Tort* (first published in 1937) was based on the idea that it was possible to draw a firm line between duties imposed by law and duties imposed by the parties themselves. In the twentieth century, one result of this was to impose a limitation on the scope of contractual liability in cases which were difficult to fit into the orthodox formulations of the classical model. Where nineteenth-century judges had, without too much trouble, imposed liability on a railway company whose trains were cancelled without warning, or on an auctioneer who advertised goods for sale without reserve,[26] twentieth-century lawyers began to see these results as not 'really' contractual. One reaction then was to suggest that the cases were wrongly decided; but on the whole, the more general reaction in recent times has been to impose a duty but to formulate it as non-contractual. In *Nagle* v. *Feilden*,[27] for example, the plaintiff was an unsuccessful applicant for a trainer's license from the Jockey Club, who, at that time, made a policy of refusing to license women. An action was brought on her behalf which the plaintiff's counsel first attempted to formulate in contractual terms. He argued that the Jockey Club had impliedly held out to the world an offer to entertain applications for licenses, and that such an offer must be reasonably understood as containing an implied agreement not to refuse a licence capriciously or arbitrarily. At first instance this case was treated as hopeless, and struck out; the Court of Appeal was equally unhappy with the contract argument, but had no doubt that a duty not to act capriciously ought nevertheless to be imposed on the Jockey Club. In their judgments all members of the Court rejected the argument based on contract as an absurd fiction, but nevertheless upheld the plaintiff as having at least an arguable case on the ground that the defendants owed her a duty not arising from contract. I need not pursue the precise grounds on which the plaintiff succeeded. The more interesting point is why the contract argument should have been rejected as wholly fictitious. The answer clearly is that the conception of contract which the judges held was basically that derived from the classical model. In effect, says the Court, a contractual liability is based on the party's will; here the defendant had no intention of being held liable, so there can be no liability; and yet, they then proceeded to impose a liability. If it is appreciated that the nature of contractual liability is much more diffuse than this; that liability is often benefit-based or reliance-based; that it is always the law

[26] *Supra*, pp. 460-1.
[27] [1966] 2 Q.B. 633.

anyhow which imposes legal duties, including contractual duties; that such duties are imposed for a variety of reasons, and that the element of consent or agreement is merely one relevant factor in the case, then it is not so obvious that the contract argument here was unsound. It is unsound only if one starts with a basic preconception about the nature of a contract; and then, only if that preconception is drawn from the express formulations of the classical model, rather than from actual English case law.

THE FAILURE OF CLASSICAL LAW

The classical model of contract, notwithstanding its formal perpetuation to the present day as a body of general principles, was a failure. In one sense, this should already be evident from the volume of statutory interference with freedom of contract which had already been enacted by Parliament by 1870, and which I reviewed in Chapter 16. But it could be argued with some plausibility that in 1870 the general nature of the classical model still corresponded substantially with the reality of the law which was being applied, and that the instances of statutory intervention were (as they were often seen by the Parliamentarians who carried them through) exceptions to the general principle of freedom of contract and *laissez-faire*. But, as we have also seen, after 1870 the exceptional nature of such interventions gradually ceased to be acceptable as an explanation of what Parliament was doing. And certainly in the modern world, where many people see the functions of Government and Parliament as virtually limitless, it is absurd to think of society as regulated by freedom of contract subject only to limited instances of State 'interference'. In this section I propose to say a little more about the specific causes of the failure of the classical model. To a considerable extent these causes are to be found in the same problems which I have already looked at from the perspective of economic theory, that is, they are instances of the failure of the classical model to cope with externalities, with monopolies and other market failures, and with the problems of consumer ignorance.

Freedom of Contract and Third Parties

One of the most obvious examples of the failure of the classical model concerns contracts or arrangements in which third parties were more or less interested. From the earliest times the common law Courts failed adequately to take account of the extent to which the freedom of two parties to adjust their contractual relationships might have a bearing on the rights of third parties. Even where the contract itself appeared to be of no concern to any one except the parties to it, there were (and are) potential implications in nearly every case for at least two classes of third parties. First, there are the potential successors of the parties, who will normally be bound by, and entitled to the benefits of the contract; and secondly, there are the interests of other potential creditors of the parties whose rights may be affected by the depletion of the assets of one of the parties by the contract in hand. So far as the potential successors of the parties are concerned, the problem was never perceived as being a *contractual* problem at all. In so far as there was a problem it was thought to be a problem about the extent of property rights and freedom of testation. In the high noon of classical theory, as we have seen, property rights tended to be seen as absolute, and freedom of testation was generally favoured as much as freedom of contract. The result was that (except for the very rich whose estates were tied up in strict settlements) contracting parties were generally able to control the succession to their estates by an exercise of freedom of contract as much as by freedom of testation. A contract was enforceable against a man's assets after his death to the same extent as during his lifetime; and so long as no conception of family property rights existed, this meant that the interests of members of his family would be subordinated to those of his creditors. Moreover, it will be appreciated, this subordination extended necessarily to mere expectation rights of the creditor, and was not confined to reliance or restitutionary rights. The existence of strict settlements, and the refusal to enforce wholly gratuitous promises, represented limits on this subordination of the family to creditors; but the question was never raised whether mere expectation interests might not also be postponed to family interests, nor, in modern times when there has been talk of abolition of consideration, has adequate attention been paid to this conflict of interests. This is perhaps the more surprising in that legal cases involving gratuitous or quasi-gratuitous promises so often arise because of the death of the promisor, and the refusal of his successors to regard themselves as bound by such promises.[28]

More important, economically at least, has been the problem of reconciling the interests of one contracting party with those of actual or potential creditors of the other party. A wide variety of legal issues may arise from the attempts of one contracting party to give himself some form of security right over the other party's assets, which will avail him against other creditors or against a trustee in bankruptcy. It seems fair to say that, by and large, this problem was never recognized for what it was by the Courts. In the second half of the nineteenth century, in particular,

---

[28] For English cases, see, e.g., *Shadwell* v. *Shadwell* (1860) 9 C.B(N.S.) 159, 142 E.R. 62; *Re Soames* (1897) 13 T.L.R. 439; *Re Hudson* (1885) 54 L.J. Ch. 811. Similarly, many of the reliance cases of the *Dillwyn* v. *Llewellyn* (1862) 4 De G. F. & J. 517, 45 E.R. 1285 variety, arose after the death of the promisor. This is also typical of many American and Canadian cases raising questions about the enforceability of gratuitous but relied-upon promises.

the problem arose in connection with bills of sale, with charges over after-acquired property, and with the attempts to retain security rights over goods sold on credit. In these circumstances the Courts almost uniformly upheld the rights of contracting parties to determine effectively, not only their own rights *inter se*, but also their rights against third party creditors. For example, in *Holroyd* v. *Marshall*[29] and *Tailby* v. *Official Receiver*,[30] the House of Lords held that a debtor could effectively grant a charge over after-acquired property which would bind the property in his hands when subsequently received, so as to secure priority for the creditor against the interests of other creditors. In the second case, indeed, it was insisted repeatedly that the rights of the creditors of the contracting parties could be no different from those of the parties themselves. The contract thus effectively determined the rights of third parties who had not consented to them, or even been aware of their existence. It is true that one limitation was imposed on this doctrine by the Courts, namely that the creditor seeking priority in this fashion must have actually paid the consideration for the rights he thus claimed; in other words, the creditor could not claim assets in the hands of the debtor in priority to other creditors if his claim was merely based on an expectation.[31] But even so, the claim to priority was too large, and it was limited by a series of Bills of Sale Acts from 1854 onwards, which created the requirement of registration in various circumstances. Although the result then remained that the contract could effectively bind the interests of third parties, they were now at least given an opportunity of ascertaining the position by consulting the register.

A similar problem arose in connection with the sale of goods on credit, over which sellers might try to preserve security rights. So long as freedom of contract was regarded as almost absolute, this was a relatively easy matter, for the seller need only stipulate in his contract of sale that property in the goods would not pass until payment in full, and a security would thus be preserved which was binding on third parties. Property rights which can be so easily manipulated by contractual 'intentions' are a serious threat to the interests of third parties. Here again, Parliamentary intervention was forthcoming in the Factors Act 1889 which was chiefly necessitated by the threat to commercial activities presented by the practice of preserving property in goods as a security in this form. In particular, where goods were sold through documents of title, where for example, imported goods were disposed of in advance of arrival by the

---

[29] (1862) 10 H.L.C. 191, 11 E.R. 999.
[30] (1888) 13 App. Cas. 523.
[31] There is a long line of cases on this though none of them offers any significant policy justification, see, e.g., *Ex parte Nichols, in re Jones* (1883) 22 Ch.D. 782; *In re Clarke* (1887) 36 Ch.D. 348; *Wilmot* v. *Alton* [1896] 1 Q.B. 17; *In re Trytel* [1952] T.L.R. 32.

sale of bills of lading, the reservation of rights by sellers could have posed a substantial threat to commercial practice. Bankers, receiving shipping documents in good faith, and lending money on their security, might be totally unaware of previous dealings which had purported to reserve title to the vendor. It was to protect such bankers that the Factors Act was passed. But in other circumstances the traditional belief in freedom of contract can still operate to the prejudice of third parties in such cases. Indeed a very recent decision is causing serious concern in commercial areas because of the potential implications for third parties.[32]

A third area in which the same device was utilized remained free from Parliamentary intervention for over half a century. The contract of hire-purchase was invented by lawyers in the last decade of the nineteenth century as a device by which sellers of consumer goods could preserve security rights over the goods until they were paid for. Here, as in the cases previously mentioned, recognition of freedom of contract was pressed to the extent of giving the power to determine the rights of the creditor against other creditors. Yet in this instance, the Courts upheld the device both as a common law matter—indeed on the point there was no real dispute—and by holding that the Bills of Sale Acts and the Factors Act did not apply to hire-purchase transactions.[33] Now I do not wish to imply that, as a matter of public policy, these decisions were necessarily undesirable; nor that, as a matter of economic efficiency, they may have been unsound. My point is the simpler one that the Courts did not see any question to be discussed here as a matter of common law. Freedom of contract, by this time, was so absolute, that in the absence of Parliamentary intervention, it was possible for contracting parties to determine their rights, not merely *inter se*, but also against third parties.

The failure of the common law here was, perhaps, the more remarkable in that the Courts had already faced up to a not dissimilar question in the law of agency. It had (as we saw earlier)[34] already been established in the classical period that a principal could not necessarily limit his liability for the acts of an agent by 'secret instructions' of which third parties could not be aware. It is true that here also there were some signs that the Courts were disinclined to press the liability of the principal too far,[35] but the possibility of liability was plainly affirmed, and as attitudes to freedom of contract changed, the Courts were thus able to swing back to a more vigorous reliance-based liability.[36] In the twentieth century, the responsibility of a principal for the unauthorized acts of an agent, both

[32] See *Aluminium Industries* v. *Romalpa Aluminium Ltd.* [1976] 2 All E.R. 552.

[33] *Helby* v. *Mathews* [1895] A.C. 471; *McEntire* v. *Crossley Bros.* [1895] A.C. 457.

[34] *Supra*, p. 496.

[35] See, e.g., *Debenham* v. *Mellon* (1880) 6 App. Cas. 24.

[36] See, e.g., *Brocklesby* v. *Temperance Building Society* [1895] A.C. 173; *Fry* v. *Smellie* [1912] 3 K.B. 282.

in contract and in tort, have been pushed further and further, as the Courts have advanced the frontiers of non-consensual liability.[37]

Freedom of Contract and Freedom of Trade

By far the most serious failure of the classical model of contract was its inability to offer any contribution to the problems raised by monopolies and restrictive agreements. As we have seen, from the 1870s onwards, British industry entered a new phase in which the belief in competition began to decline, Trade Associations grew up, and restrictive arrangements became commonplace. Market sharing agreements, quota agreements, price fixing agreements, resale price maintenance and a variety of other arrangements began to appear from the 1870s onwards. The judicial reaction to these arrangements was, in general, to fall back on the simple principle of freedom of contract. By the 1870s the judges were so accustomed to the idea that all contracts should in principle be enforceable, at least in the absence of plain illegality or sexual immorality, that even the old common law hostility to agreements in restraint of trade had been seriously weakened. In 1875 a blatant restrictive agreement between four quarry owners that only one would tender for a contract to supply the Birmingham Corporation, and that the others would share in the contract by supplying the successful tenderer, was challenged in the Courts as an agreement in restraint of trade and an unlawful conspiracy.[38] But the judge could see nothing unlawful in the arrangements at all, and he even granted an injunction to prevent the defendant breaking the agreement although the defendant had by then secured the contract with the Birmingham Corporation, and the injunction would necessarily prevent him carrying it out. The Corporation were not even considered necessary parties to the case. Thus the contract between the suppliers was upheld to the detriment of the Corporation's interests, and perhaps also of the public interest.

This case was but a straw in the wind. The major developments were to come from the 1890s on. In 1890 the legality of one of the early shipping conferences was tested in the House of Lords, in the famous *Mogul* case.[39] This was 'the most effective and the most widespread attempt at cartelization'[40] and its *modus operandi* was simple. A group of shipping companies offered substantial ('aggregated') rebates to consignors taking part in the China tea trade, but only on condition that all

---

[37] In tort, see P. S. Atiyah, *Vicarious Liability* (London, 1967), especially Part V and Part VII; in contract, see, e.g., *Freeman and Lockyer* v. *Buckhurst Park Properties Ltd.* [1964] 2 Q.B. 480; for statutory extensions, see Consumer Credit Act 1974, sect. 75.

[38] *Jones* v. *North* (1875) L.R. 19 Eq. 426.

[39] 23 Q.B.D. 544, affirmed, 23 Q.B.D. 598, affirmed, [1892] A.C. 25. The judgments in all three Courts are instructive.

[40] P. Mathias, *The First Industrial Nation* (London, 1969), p. 390.

their goods were consigned on ships belonging to members of the cartel. The plaintiffs were a shipping company which had been excluded from the cartel and was evidently in danger of being forced out of the business altogether. They sued the cartel members claiming an injunction to restrain them from operating this agreement in restraint of trade. It will be seen that the action was not in form an action on a contract at all. The plaintiffs were, in effect, claiming that the defendants were committing a tort against them by excluding them from the tea trade, the tort of 'conspiracy'. But this claim depended on the attitude of the Courts to the restrictive agreement between the members of the cartel. If the judges had thought this agreement was illegal or contrary to the public interest, they might have upheld the plaintiff's claim. But a majority of the Court of Appeal, and a unanimous House of Lords, rejected the claim. The agreement, even if in restraint of trade, was said by the judges not to be 'illegal' in the sense of being prohibited by law, or open to complaint by a third party. The illegality, if indeed there was any (which was never decided) was only such as to render the agreement void and unenforceable between the members. The decision was undoubtedly much influenced by judicial attitudes to free trade. The judges had been brought up in the very competitive conditions of mid-nineteenth century England, and they assumed that cartels of this nature were unstable. They assumed too that free competition required them to abstain from interference in what they saw as a mere move in a competitive struggle. The defendants, even if they were reducing freight rates to commercially unprofitable levels, were merely competing to the bitter end. The judges did not see how they were to draw a line between fair and unfair competition, or normal and abnormal competition.[41] They were, anyhow, confident that if the members of the cartel attempted to exploit their monopoly position, they would be defeated by new competitors.[42] Unlike Alfred Marshall (who, as we saw earlier, appreciated the severely anti-competitive effects of aggregated rebates), the judges rejected the 'disputable assumption that, in a country of free trade, and one which is not under the iron regime of statutory monopolies, such federations can ever be really successful'.[43]

As I have observed, this decision did not strictly involve the enforceability of a cartel agreement between the parties to it, and it proceeded on the assumption that the agreement was illegal in the sense of being unenforceable. But later in the nineteenth century, even this degree of illegality began to be weakened. In the *Nordenfelt* case[44] in 1894, the House of Lords was called upon to reinterpret the law of

---

[41] See Bowen L.J. 23 Q.B.D. at 615; Fry L.J. ibid., at 625–6; Lord Halsbury, [1892] A.C. at 39.
[42] Bowen L.J. 23 Q.B.D. at 619–20; Lord Morris [1892] A.C. at 50.
[43] Bowen L.J. 23 Q.B.D. at 619–20.
[44] [1894] A.C. 535.

restraint of trade in one of the traditional areas which the law had long been dealing with, that is in the case of a covenant by the seller of a business that he would not compete with the purchaser. This type of agreement has probably never been of major economic significance, and anyhow, it is plain that there are economic arguments in favour of such agreements. Despite their short-run anti-competitive tendency, they (like the institution of property itself) furnish a long-run incentive to enterprise whose benefits often outweigh their disadvantages. But the general attitude of the Lords in this case was plainly one of much greater sympathy with freedom of contract generally, and in the early years of the twentieth century this attitude was carried over into far more serious cases. By 1901 a resale price maintenance agreement could be upheld in the Courts, and any suggested illegality was regarded as simply unarguable.[45]

The technical legal position in these restraint of trade cases continued to be stated in the traditional manner; the agreement had to contain restrictions which were no wider than was reasonable in the interests of the parties, and of the public. But in practice the attitude of the Courts had changed completely. It began to be suggested that if the parties were commercial organizations, they were the best judges of whether the agreement was reasonable in their own interests; and so far as the public interest was concerned they adopted, in a somewhat new form, the old economic theory of the harmony of interests. If the agreement was reasonable in the interests of the parties, then it was presumed to be in the interests of the public in the absence of proof to the contrary. Such proof, moreover, was almost impossible to bring forward, because the question of reasonableness was decided by the Courts as a question of law, and not on evidence, as a question of fact. And since the public was not represented in any litigation between the immediate parties to a restrictive agreement, there was no one to argue the case from the public point of view. The result was a succession of cases in which restrictive agreements were upheld. In *United Shoe Machinery Co. of Canada* v. *Brunet*[46] the Privy Council upheld an agreement by which the manufacturer of shoe-making machinery, with a virtual monopoly of such equipment, imposed on hirers of the machinery an undertaking for twenty years not to use any other shoe-making machinery. The Privy Council seemed incapable of even seeing the anti-competitive nature of the agreement, it being simply assumed once again that the parties understood their own interests best. (The same agreement came before the United States Supreme Court a few years later and was there held illegal under the

---

[45] *Elliman Sons & Co.* v. *Carrington & Son Ltd.* [1901] 2 Ch. 275.
[46] [1909] A.C. 330.

Sherman Act.)[47] In *Attorney-General of Australia* v. *Adelaide Steamship Co.*[48] the Privy Council destroyed the efficacy of an Australian Statute directed at cartel agreements designed to restrict the output and keep up the price of coal. They did not, it was said in their judgment, know of any case in which a restriction reasonable in the interests of the parties had been held contrary to the public interest. And the following year the House of Lords upheld a notorious salt cartel by which manufacturers had set up a joint pooling company to which they were obliged to sell all their salt.[49]

In the inter-war period when the power of the Trade Associations was used to eliminate or minimize competitive tendencies in almost the whole of British industry, the judicial 'hands-off' policy was continued. In *Sorrell* v. *Smith*[50] the Lords upheld the legality of collective boycotts, and in *Thorne* v. *Motor Trade Association*[51] they upheld the legality of the stop-list, and of threats to place a defaulter on a stop-list if he failed to pay a 'fine' imposed for breach of collective price maintenance agreements. It was, moreover, plain that judicial sympathies were entirely on the side of freedom of contract, no matter how anti-competitive the arrangements might be. It was not merely that the judges felt great difficulty in dealing with the economic issues involved; nor merely that in the absence of evidence or argument from a public representative, it was virtually impossible to strike down such agreements. It is quite plain that the judges' sympathies were enlisted on the side of the businessmen who were making such efforts to restrict competition. In *English Hop Growers* v. *Dering*[52], for instance, the defendant, a Kentish hop grower, attempted to break up a cartel agreement by selling his hops to a third party after agreeing to supply his whole crop to the plaintiffs, a company set up to regulate (and restrict) the supply of hops. In upholding the legality of the agreement, Scrutton L.J. expressed his views on the defendant's conduct with the unconsciously revealing remark that, 'I myself have a strong opinion as to the conduct of the defendant in this matter, but I think it better not to express it, and leave him to be judged by the Societies of Kentish Men and Men of Kent, and others prominent in the County of Kent, a county well known for honesty and good sportsmanship'.[53] Similarly, in *Berg* v. *Saddler & Moore*[54] where the plaintiff had been placed on a stop-list for selling cut-price cigarettes, an attempt by him to

[47] *U.S.* v. *United Shoe Manufacturing Co.* 258 U.S. 451 (1915).
[48] [1913] A.C. 781.
[49] *North West Salt Co. Ltd.* v. *Electrolytic Alkali Co. Ltd.* [1914] A.C. 461.
[50] [1925] A.C. 700.
[51] [1937] A.C. 797.
[52] [1928] 2 K.B. 174.
[53] At pp. 180–1.
[54] [1937] 2 K.B. 158; see also comments on this case in 54 *Law Q. Rev.* 201, 216 (1938). In the 1950s and 1960s this sort of conduct was treated as a heroic attempt to beat the price-maintainers.

purchase further supplies without disclosing the fact was stigmatized by the judges as an attempt to obtain goods by false pretences.

The culmination of this judicial sympathy with restrictive agreements is to be found in the *Crofter* case[55] in 1942, in which the Lords upheld the legality of an agreement between an employers' organization and a trade union, to embargo goods which were used by rival manufacturers. Symptomatic of the general legal attitude to such cases is the fact that this decision was generally welcomed by lawyers as representing a modern and advanced outlook.[56] In particular, it was clear that the decision accorded the same freedom to trade unions as to employers to engage in anti-competitive agreements of this nature.[57] An economist viewed these developments with a more jaundiced eye:

We knew before that a combine could charge whatever prices it saw fit and hold the public to ransom without interference from the Courts. We knew that the Court would help it to discipline its members by compelling them to obey its rules, however anti-social those rules might seem. We knew that it was free to ruin any outside trader who did not accept its dictates. Now we discover new freedoms. Businessmen seeking to advance their private trade interests may not only combine with each other, but also bring their workers into the schemes, and promise them part of the swag; even this was hardly in doubt after the decision in *Reynolds* v. *Shipping Federation Ltd.*[58] Now we know that they may use not only their own workers, but workers in any other industry who happen to belong to the same union.[59]

Thus far had the Courts assisted in the destruction of freedom of trade by their pursuit of freedom of contract. Of course, pleas in mitigation may be entered. The judges were, throughout most of this period, reflecting commercial attitudes and even public opinion on these issues; they were not out on a limb of their own. They were too compelled to decide these issues as questions of law without the assistance of evidence, a crippling handicap. And this in turn was not mere obscurantism, as some economists appear to have thought,[60] but was a result of the basic principles of civil procedure. If these issues had been treated as questions of fact, to be decided upon evidence, then they would have been decisions for the jury, and not for the judges—at least until the changes in procedure in 1934 which virtually eliminated the use of civil juries. And it is understandable that judges boggled at the thought of inviting juries

---

[55] [1942] A.C. 435.

[56] I can vouch for the fact that this was the prevailing attitude at Oxford in the early 1950s.

[57] See, e.g., W. Friedman, 'The Harris Tweed Case and Freedom of Trade', 6 *Mod. Law. Rev.* 1 (1943).

[58] [1924] 1 Ch. 28.

[59] W. Arthur Lewis, 'Monopoly and the Law: An Economist's Reflections on the *Crofter* case', 6 *Mod. Law Rev.* 97 (1943).

[60] See Alex Hunter, *Competition and the Law* (London, 1966), p. 72.

to settle the finer points of dispute between Adam Smith and his successors on issues of this nature. And then again, there was the point previously made, that the public interest was simply not represented at the Bar of the Court. But the greater share of the responsibility for these legal developments must surely be laid at the door of the traditional principle of freedom of contract. A principle which had originally been justified by the political economists was pursued by the Courts to an extent which had no economic justification.

After the Second World War, opinion began to swing against these movements. A series of statutory developments and in particular the creation of the Monopolies Commission and the Restrictive Practices Court, slowly changed the climate of opinion. The virtues of competition began (sometimes) to be preached again. Resale price maintenance was largely prohibited, collective agreements became subject to the scrutiny of a Court at which the public was entitled to be represented, and monopolies and mergers became subject to statutory control. By the 1960s the Courts were ready to take the plunge and re-enter the waters of restrictive agreements even as a matter of common law. In the *Esso Petroleum* case,[61] the Courts invalidated a tying agreement by which a petrol company agreed to supply petrol to a retailer and sought to prevent him obtaining supplies elsewhere for 21 years. Such a restraint was, they now said, unreasonable in the interests of the public; and though they still insisted on the difficulty of saying that a freely negotiated commercial agreement was unreasonable in the interests of one of the parties, they admitted that this might be the case where the parties had not been bargaining on equal terms.

Since the *Esso Petroleum* case there have been a number of other decisions in which the Lords have shown a considerable flexibility of mind on such issues. In 1974 it was possible for Lord Diplock in the House of Lords to say (even if *obiter*, and without the concurrence of the other members of the House) that the true issue in restraint of trade cases was not the public interest, but the simple question of fairness:

It is, in my view, salutary to acknowledge that in refusing to enforce provisions of a contract whereby one party agrees for the benefit of the other party to exploit or to refrain from exploiting his own earning-power, the public policy which the Court is implementing is not some nineteenth-century economic theory about the benefit to the general public of freedom of trade, but the protection of those whose bargaining power is weak against being forced by those whose bargaining power is stronger to enter into bargains that are unconscionable.[62]

---

[61] [1968] A.C. 300.
[62] *A. Schroeder Music Publishing Co. Ltd.* v. *Macaulay* [1974] 3 All E.R. 616, 623.

No doubt it is salutary to acknowledge openly that the Courts are often concerned with the fairness of a bargain. But it is not obvious why even fair agreements may not be struck down as being contrary to the public interest; not, indeed, on the ground of some nineteenth-century economic doctrine but on the ground of present-day economic doctrine.

Consumer Ignorance

We have already seen how one of the theoretical presuppositions of 'perfect competition' is 'perfect knowledge'; and how, to the extent that consumers (or even commercial organizations) lack perfect knowledge it cannot be assumed that there is any harmony of interests between private contract and the public welfare. Already in the classical period of contract there was (as we saw in Chapter 16) a considerable degree of legislative activity designed to improve the means of knowledge open to contracting parties. In particular, there was then, and has continued to the present day, a stream of legislation on such matters as weights and measures, the control of advertising, false trade descriptions, and so on. Much of this legislation is, on the face of it, only concerned to impose criminal penalties, and does not directly affect civil law rights.[63] Most of these consumer protection statutes are designed to afford better enforcement provisions where the consumer is unlikely himself to take the initiative in bringing civil proceedings, because the individual grievance does not justify the cost and trouble. To this extent these statutes supplement a serious weakness in the classical law, although there is a danger that they may be going too far. There is always a cost in enacting and enforcing such legislation, and the cost is borne by all consumers while the benefits may be confined to a small group of relatively unskilled consumers.

Workmen's Compensation

One of the earliest examples of consumer ignorance to raise serious legal-economic issues is worth noting because it reflects so clearly changing judicial attitudes as scepticism grew concerning the 'laws' of political economy. This is the area of workmen's compensation laws, now thought to be conceptually a part of the law of tort, but in the nineteenth century, universally treated as a contractual issue. We have seen already something of Bramwell's views on this issue, and these may be taken as representing the orthodox view of the political economists in the first half of the century. The workman was not in general entitled to compensation for injury incurred in the course of his employment because the wages he

---

[63] But in practice the Powers of Criminal Courts Act 1973, sect. 35 of which enables compensation orders to be made in criminal cases, is beginning to have a significant effect on civil liability.

was paid were presumed to be a sufficient compensation for the risk of injury as well as for the value of his labour. Although the legal cases may not at first have articulated this as the chief ground of decision, it does not seem unreasonable to suggest that this basic idea lay behind the early cases on the doctrine of common employment, and even more clearly behind the maxim *volenti non fit injuria* when that came to be invoked against injured workmen.[64] Certainly this was the view put by Blackburn and later by Bramwell, as we have already seen.[65]

By the 1870s the whole subject was becoming one of political importance. In 1871 the Board of Trade commissioned Courteney Ilbert, then a young barrister (later first Parliamentary Counsel and clerk to the House of Commons), to draw up a memorandum on employers' liability. A Parliamentary Select Committee investigated the issue in 1876.[66] On the whole the witnesses before the Committee divided into those who thought that the principle of vicarious liability was wrong altogether, and could not see why anyone should be able to obtain damages for the negligence of an employee; and those who accepted the principle of vicarious liability but felt that the doctrine of common employment, excluding the workers themselves from its benefits, was unjust. I have already referred to Bramwell's evidence before this Committee, and it is plain that the Committee was concerned to examine the realities behind his argument. Was it true that a part of the wages paid could be said to be a sort of premium against the risk of injury? The new representatives of the working man totally rejected the idea. 'What do you think of the argument which is to be found in cases on this subject', one of them was asked, 'that a person calculates the risk when he enters into the employment and is paid higher wages accordingly?' The answer was what might be expected:

I do not think that can be borne out by facts in any instance. It seems to me that when a man enters into employment he takes it for granted that everything has been done to make that employment safe and secure.[67]

And even among the judiciary, Bramwell did not have it all his own way. Sir Balliol Brett, later Lord Esher and Master of the Rolls, appeared as a witness, in fundamental disagreement with Bramwell. When asked his views about the notion that the workman was paid to take the risk of injury, he replied that the argument required very considerable limitation 'as to its real applicability in practice'.[68]

In the following year a test case was brought before the new Court of

---

[64] See, e.g., *Woodley* v. *Metropolitan District Rly.* (1877) 2 Ex. D. 384.
[65] *Supra*, pp. 337, 502.
[66] (1876) H.C. *Parliamentary Papers*, ix. 669.
[67] Ibid., Q. 1.
[68] Ibid., p. 690.

Appeal established under the Judicature Acts.[69] A workman, employed by a contractor, to do repairs in a railway tunnel, was injured by a train of whose approach he was unaware. He sued, not his own employers, but the railway company. The old doctrine of common employment therefore did not apply, and the question was whether the Courts would take the opportunity to limit the application of this doctrine, by giving the injured workman a right to sue a third party where negligence was proved against that third party's servants. By a majority of three to two the Court rejected the claim and justified their decision by invoking the maxim *volenti non fit injuria*. The plaintiff knew the risk, said Cockburn C.J. and carried on working: 'he must abide the consequences.'[70] Among the dissenters Mellish L.J. put the more modern view:

I think he is entitled to say, 'I know I was running a great risk, and did not like it at all, but I could not afford to give up my good place from which I get my livelihood, and I supposed that if I was injured by their carelessness I should have an action against the company and that if I was killed my wife and children would have their action also.'[71]

Here, therefore, was a head on challenge to the Bramwellian economic theory. If the workman *knew* that he had no right to sue for negligence, his wages might be held to cover the risk of injury; but did he know? Was he not entitled to say that he did not know and therefore that he assumed that his wage did not include this element of risk premium? At last it was being seriously asked whether it was sufficient merely to *assume* that everyone knew and understood the background against which contracts were made.[72]

This decision was only the beginning of a long struggle. In Parliament, the Employer's Liability Act was passed in 1880 limiting the employer's right to invoke the defence of common employment in various circumstances. The debates showed as wide a variety of views among Members of Parliament as there was among the judges. On the one hand there was A. J. Balfour, on the Conservative side, to argue very much in Bramwellian terms.[73] On the other hand there was a Mr Craig on the Government benches who replied that, 'Lord Justice Bramwell, so long as he confined himself to the exposition of the law, was clear; but so soon as he gave an opinion as to the practical effect of the proposed legislation,

---

[69] *Woodley* v. *Metropolitan District Rly.*, *supra*.

[70] At p. 388.

[71] At p. 394.

[72] It will be noted that once this assumption was questioned, it became possible to challenge the idea that all risks of past and future events were allocated by a contract. The door was thus opened to the development of doctrines of mistake and frustration, both of which date from around the 1870s.

[73] *Hansard* (3rd series), H.C., vol. 253, cols. 1405–6 (1880).

he sinks below the rank of a practical witness.'[74] Earlier, on the second reading of the Bill, the same speaker had rejected the idea that the wages included an element of risk premium. That might be true 'as an abstract proposition' he argued, and might even be true to a limited extent in practice, but generally speaking the workmen did not think of the risk of injury at all.'It is never present to his mind.'[75] A third viewpoint put by some members was that a proper system of workmen's compensation should be introduced so that workmen would be entitled to compensation whether negligence could be shown or not. This was, in effect, a plea for insuring the workman against the risks of injury, and was to become of greater importance a decade later. A fourth point of view was that of the workmen's own representatives, at this time already being expressed in Parliament by members who came from the hustings 'reeking with pledges to the working men'.[76] They totally rejected the idea of workmen's compensation insurance, which 'would have the effect of enabling employers to continue their reckless conduct; and if it were adopted, it would be to call on districts where no accidents occurred to pay for accidents which, with ordinary care and the avoidance of parsimonious management, ought not to have occurred'.[77] What they wanted was the complete abolition of the doctrine of common employment.

After the 1880 Act was passed, the subject continued to raise a number of important issues in the Courts. One of the first was the question whether it was permissible for the parties to contract out of the Act. This does not appear to have been a mere attempt at evasion by unscrupulous employers, because in truth a number of employers already operated workmen's compensation schemes on a substantial scale, for example by making contributions to a friendly society which covered the workmen against risks of injury and death. These schemes appear to have been more effective and often more generous than the provisions of the Act of 1880, and the Earl of Dudley, one of the Act's chief Parliamentary opponents, argued that he was entitled to maintain his scheme with the consent of the workmen, despite the Act. His claim was upheld by the Courts on the ground that there was no reason to suppose Parliament had intended to interfere with freedom of contract to the extent of making contracting out illegal.[78] 'If it could be shewn in the present case', said Field J. 'that large classes of workmen would be deprived of the protection which the legislature intended to give them by a decision that

---

[74] Ibid., col. 1419.
[75] Ibid., vol. 252, cols. 1105-6.
[76] Ibid., col. 1135.
[77] Ibid., col. 1110.
[78] *Griffiths* v. *Earl of Dudley* (1882) 9 Q.B.D. 357.

they could contract themselves out of the provisions of the Employers Liability Act, a strong argument against that construction would be afforded. But that cannot be shewn.'[79]

However, the more troublesome question continued to be that relating to the maxim *volenti non fit injuria*. Was the workman injured through obvious and known risks to be deprived of his claim to compensation? In *Yarmouth* v. *France*[80] and again in *Thomas* v. *Quartermaine*[81] the Court of Appeal was divided on the question as they had been in the *Woodley* case before the Act. In *Thomas* v. *Quartermaine*, Bowen L.J. although siding with the majority against the workman on the facts, was willing to limit the defence to cases where the workman truly understood the nature of the danger. '[C]arelessness is not the same thing as intelligent choice', he insisted.[82] The issue was eventually carried to the House of Lords in *Smith* v. *Charles Baker & Sons*[83] where the Bramwellian view was finally overthrown. By a majority of four to one the Lords here insisted that it was not enough to presume that the workman consented to run the risk of being injured through negligence merely because certain risks were apparent. The new view was stated by Lord Herschell in language which shows clearly how far the judges had travelled since the days when they had accepted uncritically the application of simplistic economic views to such issues:

If the employed agreed, in consideration of special remuneration, or otherwise, to work under conditions in which the care which the employer ought to bestow, by providing proper machinery or otherwise, to secure the safety of the employed, was wanting, and to take the risk of their absence, he would no doubt be held to his contract, and this whether such contract were made at the inception of the service or during its continuance. But no such case is in question here. There is no evidence that any such contract was entered into . . . I must say, for my part, that in any such case in which it was alleged that such a special contract as that suggested had been entered into I should require to have it clearly shewn that the employed had brought home to his mind the nature of the risk he was undertaking and that the accident to him arose from a danger both foreseen and appreciated.[84]

It is easy to understand, in the light of this sort of attitude, why the law began to move away, during this period, from broad and sweeping arguments of legal principle, to detailed factual examination of the

---

[79] At p. 364. But opposition to 'contracting out' became a matter of dogma and led to the foundering of a further Bill in 1893. See David G. Hanes, *The First British Workmen's Compensation Act 1897* (New Haven, Conn., and London, 1968), Chapter 5.

[80] (1884) 19 Q.B.D. 647.

[81] (1887) 18 Q.B.D. 685.

[82] At p. 698.

[83] [1891] A.C. 325.

[84] At pp. 362–3.

circumstances. It was no longer sufficient to assert sweepingly that contracting parties 'must be taken' to know this, or understand that; the facts must be investigated.

I need not here pursue the subsequent history of workmen's compensation laws beyond observing on the fact that the subject has largely passed out of the area of private contract into that of modern administrative processes. For workmen's claims for damages at common law (or at common law as amended by the removal of the doctrine of common employment) gave way largely to workmen's compensation through the medium of insurance in 1897, and from there it passed into the State social security system in 1948. Although actions for damages for negligence or breach of statutory duty remain possible (and indeed, have increased in number and importance over the past thirty years) it is difficult to believe that the future lies with the common law remedy rather than in the social security sphere.

Moneylenders and Bills of Sale

A second major area in which developments after 1870 reflected the growing appreciation of the realities of consumer bargaining was that now known as consumer credit. After the abolition of the Usury Laws in 1854 there gradually rose into prominence a new type of moneylending transaction, often entered into with people of modest means, but also sometimes with people whose primary concern was secrecy. The normal practice seems to have been for the moneylender to lend (say) £50, and take a rate of interest amounting to (say) another £50. The two sums would be added together, and a promissory note for £100 taken as security. The borrower would sign a printed contract agreeing to repay the capital and interest in equal stated instalments (as with the modern hire-purchase contract) but also providing that on any default the whole sum would become due and payable, and would carry further interest. Thus the original interest of £50, in this example, would become due at once and in advance, in the event of default, plus further penal interest on the whole. Because of the huge interest rates the moneylender was often in no hurry to take proceedings upon a default, but would use the threat of doing so to persuade the borrower to enter into a new transaction, in which all the previous interest would be capitalized, and the whole process would start again. It was thus possible, in a very short space of time, for an original loan of £50 to swell into a sum of ten or twenty times that amount, all of which was legally due under the then rules of freedom of contract. Moreover, the new (post Judicature Act) procedure for obtaining rapid judgment on promissory notes (or other negotiable instruments) meant that the moneylender could bring to bear the threat of obtaining judgment and levying execution in a very short time. Not only would this be itself a potent threat, but it was often all the more alarming because it meant that the borrower's activities would be publicized to the world.

The above procedures assumed that there was no security for the loan other than the promissory notes, but it was not uncommon for such loans to be secured by the grant of bills of sale. A bill of sale was normally an instrument by which the grantor (in substance) mortgaged personal chattels—often household furniture and other such belongings—while retaining the possession of them, and granting to the moneylender a right to seize the goods specified in the bill of sale in various circumstances, such as in the event of default in repayment of any instalment of the loan. From 1854 there had been Bills of Sale Acts on the statute book designed to protect third party purchasers of goods included in bills of sale without notice of them, but these Acts had not been designed for the protection of consumers, nor were they chiefly directed at small transactions, but at commercial ones. But section 20 of the Bills of Sale Act of 1878 had, perhaps inadvertently, greatly increased the value of registered bills by granting the holder of a registered bill priority over the claims of a trustee in bankruptcy of the grantor. Thus a registered bill of sale now became a powerful form of security, and in consequence there was a great increase in the use of such bills, particularly for small consumer-type transactions. A House of Commons Select Committee in 1881 discovered that bills of sale for under £10 had been registered to the value of only £269 in 1875, but to the value of over £64,000 in 1880.[85] The total number of registered bills had increased from some 11,000 in 1875 to over 54,000 in 1880, but the total value covered by these registered bills had barely doubled. It was thus clear that there had been a great increase in the use of small bills.

The printed forms used by moneylenders, either for simple loans or for bills of sale, were, without question, hideously harsh. A standard printed form for a bill of sale, read to the Commons Committee of 1881, provided, for example, that the grantee could seize the goods specified in it, without giving any opportunity to the grantor to remedy any default, in any one of a large number of events, including, for example, failing to keep the goods safe, doing any act jeopardizing the creditor's security, underletting the premises, quitting England, being arrested, or failing to show, on demand, receipts for rent or rates. The rates of interest, even for debts so secured, were seldom less than 50 to 60 per cent, and sometimes a great deal higher. The 1878 Act had required that the bill of sale be attested by a solicitor who was supposed to explain the effect of the instrument to

---

[85] (1881) H.C. *Parliamentary Papers*, viii. 1, pp. 13–14.

the grantor but in practice this provision seems to have been rarely complied with.[86]

It was clear that there was a real problem in distinguishing between transactions of a legitimate commercial character, such as loans made for business purposes to farmers, small factory owners, or businessmen, and secured over their stock in trade, on the one hand, and the straightforward consumer credit transaction, on the other. But after the evidence given before the 1881 Commons Committee it was difficult for anyone to doubt the need for consumer protection legislation. Those most emphatic in their demands for reform here were the County Court judges who saw the law being practically applied in their Courts by unscrupulous moneylenders who came to extract their pound of flesh. Indeed, the County Court judges wanted to repeal section 20 of the 1878 Act which made a registered bill good against a trustee in bankruptcy; they argued that most of the bills were granted after the grantor was aware that he was about to become bankrupt, and that these bills were thus in fraud of other creditors.[87] But they were also convinced that it was this degree of security which encouraged the moneylenders to make small loans on the very harsh terms commonly used, and that the repeal of the section would stamp out these loans altogether.

The Bills of Sale Act of 1882 was, in the result, something of a compromise; but at the same time, it was one of the clearest examples of consumer protection legislation which interfered with freedom of contract. It was designed in the interests of small borrowers, and not (like the 1878 Act) in the interests of third parties.[88] The Act required the use of a simple statutory form which contained the only permissible grounds for seizure; it prohibited the assignment of after acquired chattels,[89] and thus went some way towards preventing the borrower from being stripped of every chattel in his possession; it required goods to be left on the premises for five days after seizure to enable the borrower to pay off the amounts due; and it totally prohibited the use of bills of under £30. This last provision, which aroused the wrath of Bramwell,[90] was an illustration of the new type of paternalist legislation which deprived some members of the community of a valuable freedom in order to protect others from their own folly. The prudent and cautious man who might have formerly borrowed money on the security of a bill of sale for under £30, was now prohibited from doing so in order that less prudent

---

[86] Ibid., p. 64.

[87] Ibid., p. 83.

[88] The authority of Lord Herschell is usually cited for this (see *Manchester, Sheffield etc., Rly. Co.* v. *North Central Wagon Co.* (1888) 13 App. Cas. 554, 560), but in fact the whole history of the Bill bears this out.

[89] As so held in *Thomas* v. *Kelly* (1888) 13 App. Cas. 506.

[90] C. Fairfield, *Some Account of Baron Bramwell* (London, 1898), pp. 136, 137.

and less cautious people should not make fools of themselves. Inevitably, those who did require small loans now had to pay a higher rate of interest, as they were unable to grant the only security that they had formerly been able to.[91] This was a classic example of paternalist legislation passed in the interests of the majority at the expense of the minority. It was not the last.

The Act of 1882 only dealt with loans secured by bills of sale; and the growth of moneylending practices in the 1880s and 1890s showed that many of the problems continued to exist in the case of unsecured loans. The default judgment on a promissory note was almost as effective a weapon as actual security, for it enabled the creditor to threaten the debtor with imprisonment for up to six weeks under the Debtors Act 1869. Towards the end of the century, the County Court judges once again became increasingly concerned at the powers which unfettered freedom of contract conferred on moneylenders. A number of moneylenders became famous for their rapacity, among them being Isaac Gordon, who defended his conduct before a Commons Select Committee in 1897 with the arguments of the classical economists: 'I risk my money and I have a perfect right to make any bargain I think fit.'[92] Gordon admitted to charging interest of up to 3,000 and 4,000 per cent,[93] but insisted on his right to make contracts free of legal control, like 'every other trader'.[94] His activities brought him before the Court of Appeal in 1899[95] and the Court was so hostile to him that their decision against him does not seem wholly reconcilable with traditional contract doctrine. The County Court judges were, perhaps, still more hostile to these moneylenders. Even before the law was altered by Parliament they often adopted their own methods of dealing with extortionate claims. One judge, for example, ordered a defendant to pay the judgment against him at the rate of one penny per month,[96] and the Recorder of Dublin made it a practice to offer the moneylender (in Chambers) the choice between accepting judgment at once for a reasonable rate of interest, or being castigated in public by the judge and having a derisory instalment order made.[97] Several of the High Court judges who gave evidence to the Select Committee made it clear that their support for freedom of contract stopped short at that point at which unfair contracts were made.[98]

The result was the enactment of the Moneylenders Act 1900 which

[91] This was said to be 'a notorious fact' by Channel J. in *Carringtons Ltd.* v. *Smith* [1906] 1 K.B. 79, 90, although his figures do not tally with those given before the Select Committee of 1881.

[92] (1897) H.C. *Parliamentary Papers*, Minutes of Evidence, xl. 405, 553.

[93] Ibid., p. 558.

[94] Ibid., p. 564.

[95] *Gordon* v. *Street* [1899] 2 Q.B. 641.

[96] (1897) H.C. *Parliamentary Papers*, Minutes of Evidence, xl. 405, 652.

[97] (1898) H.C. *Parliamentary Papers*, x. 100.

[98] e.g. Hawkins J., (1897) H.C. *Parliamentary Papers*, xl, Q.9, pp. 537, 566; Mathews J., pp. 104-5.

gave the Courts power to reopen moneylending transactions if the rate of interest was excessive and the transaction was harsh or unconscionable or otherwise such that a Court of Equity would give relief. The reversion to the doctrines of Equity is of some interest, for it was the decline of Equity during the classical period which had led to so many of the abuses, later felt to be intolerable, in the name of freedom of contract. And I have also suggested that equitable discretions were ultimately replaced by statutory discretions. This Act provides an early example of this process.

Perhaps the most surprising aftermath of this legislation—the Bills of Sale Act and the Moneylenders Act—was that Parliament made no attempt for nearly half a century to exercise any similar control over the new type of contract which was adopted in order to evade these Acts— namely the hire-purchase contract. Here again, many of the problems which later came to light were identical with those which had been revealed by the Committees on Bills of Sale and Moneylenders. The hire- purchase contract, in particular, produced the same long list of grounds for seizure on default as the old bills of sale had done, but which had been prohibited since 1882. And although the hire-purchase contract may have differed in being primarily designed to facilitate the purchase of goods on credit, it was sometimes put to uses identical with those for which bills of sale had formerly been granted. The hire-purchase 'refinancing transaction' was invented, whereby the owner of goods sold them, and then re-acquired them on hire-purchase terms, retaining possession throughout, but giving a right to seize the goods in the usual cases. Some of these cases, it is true, still fell foul of the Bills of Sale Act; but others were allowed to stand.

But in due course, Parliament intervened here too. The first Hire- Purchase Act 1938 was designed for much the same purposes as the Bills of Sale Act 1882, though it gave more extensive discretionary powers to the Court over the payment of sums due under the agreement. Later, this body of law was extended by the Acts of 1964 and 1965, and it was eventually replaced altogether by the Consumer Credit Act of 1974 which brought together the elements of consumer protection in a variety of differing credit transactions. This Act contains a modernized and generalized version of the power originally conferred by the Moneylen- ders Act, to reopen harsh and unconscionable contracts, and it is worth quoting the language of the Act because it so clearly represents the modern attitude to the permissible extent of freedom of contract in consumer transactions. Under section 137 of the Act the Court may reopen an 'extortionate' credit bargain 'so as to do justice between the parties'. Under section 138 a credit bargain is extortionate if it requires payments 'which are grossly exorbitant', or 'otherwise grossly contravenes ordinary principles of fair dealing'. These provisions, it will be seen, reflect two important points. First, that discretion, of the old equitable type, is an essential part of the law of consumer contracts, and second, they emphatically reaffirm that the judicial process is concerned with justice, and not merely with the enforcement of contract.

Contract as an Instrument of Private Planning

I suggested above that one of the chief characteristics of the classical contract model was its stress on the executory transaction. The classical model was not merely about *exchanges*, but about *future exchanges*; it was the stress on future exchanges that brought with it the association between contract and *binding* arrangements. A man is *bound* by a contract because he is bound to some future performance. Contract was thus an instrument of planning for private parties, an instrument by which future risks could be allocated, and an instrument by which penalties and rewards were the natural result of calculation or miscalculation over such future risks. To a substantial degree, the classical model was also a failure on this question, and this failure can be attributed to a number of factors. First, the pace of change in modern societies has been such that, except for limited periods, and in limited areas, people are anxious to avoid the risk of future change in private planning. Secondly, in any area where the public interest is involved—which increasingly tends to mean virtually every sphere of human activity—there is unwillingness to allow the rewards and penalties of private planning to have their full effect; and even where there is no real element of public interest, there has often been unwillingness to stand by the system of rewards and penalties because of the basically inegalitarian tendencies of this system. Thirdly, there has been a shift in the paradigm of contractual relationship from the single, discrete transaction, to relationships of a continuing character. In such continuing relationships, the tendency is for the risks of future change to be adjusted by some kind of quasi-administrative process, rather than by standing by the letter of some original contract.

The result of these and other factors has been that, in practice, contractual relations tend increasingly to be concerned with executed or part-executed transactions. The law has become increasingly dominated by what contracting parties do, and less by what they originally agreed. A breach of contract is, increasingly, treated as something more akin to an accident than to a wilful refusal to accept a bargained-for risk. It is a misfire situation, a case where something has gone wrong, and where some equitable adjustment has to be made in order to resolve a conflict. Inevitably this process has led to a return in various respects to older ideas underlying contractual liability. The decline of the executory model, and the rise of the part-executed contract, has involved the revival of the importance of the twin elements of benefit and reliance. The notion that benefits should be fairly recompensed, and the notion that reasonable reliance should be protected, have come once again into greater prominence, as the idea of the executory contract, and of promise-based liability, have declined.

Many lawyers will instinctively dispute these conclusions and even these premises. In commercial transactions, they will claim, the executory contract remains an important instrument of private planning, and of risk-allocation. Calculation and miscalculation are still rewarded appropriately by market forces. Future risks still have to be allowed for in a wide variety of commercial arrangements, and the private sector of the economy is still subject to market principles in these respects. There is truth in this, and I do not wish to overstate the claim that the executory model of classical law has been largely a failure. But there is also distortion in this perspective, even of commercial transactions. The truth is that the classical model only continues to live because by definition, anything inconsistent with it, is eliminated from the sphere of contract. Even in commercial transactions, many of the factors listed above operate today to minimize the importance of contract as an instrument of planning. Business people (at least in England) are not significantly less risk-averse than consumers. They have no great desire to use contracts as instruments of risk allocation concerning unknown future events. The modern commercial transaction is, in practice, apt to include provision for varying the terms of exchange to suit the conditions applicable at the time of performance. Goods ordered for future delivery are likely to be supplied at prices ruling at the time of delivery; rise and fall clauses in building or construction works are the rule and not the exception; currency-variation clauses may well be included in international transactions. And even where such provisions are not included in the contract itself, business people are in practice often constrained to agree to adjustments to contractual terms where subsequent events make the original contract no longer capable of performance on a fair basis. The rewards and penalties for guessing what the future will bring are no longer automatically thought of as being the natural consequences of success or failure in the skill and expertise of business activity. For example, in Government contracts, *ex gratia* payments are typically made in fixed price contracts, 'where unforeseen circumstances have substantially raised costs and caused the contractor to suffer a loss'.[99] And conversely, contractors who make 'excessive profits' in dealings with the Government may well discover, that these are not regarded as the reward for abnormal skill and enterprise, but as the result of miscalculation by

---

[99] C. Turpin, *Government Contracts* (Harmondsworth, 1972), p. 57.

the Government which they will be compelled to hand over.[1] Nor are such occurrences peculiar to Government or other public authorities. Even between private commercial organizations, the fact that business relationships are so often continuous means that the desire to maintain the goodwill of other contracting parties is often more important than the letter of a contract.

[1] Ibid., p. 171.

22

THE WHEEL COME FULL CIRCLE

THE DECLINE OF CONTRACT

THE past century, and more particularly, the past thirty years, have seen a decline of contract from the high point which it had reached by 1870. We have already seen how in political affairs, freedom of contract had ceased to be a living issue early in the twentieth century, and although freedom of contract is by no means dead in the law Courts, even among lawyers the decline has been evident. It has, indeed, become a cliché to say that there has been a reversion from 'contract' to 'status', a movement contrary to that perceived and described by Maine in 1861.[1] But in saying that freedom of contract, or even contract itself, has declined in importance, there is a danger of oversimplifying a complex process. There are at least three separate strands involved in this decline. The first is that the economic importance, the *role* of contract in our society has declined. The second sense in which contract may be said to have waned in the past century relates to the declining importance attached to the value of free choice as a source of legal rights and liabilities, and the consequent increase in importance attached to non-voluntary rights and duties. There has thus, as we shall see, been a decline in promise-based liabilities and a growth in benefit-based and reliance-based liabilities. The third sense in which there has been a decline in contract is much less obvious though, in its way, no less important than the other two. What I contend here is that there has been a significant move away from the *executory* model of exchange, away from the use of contract as a calculated instrument for the allocation of risks. If (as I suggested earlier) we distinguish between the exchange-function and the risk-allocation function of contract, the emphasis has shifted from the latter to the former. Exchange remains as important a feature of modern society as it ever was; indeed, in a sense, it has become more important with the growth of specialized activities which the complexities of modern societies demand. But while exchange remains of such paramount importance, there is a sense in which contract as an instrument for the planning of future exchanges has been replaced by contemporaneous exchanges, or short-term exchanges or long-term relationships in which

---

[1] Kahn-Freund, 'A Note on Status and Contract in British Labour Law', 30 *Modern Law Review* 635 (1967).

exchanges can be made, but on terms which are open to continuous adjustment as long as the relationship lasts.

These three aspects of the decline of contract constitute the theme of this chapter. In one sense, the first of them is by far the most important, but curiously it is this aspect of the decline of contract which has hitherto been of least interest to the lawyer. The declining role of freedom of contract and the free market leave the lawyer's conceptual apparatus largely intact. The fact that many relationships are no longer governed by contract is of little interest to the lawyer who is concerned primarily with the relationships which still are contractual. And the fact that the market in which many contracts are made is no longer a free market, likewise is of little interest to the lawyer who still applies his concepts deriving from the classical model unless he encounters some specific statutory provision intruding upon that model. But at the same time, lawyers are busy constructing another body of law to govern many of these non-market relationships, the substance of which constitutes the new administrative law. This task, has been absorbing more and more of the lawyer's time and energies, so much so that there has been, perhaps, little opportunity yet for stepping back and appraising the work which has been going on. That is not a task to be undertaken here, but I propose at least to draw attention to the fact that much administrative law now governs exchange relationships of a non-market character, and that the distinction between market and non-market relationships ends in a murky grey area where contractual and administrative-law ideas struggle for paramountcy. In these circumstances, there must be room for some attempt, at least, to perceive the differing approaches of public and private law to essentially similar relationships. The public and private lawyers may have much to learn from each other.

The Declining Role of Contract

It is today no longer the individual but the Government which largely allocates resources in the British economy. Governments directly control, for instance, the resources to be invested in the nationalized industries, and in all the public goods and services directly supplied by the State or by other public bodies. Governments also effectively manipulate the market, by price controls, wage controls, and other legal and fiscal arrangements which depress demand for this product or stimulate demand for that one. And within the public system itself, the process of decision-making on resource allocation is delegated to Committees or corporate bodies who do not function by market methods. To take one simple example, the resources devoted to higher education are fixed by the Government, who control the level of salaries to be paid, and also the fees to be charged in Universities as well as other matters of financial policy. The actual distribution of the overall sum is largely determined by the University Grants Committee which earmarks substantial capital expenditure for particular projects (such as new buildings) but otherwise distributes sums for recurrent expenditure to each University without deciding how it is to be spent. Within each University there will then be a Committee structure which allocates the recurrent grant among departments. There will, of course, be constraints operating on this distribution by Governmental policy decisions (such as the general policy that student catering and accommodation services should be self-financing) but subject to these constraints, each University is free to decide how to allocate its resources.

Within these public bodies, and between them and the persons who work for them, directly or indirectly, some of the relationships which arise may still be the subject of legal contracts, but many of them will be almost entirely governed by administrative and not contractual processes. To continue with the example of higher education, University staff are, of course, employed under legal contracts which remain subject to many of the principles of ordinary contract law. The relationships between students and their universities are more difficult to classify; in some respects these are governed by contractual principles (for example, students may have a contractual right to take courses which were advertised to be available when they applied for entry),[2] but in other respects the relationship between student and University appears to be governed by rules of public rather than private law.[3] Then there are, within the University itself, many relationships which are plainly not governed by contractual law, or even by contractual principles. An agreement between different departments, for example, as to the teaching of a combined course, or an agreement between a higher body (say a Senate, or Council) to some proposal put forward by a University department, is plainly not subject to the law of contract. No doubt technical, doctrinal arguments in justification of this could be put forward. University departments have no corporate personality, and hence no contractual capacity; perhaps agreements of this kind are 'not intended' to be legally binding, and so on. But the reality is that contract law is thought to be inappropriate to the regulation of such relationships for a variety of reasons which may not be easy to state. Perhaps it is partly a belief that, within the confines of a hierarchical institution, the governing body of that institution is the appropriate body to regulate such matters and arbitrate on any disputes. Perhaps it is partly a belief that contract law is 'too rigid' and that an institution like a University

---

[2] *D'Mello* v. *Loughborough College of Technology*, *The Times*, 17 June 1970.

[3] *R.* v. *Aston University ex parte Roffey* [1969] 2 Q.B. 538; cf. *Herring* v. *Templeman* [1973] 3 All E.R. 569.

must reserve the right to revise previous decisions in the light of new circumstances, so that even 'agreements' cannot be treated as though they had the sanctity of contracts behind them. Perhaps it is partly due to the authoritarian attitudes likely to be engendered by a hierarchical decision-making process which makes majority decisions rather than unanimous agreements the ultimate criteria for legitimating action.

The expulsion of contract law as the regulator of such relationships does not necessarily mean that such bodies operate in a legal vacuum. Individuals whose rights are affected may, in the last resort, wish to carry internal disputes to the Queen's Courts for redress, and if they do so, it is likely these days that lawyers will classify the cases as involving questions of Administrative Law. The procedure to be followed and the law to be applied, will then be quite different from those governing contractual disputes. The whole conceptual apparatus of the lawyer changes as he moves from private to public law, from contract to administrative law. He does not, for example, think in terms of 'binding promises' or 'binding agreements'. Indeed, the administrative lawyer has trouble with the very concept of a public decision-maker binding himself to act in a particular manner because he sees this as a surrender of a duty which is owed to the public, and which can, therefore, be valid, only within carefully defined limits.[4] Similarly, the public lawyer's approach to the effect of mistake, or representation is often significantly different from that of the contract lawyer.[5] On the other hand, the duties of public authorities as to the procedures to be observed, and the matters to be considered, may well be more stringent than those normally applicable in a contractual situation. In contract, the traditional approach to the rights of the parties has been (as we saw earlier) to treat them as absolute, and not within the control of the Courts. A person's right to choose with whom he will contract, and the terms on which he will contract are still largely matters entirely within his own caprice, although we will see later that there are signs of change here. But in public law, the control of decision making by the Courts imposes greater restraints on arbitrary or capricious actions.

The growth of the activities of the State has inevitably led to a great increase in the number of situations in which relationships between the citizen and the Government, or some public authority, are now governed by public law rather than private law. And it might, therefore, be thought to be a matter of some importance that there should be some rational principle for distinguishing cases which are to be governed by public law principles from those which are to be governed by contract

---

[4] See *Ayr Harbour Trustees* v. *Oswald* (1883) 8 App. Cas. 623; *Birkdale District Electric Supply Co.* v. *Southport Corpn.* [1926] A.C. 335; *W. Cory & Son Ltd.* v. *London Corpn.* [1951] 2 K.B. 476; *British Transport Commission* v. *Westmorland C.C.* [1958] A.C. 126.

[5] See, e.g., *Norfolk C.C.* v. *Secretary of State for the Environment* [1973] 1 W.L.R. 1400.

law. Similarly, where there is a divergence between public and private law in substance, it might have been thought important that the distinctions in the substantive law should be justified by some rational argument, based upon the different functions of the two bodies of law. At the least, one might have expected that analogies from the one body of law might be relied upon in the other; cases of mistake, misrepresentations, agreement, arbitrary and capricious decision-making, and so forth are problems which arise in public and private relationships. Why should the results be so different? But in practice, these methods of thought across the traditional conceptual boundaries of the law are rarely utilized, and there appears to be little attention paid even to the question whether a particular relationship is to be treated as contractual or not. A council house tenant, for instance, is treated as having a contract with the local authority, even though the contract is of a very peculiar character, and resembles a public-law relationship rather than a normal contractual tenancy.[6] On the other hand, a television licence-holder has no contract with the Post Office (or the B.B.C.) and the relationship is governed by principles of administrative law.[7] An agreement by which the police provide additional protection, beyond what they believe to be necessary, to some citizen or corporation, is governed by contractual principles—which means that the determination of the police as to what they consider necessary is conclusive.[8] On the other hand the supply of drugs to a patient under the National Health Service involves a statutory and not a contractual arrangement.[9] A local authority cannot levy sewerage charges on householders who are not connected to the public sewers because, even though this is not strictly a contractual arrangement, it is at least governed by similar principles, so that a statutory right to demand charges for services only extends to those who avail themselves of its services.[10] On the other hand, the general power to levy rates and taxes normally involves a power to subsidise or redistribute income from one group to another.

The great extension of Governmental activities naturally raises issues in some cases as to whether the agencies of Government are operating in a contractual or an executive, or even legislative capacity. These issues have rarely been litigated in England,[11] though there are Privy Council decisions from Australia[12] and Canada[13] raising these questions in

---

[6] See *Liverpool C.C.* v. *Irwin* [1977] A.C. 239, where the question was not disputed; for public law aspects of such tenancies, see *Cannock Chase D.C.* v. *Kelly* [1978] 1 All E.R. 152.

[7] See *Congreve* v. *Home Office* [1976] Q.B. 629.

[8] *Glasbrook Bros.* v. *Glamorgan C.C.* [1925] A.C. 270.

[9] *Pfizer Corpn.* v. *Minister of Health* [1965] A.C. 512.

[10] *Daymond* v. *Plymouth City Council* [1976] A.C. 609, especially at p. 640.

[11] But one example is to be found in *Amphitrite* v. *The King* [1921] 3 K.B. 500.

[12] *Australian Woollen Mills Pty. Ltd.* v. *Commonwealth* (1955) 93 C.L.R. 546.

[13] *A. G. of British Columbia* v. *Esquimault and Nanaimo Rly. Co.* [1950] 1 D.L.R. 305.

particular circumstances. But similar questions may be raised in the political area. Ministerial pronouncements, for instance, as to the solvency of a commercial organization whose affairs have been investigated by, or are involved with those of Government, may be relied upon by members of the public in their dealing with the organization. Should the Government's confidence turn out to be unfounded, questions may arise which, at least in substance, closely resemble those involved in many private law situations.[14] Or again, when a nationalized industry conducts an advertising campaign which invites the public to spend their money in reliance on a particular pricing policy being followed, questions closely analogous to those raised by many contractual cases may arise.[15] Because of the conceptual barriers involved, because legal and political issues are always debated in entirely different manners, the similarity of the substantive issues involved is rarely examined in these situations. This is regrettable, because it often helps elucidate matters of this kind, if parties are compelled to articulate the basic premises on which they proceed. If the requirements of justice differ in contractual situations and administrative situations, it would be helpful to know how, and why they differ.

Although I have no space here for a searching account of these matters, one striking feature of the administrative process which distinguishes it from the contractual, is the extreme hostility usually displayed towards the idea that public bodies can ever become 'bound' to a policy, or to stand by their pronouncements merely because these have been relied upon and acted upon by the public. Still less can bare expectations as to future Government policy, however well based on Governmental pronouncements, be treated as conferring any kind of rights on the citizen. It is, of course, understandable that despotic and tyrannical Governments should always want to preserve their freedom of action in the future, but it would be surprising if democratic Governments, who at least pay lip service to the Rule of Law, should not feel under any obligations to respect the reasonable expectations and reasonable acts of reliance of the public. And, in practice, there are certain traditional areas in which British Governments do commonly respect the rights of the public.

The conventions against retrospective legislation, for instance, are an indication that Governments respect the rights of the people to rely on the law as it is from time to time enacted. And there are other conventions of a similar character which are almost universally respected by

---

[14] See the Fifth *Report of the Parliamentary Commissioner* for 1974–5 on the Court Line affair, H.C. 498 (1974–5); Craig, 'Representations by Public Bodies', 93 *Law Q. Rev.* 398 (1977).

[15] As in the night storage heaters case. See *Hansard* (5th series), H.C., vol. 874, cols. 769–813 (1974) and H.L., vol. 352, cols. 724–9 (1974).

Governments and Parliaments. For instance, new licensing requirements for a trade or profession almost always respect the rights of those already in the trade or profession, and changes in the law which have important practical implications for those doing business are nearly always announced in advance, or have postponed commencement dates, so as to enable those affected to adjust their practices in time. So also changes in taxation laws are usually made so as to preserve the rights of those who have entered into binding transactions before the changes are announced, even where the completion of the transaction may not be scheduled to take place for many years, as for example, in the case of life insurance policies. Similarly, there are the administrative practices, almost invariably followed, when there is any reorganization or regrading of staff in the public service. If there is one rule, better respected than any other, when such reorganization or regrading takes place, it is that no person already in service should have his position altered to his prejudice. In matters of this kind, the barest expectations may be afforded a very high degree of protection. There are, for example, many civil servants who still enjoy the leave entitlements which were current before the changes made in the 1950s, and which apply to all civil servants recruited since that date. Since it is improbable that any person acts in reliance on such long-term prospects, this 'preservation' of rights is in fact the protection of the merest expectation.

As I have said, this is not the place for a full discussion of these interesting issues. But there are at least some questions worth further examination elsewhere. In particular, there is room for a comparison between the extent to which reliance and expectations are protected by contract law on the one hand, and by public law and administrative practice on the other. Such a comparison would probably demonstrate that contract law is more inclined to protect expectations and reliance than public law and practice (except perhaps in the one area of employment) but that public law and practice generally afford a greater degree of protection than contract law against arbitrary and capricious decision-making. I suggest too, that it will be found that there are in both spheres perceptible trends in the same direction, as for example, in the increasing protection being afforded to expectations in employment, while there may be a decline in the extent to which expectations are protected elsewhere.

The growth of Government, and of the public service, has also led to another development which has minimized the role of contract in the modern world. For the internal relationships which exist within the field of Government are not regulated by contract, nor generally, even by administrative law. They are largely regulated by pure administrative and political practice. One Government department does not contract with another Government department; the Army does not contract with the Navy; central Government rarely contracts with local authorities. And although the nationalized industries are sufficiently independent, both of the Government and of each other, to enter into contracts with Government, or another nationalized board, disputes between them will rarely be litigated. Serious disagreements on policy are likely to be resolved by the Government's ultimate powers of direction, or to make new appointments to the Boards, or, in the last resort, to seek fresh legislation. And similarly, even where Government departments enter into contract-like arrangements with each other, the settlement of disputes will, in the last resort be the responsibility of the Ministers or the Cabinet.

Some of this is also true of private bodies. The internal organization of a company, or a group of companies, or even of an unincorporated association, is not regulated by market principles, nor is it generally regulated by ordinary contract law. It is true that the act of incorporation, or of creation of an unincorporated body, may often be an agreement, or at least an act done in agreement. And it is true, also, that formally speaking, the relationship of the members of an unincorporated association depends on contractual doctrines, and this is even true of some of the internal relationships within a corporation. But there are two important points about these relationships which affect the applicability of ordinary contractual principles. The first is that, even as a matter of law, the principle of majority rule often applies to them so that the consent of individual members to alterations can often be dispensed with. And the second is that an organization of this kind, especially if it is of any substantial size, develops its internal hierarchical procedures which provide their own norms, and their own dispute–settlement processes. One department of a commercial organization, for instance, does not contract with another. The employees of a company, may indeed, have contractual relations with the company itself, but in pursuit of the company's own objectives, it is the command structure of the company which settles disputes, not the norms of contract law. Naturally, as organizations become larger and larger, as groups of companies are gathered under one holding company by mergers and take-overs, the result is to eliminate a significant source of contract-making. It is true that within a large group, one subsidiary may enter into formal contracts with another, but these are essentially paper transactions. In contracts of this kind (at any rate if the subsidiaries are wholly owned) the terms of the contract are not framed by the two parties as a result of some bargaining process, in which each pursues its own interest, but are framed in the overall interests of the group, so that, for example, liabilities to tax may be minimized. Within these large organizations, relationships are conducted by administrative procedures and not by market contracts. Even the staunchest upholders of market economics are constrained to admit that companies tend to become larger because the internal arrangements of a large organization may be more efficiently conducted by administrative means then they would be if the entrepreneur had to go into the market for every requirement, and buy it from an independent contractor.[16]

As these developments have occurred, they have naturally displaced a large amount of potential contractual litigation. For not only is contract-making largely eliminated within an organization, so too is litigation. If one division of a commercial entity fails to meet the targets set by management, or fails to perform an agreement with another division, any consequences must and will be settled within the organization. Even where the two divisions of the organization possess legal personality so that there would be nothing in theory to prevent litigation between them, it is obvious that no management in its senses would normally authorise such litigation.

Developments of this kind have led to the virtual destruction of the atomistic theory of society, in which each individual was perceived as entering into free-choice relationships with others, and in which the overall social structure was made up of huge numbers of such one-to-one relationships. What we now have is a relatively small number of large organizations, who exercise more or less control over their own members, and who enter into relationships, whether commercial or otherwise, with other similar organizations. The role of the individual as the centre of a network of relationships has largely disappeared. And this is the sense in which it is correct to speak of an enormous decline in the role played by contract in modern society.

But it is not only organizations which tend to regulate their internal arrangements without the aid of contract. For the reality is that many bilateral long-term relationships tend increasingly in that direction. Indeed, there is a sense in which many long-term relationships are part of a spectrum of which the discrete contract is one end, and the complete merger or take-over which creates a single organization is at the other end. Chronologically, too, the one relationship is sometimes a preliminary to the other. Two companies which have a long standing commercial arrangement by which one provides supplies to another, may end up by merging into a single corporate entity, or group. Even when the two bodies retain a sufficiently distinct identity to enter into contractual relationships it will often be found that, in practice, contract law and contractual ideas do not in substance regulate the relationship.[17] The

---

[16] See R. H. Coase, 'The Nature of the Firm', 4 *Economica* 386 (1937).
[17] See Ian R. Macneil, 'The Many Futures of Contract', 47 *S. California Law Rev.* 691 (1974).

parties often proceed as though they were engaged on a joint venture, and not a bargain in which they have mutually irreconcilable interests. In the event of default, an adjustment of the terms of the relationship for the future is far more likely than litigation. Quasi-administrative methods (such as joint committees) are likely to be found for smoothing over disputes, or avoiding conflict.

Long-term relationships of this character vary widely. They include, for instance, the relationship between employer and employee, between a company and trade unions representing its employees, between companies and their regular suppliers, between companies and their distributive networks. In some cases—as in the case of employers and trade unions—contract law and litigation is excluded from the field by a deliberate act of policy. Collective bargaining agreements, for instance, are not generally legally enforceable as contracts at all.[18] But even where contracts are made, the relationship between the parties may fail to conform to the classical model of contract in a variety of ways. In particular, the central idea of the executory contract as a risk-allocation device does not fit many of these long-term relationships. The reality is that such relationships often involve a continued sequence of exchanges, extending perhaps over many years, and regarded as a permanent or at least an indefinite arrangement. Some of these changes have begun to influence actual legal decisions in those cases which do get litigated. We shall see, for instance, changing attitudes to continuing contracts; and we shall see too some signs of recognition that parties may owe duties of care to each other in the bargaining process, something utterly alien to the classical model of contract. But these are matters to be pursued later in this chapter.

I referred earlier to the modern cliché that there has been, in recent times, a reversion from contract to status. What I have said above should suggest that this is not a very accurate description of the process I have described. It is true that in certain respects status has become more important as a source of rights and duties than it was when Maine was writing in 1861. For example, national citizenship is today a more important legal status than it was a hundred years ago when barriers to migration were few. But Maine was, anyhow, writing mainly of personal status, matters concerning family relationships. For example, he would have regarded the changing rules about the liability of a father or husband for goods supplied to his children or his wife, as illustrative of the movement from status to contract. In this sense, there has been little sign of a reversion from contract to status.[19] It would be more accurate

---

[18] *Ford Motor Co.* v. *A.E.U.* [1969] 2 Q.B. 303. This decision was reversed by the Industrial Relations Act 1971, and restored by the Trade Union and Labour Relations Act 1974.

[19] See Kahn-Freund, 'A Note on Status and Contract', 30 *Modern Law Review* 635 (1967); Havighurst, *The Nature of Private Contract* (Evanston, Ill., 1961), p. 127.

to say that there has been a movement from contract to administration, a movement from private to public law, a movement from bilateral to multilateral relationships, a movement from single, individualized transactions to long-term relationships. There is, however, another sense in which Maine's dictum may be taken. In so far as the incidents of a voluntarily created relationship were generally seen as the result of the parties' own intentions or wills when Maine was writing, it would be correct to say that there has been a movement away from contract and back to status in modern times. For the decline in the role of consent as a source of rights and liabilities has led to a great increase in the number of relationships in which the element of consent is largely exhausted once the relationship is created. Thereafter, the results of the relationship are increasingly perceived as following from the dictates of the law. That, however, is the theme of the next section.

THE DECLINE OF FREE CHOICE AND CONSENT

I have said that the second sense in which contract has declined concerns the changing importance attached to free choice, consent, and promises as sources of rights and liabilities. During the past hundred years there has been a continuous weakening of belief in the values involved in individual freedom of choice, and this weakening has been reflected in the law. The legislation of the past century has carried to great lengths the circumstances in which the individual's freedom of decision is overridden, either in the direct interests of a majority, or to give effect to values which a majority believe to be of overriding importance. At the same time, there has been a decline in the strength of the conceptual apparatus used by the classical model of contract, in the sense that lawyers are today more willing to recognize that all the consequences of a contract do not necessarily flow from the intention of the parties. To be sure there is still a considerable faith in the classical model in its essentials. I do not contend that the overall perspective of the lawyer has yet changed significantly in that respect; but in particular circumstances, in the context of particular cases, lawyers are usually more willing to reject the individualism which was central to the classical model. Here as elsewhere, we find signs of a difference in attitude in Parliament and the Courts. In Statute law the process of overriding individual freedom of choice has been taken far beyond the lengths which most lawyers would regard as compatible with the principles of contract law.

Before I illustrate these developments, there is one objection to this perspective which needs to be considered. In one major area of life, there has been, it may be urged, a significant increase in the respect accorded to individual freedom of choice. In all matters concerned directly or indirectly with sexual morality, from homosexuality to abortion, from pornography to adultery, the trend both of social mores and of the law has been towards a greater recognition of the rights of consenting adults to lead their own private lives without interference from the State. It seems paradoxical if, while these developments have been taking place, there has been at the same time a decline in the values of individual freedom of choice in the economic or commercial sphere. But the paradox must be faced since there is no real doubt that both of these movements have been taking place over recent decades. The explanation may lie in the fact that society is in general only willing to override individual freedom of choice in respect of matters on which there is a substantial degree of public agreement about the values concerned. In the case of sexual morality it is clear that there has been, for many years, an increasing trend towards the moral pluralism referred to in Chapter 20. There is no longer a substantial majority of the public who accept the conventional sexual morality of (let us say) the Christian Church, and without that degree of support in public opinion, it is no longer possible to override the freedom of individual adults to their own private sexual behaviour. On the other hand, in a variety of other respects, particularly in the economic and commercial spheres of activity, public opinion is (it seems) sufficiently uniform to tolerate the suppression, or at least the attempted suppression, of individual free choice. Moreover, the individual free choice which is overridden in contractual matters usually involves more public activity.

Property and Contract

In Part I of this work I suggested that the concept of freedom of property was a precursor, and a necessary precursor, to the age of freedom of contract. It was the freedom to buy and sell, to manage and exploit, all forms of property which led to the demand for total freedom of contract. It is no coincidence that the decline of freedom of contract has also been closely paralleled by a decline in freedom of property. The two principal forms of property in the modern world—land and company securities— have both been severely constrained during the past century by a variety of legal and practical developments.

So far as land is concerned, the absolute rights of ownership which were demanded and (subject to the effects of the strict settlements) ceded during the eighteenth and nineteenth centuries, have largely disappeared again. The gradual extension of the rights of tenants at the expense of landlords, first in the case of agricultural land, and then in the case of urban housing, has steadily eroded the owner's powers over his land. Indeed, in most cases the owner's rights barely extend beyond the right to receive the rent, and to treat the land itself as a security for that right.

He can no longer control the amount of the rent, the use to which the land shall be put, nor even the identity of his tenant. Unless the tenant voluntarily chooses to surrender the tenancy, or in some cases, upon his death, the landlord has no power to terminate the lease. Indeed, the pressures are to erode the landlords' rights still further. Since the regulation or control of rents nearly always keeps them below the level they would reach in the free market, the law in effect deprives the landlord of part of his property rights and hands them over to the tenant. But as this situation only continues so long as the tenancy continues, there is naturally pressure to extend the tenancies. The result is a tendency for these tenancies to become inheritable. At least in the case of rent regulated dwellings the Rent Acts have long provided that the tenant's statutory rights may pass once, and in some cases, twice to new tenants.[20] But these rights are not openly saleable, nor are they capable of being left by will. The result has been the creation of a peculiar kind of property right which can only be disposed of in a black market or some equally underhand way.[21] In the case of agricultural leases, legislation has recently provided for some measure of transmissibility of the tenant's rights,[22] but so long as full rights of disposal are not accorded to the tenant, he will have no freedom of property, and neither will the landlord. Thus it can be seen how the original interference with freedom of contract tends to create a new kind of property, which is also unfree.

A not dissimilar situation exists with council house tenancies which, though not having any legally protected value, are in practice so heavily subsidised that they are of very substantial value. But these too are not saleable, though many Councils will permit 'exchanges' to be made in appropriate cases. The result has been that a tenant in one town who wishes to move to another, sometimes advertises for a council tenant who wishes to move in the opposite direction. The interference with the free market thus has the result of forcing tenants to resort to barter since this is the only kind of exchange permitted to them. It is scarcely necessary to comment on the extreme inefficiency of barter, a mode of exchange which generally disappeared with the invention of money several millenia ago. Naturally the creation of these unfree forms of property, which have not otherwise existed since the feudal era, has a tendency to freeze the existing situation, and to discourage economically desirable change.

But more fundamental even than these changes concerning leases have been the effects of the Town and Country Planning Acts. Since 1947 the rights of a landowner have been, in effect, confined to the right

[20] See the Rent Act 1968, Schedule 1.
[21] See, e.g., *Ailion* v. *Spiekermann* [1976] Ch. 158.
[22] Agriculture (Miscellaneous Provisions) Act 1976.

to the existing use of the land, or such other use as may be permitted by the planning authorities. The idea of absolute ownership of land, of the absolute right of the owner to exploit and develop the land as he thinks best, has thus entirely disappeared from English law.[23] And this disappearance is not merely a matter of legal technicalities, because it reflects a fundamental shift in opinion about the very nature of a property-owning society. The eighteenth century idea that absolute rights of ownership were the mainspring and incentive to all economic activity has thus largely disappeared. At the same time, a similar change has taken place in connection with business enterprise. Ever since Berle and Means' classic study, *The Modern Corporation and Private Property*, as far back as 1932, it has become almost a cliché to remark that big business is today run by professional managers and not by owner-entrepreneurs. The role of the owner of the business has been converted into that of mere investor, and although at least his property remains readily marketable, his rights of control over the business have, in practice, been almost entirely eroded. Even without the implementation of the Bullock Report which proposes to give industrial workers the right to equal representation with shareholders on Boards of Directors, the workers generally have a more effective voice in the control of the business than the nominal owners.

The Decline of Free Choice in Contract

The role of free choice, of consent, of promises and intentions, is a complex one, and its decline has been equally complex. As I have already suggested, the decline in some cases has been primarily in the conceptual apparatus of the law, while in others it has been a true decline in the importance attached to the element of consent or free choice, as compared with other elements of a transaction or relationship. It is worth beginning by remarking on the decline of free choice generally throughout the law; the decline has not been confined to contractual cases, or matters which are conceptually classified as contractual. Apart from those areas, concerned with sexual morality which I referred to above, it seems to be generally true that throughout the judicial process, there has been a decline in the importance attached to consent, promise or intention in the law. The whittling down of freedom of property in various directions is one illustration of this decline. Another can be found in the judicial process itself. For although the trial procedure of the common law has traditionally placed a very considerable stress on the importance of the consensual element, there have been signs that here, too, parties cannot always be held to a binding consensual arrangement. In a recent case

---

[23] Despite the decision in *Bradford Corpn.* v. *Pickles* [1895] A.C. 587, which appears in the books as though the principle in that case was still good law.

concerned with the interpretation of a Statute, for instance, the House of Lords refused to accept that the consent of the parties as to the nature of the issues involved could preclude them from examining the construction of the statute.[24] Then again, the conclusiveness of the admissions of the parties in civil[25] or even in criminal proceedings,[26] has, over the past century, been somewhat watered down. For instance, it has several times been held that even a judgment obtained by consent may be set aside in various circumstances, if the underlying obligation was one which could not have been properly enforced.[27] Likewise, modern statutory provisions relating to adoption enable a Court to make an order dispensing with the consent of a parent to an adoption order on the simple ground that it is being unreasonably withheld.[28]

Similarly, in tort law, there has been a tendency to reduce or minimise the importance of a consent as a critical factor in the imposition or non-imposition of liability. The defence of *volenti non fit injuria*, for example, widely used in early cases of injured workmen (as we saw), has almost entirely disappeared from modern law.[29] The liability of an occupier to trespassers remains, it is true, somewhat different from that which he owes to those present on his land with his consent, but the difference is becoming hard to state or to apply,[30] and the pressures are towards a reform of the law which will substantially eliminate the distinction.[31] So, too, the Motor Vehicle (Passenger Insurance) Act 1971, which made it compulsory for drivers to carry insurance against the risk of injury to their passengers, can be seen as a whittling away of a *de facto* limit on liability deriving from the vague idea that the passenger agreed to the risk involved. Likewise the gradual shift from a subjective to an objective standard of care for bailees and other gratuitous undertakers, which was not yet complete before the end of the nineteenth century,[32] indicates a similar movement.

At the level of pure theory, there has too, been a decline in support for 'implied' or 'tacit' agreements formerly so widely held to justify liabilities or immunities. Most modern social contractarians for instance, do not argue overtly for an implied, still less, a real, agreement on the part of the citizen to subject himself to the State. The source of political obligation

[24] Lord Diplock, in *Cherwell D.C.* v. *Thames Water Board* [1975] 1 W.L.R. 448.

[25] *Ex parte Lenox* (1885) 16 Q.B.D. 314; see also *R.* v. *Durham Quarter Sessions ex parte Virgo* [1953] 2 Q.B. 1.

[26] See, e.g., *R.* v. *Whitehouse* [1977] 3 All E.R. 737.

[27] See, e.g., *Dietz* v. *Lennig Chemicals Ltd.* [1969] 1 A.C. 170.

[28] Adoption Act 1958, sect. 5(1)(b), now in Children Act 1975, sect. 12(2)(b).

[29] *I.C.I. Ltd.*, v. *Shatwell* [1965] A.C. 656 is a solitary exception to this trend.

[30] See *British Railways Board* v. *Herrington* [1972] A.C. 877; *Pannett* v. *McGuiness* [1972] 2 Q.B. 599.

[31] See the Law Commission *Report on Liability for Damage or Injury to Trespassers and Related Questions of Occupiers' Liability*, Cmnd. 6428 (1976).

[32] See, e.g., *Speight* v. *Gaunt* (1883) L.R. 9 App. Cas. 1, and cf. *Gold* v. *Essex C.C.* [1942] 2 K.B. 293, *post*, p. 763.

is much more likely to be found today in the benefits which the citizen derives from his membership of society, and the belief that he must in turn accept the corresponding burdens.[33] John Rawls's *A Theory of Justice*,[34] does, it is true, make considerable use of the notion of a contract *which would be made* given the circumstances and conditions he prescribes for those in his 'original position'. But this appears to be neither a genuine nor an implied agreement; it is more of a 'constructive' agreement, as a lawyer might call it. And, as such, it is difficult to see what it adds to the arguments which Rawls believes would impel those in his original position to make their social contract. If the arguments are sound on their own, then they supply a basis for his theory of justice; if they are unsound, the basis falls. In neither case does a contract which a person might have made (but did not) add any weight to the arguments themselves.[35]

At the level of promissory theory itself, a similar development has occurred to which I have previously adverted. Nobody today believes that promises are binding because of any tacit agreement to observe promises; some, in effect, argue that promises are binding because of the benefits which the promisor receives from the practice of promising in which he takes part by making a promise himself;[36] others see promises as binding because they lead to acts of reliance which may actually make the promisee's position worse if the promise is not complied with.[37]

When we turn to contract law itself, the decline in the importance of consent, or free choice, is manifest in a variety of ways. I need not dilate on the extensive use in modern times of standardised written contracts which are drawn up by one party and merely presented for signature to the other. This phenomenon has been much written about and is now widely acknowledged to involve substantial derogations from the consensual model of contract. Frequently one party has little effective choice in the matter at all, and neither reads nor understands, nor in any real sense agrees to the terms contained in such standard documents. But it is worth pausing to ask how such documentary contracts ever came to be accepted as possessing the validity of genuine agreements. Given the importance attached to the element of consent in the classical model of contract, how was it that the judges were able to conceive of such written documents as contractual? The problem is all the greater because (it will

---

[33] See D. D. Raphael, *Problems of Political Philosophy* (London and Basingstoke, 1970), pp. 106–8.
[34] Oxford, 1972.
[35] See Dworkin, 'The Original Position', 40 *Univ. Chicago Law Rev.* 500 (1973). This argument is very close to that used by Hume against the early social contractarians.
[36] H. L. A. Hart, 'Are there any Natural Rights?', 64 *Phil. Rev.* 175 (1955); J. Rawls, 'Two Concepts of Rules', 64 *Phil. Rev.* 1 (1955).
[37] Neil MacCormick, 'Voluntary Obligations and Normative Powers', *Proc. Arist. Soc. Supplement* 59 (1972).

be recalled) in the high noon of classical theory the Courts had given a new meaning to the requirements of the Statute of Frauds. The written note or memorandum required by the Statute, they insisted, was merely evidence of an agreement; the actual binding contract rested not in the writing itself, but in the will of the parties.[38] But when, later in the nineteenth century, the Courts were faced with the new problems of printed clauses, or tickets containing references to terms contained elsewhere, there was an increasing tendency to treat the written terms, subject to certain conditions, as themselves the actual words of the contract. Blackburn J. in *Harris* v. *Great Western Rly. Co.*[39] tried to rationalize it on the ground of estoppel; by signing a written document, or otherwise doing something which led the other party to believe that the written terms were accepted, the signing party became bound by estoppel. In effect this was a rationalization based on reliance, because estoppel is a doctrine whose whole basis is to be found in the conduct of one party which leads to acts of reasonable reliance by the other.

But in practice these theoretical searches into the foundation of liability in written contracts had little impact. Rather more important was the fact that (especially in the so-called 'ticket cases') juries nearly always favoured consumers against railway companies, and the Courts felt it imperative to find some way of protecting the railway companies.[40] They thus had to shift the nature of the problem from a question of fact to one of law, which they did by raising certain presumptions concerning the status of written documents or notices where sufficient notice was given of the terms. Many of these early decisions were by no means unfair because the railway companies based their charges on the extent of their liabilities, and they did not want to undertake (nor charge for) the responsibilities of insurers. In the business world, the difference between the liabilities of a carrier and of an insurer were well enough known, and the judges tended, on these matters to side with the railway companies. Their instincts also told them that it was of the greatest importance that written contracts should not be upset by external considerations because written documents were relied upon by third parties as well as the immediate parties to the contract. This is very likely one reason why the letter of a written contract tended too to be treated as more important than its spirit.[41]

Nevertheless, the result of these developments was that, when faced with written documents, the Courts in practice looked less for signs of

---

[38] *Supra*, p. 494.

[39] (1876) 1 Q.B.D. 515.

[40] See especially *Watkins* v. *Rymill* (1883) 10 Q.B.D. 178, although this was not itself a case against a railway company.

[41] See Devlin, 'Morals and the Law of Contract', in *The Enforcement of Morals* (Oxford, 1965), p. 44.

genuine agreement, and insisted more on the external conduct of the parties. Once the document could be treated as contractual, it made the task of the Courts so much easier; the dispute could be solved by looking at the terms in the document, and there would be no need to go into the broader and more difficult questions involved in searching for 'implications', or trying still more broadly to find a just solution to the dispute. It might have been thought that this process would have led more overtly to recognition that the Courts were involved in non-consensual liabilities. If a man was liable, not because he had agreed, or promised, but because he had signed a document, or given the other party to believe that he accepted it, was this not a reliance-based liability? When the Courts began to treat negligence in the signing of documents as a ground for liability of this character, the non-consensual aspect of the matter became even stronger.[42] In *United Dominions Trust Ltd.* v. *Western*,[43] in 1975, the Court of Appeal carried this approach so far that they seem (albeit unconsciously) to have merged this part of the law of contract into the law of tort. In this case the defendant carelessly signed a form in blank, thinking that he was acquiring a car on hire-purchase terms from a dealer R. In fact the form was for a personal loan and R filled in the details contrary to the defendant's understanding, and in the result passed the form to the plaintiffs who accepted it in good faith. The Court held (in effect) that the defendant was liable on the contract because he had been guilty of negligence. They insisted that there was no distinction between signing a document in blank, and signing a completed document without reading or understanding it. 'Why', asked Megaw L.J.[44] 'should a careless act which results in the opposite party being misled as to one's contractual intentions be of less legal significance and effect than a careless act of not reading, or failing to understand, an existing completed document which is put before one to sign?' Why, indeed? But this is the language of tort, not contract. If a man is held liable on a contract because he has been negligent why should he then be liable as though he had promised? There are of course, important differences between contractual and tortious liability. For example, in contract, expectations are usually protected, while in tort cases of this kind, reliance damages only are usually recoverable. I need not pursue the point here, although it is of great importance for the future development of the law, both of contract and of tort. My purpose is to stress the movement away from consent as the basis of liability even in situations which are classified by lawyers as contractual.

It should be made clear that I do not suggest that questions of consent

---

[42] See especially *Saunders* v. *Anglia Building Society* [1971] A.C. 1004.

[43] [1975] 3 All E.R. 1017.

[44] At pp. 1022–3.

are irrelevant to liabilities such as those discussed above. A person who signs a written document, knowing that it is a document which imposes some liability upon him, does plainly consent to bear some liability, even if he does not consent to the whole liability that the document in fact imposes. But what I wish to argue is that these liabilities are not *purely* consensual, or promise-based. The elements of reliance and of reciprocity of benefit remain of the most profound importance in such circumstances. For instance, if the transaction is in fact one which provides for a fair exchange, so that the party signing the document will receive a reciprocal benefit of approximately equal value, the judicial attitude is likely to be far more favourable to maintaining the liability, than it would be if the document in fact was outrageously unfair. Yet the fairness or unfairness of the exchange is barely relevant to the question of consent. In both situations there is a vague consent to something, but the subsequent liability is at least partly benefit-based. Similarly, if there is in fact no element of reliance (for instance, if the deceived person were to attempt to withdraw from the transaction after a formal 'acceptance' but before anything had been done under it) there would, it is suggested, be a strong case for permitting such withdrawal. The reliance element in the transaction might thus be given paramountcy in such circumstances over the expectation element which would govern if this were a genuine promise-based liability.

More broadly, I suggest that there is today a growing recognition that, even where parties enter into a transaction as a result of some voluntary conduct, the resulting rights and duties of the parties are, in large part, a product of the law, and not of the parties' real agreement. Of course this does not necessarily hold true of a carefully negotiated commercial document, every clause of which is hammered out between the parties and their legal advisers. But even contracts of this character do not successfully foresee every contingency or avoid every ambiguity, and any resultant dispute must be solved by an active judicial decision, not by the purely passive interpretive process which formalism takes to be the judicial role.[45] And such contracts are anyhow the exception in life as a whole, though they may not be exceptional in the Chambers of a barrister. Perhaps more typical of everyday life is the 'implied contract' created by such acts as boarding a bus, or ordering a meal in a restaurant, or even taking up a new job. These are all actions involving some degree of consensuality. Companies do not run buses by accident, and passengers do not board buses in their sleep. But it does not follow that the classical model of contract which sees such relationships as involving 'mutual

---

[45] See e.g., Young, 'Equivocation in the Making of Agreements', 64 *Columbia Law Rev.* 619 (1964); Farnsworth, 'Meaning in the Law of Contracts', 76 *Yale Law Journal* 939 (1967); Corbin on *Contract*, revised ed., vol. iii, sect. 535 (1962).

promises' has any real validity to it. It is true that the bus company and the passenger have rights and liabilities which arise out of their relationship, and it is also true that in the great majority of cases, both parties have some notion, however hazy it may be on one side, of what those rights and duties are. But even then it does not follow that it is their consent, their joint act of will, which creates the rights and duties. It is surely more realistic to recognize that it is their actions which create the relationship, and the law which creates the rights and liabilities as a result of those actions. The 'implied promises' are often largely fictitious, and it would not matter a whit if they were proved to be non-existent. A passenger who boards a bus intending not to pay his fare is just as liable as though he had acted honestly, and it is not unlikely that the bus company's liability towards him is also the same, whether he has a ticket or not. Even where both parties concur or acquiesce in the result prescribed by the law, it would seem more accurate to follow Hume and treat these as cases of co-operative acts done 'in agreement' rather than as examples of 'making an agreement'.[46]

I cannot explore this theme at the length which its importance deserves, but it is at least worth noting that there are some slight signs of judicial movement along these lines. It will be recalled that in the classical period the Courts decided that, once a relationship involving mutual rights and duties was shown to exist, mutual promises could be implied.[47] This was not a surprising move to an intellectual tradition still under the influence of Locke and his successors, for was the social contract not itself a recognition of this sense of implied promise? In English law this idea subsequently hardened into a rigid rule of law to the effect that, wherever a contractual relation did subsist between parties, their rights and liabilities depended solely on the contract and could not be laid in tort.[48] But very recently, there have been indications that this movement has reached its limits. Lord Denning has, indeed, argued that the modern decisions are irreconcilable with *Boorman* v. *Brown*[49] which was the origin of the whole doctrine that duties arising out of reciprocal relationships could be treated as contractual.[50]

I turn now to consider a number of other illustrations of the declining importance of consent in contractual relationships. There are, first, a number of situations where a party's freedom to contract or not to contract, his freedom to choose with whom he shall contract, has been whittled down. The new anti-discrimination laws, which prohibit (in various circumstances) discrimination on grounds of racial origin, or on

[46] *Supra*, p. 56.
[47] *Supra*, p. 416.
[48] *Groom* v. *Crocker* [1939] 1 K.B. 194.
[49] (1844) 11 Cl. & F. 1, 8 E.R. 1003 *supra*, p. 416.
[50] See *Esso Petroleum* v. *Mardon* [1976] 2 All E.R. 5.

grounds of sex, are illustrations of this tendency. The arbitrary caprice of a would-be contracting party is no longer tolerable in matters of this nature, where free choice is overridden by socially set values. Refusal to enter into a contract may also be prohibited on economic grounds, as where a party refuses to supply goods to another as a result of some restrictive practice prohibited by law. A supplier cannot refuse to supply goods to a retailer, for instance, merely because the retailer refuses to abide by recommended resale prices.[51] Indeed, the whole notion that a party is the sole judge of whether he will contract with another is no longer acceptable in the commercial supply of goods. The Monopolies Commission has, in recent years, explored the possible justifications for refusal to supply goods in the commercial sphere, and has examined the cases, one by one.[52] For example, the supplier is still thought entitled to make up his own mind as to the credit-worthiness of a customer, and in this respect his judgment is absolute; but the Monopolies Commission judged it contrary to public policy for a supplier to refuse supplies because (for instance) he wants to limit the number of outlets at which his goods can be sold.

Although the Report referred to above has not been implemented by legislation, there is little doubt that the trend it reflects is one which is observable in the common law as well. The absoluteness of contractual rights, the refusal of the Courts to examine the reasons for a contracting party's decisions, which was so much a feature of the classical law, has been giving way to judicial willingness to look into the facts, to examine reasons for decisions, and to judge of their reasonableness by some objective tests. The contrasting attitudes across a century are well illustrated by a comparison of the decisions of the House of Lords in *Bowes* v. *Shand*[53] in 1877, and in *Reardon Smith Line* v. *Hansen Tangen*[54] in 1976. In the first case the Lords held that a contract for the sale of Madras rice to be shipped in March and/or April was violated because some of the rice was loaded on the ship in February, and they went on to hold that it was immaterial why the buyer rejected the rice, or why the contract was in this form. Lord Cairns, delivering the leading judgment, insisted that these were solely matters for the parties, and that it was not the business of the Courts to inquire into the reasons for the parties' actions. By contrast, in the second case a contract was made for the construction of a ship at 'Yard No. 354 at Osaka Zosen' in Japan. In fact the ship was built at a different yard, and the defendants declined to accept it although there was no suggestion that the ship did not comply

---

[51] Resale Prices Act 1976, sect. 11, first enacted in Resale Prices Act 1964.

[52] See their Report, *Refusal to Supply*, Cmnd. 4372 (1970). See too *Acrow (Automation) Ltd.* v. *Rex Chainbelt Inc.* [1971] 3 All E.R. 1175.

[53] 2 App. Cas. 455.

[54] [1976] 3 All E.R. 570.

with the contract specification. In this case the Lords did examine the circumstances of the contract in an attempt to discover why the parties had described the ship to be built in this way. And it was evident from this examination that the reference to the number and situation of the yard was of no substantial significance; the defendants were therefore held liable. It is difficult not to think that the different approaches in these two cases reflect the changes in the judicial process and the values of the Courts in the various respects I have already suggested. On the one hand, there is the much greater willingness to examine the facts of a case in detail to see where the merits lie, and on the other hand, there is no longer the same judicial willingness to accept the parties as the ultimate and sole arbiters of the importance of matters arising in the performance of a contract.

A similar example of the elimination of the absolute power of contracting parties as to the exercise of their rights is to be found in section 19 of the Landlord and Tenant Act 1927. This section provided that where a lease gave the tenant power to assign but subject to the consent of the landlord, in future the consent was not to be 'unreasonably withheld'. The consent of the landlord can thus be dispensed with where the Court regards its use as unreasonable. The landlord is deprived of the rights to choose who he is to have as his tenant, a choice which (as we have seen) is also largely taken from the landlord in the case of agricultural land or rent-controlled premises. This again involves a movement away from the broad sweeping principles of classical law, to the detailed factual inquiry so prevalent in the modern law. If the landlord's refusal of consent is to be challenged, the reasons for his actions must be inquired into. Inevitably, prolonged factual issues may be involved in such cases.

Another important statutory example of this kind of development is to be found in the new provisions against 'unfair dismissal' in contracts of employment. At common law, the power of an employer to dismiss an employee, either without notice, in the case of misconduct or breach of duty, or with notice in other cases, was entirely a matter for him; however arbitrary or capricious his actions might be, he had an absolute right to dismiss an employee subject only to the terms of the contract. Since the Industrial Relations Act 1971, however, this right is no longer untrammelled, but must be exercised subject to the discretion of the Industrial Tribunals to rule the dismissal 'unfair'. In deciding this question the Tribunal is not confined to matters of strict contract but must have regard to a variety of considerations enumerated (now) in the Trade Union and Labour Relations Act 1974.[55] In particular, the reasons for the dismissal must be inquired into, and it is for the employer to show

[55] Schedule 1, Part II.

what his reasons were, and whether they were sufficient to justify the dismissal. Another similar development may be discerned in the new law relating to consumer credit where a refusal of credit now gives certain limited rights of redress to the customer.[56]

It cannot, however, yet be said to be accepted as a principle of the common law that reasons for the exercise of contractual powers are always open to examination. Conclusive evidence clauses are still often upheld by the Courts,[57] though it seems unlikely that such a clause would now be implied in the absence of strong words to that effect. A creditor is still entitled to pursue all legal remedies against his debtor, not only in order to obtain payment of his debts, but for collateral purposes, e.g., to have him made bankrupt and so disqualified from some office.[58] A landlord may still validly give his tenant notice to quit, assuming that he otherwise has this right, even though his purpose is to punish the tenant for giving evidence against him, and thus involves a contempt of Court.[59] Some of these decisions are, perhaps, to be explained by the continued vitality of the classical model in principle, despite its general decline in practice, some perhaps are of dubious validity today. On the whole the tendency to search for the reasons behind the exercise of contractual powers has been taken a good deal further in the United States than in England.[60]

I have referred in earlier chapters to the growth of the corporate State as one of the chief characteristics of modern society. Here, as elsewhere, the increase in the number and size of corporations and other organizations has had a significant effect, in a variety of ways, on the role of consent and free choice. At common law, when a person made a contract with another individual human being, he chose the person with whom he would contract. The person had a natural identity which made it evident that he was individually chosen, and he could not pass on the benefit or the burden of the contract to others. When companies came on the scene the Courts at first treated the different nature of their identity as immaterial to the law. A company was a legal personality, and when it entered into a contract, it was the legal identity of the company which mattered. Consequently it was held (for example) that a company had no greater power to assign the benefit or burden of a contract than a private individual had.[61] As late as 1945 it was held that a company had

[56] Consumer Credit Act 1974, Part X.

[57] See, e.g., *Haagerstrand* v. *Anne Thomas S.S. Co. Ltd.* (1904) 10 Com. Cas. 67; *Tredegar* v. *Hardwood* [1929] A.C. 72; *Kaye* v. *Hoskier & Dickinson* [1972] 1 W.L.R. 146; cf. *Docker* v. *Hyams* [1969] 1 W.L.R. 1060.

[58] *Fitzroy* v. *Cave* [1905] 2 K.B. 364.

[59] *Chapman* v. *Honig* [1963] 2 Q.B. 502, but note the dissenting judgment of Lord Denning.

[60] L. Friedman, *Contract Law in America* (Madison and Milwaukee, 1965) p. 190. Cf. e.g., *Dickhurst* v. *Norton* 173 N.W. 2nd 297 (1970) with *Chapman* v. *Honig, supra.*

[61] See, e.g., *Johnson* v. *Raylton* (1881) 7 Q.B.D. 438; *Griffith* v. *Tower Publishing Co.* [1897] 1 Ch. 21.

THE DECLINE OF FREE CHOICE AND CONSENT

prima facie no right to sub-contract dry cleaning work it had undertaken on behalf of the plaintiff,[62] and in 1940 the House of Lords solemnly decided that an employee of a company could not be 'transferred' without his consent to another company as a result of an amalgamation order made in the Chancery Division.[63] 'I had fancied,' said Lord Atkin, 'that ingrained in the personal status of a citizen under our laws was the right to choose for himself who he would serve; and that this right of choice constituted the main difference between a servant and a serf.'[64] But, it is scarcely necessary to say, this somewhat passionate rhetoric had little relationship to reality, for the de facto identity of a company does not depend on its legal personality but on the persons who own or (perhaps more accurately) those who manage it. And these parties may change without affecting the contractual status of an employee, while the technical alteration of legal personality was here held to amount to a dismissal of the servant. The fact that he had been working for three months under a non-existent contract (according to the decision of the Lords) seems to have been ignored.

In other respects, the law appears to have shown a greater recognition of the realities of modern circumstances, for contracts and debts are today far more readily transferable than they have ever been before. Since the Judicature Acts, the free assignment of debts (subject to very few exceptions for genuinely personal cases) has been recognized both at law and in Equity, and in practice, the assignment of book debts (factoring, and block discounting) is a substantial form of business. In all these cases a debtor can easily find that his original creditor has disappeared and that his debt is now owed to someone of whom he had never previously heard. Even where the new creditor is someone personally known to, and obnoxious to the debtor, he has no right to complain of this procedure.[65] The transfer of contractual burdens remains technically a greater problem in English law, perhaps because of the historical hangover from the classical days when free choice was so highly rated. It remains necessary to this day for the consent of the creditor to be obtained where it is proposed to transfer a liability, even where the transfer is of a relatively technical character, as where the composition of a firm changes by the retirement of one partner and the substitution of another. In the United States, which is hardly less dedicated to the philosophy of free choice, these technical problems have largely been overcome by treating the new partner as a debtor, while preserving the liability of the old partner as a sort of guarantor for the

---

[62] *Davies* v. *Collins* [1945] 1 All E.R. 247.

[63] *Nokes* v. *Doncaster Collieries* [1940] A.C. 1014. Perhaps significantly, the only Chancery law lord dissented.

[64] p. 1026.

[65] *Fitzroy* v. *Cave, supra.*

firm's debts. In this way the position of the creditor is safeguarded against real prejudice, while in the majority of instances, where there is no risk of insolvency, the actual burdens of the contract are transferable.

Another example of the influence of corporation law on the importance of free choice and consent is the growing importance which it has given to the concept of majority rule. If several persons join together in an organization, their act of creation may be a contractual act; but the new organization, once it exists, must have executive and legislative machinery, and such machinery is usually operable only on the basis of majority rule. The result is that an individual who has joined an organization on one basis, may find himself subjected to liabilities or deprived of rights, not by virtue of any agreement to the liabilities or the deprivation of the rights, but by virtue of his agreement to the principle of majority rule. In one of the earliest cases of this nature to come before the higher Courts, *Auld* v. *Glasgow Working Men's Building Society*,[66] the defendant building society had a set of rules which provided that its members could withdraw their shares in rotation, if funds were inadequate. The society having lost a substantial amount of its capital, decided that members should no longer be entitled to withdraw their money in rotation, but that a sum should be deducted from each share. The plaintiff objected to this change, and the House of Lords (dominated by common lawyers) upheld his claim. Common law judges like Halsbury and Bramwell appear to have been shocked at the idea that one party to a contract could unilaterally alter its terms to the prejudice of the other party. To Lord Halsbury, 'it [was] utterly unarguable and impossible to insist that any such power exists. A bargain is a bargain and must be kept.'[67] Lord Macnaghten, the only Chancery member of the House, and newly appointed at that, may have been somewhat intimidated by these vigorous expressions of opinion from the leading common lawyers of the day, and he expressed his concurrence in a brief speech in which, however, he said that the Building Society's mistake was that it had tried to alter its rules in a manner not conforming to the statutory power of alteration.

After this decision, a whole series of cases came before the lower Courts, in all of which Lord Macnaghten's observations were followed, and it was held that so long as the rules were altered in accordance with the statutory procedures, no member could complain that he was being deprived of his contractual rights.[68] His rights, it was now said, must be

---

[66] (1887) 12 App. Cas. 197.

[67] p. 202.

[68] See, e.g., *R.* v. *Brabrook* (1893) 69 L.T. 718; *Rosenberg* v. *Northumberland Building Society* (1889) 22 Q.B.D. 373; *Wilson* v. *Miles Platting Building Society* (1887) 22 Q.B.D. 381n.; *Allen* v. *Gold Reefs of West Africa Ltd.* [1900] 1 Ch. 656; *Strohmenger* v. *Finsbury Permanent Building Society* [1897] 2 Ch. 469; *Pepe* v. *City and Suburban Building Society* [1893] 2 Ch. 311; *Shuttleworth* v. *Cox* [1927] 2 K.B. 9.

read subject to the statutory powers of alteration.[69] Some of these decisions today look quite outrageously unfair, such as decisions holding that borrowers from a building society were 'members' (as technically they were) and could be made, by a change in the rules, to bear a share of the losses incurred by the society.[70] It is also interesting to note that the Chancery judges nearly always seem to have been more willing to accede to the powers of the majority to bind minorities. As late as 1940 there is evidence of the persistence of this traditional distinction in attitudes between common law and Chancery judges. This case[71] was an attempt to take the earlier decisions even further, in that it sought to give the majority shareholders of a company the power, by changing the articles of association, to alter the rights of a member, not as a member, but as a director. Both in the Court of Appeal (which split, two judges to one) and the House of Lords (which divided, three to two) the majority of common lawyers upheld the sanctity of the original contract, and the Chancery judges would have upheld the power of the majority to alter the rules. The origins of this difference in attitude must surely go far back in history. As we have seen, it was the common lawyers who created the classical model of contract, and the Chancery lawyers who modified it in a variety of respects. It was the Chancery lawyers, too, with their long traditions in the drafting of strict settlements, and later deeds of partnership and company documents, who saw the need for machinery to preserve long-term institutional arrangements, while it was the common lawyers who saw contracts as discrete events, transactions made in the market place and then binding for good.

In view of my suggestions about the evidentiary role of promises in early law, it is interesting also to observe the revival of this idea in cases where a consent is given, but for one reason or another, it is not absolutely binding. For example, in cases under the Moneylenders Acts, it was held that the agreement of the borrower as to the rate of interest he was to pay, although not strictly binding, was by no means irrelevant to the fairness of the transaction. Plainly if the borrower is ignorant, or imposed upon, his agreement to pay the interest demanded may be no real evidence of its fairness. But where the borrower is well informed, and not in seriously embarrassed circumstances, his agreement may be evidence at least of a fair and equitable transaction.[72] Similarly, under the Statute

---

[69] See too Lord Loreburn's memorandum to his Cabinet colleagues arguing for the overruling of the *Osborne* case [1910] A.C. 87, printed in R. Heuston, *Lives of the Lord Chancellors 1885–1940* (Oxford, 1964), p. 615.

[70] *Wilson* v. *Miles Platting Building Society, supra.* There are signs of a revolt against these extreme decisions in *Hole* v. *Garnsey* [1930] A.C. 472.

[71] *Southern Foundries Ltd.* v. *Shirlaw* [1940] A.C. 701.

[72] See *Carrington Ltd.* v. *Smith* [1906] 1 K.B. 79, 86 approved in *Reading Trust Ltd.* v. *Spero* [1930] 1 K.B. 492.

of Frauds, cases have occurred in which parol agreements have been unenforceable under the Statute, but the terms of the agreement have nevertheless been held good evidence of the value of services actually rendered in pursuance of the unenforceable contract.[73] It is strange that lawyers feel unable or unwilling to recognize that such claims are 'truly' contractual. The doctrinal explanation of such decisions is that the 'actual' contract is void or unenforceable, but that payment is due for any services actually rendered and accepted as a quasi-contractual right. Such a right, according to the conventional doctrine has 'no relationship' with contract, and is indeed scarcely worth considering in a book on the law of contract. It is surely plain that this attitude is a historical hangover. Only to a generation of lawyers brought up to regard absolutely binding consent as the one hallmark of 'true' contract, can this explanation be regarded as satisfying. To anyone who cares to take a broader perspective, and to recognize that many contractual obligations arise under part executed transactions, and that absolutely binding consent is not necessarily the mark of contract, cases of this nature make perfectly good sense as contractual decisions.

Moreover, as previously mentioned, one of the notable features of legal developments of the past century has been the increasing number of situations in which payment may be recovered for benefits conferred, even in the absence of actual consent on the part of the beneficiary. In public law, of course, this has always been a possibility, though here too instances of its application are far more frequent than they were a hundred years ago. Although judges may continue to proclaim the contractual dogma that a person cannot claim payment for benefits thrust upon another without his choice, public law is constantly making citizens pay for benefits thrust upon them without their choice. Frequently the relationship between the benefits conferred and the payments demanded is not close, as with ordinary taxation which is levied to pay for many benefits which the citizen might reject if he had the choice. But there are other cases where the payment levied bears a direct and close relationship to the benefit offered. To take one example from many, local authorities may require the drains of a building to be connected to the main sewer, and if the owner does not have the work done, they may do it themselves and charge appropriately.

Compulsory Contracts

The decline of free choice in contracting has led to a growth in the number and variety of situations in which some form of compulsory

---

[73] *Scarisbrick v. Parkinson* (1869) 20 L.T. 175; *Way v. Latilla* [1937] 3 All E.R. 759. See too the past consideration cases where it came to be said that a subsequent promise might be evidence of the reasonable sum which the promisor was already bound to pay: *Stewart v. Casey* [1892] 1 Ch. 104.

exchange may be imposed on a party. Because of the heritage of the classical tradition, to refer to these exchanges as 'compulsory contracts' seems a solecism, a contradiction in terms. Yet the truth is that the elements of pressure which induce a person to enter into a contract vary so much that it is anyhow hard to draw a line between cases which can be said to be examples of complete free choice, and those in which there is no element of free choice at all. In the classical law this problem was solved by the peculiar uses to which will theory was put. It was assumed that all contracts were the result of 'free choice' (no matter how great the pressures might be) unless the party's will was 'overborne' so that he could not be said to exercise any real choice at all. But this analysis of the nature and effect of pressures on contracting parties has never been satisfactory. Commercial, economic, or social pressures may be such as to leave a person with no effective choice by the standards of modern life, yet these pressures were ignored by the classical law. Equally, other forms of obviously acceptable pressure were also ignored; for example, nobody ever doubted that judicial bonds or recognizances, though entered into under the threat of imprisonment for refusal, were (and are) binding. Then, too, there were certain types of compulsory transaction which were common enough to be referred to as though they were compulsory contracts. Compulsory acquisition of land, for instance, has long been called 'compulsory purchase' and a formal order for such acquisition is known as a 'compulsory purchase order'. It should be stressed that, though local authorities do have the power to acquire land against the wishes and without the consent of the owner, this procedure by no means rules out some element of consent, or some element of choice. It is, for instance, usual for a local authority to attempt to negotiate a purchase with the owner in the ordinary way prior to exercise of powers of compulsory acquisition. And even though the owner may feel he has little choice but to sell in view of these powers in the background, there may still be acquiescence, or even willingness to sell on his part. The existence of the statutory powers does not in any event ensure that they will be available when the time comes—appeals may be possible, changes of mind by the appropriate committees of the authority cannot be ruled out—so that it is not true to say that there is never any element of consent or free choice in such negotiations. And even where the owner does feel that he is being compelled to sell, and would not do so if he did not feel so compelled, there is still room for genuine agreement over the price. Here, too, of course, if there is no agreement, the matter must be decided by the appropriate authority—the Lands Tribunal—but only a minority of cases of compulsory purchase reach the Tribunal.

Now I do not wish to suggest that there is no important difference between transactions of this nature, and freely negotiated contracts in an open market; obviously there are differences, but equally there are close similarities. In both types of case an exchange takes place, and in both cases there may be some degree of assent on the part of the two parties; in the free market the element of free choice is usually stronger—though market pressures may be just as coercive as statutory powers in certain circumstances—while in the compulsory purchase case, there is machinery for ensuring an objectively fair or just price which does not exist in the free market. What I wish to suggest here is that it is no longer justifiable to insist that the bare existence or use of some powers of compulsion makes the resultant transaction so different from a free market contract that it is of no interest to a contract lawyer.[74] An example of the unreasonable results which sometimes ensue from the classical heritage, with its insistence on the paramountcy of free choice as the hall mark of contract, is to be found in *Kirkness* v. *John Hudson & Co. Ltd.* in 1955.[75] It was here held by the House of Lords that profits made by a company as a result of the compulsory acquisition of its railway wagons under the railway nationalization statute, were not taxable as profits made 'on a sale'. A sale, insisted the Lords, required a consensual transaction. This was no more consensual than robbery. 'To say of a man who has had his property taken from him against his will and been awarded compensation in the settlement of which he had no voice, to say of such a man that he has sold his property appears to me to be as far from the truth as to say of a man who has been deprived of his property without compensation that he has given it away.'[76] I suggest that this kind of language is the heritage of classical contract theory, and is now outdated. Doubtless, special considerations may affect the construction of words in a taxing statute, but the result of awarding compensation for nationalized property is so closely analogous to a freely negotiated sale, that the decision in this case appears hard to justify.

Part of the problem is, of course, definitional. If contracts are defined as transactions in which mutual consent is of the essence, then it follows that cases of outright compulsion ought not be be defined as contract. But definitions of legal concepts do not fall from heaven; they are adopted to collect together cases which have sufficient in common to make it worthwhile to categorize them under one heading. Certainly for many purposes compulsory exchanges have sufficient in common with voluntary exchanges to make it fruitful to treat them together. In both cases the exchange of benefit for benefit is the essence of the transaction. Moreover, precisely because such compulsory exchanges have not traditionally been treated as, or even as analogous to, contracts, lawyers

---

[74] See Patterson 'Compulsory Contracts in the Crystal Ball', 43 *Columbia Law Rev.* 731 (1943).
[75] [1955] A.C. 696.
[76] Lord Simonds at p. 707; cf. *post*, p. 749.

are generally unaware of the very many cases in which the law does make provision for such compulsory exchanges. Since the category of 'compulsory exchange' has never been regarded as one worth adopting in the past, the wide variety of situations in which such transactions may take place have never been brought together and their relationship to voluntary exchanges explored. I propose here to give some idea of the variety and extent of compulsory contracting in the modern law, though I have no space for a full survey.

It is perhaps, worth beginning by recalling one type of situation where lawyers have traditionally, and without qualms, treated a case as contractual even though genuine assent is absent. Cases of misunderstanding,[77] unread documents,[78] revocations which arrive too late,[79] and similar situations, may all produce a result in which one party is held to a contract to which he did not really assent. As Max Radin put the point over thirty years ago:

> If the objective theory is really as fundamental in our system as is so often said, it is hard to see why 'compulsory' contracts should seem so abhorrent to the common lawyer, who so frequently boasts of his contempt for mere verbalism. All obligatory transactions are compulsory by the fact of being obligatory. And if a man is compelled to carry out what he never meant or what he did not quite understand—and that is often implied in the 'objective theory'—merely because his words or acts might reasonably be assumed to carry certain implications, we have something not very different from contracts made for parties by statutes or regulations.[80]

Similarly, lawyers have never had any difficulty in treating obligations as contractual so long as some preliminary assent was given which can be stretched to govern the resulting liabilities. For example, a person who grants an option to purchase land or stock, or a right of pre-emption, may find himself compelled to contract when the time comes. Of course, in this situation, the original consent to the arrangements can be seen as justifying the classification of the ultimate contract as itself based on consent; but it must be borne in mind how very far this can go. We have, for instance, already seen something of the cases in which an original assent to the rules of an association have been held to justify holding a party liable on the basis of changes in the rules to which he was violently opposed. Again, the party who is compelled to enter into a contract as a result of some prior agreement may often be a successor of the party who made the previous agreement. A man who buys land which is subject to an existing option to purchase is (if the option is duly registered) bound

---

[77] See, e.g., *Riverlate Properties Ltd.* v. *Paul* [1975] Ch. 133.

[78] *Saunders* v. *Anglia Building Society* [1971] A.C. 1004, *supra*, p. 733.

[79] *Byrne* v. *Van Tienhoven* (1880) 5 C.P.D. 344.

[80] 'Contract Obligation and the Human Will', 43 *Columbia Law Rev.* 575, 575, n.4 (1943).

by the option, whether or not he knew of its existence. In due form of conveyancing, he should, of course, discover the existence of the option by searching the register, and if he buys the land, with knowledge of its existence, he may be said in a sense to agree to it. But the reality is that he has no choice in the matter if he wants to buy the land. He is bound, not because of any assent or agreement, reluctant acquiescence, or even dissent; he is bound because the option is registered, and that fact benefits the buyer in that it (probably) reduces the price he pays for the property.

The land law, indeed, is today an area in which a great deal of compulsory contracting takes place. The question of compensation for benefits conferred became a major public issue in the 1870s and 1880s in connection with agricultural tenancies, as we saw earlier. The demand of tenants' for compensation for fixtures and improvements was a demand for recompense for benefits conferred upon the landlord without his consent. We have seen too how this demand was backed by arguments based upon economic efficiency, on the ground that the absence of any right to compensation was a hindrance to the development of the land. These arguments may have been unsound, at least in theory, since there is no apparent reason why landlords and tenants should not make appropriate bargains which would supply the necessary inducement to invest. But in fact such bargains were not made, mainly as a result of customary practices, and in due course the demand for tenants' rights became too strong to be resisted. It may well be that the immediately precipitating cause in favour of the legislation was the general agricultural depression of the 1880s caused by a run of bad harvests in England, and the beginning of the arrival of cheap imported grain and other foodstuffs from the United States. The first, very modest, legislative measure was passed in 1875, but the first effective Act was the Agricultural Holdings Act of 1883, section 1 of which provided for the payment of compensation for improvements of 'such sum as fairly represents the value of the improvement to an incoming tenant'. The principle embodied in this Act, together with the tenant's right to remove (or be paid for) fixtures, has remained in the law ever since,[81] and indeed, it has been extended to other forms of leases, notably to business leases.[82]

It is worth pausing to reflect on some of the legal implications of these provisions. It will be seen, in the first place, that this legislation reflects the downgrading of the element of consent in contractual relationships. The landlord's consent in the matter of improvements and fixtures is

[81] Now in Agricultural Holdings Act 1948.

[82] Landlord and Tenant Act 1927; Landlord and Tenant Act 1954. The 1954 Act was preceded by the Report of the Committee on Leasehold. See the *Interim Report* (Cmnd. 7706, 1949) and the *Final Report* (Cmnd. 7982, 1950), especially Chapter VII.

largely treated by the Acts as unnecessary; indeed, even his express disapproval (for instance in a lease) is ineffective because contracting out of the Acts is not permissible. What matters is not whether the landlord consents to the improvements, but whether he is benefited by them. In some cases, for example, of more permanent or more substantial improvements, the landlord's consent may still be required, but even in these cases, there has been a progressive decline in the landlord's rights. Today, for example, the approval of the Agricultural Lands Tribunal will usually suffice in lieu of the landlord's consent even for major developments.

It is also worth noting one particular respect in which this legislation shows its relationship to contractual ideas and contractual doctrines. For, in the earlier Acts, at least, the tenant was specifically debarred from claiming compensation in respect of any improvements which he was under an obligation to carry out by the terms of his lease. It will be seen that this principle is, in essence, the same as the rule of contract doctrine that something which a person is already bound to do cannot constitute good consideration. It was evidently felt that no real benefit could be said to accrue to the landlord so long as he was only getting what he was already entitled to under the terms of the lease. But since the Agriculture Act 1920 this requirement has been eliminated for agricultural tenancies, though it was preserved in the case of business tenancies by the Landlord and Tenant Acts 1927 and 1954. Parliament has evidently had as much trouble as the Courts with this particular problem.

It may, of course, be said by supporters of traditional contract doctrine that these statutory changes do not affect the principles of the common law which continue to govern where no statute operates. No doubt this is true; but the values of judges can change, and they tend to change as public and Parliamentary opinion change too. Judges do not have the same extensive legislative powers as Parliament, of course, but in the interstitial legislation which they do have power to make, these values may come to predominate. Certainly, in this particular field of tenants' rights, there are signs of a growing sympathy with claims for compensation on some customary ground towards the end of the nineteenth century,[83] although in the end most of these claims were subsumed under the statutory claims.

Apart from agricultural leases the modern land law affords many instances of compulsory contracts. The protection of tenants from eviction on the expiry of a residential lease leads to a 'statutory tenancy' in which the relations of landlord and tenant continue, whatever the landlord may wish. Most landlords acquiesce in this result because they have to; but whether they acquiesce or not, the legal result is the same.

[83] See *Bradburn* v. *Foley* (1878) 3 C.P.D. 129.

Similarly, since 1954 there have been limited provisions giving business tenants the right to a renewal of a lease, against the will of the landlord. Here too, where the law is clear, landlords acquiesce and new leases may be negotiated by agreement. But it makes little difference whether the landlord agrees, or whether the tenant has to obtain a court order. The renewed lease will be binding, with or without the landlord's consent. Of course, it would make a difference if there were no statutory compulsion, for the rent to be negotiated might be significantly different in that case; that is irrelevant to the present point which is that the renewed lease will be treated by the law as having the same validity as a freely negotiated contractual lease.

Since the Leasehold Reform Act 1967 there has existed an even more drastic type of compulsory contracting, whereby a tenant of a leasehold house may acquire, in certain circumstances, and subject to various limitations, the freehold of the premises without the consent of the landlord. Of course, in these, as in many other instances of compulsory contracting, the purposes of the compulsion are to affect the price to be paid. In the case of leasehold enfranchisement, there would normally have been anyhow little problem in a tenant purchasing the freehold at a freely negotiated market price. The purpose of the statutory scheme, as was plainly admitted, was to enable the buyer to acquire the freehold at less than the market price; in fact the object was to enable the buyer to buy the freehold at the price which it would bear if the landlord had no reversionary rights to the property at the expiration of the lease. This scheme had been discussed by the Leasehold Committee in 1950 where traditional arguments about freedom of contract had had yet another airing.[84] The majority of the Committee had rejected the proposal for enfranchisement on the ground that it would simply give valuable rights to tenants at the expense of landlords for their own personal benefit, and 'this in the teeth of the bargain actually made'.[85] It was, in effect, a proposal for the expropriation of part of the landlords' assets without compensation.[86] The minority, including a former Labour Solicitor-General, Sir Lynn Ungoed-Thomas, later a judge, disagreed:[87] 'We take the view', they said, 'that there is no sanctity in a contract which is unjust. This is a principle which is deeply imbedded in the thought and the law of our country and from it sprang those equitable doctrines which provided relief against unconscionable bargains, originally in the case of expectant heirs for whom the authorities of those days were particularly tender, and later in other cases in which the parties had not met upon equal terms.'[88] It is, nevertheless, difficult to understand what is unjust

---

[84] See the *Final Report* of the Committee, Cmnd. 7982 (1950).
[85] Para. 76.   [86] Para. 89.   [87] pp. 139-44.
[88] The minority's account of this historical development is (as we have seen) somewhat misleading.

about the terms of the ordinary long lease, unless it is to be supposed that the mere relationship of landlord and tenant carries an implication of injustice. To most lawyers this would seem a preposterous idea, and yet the legislation was ultimately passed by a Parliament for whom this was presumably the case. Here, therefore, is a frankly redistributive piece of legislation. Freedom of contract was rejected because the underlying distribution of property was thought to be unjust. In its anxiety to use any weapon for redistributive purposes, Parliament unfortunately overlooks the extreme inefficiency—not to say unfairness—of redistribution by such means as these.

Company law, like the land law, provides plenty of instances of compulsory contracting. Apart from the point, previously made, that all shareholders in a company hold their shares subject to any changes which the company may make, by appropriate procedures (and sometimes by appropriate majorities), there are provisions relating to variations of class rights by special majority votes, though here there may be a right to appeal to the Court. So too, a take-over bidder who succeeds in acquiring ninety per cent of the shares in a company has a statutory right to acquire the balance of the shares, over the dissent of the owners. It seems fanciful to suggest that these forms of compulsion are justifiable on the ground of some original, shadowy assent, given by implication when a person acquires shares in a company. It is surely more satisfactory to explain these as cases in which the agreement of a large majority to particular arrangements is good evidence of the fairness of those arrangements (especially when there is some appellate judicial supervision) and that the compulsory powers are designed to overcome the arbitrary, capricious or obstinate refusal of a minority to co-operate in an arrangement for the advantage of the great majority.

Another major area in which compulsory contracting is to be found is in the very judicial process itself. The remedial powers of judges frequently extend to ordering parties to enter into contractual relations. Apart from obvious cases where the Court is merely decreeing specific performance of an agreement previously made, the Court has extensive powers in a variety of other situations, to authorise what are, in effect, compulsory contracts. One of the most striking examples of this power is to be found in section 210 of the Companies Act 1948 which enables a Court to order a party guilty of oppressive conduct towards other shareholders to buy their shares at a price fixed by the Court. In the leading case on these powers, Lord Simonds spoke without apparent qualms of the resultant transaction as a 'purchase', and of the consideration for it as the 'price'.[89]

---

[89] *Scottish Co-operative Wholesale Society* v. *Meyer* [1959] A.C. 324. Cf. Lord Simonds's views cited above, p. 744.

An instance of the power of the Courts to impose a compulsory contract on parties, which derives from their own inherent jurisdiction, and not from any statutory grant, is to be found in the practice relating to undertakings as to damages. Where a party claims an interim injunction, or other interim relief, it is today the almost invariable practice of the Courts to require the claimant to give an undertaking that, if he is subsequently found to have no right to such a remedy, he will pay compensation to the other party for the loss caused by the interim order.[90] 'Precisely because this procedure is so obviously just, it is almost universal.'[91] In effect, these orders impose a compulsory contract on the parties (or at least on the party enjoined), the one party being enjoined temporarily, and the other being required to agree to compensate him for any ensuing loss.

But there is yet another area of law in which the Courts are called upon every day to construct contracts for the parties, to impose on them some sort of a judicially sanctioned exchange. Much of the law of torts, in one sense, is designed to achieve these purposes. A party with a claim in tort can 'sell' that claim to the tortfeasor at a price to be agreed, or failing agreement, at a price to be fixed by the Court. Since the great majority of tort claims are in fact settled by agreement, it is not difficult to see a tort action as a procedure for constructing a contract by which one party is compelled to pay for the buying of the other party's rights. This is obviously a somewhat unfamiliar perspective on tort law, and it may be that it is not particularly helpful in the typical tort action of modern times, that is in the action for damages for personal injuries. It may seem artificial to see such an action as a judicially-imposed contract, but this arises chiefly from the peculiar nature of personal injury actions. These are nearly always cases in which the damage has been caused unintentionally, and they are moreover, cases involving 'goods' which have no market value. A tortfeasor who runs a pedestrian over is not, in any sense, 'buying' the injuries which he inflicts, and the pedestrian is certainly not selling them. However, that does not mean that the subsequent negotiations over the tort claim do not amount to an attempt to make a contract—indeed, they plainly do—nor does it mean that the actual trial of a tort claim is not an attempt to construct a contract for the parties. In one sense, this is precisely what the Court is engaged in doing when it assesses the damages in a tort case. Here again we observe how the maxim that the Court does not make a contract for the parties is only true by a process of definition. If the Court is engaged in making a

---

[90] For the origins of this practice see *Novello* v. *James* (1854) 5 De G. M. & G. 876, 43 E.R. 1111; *Smith* v. *Day* (1882) 21 Ch. D. 421; *Griffith* v. *Blake* (1884) 27 Ch. D. 474; *Howard* v. *Press Printers* (1904) 74 L.J. Ch. 100.

[91] *Hoffman La Roche & Co.* v. *Secretary of State* [1974] 2 All E.R. 1128 at 1146 (Lord Wilberforce).

contract for the parties, it turns out that we are in the realm of tort and not of contract.

But although this may not be a very helpful perspective in personal injury cases, there are other tort actions in which this surely is a useful point of view. Where the defendant has taken property from the plaintiff which has a measurable market value, and more especially, where he has taken property which the plaintiff might have been willing to sell, a tort action may closely resemble an arbitral agreement to fix a price. Some of the earliest cases to suggest this perspective are those in which the defendant has used the plaintiff's land in some unauthorized fashion, with resultant gain to himself. The plaintiff then has a remedy in an action of trespass, but cases may well occur in which the defendant has not significantly damaged the land by his use, or in which any damage is much less in value than the benefit which the defendant has obtained. In the last few decades of the nineteenth century there was, for instance, a series of 'way-leave' cases in which the defendant had 'taken' a benefit by exercising a right of way over the plaintiff's land without the plaintiff's consent. If such rights of way were used for business purposes (for example, for the transport of coal) the defendant might have gained significantly by the use so made, and yet the plaintiff's land might have been undamaged. An action in trespass would then seem to produce the result that the plaintiff would recover only nominal damages, a result which seemed manifestly unfair. The Courts consequently adopted a different approach to these cases, based more on unjust enrichment ideas, but in effect, constructing a contract ex post facto, whereby the defendant could be made to pay a fair price for what he had had. Not surprisingly, the attitude of the Courts differed according to whether the defendant had acted fraudulently or in good faith, but in both cases the analogy of a contract was observed. In one of the leading cases on the point, Lord Hatherley insisted that where fraud was shown the defendant would be penalized by being made to pay for the full value of what he had 'taken' without any allowance for the costs involved in doing so. But where the defendant had acted in good faith, 'the matter [was] not to be treated as a case of forced sale but as a case of a sale which [had] taken place by inadvertence.'[92] In effect, the Court here held that the inadvertent trespass by the defendant should be compensated by damages representing the sort of figure which the parties would have agreed upon if they had made a willing contract. There could scarcely be a clearer case of the Court making a contract for the parties.

It is worth observing that in cases of this nature the essential fact is that the defendant has obtained a benefit by his use of the plaintiff's property,

---

[92] *Livingstone v. Rawyards Coal Co.* (1880) 5 App. Cas. 25, 34 5. See also *Jegon v. Homfray* (1871) L.R. 6 Ch. 770; *Whitwham v. Westminster Brymbo Coal and Coke Co.* [1896] 2 Ch. 538.

and that the absence of agreement is largely immaterial to the result. The plaintiff is entitled to be compensated by an appropriate recompense for the benefit obtained by the defendant, and it is immaterial whether this is conceptually seen as a claim in tort for trespass, as a restitutionary claim for unjust enrichment, or as some sort of contract-without-consent claim.

A very similar situation may arise where a plaintiff claims damages for breach of a patent right. Here too, at least where the patent owner was exploiting the patent by licensing others to manufacture the patented goods on payment of a royalty, a claim which is nominally in tort, is in substance an action for recompense for the benefit obtained by the defendant. In a recent case before the House of Lords for example,[93] defendants had infringed the plaintiff's patent rights in the manufacture of vehicle tyres over a period of some twelve years. The whole question before the Courts was the proper method of calculating the damages, and in effect it was held that the Court's function was to ascertain what price, or royalty, would have been agreed by the parties if there had been an agreement. In searching for the terms of this hypothetical bargain, the House of Lords insisted that the Court must pay regard to the actual situation of the parties. The damages must represent the price which would probably have been agreed in a contract between these particular parties, not between some hypothetical 'reasonable' parties in a different situation. 'The "willing licensor" and "willing licensee" to which reference is often made . . . is always the actual licensor and the actual licensee who, one assumes are each willing to negotiate with the other—they bargain as they are, with their strengths and weaknesses, in the market as it exists.'[94]

Yet a third type of case where a similar situation arises is illustrated by a recent decision of the Court of Appeal in the field known as 'waiver of tort'. In this case the plaintiffs had sold goods for export to the defendant on cash-against-document terms. The defendant received the shipping documents but instead of paying for them or returning the documents, he accepted the documents, sent them on to his sub-buyers and failed to pay for them. It was plain enough that the plaintiffs were entitled to judgment for the value of the goods, but a question arose as to whether the plaintiffs were bound to elect between pursuing their claim in contract on the sale, or claiming damages in tort for conversion on the basis that the defendants had no right to deal with the documents without

---

[93] *General Tire & Rubber Co.* v. *Firestone Tyre & Rubber Co. Ltd.* [1975] 2 All E.R. 173. See too *Watson Laidlaw & Co.* v. *Pott, Cassels & Williamson* (1914) 31 R.P.C. 104.

[94] Lord Wilberforce at p. 185. Patent law also provides another instance of compulsory contracting in its provisions for the grant of a compulsory licence in certain cases, e.g., of medicines. See Report of the (Banks) Committee on *The British Patent System*, Cmnd. 4407 (1970), and Patents Act 1977, sect. 48.

paying for them. The Court held that no such election was necessary, as it was entirely immaterial whether the claim was treated as lying in contract or in tort. Thus the defendant, having received the goods, or documents of title, was liable to pay their value, whether the case was one of agreement or not. The essence of the liability was the receipt of the benefit.[95]

The importance of these cases for our purposes is that they show how, in various circumstances, the rights of the parties may be regulated in virtually the same manner when one obtains a benefit from the other, whether or not they have actually agreed on a price. Of course this does not mean that the element of consent ceases to have any significance. If, for example, a price has been agreed this will obviously provide evidence (often conclusive evidence) of what is a fair price and the court will be spared the necessity of fixing the price itself. Again, if there is evidence that the owner of the property would have refused to make any agreement at all, and that the defendant, knowing this fact, has simply helped himself to the plaintiff's property, it can be assumed that the Courts would adopt a more penal approach to the defendant's liability.

Another example of a species of compulsory contract arising out of the judicial process is to be found in cases where the Court has a discretion to award damages in lieu of an injunction for the breach of some restrictive covenant, or an easement or similar right. In one recent case,[96] for example, a number of houses were built in violation of a restrictive covenant, although there had been legal doubts about the enforceability of the covenant. In the result it was held that an injunction to demolish the houses would be refused but that the plaintiffs were entitled to damages in lieu. The assessment of damages was attended with some difficulty because the market price of the plaintiff's property was not affected, but the Court acknowledged that the plaintiffs might reasonably think the amenity value of their property was lowered. It was held that damages should be calculated on the basis of what sum might reasonably have been demanded by the plaintiffs as a quid pro quo for relaxing the covenant. This approach has, in principle, been available for many years, but the Courts have generally been wary of adopting it, principally (it seems) because it does indeed amount to making a contract for the parties.[97] If the Court, in the exercise of its discretion, chooses to grant an

---

[95] *Ernest Scragg & Son Ltd.* v. *Perseverance Banking & Trust Co.* [1973] 2 Lloyd's Rep. 101. See too Lord Pearce in *Nissan* v. *Attorney General* [1970] A.C. 179, 228: 'If an unwilling shopkeeper cannot prevent a powerful customer from carrying off something which he does not wish to sell he is entitled to sue him for the value without relying on tort. His cause of action may lie in contract . . .' How is this remarkable statement to be reconciled with definitions of contract in terms of agreement or promises?

[96] *Wrotham Park Estate Co.* v. *Parkside Homes Ltd.* [1974] 1 W.L.R. 798.

[97] See, e.g., the doubts of Lord Sumner, though dissenting, in *Leeds Industrial Co-operative Society* v. *Slack* [1924] A.C. 851.

injunction then the price of 'buying-off' the injunction will be entirely a matter for the parties. The fact that an injunction has been granted is not necessarily the end of the matter because the parties may still find it possible to come to an agreement whereby the injunction is waived in return for some consideration. Indeed, claims for breach of an easement or a restrictive covenant are commonly made, not in order to prevent the defendant from continuing with his proposed action, but in order to lay the foundation for a more powerful bargaining position.[98] A developer who wishes to build some multi-million pounds building may thus be held to ransom by some one claiming that his right to light will be infringed. In cases of this kind there are (it is suggested) good reasons for the Courts to be more willing to 'make a contract for the parties' because the situation is often a monopoly one, in which it cannot be assumed that the parties will reach agreement on a fair price. Recent cases suggest that the Courts are increasingly using this jurisdiction.[99]

The Decline of the Executory Contract

The third respect in which there has been a decline in the importance of consent in contractual matters relates to the role of the executory contract. I suggested in Part II that one of the most significant changes in contractual doctrine which marked the emergence of the classical model was the shift from the executed to the executory contract, the shift from emphasis on what the parties did, to what the parties agreed to do. I now suggest that in the last century there have been, in a variety of respects, signs of a reverse movement. Generally speaking there has been little recognition of this fact, because the hold of the classical model is still so powerful. The approach of textbooks and the whole conceptual structure of the law still places the formation of contract at the beginning of the subject, and such an approach naturally stresses the executory contract. But in these respects theory is lagging behind practice. The actual developments in the law indicate a decline in the central role of the executory contract.

I may begin by pointing to a general tendency in the law for a distinction to be drawn between a present consent and a consent to some future action, which may for convenience be referred to as a future consent. This distinction has always been present to a greater or lesser degree in parts of the law, and its importance is so manifest that only the power of the classical model of contract can explain why it has not been accorded the recognition it deserves. Consider, for instance, simple matters such as the distinction between a plea of guilty and an admission

---

[98] See, e.g., *Woollerton & Wilson Ltd.* v. *Richard Costain Ltd.* [1970] 1 All E.R. 483 where this must surely have been the case.

[99] See, e.g., *Shaw* v. *Applegate* [1978] 1 All E.R. 123.

out of Court. The former is a present consent, a present admission of the charge; the latter is a future consent, an indication of willingness to admit the charge before a Court. The former is always 'binding' (in the absence of any circumstances suggesting misunderstanding, mistake, etc.) but the latter is merely evidentiary. The fact that an accused has admitted the charge out of Court is evidence that he is indeed guilty, but it is not conclusive evidence, and it certainly does not bind him to plead guilty. A similar distinction exists between many types of void contract and valid contracts. A void contract is (usually) only void while it is executory; once executed, or (in some cases) even part executed, the transaction frequently stands. For example, betting losses cannot be sued for, but actual payment of betting losses cannot be recovered. Thus the consent of the party to a wager or bet is not binding on him, but his consent to actually parting with his money is perfectly valid. The difference is between a present and a future consent.[1] Again, a gratuitous and unrelied upon promise is not binding while still executory, but an executed gift is irrevocable.

Similarly, there are many forms of conduct to which a person may give a valid assent at the time, but as to which no binding future consent can be given. Acts of physical intimacy, for instance, can obviously be assented to at the time; but nobody would argue that such assent could be given so as to bind the party in the future. The only example of such binding future assent is to be found in the case of marriage, where, at common law, it was held that the wife irrevocably consented to sexual intercourse, so that her husband could not be guilty of rape upon her. But this example helps to illustrate the point I am making precisely because this is now felt to be an anachronism, and proposals have been made to amend the law on this point. Similarly, a person can validly consent to having a surgical operation performed upon him, but it is impossible to suppose that such a consent can be given in such a way as to make it irrevocable. All this is not to say that consent may not be given to some future conduct which will continue to be operative in the future, so long as there is no withdrawal of the consent. I merely make the point that in all these cases consent is plainly revocable, and in that sense is not binding as to the future.

Now this distinction is obviously of the greatest importance. For one thing, it is in the case of a present consent that the economic assumptions about the consumer knowing his own interest best are at their strongest. What a man consents to *now*, what he agrees to *now*, is what he *wants* to do. Plainly, the case for prohibiting him from giving such a present

---

[1] Surprisingly the *Report of the Royal Commission on Betting, Lotteries and Gaming*, Cmnd. 8190 (1949–51) fails to perceive the importance of this distinction. It is overlooked too by Devlin, *The Enforcement of Morals*, p. 54.

consent must be stronger than the case for restricting the validity of a future consent. And so too in the law of contract, the case for holding a man bound by a future consent is much weaker than the case for holding him bound by a present consent. Indeed, the very meaning of 'binding' is different in the two cases. In an executory situation, to hold a man bound is to compel him to carry through some performance, or at least to hold him liable for the consequences of not doing so. The onus is on the other party to invoke the law, if he can, to compel that performance. But to hold an executed transaction binding is, in a sense, the reverse. It is to recognize the validity of what has been done, to hold to the status quo. The onus of upsetting the transaction here is on the other party. Now a part executed transaction is obviously some way between a present and a future arrangement. The party who has already performed is seeking to hold the other party bound (or at least to recover his own performance) but there is no need to hold him bound himself. His situation is only that he cannot undo what has been done.

Now what I suggest here is that there has been, as I have said, a decline in the power of the executory contract, a growing belief that there is an important difference between a present and a future consent, a growing recognition that the opportunity to change one's mind is itself a valuable right which often outweighs the desirability of holding parties bound to some future arrangement. In the case of consumer contracts, at least, the evidence of this shift of opinion is quite striking, and has actually led to amendments of the law. In the Hire Purchase Act of 1964 provision was first made for a 'cooling-off' period in certain limited circumstances, that is where orders are obtained by door-to-door salesmen, and these provisions have been much extended by the Consumer Credit Act. But in actual practice, as opposed to law, the true position today appears to be that wholly executory consumer contracts are not in fact held binding on the consumer unless there is some specific agreement to the contrary, as for example, where an agreement provides that it is 'non-cancellable'. Generally speaking consumers today expect to have the right to cancel agreements, and while they are still wholly executory, such cancellation rights are almost invariably conceded. In some cases, extra-legal arrangements have been made which formalize (and limit) the right of cancellation. For instance, members of the British Travel Agents Association permit cancellation of holiday bookings up to six weeks before departure on forfeiture of any deposit paid. Thereafter, an increasing proportion of the price is levied, as the time of cancellation approaches the departure date. Thus 30 per cent of the cost is payable for cancellation within six weeks of departure, 45 per cent within four weeks, and 60 per cent within two weeks. But in other types of arrangements, cancellation is often permitted within broader limits.

Airlines, for instance, are very tolerant of last-minute cancellations, or even of a simple failure to appear. Hotels rarely expect to charge anything, except perhaps for last-minute cancellations where a room may be vacant as a result. Thus they expect to be protected against reliance losses (that is, the loss of the opportunity to let the room to some other person) but not against bare expectation losses (that is, the loss whether or not they could have let the room again).

There are, indeed, signs that consumers frequently expect cancellation rights even where the result is to impose reliance losses on the other party. Complaints have been made, for example, that theatres often refuse to cancel bookings once the tickets have been issued, even where the cancellation is so late that the theatre is deprived of the chance to sell the seat to someone else.[2] Similarly, consumers appear to have little notion of the costs involved in cancellation of contracts, and often expect to recover deposits even for goods which have been specially ordered. A Consumer Association official recently commented that they had 'quite a lot' of cases of this kind. '[Consumers] think that because they can claim their money back on faulty goods they can claim the money back every time. They can't. If something has been ordered—and the order put through—it all costs money. That's what a deposit is about. Such a complaint has no justice in it.'[3]

Similar issues lie at the root of a long-standing dispute about life insurance.[4] Many consumers regard life insurance as a form of investment, and they expect to be able to surrender policies and withdraw their money in much the same fashion as they can withdraw their funds from other investments. On behalf of those who surrender their policies it is said that it is difficult these days to make long-term arrangements which may involve forecasting the needs and resources of the insured and his family over a period of many years—an argument which plainly rejects the very concept of binding long-term consumer contracts. The life insurance companies, however, reject this concept of the life policy. They regard the policy as a long-term contract, and although they never refuse the consumer the right to cancel the policy, they do generally offer relatively low surrender values. The beneficiaries of this approach are, of course, the policy holders who maintain their policies throughout their whole length, and frequently obtain larger bonuses as a result of the many cancellations.

I have referred earlier to the modern conveyancing practice in England, whereby preliminary agreements for the purchase and sale of houses and land are almost always made 'subject to contract'. These words have an almost magical quality; their effect is to prevent any

---

[2] See *The Times*, 16 Oct. 1976 (correspondence columns).
[3] See *Sunday Times*, Colour Supplement, 14 Nov. 1976.
[4] See correspondence in *The Times*, February 1977 and leader, ibid., 12 Feb. 1977.

binding legal obligations attaching to the initial agreement. The theory of the matter is that the parties show by the use of this language that they do not intend to create legal relations. But it would seem more realistic to recognize that this practice was devised by the legal profession some fifty years ago, when people of relatively modest means and education began to buy houses, for the purpose of protecting purchasers from their own ignorance.[5] The purchase of a house is a significant transaction for most people, and many are unaware of the pitfalls they may encounter which may prevent them from completing a purchase. The practice of making the initial agreement 'subject to contract' and therefore not binding, ensures that in the great majority of cases the purchaser will have legal advice before he becomes finally committed. No doubt this saves many people from foolish or improvident purchases, but of course, it also suffers from the disadvantage of leaving sellers, as well as buyers, at the mercy of a change of mind on the part of the other. Those who are knowledgeable in such matters may well be aware of the significance of the words 'subject to contract' and may, indeed, 'intend' not to be bound by their initial agreement. But the truth is that even parties who understand the effects of their transactions have very little choice in the matter. A buyer or seller who insisted that he wanted a firm contract at the outset would probably have great difficulty in securing the agreement of the other party to such a departure from normal practice; and in any event the great majority of buyers and sellers probably regard the lack of binding force in their agreement as prescribed by the law, rather than as depending on their intention.[6] It seems reasonable therefore, to treat this as another illustration of the declining use made of the wholly executory contract in England.

Indeed, it does not seem too much to say that almost the whole of the doctrine which prescribes that there must be an intention to create legal relations in order to create a binding contract, is concerned with executory agreements alone. Once acts of reliance or performance are carried through a Court is much more likely to find the necessary intent than when everything remains wholly executory. The result, of course, is justified by arguing that the parties 'could hardly have intended' that they should not be bound once such-and-such has been done; but in reality the critical factor appears to be what has been done rather than what was intended.[7]

---

[5] See Law Commission *Report on 'Gazumping'* (Law Com. No. 65, 1975).

[6] This was vividly illustrated by some correspondence in *The Times* in July–October 1977. A Professor of Business Policy protested that nobody had ever told him that it was possible to make a binding legal contract for the purchase of a house as soon as the parties were agreed on terms: *The Times*, 19 Sept. 1977.

[7] See, e.g., *Rose & Frank* v. *Crompton* [1925] A.C. 30; *Jones* v. *Padavatton* [1969] 1 W.L.R. 328; *Pettit* v. *Pettit* [1970] A.C. 777.

Other illustrations of these changes can be found in matrimonial law. Although we are not here dealing with matters conventionally classified as contract, matrimonial relationships are also concerned with the effects of a binding future assent to a long-continued relationship. The gradual easing of the grounds of divorce, and still more, the total abolition of actions for breach of promise of marriage, can again be seen as cases in which the binding force of future agreements have declined. And conversely, the signs of greater recognition being afforded to stable de facto relationships, even where there is no marriage at all, may be seen as illustrating a greater emphasis on present consent over binding future arrangements.

Even when we turn to examine commercial arrangements, as opposed to consumer transactions, there are signs of the waning force of the executory contract. Certainly, there is evidence that in practice, businessmen, almost as much as consumers, often expect to have some sort of right to cancel executory contracts. Empirical studies, both in the United States, and in England,[8] suggest that businessmen usually expect, and are usually conceded, the right to cancel orders for goods prior to any expenditure by the seller; and even after such expenditure, cancellation is often permitted subject to payment of the costs incurred by the seller. In other words, reliance interests are protected but bare expectations are not. There are, too, signs of a resurgence of the unilateral contract since 1870, though some of the leading cases here are consumer ones. For example, the modern view of the relationship between a vendor and a commission agent is that the vendor is not bound unless and until the agent introduces a purchaser who actually enters into a contract with the vendor.[9] Similarly, it is from the 1870s that we can date the cases holding that a tender to supply the buyer's requirements, may not amount to a binding contract even where it is 'accepted'.[10] Sometimes, the Courts appear to have switched over so suddenly to the unilateral contract that lawyers have been taken by surprise. In *Queen* v. *Demers*,[11] for instance an agreement was made between a Colonial Government and a printer for the printing of Government documents at scheduled prices for a period of eight years. A dispute between the parties led to litigation all the way up to the Privy Council. There the case was disposed of in a one paragraph judgment, by the 'discovery' that the whole arrangement was unilateral and, in so far as it was executory, not binding on the Government at all.

[8] Macaulay, 'Non-Contractual Relations in Business: A Preliminary Study', 28 *American Soc. Rev.* 55 (1963); Beale and Dugdale 'Contracts between Businessmen: Planning and the Use of Contractual Remedies', 2 *Brit. J. of Law and Soc.* 45, 53 (1975).

[9] *Luxor* v. *Cooper* [1941] A.C. 108.

[10] *Great Northern Rly. Co.* v. *Witham* (1873) L.R. 9 C.P. 16.

[11] [1900] A.C. 103.

It may well be that decisions of this character often reflect the real understanding of contracting parties more accurately than the classical model of the executory contract. It is clear that in many situations contracting parties, particularly, but not exclusively, consumers, do not regard a contract as involving mutual promises. The legal analysis of an agreement as one in which the parties both *promise* to carry out their part is often the invention of the Courts rather than the inevitable meaning of the arrangement. Parties often 'agree' on the terms of a transaction, meaning thereby that, if and in so far as the transaction is carried out, the terms governing the performance will be those which they have agreed; such an agreement does not necessarily imply that the parties mean to commit themselves not to change their minds. This is, perhaps, particularly obvious in cases of long-term or continuing relationships. We have seen how in the classical period, a continuing contract was construed by the Courts as prima facie binding in perpetuity. This itself had been a departure from earlier law when continuing contracts such as contracts of employment, partnerships, leases and so forth were held terminable at will, or on notice. Here, too, there are marked signs of a return to the pre-classical law in many situations. The terms of a continuing arrangement may well amount to an agreement that, so long as the relation subsists, it is to be on the terms agreed; but the agreement does not necessarily carry an implication that is to be permanent. Generally speaking, it is now held that, in the absence of express provision to the contrary, such continuing contracts are terminable, either at will, or on reasonable notice.[12] Indeed, even a contract of employment on 'permanent and pensionable' terms, was only held by a bare majority of the House of Lords to be a lifetime's appointment.[13] The requirement of reasonable notice for the termination of certain relationships, for example, a gratuitous licence, itself provides a clear example of a reliance-based liability. For in such a case the licensor is *bound* by his gratuitous grant of a licence during the period of reasonable notice.[14]

Other straws in the wind can occasionally be found elsewhere in contractual cases. For example, it has sometimes been suggested that the Courts are readier to hold an agreement void for uncertainty where it is wholly executory than where it has been partly performed or acted upon.[15] Then again, there is the line of cases concerning public authorities

[12] See, e.g., *Hamilton* v. *Bryant* (1914) 30 T.L.R. 408; *Winter Garden Theatre (London) Ltd.* v. *Millenium Productions Ltd.* [1948] A.C. 173; *J. H. Milner & Son* v. *Percy Bilton Ltd.* [1966] 1 W.L.R. 1582; *Re Spenborough U.D.C.'s Agreement* [1968] Ch. 139.

[13] *McClelland* v. *Northern Ireland General Health Services Board* [1957] 1 W.L.R. 594.

[14] See the *Winter Garden Theatre* case, *supra.*

[15] Lord Denning in *F. & G. Sykes (Wessex) Ltd.* v. *Fine Fair* [1967] 2 Lloyd's Rep. 52, 57–8. Perhaps *G. Scammell & Nephew Ltd.* v. *Ouston* [1941] A.C. 251 illustrates a similar tendency, for the decision seems otherwise inexplicable.

in which it has been repeatedly held that such public bodies may be unable to bind themselves as to the future exercise of their powers.[16] These cases, too, seem to recognize the distinction between an actual exercise of a power by a public body, and a binding arrangement as to its future exercise. On the other hand, one recent development in the law may seem to contradict this trend. The rule in *Seddon* v. *North East Salt Co.*,[17] which formerly operated so as to preclude rescission of an executed contract for innocent misrepresentation was abrogated by the Misrepresentation Act 1967. If there is in truth a general move away from the binding nature of executory contracts, and towards stressing the distinction between executory and executed transactions, this development may appear somewhat paradoxical. The only explanation that can be offered for this change is that it illustrates the power of the classical model and the textbook formulations, which long after the *Seddon* case was decided, continued to criticize it. Why, it was asked, should a right to rescind for innocent misrepresentation be lost 'merely' because the contract had been executed? In retrospect, the surprising thing is that there were few defenders of the rule, for it is not hard to find good reasons for a greater readiness to set aside executory transactions.[18] In any event, the change made by the Misrepresentation Act leaves the Court a good deal of discretion in the matter, and it will be surprising if the Courts do not prove somewhat more reluctant to set aside executed than executory contracts.

Before leaving this topic, something should be said about the relationship between executory contracts and the protection of expectations. I have been at pains to stress that where a wholly executory contract is enforced by the Courts—no performance, no benefit, and no reliance having taken place—the Court is protecting a bare expectation. It is commonly said that one of the primary differences between the law of damages in contract and in tort is that expectation damages are only awarded in contract. I wish to suggest that there are marked signs of change here also. In the classical model, expectations were entitled to protection because contracts were perceived as resting on mutual promises, and a man was thought *entitled* to entertain the expectations derived from a promise. In the absence of such promises, however, a man acted at his risk, and expectations were not protected. Now I pointed out previously that this was never wholly and strictly correct, because ideas of good faith did often lead the Courts to protect expectations which were not expressly bargained for, but were nevertheless reasonably enter-

---

[16] *Supra*, p. 719.

[17] [1905] 1 Ch. 326.

[18] In the similar case of mistake, the distinction between executed and executory transactions appears (though not overtly recognized) from a comparison between *Bell* v. *Lever Bros.* [1932] A.C. 161 and *Magee* v. *Pennine Insurance* [1969] 2 Q.B. 507.

tained. In the modern law this process has continued, and in certain respects, been strengthened. A particularly interesting and striking example of this is to be found in the decision of the Lords in *Ebrahimi* v. *Westbourne Galleries Ltd.*[19] In this case E and N had been in business as partners for some years, sharing the management and profits equally. In 1958 the business was converted into a limited company, the two partners taking equal shares and being nominated the first directors of the company. Shortly afterwards N's son G was admitted as a third member of the company and was appointed a director. Disputes arose and N and his son G, who were now able to outvote E, removed him from the Board. E petitioned the Court for a winding up order on the ground that it was 'just and equitable' that the company should be wound up. In effect, he argued that his reasonable expectations about the way the business would be conducted and the profits distributed, had been frustrated. The defendants, however, relied upon the articles of association and insisted that E held his shares on the terms specified in the articles. The case thus involved a conflict between the letter of the contract (as contained in the articles) and the reasonable expectations of E. The House of Lords upheld E's claim, and insisted that due regard must be had to the reasonable expectations which he had. They rejected the argument that this would mean totally disregarding the terms of the contract, as contained in the articles. The terms of the contract were important; and regard must be had to them; but regard must also be had to equitable considerations.[20]

Given decisions of this character, it may be objected that a greater importance might be expected to be attached to the executory contract, rather than a lesser, as I have argued. That, however, is not so. The truth is that expectations are becoming more and more divorced from promises. On the one hand, certain expectations are today accorded greater recognition, because they are more powerfully held. These expectations do not necessarily arise from promises, still less from contract. They arise from the modern way of life. For example, expectations with regard to future employment and earnings are amongst the best protected of all expectations in modern times. The nature of the society in which we live means that many people tend to have very powerful expectations about their future earnings, and anything which interrupts those earnings is likely to cause serious disappointment, and even dislocation. But these expectations are not protected merely as a matter of contract. Even in tort law, damages for

[19] [1972] 2 All E.R. 492.
[20] The decision can be seen as a refutation of the argument that utilitarianism would make a promise meaningless since the promisor's obligation would always be to do what would anyhow produce the most happiness.

future earnings are awarded as a matter of everyday practice in personal injury actions; and such damages do not merely take account of what the plaintiff was earning when injured, but also what he might reasonably have expected to earn in the future (inflation apart). It is difficult to understand how the common idea has grown up that expectation damages cannot be awarded in a tort action. There are also many reliance cases (especially those which can be brought under the heading of estoppel) in which expectations are protected although they do not derive from promises.[21]

Similarly, there are other situations where the Courts have treated expectations as the foundations of liabilities without pausing to inquire whether they are contractual or other expectations. For example, one of the earliest modern cases on the liability of hospitals for medical negligence is *Gold* v. *Essex County Council*.[22] In this case Lord Greene specifically rejected the suggestion that anything turned upon whether there was any payment for the services rendered, but at the same time insisted that the issue depended upon what the plaintiff was reasonably entitled to expect when he entered the hospital.[23] There are, indeed, signs that the law will pay increasing attention to public expectations, no matter how unreasonable these may appear to a lawyer. For example, the Law Commission recently recommended the abolition of perpetual rentcharges on freehold land, simply because they are 'conceptually unacceptable' to the general public.[24] No matter that it is perfectly plain on the face of the documents that the freeholder will have to pay a rentcharge in perpetuity, and no matter that this may be carefully explained to a purchaser by his solicitor, the purchaser simply does not expect to encounter such charges when he buys a freehold interest. The 'freeholder does not expect to have to pay an annual sum not readily distinguishable from a leasehold ground rent'.[25]

What it comes to, then, is that it is no longer possible to tie the protection of expectations so closely to contractual rights. Bare expectations, arising under executory contracts, may be less well protected; other expectations, not based on contracts or promises at all, may be better protected. Nevertheless, it remains true in current law that, generally speaking, expectations are the basis of the damages which will be awarded for breach of contract where such liability does exist.

---

[21] See, e.g., *Greenwood* v. *Martin's Bank* [1933] A.C. 51. Some of these cases seem to go too far in protecting expectations where there is (perhaps) only a minor element of reliance. See Spencer-Bower and Turner, *Estoppel*, 3rd edn. (London, 1977), pp. 112-14.

[22] [1942] 1 K.B. 293.

[23] See especially at p. 302.

[24] See the Law Commission *Report on Rentcharges* (Law Com. No. 68, 1975) and the Rentcharges Act 1977.

[25] Para. 26.

Even where there has been some element of reliance, or some benefit rendered, and where it might have been thought that the damages would be confined to the element of reliance or the value of the benefit, this is not generally the case. Doubtless, there are arguments for maintaining the traditional principle here,[26] though it might be better to recognize them frankly for what they are. Frequently, the best justification for awarding such expectation damages is not that the plaintiff's expectations in fact deserve such handsome protection, but that proof of the losses flowing from reliance would be too difficult or costly, and that if the damages are excessive by way of compensation, then this is a deserved penalty on the defendant anyhow. But in view of the declining belief in the idea that the law should actually deter parties from breaking their contracts, it would not be surprising if future developments tend to show a still further whittling down of expectation damages. Only in cases where expectations tend already to be so powerful that the demand for their protection is overwhelming, as in the case of employment expectations, is it likely that there will be any increase in the protection afforded by the law.

THE RESURGENCE OF BENEFIT-BASED LIABILITIES

Parallel with the decline of consensual and promise-based liabilities over the past hundred years, there has been a resurgence of benefit-based and reliance-based liabilities. There seems no doubt that in these respects, the values underlying the trends of the past hundred years more closely resemble those of the eighteenth century than of the nineteenth century. I have here only space to sketch out some of the principal respects in which modern law has moved toward a greater recognition of benefit-based liabilities.

It should perhaps first be observed that here, as elsewhere, modern theory has not yet caught up with actual developments. The power of the classical model is still great; lawyers tend still to talk of the conferring of unsolicited benefits as officious intermeddling, they still dislike the idea that benefits should be 'thrust upon a person behind his back' and there is little disposition to analyse more closely the variety of circumstances in which such benefits are conferred in order to build a new body of theory. But despite the lagging behind of theory, it will be found that in practice, lawyers and Courts have moved toward a greater recognition of benefit-based liabilities. In many respects this move has been inherent in a number of other developments that I have previously described. For example, the increased hostility to the use of penalties and forfeitures

---

[26] See Fuller and Perdue, 'The Reliance Interest in Contract Damages', 46 *Yale Law Journal* 52 and 373 (1936).

(which I described earlier) has necessarily brought with it a greater hostility to uncovenanted benefits. And so too the decline of promise-based liabilities necessarily moves the law into other channels in the search for other bases of liability. It should also be observed that the whole trend of modern law has been to reject one of the chief objections to a greater recognition of benefit-based liabilities. There seems no doubt that in the nineteenth century one of the principal reasons for the small role allotted to such liabilities was the unwillingness, or even a perceived inability, to determine, as a question of fact, whether a person had indeed received a benefit at the hands of another.[27] Courts (like the economists and the utilitarians) felt that it was a matter for each individual to decide, on the basis of his subjective preferences, whether something was a benefit or not. It was not for the judges, or juries, to decide that what one person did for another, without his express request or agreement, was a benefit to him. Hence (as we saw previously) there had been a tendency to limit quasi-contractual liability to cases in which the Courts felt it possible to say, as a matter of law, that one person's actions were necessarily beneficial to another, as where one person discharged another's legal debts. But in modern times, this inability to determine what amounts to a benefit appears quite anachronistic. The Courts regularly decide questions of fact of much greater difficulty than this, and there are a great many fields in which objective standards are now used to decide issues which were formerly felt to be purely a matter for the individual. There is, too, a sense in which the question what is a benefit-in-fact is analogous to the question of what is a loss-in-fact, an issue constantly being decided by the Courts in the presently expanding field of tort law.

The most obvious respect in which benefit-based liabilities have become of greater importance in the past hundred years has been in the development and expansion of the law of quasi-contract, and of a variety of equitable remedies of a similar character. In 1870, as we have previously seen, the distinction between 'genuine' implied-in-fact contracts and 'fictitious' quasi-contracts was entering the textbook version of the law, though it was many years before it acquired any serious support on the Bench. But so far as the substance of the law was concerned, Pollock, as founder-editor of the *Law Quarterly Review*, noted in its first year, in 1885, that there was a 'very marked tendency' among modern judges to extend the field of quasi-contractual obligations.[28] It is true that, among many of the more conservative judges, there remained a strong hostility to the textbook idea that quasi-contract was not based

---

[27] Calabresi and Melamed, 'Property Rules, Liability Rules and Inalienability: One view of the Cathedral', 85 *Harvard Law Rev.* 1089, 1117, n. 37 (1972).

[28] 1 *Law Q. Rev.* 392 (1885) (note on *Edmunds* v. *Wallingford* (1885) 14 Q.B.D. 811).

on 'implied contracts'. In 1914 Lord Sumner was still rejecting the then 'modern' idea that quasi-contract had nothing to do with 'real contract',[29] and even in 1939 he was supported by conservative academics like Holdsworth.[30] Lord Wright, however, espoused the modern view,[31] and expressed it, in a number of cases in the 1940s.[32] But this was all a somewhat sterile controversy, and I have already suggested that the 'modern' ideas being adopted by Lord Wright were in fact Roman law ideas, imported into English law via John Austin, Henry Maine, and Martin Leake. More important than these barren conceptual arguments about the 'true' basis of a certain type of liability was the actual effect of the decisions being made, and the values on which they were being made. Even in *Sinclair* v. *Brougham* itself, the case in which Lord Sumner rejected the 'modern' version of quasi-contract, the actual decision expanded a non-consensual liability, and must, in any rational sense, be treated as a case of benefit-based liability. In this complicated case the Lords held that the depositors of money banked in the *ultra vires* activities of a building society were entitled to recover their money equally with the shareholders. It is true that they were not given priority over the shareholders (which a quasi-contractual claim might have given them) but if the *ultra vires* doctrine was assumed to have a rational purpose it was not unreasonable that both the shareholders and the depositors should suffer equally for these *ultra vires* activities. The fact that the Lords rejected a quasi-contractual claim *eo nomine*, is less important than the fact that they recognised the right of the depositors to an equitable remedy over the funds in the coffers of the building society. This was, as plainly as could be, a benefit-based liability. The building society was liable to refund the money because it would have been an outrageous case of unjust enrichment if the shareholders had kept the whole proceeds of their own *ultra vires* activities.

Moreover, it is necessary to see this case as the culmination of a long series of cases which began in the later nineteenth century, all of which flowed from the results of the *ultra vires* doctrine. When that doctrine was first laid down in 1867, classical contract theory was at its height, and the result was that the law did not overtly distinguish between an executory and an executed contract. If a contract was *ultra vires* it remained *ultra vires*, no matter that it had been performed by the other party, who might have been suing the company for breach of its part. Inevitably this gave rise to much trouble, because even classical theory could not, by this time, prevent it seeming obviously unjust that one party to an *ultra vires*

---

[29] *Sinclair* v. *Brougham* [1914] A.C. 398.

[30] See 55 *Law Q. Rev.* 37 (1939).

[31] See 55 *Law Q. Rev.* 189 referring to American legal thought as exemplified by Keener, *Law of Quasi-Contract* (1888).

[32] In particular, the *Fibrosa* case [1943] A.C. 32.

contract should retain the benefit of an actual performance and escape scot free himself. The result was a long series of decisions in which, by one means or another, the Courts upheld claims against companies in such circumstances.[33] Generally, these claims were upheld in so far as moneys borrowed by an *ultra vires* loan were used to pay off existing legal obligations of the company. Such payment plainly benefited the company, and the invalidity of the contractual arrangements was not allowed to stand in the way of recovery. But it is worth noting how difficult it sometimes became to decide whether the company was in fact benefited by the *ultra vires* borrowing. Some of these cases illustrate the (perhaps obvious) point that promissory liability often has great advantages over benefit-based liability. Where running accounts are involved, for example, it is often a matter of the greatest difficulty to say whether a payment by one party has in fact benefited the other party.[34] But at least these authorities did show some advance on the previous law. For they recognized a benefit-based liability in cases where A had (in effect) paid B's debts even where he was not compellable to pay them.[35] Where he was compellable, there was, of course, no doubt of the liability, which was reaffirmed in the twentieth century.[36]

To return to the development of modern theory, there were signs, from the 1940s onwards, that judges were at last beginning to accept the distinction between quasi-contract and implied-in-fact contract. The terminology of 'quasi-contract' began to be more regularly used, and attempts to get behind the conceptual classifications of the law and to rely on its substance, began to be made by writers and even by the Courts. One notable example was the decision of the House of Lords in *United Australia* v. *Barclays Bank Ltd.*[37] where the House of Lords stressed the fictitious nature of the 'implied contract' in a quasi-contractual claim. In 1966 a book on the *Law of Restitution* (by R. L. A. Goff and Gareth Jones) made the first systematic attempt to bring together common law and equitable remedies in this area. In this work the authors insist, with some justice, that the 'implied contract' theory of quasi-contract has little appeal, and that the basic idea of unjust enrichment underlies this branch of the law. They concede, however, that it would be more accurate to regard unjust enrichment as 'an abstract proposition of justice' rather than as a strict legal principle.[38]

---

[33] *In re Cork & Youghal Rly. Co.* (1869) L.R. 4 Ch. App. 748; *Blackburn Benefit Building Society* v. *Cunliffe* (1882) 22 Ch. D. 61; *Wenlock* v. *River Dee Co.* (1887) 19 Ch. D. 155; *In re Wrexham, Mold and Connah's Quay Rly.* [1899] 1 Ch. 440.

[34] *Bannatyne* v. *MacIver* [1906] 1 K.B. 103.

[35] See too *B. Liggett (Liverpool) Ltd.* v. *Barclays Bank Ltd.* [1938] 1 K.B. 48.

[36] *Brook's Wharf and Bull's Wharf Ltd.* v. *Goodman Bros.* [1937] 1 K.B. 534.

[37] [1941] A.C. 1.

[38] p. 12.

Nevertheless, it may be suggested that this development is as misconceived as all the earlier attempts to state the basis of the law relating to such liabilities. It is misconceived, in my view, because it fails to recognize the very substantial and close relationship between contractual and restitutionary liabilities. As I have rejected the notion that contractual liabilities are all promise-based and have insisted that where part executed contracts are enforced, the liability is primarily benefit-based or reliance-based, it is evident that I cannot support a move towards a total theoretical separation of contract from restitution.

In any case, it must be said that there is little sign yet of any wholehearted acceptance by English lawyers of a new branch of law entitled the Law of Restitution, and based on unjust enrichment ideas. The reality is that unjust enrichment has become a more important underlying idea of the law, for it is only another phrase for the concept of benefit-based liability, but the developments have been occurring interstitially in all branches of the law. In contract, in tort, in family law, in the law of property, in company law, the same development has been occurring. The various cases show little signs of coming together to cohere into one new body of law, and this may be just as well.

I need now only offer a few miscellaneous illustrations of this tendency in various branches of the law for benefit-based liabilities to be given greater recognition, especially as I have discussed many other examples in the previous pages. One good recent example of modern trends is *Greenwood* v. *Bennett* [39] where the Court of Appeal held that the plaintiff, who had carried out extensive repairs on the defendant's car (which he had bought in good faith from a thief) was entitled to recover the value of these repairs from the owner. The Court felt that it would be quite wrong for the owner to receive an uncovenanted benefit as a result of these repairs. Thus this was a case in which the owner 'had a benefit thrust upon him' and yet was not entitled to keep it; but it is to be noted that the owner here was a dealer and had resold the car before the proceedings were brought. There was nothing unjust in his being compelled to pay for the repairs, therefore. The position might, of course, have been different if the owner was a private individual who did not want to sell the car, or could not afford to pay for the repairs without being forced to sell it.

Another similar case from the law of agency is *The Swan* [40] where one R owned a motor fishing vessel which was hired to a private company owned and managed by R and his family. The company instructed the plaintiffs to carry out various works to the vessel, and these were done at

---

[39] [1973] Q.B. 195.
[40] [1968] 1 Lloyd's Rep. 5. Cf. *Godfrey Davis Ltd.* v. *Culling & Hecht* [1962] 2 Lloyd's Rep. 349; *Croter & Green Ltd.* v. *Tyrrell* [1962] 2 Lloyd's Rep. 377.

considerable cost. The company went into liquidation before payment, and the repairers sought payment personally from R. Strictly, in legal doctrine, 'the contract' was not between R and the repairers but between the company and the repairers, but it would evidently have been an outrageous case of unjust enrichment if R had been able to avoid payment. It was held that he was liable as an agent, even though prima facie an agent is not liable where he contracts for a disclosed principal. Although the judge did not place his decision on the grounds of an unjust enrichment, he concluded his judgment with words which suggest that this idea was not an irrelevant factor in his mind: 'I am not sorry [to hold the defendant liable]', he said, 'for the opposite conclusion would have meant that the plaintiffs would have been out of pocket in respect of nearly £1,500 worth of work done on the defendant's boat, while the defendant who only paid £800 for the boat originally, retained the benefit of the work in the form of the much increased value of his property without having paid a penny for it.'

Another example of benefit-based liability is to be found in the line of cases holding that a liability incurred by a person in the course of doing some act at the request of another, may entitle the party so acting to an indemnity from the other. The origins of this principle can indeed be traced back as far as 1827,[41] but it received its main development after the end of the classical period.[42] It seems quite plain that this form of liability (which the Courts have found hard to classify as contractual or quasi-contractual)[43] rests on the notion that a request is evidence that the act done will be a benefit to the party requesting it, and that if some untoward liability results from it, the party benefited ought to bear the loss.[44]

Recent developments in matrimonial property law may also be thought to illustrate the growing recognition of benefit-based liabilities. For some years now there has been a long series of cases in which, on the break up of a marriage, or even of a stable de facto relationship, the parties have disagreed about the proceeds of the matrimonial home. Prior to 1970 these disputes were often litigated under section 17 of the Married Women's Property Act 1882, but in *Pettit* v. *Pettit*[45] the House of Lords held that this Act did not empower the Courts to alter the property rights of the parties in the absence of some express or implied agreement as to the division of those rights. Thus the mere fact that one

[41] *Adamson* v. *Jarvis* (1827) 4 Bing. 66, 130 E.R. 693.
[42] See *Dugdale* v. *Lovering* (1875) L.R. 10 C.P. 196; *Sheffield Corpn.* v. *Barclay* [1905] A.C. 392. I discussed these cases in 'Misrepresentation, Warranty and Estoppel', 9 *Alberta Law Rev.* 347, 359–61, 364–5 (1971).
[43] See *Secretary of State* v. *Bank of India* [1938] 1 All E.R. 797.
[44] See especially, *Bank of England* v. *Cutler* [1908] 2 K.B. 208.
[45] [1970] A.C. 777.

spouse had, by his or her efforts, improved the value of the other spouse's property, did not, of itself, entitle the former to share in the proceeds of the property. But two years later, the House of Lords reached the conclusion that what could not be done by way of contract could be done by way of trust.[46] No fictitious common intent should be imputed to the parties, according to the earlier decision, but a (more or less) fictitious trust could be imposed, according to the second. The upshot of the decisions was that, where the wife had made some real contribution to the matrimonial property, by contributing part of the purchase price, or by contributing to household expenses and thereby freeing her husband's resources for the payment of mortgage instalments, or even by do-it-yourself activities in the house, a trust would be 'implied' or imposed by the Court. The proceeds of sale could then be divided as the Court saw fit, in all the circumstances of the case. Trifling contributions, such as would be expected of a spouse in the ordinary course of a marriage, were still to be ignored because, as in the doctrine of consideration, something which a person 'ought to do anyhow' may be no real benefit.[46A] Despite the peculiar conceptual contortions which the Courts went through, this latter decision can be said to have recognised the simple fairness of requiring the husband, if he was legal owner of the property, to pay a part of the proceeds to his wife because of the benefits contributed by her. The actual agreement of the parties was by no means irrelevant. If they expressly agreed that the property should be 'in joint names', for instance, this was material; but even in the absence of any agreement, the Courts exercised their powers to ensure an equitable division of the property. Since 1970 this jurisdiction has been confirmed and enlarged by the Matrimonial Proceedings and Property Act which specifically requires the Courts to have regard to 'the contributions made by each of the parties to the welfare of the family'.[47] It is clear that both the Courts and Parliament have recognized the whole of this area as one in which the mutual rendering of benefits is a vital consideration in the division of the matrimonial assets.

Similar developments are observable in the laws governing the inheritance of a deceased's estate. Statutory and discretionary judicial decisions have combined to recognize that a person who rendered significant benefits to the deceased (even without any express contractual arrangements) may thereby acquire a right to some provision from the deceased's estate.[47A]

---

[46] *Gissing* v. *Gissing* [1971] A.C. 886.
[46A] See in particular *Button* v. *Button* [1968] 1 W.L.R. 457, 461–2.
[47] Sect. 5(1)(*f*).
[47A] See Inheritance (Provision for Family and Dependents) Act 1975, and *Re Wilkinson* [1978] 1 All E.R. 221.

THE RESURGENCE OF RELIANCE-BASED LIABILITIES

The past hundred years have witnessed a resurgence of reliance-based liabilities, as well as of benefit-based liabilities. The two developments have run closely parallel, covering both contract law itself (as generally characterized) and other branches of the law. Thus, within the law of contract, there has been a significant move to increase liabilities based on unbargained-for reliance, and in the law of tort, as well as a number of less prominent areas, there has equally been a growth of liabilities which are based on the idea of reasonable reliance. And, as with the case of benefits, the actual movements in the law have not yet been accompanied by an adequate adjustment of theory. It is still the classical model which largely prevails in theoretical formulations. Reliance is, according to this model, only justifiable if it has been paid for, or bargained for. A person who relies on another, where such reliance is not actually part of a bargain, is still, according to this theory, acting at his own risk. In the shadow of nineteenth century individualism, lawyers still pay lip service (and sometimes more) to the fundamental belief that a man should rely on himself, and not on others. But in practice, in actual decisions, and in actual legislation, it is evident that this individualism no longer represents the values underlying the law. As Lord Reid said in *Gollins* v. *Gollins*, 'life would be impossible in modern conditions unless on the highway and in the market place we were entitled to rely on the other man behaving like a reasonable man.'[48] Once again, I have only space to sketch out some of the principal developments of the past hundred years.

One of the first areas of the law to show signs of retreat from the high water mark of Victorian individualism was the law of misrepresentation. In the last few decades of the nineteenth century, this was a much litigated area of the law, perhaps partly because of the need to reconcile the hitherto differing approaches of common law and Equity; but partly also, as I suggest, because values were changing. The older notion that a man could say what he liked to a prospective contracting party, so long only as he refrained from positively dishonest assertions of fact, seems to have come up against a new morality in the late nineteenth century. The Courts began to insist on the duty of a party not to mislead the other party by extravagant or unjustified assertions,[49] and they also seem to have been influenced by a desire to impose some form of control on the new types of advertisement now appearing in the mass press.[50] There

[48] [1964] A.C. 644.

[49] See especially *Smith* v. *Land & House Property Corpn.* (1884) 28 Ch. D. 7; *Karsberg's* case [1892] 3 Ch. 1.

[50] See *Carlill* v. *Carbolic Smoke Ball Co.* [1893] 1 Q.B. 256; *Smith* v. *Land & House Property Corpn.*, *supra*, n. 49. Advertising was much despised at this time by the upper classes, some of whom made it a point not to buy advertised products at all.

was, of course, a clash between these two moralities. The older one was still very much alive, especially among common lawyers; it led (as we saw previously) to the decision in *Derry* v. *Peek*[51] in 1889, and can also be seen to be responsible for *Heilbut* v. *Buckleton*[52] as late as 1913. But the newer ideas were also very influential from the 1870s onwards, and, indeed, in their determination to stamp out the laxer business morality which gave wide latitude to misrepresentation, the Courts decided some cases in a way which even today, may seem to go too far. *Redgrave* v. *Hurd*,[53] for example, is still regarded as a leading case on the law of misrepresentation, standing for the proposition that a man cannot escape the consequences of a misrepresentation merely because the representee could have discovered the truth by reasonable care. But the actual decision was a very strong one, for the plaintiff had bought the defendant's house and his practice as a solicitor, in reliance on some casual assertions about the value of the practice, without any examination of the books. Even today that would seem such a remarkable want of due precaution on the part of the buyer that the actual decision may well be of dubious validity.

Perhaps because of the clash of these two moralities, the law of misrepresentation unfortunately became bogged down in a mass of technicalities. Judges, and textbook writers, drew distinctions between 'statements of fact' and statements of 'mere opinion' which were difficult to apply, and anyhow did not adequately reflect the essential point that justifiable reliance depended on a much wider set of factors. Similarly, the distinctions drawn between warranties and mere representations became almost impossible of application as the Courts insisted that all depended on the 'intention of the parties'. Signs of a more realistic development, towards the idea that a person with means of knowledge should generally be held responsible for a misrepresentation as against a person without such means, appeared in *De Lassalle* v. *Guildford*,[54] but were lost sight of after the catastrophic decision in *Heilbut* v. *Buckleton*.[55] By the 1960s the law of misrepresentation had become so unsatisfactory that an attempt was made at reform by the Misrepresentation Act, 1967. Although this Act may prove a workable instrument, in that it largely gives the Court the freedom, or discretion, to treat misrepresentations as a ground for rescission, or for damages, as it sees fit, the Act has unfortunately not simplified the conceptual apparatus of the law. The distinction between misrepresentation and warranty survives, and so too

[51] 14 App. Cas. 337.
[52] [1913] A.C. 30.
[53] (1881) 20 Ch. D. 1.
[54] [1901] 2 K.B. 215.
[55] [1913] A.C. 30. See the strictures of Williston, 'Representation and Warranty in Sales—Heilbut v Buckleton' 27 *Harvard Law Rev.* 1 (1913).

does the distinction between statements of opinion and statement of fact. What has gone wrong here is the failure of lawyers to appreciate the nature of the issues raised by misrepresentation cases. Instead of asking whether, having regard to the various circumstances, the representee was justified in placing any reliance on the other party, or whether he should have rested on his own judgment (or purchased expert advice in the market) they have continued to pursue the highly technical and abstract distinctions of older cases.

But of the general trend anyhow, there can be no doubt. The recognition of the independent tort of negligent misrepresentation in the *Hedley Byrne* case[56] in 1964 is a significant pointer to the greater recognition of reliance-based liabilities. And since then the decision in *Esso Petroleum* v. *Mardon*[57] has provided one of the most fascinating examples of changing attitudes to contractual relationships. This case involved a lease of a petrol station by the plaintiffs to the defendant. The rental payable was based on an estimate of the sales potential of the petrol station, prepared by the plaintiff's own experts, and relied upon by both parties. The estimates turned out to have been carelessly prepared and were wildly over-sanguine so that in the event the defendant was unable to sell anything like the estimated quantities. He was, therefore, unable to pay the rent required, and when the plaintiffs sued for the rent, he counterclaimed for damages. He succeeded in this action on the ground that the plaintiffs owed a duty to take care in the preparation of the estimates on which it was known that the defendant would rely. The decision reflects a philosophy which is so contrary to the classical model of contract that its potential impact on contractual theory is at present hard to assess. That one party to a prospective contract should owe a duty to the other party to give him satisfactory information (or at least not to give him misleading information) on matters of estimation and judgment (as opposed to straightforward questions of fact) is utterly opposed to the basic ideas underlying the free market. The idea that each party in the market makes his own judgments and estimates, and that the striking of a bargain is a way of allocating the risks of future events as to such matters, was here tossed aside. But the decision can also be seen as a reflection of the realities of much modern business practice. First, it recognizes the unequal bargaining power, and access to sources of information, held by the parties in such relationships; secondly, it recognizes that a contract of this nature—which envisages a continuing relationship—is not an exercise in once-for-all risk allocation; and thirdly, it recognizes that business relationships of this character

---

[56] [1964] A.C. 465.
[57] [1976] 2 All E.R. 5. *English* v. *Dedham Vale Properties Ltd.* [1978] 1 All E.R. 382, may be another straw in the wind.

often partake of the nature of joint and co-operative ventures, rather than arms' length bargains. Above all, it represents a significant increase in the importance of reliance-based, rather than promise-based liability.

In cases of this nature, the increased recognition accorded to reliance-based liability is plain enough. But there is little doubt that there has, at the same time, been a much wider and more steady enlargement of reliance-based liability through the application of tort principles, in ordinary actions for negligence. Here, the changes are less easily perceptible, because the 'reasonableness' of the conduct of the plaintiff and defendant is treated as a pure question of fact, and such treatment naturally conceals the changing judicial attitudes to what is reasonable. But there are evidently many ordinary negligence actions in which the reasonableness of the conduct of the parties cannot be evaluated without regard to the extent to which reliance by one party on the other is found justifiable. On the road, drivers and pedestrians rely on each other to behave in predictable ways; even a simple road signal is (in effect) a form of representation on which others may reasonably rely, and which may create legal liability.[58] Cases of products' liability frequently hinge on the reliance of the consumer on the safety of a product, or the reasonableness of warning labels and signs.[59] In cases of this nature, it is not easy to demonstrate that there has been a trend away from self-reliance, and towards upholding the right to rely on others, but there are some cases where this seems plain enough. For example, it is now established that a person who buys a house whose construction has been negligently supervised by the inspections of the local authority, may be able to claim damages for negligence from the authority.[60] This amounts to holding that the consumer is entitled to rely on the authority to carry out its function of supervising house construction in a proper manner, and that he is not obliged (at least within these limits) to go into the market and buy advice from an expert third party, such as a surveyor. This, too, therefore, represents a shift away from the market ideal to a different kind of economic and social system.

To return again to cases generally treated as contractual, we find confirmation of the expansion of reliance-based liability in the further erosion of the old rule of *caveat emptor*. Both in the civil law, and by means of statutes such as the Trade Descriptions Act, the trend has been towards treating the consumer as entitled to rely on everything said or done by sellers or manufacturers; indeed, the trend has here gone so far that it may be wondered whether it has not been carried beyond all reason.

[58] See Seavey, 'Reliance Upon Gratuitous Promises or Other Conduct', 64 *Harv. Law Rev.* 913, 915 (1951).

[59] See, e.g., cases cited in Miller and Lovell, *Products Liability* (London, 1977), Chapter 12.

[60] *Dutton* v. *Bognor Regis U.C.* [1972] 1 Q.B. 373; *Anns* v. *Merton London Borough Council* [1977] 2 W.L.R. 1024.

Even consumer protection offices of local authorities have begun to suggest that consumerism has been carried too far. 'People are not looking at what they're buying. They're buying willy-nilly in the belief that they can always complain.'[61]

To some extent, these trends, of course, reflect the changing practice of modern business. Consumers today tend to rely on the advertising and brand names of national manufacturers rather than on their own judgment, or that of the shopkeeper. It is natural that the law should begin to reflect this fact, although the law of sale still places the primary responsibility for defective goods on the seller and not the manufacturer. But it must also be borne in mind that there are costs involved in allowing consumers to rely so heavily on others. Apart from the obvious costs which arise from policing and enforcing consumer protection statutes, there are also hidden costs which arise from curtailing the flow of information to the more discriminating buyer who may have the knowledge and judgment to make of it what it is worth. For example, the law appears to be coming very close to the stage when the seller of a second-hand vehicle will be obliged to cover over the mileage reading lest the buyer be misled into treating it as accurate. Even a warning notice that the mileage reading is not guaranteed may not be sufficient to protect the seller, either under the Trade Descriptions Act,[62] or possibly even in the civil law as a result of the Misrepresentation Act. It is thus likely that sellers may be driven to deprive buyers of this information, for what it is worth, even though it may be of some value to some buyers.

More central to the reliance idea have been the developments in the doctrine of consideration and estoppel over the past century. I argued in Parts I and II that the idea of detrimental reliance as constituting a valuable consideration, and therefore as supporting a contractual liability, really goes back to the beginnings of liability in the action of *assumpsit*. But in the classical period there were attempts to narrow liability down to cases where the reliance was bargained for as part of the price of the promise. Action in reliance on a promise which was not intended, or bargained for, even though it might have been foreseeable, was thus thought by some not to provide a proper consideration. I have also suggested that this theoretical structure was never wholly adopted by English Courts, though it had a much stronger following in the United States. For a relatively short period, around the end of the nineteenth and beginning of the twentieth century, both in America and in England, it seems to have been widely thought that this was the law, partly at least because it became part of the conventional textbook

---

[61] *Sunday Times*, colour supplement, 14 November 1976.
[62] See *R.* v. *Hammertons Cars Ltd.* [1976] 3 All E.R. 758.

formulations. In the United States, it led to a celebrated controversy between Williston and Corbin. Williston supported the 'bargain theory of consideration' (perhaps first propounded in America by Holmes) and, in the early drafts of the *Restatement of Contract*, for which Williston was reponsible, this version of the law was incorporated in the definition of consideration. But Corbin protested that this simply did not reflect the authorities, and he drew attention to a large number of cases in which subsequent action-in-reliance, even though unbargained-for, had been held sufficient consideration to make a promise actionable. The initial reaction of Williston, as of many American academics, was that these decisions were wrong, or contrary to the trend of authority, or explicable on other grounds. Corbin responded by arguing that the doctrine of consideration was the invention of the Courts and if the Courts regularly treated unbargained-for action-in-reliance as a consideration, it was not possible to say that they were wrong. The upshot of all this was a compromise. The Willistonian version of consideration was retained, but it was supplemented by a new clause in the *Restatement*, section 90, which treated action-in-reliance as giving rise, in appropriate circumstances, to a remedy by way of promissory estoppel.[63]

In England, developments followed much the same course, but more slowly, and less consciously. As we have seen, there were, even in the high noon of classical law, cases which were not reconcilable with the bargain theory of consideration. And English Courts never committed themselves to that theory. But the textbook writers favoured it,[64] and certainly by the early twentieth century it was often assumed that a plain gratuitous promise could not be made actionable by a subsequent and unbargained for action of reliance,[65] though there continued to be decisions not readily reconcilable with the theory.[66] As in American law, the gap was, to some extent filled by the development of the doctrine of estoppel which has, of course, always been a form of reliance-based liability, or at any rate responsibility. But the English developments in the doctrine of estoppel suffered from some early defects which prevented it fulfilling the expansive role which section 90 of the *Restatement* enabled it to do in America. First, there was the traditional dogma that estoppel could only be set up by way of defence, and not as a cause of action.[67]

[63] See for this story, Grant Gilmore, *The Death of Contract* (Columbus, Ohio, 1974), and Corbin, 'Recent Developments in Contracts', 50 *Harvard Law Rev.* 449 (1937).

[64] Pollock, in particular, defined consideration as the price of a promise and castigated decisions holding that unbargained-for reliance could amount to a consideration, *supra*, p. 461.

[65] For some examples, see *Re Hudson* (1885) 3 W.R. 819, 54 L.J. Ch. 811; *In re Cory* (1912) 29 T.L.R. 18. Lord Blackburn came close to adopting the bargain theory of consideration in *Maddison v. Alderson* (1883) 8 App. Cas. 467, *Harris v. Nickerson* (1873) L.R. 8 Q.B. 276, and *Brownlie v. Campbell* (1880) 5 App. Cas. 925, 952-3.

[66] See, e.g., *Boston v. Boston* [1904] 1 K.B. 124; *Starkey v. Bank of England* [1903] A.C. 114; *Sheffield Corpn. v. Barclay* [1905] A.C. 392.   [67] See especially *Low v. Bouverie* [1891] 3 Ch. 82.

And secondly, there was the decision in *Jorden* v. *Money*[68] which was generally interpreted to mean that estoppel could only be based upon a statement of fact and not a promise. The first of these two difficulties did not prove very serious, because a statement of fact could always be interpreted as a warranty if the Courts really felt it desirable to impose liability,[69] and I have argued elsewhere that the dogma that estoppel is not a cause of action is really a piece of meaningless nonsense.[70] But the second limitation, that estoppel cannot be based on a promise or statement of intention, has proved more troublesome. In 1937 the Law Revision Committee recommended that action in reliance on a promise should suffice to make a promise actionable, though that Report was not implemented. But after the Second World War a series of cases, stemming from the decision of Denning J. (as he then was) in the *High Trees* case,[71] began to develop a fresh doctrine of promissory estoppel. Although this at first was treated as a revolutionary decision, and many lawyers thought it was inconsistent with the 'true' doctrine of consideration, it now seems to have established itself thoroughly as a part of the modern law. To date, it has continued to be proclaimed that promissory estoppel cannot give rise to a cause of action but is only available by way of defence, but there are, at the time of writing, signs that even this bastion is about to crumble.[72] There are also signs of a renewed vigour in parallel reliance-based doctrines, such as 'acquiescence' as a ground for refusing injunctions.[73]

It is worth adding a word about American developments since the first *Restatement* was promulgated. The surprising result of the incorporation of section 90 in the first *Restatement* has been the huge increase in actions which are based on this clause, at the expense of ordinary contractual claims. Plainly, this indicates a resurgence of reliance-based liability at the expense of consensual liability.[74] Sometimes, this has resulted in decisions far beyond anything yet accepted in England, such as the recognition of a liability for reliance which has been succeeded, not by a contract, but by the breakdown of negotiations.[75] But in other respects

[68] (1854) 5 H.L.C. 185, 10 E.R. 868.

[69] See the cases cited *supra*, p. 776, n. 66.

[70] See 9 *Alberta Law Rev.* 347, 369–73.

[71] [1947] K.B. 130. Lord Denning here and elsewhere has insisted that no detrimental reliance need be proved, and it is sufficient if the promise is acted upon, but there is little support for this either in England or America. Why should a promisee improve his rights by acting on a promise in a manner beneficial to himself?

[72] See *Re Wyvern Developments* [1974] 1 W.L.R. 1097; *Crabb* v. *Arun D.C.* [1975] 3 All E.R. 865; K. C. T. Sutton, *Consideration Reconsidered* (St. Lucia, Queensland, 1974) especially at pp. 87–9.

[73] See, e.g., *Shaw* v. *Applegate* [1978] 1 All E.R. 123.

[74] Grant Gilmore, *The Death of Contract*; Henderson, 'Promissory Estoppel and Traditional Contract Doctrine', 78 *Yale Law Journal* 343 (1968).

[75] See, e.g., *Hoffman* v. *Red Owl Stores Inc.* 133 N.W. 2d. 267 (1965); *Wheeler* v. *White* 398 S.W. 2d. 93 (1965).

the developments have been even more striking. Courts and lawyers are tending to use promissory estoppel *in place of* contractual liability even where there has been a bargained-for reliance. The explanation for this appears to lie in the desire of the Courts to escape from some of the rigidity associated with consensual liability. Thus, cases in which they feel that expectation damages may be too generous, and that reliance damages will serve the ends of justice better, may be treated as promissory estoppel claims, instead of ordinary actions on a contract.

It remains only to indicate that in England there are other signs of the resurgence of reliance-based liabilities in a wide variety of situations. In the law of contract itself, the expansion of liability for the acts of agents, for example, both at common law,[76] and by statute,[77] shows this trend; though it is also true that adherence to the classical model of contract, and consensual ideas of liability, sometimes still serve to prevent such developments.[78] In Equity, there has been much development of the doctrine of estoppel in cases where a person 'stands by' and allows another to spend money on a property not belonging to him, or otherwise act to his prejudice.[79] There has also been an entirely new branch of the law growing up around the concept of breach of confidence which shows strong signs of a reliance-basis.[80] In the law of quasi-contract, there are signs of a revival of the idea that a payee who changes his position in reliance on a payment made to him of a sum which is not due, may have a defence to a claim for its recovery.[81]

THE NEED FOR A NEW THEORY

I may conclude by suggesting that the time is plainly ripe for a new theoretical structure for contract, which will place it more firmly in association with the rest of the law of obligations. The present conceptual

---

[76] See, e.g., *Freeman & Lockyer* v. *Buckhurst Park Properties* [1964] 2 Q.B. 480.

[77] Consumer Credit Act 1974, Sect. 75, replacing provisions first enacted by the Hire Purchase Act 1964.

[78] See *Branwhite* v. *Worcester Works Finance Ltd.* [1969] A.C. 552, where Lord Wilberforce, dissenting, would have imposed liability plainly based on reasonable reliance.

[79] The modern developments here stem from *Errington* v. *Errington* [1952] 1 K.B. 290, through *Inwards* v. *Baker* [1965] 2 Q.B. 29, down to *Ward* v. *Kirkland* [1967] Ch. 194 and *E. R. Ives Investment Ltd.* v. *High* [1967] 2 Q.B. 379.

[80] See, e.g., *Vokes Ltd.* v. *Heather* (1945) 62 R.P.C. 135, 141–2; *Saltman Engineering Co.* v. *Campbell Engineering Co.* (1948) 65 R.P.C. 203 also in [1963] 2 All E.R. 413; *Terrapin Ltd.* v. *Builders' Supply Co.* (1960) R.P.C. 128; *Argyll* v. *Argyll* [1967] Ch. 302. See too the Law Commission Working Paper (No. 58) *Breach of Confidence* which displays an interesting confusion of contractual and tortious ideas.

[81] See *United Overseas Bank* v. *Jiwani* [1977] 1 All E.R. 733, where although the defence failed, the Court seems to have been more sympathetic to it than in many earlier cases. See too Gareth Jones, 'Change of Circumstances in Quasi-Contract', 73 *Law Q. Rev.* 48 (1957). *Jones Ltd.* v. *Waring & Gillow* [1926] A.C. 670 still represents the older tradition, but even here it is interesting to note that the payees abandoned their claim to retain all the money, and argued only for a right to keep what they had lost by their (alleged) actions in reliance.

apparatus of the law is, I suggest, still essentially that of the classical model, and for the reasons I have given no longer accords with the way the law is developing, nor with the value systems underlying present day ideas. This new structure must, I suggest, rest on the three basic pillars of the law of obligations, the idea of recompense for benefit, of protection of reasonable reliance, and of the voluntary creation and extinction of rights and liabilities. In the process of redrawing the conceptual categories of the law, it will necessarily be found that many of the most important and difficult issues in the law arise where there are conflicts between these three basic notions. Should liabilities be imposed where benefits are conferred without consent? Is reliance to be protected where there are no mutual benefits? To what extent (if at all) should rights be created or extinguished by mere intention, or expressed intention, where there is no reliance and no element of benefit? This new approach must also take account of the important problems, hitherto neglected, involved in the distinctions between a present and a future consent, between a present and a future exchange, and between the evidentiary and substantive role of promises. So too, the role of expections, their relationship to promises, and their importance even where they arise without promises, must be re-examined. Room, too, must be found in this new approach, for an adequate analysis of the extent to which, and the methods by which, the law attempts to ensure fairness of exchange.

The task is one to which I hope to return.

INDEX